Lecture Notes in Computer Science 10946

Commenced Publication in 1973
Founding and Former Series Editors:
Gerhard Goos, Juris Hartmanis, and Jan van Leeuwen

More information about this series at http://www.springer.com/series/7410

Willy Susilo · Guomin Yang (Eds.)

Information Security and Privacy

23rd Australasian Conference, ACISP 2018
Wollongong, NSW, Australia, July 11–13, 2018
Proceedings

Springer

Editors
Willy Susilo
University of Wollongong
Wollongong, NSW
Australia

Guomin Yang
University of Wollongong
Wollongong, NSW
Australia

ISSN 0302-9743 ISSN 1611-3349 (electronic)
Lecture Notes in Computer Science
ISBN 978-3-319-93637-6 ISBN 978-3-319-93638-3 (eBook)
https://doi.org/10.1007/978-3-319-93638-3

Library of Congress Control Number: 2018947318

LNCS Sublibrary: SL4 – Security and Cryptology

This Springer imprint is published by the registered company Springer Nature Switzerland AG
The registered company address is: Gewerbestrasse 11, 6330 Cham, Switzerland

Preface

This volume contains the papers presented at ACISP 2018 – the 23rd Australasian Conference on Information Security and Privacy held during July 11–13, 2018, in Wollongong, Australia. The conference was organized by the Institute of Cybersecurity and Cryptology at the University of Wollongong, which provided wonderful facilities and support.

This year we received 136 submissions of excellent quality from 23 countries around the world. Each submission was allocated to at least three Program Committee members and each paper received on average 2.8 reviews. The submission and review process was supported by the EasyChair conference submission server. In the first stage of the review process, the submitted papers were evaluated by the Program Committee members. In the second stage, the papers were scrutinized during an extensive discussion. Finally, the committee decided to accept 41 regular papers and ten short papers.

Among the accepted regular papers, four papers were nominated as candidates for the Best Paper Award and five papers were nominated as candidates for the Best Student Paper Award. The Program Committee voted for both awards. For the Best Paper Award, two papers were the preferred options with no clear winner and we decided to award the Best Paper to both papers:

- "Secure Publicly Verifiable Computation with Polynomial Commitment in Cloud Computing" by Jian Shen, Dengzhi Liu, Xiaofeng Chen, Xinyi Huang, Jiageng Chen, and Mingwu Zhang
- "Decentralized Blacklistable Anonymous Credentials with Reputation" by Rupeng Yang, Man Ho Au, Qiuliang Xu, and Zuoxia Yu

The Best Student Paper was awarded to the paper:

- "Asymmetric Subversion Attacks on Signature Schemes" by Chi Liu, Rongmao Chen, Yi Wang, and Yongjun Wang

The Jennifer Seberry Lecture this year was delivered by Prof. Wanlei Zhou from the University of Technology Sydney, Australia. The program also included three invited talks presented by Prof. Robert Deng from Singapore Management University, Singapore; Prof. Patrizio Campisi from the Roma Tre University, Italy; and Dr. Surya Nepal from CSIRO/Data61, Australia.

We would like to thank the Program Committee members and the external reviewers for their effort and time to evaluate the submissions, and our sponsors — School of Computing and Information Technology at the University of Wollongong, Springer, DATA61, Australian Government Department of Defence Science and Technology

(DST), *Cryptography* - Open Access Journal by MDPI, and New South Wales (NSW) Cyber Security Network, Australia, NSW Office of the Chief Scientist and Engineer, iTree and Thinking Studio — for their generous support to the conference. We are indebted to the team at Springer for their continuous support of the conference and for their help in the production of the conference proceedings.

July 2018

Willy Susilo
Guomin Yang

ACISP 2018

The 23rd Australasian Conference on Information Security and Privacy
University of Wollongong, Australia
July 11–13, 2018

Program Chairs

Willy Susilo	University of Wollongong, Australia
Guomin Yang	University of Wollongong, Australia

General Chairs

Yi Mu	University of Wollongong, Australia
Fuchun Guo	University of Wollongong, Australia

Publication Chairs

Joonsang Baek	University of Wollongong, Australia
Yang-Wai Chow	University of Wollongong, Australia

Organization Chair

Jianchang Lai	University of Wollongong, Australia

Program Committee

Masayuki Abe	NTT, Japan
Cristina Alcaraz	University of Malaga, Spain
Man Ho Au	Hong Kong Polytechnic University, SAR China
Shi Bai	Florida Atlantic University, USA
Zubair Baig	Edith Cowan University, Australia
Paulo Barreto	University of Washington, USA
Colin Boyd	Norwegian University of Science and Technology, Norway
Aniello Castiglione	University of Salerno, Italy
Jinjun Chen	Swinburne University of Technology, Australia
Liqun Chen	University of Surrey, UK
Rongmao Chen	National University of Defense Technology, China
Xiaofeng Chen	Xidian University, China
Kim-Kwang Raymond Choo	University of Texas at San Antonio, USA

Ernesto Damiani	University of Milan, Italy
Naccache David	Ecole Normale Suprieure, France
Yvo Desmedt	University of Texas at Dallas, USA
Josep Domingo-Ferrer	Universitat Rovira i Virgili, Spain
Ernest Foo	Queensland University of Technology, Australia
David Galindo	University of Birmingham, UK
Jian Guo	Nanyang Technological University, Singapore
Gerhard Hancke	City University of Hong Kong, SAR China
Qiong Huang	South China Agricultural University, China
Xinyi Huang	Fujian Normal University, China
Dong Seong Kim	University of Canterbury, New Zealand
Jongkil Kim	University of Wollongong, Australia
Noboru Kunihiro	The University of Tokyo, Japan
Fabien Laguillaumie	Université de Lyon 1/LIP, France
Dongxi Liu	CSIRO/Data61, Australia
Joseph Liu	Monash University, Australia
Zhe Liu	Nanjing University of Aeronautics and Astronautics, China
Zhen Liu	Shanghai Jiao Tong University, China
Javier Lopez	University of Malaga, Spain
Hui Ma	Chinese Academy of Sciences, China
Mark Manulis	University of Surrey, UK
Mitsuru Matsui	Mitsubishi Electric, Japan
Kazuhiko Minematsu	NEC Corporation, Japan
Chris Mitchell	Royal Holloway, University of London, UK
Khoa Nguyen	Nanyang Technological University, Singapore
Thomas Peyrin	Nanyang Technological University, Singapore
Duong Hieu Phan	XLIM (Limoges University), France
Josef Pieprzyk	CSIRO/Data61, Australia
Reza Reyhanitabar	Katholieke Universiteit Leuven, Belgium
Reyhaneh Safavi-Naini	University of Calgary, Canada
Pierangela Samarati	University of Milan, Italy
Marcos Simplicio	University of São Paulo, Brazil
Leonie Simpson	Queensland University of Technology, Australia
Ron Steinfeld	Monash University, Australia
Atsushi Takayasu	University of Tokyo, Japan
Qiang Tang	Cornell University, USA
Damien Vergnaud	Université Pierre et Marie Curie/Institut Universitaire de France, France
Huaxiong Wang	Nanyang Technological University, Singapore
Qianhong Wu	Beihang University, China
Yong Yu	Shaanxi Normal University, China
Yu Yu	Shanghai Jiao Tong University, China
Jiang Zhang	Chinese Academy of Sciences, China
Mingwu Zhang	Hubei University of Technology, China
Rui Zhang	Chinese Academy of Sciences, China

Additional Reviewers

Acien, Antonio
Al Maqbali, Fatma
Andrade, Ewerton
Anglès-Tafalla, Carles
Avizheh, Sepideh
Baek, Joonsang
Banik, Subhadeep
Bao, Zhenzhen
Bert, Pauline
Blanco-Justicia, Alberto
Bouvier, Cyril
Chen, Haixia
Chen, Long
Chengjun Lin
Chotard, Jérémy
Cominetti, Eduardo
Cui, Yuzhao
Dragan, Constantin Catalin
Du, Jiangyi
Duong, Tuyet
Gaborit, Philippe
Germouty, Paul
Gong, Junqing
Guo, Chun
Guo, Fuchun
Guo, Qingwen
Haitao, Xie
Han, Jinguang
Han, Shangbin
Hauteville, Adrien
Herold, Gottfried
Herranz, Javier
Hu, Kexin
Hu, Zhi
Huang, Jianye
Isshiki, Toshiyuki
Jha, Sonu
Jiang, Linzhi
Jiang, Shaoquan
Jiang, Yan
Jiao, Lin
Karati, Sabyasachu
Katsumata, Shuichi
Kim, Jongkil
Kito, Keisuke
Lai, Jianchang
Leontiadis, Iraklis
Li, Hongbo
Li, Shuai
Li, Sujuan
Li, Xiangxue
Li, Yalan
Li, Yannan
Lin, Changlu
Lin, Cheng-Jun
Lin, Fuchun
Liu, Guozhen
Liu, Hanlin
Liu, Yihuan
Liu, Zhiqiang
Lu, Xingye
Lu, Yuan
Murilo, Cezar
Naito, Yusuke
Nitaj, Abderrahmane
Ohigashi, Toshihiro
Pan, Yanbin
Parra-Arnau, Javier
Parry, Jack
Qin, Baodong
Ribes-González, Jordi
Ricardini, Jefferson E.
Ricci, Sara
Rios, Ruben
Rossetti, Jonatas
Ruan, Ou
Rubio, Juan E.
Sakai, Yusuke
Sakzad, Amin
Sehrawat, Vipin
Sen Gupta, Sourav
Sharifian, Setareh
Shen, Hua
Shuangyu, He
Silva, Marcos
Soria-Comas, Jordi

Sriskandarajah, Shriparen
Sun, Shuo
Suzuki, Daisuke
Takahashi, Akira
Takashima, Katsuyuki
Tan, Benjamin Hong Meng
Tan, Gaosheng
Tang, Wenyi
Tao, Yang
Thorncharoensri, Pairat
Tomida, Junichi
Trinh, Viet Cuong
Wang, Binfeng
Wang, Hao
Wang, Haoyang
Wang, Weijia
Wang, Xi
Wang, Yi
Wu, Ge
Wu, Tong
Xu, Yanhong
Yamada, Shota
Yamamoto, Takumi
Yang, Kang
Yang, Rupeng
Yang, Shao-Jun
Yu, Zuoxia
Zhang, Kai
Zhang, Ren
Zhang, Yanhua
Zhang, Yuexin
Zhao, Lan
Zhou, Sufang

Contents

Foundation

A Deterministic Algorithm for Computing Divisors in an Interval 3
Liqiang Peng, Yao Lu, Noboru Kunihiro, Rui Zhang, and Lei Hu

Reusable Fuzzy Extractor from LWE. 13
Yunhua Wen and Shengli Liu

A Reusable Fuzzy Extractor with Practical Storage Size: Modifying Canetti *et al.*'s Construction 28
Jung Hee Cheon, Jinhyuck Jeong, Dongwoo Kim, and Jongchan Lee

21 - Bringing Down the Complexity: Fast Composable Protocols for Card Games Without Secret State 45
Bernardo David, Rafael Dowsley, and Mario Larangeira

Efficient Bit-Decomposition and Modulus-Conversion Protocols with an Honest Majority 64
Ryo Kikuchi, Dai Ikarashi, Takahiro Matsuda, Koki Hamada, and Koji Chida

Verifiable Secret Sharing Based on Hyperplane Geometry with Its Applications to Optimal Resilient Proactive Cryptosystems. 83
Zhe Xia, Liuying Sun, Bo Yang, Yanwei Zhou, and Mingwu Zhang

Towards Round-Optimal Secure Multiparty Computations: Multikey FHE Without a CRS 101
Eunkyung Kim, Hyang-Sook Lee, and Jeongeun Park

Robust Multiparty Computation with Faster Verification Time 114
Souradyuti Paul and Ananya Shrivastava

Symmetric-Key Cryptography

Distributed Time-Memory Tradeoff Attacks on Ciphers (with Application to Stream Ciphers and Counter Mode) 135
Howard M. Heys

New Iterated RC4 Key Correlations 154
Ryoma Ito and Atsuko Miyaji

A New Framework for Finding Nonlinear Superpolies in Cube Attacks Against Trivium-Like Ciphers 172
Chendong Ye and Tian Tian

Differential Attacks on Reduced Round LILLIPUT 188
Nicolas Marrière, Valérie Nachef, and Emmanuel Volte

Bounds on Differential and Linear Branch Number of Permutations 207
Sumanta Sarkar and Habeeb Syed

Keyed Sponge with Prefix-Free Padding: Independence Between Capacity and Online Queries Without the Suffix Key 225
Yusuke Naito

Public-Key Cryptography

Forward-Secure Linkable Ring Signatures 245
Xavier Boyen and Thomas Haines

Revocable Identity-Based Encryption from the Computational Diffie-Hellman Problem 265
Ziyuan Hu, Shengli Liu, Kefei Chen, and Joseph K. Liu

Private Functional Signatures: Definition and Construction 284
Shimin Li, Bei Liang, and Rui Xue

Linkable Group Signature for Auditing Anonymous Communication 304
Haibin Zheng, Qianhong Wu, Bo Qin, Lin Zhong, Shuangyu He, and Jianwei Liu

Auditable Hierarchy-Private Public-Key Encryption 322
Lin Zhong, Qianhong Wu, Bo Qin, Haibin Zheng, and Jianwei Liu

Key-Updatable Public-Key Encryption with Keyword Search: Models and Generic Constructions 341
Hiroaki Anada, Akira Kanaoka, Natsume Matsuzaki, and Yohei Watanabe

Anonymous Identity-Based Encryption with Identity Recovery 360
Xuecheng Ma, Xin Wang, and Dongdai Lin

Asymmetric Subversion Attacks on Signature Schemes 376
Chi Liu, Rongmao Chen, Yi Wang, and Yongjun Wang

Cloud Security

Intrusion-Resilient Public Auditing Protocol for Data Storage in Cloud Computing 399
Yan Xu, Ran Ding, Jie Cui, and Hong Zhong

Secure Publicly Verifiable Computation with Polynomial Commitment in Cloud Computing 417
Jian Shen, Dengzhi Liu, Xiaofeng Chen, Xinyi Huang, Jiageng Chen, and Mingwu Zhang

Privacy-Preserving Mining of Association Rule on Outsourced Cloud Data from Multiple Parties 431
Lin Liu, Jinshu Su, Rongmao Chen, Ximeng Liu, Xiaofeng Wang, Shuhui Chen, and Hofung Leung

Post-quantum Cryptography

Cryptanalysis of the Randomized Version of a Lattice-Based Signature Scheme from PKC'08 455
Haoyu Li, Renzhang Liu, Abderrahmane Nitaj, and Yanbin Pan

Complete Attack on RLWE Key Exchange with Reused Keys, Without Signal Leakage 467
Jintai Ding, Scott Fluhrer, and Saraswathy Rv

Efficient Decryption Algorithms for Extension Field Cancellation Type Encryption Schemes 487
Yacheng Wang, Yasuhiko Ikematsu, Dung Hoang Duong, and Tsuyoshi Takagi

Lattice-Based Universal Accumulator with Nonmembership Arguments 502
Zuoxia Yu, Man Ho Au, Rupeng Yang, Junzuo Lai, and Qiuliang Xu

Lattice-Based Dual Receiver Encryption and More 520
Daode Zhang, Kai Zhang, Bao Li, Xianhui Lu, Haiyang Xue, and Jie Li

Anonymous Identity-Based Hash Proof System from Lattices in the Standard Model 539
Qiqi Lai, Bo Yang, Yong Yu, Yuan Chen, and Liju Dong

Post-Quantum One-Time Linkable Ring Signature and Application to Ring Confidential Transactions in Blockchain (Lattice RingCT v1.0) 558
Wilson Abel Alberto Torres, Ron Steinfeld, Amin Sakzad, Joseph K. Liu, Veronika Kuchta, Nandita Bhattacharjee, Man Ho Au, and Jacob Cheng

Security Protocol

Secure Contactless Payment 579
Handan Kılınç and Serge Vaudenay

New Attacks and Secure Design for Anonymous Distance-Bounding 598
Ahmad Ahmadi, Reihaneh Safavi-Naini, and Mamunur Akand

System and Network Security

Automatically Identifying Security Bug Reports via Multitype Features Analysis 619
Deqing Zou, Zhijun Deng, Zhen Li, and Hai Jin

A Practical Privacy Preserving Protocol in Database-Driven Cognitive Radio Networks 634
Yali Zeng, Xu Li, Xu Yang, Qikui Xu, and Dongcheng Wang

TDDAD: Time-Based Detection and Defense Scheme Against DDoS Attack on SDN Controller 649
Jie Cui, Jiantao He, Yan Xu, and Hong Zhong

Blockchain and Cryptocurrency

Fast Lottery-Based Micropayments for Decentralized Currencies 669
Kexin Hu and Zhenfeng Zhang

Z-Channel: Scalable and Efficient Scheme in Zerocash 687
Yuncong Zhang, Yu Long, Zhen Liu, Zhiqiang Liu, and Dawu Gu

Revisiting the Incentive Mechanism of Bitcoin-NG 706
Jiayuan Yin, Changren Wang, Zongyang Zhang, and Jianwei Liu

Decentralized Blacklistable Anonymous Credentials with Reputation 720
Rupeng Yang, Man Ho Au, Qiuliang Xu, and Zuoxia Yu

Short Papers

Revocable Certificateless Encryption with Ciphertext Evolution 741
Yinxia Sun, Futai Zhang, and Anmin Fu

A New Encryption Scheme Based on Rank Metric Codes 750
Terry Shue Chien Lau and Chik How Tan

Enhancing Intelligent Alarm Reduction for Distributed Intrusion Detection Systems via Edge Computing 759
Weizhi Meng, Yu Wang, Wenjuan Li, Zhe Liu, Jin Li, and Christian W. Probst

Live Path CFI Against Control Flow Hijacking Attacks 768
Mohamad Barbar, Yulei Sui, Hongyu Zhang, Shiping Chen, and Jingling Xue

Security Analysis and Modification of ID-Based Encryption with Equality Test from ACISP 2017 780
Hyung Tae Lee, Huaxiong Wang, and Kai Zhang

Improving the BKZ Reduction Algorithm by Quick Reordering Technique 787
Yuntao Wang and Tsuyoshi Takagi

ANTSdroid: Automatic Malware Family Behaviour Generation and Analysis for Android Apps 796
Yeali S. Sun, Chien-Chun Chen, Shun-Wen Hsiao, and Meng Chang Chen

Constant-Size CCA-Secure Multi-hop Unidirectional Proxy Re-encryption from Indistinguishability Obfuscation 805
Junzuo Lai, Zhengan Huang, Man Ho Au, and Xianping Mao

Practical Signatures from the Partial Fourier Recovery Problem Revisited: A Provably-Secure and Gaussian-Distributed Construction 813
Xingye Lu, Zhenfei Zhang, and Man Ho Au

CRT-KPS: A Key Predistribution Schemes Using CRT 821
Pinaki Sarkar, Mayank Baranwal, and Sukumar Nandi

Correction to: Fast Lottery-Based Micropayments for Decentralized Currencies C1
Kexin Hu and Zhenfeng Zhang

Author Index 831

Foundation

A Deterministic Algorithm for Computing Divisors in an Interval

Liqiang Peng[1,2], Yao Lu[1,2,3](✉), Noboru Kunihiro[3], Rui Zhang[1], and Lei Hu[1,2]

[1] State Key Laboratory of Information Security, Institute of Information Engineering, Chinese Academy of Sciences, Beijing 100 093, China
{pengliqiang,r-zhang}@iie.ac.cn, hu@is.ac.cn

[2] Data Assurance and Communication Security Research Center, Chinese Academy of Sciences, Beijing 100 093, China

[3] The University of Tokyo, Tokyo, Japan

Abstract. We revisit the problem of finding a nontrivial divisor of a composite integer when it has a divisor in an interval $[\alpha, \beta]$. We use Strassen's algorithm to solve this problem. Compared with Kim-Cheon's algorithms (Math Comp 84(291): 339–354, 2015), our method is a deterministic algorithm but with the same complexity as Kim-Cheon's probabilistic algorithm, and our algorithm does not need to impose that the divisor is prime. In addition, we can further speed up the theoretical complexity of Kim-Cheon's algorithms and our algorithm by a logarithmic term $\log(\beta - \alpha)$ based on the peculiar property of polynomial arithmetic we consider.

Keywords: Integer factorization · Divisors in an interval
Polynomial arithmetic

1 Introduction

RSA is the most widely deployed public-key cryptosystem. Its security relies on the difficulty of factoring large composite integer: if integer factorization is solved then RSA is broken. Factoring large numbers is long been believed as a mathematical hard problem in computational number theory. Now it is conjectured that integer factorization cannot be solved in polynomial-time without quantum computers.

However, even if integer factorization is indeed difficult to solve, one has to be very careful against the side-channel attacks, which is any attack based on information gained from the physical implementation of cryptosystems.

In this paper, we focus on the problem of integer factorization given the approximation of divisors. More precisely, we mainly focus on finding a nontrivial divisor of a composite integer N when it has a divisor in an interval $[\alpha, \beta]$.

It is clear that this problem can be solved in $\mathcal{O}(\beta - \alpha)$ time with trial division. However, based on the bit-size of parameters α and β, more efficient algorithms exist.

W. Susilo and G. Yang (Eds.): ACISP 2018, LNCS 10946, pp. 3–12, 2018.
https://doi.org/10.1007/978-3-319-93638-3_1

- For sufficiently small interval bit-size $\beta - \alpha$: Using Coppersmith's method [5] of finding small roots of modular polynomial equations, we can recover all divisors in the interval in polynomial time in $\log N$.
- For relatively small α and large β: Using Pollard's rho method [12], we can find a nontrivial divisor in $\mathcal{O}(\beta^{1/2})$ time.
- For large α and large $\beta - \alpha$: Using Kim-Cheon's algorithms [10], we can recover a nontrivial divisor in $\widetilde{\mathcal{O}}((\beta - \alpha)^{1/2})$ time.

Specifically, in [10], Kim and Cheon proposed two algorithms, one is probabilistic and the other is its deterministic version, for achieving birthday complexity in finding a divisor in an interval. Using their proposed algorithms, one can check the existence of prime divisors in the interval, and if they exist, one can find all such prime divisors.

Compared with Kim-Cheon's probabilistic algorithm, their deterministic algorithm is more complex, difficult to understand, and needs more time complexity. Besides, for the case of composite divisors, their probabilistic algorithm works well, but their deterministic algorithm fails. Therefore, Kim and Cheon posted as an open problem to design a deterministic algorithm for composite divisors.

1.1 Our Contributions

In this paper, we propose a deterministic algorithm to find a nontrivial divisor of a composite integer N when it has a divisor in an interval $[\alpha, \beta]$. Our deterministic algorithm has the same time complexity as Kim-Cheon's probabilistic algorithm, and also works for the case of composite divisors. In addition, we can further speed up the theoretical complexity of Kim-Cheon's algorithms and our algorithm by a logarithmic term $\log(\beta - \alpha)$ based on the peculiar property of polynomial arithmetic we consider.

Technically, recall that Kim-Cheon's algorithm reduces the target problem to solving a discrete logarithm problem over $(\mathbb{Z}/n\mathbb{Z})^*$, where n is an unknown divisor of the known integer N. We view the original problem from a different perspective: we relate the original problem to a variant of deterministic integer factorization problem, and then use Strassen's algorithm [13,14] to solve it. More precisely, let $p = \beta - x$ be a divisor of N in the interval $[\alpha, \beta]$, where $x \in [0, \beta - \alpha]$ is unknown. Then the problem of finding p can be transformed to computing $\gcd(N, \beta - x)$. Although x is unknown, we can use $\gcd\left(N, \prod_{i=0}^{\beta-\alpha}(\beta - i) \pmod{N}\right)$ to find p. Therefore, how to calculate $\prod_{i=0}^{\beta-\alpha}(\beta - i) \pmod{N}$ efficiently becomes the key point of the complexity.

Moreover, recently Chen and Nguyen [4] used a similar algorithm as Strassen's algorithm to solve Approximate Common Divisor Problem, the later was introduced by Howgrave-Graham [9] in CaLC 2001.

2 Preliminaries

Let a and b be integers. Let $\nu_a(b)$ denote the nonnegative integer such that $a^{\nu_a(b)} \mid b$ and $a^{\nu_a(b)+1} \nmid b$. Denote $[\alpha, \beta]$ as the set of all integers $\alpha \leq i \leq \beta$. Let $|\beta - \alpha|_2$ denote the bit-size of $\beta - \alpha$. We will use log for the binary (base 2) logarithm. Let $M(d)$ be the complexity of the multiplication of two polynomial with degree d [1]:

$$M(d) = \mathcal{O}(d \log d \log \log d).$$

In this paper, we consider the univariate polynomial $f(x) \in \mathbb{Z}_N[x]$ with N an arbitrary integer. We will use two polynomial arithmetic algorithms, $\mathbf{Alg}_{Poly}$ (compute a polynomial given as a product of d terms) and $\mathbf{Alg}_{MPE}$ (evaluate a univariate polynomial with degree d at d points), as subroutines. It is clear that we can solve them using $\mathcal{O}(d^2)$ additions and multiplications in $\mathbb{Z}_N$. However, there are classic algorithms with quasi-linear complexity operations in $\mathbb{Z}_N$ using a divide-and-conquer approach. Recently these two algorithms have been used in various area of public-key cryptanalysis [4,6,8]. We give the basic information of these two algorithms as follows:

$\mathbf{Alg}_{Poly}$: Takes integer N and d points (suppose that $a_0, \ldots, a_{d-1}$) as inputs; outputs a monic degree d polynomial over $\mathbb{Z}_N$ having d points as roots: $f(X) = \prod_{i=0}^{d-1}(X - a_i) (\bmod N)$. According to a classic result [1], the time complexity is $\mathcal{O}(\log d M(d))$ operations modulo N, and the storage requirement is $\mathcal{O}(d \log d)$ elements in $\mathbb{Z}_N$.

$\mathbf{Alg}_{MPE}$: Takes integer N, a polynomial $f(x)$ with degree d over $\mathbb{Z}_N$ and d points (suppose that $c_0, \ldots, c_{d-1}$) as inputs; outputs the evaluation of $f(x)$ at d input points: $f(c_0), \ldots, f(c_{d-1}) (\bmod N)$. According to a classic result [1], the time complexity is $\mathcal{O}(\log d M(d))$ operations modulo N, and the storage requirement is $\mathcal{O}(d \log d)$ elements in $\mathbb{Z}_N$.

3 Review Kim-Cheon's Algorithms

In this section, we will review Kim-Cheon's two algorithms: one is probabilistic and the other is its deterministic version. Their algorithms essentially work by solving the discrete logarithm problem over $(\mathbb{Z}/n\mathbb{Z})^*$, where n is an unknown divisor of the target composite integer N. Before given the full description of Kim-Cheon's algorithms, we would like to introduce a lemma from [10]:

Lemma 1. *There exists an algorithm FINDING which, given as input positive integers N, g, h, and δ with $1 < g, h < N$, $\gcd(gh, N) = 1$, outputs an integer $x \in [1, \delta]$ with $\gcd(g^x - h, N) > 1$ or shows that no such x exists in*

$$\mathcal{O}\left(M(\delta^{1/2}) \log \delta\right)$$

operations modulo N by using storage $\mathcal{O}(\delta^{1/2} \log \delta)$ elements in $\mathbb{Z}_N$.

We recall the *FINDING* algorithm, given as Algortihm 1.

Algorithm 1. $x \leftarrow FINDING(N, g, h, \delta)$

Input: Positive integers N, g, h and δ with $1 < g, h < N$, $\gcd(gh, N) = 1$.
Output: An integer $x \in [1, \delta]$ satisfying $\gcd(g^x - h, N) > 1$.

Set $L := \lceil \delta^{1/2} \rceil$.
Compute the polynomial

$$F(X) = \prod_{0 \leq i \leq L-1} (X - hg^i) \bmod N$$

using Algorithm $\mathbf{Alg}_{Poly}$.
Evaluate $F(X)$ at multiple points g^{jL} for all $1 \leq j \leq L$ using Algorithm $\mathbf{Alg}_{MPE}$
$j := 1$
while $j \leq L$ **do**
  $d_j = \gcd(F(g^{jL}), N)$
  if $d_j > 1$ **then**
    Find the great u satisfying $\gcd(g^{jL} - hg^u, N) > 1$.
    Output $x := jL - u$ and stop.
  end if
  $j := j + 1$
end while
Output "there is no such x" and stop.

The complexity of Algorithm *FINDING* mainly relies on the complexity of $\mathbf{Alg}_{Poly}$ and $\mathbf{Alg}_{MPE}$, thus the overall complexity is $\mathcal{O}\left(\log \delta M(\delta^{1/2})\right)$ operations modulo N with using storage $\mathcal{O}(\delta^{1/2} \log \delta)$ elements in $\mathbb{Z}_N$.

Now we review Kim-Cheon's probabilistic algorithm for computing a nontrivial divisor of a composite integer N, given as Algortihm 2.

Algortihm 2 takes $\mathcal{O}\left(M((\beta - \alpha)^{1/2}) \log(\beta - \alpha)\right)$ operations modulo N. The storage requirement is $\mathcal{O}((\beta - \alpha)^{1/2} \log(\beta - \alpha))$ elements in $\mathbb{Z}_N$. In [10], Kim and Cheon showed that Algortihm 2 succeeds with a probability of at least 1/2.

Kim-Cheon's Deterministic Algorithm. Since we do not know exactly how many a's are to be tested or how to choose a to split N in Algortihm 2, hence, the algorithm works probabilistically. Therefore, Kim and Cheon proposed a deterministic algorithm to overcome this problem, the key tool of their deterministic algorithm was the distribution of smooth numbers, which was originally used for devising a deterministic primality test under some condition by Konyagin and Pomerance [11]. We omit the details of their algorithm here, instead, we refer to [10]. Obviously, Kim-Cheon's probabilistic algorithm performs better than their deterministic algorithm.

4 Our Deterministic Algorithm

In this section, we propose a deterministic algorithm to find a nontrivial divisor of a composite integer N when it has a divisor in an interval $[\alpha, \beta]$. Our algorithm

Algorithm 2. Kim-Cheon's probabilistic algorithm for computing a nontrivial divisor of a composite integer N

Input: A composite integer N with unknown factorization and an interval $[\alpha, \beta]$.
Output: A nontrivial divisor of N when it has a divisor in an interval $[\alpha, \beta]$.

Choose an integer a uniformly at random in $\{2, \ldots, N-1\}$.
if $\gcd(a, N) > 1$ **then**
  output $\gcd(a, N)$ and stop.
end if
Compute $x_a \in [1, \beta - \alpha]$ such that $d = \gcd(a^{x_a} - a^{\beta-1} \mod N, N) > 1$ by applying subalgorithm *FINDING* (**Alg.1**).
if there is no such x_a **then**
  output "N has no prime divisor in the interval $[\alpha, \beta]$)" and stop.
end if
if $d < N$ **then**
  output d and stop.
end if
if $d = N$ and $y_a := \beta - 1 - x_a$ is even **then**
  $i := 1$
  while $i \leq \nu_2(y_a)$ **do**
    compute $d_i = \gcd(a^{y_a/2^i} - 1, N)$
    if $1 < d_i < N$ **then**
      output d_i and stop
    end if
    $i := i + 1$
  end while
end if
Output "failure" and stop.

has the same time complexity as Kim-Cheon's probabilistic algorithm, and also works for the case of composite divisors.

4.1 Algorithmic Details

Now we show how to reduce the target problem to a variant of integer factorization problem. Let p be the divisor of N in the interval $[\alpha, \beta]$. At first, we can write p as

$$p = \beta - x$$

where x is an unknown variable satisfying $0 \leq x \leq \beta - \alpha$. Then in this case, we are given one exact multiple $N (N \equiv 0 \bmod p)$ and one integer $\beta = p + x$, and the goal is to learn the divisor p. Here, we do not require that p is prime.

Next we give our algorithm based on Strassen's algorithm [13,14] for solving the integer factorization problem. It is clear that

$$p = \gcd\left(N, \prod_{i=0}^{\beta-\alpha} (\beta - i) \ (\bmod N)\right)$$

The key problem is how to calculate $\prod_{i=0}^{\beta-\alpha}(\beta-i) \pmod N$ faster.

To calculate faster, we require the degree of polynomial be a power of two. Let $|\beta-\alpha|_2 = l$. Therefore, we focus on

$$p = \gcd\left(N, \prod_{i=0}^{2^l-1}(\beta-i) \pmod N\right)$$

Set $l^* = \lceil l/2 \rceil$, we can rewrite it as

$$\prod_{i=0}^{2^l-1}(\beta-i) \pmod N = \prod_{i=0}^{2^{l^*-(l \bmod 2)}-1}\prod_{j=0}^{2^{l^*}-1}(\beta-2^{l^*}i-j) \pmod N$$

We define the polynomial $f_j(x)$ of degree j modulo integer N:

$$f_j(x) = \prod_{k=0}^{j-1}(\beta-x-k) \pmod N$$

Therefore, we have

$$\prod_{i=0}^{2^l-1}(\beta-i) \pmod N = \prod_{i=0}^{2^{l^*-(l \bmod 2)}-1} f_{2^{l^*}}(2^{l^*}i) \pmod N$$

which means

$$p = \gcd\left(N, \prod_{i=0}^{2^{l^*-(l \bmod 2)}-1} f_{2^{l^*}}(2^{l^*}i) \pmod N\right)$$

We need to compute the polynomial $f_{2^{l^*}}(x)$ explicitly and evaluate this polynomial at $2^{l^*-(l \bmod 2)}$ points, which can fortunately be done using $\mathbf{Alg}_{Poly}$ and $\mathbf{Alg}_{MPE}$. We give a full description of our algorithm as follows.

In our algorithm, the condition $d = 1$ means that there is no divisor in the interval $[\alpha, \beta]$ and if $1 < d \leq \beta$, d is the divisor what we want. However, if there are more than one divisors in the interval $[\alpha, \beta]$, we will obtain that $d > \beta$. According to the Strassen's algorithm, for this case we can use a trick of computing greatest common divisor based on a product tree to determine which $f_{2^{l^*}}(2^{l^*}k)$, where $1 \leq k \leq 2^{l^*-(l \bmod 2)}$ has only one divisor. Algorithm 4 gives a brief description of this trick. Note that, if it is still that $\gcd(N, f_{2^{l^*}}(2^{l^*}k)) > \beta$ which means there are still more than one divisors of N fall in the same interval $[\beta - 2^{l^*}(k+1)+1, \beta - 2^{l^*}k]$, we can further use same trick as Algorithm 4 to construct a product tree based on the following expression

$$f_{2^{l^*}}(2^{l^*}k) = \prod_{i=0}^{2^{l^*}-1}(\beta - 2^{l^*}k - i) \pmod N.$$

Algorithm 3. Our deterministic algorithm for computing a nontrivial divisor of a composite integer N

Input: A composite integer N with unknown factorization and an interval $[\alpha, \beta]$.
Output: A nontrivial divisor of N when it has a divisor in an interval $[\alpha, \beta]$.

```
Set l* = ⌈|β − α|_2/2⌉.
Compute the polynomial f_{2^{l*}}(x) using Alg_Poly.
Evaluate f_{2^{l*}}(x) at multiple points 2^{l*}k for all 1 ≤ k ≤ 2^{l* − (l mod 2)} using
    Alg_MPE.
Compute d = gcd(N, f_{2^{l*}}(1) f_{2^{l*}}(2) ··· f_{2^{l*}}(2^{l* − (l mod 2)}) mod N).
if d = 1 then
    output "there is no divisor in interval [α, β]" and stop.
end if
if 1 < d ≤ β then
    output d and stop.
end if
if β < d ≤ N then
    compute a divisor in an interval [α, β], using Algorithm 4.
end if
```

Then the divisor in the interval $[\alpha, \beta]$ can be finally determined.

Now, we analyze the complexity of Algorithm 3. The complexity of $\mathbf{Alg}_{Poly}$ and $\mathbf{Alg}_{MPE}$ takes $\mathcal{O}\left(\log(\beta-\alpha) M((\beta-\alpha)^{1/2})\right)$ operations modulo N and the storage requirement is $\mathcal{O}((\beta-\alpha)^{1/2}\log(\beta-\alpha))$ elements in $\mathbb{Z}_N$. In addition, we need GCD computations at most $2\log(\beta-\alpha)^{1/2}$ times and $\mathcal{O}((\beta-\alpha)^{1/2})$ multiplications on modulo N. Therefore, the complexity of our algorithm mainly relies on the complexity of $\mathbf{Alg}_{Poly}$ and $\mathbf{Alg}_{MPE}$, just like Kim-Cheon's probabilistic algorithm our deterministic algorithm takes $\mathcal{O}\left(\log(\beta-\alpha) M((\beta-\alpha)^{1/2})\right)$ operations modulo N.

4.2 Logarithmic Speedup

The complexity of Kim-Cheon's algorithms and our algorithm mainly relies on $\mathbf{Alg}_{Poly}$ and $\mathbf{Alg}_{MPE}$. However, since the peculiar property of these polynomials we consider, hence more efficient algorithms exist. Thus, we can speed up the theoretical complexity of Kim-Cheon's algorithms and our algorithm by a logarithmic term $\log(\beta-\alpha)$.

Revisiting Kim-Cheon's Algorithms. In Algortihm 1, they want to compute the polynomial $F(X) = \prod_{0 \le i \le L-1}(X - hg^i) \bmod N$ and evaluate $F(x)$ at points $g^L, g^{2L}, \ldots, g^{L^2}$. Notice that both (hg^i) and (g^{iL}) are geometric progressions, hence we can use more efficient algorithm of Bostan et al. [3] to compute polynomial interpolation and polynomial evaluation at a geometric progression. Bostan gave his pseudocode in [2]. This technique can speed up the overall complexity of Kim-Cheon's algorithms by a logarithmic term $\log(\beta-\alpha)$.

Algorithm 4. RecursiveFinding(N, A)

Input: A composite integer N and a set of numbers $\{a_1, \ldots, a_n\}$.
Output: A nontrivial divisor of N in the interval $[\alpha, \beta]$.

```
n' := ⌈n/2⌉
Compute d = gcd(N, ∏_{i=1}^{n'} a_i)
if 1 < d ≤ β then
    output d and stop.
end if
if d = 1 then
    RecursiveFinding(N, {a_{n'+1}, ..., a_n})
end if
if β < d ≤ N then
    RecursiveFinding(N, {a_1, ..., a_{n'}})
end if
```

Revisiting Our Algorithm. Likewise, our deterministic algorithm can also been improved by using a smarter way to calculate the evaluation of function $f_{2^{l^*}}(x)$ at $2^{l^*-(l \bmod 2)}$ points. We use Chen-Nguyen's technique, which based on Bostan, Gaudry and Schost's result [3], to speed up Algortihm 3.

More specifically, Bostan, Gaudry and Schost's result can be described as follows:

Theorem 1 *(Theorem 5 of* [3]*). Let a, b be in ring $\mathbb{R}$ and d be in $\mathbb{N}$ such that $\mathbf{d}(a, b, d)$ is invertible, with $\mathbf{d}(a, b, d) = b \cdot 2 \cdots d \cdot (a - db) \cdots (a + db)$, and suppose that the inverse of $\mathbf{d}(a, b, d)$ is known. Let $F(x)$ be in $\mathbb{R}[X]$ of degree at most d and $r \in \mathbb{R}$. Given $F(r), F(r + b), \ldots, F(r + db)$, one can compute $F(r + a), F(r + a + b), \ldots, F(r + a + db)$ in time $2M(d) + \mathcal{O}(d)$ time and space $\mathcal{O}(d)$. Here, $M(d)$ is the time of multiplying two polynomial of degree at most d.*

Define set $S(k_1, \ldots, k_j) := \{\sum_{i=1}^{j} p_{k_i} 2^{k_i} \mid p_{k_i} \in \{0, 1\}\}$. Suppose that we already have the evaluation of $f_{2^j}(x)$ at points $S(k_{l-j+1}, \ldots, k_l)$, if we can calculate the evaluation of $f_{2^{j+1}}(x)$ at points $S(k_{l-j}, \ldots, k_l)$, then with each iteration, we can evaluate the $f_{2^{l^*}}(x)$ at $2^{l^*-(l \bmod 2)}$ points closer until $j = 2^{l^*}$.

The key technique is how to calculate the evaluation of $f_{2^{j+1}}(x)$ at points $S(k_{l-j}, \ldots, k_l)$ using Theorem 1. For every $X \in S(k_{l-j}, \ldots, k_l)$, we have

$$f_{2^{j+1}}(X) = f_{2^j}(X) \cdot f_{2^j}(X + 2^{j+1})$$

We can easily calculate $f_{2^j}(X)$ and $f_{2^j}(X + 2^{j+1})$ using Theorem 1, and evaluate $f_{2^{j+1}}(x)$ at points $S(k_{l-j}, \ldots, k_l)$.

Note that, our algorithm does not need to impose that the divisor in the interval is prime. However, if we impose that the divisor is prime, we can use the method of [7], proposed by Costa and Harvey, to further speed up the theoretical complexity by removing some elements in the interval that do not contribute any useful information.

5 Conclusion

In this paper we revisit the problem of finding a nontrivial divisor of a composite integer N when it has a divisor in an interval $[\alpha, \beta]$. We present a deterministic algorithm to solve this problem, and our algorithm has the same complexity with Kim-Cheon's probabilistic algorithm. Besides, based on the special structure of polynomial, we give a method to speed up the theoretical complexity of Kim-Cheon's algorithm and our algorithm by a logarithmic term $\log(\beta - \alpha)$.

Acknowledgements. This research was supported the National Natural Science Foundation of China (Grants 61702505, 61472417, 61732021, 61772520), National Cryptography Development Fund (MMJJ20170115, MMJJ20170124) and the Fundamental Theory and Cutting Edge Technology Research Program of Institute of Information Engineering, CAS (Grants Y7Z0341103, Y7Z0321102), JST CREST Grant Number JPMJCR14D6, JSPS KAKENHI Grant Number 16H02780.

References

1. Bluestein, L.I.: A linear filtering approach to the computation of the discrete fourier transform. IEEE Trans. Electroacoust. **18**, 451–466 (1970)
2. Bostan, A.: Algorithmique efficace pour des opérations de base en calcul formel. Ph.D. thesis (2003). École polytechnique (in English)
3. Bostan, A., Gaudry, P., Schost, E.: Linear recurrences with polynomial coefficients and application to integer factorization and Cartier-Manin operator. SIAM J. Comput. **36**(6), 1777–1806 (2007)
4. Chen, Y., Nguyen, P.Q.: Faster algorithms for approximate common divisors: breaking fully-homomorphic-encryption challenges over the integers. In: Pointcheval, D., Johansson, T. (eds.) EUROCRYPT 2012. LNCS, vol. 7237, pp. 502–519. Springer, Heidelberg (2012). https://doi.org/10.1007/978-3-642-29011-4_30
5. Coppersmith, D.: Small solutions to polynomial equations, and low exponent RSA vulnerabilities. J. Cryptol. **10**(4), 233–260 (1997)
6. Coron, J.-S., Joux, A., Mandal, A., Naccache, D., Tibouchi, M.: Cryptanalysis of the RSA subgroup assumption from TCC 2005. In: Catalano, D., Fazio, N., Gennaro, R., Nicolosi, A. (eds.) PKC 2011. LNCS, vol. 6571, pp. 147–155. Springer, Heidelberg (2011). https://doi.org/10.1007/978-3-642-19379-8_9
7. Costa, E., Harvey, D.: Faster deterministic integer factorization. Math. Comput. **83**(285), 339–345 (2014)
8. Fouque, P.-A., Tibouchi, M., Zapalowicz, J.-C.: Recovering private keys generated with weak PRNGs. In: Stam, M. (ed.) IMACC 2013. LNCS, vol. 8308, pp. 158–172. Springer, Heidelberg (2013). https://doi.org/10.1007/978-3-642-45239-0_10
9. Howgrave-Graham, N.: Approximate integer common divisors. In: Silverman, J.H. (ed.) CaLC 2001. LNCS, vol. 2146, pp. 51–66. Springer, Heidelberg (2001). https://doi.org/10.1007/3-540-44670-2_6
10. Kim, M., Cheon, J.H.: Computing prime divisors in an interval. Math. Comp. **84**(291), 339–354 (2015)
11. Konyagin, S., Pomerance, C.: On primes recognizable in deterministic polynomial time. In: Graham, R.L., Nešetřil, J. (eds.) The mathematics of Paul Erdős I. Springer, Heidelberg (1997)

12. Pollard, J.M.: Monte Carlo methods for index computation (mod p). Math. Comp. **32**(143), 918–928 (1978)
13. Pollard, J.M.: Theorems on factorization and primality testing. In: Proceedings of the Cambridge Philosophical Society, vol. 76, pp. 521–528 (1974)
14. Strassen, V.: Einige Resultate *über* Berechnungskomplexit*ät*. Jber. Deutsh. Math. -Verein. **78**(1), 1–8 (1976/1977)

Reusable Fuzzy Extractor from LWE

Yunhua Wen[1,2] and Shengli Liu[1,2,3](✉)

[1] Department of Computer Science and Engineering, Shanghai Jiao Tong University, Shanghai 200240, China
{happyle8,slliu}@sjtu.edu.cn
[2] State Key Laboratory of Cryptology, P.O. Box 5159, Beijing 100878, China
[3] Westone Cryptologic Research Center, Beijing 100070, China

Abstract. Fuzzy extractor converts the reading of a noisy non-uniform source to a reproducible and almost uniform output R. The output R in turn is used in some cryptographic system as a secret key. To enable multiple extractions of keys $\mathsf{R}_1, \mathsf{R}_2, \ldots, \mathsf{R}_\rho$ from the same noisy non-uniform source and applications of different R_i, the concept of reusable fuzzy extractor is proposed to guarantee the pseudorandomness of R_i even conditioned on other extracted keys R_j (from the same source).

In this work, we construct a reusable fuzzy extractor from the Learning With Errors (LWE) assumption. Our reusable fuzzy extractor provides resilience to linear fraction of errors. Moreover, our construction is simple and efficient and imposes no special requirement on the statistical structure of the multiple readings of the source.

Keywords: Fuzzy extractor · Reusability · The LWE assumption

1 Introduction

In a cryptographic system, it is assumed that the secret key is sampled from a random source and uniformly distributed, since the security of the system heavily relies on the uniformity of the secret key. In reality, such a uniform secret key is hard to create, remember or store by users of the system. On the other hand, there are lots of random sources available like biometric data (fingerprint, iris, etc.), physical unclonable function (PUF) [17,18], or quantum information [4,19]. These sources do not provide uniform distributions though they may possess high entropy. Moreover, the readings of the source may introduce errors and only result in noisy versions. To address the issues, *fuzzy extractor* [10] is proposed to allow for reproducible extraction of an almost uniform key from a noisy non-uniform source.

Fuzzy Extractor. A fuzzy extractor consists of two algorithms ($\mathsf{Gen}, \mathsf{Rep}$). The generation algorithm Gen takes as input w (a reading of the source), and outputs a string R and a public helper string P. The reproduction algorithm Rep will reproduce R from w' with the help of P if the distance between w' and w is smaller enough. Note that the difference between w' and w is caused by errors and the

W. Susilo and G. Yang (Eds.): ACISP 2018, LNCS 10946, pp. 13–27, 2018.
https://doi.org/10.1007/978-3-319-93638-3_2

distance of w' and w evaluates the number of errors. Let n be the bit-length of w. We say that the fuzzy extractor supports linear fraction errors if it can correct up to $O(n)$ bits of errors. The security of fuzzy extractor guarantees that if w has enough min-entropy, then R is almost uniform or at least pseudorandom conditioned on P.

With a fuzzy extractor, it is convenient to implement key management for a cryptosystem. For example, a user can distill a uniform and accurately reproducible key R from his biometric data, via the generation algorithm of a fuzzy extractor, i.e., $(\mathsf{P}, \mathsf{R}) \leftarrow \mathsf{Gen}(\mathsf{w})$. Then he uses key R for cryptographic applications. When R is needed again, the user does another reading w' of his biometric data and reproduces R by the Rep algorithm with the help of P, i.e., $\mathsf{R} \leftarrow \mathsf{Rep}(\mathsf{P}, \mathsf{w}')$. During the application, the user never stores R. The public helper string P suffices for the reproduction of R.

Given a source W, multiple extractions of W by the generation algorithm result in multiple distilled key R_j and public helper strings P_j. When those keys R_j are employed in different cryptosystems, it is not desirable that the corruption of R_j endangers the usage of R_i. However, the distilled keys $\{\mathsf{R}_1, \ldots, \mathsf{R}_\rho\}$ are correlated via W. Information theoretically, given $\{(\mathsf{P}_j, \mathsf{R}_j)\}_{j \neq i}$, there might be no entropy left in R_i. Therefore most of the fuzzy extractors do not support multiple extractions of the same source [5–7,16]. This gives rise to another issue: how to support multiple extractions of the same source data? This issue is addressed by *reusable fuzzy extractor.*

Reusable Fuzzy Extractor. Reusable fuzzy extractor was first formalized by Boyen [7]. For multiple correlated samples $(\mathsf{w}, \mathsf{w}_1, \cdots, \mathsf{w}_\rho)$ of the same source, say biometric iris, applying the generation algorithm of reusable fuzzy extractor to $(\mathsf{w}, \mathsf{w}_1, \cdots, \mathsf{w}_\rho)$ respectively results in multiple pairs $(\mathsf{P}, \mathsf{R}), (\mathsf{P}_1, \mathsf{R}_1), \cdots, (\mathsf{P}_\rho, \mathsf{R}_\rho)$. The security of reusable fuzzy extractor asks for the (pseudo)randomness of R conditioned on $(\mathsf{P}, \mathsf{P}_1, \mathsf{R}_1, \cdots, \mathsf{P}_\rho, \mathsf{R}_\rho)$.

In [7], two constructions of reusable fuzzy extractor were presented. One achieves outsider security in the information theoretical setting, the other achieves insider security based on the random oracle model. Both constructions require that the difference $\delta_i = \mathsf{w}_i - \mathsf{w}$ is independent of w. Outsider security is weak in the sense that it only guarantees the randomness of R conditioned on the public helper string $(\mathsf{P}, \mathsf{P}_1, \cdots, \mathsf{P}_\rho)$.

Canetti et al. [8] constructed a reusable fuzzy extractor from a powerful tool "digital locker", and there is no assumption on how multiple readings are correlated. However, their construction can only tolerate sub-linear fraction of errors. Following the paradigm of constructing reusable fuzzy extractor from digital locker [8], Alamélou et.al. [2] built a reusable fuzzy extractor which can tolerate linear fraction of errors. However, "digital locker" is too powerful to find good instantiations. The available digital locker is either instantiated with a hash function modeled as a random oracle or based on a non-standard assumption.

As a promising post-quantum hard problem, the learning with errors (LWE) problem attracts lots of attentions from cryptographers. Great efforts have been and are devoted to the designs of a variety of cryptographic primitives from the

LWE assumption. The first fuzzy extractor from the LWE assumption is due to Fuller et al. [11]. Later, Apon et al. [3] extended the construction of fuzzy extractor to a reusable one. In their security model of reusable fuzzy extractor, the error δ_i can be adaptively manipulated by a probabilistic polynomial-time (PPT) adversary. As their construction uses the same error correction algorithm as [11], it can only tolerate logarithmic fraction of errors, i.e., for an input w of length n, it tolerates $O(\log n)$ errors. Another restriction of their construction is that components of $\mathsf{w} = (\mathsf{w}[1], \mathsf{w}[2], \ldots, \mathsf{w}[n]) \in \mathbb{Z}_q^n$ must be independently chosen according to some distribution χ, where χ is the error distribution in the LWE problem. It is hard to imagine that our biometric data follow discrete Gaussian distributions. Therefore this restriction is unreasonable.

Up to now, no construction is available for reusable fuzzy extractor, which is based on the LWE assumption and supports linear fraction of errors.

1.1 Our Contribution

In this work, we propose a simple and efficient construction of reusable fuzzy extractor based on the LWE assumption. Our security model is similar to [3], where the difference δ_i between the readings is adaptively chosen by a PPT adversary. Compared with the work of Apon et al. [3] which gave the only reusable fuzzy extractor based on the LWE assumption, our construction enjoys the following nice properties.

- Our construction is resilient to linear fraction of errors, whereas the fuzzy extractor in [3] can only tolerate logarithm fraction of errors.
- Our construction imposes no special structure requirement on the input w except that w should have enough entropy (as fuzzy extractors always required). Recall that for an input $\mathsf{w} \in \mathbb{Z}_q^n$, reusable fuzzy extractor by Apon et al. requires that each coordinate of w is chosen independently according to χ, which is the error distribution in the LWE problem.

We stress that our construction is the first reusable fuzzy extractor resilient to linear fraction of errors based on the LWE assumption. In Table 1, we compare our work with previous fuzzy extractor with reusability or from the LWE assumption.

Our Approach. Our construction makes use of a universal hash function and a secure sketch [9]. A secure sketch consists of a pair of algorithms (SS.Gen, SS.Rec) and works as follows. The generation algorithm SS.Gen on input w, outputs a sketch s; the recovery algorithm SS.Rec, on input s, can recover w from w' if w' is close to w. The security of secure sketch guarantees that s does not leak too much information of w.

- To correct errors, we apply secure sketch to w to generate a sketch s.
- To distill a random string, we apply the universal hash function $\mathsf{H_i}$ to w.

Observe that if w has enough min-entropy, then by the security of the secure sketch and the leftover hash lemma, $\mathsf{H_i}(w)$ is statistically indistinguishable from

Table 1. Comparison with some known fuzzy extractor schemes. "Reusability?" asks whether the fuzzy extractor achieves reusability; "Standard Assumption?" asks whether the fuzzy extractor is based on standard assumptions. "Linear Fraction of Errors?" asks whether the scheme can correct linear fraction of errors. "–" represents the scheme is an information theoretical one.

FE Schemes	Reusabiliy?	Standard Assumption?	Linear Fraction of Errors?
FMR13 [11]	✗	✔ (LWE)	✗
DRS04 [10], Boy04 [7]	Weak	—	✔
CFPRS16 [8]	✔	✗	✗
Boy04 [7] ABCG16 [2]	✔	✗	✔
ACEK17 [3]	✔	✔ (LWE)	✗
Ours	✔	✔ (LWE)	✔

uniformly random. However, for multiples readings $(\mathsf{w}, \mathsf{w}_1, \cdots, \mathsf{w}_\rho)$ of the same source, if two reading are identical then the outputs of the hash function will be identical as well. Obviously, this approach is impossible to achieve reusability.

To solve this problem, we do not use the output of the universal hash function $\mathsf{H}_\mathsf{i}(\mathsf{w})$ as the final output of fuzzy extractor. Instead, we use $\mathsf{H}_\mathsf{i}(\mathsf{w})$ as the secret key of a symmetric LWE-based encryption scheme. Then the LWE-based scheme encrypts a randomly distributed string R which serves as the extracted key, and the ciphertext and sketch serve as the public helper string P. At the same time, we require that the universal hash function and secure sketch should be homomorphic. This helps our fuzzy extractor to achieve reusability.

2 Preliminaries

Let λ be the security parameter. Vectors are used in the column form. We use boldface letters to denote vectors or matrices. For a column vector $\mathbf{x}$, let $\mathbf{x}[i]$ denote the i-th element of $\mathbf{x}$. Let $\mathbf{I}_l$ denote the identity matrix of $l \times l$. For a real number x, let $\lfloor x \rceil$ denote the integer closest to x. By $[\rho]$, we denote set $\{1, 2 \cdots, \rho\}$. "PPT" is short for probabilistic polynomial-time. For a distribution X, let $x \leftarrow X$ denote the process of sampling x according to X. For a set $\mathcal{X}$, $x \leftarrow_\$ \mathcal{X}$ denotes choosing x from $\mathcal{X}$ uniformly at random and $|\mathcal{X}|$ denotes the cardinality of the set. We use game-based security proof. Let the notation $\mathsf{G} \Rightarrow 1$ denote the event that game G returns 1, and notion $x \stackrel{\mathsf{G}}{=} y$ denote that x equals y or is computed as y in game G.

2.1 Metric Spaces

A metric space is a set $\mathcal{M}$ with a distance function $\mathsf{dis} \colon \mathcal{M} \times \mathcal{M} \mapsto \mathbb{Z}^+ \cup \{0\}$. In this paper, we consider $\mathcal{M} = \mathcal{F}^n$ for some alphabet $\mathcal{F}$ equipped with the Hamming distance. For any two elements $\mathsf{w}, \mathsf{w}' \in \mathcal{M}$, the Hamming distance $\mathsf{dis}(\mathsf{w}, \mathsf{w}')$ is the number of coordinates in which they differ.

2.2 Min-Entropy and Statistical Distance

Definition 1 (Average Min-Entropy). *For two random variables X and Y, the* average min-entropy *of X given Y is defined by*

$$\widetilde{H}_\infty(X \mid Y) := -\log\left[\mathbb{E}_{y\leftarrow Y}(\max_x \Pr[X = x \mid Y = y])\right].$$

Definition 2 (Statistical Distance). *For two random variables X and Y over a set $\mathcal{M}$, the* statistical distance *of X and Y is given by* $\mathbf{SD}(X, Y) := \frac{1}{2}\sum_{\mathsf{w}\in\mathcal{M}} |\Pr[X = \mathsf{w}] - \Pr[Y = \mathsf{w}]|$. *If $\mathbf{SD}(X, Y) \le \varepsilon$, X and Y are called* ε-statistically indistinguishable, *denoted by $X \overset{\varepsilon}{\approx} Y$.*

2.3 Universal Hashing

Definition 3 (Universal Hash Functions[9]). *A family of hash functions $\mathcal{H} = \{\mathsf{H_i} : \mathcal{X} \to \mathcal{Y} \mid \mathsf{i} \in \mathcal{I}\}$ is universal, if for all $x \ne x' \in \mathcal{X}$, it holds that $\Pr_{\mathsf{i}\leftarrow_\$\mathcal{I}}[\mathsf{H_i}(x) = \mathsf{H_i}(x')] \le \frac{1}{|\mathcal{Y}|}$.*

Concrete Construction of Universal Hash Functions. Let q be a prime. For $\mathbf{w} \in \mathbb{Z}_q^{l'}$, $\mathbf{A} \in \mathbb{Z}_q^{nl\times l'}$, define

$$\mathsf{H}_\mathbf{A}(\mathbf{w}) := \mathbf{A}\mathbf{w}, \tag{1}$$

then $\mathcal{H} = \{\mathsf{H}_\mathbf{A} : \mathbb{Z}_q^{l'} \to \mathbb{Z}_q^{nl} \mid \mathbf{A} \in \mathbb{Z}_q^{nl\times l'}\}$ is a family of universal hash functions.

Note that the above hash function is homomorphic in the sense that

$$\mathsf{H}_\mathbf{A}(\mathbf{w} + \mathbf{w}') = \mathbf{A}(\mathbf{w} + \mathbf{w}') = \mathbf{A}\mathbf{w} + \mathbf{A}\mathbf{w}' = \mathsf{H}_\mathbf{A}(\mathbf{w}) + \mathsf{H}_\mathbf{A}(\mathbf{w}'). \tag{2}$$

One can easily interpret a vector in $\mathbb{Z}_q^{nl}$ as a matrix in $\mathbb{Z}_q^{n\times l}$. Thus we get a family of homomorphic universal hash functions $\mathcal{H} = \{\mathsf{H}_\mathbf{A} : \mathbb{Z}_q^{l'} \to \mathbb{Z}_q^{n\times l} \mid \mathbf{A} \in \mathbb{Z}_q^{nl\times l'}\}$.

Remark 1. The reason why we interpret a vector in $\mathbb{Z}_q^{nl}$ as a matrix in $\mathbb{Z}_q^{n\times l}$ is for the convenience of the later construction of reusable fuzzy extractor in Sect. 3.

Lemma 1 (Generalized Leftover Hash Lemma [9,15]). *If $\mathcal{H} = \{\mathsf{H_i} : \mathbb{Z}_q^{l'} \to \mathbb{Z}_q^{n\times l}, \mathsf{i} \in \mathcal{I}\}$ is a family of universal hash functions, then for any random variable W taking values in $\mathbb{Z}_q^{l'}$ and any random variable Y,*

$$\mathbf{SD}\Big((\mathsf{H}_I(W), I, Y), (U, I, Y)\Big) \le \frac{1}{2}\sqrt{2^{-\widetilde{H}_\infty(W|Y)}q^{nl}},$$

where I and U are uniformly distributed over $\mathcal{I}$ and $\mathbb{Z}_q^{n\times l}$, respectively.

2.4 Secure Sketch

Definition 4 (Secure Sketch [9]**).** *An* $(\mathcal{M}, \mathfrak{m}, \hat{\mathfrak{m}}, t)$*-secure sketch (SS)* $\mathsf{SS} = (\mathsf{SS.Gen}, \mathsf{SS.Rec})$ *for metric space* $\mathcal{M}$ *with distance function* dis*, consists of a pair of PPT algorithms and satisfies correctness and security.*

- $\mathsf{SS.Gen}$ *on input* $\mathsf{w} \in \mathcal{M}$*, outputs a sketch* s.
- $\mathsf{SS.Rec}$ *takes as input a sketch* s *and* $\mathsf{w}' \in \mathcal{M}$*, and outputs* $\widetilde{\mathsf{w}}$.

Correctness. *For any* $\mathsf{w} \in \mathcal{M}$*, any* $s \leftarrow \mathsf{SS.Gen}(\mathsf{w})$*, if* $\mathsf{dis}(\mathsf{w}, \mathsf{w}') \le t$*, then* $\mathsf{SS.Rec}(s, \mathsf{w}') = \mathsf{w}$.

Security. *For any random variable* W *over* $\mathcal{M}$ *with min-entropy* $\mathfrak{m}$*, we have* $\widetilde{H}_\infty(W \mid \mathsf{SS.Gen}(W)) \ge \hat{\mathfrak{m}}$.

A secure sketch is homomorphic if $\mathsf{SS.Gen}(\mathsf{w} + \mathsf{w}') = \mathsf{SS.Gen}(\mathsf{w}) + \mathsf{SS.Gen}(\mathsf{w}')$.

An efficient $[n, k, 2t+1]_{\mathbb{F}}$-linear error correcting code $\mathcal{E}$ over $\mathbb{F}^n$ is a subspace of $\mathbb{F}^n$ and $\mathcal{E} = \{\mathsf{w} \in \mathbb{F}^n | \mathbf{H}\mathsf{w} = 0\}$, where matrix $\mathbf{H}$ is the $(n-k) \times n$ parity-check matrix of $\mathcal{E}$. For $\mathsf{w} \in \mathbb{F}^n$, define syndrome $\mathsf{syn}(\mathsf{w}) = \mathbf{H}\mathsf{w}$. For any $\mathbf{c} \in \mathcal{E}$, $\mathsf{syn}(\mathbf{c}+\mathbf{e}) = \mathsf{syn}(\mathbf{c}) + \mathsf{syn}(\mathbf{e}) = \mathsf{syn}(\mathbf{e})$. The syndrome captures all the information necessary for decoding.

As suggested in [9], based on an $[n, k, 2t+1]_{\mathbb{F}}$-linear error correcting code, a syndrome-based secure sketch can be constructed as follows.

Syndrome-Based Construction of Secure Sketch. [9] Define

$$\mathsf{SS.Gen}(\mathsf{w}) := \mathsf{syn}(\mathsf{w}) = \mathbf{H}\mathsf{w} = \mathsf{s}, \quad \mathsf{SS.Rec}(\mathsf{s}, \mathsf{w}') := \mathsf{w}' - \mathbf{e}, \tag{3}$$

where $\mathbf{e}$ is the unique vector of Hamming weight less than t such that $\mathsf{syn}(\mathbf{e}) = \mathsf{syn}(\mathsf{w}') - \mathsf{s}$.

Lemma 2. [9] *Given an* $[n, k, 2t+1]_{\mathbb{F}}$ *error-correcting code, one can construct an* $(\mathbb{F}^n, \mathfrak{m}, \mathfrak{m} - (n-k)|\mathbb{F}|, t)$ *secure sketch, which is efficient if encoding and decoding are efficient.*

Since there exist efficient $[n, k, 2t+1]_{\mathbb{F}}$-linear error correcting codes such that $t = O(n)$, the syndrome-based Secure Sketch can correct up to linear fraction of errors. Meanwhile, the fact that $\mathsf{SS.Gen}(\mathsf{w} + \mathsf{w}') := \mathsf{syn}(\mathsf{w} + \mathsf{w}') = \mathbf{H}(\mathsf{w} + \mathsf{w}') = \mathbf{H}\mathsf{w} + \mathbf{H}\mathsf{w}'$ suggests that the syndrome-based Secure Sketch is also homomorphic.

2.5 Learning with Error (LWE) Problem

The learning with errors (LWE) problem was introduced by Regev [13,14].

Definition 5 (Learning with errors (LWE) problem). *Let integers* $n = n(\lambda)$*,* $m = m(\lambda)$ *and* $q = q(\lambda) \ge 2$*. Let* $\chi(\lambda)$ *be a distribution over* $\mathbb{Z}_q$*. The decisional* $\mathsf{LWE}_{n,m,q,\chi}$ *problem is to distinguish* $(\mathbf{A}, \mathbf{A}\mathbf{s} + \mathbf{e})$ *from* $(\mathbf{A}, \mathbf{u})$*, where* $\mathbf{A} \leftarrow_{\$} \mathbb{Z}_q^{m \times n}$*,* $\mathbf{s} \leftarrow_{\$} \mathbb{Z}_q^n$*,* $\mathbf{e} \leftarrow \chi^m$ *and* $\mathbf{u} \leftarrow_{\$} \mathbb{Z}_q^m$.

The decisional $\mathsf{LWE}_{n,m,q,\chi}$ *problem is* ϵ*-hard if for any PPT adversary* $\mathcal{A}$*, its advantage* $\mathsf{Adv}^{n,m,q,\chi}_{\mathsf{LWE},\mathcal{A}}(\lambda)$ *is upper bounded by* ϵ*, i.e.,*

$$\mathsf{Adv}^{n,m,q,\chi}_{\mathsf{LWE},\mathcal{A}}(\lambda) := |\Pr[\mathcal{A}^{\mathcal{O}_{\mathsf{LWE}}(\mathbf{s})} = 1] - \Pr[\mathcal{A}^{\mathcal{O}_U} = 1]| \leq \epsilon.$$

Here the oracle $\mathcal{O}_{\mathsf{LWE}}$ *returns* $(\mathbf{A}, \mathbf{As}+\mathbf{e})$ *where* $\mathbf{A} \leftarrow_\$ \mathbb{Z}_q^{m\times n}$, $\mathbf{s} \leftarrow_\$ \mathbb{Z}_q^n$, $\mathbf{e} \leftarrow \chi^m$ *and the oracle* $\mathcal{O}_U$ *returns* $(\mathbf{A}, \mathbf{u})$ *where* $\mathbf{A} \leftarrow_\$ \mathbb{Z}_q^{m\times n}$ *and* $\mathbf{u} \leftarrow_\$ \mathbb{Z}_q^m$*, and* $\mathcal{A}$ *is limited to make at most one call to the oracle. The decisional* $\mathsf{LWE}_{n,m,q,\chi}$ *problem is hard if for any PPT adversary* $\mathcal{A}$*, its advantage* $\mathsf{Adv}^{n,m,q,\chi}_{\mathsf{LWE},\mathcal{A}}(\lambda)$ *is negligible.*

The decisional $\mathsf{LWE}_{n,m,l,q,\chi}$ problem is to distinguish $(\mathbf{A}, \mathbf{AS}+\mathbf{E})$ from $(\mathbf{A}, \mathbf{U})$, where $\mathbf{A} \leftarrow_\$ \mathbb{Z}_q^{m\times n}$, $\mathbf{S} \leftarrow_\$ \mathbb{Z}_q^{n\times l}$, $\mathbf{E} \leftarrow \chi^{m\times l}$ and $\mathbf{U} \leftarrow_\$ \mathbb{Z}_q^{m\times l}$. By a simple hybrid argument, one can show that the decisional $\mathsf{LWE}_{n,m,l,q,\chi}$ problem is hard if the decisional $\mathsf{LWE}_{n,m,q,\chi}$ problem is hard.

Lemma 3. [12] *If the decisional* $\mathsf{LWE}_{n,m,q,\chi}$ *problem is* ϵ*-hard, then the decisional* $\mathsf{LWE}_{n,m,l,q,\chi}$ *problem is* $\epsilon \cdot l$*-hard. More precisely,*

$$\mathsf{Adv}^{n,m,l,q,\chi}_{\mathsf{LWE},\mathcal{A}}(\lambda) := |\Pr[\mathcal{A}^{\mathcal{O}_{\mathsf{LWE}}(\mathbf{S})} = 1] - \Pr[\mathcal{A}^{\mathcal{O}_U} = 1]| \leq \epsilon \cdot l.$$

Here the oracle $\mathcal{O}_{\mathsf{LWE}}$ *returns* $(\mathbf{A}, \mathbf{AS}+\mathbf{E})$ *where* $\mathbf{A} \leftarrow_\$ \mathbb{Z}_q^{m\times n}$, $\mathbf{S} \leftarrow_\$ \mathbb{Z}_q^{n\times l}$, $\mathbf{E} \leftarrow \chi^{m\times l}$ *and the oracle* $\mathcal{O}_U$ *returns* $(\mathbf{A}, \mathbf{U})$ *where* $\mathbf{A} \leftarrow_\$ \mathbb{Z}_q^{m\times n}$ *and* $\mathbf{U} \leftarrow_\$ \mathbb{Z}_q^{m\times l}$*, and* $\mathcal{A}$ *is limited to make at most one call to the oracle.*

If $m = \rho m'$ with $m, m', \rho \in \mathbb{Z}^+$, the above lemma has an equivalent form.

Lemma 4. [12] *Let* $m = \rho m'$ *with* $m, m', \rho \in \mathbb{Z}^+$*. If the decisional* $\mathsf{LWE}_{n,m,q,\chi}$ *problem is* ε*-hard, then the decisional* $\mathsf{LWE}_{n,m,l,q,\chi}$ *problem is* $\epsilon \cdot l$*-hard. More precisely,*

$$\mathsf{Adv}^{n,m,l,q,\chi}_{\mathsf{LWE},\mathcal{A}}(\lambda) := |\Pr[\mathcal{A}^{\mathcal{O}_{\mathsf{LWE}}(\mathbf{S})} = 1] - \Pr[\mathcal{A}^{\mathcal{O}_U} = 1]| \leq \epsilon \cdot l.$$

Here the oracle $\mathcal{O}_{\mathsf{LWE}}$ *returns* $(\mathbf{A}, \mathbf{AS}+\mathbf{E})$ *where* $\mathbf{A} \leftarrow_\$ \mathbb{Z}_q^{m'\times n}$, $\mathbf{S} \leftarrow_\$ \mathbb{Z}_q^{n\times l}$, $\mathbf{E} \leftarrow \chi^{m'\times l}$ *and the oracle* $\mathcal{O}_U$ *returns* $(\mathbf{A}, \mathbf{U})$ *where* $\mathbf{A} \leftarrow_\$ \mathbb{Z}_q^{m'\times n}$ *and* $\mathbf{U} \leftarrow_\$ \mathbb{Z}_q^{m'\times l}$*, and* $\mathcal{A}$ *is limited to make at most* ρ *calls to the oracle.*

Consider a real parameter $\alpha = \alpha(n) \in (0, 1)$ and a prime q. Denote by $\mathbb{T} = \mathbb{R}/\mathbb{Z}$, i.e., the group of reals [0, 1) with modulo 1 addition. Define Ψ_α to be the distribution on $\mathbb{T}$ of a normal variable with mean 0 and standard deviation $\alpha/\sqrt{2\pi}$ reduced modulo 1. We denote by $\bar{\Psi}_\alpha$ the discrete distribution over $\mathbb{Z}_q$ of the random variable $\lfloor qX \rceil \mod q$ where the random variable X has distribution Ψ_α.

Lemma 5. [13] *If there exists an efficient, possibly quantum, algorithm for the decisional* $\mathsf{LWE}_{n,m,q,\bar{\Psi}_\alpha}$ *problem for* $q > 2\sqrt{n/\alpha}$*, then there exists an efficient quantum algorithm for approximating the SIVP and GapSVP problems, to within* $O((n/\alpha) \cdot \log^c n)$ *factors in the* l_2 *norm, in the worst case.*

Lemma 6. [1] *Let* $\mathbf{x}$ *be some vector in* $\{0, 1\}^m$ *and let* $\mathbf{e} \leftarrow \bar{\Psi}_\alpha^m$*. Then the quantity* $|\mathbf{x}^\top \mathbf{e}|$ *treated as an integer in* $[0, q-1]$ *satisfies*

$$|\mathbf{x}^\top \mathbf{e}| \leq \sqrt{m} q\alpha\omega(\sqrt{\log m}) + m/2$$

with all but negligible probability in m*.*

3 Reusable Fuzzy Extractor

Definition 6 (Reusable Fuzzy Extractor). *An* $(\mathcal{M}, \mathfrak{m}, \mathcal{R}, t, \varepsilon, \rho)$-resuable fuzzy extractor (rFE) *for metric space* $\mathcal{M}$ *consists of three PPT algorithms* $(\mathsf{Init}, \mathsf{Gen}, \mathsf{Rep})$,

- $\mathsf{Init}(1^\lambda)$: *the initialization algorithm takes as input the security parameters and outputs the public parameters* pp.
- $\mathsf{Gen}(\mathsf{pp}, \mathsf{w})$: *the generation algorithm takes as input the public parameters* pp *and* $\mathsf{w} \in \mathcal{M}$. *It outputs a public helper string* P *and an extracted string* $\mathsf{R} \in \mathcal{R}$.
- $\mathsf{Rep}(\mathsf{pp}, \mathsf{P}, \mathsf{w}')$: *the reproduction algorithm takes as input the public parameters* pp, *public helper string* P *and* $\mathsf{w}' \in \mathcal{M}$, *and outputs an extracted string* R *or* $\perp$.

It satisfies the following properties.

Correctness. *For all* $\mathsf{w}, \mathsf{w}' \in \mathcal{M}$ *with* $\mathsf{dis}(\mathsf{w}, \mathsf{w}') \leq t$, *for all* $\mathsf{pp} \leftarrow \mathsf{Init}(1^\lambda)$, $(\mathsf{P}, \mathsf{R}) \leftarrow \mathsf{Gen}(\mathsf{pp}, \mathsf{w})$ *and* $\widetilde{\mathsf{R}} \leftarrow \mathsf{Rep}(\mathsf{pp}, \mathsf{P}, \mathsf{w}')$, *it holds that* $\widetilde{\mathsf{R}} = \mathsf{R}$ *with overwhelming probability.*

Reusability. *For any distribution* W *over metric space* $\mathcal{M}$ *with* $H_\infty(W) \geq \mathfrak{m}$, *any PPT adversary* $\mathcal{A}$, *its advantage defined below satisfies*

$$\mathsf{Adv}^{\mathsf{reu}}_{\mathsf{rFE},\mathcal{A}}(1^\lambda) := |\Pr[\mathsf{Exp}^{\mathsf{reu}}_{\mathsf{rFE},\mathcal{A}}(1) \Rightarrow 1] - \Pr[\mathsf{Exp}^{\mathsf{reu}}_{\mathsf{rFE},\mathcal{A}}(0) \Rightarrow 1]| \leq \varepsilon,$$

where $\mathsf{Exp}^{\mathsf{reu}}_{\mathsf{rFE},\mathcal{A}}(\beta)$, $\beta \in \{0,1\}$, *describes the reusability experiment played between a challenger* $\mathcal{C}$ *and an adversary* $\mathcal{A}$.

$\mathsf{Exp}^{\mathsf{reu}}_{\mathsf{rFE},\mathcal{A}}(\beta)$: $\quad // \ \beta \in \{0,1\}$

1. *Challenger* $\mathcal{C}$ *invokes* $\mathsf{pp} \leftarrow \mathsf{Init}(1^\lambda)$ *and returns* pp *to* $\mathcal{A}$.
2. *Challenger* $\mathcal{C}$ *samples* $\mathsf{w} \leftarrow W$ *and invokes* $(\mathsf{P}, \mathsf{R}) \leftarrow \mathsf{Gen}(\mathsf{pp}, w)$. *If* $\beta = 1$, $\mathcal{C}$ *returns* (P, R) *to* $\mathcal{A}$; *if* $\beta = 0$, *it chooses* $U \leftarrow_\$ \mathcal{R}$ *and returns* (P, U) *to* $\mathcal{A}$.
3. $\mathcal{A}$ *may adaptively make at most* ρ *queries of the following form:*
   - $\mathcal{A}$ *submits a shift* $\delta_i \in \mathcal{M}$ *to* $\mathcal{C}$.
   - $\mathcal{C}$ *invokes* $(\mathsf{P}_i, \mathsf{R}_i) \leftarrow \mathsf{Gen}(\mathsf{pp}, \mathsf{w} + \delta_i)$, *and returns* $(\mathsf{P}_i, \mathsf{R}_i)$ *to* $\mathcal{A}$.
4. *As long as* $\mathcal{A}$ *outputs a guessing bit* β', *the experiment outputs* β'.

3.1 Construction of Reusable Fuzzy Extractor from LWE

Our construction of reusable fuzzy extractor $\mathsf{rFE} = (\mathsf{Init}, \mathsf{Gen}, \mathsf{Rep})$ is shown in Fig. 1, which uses the following building blocks.

- A homomorphic $(\mathbb{Z}_q^{l'}, \mathfrak{m}, \hat{\mathfrak{m}}, t)$-secure sketch $\mathsf{SS} = (\mathsf{SS.Gen}, \mathsf{SS.Rec})$.
- A family of universal hash functions $\mathcal{H} = \{\mathsf{H_i} \colon \mathbb{Z}_q^{l'} \rightarrow \mathbb{Z}_q^{n \times l}, \mathsf{i} \in \mathcal{I}\}$ with homomorphic property as defined by (2).

$\underline{\mathsf{pp} \leftarrow \mathsf{Init}(1^\lambda)}$: $\mathsf{H_i} \leftarrow_{\$} \mathcal{H}$. $\mathsf{pp} := \mathsf{H_i}$. Return pp.	$\underline{(\mathsf{P}, \mathsf{R}) \leftarrow \mathsf{Gen}(\mathsf{pp}, \mathsf{w})}$: $\quad // \mathsf{w} \in \mathbb{Z}_q^{l'}$ $s \leftarrow \mathsf{SS.Gen}(\mathsf{w})$. $\mathbf{S} := \mathsf{H_i}(\mathsf{w}) \in \mathbb{Z}_q^{n \times l}$. $\mathbf{A} \leftarrow_{\$} \mathbb{Z}_q^{m \times n}$. $\mathbf{E} \leftarrow \chi^{m \times l}$. $\mathbf{B} := (\mathbf{A}, \mathbf{A} \cdot \mathbf{S} + \mathbf{E}) \in \mathbb{Z}_q^{m \times (n+l)}$ $\mathbf{x} \leftarrow_{\$} \{0,1\}^m$. $\mathbf{m} \leftarrow_{\$} \{0,1\}^l$. $\mathbf{c}^\top = \mathbf{x}^\top \mathbf{B} + (\mathbf{0}^\top, \mathbf{m}^\top \cdot \lfloor \frac{q}{2} \rceil)$. $\mathsf{P} := (s, \mathbf{c})$, $\mathsf{R} := \mathbf{m}$. Return (P, R).	$\underline{\mathsf{R} \leftarrow \mathsf{Rep}(\mathsf{pp}, \mathsf{P}, \mathsf{w}')}$: Parse $\mathsf{P} = (s, \mathbf{c})$. $\widetilde{\mathsf{w}} \leftarrow \mathsf{SS.Rec}(s, \mathsf{w}')$. $\mathbf{S} := \mathsf{H_i}(\widetilde{\mathsf{w}}) \in \mathbb{Z}_q^{n \times l}$. $\mathbf{d} = \mathbf{c}^\top \cdot \begin{pmatrix} -\mathbf{S} \\ \mathbf{I}_l \end{pmatrix} \in \mathbb{Z}_q^l$. For $i = 1$ to l $\mathbf{m}[i] = \begin{cases} 1 & \text{if } \mathbf{d}[i] \in [\frac{1}{4}q, \frac{3}{4}q] \\ 0 & \text{else} \end{cases}$ $\mathsf{R} := \mathbf{m}$. Return R.

Fig. 1. Construction of rFE from LWE.

Remark 2. The content in the dashed frame is an LWE-based symmetric encryption scheme which is adapted from [12], the secret key is $\mathbf{S}$ and the message is $\mathbf{m}$.

Theorem 1. *If* SS *is a homomorphic* $(\mathbb{Z}_q^{l'}, \mathfrak{m}, \hat{\mathfrak{m}}, t)$*-secure sketch,* $\mathcal{H}$ *is a universal family of hash functions* $\mathcal{H} = \{\mathsf{H_i} \colon \mathbb{Z}_q^{l'} \to \mathbb{Z}_q^{n \times l}, \mathsf{i} \in \mathcal{I}\}$ *with homomorphic property as defined by (2), it satisfies* $\hat{\mathfrak{m}} - nl \log q \geq \omega(\log \lambda)$*, and the* $\mathsf{LWE}_{n,(\rho+1)m,l,q,\chi}$ *problem is* ϵ*-hard, where* χ *is the discrete Gaussian distribution* $\bar{\Psi}_\alpha$*,* $q \geq 4m$*,* $\alpha \leq 1/(8 \cdot \sqrt{m} \cdot g(n))$ *for any* $g(n) = \omega(\sqrt{\log n})$ *and* $m \geq (n + l) \log q + \omega(\log \lambda)$*, then* rFE *in Fig. 1 is an* $(\mathbb{Z}_p^{n \times l'}, \mathfrak{m}, \{0,1\}^l, t, \varepsilon, \rho)$*-reusable fuzzy extractor, where* $\varepsilon \leq 2^{-\omega(\log \lambda)} + 2\epsilon$*.*

Proof. Let us analyze the correctness first. If $\mathsf{dis}(\mathsf{w}, \mathsf{w}') \leq t$, then by the correctness of SS, we have $\mathsf{w} = \widetilde{\mathsf{w}}$, where $\widetilde{\mathsf{w}} \leftarrow \mathsf{SS.Rec}(s, \mathsf{w}')$ and $s = \mathsf{SS.Gen}(\mathsf{w})$. As a consequence, $\mathbf{S}$ can be correctly recovered. Next, we have

$$\begin{aligned} \mathbf{d} = \mathbf{c}^\top \cdot \begin{pmatrix} -\mathbf{S} \\ \mathbf{I}_l \end{pmatrix} &= \left(\mathbf{x}^\top \mathbf{B} + (\mathbf{0}^\top, \mathbf{m}^\top \cdot \left\lfloor \frac{q}{2} \right\rceil)\right) \cdot \begin{pmatrix} -\mathbf{S} \\ \mathbf{I}_l \end{pmatrix} \\ &= \left(\mathbf{x}^\top (\mathbf{A}, \mathbf{A} \cdot \mathbf{S} + \mathbf{E}) + (\mathbf{0}^\top, \mathbf{m}^\top \cdot \left\lfloor \frac{q}{2} \right\rceil)\right) \cdot \begin{pmatrix} -\mathbf{S} \\ \mathbf{I}_l \end{pmatrix} \\ &= \mathbf{x}^\top \mathbf{E} + \mathbf{m}^\top \cdot \left\lfloor \frac{q}{2} \right\rceil. \end{aligned}$$

Denote $\mathbf{E} = (\mathbf{e}_1, \cdots, \mathbf{e}_l)$, where $\mathbf{e}_i \leftarrow \chi^m$. Since $q \geq 4m$, $\alpha \leq 1/(8 \cdot \sqrt{m} \cdot g(n))$ for any $g(n) = \omega(\sqrt{\log n})$ and $\chi = \bar{\Psi}_\alpha$, by Lemma 6, we have $|\mathbf{x}^\top \mathbf{e}_i| \leq q/4$ with overwhelming probability. Consequently, $\mathbf{m}$ can be correctly reproduced with overwhelming probability. The correctness of rFE follows.

Now we show its reusability by defining a sequence of games, and proving the adjacent games indistinguishable. The differences between adjacent games will be highlighted by underline.

Game G_0 : It is the game $\mathsf{Exp}_{\mathsf{rFE},\mathcal{A}}^{\mathsf{reu}}(1)$. More precisely,

1. Challenger $\mathcal{C}$ samples $\mathsf{H_i} \leftarrow_\$ \mathcal{H}$, sets $\mathsf{pp} := \mathsf{H_i}$, and returns pp to $\mathcal{A}$.
2. Challenger $\mathcal{C}$ samples $\mathsf{w} \leftarrow W$, invokes $s \leftarrow \mathsf{SS.Gen(w)}$, $\mathbf{S} := \mathsf{H_i(w)}$, samples $\mathbf{A} \leftarrow_\$ \mathbb{Z}_q^{m\times n}$, $\mathbf{E} \leftarrow \chi^{m\times l}$, sets $\mathbf{B} := (\mathbf{A}, \mathbf{A}\cdot\mathbf{S}+\mathbf{E})$, samples $\mathbf{x} \leftarrow_\$ \{0,1\}^m$, $\mathbf{m} \leftarrow_\$ \{0,1\}^l$, sets $\mathbf{c}^\top := \mathbf{x}^\top\mathbf{B} + (\mathbf{0}^\top, \mathbf{m}^\top \cdot \lfloor \frac{q}{2} \rceil)$, $\mathsf{P} := (s, \mathbf{c})$ and $\mathsf{R} := \mathbf{m}$. Finally, it returns (P, R) to $\mathcal{A}$.
3. Upon receiving a shift $\delta_i \in \mathcal{M}$ from $\mathcal{A}$, challenger $\mathcal{C}$ invokes $s_i \leftarrow \mathsf{SS.Gen}(\mathsf{w} + \delta_i)$, $\mathbf{S}_i := \mathsf{H_i}(\mathsf{w} + \delta_i)$, samples $\mathbf{A}_i \leftarrow_\$ \mathbb{Z}_q^{m\times n}$, $\mathbf{E}_i \leftarrow \chi^{m\times l}$, sets $\mathbf{B}_i := (\mathbf{A}_i, \mathbf{A}_i\cdot\mathbf{S}_i+\mathbf{E}_i)$, samples $\mathbf{x}_i \leftarrow_\$ \{0,1\}^m$, $\mathbf{m}_i \leftarrow_\$ \{0,1\}^l$, sets $\mathbf{c}_i^\top := \mathbf{x}_i^\top\mathbf{B}_i + (\mathbf{0}^\top, \mathbf{m}_i^\top \cdot \lfloor \frac{q}{2} \rceil)$, $\mathsf{P}_i := (s_i, \mathbf{c}_i)$ and $\mathsf{R}_i := \mathbf{m}_i$. Finally, it returns $(\mathsf{P}_i, \mathsf{R}_i)$ to $\mathcal{A}$.
4. As long as $\mathcal{A}$ outputs a guessing bit β', the experiment outputs β'.

Clearly, we have

$$\Pr[\mathsf{G}_0 \Rightarrow 1] = \Pr[\mathsf{Exp}^{\mathsf{reu}}_{\mathsf{rFE},\mathcal{A}}(1) \Rightarrow 1]. \tag{4}$$

Game G_1 : It is the same as G_0, except that $s_i \leftarrow \mathsf{SS.Gen}(\mathsf{w}+\delta_i)$ now is changed to $s_i = s + \mathsf{SS.Gen}(\delta_i)$ and $\mathbf{S}_i = \mathsf{H_i}(\mathsf{w}+\delta_i)$ now is changed to $\mathbf{S}_i = \mathbf{S} + \mathsf{H_i}(\delta_i)$ in step 3. More precisely,

3. Upon receiving a shift $\delta_i \in \mathcal{M}$ from $\mathcal{A}$, challenger $\mathcal{C}$ computes $s_i = s + \mathsf{SS.Gen}(\delta_i), \mathbf{S}_i := \mathbf{S} + \mathsf{H_i}(\delta_i)$, samples $\mathbf{A}_i \leftarrow_\$ \mathbb{Z}_q^{m\times n}$, $\mathbf{E}_i \leftarrow \chi^{m\times l}$, sets $\mathbf{B}_i := (\mathbf{A}_i, \mathbf{A}_i\cdot\mathbf{S}_i+\mathbf{E}_i)$, samples $\mathbf{x}_i \leftarrow_\$ \{0,1\}^m$, $\mathbf{m}_i \leftarrow_\$ \{0,1\}^l$, sets $\mathbf{c}_i^\top := \mathbf{x}_i^\top\mathbf{B}_i + (\mathbf{0}^\top, \mathbf{m}_i^\top \cdot \lfloor \frac{q}{2} \rceil)$, $\mathsf{P}_i := (s_i, \mathbf{c}_i)$ and $\mathsf{R}_i := \mathbf{m}_i$. Finally, it returns $(\mathsf{P}_i, \mathsf{R}_i)$ to $\mathcal{A}$.

Lemma 7. $\Pr[\mathsf{G}_0 \Rightarrow 1] = \Pr[\mathsf{G}_1 \Rightarrow 1]$.

Proof. By the homomorphic property of SS, we have

$$s_i \overset{\mathsf{G}_0}{=} \mathsf{SS.Gen}(\mathsf{w}+\delta_i) = \mathsf{SS.Gen}(\mathsf{w}) + \mathsf{SS.Gen}(\delta_i) = s + \mathsf{SS.Gen}(\delta_i) \overset{\mathsf{G}_1}{=} s_i.$$

By the homomorphic property of $\mathsf{H_i}$, we have

$$\mathbf{S}_i \overset{\mathsf{G}_0}{=} \mathsf{H_i}(\mathsf{w}+\delta_i) = \mathsf{H_i}(\mathsf{w}) + \mathsf{H_i}(\delta_i) = \mathbf{S} + \mathsf{H_i}(\delta_i) \overset{\mathsf{G}_1}{=} \mathbf{S}_i.$$

As a result, the changes from G_0 to G_1 are just conceptual, thus

$$\Pr[\mathsf{G}_0 \Rightarrow 1] = \Pr[\mathsf{G}_1 \Rightarrow 1]. \qquad \square$$

Game G_2 : It is the same as G_1, except that in G_2, $\mathbf{S}$ is uniformly chosen from $\mathbb{Z}_q^{n\times l}$ instead of $\mathbf{S} = \mathsf{H_i(w)}$ in step 2. More precisely,

2. Challenger $\mathcal{C}$ samples $\mathsf{w} \leftarrow W$, invokes $s \leftarrow \mathsf{SS.Gen(w)}$, $\mathbf{S} \leftarrow_\$ \mathbb{Z}_q^{n\times l}$, samples $\mathbf{A} \leftarrow_\$ \mathbb{Z}_q^{m\times n}$, $\mathbf{E} \leftarrow \chi^{m\times l}$, sets $\mathbf{B} := (\mathbf{A}, \mathbf{A}\cdot\mathbf{S}+\mathbf{E})$, samples $\mathbf{x} \leftarrow_\$ \{0,1\}^m$, $\mathbf{m} \leftarrow_\$ \{0,1\}^l$, sets $\mathbf{c}^\top := \mathbf{x}^\top\mathbf{B} + (\mathbf{0}^\top, \mathbf{m}^\top \cdot \lfloor \frac{q}{2} \rceil)$, $\mathsf{P} := (s, \mathbf{c})$ and $\mathsf{R} := \mathbf{m}$. Finally, it returns (P, R) to $\mathcal{A}$.

Lemma 8.

$$|\Pr[\mathsf{G}_1 \Rightarrow 1] - \Pr[\mathsf{G}_2 \Rightarrow 1]| \le 2^{-\omega(\log\lambda)}.$$

Proof. We consider the information about the source w that is used in G_1.

- In step 1, challenger $\mathcal{C}$ does not need w.
- In step 2, challenger $\mathcal{C}$ uses w to generate the sketch s and extract $\mathbf{S}$, where $s \leftarrow \mathsf{SS.Gen}(\mathsf{w})$, $\mathbf{S} = \mathsf{H_i}(\mathsf{w})$.
- In step 3, upon receiving a shift δ_i from $\mathcal{A}$, challenger $\mathcal{C}$ computes $s_i = s + \mathsf{SS.Gen}(\delta_i)$, $\mathbf{S}_i = \mathbf{S} + \mathsf{H_i}(\delta_i)$. In this step, challenger $\mathcal{C}$ can perfectly answer adversary $\mathcal{A}$'s query with s and $\mathbf{S}$, and does not need w anymore.
- In step 4, challenger $\mathcal{C}$ does not need w.

From above analysis, we observe that all the information about w leaked to the adversary $\mathcal{A}$, except $\mathbf{S}$, is by the sketch $s \leftarrow \mathsf{SS.Gen}(\mathsf{w})$. Since our SS is $(\mathbb{Z}_q^l, \mathfrak{m}, \hat{\mathfrak{m}}, t)$-secure sketch and $\widetilde{H}(W) \geq \mathfrak{m}$, we have

$$\widetilde{H}(W|\mathsf{SS.Gen}(W)) \geq \hat{\mathfrak{m}}. \tag{5}$$

By the leftover hash lemma (Lemma 1), we have the statistical distance between $\mathbf{S}$ and $\mathbf{U}$ is less than $2^{-\omega(\log\lambda)}$, where $\mathbf{S} \leftarrow \mathsf{H_i}(\mathsf{w})$ and $\mathbf{U} \leftarrow_{\$} \mathbb{Z}_q^{n\times l}$. The lemma follows. □

<u>Game G_3 :</u> It is the same as G_2, except that in G_3, $\mathbf{B}, \mathbf{B}_i$ are uniformly sampled from $\mathbb{Z}_q^{m\times(n+l)}$. More precisely,

2. Challenger $\mathcal{C}$ samples $\mathsf{w} \leftarrow W$, invokes $s \leftarrow \mathsf{SS.Gen}(\mathsf{w})$, samples $\mathbf{S} \leftarrow_{\$} \mathbb{Z}_q^{n\times l}$, $\underline{\mathbf{B} \leftarrow_{\$} \mathbb{Z}_q^{m\times(n+l)}}$, $\mathbf{x} \leftarrow_{\$} \{0,1\}^m$, and $\mathbf{m} \leftarrow_{\$} \{0,1\}^l$, sets $\mathbf{c}^\top := \mathbf{x}^\top\mathbf{B} + (\mathbf{0}^\top, \mathbf{m}^\top \cdot \lfloor \frac{q}{2} \rceil)$, $\mathsf{P} := (s, \mathbf{c})$ and $\mathsf{R} := \mathbf{m}$. Finally, it returns (P, R) to $\mathcal{A}$.
3. Upon receiving a shift $\delta_i \in \mathcal{M}$ satisfying $\mathsf{dis}(\delta_i) \leq t$ from $\mathcal{A}$, challenger $\mathcal{C}$ invokes $s_i = s + \mathsf{SS.Gen}(\delta_i)$, $\mathbf{S}_i = \mathbf{S} + \mathsf{H_i}(\delta_i)$, $\underline{\text{samples}\mathbf{B}_i \leftarrow_{\$} \mathbb{Z}_q^{m\times(n+l)}}$, $\mathbf{x}_i \leftarrow_{\$} \{0,1\}^m$ and $\mathbf{m}_i \leftarrow_{\$} \{0,1\}^l$, sets $\mathbf{c}_i^\top := \mathbf{x}_i^\top\mathbf{B}_i + (\mathbf{0}^\top, \mathbf{m}_i^\top \cdot \lfloor \frac{q}{2} \rceil)$, $\mathsf{P}_i := (s_i, \mathbf{c}_i)$ and $\mathsf{R}_i := \mathbf{m}_i$. Finally, it returns $(\mathsf{P}_i, \mathsf{R}_i)$ to $\mathcal{A}$.

Lemma 9.

$$|\Pr[\mathsf{G}_2 \Rightarrow 1] - \Pr[\mathsf{G}_3 \Rightarrow 1]| \leq \mathsf{Adv}_{\mathsf{LWE},\mathcal{B}}^{n,(\rho+1)m,l,q,\chi}(\lambda).$$

Proof. We prove this lemma by showing that if there exists a PPT adversary $\mathcal{A}$ such that $|\Pr[\mathsf{G}_2 \Rightarrow 1] - \Pr[\mathsf{G}_3 \Rightarrow 1]| = \epsilon$, then we can construct a PPT algorithm $\mathcal{B}$, which can solve the decisional $\mathsf{LWE}_{n,(\rho+1)m,l,q,\chi}$ problem with the same probability ϵ. Algorithm $\mathcal{B}$ proceeds as follows.

1. Algorithm $\mathcal{B}$ samples $\mathsf{H_i} \leftarrow_{\$} \mathcal{H}$, sets $\mathsf{pp} := \mathsf{H_i}$, and returns pp to $\mathcal{A}$.
2. Algorithm $\mathcal{B}$ queries its own oracle to obtain $\mathbf{B}$. Then it samples $\mathsf{w} \leftarrow W$, invokes $s \leftarrow \mathsf{SS.Gen}(\mathsf{w})$, samples $\mathbf{x} \leftarrow_{\$} \{0,1\}^m$ and $\mathbf{m} \leftarrow_{\$} \{0,1\}^l$, sets $\mathbf{c}^\top := \mathbf{x}^\top\mathbf{B} + (\mathbf{0}^\top,\ \mathbf{m}^\top \cdot \lfloor \frac{q}{2} \rceil)$, $\mathsf{P} := (s, \mathbf{c})$ and $\mathsf{R} := \mathbf{m}$. Finally, it returns (P, R) to $\mathcal{A}$.

3. Upon receiving a shift $\delta_i \in \mathcal{M}$ from $\mathcal{A}$, algorithm $\mathcal{B}$ computes $\mathbf{S}'_i = \mathsf{H_i}(\delta_i)$ and sets $s_i = s + \mathsf{SS.Gen}(\delta_i)$, then queries its own oracle to obtain $\mathbf{B}'_i = (\mathbf{A}_i,\ \mathbf{C}_i)$, sets $\mathbf{B}_i = (\mathbf{A}_i,\ \mathbf{C}_i + \mathbf{A}_i\mathbf{S}'_i)$, samples $\mathbf{x}_i \leftarrow_\$ \{0,1\}^m$ and $\mathbf{m}_i \leftarrow_\$ \{0,1\}^l$, sets $\mathbf{c}_i^\top := \mathbf{x}_i^\top \mathbf{B}_i + (\mathbf{0}^\top, \mathbf{m}_i^\top \cdot \lfloor \frac{q}{2} \rceil)$, $\mathsf{P}_i := (s_i, \mathbf{c}_i)$ and $\mathsf{R}_i := \mathbf{m}_i$. Finally, it returns $(\mathsf{P}_i, \mathsf{R}_i)$ to $\mathcal{A}$.
4. As long as $\mathcal{A}$ outputs a guessing bit β', $\mathcal{B}$ outputs β' as its own guess.

Now we analyse the advantage of $\mathcal{B}$.

- If $\mathcal{B}$'s oracle is $\mathcal{O}_{\mathsf{LWE}}(\mathbf{S})$, the oracle will return LWE samples $\mathbf{B} = (\mathbf{A},\ \mathbf{AS} + \mathbf{E})$ and $\mathbf{B}'_i = (\mathbf{A}_i,\ \mathbf{A}_i\mathbf{S} + \mathbf{E}_i)$, where $\mathbf{A} \leftarrow_\$ \mathbb{Z}_q^{m\times n}$, $\mathbf{S} \leftarrow_\$ \mathbb{Z}_q^{n\times l}$, $\mathbf{E} \leftarrow \chi^{m\times l}$, $\mathbf{A}_i \leftarrow_\$ \mathbb{Z}_q^{m\times n}$ and $\mathbf{E}_i \leftarrow \chi^{m\times l}$, then $\mathbf{B}_i = (\mathbf{A}_i,\ \mathbf{C}_i + \mathbf{A}_i\mathbf{S}'_i) = (\mathbf{A}_i,\ \mathbf{A}_i\mathbf{S} + \mathbf{E}_i + \mathbf{A}_i\mathsf{H_i}(\delta_i)) = (\mathbf{A}_i,\ \mathbf{A}_i(\mathbf{S} + \mathsf{H_i}(\delta_i)) + \mathbf{E}_i) = (\mathbf{A}_i,\ \mathbf{A}_i\mathbf{S}_i + \mathbf{E}_i)$. In this case, algorithm $\mathcal{B}$ perfectly simulates G_2 for $\mathcal{A}$.
- If $\mathcal{B}$'s oracle is $\mathcal{O}_{\mathsf{U}}$, the oracle will return uniform samples $\mathbf{B}$, $\mathbf{B}'_i$, where $\mathbf{B} \leftarrow_\$ \mathbb{Z}_q^{m\times(n+l)}$, $\mathbf{B}'_i \leftarrow_\$ \mathbb{Z}_q^{m\times(n+l)}$, then $\mathbf{B}_i = (\mathbf{A}_i,\ \mathbf{C}_i + \mathbf{A}_i\mathbf{S}'_i) = (\mathbf{A}_i,\ \mathbf{C}_i) + (0,\ \mathbf{A}_i\mathbf{S}'_i) = \mathbf{B}'_i + (0,\ \mathbf{A}_i\mathbf{S}'_i)$ is uniformly distributed in $\mathbb{Z}_q^{m\times(n+l)}$. In this case, algorithm $\mathcal{B}$ perfectly simulates G_3 for $\mathcal{A}$.

Consequently, $|\Pr[\mathsf{G}_2 \Rightarrow 1] - \Pr[\mathsf{G}_3 \Rightarrow 1]| \leq \mathsf{Adv}_{\mathsf{LWE},\mathcal{B}}^{n,(\rho+1)m,q,\chi}(\lambda)$. □

<u>Game G_4</u> : It is the same as G_3, except that in G_4, the challenger uniformly chooses U from $\{0,1\}^l$, and returns (P, U) to $\mathcal{A}$ instead of returning (P, R) to $\mathcal{A}$.

Lemma 10. $|\Pr[\mathsf{G}_3 \Rightarrow 1] - \Pr[\mathsf{G}_4 \Rightarrow 1]| \leq 2^{-\omega(\log\lambda)}$.

Proof. We will show that G_4 is statistically indistinguishable from the G_3. Note that in G_4, $\mathbf{B}$ is uniformly chosen from $\mathbb{Z}_q^{m\times(n+l)}$ and $\mathbf{x} \leftarrow_\$ \{0,1\}^m$, since $m \geq (n+l)\log q + \omega(\log\lambda)$, by the leftover hash lemma (Lemma 1), we have $\mathbf{x}^\top\mathbf{B}$ is $2^{-\omega(\log\lambda)}$ statistically close to the uniform distribution over $\mathbb{Z}_q^{n+l}$. Consequently, $\mathsf{R} := \mathbf{m}$ is concealed, and $|\Pr[\mathsf{G}_3 \Rightarrow 1] - \Pr[\mathsf{G}_4 \Rightarrow 1]| \leq 2^{-\omega(\log\lambda)}$ follows. □

<u>Game G_5</u> : It is the same as G_4, except that in G_5, $\mathbf{B}, \mathbf{B}'_i$ are changed back to LWE samples.

Lemma 11.

$$|\Pr[\mathsf{G}_4 \Rightarrow 1] - \Pr[\mathsf{G}_5 \Rightarrow 1]| \leq \mathsf{Adv}_{\mathsf{LWE},\mathcal{B}}^{n,(\rho+1)m,l,q,\chi}(\lambda).$$

Proof. The proof is similar to the proof of Lemma 9. We omit it here. □

<u>Game G_6</u> : It is the same as G_5, except that $\mathbf{S} \leftarrow_\$ \mathbb{Z}_q^{n\times l}$ in G_5 is changed back to $\mathbf{S} := \mathsf{H_i}(\mathsf{w})$ in G_6.

Lemma 12.

$$|\Pr[\mathsf{G}_5 \Rightarrow 1] - \Pr[\mathsf{G}_6 \Rightarrow 1]| \leq 2^{-\omega(\log\lambda)}.$$

Proof. The proof is similar to the proof of Lemma 8. We omit it here.

Game G_7 : It is the same as G_6, except that

- $s_i := s + \mathsf{SS.Gen}(\delta_i)$ now is changed back to $s_i \leftarrow \mathsf{SS.Gen}(\mathsf{w} + \delta_i)$.
- $\mathbf{S}_i := \mathbf{S} + \mathsf{H_i}(\delta_i)$ now is changed back to $\mathbf{S}_i := \mathsf{H_i}(\mathsf{w} + \delta_i)$.

Lemma 13. $\Pr[\mathsf{G}_6 \Rightarrow 1] = \Pr[\mathsf{G}_7 \Rightarrow 1]$.

Proof. The proof is identical to the proof of Lemma 7. We omit it here. □

Observe that G_7 is identical to $\mathsf{Exp}^{\mathsf{reu}}_{\mathsf{rFE},\mathcal{A}}(0)$, as a result

$$\Pr[\mathsf{G}_7 \Rightarrow 1] = \Pr[\mathsf{Exp}^{\mathsf{reu}}_{\mathsf{rFE},\mathcal{A}}(0) \Rightarrow 1]. \tag{6}$$

Combining Eq. (4), Lemmas 7–13 and Eq. (6) together, we have

$$\mathsf{Adv}^{\mathsf{reu}}_{\mathsf{rFE},\mathcal{A}}(1^\lambda) \leq 2^{-\omega(\log \lambda)} + 2\mathsf{Adv}^{n,(\rho+1)m,l,q,\chi}_{\mathsf{LWE},\mathcal{B}}(\lambda).$$

This completes the proof of Theorem 1. □

If we instantiate SS and $\mathsf{H_i}$ with the syndrome-based secure sketch as defined in (3) and homomorphic universal hashing as defined in (1), the construction of rFE in Fig. 1 results in a reusable fuzzy extractor from the LWE assumption, which is resilient to linear fraction of errors.

4 Conclusion

Traditional fuzzy extractor distills an almost uniform output from a non-uniform noisy source, but the distillation is implemented only once. In this paper, we study on reusable fuzzy extractor which enables multiple distillations from the same non-uniform noisy source and provide the first reusable fuzzy extractor which is resilient to linear fraction of errors from the LWE assumption. In the construction, a secure sketch is used to correct errors, an LWE-type encryption is used to break the correlations between multiple distilled strings, and universal hashing is used to extract uniform strings. The reusability of our construction benefits from the LWE assumption and the homomorphic properties of secure sketch and universal hashing.

Acknowledgements. This work was supported by the National Natural Science Foundation of China (NSFC No. 61672346).

References

1. Agrawal, S., Boneh, D., Boyen, X.: Efficient lattice (H)IBE in the standard model. In: Gilbert, H. (ed.) EUROCRYPT 2010. LNCS, vol. 6110, pp. 553–572. Springer, Heidelberg (2010). https://doi.org/10.1007/978-3-642-13190-5_28
2. Alamélou, Q., Berthier, P.E., Cachet, C., Cauchie, S., Fuller, B., Gaborit, P., Simhadri, S.: Pseudoentropic isometries: a new framework for fuzzy extractor reusability (2016). http://eprint.iacr.org/2016/1100
3. Apon, D., Cho, C., Eldefrawy, K., Katz, J.: Efficient, reusable fuzzy extractors from LWE. In: Dolev, S., Lodha, S. (eds.) CSCML 2017. LNCS, vol. 10332, pp. 1–18. Springer, Cham (2017). https://doi.org/10.1007/978-3-319-60080-2_1
4. Bennett, C.H., Brassard, G., Robert, J.: Privacy amplification by public discussion. SIAM J. Comput. **17**(2), 210–229 (1988). https://doi.org/10.1137/0217014
5. Blanton, M., Aliasgari, M.: On the (non-)reusability of fuzzy sketches and extractors and security in the computational setting. In: Lopez, J., Samarati, P. (eds.) SECRYPT 2011, pp. 68–77. SciTePress (2011)
6. Blanton, M., Aliasgari, M.: Analysis of reusability of secure sketches and fuzzy extractors. IEEE Trans. Inf. Forensics Secur. **8**(9), 1433–1445 (2013). https://doi.org/10.1109/TIFS.2013.2272786
7. Boyen, X.: Reusable cryptographic fuzzy extractors. In: Atluri, V., Pfitzmann, B., McDaniel, P.D. (eds.) CCS 2004, pp. 82–91. ACM, New York (2004). https://doi.org/10.1145/1030083.1030096
8. Canetti, R., Fuller, B., Paneth, O., Reyzin, L., Smith, A.: Reusable fuzzy extractors for low-entropy distributions. In: Fischlin, M., Coron, J.-S. (eds.) EUROCRYPT 2016. LNCS, vol. 9665, pp. 117–146. Springer, Heidelberg (2016). https://doi.org/10.1007/978-3-662-49890-3_5
9. Dodis, Y., Ostrovsky, R., Reyzin, L., Smith, A.D.: Fuzzy extractors: how to generate strong keys from biometrics and other noisy data. SIAM J. Comput. **38**(1), 97–139 (2008)
10. Dodis, Y., Reyzin, L., Smith, A.: Fuzzy extractors: how to generate strong keys from biometrics and other noisy data. In: Cachin, C., Camenisch, J. (eds.) EUROCRYPT 2004. LNCS, vol. 3027, pp. 523–540. Springer, Heidelberg (2004). https://doi.org/10.1007/978-3-540-24676-3_31
11. Fuller, B., Meng, X., Reyzin, L.: Computational fuzzy extractors. In: Sako, K., Sarkar, P. (eds.) ASIACRYPT 2013. LNCS, vol. 8269, pp. 174–193. Springer, Heidelberg (2013). https://doi.org/10.1007/978-3-642-42033-7_10
12. Peikert, C., Vaikuntanathan, V., Waters, B.: A framework for efficient and composable oblivious transfer. In: Wagner, D. (ed.) CRYPTO 2008. LNCS, vol. 5157, pp. 554–571. Springer, Heidelberg (2008). https://doi.org/10.1007/978-3-540-85174-5_31
13. Regev, O.: On lattices, learning with errors, random linear codes, and cryptography. In: Gabow, H.N., Fagin, R. (eds.) STOC 2005, pp. 84–93. ACM, New York (2005). https://doi.org/10.1145/1060590.1060603
14. Regev, O.: The learning with errors problem (invited survey). In: CCC 2010, pp. 191–204. IEEE Computer Society (2010). https://doi.org/10.1109/CCC.2010.26
15. Shoup, V.: A Computational Introduction to Number Theory and Algebra. Cambridge University Press, Cambridge (2006)
16. Simoens, K., Tuyls, P., Preneel, B.: Privacy weaknesses in biometric sketches. In: 30th IEEE Symposium on Security and Privacy, pp. 188–203. IEEE Computer Society (2009). https://doi.org/10.1109/SP.2009.24

17. Tanamoto, T., Yasuda, S., Takaya, S., Fujita, S.: Physically unclonable function using an initial waveform of ring oscillators. IEEE Trans. Circuits Syst. **64**(7), 827–831 (2017). https://doi.org/10.1109/TCSII.2016.2602828
18. Valsesia, D., Coluccia, G., Bianchi, T., Magli, E.: User authentication via PRNU-based physical unclonable functions. IEEE Trans. Inf. Forensics Secur. **12**(8), 1941–1956 (2017). https://doi.org/10.1109/TIFS.2017.2697402
19. Wilde, M.M.: Quantum Information Theory. Cambridge University Press, Cambridge (2017). https://doi.org/10.1017/9781316809976

A Reusable Fuzzy Extractor with Practical Storage Size: Modifying Canetti *et al.*'s Construction

Jung Hee Cheon, Jinhyuck Jeong(✉), Dongwoo Kim, and Jongchan Lee

Department of Mathematical Sciences, Seoul National University, Seoul, Korea
{jhcheon,wlsyrlekd,dwkim606,jclee0208}@snu.ac.kr

Abstract. After the concept of a Fuzzy Extractor (FE) was first introduced by Dodis *et al.*, it has been regarded as one of the candidate solutions for key management utilizing biometric data. With a noisy input such as biometrics, FE generates a public helper value and a random secret key which is reproducible given another input *similar* to the original input. However, "helper values" may cause some leakage of information when generated repeatedly by correlated inputs, thus *reusability* should be considered as an important property. Recently, Canetti *et al.* (Eurocrypt 2016) proposed a FE satisfying both *reusability* and *robustness* with inputs from low-entropy distributions. Their strategy, the so-called Sample-then-Lock method, is to sample many partial strings from a noisy input string and to lock one secret key with each partial string independently.

In this paper, modifying this reusable FE, we propose a new FE with size-reduced helper data hiring a threshold scheme. Our new FE also satisfies both reusability and robustness, and requires much less storage memory than the original. To show the advantages of this scheme, we analyze and compare our scheme with the original in concrete parameters of the biometric, IrisCode. As a result, on 1024-bit inputs, with false rejection rate 0.5 and error tolerance 0.25, while the original requires about 1 TB for each helper value, our scheme requires only 300 MB with an additional 1.35 GB of common data which can be used for all helper values.

Keywords: Fuzzy extractors · Reusability · Key derivation
Digital lockers · Threshold scheme · Biometric authentication

1 Introduction

Biometrics are metrics derived from biological characteristics inherent to each individual, such as fingerprints, iris patterns, facial features, gait, etc. A noteworthy property of this biometric information is inseparability. Biometric information cannot be separated from its owner, and can be used to authenticate a person without requiring other keys or passwords. However, biometric authentication

W. Susilo and G. Yang (Eds.): ACISP 2018, LNCS 10946, pp. 28–44, 2018.
https://doi.org/10.1007/978-3-319-93638-3_3

has its problems; First, once biometric information is leaked to an adversary it is not easy to revoke. This makes protecting biometric information more crucial. Second, whenever one generates biometric data from their biological source using a device, small errors occur naturally because of the various environments and conditions.

This obstacle causes much harder problems in "Privacy-preserving Biometric Authentication" since classical cryptographic systems are constructed so that even little errors in inputs lead to huge errors in outputs. For privacy-preserving biometric authentication, there are recent works [1–4] using cryptographic tools, especially, homomorphic encryption. They propose a secure biometric authentication system which is executed with encrypted biometrics, to prevent an adversary from obtaining any information about the biometrics. Such an authentication system, however, may lose its power if the secret key is leaked and thus secret key management is a subject of major concern. Storing the secret key in secure memory and tamper-resistant hardware such as TrustZone and SoftwareGuardExtensions might be a solution, but these hardwares are too expensive, and/or can be vulnerable to physical attacks. For these reasons, generating a secret key whenever biometrics are scanned was proposed as an alternative solution, and the notion of Fuzzy Extractors (FE) was introduced by Dodis *et al.* It is a cryptographic primitive which extracts the same key from noisy inputs [5,6].

More precisely, a fuzzy extractor consists of two algorithms; a generating algorithm (Gen) and a reproducing algorithm (Rep). Gen generates a random secret key and a public helper value from input biometrics. Rep reproduces the same key from the helper value and a biometric, when it is sufficiently similar to the original used in the Gen algorithm.

For the security of a FE, there are some important properties such as *robustness* and *reusability*. A fuzzy extractor is robust if an adversary cannot forge a given helper value in a way that Rep outputs a wrong key even though the input biometric is legitimate. This robustness is quite important, since in a non-robust FE, a user cannot trust the key generated by Rep, rendering the FE meaningless. On the other hand, a FE is reusable if it remains secure even if several pairs (random key, and related helper value) issued from correlated inputs are revealed to an adversary. Considering biometric authentication via FE, reusability guarantees that the authentication system is still safe for future use even if some helper values and related keys of a user have been compromised.

In [7], Apon *et al.* modified the construction of [8] based on the LWE-assumption making it reusable with a common matrix for every input of Gen. Unfortunately, it fails to satisfy robustness since it is susceptible to trivial forgery. In Eurocrypt 2016, Canetti *et al.* proposed a reusable fuzzy extractor [9]. It is the first reusable robust fuzzy extractor without assumptions on correlations of multiple readings of the source, applying the sample-then-lock method with cryptographic digital lockers. It can tolerate $\frac{cn \ln n}{k}$ errors in a given n-bit input allowing running time in n^c with a security parameter of at most k. However, some biometrics such as IrisCode have error linear (20%–30%) in n.

In this paper, we point out that Canetti *et al.*'s fuzzy extractor is inappropriate for these cases; it requires too much storage space for the helper value. In their construction, each locker acts as an oracle to check each partial substring of the input biometric, outputting the original secret key if that substring is correct. Therefore, a smaller substring size directly leads to a decrease in the security of the fuzzy extractor. Without diminishing the size of substrings, the number of lockers should increase exponentially, leading to impractical storage requirement in cases with linear errors of input.

The main idea of our construction is to overcome this oracle by modifying the digital lockers and using shorter substrings. We also exploit a (perfect) threshold scheme to divide each locker, preserving security. More precisely, we provide m modified lockers, and each unordered τ-pair of them is applied with a recovery algorithm of a threshold scheme for reproducing the secret key. As a result, the probability that each modified locker is unlocked successfully becomes larger under the same security, leading to a crucial decrease of storage for the helper values. Although time consumption increases as a side-effect, this trade-off is favorable because it can be relieved with parallel computing. More precisely, our contribution can be summarized as follows;

- Combining the reusable FE of [9] and a threshold scheme, we propose a new size-reduced reusable fuzzy extractor satisfying robustness.[1] Our construction is based on the same or weaker conditions on the biometric source distribution than Canetti *et al.*'s construction.
- We analyze this new FE and the original with concrete parameters focusing on the biometric IrisCode. As a result, we highly reduced the amount of storage space required. For example, when using a 1024 bit biometric with false rejection rate[2] 0.5, the original requires about 6 GB of each helper value for error tolerance 0.2, 1 TB for 0.25, and 270 TB for 0.3. On the other hand, our scheme requires only 1.6 MB for 0.2, 300 MB for 0.25, and 111 GB for 0.3 with an additional 1.35 GB of common data which is commonly used for every helper value. One can find more information in Tables 1 and 2.
- In fact, there is a trade-off between required time and storage space; approximately, a decrease by a factor of 10^3 in storage space causes an tenfold increase in required time. We implement our scheme as a proof-of-concept with parallel computing via Cuda, and show that the trade-off can be relieved outstandingly.

Road Map. In Sect. 2, we provide some preliminaries for our work. In Sect. 3, we briefly introduce the reusable fuzzy extractor of Canetti *et al.* with concrete analysis. In Sect. 4, we give our construction of new fuzzy extractor and analysis of it.

---

[1] Robustness can easily be satisfied by the random-oracle-based transform of [10] as mentioned in [9]. Thus, we only focus on the reusability in this paper.

[2] The false rejection rate is the probability that the reproducing algorithm Rep fails to regenerate the secret value even though a legitimate input is given.

2 Preliminaries

Through this paper, for a natural number a, $|a|$ denotes the bit size of a. Here we mostly adhere to the notations used by Canetti *et al.*, for convenience.

2.1 Entropy

Let X_i be a random variable over some alphabet $\mathcal{Z}$ for $i = 1, \ldots, n$. We denote by a random variable $X = X_1, \ldots, X_n := (X_1, \ldots, X_n)$. The *minentropy* $H_\infty(X)$ of X is defined as

$$H_\infty(X) = -\log[\max_x Pr(X = x)],$$

and the *average (conditional) minentropy* $\tilde{H}_\infty(X|Y)$ of X given Y defined as

$$\tilde{H}_\infty(X|Y) = -\log[\mathbb{E}_y \max_x Pr(X = x|Y = y)].$$

The *computational distance* between variables X and Y is defined by $\delta^D(X, Y) = |\mathbb{E}[D(X)] - \mathbb{E}[D(Y)]|$ for a given distinguisher D, and for a class of distinguishers $\mathcal{D}$ we define $\delta^{\mathcal{D}}(X, Y) = \max_{D \in \mathcal{D}} \delta^D(X, Y)$. We will consider the class $\mathcal{D}_s$ of distinguishers (circuit) of size at most s which output a single bit.

2.2 Fuzzy Extractor and Reusability

Fuzzy extractors (FE) consist of two algorithms; Gen and Rep. Gen takes an input w such as biometric data and outputs an extracted string r and a helper value $p \in \{0,1\}^*$. Rep takes as input w' and p and outputs the previous r whenever w' is similar to w. In this work, we focus on computational fuzzy extractors. (For the information-theoretic notions, see [6]). The formal definition of computational fuzzy extractors and their notion of security follows.

Definition 1 (Computational Fuzzy Extractors [8]**).** *Given a metric space* $(\mathcal{M}, \mathsf{dis})$, *let* $\mathcal{W}$ *be a family of probability distributions over* $\mathcal{M}$. *A pair of randomized procedures "generate" (*Gen*) and "reproduce" (*Rep*) is an* $(\mathcal{M}, \mathcal{W}, \kappa, t)$-*computational fuzzy extractor that is* $(\varepsilon_{sec}, s_{sec})$-*hard with error* δ *if* Gen *and* Rep *satisfy the following properties:*

- *The generate procedure* Gen *on input* $w \in \mathcal{M}$ *outputs an extracted string* $r \in \{0,1\}^\kappa$ *and a helper string* $p \in \{0,1\}^*$.
- ***Correctness*** *The reproduction procedure* Rep *takes an element* $w' \in \mathcal{M}$ *and a bit string* $p \in \{0,1\}^*$ *as inputs. The correctness property guarantees that if* $\mathsf{dis}(w, w') \leq t$ *and* $(r, p) \leftarrow \mathsf{Gen}(w)$, *then* $\Pr[\mathsf{Rep}(w', p) = r] \geq 1 - \delta$ *where the probability is over the randomness of (*Gen, Rep*).*
- ***Security*** *For any distribution* $W \in \mathcal{W}$, *the string* r *is pseudorandom conditioned on* p, *that is* $\delta^{D_{s_{sec}}}((R, P), (U_\kappa, P)) \leq \varepsilon_{sec}$.

Fuller *et al.* proposed a computational fuzzy extractor based on the Learning with Error (LWE) problem [8]. However, their construction does not satisfy *robustness* and *reusability*, which mean the security against an adversary forging a given helper value while avoiding detection,[3] and the security of a reissued pair $(r, p) \leftarrow \mathsf{Gen}(w)$ when an adversary has extorted some pairs $(r_i, p_i) \leftarrow \mathsf{Gen}(w_i)$ for correlated w and w_i's, respectively.

The formal definition of a reusable fuzzy extractor is as follows:

Definition 2 (Reusable Fuzzy Extractor [9]**).** *Let $\mathcal{W}$ be a family of distributions over $\mathcal{M}$. Let (*Gen, Rep*) be a $(\mathcal{M}, \mathcal{W}, \kappa, t)$-computational fuzzy extractor that is $(\varepsilon_{sec}, s_{sec})$-hard with error δ. Let $(W^1, W^2, \dots, W^\rho)$ be ρ correlated random variables such that each $W^j \in \mathcal{W}$. Let D be an adversary. Define the following game for all $j = 1, \dots, \rho$:*

- ***Sampling*** *The challenger samples $w^j \leftarrow W^j$ and $u \leftarrow \{0,1\}^\kappa$.*
- ***Generation*** *The challenger computes $(r^j, p^j) \leftarrow \mathsf{Gen}(w^j)$.*
- ***Distinguishing*** *The advantage of D is*

$$\begin{aligned} Adv(D) := \Pr[&D(r^1, \dots, r^{j-1}, r^j, r^{j+1}, \dots, r^\rho, p^1, \dots, p^\rho) = 1] \\ - \Pr[&D(r^1, \dots, r^{j-1}, u, r^{j+1}, \dots, r^\rho, p^1, \dots, p^\rho) = 1]. \end{aligned}$$

$(\mathsf{Gen}, \mathsf{Rep})$ *is $(\rho, \varepsilon_{sec}, s_{sec})$-reusable if for all $D \in \mathcal{D}_{s_{sec}}$ and for all $j = 1, \dots, \rho$, the advantage is at most ε_{sec}.*

The first reusable fuzzy extractor without assumptions about the correlations on multiple readings of the source is proposed by Canetti *et al.* in Eurocrypt 2016 using the digital lockers with sample-then-lock construction [9]. We analyze this scheme with concrete parameters focusing on the biometric IrisCode. It requires too much storage space to tolerate up to 20% or more errors in 1024-bit iris code. To overcome this problem, we propose a modified FE exploiting threshold scheme, which satisfies both robustness and reusability. More details including Canetti *et al.*'s construction and analysis of it are in Sect. 3. Construction of our new fuzzy extractor is in Sect. 4.

On the other hand, recently, another reusable fuzzy extractor has been proposed by [7] adapting the LWE-based FE [8]. They presented a generic technique for converting any weakly reusable FE to a strongly reusable one in the random-oracle model, and made a (strongly) reusable FE by modifying the original LWE-based FE into a weakly reusable one. Furthermore, they provided a construction of a strongly reusable FE based on the LWE assumption, not relying on the random oracles. However, it does not satisfy robustness. On the contrary, Canetti *et al.* [9]'s constructions can easily be made robust by the random-oracle-based transform of [10], and so can our modification.

[3] We refers the formal definition of robustness to [11].

2.3 (τ, m)-Threshold Scheme

The (τ, m)-threshold scheme is a secret sharing scheme with participants m and threshold τ. It consists of a Distribution Algorithm $\mathsf{DA}_{\tau,m}$ and a Recovery Algorithm $\mathsf{RA}_{\tau,m}$. $\mathsf{DA}_{\tau,m}$ takes a secret s, and divides it into m shares which are distributed to each participant. $\mathsf{RA}_{\tau,m}$ takes τ inputs, and outputs the original secret s only if each τ input is the corresponding share generated by $\mathsf{DA}_{\tau,m}(s)$. For the security of this threshold scheme, an adversary with less than τ shares should not be able to obtain any information about the secret.

The basic idea of a secret sharing scheme was introduced by Shamir and Blakely independently [12,13]. Shamir's scheme is based on polynomial interpolation, and it requires heavy computation for $\mathsf{DA}_{\tau,m}$ and $\mathsf{RA}_{\tau,m}$ due to the employment of a τ-degree polynomial. To reduce computational costs, a new secret sharing scheme using just EXCLUSIVE-OR (XOR) operations was proposed for special cases, such as $(2,3), (2,m), (3,m)$-threshold schemes by Ishizu *et al.*, Fujii *et al.*, Kuihara *et al.*, respectively [14–16]. Finally, Kurihara *et al.* proposed a (τ, m)-threshold scheme [17] generalizing previous schemes.

Perfect (τ, m)-Threshold Scheme. In the (τ, m)-threshold scheme, leakage of information about the secret can be measured by entropy. Let $H(X)$ denote the Shannon entropy of a random variable X. Let $s \in \mathcal{S}$ and $s_i \in \mathcal{S}_i$ be a secret and a share respectively, and S, S_i be the random variables of secrets and shares, respectively.

A (τ, m)-secret sharing scheme is *perfect* if

$$H(S|S_I) = \begin{cases} 0 & \text{if } I \text{ contains } k \text{ or more elements} \\ H(S) & \text{otherwise} \end{cases}$$

where $I = \{i_1, i_2, \ldots, i_j\} \subseteq \{1, 2, \ldots, N\}$, and $S_I = S_{i_1} S_{i_2} \ldots S_{i_j} := (S_{i_1}, S_{i_2}, \ldots, S_{i_j})$.

Kurihara *et al.*'s (τ, m)-Threshold Scheme [17]. In fact, our scheme can be instantiated with any *perfect* secret sharing scheme. For the clarity of description and the concrete parameter comparison with Canetti *et al.*, we utilize Kurihara *et al.*'s (τ, m)-threshold scheme [17]. As far as we know, it is one of the most efficient (τ, m)-threshold schemes which are *perfect.* From now on, (τ, m)-threshold scheme refers to Kurihara *et al.*'s (τ, m)-threshold scheme. In the following, we list some properties of $\mathsf{DA}_{\tau,m}$ and $\mathsf{RA}_{\tau,m}$ of Kurihara *et al.*'s scheme used in this paper.

1. $\mathsf{DA}_{\tau,m}$ can only be constructed for a prime m. For a general m, one can take a prime m_p larger than m, run DA_{τ,m_p}, and discard the surplus shares.
2. For a fixed $D \in \mathbb{Z}_{>0}$, and an input secret $s \in \{0,1\}^{D(m_p-1)}$, $\mathsf{DA}_{\tau,m}(s)$ outputs $s_i \in \{0,1\}^{D(m_p-1)}$ for $i = 1, 2, \ldots, m_p$.
3. $\mathsf{RA}_{\tau,m}$ takes as input τ shares of secrets, and outputs s if all τ inputs are correct shares.
   For a set $S' = \{s'_1, \ldots, s'_\tau\}$, we denote $\mathsf{RA}_{\tau,m}(S') := \mathsf{RA}_{\tau,m}(s'_1, \ldots, s'_\tau)$.
4. $\mathsf{DA}_{\tau,m}$ requires at most $\tau D m_p(m_p - 1)$ XOR operations.

5. Each $\mathsf{RA}_{\tau,m}$ requires at most $\tau D m_p(m_p-1)$ XOR operations given $D(m_p-1)$ by $\tau D(m_p-1)$ binary matrices. (Each of which can be generated by $O(\tau^3 m_p^3)$ bitwise XOR operations).

3 Canetti *et al.*'s Reusable Fuzzy Extractor

As mentioned before, Canetti *et al.* proposed a reusable fuzzy extractor using digital lockers and sample-then-lock construction. In this section, we review their construction and give an analysis on concrete parameters focusing on the case when the input biometric is IrisCode.

3.1 Sources with α-Entropy k-Samples

As in the Canetti *et al.*'s construction [9], we assume that the source $W = W_1 W_2 \ldots W_n$, consisting of strings of length n over some alphabet $\mathcal{Z}$ is a source with *α-entropy k-samples*, i.e., $\tilde{H}_\infty(W_{j_1} W_{j_2} \ldots W_{j_k} | j_1, j_2, \ldots j_k) \geq \alpha$ for k uniformly random indices $1 \leq j_1, j_2, \ldots, j_k \leq n$.

3.2 Digital Lockers

A digital locker is a kind of symmetric encryption scheme which is secure even if many correlated keys have already been used before [18]. It is composed of two algorithms; lock, and unlock. The lock algorithm encrypts val (a value) with key (a key), and outputs $\mathsf{lock}(\mathsf{key}, \mathsf{val})$. The unlock algorithm decrypts $\mathsf{lock}(\mathsf{key}, \mathsf{val})$ with given key', outputs val if $\mathsf{key} = \mathsf{key}'$, and aborts ($\perp$) otherwise. The digital locker can be instantiated as $\mathsf{lock}(\mathsf{key}, \mathsf{val}) = (\mathsf{nonce}, H(\mathsf{nonce}, \mathsf{key}) \oplus (\mathsf{val} \| 0^s))$ where nonce is a nonce, $\|$ denotes concatenation, and s is a security parameter. unlock is instantiated by XORing($\oplus$) $H(\mathsf{nonce}, \mathsf{key}')$ with $\mathsf{lock}(\mathsf{key}, \mathsf{val})$. H can be a random oracle [19], or a cryptographic hash function with specific properties [20]. Note that nonce is usually different for each lock, and by hashing it with key, the correlation between keys disappears. For the following definition of digital lockers, let $\mathsf{idealUnlock}(\mathsf{key}, \mathsf{val})$ be the oracle that returns val when given key, and $\perp$ otherwise.

Definition 3 (Digital locker). *The pair of algorithms* $(\mathsf{lock}, \mathsf{unlock})$ *with security parameter* λ *is an* ℓ*-composable secure digital locker with error* γ *if the following holds:*

- ***Correctness*** *For all* key *and* val, $\Pr[\mathsf{unlock}(\mathsf{key}, \mathsf{lock}(\mathsf{key}, \mathsf{val})) = \mathsf{val}] \geq 1-\gamma$. *Furthermore, for any* $\mathsf{key}' \neq \mathsf{key}$, $\Pr[\mathsf{unlock}(\mathsf{key}', \mathsf{lock}(\mathsf{key}, \mathsf{val})) = \perp] \geq 1-\gamma$.
- ***Security*** *For every PPT adversary A and every positive polynomial p, there exists a (possibly inefficient) simulator S and a polynomial* $q(\lambda)$ *such that for any sufficiently large* s, *any polynomial-long sequence of values* $(\mathsf{val}_i, \mathsf{key}_i)$ *for* $i = 1, \ldots, \ell$, *and any auxiliary input* $z \in \{0,1\}^*$,

$$\left| \Pr\left[A\left(z, \{\mathsf{lock}\left(\mathsf{key}_i, \mathsf{val}_i\right)\}_{i=1}^{\ell}\right) = 1\right] - \Pr\left[S\left(z, \{|\mathsf{key}_i|, |\mathsf{val}_i|\}_{i=1}^{\ell}\right) = 1\right] \right| \leq \frac{1}{p(\mathsf{s})}$$

where S is allowed $q(\lambda)$ *oracle queries to the oracles* $\{\mathsf{idealUnlock}(\mathsf{key}_i, \mathsf{val}_i)\}_{i=1}^{\ell}$.

3.3 Description

The main idea of Canetti *et al.*'s scheme [9] is that a random string $r \in \{0,1\}^\kappa$ is locked multiple times by some substrings $v_1, \ldots, v_\ell$ of an input string w and thus each locked value can be unlocked only with $v_1, \ldots, v_\ell$, respectively. To reproduce the same r, one must extract substrings $v'_1, \ldots, v'_\ell$ corresponding to $v_1, \ldots, v_\ell$, at least one of which must be identical to its counterpart, and proceed to unlock with those substrings.

Construction (Sample-then-Lock, [9]). Let $\mathcal{M} = \{0,1\}^n$ be an input space and $w = w_1 \ldots w_n \in \mathcal{M}$, where $w_i \in \{0,1\}$. Let ℓ be a positive integer and let $(\mathsf{lock}, \mathsf{unlock})$ be an ℓ-composable secure digital locker with error γ. To recover the random value r in Rep, information on how the substrings are generated should be stored. Thus a helper value p containing the indices of the bits of $w = w_1 \ldots w_n$ which are used for each substring is generated along with r in Gen. The algorithms are in the next table.

Algorithm 1: Gen and Rep of Canetti *et al.*'s Reusable Fuzzzy Extractor

Gen	Rep
Input: $w = w_1 \ldots w_n$	**Input**: $w' = w'_1 \ldots w'_n$, $p = p_1 \ldots p_\ell$
1. Sample $r \xleftarrow{\$} \{0,1\}^\kappa$	
2. For $i = 1, \ldots, \ell$	1. For $i = 1, \ldots, \ell$
(i) Uniformly choose $j_{i,m} \xleftarrow{\$} \{1, \ldots, n\}$ for each $1 \le m \le k$	(i) Parse p_i as $c_i, (j_{i,1}, \ldots, j_{i,k})$
	(ii) $v'_i \leftarrow w'_{j_{i,1}} \ldots w'_{j_{i,k}}$
(ii) $v_i \leftarrow w_{j_{i,1}} \ldots w_{j_{i,k}}$	(iii) $r_i \leftarrow \mathsf{unlock}(v'_i, c)$
(iii) $c_i \leftarrow \mathsf{lock}(v_i, r)$	If $r_i \neq \perp$, then output r_i.
(iv) $p_i \leftarrow c_i, (j_{i,1}, \ldots, j_{i,k})$	
3. Output (r, p) where $p = p_1 \ldots p_\ell$	2. Output $\perp$

3.4 Analysis on Concrete Parameters

In this subsection, we give an analysis of Canetti *et al.*'s fuzzy extractor with concrete parameters with IrisCode as the input biometric. To make the False Rejection Rate (FRR) less than δ, it requires the following condition:

$$\left(1 - \left(1 - \frac{t}{n}\right)^k\right)^\ell + \ell \cdot \gamma \le \delta.$$

Using the approximation $e^x \approx 1 + x$, they suggested parameter conditions $\ell \cdot \gamma \le \delta/2$, $tk = cn \log n$, and $\ell \approx n^c \log \frac{2}{\delta}$ for some constant c. Note that under these parameter conditions, we have $\left(1 - (1 - \frac{t}{n})^k\right)^\ell \approx (1 - e^{-\frac{tk}{n}})^\ell \approx \exp(-\ell e^{-\frac{tk}{n}}) \approx \delta/2$ where e is the natural constant.

However, if $\mathsf{lock}(\mathsf{key}, \mathsf{val}) = (\mathsf{nonce}, H(\mathsf{nonce}, \mathsf{key}) \oplus \mathsf{val}||0^s)$ where H is a hash function, we can set better parameters since $\gamma = 2^{-s}$ is small enough. In our parameter setting, we set $\delta = 1/2$, $\kappa = 128$, and use SHA2[4] with 224-bit output as an instantiation of H. Then, $\mathsf{lock}(v_i, r)$ has an error rate $\gamma \approx 2^{128-224} = 2^{-96}$, and $\ell \cdot \gamma$ is negligible. Therefore, we set parameters so that the first term of the above condition is slightly smaller than $\delta = 1/2$, instead of $\delta/2$. Now, we have $\left(1 - \left(1 - \frac{t}{n}\right)^k\right)^\ell \approx \exp(-\ell e^{-\frac{tk}{n}}) \lesssim \delta$ from $\ell \approx n^c \log \frac{1}{\delta} = e^{\frac{tk}{n}}$ and $tk = cn \log n$.[5]

Error Tolerance. Many researches have indicated that the Threshold Hamming Distance $T := \frac{t}{n}$ of IrisCode should lie between 20% and 35% [21–23]. According to this, we set $T = 0.2, 0.25, 0.3, 0.35$.

Security. With the helper value p, an adversary without biometric information can run a brute force attack on digital locker $\mathsf{lock}(v_i, r)$ with an exhaustive search for v_i which is a partial biometric of a user. Therefore, $k = |v_i|$ must be larger than at least the security parameter λ. We set $k = \lambda = 80$.[6]

Iteration Number. Given $T = t/n$, k, and $\delta = 0.5$, we set iteration number $\ell \approx e^{\frac{tk}{n}}$ so that the false rejection rate is smaller than 0.5.

Storage Space. The helper value p consists of two parts; indices and locks for each iteration. The indices for each iteration represent k among n bit positions of the biometric, and requires $(k \log n)$-bits of storage space. On the other hand, since we use SHA2-224, $|r| = \kappa = 128$, $k = 80$, and the output size of hash function is 224 bits. We set the nonce for the hash input to 144 bits[7]. As we need ℓ iterations, the total storage space for lockers is $\ell \cdot (k \log n + 368)$ bits.

Time Consumption. To measure actual time consumption, we implemented Canetti *et al.*'s reusable fuzzy extractor as a C++ program. We used g++ 5.4.0 to compile C++ source codes under the C++ 11 standard and ran them on a GNU/Linux ubuntu 4.4.0-62-generic machine that has a Intel(R) Xeon(R) E5-2620 v4 2.10 GHz CPU with a 64 GB RAM and a x86_64 architecture. We measured the average time for 1 unlock under various sets of parameters, and obtained results as displayed in the table below.

---

4 One can also use SHA3 or other hash functions.

5 We take $\delta = 1/2$ for convenience. One can achieve $\delta = 1/2^b$ increasing ℓ to $b\ell$.

6 In fact, we should take into account the min-entropy of the partial biometric, but we will assume that the min-entropy is k for simplicity.

7 In fact, we should take the size of nonce so that the resulting locker is ℓ-composable, i.e., no collision occurs among ℓ nonces. In our cases, 144 (= 224−80) bit is sufficient for the size of nonce.

Table 1. Security, storage space and time consumption with $\delta = 1/2$, $\kappa = 128$, SHA2-224.

Security k	Biometric n	Error tolerance T	Iterations ℓ	Storage space (Byte)			Rep Time (unlock) (μs)
				Index	Lock	Total	
80	512	0.20	4.41×10^7	3.97 G	2.03 G	6.00 G	12.6
80	512	0.25	6.85×10^9	617 G	315 G	932 G	12.6
80	512	0.30	1.87×10^{12}	168 T	86.0 T	254 T	12.6
80	512	0.35	7.79×10^{14}	70.1 P	35.8 P	106 P	12.6
80	1024	0.20	4.00×10^7	4.00 G	1.84 G	5.84 G	13.9
80	1024	0.25	6.85×10^9	685 G	315 G	1 T	13.9
80	1024	0.30	1.87×10^{12}	187 T	86.0 T	273 T	13.9
80	1024	0.35	6.90×10^{14}	69.0 P	31.8 P	101 P	13.9
80	2048	0.20	4.00×10^7	4.40 G	1.84 G	6.24 G	15.5
80	2048	0.25	6.85×10^9	754 G	315 G	1.07 T	15.5
80	2048	0.30	1.77×10^{12}	194 T	81.3 T	276 T	15.5
80	2048	0.35	6.50×10^{14}	71.5 P	29.9 P	101 P	15.5

In Table 1, we present security, storage space, and time required for each unlock with concrete parameters.[8] The maximum required time of Rep is $\ell \times$ Time(unlock). As fully carrying out all ℓ iterations of Rep is unfeasible for most parameter sets due to the large storage space requirements, we ran Rep for a much smaller number of iterations and computed the average running time for each single iteration of Rep and measured the storage memory theoretically.

The form of digital lockers are the same for all cases, and time for unlock changes little by input size. Note that the iteration ℓ and Storage space highly (exponentially) depends on T, but not on n.

4 Our Construction and Analysis

Note that, in Canetti *et al.*'s scheme, $tk = cn \log n$ and $l \approx n^c \log \frac{2}{\delta}$ give large ℓ values, leading to large storage space for $T \in [0.2, 0.35]$. One easy strategy for reducing memory requirements is reducing k. However, a smaller k value implies less security, since an adversary can easily unlock $\mathsf{lock}(\mathsf{key}, \mathsf{val})$ if $k = |\mathsf{key}|$ is small.

We solve this problem by preventing adversaries from checking their guesses on each individual lock. For this purpose, we use a modified digital locker $(\mathsf{lock}', \mathsf{unlock}')$. It is a symmetric encryption scheme very similar to the original digital locker except for one difference; unlock' outputs a random string instead of $\perp$ when $\mathsf{key}' \neq \mathsf{key}$. With this modified digital locker, adversaries can not check whether their guesses are right or not, since they can not distinguish a random string from val in our construction.

[8] Canetti *et al.* [9] mentioned that with sophisticated samplers, one can decrease the required storage. However, it can only decrease the storage for index, and the storage for locks can not be decreased.

However, a fuzzy extractor must output $\perp$ when the input is not legitimate. We additionally exploit a (τ, m)-threshold scheme to enable legitimacy checking. More precisely, we encrypt each share with the modified lock, so that the adversary can recover the original secret s only if he or she has found τ or more correct shares by unlocking corresponding lock's with their correct keys. Then, the legitimacy check of the recovered secret s' is done by $\mathsf{unlock}(s', \mathsf{lock}(s, r))$.

4.1 Construction

The details of our construction are as follows. First, the modified digital locker can be instantiated as the original digital locker with the reduction of the zero-padding portion, i.e., $\mathsf{lock}'(\mathsf{key}, \mathsf{val}) := (\mathsf{nonce}, \pi \circ H(\mathsf{nonce}, \mathsf{key}) \oplus \mathsf{val})$ for $\mathsf{val} \in \{0,1\}^v$ and $\mathsf{key} \in \{0,1\}^k$, where $\pi : \{0,1\}^\mu \longrightarrow \{0,1\}^v$ is the canonical projection of the first v bits of vectors in $\{0,1\}^\mu$, the output space of hash H. Unlock' is similar to unlock, XORing $(\oplus)$ lock' with $\pi \circ H(\mathsf{nonce}, \mathsf{key}')$. The notion of security for the modified digital locker is the same as that of the original digital locker, except that if $\mathsf{key}' \neq \mathsf{key}$, $\mathsf{unlock}'(\mathsf{key}', \mathsf{lock}(\mathsf{key}, \mathsf{val}))$ outputs $\mathsf{val}' \neq \mathsf{val}$ which is indistinguishable from a uniformly random string. H can be a random oracle or the same cryptographic hash function H as in the original digital locker.

The Gen algorithm takes as input a bit string w with length n. For a divisor d of n,[9] we consider the set $\mathbb{P}_d(n)$ of partitions $\mathcal{P} = \{B_j : |B_j| = d\}_{j=1}^m$ of $[n] = \{1, \ldots, n\}$ where $m = n/d$.[10] For a partition $\mathcal{P}_i \in \mathbb{P}_d(n)$, we denote $v_{i,j} = w_{B_j} := w_{j_1}, \ldots, w_{j_d}$, where $B_j = \{j_1, \ldots, j_d\} \in \mathcal{P}_i$. We first choose a random string $r \in \{0,1\}^\kappa$ and lock it with a random secret $s_i \in \{0,1\}^k$ resulting in $\mathsf{lock}(s_i, r)$.[11]

Next we split this s_i into several shares $\{s_{i,j}\}_{j=1}^m$ using the Distribution Algorithm $\mathsf{DA}_{\tau,m}$ of the (τ, m)–threshold scheme. We now choose a random partition $\mathcal{P}_i \in \mathbb{P}_d(n)$, which specifies $v_{i,j}$'s for $j = 1, \ldots, m$. Finally, lock the shares $s_{i,j}$ with the substrings $v_{i,j}$ of w using the modified locker, resulting in $\mathsf{lock}'(v_{i,j}, s_{i,j})$. We iterate this process N times, and output the public helper value which can be represented by $\{\mathsf{lock}(s_i, r), \mathsf{lock}'(v_{i,j}, s_{i,j})|_{j=1}^m, \mathcal{P}_i\}_{i=1}^N$.

The Rep algorithm is simple. Each partition $\mathcal{P}_i$ in the helper value specifies $v_{i,j}^*$'s from the input w^*. Unlock all modified $\mathsf{lock}'(v_{i,j}, s_{i,j})$'s with $v_{i,j}^*$'s. Finally, use Recovery Algorithm $\mathsf{RA}_{\tau,m}$ to recover s_i from $s_{i,j}^*$, and check if the recovered s_i^* is correct by unlocking $\mathsf{lock}(s_i, r)$. Output r if at least one of such unlocks was successful, and output $\perp$ otherwise.

---

9 We can also consider a divisor d of $n' \leq n$, and follow the construction taking n' instead of n.

10 For convenience, we only consider the partitions whose elements have the same cardinality. An analogous statement can be made for more general partitions.

11 Note that, in (τ, m) threshold scheme, the size of secret k is $D(m_p - 1)$ for some $D \in \mathbb{Z}_{>0}$. We take D satisfying proper security.

Algorithm 2 :Gen and Rep of our RFE

Gen	Rep
Input: $w = w_1 \dots w_n$	**Input**: $w^* = w_1^* \dots w_n^*$, $p = (p_1 \dots p_N)$
1. Sample $r \xleftarrow{\$} \{0,1\}^\kappa$	
2. For $i = 1, \dots, N$	1. For $i = 1, \dots, N$
(i) Choose $\mathcal{P}_i \in \mathbb{P}_d(n)$, sample $s_i \xleftarrow{\$} \{0,1\}^k$	(i) Parse p_i as $c_{i,1}, \dots, c_{i,m}, \mathcal{P}_i, d_i$
(ii) $s_{i,1}, \dots, s_{i,m} \leftarrow \mathsf{DA}_{\tau,m}(s_i)$, $(m = n/d)$	(ii) For $j = 1, \dots, m$
(iii) for $j = 1, \dots, m$ with $\{B_j\}_{j=1}^m = \mathcal{P}_i$	(ii)-1 $v_{i,j}^* = w_{B_j}^*$, where $\{B_1, \dots, B_m\} = \mathcal{P}_i$
(iii)-1 $v_{i,j} = w_{B_j}$	
(iii)-2 $c_{i,j} \leftarrow \mathsf{lock}'(v_{i,j}, s_{i,j})$	(ii)-2 $s_{i,j}^* \leftarrow \mathsf{unlock}'(v_{i,j}^*, c_{i,j})$
	(iii) For each $S \subseteq \{s_{i,j}^*\}_{j=1}^m$ s.t. $\lvert S \rvert = \tau$,
(iv) $d_i \leftarrow \mathsf{lock}(s_i, r)$	(iii)-1 $s_i^* \leftarrow \mathsf{RA}_{\tau,m}(S)$
(v) $p_i \leftarrow c_{i,1}, \dots, c_{i,m}, \mathcal{P}_i, d_i$	(iii)-2 $r_i^* \leftarrow \mathsf{unlock}(s_i^*, d_i)$, and if $r_i^* \neq \perp$ then output r_i^*.
3. Output (r, p) where $p = (p_1 \dots p_N)$	2. Output $\perp$

4.2 Parameters and Security Analysis

Correctness and Security. To ensure correctness of the FE, the parameters must satisfy

$$\mathsf{FRR} := \Pr[\perp \leftarrow \mathsf{Rep}(w^*) | \mathsf{dis}(w, w^*) \leq t] \leq \delta.$$

To compute this probability, for fixed $\mathcal{P}_i$ and w^* with $\mathsf{dis}(w, w^*) = t$, let

$$q = \Pr\left[s = s_i^* | s_i^* \leftarrow \mathsf{RA}_{\tau,m}(S) \text{ for some } S \in \mathbb{P}_\tau(\{s_{i,j}^*\}_{j=1}^m)\right]. \quad (1)$$

Note that q is independent from the index i. Then, FRR is at most $(1-q)^N + N \cdot \gamma$ considering incorrectness arising from error γ in the lockers. As in Sect. 3.4 we ignore $N \cdot \gamma$ and set $(1-q)^N \approx 1 - qN \lesssim \delta = 1/2$.

Here, we state a lemma calculating the exact value of q. All proofs of lemmas and theorems in this subsection are given in the full version of this paper, which will be uploaded in ePrint.[12]

Lemma 4. *Let $\mathcal{M} = \{0,1\}^n$ be the input space of the reusable fuzzy extractor in Construction with parameters $n, d, \lambda, \tau, \delta, t$ as previously defined. For an input $w = w_1 w_2 \dots w_n$, let $(r, p) \leftarrow Gen(W)$. If a certifier has a query input $w^* = w_1^* \dots w_n^*$ with $\mathsf{dis}(w, w^*) = t$,*

$$q := \Pr(r_i^* = r) = \frac{{}_{\tau m}C_\tau}{{}_nC_t} \sum_{\eta=\tau}^{m} (-1)^{\eta-\tau} \cdot \frac{{}_{m-\tau}C_{\eta-\tau} \times {}_{n-\eta d}C_t}{\eta} \text{ for all } i = 1, \dots, N.$$

Here ${}_aC_b$ denotes the usual binomial coefficient $\frac{a!}{b!(a-b)!}$ for integers a, b such that $0 \leq b \leq a$.

---

[12] https://eprint.iacr.org/.

We can easily see that our fuzzy extractor is reusable, as is Canetti *et al.*'s.

Theorem 5. *Let λ be a security parameter and $\mathcal{W}$ be a family of sources with α-entropy k-samples over $\mathcal{Z}^n$ where $\alpha = \omega(\log \lambda)$. Then for any $s_{sec} = \mathsf{poly}(\lambda)$ there exists an $\epsilon_{sec} = \mathsf{ngl}(\lambda)$ such that Construction is a $(\mathcal{Z}^n, \mathcal{W}, \kappa, t)$- computational fuzzy extractor that is $(\epsilon_{sec}, s_{sec})$-hard with error $\delta = (1-q)^N + mN \cdot \gamma$, where the formula for q is given in Lemma 4.*

Reusability. As in [9], reusability follows easily from the security of digital lockers. To enable ρ reuses, we need $N(m+1)\cdot\rho$ composable digital lockers. Then we can simulate an adversary given $r^1, \ldots, r^{i-1}, r^{i+1}, \ldots, r^\rho$, and $p^1, \ldots, p^\rho$ as a simulator with $r^1, \ldots, r^{i-1}, r^{i+1}, \ldots, r^\rho$ as auxiliary input in the security of digital locker (see Definition 3). Now, we can prove the reusability similarly to Theorem 5.

Theorem 6. *Fix ρ and let all the variables be as in Theorem 5, except that* $(\mathsf{lock}, \mathsf{unlock})$ *is $N(m+1)\cdot\rho$ - composable instead of $N(m+1)$ - composable*[13] *(for κ-bit values and keys over $\mathcal{Z}^k$). Then for all $s_{sec} = \mathsf{poly}(n)$ there exists some $\epsilon_{sec} = \mathsf{ngl}(n)$ such that Construction is a $(\rho, \epsilon_{sec}, s_{sec})$-reusable fuzzy extractor.*

Comparison with [9]. In Canetti *et al.*'s work [9], they used the subsets of strings (biometrics) to lock and take multiple samples for correctness. However, for reliable error tolerance, they required too many samples, resulting in the use of enormous amounts of memory space as displayed in Table 1. We divide said subsets into small pieces and use the threshold scheme to diminish storage space requirement. As a result, our scheme consumes more time as it requires multiple RA operations in recovering the secret. We will show that this can be resolved through the use of parallel computing. In [9], the source of w needed to be *α-entropy k-samples*, i.e., $\tilde{H}_\infty(W_{j_1} W_{j_2} \ldots W_{j_k} | j_1, j_2, \ldots j_k) \geq \alpha$ for k uniformly random indices $1 \leq j_1, j_2, \ldots, j_k \leq n$. Our construction requires a slightly different condition regarding the distribution of the source : $\tilde{H}_\infty(W_{j_1} W_{j_2} \ldots W_{j_k} | j_1, j_2, \ldots j_k) \geq \alpha$ for k uniformly random indices $1 \leq j_1, j_2, \ldots, j_k \leq n$ selected without repetition.

4.3 Analysis on Concrete Parameters

To analyze our scheme as in Sect. 3.4 with concrete parameters, we calculated the storage space and number of operations needed when employing Kurihara *et al.*'s threshold scheme. We set $\delta = 1/2$, $\kappa = 128$, $T = \frac{t}{n} = 0.2, 0.25, 0.3$, $\tilde{k} := \tau d \geq \lambda = 80$ and used SHA2-224 as the hash function as in Sect. 3.4.

Security. To recover r, an adversary equipped with helper value p must correctly guess at least τ of the $d-$bit keys for lock''s. Therefore, $\tau \cdot d$ should be at least $\lambda = 80$, the security parameter. (Note that as in Canetti *et al.*'s scheme, we should consider the min-entropy of the partial biometric of length τd.)

[13] Canetti *et al.*'s construction requires ℓ or $\ell\rho$ -composable digital lockers, and $\ell \geq N(m+1)$ in our parameter settings.

Iteration Number. For given $T = \frac{t}{n}$, $\tilde{k} = \tau d$, and $\delta = 0.5$, we can find iteration number N such that FRR $\leq (1-q)^N + N \cdot \gamma \leq 0.5$ where q is defined in Lemma 4. As in Sect. 3.4, $N\gamma$ is negligible.

Storage Space. The helper value p again consists of two parts; indices and digital lockers. Indices for each iteration indicate which among m sets in a partition of $[n]$ each biometric bit belongs to, and take up roughly $(n \log m)$-bits of memory space. The size of a locker (of either type) is the sum of the output size 224 bits of hash function SHA2-224 and that of the nonce in the hash input which is 144 bits. Since we need $m+1$ lockers (1 for $\mathsf{lock}(s_i, r)$) each for a total of N iterations, the total memory required for p is $N \cdot (n \log m + (224+144) \cdot (m+1))$ bits. This is denoted as "Help.val." in Table 2. For efficient computation of the secret sharing scheme, we will additionally store $\binom{m}{\tau}$ precomputed $(m_p - 1) \times \tau(m_p - 1)$ binary matrices needed for each of the $\binom{m}{\tau}$ recovery algorithms. The matrices are reused for all N iterations. The amount of memory space dedicated to these matrices is denoted as "Mat." in Table 2.

Time Consumption. We implemented our fuzzy extractor in the same environment as in Sect. 3.4.

Here we give a table for the required storage space, time consumption, and security of our reusable fuzzy extractor. Again, we did not run the program for all N iterations, but instead ran it for a smaller number of iterations multiple times to obtain average values of the time costs of the unlock' and $(\mathsf{RA} + \mathsf{unlock})$ operations. "All unlock'" denotes the time for *(ii)*, and "$1(\mathsf{RA}+\mathsf{unlock})$" denotes the time for each subset S in *(iii)* of Rep (Algorithm 2).

In our FE, Rep takes at most $N \cdot (\binom{m}{\tau} \cdot \mathsf{Time}(\mathsf{RA} + \mathsf{unlock}) + \mathsf{Time}(\mathsf{All\ unlock}'))$ time. The maximum time for Gen is $N \cdot (\mathsf{Time}(\mathsf{DA} + \mathsf{lock}) + \mathsf{Time}(\mathsf{All\ lock}'))$.[14]

We visualized the trade-off between time and helper value storage space in Fig. 1.[15] Every point in the figure comes from either Table 1 or Table 2. The amount of required memory tends to decrease by a factor of approximately 10^3, i.e. from GB to MB(or TB to GB) whenever time consumption increases tenfold. Although time consumption seems impractical for both FEs, this can be solved with parallel computing methods since Rep consists of mutually independent iterative routines. We actually implemented our scheme with parallel computing using CUDA as proof of this (though not optimized), and the obtained positive results. We compiled CUDA and C++(test driver) codes using nvcc v7.5.17 with the SM53 architecture and under the C++ 11 standard. Then we ran the program on the aforementioned GNU/Linux machine with the same CPU, with an additional NVIDIA GeForce GTX 1080 GPU attached for the parallel

[14] Since $\mathsf{Time}(\mathsf{RA}) \approx \mathsf{Time}(\mathsf{DA})$, maximal time of Rep is much bigger than that of Gen, and we only consider the time of Rep.

[15] The space for "Mat. for DA" is excluded since it is a common data for every users. It doesn't affect the tendency in this graph overall.

Table 2. The table for the storage space, time consumption and security of our scheme. The column $\tilde{k}$ and T means the security parameter and the error tolerance, respectively.

$\tilde{k}$	Bio. n	T	d	τ	m	Iter. N	Storage space (Byte)				Time/iteration (μs)	
							Mat.	Index	Lock	Help.val.	All unlock′	1(RA+unlock)
80	512	0.2	16	5	32	1674	1.47 G	0.54 M	2.45 M	3.00 M	184	25.2
80	512	0.2	20	4	25	38612	44.6 M	11.5 M	44.4 M	55.9 M	146	16.3
80	512	0.25	16	5	32	$3.82 \cdot 10^5$	1.47 G	122 M	562 M	685 M	184	25.2
80	512	0.3	16	5	32	$1.98 \cdot 10^8$	1.47 G	63.5 G	292 G	355 G	184	25.2
80	1024	0.2	20	4	51	516	1.35 G	0.37 M	1.21 M	1.59 M	292	39.0
81	1024	0.2	27	3	37	26786	34.0 M	17.9 M	45.6 M	63.5 M	428	18.8
80	1024	0.25	20	4	51	97751	1.35 G	71.0 M	228 M	300 M	292	39.0
80	1024	0.3	20	4	51	$3.63 \cdot 10^7$	1.35 G	26.3 G	85.1 G	111G	292	39.0
81	2048	0.2	27	3	75	1546	616 M	2.47 M	5.33 M	7.80 M	440	60.9
81	2048	0.25	27	3	75	$3.26 \cdot 10^5$	616 M	520 M	1.12 G	1.64G	440	60.9

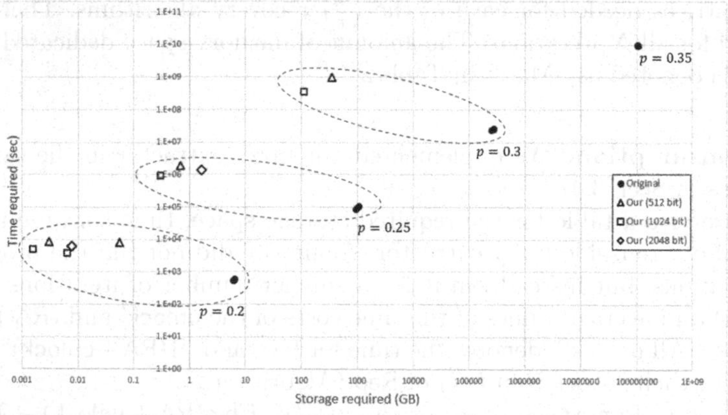

Fig. 1. A log-scaled graph of storage space for helper values and time (Original and Ours)

computing. For the case $(n, p, d, \tau, m) = (1024, 0.2, 27, 3, 37)$, the algorithm Rep takes only 151 s, which is 20 times faster than without parallelization.

5 Conclusion

We analyzed the reusable fuzzy extractor of Canetti *et al.* with concrete parameters regarding iris authentication with IrisCode and found out that the required storage space is too large to be used in practice. To solve this problem, we propose a modified reusable fuzzy extractor using a perfect threshold scheme. Our modification cuts down the memory cost by a considerable amount. Though this approach yields a trade-off between memory and time costs, this can be resolved through parallel computing, since Rep consists of independent subroutines. When fully parallelized, our scheme reduces memory requirements from GB or TB to MB in many cases, while still operating in reasonable time.

Acknowledgements. The authors would like to thank the anonymous reviewers of ACISP 2018 for their valuable comments. This work were supported by Samsung Electronics, Co., Ltd. (No. 0536-20160013).

References

1. Erkin, Z., Franz, M., Guajardo, J., Katzenbeisser, S., Lagendijk, I., Toft, T.: Privacy-preserving face recognition. In: Goldberg, I., Atallah, M.J. (eds.) PETS 2009. LNCS, vol. 5672, pp. 235–253. Springer, Heidelberg (2009). https://doi.org/10.1007/978-3-642-03168-7_14
2. Kulkarni, R., Namboodiri, A.M.: Secure hamming distance based biometric authentication. In: International Conference on Biometrics, ICB 2013, pp. 1–6 (2013). https://doi.org/10.1109/ICB.2013.6613008
3. Karabat, C., Kiraz, M.S., Erdogan, H., Savas, E.: THRIVE: threshold homomorphic encryption based secure and privacy preserving biometric verification system. EURASIP J. Adv. Sig. Process. **2015**, 71 (2015). https://doi.org/10.1186/s13634-015-0255-5
4. Cheon, J.H., Chung, H., Kim, M., Lee, K.: Ghostshell: secure biometric authentication using integrity-based homomorphic evaluations. IACR Cryptology ePrint Archive 2016, 484 (2016)
5. Dodis, Y., Reyzin, L., Smith, A.: Fuzzy extractors: how to generate strong keys from biometrics and other noisy data. In: Cachin, C., Camenisch, J.L. (eds.) EUROCRYPT 2004. LNCS, vol. 3027, pp. 523–540. Springer, Heidelberg (2004). https://doi.org/10.1007/978-3-540-24676-3_31
6. Dodis, Y., Ostrovsky, R., Reyzin, L., Smith, A.D.: Fuzzy extractors: how to generate strong keys from biometrics and other noisy data. SIAM J. Comput. **38**(1), 97–139 (2008). https://doi.org/10.1137/060651380
7. Apon, D., Cho, C., Eldefrawy, K., Katz, J.: Efficient, reusable fuzzy extractors from LWE. In: Dolev, S., Lodha, S. (eds.) CSCML 2017. LNCS, vol. 10332, pp. 1–18. Springer, Cham (2017). https://doi.org/10.1007/978-3-319-60080-2_1
8. Fuller, B., Meng, X., Reyzin, L.: Computational fuzzy extractors. In: Sako, K., Sarkar, P. (eds.) ASIACRYPT 2013. LNCS, vol. 8269, pp. 174–193. Springer, Heidelberg (2013). https://doi.org/10.1007/978-3-642-42033-7_10
9. Canetti, R., Fuller, B., Paneth, O., Reyzin, L., Smith, A.: Reusable fuzzy extractors for low-entropy distributions. In: Fischlin, M., Coron, J.-S. (eds.) EUROCRYPT 2016. LNCS, vol. 9665, pp. 117–146. Springer, Heidelberg (2016). https://doi.org/10.1007/978-3-662-49890-3_5
10. Boyen, X., Dodis, Y., Katz, J., Ostrovsky, R., Smith, A.: Secure remote authentication using biometric data. In: Cramer, R. (ed.) EUROCRYPT 2005. LNCS, vol. 3494, pp. 147–163. Springer, Heidelberg (2005). https://doi.org/10.1007/11426639_9
11. Dodis, Y., Kanukurthi, B., Katz, J., Reyzin, L., Smith, A.D.: Robust fuzzy extractors and authenticated key agreement from close secrets. IEEE Trans. Inf. Theory **58**(9), 6207–6222 (2012). https://doi.org/10.1109/TIT.2012.2200290
12. Shamir, A.: How to share a secret. Commun. ACM **11**, 612–613 (1979). https://doi.org/10.1145/359168.359176
13. Blakley, G.R.: Safeguarding cryptographic keys. In: Proceedings of the AFIPS 1979 National Computer Conference, pp. 313–317 (1979). https://doi.org/10.1109/AFIPS.1979.98

14. Ishizu, H., Ogihara, T.: A study on long-term storage of electronic data. In: Proceedings of the IEICE General Conference, vol. D-9-10, no. 1, p. 125 (2004)
15. Fujii, Y.: A fast (2, n)-threshold scheme and its application. In: Proceedings of the CSS 2005, pp. 631–636 (2005)
16. Kurihara, J., Kiyomoto, S., Fukushima, K., Tanaka, T.: A fast (3, n)-threshold secret sharing scheme using exclusive-OR operations. IEICE Trans. Fundam. Electron. Commun. Comput. Sci. **91**(1), 127–138 (2008). https://doi.org/10.1093/ietfec/e91-a.1.127
17. Kurihara, J., Kiyomoto, S., Fukushima, K., Tanaka, T.: A New (k, n)-threshold secret sharing scheme and its extension. In: Wu, T.-C., Lei, C.-L., Rijmen, V., Lee, D.-T. (eds.) ISC 2008. LNCS, vol. 5222, pp. 455–470. Springer, Heidelberg (2008). https://doi.org/10.1007/978-3-540-85886-7_31
18. Canetti, R., Tauman Kalai, Y., Varia, M., Wichs, D.: On symmetric encryption and point obfuscation. In: Micciancio, D. (ed.) TCC 2010. LNCS, vol. 5978, pp. 52–71. Springer, Heidelberg (2010). https://doi.org/10.1007/978-3-642-11799-2_4
19. Lynn, B., Prabhakaran, M., Sahai, A.: Positive results and techniques for obfuscation. In: Cachin, C., Camenisch, J.L. (eds.) EUROCRYPT 2004. LNCS, vol. 3027, pp. 20–39. Springer, Heidelberg (2004). https://doi.org/10.1007/978-3-540-24676-3_2
20. Canetti, R., Dakdouk, R.R.: Obfuscating point functions with multibit output. In: Smart, N. (ed.) EUROCRYPT 2008. LNCS, vol. 4965, pp. 489–508. Springer, Heidelberg (2008). https://doi.org/10.1007/978-3-540-78967-3_28
21. Hollingsworth, K.P., Bowyer, K.W., Flynn, P.J.: Improved iris recognition through fusion of hamming distance and fragile bit distance. IEEE Trans. Pattern Anal. Mach. Intell. **33**(12), 2465–2476 (2011). https://doi.org/10.1109/TPAMI.2011.89
22. Daugman, J.: Probing the uniqueness and randomness of iriscodes: results from 200 billion iris pair comparisons. Proc. IEEE **94**(11), 1927–1935 (2006). https://doi.org/10.1109/JPROC.2006.884092
23. Desoky, A.I., Ali, H.A., Abdel-Hamid, N.B.: Enhancing iris recognition system performance using templates fusion. Ain Shams Eng. J. **3**(2), 133–140 (2012). https://doi.org/10.1109/ISSPIT.2010.5711758

21 - Bringing Down the Complexity: Fast Composable Protocols for Card Games Without Secret State

Bernardo David[1,3(✉)], Rafael Dowsley[2,3], and Mario Larangeira[1,3]

[1] Tokyo Institute of Technology, Tokyo, Japan
{bernardo,mario}@c.titech.ac.jp
[2] Aarhus University, Aarhus, Denmark
[3] IOHK, Hong Kong, China
rafael@cs.au.dk

Abstract. While many cryptographic protocols for card games have been proposed, all of them focus on card games where players have some state that must be kept secret from each other, *e.g* closed cards and bluffs in Poker. This scenario poses many interesting technical challenges, which are addressed with cryptographic tools that introduce significant computational and communication overheads (*e.g.* zero-knowledge proofs). In this paper, we consider the case of games that do not require any secret state to be maintained (*e.g.* Blackjack and Baccarat). Basically, in these games, cards are chosen at random and then publicly advertised, allowing for players to publicly announce their actions (before or after cards are known). We show that protocols for such games can be built from very lightweight primitives such as digital signatures and canonical random oracle commitments, yielding constructions that far outperform all known card game protocols in terms of communication, computational and round complexities. Moreover, in constructing highly efficient protocols, we introduce a new technique based on verifiable random functions for extending coin tossing, which is at the core of our constructions. Besides ensuring that the games are played correctly, our protocols support financial rewards and penalties enforcement, guaranteeing that winners receive their rewards and that cheaters get financially penalized. In order to do so, we build on blockchain-based techniques that leverage the power of stateful smart contracts to ensure fair protocol execution.

1 Introduction

Cryptographic protocols for securely playing card games among mutually distrustful parties have been investigated since the seminal work of Shamir

B. David and M. Larangeira—This work was supported by the Input Output Cryptocurrency Collaborative Research Chair, which has received funding from Input Output HK.

R. Dowsley—This project has received funding from the European research Council (ERC) under the European Unions's Horizon 2020 research and innovation programme (grant agreement No 669255).

W. Susilo and G. Yang (Eds.): ACISP 2018, LNCS 10946, pp. 45–63, 2018.
https://doi.org/10.1007/978-3-319-93638-3_4

et al. [20] in the late 1970s, which initiated a long line of research [3,4,8,10–12,14,17–19,21–24]. Not surprisingly, all of these previous works have focused on obtaining protocols suitable for implementing a game of Poker, which poses several interesting technical challenges. Intuitively, in order to protect a player's "poker face" and allow him to bluff, all of his cards might need to be kept private throughout (and even after) protocol execution. In previous works, ensuring this level of privacy required several powerful but expensive cryptographic techniques, such as the use of zero-knowledge proofs and threshold cryptography. However, not all popular card games require a secret state (*e.g.* private cards) to be maintained, which is the case of the popular games of Blackjack (or 21) and Baccarat. In this work, we investigate how to exploit this fundamental difference to construct protocols specifically for games without secret state that achieve higher efficiency than those for Poker.

Games Without Secret State: In games such as Baccarat and Blackjack, no card is privately kept by any player at any time. Basically, in such games, cards from a shuffled deck of closed cards (whose values are unknown to all players) are publicly opened, having their value revealed to all players. We say these are *games without secret state*, since no player possesses any secret state (*i.e.* private cards) at any point in the game, as opposed to games such as Poker, where the goal of the game is to leverage private knowledge of one's card's values to choose the best strategy. An immediate consequence of this crucial difference is that the heavy cryptographic machinery used to guarantee the secrecy and integrity of privately held cards can be eliminated, facilitating the construction of highly efficient card game protocols.

Security Definitions: Even though protocol for secure card games (and specially Poker) have been investigated for several decades, formal security definitions have only been introduced very recently in Kaleidoscope [12] (for the case of Poker protocols) and Royale [14] (for the case of protocols for general card games). Concrete security issues and cases of cheating when trusting online casinos for playing card games are also analysed in [12]. The lack of formal security definitions in previous works has not only made their security guarantees unclear but resulted in concrete security issues, such as the ones in [3,8,23,24], as pointed out in [12,19]. Hence, it is important to provide security definitions that capture the class of protocols for card games without secret state. Adapting the approach of Royale [14] for defining security of protocols for general card games with secret state in the Universal Composability framework of [6] is a promising direction to tackle this problem. Besides clearly describing the security guarantees of a given protocol, a security definition following the approach of Royale also ensures that protocols are *composable*, meaning that they can be securely used concurrently with copies of themselves or other protocols.

Enforcing Financial Rewards and Punishment: One of the main issues in previous protocols for card games is ensuring that winners receive their rewards while preventing cheaters to keep the protocol from reaching an outcome. This problem was recently solved by Andrychowicz *et al.* [1,2] through an approach based on decentralized cryptocurrencies and blockchain protocols. They construct a mechanism that ensures that honest players receive financial rewards and financially punishes cheaters (who abort the protocol or provide invalid messages). The main idea is to have all players provide deposits of betting and collateral funds, forfeiting their collateral funds if they are found to be cheating. A cheater's collateral funds are then used to compensate honest players. Their general approach has been subsequently improved and applied to poker protocols by Kumaresan *et al.* [17] and Bentov *et al.* [4]. However, protocols for Poker (resp., for general card games) using this approach have only been formally analysed in Kaleidoscope [12] (resp., Royale [14]), where fine tuned *checkpoint witnesses* of correct protocol execution are also proposed as means of improving the efficiency of the mechanism for enforcing rewards/penalties. Such an approach can be carried over to the case of games without secret state.

1.1 Our Contributions

We introduce a general model for reasoning about the composable security of protocols for games without secret state and a protocol that realizes our security definitions with support to financial rewards/penalties. We also introduce optimizations of our original protocol that achieve better round and communication complexities at the expense of a cheap preprocessing phase (in either the Check-in or Create Shuffled Deck procedures). Our protocols do not require expensive card shuffling operations that rely on zero-knowledge proofs, achieving much higher concrete efficiency than all previous works that support card games with secret state (*e.g.* Poker). Our contributions are summarized below:

- The first ideal functionality for general card games without secret state: $\mathcal{F}_{\mathsf{CG}}$.
- An analysis showing that that Baccarat and Blackjack can be implemented by our general protocol ,*i.e.* in the $\mathcal{F}_{\mathsf{CG}}$-hybrid model (Sect. 3).
- A highly efficient protocol π_{CG} for card games which realizes $\mathcal{F}_{\mathsf{CG}}$ along with optimized Protocols $\pi_{\mathsf{CG-PRE}}$ and $\pi_{\mathsf{CG-VRF}}$ (Theorems 1, 2 and 3).
- A novel technique for coin tossing "extension" based on verifiable random functions (VRF) that is of independent interest (Sect. 5).

We start by defining $\mathcal{F}_{\mathsf{CG}}$, an ideal functionality that captures only games without secret state, which is adapted from the functionality for general card games with secret state proposed in Royale [14]. In order to show that such a restricted functionality still finds interesting applications, we show that the games of Blackjack and Baccarat can be implemented by $\mathcal{F}_{\mathsf{CG}}$. Leveraging the fact the $\mathcal{F}_{\mathsf{CG}}$ only captures games without secret state, we construct protocols that rely on cheap primitives such as digital signatures and canonical random oracle based commitments, as opposed to the heavy zero knowledge and threshold cryptography machinery employed in previous works. Most notably, our approach eliminates the need for expensive card shuffling procedure relying on zero-knowledge proofs of shuffle correctness. In fact, no card shuffling procedure is needed in Protocol π_{CG} and Protocol $\pi_{\mathsf{CG-VRF}}$, where card values are selected on the fly during the Open Card procedure. Our basic protocol π_{CG} simply selects the value of each (publicly) opened card from a set of card values using randomness obtained by a simple commit-and-open coin tossing, which requires two rounds. Later we show that we perform the Open Card operation in one sigle round given a cheap preprocessing phase. In order to perform this optimization, we introduce a new technique that allows for a single coin tossing performed during the Check-in procedure to be later "extended" in a single round with the help of a VRF, obtaining fresh randomness for each Open Card operation.

Related Works. Our results are most closely relate to Royale [14], the currently most efficient protocol for general card games with secret state, which employs a mechanism for enforcing financial rewards and penalties following the stateful contract approach of Bentov *et al.* [4]. In our work, we restrict the model of Royale to capture only games without secret state but maintain the same approach for rewards/penalties enforcement based on stateful contracts. As an advantage of restricting our model to this specific class of games, we eliminate the need for expensive card suffling procedures while constructing very cheap Open Card procedures. Moreover, we are able to construct protocols that only require digital signatures and simple random oracle based commitments (as well as VRFs for one of our optimizations), achieving much higher efficiency than Royale, as shown in Sect. 6. Our protocols enjoy much better efficiency for the recovery phase than Royale, since we employ the same compact checkpoint witnesses but achieve much lower communication complexity, meaning that the protocol messages that must be sent to the stateful contract (*i.e.* posted on a blockchain) are much shorter than those of Royale.

2 Preliminaries

We denote the security parameter by κ. For a randomized algorithm F, $y \stackrel{\$}{\leftarrow} F(x;r)$ denotes running F with input x and its random coins r, obtaining an output y. If r is not specified it is assumed to be sampled uniformly at random. We denote sampling an element x uniformly at random from a set $\mathcal{X}$ (resp. a distribution $\mathcal{Y}$) by $x \stackrel{\$}{\leftarrow} \mathcal{X}$ (resp. $y \stackrel{\$}{\leftarrow} \mathcal{Y}$). We denote two *computationally indistinguishable* ensembles of binary random variables X and Y by $X \approx_c Y$.

Security Model: We prove our protocols secure in the Universal Composability (UC) framework introduced by Canetti in [6]. We consider *static malicious* adversaries, who can arbitrarily deviate from the protocol but must corrupt parties before execution starts, having the corrupted (or honest) parties remain so throughout the execution. It is a well-known fact that UC-secure two-party and multiparty protocols for non trivial functionalities require a setup assumption [7]. We assume that parties have access to a random oracle functionality $\mathcal{F}_{\mathsf{RO}}$, a digital signature functionality $\mathcal{F}_{\mathsf{DSIG}}$, a verifiable random function functionality $\mathcal{F}_{\mathsf{VRF}}$ and a smart contract functionality $\mathcal{F}_{\mathsf{SC}}$. For further details on the UC framework as well as on the ideal functionalities, we refer the reader to [6] and to the full version of this paper [13].

Verifiable Random Functions: Verifiable random functions (VRF) are a key ingredient of one of our optimized protocols. In order to provide a modular construction in the UC framework, we model VRFs as an ideal functionality $\mathcal{F}_{\mathsf{VRF}}$ that captures the main security guarantees for VRFs, which are usually modeled in game based definitions. While a VRF achieving the standard VRF security definition or even the simulatable VRF notion of [9] is not sufficient to realize $\mathcal{F}_{\mathsf{VRF}}$, it has been shown in [15] that this functionality can be realized in the random oracle model under the CDH assumption by a scheme based on the 2-Hash-DH verifiable oblivious pseudorandom function construction of [16]. We refer interested readers to [15] and the full version of this paper [13] for the definition of functionality $\mathcal{F}_{\mathsf{VRF}}$ and further discussion of its implementation.

Stateful Contracts: We employ an ideal functionality $\mathcal{F}_{\mathsf{SC}}$ that models a *stateful contract*, following the approach of Bentov *et al.* [4]. We use the functionality $\mathcal{F}_{\mathsf{SC}}$ defined in [14] and presented in Fig. 1. This functionality is used to ensure correct protocol execution, enforcing rewards distribution for honest parties and penalties for cheaters. Basically, it provides a "Check-in" mechanism for players to deposit betting and collateral funds, a "Check-out" mechanism for ensuring that players receive their rewards according to the game outcome and a Recovery mechanism for identifying (and punishing) cheaters. After check-in, if a player suspects cheating, it can complain to $\mathcal{F}_{\mathsf{SC}}$ by requesting the Recovery phase to be activated, during which $\mathcal{F}_{\mathsf{SC}}$ mediates protocol execution, verifying that each player generates valid protocol messages. If any player is found to be cheating, $\mathcal{F}_{\mathsf{SC}}$ penalizes the cheaters, distributing their collateral funds among the honest players and ending the execution. It is important to emphasize that the $\mathcal{F}_{\mathsf{SC}}$ functionality can be easily implemented via smart contracts over a blockchain, such as Ethereum [5]. Moreover, our construction (Protocol π_{CG}) requires only simple operations, *i.e.* verification of signatures and of random oracle outputs. A regular honest execution of our protocol is performed entirely off-chain, without intervention of the contract.

3 Modeling Card Games Without Secret State

Before presenting our protocols, we must formally define security for card games without secret state. We depart from the framework introduced in Royale [14] for modeling general card games (which can include secret state), restricting the model to the case of card games without secret state. In order to showcase

Functionality $\mathcal{F}_{SC}$

The functionality is executed with players $\mathcal{P}_1, \ldots, \mathcal{P}_n$ and is parametrized by a timeout limit τ, and the values of the initial stake t, the compensation q and the security deposit $d \geq (n-1)q$. There is an embedded program GR that represents the game's rules and a protocol verification mechanism pv.

Players Check-in: When execution starts, $\mathcal{F}_{SC}$ waits to receive from each player $\mathcal{P}_i$ the message (CHECKIN, $sid, \mathcal{P}_i, \mathsf{coins}(d+t), \mathsf{SIG}.vk_i$) containing the necessary coins and its signature verification key. Record the values and send (CHECKEDIN, $sid, \mathcal{P}_i, \mathsf{SIG}.vk_i$) to all players. If some player fails to check-in within the timeout limit τ or if a message (CHECKIN-FAIL, sid) is received from any player, then send (COMPENSATION, $\mathsf{coins}(d+t)$) to all players who checked in and halt.

Player Check-out: Upon receiving (CHECKOUT-INIT, $sid, \mathcal{P}_j$) from $\mathcal{P}_j$, send (CHECKOUT-INIT, $sid, \mathcal{P}_j$) to all players. Upon receiving (CHECKOUT, sid, $\mathcal{P}_j, \mathsf{payout}, \sigma_1, \ldots, \sigma_n$) from $\mathcal{P}_j$, verify that $\sigma_1, \ldots, \sigma_n$ are valid signatures by the players $\mathcal{P}_1, \ldots, \mathcal{P}_n$ on ($\mathsf{CHECKOUT}|\mathsf{payout}$) with respect to $\mathcal{F}_{\mathsf{DSIG}}$. If all tests succeed, for $i = 1, \ldots, n$, send (PAYOUT, $sid, \mathcal{P}_i, \mathsf{coins}(w)$) to $\mathcal{P}_i$, where $w = \mathsf{payout}[i] + d$, and halt.

Recovery: Upon receiving a recovery request (RECOVERY, sid) from a player $\mathcal{P}_i$, send the message (REQUEST, sid) to all players. Upon getting a message (RESPONSE, $sid, \mathcal{P}_j, \mathsf{Checkpoint}_j, \mathsf{proc}_j$) from some player $\mathcal{P}_j$ with checkpoint witnesses (which are not necessarily relative to the same checkpoint as the ones received from other players) and witnesses for the current procedure; or an acknowledgement of the witnesses previous submitted by another player, forward this message to the other players. Upon receiving replies from all players or reaching the timeout limit τ, fix the current procedure by picking the most recent checkpoint that has valid witnesses (*i.e.* the most recent checkpoint witness signed by all players $\mathcal{P}_i$). Verify the last valid point of the protocol execution using the current procedure's witnesses, the rules of the game GR, and pv. If some player $\mathcal{P}_i$ misbehaved in the current phase (by sending an invalid message), then send (COMPENSATION, $\mathsf{coins}(d + q + \mathsf{balance}[j] + \mathsf{bets}[j])$) to each $\mathcal{P}_j \neq \mathcal{P}_i$, send the leftover coins to $\mathcal{P}_i$ and halt. Otherwise, proceed with a mediated execution of the protocol until the next checkpoint using the rules of the game GR and pv to determine the course of the actions and check the validity of the answer. Messages (NXT-STP, $sid, \mathcal{P}_i, \mathsf{proc}, \mathsf{round}$) are used to request from player $\mathcal{P}_i$ the protocol message for round round of procedure proc according to the game's rules specified in GR, who answer with messages (NXT-STP-RSP, $sid, \mathcal{P}_i, \mathsf{proc}, \mathsf{round}, \mathsf{msg}$), where msg is the requested protocol message. All messages (NXT-STP, $sid, \ldots$) and (NXT-STP-RSP, $sid, \ldots$) are delivered to all players. If during this mediated execution a player misbehaves or does not answer within the timeout limit τ, penalize him and compensate the others as above, and halt. Otherwise send (RECOVERED, sid, proc, Checkpoint), to the parties once the next checkpoint Checkpoint is reached, where proc is the procedure for which Checkpoint was generated.

Fig. 1. The stateful contract functionality used by the secure protocol for card games based on Royale [14].

the applicability of our model to popular games, we further present game rule programs for Blackjack and Baccarat, which paramterize our general card game functionality for realizing these games.

Modeling General Games Without Secret State. We present an ideal functionality $\mathcal{F}_{\mathsf{CG}}$ for card games without secret state in Fig. 2. Our ideal functionality is heavily based on the $\mathcal{F}_{\mathsf{CG}}$ for games with secret state presented in Royale [14]. We define a version of $\mathcal{F}_{\mathsf{CG}}$ that only captures games without secret state, allowing us to realize it with a lightweight protocol. This version has the same structure and procedures as the $\mathcal{F}_{\mathsf{CG}}$ presented in Royale, except for the procedures that require secret state to be maintained. Namely, we model game rules with an embedded program GR that encodes the rules of the game to be implemented. $\mathcal{F}_{\mathsf{CG}}$ offers mechanisms for GR to specify the distribution of rewards and financially punish cheaters. Additionally, it offers a mechanism for GR to communicate with the players in order to request actions (*e.g.* bets) and publicly register their answers to such requests. In contrast to the model of Royale and previous protocols focusing on poker, $\mathcal{F}_{\mathsf{CG}}$ only offers two main card operations: shuffling and *public* opening of cards. Restricting $\mathcal{F}_{\mathsf{CG}}$ to these operations captures the fact that only games without secret state can be instantiated and allows for realizing this functionality with very efficient protocols. Notice that all actions announced by players are publicly broadcast by $\mathcal{F}_{\mathsf{CG}}$ and that players cannot draw closed cards (which might never be revealed in the game, constituting a secret state). As in Royale, $\mathcal{F}_{\mathsf{CG}}$ can be extended with further operations (*e.g.* randomness generation), incorporating ideal functionalities that model these operations. However, differently from Royale, these operations cannot rely on the card game keeping a secret state.

Formalizing and Realizing Blackjack and Baccarat. In order to illustrate the usefulness of our general functionality $\mathcal{F}_{\mathsf{CG}}$ for games without secret state, we show that it can be used to realize the games of Blackjack and Baccarat. In the full version of this work [13], we define game rule programs $\mathsf{GR}_{\mathsf{blackjack}}$ and $\mathsf{GR}_{\mathsf{blackjack}}$ for Blackjack and Baccarat, respectively, which parameterize $\mathcal{F}_{\mathsf{CG}}$ to realize these games. Both these games requires a special player that acts as the "dealer" or "house", providing funds that will be used to reward the other players in case they win bets. We remark that the actions taken by this special player are pre-determined in both $\mathsf{GR}_{\mathsf{blackjack}}$ and $\mathsf{GR}_{\mathsf{blackjack}}$, meaning that the party representing the "dealer" or "house" does not need to provide inputs (*e.g.* bets or actions) to the protocol, except for providing its funds. While $\mathsf{GR}_{\mathsf{blackjack}}$ and $\mathsf{GR}_{\mathsf{blackjack}}$ model the behavior of this special player as an individual party (which would be required to provide the totality of such funds), these programs can be trivially modified to require each player to provide funds that will be pooled to represent the "dealer's" or "house's" funds, since all of their actions are deterministic and already captured by $\mathsf{GR}_{\mathsf{blackjack}}$ and $\mathsf{GR}_{\mathsf{blackjack}}$.

Functionality $\mathcal{F}_{\mathsf{CG}}$

The functionality is executed with players $\mathcal{P}_1, \ldots, \mathcal{P}_n$ and is parameterized by a timeout limit τ, and the values of the initial stake t, the security deposit d and of the compensation q. There is an embedded program GR that represents the rules of the game and is responsible for mediating the execution: it requests actions from the players, processes their answers, and invokes the procedures of $\mathcal{F}_{\mathsf{CG}}$. $\mathcal{F}_{\mathsf{CG}}$ provides a check-in procedure that is run in the beginning of the execution, a check-out procedure that allows a player to leave the game (which is requested by the player via GR) and a compensation procedure that is invoked by GR if some player misbehaves/aborts. It also provides a channel for GR to request public actions from the players and card operations as described below. GR is also responsible for updating the vectors balance and bets. Whenever a message is sent to $\mathcal{S}$ for confirmation or action selection, $\mathcal{S}$ should answer, but can always answer (ABORT, sid), in which case the compensation procedure is executed; this option will not be explicitly mentioned in the functionality description henceforth.

Check-in: Executed during the initialization, it waits for a check-in message (CHECKIN, sid, $\mathsf{coins}(d+t)$) from each $\mathcal{P}_i$ and sends (CHECKEDIN, sid, $\mathcal{P}_i$) to the remaining players and GR. If some player fails to check-in within the timeout limit τ, then allow the players that checked-in to dropout and reclaim their coins. Initialize vectors $\mathsf{balance} = (t, \ldots, t)$ and $\mathsf{bets} = (0, \ldots, 0)$.

Check-out: Whenever GR requests the players's check-out with payouts specified by vector payout, send (CHECKOUT, sid, payout) to $\mathcal{S}$. If $\mathcal{S}$ answers (CHECKOUT, sid, payout), send (PAYOUT, sid, $\mathcal{P}_i$, $\mathsf{coins}(d + \mathsf{payout}[i])$) to each $\mathcal{P}_i$ and halt.

Compensation: This procedure is triggered whenever $\mathcal{S}$ answers a request for confirmation of an action with (ABORT, sid). Send (COMPENSATION, sid, $\mathsf{coins}(d + q + \mathsf{balance}[i] + \mathsf{bets}[i])$) to each active honest player $\mathcal{P}_i$. Send the remaining locked coins to $\mathcal{S}$ and stop the execution.

Request Action: Whenever GR requests an action with description $act-desc$ from $\mathcal{P}_i$, send a message (ACTION, sid, $\mathcal{P}_i$, $act-desc$) to the players. Upon receiving (ACTION-RSP, sid, $\mathcal{P}_i$, $act-rsp$) from $\mathcal{P}_i$, forward it to all other players and GR.

Create Shuffled Deck: Whenever GR requests the creation of a shuffled deck of cards containing cards with values $v_1, \ldots, v_m$, choose the next m free identifiers $\mathsf{id}_1, \ldots, \mathsf{id}_m$, representing cards as pairs $(\mathsf{id}_1, v_1), \ldots, (\mathsf{id}_m, v_m)$. Choose a random permutation Π that is applied to the values $(v_1, \ldots, v_m)$ to obtain the updated cards $(\mathsf{id}_1, v_1'), \ldots, (\mathsf{id}_m, v_m')$ such that $(v_1', \ldots, v_m') = \Pi(v_1, \ldots, v_m)$. Send the message (SHUFFLED, sid, $v_1, \ldots, v_m, \mathsf{id}_1, \ldots, \mathsf{id}_m$) to all players and GR.

Open Card: Whenever GR requests to reveal the card (id, v) in public, read the card (id, v) from the memory and send the message (CARD, sid, id, v) to $\mathcal{S}$. If $\mathcal{S}$ answers (CARD, sid, id, v), forward this message to all players and GR.

Fig. 2. Functionality for card games without secret state $\mathcal{F}_{\mathsf{CG}}$ based on [14].

Protocol π_{CG} (Part 1)

Protocol π_{CG} is parametrized by a security parameter 1^κ, a timeout limit τ, the values of the initial stake t, the compensation q, the security deposit $d \geq (n-1)q$ and an embedded program GR that represents the rules of the game. In all queries (SIGN, sid, m) to $\mathcal{F}_{\mathsf{DSIG}}$, the message m is implicitly concatenated with $\mathtt{NONCE}$ and $\mathtt{cnt}$, where $\mathtt{NONCE} \xleftarrow{\$} \{0,1\}^\kappa$ is a fresh nonce (sampled individually for each query) and $\mathtt{cnt}$ is a counter that is increased after each query. Every player $\mathcal{P}_i$ keeps track of used $\mathtt{NONCE}$ values (rejecting signatures that reuse nonces) and implicitly concatenate the corresponding $\mathtt{NONCE}$ and $\mathtt{cnt}$ values with message m in all queries $(\text{VERIFY}, sid, m, \sigma, \mathsf{SIG}.vk')$ to $\mathcal{F}_{\mathsf{DSIG}}$. Protocol π_{CG} is executed by players $\mathcal{P}_1, \ldots, \mathcal{P}_n$ interacting with functionalities $\mathcal{F}_{\mathsf{SC}}$, $\mathcal{F}_{\mathsf{RO}}$ and $\mathcal{F}_{\mathsf{DSIG}}$ as follows:

- **Checkpoint Witnesses:** After the execution of a procedure, the players store a checkpoint witness that consists of the lists $\mathcal{C}_O$ and $\mathcal{C}_C$, the vectors $\mathsf{balance}$ and bets as well as a signature by each of the other players on the concatenation of all these values. Each signature is generated using $\mathcal{F}_{\mathsf{DSIG}}$ and all players check all signatures using the relevant procedure of $\mathcal{F}_{\mathsf{DSIG}}$. Old checkpoint witnesses are deleted. If any check fails for $\mathcal{P}_i$, he proceeds to the recovery procedure.

- **Recovery Triggers:** All signatures and proofs in received messages are verified by default. Players are assumed to have loosely synchronized clocks and, after each round of the protocol starts, players expect to receive all messages sent in that round before a timeout limit τ. If a player $\mathcal{P}_i$ does not receive an expected message from a player $\mathcal{P}_j$ in a given round before the timeout limit τ, $\mathcal{P}_i$ considers that $\mathcal{P}_j$ has aborted. After the check-in procedure, if any player receives an invalid message or considers that another player has aborted, it proceeds to the recovery procedure.

- **Check-in:** Every player $\mathcal{P}_i$ proceeds as follows:
  1. Send (KEYGEN, sid) to $\mathcal{F}_{\mathsf{DSIG}}$, receiving $(\text{VERIFICATION KEY}, sid, \mathsf{SIG}.vk_i)$.
  2. Send $(\text{CHECKIN}, sid, \mathcal{P}_i, \mathsf{coins}(d+t), \mathsf{SIG}.vk_i)$ to $\mathcal{F}_{\mathsf{SC}}$.
  3. Upon receiving $(\text{CHECKEDIN}, sid, \mathcal{P}_j, \mathsf{SIG}.vk_j)$ from $\mathcal{F}_{\mathsf{SC}}$ for all $j \neq i$, $j = 1, \ldots, n$, initialize the internal lists of open cards $\mathcal{C}_O$ and closed cards $\mathcal{C}_C$. We assume parties have a sequence of unused card id values (*e.g.* a counter). Initialize vectors $\mathsf{balance}[j] = t$ and $\mathsf{bets}[j] = 0$ for $j = 1, \ldots, n$. Output $(\text{CHECKEDIN}, sid)$.
  4. If $\mathcal{P}_i$ fails to receive $(\text{CHECKEDIN}, sid, \mathcal{P}_j, \mathsf{SIG}.vk_j)$ from $\mathcal{F}_{\mathsf{SC}}$ for another party $\mathcal{P}_j$ within the timeout limit τ, it requests $\mathcal{F}_{\mathsf{SC}}$ to dropout and receive its coins back.

- **Compensation:** This procedure is activated if the recovery phase of $\mathcal{F}_{\mathsf{SC}}$ detects a cheater, causing honest parties to receive refunds plus compensation and the cheater to receive the remainder of its funds after honest parties are compensated. Upon receiving $(\text{COMPENSATION}, sid, \mathcal{P}_i, \mathsf{coins}(w))$ from $\mathcal{F}_{\mathsf{SC}}$, a player $\mathcal{P}_i$ outputs this message and halts.

Fig. 3. Part 1 of Protocol π_{CG}.

Protocol π_{CG} (Part 2)

- **Check-out:** A player $\mathcal{P}_j$ can initiate the check-out procedure and leave the protocol at any point that GR allows, in which case all players will receive the money that they currently own plus their collateral refund. The players proceed as follows:
  1. $\mathcal{P}_j$ sends $(\text{CHECKOUT-INIT}, sid, \mathcal{P}_j)$ to $\mathcal{F}_{SC}$.
  2. Upon receiving $(\text{CHECKOUT-INIT}, sid, \mathcal{P}_j)$ from $\mathcal{F}_{SC}$, each $\mathcal{P}_i$ (for $i = 1, \ldots, n$) sends $(\text{SIGN}, sid, (\mathsf{CHECKOUT}|\mathsf{payout}))$ to $\mathcal{F}_{DSIG}$ (where payout is a vector containing the amount of money that each player will receive according to GR), obtaining $(\text{SIGNATURE}, sid, (\mathsf{CHECKOUT}|\mathsf{payout}), \sigma_i)$ as answer. Player $\mathcal{P}_i$ sends σ_i to $\mathcal{P}_j$.
  3. For all $i \neq j$, $\mathcal{P}_j$ sends $(\text{VERIFY}, sid, (\mathsf{CHECKOUT}|\mathsf{payout}), \sigma_i, \mathsf{SIG}.vk_i)$ to $\mathcal{F}_{DSIG}$, where payout is computed locally by $\mathcal{P}_j$. If $\mathcal{F}_{DSIG}$ answers all queries $(\text{VERIFY}, sid, (\mathsf{CHECKOUT}|\mathsf{payout}), \sigma_i, \mathsf{SIG}.vk_i)$ with $(\text{VERIFIED}, sid, (\mathsf{CHECKOUT}|\mathsf{payout}), 1)$, $\mathcal{P}_j$ sends $(\text{CHECKOUT}, sid, \mathsf{payout}, \sigma_1, \ldots, \sigma_n)$ to $\mathcal{F}_{SC}$. Otherwise, it proceeds to the recovery procedure.
  4. Upon receiving $(\text{PAYOUT}, sid, \mathcal{P}_i, \mathsf{coins}(w))$ from $\mathcal{F}_{SC}$, $\mathcal{P}_i$ outputs this message and halts.
- **Executing Actions:** Each $\mathcal{P}_i$ follows GR that represents the rules of the game, performing the necessary card operations in the order specified by GR. If GR request an action with description $act - desc$ from $\mathcal{P}_i$, all the players output $(\text{ACT}, sid, \mathcal{P}_i, act - desc)$ and $\mathcal{P}_i$ executes any necessary operations. $\mathcal{P}_i$ broadcasts $(\text{ACTION-RSP}, sid, \mathcal{P}_i, act - rsp, \sigma_i)$, where $act - rsp$ is his answer and σ_i his signature on $act - rsp$, and outputs $(\text{ACTION-RSP}, sid, \mathcal{P}_i, act - rsp)$. Upon receiving this message, all other players check the signature, and if it is valid output $(\text{ACTION-RSP}, sid, \mathcal{P}_i, act - rsp)$. If a player $\mathcal{P}_j$ believes cheating is happening, he proceeds to the recovery procedure.
- **Tracking Balance and Bets:** Every player $\mathcal{P}_i$ keeps a local copy of the vectors balance and bets, such that $\mathsf{balance}[j]$ and $\mathsf{bets}[j]$ represent the balance and current bets of each player $\mathcal{P}_j$, respectively. In order to keep balance and bets up to date, every player proceeds as follows:
  - At each point that GR specifies that a betting action from $\mathcal{P}_i$ takes place, player $\mathcal{P}_i$ broadcasts a message $(\text{BET}, sid, \mathcal{P}_i, bet_i)$, where bet_i is the value of its bet. It updates $\mathsf{balance}[i] = \mathsf{balance}[i] - b_i$ and $\mathsf{bets}[i] = \mathsf{bets}[i] + b_i$.
  - Upon receiving a message $(\text{BET}, sid, \mathcal{P}_j, bet_j)$ from $\mathcal{P}_j$, player $\mathcal{P}_i$ sets $\mathsf{balance}[j] = \mathsf{balance}[j] - b_j$ and $\mathsf{bets}[j] = \mathsf{bets}[j] + b_j$.
  - When GR specifies a game outcome where player $\mathcal{P}_j$ receives an amount pay_j and has its bet amount updated to b'_j, player $\mathcal{P}_i$ sets $\mathsf{balance}[j] = \mathsf{balance}[j] + pay_j$ and $\mathsf{bets}[j] = b'_j$.
- **Create Shuffled Deck:** When requested by GR to create a shuffled deck of cards containing cards with values $v_1, \ldots, v_m$, each player $\mathcal{P}_i$ chooses the next m free identifiers $\mathsf{id}_1, \ldots, \mathsf{id}_m$ and, for $j = 1, \ldots, m$, stores $(\mathsf{id}_j, \perp)$ in $\mathcal{C}_O$ and v_j in $\mathcal{C}_C$. $\mathcal{P}_i$ outputs $(\text{SHUFFLED}, sid, v_1, \ldots, v_m, \mathsf{id}_1, \ldots, \mathsf{id}_m)$.

Fig. 4. Part 2 of Protocol π_{CG}.

Protocol π_{CG} (Part 3)

– **Open Card:** Every player $\mathcal{P}_i$ proceeds as follows to open card with id id:
1. Organize the card values in $\mathcal{C}_C$ in alphabetic order obtaining an ordered list $\mathcal{C}_C = \{v_1, \ldots, v_m\}$.
2. Sample a random $r_i \xleftarrow{\$} \{0,1\}^\kappa$ and send (sid, r_i) to $\mathcal{F}_{\text{RO}}$, receiving (sid, h_i) as response. Broadcast (sid, h_i).
3. After all (sid, h_j) for $j \neq i$ and $j = 1, \ldots, n$ are received, broadcast (sid, r_i).
4. For $j = 1, \ldots, n$ and $j \neq i$, send (sid, r_j) to $\mathcal{F}_{\text{RO}}$, receiving (sid, h'_j) as response and checking that $h_j = h'_j$. If all checks succeed, compute $k = \sum_i r_i \bmod m$, proceeding to the Recovery phase otherwise. Define the opened card value as v_k, remove v_k from $\mathcal{C}_C$ and update $(\mathsf{id}, \perp)$ in $\mathcal{C}_O$ to (id, v_k).

– **Recovery:** Player $\mathcal{P}_i$ proceeds as follows:
- Starting Recovery: Player $\mathcal{P}_i$ sends (RECOVERY, sid) to $\mathcal{F}_{\text{SC}}$ if it starts the procedure.
- Upon receiving a message (REQUEST, sid) from $\mathcal{F}_{\text{SC}}$, every player $\mathcal{P}_i$ sends (RESPONSE, $sid, \mathcal{P}_i$, $\mathsf{Checkpoint}_i$, proc_i) to $\mathcal{F}_{\text{SC}}$, where $\mathsf{Checkpoint}_i$ is $\mathcal{P}_i$'s latest checkpoint witness and proc_i are $\mathcal{P}_i$'s witnesses for the protocol procedure that started after the latest checkpoint; or acknowledges the witnesses sent by another party if it is the same as the local one.
- Upon receiving a message (NXT-STP, $sid, \mathcal{P}_i$, proc, round) from $\mathcal{F}_{\text{SC}}$, player $\mathcal{P}_i$ sends (NXT-STP-RSP, $sid, \mathcal{P}_i$, proc, round, msg) to $\mathcal{F}_{\text{SC}}$, where msg is the protocol message that should be sent at round round of procedure proc of the protocol according to GR.
- Upon receiving a message (NXT-STP-RSP, $sid, \mathcal{P}_j$, proc, round, msg) from $\mathcal{F}_{\text{SC}}$, every player $\mathcal{P}_i$ considers msg as the protocol message sent by $\mathcal{P}_j$ in round of procedure proc and take it into consideration for future messages.
- Upon receiving a message (RECOVERED, sid, proc, Checkpoint) from $\mathcal{F}_{\text{SC}}$, every player $\mathcal{P}_i$ records Checkpoint as the latest checkpoint and continues protocol execution according to the game rules GR.

Fig. 5. Part 3 of Protocol π_{CG}.

4 The Framework

Our framework can be used to implement any card game without secret state where cards that were previously randomly shuffled are publicly revealed. Instead of representing cards as ciphertexts as in previous works, we exploit the fact that publicly opening a card from a set of previously randomly shuffled cards is equivalent to randomly sampling card values from an initial set of card values. The main idea is that each opened card has its value randomly picked from a list of "unopened cards" using randomness generated by a coin tossing protocol executed by all parties. This protocol requires no shuffling procedure per se and requires 2 rounds for opening each card (required for executing coin tossing). Later on, we will show that this protocol can be optimized in different ways, but its simple structure aids us in describing our basic approach.

When the game rules GR specify that a card must be created, it is added to a list of cards that have not been opened $\mathcal{C}_C$. When a card is opened, the parties execute a commit-and-open coin tossing protocol to generate randomness that is used to uniformly pick a card from the list of unopened cards $\mathcal{C}_C$, removing the selected card from $\mathcal{C}_C$ and adding it to a list of opened cards $\mathcal{C}_O$. This technique works since every card is publicly opened and no player gets to privately learn the value of a card with the option of not revealing it to the other players, which allows the players to keep the list of unopened cards up-to-date. We implement the necessary commitments with the canonical efficient random oracle based construction, where a commitment is simply an evaluation of the random oracle on the commitment message concatenated with some randomness and the opening consists of the message and randomness themselves. This simple construction achieves very low computational and communication complexities as computing a commitment (and verifying and opening) requires only a single call to the random oracle and the commitment (and opening) can be represented by a string of the size of the security parameter. Besides being compact, these commitments are publicly verifiable, meaning that any third party party can verify the validity of an opening, which comes in handy for verifying that the protocol has been correctly executed.

In order to implement financial rewards/penalties enforcement, our protocol relies on a stateful contract functionality $\mathcal{F}_{\mathsf{SC}}$ that provides a mechanism for the players to deposit betting and collateral funds, enforcing correct distribution of such funds according to the protocol execution. If the protocol is correctly executed, the rewards corresponding to a game outcome are distributed among the players. Otherwise, if a cheater is detected, $\mathcal{F}_{\mathsf{SC}}$ distributes the cheater's collateral funds among honest players, who also receive a refund of their betting and collateral funds. After each game action (*e.g.* betting and card opening), all players cooperate to generate a *checkpoint witness* showing that the protocol has been correctly executed up to that point. This compact checkpoint witness is basically a set of signatures generated under each player's signing key on the opened and unopened cards lists and vectors representing the players' balance and bets. In case a player suspects cheating, it activates the recovery procedure of $\mathcal{F}_{\mathsf{SC}}$ with its latest checkpoint witness, requiring players to provide their most up-to-date checkpoint witnesses to $\mathcal{F}_{\mathsf{SC}}$ (or agree with the one that has been provided). After this point, $\mathcal{F}_{\mathsf{SC}}$ mediates protocol execution, receiving from all players the protocol messages to be sent after the latest checkpoint witness, ensuring their validity and broadcasting them to all players. If the protocol proceeds until next checkpoint witness is generated, the execution is again carried out directly by the players without involving $\mathcal{F}_{\mathsf{SC}}$. Otherwise, if a player is found to be cheating (by failing to provide their messages or providing invalid ones), $\mathcal{F}_{\mathsf{SC}}$ refunds the honest parties and distributes among them the cheater's collateral funds. Protocol π_{CG} is presented in Figs. 3, 4 and 5.

Security Analysis: The security of protocol π_{CG} in the Universal Composability framework is formally stated in Theorem 1. In order to prove this theorem we construct a simulator such that an ideal execution with this simulator and functionality $\mathcal{F}_{\mathsf{CG}}$ is indistinguishable from a real execution of π_{CG} with any adversary. The main idea behind this simulator is that it learns from $\mathcal{F}_{\mathsf{CG}}$ the value of each opened card, "cheating" in the commit-and-open coin tossing procedure in order to force it to yield the right card value. The simulator can do that since it knows the values that each player has committed to with the random oracle based commitments and it can equivocate the opening of its own commitment, forcing the coin tossing to result in an arbitrary output, yielding an arbitrary card value. The simulation for the mechanisms for requesting players actions and enforcing financial rewards/penalties follows the same approach as in Royale [14]. Namely, the simulator follows the steps of an honest user and makes $\mathcal{F}_{\mathsf{CG}}$ fail if a corrupted party misbehaves, subsequently activating the recovery procedure that results in cheating parties being penalized and honest parties being compensated.

Theorem 1. *For every static active adversary $\mathcal{A}$ who corrupts at most $n-1$ parties, there exists a simulator $\mathcal{S}$ such that, for every environment $\mathcal{Z}$, the following relation holds:*

$$\mathsf{IDEAL}_{\mathcal{F}_{\mathsf{CG}},\mathcal{S},\mathcal{Z}} \approx_c \mathsf{HYBRID}^{\mathcal{F}_{\mathrm{RO}},\mathcal{F}_{\mathsf{DSIG}},\mathcal{F}_{\mathsf{SC}}}_{\pi_{\mathsf{CG}},\mathcal{A},\mathcal{Z}}.$$

The proof is presented in the full version of this work [13].

5 Optimizing Our Protocol

In this section, we construct optimized protocols that improve on the round complexity of the open card operation, which represents the main efficiency bottleneck of our framework. The basic protocol constructed in the previous section requires a whole "commit-then-open" coin tossing to be carried out for each card that is opened. Even though this coin tossing can be implemented efficiently in the random oracle model, its inherent round complexity implies that each card opening requires 2 rounds. We show how the open card operation can be executed with only 1 round while also improving communication complexity but incurring a higher local space complexity (linear in the number of cards) for each player in the Shuffle Card operation. Next, we show how to achieve the same optimal round complexity with a low constant local space complexity.

Lower Round and Communication Complexities: A straightforward way to execute the Open Card operation in one round is to pre-process the necessary commitments during the Shuffle Cards operation. Basically, in order to pre-process the opening of m cards, all players broadcast m commitments to random values in the Shuffle Cards phase. Later on, every time the Open Card operation is executed, each player broadcasts an opening to one of their previously sent commitments. Besides making it possible to open cards in only one round, this simple technique reduces the communication complexity of

Protocol $\pi_{\mathsf{CG-PRE}}$

- **Create Shuffled Deck:** When requested by GR to create a shuffled deck of cards containing cards with values $v_1, \ldots, v_m$, each player $\mathcal{P}_i$ creates $\mathcal{C}_O = \{(\mathsf{id}_1, \perp), \ldots, (\mathsf{id}_m, \perp)\}$ and $\mathcal{C}_C = \{v_1, \ldots, v_m\}$ following the instructions of π_{CG}. Moreover, for $l = 1, \ldots, m$, $\mathcal{P}_i$ samples a random $r_{i,l} \xleftarrow{\$} \{0,1\}^\kappa$ and sends $(sid, r_{i,l})$ to $\mathcal{F}_{\mathrm{RO}}$, receiving (sid, h_i) in response. $\mathcal{P}_i$ broadcasts $(sid, h_{i,1}, \ldots, h_{i,m})$. After all $(sid, h_{j,1}, \ldots, h_{j,m})$ for $j \neq i$ and $j = 1, \ldots, n$ are received, $\mathcal{P}_i$ outputs $(\text{SHUFFLED}, sid, v_1, \ldots, v_m, \mathsf{id}_1, \ldots, \mathsf{id}_m)$.
- **Open Card:** Each player $\mathcal{P}_i$ proceeds as follows to open card with id id:
  1. Organize the card values in $\mathcal{C}_C$ in alphabetic order obtaining an ordered list $\mathcal{C}_C = \{v_1, \ldots, v_m\}$.
  2. Broadcast $(sid, r_{i,l})$, where $h_{i,l}$ is the next available (still closed) commitment generated in the Shuffle Cards operation.
  3. For $j = 1, \ldots, n$ and $j \neq i$, send $(sid, r_{j,l})$ to $\mathcal{F}_{\mathrm{RO}}$, receiving $(sid, h'_{j,l})$ in response and checking that $h_{j,l} = h'_{j,l}$. If all checks succeed, compute $k = \sum_i r_i \mod m$, proceeding to the Recovery phase otherwise. Define the opened card value as v_k, remove v_k from $\mathcal{C}_C$ and update $(\mathsf{id}, \perp)$ in $\mathcal{C}_O$ to (id, v_k).

Fig. 6. Protocol $\pi_{\mathsf{CG-PRE}}$ (only phases that differ from Protocol π_{CG} are described).

the Open Card operation, since each player only broadcasts one opening per card (but no commitment). However, it requires each player to store $(n-1)m$ commitments (received from other players) as all well as m openings (for their own commitments). Protocol $\pi_{\mathsf{CG-PRE}}$ is very similar to Protocol π_{CG}, only differing in the Shuffle Card and Open Card operations, which are presented in Fig. 6. The security of this protocol is formally stated in Theorem 2.

Theorem 2. *For every static active adversary $\mathcal{A}$ who corrupts at most $n-1$ parties, there exists a simulator $\mathcal{S}$ such that, for every environment $\mathcal{Z}$, the following relation holds:*

$$\mathsf{IDEAL}_{\mathcal{F}_{\mathsf{CG}}, \mathcal{S}, \mathcal{Z}} \approx_c \mathsf{HYBRID}^{\mathcal{F}_{\mathrm{RO}}, \mathcal{F}_{\mathsf{DSIG}}, \mathcal{F}_{\mathsf{SC}}}_{\pi_{\mathsf{CG-PRE}}, \mathcal{A}, \mathcal{Z}}.$$

The proof is very similar to that of Theorem 1, a sketch is presented in the full version of this work [13].

Lower Round and Space Complexities via Coin Tossing Extension: Even though the previous optimization reduces the round complexity of our original protocol, it introduces a high local space complexity overhead, since each party needs to store the preprocessed commitments. In order to achieve low round complexity without a space complexity overhead, we show that a single coin tossing can be "extended" to open an unlimited number of cards. With this technique, we first run a coin tossing in the Check-in phase, later extending it to obtain new randomness used to pick each card that is opened.

Protocol $\pi_{\mathsf{CG-VRF}}$

- **Check-in:** When requested by GR to shuffle cards with identifiers $(\mathsf{id}_1, \ldots, \mathsf{id}_m)$ to be shuffled, each $\mathcal{P}_i$ proceeds as follows:
  1. Execute the steps of the Check-in phase of π_{CG}.
  2. Send (KEYGEN, sid) to $\mathcal{F}_{\mathsf{VRF}}$, receiving $(\text{VERIFICATION KEY}, sid, \mathsf{VRF}.vk_i)$ in response. Sample a random $\mathtt{seed}_i \xleftarrow{\$} \{0,1\}^{\kappa}$ and send $(sid, \mathtt{seed}_i)$ to $\mathcal{F}_{\mathrm{RO}}$, receiving (sid, h_i) in response. Broadcast $(sid, \mathsf{VRF}.vk_i, h_i)$.
  3. After all $(sid, \mathsf{VRF}.vk_j, h_j)$ for $j \neq i$ and $j = 1, \ldots, n$ are received, broadcast $(sid, \mathtt{seed}_i)$.
  4. For $j = 1, \ldots, n$ and $j \neq i$, send $(sid, \mathtt{seed}_j)$ to $\mathcal{F}_{\mathrm{RO}}$, receiving (sid, h'_j) in response and checking that $h_j = h'_j$. If all checks succeed, compute $\mathtt{seed} = \sum_i \mathtt{seed}_i$, proceeding to the Recovery phase otherwise. Set $\mathtt{cnt} = 1$ and broadcast message $(\text{SHUFFLED}, sid, \mathsf{id}_1, \ldots, \mathsf{id}_m)$.
- **Open Card:** Every player $\mathcal{P}_i$ proceeds as follows to open card with id id:
  1. Organize the card values in $\mathcal{C}_C$ in alphabetic order obtaining an ordered list $\mathcal{C}_C = \{v_1, \ldots, v_m\}$.
  2. Send $(\text{EVALPROVE}, sid, \mathtt{seed}|\mathtt{cnt})$ to $\mathcal{F}_{\mathsf{VRF}}$, receiving $(\text{EVALUATED}, sid, y_i, \pi_i)$ in response. Broadcast (sid, y_i, π_i).
  3. For $j = 1, \ldots, n$ and $j \neq i$, send $(\text{VERIFY}, sid, \mathtt{seed}|\mathtt{cnt}, y_j, \pi_j, \mathsf{VRF}.vk_j)$ to $\mathcal{F}_{\mathsf{VRF}}$, checking that $\mathcal{F}_{\mathsf{VRF}}$ answers with $(\text{VERIFIED}, sid, \mathtt{seed}|\mathtt{cnt}, y_j, \pi_j, 1)$. If all checks succeed, compute $k = \sum_i y_i \mod m$, proceeding to the Recovery phase otherwise. Define the opened card value as v_k, remove v_k from $\mathcal{C}_C$, update $(\mathsf{id}, \perp)$ in $\mathcal{C}_O$ to (id, v_k) and increment the counter $\mathtt{cnt}$.

Fig. 7. Protocol $\pi_{\mathsf{CG-VRF}}$ (only phases that differ from Protocol π_{CG} are described).

We develop a new technique for extending coin tossing based on verifiable random functions, which is at the core of our optimized protocol. The main idea is to first have all parties broadcast their VRF public keys and execute a single coin tossing used to generate a seed. Every time a new random value is needed, each party evaluates the VRF under their secret key using the seed concatenated with a counter as input, broadcasting the output and accompanying proof. Upon receiving all the other parties' VRF output and proof, each party verifies the validity of the output and defines the new random value as the sum of all outputs. Protocol $\pi_{\mathsf{CG-VRF}}$ is very similar to Protocol π_{CG}, only differing in the Shuffle Card and Open Card operations, which are presented in Fig. 7. The security of this protocol is formally stated in Theorem 3.

Theorem 3. *For every static active adversary $\mathcal{A}$ who corrupts at most $n - 1$ parties, there exists a simulator $\mathcal{S}$ such that, for every environment $\mathcal{Z}$, the following relation holds:*

$$\mathsf{IDEAL}_{\mathcal{F}_{\mathsf{CG}}, \mathcal{S}, \mathcal{Z}} \approx_c \mathsf{HYBRID}^{\mathcal{F}_{\mathrm{RO}}, \mathcal{F}_{\mathsf{DSIG}}, \mathcal{F}_{\mathsf{VRF}}, \mathcal{F}_{\mathsf{SC}}}_{\pi_{\mathsf{CG-VRF}}, \mathcal{A}, \mathcal{Z}}.$$

The proof is very similar to that of Theorem 1, a sketch is presented in the full version of this work [13].

6 Concrete Complexity Analysis

In this section, we analyse our protocols' computational, communication, round and space complexities, showcasing the different trade-offs obtained by each optimization. We compare our protocols with Royale [14], which is the currently most efficient protocol for general card games (with secret state) that enforces financial rewards and penalties. We focus on the Create Shuffled Deck and Open Card operations, which represent the main bottlenecks in card game protocols. Interestingly, our protocols eliminate the need for expensive zero knowledge proofs of shuffle correctness in the Create Shuffled Card, which are the most expensive components in previous works. Protocol π_{CG} only requires a simple coin tossing to perform the Open Card procedure at the cost of one extra round (in comparison to previous protocols), while our optimized protocols $\pi_{\mathsf{CG-PRE}}$ and $\pi_{\mathsf{CG-VRF}}$ implement this operation with a single round.

Table 1. Complexity comparison of the Shuffle Cards and Open Card operation of Protocols π_{CG}, $\pi_{\mathsf{CG-PRE}}$ and $\pi_{\mathsf{CG-VRF}}$ with n and m cards, excluding checkpoint witness signature generation costs. The cost of calling the random oracle is denoted by H and the cost of a modular exponentiation is denoted by Exp. The size of elements of $\mathbb{G}$ and $\mathbb{Z}$ are denoted by $|\mathbb{G}|$ and $|\mathbb{Z}|$, respectively.

Operation	Protocol	Computational	Communication	Space	Rounds
Open card	π_{CG}	$n\ \mathsf{H}$	$2n\kappa$	0	2
	$\pi_{\mathsf{CG-PRE}}$	$(n-1)\ \mathsf{H}$	$n\kappa$	$nm\kappa$	1
	$\pi_{\mathsf{CG-VRF}}$	$3n\ \mathsf{H}$ $+(4n-1)\ Exp$	$3n\kappa + n\ \lvert\mathbb{Z}\rvert)$	$n\ \lvert\mathbb{G}\rvert + \kappa$	1
	Royale [14]	$n\ \mathsf{H}\ +4n\ Exp$	$n\ \lvert\mathbb{G}\rvert + 2n\ \lvert\mathbb{Z}\rvert$	$2m\ \lvert\mathbb{G}\rvert$	1
Create shuffled deck	π_{CG}	0	0	0	0
	$\pi_{\mathsf{CG-PRE}}$	$m\ \mathsf{H}$	$nm\kappa$	0	1
	$\pi_{\mathsf{CG-VRF}}$	0	0	0	0
	Royale [14]	$n\ \mathsf{H}+$ $(2\log(\lceil\sqrt{m}\rceil)$ $+4n-$ $2)m\ Exp$	$n(2m+\lceil\sqrt{m}\rceil)\ \mathbb{G}$ $+5n\lceil\sqrt{m}\rceil\ \mathbb{Z}$	0	n

We estimate the computational complexity of the Shuffle Cards and Open Card operations of our protocols in terms of the number of RO calls and modular exponentiations. We present complexity estimates excluding the cost of generating the checkpoint witness signatures, since these costs are the same in both Royale and our protocols (1 signature generation and $n-1$ signature verifications). The communication and space complexities are estimated in terms of the number of strings of size κ, and elements from $\mathbb{G}$ and $\mathbb{Z}$. In order to estimate concrete costs, we assume that $\mathcal{F}_{\mathsf{RO}}$ is implemented by a hash function with κ

bits outputs. Moreover, we assume that $\mathcal{F}_{\mathsf{VRF}}$ is implemented by the 2-Hash-DH verifiable oblivious pseudorandom function construction of [16] as discussed in Sect. 2. This VRF construction requires 1 modular exponentiation to generate a key pair, 3 modular exponentiations and 3 calls to the random oracle to evaluate an input and generate a proof, and 4 modular exponentiations and 3 calls to the random oracle to verify an output given a proof. A verification key is one element of a group $\mathbb{G}$ and the output plus proof consist of 3 random oracle outputs and an element of a ring $\mathbb{Z}$ of same order as $\mathbb{G}$. The estimates for Royale are taken from [14].

Our concrete complexity estimates are presented in Table 1. Notice that our basic protocol π_{CG} and our optimized protocol $\pi_{\mathsf{CG-VRF}}$ do not require a Create Shuffled Deck operation at all, while Protocol $\pi_{\mathsf{CG-PRE}}$ requires a cheap Create Shuffled Cards operation where a batch of commitments to random values are performed. In fact, our protocols eliminate the need for expensive zero knowledge proofs of shuffle correctness, which is the main bottleneck in previous works such as Royale [14], the currently most efficient protocol for card games with secret state. Protocol $\pi_{\mathsf{CG-PRE}}$ improves on the round complexity of the Open Card operation of protocol π_{CG}, requiring only 1 round and the same computational complexity but incurring in a larger space complexity as each player must locally store $nm\kappa$ bits to complete this operation, since they need to store a number of pre-processed commitments that depends on both the number of players and the number of cards in the game. We solve this local storage issue with Protocol $\pi_{\mathsf{CG-VRF}}$, which employs our "coin tossing extension" technique to achieve local space complexity independent of the number of cards, which tends to be much larger than the number of players. We remark that the computational complexity of the Open Card operation of $\pi_{\mathsf{CG-VRF}}$ is equivalent to that of Royale [14], while the communication and space complexities are much lower.

References

1. Andrychowicz, M., Dziembowski, S., Malinowski, D., Mazurek, Ł.: Fair two-party computations via bitcoin deposits. In: Böhme, R., Brenner, M., Moore, T., Smith, M. (eds.) FC 2014. LNCS, vol. 8438, pp. 105–121. Springer, Heidelberg (2014). https://doi.org/10.1007/978-3-662-44774-1_8
2. Andrychowicz, M., Dziembowski, S., Malinowski, D., Mazurek, L.: Secure multiparty computations on bitcoin. In: 2014 IEEE Symposium on Security and Privacy, pp. 443–458. IEEE Computer Society Press, May 2014
3. Barnett, A., Smart, N.P.: Mental poker revisited. In: Paterson, K.G. (ed.) Cryptography and Coding 2003. LNCS, vol. 2898, pp. 370–383. Springer, Heidelberg (2003). https://doi.org/10.1007/978-3-540-40974-8_29
4. Bentov, I., Kumaresan, R., Miller, A.: Instantaneous decentralized poker. In: Takagi, T., Peyrin, T. (eds.) ASIACRYPT 2017. LNCS, vol. 10625, pp. 410–440. Springer, Cham (2017). https://doi.org/10.1007/978-3-319-70697-9_15
5. Buterin, V.: White paper (2013). https://github.com/ethereum/wiki/wiki/White-Paper. Accessed 12 May 2017

6. Canetti, R.: Universally composable security: a new paradigm for cryptographic protocols. In: 42nd FOCS, pp. 136–145. IEEE Computer Society Press, October 2001
7. Canetti, R., Fischlin, M.: Universally composable commitments. In: Kilian, J. (ed.) CRYPTO 2001. LNCS, vol. 2139, pp. 19–40. Springer, Heidelberg (2001). https://doi.org/10.1007/3-540-44647-8_2
8. Castellà-Roca, J., Sebé, F., Domingo-Ferrer, J.: Dropout-tolerant TTP-free mental poker. In: Katsikas, S., López, J., Pernul, G. (eds.) TrustBus 2005. LNCS, vol. 3592, pp. 30–40. Springer, Heidelberg (2005). https://doi.org/10.1007/11537878_4
9. Chase, M., Lysyanskaya, A.: Simulatable VRFs with applications to multi-theorem NIZK. In: Menezes, A. (ed.) CRYPTO 2007. LNCS, vol. 4622, pp. 303–322. Springer, Heidelberg (2007). https://doi.org/10.1007/978-3-540-74143-5_17
10. Crépeau, C.: A secure poker protocol that minimizes the effect of player coalitions. In: Williams, H.C. (ed.) CRYPTO 1985. LNCS, vol. 218, pp. 73–86. Springer, Heidelberg (1986). https://doi.org/10.1007/3-540-39799-X_8
11. Crépeau, C.: A zero-knowledge poker protocol that achieves confidentiality of the players' strategy *or* how to achieve an electronic poker face. In: Odlyzko, A.M. (ed.) CRYPTO 1986. LNCS, vol. 263, pp. 239–247. Springer, Heidelberg (1987). https://doi.org/10.1007/3-540-47721-7_18
12. David, B., Dowsley, R., Larangeira, M.: Kaleidoscope: an efficient poker protocol with payment distribution and penalty enforcement. Cryptology ePrint Archive, Report 2017/899 (2017). http://eprint.iacr.org/2017/899
13. David, B., Dowsley, R., Larangeira, M.: 21 - bringing down the complexity: fast composable protocols for card games without secret state. Cryptology ePrint Archive, Report 2018/303 (2018). https://eprint.iacr.org/2018/303
14. David, B., Dowsley, R., Larangeira, M.: ROYALE: a framework for universally composable card games with financial rewards and penalties enforcement. Cryptology ePrint Archive, Report 2018/157 (2018). https://eprint.iacr.org/2018/157
15. David, B., Gaži, P., Kiayias, A., Russell, A.: Ouroboros praos: an adaptively-secure, semi-synchronous proof-of-stake protocol. Cryptology ePrint Archive, Report 2017/573 (2017). https://eprint.iacr.org/2017/573. (to appear in Eurocrypt 2018)
16. Jarecki, S., Kiayias, A., Krawczyk, H.: Round-optimal password-protected secret sharing and T-PAKE in the password-only model. In: Sarkar, P., Iwata, T. (eds.) ASIACRYPT 2014. LNCS, vol. 8874, pp. 233–253. Springer, Heidelberg (2014). https://doi.org/10.1007/978-3-662-45608-8_13
17. Kumaresan, R., Moran, T., Bentov, I.: How to use bitcoin to play decentralized poker. In: Ray, I., Li, N., Kruegel, C. (eds.) ACM CCS 2015, pp. 195–206. ACM Press, New York (2015)
18. Schindelhauer, C.: A toolbox for mental card games. Technical report, University of Lübeck (1998)
19. Sebe, F., Domingo-Ferrer, J., Castella-Roca, J.: On the security of a repaired mental poker protocol. In: Third International Conference on Information Technology: New Generations, pp. 664–668 (2006)
20. Shamir, A., Rivest, R.L., Adleman, L.M.: Mental poker. In: Klarner, D.A. (ed.) The Mathematical Gardner, pp. 37–43. Springer, Boston (1981). https://doi.org/10.1007/978-1-4684-6686-7_5
21. Wei, T.: Secure and practical constant round mental poker. Inf. Sci. **273**, 352–386 (2014)
22. Wei, T., Wang, L.-C.: A fast mental poker protocol. J. Math. Cryptol. **6**(1), 39–68 (2012)

23. Zhao, W., Varadharajan, V.: Efficient TTP-free mental poker protocols. In: International Conference on Information Technology: Coding and Computing (ITCC 2005) - Volume II, vol. 1, pp. 745–750, April 2005
24. Zhao, W., Varadharajan, V., Mu, Y.: A secure mental poker protocol over the internet. In: Proceedings of the Australasian Information Security Workshop Conference on ACSW Frontiers 2003 - Volume 21, ACSW Frontiers 2003, pp. 105–109, Darlinghurst, Australia. Australian Computer Society Inc. (2003)

Efficient Bit-Decomposition and Modulus-Conversion Protocols with an Honest Majority

Ryo Kikuchi[1(✉)], Dai Ikarashi[1], Takahiro Matsuda[2], Koki Hamada[1], and Koji Chida[1]

[1] NTT Corporation, Tokyo, Japan
kikuchi_ryo@fw.ipsj.or.jp,
{ikarashi.dai,hamada.koki,chida.koji}@lab.ntt.co.jp
[2] National Institute of Advanced Industrial Science and Technology (AIST), Tokyo, Japan
t-matsuda@aist.go.jp

Abstract. In this paper, we propose secret-sharing-based bit-decomposition and modulus-conversion protocols for a prime order ring $\mathbb{Z}_p$ with an honest majority: an adversary can corrupt $k-1$ parties of n parties and $2k-1 \leq n$. Our protocols are secure against passive and active adversaries depending on the components of our protocols. We assume a secret is an ℓ-bit element and $2^{\ell+\lceil \log m \rceil} < p$, where $m = k$ in the passive security and $m = \binom{n}{k-1}$ in the active security. The outputs of our bit-decomposition and modulus-conversion protocols are ℓ tuple of shares in $\mathbb{Z}_2$ and a share in $\mathbb{Z}_{p'}$, respectively, where p' is the modulus after the conversion. If k and n are small, the communication complexity of our passively secure bit-decomposition and modulus-conversion protocols are $O(\ell)$ bits and $O(\lceil \log p' \rceil)$ bits, respectively. Our key observation is that a quotient of additive shares can be computed from the *least* significant $\lceil \log m \rceil$ bits. If a secret a is "shifted" and additively shared as x_is so that $2^{\lceil \log m \rceil} a = \sum_{i=0}^{m-1} x_i = 2^{\lceil \log m \rceil} a + qp$, the least significant $\lceil \log m \rceil$ bits of $\sum_{i=0}^{m-1} x_i$ determine q since p is an odd prime and the least significant $\lceil \log m \rceil$ bits of $2^{\lceil \log m \rceil} a$ are 0s.

Keywords: Bit decomposition · Modulus conversion
Secure computation · Secret sharing · Honest majority

1 Introduction

Secure computation enables *parties* with inputs to compute a function on the inputs while keeping them secret. There are security notions that secure computation should satisfy, e.g., privacy, meaning the protocol reveals nothing except the output, and correctness, meaning the protocol computes the desired function. These notions should be satisfied in the presence of an adversary, and there are two classical adversary models according to adversaries' behaviors: passive

W. Susilo and G. Yang (Eds.): ACISP 2018, LNCS 10946, pp. 64–82, 2018.
https://doi.org/10.1007/978-3-319-93638-3_5

(i.e., semi-honest) and active (i.e., malicious). Passive security means an adversary follows the protocol but may try to learn something from the protocol transcript, and active security means the adversary tries to cheat with an arbitrary strategy including deviating from the protocol. Active security provides stronger security guarantee but passive security is sufficient in some cases, e.g., each party somewhat trusts each other but cannot share their information due to privacy regulations, parties cannot tamper with an installed program of secure computation, and the only thing they can do is seeing the input and output.

An adversary can corrupt a party to see its input and output and control its behavior. There are two major settings specifying the number of parties the adversary can corrupt. Honest majority means an adversary can corrupt less than half the parties, and dishonest majority means it can corrupt more than half. Security with a dishonest majority provides stronger security guarantee but security with an honest majority is sufficient in some cases, for example, each party is a "somewhat" trusted authority, such as a government agency of a different country that may not collude with other agencies.

Secure computation can accelerate an application of sensitive data since one can analyze data while they are secret by using secure computation, e.g., detecting tax fraud [3] and aggregating clinical information [14]. Despite the advantage of secure computation, it has not been widely used in practice. One of main reasons is its inefficiency. Secure computation tends to require heavy computations and communication; thus, its performance is typically much lower than that of local computation when the same function is computed. Therefore, to achieve better performance is one of the main challenges in secure computation.

1.1 Bit Decomposition and Modulus Conversion

When we are interested in secure computation on an integer input $a \in \mathbb{Z}_p$, there are two major representations to describe an intended function: an arithmetic circuit and a Boolean circuit. An input and output of an arithmetic circuit are represented as elements in $\mathbb{Z}_p$, while those of a Boolean circuit are in $\mathbb{Z}_2$.

Secure computation in better suited representation provides better performance. For example, addition and multiplication (in $\mathbb{Z}_p$) can be computed efficiently by an arithmetic circuit, while not by a Boolean circuit. In contrast, bit-operations, such as comparison and calculating Hamming weight, can be computed efficiently by a Boolean circuit, while those operations are non-trivial tasks for an arithmetic circuit.

To bridge these two representations, Damgård et al. [7] and Schoenmakers and Tuyls [18] proposed bit-decomposition protocols to convert the integer representation into the binary one. The former is a secret-sharing (SS)-based protocol and unconditionally secure with an honest majority, while the latter is a homomorphic-encryption-based protocol and computationally secure without an honest majority. In the honest majority case, several subsequent works have improved the efficiency [4,8,16,17,20].

There are two types in SS-based bit-decomposition protocols based on whether each bit of the bit-decomposition result of an original secret is in $\mathbb{Z}_p$

or in $\mathbb{Z}_2$. If these bits are shared in $\mathbb{Z}_p$, it is easy to convert the bit representation into an integer representation after computations with a Boolean circuit. In contrast, if these bits are shared in $\mathbb{Z}_2$, a Boolean circuit can be computed efficiently since the parties can *locally* compute an XOR gate. In this paper, we focus on the latter type of output; the output of the bit-decomposition protocol is shares in $\mathbb{Z}_2$.

A modulus-conversion protocol is a related protocol that converts a share in $\mathbb{Z}_p$ into that in $\mathbb{Z}_{p'}$ (with $p \neq p'$) without changing an original secret. This protocol corresponds to a type-casting operation (i.e., type conversion) for ordinary computers. In many applications, a user of secure computation may want to obtain values that are *not* reduced by modulus. For example, if we intend to obtain the sum of shared secrets, we want to obtain $\sum a_i$, not $\sum a_i \mod p$. In this case, we have to manage the shared values not to exceed the modulus p. However, if we do not know which function will be computed with shared secrets, we cannot determine beforehand how large p should be. Even if we use a large enough p for most functions, the communication complexity of secure computation is at least proportional to $\log p$ and the efficiency therefore decreases. The modulus-conversion protocol can be a solution of this problem; namely, when an output of secure computation will exceed p, we can change p into p', which is large enough to represent the output. Another application of a modulus-conversion protocol is the inverse of a bit-decomposition protocol by setting $p = 2$.

1.2 Our Contribution

We propose an SS-based bit-decomposition protocol for $\mathbb{Z}_p$ and modulus-conversion protocol from $\mathbb{Z}_p$ to $\mathbb{Z}_{p'}$ with low communication complexity and an honest majority, where p and p' are prime numbers. Our basic protocols are passively secure, but can be made actively secure if the number of parties is small. In this paper, we consider active security *with abort* in which an honest party will abort if an adversary cheats. In our protocols, it is assumed that the parties know the bit-length ℓ of a secret, i.e., a secret a satisfies $a < 2^{\ell+1}$. Therefore, the output of our bit-decomposition protocol is ℓ shares in $\mathbb{Z}_2$.[1] We also assume $\ell + \lceil \log m \rceil < \lceil \log p \rceil$, where $m = k$ in the passive security case and $m = \binom{n}{k-1}$ in the active security case, where k is the number of parties who can reconstruct the secret and n is the number of all parties. It seems natural that $\lceil \log p \rceil$ is somewhat larger than ℓ and the parties know ℓ to prevent an output of secure computation from exceeding p; nevertheless, our protocol supports neither full extraction of the bits of secret nor too many parties in which $\ell + \lceil \log m \rceil \geq \lceil \log p \rceil$. In addition, $\binom{n}{k-1}$ is exponential in n so our actively secure protocol is only for a small number of parties.

Our protocols consist of bit-wise share generation, random share generation, and Boolean circuit evaluation. If p is a Merssene prime, both of our protocols can be simplified and their communication complexity is improved in a constant factor. By using ordinary circuits and regarding k and n as constants, the

[1] If one wants to use Shamir's SS scheme, $\mathrm{GF}(2^{\lceil \log n \rceil + 1})$ can be an alternative option.

communication complexity of our bit-decomposition protocol is $O(\ell)$ bits, which seems optimal since the output is an ℓ-tuple of $\mathbb{Z}_2$. For the specific parameters of $(k,n) = (2,3)$ and when p is a Merssene prime, the communication complexity is $10\ell + 4$ bits, which is smaller than the best known result [4] of $17\lceil \log p \rceil + 12\lceil \log \lceil \log p \rceil \rceil$ bits, while [4] supports full extraction of bits and uses a different ring $p = 2^d$. Our modulus-conversion protocol has a similar structure, and the communication complexity is $O(\lceil \log p' \rceil)$ bits, which seems also optimal since the output of the protocol is a share in $\mathbb{Z}_{p'}$. We note that out protocols are not constant-round protocols. Nonetheless, the round complexity is comparable to that of constant-round protocols when $(k,n) = (2,3)$.

1.3 Technical Overview

A common difficulty in constructing bit-decomposition and modulus-conversion protocols is secure computation of a *quotient*. Let $a \in \mathbb{Z}_p$ be a secret and assume a is *additively* shared as $a = \sum_{i=0}^{m-1} x_i \mod p$. When we intend to obtain a share of a in $\mathbb{Z}_2$, one may try to replace x_i with $x_i \mod 2$. However, it does not work since $\sum_{i=0}^{m-1} x_i \mod 2 = a + qp \mod 2 = a + (q \mod 2)(p \mod 2) \neq a$. Here, p is public, but q is unknown and thus q should be securely computed. A naïve way to obtain q is to securely compute $\sum_{i=0}^{m-1} x_i$ by a Boolean circuit and compare $\sum_{i=0}^{m-1} x_i$ with p. However, this naïve method requires $O(\lceil \log p \rceil)$-bit communication to compute $\sum_{i=0}^{m-1} x_i$ by a Boolean circuit.

Our key observation is that a quotient of additive shares can be computed from the *least* significant u bits, and we call this property the *quotient transfer*. In both of our protocols, we first additively share $2^u a$ rather than a, i.e., $\sum_{i=0}^{m-1} x_i = 2^u a + qp$. Recall that we assume $\ell + u \leq \lceil \log p \rceil$, and thus $2^u a \mod p = 2^u a$. We observe that the least significant u bits of $\sum_{i=0}^{m-1} x_i$ represents q since p is an odd prime and the least significant u bits of $2^u a$ are 0s. Therefore, we can obtain q by securely computing the least significant u bits of $\sum_{i=0}^{m-1} x_i$. By using the quotient transfer, $\ell + u$ bits and $\lceil \log p' \rceil + u$ bits of $\sum_{i=0}^{m-1} x_i$ are sufficient for our bit-decomposition and modulus-conversion protocols, respectively.

1.4 Related Work

Damgård et al. [7] proposed a constant round bit-decomposition protocol, which was simplified by Nishide and Ohta [16]. Toft proposed another bit-decomposition protocol [20] with almost linear communication complexity, and Reistad and Toft [17] proposed a bit-decomposition protocol with linear communication complexity while admitting statistical privacy. In these works, the output of a bit-decomposition protocol is shares in $\mathbb{Z}_p$, and linear communication complexity means that the number of invocations of a multiplication protocol is linear in $\lceil \log p \rceil$. In this paper, we measure the communication complexity in bits among all the parties. With respect to the communication complexity in bits, the above mentioned existing protocols incur at least $O(\lceil \log p \rceil^2)$ since a multiplication protocol requires $O(\lceil \log p \rceil)$-bit communication.

A bit-decomposition protocol that outputs XOR-free shares was proposed by From and Jakobson [8]. They use a share in GF(2^{256}) as an output. Bogdanov et al. [4] proposed a bit-decomposition protocol that is dedicated to the replicated SS scheme [6,13] with $(k, n) = (2, 3)$ and $p = 2^d$ for some positive integer d. The output of their bit-decomposition protocol is $\lceil \log p \rceil$ shares in $\mathbb{Z}_2$ since they support full extraction.

Regarding modulus conversion, Bogdanov et al. [4] proposed a specific case of a modulus-conversion protocol from $\mathbb{Z}_2^{\lceil \log p \rceil}$ into $\mathbb{Z}_p$. This protocol is also dedicated to the replicated SS scheme with $(k, n) = (2, 3)$ and $p = 2^d$ for some positive integer d. This protocol is the inverse of a bit-decomposition protocol.

2 Preliminaries

Let $a := b$ denote that a is defined by b, and $a \| b$ denote the concatenation of a and b. If a is an ℓ-bit element, $a^{(i)}$ denotes the i-th bit of a, where we count the indices in the right-to-left order with 0 being the initial index, i.e., $a := a^{(\ell-1)} \| \cdots \| a^{(0)}$. If A is a probabilistic algorithm, $a \leftarrow \mathsf{A}(b)$ means a is the output of A on input b. The notations $\mathscr{R}$, $\mathbb{Z}$, $\mathbb{Z}_p$, and $\mathbb{Z}_p^m$ denote a ring, the set of integers, $\mathbb{Z}/p\mathbb{Z}$, and m-tuple of the elements in $\mathbb{Z}_p$, respectively. For a relation R, $\langle R \rangle$ denotes 1 if R is true and 0 otherwise. For example, $\langle a <_? b \rangle$ denotes 1 if $a < b$ and 0 otherwise.

2.1 Mersenne Prime

A Mersenne prime is a prime number of the form $p = 2^e - 1$ for some integer e. It provides efficient modular arithmetic, e.g., [5], since modulo a Mersenne prime can be computed by bit-shifting and addition: If $a = a_0 2^e + a_1$, then $a \bmod p = a_0 2^e + a_1 \bmod p = a_0 + a_1 \bmod p$ holds since $2^e - 1 = 0 \bmod p$.

2.2 Security Model and Definition

We consider SS-based secure computation with an honest majority. In this setting, there are n parties $P_0, \ldots, P_{n-1}$, a secret is shared among the n parties via SS, any k parties can reconstruct the secret from their shares, and an adversary corrupts up to $k-1$ parties at the beginning of the protocol, where $2k - 1 \leq n$.

We consider the client/server model. This model is used to outsource secure computation, where any number of clients send shares of their inputs to the servers. Therefore, both the input and output of the servers are shares, and both of our protocols are therefore share-input and share-output protocols.

Regarding adversarial behaviors, we consider two security models: passive and active security with abort. We prove the security of our protocols in a hybrid model, where parties run a protocol with real messages and also have access to a trusted party computing a subfunctionality for them. When the subfunctionality is g, we say that the protocol works in the *g-hybrid model*. We give a brief explanation here and the formal definitions of security will appear in the full version.

Passive Security. In passive security, corrupted parties follow a protocol. Therefore, a passive adversary tries to obtain information about a secret from transcripts that the corrupted parties have. Formally, we say that a protocol is passively secure if there is a simulator that simulates the view of the corrupted parties from the inputs and outputs of the protocol [11].

Active Security with Abort. In this paper, an actively secure protocol is a secure computation *with abort.* This means that if an adversary cheats, an honest party will abort. This security model does not guarantee fairness: An adversary may obtain the outputs of corrupted parties while the honest parties do not.[2] Note that we do not care about fairness even it is possible with an honest majority. This is because efficient circuit evaluation protocols are known [9,10] in this security model, and it may be difficult to reveal a secret without abort efficiently. From here on, in this paper, active security means active security with abort.

2.3 Secret Sharing

We use an unconditionally secure linear SS scheme [2] that supports the following algorithms, protocols, and local operations.

- Share: On input $a \in \mathscr{R}$, this algorithm outputs shares of a. The notation $[a]_i$ denotes P_i's share and $[a]$ denotes a sharing, which is a tuple of all shares. Several rings will appear, and thus we explicitly indicate the ring to which shares/sharings belong. For example, $[a]^{\mathbb{Z}_p}$ denotes a sharing of a in $\mathbb{Z}_p$, while $[a]^{\mathbb{Z}_2}$ denotes a sharing of a in $\mathbb{Z}_2$. In addition, $[a]^{\mathbb{Z}_2^m}$ denotes a tuple of sharings $([a_0]^{\mathbb{Z}_2}, \dots, [a_{m-1}]^{\mathbb{Z}_2})$, where $a = \sum_{i=0}^{m-1} 2^i a_i$.
- Reconstruction: On input k shares, this algorithm outputs a secret. For any linear SS scheme, a secret can be reconstructed by a linear combination of k shares. For example, we denote the linear combination of the shares of $P_0, \dots, P_{k-1}$ as $a = \sum_{i=0}^{k-1} \lambda_i [a]_i$ for some λ_i.[3]
- Reveal: This is a protocol for reconstructing a secret from its shares. The requirements of this protocol are different depending on considered security models. In the presence of a passive adversary, given a sharing of a, this protocol guarantees that at the end of the execution, all the parties obtain a. When we consider an active adversary, this protocol guarantees that at the end of the execution, if $[a]$ is not correct, i.e., either a secret reconstructed from some k shares is $\perp$ or does not equal to that from other k shares, then all the honest parties will abort. Otherwise, if $[a]$ is correct, then each party will either output a or abort.

---

[2] The outputs of our protocols are shares, so the adversary cannot obtain any secret information.

[3] This is a slightly small class of SS schemes compared to [2] with respect that each party has a single share.

- Local operations: Given sharings $[a]$ and $[b]$ and a scalar $\alpha \in \mathscr{R}$, the parties can generate sharings of $[a+b]$, $[\alpha a]$, and $[\alpha + a]$ using only local operations. The notations $[a] + [b]$, $\alpha[a]$, and $\alpha + [a]$ denote these local operations, respectively.
- Multiplication protocol and secure circuit evaluation: Given sharings $[a]$ and $[b]$, the parties can generate $[ab]$ by the multiplication protocol. Combining local operations with the multiplication protocol, we can compute any Boolean circuit over shared data.

Concrete examples of a linear SS scheme are Shamir's scheme [19] and the replicated SS scheme [6,13]. In this paper, we use $\mathbb{Z}_p$, $\mathbb{Z}_{p'}$, and $\mathbb{Z}_2$ as instantiations of a ring, where p and p' are prime numbers. We especially say that a is *additively* shared in $\mathbb{Z}_p$ if $a = \sum_{i=0}^{m-1} x_i \mod p$ for some m, and we call x_i a *sub-share*.

Although an input and output of our protocols can be shares of any linear SS scheme, the shares have to be converted into one of the replicated SS scheme in our actively secure protocols. The share size of the replicated SS scheme is exponential in n; therefore, our protocols with active security are suitable only for a small number of parties, whereas our protocols with passive security do not have this restriction.

Replicated Secret Sharing Scheme. The replicated SS scheme [6,13] is an SS scheme in which a secret is represented as an addition of sub-shares and each sub-share corresponds to a maximal unqualified set of parties.

Protocol 1. Share conversion from a linear SS scheme into the replicated SS scheme

---

Input: $[a]^{\mathbb{Z}_p}$
Output: $[\![a]\!]^{\mathbb{Z}_p}$
1: The parties call $\mathcal{F}_{\text{rand}}$ and receive $[\![r]\!]^{\mathbb{Z}_p}$.
2: The parties locally convert $[\![r]\!]^{\mathbb{Z}_p}$ into $[r]^{\mathbb{Z}_p}$.
3: The parties reveal $[a-r]^{\mathbb{Z}_p}$ and obtain $a-r$.
4: $[\![a]\!]^{\mathbb{Z}_p} := (a-r) + [\![r]\!]$.
5: The parties output $[\![a]\!]^{\mathbb{Z}_p}$.

Let $m := \binom{n}{k-1}$ and $\mathbb{T} = \{\mathbb{T}_0, \ldots, \mathbb{T}_{m-1}\}$ be the family of all $(k-1)$-subsets of $\{0, \ldots, n-1\}$. We especially use the notation $[\![\cdot]\!]_i$ (resp. $[\![\cdot]\!]$) for a share (resp. a sharing) of the replicated SS scheme. Shares of the replicated SS scheme in $\mathbb{Z}_p$ are generated as follows. A secret a is additively shared into m sub-shares as $a = \sum_{i=0}^{m-1} x_i \mod p$, and a share for P_i is $[\![a]\!]_i = \{x_j \mid i \notin \mathbb{T}_j, \mathbb{T}_j \in \mathbb{T}\}$. Here, $k-1$ parties cannot obtain any information about a since there exists $\mathbb{T}_j$ that contains all the corrupted parties, and an adversary cannot know x_j.

The size of a share of the replicated SS scheme becomes very large for a large number of parties since each party has $\binom{n-1}{k-1}$ sub-shares. However, the replicated SS scheme has an attractive property that the parties can generate a share of a random number *without interaction*, which is called pseudorandom secret sharing (PRSS) [6]. Formally, PRSS securely computes the following functionality $\mathcal{F}_{\text{rand}}$.

FUNCTIONALITY 2.1 ($\mathcal{F}_{\text{rand}}$ – **Generating shares of a random value**)
Upon receiving *id* from P_i for $0 \leq i < n$, sample $r \leftarrow \mathbb{Z}_p$, generate $[\![r]\!]^{\mathbb{Z}_p}$ by the sharing algorithm, and send $[\![r]\!]_i^{\mathbb{Z}_p}$ to P_i

Share Conversion Among SS Schemes. It is known that shares can be converted among additive shares, a linear SS scheme, and the replicated SS scheme.

A share of a linear SS scheme $[a]_i$ can be locally converted to additive shares with k sub-shares by setting $x_i := \lambda_i[a]_i$, where P_i has x_i for $0 \leq i < k$. On the contrary, when P_i for $0 \leq i < k$ has an additive share x_i, the shares can be converted by sharing all the sub-shares x_i via a linear SS scheme and adding them all.

A share of the replicated SS scheme can be locally converted into that of a linear SS scheme [6]. On the contrary, a share of a linear SS scheme can be converted into that of the replicated SS scheme by using Protocol 1. This protocol is actively secure in the $\mathcal{F}_{\text{rand}}$-hybrid model since we assume that the reveal protocol is actively secure.

Secure Circuit Evaluation on Linear SS. In our protocols, several circuits are securely computed. We consider the sum, carryless-sum, and zero-test circuits. The sum circuit on input m ℓ-bit elements, outputs $(\lceil \log m \rceil + \ell)$-bit element that is the sum of the inputs. The carryless-sum circuit is the same as the sum circuit except the output is ℓ-bit element by discarding the most significant $\lceil \log m \rceil$ bits. The zero-test circuit on input m 1-bit elements, outputs 0 if all the inputs are 0, and 1 otherwise. We construct our protocols in a modular way using the functionalities $\mathcal{F}_{\text{sum}}$, $\mathcal{F}_{\text{clsum}}$, and $\mathcal{F}_{\text{zero}}$ that correspond to the sum, carryless-sum, and zero-test circuits, respectively. The formal descriptions of those functionalities will appear in the full version.

3 Quotient Transfer

In this section, we show our key observation that we call *quotient transfer*. Informally, quotient transfer means that, if a "shifted" secret $2^u a$ is additively shared as $\sum_{i=0}^{m-1} x_i = 2^u a + qp$, the parties can compute the quotient q from the least significant u bits of $\sum_{i=0}^{m-1} x_i$, where $u = \lceil \log m \rceil$.

Theorem 3.1. *Let m be a positive integer, $u = \lceil \log m \rceil$, and $2^u < p$. Let $(x_0, \ldots, x_{m-1})$ be a tuple of elements in $\mathbb{Z}_p$ satisfying $\sum_{i=0}^{m-1} x_i = 2^u a + qp$. Then, the quotient q satisfies*

$$q = (p \mod 2^u)^{-1} \sum_{i=0}^{m-1} x_i \mod 2^u. \quad (1)$$

Proof. We observe

$$\sum_{i=0}^{m-1} x_i \mod 2^u = 2^u a + qp \mod 2^u = q(p \mod 2^u) \mod 2^u$$

since $q \leq m - 1 < 2^u$. In addition, 2^u and $(p \mod 2^u)$ are co-prime, and thus $(p \mod 2^u)^{-1}$ exists. ∎

The prime number p is public, and thus $(p \mod 2^u)^{-1}$ can be computed by every party. Therefore, Eq. 1 means that the quotient q can be computed from the least significant u bits of $\sum_{i=0}^{m-1} x_i$.

For practical applications, protocols with a small number of parties may be used, and we will later consider the case $m = 2$ (i.e. three-party case). Furthermore, for performance reasons, a Mersenne prime is used for p. Therefore, in the following, we give specific cases of Theorem 3.1 for these cases. The second equation below shows that the parties can compute the quotient q from the LSB of $\sum_{i=0}^{m-1} x_i$ in a secure three-party computation when p is a Mersenne prime.

Corollary 3.2. *If p is a Mersenne prime, i.e., $p = 2^e - 1$, Eq. (1) is*

$$q = -\sum_{i=0}^{m-1} x_i \mod 2^u$$

since $p \mod 2^u = -1$. Furthermore, when $m = 2$,

$$q = x_0 + x_1 \mod 2.$$

4 Bit-Decomposition Protocol

In this section, we first show a useful equation for our proposed protocols, then show our passively secure bit-decomposition protocol. After that, we discuss a technique to achieve active security. Here, we show the protocol in which p is a Mersenne prime, and will give a general protocol in the full version.

4.1 Equation for Bit Decomposition

The following equation can be derived from quotient transfer.

Theorem 4.1. *Let $m, u, p, a, (x_0, \ldots, x_{m-1})$ be the same as Theorem 3.1, and ℓ be a positive integer such that $\ell + u \leq |p|$ and $a < 2^{\ell+1}$. Let $r_u = \sum_{i=0}^{m-1} x_i \mod 2^u$, $\tilde{p} = (p \mod 2^u)^{-1} \mod 2^u$, and q_u, z, and z' be the quotients of $\sum_{i=0}^{m-1} x_i / 2^u$, $\tilde{p} \sum_{i=0}^{m-1} x_i / 2^u$, and $p\tilde{p}/2^u$ in modulo $2^{\ell+u}$, respectively. Then,*

$$a = q_u - z' r_u - zp \mod 2^\ell.$$

Proof. Let q be a quotient of $\sum_{i=0}^{m-1} x_i$ divided by p, i.e., $\sum_{i=0}^{m-1} x_i = qp + 2^u a$. Here, $2^u a = \sum_{i=0}^{m-1} x_i - qp$ in $\mathbb{Z}$, therefore, $2^u a = -qp + \sum_{i=0}^{m-1} x_i \mod 2^{\ell+u}$. Recall that $\tilde{p} = (p \mod 2^u)^{-1}$ in modulo 2^u. From Theorem 3.1,

$$\begin{aligned} &-qp + \sum_{i=0}^{m-1} x_i \mod 2^{\ell+u} \\ &= -(\tilde{p}\sum_{i=0}^{m-1} x_i \mod 2^u)(p \mod 2^{\ell+u}) + \sum_{i=0}^{m-1} x_i \mod 2^{\ell+u}. \qquad (2) \end{aligned}$$

Recall that $r_u = \sum_{i=0}^{m-1} x_i \mod 2^u$ and z is the quotient of $\tilde{p}\sum_{i=0}^{m-1} x_i/2^u \mod 2^{\ell+u}$. Then, Eq. (2) is equal to

$$\begin{aligned} &-(\tilde{p}r_u \mod 2^u)(p \mod 2^{\ell+u}) + \sum_{i=0}^{m-1} x_i \mod 2^{\ell+u} \\ &= -(\tilde{p}r_u - z2^u \mod 2^{\ell+u})(p \mod 2^{\ell+u}) + \sum_{i=0}^{m-1} x_i \mod 2^{\ell+u} \\ &= -p\tilde{p}r_u - zp2^u + \sum_{i=0}^{m-1} x_i \mod 2^{\ell+u}. \qquad (3) \end{aligned}$$

Recall that q_u and z' are the quotients of $\sum_{i=0}^{m-1} x_i/2^u \mod 2^{\ell+u}$ and $p\tilde{p}/2^u \mod 2^{\ell+u}$, respectively. In addition, $p\tilde{p} = 1 \mod 2^u$. Then, Eq. (3) is equal to

$$-(z'2^u + 1)r_u - zp2^u + q_u 2^u + r_u \mod 2^{\ell+u} = (q_u - z'r_u - zp)2^u \mod 2^{\ell+u}.$$

Consequently, we obtain $2^u a = (q_u - z'r_u - zp)2^u \mod 2^{\ell+u}$. By dividing both sides by 2^u, We finally obtain

$$a = q_u - z'r_u - zp \mod 2^\ell.$$

This concludes the proof. ■

We give a specific case of Theorem 4.1 in which p is a Mersenne prime as follows.

Corollary 4.2. *Under the same setting as in Theorem 4.1, if p is a Mersenne prime, i.e., $p = 2^e - 1$ for some integer e, it holds that*

$$a = q_u + \langle r_u \neq_? 0 \mod 2^u \rangle \mod 2^\ell. \qquad (4)$$

Proof. If $p = 2^e - 1$, then $\tilde{p} = 2^u - 1 \mod 2^{\ell+u}$. In addition, $z' = -1 \mod 2^{\ell+u}$ holds since $p\tilde{p} = (2^e - 1)(2^u - 1) \mod 2^{\ell+u} = -2^u + 1 \mod 2^{\ell+u}$.

Recall that z satisfies $\tilde{p}r_u \mod 2^u = \tilde{p}r_u - z2^u \mod 2^{\ell+u}$. By substituting $\tilde{p} = 2^e - 1 \mod 2^{\ell+u}$,

$$-r_u \mod 2^u = (2^u - 1)r_u - z2^u \mod 2^{\ell+u}$$

and

$$z2^u \mod 2^{\ell+u} = r_u 2^u - (-r_u \mod 2^u) - r_u \mod 2^{\ell+u}.$$

Here,

$$-r_u \mod 2^u = -\sum_{i=0}^{m-1} x_i \mod 2^u = \begin{cases} 0 & \text{if } \sum_{i=0}^{m-1} x_i \mod 2^u = 0, \\ 2^u - 1 & \textit{otherwise.} \end{cases}$$

Therefore, if $r_u = 0$, then $z = r_u$; otherwise, $z = r_u - 1$. This is equivalent to $z = r_u - \langle r_u \neq_? 0 \rangle$. By substituting the above into Theorem 4.1, we conclude the proof. ■

Theorem 4.1 and Corollary 4.2 show that a can be represented from the $\ell + u$ bits of $\sum_{i=0}^{m-1} x_i$. We further obtain the following corollary since it is convenient that an equation is represented by bit-operations of sub-shares. The following corollary is in fact securely computed in our bit-decomposition protocol.

Corollary 4.3. *Let $m, u, p, a, (x_0, \ldots, x_{m-1})$ be the same as Theorem 4.1. Let q_i and r_i be the bits of x_i larger than $u - 1$ bit and those smaller than u bit, respectively, and q_u and r_u be the bits of $\sum_{i=0}^{m-1} r_i$ larger than $u - 1$ bit and those smaller than u bit, respectively. Then,*

$$a = \sum_{i=0}^{m-1} q_i + q_u + \langle r_u \neq_? 0 \rangle \mod 2^\ell.$$

4.2 Passively Secure Bit-Decomposition Protocol

Our passively secure bit-decomposition protocol for $\mathbb{Z}_p$ with a Mersenne prime p, is derived from Corollary 4.3 as Protocol 2.

Security Against a Passive Adversary. Protocol 2 consists of share generation and circuit evaluation, and the security of the protocol is therefore directly reduced to them. Informally, share generation does not reveal any information about a secret since SS is unconditionally secure. Therefore, Protocol 2 is passively secure in the $(\mathcal{F}_{\text{sum}}, \mathcal{F}_{\text{clsum}}, \mathcal{F}_{\text{zero}})$-hybrid model.

4.3 Efficiency

The communication complexity of our bit-decomposition protocol is $k(\ell + u)\texttt{share}_{\mathbb{Z}_2} + \texttt{sum}_{u,k} + \texttt{clsum}_{\ell,k+2} + \texttt{zerotest}_u$ bits, where $\texttt{share}_{\mathbb{Z}_2}$ denotes the communication complexity to share a bit, $\texttt{sum}_u$ denotes that to securely compute the sum on input k u-bit elements, $\texttt{clsum}_{\ell,k+2}$ denotes that to securely compute the carryless-sum circuit on input $(k+2)$ ℓ-bit elements[4], and $\texttt{zerotest}_u$ denotes that to securely compute the zero-test circuit on input u 1-bit elements. If k (and u) is regarded as a constant, the communication complexity is $O(\ell)$ bits since

[4] Precisely, k ℓ-bit elements, one u-bit element, and one 1-bit element are summed up.

Protocol 2. Passively secure bit-decomposition protocol

Input: $[a]^{\mathbb{Z}_p}$

Output: $[a]^{\mathbb{Z}_2^\ell}$

1: P_i computes $x_i := 2^u \lambda_i [a]_i \mod p$ for $u = \lceil \log k \rceil$ and $0 \le i < k$, and let the j-th bit of x_i be $x_i^{(j)}$.
2: **for** $0 \le i < k$ **do**
3: P_i shares $x_i^{(0)}, \ldots, x_i^{(u-1)}$ bit-by-bit in $\mathbb{Z}_2$, and the parties regard them as $[r_i]^{\mathbb{Z}_2^u}$.
4: P_i shares $x_i^{(u)}, \ldots, x_i^{(\ell+u-1)}$ bit-by-bit in $\mathbb{Z}_2$, and the parties regard them as $[q_i]^{\mathbb{Z}_2^\ell}$.
5: The parties call $\mathcal{F}_{\text{sum}}$ on input $[r_i]^{\mathbb{Z}_2^u}$ for $0 \le i < k$, and receive $[\sum_{i=0}^{k-1} r_i]^{\mathbb{Z}_2^{2u}}$. ($k$ additions yield $2u$-bit output).
6: The parties regard the least u bits of $[\sum_{i=0}^{k-1} r_i]^{\mathbb{Z}_2^{2u}}$ as $[r_u]^{\mathbb{Z}_2^u}$, and the others as $[q_u]^{\mathbb{Z}_2^u}$.
7: The parties call $\mathcal{F}_{\text{zero}}$ on input $[r_u]^{\mathbb{Z}_2^u}$, and receive $[(r_u \neq_? 0)]^{\mathbb{Z}_2}$.
8: The parties call $\mathcal{F}_{\text{clsum}}$ on input $[q_0]^{\mathbb{Z}_2^\ell}, \ldots, [q_{k-1}]^{\mathbb{Z}_2^\ell}$, $[q_u]^{\mathbb{Z}_2^u}$, and $[(r_u \neq_? 0)]^{\mathbb{Z}_2}$, and receive $[a]^{\mathbb{Z}_2^\ell} := [\sum_{i=0}^{k-1} q_i + q_u + (r_u \neq_? 0)]^{\mathbb{Z}_2^\ell}$.
9: The parties output $[a]^{\mathbb{Z}_2^\ell}$.

$\mathtt{share}_{\mathbb{Z}_2}$ is constant, $\mathtt{clsum}_{\ell,k+2}$ invokes $O(\ell)$ multiplication protocols in $\mathbb{Z}_2$, and a multiplication protocol in $\mathbb{Z}_2$ requires $O(1)$-bits communication per invocation.

For concrete comparison in a specific parameter, we give a precise communication complexity when $(k,n) = (2,3)$ and use the replicated SS scheme to share $\mathbb{Z}_2$. We assume that sum and carryless-sum circuits compute a full adder sequentially, and zerotest circuit computes an AND gate sequentially. Here, $u = \lceil \log k \rceil = 1$, $\mathtt{share} = 2$,[5] $\mathtt{sum}_{1,2}$ is $\mathtt{Mult}_{\mathbb{Z}_2}$, $\mathtt{clsum}_{\ell,4}$ is $(\ell-1)\mathtt{Mult}_{\mathbb{Z}_2}$, and $\mathtt{zerotest}_u$ requires no communication since $[(r_u \neq_? 0)]^{\mathbb{Z}_2} = [r_u]^{\mathbb{Z}_2} + [q_u]^{\mathbb{Z}_2}$, where $\mathtt{Mult}_{\mathbb{Z}_2}$ denotes the communication complexity of a multiplication protocol in $\mathbb{Z}_2$. If we use the replicated SS scheme, $\mathtt{Mult}_{\mathbb{Z}_2} = 6$ per invocation [12]. Therefore, the communication complexity is $4(\ell+1)+6+6(\ell-1) = 10\ell+4$ bits. This means that, if $\ell \approx \lceil \log p \rceil / 2$, the communication complexity of our bit-decomposition protocol is as large as that of a multiplication protocol in $\mathbb{Z}_p$, which is $6\lceil \log p \rceil$.

There is no bit-decomposition protocol in which $\ell + u < \lceil \log p \rceil$ is assumed and which outputs $[a]^{\mathbb{Z}_2^\ell}$, and thus our protocol is formally incomparable to existing bit-decomposition protocols. If we try to compare our bit-decomposition protocol with existing ones, the most efficient bit-decomposition protocol is [4] and its communication complexity is $5\lceil \log p \rceil + 12(\lceil \log \lceil \log p \rceil \rceil + 1)\lceil \log p \rceil = 17\lceil \log p \rceil + 12\lceil \log \lceil \log p \rceil \rceil$ bits. Even regarding $\lceil \log p \rceil = \ell$, our protocol is about three times faster. However, [4] supports full extraction and $p = 2^m$, and thus it is difficult to simply compare with ours.

The round complexity of our bit-decomposition protocol is $1 + sum_{u,k} + clsum_{\ell,k+2} + zerotest_u$, where $sum_{u,k}$, $clsum_{\ell,k+2}$, and $zerotest_u$ are the round complexities of protocols instantiating $\mathcal{F}_{\text{sum}}$, $\mathcal{F}_{\text{zero}}$, and $\mathcal{F}_{\text{zero}}$, respectively. If

[5] This comes from a communication-efficient sharing given in the full version.

$(k, n) = (2, 3)$, the round complexity of our bit-decomposition protocol is $1+1+(\ell-1)+0 = \ell+1$ if we use the same circuits in evaluating the communication complexity.

4.4 Achieving Active Security Using Replicated SS

We show how to make Protocol 2 secure against an active adversary. Step 1 of the protocol is local computation; therefore, it is secure even against an active adversary. In addition, the steps from Step 5 are secure circuit evaluation. Therefore, if we use an actively secure circuit evaluation protocol, such as [1,10,12,15], these steps are secure against an active adversary, as desired.

The remaining steps are Steps 2, 3, and 4. In general, an adversary may corrupt P_i and share an incorrect $\tilde{x}_i$, and it is difficult to detect it. Therefore, we prevent the adversary from mounting such an attack by making these steps consist only of *local* computations. We show that if a secret is shared via the replicated SS scheme, we can generate a bit-wise share of sub-shares by local computations.

Consequently, our bit-decomposition protocol can be actively secure in the $(\mathcal{F}_{\mathsf{sum}}, \mathcal{F}_{\mathsf{zero}}, \mathcal{F}_{\mathsf{clsum}})$-hybrid model by converting a share by Protocol 1 at first, and then performing local share generation of sub-shares.

The communication complexity of the actively secure version of our protocol is at least $O(\lceil \log p \rceil)$ bits since revealing in Protocol 1 incurs this amount of communication. Therefore, only if a secret is shared via the replicated SS scheme from the beginning, the communication complexity of our actively secure bit-decomposition protocol is $O(\ell)$ bits, while $O(\lceil \log p \rceil)$ for a general linear SS scheme.

Local Share Generation of Sub-shares in Replicated SS. In the replicated SS scheme, each sub-share x_i is held by $n-k+1$ parties. To obtain a share of the j-th bit of x_i, each of the $n-k+1$ parties sets his sub-share x'_i as the j-th bit of x_i, and the parties set all the other sub-shares as 0. It trivially holds that $\sum_{i=0}^{m-1} x'_i = x_i$. In general, the parties can locally generate an additive share of $f(x_i) \mod p'$, where f is an arbitrary function. We give the algorithm in Algorithm 3.

Algorithm 3. Local share generation of sub-shares in replicated SS

Input: The $n-k+1$ parties have $x_i \in \mathbb{Z}_p$
Output: Each P_i has $[\![f(x)]\!]_i^{\mathbb{Z}_{p'}}$
1: The $n-k+1$ parties who have x_i compute $x'_i = f(x_i) \mod p'$.
2: The parties set the all sub-shares x'_j as 0 except x'_i.
3: Each P_i outputs $[\![f(x)]\!]_i = \{x'_j \mid i \notin \mathbb{T}_j, \mathbb{T}_j \in \mathbb{T}\}$.

We give an example to obtain a bit-wise share of sub-shares in the case of $(k, n) = (2, 3)$ and $p' = 2$: Before starting the protocol, P_0 has (x_0, x_1), P_1 has

(x_1, x_2), and P_2 has (x_2, x_0), where $a = x_0 + x_1 + x_2 \mod p$. The parties P_0, P_1, and P_2 regard $(x_0^{(0)}, 0)$, $(0, 0)$, $(0, x_0^{(0)})$ as their shares of $x_0^{(0)}$, respectively. By recursively doing the same procedure for the other bits, the parties obtain the bit-by-bit shares of x_0, x_1, and x_2.

5 Modulus-Conversion Protocol

When we consider modulus conversion, computing the quotient also has an important role. Let us consider the case in which we want to convert a share of a in $\mathbb{Z}_p$ into a share of a in $\mathbb{Z}_{p'}$, and a is additively shared, i.e., $a := \sum_{i=0}^{m-1} x_i \mod p$. In this case, $\sum_{i=0}^{m-1} x_i \mod p' = qp + a \mod p' = (q \mod p')(p \mod p') + (a \mod p')$. Here, $p \mod p'$ can be computed from the public modulus and thus $q \mod p'$ is the only unknown value. Therefore, by computing q using quotient transfer, we can obtain an efficient modulus-conversion protocol.

In this section, we first give a definition and instantiation of the functionality we use in our modulus-conversion protocols. We then propose a special case of our modulus-conversion protocol from $\mathbb{Z}_2^u$ to $\mathbb{Z}_{p'}$. After that, we propose our modulus-conversion protocol from $\mathbb{Z}_p$ to $\mathbb{Z}_{p'}$.

5.1 Generating a Pair of Random Shares

In our modulus-conversion protocol, we have to generate $([r]^{\mathbb{Z}_2}, [r]^{\mathbb{Z}_{p'}})$ for $r \leftarrow \mathbb{Z}_2$. The functionality that should be realized by such a protocol is defined as $\mathcal{F}_{\text{doublerand}}$ described below. This can be instantiated with $O(\lceil \log p' \rceil)$ bits communication by combining a protocol generating $[r]^{\mathbb{Z}_p}$ (RAN$_2$() in [7]) and our bit-decomposition protocol. We will further give a more efficient and actively secure version of our modulus-conversion protocol for a small number of parties in the full version.

FUNCTIONALITY 5.1 ($\mathcal{F}_{\text{doublerand}}$ – Generating pair of random shares)
Upon receiving *id* from each party P_i, sample $r \leftarrow \mathbb{Z}_2$, generate $([r]^{\mathbb{Z}_2}, [r]^{\mathbb{Z}_{p'}})$ via the sharing algorithms, and send $([r]_i^{\mathbb{Z}_2}, [r]_i^{\mathbb{Z}_{p'}})$ to each party P_i.

5.2 Modulus-Conversion Protocol from $\mathbb{Z}_2^u$ to $\mathbb{Z}_p$

We now give the formal description of Protocol 4, which is a special case of modulus conversion in which shares $[a]^{\mathbb{Z}_2^u}$ can be converted to $[a]^{\mathbb{Z}_{p'}}$.

Protocol 4 consists of local operations, revealing, and $\mathcal{F}_{\text{doublerand}}$. Recall that we assume revealing is secure against an active adversary. Therefore, Protocol 4 is also actively secure in the $\mathcal{F}_{\text{doublerand}}$-hybrid model.

The communication complexity is $u(\texttt{drand}_{\mathbb{Z}_{p'}} + \texttt{reveal}_{\mathbb{Z}_2})$, where $\texttt{drand}_{\mathbb{Z}_{p'}}$ and $\texttt{reveal}_{\mathbb{Z}_2}$ are the communication complexities of generating $([r]^{\mathbb{Z}_2}, [r]^{\mathbb{Z}_{p'}})$ for $r \leftarrow \mathbb{Z}_2$ and revealing a share in $\mathbb{Z}_2$. If we regard the number of parties as a constant, it is $O(\log \lceil p' \rceil)$ bits. The round complexity is *drand* + 1, where *drand* is that of a protocol for realizing $\mathcal{F}_{\text{doublerand}}$.

Protocol 4. modulus-conversion protocol from $\mathbb{Z}_2^u$ to $\mathbb{Z}_{p'}$

Input: $[a]^{\mathbb{Z}_2^u}$
Output: $[a]^{\mathbb{Z}_{p'}}$

for $0 \le i < u$ **do**
  The parties call $\mathcal{F}_{\text{doublerand}}$ and receive $([r^{(i)}]^{\mathbb{Z}_2}, [r^{(i)}]^{\mathbb{Z}_{p'}})$.
  The parties reveal $[a^{(i)} - r^{(i)}]^{\mathbb{Z}_2} = [a^{(i)}]^{\mathbb{Z}_2} - [r^{(i)}]^{\mathbb{Z}_2}$ to obtain $a^{(i)} - r^{(i)}$.
  if $a^{(i)} - r^{(i)} = 0$ **then**
    The parties set $[a^{(i)}]^{\mathbb{Z}_{p'}} = [r^{(i)}]^{\mathbb{Z}_{p'}}$.
  else
    The parties set $[a^{(i)}]^{\mathbb{Z}_{p'}} = (1 - [r^{(i)}]^{\mathbb{Z}_{p'}})$.
$[a]^{\mathbb{Z}_{p'}} := \sum_{i=0}^{u-1} 2^i [a^{(i)}]^{\mathbb{Z}_{p'}} \mod p'$.
The parties output $[a]^{\mathbb{Z}_{p'}}$.

5.3 Equation for Modulus Conversion

Similarly to our bit-decomposition protocol, we first show a useful equation for our protocol.

Theorem 5.2. *Let $m, p, a, (x_0, \ldots, x_{m-1}), \tilde{p}$ be the same as Theorem 3.1, p' be a prime number, and ℓ be a positive integer such that $\ell + u \le |p|$. Then,*

$$a = 2^{-u}\left(\sum_{i=0}^{m-1} x_i - (\tilde{p}\sum_{i=0}^{m-1} x_i \mod 2^u)p\right) \mod p'.$$

Proof. It directly follows from Theorem 3.1 and the fact that 2^u and p' are co-prime,

$$\sum_{i=0}^{m-1} x_i - (\tilde{p}\sum_{i=0}^{m-1} x_i \mod 2^u)p = \sum_{i=0}^{m-1} x_i - qp = (2^u a + qp) - qp = 2^u a.$$

■

We obtain the following corollary when p is a Mersenne prime.

Corollary 5.3. *Let $m, u, p, a, (x_0, \ldots, x_{m-1})$ be the same as Corollary 4.3. Let r_i be the bits of $-x_i \mod 2^u$ smaller than u bit and a be an ℓ-bit input and $\hat{a} := a2^\ell$. Then,*

$$a = 2^{-u}\left(\sum_{i=0}^{m-1} x_i - p(\sum_{i=0}^{m-1} r_i \mod 2^u)\right) \mod p'.$$

5.4 Our Modulus-Conversion Protocol

In this subsection, we give *two* modulus-conversion protocols with a Mersenne prime p. The first protocol is passively secure, and the second one is actively secure if the components are actively secure, while the latter assumes the small number of parties due to the use of the replicated SS scheme. A protocol for a general prime will appear in the full version.

The first protocol is as described in Protocol 5. The protocol uses Protocol 4 and share conversion from additive shares to a linear SS scheme. Protocol 5 is passively secure in the $(\mathcal{F}_{\text{clsum}}, \mathcal{F}_{\text{doublerand}})$-hybrid model since the protocol consists of sharing and $\mathcal{F}_{\text{clsum}}$, and Protocol 5 uses $\mathcal{F}_{\text{doublerand}}$.

Protocol 5. Passively secure modulus-conversion protocol

Input: $[a]^{\mathbb{Z}_p}$
Output: $[a]^{\mathbb{Z}_{p'}}$

1: P_i computes $x_i := 2^u \lambda_i [a]_i \mod p$ for $u = \lceil \log k \rceil$ and $0 \le i < k$.
2: $\hat{x}_i := -x_i \mod 2^u$ and let the j-th bit of $\hat{x}_i$ be $\hat{x}_i^{(j)}$.
3: **for** $0 \le i < k$ **do**
4: P_i shares $\hat{x}_i^{(0)}, \ldots, \hat{x}_i^{(u-1)}$ bit-by-bit in $\mathbb{Z}_2$, and the parties regard them as $[r_i]^{\mathbb{Z}_2^u}$.
5: The parties call $\mathcal{F}_{\text{clsum}}$ on input $[r_i]^{\mathbb{Z}_2^u}$ for $0 \le i < k$, and regard the received value as $[q]^{\mathbb{Z}_2^u} := [\sum_{i=0}^{k-1} r_i]^{\mathbb{Z}_2^u}$.
6: The parties convert $[q]^{\mathbb{Z}_2^u}$ into $[q]^{\mathbb{Z}_{p'}}$ via Protocol 4.
7: P_i computes $x_i := x_i \mod p'$ and shares x_i via sharing algorithm of a linear SS scheme in $\mathbb{Z}_{p'}$ for $0 \le i < k$.
8: The parties add the received shares as $[\sum_{i=0}^{k-1} x_i]^{\mathbb{Z}_{p'}} = \sum_{i=0}^{k-1} [x_i]^{\mathbb{Z}_{p'}}$.
9: The parties locally compute $[a]^{\mathbb{Z}_{p'}} := 2^{-u}([\sum_{i=0}^{k-1} x_i]^{\mathbb{Z}_{p'}} - p[q]^{\mathbb{Z}_{p'}}) \mod p'$.
10: Each P_i outputs $[a]_i^{\mathbb{Z}_{p'}}$.

The second protocol is as described in Protocol 6. This protocol uses the same idea as our bit-decomposition protocol. We first convert $[a]^{\mathbb{Z}_p}$ into $[\![a]\!]^{\mathbb{Z}_p}$, and locally generate bit-wise shares. Protocol 6 is passively/actively secure in $(\mathcal{F}_{\text{clsum}}, \mathcal{F}_{\text{doublerand}}, \mathcal{F}_{\text{rand}})$ hybrid model since Protocols 1 and 4 use $\mathcal{F}_{\text{rand}}$ and $\mathcal{F}_{\text{doublerand}}$.

5.5 Efficiency

The communication complexity of Protocol 5 is u $\texttt{share}_{\mathbb{Z}_2} + \texttt{clsum}_{u,k} + u(\texttt{drand}_{\mathbb{Z}_{p'}} + \texttt{reveal}_{\mathbb{Z}_2}) + k$ $\texttt{share}_{\mathbb{Z}_{p'}}$. If the number of parties is small and regarded as a constant, the communication complexity of u $\texttt{share}_{\mathbb{Z}_2}$, $\texttt{clsum}_{u,k}$, and $\texttt{reveal}_{\mathbb{Z}_2}$ are $O(1)$, $\texttt{drand}_{\mathbb{Z}_{p'}}$ is $O(\lceil \log p' \rceil)$, and $\texttt{share}_{\mathbb{Z}_{p'}}$ is $O(\lceil \log p' \rceil)$, respectively. Therefore, the total communication complexity is $O(\lceil \log p' \rceil)$.

The communication complexity of Protocol 6 is $\texttt{toRep}_{\mathbb{Z}_p} + \texttt{clsum}_{u,m} + u(\texttt{drand}_{\mathbb{Z}_{p'}} + \texttt{reveal}_{\mathbb{Z}_2})$, where $\texttt{toRep}_{\mathbb{Z}_p}$ is that of Protocol 1. If the number of parties is regarded as a constant, the total communication complexity is $O(\lceil \log p \rceil + \lceil \log p' \rceil)$ due to $\texttt{toRep}_{\mathbb{Z}_p}$. However, if $p' > p$, Protocol 6 can be more efficient than Protocol 5. The number of rounds is $(rand + 1) + 1 + (1 + drand) + 1 = 4 + rand + drand$, where $rand$ and $drand$ are the number of rounds to instantiate $\mathcal{F}_{\text{rand}}$ and $\mathcal{F}_{\text{doublerand}}$, respectively.

Protocol 6. Modulus-conversion protocol for a small number of parties

Input: $[a]^{\mathbb{Z}_p}$

Output: $[a]^{\mathbb{Z}_{p'}}$

1: The parties invoke Protocol 1 on input $[a]^{\mathbb{Z}_p}$ and receive $[\![a]\!]^{\mathbb{Z}_p}$, where $m = \binom{n}{k-1}$ and $a = \sum_{i=0}^{m-1} x_i \mod p$.
2: The parties set $\hat{x}_i := -x_i \mod 2^u$ and let the j-th bit of $\hat{x}_i$ be $\hat{x}_i^{(j)}$.
3: The parties obtain $[\![\hat{x}_i]\!]^{\mathbb{Z}_2^u}$ for $0 \leq i < m$ by Algorithm 3.
4: The parties call $\mathcal{F}_{\mathsf{clsum}}$ on input $[\![r_i]\!]^{\mathbb{Z}_2^u}$ for $0 \leq i < m$, and regard the received value as $[\![q]\!]^{\mathbb{Z}_2^u} := [\![\sum_{i=0}^{m-1} r_i]\!]^{\mathbb{Z}_2^u}$.
5: The parties convert $[q]^{\mathbb{Z}_2^u}$ into $[q]^{\mathbb{Z}_{p'}}$ via Protocol 4.
6: The parties locally compute $x_j := x_j \mod p'$ for all their own sub-shares, and regard them as $[\![\sum_{i=0}^{m-1} x_i]\!]^{\mathbb{Z}_{p'}}$.
7: The parties compute $[\![a]\!]^{\mathbb{Z}_{p'}} := 2^{-u}([\![\sum_{i=0}^{m-1} x_i]\!]^{\mathbb{Z}_{p'}} - p[\![q]\!]^{\mathbb{Z}_{p'}}) \mod p'$.
8: The parties locally convert $[\![a]\!]^{\mathbb{Z}_{p'}}$ into $[a]^{\mathbb{Z}_{p'}}$.
9: The parties output $[a]^{\mathbb{Z}_{p'}}$.

6 Experiments

We implemented our bit-decomposition and modulus-conversion protocols and compare their efficiency with existing results. As we stated, to the best of our knowledge, there is no bit-decomposition protocol in which $\ell + u < \lceil \log p \rceil$ is assumed and which outputs $[a]^{\mathbb{Z}_2^\ell}$. Therefore, our bit-decomposition protocols are formally incomparable to existing ones. In this paper, we compare experimental results with those of [4] as reference, since it is the most efficient bit-decomposition protocol. We implemented our bit-decomposition protocol with several optimizations that will appear in the full version. Those optimizations affect the constant factor of the communication complexity.

The details of the machines and network environments used in the experiment are as follows. Each machine had an Intel® Core™ i7 6900K 3.2 GHz × 8 cores. For a gigabit network, we used Intel® I218-LM star network via an L2 Gigabit hub. The ping latency was 0.19 ms.

The experimental results are listed in Table 1. It shows the experimental result of passively secure bit-decomposition protocols in a gigabit network. We measured the processing time of the bit-decomposition protocol of 10^7 ℓ-bit elements. To align the setting to [4]. we used $(k, n) = (2, 3)$. Our protocol uses $p = 2^{61} - 1$, and $\ell = 32$, 20, and 2. The setting of $\ell = 32$ is the same message space as [4], while $\ell = 20$ and 2 are favorable for our bit-decomposition protocol. The input and output of our protocol were shares of Shamir's scheme, while those of [4] were shares of the replicated SS scheme.

As shown in Table 1, our bit-decomposition protocol achieves higher performance than that of [4]. Further experiments including modular-conversion protocols will appear in the full version.

Table 1. Processing time (ms) for 10^7 records in passively secure bit-decomposition protocols in Gigabit network

	Modulus (p)	Bit-length of secret (ℓ)	Processing time (ms)
[4]	2^{32}	32	200,000
Our bit-decomposition protocol	$2^{61}-1$	32	1,194
	$2^{61}-1$	20	759
	$2^{61}-1$	2	123

7 Conclusion

We proposed secret-sharing-based bit-decomposition and modulus-conversion protocols for $\mathbb{Z}_p$ with an honest majority. Our protocols are secure against passive and active adversaries depending on the components of our protocols. If k and n are small, the communication complexity of our passively secure bit-decomposition and modulus-conversion protocols are $O(\ell)$ bits and $O(\lceil \log p' \rceil)$ bits, respectively. While some settings are different from existing works, the communication complexity is smaller than the current best result [4]. Furthermore, we also confirmed with the experimental results that our protocols are highly efficient.

References

1. Araki, T., Furukawa, J., Lindell, Y., Nof, A., Ohara, K.: High-throughput semi-honest secure three-party computation with an honest majority. In: Weippl, E.R., Katzenbeisser, S., Kruegel, C., Myers, A.C., Halevi, S. (eds.) ACM CCS, pp. 805–817. ACM (2016)
2. Beimel, A.: Secure schemes for secret sharing and key distribution. Ph.D. thesis, Israel Institute of Technology (1996)
3. Bogdanov, D., Jõemets, M., Siim, S., Vaht, M.: Privacy-preserving tax fraud detection in the cloud with realistic data volumes. Cybernetica research report (2016)
4. Bogdanov, D., Niitsoo, M., Toft, T., Willemson, J.: High-performance secure multi-party computation for data mining applications. Int. J. Inf. Sec. **11**(6), 403–418 (2012)
5. Bos, J.W., Kleinjung, T., Lenstra, A.K., Montgomery, P.L.: Efficient SIMD arithmetic modulo a Mersenne number. In: Antelo, E., Hough, D., Ienne, P. (eds.) 20th IEEE Symposium on Computer Arithmetic, ARITH 2011, 25–27 July 2011, Tübingen, Germany, pp. 213–221. IEEE Computer Society (2011)
6. Cramer, R., Damgård, I., Ishai, Y.: Share conversion, pseudorandom secret-sharing and applications to secure computation. In: Kilian, J. (ed.) TCC 2005. LNCS, vol. 3378, pp. 342–362. Springer, Heidelberg (2005). https://doi.org/10.1007/978-3-540-30576-7_19
7. Damgård, I., Fitzi, M., Kiltz, E., Nielsen, J.B., Toft, T.: Unconditionally secure constant-rounds multi-party computation for equality, comparison, bits and exponentiation. In: Halevi, S., Rabin, T. (eds.) TCC 2006. LNCS, vol. 3876, pp. 285–304. Springer, Heidelberg (2006). https://doi.org/10.1007/11681878_15

8. From, S.L., Jakobsen, T.: Secure multi-party computation on integers. Ph.D. thesis, University of Aarhus (2006)
9. Furukawa, J., Lindell, Y., Nof, A., Weinstein, O.: High-throughput secure three-party computation for malicious adversaries and an honest majority. In: Coron, J.-S., Nielsen, J.B. (eds.) EUROCRYPT 2017. LNCS, vol. 10211, pp. 225–255. Springer, Cham (2017). https://doi.org/10.1007/978-3-319-56614-6_8
10. Genkin, D., Ishai, Y., Prabhakaran, M., Sahai, A., Tromer, E.: Circuits resilient to additive attacks with applications to secure computation. In: Shmoys, D.B. (ed.) STOC, pp. 495–504. ACM (2014)
11. Goldreich, O.: The Foundations of Cryptography: Basic Applications, vol. 2. Cambridge University Press, Cambridge (2004)
12. Ikarashi, D., Kikuchi, R., Hamada, K., Chida, K.: Actively private and correct MPC scheme in $t < n/2$ from passively secure schemes with small overhead. IACR Cryptology ePrint Archive, vol. 2014, p. 304 (2014)
13. Ito, M., Saito, A., Nishizeki, T.: Secret sharing scheme realizing general access structure. IEICE Trans. **72**, 56–64 (1989)
14. Kimura, E., Hamada, K., Kikuchi, R., Chida, K., Okamoto, K., Manabe, S., Kuroda, T., Matsumura, Y., Takeda, T., Mihara, N.: Evaluation of secure computation in a distributed healthcare setting. In: Proceedings of MIE2016 at HEC2016, pp. 152–156 (2016)
15. Lindell, Y., Nof, A.: A framework for constructing fast MPC over arithmetic circuits with malicious adversaries and an honest-majority. In: Thuraisingham, B.M., Evans, D., Malkin, T., Xu, D. (eds.) ACM CCS 2017, pp. 259–276. ACM (2017)
16. Nishide, T., Ohta, K.: Multiparty computation for interval, equality, and comparison without bit-decomposition protocol. In: Okamoto, T., Wang, X. (eds.) PKC 2007. LNCS, vol. 4450, pp. 343–360. Springer, Heidelberg (2007). https://doi.org/10.1007/978-3-540-71677-8_23
17. Reistad, T., Toft, T.: Linear, constant-rounds bit-decomposition. In: Lee, D., Hong, S. (eds.) ICISC 2009. LNCS, vol. 5984, pp. 245–257. Springer, Heidelberg (2010). https://doi.org/10.1007/978-3-642-14423-3_17
18. Schoenmakers, B., Tuyls, P.: Efficient binary conversion for Paillier encrypted values. In: Vaudenay, S. (ed.) EUROCRYPT 2006. LNCS, vol. 4004, pp. 522–537. Springer, Heidelberg (2006). https://doi.org/10.1007/11761679_31
19. Shamir, A.: How to share a secret. Commun. ACM **22**(11), 612–613 (1979)
20. Toft, T.: Constant-rounds, almost-linear bit-decomposition of secret shared values. In: Fischlin, M. (ed.) CT-RSA 2009. LNCS, vol. 5473, pp. 357–371. Springer, Heidelberg (2009). https://doi.org/10.1007/978-3-642-00862-7_24

Verifiable Secret Sharing Based on Hyperplane Geometry with Its Applications to Optimal Resilient Proactive Cryptosystems

Zhe Xia[1], Liuying Sun[1], Bo Yang[2(✉)], Yanwei Zhou[2], and Mingwu Zhang[3]

[1] School of Computer Science, Wuhan University of Technology, Wuhan, China
xiazhe@whut.edu.cn, liuyingsunwhut@gmail.com

[2] School of Computer Science, Shaanxi Normal University, Xi'an, China
byang@snnu.edu.cn, zyw@snnu.edu.cn

[3] School of Computers, Hubei University of Technology, Wuhan, China
csmwzhang@gmail.com

Abstract. Secret sharing, first introduced by Shamir and Blakley independently, is an important technique to ensure secrecy and availability of sensitive information. It is also an indispensable building block in various cryptographic protocols. In the literature, most of these existing protocols are employing Shamir's secret sharing, while Blakley's one has attracted very little attention. In this paper, we revisit Blakley's secret sharing that is based on hyperplane geometry, and illustrate that some of its potentials are yet to be employed. In particular, it has an appealing property that compared with Shamir's secret sharing, it not only handles (t, n) secret sharing with similar computational costs, but also handles (n, n) secret sharing with better efficiency. We further apply this property to design a provably secure and optimal resilient proactive secret sharing scheme. Our proposed protocol is versatile to support proactive cryptosystems based on various assumptions, and it employs only one type of verifiable secret sharing as the building block. By contrast, the existing proactive secret sharing schemes with similar properties all employ two different types of verifiable secret sharing. Finally, we briefly discuss some possible extensions of our proposed protocol as well as how to explore more potentials of Blakley's secret sharing.

1 Introduction

Secret sharing allows the secret to be shared among a number of participants, so that a quorum or more of these participants can work together to recover the secret, but less participants cannot learn any information of the secret. Therefore, either to learn the secret or to destroy it, the adversary needs to compromise multiple of these participants instead of a single one, and this helps to enhance both secrecy and availability of the secret. Moreover, secret sharing is an important

W. Susilo and G. Yang (Eds.): ACISP 2018, LNCS 10946, pp. 83–100, 2018.
https://doi.org/10.1007/978-3-319-93638-3_6

building block for various cryptographic protocols, such as distributed key generation [6,15], threshold cryptosystems [11,27], attribute-based encryptions [24], secure multi-party computation [4,10], and so on.

The earliest two secret sharing schemes were proposed by Shamir [26] and Blakley [5] independently, where Shamir's scheme is based on polynomial interpolation and Blakley's one is based on hyperplane geometry. Although their technical details appear to be different, their ideas are closely related. As pointed out by Kothari [20], Blakley's scheme is the generalisation of Shamir's one. To see this relationship, recall that in a (t, n) Blakley's secret sharing scheme, the secret is treated as some coordinate of a point P in a t-dimensional space. Each of the n participants is given a secret share as an independent t-dimensional hyperplane in the space that crosses over P. Note that the coefficients of each hyperplane form a t-dimensional vector, and in addition, all these vectors form an $n \times t$ matrix M. When t or more participants work together, they can combine their hyperplanes to retrieve the secret by solving a system of equations. But less than t participants are unable to learn any information of the secret. Shamir's secret sharing is a special case of Blakley's one when the matrix M is initialised using some Vandermonde matrix. In this case, the different coordinates of P can be treated as the coefficients of some polynomial $f(\cdot)$ with degree $t-1$. And $f(\cdot)$ can be reconstructed through polynomial interpolation when t or more of the secret shares are revealed. Moreover, the Vandermonde matrix and polynomial interpolation have some extra properties, making Shamir's secret sharing very easy to use. Firstly, when using the Vandermonde matrix, only n unique values are needed to represent the entire $n \times t$ matrix M, and this helps to reduce the size of the public parameters. Secondly, knowing t or more secret shares, polynomial interpolation allows to retrieve the unknown secret shares directly without recovering $f(\cdot)$, and this is very useful in the security proofs during simulation. At the moment, thanks to its simplicity and elegance, Shamir's secret sharing has gained wide acceptance and it has been employed in most of the existing cryptographic protocols where threshold secret sharing is needed. By contrast, Blakley's secret sharing has attracted very little attention.

Our Contributions. In this paper, we revisit Blakley's secret sharing, illustrating that it has some potentials yet to be employed. Our idea is very simple. Since Blakley's secret sharing is the generalisation of Shamir's one, we are not restricted to initialise the matrix M using the Vandermonde matrix. Instead, we could explore some other special matrices with unique properties, and then use them to design new cryptographic protocols or extend the existing ones.

One such special matrix we have found is the Hadamard matrix, which is a square matrix satisfying the following property. Let H be a Hadamard matrix of order n. Then, the transpose of H is closely related to its inverse as: $\mathsf{H} \times \mathsf{H}^T = n \cdot \mathsf{I}_n$, where H^T denotes the transpose of H and I_n denotes the $n \times n$ identity matrix. Note that to recover the secret in Blakley's secret sharing, the most expensive computation is to invert a square matrix (i.e. some submatrix of M). Therefore, when using the Hadamard matrix, such a computation is almost for free. This makes Blakley's secret sharing much more efficient than Shamir's one when handling (n, n) secret sharing, because the computational complexity of the secret reconstruction phase can be reduced from $O(n^2)$ to $O(n)$. To the best of our knowledge, this property has not been employed in the existing cryptographic protocols.

We further apply the above findings to propose a provably secure and optimal resilient proactive secret sharing scheme. Our proposed scheme is versatile to support proactive cryptosystems based on various assumptions, and it is as efficient as the existing schemes with similar properties. But it can be designed using less building blocks: our scheme employs only one type of verifiable secret sharing, while the existing schemes all require two different types of verifiable secret sharing. Note that the proposed scheme should be treated as a proof of concept, demonstrating the potentials of secret sharing based on hyperplane geometry. We are not suggesting that it should be used to replace the existing schemes in practice, but we assume that these discovered potentials may find applications in other cryptographic protocols.

Outline of the Paper. The rest of the paper is organised as follows: some related works are briefly reviewed in Sect. 2. In Sect. 3, we describe a verifiable secret sharing scheme based on hyperplane geometry. And the proposed proactive secret sharing scheme is presented in Sect. 4. Finally, we discuss some possible extensions of our proposed scheme and conclude in Sect. 5.

2 Related Works

Blakley's Secret Sharing. Blakley's secret sharing is based on hyperplane geometry [5]. Although it has been introduced for decades, not many applications of it can be found in the literature. Recently, Xia et al. [29] have shown that threshold Paillier encryption can be designed using secret sharing based on hyperplane geometry such that the "interpolating over $\mathbb{Z}_{\phi(N)}$ problem" (N is the RSA modulus and ϕ is the Euler's totient function) can be completely avoided. And this method could have some tiny computational advantages over Shoup's trick [27]. Note that Xia's work in [29] can be considered as the complement of this paper. Both these two papers aim to illustrate some potentials of secret sharing based on hyperplane geometry, but the explored properties are different and their applications are different as well.

Verifiable Secret Sharing. Verifiable secret sharing (VSS) ensures that dishonest behaviour in the secret sharing schemes can be detected. In particular, it not only prevents the dealer from distributing inconsistent secret shares in the share distribution phase, but also prevents the participants from revealing invalid secret shares in the secret reconstruction phase. The two most widely used VSS schemes were introduced by Feldman [12] and Pedersen [22] respectively, and both these schemes are based on polynomial interpolation. Although it is straightforward to design VSS schemes based on hyperplane geometry, it seems that no such work exists in the literature. In Sect. 3, we adapt the ideas of Feldman's VSS and present a new VSS scheme that is based on hyperplane geometry. This VSS serves for two purposes. Firstly, it will be used as a building block in the proposed proactive scheme in Sect. 4. Secondly, we need the guarantee that different matrices with special properties can be used in Blakley's secret sharing without sacrificing its security, and the security proofs of this VSS provide such an assurance.

Proactive Secret Sharing. In some circumstances, the secret needs to be kept for a very long time, e.g. crypto master keys, legal documents and medical records. In these cases, traditional secret sharing is insufficient to protect the secret. This is because the adversary can break into the participants in the monotonic fashion, and she has a very long time to mount the attack. In this way, the adversary may gradually compromise enough participants to learn its information or destroy it [21].

To address this problem, proactive secret sharing has been introduced. The key idea is to divide the entire lifetime of the secret into multiple time periods. At the beginning of each time period, the participants jointly update their secret shares, while leaving the original secret unchanged. The update phase is composed of a *share recovery* protocol followed by a *share refreshment* protocol. In the share recovery protocol, the lost or tampered secret shares are recovered for the corresponding participants respectively without being disclosed to the others. In the share refreshment protocol, the participants jointly compute new secret shares among themselves and erase the old ones. The requirement is that the new secret shares are independent to the old ones. Therefore, if the adversary cannot compromise enough participants in a single time period, after the update phase, her obtained secret shares will be obsolete. Informally, a proactive secret sharing scheme is said to be *optimal resilient* if it is robust against any minority of corrupted participants. Note that this threshold is the maximum number of corrupted participants that are allowed in secret sharing schemes.

In the literature, there are three major approaches to design provably secure and optimal resilient proactive secret sharing schemes:

- **Herzberg's approach** [19]: before the update, the secret s is shared among the participants in a (t, n) threshold fashion using a $t-1$ degree polynomial $f(x)$ such that $f(0) = s$. To update the secret shares, the participants jointly generate a random $t-1$ degree polynomial $\delta(x)$ with $\delta(0) = 0$. After the update, each participant holds a new secret share of the $t-1$ degree polynomial $f'(x) = f(x) + \delta(x)$. Because, $f'(0) = f(0) + \delta(0) = s$, the secret shares have been updated without changing the original secret.
- **Frankel's approach** [13]: before the update, the secret is also shared among the participants in a (t, n) threshold fashion. To update the secret shares, the participants first jointly transform the (t, n) polynomial sharing of the secret into an (n, n) additive sharing of the secret. To achieve optimal resilience, each secret share of the (n, n) additive sharing is further shared among the participants in the (t, n) threshold fashion. Then, the participants jointly transform the (n, n) additive sharing of the secret back to an independent (t, n) polynomial sharing of the secret. Note that in both transformations, the secret is not revealed to any individual participant.

- **Rabin's approach** [23]: before the update, the secret is (n, n) additively shared among the participants. To achieve optimal resilience, each of these secret shares is further shared among the participants in the (t, n) threshold fashion. To update the secret shares, each participant first shares her old secret share among all the participants using another (n, n) additive sharing. In this process, each participant will receive a sub-share of the old secret share from every other participant. Then, each participant sums the received sub-shares, obtaining the new secret share of the secret. For optimal resilience, each participant also needs to further share this new secret share among the participants in the (t, n) threshold fashion. Now, the new secret shares form an independent (n, n) additive sharing of the original secret.

Based on the above three approaches, many extensions of proactive secret sharing have been proposed over the last two decades. For example, Zhou et al. [30] and Schultz et al. [25] have introduced proactive secret sharing schemes that are also dynamic. This property allowes the threshold to be changed dynamically, and this property is very useful when secret sharing is used for key management in ad hoc networks. Canetti et al. [9], followed by Frankel et al. [14] and Almansa et al. [1], have designed proactive secret sharing schemes that are adaptively secure. In these schemes, the adversary is not required to choose the set of corrupted participants at the beginning of protocol, but she could decide which participants to corrupt at anytime throughout the protocol, based on the information she gathered during the run of the protocol. Cachin et al. [7] have considered proactive secret sharing in the asynchronous networks, in which the messages sent by participants might be delayed. Stinson and Wei [28] and Baron et al. [2,3] have proposed proactive secret sharing schemes that are information theoretically secure. To detect dishonest participants, error-correction codes and hyper-invertible matrices are used in Stinson's scheme and Baron's schemes, respectively. Note that when considering asynchronous networks or information theoretically security, the proactive secret sharing schemes can only tolerate less than a third of cheating participants. The majority of the above schemes prove their security in the traditional way, considering the secrecy and robustness properties separately. But some schemes, e.g. [1,2], prove their security in the UC model [8], demonstrating that the proposed scheme is indistinguishable from an idea scheme which has all the desired properties.

In this paper, to design the proposed proactive secret sharing scheme, we will not consider any of the extensions mentioned above. The purpose is to clearly present the features that we believe are most useful to demonstrate the potentials of secret sharing based on hyperplane geometry. Therefore, we will only compare our proposed scheme with the three basic approaches. Note that in these three schemes, Herzberg's one only employs the (t, n) secret sharing as the building block. But its limitation is that when designing proactive cryptosystems, it only supports schemes based on the discrete logarithm assumption [18]. Frankel's and Rabin's schemes require both (t, n) secret sharing and (n, n) secret sharing. The (t, n) part is realised using Shamir's secret sharing, while the (n, n) part is realised by secret splitting for the sake of efficiency[1]. Therefore, both Frankel's and Rabin's schemes have employed two types of secret sharing schemes. But they are able to support proactive cryptosystems based on various assumptions, including the factoring assumption. It is still an open question whether proactive cryptosystems that are versatile to support various assumptions can be designed using just one type of secret sharing. In this paper, we answer this question affirmatively by employing the special properties of secret sharing based on hyperplane geometry.

3 Verifiable Secret Sharing Based on Hyperplane Geometry

3.1 Model and Assumptions

System Model: The players include a dealer $\mathcal{D}$, n participants $\{P_1, P_2, \ldots, P_n\}$ and an adversary $\mathcal{A}$. We assume that all these players are computationally bounded. Among the n participants, at least t of them are honest, where $n = 2t - 1$. The adversary $\mathcal{A}$ is assumed to be static: it can corrupt up to $t - 1$ participants at the beginning of the protocol. If a participant is compromised, $\mathcal{A}$ not only learns its private information, but also controls it to divert from the specified protocol in any way.

Communication Channel: We assume that there exists a secure channel between the dealer $\mathcal{D}$ and every participant, so that the secret shares can be distributed privately. Moreover, we assume that every player is connected to a common broadcast channel, where any message sent through this channel can be heard by the other players.

Definition 1 (Robustness): *A verifiable secret sharing scheme is robust if (1) the dealer $\mathcal{D}$ cannot distribute inconsistent secret shares among the participants, and (2) the secret can be correctly reconstructed even if there exists some dishonest participants.*

Definition 2 (Secrecy): *A verifiable secret sharing scheme is secret if the adversary $\mathcal{A}$ cannot learn any information of the secret.*

3.2 Verifiable Secret Sharing Based on Hyperplane Geometry

The verifiable secret sharing (VSS) based on hyperplane geometry is consisted of the following three phases: initialisation phase, share distribution phase and secret reconstruction phase.

[1] In secret splitting, the sum of the secret shares directly reveals the secret. When recovering the secret in (n, n) secret sharing, the computational complexity is $O(n^2)$ in Shamir's scheme and $O(n)$ in secret splitting.

Initialisation Phase: Denote G as a group in which the discrete logarithm is hard and g is a generator of G. To share the secret $s = a_1$, the dealer $\mathcal{D}$ randomly selects $t-1$ values $\{a_2, a_3, \ldots, a_t\}$, and publishes $A_i = g^{a_i}$ for $i = 1, 2, \ldots, t$. Moreover, $\mathcal{D}$ generates and broadcasts an $n \times t$ matrix M such that all its rows are linearly independent. The (i, j)-th entry of M is denoted as $b_{i,j}$.

Share Distribution Phase: $\mathcal{D}$ computes the secret shares $s_i = b_{i,1}a_1 + b_{i,2}a_2 + \cdots + b_{i,t}a_t$ for $i = 1, 2, \ldots, n$, and sends s_i to the participant P_i through the secure channel. Now, each participant P_i can verify whether its received secret share s_i is valid by checking the following equation:

$$g^{s_i} = \prod_{j=1}^{t} A_j{}^{b_{i,j}} \tag{1}$$

Secret Reconstruction Phase: Each participant P_i broadcasts its secret share s_i. Anyone can also use the Eq. (1) to verify the validity of s_i. Without loss of generality, we assume that the participants $\{P_1, P_2, \ldots P_t\}$ are honest, and their corresponding rows in M form a $t \times t$ matrix $\mathsf{M}_{\mathcal{S}}$. Denote $\mathsf{M}_{\mathcal{S}}{}^{-1}$ as the inverse matrix of $\mathsf{M}_{\mathcal{S}}$ with the (i, j)-th entry as $c_{i,j}$. Then, the secret can be reconstructed using the first row of $\mathsf{M}_{\mathcal{S}}{}^{-1}$ as $s = \sum_{i=1}^{t} c_{1,i}s_i$.

3.3 Security Analysis

Robustness: Firstly, if all the players are honest, it is obvious that the proposed VSS protocol will always deliver the correct result. In case if the dealer $\mathcal{D}$ distributes inconsistent secret shares, at least one honest participant will receive a secret share that $s_i \neq \sum_{j=1}^{t} b_{i,j}a_j$. In this case, P_i's verification of the Eq. (1) will fail, and P_i can make an accusation against $\mathcal{D}$. In the secret reconstruction phase, if some participants reveal invalid secret shares, the verification of the Eq. (1) will also fail. In this case, we can simply ignore these invalid secret shares, and use the remaining ones to recover the secret. Therefore, the proposed VSS protocol satisfies the robustness property.

Secrecy: We prove this property by simulation. Suppose there exists a probabilistic polynomial time (PPT) simulator $\mathcal{S}$. Without the knowledge of the secret, $\mathcal{S}$ can simulate the adversary $\mathcal{A}$'s view of the protocol, and $\mathcal{A}$ cannot distinguish a real run of the protocol from a simulated one. Because the simulated protocol does not contain any information of the secret, this proves that the real protocol reveals no information of the secret.

Without loss of generality, we assume that the participants $\{P_1, P_2, \ldots, P_{t-1}\}$ are controlled by $\mathcal{A}$. In the simulation, $\mathcal{S}$ first selects $t-1$ random values $\{s_1, s_2, \ldots s_{t-1}\}$. Then, $\mathcal{S}$ knows that these random values satisfy the following relationships, although $\mathcal{S}$ does not know the secret $s = a_1$.

$$\begin{pmatrix} 1 & 0 & \dots & 0 \\ b_{1,1} & b_{1,2} & \dots & b_{1,t} \\ b_{2,1} & b_{2,2} & \dots & b_{2,t} \\ \vdots & & \vdots & \\ b_{t-1,1} & b_{t-1,2} & \dots & b_{t-1,t} \end{pmatrix} \cdot \begin{pmatrix} a_1 \\ a'_2 \\ \vdots \\ a'_t \end{pmatrix} = \begin{pmatrix} a_1 \\ s_1 \\ s_2 \\ \vdots \\ s_{t-1} \end{pmatrix}$$

Denote the matrix on the left hand side of the above equation as M', and in its inverse matrix the (i, j)-th entry is denoted as $d_{i,j}$. Then, $\mathcal{S}$ can simulate $A'_i = g^{a'_i} = A_1{}^{d_{i,1}} \prod_{j=2}^{t} g^{d_{i,j} s_{j-1}}$ for $i = 2, \dots, t$.

The simulated protocol runs as follows: in the initialisation phase, $\mathcal{S}$ first publishes $A_1 = g^{a_1}$ as well as the values A'_i for $i = 2, \dots, t$. Then, $\mathcal{S}$ broadcasts exactly the same matrix M that is used in the real run of the protocol. In the share distribution phase, $\mathcal{S}$ sends the values $\{s_1, s_2, \dots, s_{t-1}\}$ to the adversary $\mathcal{A}$. From $\mathcal{A}$'s point of view, the values published by $\mathcal{S}$ in the initialisation phase are distributed identically as in the real protocol. This is because the same A_1 value and the same matrix M are used, and the other values are randomly distributed in both protocols. In the share distribution phase, $\mathcal{A}$ will receive $t - 1$ random values in both protocols, and all these values satisfy the Eq. (1). Hence, $\mathcal{A}$'s view in this phase is identical as well. Therefore, the adversary $\mathcal{A}$ cannot distinguish the real protocol from a simulated one, and the proposed VSS protocol satisfies the secrecy property.

3.4 Some Observations

A key observation of the above VSS protocol is that the matrix M can be initialised arbitrarily subject to the condition that its rows are linearly independent. Therefore, apart from the Vandermonde matrix that is widely used in existing secret sharing schemes, we can also use some other special matrices with unique properties. For example, in (t, n) secret sharing, the proposed VSS scheme is as efficient as Feldman's VSS [12]: the computational complexity of the share distribution phase and the secret reconstruction phase is $O(t)$ and $O(t^2)$ respectively. In (n, n) secret sharing, if the Hadamard matrix was used to initialise M in the proposed VSS scheme, the computational complexity of the secret reconstruction phase can be reduced to $O(n)$, which is more efficient than Feldman's VSS. This is because the transpose of the Hadamard matrix has a very close relationship with its inverse matrix, making the computation of the inverse matrix almost for free. In the next section, we use this property to introduce a new proactive secret sharing scheme that is provably secure and optimal resilient.

4 A Proactive Secret Sharing Scheme

4.1 Model and Assumptions

System Model: The players include n participants $\{P_1, P_2, \dots, P_n\}$ and a mobile adversary $\mathcal{A}_M$. We assume that all these players have computational resources. Besides, the system is assumed to be synchronised: the players can access to some common global clock, and each player has a local source of randomness. Moreover, it is assumed that $n = 2t - 1$, where t is the threshold.

Time Periods: The entire lifetime of the secret can be divided into many short time periods (e.g. a day or a week), which is determined by the common global clock. At the beginning of the first time period, there is a share distribution phase in which the secret is shared among the participants either by a trusted dealer or in a distributed fashion [15]. For all the other time periods, there is an update phase at the beginning of each time period. The update includes a share recovery protocol and a share refreshment protocol. After the update, the participants hold new shares of the secret and the old shares are erased. When some participants are corrupted at the update phase, it is assumed that they are corrupted in both the adjacent time periods.

The Mobile Adversary: Following [21], the mobile adversary $\mathcal{A}_M$ can be envisioned as follows: it has $t-1$ pebbles, and at the beginning of each time period, $\mathcal{A}_M$ will place the pebbles on any $t-1$ participants. If a pebble was placed on a participant, this participant is compromised by $\mathcal{A}_M$. Corrupting a participant means learning its private information, changing its intended behaviour, disconnecting it, and etc. When the pebble is removed from a participant, this participant will be "rebooted" to the safe state at the beginning of the next time period, and its share will be jointly recovered by the share recovery protocol. After each time period, $\mathcal{A}_M$ can move pebbles from a set of participants to another set of participants. Therefore, the mobile adversary $\mathcal{A}_M$ has more power than the ordinary adversary in traditional secret sharing schemes, because $\mathcal{A}_M$ can compromise all participants or compromise some participants multiple times throughout the entire lifetime of the secret. The restriction is that $\mathcal{A}_M$ can only compromise up to $t-1$ participants in any time period.

Communication Model: We assume that all players are connected to an authenticated broadcast channel $\mathcal{C}$, such that any message sent through $\mathcal{C}$ can be heard by the other players. The mobile adversary $\mathcal{A}_M$ can neither modify messages send by an uncorrupted participant through $\mathcal{C}$, nor prevent an uncorrupted participant from receiving messages from $\mathcal{C}$. Moreover, we assume that there are secure pairwise channels among the participants, and $\mathcal{A}_M$ cannot tamper or intercept messages sent through these secure channels. With these assumptions, we can focus our description without considering the low level technical details. Note that these assumed authenticated broadcast channel and secure pairwise channels can be implemented using standard cryptographic techniques such as encryptions and digital signatures.

Definition 3 (Robustness): *A proactive secret sharing scheme is robust if in the presence of the mobile adversary, the secret can be correctly recovered in any time period throughout the entire lifetime of the secret.*

Definition 4 (Secrecy): *A proactive secret sharing scheme is secret if after polynomially many updates, the mobile adversary still cannot learn any information of the secret.*

Definition 5 (Optimal resilience): *A proactive secret sharing scheme is optimal resilient if it is robust against the mobile adversary who has the ability to corrupt any minority of the participants.*

4.2 The Proposed Scheme

Denote M as an $n \times t$ matrix with the (i, j)-th element as $b_{i,j}$, and all the rows of M are linearly independent. When t of its rows are selected, these rows form a $t \times t$ matrix M_S. In the reverse matrix of M_S, the (i, j)-th element is denoted as $c_{i,j}$. Moreover, denote H as an $t \times t$ Hadamard matrix with the (i, j)-th element as $h_{i,j}$.

In the k-th time period, the secret $s = a_1^{(k)}$ is shared among the participants $\{P_1, P_2, \ldots, P_n\}$ using the point $\mathsf{P}^{(k)}$ in the t-dimensional space with its coordinates as a vector $(a_1^{(k)}, a_2^{(k)}, \ldots a_t^{(k)})$. And the values $A_i^{(k)} = g^{a_i^{(k)}}$ for $i = 1, 2, \ldots, t$ are broadcast through the channel $\mathcal{C}$. The participant P_i's secret share satisfies $s_i^{(k)} = b_{i,1}a_1^{(k)} + b_{i,2}a_2^{(k)} + \ldots + b_{i,t}a_t^{(k)}$. At the beginning of the $(k+1)$-th time period, the participants will jointly update their secret shares. The update phase consists a share recovery protocol and a share refreshment protocol as follows.

Share Recovery Protocol. The set of participants in Λ, where $|\Lambda| \geq t$, jointly recover the lost share $s_r^{(k)}$ for the participant P_r as follows:

1. The participant P_i randomly selects a vector $(\delta_{i,1}, \delta_{i,2}, \ldots, \delta_{i,t})$. The requirement is that $0 = b_{r,1}\delta_{i,1} + b_{r,2}\delta_{i,2} + \ldots + b_{r,t}\delta_{i,t}$. Moreover, P_i publishes the values $\Delta_{i,j} = g^{\delta_{i,j}}$ for $j = 1, 2, \ldots, t$. Note that the condition can be checked using the following equation
$$1 = \Delta_{i,1}^{b_{r,1}} \cdot \Delta_{i,2}^{b_{r,2}} \cdots \Delta_{i,t}^{b_{r,t}}$$
2. P_i computes $u_{i,j} = b_{j,1}\delta_{i,1} + b_{j,2}\delta_{i,2} + \ldots + b_{j,t}\delta_{i,t}$, and sends it to each other participant P_j through the secure channel. P_j can verify whether the received value $u_{i,j}$ is valid by checking
$$g^{u_{i,j}} = \Delta_{i,1}^{b_{j,1}} \cdot \Delta_{i,2}^{b_{j,2}} \cdots \Delta_{i,t}^{b_{j,t}}$$
3. P_i computes $s_i' = s_i^{(k)} + \sum_{j \in \Lambda} u_{j,i}$, and sends this value to P_r through the secure channel. P_r can verify whether the received value s_i' is valid by checking
$$g^{s_i'} = \prod_{l=1}^{t} {A_l^{(k)}}^{b_{i,l}} \cdot \prod_{j \in \Lambda} \prod_{k=1}^{t} \Delta_{j,k}^{b_{i,k}}$$
4. Finally, P_r selects t valid values of s_i' and solves a system of equations to recover a vector $(a_1', a_2', \ldots a_t')$, where $a_i' = a_i^{(k)} + \sum_{j \in \Lambda} \delta_{j,i}$. Then, P_r's lost secret share can be computed as $s_r^{(k)} = b_{r,1}a_1' + b_{r,2}a_2' + \ldots + b_{r,t}a_t'$.

Share Refreshment Protocol. Here, we follow Frankel's approach [13] to divide the share refreshment protocol into two sub-protocols: *Poly-to-Sum* and *Sum-to-Poly*. Note that we can also design the share refreshment protocol following Rabin's approach [23], in which the secret is always additively shared.

1. **Poly-to-Sum:** the set of participants in Γ, where $|\Gamma| = t$, jointly transform the polynomial sharing of the secret into an additive sharing of the secret.
   (a) Each participant P_i computes $\sigma_{i,1} = c_{1,i}s_i^{(k)}$, and selects $t-1$ random values $(\sigma_{i,2}, \sigma_{i,3}, \ldots, \sigma_{i,t})$. Moreover, P_i publishes $\Sigma_{i,j} = g^{\sigma_{i,j}}$ for $j = 1, 2, \ldots, t$. Anyone can verify the validity of $\Sigma_{i,1}$ by
   $$\Sigma_{i,1} = (A_1^{(k)^{b_{i,1}}} \cdot A_2^{(k)^{b_{i,2}}} \cdots A_t^{(k)^{b_{i,t}}})^{c_{1,i}}$$
   (b) Then, each P_i computes $w_{i,j} = h_{j,1}\sigma_{i,1} + h_{j,2}\sigma_{i,2} + \cdots + h_{j,t}\sigma_{i,t}$ for $j = 1, 2, \ldots, t$, and sends $w_{i,j}$ to each other participant P_j through the secure channel. The receiver P_j can verify whether its received value $w_{i,j}$ is valid by
   $$g^{w_{i,j}} = \Sigma_{i,1}^{h_{j,1}} \cdot \Sigma_{i,2}^{h_{j,2}} \cdots \Sigma_{i,t}^{h_{j,t}}$$
   (c) Each P_i, for $i = 1, 2, \ldots, t$, computes $s'_i = (\sum_{j \in \Gamma} w_{j,i}) \cdot h_{i,1} \cdot t^{-1}$. At this moment, the values $(s'_1, s'_2, \ldots, s'_t)$ form an additive sharing of the secret.
2. **Sum-to-Poly:** the set of participants in Γ, where $|\Gamma| = t$, jointly transform the additive sharing of the secret back to an independent polynomial sharing of the secret.
   (a) Denote $\psi_{i,1} = s'_i$. Each P_i selects $t-1$ random values $(\psi_{i,2}, \psi_{i,3}, \ldots, \psi_{i,t})$. Moreover, P_i publishes $\Psi_{i,j} = g^{\psi_{i,j}}$ for $j = 1, 2, \ldots, t$. Anyone can verify the validity of $\Psi_{i,1}$ by
   $$\Psi_{i,1} = (\prod_{j \in \Gamma} \prod_{l=1}^{t} \Sigma_{j,l}^{h_{i,l}})^{h_{i,1} \cdot t^{-1}}$$
   (b) Then, each P_i computes $v_{i,j} = b_{j,1}\psi_{i,1} + b_{j,2}\psi_{i,2} + \ldots + b_{j,t}\psi_{i,t}$ for $j = 1, 2, \ldots, n$, and sends $v_{i,j}$ to each other participant P_j through the secure channel. The receiver P_j can verify whether its received value $v_{i,j}$ is valid by
   $$g^{v_{i,j}} = \Psi_{i,1}^{b_{j,1}} \cdot \Psi_{i,2}^{b_{j,2}} \cdots \Psi_{i,t}^{b_{j,t}}$$
   (c) Each P_i sums its received values, resulting the updated secret share $s_i^{(k+1)} = \sum_{j \in \Gamma} v_{j,i}$. At this moment, we have
   $$g^{s_i^{(k+1)}} = \prod_{j \in \Gamma} \prod_{l=1}^{t} \Psi_{j,l}^{b_{i,l}}$$
   where $i = 1, 2, \ldots n$. Using these values, anyone can compute the commitments $A_i^{(k+1)}$ for the $(k+1)$-th time period as
   $$A_i^{(k+1)} = g^{a_i^{(k+1)}} = (g^{s_1^{(k+1)}})^{c_{i,1}} \cdot (g^{s_2^{(k+1)}})^{c_{i,2}} \cdots (g^{s_t^{(k+1)}})^{c_{i,t}}$$
   where $i = 1, 2, \ldots, t$.

4.3 Security Analysis

Theorem 1. *The proposed proactive secret sharing scheme satisfies robustness, secrecy and optimal resilience.*

Proof. **Robustness and optimal resilience:** Firstly, we show that if the participants are honest, the share recovery protocol will recover the correct secret shares for the corresponding participants and the share refreshment protocol will refresh the secret shares without changing the secret.

Before the share recovery protocol, the secret shares $(s_1^{(k)}, s_2^{(k)}, \ldots, s_n^{(k)})$ can be used to recover the point $\mathsf{P}^{(k)}$ with coordinates $(a_1^{(k)}, a_2^{(k)}, \ldots a_t^{(k)})$. Then, each participant P_i serves as the dealer to share a random point with coordinates $(\delta_{i,1}, \delta_{i,2}, \ldots, \delta_{i,t})$ among the participants. The requirement is that the r-th secret share for each of these random points is 0. Thanks to the additive homomorphic property of secret sharing by hyperplane geometry [20], the sum of the secret shares (secret shares with the same index are summed together) can be used to recover the sum of the points (coordinates with the same index are summed together). Therefore, the secret share in the r-th position remains unchanged, but all the other secret shares are randomised. With t of these summed secret shares, P_r can recover the summed point. And then, the r-th secret share can be computed by P_r. Moreover, because each of the point $(\delta_{i,1}, \delta_{i,2}, \ldots, \delta_{i,t})$ is randomly chosen, P_r cannot learn the original point $(a_1^{(k)}, a_2^{(k)}, \ldots a_t^{(k)})$, although P_r has seen the summed point. This implies that P_r cannot learn the secret $s = a_1^{(k)}$. And because the summed secret shares are sent to P_r through secure channels, the secret share $s_r^{(k)}$ is not disclosed to the other participants.

At the beginning of the share refreshment protocol, the secret $s = a_1^{(k)}$ is polynomially shared among the n participants, where each participant P_i possesses the secret share $s_i^{(k)}$. In the Poly-to-Sum part, each participant serves as a dealer to share the value $c_{1,i}s_i^{(k)}$ among all participants in the additive fashion. Because the sum of these $c_{1,i}s_i^{(k)}$ values equals the secret, if each participant sums its received sub-shares, the secret is now additively shared among these participants. In the Sum-to-Poly part, each participant serves as a dealer to share its secret share among the participants in the polynomial fashion. Recall that the sum of these secret shares equals the secret. If each participant sums its received sub-shares, the secret is polynomially shared among the participants. Considering the point before the refreshment as $\mathsf{P}^{(k)}$ with coordinates $(a_1^{(k)}, a_2^{(k)}, \ldots a_t^{(k)})$ and the point after the refreshment as $\mathsf{P}^{(k+1)}$ with coordinates $(a_1^{(k+1)}, a_2^{(k+1)}, \ldots a_t^{(k+1)})$, we have $a_1^{(k)} = a_1^{(k+1)}$, but all the other coordinates are independent. Therefore, after the share refreshment protocol, the secret shares have been updated without changing the secret.

Moreover, all the steps of the proposed scheme are verifiable. For example, in the share recovery protocol, P_r can verify whether its received value s_i' is valid. And because P_r only needs t of these values to recover its lost secret share, based on our assumption that $n = 2t - 1$ and t is the threshold, P_r

can always recover its lost secret share. In the share refreshment protocol, one can verify whether each participant has shared the correct value and whether this value has been shared consistently. If any cheating behaviour is detected, the dishonest participants will be removed and the protocol will restart. In the worst case, after $t-1$ trials, the protocol will end successfully. Therefore, even if there exists some minority of dishonest participants, both the share recovery protocol and the share refreshment protocol always output the correct results. In other words, the proposed protocol satisfies robustness and optimal resilience.

Secrecy: We prove the secrecy property by simulation. Assume there exists a PPT simulator $\mathcal{S}$. We show that $\mathcal{S}$ can simulate the mobile adversary's view in our proposed scheme. And $\mathcal{A}_M$, who corrupts up to $t-1$ participants, cannot distinguish a real run of the protocol from a simulated one.

Simulation of the Share Recovery Protocol. We assume that P_r is not corrupted by $\mathcal{A}_M$, and $\mathcal{S}$ has the knowledge of secret shares processed by the corrupted participants.

1. For each participant P_i, $\mathcal{S}$ randomly selects $(\delta_{i,1}, \delta_{i,2}, \ldots, \delta_{i,t})$ such that $0 = b_{r,1}\delta_{i,1} + b_{r,2}\delta_{i,2} + \ldots + b_{r,t}\delta_{i,t}$. $\mathcal{S}$ then publishes $\Delta_{i,j} = g^{\delta_{i,j}}$ for $j = 1, 2, \ldots, t$. If P_i is corrupted, $\mathcal{S}$ also sends the vector $(\delta_{i,1}, \delta_{i,2}, \ldots, \delta_{i,t})$ to $\mathcal{A}_M$.
2. For each participant P_i, $\mathcal{S}$ computes $u_{i,j} = b_{j,1}\delta_{i,1} + b_{j,2}\delta_{i,2} + \ldots + b_{j,t}\delta_{i,t}$ for $j \in \Lambda$. If P_i is corrupted, $\mathcal{S}$ sends all these $u_{i,j}$ values to $\mathcal{A}_M$. Otherwise, $\mathcal{S}$ only sends those $u_{i,j}$ values to $\mathcal{A}_M$, where P_j is corrupted by $\mathcal{A}_M$.
3. For the corrupted participants, $\mathcal{S}$ computes $s'_i = s_i^{(k)} + \sum_{j\in\Lambda} u_{j,i}$, and sends these values to $\mathcal{A}_M$.

Note that all the above steps follow the original protocol exactly. Therefore, the simulated protocol is perfectly indistinguishable from the real one in $\mathcal{A}_M$'s view, and $\mathcal{A}_M$ can learn no information of the recovered secret share $s_r^{(k)}$.

Simulation of the Share Refreshment Protocol. The share refreshment protocol consists two parts. Here, we only prove the Sum-to-Poly part, and the security proof for the Poly-to-Sum part can be derived similarly.

1. If the participant P_i is corrupted, $\mathcal{S}$ firstly sets $\psi_{i,1} = s'_i$, then randomly selects $(\psi_{i,2}, \psi_{i,3}, \ldots, \psi_{i,t})$, and finally publishes $\Psi_{i,j} = g^{\psi_{i,j}}$ for $j = 1, 2, \ldots, t$. In this case, $\mathcal{S}$ also sends the the vector $(\psi_{i,1}, \psi_{i,2}, \ldots, \psi_{i,t})$ to $\mathcal{A}_M$. Otherwise, if the participant P_i is not corrupted, $\mathcal{S}$ first randomly selects $t-1$ values $(v_{i,1}, v_{i,2}, \ldots v_{i,t-1})$. Moreover, denote the matrix M' as

$$\mathsf{M}' = \begin{pmatrix} 1 & 0 & \ldots & 0 \\ b_{1,1} & b_{1,2} & \ldots & b_{1,t} \\ b_{2,1} & b_{2,2} & \ldots & b_{2,t} \\ \vdots & & & \vdots \\ b_{t-1,1} & b_{t-1,2} & \ldots & b_{t-1,t} \end{pmatrix}$$

and the (i,j)-th entry of its inverse matrix as $d_{i,j}$. Then, $\mathcal{S}$ publishes the same $\Psi_{i,1}$ value as in the real protocol, and publishes the other $\Psi_{i,j}$ values for

$j = 2, 3, \ldots, t$ as

$$\Psi_{i,j} = \Psi_{i,1}^{d_{j,1}} \cdot \prod_{l=2}^{t} g^{d_{j,l} \cdot v_{i,l-1}}$$

2. If P_i is corrupted, $\mathcal{S}$ computes $v_{i,j} = b_{j,1}\psi_{i,1} + b_{j,2}\psi_{i,2} + \cdots + b_{j,t}\psi_{i,t}$, and sends these values to $\mathcal{A}_M$. Otherwise, if P_i is not corrupted, $\mathcal{S}$ sends the values $(v_{i,1}, v_{i,2}, \ldots v_{i,t-1})$ selected in the previous step to $\mathcal{A}_M$.
3. For the corrupted participants, $\mathcal{S}$ computes $s_i^{(k+1)} = \sum_{j \in \Gamma} v_{j,i}$, and sends these values to $\mathcal{A}_M$.

In the above simulation, when the participant P_i is corrupted, the simulated steps follow the original protocol exactly. Otherwise, when the participant P_i is not corrupted, the random values $(v_{i,1}, v_{i,2}, \ldots v_{i,t-1})$ are distributed identically as in the real protocol. Moreover, they satisfy the verification $g^{v_{i,j}} = \Psi_{i,1}^{b_{j,1}} \cdot \Psi_{i,2}^{b_{j,2}} \cdots \Psi_{i,t}^{b_{j,t}}$. Therefore, $\mathcal{A}_M$ cannot distinguish the simulated protocol from a real one, and this proves that $\mathcal{A}_M$ cannot learn any information of the secret in the Sum-to-Poly part.

Note that similar results also can be obtained for the Poly-to-Sum part. When putting everything together, we can prove that $\mathcal{A}_M$ cannot learn any information of the secret in the proposed proactive secret sharing scheme, and this completes the proof of the secrecy property.

4.4 Efficiency Analysis

We now compare the computational costs of our proposed scheme with some existing schemes. The share recovery protocol will be compared with the one in Herzberg's scheme [19]. This is because both Frankel's scheme [13] and Rabin's scheme [23] only focus on the share refreshment protocol, and they assume that Herzberg's share recovery protocol can be used in their works. The share refreshment protocol will be compared with the one in Frankel's scheme.

In the share recovery protocol, in steps 1 and 2, each participant serves as the dealer to share some random value among the participants. Recall that in both secret sharing based on polynomial interpolation and secret sharing based on hyperplane geometry, the computational complexity of the share distribution phase is $O(n)$. Hence, in these two steps, each participant's computational cost is similar as in Herzberg's scheme. In step 3, each participant just sums the received sub-shares and sends the result to P_r. The computational cost is similar in this step as well. In step 4, P_r recovers its lost secret share. The computational complexity for this step is $O(n^2)$ both in Herzberg's scheme and our proposed scheme. Therefore, our proposed scheme has similar computational costs as in Herzberg's scheme regarding the share recovery protocol.

In the share refreshment protocol, the Poly-to-Sum part requires each participant to share some value among the participants through additive secret sharing. In Frankel's scheme, the additive secret sharing is implemented using the secret splitting method. And in our proposed scheme, it is implemented using secret sharing based on hyperplane geometry in which M is initialised using the Hadamard matrix. Although our proposed scheme is slightly less efficient, the computational complexity is $O(n)$ in both schemes[2]. In the Sum-to-Poly part, each participant serves as the dealer to share some value among the participants through polynomial secret sharing. And the computational costs are similar in both schemes. In summary, our proposed scheme and Frankel's scheme have similar computational complexity regarding the share refreshment protocol. But we have used only one type of secret sharing (i.e. secret sharing based on hyperplane geometry) while Frankel's scheme has employed two different types of secret sharing (i.e. secret sharing based on polynomial interpolation and secret splitting). Note that the proposed scheme also can be designed following Rabin's approach [23]. In this case, its computational complexity will be similar as in Rabin's scheme, but it uses less secret sharing as the building block as well.

5 Discussion and Conclusion

In this paper, we have renovated an existing proactive secret sharing scheme using a different mathematical structure. The appealing feature of our proposed scheme is that it only requires one type of secret sharing as the building block, while the existing schemes with similar properties require two types of secret sharing. This improvement is due to the special property found in secret sharing based on hyperplane geometry. In particular, secret sharing based on hyperplane geometry handles (t, n) secret sharing as efficient as the one based on polynomial interpolation, but it can handle (n, n) secret sharing more efficiently. We assume that this property may find other applications in cryptographic protocols as well.

Moreover, one can further explore some other special matrices with unique properties and apply them with secret sharing based on hyperplane geometry. This may uncover some still unknown features of secret sharing. We will further investigate this in the future work.

Finally, we note that the proposed scheme could be extended in various aspects. We have deliberately avoided mentioning these extensions in the previous section in order to make the explanation concise. Here, we briefly discuss how the extensions can be applied to our proposed scheme.

- **Dynamic property.** With minor modifications, our proposed scheme could achieve the dynamic property [30], allowing the threshold to be changed dynamically. For example, suppose that the threshold needs to be changed from t to t', then the share refreshment protocol can be modified as follows: it first transforms the (t, n) polynomial secret sharing into the (t, t) additive secret sharing, and then it transforms the (t, t) additive secret sharing into a (t', n) polynomial secret sharing.

[2] In Frankel's scheme, each participant just sums the received sub-shares, while in our proposed scheme, each participant needs to sum the received sub-shares and then multiplies the result by some constant values. Although our proposed scheme has an additional multiplicaiton step, the computational complexity is asymptotically similar in both schemes.

- **Adaptive security.** Our proposed scheme can be extended to satisfy the adaptive security. The major challenge in designing adaptively secure distributed protocols is that the adversary can corrupt the participants at any time throughout the protocol, and the corrupted participants have to reveal their internal states that are consistent with the public information. One feasible solution is to use Canetti's trick of Single Inconsistent Participant (SIP) [9]. In the protocol, the Feldman's VSS [12] needs to be replaced by Pedersen's VSS [22] so that the public commitments are binded softly. In the simulation, the simulator $\mathcal{S}$ fully controls $n-1$ participants, and the remaining one, called *special participant*, is used to ensure that the public parameters are consistent as in the real protocol. Moreover, zero-knowledge proofs [16,17] are used to verify the participants' behaviour. In this way, although $\mathcal{S}$ has no knowledge of the special participant's internal state, its corresponding zero-knowledge proof can be simulated. Therefore, if the special participant was corrupted by the adversary (with probability roughly 50%), the simulation terminates and rewinds. Otherwise, $\mathcal{S}$ can generate the adversary's view that is indistinguishable from a real run of the protocol.
- **Asynchronous networks.** The technical difficulty in the asynchronous networks model is that when the receiver did not receive the messages from the sender as expected, it is hard to judge whether this is caused by the network delay or by a dishonest sender. Similar techniques as in [7] can be applied to adapt our proposed scheme in the asynchronous networks model. However, such a scheme is no more optimal resilient, as it only tolerates less than one third of dishonest participants.
- **Proofs in the UC model.** It is possible to prove the proposed scheme in the UC model [8], and this may demonstrate another advantage of our proposed scheme. Recall that the general goal of the UC model is as follows: suppose that protocols $\rho_1, \rho_2, \ldots, \rho_m$ securely evaluate functions $f_1, f_2, \ldots, f_m$ respectively, and the n-party protocol π securely evaluates an n-party function g with subroutine calls to $f_1, f_2, \ldots, f_m$, then the protocol $\pi^{\rho_1, \rho_2, \ldots, \rho_m}$ derived from π by replacing the subroutine calls to $f_1, f_2, \ldots, f_m$ with invocations of $\rho_1, \rho_2, \ldots, \rho_m$ also securely evaluates g. Therefore, when the protocol π is designed with fewer building blocks, less subroutine protocols needs to be considered, and this helps to simplify the security proof in the UC model.

Acknowledgement. This work was partially supported by the National Natural Science Foundation of China (Grant No. 61572303, 61772326, 61672010, 61672398), and Natural Science Foundation of Hubei Province (Grant No. 2017CFB303, 2017CFA012). We are also grateful to the anonymous reviewers for their valuable comments on the paper.

References

1. Almansa, J.F., Damgård, I., Nielsen, J.B.: Simplified threshold RSA with adaptive and proactive security. In: Vaudenay, S. (ed.) EUROCRYPT 2006. LNCS, vol. 4004, pp. 593–611. Springer, Heidelberg (2006). https://doi.org/10.1007/11761679_35
2. Baron, J., El Defrawy, K., Lampkins, J., Ostrovsky, R.: How to withstand mobile virus attacks, revisited. In: Proceedings of the 2014 ACM Symposium on Principles of Distributed Computing, pp. 293–302. ACM (2014)
3. Baron, J., Defrawy, K.E., Lampkins, J., Ostrovsky, R.: Communication-optimal proactive secret sharing for dynamic groups. In: Malkin, T., Kolesnikov, V., Lewko, A.B., Polychronakis, M. (eds.) ACNS 2015. LNCS, vol. 9092, pp. 23–41. Springer, Cham (2015). https://doi.org/10.1007/978-3-319-28166-7_2
4. Ben-Or, M., Goldwasser, S., Wigderson, A.: Completeness theorems for non-cryptographic fault-tolerant distributed computation. In: Proceedings of the Twentieth Annual ACM Symposium on Theory of Computing, pp. 1–10. ACM (1988)
5. Blakley, G.R., et al.: Safeguarding cryptographic keys. In: Proceedings of the National Computer Conference, vol. 48, pp. 313–317 (1979)
6. Boneh, D., Franklin, M.: Efficient generation of shared RSA keys. In: Kaliski, B.S. (ed.) CRYPTO 1997. LNCS, vol. 1294, pp. 425–439. Springer, Heidelberg (1997). https://doi.org/10.1007/BFb0052253
7. Cachin, C., Kursawe, K., Lysyanskaya, A., Strobl, R.: Asynchronous verifiable secret sharing and proactive cryptosystems. In: Proceedings of the 9th ACM Conference on Computer and Communications Security, pp. 88–97. ACM (2002)
8. Canetti, R.: Universally composable security: a new paradigm for cryptographic protocols. In: 42nd IEEE Symposium on Foundations of Computer Science, 2001. Proceedings, pp. 136–145. IEEE (2001)
9. Canetti, R., Gennaro, R., Jarecki, S., Krawczyk, H., Rabin, T.: Adaptive security for threshold cryptosystems. In: Wiener, M. (ed.) CRYPTO 1999. LNCS, vol. 1666, pp. 98–116. Springer, Heidelberg (1999). https://doi.org/10.1007/3-540-48405-1_7
10. Chaum, D., Crépeau, C., Damgard, I.: Multiparty unconditionally secure protocols. In: Proceedings of the Twentieth Annual ACM Symposium on Theory of Computing, pp. 11–19. ACM (1988)
11. Desmedt, Y.: Threshold cryptosystems. In: Seberry, J., Zheng, Y. (eds.) AUSCRYPT 1992. LNCS, vol. 718, pp. 1–14. Springer, Heidelberg (1993). https://doi.org/10.1007/3-540-57220-1_47
12. Feldman, P.: A practical scheme for non-interactive verifiable secret sharing. In: 1987 28th Annual Symposium on Foundations of Computer Science, pp. 427–438. IEEE (1987)
13. Frankel, Y., Gemmell, P., MacKenzie, P.D., Yung, M.: Optimal-resilience proactive public-key cryptosystems. In: 38th Annual Symposium on Foundations of Computer Science, 1997. Proceedings, pp. 384–393. IEEE (1997)
14. Frankel, Y., MacKenzie, P., Yung, M.: Adaptively-secure optimal-resilience proactive RSA. In: Lam, K.-Y., Okamoto, E., Xing, C. (eds.) ASIACRYPT 1999. LNCS, vol. 1716, pp. 180–194. Springer, Heidelberg (1999). https://doi.org/10.1007/978-3-540-48000-6_15
15. Gennaro, R., Jarecki, S., Krawczyk, H., Rabin, T.: Secure distributed key generation for discrete-log based cryptosystems. J. Cryptol. **20**(1), 51–83 (2007)
16. Goldreich, O., Micali, S., Wigderson, A.: Proofs that yield nothing but their validity or all languages in NP have zero-knowledge proof systems. J. ACM (JACM) **38**(3), 690–728 (1991)

17. Goldwasser, S., Micali, S., Rackoff, C.: The knowledge complexity of interactive proof systems. SIAM J. Comput. **18**(1), 186–208 (1989)
18. Herzberg, A., Jakobsson, M., Jarecki, S., Krawczyk, H., Yung, M.: Proactive public key and signature systems. In: Proceedings of the 4th ACM Conference on Computer and Communications Security, pp. 100–110. ACM (1997)
19. Herzberg, A., Jarecki, S., Krawczyk, H., Yung, M.: Proactive secret sharing or: how to cope with perpetual leakage. In: Coppersmith, D. (ed.) CRYPTO 1995. LNCS, vol. 963, pp. 339–352. Springer, Heidelberg (1995). https://doi.org/10.1007/3-540-44750-4_27
20. Kothari, S.C.: Generalized linear threshold scheme. In: Blakley, G.R., Chaum, D. (eds.) CRYPTO 1984. LNCS, vol. 196, pp. 231–241. Springer, Heidelberg (1985). https://doi.org/10.1007/3-540-39568-7_19
21. Ostrovsky, R., Yung, M.: How to withstand mobile virus attacks. In: Proceedings of the Tenth Annual ACM Symposium on Principles of Distributed Computing, pp. 51–59. ACM (1991)
22. Pedersen, T.P.: Non-interactive and information-theoretic secure verifiable secret sharing. In: Feigenbaum, J. (ed.) CRYPTO 1991. LNCS, vol. 576, pp. 129–140. Springer, Heidelberg (1992). https://doi.org/10.1007/3-540-46766-1_9
23. Rabin, T.: A simplified approach to threshold and proactive RSA. In: Krawczyk, H. (ed.) CRYPTO 1998. LNCS, vol. 1462, pp. 89–104. Springer, Heidelberg (1998). https://doi.org/10.1007/BFb0055722
24. Sahai, A., Waters, B.: Fuzzy identity-based encryption. In: Cramer, R. (ed.) EUROCRYPT 2005. LNCS, vol. 3494, pp. 457–473. Springer, Heidelberg (2005). https://doi.org/10.1007/11426639_27
25. Schultz, D., Liskov, B., Liskov, M.: MPSS: mobile proactive secret sharing. ACM Trans. Inf. Syst. Secur. (TISSEC) **13**(4), 34 (2010)
26. Shamir, A.: How to share a secret. Commun. ACM **22**(11), 612–613 (1979)
27. Shoup, V.: Practical threshold signatures. In: Preneel, B. (ed.) EUROCRYPT 2000. LNCS, vol. 1807, pp. 207–220. Springer, Heidelberg (2000). https://doi.org/10.1007/3-540-45539-6_15
28. Stinson, D.R., Wei, R.: Unconditionally secure proactive secret sharing scheme with combinatorial structures. In: Heys, H., Adams, C. (eds.) SAC 1999. LNCS, vol. 1758, pp. 200–214. Springer, Heidelberg (2000). https://doi.org/10.1007/3-540-46513-8_15
29. Xia, Z., Yang, X., Xiao, M., He, D.: Provably secure threshold paillier encryption based on hyperplane geometry. In: Liu, J.K., Steinfeld, R. (eds.) ACISP 2016. LNCS, vol. 9723, pp. 73–86. Springer, Cham (2016). https://doi.org/10.1007/978-3-319-40367-0_5
30. Zhou, L., Schneider, F.B., Van Renesse, R.: APSS: proactive secret sharing in asynchronous systems. ACM Trans. Inf. Syst. Secur. (TISSEC) **8**(3), 259–286 (2005)

Towards Round-Optimal Secure Multiparty Computations: Multikey FHE Without a CRS

Eunkyung Kim[1], Hyang-Sook Lee[2(✉)], and Jeongeun Park[2]

[1] Institute of Mathematical Sciences, Ewha Womans University, Seoul, Republic of Korea
ekim410@ewha.ac.kr

[2] Department of Mathematics, Ewha Womans University, Seoul, Republic of Korea
hsl@ewha.ac.kr, jungeun7430@ewhain.net

Abstract. Multikey fully homomorphic encryption (MFHE) allows homomorphic operations between ciphertexts encrypted under different keys. In applications for secure multiparty computation (MPC) protocols, MFHE can be more advantageous than usual fully homomorphic encryption (FHE) since users do not need to agree with a common public key before the computation when using MFHE. In EUROCRYPT 2016, Mukherjee and Wichs constructed a secure MPC protocol in only two rounds via MFHE which deals with a common random/reference string (CRS) in key generation. After then, Brakerski et al. replaced the role of CRS with the distributed setup for CRS calculation to form a four round secure MPC protocol. Thus, recent improvements in round complexity of MPC protocols have been made using MFHE.

In this paper, we go further to obtain round-efficient and secure MPC protocols. The underlying MFHE schemes in previous works still involve the common value, CRS, it seems to weaken the power of using MFHE to allow users to independently generate their own keys. Therefore, we resolve the issue by constructing an MFHE scheme without CRS based on LWE assumption, and then we obtain a secure MPC protocol against semi-malicious security in three rounds.

1 Introduction

Multikey Fully Homomorphic Encryption. *Fully homomorphic encryption (FHE)* scheme $(\mathsf{KeyGen}, \mathsf{Enc}, \mathsf{Dec}, \mathsf{Eval})$ is a public key encryption scheme with the additional algorithm Eval that allows *homomorphic operations* on ciphertexts: for any $(\mathsf{pk}, \mathsf{sk}) \leftarrow \mathsf{KeyGen}(1^\lambda)$, a function f, and two ciphertexts c, c' encrypted with pk, Eval algorithm takes $(\mathsf{pk}, f, \langle c, c' \rangle)$ as input and returns a new ciphertext c^* such that

$$\mathsf{Dec}(\mathsf{sk}, c^*) = f(\mathsf{Dec}(\mathsf{sk}, c), \mathsf{Dec}(\mathsf{sk}, c')).$$

FHE is a very useful cryptographic primitive, and there has been profound progress after the first construction of FHE by Gentry [4]. *Multikey fully homomorphic encryption (MFHE)*, introduced in [6], is part of that progress. MFHE

W. Susilo and G. Yang (Eds.): ACISP 2018, LNCS 10946, pp. 101–113, 2018.
https://doi.org/10.1007/978-3-319-93638-3_7

is a generalization of FHE which supports homomorphic operations between ciphertexts encrypted with *different* keys: with abbreviated notation, Eval algorithm of an MFHE scheme takes c and c' encrypted with pk and pk′, respectively, and then returns a new ciphertext c^* such that[1]

$$\mathsf{Dec}(\langle \mathsf{sk}, \mathsf{sk}' \rangle, c^*) = f(\mathsf{Dec}(\mathsf{sk}, c), \mathsf{Dec}(\mathsf{sk}', c')).$$

MFHE can be applied to construct *secure multiparty computation (MPC)* protocols, which is our main concern.

Secure Multiparty Computation via MFHE. Secure multiparty computation (MPC) can be very helpful for those who want to evaluate a function on their personal data in cooperation with untrusted parties. More specifically, suppose that N parties hold the private input $x_1, \cdots, x_N$, respectively, and that they do not believe one another at all but must evaluate a function f. Then secure MPC protocol allows the parties to compute $f(x_1, \cdots, x_N)$ without disclosing their secret inputs to other users.

MPC protocols can be realized by MFHE schemes easily: each user encrypts the data x_i with its own public key pk_i, and sends the ciphertext $c_i \leftarrow \mathsf{Enc}(\mathsf{pk}_i, x_i)$ to other users. On receiving all the public keys $\mathsf{pk}_1, \cdots, \mathsf{pk}_N$ and all the ciphertexts $c_1, \cdots, c_N$, users run Eval algorithm of MFHE with inputs $(\{\mathsf{pk}_i\}_{i\in[N]}, \{c_i\}_{i\in[N]}, f)$ to obtain a new ciphertext c^* which encrypts the function value $f(x_1, \cdots, x_N)$. These MPC protocols are not only secure by MFHE, but also highly efficient in terms of round complexity: Mukherjee and Wichs [8] constructed an MFHE scheme based on LWE which simplified the scheme of Clear and McGoldrick [3] to obtain a MPC protocol in only two rounds with a common random/reference string (CRS). They also achieved semi-malicious security for their MPC protocol based on LWE assumption, and fully-malicious security with additional NIZK. And then, Brakerski et al. [2] replaced the CRS in their MFHE scheme with a distributed setup for deriving the CRS, and obtained a three round semi-mailiciously secure MPC protocol and a four round fully-maliciously secure MPC protocol.

However, since these protocols are constructed from MFHE scheme associated with the CRS, either a trusted setup in which all parties get access to the same string CRS (see [8]), or a complex setup for generating the CRS that adds one more round in the protocol (see [2]) is needed. This may weaken the power of using MFHE. Therefore, in order to get a secure MPC protocol which is also simple and round-efficient, it is important to construct an MFHE scheme without CRS.

Previous Work. Let us briefly review the MFHE scheme by Mukherjee and Wichs [8] with N parties. Given a common random public matrix $\mathbf{B} \in \mathbb{Z}_q^{(n-1)\times m}$ as a CRS (m and n will be specified later), for $i \in [N]$, i-th party P_i generates a key pair $(\mathsf{pk}_i, \mathsf{sk}_i) = (\mathbf{A}_i, \mathbf{t}_i)$ where $\mathbf{A}_i = (\mathbf{B}, \mathbf{b}_i)^T \in \mathbb{Z}_q^{n\times m}$, $\mathbf{t}_i \in \mathbb{Z}_q^n$ and $\mathbf{t}_i\mathbf{A}_i \approx_q$

[1] Both of secret keys sk and sk′ are needed to decrypt the *multikey ciphertext* c^* for the semantic security.

$\mathbf{0}$ (i.e. $\mathbf{t}_i\mathbf{A}_i - \mathbf{0}$ is short in $\mathbb{Z}_q^m$). Define the *multi-secret key* $\hat{\mathbf{t}} = (\mathbf{t}_1, \cdots, \mathbf{t}_N) \in \mathbb{Z}_q^{nN}$ which is required for the semantic security. Then a valid *multi-key ciphertext* of a bit $\mu \in \{0,1\}$, which requires all the secret keys $\mathsf{sk}_1, \cdots, \mathsf{sk}_N$ to decrypt, is a matrix $\hat{\mathbf{C}}_i \in \mathbb{Z}_q^{nN\times mN}$ such that $\hat{\mathbf{t}}\hat{\mathbf{C}}_i \approx_q \mu\hat{\mathbf{t}}\hat{\mathbf{G}}$ (i.e. $\hat{\mathbf{t}}\hat{\mathbf{C}}_i - \mu\hat{\mathbf{t}}\hat{\mathbf{G}}$ is short in $\mathbb{Z}_q^{mN}$) where $\mathbf{G} \in \mathbb{Z}_q^{n\times m}$ is a fixed public matrix and $\hat{\mathbf{G}} = diag(\mathbf{G}, \cdots, \mathbf{G}) \in \mathbb{Z}_q^{nN\times mN}$ is an expanded matrix having the matrix $\mathbf{G}$ as diagonal components. To do this, they built a polynomial time algorithm GSW. Lcomb (see Property 5.3 in [8]) that links $\mathsf{pk}_i = \mathbf{A}_i$ and $\mathsf{sk}_j = \mathbf{t}_j$ for $i \neq j$ which is possible thanks to the CRS matrix $\mathbf{B}$. Then the multi-key ciphertext $\hat{\mathbf{C}}_i$ is obtained from a *single-key ciphertext* $\mathbf{C}_i$, which can be decrypted by all parties' secret keys. Then they use the MFHE scheme to construct a two round MPC protocol which is secure in the fully-malicious model. See [8] for details.

Our Contribution. In this work, we give an important stepping stone to get a simple and round-efficient MPC protocol. Namely, we construct a three round MPC protocol, that is secure in the semi-malicious model, without a CRS from an MFHE scheme that use neither a CRS nor a complex setup for inducing a CRS. This is interesting mainly for two reasons. (i) A MPC protocol without a CRS means that no longer a trusted setup (for example, banks, or any certificate authorities) for distributing the CRS is needed, and this fits the recent trends in cryptography such as the famous digital currency Bitcoin. (ii) Three-round seems to be a lower bound when we do not use a CRS: Firstly, since there is no CRS, each user generates its own key pair independently and sends it to other users prior to the protocol, which requires at least one round. Next, once the ciphertexts and public keys are transferred, the computation can be done by the evaluation algorithm of MFHE. Thus, it takes at least one more round to transfer the information. Finally, since the decryption algorithm of MFHE requires all the secret keys $(\mathsf{sk}_1, \cdots, \mathsf{sk}_N)$ as input due to the semantic security, at least one more round is needed in order for each user to send an intermediate decrypted value involving only its secret key to another users.

To do this, we generalize the MFHE scheme by Mukherjee and Wichs [8] to construct an MFHE scheme without a CRS. In our scheme, P_i freely generates its key pair $(\mathsf{pk}_i, \mathsf{sk}_i) = (\mathbf{A}_i, \mathbf{t}_i)$ by choosing its own random matrix $\mathbf{B}_i \in \mathbb{Z}_q^{(n-1)\times m}$, instead of the CRS matrix $\mathbf{B}$. Namely, we have $\mathsf{pk}_i = \mathbf{A}_i = (\mathbf{B}_i, \mathbf{b}_i)^T \in \mathbb{Z}_q^{n\times m}$. Since pk_i's no longer contain the common matrix $\mathbf{B}$, we cannot apply GSW. Lcomb algorithm directly to link $\mathsf{pk}_i = \mathbf{A}_i$ and $\mathsf{sk}_j = \mathbf{t}_j$ for $i \neq j$. Instead, we give a polynomial time algorithm LinkAlgo that generalizes GSW. Lcomb algorithm. Then we use LinkAlgo algorithm to transform a single-key ciphertext $\mathbf{C}_i$ into a multi-key ciphertext $\hat{\mathbf{C}}_i$ as in [8]. Since our single key encryption step is independent of the LinkAlgo algorithm, one can use our scheme for single key FHE and then just expand it freely with multi parties if she wants to use it for MFHE or MPC.

Organization. In Sect. 2, we introduce notation used throughout the paper, and review important definitions, including the learning with errors (LWE) problem and Multikey fully homomorphic encryption (MFHE) schemes. In Sect. 3, as our first main result, we present LinkAlgo algorithm for transforming a single-key ciphertext to the related multi-key ciphertext. Based on the first result, in Sect. 4, we construct an MFHE scheme without a CRS, and obtain a three round MPC protocol that is secure in the semi-malicious model.

2 Preliminaries

Notations. We denote κ the *security parameter*. A function $\mathbf{negl}(\kappa)$ is negligible if for every positive polynomial $p(\kappa)$ it holds that $\mathbf{negl}(\kappa) < \frac{1}{p(\kappa)}$. We denote $\mathbb{Z}/q\mathbb{Z}$ as $\mathbb{Z}_q$ and its elements are integer in the range of $(-q/2, q/2]$. Now we define the notation of vectors and matrices. For a vector $\mathbf{x} = (x_1, x_2, \ldots, x_n) \in \mathbb{Z}^n$, $\mathbf{x}[i]$ denotes the i-th component scalar. For a matrix $\mathbf{M} \in \mathbb{Z}^{n \times m}$, $\mathbf{M}[i, j]$ denotes the i-th row and the j-th column element of $\mathbf{M}$. Also we use the notation $\mathbf{M}_i^{row}$ which is denoted as i-th row of $\mathbf{M}$ and similarly, $\mathbf{M}_j^{col}$ is denoted as j-th column of $\mathbf{M}$. We use row representation of matrices and define the infinity norm of a vector $\mathbf{x}$ as $\|\mathbf{x}\|_\infty = max_i(\mathbf{x}[i])$ and that of a matrix $\mathbf{M}$ is defined as $max_i(\sum_j \mathbf{M}[i, j])$. Dot product of two vectors $\mathbf{v}, \mathbf{w}$ is denoted by $< \mathbf{v}, \mathbf{w} >$. We also denote the set $\{1, \ldots, n\}$ by $[n]$.

Let X and Y be two distributions over a finite domain. We write $X \overset{comp}{\approx} Y$ if they are computationally indistinguishable. For an integer bound $B_\chi = B_\chi(\kappa)$, we say that a distribution ensemble $\chi = \chi(\kappa)$ is B_χ-bounded if $Pr_{x \leftarrow \chi(\kappa)}[|x| > B_\chi(\kappa)] \le \mathbf{negl}(\kappa)$. Throughout this paper, we use the notation $\approx_q$ to emphasize that the two values are almost equal in $\mathbb{Z}_q$ except for *short* differences.

The Learning with Errors Problem. We recall the learning with errors (LWE) problem, a representative hard problem on lattices introduced by Regev [9]

Definition 1. *Let κ be the security parameter, $n = n(\kappa), q = q(\kappa)$ be integers and let $\chi = \chi(\kappa)$, be distributions over $\mathbb{Z}$. Given a matrix $\mathbf{A} \in \mathbb{Z}_q^{m \times n}$ and a vector $\mathbf{b} \in \mathbb{Z}_q^n$, the decisional learning with error (LWE) problem is determining whether $\mathbf{b}$ has been sampled uniformly at random from $\mathbb{Z}_q^n$ or $\mathbf{b} = \mathbf{sA} + \mathbf{e}$ for some small random $\mathbf{s} \in \mathbb{Z}_q^m$ and $\mathbf{e} \in \chi^n$ for any polynomial $m = m(\kappa)$.*

The parameter setting for our version of the LWE assumption is that for any polynomial $p = p(\kappa)$ there is a polynomial $n = n(\kappa)$, a modulus $q = q(\kappa)$ of singly-exponential size, and a B_χ bounded distribution $\chi = \chi(\kappa)$ and $q \ge 2^p B_\chi$.

Multikey FHE (MFHE). We give a formal definition of Multikey FHE (MFHE) [8] which is an adaptation from the original concept [6].

Definition 2. *A multikey (Leveled) FHE scheme is a tuple of algorithms* MFHE = (Setup, KeyGen, Enc, Expand, Expand, Dec) *described as follows.*

- Setup($1^\kappa, 1^d$) → params*: It takes κ is a security parameter and d is the circuit depth as inputs and it outputs the system parameters* params.

- $\mathsf{KeyGen}(\mathsf{params}) \rightarrow (\mathsf{pk}, \mathsf{sk})$: *It takes* params *and outputs a key pair* (pk, sk).
- $\mathsf{Enc}(\mathsf{pk}, \mu) \rightarrow c$: *On input* pk *and a message* μ, *outputs a ciphertext* c. *we call it by a fresh ciphertext.*
- $\mathsf{Expand}((\mathsf{pk}_1, \ldots, \mathsf{pk}_N), c, i) \rightarrow \hat{c}_i$: *Given a sequence of* N *public-keys, and a fresh ciphertext* c *under* i*-th key* pk_i, *it outputs an expanded ciphertext* $\hat{c}$.
- $\mathsf{Eval}(\mathsf{params}, \mathcal{C}, (\hat{c}_1, \ldots, \hat{c}_\ell)) \rightarrow \hat{c}$: *Given a boolean circuit* $\mathcal{C}$ *of depth* $\leq d$ *along with* ℓ *expanded ciphertexts, it outputs an evaluated ciphertext* $\hat{c}$.
- $\mathsf{Dec}(\mathsf{params}, \hat{c}, (\mathsf{sk}_1, \ldots, \mathsf{sk}_N)) \rightarrow \mu$: *On input a ciphertext (possibly evaluated)* $\hat{c}$ *and a sequence of* N *secret keys, it outputs the message* μ. *This decryption procedure can be done by the one round threshold distributed decryption:*
  - $\mathsf{PartDec}(\hat{c}, i, \mathsf{sk}_i)$: *On input a ciphertext (possibly evaluated) under a sequence of* N *public keys and* i*-th secret key, it outputs a partial decryption* p_i.
  - $\mathsf{FinDec}(p_1, \ldots, p_N)$: *On input* N *partial decryptions, it outputs the message* μ.

GSW FHE Scheme. Our MFHE scheme is similar to [8] apart from the existence of a trusted setup and a few algorithms. Here we describe the GSW fully homomorphic encryption scheme [5] following the notation of [8]. Note that we take the matrix $\mathbf{B}$ in KeyGen as with the original GSW encryption scheme instead Mukherjee and Wichs [8] gets the matrix $\mathbf{B}$ from Setup, hence consider it as a CRS.

- $\mathsf{GSW.Setup}(1^\kappa, 1^d) \rightarrow (\mathsf{params})$: The needed parameters for this scheme to satisfy the LWE assumption are $n, m, q, \mathbf{G}, \chi$ where $\mathbf{G} \in \mathbb{Z}_q^{n \times m}$ is a trapdoor matrix [7], B_χ-bounded error distribution $\chi = \chi(\kappa, d)$, a modulus $q = B_\chi 2^{\omega(d\kappa log\kappa)}$, and $m = n \log q + \omega \log(\kappa)$. and It outputs $\mathsf{params} := (n, m, q, \mathbf{G}, \chi, B_\chi)$.
- $\mathsf{GSW.KeyGen}(\mathsf{params}) \rightarrow (\mathsf{pk}, \mathsf{sk})$: generates a secret key and the corresponding public key respectively. Sample $\mathbf{s} \xleftarrow{\$} \mathbb{Z}_q^{n-1}$. A secret key $\mathsf{sk} = \mathbf{t} := (-\mathbf{s}, 1) \in \mathbb{Z}_q^n$. Sample $\mathbf{e} \xleftarrow{\$} \chi^m$ and $\mathbf{B} \xleftarrow{\$} \mathbb{Z}_q^{(n-1) \times m}$. Set $\mathbf{b} = \mathbf{sB} + \mathbf{e} \in \mathbb{Z}_q^m$. The corresponding $\mathsf{pk} = \mathbf{A} \in \mathbb{Z}_q^{n \times m}$ is defined as $\mathbf{A} := \begin{pmatrix} \mathbf{B} \\ \mathbf{b} \end{pmatrix}$.
  - The important relation between pk and sk is $\mathbf{tA} \approx_q 0$, which is because $\mathbf{tA} = (-\mathbf{s}, 1) \begin{pmatrix} \mathbf{B} \\ \mathbf{b} \end{pmatrix} = -\mathbf{sB} + \mathbf{b} = \mathbf{e}$: small(i.e.$\|\mathbf{e}\|_\infty \leq B_\chi$).
- $\mathsf{GSW.Enc}(\mathsf{pk}, \mu) \rightarrow (\mathbf{C})$: Choose a short random matrix $\mathbf{R} \xleftarrow{\$} \{0,1\}^{m \times m}$ then encrypt a bit message $\mu \in \{0,1\}$ under the public key pk as $\mathbf{C} \in \mathbb{Z}_q^{n \times m}$, where

$$\mathbf{C} := \mathbf{AR} + \mu\mathbf{G}$$

  Here, $\mathbf{tC} = \mathbf{e}' + \mu\mathbf{tG}$ where $\mathbf{e}' = \mathbf{eR}$ implies $\|\mathbf{e}'\|_\infty \leq mB_\chi$.
- $\mathsf{GSW.Eval}(\mathbf{C}_1, \mathbf{C}_2) \rightarrow (\mathbf{C}^*)$: Let $\mathbf{C}_1, \mathbf{C}_2 \in \mathbb{Z}_q^{n \times m}$ be two GSW encryption of μ_1, μ_2 under the pk respectively, so that: $\mathbf{tC}_1 = \mu_1\mathbf{tG} + \mathbf{e}_1$ and $\mathbf{tC}_2 = \mu_1\mathbf{tG} + \mathbf{e}_2$. We can do homomorphic operations(addition, multiplication) as following:

- $\mathsf{GSW.Add}(\mathbf{C}_1, \mathbf{C}_2)$: $\mathbf{C}_1 + \mathbf{C}_2$.
- $\mathsf{GSW.Mult}(\mathbf{C}_1, \mathbf{C}_2)$: $\mathbf{C}_1\mathbf{G}^{-1}(\mathbf{C}_2) \in \mathbb{Z}_q^{n\times m}$.

– $\mathsf{GSW.Dec}(\mathsf{sk}, \mathbf{C}) \to (\mu)$: On input as sk, $\mathbf{C}$, set $\mathbf{w} = (0, \ldots, 0, \lfloor q/2 \rceil) \in \mathbb{Z}_q^n$ and compute $\mathbf{v} = \mathbf{t}\mathbf{C}\mathbf{G}^{-1}(\mathbf{w}^T) = \bar{\mathbf{e}} + \mu(q/2) \in \mathbb{Z}_q$ such that $\bar{\mathbf{e}} =< \mathbf{e}, \mathbf{G}^{-1}(\mathbf{w}^T) >$. Output $||\lfloor \frac{\mathbf{v}}{q/2} \rceil||$ checking if the value is close to 0 or q/2.

The function $\mathbf{G}^{-1}(\cdot)$ introduced in [7] takes any matrix $\mathbf{M} \in \mathbb{Z}_q^{n\times m'}$ (for any $m' \in \mathbb{N}$) and outputs a matrix whose all elements are in the set {0,1}. This function satisfies $\mathbf{G}\mathbf{G}^{-1}(\mathbf{M}) = \mathbf{M}$.

The semantic security of GSW FHE scheme under the LWE assumption (with proper parameters) is proved in [5]. To analyze the correctness, we follow the notion of β-noisy ciphertext [8].

Definition 3. *A β-noisy ciphertext of a message μ under a secret key* $\mathsf{sk}(= \mathbf{t}) \in \mathbb{Z}_q^n$ *is a matrix* $\mathbf{C} \in \mathbb{Z}_q^{n\times m}$ *satisfying* $\mathbf{tC} = \mu\mathbf{tG} + \mathbf{e}$ *for some* $\mathbf{e}$ *with* $\|\mathbf{e}\|_\infty \leq \beta$.

To recover the original message correctly, the maximum size of the error generated during the decryption procedure should be less than $q/4$. Recall that the depth of the circuit is d and let the fresh ciphertext is β-noisy ciphertext. Then β is mB_χ. And evaluated ciphertext is at most $(m+1)^d\beta$-noisy. Finally during the GSW-decryption procedure, the error is multiplied by m. Therefore, the error would become at most $m^2(m+1)^dB_\chi$, which is less than $q/4$ because of our choice of parameters.

3 MFHE Scheme Without a CRS

3.1 Single-Key Ciphertext to Multi-key Ciphertext

An MFHE scheme allows homomorphic operations between ciphertexts under different keys, but the GSW scheme from the previous section is not enough for such operations. This is due to the fact that there is no relation between two different users' keys. In this section, we present a polynomial time algorithm LinkAlgo that links two different keys by giving a relation between them. And then we will use LinkAlgo to transform a *single-key* GSW *ciphertext* into a *multi-key ciphertext*, and finally to obtain an MFHE scheme.

Let $R \in \{0,1\}^{m\times m}$ be a 0-1 matrix, and $V^{(s,t)}$ be a β-noisy GSW ciphertext of $R[s,t]$ (s-th row and t-th column of $\mathbf{R}$) under $(\mathsf{pk}, \mathsf{sk}) = (\mathbf{A}, \mathbf{t})$ for all $s, t \in [m]$. Let $(\mathsf{pk}', \mathsf{sk}')$ be another, or possibly same, GSW key pair. Then LinkAlgo takes pk' and encryptions $V^{(s,t)}$'s, and returns a matrix $\mathbf{X}$ as follows:

Proposition 4. *We have* $\mathbf{tX} = \mathbf{tA}'\mathbf{R} + \mathbf{e}$, *where* $\|\mathbf{e}\|_\infty \leq m^3\beta$.

Proof. Since $\mathbf{V}^{(s,t)}$ is a β-noisy encryption of $\mathbf{R}[s,t]$ under $(\mathsf{pk}, \mathsf{sk}) = (\mathbf{A}, \mathbf{t})$, we have $\mathbf{tV}^{(s,b)} = \mathbf{R}[s,t]\mathbf{tG} + \mathbf{e}_{s,t}$ for some $\mathbf{e}_{s,t}$ with $\|\mathbf{e}_{s,t}\|_\infty \leq \beta$. Hence, it holds

Algorithm 1. LinkAlgo algorithm

Input: pk' and $\{V^{(s,t)}\}_{s,t\in[m]}$
Output: $\mathbf{X} \in \mathbb{Z}_q^{n\times m}$

1. Define $\mathbf{L}_{s,t} \in \mathbb{Z}_q^{n\times m}$ for all $s,t \in [m]$ by

$$\mathbf{L}_{s,t}[a,b] = \begin{cases} \mathbf{A}'[a,s] & \text{if t=b} \\ 0 & \text{otherwise} \end{cases}$$

2. Output $\mathbf{X} = \sum_{s=1}^{m} \sum_{t=1}^{m} \mathbf{V}^{(s,t)}\mathbf{G}^{-1}(\mathbf{L}_{s,t}) \in \mathbb{Z}_q^{n\times m}$.

that

$$\begin{aligned} \mathbf{tX} &= \sum_{s,t} \mathbf{tV}^{(s,t)}\mathbf{G}^{-1}(\mathbf{L}_{s,t}) \\ &= \sum_{s,t} (\mathbf{R}[s,t]\mathbf{tG} + \mathbf{e}_{s,t})\mathbf{G}^{-1}(\mathbf{L}_{s,t}) \\ &= \sum_{s,t} (\mathbf{R}[s,t]\mathbf{tL}_{s,t} + \mathbf{e}'_{s,t}) \\ &= \mathbf{t}\sum_{s,t} \mathbf{R}[s,t]\mathbf{L}_{s,t} + \sum_{s,t}^{m} \mathbf{e}'_{s,t}, \end{aligned}$$

where $\mathbf{e}'_{s,t} := \mathbf{e}_{s,t}\mathbf{G}^{-1}(\mathbf{L}_{s,t})$ has a norm $\|\mathbf{e}'_{s,t}\| \leq m\beta$.

Now it suffices to show that $\sum_{s=1}^{m} \sum_{t=1}^{m} \mathbf{R}[s,t]\mathbf{L}_{s,t} = \mathbf{A}'\mathbf{R}$. Note that $\mathbf{L}_{s,t}$ has s-th column of $\mathbf{A}'$ on the t-th column and 0 elsewhere.

$$\begin{aligned} \sum_{s=1}^{m}\sum_{t=1}^{m} \mathbf{R}[s,t]\mathbf{L}_{s,t} &= \sum_{t=1}^{m}\sum_{s=1}^{m} \begin{pmatrix} 0 \cdots \mathbf{R}[s,t]\mathbf{A}'[1,s] \cdots 0 \\ \vdots \ddots \mathbf{R}[s,t]\mathbf{A}'[2,s] \cdots 0 \\ \vdots \;\vdots \quad \vdots \quad \cdots \vdots \\ 0 \cdots \mathbf{R}[s,t]\mathbf{A}'[n,s] \cdots 0 \end{pmatrix} \\ &= \sum_{t=1}^{m} \begin{pmatrix} 0 \cdots \sum_{s=1}^{m} \mathbf{R}[s,t]\mathbf{A}'[1,s] \cdots 0 \\ \vdots \ddots \sum_{s=1}^{m} \mathbf{R}[s,t]\mathbf{A}'[2,s] \cdots 0 \\ \vdots \;\vdots \quad \vdots \quad \cdots \vdots \\ 0 \cdots \sum_{s=1}^{m} \mathbf{R}[s,t]\mathbf{A}'[n,s] \cdots 0 \end{pmatrix} \\ &= \sum_{t=1}^{m} \begin{pmatrix} 0 \cdots < \mathbf{A}_1'^{row}, \mathbf{R}_t^{col} > \cdots 0 \\ \vdots \ddots < \mathbf{A}_2'^{row}, \mathbf{R}_t^{col} > \cdots 0 \\ \vdots \;\vdots \quad \vdots \quad \cdots \vdots \\ 0 \cdots < \mathbf{A}_m'^{row}, \mathbf{R}_t^{col} > \cdots 0 \end{pmatrix} = \mathbf{A}'\mathbf{R}, \end{aligned}$$

where $\mathbf{A}_\ell'^{row}$ denotes the ℓ-th row of $\mathbf{A}'$ and $\mathbf{R}_\ell^{col}$ denotes the ℓ-th colum of $\mathbf{R}$.

To sum up,

$$\mathbf{tX} = \mathbf{t}\sum_{s,t}^{m} \mathbf{R}[s,t]\mathbf{L}_{s,t} + \sum_{s,t} \mathbf{e}'_{s,t} = \mathbf{tA}'\mathbf{R} + \mathbf{e},$$

where $\mathbf{e} := \sum_{s=1}^{m} \sum_{t=1}^{m} \mathbf{e}'_{s,t}$ has norm $\|\mathbf{e}\|_\infty \leq m^3\beta$. □

3.2 Our Leveled MFHE Scheme

Let $\mathbf{G}$ be the matrix and $\mathbf{G}^{-1}(\cdot)$ be the function as we described in Sect. 2. Following the notation of [8], we expand $\mathbf{G}$ as $\hat{\mathbf{G}}_N = diag(\mathbf{G}, \cdots, \mathbf{G}) \in \mathbb{Z}_q^{nN \times mN}$ and let $\hat{\mathbf{G}_N}^{-1}(\cdot)$ be the corresponding function of $\hat{\mathbf{G}}_N$.

Define a tuple of algorithms
(MFHE . Setup, MFHE . KeyGen, MFHE . Enc, MFHE . Expand, MFHE . Eval, MFHE . Dec)
as follows:

- $\mathsf{MFHE.Setup}(1^\lambda, 1^d) \rightarrow (\mathsf{params})$
  1. Run $\mathsf{GSW.Setup}(1^\lambda, 1^d)$
  2. Output params.
- $\mathsf{MFHE.KeyGen}(\mathsf{params}) \rightarrow (\mathsf{pk}, \mathsf{sk})$
  1. Run GSW . KeyGen(params)
  2. Output $(\mathsf{pk}, \mathsf{sk}) = \left(\begin{pmatrix} \mathbf{B} \\ \mathbf{b} \end{pmatrix}, \mathbf{t} \right)$.
- $\mathsf{MFHE.Enc}(\mathsf{pk}, \mu) \rightarrow (\mathbf{C})$
  1. Run $\mathsf{GSW.Enc}(\mathsf{pk}, \mu)$.
  2. Output $\mathbf{C}$ (i.e. $\mathbf{C} = \mathbf{AR} + \mu\mathbf{G}$).
- $\mathsf{MFHE.Expand}((\mathsf{pk}_1, \mathsf{pk}_2, \ldots, \mathsf{pk}_N), i, \mathbf{C}) \rightarrow (\hat{\mathbf{C}}_i)$ On other's public keys and a fresh ciphertext $\mathbf{C}$, the execution is following:
  1. $\{\mathbf{V}_{i,j}^{(s,t)}\}_{s,t\in[m]} \leftarrow \{\mathsf{GSW.Enc}(\mathbf{R}[s,t], \mathsf{pk}_j)\}_{s,t\in[m]}$ for $j \in [N]$.
  2. Compute $\mathbf{X}_i^j \leftarrow \mathsf{LinkAlgo}(\{\mathbf{V}_{i,j}^{(s,t)}\}_{s,t\in[m]}, \mathsf{pk}_i)$ for $j \in [N]$.
  3. Define a matrix $\hat{\mathbf{C}}_i \in \mathbb{Z}_q^{nN \times mN}$ as

$$\hat{\mathbf{C}}_i := \begin{bmatrix} \mathbf{C}_i - \mathbf{X}_i^1 & 0 & \ldots 0 & 0 \\ 0 & \mathbf{C}_i - \mathbf{X}_i^2 & \ldots 0 & 0 \\ \vdots & \vdots & \vdots \;\; \vdots & \vdots \\ \mathbf{X}_i^i & \ldots & \mathbf{C}_i \ldots & \mathbf{X}_i^i \\ \vdots & \vdots & \vdots & \vdots \\ 0 & 0 & \ldots 0 & \mathbf{C}_i - \mathbf{X}_i^N \end{bmatrix}$$

  which is concatenated by N^2 number of $n \times m$ sub-matrices. The diagonal sub-matrix of $\hat{\mathbf{C}}_i$ is $\mathbf{C}_i - \mathbf{X}_i^j$ for j∈ $[N]\setminus \{i\}$ and the i-th diagonal sub-matrix is just $\mathbf{C}_i$. Lastly, $\mathbf{X}_i^i$ is on the i-th row and zero matrix $0^{n\times m}$ is elsewhere.
  4. Output $\hat{\mathbf{C}}_i$.

- $\mathsf{MFHE.Eval}(\mathsf{params}, f, \hat{\mathbf{C}}_1, \ldots, \hat{\mathbf{C}}_\ell) \rightarrow (\hat{\mathbf{C}}^*)$
  1. Given ℓ expanded ciphertexts, run the GSW homomorphic evaluation algorithm working with the expanded dimension nN, mN and $\hat{\mathbf{G}}_N, \hat{\mathbf{G}^{-1}}_N$.
  2. Output $\hat{\mathbf{C}}^*$.
- $\mathsf{MFHE.Dec}(\mathsf{params}, (\mathsf{sk}_1, \ldots, \mathsf{sk}_N), \hat{\mathbf{C}}_i) \rightarrow (\mu)$
  1. Given the sequence of secret keys($\mathsf{sk}_1 = \mathbf{t}_1, \ldots, \mathsf{sk}_N = \mathbf{t}_N$) and an expanded ciphertext $\hat{\mathbf{C}}_i$, set a vector $\hat{\mathbf{t}}{:=}[t_1, t_2, \ldots, t_N] \in \mathbb{Z}_q^{nN}$.
  2. Run $\mathsf{GSW.Dec}$ algorithm with $\hat{\mathbf{G}}_N$ and $\hat{\mathbf{G}}_N^{-1}$.
  3. Output μ.

To obtain a multi-key version of GSW scheme, Mukherjee and Wich's scheme [8] used a slightly modified versions of setup and key generation algorithms. Namely, they modified GSW setup algorithm to contain a random matrix $\mathbf{B}$ which is originally chosen during key generation. By doing this, one can consider $\mathbf{B}$ as a CRS, and can guarantee that all parties use the same $\mathbf{B}$ to generate public keys. Then they added a component to ciphertext for multi-key setting.

On the other hand, we use the exactly same setup, key generation and encryption algorithms as GWS scheme. There is no need to modify the setup algorithm to contain a random matrix (a CRS). Instead, each party can choose a random matrix to generate its key pair as in the original GSW scheme. This means that one can use the single-key GSW scheme as usual, and can easily start multi-key homomorphic operation with anyone when it is needed. All you have to do to start a multi-key homomorphic operation is to find public key of whoever you want to communicate, and to use our link algorithm.

Note that the decryption algorithm $\mathsf{MFHE.Dec}$ can be done by threshold decryption, described in Sect. 2.

- $\mathsf{MFHE.PartDec}(c, \mathsf{sk}_i) \rightarrow (p_i)$:
  1. Given an expanded ciphertext $c = \hat{\mathbf{C}}$ and i-th $\mathsf{sk}_i = \mathbf{t}_i \in \mathbb{Z}_q^n$, break $\hat{\mathbf{C}}$ into N row sub matrices $\hat{\mathbf{C}}_i$ (i.e. $\hat{\mathbf{C}} = (\hat{\mathbf{C}}_1^T, \ldots, \hat{\mathbf{C}}_N^T)$ where $\hat{\mathbf{C}}_i \in \mathbb{Z}^{n \times mN}$.
  2. Fix a vector $\hat{\mathbf{w}} = [0, \ldots, 0, \lceil q/2 \rceil] \in \mathbb{Z}_q^{nN}$.
  3. compute $\gamma_i = \mathbf{t}_i \hat{\mathbf{C}}_i \hat{\mathbf{G}}^{-1}(\hat{\mathbf{w}}^T) \in \mathbb{Z}_q$
  4. Output $p_i = \gamma_i + e_i^{sm}$ where $e_i^{sm} \xleftarrow{\$} [-\mathbf{B}_{smdg}^{dec}, \mathbf{B}_{smdg}^{dec}]$ is small randon noise with $\mathbf{B}_{smdg}^{dec} = 2^{d\lambda log\lambda} B_\chi$.
- $\mathsf{MFHE.FinDec}(p_1, \ldots, p_N) \rightarrow (\mu)$:
  1. Given $p_1, \ldots, p_N$, just sum $p = \sum_{i=1}^N p_i$.
  2. Output $\mu = |\lceil \frac{p}{q/2} \rfloor|$.

Correctness of Expansion. Let $\hat{\mathbf{C}}$ be the multi-key ciphertext of a bit μ obtained by i-th user from $\mathsf{MFHE.Expand}$ algorithm:

$$\hat{\mathbf{C}} \leftarrow \mathsf{MFHE.Expand}((\mathsf{pk}_1, \cdots, \mathsf{pk}_N), i, \mathbf{C})$$

where $\mathbf{C}$ is a GSW encryption of μ under $(\mathsf{pk}_i, \mathsf{sk}_i) = (\mathbf{A}_i, \mathbf{t}_i)$ and $\mathbf{R}_i$ is the relevant random matrix. For the multi-secret key $\hat{\mathbf{t}} = [\mathbf{t}_1, \cdots, \mathbf{t}_N]$ and the public matrix $\hat{\mathbf{G}_N}$, if $\hat{\mathbf{C}}$ satisfies the relation $\hat{\mathbf{t}}\hat{\mathbf{C}} \approx_q \mu\hat{\mathbf{t}}\hat{\mathbf{G}_N}$, then we can naturally generalize the arguments of GSW FHE scheme. Namely, we can achieve the correctness of encryption, correctness of evaluation, simulatability of partial decryption, and hence a valid MFHE scheme as in [8].

Recall that for a valid GSW key pair $(\mathsf{pk}, \mathsf{sk}) = (\mathbf{A}, \mathbf{t})$ it holds that $\mathbf{tA} = -\mathbf{sB}+\mathbf{b} = \mathbf{e}$ for some $\|\mathbf{e}\|_\infty \leq B_\chi$. For a valid GSW ciphertext $\mathbf{C}$ of μ under $(\mathsf{pk}, \mathsf{sk}) = (\mathbf{A}, \mathbf{t})$ it holds that $\mathbf{tC} = \mu\mathbf{tG} + \mathbf{e}'$ for some $\|\mathbf{e}'\|_\infty \leq \beta_{init} = mB_\chi$. We also recall that for a valid output $\mathbf{X}$ from $\mathsf{LinkAlgo}(\{\mathbf{V}^{(a,b)}\}_{a,b}, \mathsf{pk}' = \mathbf{A}')$ with respect to a 0-1 matrix $\mathbf{R}$ we have $\mathbf{tX} = \mathbf{tA}'\mathbf{R} + \mathbf{e}''$ for some $\|\mathbf{e}''\|_\infty \leq m^3\beta_{init} = m^4B_\chi$.

Now, we are ready to prove the correctness of expansion. By the definition, we have

$$\begin{aligned}\hat{\mathbf{t}}\hat{\mathbf{C}} &= [\mathbf{t}_1(\mathbf{C} - \mathbf{X}_i^1) + \mathbf{t}_i\mathbf{X}_i^i, \mathbf{t}_2(\mathbf{C} - \mathbf{X}_i^2) + \mathbf{t}_i\mathbf{X}_i^i, \cdots, \mathbf{t}_i\mathbf{C}, \cdots, \mathbf{t}_N(\mathbf{C} - \mathbf{X}_i^N) + \mathbf{t}_i\mathbf{X}_i^i] \\ &= [\mathbf{t}_1\mathbf{C} - \mathbf{t}_1\mathbf{X}_i^1 + \mathbf{t}_i\mathbf{X}_i^i, \mathbf{t}_2\mathbf{C} - \mathbf{t}_2\mathbf{X}_i^2 + \mathbf{t}_i\mathbf{X}_i^i, \cdots, \mathbf{t}_i\mathbf{C}, \cdots, \mathbf{t}_N\mathbf{C} - \mathbf{t}_N\mathbf{X}_i^N + \mathbf{t}_i\mathbf{X}_i^i].\end{aligned}$$

The only thing left is the term $\mathbf{t}_j\mathbf{C}$ for $j \neq i$. This will be $\mathbf{t}_j\mathbf{C} = \mathbf{t}_j(\mathbf{A}_i\mathbf{R}_i + \mu\mathbf{G}) = \mathbf{t}_j\mathbf{A}_i\mathbf{R}_i + \mu\mathbf{t}_j\mathbf{G}$. Then, for $j \neq i$,

$$\begin{aligned}\mathbf{t}_j\mathbf{C} - \mathbf{t}_j\mathbf{X}_i^j + \mathbf{t}_i\mathbf{X}_i^i &= (\mathbf{t}_j\mathbf{A}_i\mathbf{R}_i + \mu\mathbf{t}_j\mathbf{G}) - (\mathbf{t}_j\mathbf{A}_i\mathbf{R}_i + \mathbf{e}_j') + (\mathbf{t}_i\mathbf{A}_i\mathbf{R}_i + \mathbf{e}_i) \\ &= \mu\mathbf{t}_j\mathbf{G} + \tilde{\mathbf{e}_j}\end{aligned}$$

where $\tilde{\mathbf{e}_j} = -\mathbf{e}_j' + \mathbf{t}_i\mathbf{A}_i\mathbf{R}_i + \mathbf{e}_i \leq m^4B_\chi + (mB_\chi + m^4B_\chi) + mB_\chi = 2(m^4 + m)B_\chi$. And $\mathbf{t}_i\mathbf{C} = \mu\mathbf{t}_i\mathbf{G} + \mathbf{e}'$ with $\|\mathbf{e}'\|_\infty \leq mB_\chi$. Therefore, we have $\hat{\mathbf{t}}\hat{\mathbf{C}} = \mu\hat{\mathbf{t}}\hat{\mathbf{G}}_N + \mathbf{e}$ where $\mathbf{e} = [\tilde{\mathbf{e}_1}, \cdots, \mathbf{e}', \cdots, \tilde{\mathbf{e}_N}]$ and $\|\mathbf{e}\|_\infty \leq 2(m^4+m)B_\chi$. Thus, one can think of $\hat{\mathbf{C}}$ as a GSW encryption under the secret key $\hat{\mathbf{t}}$, and the correctness of decryption is guaranteed if we have $2(m^4 + m)B_\chi < q/(4mN)$. This particularly holds by the choice of $q = B_\chi 2^{\omega(d\kappa log\kappa)}$.

4 A Three Round MPC Protocol: Semi-malicious Security

In the previous section, we give the $\mathsf{LinkAlgo}$ algorithm to have a relation between two key pairs $(\mathsf{pk}, \mathsf{sk})$ and $(\mathsf{pk}', \mathsf{sk}')$. In this section, we make use of the relation obtained by $\mathsf{LinkAlgo}$ algorithm to construct our MFHE scheme, and then we introduce a three round MPC protocol that is secure against semi-malicious adversary from the MFHE scheme. This type of adversary is weaker than standard active malicious adversary but stronger than semi honest adversary who just follows a protocol honestly albeit it wants to know other parties' inputs. We give a definition of *Semi-malicious* adversary model which is introduced in [1].

Semi-malicious Adversary. A semi-malicious adversary can corrupt arbitrary number of honest parties. It can deviate a protocol to some extent. In other words, he can choose the randomness of input by himself arbitrarily and adaptively in each round. This choice must explain the message sent by the adversary. It must follow the correct behavior of the honest protocol with inputs and randomness that it knows. We assume that it can be rushing (i.e. after seeing messages from honest parties, it may choose its message.) and also the adversarial parties may abort at any point of the protocol. The proof of the security goes on in the usual way showing that the real model's distribution $\overset{comp}{\approx}$ the ideal one.

4.1 A Three Round MPC Protocol via MFHE

Let $f : (\{0,1\})^N \to \{0,1\}$ be the function to compute. Let d the depth of the circuit for computing f.

Preprocessing. Run $\mathsf{params} \leftarrow \mathsf{MFHE.Setup}(1^\lambda, 1^d)$. Make sure that all the parties have params.

Input: For $i \in [N]$, each party P_i holds input $x_i \in \{0,1\}$, and wants to compute $f(x_1, \cdots, x_N)$.

Round I. *(Round for public key)* Each party P_i executes the following steps:
- Generate its key pair $(\mathsf{pk}_i, \mathsf{sk}_i) \leftarrow \mathsf{MFHE.KeyGen}(\mathsf{params})$.
- Broadcast the public key pk_i.

Round II. *(Round for multi-key ciphertext)* Each party P_i for $i \in [N]$ on receiving public keys $\{\mathsf{pk}_k\}_{k \neq i}$ executes the following steps:
- Encrypt the message x_i with its public key pk_i to get a single-key ciphertext $\mathbf{C}_i \leftarrow \mathsf{MFHE.Enc}(\mathsf{pk}_i, x_i)$. Keep the relevant random matrix $\mathbf{R}_{i,j} \in \{0,1\}^{m \times m}$ to C_i which will be need for $\mathsf{MFHE.Expand}$.
- Run the expand algorithm to get a multi-key ciphertext:

$$\hat{\mathbf{C}}_i \leftarrow \mathsf{MFHE.Expand}((\mathsf{pk}_1, \cdots, \mathsf{pk}_N), i, \mathbf{C}_i)$$

- Broadcast the multi-key ciphertext $\hat{\mathbf{C}}_i$.

Round III. *(Round for partial decryptions)* Each party P_i for $i \in [N]$ on receiving ciphertexts $\{\hat{\mathbf{C}}_k\}_{k \neq i}$ executes the following steps:
- Run the evaluation algorithm to get the evaluated ciphertext:

$$\hat{\mathbf{C}}^* \leftarrow \mathsf{MFHE.Eval}(f, (\hat{\mathbf{C}}_1, \cdots, \hat{\mathbf{C}}_N))$$

- Run the partial decryption algorithm on $\hat{\mathbf{C}}^*$:

$$p_i \leftarrow \mathsf{MFHE.PartDec}(\hat{\mathbf{C}}^*, (\mathsf{pk}_1, \cdots, \mathsf{pk}_N), i, \mathsf{sk}_i)$$

- Broadcast the partial decryption p_i of $\hat{\mathbf{C}}^*$.

Output: On receiving all the values $\{p_k\}_{k \neq i}$, run the final decryption algorithm to obtain the function value $f(x_1, \cdots, x_N)$:

$$y \leftarrow \mathsf{MFHE.FinDec}(p_1, \cdots, p_N),$$

and output $y = f(x_1, \cdots, x_N)$.

Security. The security proof of the above MPC protocol against semi-malicious adversaries is similar to that of the previous work [8]. The proof heavily depends on the simulatability of partial decryption and the semantic security of GSW encryption. By the correctness of expansion in Sect. 4, our MFHE scheme inherits the simulatability of [8]. They proved the MPC protocol is secure against any static semi-malicious adversaries who corrupt exactly $N-1$ parties at first because of their simulator of the threshold decryption. Then they proved the security against those who corrupt arbitrary number of parties using only pseudorandom functions. We adapt their way apart from the messages of each round, i.e. the simulator's the first round behavior of [8] works in our second round and that of the second round works in our third round.

5 Conclusion

We have presented an MFHE scheme without a CRS (in public key), based on the LWE assumption. As an important application, we have constructed a three round MPC protocol which is secure against semi-malicious adversaries. This seems to be round-optimal among all MPC from MFHE without CRS as we mentioned in introduction. Our construction also has a strong point that one can use its key pair for both multi-key setting and single-key setting since we separate the component for multi-key operation from ciphertext. Furthermore, with public key infrastructure (PKI), the round complexity is reduced to 2 since the first round of our MPC protocol is only for broadcasting public keys. In this work, we also have suggested an important stepping stone to get secure MPC protocol, without any trusted setup, against fully malicious adversaries.

Acknowledgement. The authors were supported by Basic Science Research Program through the National Research Foundation of Korea (NRF) funded by the Ministry of Science, ICT and Future Planning (Grant Number: 2015R1A2A1A15054564)

References

1. Asharov, G., Jain, A., López-Alt, A., Tromer, E., Vaikuntanathan, V., Wichs, D.: Multiparty computation with low communication, computation and interaction via threshold FHE. In: Pointcheval, D., Johansson, T. (eds.) EUROCRYPT 2012. LNCS, vol. 7237, pp. 483–501. Springer, Heidelberg (2012). https://doi.org/10.1007/978-3-642-29011-4_29
2. Brakerski, Z., Halevi, S., Polychroniadou, A.: Four round secure computation without setup. In: Kalai, Y., Reyzin, L. (eds.) TCC 2017. LNCS, vol. 10677, pp. 645–677. Springer, Cham (2017). https://doi.org/10.1007/978-3-319-70500-2_22
3. Clear, M., McGoldrick, C.: Multi-identity and multi-key leveled FHE from learning with errors. In: Gennaro, R., Robshaw, M. (eds.) CRYPTO 2015. LNCS, vol. 9216, pp. 630–656. Springer, Heidelberg (2015). https://doi.org/10.1007/978-3-662-48000-7_31
4. Gentry, C.: A fully homomorphic encryption scheme. Stanford University (2009)

5. Gentry, C., Sahai, A., Waters, B.: Homomorphic encryption from learning with errors: conceptually-simpler, asymptotically-faster, attribute-based. In: Canetti, R., Garay, J.A. (eds.) CRYPTO 2013. LNCS, vol. 8042, pp. 75–92. Springer, Heidelberg (2013). https://doi.org/10.1007/978-3-642-40041-4_5
6. LópezAlt, A., Tromer, E., Vaikuntanathan, V.: On-the-fly multiparty computation on the cloud via multikey fully homomorphic encryption. In: Proceedings of the Forty-Fourth Annual ACM Symposium on Theory of Computing, pp. 1219–1234. ACM (2012)
7. Micciancio, D., Peikert, C.: Trapdoors for lattices: simpler, tighter, faster, smaller. In: Pointcheval, D., Johansson, T. (eds.) EUROCRYPT 2012. LNCS, vol. 7237, pp. 700–718. Springer, Heidelberg (2012). https://doi.org/10.1007/978-3-642-29011-4_41
8. Mukherjee, P., Wichs, D.: Two round multiparty computation via multi-key FHE. In: Fischlin, M., Coron, J.-S. (eds.) EUROCRYPT 2016. LNCS, vol. 9666, pp. 735–763. Springer, Heidelberg (2016). https://doi.org/10.1007/978-3-662-49896-5_26
9. Regev, O.: On lattices, learning with errors, random linear codes, and cryptography. J. ACM (JACM) **56**(6), 34 (2009)

Robust Multiparty Computation with Faster Verification Time

Souradyuti Paul[1] and Ananya Shrivastava[2(✉)]

[1] Indian Institute of Technology Bhilai, Raipur, India
souradyuti@iitbhilai.ac.in
[2] Indian Institute of Technology Gandhinagar, Gandhinagar, India
ananya.shrivastava@iitgn.ac.in

Abstract. In Eurocrypt 2016, Kiayias, Zhou and Zikas (KZZ) have designed a multiparty protocol for computing an *arbitrary* function, which they prove to be secure in the malicious model with identifiable abort supporting robustness property. In their algorithm, the total transaction verification time has turned out to be $O(n^6)$, where n is the number of parties participating in the protocol. The main contribution of this paper is the improvement of their verification time to $O(n^3 \log n)$. We achieve this by observing that a deposit transaction created by a party in KZZ can be generated simply from the information contained in a *different* deposit transaction. This observation coupled with a host of novel techniques for addition and elimination of elements on a set relevant for our protocol is primarily the reason we were able to improve the verification time complexity of the KZZ protocol. Our trick can potentially be applied to speed up many other similar protocols (as much as it is prohibitive in some other specific scenarios). We compare our protocol with the others, based on various performance and security parameters, and, finally discuss the feasibility of implementing this in the Ethereum platform.

Keywords: Blockchain · Fairness · Robustness
Multi-party computation · Ethereum

1 Introduction

In a secure multiparty computation, a set of mutually distrusting n parties – denotes P_1, P_2, $\cdots$, P_n – compute the output of a publicly known function $f(x_1, x_2, \cdots, x_n)$, where x_i is private to P_i. This line of research on design and security analyses of various multiparty protocols (MPP), initiated in the seminal works of Yao [30] and Goldreich *et al.* [14], has now become a hot pursuit among the cryptographers, due to its enormous potential to solve various hard and practically useful problems. While privacy is the most important property of an MPP, it is still not sufficient for the protocol's practical adoption into a real-world application. In this context, a property named *fairness* takes the center stage that guarantees that, after the execution of the protocol, either all

W. Susilo and G. Yang (Eds.): ACISP 2018, LNCS 10946, pp. 114–131, 2018.
https://doi.org/10.1007/978-3-319-93638-3_8

parties learn the output, or nobody does. However, Cleve has shown that *fairness* is impossible to achieve, if the number of dishonest parties is more than $n/2$ [10]. This has led the researchers to investigate a slightly diluted version of the property, known as *fairness with compensation* which ensures that, if a party aborts the protocol after knowing the output, he has to pay fine to the honest parties [7]. Interestingly, it also turns out that this diluted version is still not enough in various practical applications, since this property fails to penalize a dishonest party if he aborts right after the *start* of the protocol (but before knowing the output); this can lead to a scenario where the honest parties ended up wasting their time and resources without knowing the output until the end of the protocol, and the dishonest parties responsible for the abort did not pay any fine. The *robustness* property addresses this issue and guarantees that either the honest parties obtain the output, or they are compensated, no matter the point during the execution at which they abort the protocol [16].

With the advent of the decentralized cryptocurrencies like Bitcoin and Ethereum, achieving *fairness with compensation* becomes a realistic goal [21,29]. A number of papers emerged that implemented several multiparty protocols with monetary penalty [2,7,17–19]. Although these protocols achieve fine-based compensation, they still lack the *robustness* property as discussed above. In [16], the authors introduced this new notion, and provided a compiler that transforms any multiparty protocol π_{mal}, which is secure in the malicious model with identifiable abort, to a protocol which is *robust* as well as secure in the malicious model with identifiable abort. Their compiler is based on the following novel ideas: (1) Broadcasting the commitments of the setup strings using deposit phase; (2) The function evaluation is done after the deposit phase; (3) Finally, the robustness is achieved through creation of *islands* for all parties; an *island* of a party is a set of parties who have created similar type of deposit transactions for all the parties.

Our Contribution. In this paper, we propose a faster technique for computing *islands* required for achieving robustness property; as a result, we improve the verification time of the KZZ compiler from $O(n^6)$ to $O(n^3 \log n)$. Our technique takes advantage of the following crucial observation: the information contained in the deposit transactions are not independent; in particular, information of a deposit transaction of one party can be generated from the deposit transaction of another party. Note that this technique can *only* be applied to a protocol where the embedded commitments as well as the predicates of all the deposit transactions can be computed from the information contained in the other deposit transactions. We also observe that this technique is unique and cannot be universally applied to all protocols such as those in [7,18,19]. To complete the protocol, we have used three new *efficient* predicates to store, update and check the existence of appropriate transactions, study of which may be of independent research interest. We have also described the feasibility of implementing our protocol in Ethereum. Finally, we compare our protocol with other multiparty protocols with respect to various security and performance parameters in Table 1.

Table 1. Comparison between various protocols implementing multi-party computation of an arbitrary function. Here, n = # of parties, λ = security parameter, T = size of the transcript in the protocol. The Script complexity also reflects the communication complexity. The Setup time for all the schemes is $O(1)$.

Scheme	On-Chain Trans.	Script Comp.	Ledger Rounds	Verification Time	Fairness Prop.	Robustness Prop.
BK [7]	$O(n)$	$O(n^2)$	$O(n)$	$O(n)$	Yes	No
KVN1 [19]	$O(n)$	$O(n\lambda)$	$O(n)$	$O(1)$	Yes	No
BKM [18]	$O(n^2)$	$O(n^2T)$	$O(n^2)$	$O(n)$	Yes	No
KVN2 [19]	$O(n)$	$O(nT)$	$O(n)$	$O(1)$	Yes	No
KZZ [16]	$O(n^2)$	$O(n^4)$	$O(1)$	$O(n^6)$	Yes	Yes
This paper	$\boldsymbol{O(n^2)}$	$\boldsymbol{O(n^4)}$	$\boldsymbol{O(1)}$	$\boldsymbol{O(n^3 \log n)}$	**Yes**	**Yes**

Related Work. The subject of fairness with compensation has been the theme of various other papers [2,3,7,17–19]. In addition, Ruffing, Kate and Schröder recently addressed the equivocation issue in the Bitcoin, i.e., making conflicting statements to others in a distributed protocol, via penalty mechanism [26]. Fairness can be viewed from *resource* and *optimistic* perspectives that guarantee fairness with high probability at the cost of running time of the protocol cf. [5,8,9,13]. Contrary to our work, there are several other works that try to achieve the fairness property in MPC using alternate models: reputation system to measure the reliability of each party in the protocol [4]; exploiting the rational adversarial power to design protocol using game-theoretic equilibrium setting for the parties [12]. Another related work is done in [6,20], where they focus on reducing the collateral amount deposited in the multiparty lottery protocol. However, these protocols are designed for computing a specific function and cannot be trivially extended for computing any arbitrary function.

Organization. We start with preliminaries in Sect. 2. Then in Sects. 3.1 and 3.2, we described the predicates and the sub-protocols to be used in our protocol. In Sect. 3.3, we present the full description of our protocol that will reduce the verification time as compared to [16]. In Sect. 3.4, we highlight the difference between the KZZ and our compilers. Implementation of our protocol in the Ethereum platform is discussed in Sect. 4. In Sect. 5, we provide the security analysis of the robustness property of our protocol. Finally, we conclude in Sect. 6.

2 Preliminaries

Notation. Throughout the paper, we assume an (often implicit) security parameter denoted as k. For a number $n \in \mathbb{N}$ we denote by $[n]$ the set $[n] = \{1, \cdots, n\}$. We define *Ledger* as a publicly-verifiable database which stores all the valid transactions in the form of a block. Let max_{Ledger} denote the maximum time taken by the network to verify a transaction and include it in the *Ledger*. The *state* is defined as a set of valid transactions stored in the *Ledger*. Let RoundTime(1) denote the time at which the parties have agreed to start the protocol execution. We define $\text{RoundTime}(\rho) = \text{RoundTime}(1) + \rho \times \max_{Ledger}$.

Definition 1 (Script Complexity [17,19]**).** *Let Π be a protocol among n parties $P_1, \cdots, P_n$ in the $\mathcal{F}^*_{CR}$-hybrid model. For circuit ϕ, let $|\phi|$ denote its circuit complexity. For a given execution of Π, starting from a particular initialization Ω of parties' inputs, random tapes and distribution of coins, let $V_{\Pi,\Omega}$ denote the sum of all $|\phi|$'s, such that some honest party claimed an $\mathcal{F}^*_{CR}$ transaction by producing a witness for ϕ during an execution of Π. Then the script complexity of Π, denoted V_Π, equals $max_\Omega(V_{\Pi,\Omega})$.*

Definition 2 (Q-robustness [16]**).** *We say protocol π realizes functionality $\mathcal{F}$ with $Q_{\bar{\mathcal{G}}}$-robustness with respect to global functionality $\bar{\mathcal{G}}$, provided the following statement is true. There exists a threshold T such that for all adversaries $\mathcal{A}$, there is a simulator $\mathcal{S}$ so that for all environments $\mathcal{Z}$ it holds:*

$$\text{Exec}^{\bar{\mathcal{G}}}_{\pi,\mathcal{A},\mathcal{Z}} \approx \text{Exec}^{\bar{\mathcal{G}},\mathcal{W}^T_{Q,\mathcal{G}}(\mathcal{F})}_{\mathcal{S},\mathcal{Z}}$$

Moreover, whenever the wrapper $\mathcal{W}$ reaches its termination limit, then the state state *of the global setup $\bar{\mathcal{G}}$ upon termination holds that $Q^{Dlv}_{\bar{\mathcal{G}}}(sid, P, R^{pub}_{P,sid}, \text{state})$*[1] *for every party $P \in \mathcal{P}$, where* sid *denotes the protocol ID; $R^{pub}_{P,sid}$ denotes the public component of party P.*

Correlated Randomness as a Sampling Functionality [16]**.** Our protocol is in the *correlated randomness model.* In this model, we assume that the parties initially, before receiving their inputs, receive appropriately correlated random strings. It is parameterized by a sampling distribution $\mathcal{D}$ and the player set $\mathcal{P} = \{P_1, \cdots, P_n\}$. In this model, the parties jointly hold a vector $\boldsymbol{R} = (R_1, \cdots, R_n) \in (\{0,1\}^*)^n$, where P_i holds R_i, drawn from a given efficiently samplable distribution $\mathcal{D}$. This is, as usual, captured by giving the parties initial access to an ideal functionality $\mathcal{F}^{\mathcal{D}}_{CORR}$, known as a *sampling functionality* (see Fig. 1 for details). Hence, a protocol in the correlated randomness model is formally an $\mathcal{F}^{\mathcal{D}}_{CORR}$-hybrid protocol.

Functionality $\mathcal{F}^{\mathcal{D}}_{CORR}(\mathcal{P}, \text{REQUEST}, \text{sid})$

- Wait to receive the message (REQUEST, sid) from any party or the adversary $\mathcal{S} \in \mathcal{P}$. Set $\boldsymbol{R} = (R_1, \cdots, R_n) \leftarrow \mathcal{D}$.
- For all $i \in [n]$, output (REQUEST, sid, R_i) to P_i (or to the adversary if P_i is corrupted).

Fig. 1. The correlated randomness functionality $\mathcal{F}^{\mathcal{D}}_{CORR}$ in the malicious model.

[1] It ensures that the honest parties do not lose money during execution of the protocol.

Information-Theoretic Signatures [15,27,28]. Our protocol uses information-theoretic signatures to commit a party to messages it sends. Informally, the *signer*, P_i, sends his signature σ on a message m to the *receiver*, P_j, such that P_j can later verify that the message was indeed sent from P_i [15]. Note that in order to achieve information-theoretic security the verification key is not known publicly to all the parties. Rather, each *receiver*, P_i, knows private verification key vk_i corresponding to the signing key sk.

Security with Identifiable abort [15]. *Secure multi-party computation with identifiable abort*, also referred to as *Identifiable* MPC (ID-MPC), ensures that, if a protocol π aborts, then all the parties agree on the identity of the aborting (or corrupted) party P_i. We say that *the parties aborted with* P_i. Consider any arbitrary functionality $\mathcal{F}$; we define a new functionality $[\mathcal{F}]_{\perp}^{\mathrm{ID}}$ that behaves exactly as $\mathcal{F}$ with the following modification: upon receiving from the simulator a special command (abort, P_i), where P_i is a corrupted party, $[\mathcal{F}]_{\perp}^{\mathrm{ID}}$ sets the outputs of all (honest) parties to (abort, P_i).

Definition 3 ([15]). *Let $\mathcal{F}$ be a functionality and $[\mathcal{F}]_{\perp}^{ID}$ be the corresponding functionality with identifiable abort. We say that a protocol π securely realizes $\mathcal{F}$ with identifiable abort if π securely realizes the functionality $[\mathcal{F}]_{\perp}^{ID}$.*

Overview of Blockchain. The Blockchain is a *decentralized*, *immutable*, *public* ledger of transactions. It relies on the idea of computationally hard cryptographic puzzle – a.k.a. moderately hard functions or proofs of work – put forth by Dwork and Naor [11]. It attempts to provide robustness as long as *more than half of the computing power* is held by the honest participants [23]. A plethora of similar-looking currencies like [1,22,24,25] fundamentally use Blockchain as its underlying technology. Very briefly, the main idea behind the Blockchain technology is storing and aggregating multiple transactions between the nodes of the network in the form of a block, and afterwards joining these blocks in a linear chain. However, the aspect that makes this technology different from all previous secure storage techniques, is that it is able to correctly verify all these transactions *even when the nodes in the network are not trustworthy.* For more technical details regarding Blocks and Blockchain, please refer to [21].

Overview of Ethereum. Ethereum is a blockchain based distributed computing platform supporting a Turing-complete scripting language [29]. It can also be viewed as transaction-based state machine. In Ethereum, the state is comprised of many small objects called *"accounts"* that transition the state by transferring values and information from one account to other. There are two types of account: (1) *Externally owned account* which are controlled by private keys and have no code associated with them. (2) *Contract account* which are controlled by their contract code and have code associated with them. Transactions in ethereum are of two types: those which result in message calls and those which result in the creation of new accounts with associated code (known informally as 'contract creation'). Each transaction contains recipient account, a signature identifying the sender, the amount of ether as well as gasLimit and gasPrice. gasPrice represents the cost per computational step and gasLimit represents the maximum amount of gas that should be used in executing this transaction. A contract when executed can change its local state as well as generate new transactions. For a transaction to be considered valid, it must go through a validation process known as mining. The contract is executed by the miner that processes an incoming transaction as part of the state update function of the Ethereum blockchain. Once the validation is done, the state is updated and respective amount is debited from sender's account and updated in receiver's account. If the value transfer failed because the sender did not have enough money, or the code execution ran out of gas, all state changes are reverted back except the payment of the fees which is added in the miner's account. Ethereum makes use a special kind of data structure, called Merkle-patricia-tree (trie), that can store state in the form of keys and values. Ethereum makes use a special kind of data structure, called Merkle Patricia Trees, that can store cryptographically authenticated data in the form of keys and values. A Merkle Patricia Tree with a certain group of keys and values can only be constructed in a single way. In other words, given the same set of keys and values, two Merkle Patricia Trees constructed independently will result in the same structure bit-by-bit. For our work, the Merkle aspect of the trees are what matter in Ethereum. Rather than keeping the whole tree inside a block, the hash of its root node is embedded in the block. If some malicious node were to tamper with the state of the blockchain, it would become evident as soon as other nodes computed the hash of the root node using the tampered data [29].

3 Description of the Compiler KZZ′

Let π_{mal} be a protocol implementing an arbitrary function $f(\cdot)$ that is secure in the *malicious model with identifiable abort*. The KZZ′ is a compiler that takes π_{mal} as an input and outputs the protocol π_{rob} which is *robust* and secure in the *malicious model with identifiable abort*. The naming of KZZ′ is due to the fact that it is a more efficient version of the compiler KZZ, named after their authors Kiayias, Zhou and Zikas. The difference between KZZ and KZZ′ is described in Sect. 3.4. In the description, the difference of our protocol with KZZ has been identified in blue color.

Suppose, $\mathcal{P} = \{P_1, \cdots, P_n\}$ is the set of parties who want to compute the function $f(x_1, \cdots, x_n)$, where x_i is the private input of party P_i. Let ρ_c be the number of rounds of the protocol π_{mal}.

We describe the protocol by dividing it into three parts: (A) we give the description of the predicates to be used in various transactions; (B) then, we use the sub-protocol such as Dep_Ref(·) and Claim(·) for deposit and claim using (A); (C) and finally, we give the full description of our compiler KZZ′ based on (B).

3.1 Description of the Predicates Used in KZZ′ Transactions

Predicates associated with creation and update of *islands*. The following three predicates – namely, set_un(·), update(·) and exist(·) – work on creation and update of islands and sub-islands, and hence, are to be studied together. Let $\mathcal{P}'_{ia_j} = \{P_{a_j}\}$ denote the sub-island of P_i. The $\mathcal{P}'_i = \{P_i\} \bigcup_{\forall j \in [m]} \mathcal{P}'_{ia_j}, \forall i \in [n]$, denotes the island of P_i (see Fig. 2).

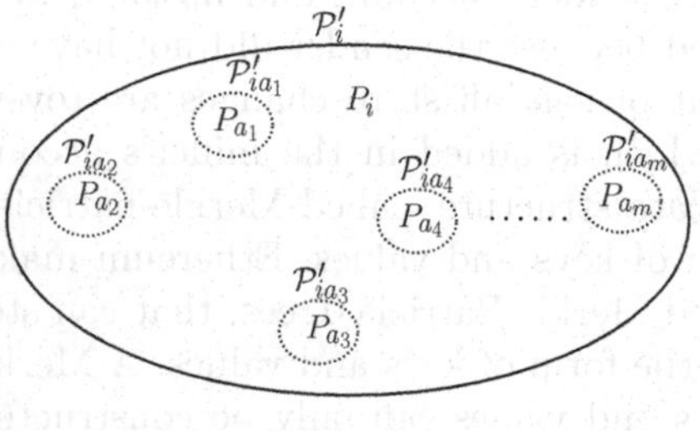

Fig. 2. $\mathcal{P}'_i$, represented by the solid oval, denotes the island of P_i. The dotted circles represent the sub-islands $\mathcal{P}'_{ia_j}, \forall j \in [m]$.

set_un(s, i). The predicate returns 1 after creating the sub-island $\mathcal{P}'_{si}$.

update(s, i). The predicate returns 1 if, for a pair of parties (P_s, P_i) and their respective sub-island $(\mathcal{P}'_{si}, \mathcal{P}'_{is})$:

1. *If* $\left(P_s \in \mathcal{P}'_{is} \wedge \mathcal{P}'_{si} = \{\}\right)$ *then* update $\mathcal{P}'_{is} = \{\}$.
2. *If* $\left(P_i \in \mathcal{P}'_{si} \wedge \mathcal{P}'_{is} = \{\}\right)$ *then* update $\mathcal{P}'_{si} = \{\}$.

The predicate ensures that if a pair of parties doesn't exist in each other's sub-islands, then they should be removed from the sub-islands. This strategy will help in removing an honest party from a corrupt party's island.

exist(s, i). The predicate is verified by executing the following: Check if $P_i \in \mathcal{P}'_{si}$.

The predicate will be used to ensure that a *claimant* P_i can only redeem the deposit transactions if he exists in the sub-island of the *depositor* P_s.

Predicate $\boldsymbol{\phi_\rho\left(\alpha, \beta, h^{(\rho-1)}; \{Com_j\}_{j\in[n]}\right)}$. Let α, β and $h^{(\rho-1)}$ denote the message, the NIZK proof of the secret and the random number of a party, and the history of the protocol at round $\rho-1$ respectively. The predicate is verified if α is the correct round-ρ-message in the protocol corresponding to the proof β, the history of the protocol $h^{(\rho-1)}$ at round $\rho-1$, and the commitments $\{Com_j\}_{j\in[n]}$ (for more details see [15]).

The predicate ensures that parties are executing the protocol correctly by asking them to provide zero-knowledge proof of the secret and the random numbers that prove that the revealed witness is consistent with the *history* of the protocol so far. If any party sends an inconsistent message then the protocol aborts and each party knows the identity of the aborter.

Predicate $\phi_i'\Big(\mathtt{D}; n-1, \{Com_j\}_{j\in[n]}\Big)$**.** Let D denote the set of all deposit transactions created by a party. The predicate is verified by executing the following: It will first check whether $|\mathtt{D}| = n-1$; then, check whether all the transactions in D are created by P_i, that is whether $\mathsf{Ver}_i(\cdot) = 1$. Now $\forall x \in \mathtt{D}$, check if the output script contains the predicate $\phi_\rho(\cdot)$.

This is the most important and newly designed predicate. The predicate check if the supplied deposit transactions have similar setup as the current deposit transaction. This strategy will help in creating island for parties having similar deposit transactions.

3.2 Description of the Sub-protocols Dep_Ref(·) and Claim(·)

In any protocol supporting fairness with compensation, the major two operations are deposit and claim of money by creation of transactions and verifying them against conditions, also known as predicates. The following protocols, namely, Dep_Ref(·) and Claim(·) are used by the parties for depositing the money and claiming them back later. The algorithmic description is given in Fig. 3.

Dep_Ref(·). The protocol takes following parameters as an input: sid = protocol id, s = the creator of the transaction, i = the receiver of the transaction, v = the amount to be deposited and ρ = round of a synchronous protocol π.

The protocol proceeds as follows: A party P_s sends some amount v to P_i by creating a transaction $\mathtt{Tx}^{(d)}$ which can be redeemed if he satisfies the following conditions. (1) If P_i posts the claim transaction within the *time* interval $(\tau_\rho^-, \tau_\rho^+)$, where $\tau_\rho^- = \text{RoundTime}(\rho)$ and $\tau_\rho^+ = \text{RoundTime}(\rho) + \mathsf{max}_{Ledger} - 1$, (2) If the supplied NIZK proof proves that the message is consistent with the view of the protocol so far, (3) If the claim is done for first round of the protocol π, then check if the claimant has created his own deposit transactions then add him into the depositor's island, (4) Otherwise, check if the claimant exists in the depositor's island, (5) If the claim is not done within the specified time interval then the money will be refunded back to P_s, if he supplies both P_i and P_s signatures. Now, for P_s to redeem his deposited money back to himself, he creates a partially complete refund transaction $\mathtt{Tx}^{(r)}$ and sends it to P_i. P_i will then sign on this refund transaction, before sending it back to P_s. This ensures that P_s can redeem his money only after time τ_ρ^+.

Claim(·). The protocol takes following parameters as an input: sid = protocol id, i = the creator of the transaction, s = the party who has pledged the amount to party i, v = the amount to be deposited, ρ = round of a synchronous protocol $\pi, m = \rho^{\text{th}}$ round message of $\pi, p =$ NIZK proof of secret and message generated in $\pi, h =$ history of the protocol π at round $\rho - 1$.

The protocol starts by collecting all the deposit transactions created by party P_i inside the set D. P_i then redeems the deposit transaction $\texttt{Tx}^{(d)}$ made to him by P_s by supplying the relevant secrets values inside the data field of his claim transaction $\texttt{Tx}^{(c)}$. If the claim transaction is created for the first round ($\rho = 1$) of the synchronous protocol π then the relevant data values will be (m, p, h and the set D), if $\rho > 1$ then the relevant data values will be (m, p, h) else the set D.

$\mathsf{Dep\_Ref}(\mathsf{sid}, s, i, v, \rho)$

1. P_s creates a transaction with ID $\texttt{Tx}^{(d)}$, and stores, having the following parameters:
   - protocol id: sid
   - output script/contract code:
     $$\underbrace{\rho = 1 \wedge \tau_1^- \leq time < \tau_1^+ \wedge \mathsf{Ver}_i(\cdot) \wedge \phi_\rho(\cdot) \wedge \phi_i'(\cdot) \wedge \texttt{Tx}^{(\texttt{isl})}.\mathsf{set\_un}(s, i)}_{\text{for } P_i}$$
     $$\bigvee \underbrace{\rho > 1 \wedge \tau_\rho^- \leq time < \tau_\rho^+ \wedge \mathsf{Ver}_i(\cdot) \wedge \phi_\rho(\cdot) \wedge \texttt{Tx}^{(\texttt{isl})}.\mathsf{exist}(s, i)}_{\text{for } P_i}$$
     $$\bigvee \underbrace{\rho = \perp \wedge \tau_\perp^- \leq time < \tau_\perp^+ \wedge \mathsf{Ver}_i(\cdot) \wedge \phi_i'(\cdot) \wedge \texttt{Tx}^{(\texttt{isl})}.\mathsf{update}(s, i)}_{\text{for } P_i}$$
     $$\bigvee \underbrace{time \geq \tau_\rho^+ \wedge \mathsf{Ver}_s(\cdot) \wedge \mathsf{Ver}_i(\cdot)}_{\text{for } P_s}$$
   - value: v
   - input transaction ID: Tx
   - inputscript: $\mathsf{sig}_s(\mathsf{sid} \,\|\langle\text{output script}\rangle\|v\|\texttt{Tx})$
2. P_s also creates a partially complete transaction with ID $\texttt{Tx}^{(r)}$ having the following parameters:
   - protocol id: sid
   - output script/contract code: $\mathsf{Ver}_s(\cdot)$
   - value: v
   - input transaction ID: $\texttt{Tx}^{(d)}$
   - inputscript: ?
3. P_s sends $\texttt{Tx}^{(d)}$ and $\texttt{Tx}^{(r)}$ to P_i who adds his signature σ_1 on $\texttt{Tx}^{(r)}$, before returning it to P_s. P_s then adds his signature σ_2 on $\texttt{Tx}^{(r)}$. Therefore, finally, inputscript $= \sigma_1, \sigma_2$.
4. Release the transaction $\texttt{Tx}^{(r)}$ after time τ_ρ^+ in the network.

$\mathsf{Claim}(\mathsf{sid}, i, s, v, \rho, m, p, h)$

1. If $\rho = \perp$, D = set of all deposit transactions created by P_i in Step 4 of Fig. 4.
2. Otherwise, D = set of all deposit transactions created by P_i in Step 3 of Fig. 4.
3. P_i creates a transaction with ID $\texttt{Tx}^{(c)}$ having the following parameters:
   - protocol id: sid
   - output script/contract code: $\mathsf{Ver}_i(\cdot)$
   - value: v
   - input transaction ID: $\texttt{Tx}^{(d)}$
   - input script: $\mathsf{sig}_i(\mathsf{sid} \,\|\langle\text{output script}\rangle\|v\|\texttt{Tx}^{(d)})$
   - data: $\begin{cases} m, p, h, \texttt{D} & \text{if } \rho = 1 \\ m, p, h & \text{if } \rho > 1 \\ \texttt{D} & \text{if } \rho = \perp \end{cases}$

Fig. 3. Algorithmic description of the protocols $\mathsf{Dep\_Ref}(\cdot)$ and $\mathsf{Claim}(\cdot)$. For details see Sect. 3.2.

$\pi_{rob} = \mathsf{KZZ}'(\pi_{mal}, v)$

Global variable: state state; set of parties $\mathcal{P}$.
Input: int v, protocol π_{mal}.
Output: π_{rob}.

1. [*Setup*] (At τ_{-3} = RoundTime(1) − 2). For all $i \in [n]$:
   - Party $P_i \in \mathcal{P}$ invokes the *sampling functionality* $\mathcal{F}^{\mathcal{D}}_{CORR}$ (as described in Sect. 2) by sending message (REQUEST, sid), where sid is the protocol's session ID .
   - Output received by P_i from $\mathcal{F}^{\mathcal{D}}_{CORR}$ is (R^{priv}_i, R^{pub}). Here, R^{priv}_i = random coins required in the protocol$\|\mathsf{OTP}_i\|sk_i$, where OTP_i is the *One-Time Pad*, sk_i is the signing key; $R^{pub} = (Com_1, \cdots, Com_n)\|(vk_1, \cdots, vk_n)\|\mathsf{CRS}$, where: Com_i is the commitment on R^{priv}_i; vk_i is the verification key corresponding to sk_i; and CRS is the common reference string.
   - Create a transaction, namely, $\mathsf{Tx}^{(\mathsf{isl})}$ with predicates set_un(·), update() and exist(·). This transaction also contains variables $\mathcal{P}'_{ij}$, where $\mathcal{P}'_{ij}$ is initially empty, $i \neq j$, and $\mathcal{P}'_{ii}$ is initialized to $\{P_i\}$, $\forall i, j \in [n]$.
   - P_i sets his public key address $address_i := vk_i$.
2. [Checking Balance] (At τ_{-1} = RoundTime(1) − 1). Let ρ_c be the number of *rounds* of the protocol π_{mal}. If a party $P \in \mathcal{P}$ has less than $(n-1) \times v \times \rho_c$ unspent coins in the state, then it broadcasts ⊥, and every party aborts the protocol execution with output ⊥.
3. [Deposit1] For all $(s, \rho) \in [n] \times [\rho_c]$, execute the following:
   - (At τ_0 = RoundTime(1)) For all $i \in [n]$, $i \neq s$: invoke Dep_Ref(sid, s, i, v, ρ). (Details of the protocol are in Fig. 3.)
4. [Deposit2] (At τ_1 = RoundTime(2)) For all $s, i \in [n]$, $i \neq s$: invoke Dep_Ref(sid, s, i, v, ⊥). (Details of the protocol are in Fig. 3.)
5. [Claim Loop plus execution of π_{mal}] All parties together execute the following steps (sequentially) :
   - (At τ_2 = RoundTime(3)) Invoke $\pi^{(1)}_{mal}\left(\mathcal{P}, \{x_i, R^{priv}_i\}_{i\in[n]}\right) \rightarrow \{(m_{s,1}, p_{s,1}) : s \in [n]\}$, where $m_{s,1} = x_s \oplus \mathsf{OTP}_s$, and $p_{s,1}$ = NIZK proof of (x_s, OTP_s). Here, x_s is the private input of P_s.
   - (At τ_3 = RoundTime(4)) For all $s, i \in [n], i \neq s$, invoke Claim(sid, i, s, v, 1, $m_{s,1}$, $p_{s,1}$, {}).
   - (At τ_4 = RoundTime(5)) For all $s, i \in [n], i \neq s$, invoke Claim(sid, i, s, v, ⊥, ⊥, ⊥, ⊥). [After execution of this round, the island $\mathcal{P}'_s$ is computed as $P_s \bigcup_{\forall j\in[n]} \mathcal{P}'_{sj}, \forall s \in [n]$.]
   - For $\rho = 2, \cdots, \rho_c$:
     (a) (At $\tau_{\rho+3}$ = RoundTime(ρ+4)) If the state is not *aborting*, that is, there are no missing claim transactions in the previous round* then execute the following:
       i. (At $\tau_{\rho+4}$ = RoundTime(ρ + 5)) Invoke $\pi^{(\rho)}_{mal}\left(\mathcal{P}'_s, \{(m_{a_j,\rho-1}, p_{a_j,\rho-1}) : j \in [m]\}, \{R^{priv}_j\}_{j\in[m]}\right) \rightarrow \{(m_{a_k,\rho}, p_{a_k,\rho}) : k \in [m]\}$
       ii. (At $\tau_{\rho+5}$ = RoundTime(ρ + 6)) For all $i, k \in [m], i \neq k$, invoke Claim$\left(\mathsf{sid}, u_i, u_k, v, \rho, m_{a_k,\rho}, p_{a_k,\rho}, h^{(\rho-1)}_{\pi_{mal}}\right)$. Here, $h^{(\rho-1)}_{\pi_{mal}}$ = history of the protocol π_{mal} at round $\rho - 1$.
     (b) If the state is *aborting* then break.
6. Every party broadcasts the output of the function $f(x_1, \cdots, x_n)$ (or outputs ⊥ in case of *abort*) and halts.

*In case, $\rho = 2$, two previous rounds are considered.

Fig. 4. Algorithmic description of the KZZ′ compiler. For details see Sect. 3.3.

3.3 Constructing KZZ′ Using Dep_Ref(·) and Claim(·)

In this section, we will give the full description of our compiler KZZ′ using the sub-protocols described in Sect. 3.2. The algorithmic description is given in Fig. 4 (and pictorially in Fig. 5).

The KZZ′ compiler is an $\mathcal{F}^{\mathcal{D}}_{CORR}$-hybrid protocol that transforms π_{mal} into π_{rob} which is secure in the malicious model with identifiable abort having the robustness property, where π_{mal} lacks the robustness property (see Sect. 2 for

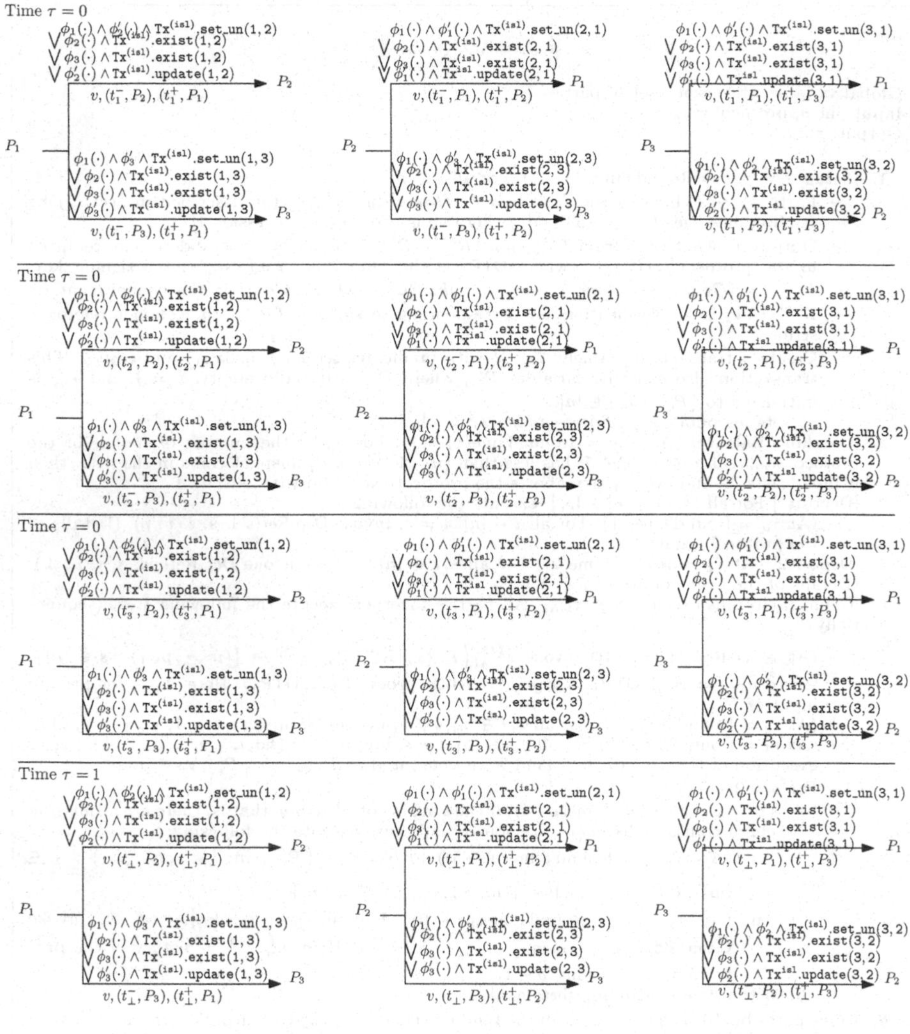

Fig. 5. Pictorial representation of the deposit phase of the KZZ′ compiler.

more details). The KZZ′ compiler consists of following components: (1) *Setup* protocol (2) The MPC execution of π_{mal}, (3) Blockchain execution, namely Dep_Ref(·) and Claim(·).

Suppose, $\mathcal{P} = \{P_1, \cdots, P_n\}$ is the set of parties who want to compute the function $f(x_1, \cdots, x_n)$, where x_i is the private input of party P_i. Let ρ_c be the number of rounds of the protocol π_{mal}.

The general idea of our protocol is that each party first commits to their setup string by creating a deposit transaction for the remaining parties for each round of π_{mal}. This is done before the execution of the π_{mal}. Depending upon the parties who have created the transactions in deposit phase, the protocol creates an island of parties after the first round of claim phase and proceeds among them. Each party can claim the "committed" transactions in some round ρ only if he satisfies the following conditions: (1) the claim transaction is posted corresponding to round ρ, (2) the party has claimed all the previous "committed" transactions made for him, (3) the claim transaction contains valid message for round ρ, and (4) the party has created his deposit transactions for all the rounds.

The protocol proceeds as follows: In a pre-processing (or setup) phase (before choosing their inputs), each party invokes the sampling functionality $\mathcal{F}^{\mathcal{D}}_{CORR}$ (described in Sect. 2) to receive all the random numbers required in the protocol, the *One-time Pad* OTP and the signing key sk_i. The parties also create a transaction $\mathtt{Tx}^{(isl)}$, which creates the *island* for each party. These are done by executing the *Setup* phase, as described in Fig. 4. Every party $P_i \in \mathcal{P}$ checks if it has sufficient fund to execute the protocol. If P_i has insufficient balance, then it broadcasts $\perp$ and every party aborts the protocol execution with output $\perp$. Now, for each round $\rho \in [\rho_c]$ of π_{mal}, each party creates a deposit transaction by invoking $\mathsf{Dep\_Ref}(\cdot)$ (as described in Fig. 3) which commits their randomness for the remaining parties. A party can only claim it if he supplies the proof of existence of his transaction, i.e., he has executed $\mathsf{Dep\_Ref}(\cdot)$ protocol, along with a NIZK proof of statement that the message is correct, i.e., he knows the input and randomness that are consistent with the commitments, $\{Com_j\}_{j\in[n]}$ and the history of the protocol so far, $h^{(\rho-1)}_{\pi_{mal}}$. Each party also creates a separate set of deposit transactions for the remaining parties which can be claimed if they update islands for each party. After creating deposit transactions, each honest party invokes the first-round message of $\pi^{(1)}_{mal}$ and $\mathsf{Claim}(\cdot)$. After execution of this round, the island is computed as $\mathcal{P}'_s = P_s \bigcup_{\forall j\in[n]} \mathcal{P}'_{sj}, \forall s \in [n]$. However, some of the honest parties are added in the corrupt parties island. To remove them from the island, each party updates the island for each pair of parties by creating respective claim transactions. The parties, then, execute $\pi^{(\rho)}_{mal}|_{\mathcal{P}'_i}$ and $\mathsf{Claim}(\cdot)$ round-by-round by revealing the secrets along with the proof of the existence of transactions created by them in deposit phase. If a party $P_{a_k} \in \mathcal{P}'_s$ aborts in some round ρ of claim phase, then every honest party stops executing the protocol, and after the timelock τ^+_ρ, all the deposits from round ρ till ρ_c will be refunded back to the honest parties.

3.4 Comparing the Verification Times of KZZ and KZZ′ Compilers

Verification Time of KZZ. In KZZ protocol [16], for each deposit transaction created by party P_i we will execute the algorithm $\mathsf{Island}(\cdot)$ as described in Algorithm 1. Since, the number of parties and the number of transactions per party are both $O(n)$, the total number of invocations of the algorithm is $O(n^2)$. The time complexity of the Algorithm 1 is $O(n^4)$ which is computed as follows: Line 3 is a loop on round ρ_c that requires $O(1)$ time. Lines 4 and 5 constitute a loop on the number of parties that require $O(n)$ time. Line 6 is a condition to search transactions in *state* that requires $O(n^2)$ time. Therefore, the total verification time of the KZZ compiler: $O(n^4) \times \#$ of invocations $= O(n^6)$.

Algorithm 1. $\mathsf{Island}(\mathsf{sid}, \mathcal{P}, P_{n+1}, \rho_c, i)$

1 $\mathcal{P}^{+1} = \mathcal{P} \cup \{P_{n+1}\}$
2 $\mathcal{P}_i^{+1} = \mathcal{P}^{+1}$
3 **for** $\rho = 1, \rho \leq \rho_c, \rho++$ **do**
4   **for** k *in* $\mathcal{P}_i^{+1}$ **do**
5   **for** j *in* $\mathcal{P}$ **do**
6   **if** *state does not contain transaction with* $\mathsf{arg1}_{k,j,\rho} = (RoundTime(\rho) + \mathsf{max}_{Ledger}, RoundTime(\rho) + 2 \cdot \mathsf{max}_{Ledger} - 1)$, $\mathsf{arg2}_{k,j,\rho} = (\mathsf{sid}, k, j, \rho)$, *and* $\mathsf{aux}_{k,j,\rho} = R^{pub}$ **then**
7   update $\mathcal{P}_i^{+1} = \mathcal{P}_i^{+1} \setminus \{k\}$
8   go to 4
9   **end**
10   **end**
11   **end**
12 **end**

Verification time of KZZ′. In our protocol, for each deposit transaction created by party P_i we will execute the algorithm $\mathsf{Island}'(\cdot)$ as described in Algorithm 2. Since, the number of parties and the number of transactions per party are both $O(n)$, the total number of invocations of the algorithm is $O(n^2)$. The time complexity of the Algorithm 2 is $O(n \log n)$ which is computed as follows: Line 2 is a loop on the set of all deposit transactions $\mathtt{D}$, created by party P_i in Step 3 of Fig. 4, that requires $O(n)$ time. Line 4 is a condition to search transactions in *state* that requires $O(\log n)$ time. Line 5 is adding element by calling $\mathtt{Tx}^{(isl)}\mathtt{.set\_un(i,k)}$ that requires $O(1)$ time. Therefore, the total verification time for island creation: $O(n \log n) \times \#$ of invocations $= O(n^3 \log n)$.

In this way, all the (honest) parties will remain in the island $\mathcal{P}_i' = \{P_i\} \bigcup_{\forall j \in [m]} \mathcal{P}_{ia_j}', \forall i \in [n]$. However, this strategy may add some of the honest parties into the corrupt party's island. This can be handled by executing the algorithm $\mathsf{Update\_Island}'(\cdot)$ as described in Algorithm 3. Since, the number of parties and the number of transactions per party are both $O(n)$, the total number of invocations of the algorithm is $O(n^2)$. The time complexity of the Algorithm 3 is $O(n \log n)$ which is computed as follows: Line 1 is a loop on the set of all deposit transactions $\mathtt{D}'$, created by party P_i in Step 4 of Fig. 4, that requires $O(n)$ time. Line 3 is a condition to search transactions in *state* that requires $O(\log n)$ time. Line 4 is updating the sub-island by calling $\mathtt{Tx}^{(isl)}\mathtt{.update(i,k)}$ that requires $O(1)$ time. Therefore, the total verification time for updating island: $O(n \log n) \times \#$ of invocations $= O(n^3 \log n)$. Therefore, the total verification time of our protocol: Verification time for island creation + Verification time for updating island $= O(n^3 \log n)$.

Algorithm 2. $\mathsf{Island}'(\mathsf{sid}, \mathcal{P}, \rho_c, i, \mathtt{D}, \mathtt{Tx}^{(\mathtt{isl})})$

For all $i, s \in [n], \begin{cases} \mathcal{P}'_{is} = \{\}, & \text{if } i \neq s \\ \mathcal{P}'_{ii} = \{P_i\}, & \text{if } i = s \end{cases}$

for d *in* $\mathtt{D}$ **do**

  Determine P_k and ρ from d

  if *state contains transaction with* $\mathit{arg1}_{i,k,\rho} = (\mathit{RoundTime}(\rho) + \mathsf{max}_{\mathit{Ledger}}, \mathit{RoundTime}(\rho) + 2 \cdot \mathsf{max}_{\mathit{Ledger}} - 1)$, $\mathit{arg2}_{i,k,\rho} = (\mathit{sid}, i, k, \rho)$, *and predicate* $\phi_\rho(\cdot)$ **then**

    call $\mathtt{Tx}^{(\mathtt{isl})}.\mathtt{set\_un}(\mathtt{i}, \mathtt{k})$

  end

end

Algorithm 3. $\mathsf{Update\_Island}'(\mathsf{sid}, \mathcal{P}, \rho_c, i, \mathtt{D}, \mathtt{Tx}^{(\mathtt{isl})})$

---

for d *in* $\mathtt{D}'$ **do**

  Determine P_k and ρ from d

  if *state contains transaction with* $\mathit{arg1}_{i,k,\rho} = (\mathit{RoundTime}(\rho) + \mathsf{max}_{\mathit{Ledger}}, \mathit{RoundTime}(\rho) + 2 \cdot \mathsf{max}_{\mathit{Ledger}} - 1)$, $\mathit{arg2}_{i,k,\rho} = (\mathit{sid}, i, k, \rho)$, *and predicate* $\phi_\rho(\cdot)$ **then**

    call $\mathtt{Tx}^{(\mathtt{isl})}.\mathtt{update}(\mathtt{i}, \mathtt{k})$

  end

end

---

4 Feasibility of Implementing KZZ′ Using Ethereum Contracts

In this section, we will mention the feasibility of implementing our construction using Ethereum smart contracts. First, we note that, unlike KZZ, our protocols $\mathsf{Dep\_Ref}(\cdot)$ and $\mathsf{Claim}(\cdot)$ can be directly executed in ethereum by creating an *externally-owned* account and *contract* account.

In order to create deposit transactions, each party will create a *contract* account that will transfer v ether to the receiver if he satisfies the predicates. The special features of our deposit transactions are (1) $\mathtt{Tx}^{(\mathtt{isl})}$ stores data inside its contract which can be accessed using $(\mathsf{Tx}^{(\mathsf{isl})}.\mathsf{storage}[\cdot])$, (2) It calls another *contract* account in response to the claim transactions that they receive. The refund/claim transactions can be, simply, created in the form of *externally-owned* account as they have no code associated with them.

Now, we will describe how transactions are validated and processed in ethereum. Claim transactions (or *message-call* transaction) are processed by the miners in a straight-forward manner by debiting v ether from $\mathit{address}_s$ account and crediting to $\mathit{address}_i$ account if the supplied signature σ_i and witnesses are valid. Time-locked transactions having time-intervals $(\tau_\rho^-, \tau_\rho^+)$ are put on hold for verification until the specified time-interval (however no credit or debit is applied). If a claim transaction has been issued between time-interval $(\tau_\rho^-, \tau_\rho^+)$

and all the witnesses are valid then the amount v is removed from hold, debited from $address_s$ account and credited in the $address_i$ account. Otherwise, after $time = \tau_\rho^+$, the refund transaction becomes valid, and the amount v is debited from $address_s$ account and credited to $address_s$ account.

5 Robustness Proof of KZZ′ Compiler

The main ingredient for proving the robustness property of KZZ′ is the following lemma.

Lemma 1. *In the protocol π_{rob}, any party P_i can claim a deposit transaction T_y, created by party P_j, $j \neq i$, if he has created his deposit transaction with appropriate setup.*

Proof sketch. In order to prove that a particular transaction, say T_x, is P_i's deposit transaction, the following statements need to be verified.

1. P_i has indeed created T_x.
2. The output script of T_x contains the predicate $\phi_\rho(\cdot)$.
3. P_i is added in the sub-island $\mathcal{P}'_{ji}$ (i.e., $\mathtt{Tx}^{(\mathtt{isl})}.\mathsf{set\_un}(j,i)$ has returned 1).

OR P_i exists in the sub-island $\mathcal{P}'_{ji}$ (i.e., $\mathtt{Tx}^{(\mathtt{isl})}.\mathsf{exist}(j,i)$ has returned 1).

If P_i is able to claim the deposit transaction then it implies that the above statements are true. This automatically implies that P_i has created his deposit transaction similar to P_j's deposit transaction. Thus, the lemma is proved. □

Theorem 1 (Robustness Property [16]**).** *Let $\mathcal{F}$ be the functionality that realizes an arbitrary function $f(\cdot)$ in the ideal world. Suppose $\mathcal{W}(\mathcal{F})$ is the wrapper functionality of $\mathcal{F}$. The π_{rob} protocol, as described in Fig. 4, in the $\mathcal{F}_{CORR}^{\mathcal{D}}$-hybrid world realizes the wrapper functionality $\mathcal{W}(\mathcal{F})$ with robust compensation.*

Proof sketch. We first sketch the simulator $\mathcal{S}$, and prove that the π_{rob} protocol is simulatable, that is, for all PPT adversary $\mathcal{A}$ and the environment $\mathcal{Z}$, the execution of π_{rob} in the $\mathcal{F}_{\text{CORR}}^{\mathcal{D}}$-hybrid world and the simulated execution in the ideal world are indistinguishable. The simulator $\mathcal{S}$ simulates in the ideal world as follows: If the protocol aborts, as some party has insufficient unspent coins, before the parties make their transactions, then the simulator can easily simulate such an abort, as he just needs to check the state and see, if all the honest parties have sufficient coins to play the protocol. Now, we will show the simulation for the remainder of the protocol. Initially, the simulator $\mathcal{S}$ internally simulates the sampling functionality, and computes the islands for all parties. It is sufficient to provide a simulator for honest party's island as there is no guarantee given for corrupt party's island by Q-robustness. Now to execute π_{mal}, the simulator invokes $\mathsf{S}_{\pi_{mal}}$ that computes the messages for honest parties (note that the simulator receives the messages for the corrupt parties from the adversary $\mathcal{A}$). If $\mathsf{S}_{\pi_{mal}}$ sends "abort" then the simulator $\mathcal{S}$ sends "abort" to the wrapped functionality $\mathcal{W}(\mathcal{F})$, and all the honest parties will claim their money back. The soundness of the simulation of $\mathsf{S}_{\pi_{mal}}$ ensures that the output of the parties and the contents of the state in the real and the ideal worlds are indistinguishable. Now, to complete the simulation, and to deliver the relevant output to the honest parties, we need to ensure the following. (1) If the state is not *aborting* within the island, then all the honest parties will claim all the transactions made for them by the parties in the island, and will have zero balance, (2) If a (corrupt) party is not there in an honest party's island, then he will not be able to claim the transaction made to him by the honest party (because of Lemma 1). Hence, all the transactions will be refunded to the honest parties. (3) If the state is *aborting* within the island, then there can be two possible cases: (i) Some party P_i has broadcast an inconsistent message in round ρ. In other words, the verification of the predicate $\phi_\rho(\cdot)$ using (private) verification key of P_j has returned 0. In this case, all the honest parties know the identity of the aborting party P_i; (ii) Some party P_i has *not* created the claim transaction in round ρ. In both the cases, all the honest parties will claim all the deposit transactions made to them in round ρ (as they honestly execute their protocol) while P_i will not be able to claim the transactions made to him in round ρ, hence, each honest party will gain v coins. Since the protocol aborted because of P_i in round ρ, hence, the honest parties will get a refund of all the transactions that they made for rounds $\rho, \rho+1, \cdots, \rho_c$. Thus, the honest parties will gain at least v coins as required by Q-robustness. □

6 Conclusion

In this paper, we have improved the verification time of KZZ protocol that computes an arbitrary function in a multiparty setting. We achieve this by observing a crucial property that deposit transactions of KZZ can be generated from each other; thereby, the verification time can be sped up by bypassing the exhaustive searches at certain points on the execution path of KZZ. This trick can potentially be used in various other similar protocols. As much as it is useful in certain cases, unfortunately, these methods are prohibitive in various other scenarios, especially, where deposit transactions contain independent information, that is, they cannot be generated from one another.

Acknowledgement. The second author is supported by Tata Consultancy Services (TCS) research fellowship. We thank anonymous reviewers for their constructive comments.

References

1. Litecoin. https://litecoin.org/. Accessed 15 Apr 2018
2. Andrychowicz, M., Dziembowski, S., Malinowski, D., Mazurek, Ł.: Fair two-party computations via bitcoin deposits. In: Böhme, R., Brenner, M., Moore, T., Smith, M. (eds.) FC 2014. LNCS, vol. 8438, pp. 105–121. Springer, Heidelberg (2014). https://doi.org/10.1007/978-3-662-44774-1_8

3. Andrychowicz, M., Dziembowski, S., Malinowski, D., Mazurek, Ł.: Secure multiparty computations on bitcoin. In: 2014 IEEE Symposium on Security and Privacy (SP), pp. 443–458. IEEE (2014)
4. Asharov, G., Lindell, Y., Zarosim, H.: Fair and efficient secure multiparty computation with reputation systems. In: Sako, K., Sarkar, P. (eds.) ASIACRYPT 2013. LNCS, vol. 8270, pp. 201–220. Springer, Heidelberg (2013). https://doi.org/10.1007/978-3-642-42045-0_11
5. Asokan, N., Schunter, M., Waidner, M.: Optimistic protocols for fair exchange. In: Proceedings of the 4th ACM Conference on Computer and Communications Security, pp. 7–17. ACM (1997)
6. Bartoletti, M., Zunino, R.: Constant-deposit multiparty lotteries on bitcoin. In: Brenner, M., Rohloff, K., Bonneau, J., Miller, A., Ryan, P.Y.A., Teague, V., Bracciali, A., Sala, M., Pintore, F., Jakobsson, M. (eds.) FC 2017. LNCS, vol. 10323, pp. 231–247. Springer, Cham (2017). https://doi.org/10.1007/978-3-319-70278-0_15
7. Bentov, I., Kumaresan, R.: How to use bitcoin to design fair protocols. In: Garay, J.A., Gennaro, R. (eds.) CRYPTO 2014. LNCS, vol. 8617, pp. 421–439. Springer, Heidelberg (2014). https://doi.org/10.1007/978-3-662-44381-1_24
8. Boneh, D., Naor, M.: Timed commitments. In: Bellare, M. (ed.) CRYPTO 2000. LNCS, vol. 1880, pp. 236–254. Springer, Heidelberg (2000). https://doi.org/10.1007/3-540-44598-6_15
9. Cachin, C., Camenisch, J.: Optimistic fair secure computation. In: Bellare, M. (ed.) CRYPTO 2000. LNCS, vol. 1880, pp. 93–111. Springer, Heidelberg (2000). https://doi.org/10.1007/3-540-44598-6_6
10. Cleve, R.: Limits on the security of coin flips when half the processors are faulty. In: Proceedings of the Eighteenth Annual ACM Symposium on Theory of Computing, pp. 364–369. ACM (1986)
11. Dwork, C., Naor, M.: Pricing via processing or combatting junk mail. In: Brickell, E.F. (ed.) CRYPTO 1992. LNCS, vol. 740, pp. 139–147. Springer, Heidelberg (1993). https://doi.org/10.1007/3-540-48071-4_10
12. Garay, J., Katz, J., Maurer, U., Tackmann, B., Zikas, V.: Rational protocol design: cryptography against incentive-driven adversaries. In: 2013 IEEE 54th Annual Symposium on Foundations of Computer Science (FOCS), pp. 648–657. IEEE (2013)
13. Garay, J., MacKenzie, P., Prabhakaran, M., Yang, K.: Resource fairness and composability of cryptographic protocols. In: Halevi, S., Rabin, T. (eds.) TCC 2006. LNCS, vol. 3876, pp. 404–428. Springer, Heidelberg (2006). https://doi.org/10.1007/11681878_21
14. Goldreich, O., Micali, S., Wigderson, A.: How to play any mental game. In: Proceedings of the Nineteenth Annual ACM Symposium on Theory of Computing, pp. 218–229. ACM (1987)
15. Ishai, Y., Ostrovsky, R., Zikas, V.: Secure multi-party computation with identifiable abort. In: Garay, J.A., Gennaro, R. (eds.) CRYPTO 2014. LNCS, vol. 8617, pp. 369–386. Springer, Heidelberg (2014). https://doi.org/10.1007/978-3-662-44381-1_21
16. Kiayias, A., Zhou, H.-S., Zikas, V.: Fair and Robust multi-party computation using a global transaction ledger. In: Fischlin, M., Coron, J.-S. (eds.) EUROCRYPT 2016. LNCS, vol. 9666, pp. 705–734. Springer, Heidelberg (2016). https://doi.org/10.1007/978-3-662-49896-5_25
17. Kumaresan, R., Bentov, I.: How to use bitcoin to incentivize correct computations. In: Proceedings of the 2014 ACM SIGSAC Conference on Computer and Communications Security, pp. 30–41. ACM (2014)

18. Kumaresan, R., Moran, T., Bentov, I.: How to use bitcoin to play decentralized poker. In: Proceedings of the 22nd ACM SIGSAC Conference on Computer and Communications Security, pp. 195–206. ACM (2015)
19. Kumaresan, R., Vaikuntanathan, V., Vasudevan, P.N.: Improvements to secure computation with penalties. In: Proceedings of the 2016 ACM SIGSAC Conference on Computer and Communications Security, pp. 406–417. ACM (2016)
20. Miller, A., Bentov, I.: Zero-collateral lotteries in bitcoin and ethereum. In: 2017 IEEE European Symposium on Security and Privacy Workshops (EuroS&PW), pp. 4–13. IEEE (2017)
21. Nakamoto, S.: Bitcoin: a peer-to-peer electronic cash system. Consulted **1**(2012), 28 (2008)
22. Pass, R., Shelat, A.: Micropayments for decentralized currencies. In: Proceedings of the 22nd ACM SIGSAC Conference on Computer and Communications Security, pp. 207–218. ACM (2015)
23. Pass, R., Seeman, L., Shelat, A.: Analysis of the Blockchain protocol in asynchronous networks. In: Coron, J.-S., Nielsen, J.B. (eds.) EUROCRYPT 2017. LNCS, vol. 10211, pp. 643–673. Springer, Cham (2017). https://doi.org/10.1007/978-3-319-56614-6_22
24. Peyrott, S.: An introduction to ethereum and smart contracts: a programmable blockchain. https://auth0.com/blog/an-introduction-to-ethereum-and-smart-contracts-part-2/. Accessed 30 Jan 2018
25. Poon, J., Dryja, T.: The bitcoin lightning network: Scalable off-chain instant payments. Draft version 0.5, 14 January 2016
26. Ruffing, T., Kate, A., Schröder, D.: Liar, liar, coins on fire!: penalizing equivocation by loss of bitcoins. In: Proceedings of the 22nd ACM SIGSAC Conference on Computer and Communications Security, pp. 219–230. ACM (2015)
27. Seito, T., Aikawa, T., Shikata, J., Matsumoto, T.: Information-theoretically secure key-insulated multireceiver authentication codes. In: Bernstein, D.J., Lange, T. (eds.) AFRICACRYPT 2010. LNCS, vol. 6055, pp. 148–165. Springer, Heidelberg (2010). https://doi.org/10.1007/978-3-642-12678-9_10
28. Swanson, C.M., Stinson, D.R.: Unconditionally secure signature schemes revisited. In: Fehr, S. (ed.) ICITS 2011. LNCS, vol. 6673, pp. 100–116. Springer, Heidelberg (2011). https://doi.org/10.1007/978-3-642-20728-0_10
29. Wood, G.: Ethereum: a secure decentralised generalised transaction ledger. Ethereum Proj. Yellow Pap. **151**, 1–32 (2014)
30. Yao, A.C.: Protocols for secure computations. In: FOCS, pp. 160–164. IEEE (1982)

Symmetric-Key Cryptography

Distributed Time-Memory Tradeoff Attacks on Ciphers
(with Application to Stream Ciphers and Counter Mode)

Howard M. Heys(✉)

Memorial University of Newfoundland, St. John's, Canada
hheys@mun.ca

Abstract. In this paper, we consider the implications of parallelizing time-memory tradeoff attacks using a large number of distributed processors. It is shown that Hellman's original tradeoff method and the Biryukov-Shamir attack on stream ciphers, which incorporates data into the tradeoff, can be effectively distributed to reduce both time and memory, while other approaches are less advantaged in a distributed approach. Distributed tradeoff attacks are specifically discussed as applied to stream ciphers and the counter mode operation of block ciphers, where their feasibility is considered in relation to distributed exhaustive key search. In particular, for counter mode with an unpredictable initial count, we show that distributed tradeoff attacks are applicable, but can be made infeasible if the entropy of the initial count is at least as large as the key. In general, the analyses of this paper illustrate the effectiveness of a distributed tradeoff approach and show that, when enough processors are involved in the attack, it is possible some systems, such as lightweight cipher implementations, may be susceptible to attack in practice.

Keywords: Cryptanalysis · Time-memory tradeoff attacks
Block ciphers · Stream ciphers · Counter mode

1 Introduction

Time-memory tradeoff (TMTO) attacks were first introduced by Hellman [1] to attack block ciphers using a chosen plaintext or easily predicted known plaintext. The basic concept involves two phases: Before system operation begins, the *preprocessing* (or offline) phase prepares a compact table from chains representing information from (almost) all keys, while the *online* phase efficiently searches the table in an attempt to identify which key is used to encrypt during system operation. Following Hellman's work, Babbage [2] and Golić [3] independently showed that a time-memory-data tradeoff based on the birthday paradox was applicable to stream ciphers by attacking the stream cipher state, rather than the key. This was subsequently combined with Hellman's approach by Biryukov and Shamir [4] to develop another, more flexible, tradeoff involving data and

W. Susilo and G. Yang (Eds.): ACISP 2018, LNCS 10946, pp. 135–153, 2018.
https://doi.org/10.1007/978-3-319-93638-3_9

targeting the stream cipher state. This approach was then extended by Hong and Sarkar [5] to attack directly the key and initialization vector (IV) of stream ciphers, as well as being applied to some block cipher modes.

Numerous papers have refined Hellman's approach trying various methods to improve the success rate and reduce the attack complexity. Most notably, the distinguished points method, attributed to Rivest in [6], can be used to minimize costly memory accesses, while the rainbow table method can be used to minimize memory accesses and improve the speed of the table search [7].

Although the concept of distributed cryptanalytic attacks is well known, no paper has systematically characterized the value of distributed time-memory tradeoff attacks. In this paper, we examine tradeoff expressions for a number of distributed TMTO approaches using the number of processors as a tradeoff parameter. Further, we explicitly examine the applicability of distributed TMTO attacks to stream ciphers and the counter mode operation of block ciphers.

2 Background on Time-Memory Tradeoff Attacks

In our discussion, complexities are given for time, memory, and data and the units of these complexities may differ by a modest multiplicative constant when comparing approaches. Time and memory complexities are often represented in units equivalent to the number of encryption operations and the number of key pairs stored, respectively, while data complexities are sometimes expressed as the number of contiguous bits of data or the number of data blocks, with each block corresponding to a unique IV. Also, as is usually done, we assume that when an algorithm complexity involves a factor that is logarithmic in a parameter, this factor is small enough to be ignored.

2.1 Hellman's Attack

The basic TMTO attack on block ciphers introduced by Hellman [1] works because memory is saved by storing in a table just the start and end of chains generated during the preprocessing phase, such that, in the online phase, the table can be efficiently searched while walking through a chain starting with the data captured from the system. As a result, the preprocessing phase requires a time complexity that is equivalent to the size of the key space, while the online time complexity and the memory complexity can be substantially less than the size of the key space.

The preprocessing phase of Hellman's approach involves constructing a table consisting of t subtables, each subtable consisting of m chains of keys of length t. Each chain is constructed by using a chaining function to map a cipher output to the next key input, using a fixed plaintext as input to the cipher in each step. Each subtable uses a different chaining function and picks m arbitrary keys as starting points for the chains. Only the first and last keys in a chain need to be stored, with the key pairs in a subtable sorted according to the last key, for easy search during the online phase of the attack. The table should cover most of the key space, thus requiring a so-called stopping criterion of $mt^2 = K$, where K is the size of the key space. Because only the start and end of each chain is stored, the table requires a memory complexity of $M = mt$.

During the online phase, a subtable is searched by producing a chain of length t, starting from the intercepted ciphertext (produced by the plaintext used to the build the table). At each step in the chain, if the key is found to be one of the stored last keys of a chain in the subtable, then the cipher key can be determined by proceeding from the starting key of the chain until the ciphertext is generated. The corresponding key is very likely to be the correct cipher key. A chain is built for each of t subtables and, hence, the online time complexity is given by $T = t^2$.

Subsequently, it can be derived that the following tradeoff exists:

$$TM^2 = K^2. \tag{1}$$

The preprocessing time, P, is determined by the time to construct the table given by mt^2, and, hence, due to the stopping criterion relationship, $P = K$. Hellman uses the example that, if $T = M$, then both online time and memory are smaller than the key space and, in fact, $T = M = K^{2/3}$.

2.2 Babbage-Golić (BG) Tradeoff

Both Babbage [2] and Golić [3] independently proposed a tradeoff attack on stream ciphers, referred to as the BG attack. Assume that the size of the stream cipher's state space is N. A keystream prefix is a $\log_2 N$ sequence of keystream bits corresponding to the state at which the prefix starts. The BG tradeoff works by constructing, during preprocessing, a table of N/D pairs of the state and the corresponding keystream prefix. A total of $D + \log_2 N - 1 \approx D$ bits of keystream are acquired in the online phase resulting in the determination of D keystream prefixes, using a sliding window. Due to the birthday paradox, with high probability, one of the D keystream prefixes can be found in the table and the corresponding state derived, thus breaking the cipher.

For this attack, the tradeoff expression, involving online time complexity T and memory complexity M, is

$$TM = N \tag{2}$$

where $T = D$, $M = N/D$, and the preprocessing time complexity is $P = N/D$. Due to this attack, it is prudent to ensure that the state of the stream cipher (in bits) should be at least twice as large as the key (in bits) (i.e., $N \geq K^2$) to ensure that $T \geq K$ or $M \geq K$.

Note that a recent direction of research in the design of stream ciphers is to develop structures to provide security using a state with a size that is less than double the key size. The objective of such research is to minimize the hardware complexity of the ciphers. Designs to do this have been proposed by having the state update be a function of key [8,9] or by using a specific initialization approach and applying packet mode where the amount of keystream generated under one IV is constrained [10]. We do not address these designs in our discussion.

2.3 Biryukov-Shamir (BS) Tradeoff

In [4], Biryukov and Shamir combined Hellman's table and the BG tradeoff use of data to develop a new tradeoff involving time, memory, and data, applicable to stream ciphers. In the BS tradeoff, the Hellman table is derived from chains on the cipher state, rather than the key. During preprocessing, a total of t/D subtables are constructed, with each covering m chains of length t, for which only the first and last states are stored. Variable D represents the amount of data in the form of contiguous keystream bits used in the attack and now the memory complexity is $M = mt/D$. The preprocessing complexity is thus $P = N/D$, where $mt^2 = N$ is the stopping criterion for constructing the table.

During the online phase, t steps through the chain must be executed, with each of the t/D subtables being searched and this must be done for each of the D prefixes derived from a sliding window over the D bits. Hence, the online time takes $T = t(t/D)D = t^2$. As a result, the tradeoff in this case becomes

$$TM^2D^2 = N^2. \tag{3}$$

It should be noted that to ensure there is at least one complete subtable, it is assumed that $D \leq t$ and therefore the restriction of $D^2 \leq T$ exists. Letting $N \geq K^2$ results in $T \geq K$ or $M \geq K$, thereby ensuring that a BS TMTO attack cannot do better than exhaustive key search.

2.4 Hong-Sarkar (HS) Tradeoff

In [5], Hong and Sarkar explicitly relate the BS tradeoff for stream ciphers to the key and the IV, rather than the state. The key is secret and unknown when building the table during preprocessing and, while the IV is typically public and known during the online phase, it may be unpredictable and therefore also unknown when building the table during preprocessing. The HS tradeoff approach treats the input to be discovered in the tradeoff attack to be the key/IV combination. If the size of the IV space is defined to be V and the IVs to be used by the system are unknown during preprocessing, then the HS approach can be applied to a stream cipher with the tradeoff being

$$TM^2D_{iv}^2 = (KV)^2 \tag{4}$$

where the preprocessing complexity is given by $P = KV/D_{iv}$. The attack has a similar data restriction of $D_{iv}^2 \leq T$ as the BS approach. Note that the D term used in the BS tradeoff of (3) has been replaced by D_{iv} in (4) to emphasize that, rather than D contiguous bits, in fact, D_{iv} represents the number of $\log_2(KV)$ bit prefixes at the start of the keystream for different key/IV combinations.

In theory, each prefix used in the attack must be collected from different key/IV combinations and, hence, success in the attack may mean finding one key from among a number of keys used in encryption. In the single-key scenario, where it is assumed that data is only available from one key, if unpredictable IVs are to be used, then data could be collected from different IVs and the target key. Then the tradeoff of (4) can be applied, where D_{iv} represents the number of IVs under the one key and, hence, $D_{iv} \leq V$.

2.5 Dunkelman-Keller (DK) Approach

The HS tradeoff approach assumes that preprocessing is structured to consider the combination of key and IV as one input and builds the table based on this, resulting in the restriction on data. However, the HS method of attack does not take advantage of the fact that, during the online phase, the IV is known and only the key needs to be discovered. In [11], Dunkelman and Keller modify the HS approach by separating the key and IV in the attack. The preprocessing phase then builds a number of Hellman tables to cover keys, with each table built for a particular IV. This allows the online phase of the attack to simply consider whether an intercepted IV has been used to build a table. If so, the table corresponding to this IV can be searched for the key. In this approach, which we refer to as the DK approach, assuming equally likely occurences of any IV, if V/D_{iv} tables, each corresponding to a different IV, are built during preprocessing, then collected data from D_{iv} IVs during the online phase should result in one of the intercepted IVs being used in the tables with high probability. For this tradeoff, $M = (V/D_{iv})mt$ and $T = t^2$, where the stopping criterion of $mt^2 = K^2$ applies to the Hellman tables. Hence, the DK method has the tradeoff expression of (4) if the IV is unpredictable, but now has no restriction on the data, D_{iv}, other than $D_{iv} \leq V$ in the single-key scenario. Further, this approach has an advantage for applications where the IV is unpredictable but not equally likely in distribution, as this knowledge can be used to build tables for the most likely IVs.

2.6 Other Work on TMTO Attacks

We shall consider in our work both the distinguished points and rainbow table refinements of Hellman's TMTO attack. These refinements and their relative merits in terms of probability of success, detailed complexity analyses, and other practical performance related issues, are studied in a number of papers including [12–14]. The results of these comparisons indicate that these practical performance issues do not seem to have substantial implications (i.e., orders of magnitude effects on complexity) and, hence, we do not consider them significant for our discussion on distributed TMTO attacks.

It is known that it is possible to parallelize TMTO attacks. For example, distributed attacks are mentioned in [15] where it is noted that it is possible to divide the Hellman subtables into groupings and circulate to participating processors. Parallelizing TMTO attacks is further studied in [16,17]. However, no work has yet systematically characterized the tradeoff aspects of multiple processors. In our work, we will thoroughly characterize the distributed approach to various forms of time-memory tradeoffs.

3 Distributed Hellman Attack

We now consider the parallelization of Hellman's attack using distributed processors, as well as the related approaches of distinguished points and the rainbow table. We assume that W processors, with independent memory, are available. This might represent, for example, W computers on the Internet with users willing to participate, or being duped into participating, in attacking some cryptographic system. We assume that any necessary communication complexity between these processors and a central controlling processor are negligible in comparison to the time and memory complexities associated with the attack.

In our discussion, we let T_0, M_0, and P_0 represent the online time complexity, memory complexity, and preprocessing time complexity, respectively, for an individual processor. It is these quantities, along with W, which determine the efficacy of the attack, since it is assumed that the individual processors can operate concurrently. For example, while a non-distributed attack might require an online time complexity of T, if it is possible to spread this work evenly between W processors, each processor would only require a time of $T_0 = T/W$, which could be done concurrently for all processors, and thus the overall duration of the attack could be dramatically reduced if W is large. As a point of comparison for distributed tradeoff attacks, we consider distributed exhaustive key search, which is expected to have a time complexity for an individual processor of $T_0 = K/W$ (with, of course, no preprocessing phase and negligible memory complexity).

3.1 Distributed Approach to the Original Hellman Attack

A distributed approach to Hellman's TMTO attack can proceed by distributing the responsibility for generating the t subtables to the W processors, so that each processor generates t/W subtables independently. When the necessary ciphertext data is captured during system operation, it will be distributed to all processors. Each processor will require a memory of M_0, where $M_0 = m(t/W) = M/W$ and M is the total memory requirement for the attack, with $W \leq t$ in order to ensure that each processor generates one or more subtables.

Since each processor only needs to implement t encryptions for each of t/W subtables, the time taken in a processor (and, if all processors operate concurrently, the overall time to search the full Hellman table) is $T_0 = t(t/W) = T/W$, where T is the time required for the non-distributed attack. When a key is found by a processor in its share of the table, it must communicate this back to the central processor that is overseeing the cryptanalytic process and that will be able to announce the successful completion of the attack.

Now $T_0 M_0^2 = (t^2/W)(mt/W)^2 = (mt^2)^2/W^3$ and assuming the Hellman stopping criterion of $mt^2 = K$ results in the tradeoff for an individual processor to be

$$T_0 M_0^2 W^3 = K^2 \tag{5}$$

where the constraint $W \leq t$, or equivalently $W \leq T_0$, applies. This expression captures the tradeoff of interest in a distributed Hellman attack and reflects that both time and memory can be improved by a factor of W. The preprocessing time for an individual processor is $P_0 = K/W$ and is improved by a factor of W over the time required in the non-distributed attack, since each processor only needs to construct chains covering a fraction of the table. Although we notate this as the preprocessing cost of the individual processor, if we assume that all processors compute their tables concurrently, it also reflects the overall time complexity to prepare for the attack.

It is clear that using a number of processors to implement the attack potentially provides a very significant advantage and may actually make the attack possible in some practical scenarios. Although exhaustive key search can also be improved by a distributed approach, a distributed TMTO attack preserves the possibility for a significantly faster online processing time at the expense of more memory. Consider the following example applying to an implementation of AES-128 for which $K = 2^{128}$. Letting $W = 2^{20}$, the non-distributed exhaustive key search would require $T = 2^{128}$, while the distributed exhaustive key search would require $T_0 = 2^{108}$. In the case of a Hellman TMTO attack with equal online time and memory complexity, the non-distributed attack would take $T = M = 2^{85.3}$ (with $P = 2^{128}$), while the distributed approach would require $T_0 = M_0 = 2^{65.3}$ (with $P_0 = 2^{108}$). As another example, consider a lightweight block cipher with an 80-bit key so that $K = 2^{80}$. In this case, with $W = 2^{20}$, a distributed TMTO attack exists with $T_0 = M_0 = 2^{33.3}$ (and $P_0 = 2^{60}$), which is substantially less complex than the $T_0 = 2^{60}$ required for a distributed exhaustive key search.

3.2 Distributed Distinguished Points (DP) Method

One of the issues identified for the Hellman TMTO attack is that the cost of a memory access can vary by orders of magnitude depending on whether the access is to internal memory (RAM) or to an external memory (e.g. hard disk drive or a solid state drive) [18]. In order to mitigate the cost of slow memory accesses, the distinguished points (DP) method was proposed by Rivest [6]. In this approach, rather than build chains of fixed length t when constructing a Hellman table, the preprocessing phase can build a chain which terminates when a particular pattern (e.g. all zeroes) is recognized in the first $\log_2 t$ bits of the key. This means the length of a chain is variable but will be a length of t on average. When executing the online portion of the attack, since the end point of a chain must start with $\log_2 t$ zeroes, only about $1/t$ encryptions needs a look up to be executed in the subtable (which is likely stored in slow access external memory).

In the distributed Hellman attack, it is fully possible to execute the distinguished points approach to the attack. The amount of memory in a processor is still fixed at $M_0 = mt/W$, since there are t subtables split between the W processors. However, the time required to finish the concurrent computations of W processors is now more complex. Since there is an average of t steps in each chain, the number of encryptions per subtable must be more than t to cope with chains having more than t steps. Assume that, at most, γt encryptions are executed for each subtable. The DP method is likely to set γ to be a modest value, to keep the time complexity of the attack constrained. When preparing the table during the preprocessing phase, the DP method will stop a chain when a distinguished point is found or when γt steps in a chain have been reached without hitting a distinguished point. Similarly, during the online process, if, after γt encryptions, a distinguished point is not reached for a subtable, the subtable is assumed to not contain the key. Of course, the value used for γ affects the probability of success, but as shown in [13], γ can effectively be a small constant. Hence, the online time complexity can be no worse than the maximum chain length, γt, multiplied by the number of subtables to search through, t/W, and, hence, $T_0 = \gamma t^2/W$ where T_0 now represents the maximum possible time taken at an individual processor.

This leads to a tradeoff of the form $T_0 M_0^2 W^3 = \gamma K^2$ which is slightly worse than the distributed Hellman tradeoff of (5). However, it is quite possible that implementing the distinguished points method when using a distributed approach will not be necessary. Since the memory size needed in the individual processors in a distributed attack is reduced by a factor of W, it is quite conceivable for some parameters that the processor memory complexity of M_0 is small enough that the processor's complete table portion could be stored in internal memory and slow accesses to external memory are not needed. In such a case, there would be no need to implement the DP approach.

3.3 Distributed Rainbow Table Method

In [7], Oechslin proposed an alternate formulation to represent the key chains in the TMTO attack. Hellman's approach was to use one chaining function for every step of a chain and for all the chains in one subtable, with different subtables then using different chaining functions. In contrast, the rainbow table approach uses a different chaining function for each step of the chain and then builds one table of such chains. It is argued that there are improvements to Hellman's approach [7,19]. For the online phase, t partial chains of length $\leq t$ are produced, starting with the intercepted ciphertext, requiring $t^2/2$ encryptions in total. Ignoring the somewhat insignificant factor of $1/2$ in the number of encryptions gives $T \approx t^2$ and results in the same tradeoff expression as in (1). However, since only at the end of one of the partial chains is it necessary to look up in the table, only t memory accesses to the table are required.

The distributed rainbow table approach can be accomplished by distributing the table so that $M_0 = mt/W = M/W$. However, for each processor, the time complexity involves reproducing t partial chains for a total of $T_0 = t^2/2 \approx t^2$ encryptions required in each processor. Hence, the time complexity cannot be improved by distributing the table since each processor must take $\sim t^2$ to consider their portion of the table, i.e., $T_0 = T$. The resulting tradeoff expression is

$$T_0 M_0^2 W^2 = K^2. \tag{6}$$

Rather than divide up the rainbow table between processors, an alternative approach for a distributed rainbow table attack would be to distribute the computation of t partial chains between W processors. In this case, $T_0 \approx t(t/W)$ would represent the online time complexity (again ignoring the factor of $1/2$). However, the resulting distributed computations would need to be checked in one central table. In this case, $T_0 = T/W$, but $M_0 = M = mt$. Hence, the tradeoff becomes even worse as

$$T_0 M_0^2 W = K^2. \quad (7)$$

For the rainbow table approach, distributing the table and the computations is not feasible, since the end of each partial chain must be looked up in the full table. Hence, the distributed rainbow table approach is inferior to the distributed version of the original Hellman TMTO approach. In addition, when applying a distributed approach to time-memory tradeoffs, since the memory requirements could be substantially smaller on a per processor basis, reducing memory accesses (one of the advantages of the rainbow table) may not be important, since the necessary subtables of the Hellman approach may fit within a processor's RAM.

4 Applying Distributed TMTO Attacks on Stream Ciphers

In this section, we consider the application of distributed TMTO attacks to stream ciphers.

4.1 Distributed BG Attack

We first consider the distributed BG attack, which makes use of data collected and assumes D bits of keystream are available. In this case, the attack can be distributed by dividing up the work to prepare, and the memory to store, the BG table to W processors, so that $P_0 = N/(DW)$ and $M_0 = N/(DW)$. The time required in a processor during the online phase is directly proportional to the processing of all D prefixes, so that $T_0 = D$, which is unchanged from the non-distributed case. As a result, it can be shown that

$$T_0 M_0 W = N. \quad (8)$$

For a non-distributed attack, letting $N \geq K^2$ ensures that the BG tradeoff does not lead to a better attack than exhaustive key search. Placing this constraint on the stream cipher leads to the following proposition for the distributed BG attack.

Proposition 1
If $N \geq K^2$, there is no value of W for which a distributed BG TMTO attack on a stream cipher has a lower complexity for both online time and memory than the complexity of distributed exhaustive key search.

Proof
A distributed exhaustive key search has a complexity of K/W. Let $N = aK^2$, where $a \geq 1$. We can now adjust (8) to be $T_0 M_0 W = aK^2$. For the best TMTO

attack, we can minimize the maximum of either T_0 or M_0 in this equation by letting $T_0 = M_0$, leading to

$$T_0 = \frac{a^{1/2}K}{W^{1/2}} \tag{9}$$

which clearly implies $T_0 \geq K/W$ and $M_0 \geq K/W$ for all values of W. Since other tradeoffs lead to one of T_0 or M_0 being larger, there will always be at least one of T_0 or M_0 being at least as large as K/W. Hence, clearly the distributed BG tradeoff cannot have a lower complexity than distributed exhaustive key search for any number of processors. □

4.2 Distributed BS Attack

Consider now the distributed BS attack. With W processors and D contiguous data bits of keystream, the t/D subtables needed in the BS approach can be divided into W groups, resulting in the memory for individual processors being $M_0 = mt/(DW)$, where $W \leq t/D$ in order for each processor to have one or more subtables. The time in an individual processor to process the data and recover the state is given by $T_0 = t{\cdot}(t/(DW)){\cdot}D = t^2/W$, where the first term represents the t encryptions to reproduce a chain from the starting point of the captured data, the middle bracketed term represents the number of subtables to process in each processor, and the last term represents the data that each processor must consider. Combining the expressions for M_0 and T_0 leads to the following tradeoff:

$$T_0 M_0^2 D^2 W^3 = N^2 \tag{10}$$

where the amount of data and the number of processors must satisfy $D^2 W \leq T_0$ (which is derived by combining the constraint on W with the expression for T_0). Since deriving the required subtables determines the preprocessing time in an individual processor, we also have $P_0 = N/(DW)$.

In the following proposition, we show that the constraint of $N \geq K^2$ ensures that the distributed BS attack performs no better than distributed exhaustive key search.

Proposition 2
If $N \geq K^2$, there is no value of W for which a distributed BS TMTO attack on a stream cipher, satisfying the constraint $D^2 W \leq T_0$, has a lower complexity for both online time and memory than the complexity of distributed exhaustive key search.

Proof
Let $N = aK^2$, where $a \geq 1$. Minimizing T_0 and M_0 in the application of the BS tradeoff is done by maximizing the data in the tradeoff. Using the upper bound of $D \leq (T_0/W)^{1/2}$, it can be shown that (10) is equivalent to the tradeoff of $T_0 M_0 W = aK^2$. This is now identical in form to the distributed BG tradeoff of (8) and, hence, the remainder of the proof can follow similarly to the proof of Proposition 1. □

4.3 Distributed HS and DK Attacks

Targeting a stream cipher system which uses a single key and numerous IVs and applying a distributed HS approach results in the tradeoff

$$T_0 M_0^2 D_{iv}^2 W^3 = (KV)^2, \tag{11}$$

where D_{iv} represents the number of prefixes that are derived from the first $\log_2(KV)$ bits of the initial cipher state following the reinitialization from different IVs. The constraints $D_{iv}^2 W \le T_0$ and $D_{iv} \le V$ apply and the preprocessing complexity is $P_0 = (KV)/(D_{iv}W)$.

The distributed DK approach, which builds V/D_{iv} Hellman tables for different IVs results in the same tradeoff as (11), as well as the same constraint of $D_{iv} \le V$ and the same preprocessing complexity of $P_0 = (KV)/(D_{iv}W)$. However, since the DK approach builds a Hellman table to cover just keys (rather than key/IV combinations), we can assume that each processor contains t/W of the Hellman subtables for all of the V/D_{iv} IVs. In this case, $M_0 = (V/D_{iv})m(t/W)$ and $T_0 = t(t/W)$, resulting in (11) with the contraint that $W \le t$, or equivalently $W \le T_0$, since at least one full subtable per IV must be stored in a processor.

Note that the HS and DK approaches of (11) require a total number of bits of data to be about $D_{total} = D_{iv}\mu_{iv}$, where μ_{iv} represents the average number of bits encrypted under one IV (although only the first $\log_2(KV)$ bits of each IV's keystream are used in the attack). Hence, substituting into (11) results in

$$TM^2 D_{total}^2 W^3 = (KV\mu_{iv})^2 \tag{12}$$

where D_{total} is the number of bits collected (although many are discarded) and, while it represents data collected from multiple IVs, it is similar to the D term in (10), implying that (12) is a better tradeoff when $KV\mu_{iv} < N$. In cases where $N = K^2$, which ensures security against BG and BS attacks and minimizes cipher implementation complexity, (12) is the better tradeoff when $V\mu_{iv} < K$. These arguments apply equally to the non-distributed and distributed HS and DK approaches.

5 Applying Distributed TMTO Attacks to Counter Mode

In this section, we describe how distributed TMTO attacks can be applied to counter mode [20]. This is of interest because when a block cipher operates in counter mode, in addition to the key, the initial count value can be unpredictable during the preprocessing phase of TMTO attacks, making the building of the Hellman table more challenging, even when a chosen plaintext approach can be applied during the online phase. When counter mode is operated with a predictable initial count, Hellman's TMTO attack (distributed or non-distributed) can be directly applied by constructing tables for this known initial count.

5.1 Distributed Attack Without Data

In this section, we consider the application of a distributed TMTO attack to counter mode with a single key and an unpredictable initial count. (The non-distributed attack can be considered by simply letting $W = 1$.) Here, we shall use the term IV to refer to the unpredictable portion of the initial count and assume that the non-IV portion is fixed and predictable. We let V represent the number of possible values for the IV and to apply the attack, V Hellman tables to cover the keys are built (using appropriate chaining functions to map the cipher operation output to the next key input), one for each IV. An attack which does not use data in the tradeoff can be performed by dividing the t subtables of the V Hellman tables between the W processors. Letting $\log_2 V$ represent the size of the IV, the tradeoff used in this approach would be a simple modification of (5), where K is replaced by KV:

$$T_0 M_0^2 W^3 = (KV)^2 \tag{13}$$

with $W \leq T_0$ and preprocessing requiring $P_0 = KV/W$ to cover all key/IV combinations across all processors. We now consider an expression which indicates the size of W necessary to allow a TMTO attack to outperform a distributed exhaustive key search. This is equivalent to saying that the online time complexity and memory complexity of the TMTO attack should both be less than K/W. The resulting analysis leads to Proposition 3.

Proposition 3
Consider counter mode such that the key and the IV portion of the initial count are unpredictable during the preprocessing phase and assumed to be randomly drawn from the K and V possible values, respectively. With $T_0 = M_0^r$, a distributed tradeoff approach can be applied to obtain an attack with an online time complexity and memory complexity less than the complexity of distributed exhaustive key search for the following conditions on W:

$$W > \begin{cases} V^{\frac{2}{1-r}}/K^{\frac{r}{1-r}} & ,r < 1 \\ 0 & ,r = 1,\ \text{if } V < K^{1/2} \\ \infty & ,r = 1,\ \text{if } V \geq K^{1/2} \\ K^{\frac{r-2}{2r-2}} V^{\frac{2r}{2r-2}} & ,r > 1 \end{cases} \tag{14}$$

Proof
We need to show the conditions on W for which $T_0 < K/W$ and $M_0 < K/W$. The proof considers the three cases for r. For $r > 1$, $T_0 > M_0$ and, hence, it is sufficient to consider scenarios for $T_0 < K/W$, while for $r < 1$, $M_0 > T_0$, and, therefore, it is sufficient to consider $M_0 < K/W$. For the case of $r = 1$, $T_0 = M_0$ and we can consider a bound on either T_0 or M_0.

From (13), it can be shown that, if $r > 1$, then

$$T_0 = \frac{(KV)^{\frac{2r}{r+2}}}{W^{\frac{3r}{r+2}}} \tag{15}$$

which, when letting $T_0 < K/W$, leads to the result for $r > 1$.

Similarly, for $r < 1$,

$$M_0 = \frac{(KV)^{\frac{2}{r+2}}}{W^{\frac{3}{r+2}}} \tag{16}$$

which, when letting $M_0 < K/W$, leads to the result for $r < 1$.

Finally, letting $T_0 = M_0$, gives

$$T_0 = \frac{(KV)^{2/3}}{W} \tag{17}$$

which, when compared to K/W, results in an inequality not involving W, but which shows that, for $V < K^{1/2}$, the TMTO attack can improve upon distributed exhaustive key search for any W, while, for $V \geq K^{1/2}$, the TMTO attack cannot improve upon distributed exhaustive key search for any W. □

The interpretation of Proposition 3 can be demonstrated by considering the following example where we let $K = 2^{128}$ and $V = 2^{32}$. From Proposition 3, we can determine: (1) if $T_0 = M_0$, then $W > 0$, (2) if $T_0 = M_0^{1/2}$, then $W > 1$, and (3) if $T_0 = M_0^2$, $W > 2^{64}$. So we can conclude that a distributed TMTO attack can be made more efficient than distributed exhaustive key search for cases 1 and 2 by using as few as 1 and 2 processors, respectively, while for case 3, the number of processors must be more than 2^{64}, an impractically large requirement. Hence, for case 3, although it may be theoretically possible to mount a distributed TMTO attack, it is not practical to do so. Other examples for values of K, V and r can be considered to determine their practicality in terms of the number of required processors in a distributed attack.

The following proposition gives the relationship between K and V in order to ensure that it is impossible for a distributed TMTO attack to outperform distributed exhaustive key search for any tradeoff of time and memory (i.e., any r).

Proposition 4

Consider counter mode such that the key and the IV portion of the initial count are unpredictable during the preprocessing phase and assumed to be randomly drawn from the K and V possible values, respectively. If $V \geq K^{1/2}$, the online time complexity or the memory complexity of a distributed TMTO attack (which does not use multiple data) is at least as large as the complexity of a distributed exhaustive key search.

Proof

The best tradeoff from (13) occurs when we minimize the maximum of either T_0 or M_0, which occurs for $T_0 = M_0$, leading to $T_0 = (KV)^{2/3}/W$. If $V \geq K^{1/2}$, in this case clearly $T_0 \geq K/W$ and $M_0 \geq K/W$ for any W, where K/W is the complexity of a distributed exhaustive key search. Reducing T_0 at the expense of M_0 (or vice versa) still clearly results in M_0 (or T_0) being at least K/W. □

Proposition 4 implies that the entropy of the initial count (which is $\log_2 V$ for a random IV) should be at least half the size of the key to ensure security against distributed TMTO attacks, which do not use data. This is also true for non-distributed TMTO attacks, where $W = 1$.

5.2 Incorporating Data into the Attack

Consider now incorporating the use of data into the distributed TMTO attack on a single-key implementation of counter mode. In doing so, the distributed DK approach can be applied and, hence, the tradeoff of (11) can be used, with the constraints $W \leq T_0$ and $D_{iv} \leq V$, and $P_0 = KV/(D_{iv}W)$. Extending Proposition 4 leads to the following proposition.

Proposition 5
Consider counter mode such that the key and the IV portion of the initial count are unpredictable during the preprocessing phase and assumed to be randomly drawn from the K and V possible values, respectively. Assume that a distributed TMTO attack on a single-key system is applied with data available from D_{iv} IVs, where $D_{iv} \leq V$. If $V/D_{iv} \geq K^{1/2}$, the online time complexity or the memory complexity of a distributed TMTO attack is at least as large as the complexity of a distributed exhaustive key search.

Proof
We can simply follow the proof of Proposition 4, but base it on the distributed DK tradeoff of (11), which can be rewritten to be

$$T_0 M_0^2 W^3 = (K[V/D_{iv}])^2. \tag{18}$$

This equation is similar to (13) used in the proof of Proposition 4, except that we have substituted V with V/D_{iv}. Proposition 4 now follows with the same substitution, resulting in the distributed TMTO attack with data not being able to improve on distributed exhaustive key search when $V/D_{iv} \geq K^{1/2}$. □

Proposition 5 increases the lower bound on V for which the distributed TMTO attack becomes infeasible. Assuming that it is impractical for $D_{iv} > K^{1/2}$, then letting $V \geq K$ is sufficient to ensure security against TMTO attacks which make use of data. Now if $D_{iv}W = \alpha V$, where $\alpha > 1$, then $P_0 < K$, meaning the preprocessing time is better than exhaustive search on a cipher with key space K. Further, $T_0 M_0^2 = K^2/(\alpha^2 W) < K^2/W$, which could be substantially better than the tradeoff of the non-distributed approach. Consider the following case of counter mode using AES-128: $K = 2^{128}$, $V = 2^{32}$ and $W = 2^{20}$. If we let $T_0 = M_0$ and $D_{iv} = 2^{20}$ (so that $\alpha = 256$), we get $T_0 = M_0 = 2^{73.3}$, with $P_0 = 2^{120}$. Hence, the complexity of the online phase of the distributed TMTO attack is much better than the complexity of distributed exhaustive key search, which would be $K/W = 2^{108}$. Of course, collecting more data D_{iv} and/or involving more processors W could be used to improve the attack even further, but is still subject to the DK approach constraints of $D_{iv} \leq V$ and $W \leq T_0$.

To this point, we have only considered single-key systems. Note that the concept of attacking a multi-key block cipher system [5, 21] where the cipher uses counter mode can result in the tradeoff (11) targeting the key and unpredictable initial count and may result in some systems being vulnerable.

6 Conclusions

In this paper, we have discussed the characterization of distributed TMTO attacks on ciphers. A summary of the characteristics of tradeoff attacks, including the distributed versions discussed in this paper, is presented in Appendix A. In Appendix B, numerical examples are used to illustrate the effectiveness of the attacks against a lightweight cipher (80-bit key) and an AES-level cipher (128-bit key).

Not surprisingly, distributing Hellman's approach can be highly effective, scaling both time and memory by the number of processors. Other tradeoff approaches such as the rainbow table method and the BG method are not as well suited to a distributed approach. The BS method benefits from a distributed approach in both time and memory, but the benefit of data in the tradeoff is not scaled by the number of processors involved. We have also described the application of distributed tradeoff attacks in relation to stream ciphers and have shown that distributed TMTO approaches can be effectively applied to counter mode in scenarios where the entropy of the initial count is too small. In particular, distributed TMTO attacks are of concern in the context of lightweight cryptography, where key sizes are smaller and the cryptanalytic gain of distributing the attacks could seriously compromise the security of some systems.

Appendix A: Summary of Tradeoffs

Table 1 contains a summary of all tradeoffs discussed and applied in this paper. Tradeoff expressions and preprocessing complexity, as well as target applications and meaningful restrictions on tradeoff parameters, are presented.

Appendix B: Numerical Results for Some Tradeoffs

In this section, we highlight a few cases to illustrate the applicability of the distributed TMTO attack. The data presented considers two key sizes of 80 bits (Table 2) and 128 bits (Table 3) and represents results for both stream ciphers and block ciphers using counter mode. A key size of 80 bits is consistent with the typical use of a lightweight block or stream cipher, while the 128-bit key represents an application that uses AES-128 level security. The results in the tables represent a tradeoff attack using the DK approach of a single-key system and the table values assume equal complexity for the online time and memory,

Table 1. Summary of Tradeoffs

	Tradeoff	Preprocessing	Target applications and restrictions
Exhaustive Key Search	$T = K$, $M = 1$	$P = 0$	block cipher key stream cipher key
Full Dictionary Attack	$T = 1$, $M = K$	$P = K$	block cipher key stream cipher key
Hellman	$TM^2 = K^2$	$P = K$	block cipher key
BG	$TM = N$	$P = N/D$	stream cipher state $D = T$
BS	$TM^2D^2 = N^2$	$P = N/D$	stream cipher state $D^2 \leq T$
HS	$TM^2D_{iv}^2 = (KV)^2$	$P = KV/D_{iv}$	stream cipher key/IV counter mode key/IV $D_{iv}^2 \leq T$
DK	$TM^2D_{iv}^2 = (KV)^2$	$P = KV/D_{iv}$	stream cipher key counter mode key $D_{iv} \leq V$ for single-key
Distributed Exh Key Srch	$T_0 = K/W$, $M_0 = 1$	$P_0 = 0$	block cipher key stream cipher key
Distributed Full Dict Att	$T_0 = 1$, $M_0 = K/W$	$P_0 = K/W$	block cipher key stream cipher key
Distributed Hellman	$T_0M_0^2W^3 = K^2$	$P_0 = K/W$	block cipher key $W \leq T_0$
Distributed BG	$T_0M_0W = N$	$P_0 = N/(DW)$	stream cipher state $D = T_0$
Distributed BS	$T_0M_0^2D^2W^3 = N^2$	$P_0 = N/(DW)$	stream cipher state $D^2W \leq T_0$
Distributed HS	$T_0M_0^2D_{iv}^2W^3 = (KV)^2$	$P_0 = KV/(D_{iv}W)$	stream cipher key/IV counter mode key/IV $D_{iv}^2W \leq T_0$ $D_{iv} \leq V$ for single-key
Distributed DK	$T_0M_0^2D_{iv}^2W^3 = (KV)^2$	$P_0 = KV/(D_{iv}W)$	stream cipher key counter mode key $W \leq T_0$ $D_{iv} \leq V$ for single-key

i.e., $T_0 = M_0$. The tradeoff expression of (11) is applied and the constraints $D_{iv} \leq V$ and $W \leq T_0$ are satisfied. For $V > 1$, $P_0 = KV/(D_{iv}W)$ resulting in

$$T_0 = \frac{P_0^{2/3}}{W^{1/3}} \tag{19}$$

which can be used to derive the values in the tables. However, for the case of $V = 1$ (that is, a predictable initial count in counter mode or a stream cipher with no IV), data cannot be used in the tradeoff and $P_0 = KV/W$ with (19) still suitable.

For both key sizes, various IV sizes are given and the complexity presented for cases of differing amounts of data, D_{iv}, and number of processors, W. For reference, the appropriate distributed exhaustive key search complexity (DEKS) is also presented for each case. Each TMTO case given in the tables has the online time complexity and the preprocessing complexity for an individual processor presented in the format "T_0/P_0".

It is obvious from the tables that there are many scenarios in which distributed TMTO attacks could be made more effective than a distributed exhaustive key search. Most notably, if $V = 1$, one Hellman table can be constructed straightforwardly to cover just the keys. In this case, although the use of data from multiple IVs is not applicable, applying a distributed approach can result in extremely small online time complexities - as low as $2^{33.3}$ for a lightweight cipher with an 80-bit key using 2^{20} processors. For cases with $V > 1$, using data drawn from a modest number of IVs can result in a compromise of the security of the cipher. For example, with $K = 2^{128}$ and $V = 2^{32}$, using data from only 2^{20} IVs and applying 2^{20} processors results in a TMTO attack with an online time complexity of $2^{73.3}$ and a preprocessing time complexity of 2^{120}. Hence, the online time complexity is substantially better than the distributed exhaustive key search complexity of 2^{108}, while the preprocessing complexity is only slightly worse.

Table 2. TMTO Results T_0/P_0 for 80-bit Keys

$K = 2^{80}$	DEKS	$V = 1$	$V = 2^{20}$	$V = 2^{40}$
$W = 1,\ D_{iv} = 1$	2^{80}	$2^{53.3}/2^{80}$	$2^{66.7}/2^{100}$	$2^{80}/2^{120}$
$W = 1,\ D_{iv} = 2^{10}$	2^{80}	$2^{53.3}/2^{80}$	$2^{60}/2^{90}$	$2^{73.3}/2^{110}$
$W = 2^{20},\ D_{iv} = 1$	2^{60}	$2^{33.3}/2^{60}$	$2^{46.7}/2^{80}$	$2^{60}/2^{100}$
$W = 2^{20},\ D_{iv} = 2^{10}$	2^{60}	$2^{33.3}/2^{60}$	$2^{40}/2^{70}$	$2^{53.3}/2^{90}$

Table 3. TMTO Results T_0/P_0 for 128-bit Keys

$K = 2^{128}$	DEKS	$V = 1$	$V = 2^{32}$	$V = 2^{64}$
$W = 1,\ D_{iv} = 1$	2^{128}	$2^{85.3}/2^{128}$	$2^{106.7}/2^{160}$	$2^{128}/2^{192}$
$W = 1,\ D_{iv} = 2^{20}$	2^{128}	$2^{85.3}/2^{128}$	$2^{93.3}/2^{140}$	$2^{114.7}/2^{172}$
$W = 2^{20},\ D_{iv} = 1$	2^{108}	$2^{65.3}/2^{108}$	$2^{86.7}/2^{140}$	$2^{108}/2^{172}$
$W = 2^{20},\ D_{iv} = 2^{20}$	2^{108}	$2^{65.3}/2^{108}$	$2^{73.3}/2^{120}$	$2^{94.7}/2^{152}$

References

1. Hellman, M.E.: A cryptanalytic time-memory trade-off. IEEE Trans. Inf. Theory **26**(4), 401–406 (1980)
2. Babbage, S.: A space/time tradeoff in exhaustive search attacks on stream ciphers. In: European Convention on Security and Detection, IEEE Conference Publication No. 408, pp. 161–166 (1995)
3. Golić, J.D.: Cryptanalysis of alleged A5 stream cipher. In: Fumy, W. (ed.) EUROCRYPT 1997. LNCS, vol. 1233, pp. 239–255. Springer, Heidelberg (1997). https://doi.org/10.1007/3-540-69053-0_17
4. Biryukov, A., Shamir, A.: Cryptanalytic time/memory/data tradeoffs for stream ciphers. In: Okamoto, T. (ed.) ASIACRYPT 2000. LNCS, vol. 1976, pp. 1–13. Springer, Heidelberg (2000). https://doi.org/10.1007/3-540-44448-3_1
5. Hong, J., Sarkar, P.: New applications of time memory data tradeoffs. In: Roy, B. (ed.) ASIACRYPT 2005. LNCS, vol. 3788, pp. 353–372. Springer, Heidelberg (2005). https://doi.org/10.1007/11593447_19
6. Denning, D.E.: Cryptography and Data Security. Addison-Wesley, Boston (1982)
7. Oechslin, P.: Making a faster cryptanalytic time-memory trade-off. In: Boneh, D. (ed.) CRYPTO 2003. LNCS, vol. 2729, pp. 617–630. Springer, Heidelberg (2003). https://doi.org/10.1007/978-3-540-45146-4_36
8. Armknecht, F., Mikhalev, V.: On lightweight stream ciphers with shorter internal states. In: Leander, G. (ed.) FSE 2015. LNCS, vol. 9054, pp. 451–470. Springer, Heidelberg (2015). https://doi.org/10.1007/978-3-662-48116-5_22
9. Mikhalev, V., Armknecht, F., Müller, C.: On ciphers that continuously access the non-volatile key. IACR Trans. Symmetric Cryptol. **2016**(2), 52–79 (2016)
10. Hamann, M., Krause, M., Meier, W.: LIZARD - a lightweight stream cipher for power-constrained devices. IACR Trans. Symmetric Cryptol. **2017**(1), 45–79 (2017)
11. Dunkelman, O., Keller, N.: Treatment of the initial value in time-memory-data tradeoff attacks on stream ciphers. Inf. Process. Lett. **107**(5), 133–137 (2008)
12. Avoine, G., Junod, P., Oechslin, P.: Characterization and improvement of time-memory trade-off based on perfect tables. ACM Trans. Inf. Syst. Secur. **11**(4), 17:1–17:22 (2008)
13. Hong, J., Moon, S.: A comparison of cryptanalytic tradeoff algorithms. J. Cryptol. **26**(4), 559–637 (2013)
14. van den Broek, F., Poll, E.: A comparison of time-memory trade-off attacks on stream ciphers. In: Youssef, A., Nitaj, A., Hassanien, A.E. (eds.) AFRICACRYPT 2013. LNCS, vol. 7918, pp. 406–423. Springer, Heidelberg (2013). https://doi.org/10.1007/978-3-642-38553-7_24
15. Borst, J., Preneel, B., Vandewalle, J.: On the time-memory tradeoff between exhaustive key search and table precomputation. In: Proceedings of the 19th Symposium in Information Theory in the Benelux, WIC, pp. 111–118 (1998)
16. Hong, J., Lee, G.W., Ma, D.: Analysis of the parallel distinguished point tradeoff. In: Bernstein, D.J., Chatterjee, S. (eds.) INDOCRYPT 2011. LNCS, vol. 7107, pp. 161–180. Springer, Heidelberg (2011). https://doi.org/10.1007/978-3-642-25578-6_14
17. Kim, J.W., Seo, J., Hong, J., Park, K., Kim, S.-R.: High-speed parallel implementations of the rainbow method based on perfect tables in a heterogeneous system. Softw. Pract. Exper. **45**(6), 837–855 (2015)

18. Avoine, G., Carpent, X., Kordy, B., Tardif, F.: How to Handle Rainbow Tables with External Memory. In: Pieprzyk, J., Suriadi, S. (eds.) ACISP 2017. LNCS, vol. 10342, pp. 306–323. Springer, Cham (2017). https://doi.org/10.1007/978-3-319-60055-0_16
19. Lee, G.W., Hong, J.: Comparison of perfect table cryptanalytic tradeoff algorithms. Des. Codes Crypt. **80**(3), 473–523 (2016)
20. National Institute of Standards and Technology. NIST Special Publication 800–38A: Recommendation for Block Cipher Modes of Operation, December 2001. https://csrc.nist.gov/publications/detail/sp/800-38a/final
21. Biryukov, A., Mukhopadhyay, S., Sarkar, P.: Improved time-memory trade-offs with multiple data. In: Preneel, B., Tavares, S. (eds.) SAC 2005. LNCS, vol. 3897, pp. 110–127. Springer, Heidelberg (2006). https://doi.org/10.1007/11693383_8

New Iterated RC4 Key Correlations

Ryoma Ito[(✉)] and Atsuko Miyaji

Osaka University, 2-1 Yamadaoka, Suita-shi, Osaka 565-0871, Japan
ito@cy2sec.comm.eng.osaka-u.ac.jp, miyaji@comm.eng.osaka-u.ac.jp

Abstract. This paper investigates key correlations of the keystream generated from RC4, and then presents significant improvements for a plaintext recovery attack on WPA-TKIP from the attack by Isobe et al. at FSE 2013. We first discuss newly discovered key correlations between 2 bytes of the RC4 key and a keystream byte in each round. Such correlations are referred as *iterated RC4 key correlations*. We further apply our iterated RC4 key correlations to the plaintext recovery attack on WPA-TKIP in the same way as the attack by Sen Gupta et al. at FSE 2014, and achieve significant improvements for recovering 8 bytes of a plaintext from the attack by Isobe et al. at FSE 2013. Our result implies that WPA-TKIP further lowers the security level of generic RC4.

Keywords: RC4 · WPA-TKIP · Bias · Key correlations
Plaintext recovery

1 Introduction

The stream cipher RC4 was designed by Rivest in 1987, and is widely used in various security protocols such as Secure Socket Layer/Transport Layer Security (SSL/TLS), Wired Equivalent Privacy (WEP), and Wi-fi Protected Access - Temporal Key Integrity Protocol (WPA-TKIP). After the disclosure of RC4 algorithm in 1994, RC4 has been intensively analyzed over the past two decades due to its popularity and simplicity.

There are mainly two approaches to the cryptanalysis of RC4. One is to demonstrate the existence of certain events with statistical weaknesses known as a *bias* involving the RC4 key, the internal state variables, and the output pseudo-random sequence (keystream) bytes [Roo95,MS02,IOWM14]. Now, we refer to the event with significantly higher or lower than random association as a *positive bias* or a *negative bias*, respectively. The other is to recover an RC4 key (a *key recovery attack*) [PM07,SVV11], an internal state (a *state recovery attack*) [KMP+98,MK08] and a plaintext (a *plaintext recovery attack*) [MS02,IOWM14] using various biases. In addition, many cryptanalyses of the security protocols have been reported such as the plaintext recovery attacks on SSL/TLS [IOWM14,VP15] and WPA-TKIP [GMM+15,VP15], and the key recovery attacks on WEP [FMS01,VV07]. From these attacks, the usage of RC4 cipher suites was prohibited in all SSL/TLS versions in 2015 [Pop15], and is not

W. Susilo and G. Yang (Eds.): ACISP 2018, LNCS 10946, pp. 154–171, 2018.
https://doi.org/10.1007/978-3-319-93638-3_10

recommended in both WEP and WPA-TKIP. On the other hand, around 21% of all Web browsers/servers for SSL/TLS remain supporting RC4 cipher suites as of February 2018[1]. Furthermore, a downgrade attack in Wi-Fi network is still real threat [VP16]. In summary, many people may continue to use RC4 in the security protocols, and thus we need to pay attention to RC4 from now on.

1.1 Description of RC4

RC4 consists of two algorithms: a Key Scheduling Algorithm (KSA) and a Pseudo Random Generation Algorithm (PRGA). We describe the KSA and the PRGA as Algorithm 1 and Algorithm 2, respectively. Both the KSA and the PRGA update secret internal states S^K and S which are permutations of all possible bytes N (typically, $N = 2^8$) and two 8-bit indices i and j. The KSA generates the initial state S_0 $(= S_N^K)$ from a secret key K of ℓ bytes to become an input of the PRGA. Once the initial state S_0 is generated from the KSA, the PRGA outputs a keystream byte $\{Z_1, Z_2, \ldots, Z_r\}$ in each round, where r is the number of rounds. All additions in both the KSA and the PRGA are arithmetic addition modulo N. We use this notation throughout the remainder of this paper.

Algorithm 1. KSA

for $i = 0$ to $N - 1$ **do**
    $S_0^K[i] \leftarrow i$
end for
$j_0^K \leftarrow 0$
for $i = 0$ to $N - 1$ **do**
    $j_{i+1}^K \leftarrow j_i^K + S_i^K[i] + K[i \bmod \ell]$
    Swap$(S_i^K[i], S_i^K[j_{i+1}^K])$
end for

Algorithm 2. PRGA

$r \leftarrow 0$, $i_0 \leftarrow 0$, $j_0 \leftarrow 0$
loop
    $r \leftarrow r + 1$, $i_r \leftarrow i_{r-1} + 1$
    $j_r \leftarrow j_{r-1} + S_{r-1}[i_r]$
    Swap$(S_{r-1}[i_r], S_{r-1}[j_r])$
    Output: $Z_r \leftarrow S_r[S_r[i_r] + S_r[j_r]]$
end loop

1.2 Description of WPA-TKIP

WPA is a security protocol for IEEE 802.11 wireless network standardized as a substitute for WEP in 2003. WPA improves a 16-byte RC4 key setting, which is known as TKIP, from that in WEP. TKIP includes a key management scheme, a temporal key hash function [HWF02], and a message integrity code function. The key management scheme generates a 16-byte Temporal Key (TK) after the IEEE 802.1X authentication. After that, the temporal key hash function outputs a 16-byte RC4 key from the TK, a 6-byte Transmitter Address, and a 48-bit Initialization Vector (IV), which is a sequence counter. In addition, TKIP uses MICHAEL [FM02] to ensure integrity of a message. One of the remarkable features in TKIP is that the first 3-byte RC4 key bytes $\{K[0], K[1], K[2]\}$ are derived from the last 16-bit Initialization Vector (IV16) as follows:

$$K[0] = (\text{IV16} \gg 8) \ \&\ \text{0xFF},$$

[1] See https://www.trustworthyinternet.org/ssl-pulse/.

$$K[1] = ((\text{IV16} \gg 8) \mid \text{0x20}) \,\&\, \text{0x7F},$$
$$K[2] = \text{IV16} \,\&\, \text{0xFF}.$$

We note that the first 3-byte RC4 key bytes $\{K[0], K[1], K[2]\}$ in WPA-TKIP is known because the IV can be obtained by observing packets.

1.3 Our Contributions

In [SVV11], Sepehrdad et al. investigated correlations between the RC4 key and the keystream experimentally. We refer to such correlations as *key correlations* of the keystream. Their investigations are limited to ℓ rounds. Thus, no correlations between $K[r \bmod \ell]$ and Z_r for $r \geq \ell$ have been investigated although $K[r \bmod \ell]$ may be iterated to use to produce Z_r for $r \geq \ell$.

In this paper, we focus on the key correlations of the keystream, and investigate them in detail. We first discuss new key correlations that events $Z_r = K[0] - K[r \bmod \ell] - r$ for any arbitrary round r induce positive biases, where $(K[0], K[r \bmod \ell])$ pairs in our key correlations are *iterated* every ℓ rounds. This is why we hereinafter refer to the newly discovered key correlations as *iterated RC4 key correlations.*

By combining our key correlations with the previous ones, e.g., $Z_1 = K[0] - K[1] - 1$ and $Z_{x \cdot \ell} = -x \cdot \ell$ $(x = 1, 2, \ldots, 7)$, we can integrate the iterated RC4 key correlations completely. Our contributions can be summarized as follows:

- Theorem 7 shows that events $Z_r = K[0] - K[r \bmod \ell] - r$ induce positive biases in both generic RC4 and WPA-TKIP except when $r = 1, 2, x \cdot \ell$ $(x = 1, 2, \ldots, 7)$.
- Theorem 9 shows that an event $Z_1 = K[0] - K[1] - 1$ induces an negative bias in only WPA-TKIP.
- Theorem 10 shows that an event $Z_2 = K[0] - K[2] - 2$ does not induce a bias in both generic RC4 and WPA-TKIP.

We further present how to apply our iterated RC4 key correlations to the plaintext recovery attack on WPA-TKIP. In [GMM+15], Sen Gupta et al. extended the plaintext recovery attack on generic RC4 by Isobe et al. in [IOWM14], and improved to recover 4 bytes of a plaintext $\{P_1, P_3, P_{256}, P_{257}\}$ on WPA-TKIP. Their improvements can be achieved by using key correlations of the keystream based on the first 3-byte RC4 key bytes $\{K[0], K[1], K[2]\}$, which are known values of WPA-TKIP. In the same way as the attack by Sen Gupta et al., our new iterated RC4 key correlations demonstrate significant improvements for recovering 8 bytes of a plaintext on WPA-TKIP from [IOWM14]. In fact, the number of samples for recovering P_{17}, P_{18}, P_{33}, P_{34}, P_{49}, P_{50}, P_{66}, and P_{82} on WPA-TKIP can be reduced to $2^{17.727}$, $2^{17.800}$, $2^{18.955}$, $2^{19.035}$, $2^{20.297}$, $2^{20.386}$, $2^{21.869}$, and $2^{23.505}$ from $2^{23.178}$, $2^{23.210}$, $2^{23.770}$, $2^{23.791}$, $2^{24.114}$, $2^{24.135}$, $2^{24.479}$, and $2^{24.820}$, respectively. Our result implies that WPA-TKIP further lowers the security level of generic RC4.

1.4 Organization of This Paper

This paper is organized as follows: Sect. 2 summarizes the previous works for both key correlations and attacks. Section 3 shows theoretical proofs of the iterated RC4 key correlations and its experimental results. Section 4 demonstrates significant improvements of the plaintext recovery attack on WPA-TKIP from [IOWM14] using our iterated RC4 key correlations. Section 5 concludes this paper.

2 Previous Works

2.1 Known Key Correlations

In [Sar14], Sarkar proved key correlations of the keystream $\{Z_1, Z_3, Z_4\}$ reported in [SVV11] theoretically. Their key correlations are given as follows:

Theorem 1 ([Sar14, Theorem 4]). *For any arbitrary secret key K, a key correlation of the keystream Z_1 is given by*

$$\Pr(Z_1 = K[0] - K[1] - 1) \approx \alpha_1 + \tfrac{1}{N}(1 - \alpha_1),$$

where $\alpha_1 = \frac{1}{N^2} \cdot (1 - \frac{2}{N}) \cdot (1 - \frac{1}{N})^{N-2} \sum_{x=2}^{N-1} (1 - \frac{1}{N})^x \cdot (1 - \frac{1}{N})^{x-2} \cdot (1 - \frac{2}{N})^{N-x-1}$.

Proposition 1 ([Sar14, Theorem 8]). *For any arbitrary secret key K, a key correlation of the keystream Z_3 is given by*

$$\Pr(Z_3 = K[0] - K[3] - 3) \approx \alpha_3 + \tfrac{1}{N}(1 - \alpha_3),$$

where $\alpha_3 = \frac{N^3-11N^2+42N-55}{N^4} \cdot (1 - \frac{1}{N})^{N-4} \cdot \frac{N^2-3N+2}{N^2}) \cdot \frac{1}{N} \sum_{x=4}^{N-1} (1 - \frac{1}{N})^x \cdot (1 - \frac{1}{N})^{x-4} \cdot (1 - \frac{2}{N})^{N-x-1}$.

Proposition 2 ([Sar14, Theorem 9]). *For any arbitrary secret key K, a key correlation of the keystream Z_4 is given by*

$$\Pr(Z_4 = K[0] - K[4] - 4) \approx \alpha_4 + \tfrac{1}{N}(1 - \alpha_4),$$

where $\alpha_4 = \frac{N^4-18N^3+124N^2-385N+452}{N^5} \cdot (1 - \frac{1}{N})^{N-5} \cdot \frac{N^3-8N^2+21N-18}{N^3} \cdot \frac{1}{N} \sum_{x=5}^{N-1} (1 - \frac{1}{N})^x \cdot (1 - \frac{1}{N})^{x-5} \cdot (1 - \frac{2}{N})^{N-x-1}$.

In [IOWM14], Isobe et al. showed keylength-dependent biases as follows:

Theorem 2 ([IOWM14, Theorem 9]). *When $r = x \cdot \ell$ $(x = 1, 2, \ldots, 7)$, the probability of* $\Pr(Z_r = -r)$ *is approximately*

$$\Pr(Z_r = -r) \approx \tfrac{1}{N^2} + \left(1 - \tfrac{1}{N^2}\right) \cdot \gamma_r + (1 - \delta_r) \cdot \tfrac{1}{N},$$

where $\gamma_r = \frac{1}{N^2} \cdot (1 - \frac{r+1}{N})^y \cdot \sum_{y=r+1}^{N-1} (1 - \frac{1}{N}) \cdot (1 - \frac{2}{N})^{y-r} \cdot (1 - \frac{3}{N})^{N-y+2r-4}$, $\delta_r = \Pr(S_{r-1}[r] = 0)$.

Their keylength-dependent biases are similar to the key correlations proved by Sarkar because $Z_{x \cdot \ell} = K[0] - K[x \cdot \ell \bmod \ell] - x \cdot \ell = K[0] - K[0] - x \cdot \ell = -x \cdot \ell$.

2.2 Known Attacks in the Broadcast Setting

In [MS02], Mantin and Shamir demonstrated how to recover the second byte of a plaintext in the broadcast setting as follows:

Theorem 3 ([MS02, Theorem 1]). *Assume that the initial state S is randomly chosen from the set of all possible permutations of $\{0, \ldots, N-1\}$. Then, the probability that the second byte of the keystream Z_2 is 0 is approximately $\frac{2}{N}$.*

Theorem 4 ([MS02, Theorem 2]). *Let X and Y be two distributions, and suppose that the event e occurs in X with a probability p and Y with a probability $p \cdot (1+q)$. Then, for small p and q, $\mathcal{O}(\frac{1}{p \cdot q^2})$ samples suffice to distinguish X from Y with a constant probability of success.*

Let X be a distribution of a random sequence, and let Y be a distribution of the second byte of the keystream Z_2 generated form RC4. Then, the number of samples required to distinguish X from Y is around N because p and q are given as $p = \frac{1}{N}$ and $q = 1$.

Theorem 5 ([MS02, Theorem 3]). *Let P be a plaintext, and let $C^{(1)}, \ldots, C^{(k)}$ be the RC4 encryptions of P under k randomly chosen keys. Then, if $k = \Omega(N)$, the second byte of P can be reliably extracted from $C^{(1)}, \ldots, C^{(k)}$.*

If $Z_2^{(i)} = 0$, then P_2 has the same value as $C_2^{(i)}$ because P_2 is XORed with $Z_2^{(i)}$ to output $C_2^{(i)}$ in the RC4 encryptions. From Theorem 3, the event $Z_2 = 0$ occurs with pretty high probability in comparison with the other events. Thus, we can recover P_2 by exploiting the most frequent value in the distribution of $C_2^{(1)}, \ldots, C_2^{(k)}$. From Theorem 4, the number of samples for recovering P_2 requires more than N ciphertexts encrypted by randomly chosen keys.

In [IOWM14], Isobe et al. presented a set of the strongest biases in the first 257 bytes of the keystream including their newly discovered biases. They further demonstrated a practical plaintext recovery attack using their set of the strongest biases as the following 3 steps:

Step 1. Randomly generate a target plaintext P.
Step 2. Obtain 2^x ciphertexts C by encrypting P with randomly chosen keys.
Step 3. Exploit the most frequent value in the distribution of C_r, and recover P_r using the set of the strongest biases of keystream bytes Z_r.

From their experimental results, the first 257 bytes of the plaintext could be recovered with a probability of more than 0.8 using 2^{32} ciphertexts encrypted by randomly chosen keys.

In [GMM+15], Sen Gupta et al. investigated for significant key correlations of the keystream Z_r experimentally using certain linear combinations of the known RC4 key bytes $\{K[0], K[1], K[2]\}$. If the exploited key correlations induce higher biases than certain events used in the attack by Isobe et al., then the key correlations improve the plaintext recovery attack on WPA-TKIP in the same way as the existing attacks [MS02,IOWM14]. Table 1 presents their experimental results for the plaintext recovery attack on WPA-TKIP. Their results show significant improvements for recovering 4 bytes of a plaintext $\{P_1, P_3, P_{256}, P_{257}\}$, where the existing attack requires around 2^{30} ciphertexts encrypted by randomly chosen keys to achieve the same probability of success.

Table 1. Experimental results for recovering 4 bytes of a plaintext on WPA-TKIP. The probability of success in each case is around 1.

Round	Key correlations	# of ciphertexts
1	$Z_1 = -K[0] - K[1]$	$5 \cdot 2^{13} \approx 2^{15.322}$
	$Z_1 = K[0] + K[1] + K[2] + 3$	
3	$Z_3 = K[0] + K[1] + K[2] + 3$	2^{19}
256	$Z_{256} = -K[0]$	2^{19}
257	$Z_{257} = -K[0] - K[1]$	2^{21}

3 New Iterated RC4 Key Correlations

3.1 Our Observations

This section shows new key correlations of the keystream in both generic RC4 and WPA-TKIP. In [SVV11], Sepehrdad et al. investigated some key correlations of the keystream by using a linear form

$$(a_0 \cdot K[0] + \cdots + a_{\ell-1} \cdot K[\ell-1] + a_\ell \cdot Z_1 + \cdots + a_{2\ell-1} \cdot Z_\ell) \bmod N = b, \quad (1)$$

where $a_i \in \{-1, 0, 1\}$ for $0 \leq i \leq 2\ell - 1$. However, they did not investigate key correlations of the keystream over ℓ rounds. In addition, we focus on the key correlations of the keystream $\{Z_1, Z_3, Z_4\}$ proved by Sarkar in [Sar14], and predict that there might exist correlations between $(K[0], K[r \bmod \ell])$ pairs and Z_r. Then, we have executed experiments for investigating correlations based on $(K[0], K[r \bmod \ell])$ pairs with 256 bytes of the keystream generated from N^4 randomly chosen keys.

Figures 1 and 2 show our experimental observations in both generic RC4 and WPA-TKIP, respectively. From our experimental results, we have observed new key correlations of the keystream as follows:

Observation 1. For any arbitrary secret key K, the following key correlations of the keystream Z_r in both generic RC4 and WPA-TKIP induce biases:

$$Z_r = K[0] - K[r \bmod \ell] - r.$$

Predictably, we have demonstrated that there exist key correlations between $(K[0], K[r \bmod \ell])$ pairs and Z_r. $(K[0], K[r \bmod \ell])$ pairs are iterated every ℓ rounds. Therefore, we refer to our newly observed key correlations as *iterated RC4 key correlations*. By combining our key correlations with the previous ones, we can integrate the iterated RC4 key correlations completely. Our motivation is to prove the iterated RC4 key correlations theoretically.

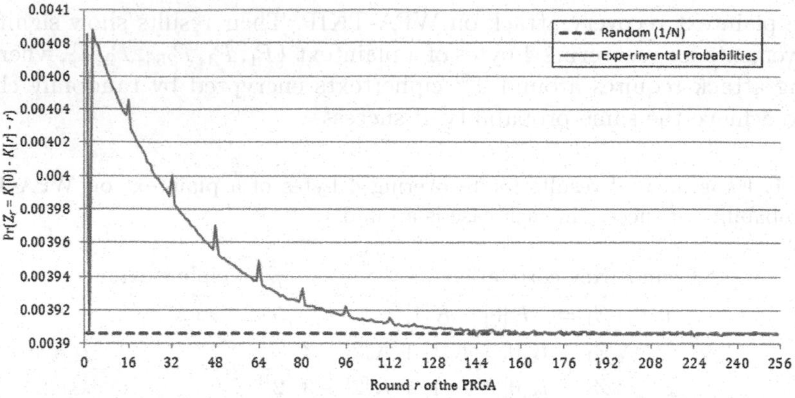

Fig. 1. Our experimental observations in generic RC4.

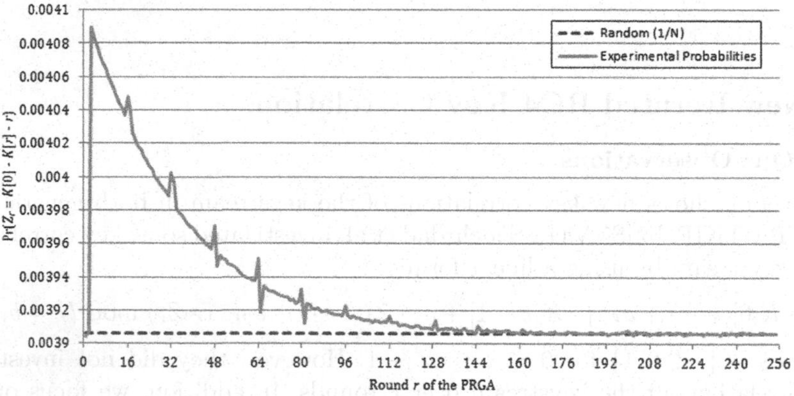

Fig. 2. Our experimental observations in WPA-TKIP.

3.2 Proofs

This section provides theoretical proofs of Observation 1 as Theorems 7, 9 and 10. Theorem 7 shows that events $Z_r = K[0] - K[r \bmod \ell] - r$ induce positive biases in both generic RC4 and WPA-TKIP except when $r = 1, 2, x \cdot \ell$ $(x = 1, 2, \ldots, 7)$. We note that Theorem 7 includes the precise proofs of Propositions 1 and 2. Theorem 9 shows that an event $Z_1 = K[0] - K[1] - 1$ induces a negative bias in only WPA-TKIP, and a positive bias in generic RC4 as Theorem 1. Theorem 10 shows that an event $Z_2 = K[0] - K[2] - 2$ does not induce a bias in both generic RC4 and WPA-TKIP. As a result, by combining Theorems 7, 9 and 10 with Theorems 1 and 2, Observation 1 can be proven completely.

In our proofs, we assume that certain events with no significant bias occur with a probability of random association, whose probability is $\frac{1}{N}$. These assumptions are confirmed experimentally. We also assume that the RC4 key K is generated uniformly at random in both generic RC4 and WPA-TKIP, except the first 3-byte RC4 key bytes $\{K[0], K[1], K[2]\}$ in WPA-TKIP generated by IV using a sequence counter.

Before showing the proof of Theorem 7, the non-randomness of the initial state S_0 is given as Theorem 6. In [Man01], Mantin showed that the initial state S_0 generated from the KSA is non-randomness.

Theorem 6 ([Man01, Theorem 6.2.1]). *In the initial state of the PRGA for* $0 \le u \le N-1$, $0 \le v \le N-1$, *we have*

$$\Pr(S_0[u] = v) = \begin{cases} \frac{1}{N}\left(\left(1-\frac{1}{N}\right)^v + \left(1-\left(1-\frac{1}{N}\right)^v\right)\left(1-\frac{1}{N}\right)^{N-u-1}\right) & \textit{if } v \le u, \\ \frac{1}{N}\left(\left(1-\frac{1}{N}\right)^{N-u-1} + \left(1-\frac{1}{N}\right)^v\right) & \textit{if } v > u. \end{cases}$$

By using Theorem 6, which is denoted by $\zeta_{u,v} = \Pr(S_0[u] = v)$, Theorem 7 is proved as follows:

Theorem 7. *For any arbitrary secret key K and round r except when $r = 1, 2, x \cdot \ell$ $(x = 1, 2, \ldots, 7)$, key correlations of the keystream Z_r in both generic RC4 and WPA-TKIP are given by*

$$\Pr(Z_r = K[0] - K[r \bmod \ell] - r) \approx \alpha_r + \tfrac{1}{N}(1 - \alpha_r),$$

where α_r, β_r, γ_r and δ_r are given by

$$\alpha_r \approx \left(\beta_r + \tfrac{1}{N(N-1)}(1-\beta_r)\right) \cdot \gamma_r \cdot \left(\delta_r + \tfrac{1}{N}(1-\delta_r)\right),$$

$$\beta_r \approx \tfrac{1}{N} \cdot \tfrac{N-r-1}{N} \cdot \prod_{x=3}^{r}(N-x-1) / \prod_{x=0}^{r-3}(N-x),$$

$$\gamma_r \approx \left(1-\tfrac{1}{N}\right)^{N-r-1} \cdot \tfrac{1}{N} \cdot \sum_{x=r+1}^{N-1}\left(1-\tfrac{1}{N}\right)^x \cdot \left(1-\tfrac{1}{N}\right)^{x-r-1} \cdot \left(1-\tfrac{2}{N}\right)^{N-x-1},$$

$$\delta_r \approx \left(1 - \sum_{v=2}^{r}\zeta_{1,v} - \sum_{x=r+1}^{N-1}\tfrac{\zeta_{1,x}}{N-r-2}\right) \cdot \tfrac{N-r+1}{N-1}.$$

Proof. We consider the following three phases to prove the major path for the target event. In the following proof, $f_i = \frac{i(i+1)}{2} + \sum_{x=0}^{i} K[x \bmod \ell]$ for $i \ge 0$.

Phase 1. From the initial to the $(r+1)$-th round of the KSA, we assume that all of the following events hold:

$$j_1^K = K[0] = f_0 \notin \{1, 2, \ldots, r-1, r, f_{r-1}\},$$
$$j_2^K = K[0] + K[1] + S_1^K[1] = f_1 \notin \{2, 3, \ldots, r-1, r, f_0, f_{r-1}\},$$
$$j_3^K = K[0] + \sum_{x=1}^{2}(K[x] + S_x^K[x]) = f_2 \notin \{3, 4, \ldots, r-1, r, f_0, f_{r-1}\},$$
$$\vdots$$
$$j_{r-1}^K = K[0] + \sum_{x=1}^{r-2}(K[x \bmod \ell] + S_x^K[x]) = f_{r-2} \notin \{r-1, r, f_0, f_{r-1}\},$$

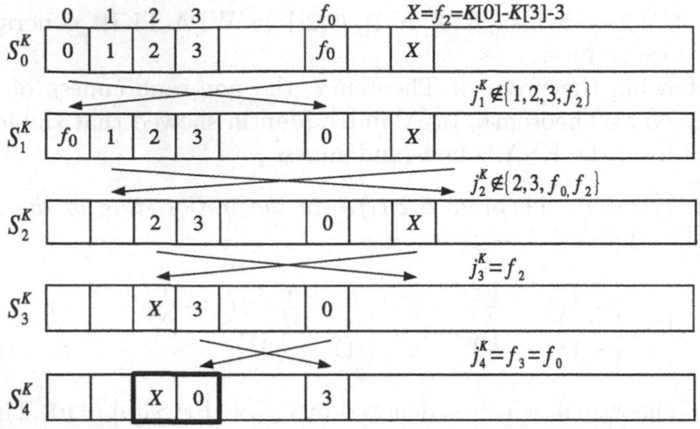

Fig. 3. State transition diagram of the major path in Phase 1 when $r = 3$.

$$j_r^K = K[0] + \sum_{x=1}^{r-1} (K[x \bmod \ell] + S_x^K[x]) = f_{r-1},$$
$$j_{r+1}^K = K[0] + \sum_{x=1}^{r} (K[x \bmod \ell] + S_x^K[x]) = f_r = f_0.$$

Figure 3 shows a state transition when the above assumptions hold and $r = 3$. We note that $f_{r-1} = f_{r-1} - (f_r - f_0) = K[0] - K[r \bmod \ell] - r$ when the event $f_r = f_0$ holds. Under the assumptions, both $S_{r+1}^K[r-1] = K[0] - K[r \bmod \ell] - r$ and $S_{r+1}^K[r] = 0$ always hold simultaneously after the $(r+1)$-th round of the KSA. Now, we can rewrite $S_x^K[x]$ into $S_1[x]$ for $x \in [1, r-1]$ as follows:

$$j_1^K = K[0] = f_0 \notin \{1, 2, \ldots, r-1, r, f_{r-1}\} \text{ w.p. } \tfrac{N-r-1}{N},$$
$$j_2^K = K[0] + K[1] + S_1^K[1] = f_1 \notin \{2, 3, \ldots, r-1, r, f_0, f_{r-1}\} \text{ w.p. } \tfrac{N-r-1}{N},$$
$$j_3^K = K[0] + \sum_{x=1}^{2} (K[x] + S_1^K[x]) = f_2 \notin \{3, 4, \ldots, r-1, r, f_0, f_{r-1}\} \text{ w.p. } \tfrac{N-r}{N-1},$$
$$\vdots$$
$$j_{r-1}^K = K[0] + \sum_{x=1}^{r-2} (K[x \bmod \ell] + S_1^K[x]) = f_{r-2} \notin \{r-1, r, f_0, f_{r-1}\} \text{ w.p. } \tfrac{N-4}{N-r+3},$$
$$j_r^K = K[0] + \sum_{x=1}^{r-1} (K[x \bmod \ell] + S_1^K[x]) = f_{r-1} \text{ w.p. } 1,$$
$$j_{r+1}^K = K[0] + \sum_{x=1}^{r} (K[x \bmod \ell] + S_1^K[x]) = f_r = f_0 \text{ w.p. } \tfrac{1}{N}.$$

This is because $S_1^K[x]$ is never swapped during the first x rounds when all of the individual events hold. These occur with each of probabilities in the above events because the internal state in RC4 is a permutation. Therefore, the probability that all events happen simultaneously is given by

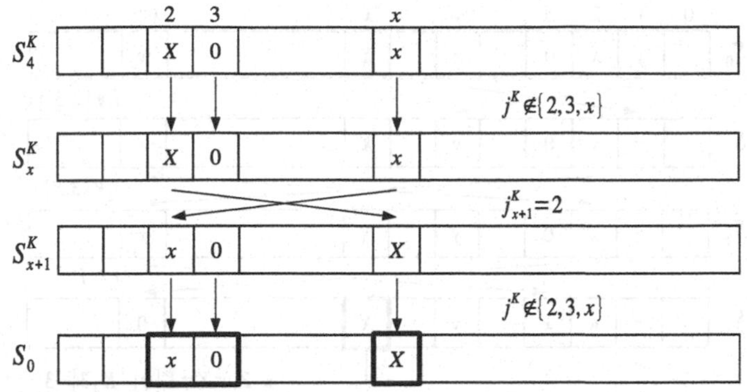

Fig. 4. State transition diagram of the major path in Phase 2 when $r = 3$.

$$\beta_r \approx \frac{1}{N} \cdot \frac{N-r-1}{N} \cdot \prod_{x=3}^{r} (N - x - 1) / \prod_{x=0}^{r-3} (N - x).$$

On the other hand, if any individual event does not hold, we then assume that both $S_{r+1}^K[r-1] = K[0] - K[r \bmod \ell] - r$ and $S_{r+1}^K[r] = 0$ hold simultaneously with a probability of random association. The probability of random association is $\frac{1}{N(N-1)}$ because the internal state in RC4 is a permutation. Therefore, the probability in that case is given by $\frac{1}{N(N-1)}(1 - \beta_r)$.

Phase 2. From the $(r+2)$-th round to the end of the KSA, we assume that all of the following events hold:

- From the $(r+2)$-th round to the end of the KSA, we assume that the values of j^K are not equal to r. This event occurs with a probability of $(1 - \frac{1}{N})^{N-r-1}$.
- For an index $x \in [r+1, N-1]$, we assume that $S_x^K[x] = x$. This event occurs with a probability of $(1 - \frac{1}{N})^x$.
- From the $(r+2)$-th to the x-th round of the KSA, we assume that the values of j^K are not equal to $r-1$. This event occurs with a probability of $(1 - \frac{1}{N})^{x-r-1}$.
- At the $(x+1)$-th round of the KSA, we assume that $j_{x+1}^K = r - 1$. This event occurs with a probability of $\frac{1}{N}$. Thus, $S_{x+1}^K[r-1] = x$ due to the swap operation.
- For the remaining $N - x - 1$ rounds of the KSA, we assume that the values of j^K do not touch the indices $r-1$ and x. This event occurs with a probability of $(1 - \frac{2}{N})^{N-x-1}$.

Figure 4 shows a state transition when the above assumptions hold and $r = 3$. Under the above assumptions, all of $S_0[r-1] = x$, $S_0[r] = 0$ and $S_0[x] = K[0] - K[r \bmod \ell] - r$ always hold simultaneously after the end of the KSA. Therefore, the probability that all events occur simultaneously is given by

$$\gamma_r \approx \left(1 - \frac{1}{N}\right)^{N-r-1} \cdot \frac{1}{N} \cdot \sum_{x=r+1}^{N-1} \left(1 - \frac{1}{N}\right)^x \cdot \left(1 - \frac{1}{N}\right)^{x-r-1} \cdot \left(1 - \frac{2}{N}\right)^{N-x-1}.$$

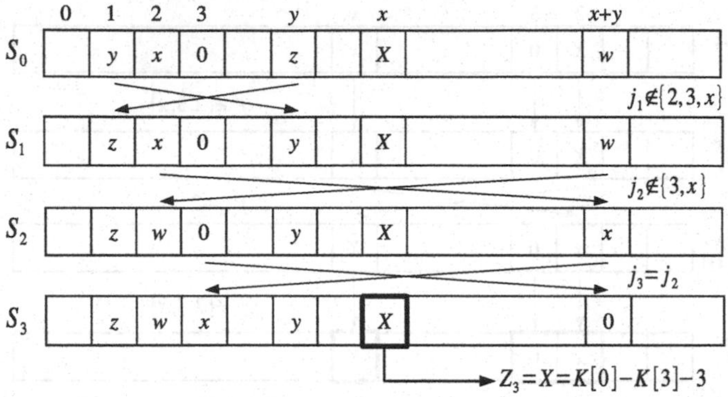

Fig. 5. State transition diagram of the major path in Phase 3 when $r = 3$.

Phase 3. From the initial to the $(r-1)$-th round of the PRGA, we assume that all of the following events hold:

$$j_1 = S_0[1] \notin \{2, 3, \ldots, r-1, r, x\},$$

$$j_2 = \sum_{u=0}^{1} S_u[u+1] \notin \{3, 4, \ldots, r-1, r, x\},$$

$$\vdots$$

$$j_{r-2} = \sum_{u=0}^{r-3} S_u[u+1] \notin \{r-1, r, x\},$$

$$j_{r-1} = \sum_{u=0}^{r-2} S_u[u+1] \notin \{r, x\}.$$

Figure 5 shows a state transition when the above assumptions hold and $r = 3$. We note that the values of j do not touch the index r and $x \in [r+1, N-1]$ from the initial to the $(r-1)$-th round of the PRGA. Under the above assumptions, both $S_r[r] = S_{r-1}[j_r] = S_{r-1}[j_{r-1}] = S_{r-2}[r-1] = S_0[r-1] = x$ and $S_r[j_r] = S_{r-1}[r] = S_0[r] = 0$ always hold simultaneously after the $(r-1)$-th round of the PRGA. After that, the PRGA outputs $Z_r = S_r[S_r[r] + S_r[j_r]] = S_r[x] = S_0[x] = K[0] - K[r \bmod \ell] - r$. Now, as with the discussion in Step 1, we can rewrite S_u into S_0 as follows[2]:

$$j_1 = S_0[1] \notin \{2, 3, \ldots, r-1, r, x\} \text{ w.p. } 1 - \sum_{v=2}^{r} \zeta_{1,v} - \sum_{x=r+1}^{N-1} \frac{\zeta_{1,x}}{N-r-2},$$

$$j_2 = \sum_{u=0}^{1} S_0[u+1] \notin \{3, 4, \ldots, r-1, r, x\} \text{ w.p. } \frac{N-r+1}{N-1},$$

$$\vdots$$

$$j_{r-2} = \sum_{u=0}^{r-3} S_0[u+1] \notin \{r-1, r, x\} \text{ w.p. } \frac{N-3}{N-r+3},$$

[2] $\Pr(S_0[1] = x)$ is an average probability because the range of x is from $r+1$ to $N-1$.

$$j_{r-1} = \sum_{u=0}^{r-2} S_0[u+1] \notin \{r, x\} \quad \text{w.p. } \tfrac{N-2}{N-r+2}.$$

These occur with each of probabilities in the above events because the internal state in RC4 is a permutation. Therefore, the probability that all of the above events occur simultaneously is given by

$$\delta_r \approx \Big(1 - \sum_{v=2}^{r} \zeta_{1,v} - \sum_{x=r+1}^{N-1} \tfrac{\zeta_{1,x}}{N-r-2}\Big) \cdot \prod_{y=2}^{r-1}(N-y) / \prod_{y=1}^{r-2}(N-y)$$

$$= \Big(1 - \sum_{v=2}^{r} \zeta_{1,v} - \sum_{x=r+1}^{N-1} \tfrac{\zeta_{1,x}}{N-r-2}\Big) \cdot \tfrac{N-r+1}{N-1}.$$

On the other hand, if any individual event does not hold, we then assume that the PRGA outputs $Z_r = K[0] - K[r \bmod \ell] - r$ with a probability of random association $\frac{1}{N}$. Therefore, the probability in that case is given by $\frac{1}{N}(1 - \delta_r)$.

We assume that all events in the above three phases are mutually independent. Therefore, we obtain the probability of the major path as

$$\alpha_r \approx \big(\beta_r + \tfrac{1}{N(N-1)}(1 - \beta_r)\big) \cdot \gamma_r \cdot \big(\delta_r + \tfrac{1}{N}(1 - \delta_r)\big).$$

If any phase does not hold, we then assume that $Z_r = K[0] - K[r \bmod \ell] - r$ with a probability of random association $\frac{1}{N}$. In summary, we obtain

$$\Pr(Z_r = K[0] - K[r \bmod \ell] - r) \approx \alpha_r + \tfrac{1}{N}(1 - \alpha_r).$$

□

Before showing the proof of Theorem 9, a distribution of $K[0]+K[1]$ in WPA-TKIP is given as Theorem 8. In [GMM+15], Sen Gupta et al. demonstrated a distribution of $K[0]+K[1]$, which is based on a relation between $K[0]$ and $K[1]$ in WPA-TKIP.

Theorem 8 ([GMM+15, Theorem 1]). *For $0 \le v \le N-1$, the sum v of $K[0]$ and $K[1]$ in WPA-TKIP is distributed as follows:*

$$\Pr(K[0]+K[1]=v) = 0 \quad \text{if } v \text{ is odd},$$
$$\Pr(K[0]+K[1]=v) = 0 \quad \text{if } v \text{ is even and } v \in [0,31] \cup [128,159],$$
$$\Pr(K[0]+K[1]=v) = \tfrac{2}{N} \quad \text{if } v \text{ is even and } v \in [32,63] \cup [96,127] \cup [160,191] \cup [224,255],$$
$$\Pr(K[0]+K[1]=v) = \tfrac{4}{N} \quad \text{if } v \text{ is even and } v \in [64,95] \cup [192,223].$$

By using Theorem 8, Theorem 9 is proved as follows:

Theorem 9. *For any arbitrary secret key K, a key correlation of the keystream Z_1 in WPA-TKIP is given by*

$$\Pr(Z_1 = K[0] - K[1] - 1) \approx \tfrac{1}{N}(1 - \alpha_1),$$

where $\alpha_1 \approx \frac{1}{N^2} \cdot (1 - \frac{2}{N}) \cdot (1 - \frac{1}{N})^{N-2} \cdot \sum_{x=2}^{N-1} (1 - \frac{1}{N})^{x} \cdot (1 - \frac{1}{N})^{x-2} \cdot (1 - \frac{2}{N})^{N-x-1}$.

Proof. The major path for the target event is as follows:

- We assume that $K[0] \neq 0, 1$ and $K[1] = 255$. This event occurs with a probability of $\frac{2}{N}(1 - \frac{1}{N})$.
- After the second round of the KSA, $S_2^K[1] = 0$ because $j_2^K = K[0]+K[1]+1 = K[0]$.
- From the third round to the end of the KSA, we assume that the values of j^K are not equal to 1. This event occurs with a probability of $(1 - \frac{1}{N})^{N-2}$.
- For an index $x \in [2, N-1]$, we assume that $S_x^K[x] = x$. This event occurs with a probability of $(1 - \frac{1}{N})^x$.
- For the third to the x-th round of the KSA, we assume that the values of j^K are not equal to 0. This event occurs with a probability of $(1 - \frac{1}{N})^{x-2}$.
- At the $(x+1)$-th round of the KSA, we assume that $j_{x+1}^K = 0$. This event occurs with a probability of $\frac{1}{N}$. Thus, $S_{x+1}^K[r-1] = x$ due to the swap operation.
- For the remaining $N - x - 1$ rounds of the KSA, we assume that the values of j^K do not touch the indices 0 and x. This event occurs with a probability of $(1 - \frac{2}{N})^{N-x-1}$.

If all of the individual events hold, all of $S_0[0] = x$, $S_0[1] = 0$ and $S_0[x] = K[0]$ always hold simultaneously after the end of the KSA, and then the PRGA outputs $Z_1 = K[0] = K[0] - K[1] - 1$ as $K[1] = 255$. We assume that the individual events in the major path become mutually independent. Then, all events occur with a probability of $\alpha_1 \approx \frac{1}{N^2} \cdot (1 - \frac{2}{N}) \cdot (1 - \frac{1}{N})^{N-2} \sum_{x=2}^{N-1} (1 - \frac{1}{N})^x \cdot (1 - \frac{1}{N})^{x-2} \cdot (1 - \frac{2}{N})^{N-x-1}$. However, Theorem 8 shows that the range of $K[1]$ is limited to either from 32 to 63 or from 96 to 127 in WPA-TKIP. Thus, the target event never occurs because $K[1] \neq 255$ in WPA-TKIP.

On the other hand, we assume that $Z_1 = K[0] - K[1] - 1$ with a probability of random association $\frac{1}{N}$ except the major path. Therefore, we obtain $\Pr(Z_1 = K[0] - K[1] - 1) \approx \frac{1}{N}(1 - \alpha_1)$. □

Theorem 10. *For any arbitrary secret key K, a key correlation of the keystream Z_2 in both generic RC4 and WPA-TKIP is given by*

$$\Pr(Z_2 = K[0] - K[2] - 2) \approx \frac{1}{N}.$$

Proof. We can prove the major path for the target event in the same way as the proof of Theorem 7 when $r = 2$. After the end of the KSA, all of $S_0[1] = x$, $S_0[2] = 0$ and $S_0[x] = K[0] - K[2] - 2$ hold simultaneously (see Step 2 in the proof of Theorem 7). In addition, $S_0[1] \neq 2$ always hold because $x \in [3, N-1]$ during Step 2 in the proof of Theorem 7. Figure 6 shows a state transition from the initial to the second round of the PRGA. According to the state transition, the PRGA outputs $Z_2 = 0$. Then, the target event occurs only when $K[0] - K[2] - 2 = 0$, whose probability is $\frac{1}{N}$ because the RC4 key is generated uniformly at random. Therefore, we obtain the probability of the major path as $\frac{1}{N}\alpha_2$.

On the other hand, we assume that the target event occurs with a probability of random association $\frac{1}{N}$ except the major path. In summary, we obtain

$$\Pr(Z_2 = K[0] - K[2] - 2) \approx \frac{1}{N}\alpha_2 + \frac{1}{N}(1 - \alpha_2) = \frac{1}{N},$$

where $\alpha_2 \approx \frac{1}{N^2} \cdot (1 - \frac{3}{N}) \cdot (1 - \frac{1}{N})^{N-3} \sum_{x=3}^{N-1} (1 - \frac{1}{N})^x \cdot (1 - \frac{1}{N})^{x-3} \cdot (1 - \frac{2}{N})^{N-x-1}$. □

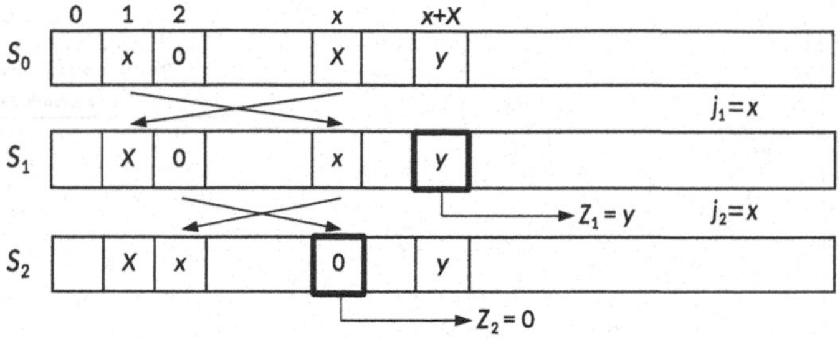

Fig. 6. State transition diagram of the major path in the case of Z_2.

3.3 Experimental Results

We have executed experiments on Theorems 7, 9 and 10 in order to confirm the accuracy of theoretical values. The following is experimental environment: Intel(R) Xeon(R) CPU E5-1680 v3 with 3.20 GHz, 32.0 GB memory, gcc 5.4.0 compiler and C language. Our experiments have used N^5 samples generated from randomly chosen keys in generic RC4 and WPA-TKIP. Because each of the iterated RC4 key correlations has a relative bias with a probability of at least $\mathcal{O}(\frac{1}{N})$. Then, the number of samples to distinguish each of the iterated RC4 key correlations from random distribution is at least $\mathcal{O}(N^3)$ according to Theorem 4. We have also evaluated the percentage of the relative error ϵ of the experimental values compared with the theoretical values:

$$\epsilon = \frac{|\text{experimental value} - \text{theoretical value}|}{\text{experimental value}} \times 100(\%).$$

Figures 7, 8 and 9 show comparison between the experimental and the theoretical probabilities in both generic RC4 and WPA-TKIP, and the percentage of the relative error ϵ, respectively.

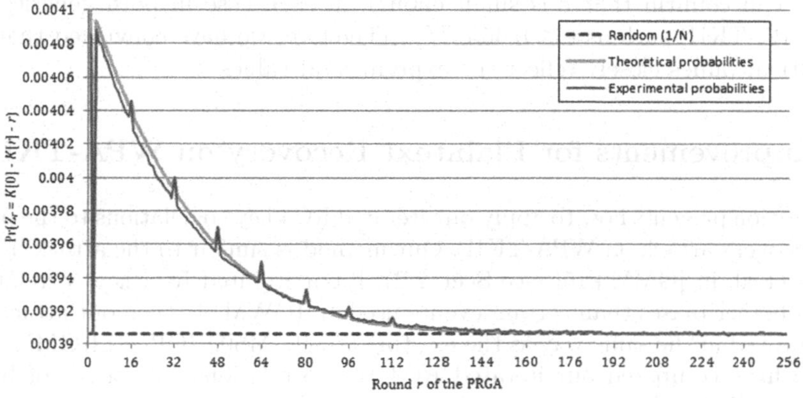

Fig. 7. Comparison between experimental and theoretical probabilities in generic RC4.

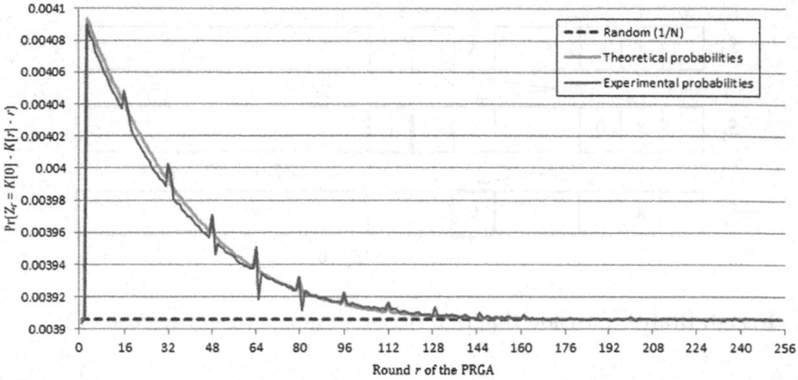

Fig. 8. Comparison between experimental and theoretical probabilities in WPA-TKIP.

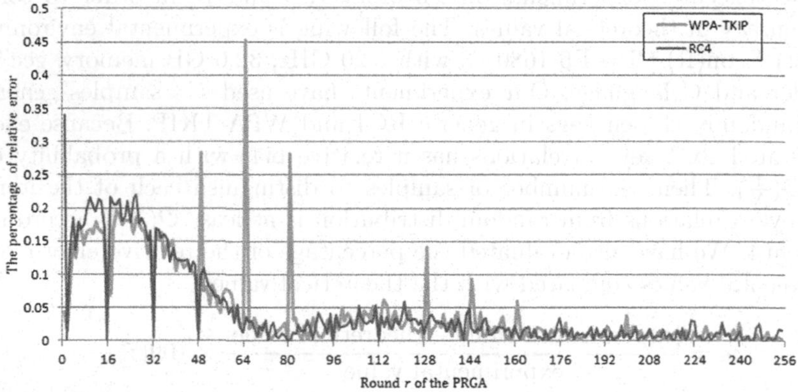

Fig. 9. The percentage of relative error ϵ between experimental and theoretical probabilities in both generic RC4 and WPA-TKIP.

We can confirm that ϵ is small enough in each case in both generic RC4 and WPA-TKIP such as $\epsilon \leq 0.453$ (%). Therefore, we have convinced that the theoretical values closely reflect the experimental values.

4 Improvements for Plaintext Recovery on WPA-TKIP

This section presents how to apply our iterated RC4 key correlations to the plaintext recovery attack on WPA-TKIP. Our method is similar to the attack by Sen Gupta et al. in [GMM+15] (see Sect. 2.2). If our iterated RC4 key correlations induce higher biases than certain events used in [IOWM14], then our attack can be improved in the same way as the existing attack [MS02,IOWM14,GMM+15].

We have compared our iterated RC4 key correlations with a set of biases used in [IOWM14]. Our iterated RC4 key correlations of the keystream $\{Z_{17}, Z_{18}, Z_{33}, Z_{34}, Z_{49}, Z_{50}, Z_{66}, Z_{82}\}$ induce higher biases than the corresponding events used in [IOWM14]. Thus, we can reduce the number of ciphertexts for recovering the corresponding bytes of a plaintext on WPA-TKIP according to Theorem 4. Table 2 shows significant improvements for recovering 8 bytes of a plaintext on WPA-TKIP from [IOWM14].

To summarize our result, by using our iterated RC4 key correlations instead of the corresponding events used in [IOWM14], the number of ciphertexts for recovering P_{17}, P_{18}, P_{33}, P_{34}, P_{49}, P_{50}, P_{66}, and P_{82} on WPA-TKIP can be reduced to $2^{17.727}$, $2^{17.800}$, $2^{18.955}$, $2^{19.035}$, $2^{20.297}$, $2^{20.386}$, $2^{21.869}$, and $2^{23.505}$ from $2^{23.178}$, $2^{23.210}$, $2^{23.770}$, $2^{23.791}$, $2^{24.114}$, $2^{24.135}$, $2^{24.479}$, and $2^{24.820}$, respectively.

Table 2. Significant improvements for recovering 8 bytes of a plaintext on WPA-TKIP from [IOWM14].

Round	Iterated RC4 key correlations			Biases used in [IOWM14]		
	Event	Probability	# of ciphertexts	Event	Probability	# of ciphertexts
17	$Z_{17} = K[0] - K[1] - 17$	$2^{-8} \cdot (1 + 2^{-4.863})$	$2^{17.727}$	$Z_{17} = 17$	$2^{-8} \cdot (1 + 2^{-7.589})$	$2^{23.178}$
18	$Z_{18} = K[0] - K[2] - 18$	$2^{-8} \cdot (1 + 2^{-4.900})$	$2^{17.800}$	$Z_{18} = 18$	$2^{-8} \cdot (1 + 2^{-7.605})$	$2^{23.210}$
33	$Z_{33} = K[0] - K[1] - 33$	$2^{-8} \cdot (1 + 2^{-5.477})$	$2^{18.955}$	$Z_{33} = 0$	$2^{-8} \cdot (1 + 2^{-7.885})$	$2^{23.770}$
34	$Z_{34} = K[0] - K[2] - 34$	$2^{-8} \cdot (1 + 2^{-5.518})$	$2^{19.035}$	$Z_{34} = 0$	$2^{-8} \cdot (1 + 2^{-7.896})$	$2^{23.791}$
49	$Z_{49} = K[0] - K[1] - 49$	$2^{-8} \cdot (1 + 2^{-6.149})$	$2^{20.297}$	$Z_{49} = 0$	$2^{-8} \cdot (1 + 2^{-8.057})$	$2^{24.114}$
50	$Z_{50} = K[0] - K[2] - 50$	$2^{-8} \cdot (1 + 2^{-6.193})$	$2^{20.386}$	$Z_{50} = 0$	$2^{-8} \cdot (1 + 2^{-8.068})$	$2^{24.135}$
66	$Z_{66} = K[0] - K[2] - 66$	$2^{-8} \cdot (1 + 2^{-6.934})$	$2^{21.869}$	$Z_{66} = 0$	$2^{-8} \cdot (1 + 2^{-8.239})$	$2^{24.479}$
82	$Z_{82} = K[0] - K[2] - 82$	$2^{-8} \cdot (1 + 2^{-7.752})$	$2^{23.505}$	$Z_{82} = 0$	$2^{-8} \cdot (1 + 2^{-8.410})$	$2^{24.820}$

5 Conclusion

This paper has focused on key correlations of the keystream, and investigated correlations between $(K[0], K[r \bmod \ell])$ pairs and Z_r based on the previous works in [SVV11, Sar14]. Then, we have provided theoretical proofs of newly observed key correlations of the keystream. Combining our key correlations with the previous ones can be integrated as the *iterated RC4 key correlations* completely, i.e., $Z_r = K[0] - K[r \bmod \ell] - r$ for any arbitrary round r.

Furthermore, this paper has presented how to apply our iterated RC4 key correlations to the plaintext recovery attack on WPA-TKIP. Our iterated RC4 key correlations of the keystream $\{Z_{17}, Z_{18}, Z_{33}, Z_{34}, Z_{49}, Z_{50}, Z_{66}, Z_{82}\}$ induce higher biases than the corresponding events used in [IOWM14]. Then, our attack has demonstrated significant improvements for recovering the corresponding 8 bytes of a plaintext on WPA-TKIP from [IOWM14].

Our work could be further extended in the following directions, which remain open problems in the future:

- In [SVV11], Sepehrdad et al. discovered new key correlations of the keystream experimentally, and applied these key correlations to the theoretical key recovery attack on generic RC4. Similarly, new iterated RC4 key correlations might contribute to the improvements for recovering full bytes of an RC4 key on both generic RC4 and WPA-TKIP.

- In [OIWM15], Ohigashi et al. proposed full plaintext recovery against generic RC4 with the help of around 2^{35} ciphertexts. In [PPS15] and [VP15], Paterson et al. and Vanhoef et al. presented practical impact of the plaintext recovery attacks against WPA-TKIP, respectively. Our iterated RC4 key correlations might be applied to the attacks against both generic RC4 and WPA-TKIP, and reduce the number of ciphertexts for recovering full bytes of a plaintext.
- In [IM17], Ito et al. proposed secure IV setting for WPA-TKIP in such a way that it can keep the security level of generic RC4. Similarly, we would like to suggest some minimal improvement to the RC4 key schedule that makes plaintext recovery attacks more difficult.

Acknowledgements. This work is partially supported by JSPS KAKENHI Grant (C) (JP15K00183) and (JP15K00189) and Japan Science and Technology Agency, CREST (JPMJCR1404) and Infrastructure Development for Promoting International S&T Cooperation and Project for Establishing a Nationwide Practical Education Network for IT Human Resources Development, Education Network for Practical Information Technologies.

References

[FM02] Ferugson, N., MacFergus: Michael: an improved MIC for 802.11 WEP. doc.: IEEE 802.11-02/020r0, April 2002

[FMS01] Fluhrer, S., Mantin, I., Shamir, A.: Weaknesses in the key scheduling algorithm of RC4. In: Vaudenay, S., Youssef, A.M. (eds.) SAC 2001. LNCS, vol. 2259, pp. 1–24. Springer, Heidelberg (2001). https://doi.org/10.1007/3-540-45537-X_1

[GMM+15] Sen Gupta, S., Maitra, S., Meier, W., Paul, G., Sarkar, S.: Dependence in IV-related bytes of RC4 key enhances vulnerabilities in WPA. In: Cid, C., Rechberger, C. (eds.) FSE 2014. LNCS, vol. 8540, pp. 350–369. Springer, Heidelberg (2015). https://doi.org/10.1007/978-3-662-46706-0_18

[HWF02] Housley, R., Whiting, D., Ferguson, N.: Alternate temporal key hash. doc.: IEEE 802.11-02/282r2, April 2002

[IM17] Ito, R., Miyaji, A.: Refined construction of RC4 key setting in WPA. IEICE Trans. Fundam. **E100–A**(1), 138–148 (2017)

[IOWM14] Isobe, T., Ohigashi, T., Watanabe, Y., Morii, M.: Full plaintext recovery attack on broadcast RC4. In: Moriai, S. (ed.) FSE 2013. LNCS, vol. 8424, pp. 179–202. Springer, Heidelberg (2014). https://doi.org/10.1007/978-3-662-43933-3_10

[KMP+98] Knudsen, L.R., Meier, W., Preneel, B., Rijmen, V., Verdoolaege, S.: Analysis methods for (Alleged) RC4. In: Ohta, K., Pei, D. (eds.) ASIACRYPT 1998. LNCS, vol. 1514, pp. 327–341. Springer, Heidelberg (1998). https://doi.org/10.1007/3-540-49649-1_26

[Man01] Mantin, I.: Analysis of the Stream Cipher RC4. Master's thesis, The Weizmann Institute of Science, Israel (2001). http://edge.cs.drexel.edu/regli/Classes/CS680/Papers/802.11/Security/RC4/Mantin1.ps

[MK08] Maximov, A., Khovratovich, D.: New state recovery attack on RC4. In: Wagner, D. (ed.) CRYPTO 2008. LNCS, vol. 5157, pp. 297–316. Springer, Heidelberg (2008). https://doi.org/10.1007/978-3-540-85174-5_17

[MS02] Mantin, I., Shamir, A.: A practical attack on broadcast RC4. In: Matsui, M. (ed.) FSE 2001. LNCS, vol. 2355, pp. 152–164. Springer, Heidelberg (2002). https://doi.org/10.1007/3-540-45473-X_13

[OIWM15] Ohigashi, T., Isobe, T., Watanabe, Y., Morii, M.: Full plaintext recovery attacks on RC4 using multiple biases. IEICE Trans. Fundam. **E98–A**(1), 81–91 (2015)

[PM07] Paul, G., Maitra, S.: Permutation after RC4 key scheduling reveals the secret key. In: Adams, C., Miri, A., Wiener, M. (eds.) SAC 2007. LNCS, vol. 4876, pp. 360–377. Springer, Heidelberg (2007). https://doi.org/10.1007/978-3-540-77360-3_23

[Pop15] Popov, A.: Prohibiting RC4 cipher suites. Internet Engineering Task Force - IETF, Request for Comments, 7465, February 2015

[PPS15] Paterson, K.G., Poettering, B., Schuldt, J.C.N.: Plaintext recovery attacks against WPA/TKIP. In: Cid, C., Rechberger, C. (eds.) FSE 2014. LNCS, vol. 8540, pp. 325–349. Springer, Heidelberg (2015). https://doi.org/10.1007/978-3-662-46706-0_17

[Roo95] Roos, A.: A class of weak keys in the RC4 stream cipher. Posts in sci.crypt (1995). http://marcel.wanda.ch/Archive/WeakKeys

[Sar14] Sarkar, S.: Proving empirically key-correlations in RC4. Inf. Process. Lett. **114**(5), 234–238 (2014)

[SVV11] Sepehrdad, P., Vaudenay, S., Vuagnoux, M.: Discovery and exploitation of new biases in RC4. In: Biryukov, A., Gong, G., Stinson, D.R. (eds.) SAC 2010. LNCS, vol. 6544, pp. 74–91. Springer, Heidelberg (2011). https://doi.org/10.1007/978-3-642-19574-7_5

[VP15] Vanhoef, M., Piessens, F.: All your biases belong to Us: breaking RC4 in WPA-TKIP and TLS. In: USENIX Security Symposium 2015, pp. 97–112 (2015)

[VP16] Vanhoef, M., Piessens, F.: Predicting, decrypting, and abusing WPA2/802.11 group keys. In: USENIX Security Symposium (2016)

[VV07] Vaudenay, S., Vuagnoux, M.: Passive–Only key recovery attacks on RC4. In: Adams, C., Miri, A., Wiener, M. (eds.) SAC 2007. LNCS, vol. 4876, pp. 344–359. Springer, Heidelberg (2007). https://doi.org/10.1007/978-3-540-77360-3_22

A New Framework for Finding Nonlinear Superpolies in Cube Attacks Against Trivium-Like Ciphers

Chendong Ye and Tian Tian(✉)

National Digital Switching System Engineering and Technological Research Center, P.O. Box 407, 62 Kexue Road, Zhengzhou 450001, China
tiantian_d@126.com

Abstract. In this paper, we focus on traditional cube attacks against Trivium-like ciphers in which linear and nonlinear superpolies are experimentally tested. We provide a new framework on nonlinear superpoly recoveries by exploiting a kind of linearization technique. It worth noting that, in this new framework, the complexities of testing and recovering nonlinear superpolies are almost the same as those of testing and recovering linear superpolies. Moreover, extensive experiments show that by making use of the new framework, the probability to find a quadratic superpoly is almost twice as large as that to find a linear superpoly for Kreyvium and they are almost the same for Trivium. Hopefully, this new framework would provide some new insights on cube attacks against NFSR-based ciphers, and in particular make nonlinear superpolies potentially useful in the future cube attacks.

Keywords: Cube attacks · Linearity tests · Quadracity tests Trivium-like ciphers

1 Introduction

Trivium [3] is a bit oriented synchronous stream cipher designed by Cannière and Preneel, which is one of the eSTREAM hardware-oriented finalists and an International Standard under ISO/IEC 29192-3:2012.

Since proposed, Trivium has attracted a lot of attention for its simplicity. As a result, there are many cryptanalytic results on Trivium such as key recovery attacks based on cube attacks [7,8,12,14,17,19], distinguishing attacks based on cube attacks [10,11,15,18,22], conditional differential attacks [9], and internal state recovery attacks [13]. Among these various cryptanalytic techniques, cube attacks are one of the most powerful tool against Trivium. It was proposed by Dinur and Shamir [7]. In [7], the authors recovered 35 linear superpolies of the 767-round Trivium. In [14], Mroczkowski and Szmidt applied cube attacks to the 709-round Trivium, and firstly reported quadratic superpolies. In specific,

Supported by National Natural Science Foundation of China 61672533.

W. Susilo and G. Yang (Eds.): ACISP 2018, LNCS 10946, pp. 172–187, 2018.
https://doi.org/10.1007/978-3-319-93638-3_11

they found 41 linear superpolies and 22 quadratic superpolies. In [8], two new ideas are proposed concerning cube attacks against Trivium. One is a recursive method to construct useful cubes. The other is simultaneously testing a lots of subcubes of a large cube using the Meobius transformation. They found 12 linear superpolies and 6 quadratic superpolies for the 799-round Trivium. In [17], Todo et al. applied the division property to cube attacks. Based on the division property, attackers could identify the key variables involved in the superpoly of a given cube by solving corresponding MILP models instead of performing linearity/quadraticity tests. As a result, for the 832-round Trivium, they provide a cube of size 72 whose superpoly involves at most 5 key bits. Hence, they could recover at most one key bit of the secret key with an impractical attack complexity 2^{77}. In [19], the authors proposed a technique to reduce the complexity of superpoly recovery based on the work of [17]. Very recently, in [7], Liu et al. proposed a new variant of cube attack called correlation cube attack, which exploits conditional correlation properties between the superpoly of a cube and a specific set of low-degree polynomials. A major difference between [7] and the previous cube attacks is that secret information is recovered by solving a system of probabilistic equations rather than deterministic equations. As a result, they could recover about 7 key bits and 5 key bits of the 805- and 835-round Trivium with time complexity 2^{44}, using 2^{45} keystream bits and preprocessing time 2^{51}.

Due to the simplicity and the established security of Trivium, some recently proposed crypto primitives adopt similar designs, such as Kreyvium [4] and TriviA-SC [5,6].

Kreyvium is designed for the efficient homomorphic-ciphertext compression in homomorphic encryptions. In [10], based on a cube of size 61, Liu presented a distinguisher on the 872-round Kreyvium. In [19], for the 888-round Kreyvium, the authors provided a key recovery attack based on a cube of size 102. In [20], with 24-th and 25-th order conditional characteristics, the authors proposed distinguishers on 899-round Kreyvium.

TriviA-SC is the base component of the authenticated encryption algorithm TriviA which was a second-round candidate of CAESAR competition. It has two versions, i.e., TriviA-SC-v1 and TriviA-SC-v2. Hereinafter, TriviA-SC means its both versions, if not specified. In [15], the authors proposed distinguishers for the 930-round TriviA-SC-v1 and the 950-round TriviA-SC-v2 respectively. Furthermore, the authors provided a slide attack on the full TriviA-SC-v2. In [10], based on cubes of sizes around 63, the author proposed distinguishers of the 1035-round TriviA-SC-v1, the 1046-round TriviA-SC-v2, and the full 1152-round of simplified TriviA-SC where the nonlinear term in the output bit was removed. In [21], for the full 1152 rounds simplified TriviA-SC, the authors found a linear distinguisher with a complexity of 2^{120}.

Before the work of [17], cube attacks utilize linearity/quadraticity tests to find desirable superpolies, which is called traditional cube attacks to distinguish from division property based cube attacks and correlation cube attacks. In this paper, we are concerned with traditional cube attacks and provide a new idea on nonlinear superpoly recoveries.

1.1 Our Contributions

The inspiration of this paper comes from our observations of cube attacks against Trivium. In particular, it is observed that the algebraic normal forms (ANFs) of quadratic superpolies recovered in cube attacks against Trivium have fixed forms. Besides, this observation is also true for other Trivium-like ciphers. Hence, we propose to treat some nonlinear key expressions as a whole, and regard the first output bit as a function on these nonlinear key expressions not key variables themselves. Thus, nonlinear superpolies could be recovered by testing linearity on nonlinear key expressions. Based on this idea, we propose a generic framework to recover nonlinear superpolies using linearity test principles for Trivium-like ciphers.

As illustrations, we perform extensive experiments on Trivium, Kreyvium, and TriviA-SC-v2 with our new framework. To show the correctness and effectiveness of our framework, for each of the variants with from 600 to 700 initialization rounds of these three ciphers, we search for linear and nonlinear superpolies based on 100 randomly chosen cubes. Table 1 shows the total number of nonlinear and linear superpolies that we find. Note that, in the case of Trivium and Kreyvium, the number of nonlinear superpolies is close to or even twice as large as that of linear superpolies.

Moreover, with our framework we find several new superpoies for variants with relatively high initialization rounds. First, we reveal some new quadratic supeprolies of the 784- and the 799-round Trivium. Besides, we recover 5 linear superpolies and 2 quadratic superploies of the 802-round Trivium. Second, with a cube of size 38, we find 8 different quadratic superpolies but no linear superpolies for the 776-round Kreyvium. Third, we gain linear and quadratic superpolies for the 864-round TriviA-SC-v2 and the 992-round simplified TriviA-SC-v2, respectively. Table 2 lists our results.

Table 1. The distribution of nonlinear and linear superpolies

Stream ciphers	# of nonlinear superpolies	# of linear superpolies	Ratios
Trivium	7517944	8155985	0.92
Krevium	2538591	1194480	2.13
TrivA-SC-v2	491551	4074914	0.12

Table 2. Results on round-reduced Trivium-like stream ciphers

Ciphers	# of rounds	# of superpolies
Trivium	802	5 linear, 2 quadratic
Kreyvium	776	8 quadratic
TriviA-SC-v2	864	12 linear, 3 quadratic
TriviA-SC-v2 simplified	992	14 linear, 2 quadratic

1.2 Organization

The rest of this paper is structured as follows. In Sect. 2, we introduce some basic definitions and facts. In Sect. 3, we propose a new framework to find nonlinear superpolies with a low complexity. In Sect. 4, our new framework is applied to Trivium-like stream ciphers. In Sect. 5, we summarize our work.

2 Preliminaries

2.1 Trivium-Like Stream Ciphers

The main building block of a Trivium-like cipher is a Galois nonlinear feedback shift register, such that for every clock cycle there are three internal state bits updated by quadratic feedback functions and all the other internal sate bits are updated by shifting. In specific, let A, B and C be three shift registers of length L_A, L_B, and L_C respectively. For $t \geq 0$, let $A_t = (x_t, \dots, x_{t+L_A-1})$, $B_t = (y_t, \dots, y_{t+L_B-1})$, and $C_t = (z_t, \dots, z_{t+L_C-1})$ denote the t-th state of A, B and C respectively. Then the internal state of a Trivium-like cipher at time instance t is given by $s_t = (A_t, B_t, C_t)$, and the state update function could be described as

$$\begin{aligned} x_t &= z_{t-r_c-1} \cdot z_{t-r_c} + l_A(s_{t-1}), \\ y_t &= x_{t-r_a-1} \cdot x_{t-r_a} + l_B(s_{t-1}), \\ z_t &= y_{t-r_b-1} \cdot y_{t-r_b} + l_C(s_{t-1}), \end{aligned}$$

where l_λ is a linear function and $1 \leq r_\lambda \leq L_\lambda$ for $\lambda \in \{A, B, C\}$. After N initialization rounds, a filtering function f is used to compute a keystream bit from the current internal state, i.e., $z_t = f(s_t)$ for $t \geq N$.

There are three well-known Trivium-like ciphers, say Trivium [3], Kreyvium [4], and TriviA-SC [5,6]. The first two algorithms well fulfill the description above, while the last algorithm uses two extra registers K^* and V^*, which are padded with key bits and IV bits respectively, to XOR the key bits and IV bits to the feedback function. Besides, the filtering functions of Trivium and Keryvium are linear, while that of TriviA-SC is quadratic.

2.2 Cube Attacks

The idea of cube attack was first proposed by Dinur and Shamir in [7]. In the cube attack against stream ciphers, an output bit z is described as a tweakable Boolean function f on secret key variables $Key = (k_0, k_1, \dots, k_{n-1})$ and public IV variables $IV = (iv_0, iv_1, \dots, iv_{m-1})$, i.e.,

$$z = f(Key, IV).$$

Let I be a subset of d public variables, where $1 \leq d \leq m$. Without loss of generality, we assume that $I = \{iv_0, iv_1, \dots, iv_{d-1}\}$. Then the function f can be rewritten

$$f(Key, IV) = t_I \cdot p_I(Key, iv_d, iv_{d+1}, \dots, iv_{m-1}) \oplus q(Key, IV),$$

where $t_I = \prod_{i=0}^{d-1} iv_i$, p_I does not contain any variable in I, and each term in q is not divisible by t_I. It can be seen that the summation of the 2^d functions derived from f by assigning all the possible values to the d variables in I is equal to p_I. The variables in the set I are called *cube variables*, the set C_I of all 2^d possible assignments of the cube variables in I is called a *d-dimensional cube*, and the polynomial p_I is called the *superpoly* of I. Furthermore, fixing each non-cube variable to be a constant, the superpoly p_I becomes a polynomial with secret key variables only. **In this paper, all non-cube variables are fixed to be 0's.**

A cube attack consists of two phases: a preprocessing phase which is independent of the secret key and a online phase which should be carried out for every secret key. In the preprocessing phase, attackers should find some useful superpolies to recover the secret key. In the online phase, by solving a system of equations derived from previously found superpolies under the real key, some information of the real key could be revealed.

2.3 Linearity and Quadraticity Tests

Let $f(x_1, x_2, \ldots, x_n)$ be a black-box Boolean function, whose explicit representation is unknown, but the value $f(\boldsymbol{a})$ for any input vector $\boldsymbol{a} \in \mathbb{F}_2^n$ can be queried. In the following, we would recall how to do linearity [2]/quadraticity [1] tests of f.

The BLR Linearity Test. Choose $\boldsymbol{a}, \boldsymbol{b} \in \mathbb{F}_2^n$ uniformly and independently, and verify

$$f(\boldsymbol{a} \oplus \boldsymbol{b}) \oplus f(\boldsymbol{a}) \oplus f(\boldsymbol{b}) = f(\boldsymbol{0}). \tag{1}$$

If f is linear, then the test will succeed, whereas if $\deg(f) \geq 2$, then the test may fail with a certain probability. Thus the test should be repeated sufficiently many times to make sure that f is very close to being linear. If f passes through the linearity test, then its ANF could be recovered by $n+1$ more queries. The constant term of f is given by $f(\boldsymbol{0})$. Then the coefficient of the variable x_i in f for $1 \leq i \leq n$ is given by

$$c_i = f(\boldsymbol{e}_i) \oplus f(\boldsymbol{0}),$$

where $e_i \in \mathbb{F}_2^n$ whose elements are 0 except the i-th elements.

The Quadraticity Test. Choose $\boldsymbol{a}, \boldsymbol{b}, \boldsymbol{c} \in \mathbb{F}_2^n$ uniformly and independently, and verify

$$f(\boldsymbol{a} \oplus \boldsymbol{b} \oplus \boldsymbol{c}) \oplus f(\boldsymbol{a} \oplus \boldsymbol{b}) \oplus f(\boldsymbol{a} \oplus \boldsymbol{c}) \oplus f(\boldsymbol{b} \oplus \boldsymbol{c}) \oplus f(\boldsymbol{a}) \oplus f(\boldsymbol{b}) \oplus f(\boldsymbol{c}) = f(\boldsymbol{0}). \tag{2}$$

Similarly if f is quadratic, then the test succeeds, whereas if $\deg(f) > 2$, then the test may fail. Thus the test should be repeated sufficiently many times to make sure that f is very close to being quadratic. If f passes through the quadraticity test, then the coefficient of a quadratic term $x_i x_j$ in f for $1 \leq i < j \leq n$ is given by $f(\boldsymbol{e}_i \oplus \boldsymbol{e}_j) \oplus f(\boldsymbol{e}_i) \oplus f(\boldsymbol{e}_j) \oplus f(\boldsymbol{0})$.

3 A New Framework to Find Nonlinear Superpolies

3.1 Motivations

The motivations of this paper come from the following observations on the extensive superpolies recovered by the previous traditional cube attacks against Trivium. Please refer to [7,8,14] for a large number of instances of superpolies for Trivium variants.

Our first observation is **the sparsity of nonlinear superpolies**. It can be easily observed that the ANFs of all recovered superpolies are very sparse, most of which have less than five terms. Accordingly, the systems of nonlinear equations in key variables defined by these superpolies are easy to solve during the online phase, see [14] for an example.

Our second observation is that **some key variables are missing in linear superpolies**. It can be observed that none of the linear superpolies were found so far involving the key variables between k_{69} and k_{79}. This phenomenon is also mentioned in [8]. Hence, to recover the information of the key variables between k_{69} and k_{79}, linear superpolies are not sufficient.

Accordingly, nonlinear superpolies are as useful as linear superpolies in cube attacks against Trivium, and exploiting nonlinear superpolies could definitely bring some merits to mounting cube attacks. However, compared with linear superpolies, it needs much more queries to find nonlinear superpolies. For instance, eight queries are needed to do one verification in quadraticity tests (see (2)), while only four queries are needed to do one verification in linear tests (see (1)). When the dimension of a cube becomes large, it would be much more difficult to find nonlinear superpolies than linear superpolies.

Our third observation is **the fixed forms of nonlinear superpolies**. It is interesting to find that the ANFs of all nonlinear superpolies recovered in cube attacks against Trivium have very specific forms. It can be observed that most of the published quadratic superpolies only have one quadratic monomial of the form $x_i x_{i+1}$ accompanied by two degree 1 monomials. This observation was also mentioned in [8, Section 4.2].

We remark that since TriviA-SC-v2 and Kreyvium are designed based on Trivium, the three observations also hold for TriviA-SC-v2 and the first and the third observations hold for Kreyvium (This maybe due to that Kreyvium has an independent Key register whose output is continuously xored to the feedback of the main register.) Inspired by the third observation, we propose a new framework to find and recover nonlinear superpolies with low complexities. In the new framework, we fix some nonlinear key expressions, and find superpolies which are linear about these fixed nonlinear key expressions. Note that linear superpolies in this sense are *nonlinear* on key variables. There are two key points involved in the new framework. One is how to do linearity tests on superpolies about the fixed nonlinear key expressions. The other is how to choose useful nonlinear key expressions. We shall explain these two points in detail in the following two subsections respectively.

3.2 A Generic Technique for Linearity Tests of Composite Functions

Let $g(y_0, y_1, \ldots, y_{m-1})$ be a Boolean function on the variables $y_0, y_1, \cdots, y_{m-1}$. For $0 \leq i \leq m-1$, let $h_i(x_0, x_1, \ldots, x_{n-1})$ be a Boolean function on the variables $x_0, x_1, \cdots, x_{n-1}$. Then

$$f(x_0, x_1, \ldots, x_{n-1}) = g(h_0(x_0, x_1, \ldots, x_{n-1}), \ldots, h_{m-1}(x_0, x_1, \ldots, x_{n-1}))$$

is a composite function of $g(y_0, y_1, \ldots, y_{m-1})$ and $h_i(x_0, x_1, \ldots, x_{n-1})$. Note that when f is nonlinear on the variables $x_0, x_1, \ldots, x_{n-1}$, it is not necessary that f is nonlinear on the expressions $h_0, h_1, \ldots, h_{m-1}$.

Example 1. Let $f = x_0 \cdot x_1 \oplus x_2 \cdot x_3$ be a Boolean function. Let $h_0 = x_0 \cdot x_1$ and $h_1 = x_2 \cdot x_3$. It is clear that $f = h_0 \oplus h_1$. Hence f is linear on the expressions h_0 and h_1, but nonlinear on the variables x_0, x_1, x_2, x_3.

In Example 1, the ANF of $f(x_0, x_1, x_2, x_3)$ is known, and so it is easy to see whether f is linear on h_0 and h_1. Now the problem is when $f(x_0, x_1, \ldots, x_{n-1})$ is a black-box Boolean function, how to test whether f is a linear Boolean function on $h_0, h_1, \ldots, h_{m-1}$. Note that f could be queried only by assigning values to the variables $x_0, x_1, \ldots, x_{n-1}$. We formally present this problem in the following.

Problem 1. Let $f(x_0, x_1, \ldots, x_{n-1})$ be a black-box Boolean function. Assume that $h_0, h_1, \ldots, h_{m-1}$ are m Boolean functions on the variables $x_0, x_1, \ldots, x_{n-1}$ such that there is a Boolean function $g(y_0, y_1, \cdots, y_{m-1})$ satisfying $f = g(h_0, h_1, \ldots, h_{m-1})$. How to test whether f is linear about $h_0, h_1, \ldots, h_{m-1}$ by querying $f(x_0, x_1, \ldots, x_{n-1})$?

The difference between Problem 1 and the traditional linearity test of black-box Boolean functions lies in that we ask the linearity of a set of nonlinear expressions of inputting variables not simply inputting variables themselves. This general problem is open. In the following we give a simple technique to tackle some instances of the problem which is useful in the following attacks. Our basic idea is still the BLR linearity test.

Theorem 1. *Let $f, h_0, \ldots, h_{m-1}$ be as described in Problem 1. If the mapping*

$$H : \boldsymbol{a} = (a_0, a_1, \ldots, a_{n-1}) \mapsto (h_0(\boldsymbol{a}), h_1(\boldsymbol{a}), \ldots, h_{m-1}(\boldsymbol{a})), \boldsymbol{a} \in \mathbb{F}_2^n,$$

is surjective with $H(\mathbf{0}) = \mathbf{0}$, then Algorithm 1 is a one-sided tester for f being linear on the expressions $h_0, h_1, \ldots, h_{m-1}$. In particular, if Algorithm 1 returns reject, then f is not linear on the expressions $h_0, h_1, \ldots, h_{m-1}$ with probability 1.

Proof. Since f is a composite function of the form

$$f = g(h_0, h_1, \ldots, h_{m-1}),$$

it follows that f being linear on the given expressions $h_0, h_1, \ldots, h_{m-1}$ is equivalent to $g(y_0, y_1, \cdots, y_{m-1})$ is linear. Thus it suffices to show Algorithm 1 is actually a BLR linearity test on $g(y_0, y_1, \cdots, y_{m-1})$.

Algorithm 1. Linearity test of composite functions

Require: a black-box function f on $X = (x_0, x_1, \ldots, x_{n-1})$ and a vectorial Boolean function $H = (h_0(X), h_1(X), \ldots, h_{m-1}(X))$.
1: choose $\boldsymbol{a}$ and $\boldsymbol{b}$ randomly and uniformly in $\mathbb{F}_2^m$;
2: compute X_1, X_2, X_3 satisfying $H(X_1) = \boldsymbol{a}$, $H(X_2) = \boldsymbol{b}$, and $H(X_3) = \boldsymbol{a} \oplus \boldsymbol{b}$, respectively;
3: compute $v = f(X_1) \oplus f(X_2) \oplus f(X_3) \oplus f(\boldsymbol{0})$
4: **if** $v \neq 0$ **then**
5:     **return** reject;
6: **else**
7:     **return** accept;
8: **end if**

Let $\boldsymbol{a}$, $\boldsymbol{b}$, $\boldsymbol{c}$, X_1, X_2, and X_3 be as described in Algorithm 1, where the existence of X_1, X_2, X_3 can be deduced from the hypothesis that H is surjective. Then we have

$$f(X_1) = g(\boldsymbol{a}), f(X_2) = g(\boldsymbol{b}) \text{ and } f(X_3) = \boldsymbol{a} \oplus \boldsymbol{b}.$$

It follows that

$$f(X_1) \oplus f(X_2) \oplus f(X_3) \oplus f(\boldsymbol{0}) = g(\boldsymbol{a}) \oplus g(\boldsymbol{b}) \oplus g(\boldsymbol{a} \oplus \boldsymbol{b}) \oplus g(\boldsymbol{0}).$$

Hence it can be seen that line 3 in Algorithm 1 is a BLR linearity test for $g(y_0, y_1, \ldots, y_{m-1})$.

Remark 1. The probability that Algorithm 1 rejects a function f which is nonlinear on $h_0, h_1, \ldots, h_{m-1}$ is equal to the probability that the algorithm in [1] rejecting the corresponding function g which is nonlinear.

Algorithm 1 needs repeating sufficient times to make sure that f is very close to being linear on $h_0, h_1, \ldots, h_{m-1}$. When we make sure that f is linear on $h_0, h_1, \ldots, h_{m-1}$, we could recover the ANF of f using only $m + 1$ queries like recovering a linear Boolean function. It can be seen that the complexities of doing linearity tests on f and the ANF recovery of f are almost the same as that of linearity tests and linear Boolean functions recovery except the time spent on finding a preimage of the mapping H. When the system of equations defined by $h_0, h_1, \ldots, h_{m-1}$ is sparse and simple, a preimage of the mapping H could be found efficiently. That is the case in our attacks, and it costs less than one second to find a preimage for H in our experiment.

3.3 A Generic Method of Choosing Useful Nonlinear Key Expressions

When it comes to cube attacks, the composite function f discussed in the last subsection is a superpoly p_I of some chosen cube C_I. Traditionally, p_I is seen as a black-box Boolean function on key variables, say $k_0, k_1, \ldots, k_{n-1}$, and attackers try to recover linear superpolies on $k_0, k_1, \ldots, k_{n-1}$. If there exists a set of nonlinear expressions $h_0, h_1, \ldots, h_{m-1}$ in key variables such that p_I could be represented as a composite function $p_I = g(h_0, h_1, \ldots, h_{m-1})$ for some function g, then our new technique could efficiently test whether p_I is linear on the expressions $h_0, h_1, \ldots, h_{m-1}$ resulting in a desirable nonlinear superpoly in key variables.. In the following, we shall show a generic method to find such useful nonlinear expressions in key variables.

During the initialization process of stream ciphers, key variables are gradually mixed with IV variables, and so in some early rounds, when the mixture is not sufficient, they may not be multiplied together. Namely, at some time instance t, each internal state bit s_t^i could be written as

$$s_t^i = g_{i,1}(IV) \oplus g_{i,2}(Key)(0 \leq i \leq l-1),$$

where l is the size of the internal state and $g_{i,1}$ and $g_{i,2}$ may be equal to 0. Since the internal state is updated iteratively, in cube attacks, when all the non-cube variables are set to constant values, the superpoly p_I of a given cube C_I could be naturally seen as a Boolean function on the expressions in the set

$$G = \{g_{i,2}(Key) \mid 0 \leq i \leq l-1\}.$$

Hence, p_I may be nonlinear on key variables but linear on the expressions in G which is the case we desire. By reasonably classifying the set G, attackers can choose several subsets of G satisfying the surjective condition in Theorem 1.

Finally, recall that the third observation given in Subsect. 3.1 points out that Trivium's nonlinear superpolies have fixed forms. In fact, such fixed forms are in accordance with our choosing method, which will be clearly seen in Subsect. 4.2. Hence, this method for choosing useful nonlinear expressions in our new framework is very reasonable.

4 Application to Trivium-Like Stream Ciphers

In this section, we discuss specific applications of our new framework to cube attacks against Trivium-like ciphers including Trivium, Keryvium, and TriviA-SC-v2.

4.1 Some Notes

We give some remarks on implementation details about our framework being used in traditional cube attacks to recover nonlinear superpolies.

First, we suggest to solve the involved systems of nonlinear equations by SAT solvers such as CryptoMiniSat-2.9.5 developed by Soos [16]. There are two main reasons for using CryptoMiniSat not Gröbner basis algorithms or other algebraic methods. The first one is that we only need one solution not all solutions for each system of equations. The second one is that CryptoMiniSat is experimentally fast for sparse equations.

Second, recall that in [8], the Moebius transformation was used to search all the subcubes of a large cube to find linear and quadratic superpolies. Our new framework for recovering nonlinear superpolies could be combined with the Moebius transformation if one has enough memory.

Third, for a stream cipher, useful nonlinear expressions are classified into several groups according to the hypothesis of Theorem 1. Reusing $f(X_1)$ and $f(X_2)$ described in Algorithm 1 for each group test could reduce lots of queries. Besides, when there is only one set of useful nonlinear expressions, $f(X_1)$ and $f(X_2)$ can be reused to find linear superpolies.

4.2 Experimental Results

Results of Trivium. Every internal state bit of Trivium is seen as a Boolean function of key and IV variables. By observing the internal states after 91 initialization rounds, we choose the following two sets of nonlinear expressions in Table 3. There are mainly two reasons for choosing these two sets of nonlinear expressions. Firstly, these two sets of nonlinear expressions satisfy the condition mentioned in Theorem 1 perfectly. Secondly, these two sets could cover all the quadratic expressions appearing in the internal state after 91 initialization rounds.

Table 3. The chosen nonlinear expressions for Trivium

Ciphers	Set	Chosen nonlinear expressions
Trivium	Set A	$k_{i+25}k_{i+26} \oplus k_{i+27} \oplus k_i (0 \le i \le 52)$
	Set B	$k_0k_1 \oplus k_2 \oplus k_{44}$ $k_ik_{1+i} \oplus k_{2+i} \oplus k_{44+i} \oplus k_{53+i}(1 \le i \le 12)$ $k_ik_{1+i} \oplus k_{2+i} \oplus k_{44+i}(13 \le i \le 24)$

To show the correctness and effectiveness of finding nonlinear superpolies using our new framework, we do extensive experiments on the Trivium variants with from 600 to 700 initialization rounds. For each variant, we randomly choose 100 cubes to search linear superpolies and superpolies which are linear about expressions in Set A or B. As a result, we totally obtain 8155985 linear superpolies and 7517944 quadratic superpolies for all these 100 variants. It worth noting that the number of quadratic superpolies is very close to that of linear superpolies. It indicates that quadratic superpolies could be found as easily as linear superpolies with our new framework. Namely, our new framework would make quadratic superpolies play a more important role in cube attacks against Trivium.

Second, we try our framework for Trivium variants with up to 802 initialization rounds. Some new cubes and superpolies for the 784, 799 and 802-round Trivium are listed in Table 5 in the Appendix. To the best of our knowledge, for Trivium variants, it is the first time that traditional cube attacks could reach 802 initialization rounds.

Results of Kreyvium. According to the internal state after 66 initialization rounds and the condition mentioned in Theorem 1, we choose the following nonlinear key expressions

$$k_i \oplus k_{25+i}k_{26+i} \oplus k_{27+i}(0 \leq i \leq 65).$$

Certainly, there may exist other sets of useful nonlinear expressions.

We do similar experiments as those of Trivium on Kreyvium variants with from 600 to 700 initialization rounds. We totally find 1194480 linear superpolies and 2538591 quadratic superpolies for all these 100 variants. Note that the number of quadratic superpolies is more than twice as large as that of linear superpolies. It indicates that quadratic superpolies could be found more easily than linear superpolies. Then, we apply our new framework to search linear superpolies and quadratic superpolies for Kreyvium variants with a higher number of initialization rounds. Consequently, for the 776-round Kreyvium, we gain 8 different quadratic superpolies but no linear superpolies based on a cube of size 38, see Table 6 in the Appendix.

Results of TriviA-SC-v2. According to the internal state of TriviA-SC-v2 after 96 initialization rounds and the condition mentioned in Theorem 1, we choose the following two sets of expressions in Table 4.

First, we perform similar experiments as those of Trivium on the TriviA-SC-v2 variants with from 600 to 700 initialization rounds. For all these 100 variants, we gain 4074914 linear superpolies and 491551 quadratic superpolies. It can be seen that the number of quadratic superpolies is non-ignorable. Namely, finding quadratic superpolies with our framework would bring non-ignorable

Table 4. The nonlinear expressions chosen for of TriviA-SC-v2

Ciphers	Set	Chosen nonlinear expressions
TriviA-SC-v2	Set A	$k_i \oplus k_{64+i}k_{65+i} \oplus k_{66+i}(0 \leq i \leq 61)$ $k_{62} \oplus k_{126}k_{127}$
	Set B	$k_{35+i} \oplus k_{36+i}k_{37+i} \oplus k_{47+i}(0 \leq i \leq 29)$

benefits to traditional cube attacks on TriviA-SC-v2. Then, based on the chosen nonlinear expressions, we attack TriviA-SC-v2 variants with more initialization rounds with our new framework. As a result, we find several linear superpolies and quadratic superpolies for the 864-round TriviA-SC-v2 and the 992-round simplified TriviA-SC-v2, see Table 7 in the Appendix.

5 Conclusion

In this paper, we study traditional cube attacks against Trivium-like stream ciphers, and propose a new framework to find nonlinear superpolies using linearity tests principle. Based on the extensive experiments, it is interesting to find that the probability of finding a quadratic superpoly is twice as large as that of finding a linear suppoly for Kreyvium. That is to find a nonlinear superpoly is easier than to find a linear superpoly for Keryvium. The reason for this and further implications on the security of Kreyvium will be one subject of future work.

Although we only performed lots of experiments on quadratic superpolies for Trivium-like stream ciphers, cubic superpolies and superpolies with degree larger than three are also applicable. In such cases, more careful analysis is needed to choose useful key expressions. This also will be one subject of our future work.

Appendix

In this paper, all our programs are implemented with CUDA and we perform experiments on a PC with an Intel(R) Core i7-4790k @4.00 GHZ CPU, 32 G memory and a GTX-1080 GPU. In the following, we list all the experimental results in details.

Table 5. New superpolies of round-reduced Trivium variants

# of rounds	Superpolies	Cube index
784	$k_{38} \oplus k_{63}k_{64} \oplus k_{65}$	2,4,6,8,10,12,13,15,19,22,24,28,29,32,34,37,38, 40,41,44,47,49,51,53,55,57,65,68,70,73,74,76,78
	$k_{46} \oplus k_{71}k_{72} \oplus k_{73}$	2,4,6,8,10,12,13,15,19,24,28,29,32,34,37,40,41,44, 47,49,51,53,55,57,59,62,65,70,72,73,74,76,78
	$k_{48} \oplus k_{73}k_{74} \oplus k_{75}$	2,4,6,8,10,12,13,15,19,24,28,29,32,34,37,38,40, 41,44,47,49,51,53,55,57,59,68,70,72,73,74,76,78
799	$k_2 \oplus k_{27}x_{28} \oplus k_{29}$	0,2,4,5,6,7,9,11,13,15,18,20,22,24,26,30,32, 35,37,39,42,44,46,52,53,57,62,68,70,72,74,79
	$k_{46} \oplus k_{71}k_{72} \oplus k_{73}$	0,2,4,5,6,7,9,11,13,14,15,18,20,22,24,26,32,35, 37,39,42,44,48,52,53,55,57,61,62,68,70,74,79
802	k_{47}	2,3,4,6,8,10,11,12,15,17,19,21,23,25,29,30,32,34,36, 39,41,43,45,48,50,54,57,58,65,67,69,76,49,59,73,79
	k_{55}	5,7,9,11,13,16,18,20,22,24,26,28,30,31,33,35,37,40, 42,44,46,47,49,51,53,56,60,62,64,66,68,70,74,76,79
	k_{56}	2,4,6,8,10,11,15,17,19,21,23,25,29,30,32,34,36,39, 41,43,45,50,52,54,57,58,67,69,76,49,59,71,73,79
	k_{57}	5,7,9,11,13,16,18,20,22,24,26,28,30,31,33,35,37,40, 42,44,46,49,51,53,55,60,62,64,66,68,70,74,76,79
	k_{59}	5,7,9,11,13,16,18,20,22,24,26,28,30,31,33,35,37,38, 40,42,44,49,51,55,56,60,62,64,66,68,72,74,76,79
	k_{61}	5,7,9,11,13,16,18,20,22,24,26,28,30,31,33,35,37,38, 40,42,46,49,51,53,55,56,60,62,64,66,68,72,74,76,79
	$k_{13} \oplus k_{38}k_{39} \oplus k_{40}$	0,5,7,9,11,13,16,18,20,22,24,26,28,30,31,33,35, 37,40,42,44,46,47,49,51,53,60,62,64,66,72,74,76,79
	$k_{36} \oplus k_{61}k_{62} \oplus k_{63}$	1,2,3,4,6,8,10,12,15,17,19,21,23,25,29,30,32,34,36, 39,41,43,45,50,52,54,57,58,65,67,69,76,49,59,73,79

Table 6. Superpolies of the 776-round Kreyvium

Superpolies	Cube index
$k_4 \oplus k_{29}k_{30} \oplus k_{31}$	2,5,7,9,13,17,19,22,24,28,30,37,39,41,43,45,52,54,58, 64,69,71,73,77,81,83,87,92,97,103,106,109,117,121
$k_5 \oplus k_{30}k_{31} \oplus k_{32}$	0,2,5,7,9,13,19,22,24,28,30,37,39,41,43,45,52,54,58,66, 69,71,73,77,81,83,87,92,97,103,106,109,117,121,127
$k_6 \oplus k_{31}k_{32} \oplus k_{33}$	0,2,5,7,9,13,17,19,22,24,28,30,37,39,41,43,45,49,52, 54,64,66,69,71,73,77,81,83,97,103,106,117,121,127
$k_{26} \oplus k_{51}k_{52} \oplus k_{53}$	2,5,7,9,13,17,19,22,24,28,30,37,39,41,43,45,49,52,64, 66,69,71,73,77,81,83,87,92,97,103,106,109,117,121
$k_{38} \oplus k_{63}k_{64} \oplus k_{65}$	0,2,5,7,9,13,17,19,22,24,28,30,37,39,41,43,45,49,52, 54,64,66,69,71,73,77,81,83,87,92,97,103,106,117,127
$k_{39} \oplus k_{64}k_{65} \oplus k_{66}$	0,2,5,7,13,17,19,22,24,28,30,37,41,43,45,49,52,54,58, 64,66,71,73,77,81,83,87,92,97,103,106,109,117,121,127
$k_{46} \oplus k_{71}k_{72} \oplus k_{73}$	0,2,5,7,9,13,17,19,22,24,28,30,37,39,41,43,45,52,54, 64,66,69,71,73,77,81,83,87,92,97,103,106,109,117,127
$k_{58} \oplus k_{83}k_{84} \oplus k_{85}$	2,5,7,9,13,17,19,22,24,28,30,37,39,41,43,45,52,54, 58,64,66,69,71,73,77,81,83,87,97,103,109,117,121,127

Table 7. Superpolies of round-reduce TriviA-SC-v2 variants

ciphers	# of rounds	superpolies	cube indexes
TriviA-v2	864	k_1	0,2,8,12,15,18,22,25,30,33,40,47,50,69,72,86,89,92,95,98, 104,111,115,120,127
		k_{20}	0,2,8,12,18,22,25,30,33,40,55,60,66,69,72,86,89,98, 100, 104,111,115,120,127
		k_{21}	0,2,8,15,18,22,25,30,33,40,47,55,66,69,72,86,92,95,98,100, 111,115,120,127
		$k_{22} \oplus 1$	0,2,8,12,18,22,25,30,33,47,50,55,66,69,72,86,89,92,95,98, 104,111,115,120,127
		k_{35}	0,2,8,15,18,22,25,27,30,33,47,55,60,66,69,72,86,89,95,100, 104,111,115,120,127
		k_{37}	0,8,12,15,18,22,27,30,33,47,50,55,66,69,72,86,89,92,98, 100,104,111,115,120,127
		k_{46}	0,2,8,12,15,18,22,30,33,40,44,47,55,60,66,69,72,86,89,92, 98,100,104,111,115,127
		k_{50}	0,2,8,12,15,18,22,25,30,33,40,47,50,60,69,86,89,92,98,100, 104,111,115,120,127
		$k_{52} \oplus 1$	0,2,8,12,18,22,25,30,33,44,47,50,66,69,72,86,89,92,98,100, 104,111,115,120,127
		k_{54}	0,2,8,12,15,18,22,25,30,33,40,50,60,66,69,72,86,89,92,98, 100,104,115,120,127
		k_{56}	0,2,8,12,15,18,22,25,30,33,40,55,66,69,72,86,89,92,100, 104,111,115,120,127
		k_{64}	0,2,8,12,15,18,22,25,30,33,40,50,55,69,72,86,92,95,98,100, 104,111,115,120,127
		$k_{32} \oplus k_{96}k_{97} \oplus k_{98}$	0,2,8,15,22,22,25,30,33,40,44,55,60,66,69,72,86,89,92,100, 111,115,120,127
		$k_{47} \oplus k_{111}k_{112} \oplus k_{113}$	0,2,12,15,18,22,25,30,33,40,47,55,60,69,72,86,89,92,95,98, 100,104,111,115,120,127
		$k_{61} \oplus k_{125}k_{126} \oplus k_{127}$	0,2,8,12,15,22,25,30,33,47,50,55,66,69,72,86,89,92,98,100, 111,115,120
TriviA-v2(simplified)	992	k_2	0,2,5,10,13,16,23,29,34,40,45,49,51,59,66,78,88,90,98,104, 108,110,114,117,119,121,123,125,127
		k_{25}	0,2,5,10,13,19,23,29,34,40,45,49,55,59,66,71,78,85,88,90, 94,98,104,110,112,114,119,121,123,125,
		k_{26}	0,2,5,10,13,16,19,23,29,34,40,45,49,55,59,66,71,78,85,88, 90,94,104,110,112,114,119,121,123,125
		k_{27}	0,2,5,10,13,16,19,23,29,34,40,45,49,55,59,62,71,78,85,90, 94,98,104,108,110,112,114,117,119,121,123,125,
		k_{41}	0,2,10,13,16,19,23,29,40,45,49,55,59,66,71,78,85,88,90,94, 98,104,108,110,112,114,117,121,123,125
		$k_{41} + k_{63}$	0,2,10,13,16,19,23,29,40,45,49,51,55,59,71,78,85,88,90,94, 98,104,108,110,112,114,119,121,123,125
		k_{48}	0,2,5,10,13,16,23,29,40,45,49,51,55,59,66,71,78,88,90,94, 98,104,110,114,117,119,121,123,125
		k_{50}	0,2,5,10,13,16,19,23,29,40,45,49,55,59,66,71,78,85,88,90, 98,104,110,112,114,119,121,123,125,127
		$k_{53} \oplus 1$	0,2,5,10,13,16,19,23,29,34,40,45,49,55,59,66,71,78,85,88, 90,94,98,104,110,112,114,119,121,123
		k_{56}	0,5,10,13,16,19,23,29,40,45,49,55,59,66,71,78,85,88,90, 94,98,104,110,117,119,121,125,127
		k_{57}	2,5,10,13,16,19,23,29,34,40,45,49,55,59,66,71,78,85,88,90, 94,98,104,110,112,114,117,119,121,123,125
		k_{59}	0,2,5,10,13,16,19,23,29,40,45,49,51,55,59,62,66,71,78,85, 94,104,110,112,114,117,119,121,123
		k_{61}	0,2,5,10,13,16,19,23,29,34,40,45,51,55,59,66,71,78,85,90, 94,98,104,108,110,112,114,117,119,121,125
		k_{72}	0,5,10,13,16,19,23,29,40,45,55,59,62,66,71,78,85,90,94, 98,104,110,112,114,117,121,123,125,127
		$k_{33} \oplus k_{97}k_{98} \oplus k_{99}$	0,2,5,10,13,19,23,29,40,45,49,51,55,59,66,71,78,85,88,90, 98,104,108,110,117,119,121,127
		$k_{61} \oplus k_{125}k_{126} \oplus k_{127}$	0,5,10,13,16,19,23,29,34,40,45,49,55,59,62,66,71,78,88, 90,94,98,104,108,110,112,119,121,123,127

References

1. Alon, N., Kaufman, T., Krivelevich, M., Litsyn, S., Ron, D.: Testing low-degree polynomials over $GF(2)$. In: Arora, S., Jansen, K., Rolim, J.D.P., Sahai, A. (eds.) APPROX/RANDOM -2003. LNCS, vol. 2764, pp. 188–199. Springer, Heidelberg (2003). https://doi.org/10.1007/978-3-540-45198-3_17
2. Blum, M., Luby, M., Rubinfeld, R.: Self-testing/correcting with applications to numerical problems. J. Comput. Syst. Sci. **47**(3), 549–595 (1993). https://doi.org/10.1016/0022-0000(93)90044-W
3. De Cannière, C., Preneel, B.: Trivium. In: Robshaw, M., Billet, O. (eds.) New Stream Cipher Designs. LNCS, vol. 4986, pp. 244–266. Springer, Heidelberg (2008). https://doi.org/10.1007/978-3-540-68351-3_18
4. Canteaut, A., Carpov, S., Fontaine, C., Lepoint, T., Naya-Plasencia, M., Paillier, P., Sirdey, R.: Stream ciphers: a practical solution for efficient homomorphic-ciphertext compression. In: Peyrin, T. (ed.) FSE 2016. LNCS, vol. 9783, pp. 313–333. Springer, Heidelberg (2016). https://doi.org/10.1007/978-3-662-52993-5_16
5. Chakraborti, A., Chattopadhyay, A., Hassan, M., Nandi, M.: TriviA: a fast and secure authenticated encryption scheme. In: Güneysu, T., Handschuh, H. (eds.) CHES 2015. LNCS, vol. 9293, pp. 330–353. Springer, Heidelberg (2015). https://doi.org/10.1007/978-3-662-48324-4_17
6. Chakraborti, A., Nandi, M.: Trivia-ck-v2 (2015). http://competitions.cr.yp.to/round2/triviackv2.pdf
7. Dinur, I., Shamir, A.: Cube attacks on tweakable black box polynomials. In: Joux, A. (ed.) EUROCRYPT 2009. LNCS, vol. 5479, pp. 278–299. Springer, Heidelberg (2009). https://doi.org/10.1007/978-3-642-01001-9_16
8. Fouque, P.-A., Vannet, T.: Improving key recovery to 784 and 799 rounds of trivium using optimized cube attacks. In: Moriai, S. (ed.) FSE 2013. LNCS, vol. 8424, pp. 502–517. Springer, Heidelberg (2014). https://doi.org/10.1007/978-3-662-43933-3_26
9. Knellwolf, S., Meier, W., Naya-Plasencia, M.: Conditional differential cryptanalysis of trivium and KATAN. In: Miri, A., Vaudenay, S. (eds.) SAC 2011. LNCS, vol. 7118, pp. 200–212. Springer, Heidelberg (2012). https://doi.org/10.1007/978-3-642-28496-0_12
10. Liu, M.: Degree evaluation of NFSR-based cryptosystems. In: Katz, J., Shacham, H. (eds.) CRYPTO 2017. LNCS, vol. 10403, pp. 227–249. Springer, Cham (2017). https://doi.org/10.1007/978-3-319-63697-9_8
11. Liu, M., Lin, D., Wang, W.: Searching cubes for testing boolean functions and its application to Trivium. In: IEEE International Symposium on Information Theory, ISIT 2015, 14–19 June 2015, Hong Kong, China, pp. 496–500 (2015). https://doi.org/10.1109/ISIT.2015.7282504
12. Liu, M., Yang, J., Wang, W., Lin, D.: Correlation cube attacks: from weak-key distinguisher to key recovery. To appear in EUROCRYPT 2018. Cryptology ePrint Archive, report 2018/158 (2018). https://eprint.iacr.org/2018/158
13. Maximov, A., Biryukov, A.: Two trivial attacks on TRIVIUM. In: Adams, C., Miri, A., Wiener, M. (eds.) SAC 2007. LNCS, vol. 4876, pp. 36–55. Springer, Heidelberg (2007). https://doi.org/10.1007/978-3-540-77360-3_3
14. Mroczkowski, P., Szmidt, J.: Corrigendum to: the cube attack on stream cipher Trivium and quadraticity tests. IACR Cryptology ePrint Archive, vol. 2011, p. 32 (2011). http://eprint.iacr.org/2011/032

15. Sarkar, S., Maitra, S., Baksi, A.: Observing biases in the state: case studies with Trivium and Trivia-SC. Des. Codes Crypt. **82**(1–2), 351–375 (2017). https://doi.org/10.1007/s10623-016-0211-x
16. Soos, M.: Cryptominisat-2.9.5. http://www.msoos.org/cryptominisat2/
17. Todo, Y., Isobe, T., Hao, Y., Meier, W.: Cube attacks on non-blackbox polynomials based on division property. In: Katz, J., Shacham, H. (eds.) CRYPTO 2017. LNCS, vol. 10403, pp. 250–279. Springer, Cham (2017). https://doi.org/10.1007/978-3-319-63697-9_9
18. Vardasbi, A., Salmasizadeh, M., Mohajeri, J.: Superpoly algebraic normal form monomial test on Trivium. IET Inf. Secur. **7**(3), 230–238 (2013). https://doi.org/10.1049/iet-ifs.2012.0175
19. Wang, Q., Hao, Y., Todo, Y., Li, C., Isobe, T., Meier, W.: Improved division property based cube attacks exploiting low degree property of superpoly. Cryptology ePrint Archive, report 2017/1063 (2017). https://eprint.iacr.org/2017/1063
20. Watanabe, Y., Isobe, T., Morii, M.: Conditional differential cryptanalysis for Kreyvium. In: Pieprzyk, J., Suriadi, S. (eds.) ACISP 2017. LNCS, vol. 10342, pp. 421–434. Springer, Cham (2017). https://doi.org/10.1007/978-3-319-60055-0_22
21. Xu, C., Zhang, B., Feng, D.: Linear cryptanalysis of FASER128/256 and TriviA-ck. In: Meier, W., Mukhopadhyay, D. (eds.) INDOCRYPT 2014. LNCS, vol. 8885, pp. 237–254. Springer, Cham (2014). https://doi.org/10.1007/978-3-319-13039-2_14
22. Todo, Y., Isobe, T., Hao, Y., Meier, W.: Cube attacks on non-blackbox polynomials based on division property (full version). Cryptology ePrint Archive, report 2017/306 (2017). https://eprint.iacr.org/2017/306

Differential Attacks on Reduced Round LILLIPUT

Nicolas Marrière(✉), Valérie Nachef, and Emmanuel Volte

Department of Mathematics, University of Cergy-Pontoise, CNRS UMR 8088, 2 avenue Adolphe Chauvin, 95011 Cergy-Pontoise Cedex, France
{nicolas.marriere,valerie.nachef,emmanuel.volte}@u-cergy.fr

Abstract. In SAC 2013, Berger et al. defined Extended Generalized Feistel Networks (EGFN) and analyzed their security. Later, they proposed a cipher based on this structure: *LILLIPUT*. Impossible differential attacks and integral attacks have been mounted on *LILLIPUT*. We propose a tool which has found some classical, impossible and improbable differential attacks by using the variance method. It has highlighted unusual differential conditions which lead to efficient attacks according to the complexity. Moreover, it is the first time we apply the generic variance method to a concrete cipher.

Keywords: Differential cryptanalysis
Improbable differential cryptanalysis · Automated search of attacks

1 Introduction

Lightweight cryptography has become an important field of research with the development of IoT. As a solution, a lot of block ciphers have been built. Some of them are SPN ciphers like PRESENT [8] or more recently SKINNY [2]. Others are Feistel ciphers like SIMON [1] or CLEFIA [16]. In this context, a new variant of generalized Feistel network has been designed: the Extended Generalized Feistel Network [4] (EGFN). It is based on Matrix representation and provides an efficient diffusion. In comparison to the generalized Feistel networks, the distinctive feature in the EGFN is a linear layer after the confusion step. Moreover, an efficient differential analysis method remains unknown [14] because of this linear layer. A cipher based on the EGFN structure called *LILLIPUT* [3] has been designed. It is a 30 rounds block cipher. Several kinds of attacks on *LILLIPUT* have been provided as shown in Table 1.

Differential attacks [6] consist in putting a specific difference on the inputs and looking how it propagates through the cipher into the outputs in order to highlight a bias. Differential cryptanalysis is an efficient statistical attack and some attacks are derived from it: truncated differential ones [10] or impossible differential ones [5] for example. A differential analysis based on the variance method [12] has been made on the EGFN [11]. In this article, we have applied this method to *LILLIPUT*.

W. Susilo and G. Yang (Eds.): ACISP 2018, LNCS 10946, pp. 188–206, 2018.
https://doi.org/10.1007/978-3-319-93638-3_12

Table 1. Best Attacks on *LILLIPUT*.

Variety	Distinguisher	Key recovery	Source
Impossible differential	9 rounds	N/A	[15]
Division property	13 rounds	17 rounds	[14]
Differential	8 rounds	12 rounds	Sect. 4

Our Contribution. In this paper, we provide some differential cryptanalysis attacks on *LILLIPUT*. Indeed, we provide some differential distinguishers. These attacks are NCPA (Non-Adaptive Chosen Plaintext Attack) ones. They are based on the variance method [12] that was already used on the EGFN and on some generalized Feistel network [13,19]. For the first time, we apply this generic method to a concrete cipher. These differential attacks do not rely on the key schedule but only on the *LILLIPUT* structure. Moreover, we have made a tool in Python to process an automated research of differential attacks. There are generic tools devoted to different kinds of attacks: meet-in-the-middle and impossible differential attacks in [9], or only for impossible differential attacks in [15], in [20] or in [21] for example. Contrary to others generic tools, our program is designed to apply the variance method to a concrete cipher. It can be used on some block ciphers and allows to get differential attacks, impossible differential attacks and improbable differential attacks. Indeed, we have found empirically some improbable differential attacks [17,18] and we provide explanations of how it works. Improbable differential cryptanalysis is a statistical cryptanalytic technique for which some attacks have been invalidated [7] when built from an impossible distinguisher. In the theory, an improbable differential attack is like a classical differential attack but the expected differences occur less often for a permutation generated by the studied cipher than for a random permutation. In this paper, the attacks we describe work in practice and we provide simulations of them.

This paper is organized as follow: In Sect. 2, we will describe *LILLIPUT*. Then in Sect. 3 we will detail the general structure of our attacks and describe the tool that allows to find attacks. Section 4 is devoted to the presentation of distinguishing attacks up to 8 rounds. Conclusion is given in Sect. 6.

2 LILLIPUT

The input is denoted by 16 nibbles: $I = [I_{16}, I_{15}, \cdots, I_1]$. Similarly, the output is denoted by: $S = [S_{16}, S_{15}, \cdots, S_1]$. We describe one round of *LILLIPUT* in the Fig. 1.

We can see there are three layers in a round:

- *NonLinear* layer step with the sbox. There is only one 4-bit sbox in *LILLIPUT* and we have described it in Table 2 according to the value of the input.

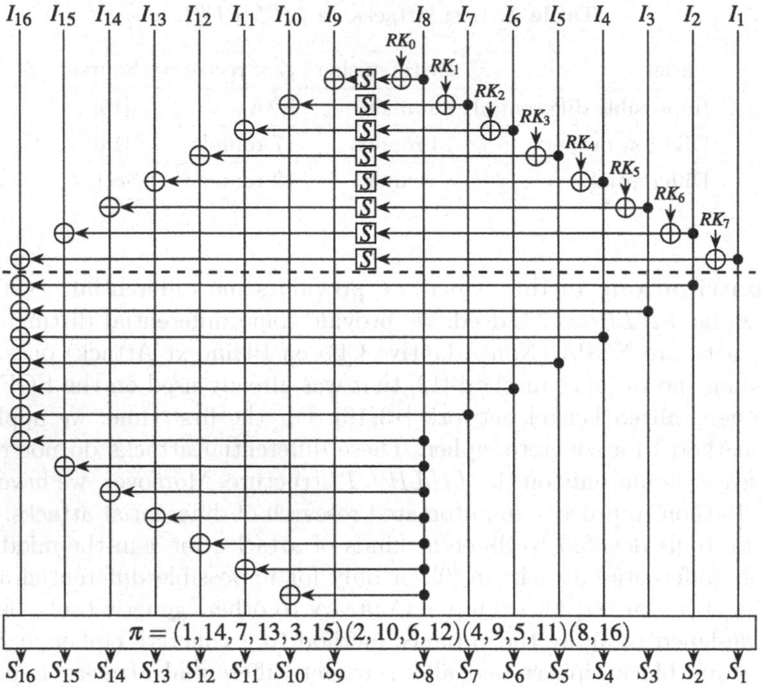

Fig. 1. One round of *LILLIPUT*.

Table 2. Sbox of *LILLIPUT*.

Input value	0	1	2	3	4	5	6	7	8	9	*A*	*B*	*C*	*D*	*E*	*F*
Ouput value	4	8	7	1	9	3	2	*E*	0	*B*	6	*F*	*A*	5	*D*	*C*

Table 3. Permutation of *LILLIPUT*.

Input	1	2	3	4	5	6	7	8	9	10	11	12	13	14	15	16
Output	14	10	15	9	11	12	13	16	5	6	4	2	3	7	1	8

- *Linear* layer step: this is a step with some xor operations between the left side branches and the right side.
- *Permutation* layer: there is a permutation step and we have described it in Table 3.

One can notice that there are two sides and the left side branches go to the right side through the permutation step and vice versa.

LILLIPUT is an instance of Extended Generalized Feistel Network, a generic family of Feistel schemes. Because of the *LinearLayer*, there are no efficient known methods to make a differential study of this scheme. As previously said, differential attacks on EGFN have already been proposed. These attacks are based on the variance method [12] that we will use on *LILLIPUT* as well. However, we can not use the same differential trails or use the same kind of relations between inputs and outputs because the sbox in *LILLIPUT* is a bijection.

3 Structure of the Attacks

3.1 Variance Method

Our attacks are based on variance method [12]. With this method, we can make a further analysis than a classical differential attack. The aim of the attack is to distinguish a permutation obtained with *LILLIPUT* from a random permutation. Just like the authors of the variance method, we will generate a lot of pairs of messages and count how many of them satisfy specific differential relations between inputs and outputs. The number of such pairs is denoted by $\mathcal{N}_{perm}$ for a random permutation and by $\mathcal{N}_L$ for a *LILLIPUT* permutation.

Then, the attack is successful if $\mathcal{N}_{perm}$ is significantly different from $\mathcal{N}_L$. If it is smaller, we obtain an impossible or an improbable differential attack and if it is greater, we have a classical differential one. But if $\mathcal{N}_L$ and $\mathcal{N}_{perm}$ are of the same order, then the attack can be successful using the expectation and standard deviation functions if $|\mathbb{E}(\mathcal{N}_L) - \mathbb{E}(\mathcal{N}_{perm})| > \max(\sigma(\mathcal{N}_{perm}), \sigma(\mathcal{N}_L))$, where $\mathbb{E}$ stands for the expectation function and σ for the standard deviation function. In that case, the attacks work thanks to the Chebychev formula, which states that for any random variable X, and any $\alpha > 0$, we have $\mathbb{P}\left(|X - \mathbb{E}(X)| \geq \alpha\sigma(x)\right) \leq \frac{1}{\alpha^2}$. Using this formula, it is then possible to construct a prediction interval for $\mathcal{N}_L$ for example, in which future computations will fall, with a good probability. It is important to notice that for our attacks, it is enough to compute $\mathbb{E}(\mathcal{N}_{perm})$, $\mathbb{E}(\mathcal{N}_L)$ and $\sigma(\mathcal{N}_{perm})$. For more details about the variance method see [12], Chap. 5 for example.

Moreover, for all attacks we will see, the condition on the outputs is an equality on 4 bits. So, it is easy to check that if m is the number of messages for a given attack, then for a random permutation: $\mathbb{E}(\mathcal{N}_{perm}) \simeq \frac{m\cdot(m-1)}{2} \times \frac{1}{2^4}$ and $\sigma(\mathcal{N}_{perm}) \simeq \sqrt{\mathbb{E}(\mathcal{N}_{perm})}$.

3.2 Conditions on the Inputs and the Outputs

There are 16 branches in *LILLIPUT*. Our attacks are differential ones, so we look for differential trails. Due to the structure of *LILLIPUT*, we look for attacks by putting conditions to the left side $[I_{16}, \cdots, I_9]$ of the inputs and looking some conditions on the left side $[S_{16}, \cdots, S_9]$ of the outputs. Indeed, one can check that, if we found an interesting distinguisher which uses the right side of the output, it leads to a distinguisher which uses the left side of the output and reaches one more round. It is because in a round the right side goes to the left side with probability 1 without changes.

We have found by hand distinguishers up to 4 rounds and for more rounds with the tool. Most attacks are based on a common structure. Each pair (m_1, m_2)

of messages that we study has to verify that: m_1 and m_2 are equal on all branches but some on the left side. Moreover, on the branches involved, the non-zero differences have to be equal. For example, this condition on branch number 9 will be written $I_9(m_1) \oplus I_9(m_2) = \Delta$ or if more simply $\Delta I_9 = \Delta$.

On the outputs, if $c_1 = LILLIPUT(m_1)$ and $c_2 = LILLIPUT(m_2)$ we will look at the xor between some branches of $c = c_1 \oplus c_2$. For example, if we are interested in the branches S_{12} and S_{10}, we will compute $S_{12} \oplus S_{10}$ on c and it is denoted by $\Delta S_{12} \oplus \Delta S_{10}$. One can notice that if one is interested in only one branch, it leads to a classical differential attack.

3.3 Complexity

In our differential attacks we use structures of messages. Let (m_1, m_2) be a pair of messages. As we have said earlier, there are 2 properties the pairs have to follow. First, m_1 and m_2 are equal on all branches but some on the left side. Then, for the non zero branches of $m_1 \oplus m_2$, the difference has to be the same. Thus, a structure is based on a message m that is randomly chosen. As we want the same difference on some branches, it leads to 15 more messages. Indeed, the non zero difference can be $\Delta \in [1 \cdots 15]$ because branches have 4 bits. So, a structure has 16 messages, and it leads to $16 \times 15/2 = 120$ pairs.

For example, if we are interested in the branches I_{10} and I_{13}, a pair will be (m_1, m_2) such that: $m_1 \oplus m_2 = [0, 0, 0, \Delta, 0, 0, \Delta, 0, 0, 0, 0, 0, 0, 0, 0, 0]$. There are exactly $2^{4 \times 14}$ of such structures.

The main drawback of our attacks is the data complexity. Indeed for a given attack which requires 2^7 messages, the number of pairs is $\frac{2^7 \times (2^7-1)}{2} = 8,128$. With our kinds of attacks, because we need the same Δ difference on several branches, we need 68 structures of 120 pairs ($68 \times 120 = 8,160$ pairs) and it corresponds to $68 \times 16 = 1,088$ messages instead of 2^7. But, thanks to these new conditions, one can see special relations between internal variables which can be used to build a differential attack.

3.4 Automated Research of Attacks

To extend this kind of attacks, we have implemented a tool[1] in Python to process an exhaustive search of such conditions. We describe it in Algorithm 1.

In order to optimise this algorithm, we test on a small number of samples and if we found an interesting result, then we test again in a more meaningful number of samples. It appears that the most efficient attacks are based on having 2 branches involved on the inputs and 2 branches involved on the ouput. We detail the best attacks we have found in Sect. 4 and some empirical results in Sect. 4.3.

---

[1] Our tool is available on the Internet at this link: github.com/NicolasCergy/Lilliput_analysis.

Algorithm 1. Automated search of attacks

for all inputCondition=Combination of branches in the left side of inputs: **do**
  Generate a sample of pairs which verify the condition on the input: Equal on all branches but the inputCondition.
  for all outputCondition=Combination of branches in the left side of outputs: **do**
    Count how many pairs verify the outputCondition: the xor between some branches of the difference of the outputs equals to 0.
    if this result is different than the one expected for a random permutation **then**
      We have found a distinguisher.
    end if
  end for
end for

4 Distinguishing Attacks

In this Section, we will describe the different distinguishers we have found by hand or thanks to the tool. We have made simulations of these attacks. Input is denoted by: $I_{16}, \cdots, I_1$. After the first *NonLinear* and *Linear* layers and before the permutation, the output is: $X_8^1, X_7^1, X_6^1, X_5^1, X_4^1, X_3^1, X_2^1, X_1^1, I_8, I_7, I_6, I_5, I_4, I_3, I_2, I_1$. Here $X_1^1, \ldots, X_8^1$ denote the internal variable that appear at round 1. More generally, X_j^i, $1 \leq j \leq 16$ represent the internal variable that are introduced at round i. To simplify the notation, we always denote by f the round functions. But, even though we always use the same bijective sbox, the entry is xored with a sub-key. For a given round, it is important to note that $f(X_j^i) = f(X_k^i)$ does not mean that $X_j^i = X_k^i$.

4.1 First Rounds

In the first rounds, we can mount differential attacks with probability 1 on *LILLIPUT* with only 2 messages. So let (m_1, m_2) be a couple of messages. We will note $c_1 = LILLIPUT(m_1)$, $c_2 = LILLIPUT(m_2)$ and $c = c_1 \oplus c_2$. We describe an attack on 5 rounds in order to show the relation between internal variables in *LILLIPUT*.

Property 1. *After r rounds ($r \geq 3$), the output is:*
$[X_8^{r-1}, X_5^{r-1}, X_7^{r-1}, X_6^{r-1}, X_2^{r-1}, X_1^{r-1}, X_4^{r-1}, X_3^{r-1}, X_8^r, X_6^r, X_2^r, X_1^r, X_3^r, X_5^r, X_4^r, X_7^r]$.
We have the following formulas:

$$\begin{aligned}
X_1^r &= X_3^{r-2} \oplus f(X_8^{r-1}) & X_5^r &= X_6^{r-2} \oplus X_8^{r-1} \oplus f(X_3^{r-1})\\
X_2^r &= X_4^{r-2} \oplus X_8^{r-1} \oplus f(X_6^{r-1}) & X_6^r &= X_7^{r-2} \oplus X_8^{r-1} \oplus f(X_5^{r-1})\\
X_3^r &= X_1^{r-2} \oplus X_8^{r-1} \oplus f(X_2^{r-1}) & X_7^r &= X_5^{r-2} \oplus X_8^{r-1} \oplus f(X_4^{r-1})\\
X_4^r &= X_2^{r-2} \oplus X_8^{r-1} \oplus f(X_1^{r-1}) & &
\end{aligned}$$

And: $X_8^r = X_8^{r-2} \oplus X_8^{r-1} \oplus X_6^{r-1} \oplus X_5^{r-1} \oplus X_4^{r-1} \oplus X_3^{r-1} \oplus X_2^{r-1} \oplus X_1^{r-1} \oplus f(X_7^{r-1})$

After five rounds, there is an NCPA attack that needs only 2 messages. As input condition we have $I_i(m_1) \neq I_i(m_2)$ only for $i \in \{9, 10\}$. Moreover, we set

$\Delta I_9 = \Delta I_{10}$. Then, one has to check if $\Delta S_9 \oplus \Delta S_{10} = 0$. This is satisfied with probability $\frac{1}{2^4}$ for a random permutation. We now explain why this is true with probability 1 for a permutation obtained with *LILLIPUT*.

According to Property 1, we have: $S_9 = X_3^4 = X_1^2 \oplus X_8^3 \oplus f(X_2^3)$ and $S_{10} = X_4^4 = X_2^2 \oplus X_8^3 \oplus f(X_1^3)$.

$$X_1^2 = I_{14} \oplus f(X_8^1) \qquad X_2^3 = X_4^1 \oplus X_8^2 \oplus f(X_6^2)$$
$$X_2^2 = I_2 \oplus X_8^1 \oplus f(X_6^1) \qquad X_1^3 = X_3^1 \oplus f(X_8^2)$$

Using the input conditions, we obtain $\Delta X_8^1 = 0, \Delta X_1^2 = 0, \Delta X_6^1$ and $\Delta X_2^2 = 0$. This gives $\Delta S_9 \oplus \Delta_{10} = \Delta f(X_2^3) \oplus \Delta f(X_1^3)$. Moreover, $\Delta X_3^1 = 0$ and $\Delta X_8^2 = \Delta X_1^1 \oplus \Delta X_2^1 = I_9 \oplus \Delta I_{10} = 0$. This implies that $\Delta f(X_1^3) = 0$. It is easy to check that we also have $\Delta f(X_2^3) = 0$. This shows that we have $\Delta S_9 \oplus \Delta S_{10} = 0$ with probability 1. Note that the tool has also found a lot of impossible differential attacks and improbable differential attacks but we have only detailled the most efficient attacks. We have found 26 of such attacks which require 2 messages.

4.2 Further Attacks

As we have said in Sect. 3, our attacks are based on a specific structure: for each pair we have equalities on all but some branches and this non zero difference is the same on the different branches. So, we will detail for each attack, the input branches involved. Similarly, we have said that the output condition is the xor between some branches of $c = c_1 \oplus c_2$. So, we will explain which output branches are involved. In order to obtain $\mathbb{E}(\mathcal{N}_L)$, we will use the mean value obtained from some samples. Thus, we will also detail the number of samples, the number of pairs for each sample and the results we have obtained.

6 Rounds. The tool has found a lot of attacks on 6 rounds.[2] We present here the most efficient ones. With only one structure (so 120 pairs of messages, this corresponds to 2^4 messages since if m is the number of messages, then we have $\frac{m(m-1)}{2}$ pairs of distinct messages) we will see that we can distinguish *LILLIPUT* from a random permutation. The output condition is $\Delta S_9 \oplus \Delta S_{15} = 0$. It is an equality on 4 bits, so for a random permutation, the mean value is expected to be $\mathbb{E}(\mathcal{N}_{perm}) = \frac{m(m-1)}{2 \cdot 2^4} = 7.5$. The results we have obtained are shown in Table 4. We notice that the number of pairs of message satisfying the conditions is 32. This provides a distinguishing attack.

Moreover, this attack is still valid with only 4 messages: the last version of our tool works with structures of messages so the minimal number is 2^4 but, one can reduce this attack to 4 messages. Indeed, the mean value of pairs which satisfy the output condition for a random permutation is then expected to be $\mathbb{E}(\mathcal{N}_{perm}) = 0.375$ and we have obtained by simulation:[3] $\mathbb{E}(\mathcal{N}_L) = 1.7128$. We now explain how the structure of *LILLIPUT* leads to this result.

[2] See Sect. 4.3.

[3] Mean value obtained in simulation with 5000 samples of 4 messages.

Table 4. Attack on 6 rounds.

Input branches	Output branches	#Sample	#Pairs in a sample	#Pairs in average
I_{10}, I_{14}	S_9, S_{15}	100	120	32

At the end of round 6 (see Property 1) we have: $S_{15} = X_5^5$ and $S_9 = X_3^5$ and

$$X_5^5 = X_6^3 \oplus X_8^4 \oplus f(X_3^4),\quad X_3^5 = X_1^3 \oplus X_8^4 \oplus f(X_2^4),$$
$$X_6^3 = X_7^1 \oplus X_8^2 \oplus f(X_5^2),\quad X_1^3 = X_3^1 \oplus f(X_8^2),$$
$$X_7^1 = I_{15} \oplus I_8 \oplus f(I_2),\quad X_3^1 = I_{11} \oplus I_8 \oplus f(I_6),$$
$$X_5^2 = I_7 \oplus X_8^1 \oplus f(X_3^1).$$

So we have: $\Delta X_7^1 = 0$, $\Delta X_3^1 = 0$, $\Delta X_5^2 = 0$. Or, $\Delta X_8^2 = \Delta I_{10} \oplus \Delta I_{14} = 0$. So, $\Delta X_1^3 = 0$ and $\Delta X_6^3 = 0$. Thus $\Delta S_9 \oplus \Delta S_{15} = \Delta f(X_2^4) \oplus \Delta f(X_3^4)$.

$$X_2^4 = X_4^2 \oplus X_8^3 \oplus f(X_6^3),\quad X_3^4 = X_1^2 \oplus X_8^3 \oplus f(X_2^3),$$
$$X_4^2 = I_6 \oplus X_8^1 \oplus f(X_1^1),\quad X_1^2 = I_4 \oplus f(X_8^1),$$
$$X_1^1 = I_9 \oplus f(I_8),\quad X_2^3 = X_4^1 \oplus X_8^2 \oplus f(X_6^2).$$

So $\Delta X_1^1 = 0$, $\Delta X_4^2 = 0$, $\Delta X_2^3 = 0$, $\Delta X_1^2 = 0$. So $\Delta f(X_2^3) = 0$, $\Delta X_3^4 = \Delta X_2^4 = \Delta X_8^3$. Or, we have:

$$\begin{aligned}\Delta X_8^3 &= \Delta X_2^2 \oplus \Delta X_3^2\\ &= \Delta f(X_6^1) \oplus \Delta f(X_2^1)\\ &= f(X_6^1) \oplus f(X_6^1 \oplus \Delta I_{14}) \oplus f(X_2^1) \oplus f(X_2^1 \oplus \Delta I_{10}).\end{aligned}$$

So we have: $\Delta S_9 \oplus \Delta S_{15} = f(X_2^4) \oplus f(X_2^4 \oplus \Delta X_8^3) \oplus f(X_3^4) \oplus f(X_3^4 \oplus \Delta X_8^3)$.

The bias is obtained if $f(X_2^4) = f(X_3^4)$ note that the round key is not the same for these two values so it does not lead to $X_2^4 = X_3^4$. We can also follow the differential trail if $X_8^3 = 0$. This happens at random or if $f(X_6^1) = f(X_2^1)$ and, similarly, it does not mean $X_6^1 = X_2^1$. Thus we are able to distinguish a random permutation from a *LILLIPUT* permutation. We can also turn this attack into a related key attack with probability 1 (see Sect. 5.2).

7 Rounds. Just like the attacks for 6 rounds, our program has found some attacks[4] and we will describe the most efficient of them. The tool found an improbable differential attack on *LILLIPUT* reduced to 7 rounds. For this attack, we use samples of 8, 160 pairs, so 68 structures of 120 pairs of messages each. This corresponds to about 2^7 messages, but with this kind of attack, about 2^{10} messages are needed (see Subsect. 3.3). The output condition is an equality on 4 bits: $\Delta S_{10} \oplus \Delta S_{12} = 0$. Thus, for a random permutation, the number of pairs verifying this condition is expected to be 510 in average, since we have $\mathbb{E}(\mathcal{N}_{perm}) \simeq \frac{m(m-1)}{2.\cdot 2^4}$ and we obtain that $\sigma(\mathcal{N}_{perm}) \simeq \sqrt{\mathbb{E}(\mathcal{N}_{perm})}$ is about

[4] See Sect. 4.3.

22.58. If we look at the values we have obtained and that are given in Table 5, we see that $|\mathbb{E}(\mathcal{N}_L) - \mathbb{E}(\mathcal{N}_{perm})| > \sigma(\mathcal{N}_{perm})$. This shows that, as explained in Sect. 3.1, the attack is successful. Moreover, since $\mathbb{E}(\mathcal{N}_L) < \mathbb{E}(\mathcal{N}_{perm})$, we have an improbable attack.

Table 5. Attack simulation on 7 rounds.

Input branches	Output branches	#Sample	#Pairs in a sample	#Pairs in average
I_{10}, I_{12}	S_{10}, S_{12}	500	8, 160	477

We describe now the details of the equations and explain why it leads to an improbable differential attack. At the end of round 6 (see Property 1) we have: $S_{10} = X_4^6$ and $S_{12} = X_2^6$.

$$\begin{aligned}
X_4^6 &= X_2^4 \oplus X_8^5 \oplus f(X_1^5), \\
X_2^4 &= X_4^2 \oplus X_8^3 \oplus f(X_6^3), \\
X_4^2 &= I_6 \oplus X_8^1 \oplus f(X_1^1), \\
X_1^1 &= I_9 \oplus f(I_8), \\
X_6^3 &= X_7^1 \oplus X_8^2 \oplus f(X_5^2), \\
X_7^1 &= I_{15} \oplus I_8 \oplus f(I_2),
\end{aligned}$$

$$\begin{aligned}
X_2^6 &= X_4^4 \oplus X_8^5 \oplus f(X_6^5), \\
X_4^4 &= X_2^2 \oplus X_8^3 \oplus f(X_1^3), \\
X_2^2 &= I_2 \oplus X_8^1 \oplus f(X_6^1), \\
X_6^1 &= I_{14} \oplus I_8 \oplus f(I_3), \\
X_1^3 &= X_3^1 \oplus f(X_8^2), \\
X_3^1 &= I_{11} \oplus I_8 \oplus f(I_6).
\end{aligned}$$

So, $\Delta X_3^1 = 0$, $\Delta X_1^3 = 0$, $\Delta X_6^1 = 0$, $\Delta X_2^2 = 0$. Similarly, $\Delta X_7^1 = 0$, $\Delta X_6^3 = 0$, $\Delta X_1^1 = 0$ and $\Delta X_4^2 = 0$. So, $\Delta X_4^6 \oplus \Delta X_2^6 = \Delta f(X_6^5) \oplus \Delta f(X_1^5)$. Moreover we have: $\Delta X_1^5 = \Delta X_3^3 \oplus \Delta f(X_8^4)$ and $\Delta X_6^5 = \Delta X_8^4 \oplus \Delta f(X_5^4)$ It is easy to check that $\Delta X_3^3 = 0$ and $\Delta X_5^4 = \Delta X_6^2 \oplus \Delta X_8^3 \oplus \Delta f(X_3^3) = \Delta X_8^3$. We also have $\Delta X_8^4 = \Delta X_8^3 \oplus \Delta X_5^3$. This gives:

$$\begin{aligned}
\Delta S_{10} \oplus \Delta S_{12} = f(X_1^5) &\oplus f\left(X_1^5 \oplus f(X_8^4) \oplus f(X_8^4 \oplus \Delta X_8^4)\right) \\
&\oplus f(X_6^5) \oplus f\left(X_6^5 \oplus \Delta X_8^4 \oplus f(X_5^4) \oplus f(X_5^4 \oplus \Delta X_8^3)\right).
\end{aligned}$$

Suppose that $\Delta X_8^3 = \Delta X_5^3$. This implies that $\Delta X_8^4 = 0$ and we have: $\Delta S_{10} \oplus \Delta S_{12} = f(X_6^5) \oplus f\left(X_6^5 \oplus f(X_5^4) \oplus f(X_5^4 \oplus \Delta X_8^3)\right)$. Since f is bijective, we obtain:

$$\Delta S_{10} \oplus \Delta S_{12} = 0 \Leftrightarrow f(X_5^4) \oplus f(X_5^4 \oplus \Delta X_8^3) = 0 \Leftrightarrow \Delta X_8^3 = 0.$$

This also gives $\Delta X_5^3 = 0$. But $\Delta X_5^3 = 0 \Leftrightarrow \Delta X_3^2 = 0 \Leftrightarrow \Delta I_{10} = 0$ which is not possible. We now compute the probabilities. We have:

$$\begin{aligned}
\mathbb{P}\left[\Delta S_{10} \oplus \Delta S_{12} = 0\right] = &\ \mathbb{P}\left[\Delta S_{10} \oplus \Delta S_{12} = 0 / \Delta X_5^3 \neq \Delta X_8^3\right] \mathbb{P}\left[\Delta X_5^3 \neq \Delta X_8^3\right] \\
&+ \mathbb{P}\left[\Delta S_{10} \oplus \Delta S_{12} = 0 / \Delta X_5^3 = \Delta X_8^3\right] \mathbb{P}\left[\Delta X_5^3 = \Delta X_8^3\right].
\end{aligned}$$

The previous computations show that: $\mathbb{P}\left[\Delta S_{10} \oplus \Delta S_{12} = 0/\Delta X_5^3 = \Delta X_8^3\right] = 0$. Thus we obtain, if m is the number of messages.

$$\mathbb{P}\left[\Delta S_{10} \oplus \Delta S_{10} = 0\right] = \mathbb{P}\left[\Delta S_{10} \oplus \Delta S_{10} = 0/\Delta X_5^3 \neq \Delta X_8^3\right] \mathbb{P}\left[\Delta X_5^3 \neq \Delta X_8^3\right]$$
$$= \frac{m(m-1)}{2 \cdot 2^4}\left(1 - \frac{1}{2^4}\right).$$

With $m = 2^7$, this is the value given in Table 5. This shows that we have here an improbable attack.

8 Rounds. The tool have found a differential attack on *LILLIPUT* reduced to 8 rounds. For this attack, we use samples of 301, 977, 600 pairs, so 2, 516, 480 structures. This corresponds to about 1.5×2^{14} messages, but with this kind of attack, about 2^{25} messages are needed (see Subsect. 3.3). The output condition is an equality on 4 bits: $\Delta S_{12} \oplus \Delta S_{14} = 0$. For a random permutation, the number of pairs verifying this condition is expected to be 18, 873, 600 in average, i.e. $\mathbb{E}(\mathcal{N}_{perm}) \simeq \frac{m(m-1)}{2 \cdot 2^4}$, and the standard deviation is about the square root of the mean value which gives: 4344. Since the mean value obtained for a *LILLIPUT* permutation is 18, 882, 219.56, we can see that $|\mathbb{E}(\mathcal{N}_L) - \mathbb{E}(\mathcal{N}_{perm})| > \sigma(\mathcal{N}_{perm})$. This shows that, as explained in Sect. 3.1, the attack is successful. The simulations described in Table 6 have taken 65.6 hours of computation on a virtual machine with a E8500 as processor and 4GB of RAM.

Table 6. Attack simulation on 8 rounds.

Input branches	Output branches	#Sample	#Pairs in a sample	#Pairs in average
I_9, I_{10}	S_{12}, S_{14}	50	301, 977, 600	18, 882, 219.56

Here are the details of the equations: $S_{12} = X_2^7$ and $S_{14} = X_7^7$.

$$\begin{aligned}
X_2^7 &= X_4^5 \oplus X_8^6 \oplus f(X_6^6), & X_7^7 &= X_5^5 \oplus X_8^6 \oplus f(X_4^6),\\
X_4^5 &= X_2^3 \oplus X_8^4 \oplus f(X_1^4), & X_5^5 &= X_6^3 \oplus X_8^4 \oplus f(X_3^4),\\
X_2^3 &= X_4^1 \oplus X_8^2 \oplus f(X_6^2), & X_6^3 &= X_7^1 \oplus X_8^2 \oplus f(X_5^2),\\
X_4^1 &= I_{12} \oplus I_8 \oplus f(I_5), & X_4^1 &= I_{12} \oplus I_8 \oplus f(I_5),\\
\Delta X_4^1 &= 0, & \Delta X_7^1 &= 0.
\end{aligned}$$

Or $\Delta f(X_5^2) = 0$ and $\Delta f(X_6^2) = 0$. So $\Delta S_{12} \oplus \Delta S_{14} = \Delta f(X_6^6) \oplus \Delta f(X_4^6) \oplus \Delta f(X_1^4) \oplus \Delta f(X_3^4)$. We can observe that the condition $\Delta S_{12} \oplus \Delta S_{14} = 0$ can be satisfied if for example: $f(X_1^4) = f(X_3^4), f(X_1^4 \oplus \Delta X_1^4) = f(X_3^4 \oplus \Delta X_3^4), f(X_4^6) = f(X_6^6)$, and $f(X_4^6 \oplus \Delta X_4^6) = f(X_6^6 \oplus \Delta X_6^6)$. But other equalities are also possible.

Table 7. Some differential and improbable differential attacks on 6 rounds.

Inputs	Condition	Result
I_9, I_{11}	$\Delta S_{10} \oplus \Delta S_{12} = 0$	1,744.584
I_9, I_{13}	$\Delta S_{12} \oplus \Delta S_{14} = 0$	2,336.416
I_9, I_{14}	$\Delta S_{10} \oplus \Delta S_{15} = 0$	1,731.616
I_{10}, I_{12}	$\Delta S_9 \oplus \Delta S_{13} = 0$	1,722.962
I_{10}, I_{14}	$\Delta S_9 \oplus \Delta S_{15} = 0$	2,364.232
I_{11}, I_{12}	$\Delta S_{12} \oplus \Delta S_{14} = 0$	625.882
I_{11}, I_{14}	$\Delta S_{11} \oplus \Delta S_{15} = 0$	638.076
I_{11}, I_{15}	$\Delta S_{12} \oplus \Delta S_{13} = 0$	671.91
I_{12}, I_{13}	$\Delta S_9 \oplus \Delta S_{14} = 0$	1,736.72

Inputs	Condition	Result
I_{10}, I_{13}	$\Delta S_9 \oplus \Delta S_{14} = 0$	391.92
I_{10}, I_{13}	$\Delta S_9 \oplus \Delta S_{15} = 0$	388.426
I_{10}, I_{14}	$\Delta S_9 \oplus \Delta S_{10} = 0$	430.186
I_{10}, I_{14}	$\Delta S_9 \oplus \Delta S_{13} = 0$	386.47
I_{10}, I_{14}	$\Delta S_{13} \oplus \Delta S_{15} = 0$	386.146
I_{11}, I_{13}	$\Delta S_{12} \oplus \Delta S_{14} = 0$	391.322
I_{11}, I_{14}	$\Delta S_{10} \oplus \Delta S_{13} = 0$	430.098
I_{11}, I_{14}	$\Delta S_{10} \oplus \Delta S_{15} = 0$	433.2
I_{12}, I_{14}	$\Delta S_9 \oplus \Delta S_{13} = 0$	426.554

Table 8. Some differential and improbable differential attacks on 7 rounds.

Inputs	Condition	Result
I_9, I_{13}	$\Delta S_9 \oplus \Delta S_{10} = 0$	133,707.05
I_9, I_{13}	$\Delta S_9 \oplus \Delta S_{12} = 0$	131,796.3
I_9, I_{14}	$\Delta S_{13} \oplus \Delta S_{14} = 0$	131,893.75
I_{10}, I_{13}	$\Delta S_{10} \oplus \Delta S_{12} = 0$	132,552.95
I_{10}, I_{14}	$\Delta S_9 \oplus \Delta S_{15} = 0$	132,127.9
I_{11}, I_{12}	$\Delta S_{12} \oplus \Delta S_{14} = 0$	133,870.55
I_{11}, I_{13}	$\Delta S_9 \oplus \Delta S_{14} = 0$	132,262.4
I_{12}, I_{14}	$\Delta S_9 \oplus \Delta S_{15} = 0$	133,746.8
I_{13}, I_{14}	$\Delta S_9 \oplus \Delta S_{15} = 0$	132,071.85

Inputs	Condition	Result
$I_9\ I_{11}$	$\Delta S_9 \oplus \Delta S_{14} = 0$	127,667.15
$I_9\ I_{13}$	$\Delta S_9 \oplus \Delta S_{13} = 0$	127,620.15
$I_9\ I_{13}$	$\Delta S_9 \oplus \Delta S_{14} = 0$	130,417.3
$I_9\ I_{13}$	$\Delta S_9 \oplus \Delta S_{15} = 0$	127,600.45
$I_9\ I_{14}$	$\Delta S_9 \oplus \Delta S_{13} = 0$	127,740.7
$I_{10}\ I_{12}$	$\Delta S_{10} \oplus \Delta S_{12} = 0$	123,372.9
$I_{10}\ I_{14}$	$\Delta S_{13} \oplus \Delta S_{15} = 0$	130,438.75
$I_{11}\ I_{13}$	$\Delta S_9 \oplus \Delta S_{10} = 0$	129,541.15
$I_{11}\ I_{13}$	$\Delta S_9 \oplus \Delta S_{12} = 0$	130,483.15

4.3 Simulation of Attacks on 6 and 7 Rounds

In this part, we describe some attacks on *LILLIPUT* reduced to 6 and 7 rounds. These attacks are based on 500 samples of 8160 couples of messages. This corresponds to 2^7 messages as explained in Sect. 3.3. We count how many couples verify a property. The average result for a random permutation is $\frac{8160}{2^4} = 510$ because it is an equality on 4 bits. In order to obtain an attack, the difference between these values is expected to be $\frac{8160}{2^8} = 32$. As said in Sect. 4, these attacks are based on an non zero difference put on two input branches. We detail the result obtained in Tables 7 and 8. The tool also found attacks for all combination $i \in \{1, \cdots, 8\}$ branches in input and $j \in \{1, \cdots, 8\}$ branches in output but $i = 2$ and $j = 2$ leads to the most relevant attacks. Note that the attacks on 7 rounds are not based on 2^7 messages but 2^{11} according to Sect. 3.3.

5 Key Recovery

In this section, we describe how the key recovery works in order to show what we can do. We process the key recovery on *LILLIPUT* reduced to 7 and 8 rounds. We have used the distinguishing attack on 6 rounds to attack 7 then 8 rounds in order to do simulations because the distinguishing attack on 8 rounds require 2^{25} messages to be processed. Nevertheless, it will work similarly for this distinguishing attack.

5.1 Key Schedule Description

LILLIPUT uses a 80-bit master key. The key schedule is managed by an internal state denoted by 20 nibbles (4-bit words): $Y_{19}, \ldots, Y_0$. It is initialized with the master key and is processed by Algorithm 2 in order to build the round keys $RK^0, \ldots, RK^{29}$. The *ExtractRoundKey* function is described in Algorithm 3. Note that the Sbox S used in the *ExtractRoundKey* function is the same as the one in *LILLIPUT*. The functions L_0, L_1, L_2 and L_3 are generalized Feistel schemes with 5 branches and a bit size of 4. They are described in Figs. 2 and 3.

Algorithm 2. LILLIPUT key schedule

$Y_{19}, \ldots, Y_0 = MasterKey$
$RK^0 = ExtractRoundKey(Y_{19}, \ldots, Y_0)$
for i in $1, \ldots, 29$ **do**
  $(Y_4, \ldots, Y_0) = L_0(Y_4, \ldots, Y_0)$
  $(Y_9, \ldots, Y_5) = L_1(Y_9, \ldots, Y_5)$
  $(Y_{14}, \ldots, Y_{10}) = L_2(Y_{14}, \ldots, Y_{10})$
  $(Y_{19}, \ldots, Y_{15}) = L_3(Y_{19}, \ldots, Y_{15})$
  $RK^i = ExtractRoundKey(Y_{19}, \ldots, Y_0)$
end for

Algorithm 3. *ExtractRoundKey* function for RK^i

Let Z, a 32-bit word such that: $Z = Y_{18}Y_{16}Y_{13}Y_{10}Y_9Y_6Y_3Y_1$
The bits of Z are denoted by: $Z_{31}, \ldots, Z_0$
$RK^0 = ExtractRoundKey(Y_{19}, \ldots, Y_0)$
for j in $0, \ldots, 7$ **do**
  $RK^i_j = S(Z_j || Z_{8+j} || Z_{16+j} || Z_{24+j})$
end for
$RK^i = RK^i \oplus (i||0)$

5.2 Related Key Attack on 6 Rounds

In this section, we describe the related key attack on *LILLIPUT* reduced to 6 rounds. To recall the attack, the input branches involved are I_{10} and I_{14}. If $c = c_1 \oplus c_2$, the output condition is $S_9(c) \oplus S_{15}(c) = 0$.

If $I_{10} = I_{14}$ and $RK^1_1 = RK^1_5$ and $RK^2_1 = RK^2_2$, the differential trail is verified with probability 1. This attack was verified in practice. The aim of the attack is to make $\Delta X^3_8 = 0$. We have seen that $\Delta X^3_8 = f(X^1_6) \oplus f(X^1_6 \oplus \Delta I_{14}) \oplus f(X^1_2) \oplus f(X^1_2 \oplus \Delta I_{10})$. Moreover, we know that $\Delta I_{14} = \Delta I_{10}$.

But, it is important to notice that $f(X_6^1) = sbox(X_6^1 \oplus RK_1^1)$. Similarly, $f(X_2^1) = sbox(X_2^1 \oplus RK_2^1)$. So, $\Delta X_8^3 = 0$ if and only if $sbox(X_2^1 \oplus RK_2^1) = sbox(X_6^1 \oplus RK_1^1)$. It can happens at random but if we have the condition on the key $RK_1^1 = RK_2^1$, then $(X_6^1 = X_2^1) \Rightarrow \Delta X_8^3 = 0$. Then, we have $X_6^1 \oplus X_2^1 = I_{14} \oplus I_{10} \oplus sbox(I_3 \oplus RK_5^0) \oplus sbox(I_7 \oplus RK_1^0)$. So if $I_{10} = I_{14}$, then $(X_6^1 \oplus X_2^1 = 0$ if and only if $I_3 \oplus RK_5^0 = I_7 \oplus RK_1^0)$. Now we will see what kind of conditions on the master key we have. The key state is denoted by 20 nibbles of 4 bits: $Y = [Y_{19}, \cdots, Y_0]$. Each round there is a 32-bit round key extracted by the extraction function. First, we have $Z = [Y_{18}, Y_{16}, Y_{13}, Y_{10}, Y_9, Y_6, Y_3, Y_1]$. Let $Z = Z_{31}, \cdots, Z_0$ the bits of Z. Then, we have:

$RK_1^1 = sbox([Z_1, Z_9, Z_{17}, Z_{25}])$ $\quad$ $RK_5^1 = sbox([Z_5, Z_{13}, Z_{21}, Z_{29}])$

$RK_1^2 = sbox([Z_1, Z_9, Z_{17}, Z_{25}]) \oplus 1$ $\quad$ $RK_2^2 = sbox([Z_2, Z_{10}, Z_{18}, Z_{26}]) \oplus 1$

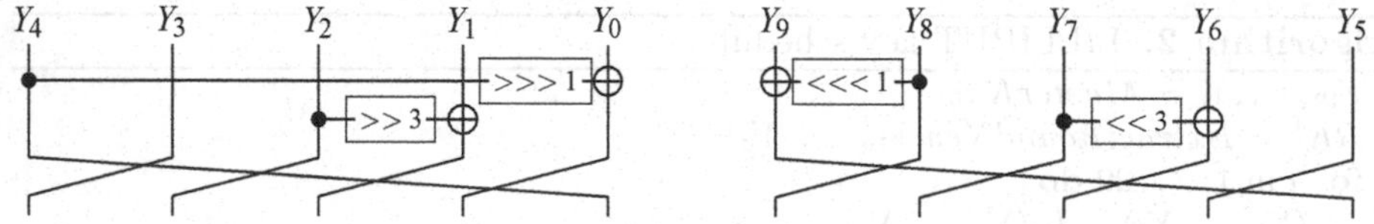

Fig. 2. L_0 and L_1 respectively

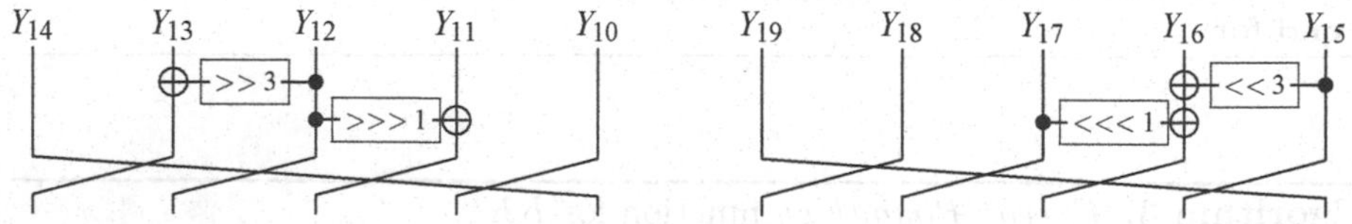

Fig. 3. L_2 and L_3 respectively

Note that the xor with 1 is processed to flip the bit at the left. $RK_1^1 = RK_5^1$ if and only if $sbox([Z_1, Z_9, Z_{17}, Z_{25}]) = sbox([Z_5, Z_{13}, Z_{21}, Z_{29}])$. So $RK_1^1 = RK_5^1$ if and only if $[Z_1, Z_9, Z_{17}, Z_{25}] = [Z_5, Z_{13}, Z_{21}, Z_{29}]$. So $RK_1^1 = RK_5^1$ if $Z_1 = Z_5$, $Z_9 = Z_{13}$, $Z_{17} = Z_{21}$ and $Z_{25} = Z_{29}$. If $K = K_{79}, \cdots, K_0$ is the master key, these conditions lead to: $K_5 = K_{13}$, $K_{25} = K_{38}$, $K_{41} = K_{53}$ and $K_{65} = K_{73}$. Similarly $RK_1^2 = RK_2^2$ if $Z_1 = Z_2$, $Z_9 = Z_{10}$, $Z_{17} = Z_{18}$ and $Z_{25} = Z_{26}$. Note that it is the Z of the second round, so the Z_9 is not the same. It leads to these conditions on the master key: $K_1 \oplus K_{18} = K_2 \oplus K_{19}$, $K_{21} = K_{22}$, $K_{58} = K_{57}$ and $K_{61} = K_{62}$. With these 8 conditions on 1 bit on the master key, we have the attack with probability 1 on *LILLIPUT* reduced to 6 rounds.

5.3 Key Recovery Analysis on 7 Rounds

This attack is based on some distinguishing attacks on 6 rounds. As usual, a plaintext structure contains 16 messages (thus 120 different pairs) which are different only on 2 branches. Moreover, the difference has to be the same on these branches.

On *LILLIPUT* reduced to 6 rounds, there are some differential attacks based on our attacks. The involved input branches are I_9 and I_{10}. On the outputs, the conditions can be: $\Delta S_9 \oplus \Delta S_{10} = 0$ or $\Delta S_9 \oplus \Delta S_{14} = 0$ or $\Delta S_{10} \oplus \Delta S_{14} = 0$. Based on one of these attacks, one can mount a key recovery attack on 7 rounds using Algorithm 4.

Algorithm 4. Key recovery on 7 rounds.

Encrypt some samples of 68 structures on 7 rounds.
for all guess of RK_0^6, RK_1^6 **do**
  Decrypt one round with the guess.
  r =Count how many pairs verify $\Delta S_9 \oplus \Delta S_{10} = 0$.
  if $r > 550$ **then**
    The guess is possible, one has to stock it.
  end if
end for

This algorithm allows to get a list of possible RK_0^6, RK_1^6. There are 2^8 possibilities for the guess. In simulations, one can find directly the correct guess (list of one element) with 5 or 10 samples. But with less samples, one get a list of several possibilities. With the knowledge of RK_0^6, RK_1^6, one get the following bits of the corresponding Z: $Z_0Z_1Z_8Z_9Z_{16}Z_{17}Z_{24}Z_{25}$. Even if there are several RK_0^6, RK_1^6, the cost of the brute-force attack is reduced from 2^{80} to about 2^{74}. Of course, one can optimize this algorithm.

Indeed, one can use several attacks in order to get a better attack. It is described in Algorithm 5. In simulations, we have always get the correct guess RK_0^6, RK_1^6 and RK_5^6. As we do not test all the possibilities for the second and third attack but only the ones which work from the previous step, the number of possibilities is lower than 3×2^8.

With Algorithm 5, one has the knowledge of RK_0^6, RK_1^6 and RK_5^6. It corresponds to the following bits of Z: $Z_0Z_1Z_5Z_8Z_9Z_{13}Z_{16}Z_{17}Z_{21}Z_{24}Z_{25}Z_{29}$. Then, the cost of the brute-force attack is reduced from 2^{80} to 2^{68}.

We can also improve Algorithm 5 by using the following improbable differential attacks: $\Delta S_9 \oplus \Delta S_{15} = 0$, $\Delta S_{10} \oplus \Delta S_{15} = 0$ and $\Delta S_{14} \oplus \Delta S_{15} = 0$. There are 2^4 possibilities for RK_6^6, the corresponding round key for S_{15}, and we test only with the possible RK_0^6, RK_1^6 and RK_5^6. Thus, the cost of the brute-force attack is reduced from 2^{80} to 2^{64}.

Starting from these attack, one can get additional details by using distinguishing attacks on *LILLIPUT* reduced to 5 rounds. Indeed, based on the same input conditions, there are the following attacks on 5 rounds: $\Delta S_{13} \oplus \Delta S_{15} = 0$, $\Delta S_{13} \oplus \Delta S_{14} = 0$ and $\Delta S_{14} \oplus \Delta S_{15} = 0$. These attacks require the previous guess RK_0^6, RK_1^6 and RK_6^6. One can use the same method from Algorithm 5 to get RK_4^5, RK_5^5 and RK_6^5. Thus, the corresponding bits of Z for the round

Algorithm 5. Key recovery on 7 rounds.

Encrypt some samples of 68 structures on 7 rounds.
for all guess of RK_0^6, RK_1^6 **do**
  Decrypt one round with the guess.
  r =Count how many pairs verify $\Delta S_9 \oplus \Delta S_{10} = 0$.
  if $r > 550$ **then**
    The guess is possible, one has to stock it in $List_0$.
  end if
end for
for all possible RK_0^6 in $List_0$ **do**
  for all guess of RK_5^6 **do**
    Decrypt one round of the ciphertexts after 7 rounds with the guess RK_0^6 and RK_5^6.
    r =Count how many pairs verify $\Delta S_9 \oplus \Delta S_{14} = 0$.
    if $r > 550$ **then**
      The guess is possible, one has to stock it in $List_1$.
    end if
  end for
end for
for all possible RK_1^6 in $List_0$ **do**
  for all possible RK_5^6 in $List_1$ **do**
    Decrypt one round of the ciphertexts after 7 rounds with the guess RK_1^6 and RK_5^6.
    r =Count how many pairs verify $\Delta S_{10} \oplus \Delta S_{14} = 0$.
    if $r > 550$ **then**
      The guess is possible, one has to stock it.
    end if
  end for
end for
Deduce the possible correct guess RK_0^6, RK_1^6, RK_5^6.

5 are: $Z_4Z_5Z_6Z_{12}Z_{13}Z_{14}Z_{20}Z_{21}Z_{22}Z_{28}Z_{29}Z_{30}$. In the key schedule, these bits correspond to Y_3, Y_9, Y_{13} and Y_{18}. Then, for the round 6, they shift to: Y_4, Y_5, Y_{14} and Y_{19}. For this step, the number of possibilities is lower than 3×2^8.

There is a efficient attack with the same input condition on *LILLIPUT* reduced to 5 rounds and we can exploit it in our key recovery attack. The output condition is $\Delta S_9 \oplus \Delta S_{10} = 0$. This condition is always verified, so we can test it on smaller samples in order to decrease the global complexity. One can look which round keys are involved from the end of round 7: RK_0^5, RK_1^5, RK_4^6 and RK_7^6. The number of possibilities is 2^{16}.

Finally, we have attacked *LILLIPUT* reduced to 7 rounds using distinguishing attacks on 6 and 5 rounds. One can see the round keys recovered in Table 9. Here is the state[5] at the end of round 6: Y_1 =??||, Y_3 = ||||, Y_6 =??||, Y_9 = ||||, Y_{10} =??||, Y_{13} = ||||, Y_{16} =??||, Y_{18} = ||||. At the end of the round 5, it is similar, we have the knowledge of: Y_1 =??||, Y_3 =?|||, Y_6 =??||, Y_9 =?|||, Y_{10} =??||, Y_{13} =?|||, Y_{16} =??||, Y_{18} =?|||. But, these bits shift for the round 6. Thus, at the end of round 6, we also have more details described in Table 10. We can see in this table that we have recovered 44 bits of the internal state. Thus, the cost of the brute-force is reduced from 2^{80} to 2^{36}. The cost for all guess is less than:

[5] '?' means unknown bit and '|' means known bit.

Table 9. Round key recovery at the end of round 5 and 6 to attack 7 rounds.

Round key	Corresponding bits on Z	Corresponding Y
RK_0^6	Z_0, Z_8, Z_{16}, Z_{24}	Y_1, Y_6, Y_{10}, Y_{16}
RK_1^6	Z_1, Z_9, Z_{17}, Z_{25}	Y_1, Y_6, Y_{10}, Y_{16}
RK_4^6	$Z_4, Z_{12}, Z_{20}, Z_{28}$	Y_3, Y_9, Y_{13}, Y_{18}
RK_5^6	$Z_5, Z_{13}, Z_{21}, Z_{29}$	Y_3, Y_9, Y_{13}, Y_{18}
RK_6^6	$Z_6, Z_{14}, Z_{22}, Z_{30}$	Y_3, Y_9, Y_{13}, Y_{18}
RK_7^6	$Z_7, Z_{15}, Z_{23}, Z_{31}$	Y_3, Y_9, Y_{13}, Y_{18}
RK_0^5	Z_0, Z_8, Z_{16}, Z_{24}	Y_1, Y_6, Y_{10}, Y_{16}
RK_1^5	Z_1, Z_9, Z_{17}, Z_{25}	Y_1, Y_6, Y_{10}, Y_{16}
RK_4^5	$Z_4, Z_{12}, Z_{20}, Z_{28}$	Y_3, Y_9, Y_{13}, Y_{18}
RK_5^5	$Z_5, Z_{13}, Z_{21}, Z_{29}$	Y_3, Y_9, Y_{13}, Y_{18}
RK_6^5	$Z_6, Z_{14}, Z_{22}, Z_{30}$	Y_3, Y_9, Y_{13}, Y_{18}

$c = 2^{16} + 6 * 2^8 + 2^4$. We can continue to use the previous rounds with more distinguishing attacks in order to reduce the complexity.

Table 10. Internal state at round 6 to attack 7 and 8 rounds respectively.

Parts of Y	Nibble state
Y_0, Y_8, Y_{12}, Y_{15}	????
$Y_1, Y_2, Y_6, Y_7, Y_{10}, Y_{11}, Y_{16}, Y_{17}$	??||
Y_4, Y_5, Y_{14}, Y_{19}	?|||
Y_3, Y_9, Y_{13}, Y_{18}	||||

Parts of Y	Nibble state
$Y_0, Y_4, Y_5, Y_7, Y_{11}, Y_{14}, Y_{15} Y_{19}$	????
Y_3, Y_9, Y_{13}, Y_{18}	??|?
Y_1, Y_6, Y_{10}, Y_{16}	??||
Y_2, Y_8, Y_{12}, Y_{17}	||?|

5.4 Key Recovery Analysis on 8 Rounds

We have seen how the key recovery works based on our attacks. Now, we will see how it can be extend. In this subsection, we will see how it works on *LILLIPUT* reduced to 8 rounds.

Table 11. Round key involved for key recovery on 8 rounds.

Branch involved	Round key and involved branches	Round key for internal variables
X_3^5	RK_0^6, X_8^6	RK_7^7
X_4^5	RK_1^6, X_6^6	RK_4^7
X_7^5	RK_5^6, X_5^6	RK_6^7
X_5^5	RK_6^6, X_4^6	RK_1^7

First, we want to use our distinguishing attack on 6 rounds: $\Delta S_9 \oplus \Delta S_{10} = 0$. If we look at the branches involved until 8 rounds, we can see which round key we have to guess. We summarize the analysis in Table 11. To mount a key recovery attack on *LILLIPUT* reduced to 8 rounds, one can use Algorithm 6. As is it described in Table 11, if one wants to exploit $\Delta S_9 \oplus \Delta S_{10} = 0$, the round key to guess will be: RK_0^6, RK_1^6, RK_7^7 and RK_4^7. Thus the number of possibilities is 2^{16}. We can use more distinguishing attacks in order to get more round keys: $\Delta S_9 \oplus \Delta S_{10} = 0$ and $\Delta S_9 \oplus \Delta S_{10} = 0$ for example. Moreover, there are the same improbable differential attacks as in the Sect. 5.3: $\Delta S_9 \oplus \Delta S_{15} = 0$, $\Delta S_{10} \oplus \Delta S_{15} = 0$ and $\Delta S_{14} \oplus \Delta S_{15} = 0$.

Algorithm 6. Key recovery on 8 rounds.

```
Encrypt some samples of 68 structures on 8 rounds.
for all guess of RK_7^7, RK_4^7 do
    Decrypt one round with the guess.
    for all guess of RK_0^6, RK_1^6 do
        r =Count how many pairs verify ΔS_9 ⊕ ΔS_10 = 0.
        if r > 550 then
            The guess is possible, one has to stock it.
        end if
    end for
end for
```

We can use the same method as Algorithm 5. Thanks to this algorithm, we have recovered 24 bits of data as described in Table 12. Then we will see how much is the cost of the brute-force attack without using previous rounds method.

Table 12. Round key recover at the end of round 6 and 7 to attack 8 rounds.

Round key	Corresponding bits on Z	Corresponding Y
RK_0^6	Z_0, Z_8, Z_{16}, Z_{24}	Y_1, Y_6, Y_{10}, Y_{16}
RK_1^6	Z_1, Z_9, Z_{17}, Z_{25}	Y_1, Y_6, Y_{10}, Y_{16}
RK_5^6	Z_4, Z_{12}, Z_{20}, Z_{28}	Y_3, Y_9, Y_{13}, Y_{18}
RK_4^7	Z_4, Z_{12}, Z_{20}, Z_{28}	Y_3, Y_9, Y_{13}, Y_{18}
RK_6^7	Z_6, Z_{14}, Z_{22}, Z_{30}	Y_3, Y_9, Y_{13}, Y_{18}
RK_7^7	Z_7, Z_{15}, Z_{23}, Z_{31}	Y_3, Y_9, Y_{13}, Y_{18}

As we can see in the Sect. 5.1, the information recovered at the end of round 7 can be go up at the end of round 6 without any condition. Thus, with an algorithm similar to Algorithm 5, we have recovered 24 bits of data for the internal state at the end of round 6 and not only split on two rounds. It is described in Table 10. The cost of the brute-force attack is reduced from 2^{80} to 2^{56}.

5.5 Key Recovery Analysis on More Rounds

We have seen how to attack 2 rounds more than the distinguisher. In order to attack more rounds, we need the internal variable on the branch I_{16}. Thus we will need to guess all the round keys for this round. So, it costs 2^{32}. Similarly, if we want to attack 4 rounds more than the distinguisher attack, it will cost 2^{64}. It is possible to reduce enough the complexity to do that but we can not process one more round with this method. Based on the distinguisher on 8 rounds, it is then possible to attack 12 rounds.

6 Conclusion

We have seen some differential attacks based on the variance method on *LILLIPUT*. This is the first time this method is applied to a concrete cipher. The tool has highlighted unusual differential conditions for which *LILLIPUT* is sensitive. Our distinguishers do not reach more rounds than the previous analysis. But, we have found our results empirically and since the last attack require 2^{25} messages, it is far from the maximum. Thus, we can look for distinguishers which reach more rounds with a devoted equipment. We also have described how the key recovery works with our attacks. Finally, we have presented improbable differential attacks which work well in simulations. This scheme can be an efficient support to study this kind of attacks.

References

1. Beaulieu, R., Shors, D., Smith, J., Treatman-Clark, S., et al.: The SIMON and SPECK families of lightweight block ciphers. Cryptology ePrint archive: 2013/404: Listing for 2013 (2013)
2. Beierle, C., Jean, J., Kölbl, S., et al.: The SKINNY family of block ciphers and its low-latency variant MANTIS. Cryptology ePrint archive: 2016/660: Listing for 2016 (2016)
3. Berger, T.P., Francq, J., Minier, M., Thomas, G.: Extended generalized feistel networks using matrix representation to propose a new lightweight block cipher: lilliput. IEEE Trans. Comput. **65**(7), 2074–2089 (2016)
4. Berger, T.P., Minier, M., Thomas, G.: Extended generalized feistel networks using matrix representation. In: Lange, T., Lauter, K., Lisoněk, P. (eds.) SAC 2013. LNCS, vol. 8282, pp. 289–305. Springer, Heidelberg (2014). https://doi.org/10.1007/978-3-662-43414-7_15
5. Biham, E., Biryukov, A., Shamir, A.: Cryptanalysis of skipjack reduced to 31 rounds using impossible differentials. In: Stern, J. (ed.) EUROCRYPT 1999. LNCS, vol. 1592, pp. 12–23. Springer, Heidelberg (1999). https://doi.org/10.1007/3-540-48910-X_2
6. Biham, E., Shamir, A.: Differential cryptanalysis of DES-like cryptosystems. J. Cryptol. **4**(1), 3–72 (1991)
7. Blondeau, C.: Improbable differential from impossible differential: on the validity of the model. In: Paul, G., Vaudenay, S. (eds.) INDOCRYPT 2013. LNCS, vol. 8250, pp. 149–160. Springer, Cham (2013). https://doi.org/10.1007/978-3-319-03515-4_10

8. Bogdanov, A., et al.: PRESENT: an ultra-lightweight block cipher. In: Paillier, P., Verbauwhede, I. (eds.) CHES 2007. LNCS, vol. 4727, pp. 450–466. Springer, Heidelberg (2007). https://doi.org/10.1007/978-3-540-74735-2_31
9. Derbez, P., Fouque, P.-A.: Automatic search of meet-in-the-middle and impossible differential attacks. In: Robshaw, M., Katz, J. (eds.) CRYPTO 2016. LNCS, vol. 9815, pp. 157–184. Springer, Heidelberg (2016). https://doi.org/10.1007/978-3-662-53008-5_6
10. Knudsen, L.R.: Truncated and higher order differentials. In: Preneel, B. (ed.) FSE 1994. LNCS, vol. 1008, pp. 196–211. Springer, Heidelberg (1995). https://doi.org/10.1007/3-540-60590-8_16
11. Nachef, V., Marrière, N., Volte, E.: Improved Attacks on extended generalized feistel networks. In: Foresti, S., Persiano, G. (eds.) CANS 2016. LNCS, vol. 10052, pp. 562–572. Springer, Cham (2016). https://doi.org/10.1007/978-3-319-48965-0_35
12. Nachef, V., Patarin, J., Volte, E.: Feistel Ciphers. Springer, Heidelberg (2017). https://doi.org/10.1007/978-3-319-49530-9
13. Nachef, V., Volte, E., Patarin, J.: Differential attacks on generalized feistel schemes. In: Abdalla, M., Nita-Rotaru, C., Dahab, R. (eds.) CANS 2013. LNCS, vol. 8257, pp. 1–19. Springer, Cham (2013). https://doi.org/10.1007/978-3-319-02937-5_1
14. Sasaki, Y., Todo, Y.: New differential bounds and division property of LILLIPUT: block cipher with extended generalized feistel network. In: Avanzi, R., Heys, H. (eds.) SAC 2016. LNCS, vol. 10532, pp. 264–283. Springer, Cham (2017). https://doi.org/10.1007/978-3-319-69453-5_15
15. Sasaki, Y., Todo, Y.: New impossible differential search tool from design and cryptanalysis aspects. In: Coron, J.-S., Nielsen, J.B. (eds.) EUROCRYPT 2017. LNCS, vol. 10212, pp. 185–215. Springer, Cham (2017). https://doi.org/10.1007/978-3-319-56617-7_7
16. Shirai, T., Shibutani, K., Akishita, T., Moriai, S., Iwata, T.: The 128-bit blockcipher clefia (extended abstract). In: Biryukov, A. (ed.) FSE 2007. LNCS, vol. 4593, pp. 181–195. Springer, Heidelberg (2007). https://doi.org/10.1007/978-3-540-74619-5_12
17. Tezcan, C.: Truncated, impossible, and improbable differential analysis of ascon. Cryptology ePrint archive: 2016/490: Listing for 2016 (2016)
18. Tezcan, C.: The improbable differential attack: cryptanalysis of reduced round CLEFIA. In: Gong, G., Gupta, K.C. (eds.) INDOCRYPT 2010. LNCS, vol. 6498, pp. 197–209. Springer, Heidelberg (2010). https://doi.org/10.1007/978-3-642-17401-8_15
19. Volte, E., Nachef, V., Marrière, N.: Automatic expectation and variance computing for attacks on feistel schemes. Cryptology ePrint archive: 2016/136: Listing for 2016 (2016)
20. Wu, S., Wang, M.: Automatic search of truncated impossible differentials for word-oriented block ciphers. In: Galbraith, S., Nandi, M. (eds.) INDOCRYPT 2012. LNCS, vol. 7668, pp. 283–302. Springer, Heidelberg (2012). https://doi.org/10.1007/978-3-642-34931-7_17
21. Luoand, Y., Wu,Z., Lai, X., Gong, G.: A unified method for finding impossible differentials of block cipher structures (2009). http://eprint.iacr.org/

Bounds on Differential and Linear Branch Number of Permutations

Sumanta Sarkar(✉) and Habeeb Syed

TCS Innovation Labs, Hyderabad, India
sumanta.sarkar1@tcs.com, habeeb.syed@tcs.com

Abstract. Nonlinear permutations (S-boxes) are key components in block ciphers. The differential branch number measures the diffusion power of a permutation, whereas the linear branch number measures resistance against linear cryptanalysis. There has not been much analysis done on the differential branch number of nonlinear permutations of $\mathbb{F}_2^n$, although it has been well studied in case of linear permutations. Similarly upper bounds for the linear branch number have also not been studied in general. In this paper we obtain bounds for both the differential and the linear branch number of permutations (both linear and nonlinear) of $\mathbb{F}_2^n$. We also prove that in the case of $\mathbb{F}_2^4$, the maximum differential branch number can be achieved only by affine permutations.

Keywords: Permutation · S-box · Differential branch number
Linear branch number · Block cipher · Griesmer bound

1 Introduction

A basic design principle of a block cipher consists of confusion and diffusion as suggested by Shannon [14]. Confusion layer makes the relation between key and the ciphertext as complex as possible, whereas diffusion layer spreads the plaintext statistics across the ciphertext. So far there have been several constructions of block ciphers, and equal efforts have been made to break them. In the process literature has been enriched by proposals of elegant cryptanalysis techniques, for instance, differential cryptanalysis [3] and linear cryptanalysis [12]. The latter two cryptanalysis methods led to the design known as wide-trail strategy [6]. This design constructs round transformations of block ciphers with efficiency and provides resistance against the differential and the linear cryptanalysis. This strategy also explains how the differential branch number is related to the number of active S-boxes.

Recently lightweight cryptography has gained huge attention from both the industry and academia. There have been several proposals of lightweight ciphers so far, which are mostly based on symmetric cryptography. In this work we are interested in block ciphers. Some examples of lightweight block ciphers are `CLEFIA` [15] and `PRESENT` [4]; both are included in the ISO/IEC 29192 standard. There are many block ciphers which follow the design of Substitution-Permutation-Network (SPN), for example, `AES` [7]. In this model, S-boxes are

W. Susilo and G. Yang (Eds.): ACISP 2018, LNCS 10946, pp. 207–224, 2018.
https://doi.org/10.1007/978-3-319-93638-3_13

used to achieve the confusion property, whereas in general MDS matrices are used as the diffusion layer of a block cipher. MDS matrices generate MDS codes which achieve the highest possible minimum distance, thus MDS matrices have the highest possible diffusion power. In the same note we find the design of PRESENT very interesting. It has removed the usual diffusion layer that is normally implemented by an MDS matrix. Thus saving a considerable amount of hardware cost. It uses a 4×4 S-box that has the following properties:

- differential branch number is 3,
- differential uniformity is 4 (the highest possible),
- nonlinearity is 4 (the highest possible),
- algebraic degree is 3.

One round function of PRESENT is comprised of 16 such S-boxes followed by a linear bit-wise permutation $L : \mathbb{F}_2^{64} \rightarrow \mathbb{F}_2^{64}$. The role of this linear permutation is to mix up the outputs of the S-boxes which become the input to the next round. As bit-wise permutation can be implemented by wires only, so this reduces the number of gates required for the whole design. Recently a lightweight block cipher GIFT [2] has also appeared which relies on the same design principle as of PRESENT (Fig. 1).

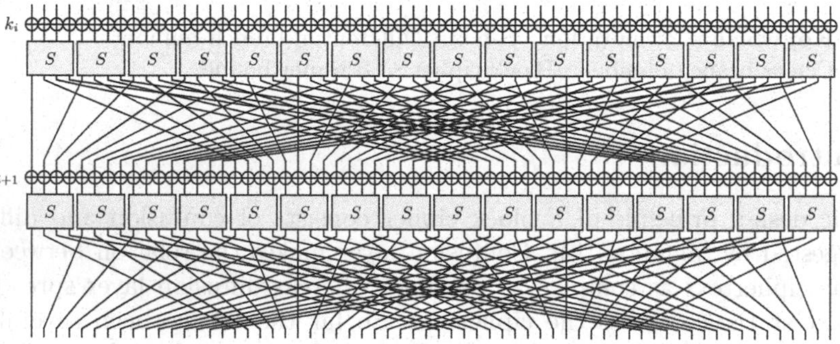

Fig. 1. Round function of PRESENT (image source: [9])

PRESENT (in 2007) used the diffusion property of an S-box. This construction idea will succeed provided the S-box has high differential branch number along with the other cryptographic properties. However after PRESENT, through the last 10 years, no attempt has been made to analyze how far an S-box can diffuse. We consider this problem and provide an upper bound for the differential branch number of permutations in general. To the best of our knowledge this is the first ever work which gives nontrivial bounds on diffusion power of S-boxes. On the other hand it is also crucial to have S-boxes with high linear branch number in order to resist the linear cryptanalysis. So we study the differential branch number of permutations in conjunction with the linear branch number. Below we summarize our contributions.

Our Contributions

In Sect. 4, we present bounds on the differential branch number of any permutation of $\mathbb{F}_2^n$. We completely characterize permutations of $\mathbb{F}_2^4$ in terms of the differential branch number. In [13] huge computational effort was made in order to characterize cryptographic properties of 4×4 S-boxes. In their search they considered 16 optimal 4×4 S-boxes from [10] and showed that the maximum possible differential branch number of such an S-box is 3. However, from this search it is not clear whether 3 is the maximum for all 4×4 S-boxes. In Theorem 4, we prove that if a permutation of $\mathbb{F}_2^4$ has differential branch number 4 then it is affine, which shows (Theorem 5) that in fact for any 4×4 S-box, the maximum possible differential branch number is 3. Further in Theorem 6, we prove that for any permutation over $\mathbb{F}_2^n$, for $n \geq 5$, its differential branch number is upper bounded by $\lceil 2\frac{n}{3} \rceil$. There is a bound known as Griesmer bound [8] which applies only to linear permutations, whereas our bound works on any permutation. We compare these two bounds in Table 3, and observe that values are very close to each other.

We also study bounds on the linear branch number of permutations of $\mathbb{F}_2^n$. It turns out that for a linear permutation of $\mathbb{F}_2^n$, the maximum value of the linear branch number matches with the maximum value of the differential branch number (see Theorem 1). For any permutation of $\mathbb{F}_2^n$, the linear branch number is upper bounded by n (see Theorem 3).

2 Preliminaries

Denote by $\mathbb{F}_2$ the finite field of two elements $\{0, 1\}$ and by $\mathbb{F}_2^n$ the n-dimensional vector space over $\mathbb{F}_2$. For any $x \in \mathbb{F}_2^n$ the Hamming weight of x, denoted by $wt(x)$ is the number of 1's in x. Bitwise XOR is denoted by $\oplus$ and for any $x, y \in \mathbb{F}_2^n$ their dot product $x^t \cdot y$ is simply the usual inner product $x_0y_0 \oplus \cdots \oplus x_{n-1}y_{n-1}$.

We now bring in some notations which will be frequently used. For $i = 0, \ldots, n-1$ denote by e_i, the element of $\mathbb{F}_2^n$ which has 1 in the i-th position, and 0 elsewhere. Note that the set $\{e_0, \ldots, e_{n-1}\}$ forms a basis of $\mathbb{F}_2^n$. Further, the element of $\mathbb{F}_2^n$ with all 1 is denoted by $\bar{e}$. To illustrate let $n = 4$, then we have $e_0 = (1, 0, 0, 0)$, $e_1 = (0, 1, 0, 0)$, $e_2 = (0, 0, 1, 0)$, $e_3 = (0, 0, 0, 1)$, and $\bar{e} = (1, 1, 1, 1)$.

An $n \times n$ S-box is a permutation $\mathrm{S} : \mathbb{F}_2^n \to \mathbb{F}_2^n$ which is (strictly) nonlinear. We denote by $\mathbb{GL}(n, \mathbb{F}_2)$ (or simply by $\mathbb{GL}(n)$) the set of linear permutations of $\mathbb{F}_2^n$. Clearly $\mathbb{GL}(n)$ is a proper subset of set of all permutations of $\mathbb{F}_2^n$ and by definition an $n \times n$ S-box is a permutation of $\mathbb{F}_2^n$ which is not in $\mathbb{GL}(n)$. For a secure design, S-box needs to satisfy several properties such as high nonlinearity, high differential uniformity, high algebraic degree, etc. [5]. We now recall the notions of correlation matrices, linear and differential branch numbers. See [7] for detailed discussion on these.

Consider a permutation ϕ of $\mathbb{F}_2^n$.

For any $\alpha, \beta \in \mathbb{F}_2^n$ the correlation coefficient of ϕ with respect to (α, β) is given by

$$\mathtt{C}_\phi(\alpha, \beta) = \sum_{x \in \mathbb{F}_2^n} (-1)^{\alpha^t \cdot x \oplus \beta^t \cdot \phi(x)} \tag{1}$$

It is easy to see that $-2^n \leq \mathtt{C}_\phi(\alpha, \beta) \leq 2^n$. See [7, Chap. 7] for detailed discussion on correlation matrices of Boolean functions and their properties. We define the correlation matrix $\mathtt{C}_\phi$ of ϕ as the $2^n \times 2^n$ matrix indexed by $\alpha, \beta \in \mathbb{F}_2^n$ in which the entry in the cell (α, β) is given by $\mathtt{C}_\phi(\alpha, \beta)$:

$$\mathtt{C}_\phi = [C_{\alpha,\beta}]_{2^n \times 2^n} \quad \text{where } C_{\alpha,\beta} = \mathtt{C}_\phi(\alpha, \beta) \tag{2}$$

Next we recall some definitions related to branch numbers of permutations.

Definition 1. *For any ϕ of $\mathbb{F}_2^n$, its differential branch number (respectively linear branch number) is denoted by $\beta_{\mathtt{d}}(\phi)$ (respectively $\beta_{\ell}(\phi)$) and defined as*

$$\beta_{\mathtt{d}}(\phi) := \min_{x, x' \in \mathbb{F}_2^n,\, x \neq x'} \{wt(x \oplus x') + wt(\phi(x) \oplus \phi(x'))\},$$

and

$$\beta_{\ell}(\phi) := \min_{\alpha, \beta \in \mathbb{F}_2^n,\, \mathtt{C}_\phi(\alpha,\beta) \neq 0} \{wt(\alpha) + wt(\beta)\}.$$

where $\mathtt{C}_\phi(\alpha, \beta)$ is the correlation coefficient as in (1).

If ϕ is a linear permutation of $\mathbb{F}_2^n$, then there exists a binary $n \times n$ invertible matrix M such that $\phi(x) = \mathrm{M}x$ for every $x \in \mathbb{F}_2^n$. In this case $\beta_{\mathtt{d}}(\phi)$ and $\beta_{\ell}(\phi)$ can be simplified as in the following lemma [7, Chap. 9].

Lemma 1. *Let ϕ be a linear permutation of $\mathbb{F}_2^n$ given by $\mathrm{M} \in \mathbb{GL}(n, \mathbb{F}_2)$. Then,*

$$\beta_{\mathtt{d}}(\phi) = \min_{\alpha \in \mathbb{F}_2^n, \alpha \neq 0} \{wt(\alpha) + wt(\mathrm{M}\alpha)\} \tag{3}$$

$$\beta_{\ell}(\phi) = \min_{\alpha \in \mathbb{F}_2^n, \alpha \neq 0} \{wt(\alpha) + wt(\mathrm{M}^t\alpha)\}. \tag{4}$$

For any $\phi \in \Pi(n)$ it is easy to see that $\beta_{\mathtt{d}}(\phi)$ is ≥ 2 and $\beta_{\ell}(\phi) \geq 2$. Also,

$$\beta_{\mathtt{d}}(\phi) = \beta_{\mathtt{d}}(\phi^{-1}) \qquad \text{and} \qquad \beta_{\ell}(\phi) = \beta_{\ell}(\phi^{-1}).$$

It is interesting to note that the differential branch number is related to the difference distribution table (DDT). DDT of a permutation ϕ of $\mathbb{F}_2^n$ denoted by $\mathcal{D}_\phi$ is a matrix of order $2^n \times 2^n$. Suppose for the input difference δ, the output difference of the permutation ϕ is Δ, i.e., $\phi(x) \oplus \phi(x \oplus \delta) = \Delta$. Let $\mathcal{D}_\phi(\delta, \Delta)$ be the number solutions of $\phi(x) \oplus \phi(x \oplus \delta) = \Delta$, then the (δ, Δ)-th element of DDT is $\mathcal{D}_\phi(\delta, \Delta)$. In Table 1, we present the difference distribution table of the S-box $\phi = $ 408235B719A6CDEF.

Then the differential branch number can be redefined as

$$\beta_{\mathtt{d}}(\phi) := \min_{\delta \neq 0, \Delta \neq 0, \mathcal{D}_\phi(\delta, \Delta) \neq 0} \{wt(\delta) + wt(\Delta)\}.$$

Table 1. DDT of S-Box 408235B719A6CDEF

δ	Δ															
	0	1	2	3	4	5	6	7	8	9	A	B	C	D	E	F
0	16	0	0	0	0	0	0	0	0	0	0	0	0	0	0	0
1	0	4	0	0	2	0	2	0	2	0	2	0	4	0	0	0
2	0	0	8	0	0	0	0	0	2	0	0	2	2	0	0	2
3	0	0	0	6	2	0	2	2	2	0	0	0	0	0	2	0
4	0	0	0	2	4	4	0	2	0	2	0	0	0	2	0	0
5	0	2	0	2	0	4	0	0	2	2	0	0	2	0	0	2
6	0	0	0	0	0	0	4	4	0	0	0	4	0	0	0	4
7	0	2	0	2	0	0	0	4	0	0	2	2	0	2	2	0
8	0	0	2	0	2	4	0	0	4	2	0	0	0	0	0	2
9	0	2	0	0	2	0	0	0	2	4	0	0	0	2	4	0
A	0	0	0	0	0	0	2	2	0	2	4	2	0	2	2	0
B	0	2	2	2	0	0	2	0	0	0	2	4	2	0	0	0
C	0	4	2	0	0	0	2	0	2	0	0	0	2	4	0	0
D	0	0	0	0	2	0	0	2	0	2	2	0	4	4	0	0
E	0	0	0	2	2	0	0	0	0	2	4	0	0	0	2	4
F	0	0	2	0	0	4	2	0	0	0	0	2	0	0	4	2

For example, it is clear from the DDT of the differential branch number of 408235B719A6CDEF is 2.

One of the basic notion in the study of permutations is that of *affine equivalence*. This equivalence preserves various cryptographic properties like nonlinearity, differential uniformity, algebraic degree (more than one), etc.

Definition 2 (Affine Equivalence). *Let ϕ, ϕ' be two permutations of $\mathbb{F}_2^n$. We say that ϕ is affine equivalent to ϕ' if there exist A, $B \in \mathbb{GL}(n, \mathbb{F}_2)$, and $c, d \in \mathbb{F}_2^n$ such that*

$$\phi'(x) = B \cdot \phi[A\,x \oplus c] \oplus d, \qquad \text{for all } x \in \mathbb{F}_2^n. \tag{5}$$

Affine equivalence preserves many properties of S-boxes, such as uniformity, nonlinearity, degree, but it does not preserve branch number in general. For instance, the following two affine equivalent S-boxes (in Table 2) have different differential branch number. Here S and S′ are related as $\mathrm{S}'(x) = B\,\mathrm{S}(x)$, where B is a matrix with the rows $\{(1,0,0,1),(0,1,0,0),(0,0,1,0),(0,0,0,1)\}$. Note that $\beta_{\mathrm{d}}(\mathrm{S}) = 3$, whereas $\beta_{\mathrm{d}}(\mathrm{S}') = 2$, although they are affine equivalent. The S-box S is used in PRESENT.

On the other hand, if A and B are permutation matrices[1] then the corresponding affine equivalence class preserves the branch number [13]. We state this as the following lemma.

[1] A matrix obtained by permuting rows (or columns) of an identity matrix.

Table 2. Affine equivalent S-boxes with different differential branch numbers.

x	0	1	2	3	4	5	6	7	8	9	A	B	C	D	E	F
S(x)	C	5	6	B	9	0	A	D	3	E	F	8	4	7	1	2
S′(x)	C	D	6	3	1	0	A	5	B	E	7	8	4	F	9	2

Lemma 2. *If ϕ and ϕ_1 are two affine equivalent permutations of $\mathbb{F}_2^n$ such that $\phi_1(x) = B\,\phi[A\,x \oplus c] \oplus d$, for all $x \in \mathbb{F}_2^n$, where A and B are $n \times n$ permutation matrix, and $c, d \in \mathbb{F}_2^n$, then $\beta_{\mathsf{d}}(\phi) = \beta_{\mathsf{d}}(\phi_1)$ and $\beta_{\ell}(\phi) = \beta_{\ell}(\phi_1)$.*

3 Bounds on Linear Branch Number

First we consider the case of linear permutations of $\mathbb{F}_2^n$. In this case we have the following connection between the linear and the differential branch numbers of such permutations.

Theorem 1. *For linear permutations of $\mathbb{F}_2^n$ the maximum differential branch number is equal to the maximum linear branch number.*

Proof. Suppose ϕ be a linear permutation of $\mathbb{F}_2^n$, then there exists a matrix $\mathrm{M} \in \mathbb{GL}(n, \mathbb{F}_2)$ such that $\phi(x) = \mathrm{M}x$ for every $x \in \mathbb{F}_2^n$. Consider the permutation ϕ^t defined as $\phi^t(x) = \mathrm{M}^t x$ for $x \in \mathbb{F}_2^n$. Using Lemma 1 we see that $\beta_{\mathsf{d}}(\phi) = \beta_{\ell}(\phi^t)$ from which the result follows. □

Remark 1. The best known bound for the differential branch number of a linear permutation is Griesmer bound (see Sect. 4). Above theorem suggests that this is also the best bound for the linear branch number of such permutations. Later in Theorem 6 we present new a bound on the differential branch number of more general permutations of $\mathbb{F}_2^n$ which is quite comparable to Griesmer bound in case linear permutations.

It is pertinent to mention here some results similar to Theorem 1 in case of permutations of $\mathbb{F}_q^n$ when $q = 2^m$ for $m > 1$. These results along with proofs can be found in [7]. We present some of them here for sake of completeness. In [7] authors consider a permutation of $\mathbb{F}_q^n$ as a "bundled" permutation of $\mathbb{F}_2^{mn}$ with bundle size m, i.e., if ψ is such permutation then it is defined as

$$\psi(x_0, \ldots, x_{n-1}) = (y_0, \ldots, y_{n-1}) \tag{6}$$

where $(x_0, \ldots, x_{n-1}), (y_0, \ldots, y_{n-1}) \in \mathbb{F}_{2^m}^n$. The notion of branch numbers (linear and differential) are defined with respect to the bundle size. With these authors prove the following theorem [7, Theorem B.1.2].

Theorem 2. *Let $\psi : \mathbb{F}_2^{mn} \longrightarrow \mathbb{F}_2^{mn}$ be a bundled permutation as in (6). Then ψ has maximal differential branch number if and only if it has maximal linear branch number.*

If ψ is a linear permutation of $\mathbb{F}_q^n$ given by $n \times n$ nonsingular matrix N over $\mathbb{F}_q$, i.e., $\psi(x) = Nx$, then Theorem 2 simply means that the matrix N is MDS if and only if its transpose is also MDS. Note that Theorem 2 goes beyond linear permutations and includes all permutation of $\mathbb{F}_q^n$. However, an important point to be noted here is that Theorem 2 is applicable for bundled permutations of $\mathbb{F}_2^{mn}$ of bundle size $m > 1$ and is not applicable to our results which involve permutations of $\mathbb{F}_2^n$. In the following we will see that such a nice connection is elusive in case of permutations of $\mathbb{F}_2^n$. To continue our results from Theorem 1 we now prove a bound on the linear branch number of general permutations.

To present our results we need some facts related to Boolean functions which we recall here. A n variable Boolean function is map $\varphi : \mathbb{F}_2^n \longrightarrow \mathbb{F}_2$. We say that φ is balanced if

$$\#\{x \in \mathbb{F}_2^n : \varphi(x) = 0\} = \#\{x \in \mathbb{F}_2^n : \varphi(x) = 1\} = 2^{n-1}.$$

The map φ is said to be r^{th} order Correlation Immune (r-CI) if

$$\sum_{x \in \mathbb{F}_2^n} (-1)^{\alpha^t \cdot x \oplus \varphi(x)} = 0, \tag{7}$$

for all $\alpha \in \mathbb{F}_2^n$ such that $1 \leq wt(\alpha) \leq r$. If φ is balanced and r-CI then it said to be $r-$resilient Boolean function. In our study Boolean functions occur as coordinate functions of a permutation ϕ of $\mathbb{F}_2^n$. The linear branch number of ϕ and the resiliency order of its coordinate functions is interconnected as follows. Suppose that ϕ is a permutation of $\mathbb{F}_2^n$ given by $\phi(x) = (\phi_0(x), \ldots, \phi_{n-1}(x))$ where $x \in \mathbb{F}_2^n$ and each of $\phi_0, \ldots, \phi_{n-1}$ is a coordinate Boolean function. If $\beta_\ell(\phi) = r$ then, by definition for any $\alpha, \beta \in \mathbb{F}_2^n$

$$\mathsf{C}_\phi(\alpha, \beta) = 0 \quad \text{whenever} \quad 2 \leq wt(\alpha) + wt(\beta) \leq r - 1.$$

In particular if we choose $\beta = e_i \subset \mathcal{B}_n$, then the above equation implies that

$$\mathsf{C}_\phi(\alpha, e_i) = \sum_{x \in \mathbb{F}_2^n} (-1)^{\alpha^t \cdot x \oplus \phi_i(x)} = 0 \quad \text{whenever} \quad 1 \leq wt(\alpha) \leq r - 2, \tag{8}$$

which means that ϕ_i is $(r-2)-$ CI Boolean function. Also, ϕ_i is balanced since it is a coordinate function of a permutation. Thus we see that each ϕ_i is a $r-2$ resilient Boolean function. In a nutshell this is our observation:

Lemma 3. *Let $\phi = (\phi_0, \ldots, \phi_{n-1})$ be a permutation of $\mathbb{F}_2^n$. For every $0 \leq i \leq n-1$ the coordinate function ϕ_i is $\beta_\ell(\phi) - 2$ resilient Boolean function.*

We also recall the notion of degree of a Boolean function. Given a Boolean function φ of n variables there exist a unique polynomial $P(X_0, \ldots, X_{n-1})$ in n variables over $\mathbb{F}_2$ such that $\varphi(x_0, \ldots, x_{n-1}) = P(x_0, \ldots, x_{n-1})$ for every $(x_0, \ldots, x_{n-1}) \in \mathbb{F}_2^n$. Such a polynomial is called *Algebraic Normal Form* of φ and the total degree of P is called algebraic degree (or simply degree) of φ. Note that $\deg(\varphi) = 0$ only for constant functions and $\deg(\varphi) = 1$ if φ is affine. For any Boolean function φ its resiliency order and its degree are connected as follows, which is known as Siegenthaler bound [16]. If φ is a n variable r−resilient Boolean function then

$$\deg(\varphi) \leq n - 1 - r. \tag{9}$$

Using the connection in Lemma 3 and (9) we obtain bounds on the linear branch number of permutations of $\mathbb{F}_2^n$.

Theorem 3. *For any nonlinear permutation ϕ of $\mathbb{F}_2^n$ we have $\beta_\ell(\phi) \leq n - 1$.*

Proof. First we show that $\beta_\ell(\phi) \leq n$ and then that only linear permutations have $\beta_\ell(\phi) = n$. Let $\phi = (\phi_0, \ldots, \phi_{n-1})$ be a permutation of $\mathbb{F}_2^n$ with coordinate Boolean functions $\{\phi_0, \ldots, \phi_{n-1}\}$. Suppose $\phi_i \in \{\phi_0, \ldots, \phi_{n-1}\}$ be any coordinate function. If $\beta_\ell(\phi) \geq n+1$ then from Lemma 3 it follows that the function ϕ_i is $r-$ resilient where $r \geq (n+1) - 2 = n - 1$. By Siegenthaler bound (9) we must have $\deg(\phi_i) \leq (n-1) - (n-1) = 0$. On the other hand, if $\deg(\phi_i) = 0$ then ϕ_i is a constant function which is impossible because ϕ_i a coordinate function of a permutation of $\mathbb{F}_2^n$ and hence need to be balanced. This contradiction shows that $\beta_\ell(\phi) \leq n$. Using same kind of argument one can easily see that if $\beta_\ell(\phi) = n$ then $\deg(\phi_i) \leq 1$ for every $0 \leq i \leq n-1$, which implies that it is affine and hence ϕ itself is affine. As a consequence it follows that if ϕ is a nonlinear permutation of $\mathbb{F}_2^n$ then $\beta_\ell(\phi) \leq n - 1$. □

Next we focus on bounds for the differential branch number of general permutations of $\mathbb{F}_2^n$.

4 Bounds on Differential Branch Number

It is trivial to check that for any permutation ϕ of $\mathbb{F}_2^n$, we have $\beta_{\mathrm{d}}(\phi) \geq 2$. For linear permutations, some upper bound can be easily obtained from coding theory. If $L : \mathbb{F}_2^n \to \mathbb{F}_2^n$ is linear permutation, then the set $\mathcal{C} = \{(x, L(x)) : x \in \mathbb{F}_2^n\}$ forms a $[2n, n]$ linear code, and its minimum distance is actually the differential branch number of L. An $[N, K]$ linear code has minimum distance $d \leq N - K + 1$ (Singleton Bound). The codes which achieve the Singleton Bound are called MDS codes. Therefore, the differential branch number of L is bounded by $n + 1$. However, it is known that there is no nontrivial binary MDS code [11], which means that there is no linear permutation defined over $\mathbb{F}_2^n$ having the differential branch number $n + 1$. Thanks to Griesmer bound we can have further bounds [8].

Lemma 4 (Griesmer Bound). *Let $[N, K]$ be a binary linear code with the minimum distance d then*

$$N \geq \sum_{i=0}^{K-1} \left\lceil \frac{d}{2^i} \right\rceil .$$

In this section we present a bound on the differential branch number of an arbitrary permutation of $\mathbb{F}_2^n$. We begin with following remark which will be useful in our proofs.

Remark 2. Let ϕ be a permutation of $\mathbb{F}_2^n$ such that $\phi(0) = c$ for some $c \neq 0 \in \mathbb{F}_2^n$. Then for the permutation ϕ' defined as $\phi'(x) = \phi(x) \oplus c$ it is easy to see that $\beta_{\mathrm{d}}(\phi) = \beta_{\mathrm{d}}(\phi')$ and $\phi'(0) = 0$. Thus while deriving bounds on the differential branch numbers we can simply consider permutations ϕ such that $\phi(0) = 0$.

Suppose q is a power of prime, and $L : \mathbb{F}_q^n \longrightarrow \mathbb{F}_q^n$ is a linear permutation. It is a well known fact [11] that $\beta_{\mathrm{d}}(L) \leq n+1$ whenever $q \neq 2$.

Next, let ϕ be a arbitrary permutation of $\mathbb{F}_2^n$. If $\beta_{\mathrm{d}}(\phi) = n+1$ then by Definition 1 and Remark 2 we get

$$wt(e_i \oplus 0) + wt(\phi(e_i) \oplus \phi(0)) = wt(e_i) + wt(\phi(e_i)) \geq n+1,$$

which implies that $wt(\phi(e_i)) \geq n$ for $i = 0, \ldots n-1$. However, this is impossible because there is precisely one element $\bar{e} \in \mathbb{F}_2^n$ with $wt(\bar{e}) = n$. Hence we must have $\beta_{\mathrm{d}}(\phi) < n+1$. This gives us a trivial bound on the differential branch number of permutations of $\mathbb{F}_2^n$ as follows.

Lemma 5. *For any permutation ϕ of $\mathbb{F}_2^n$ we have $\beta_{\mathrm{d}}(\phi) < n+1$.*

In the remaining part of this section we sharpen the bound in Lemma 5. To make proofs easy we consider the case of permutations over $\mathbb{F}_2^4$ and the case of permutations over $\mathbb{F}_2^n, n \geq 5$ separately.

4.1 Differential Branch Number of Permutations of $\mathbb{F}_2^4$

In this section we consider permutations defined on $\mathbb{F}_2^4$ which are used to design 4×4 S-boxes. Here we show that if the differential branch number of a permutation of $\mathbb{F}_2^4$ is 4 then it is necessarily affine and hence the differential branch number of any 4×4 S-box is bounded above by 3.

Lemma 6. *Suppose $\phi : \mathbb{F}_2^4 \to \mathbb{F}_2^4$ is a permutation with $\phi(0) = 0$ and $\beta_{\mathrm{d}}(\phi) = 4$. Then the following conditions hold for $x \in \mathbb{F}_2^4$*

C1. *if $wt(x) = 4$ then $wt\,(\phi(x)) = 4$,*
C2. *if $wt(x) = 1$ then $wt\,(\phi(x)) = 3$,*
C3. *if $wt(x) = 2$ then $wt\,(\phi(x)) = 2$,*
C4. *if $wt(x) = 3$ then $wt\,(\phi(x)) = 1$.*

Proof. Since $\beta_{\mathrm{d}}(\phi) = 4$, and $\phi(0) = 0$, any nonzero $x \in \mathbb{F}_2^4$ must satisfy

$$wt(x) + wt(\phi(x)) \geq 4. \tag{10}$$

Immediate consequence of this is that $wt(\phi(e_i)) = 3$ or $wt(\phi(e_i)) = 4$ as $wt(e_i) = 1$ for any $0 \leq i \leq 3$. Suppose $wt(\phi(e_i)) = 4$ for some i, then for any $j \neq i$ we have

$$wt(e_i \oplus e_j) + wt(\phi(e_i) \oplus \phi(e_j)) = 3 < 4,$$

contradicting (10). Hence C2 follows.

Next let $x \in \mathbb{F}_2^4$ with $wt(x) = 2$. Then, $2 \leq wt(\phi(x)) \leq 4$ by (10). Since ϕ maps all weight 1 elements to weight 3 elements and ϕ is a permutation, so $wt(\phi(x)) \neq 3$. Suppose that $wt(\phi(x)) = 4$. Choose e_i such that $wt(e_i \oplus x) = 1$, and since $wt(\phi(e_i)) = 3$ we must have

$$wt(e_i \oplus x) + wt(\phi(e_i) \oplus \phi(x)) = 1 + 1 = 2 < 4,$$

again contradicting (10); hence it follows that $wt(\phi(x)) = 2$. This concludes the proof of C3.

Now let's prove C4. Consider x with $wt(x) = 3$. By C2 and C3, we have $wt(S(x)) \neq 2, 3$. This leaves open the possibility that $wt(\phi(x)) = 1$ or 4. If $wt(\phi(x)) = 4$, consider an element x' with $wt(x') = 2$ and $wt(x \oplus x') = 1$. Then

$$wt(x \oplus x') + wt(\phi(x) \oplus \phi(x')) = 1 + 2 < 4,$$

a contradiction. So $wt(\phi(x)) = 1$.

Finally, C2, C3, C4 imply that $wt(\phi(x)) = 4$, when $wt(x) = 4$. □

Above theorem leads to the following characterization of permutations ϕ of $\mathbb{F}_2^4$ for which $\beta_{\mathsf{d}}(\phi) = 4$.

Theorem 4. *Let $\phi : \mathbb{F}_2^4 \longrightarrow \mathbb{F}_2^4$ be a permutation with $\beta_{\mathsf{d}}(\phi) = 4$. Then ϕ is affine.*

Proof. As per Remark 2 we prove the result for $\phi(0) = 0$. Since $\beta_{\mathsf{d}}(\phi) = 4$ and $\phi(0) = 0$, ϕ satisfies C1, C2, C3, C4 (of Lemma 6). Note that the set of 1-weight vectors $\{e_0, e_1, e_2, e_3\}$ form a basis of $\mathbb{F}_2^4$ and by C2 the corresponding image set $\{\phi(e_0), \phi(e_1), \phi(e_2), \phi(e_3)\}$ contains all the 3-weight vectors of $\mathbb{F}_2^4$. Note that $\{\phi(e_0), \phi(e_1), \phi(e_2), \phi(e_3)\}$ also forms a basis of $\mathbb{F}_2^4$. Recall that the permutation ϕ is a linear map iff

$$\phi(c_0e_0 \oplus c_1e_1 \oplus c_2e_2 \oplus c_3e_3) = c_0\phi(e_0) \oplus c_1\phi(e_1) \oplus c_2\phi(e_2) \oplus c_3\phi(e_3)$$

holds for all $(c_0, c_1, c_2, c_3) \in \mathbb{F}_2^4$.

As $wt(\phi(e_0 \oplus e_1 \oplus e_2 \oplus e_3)) = 4$ (by C1 of Lemma 6), and $wt(\phi(e_0) \oplus \phi(e_1) \oplus \phi(e_2) \oplus \phi(e_3)) = 4$, then

$$\phi(e_0 \oplus e_1 \oplus e_2 \oplus e_3) = \phi(e_0) \oplus \phi(e_1) \oplus \phi(e_2) \oplus \phi(e_3).$$

In the following we will use the fact that $\phi(e_i) \oplus \phi(e_j)$ has weight 2, and $\phi(e_i) \oplus \phi(e_j) \oplus \phi(e_k)$ has weight 1. The set $\{\phi(e_0), \phi(e_1), \phi(e_2), \phi(e_3)\}$ forms a basis and $wt(\phi(e_i \oplus e_j)) = 2$ (by C3 of Lemma 6), then $\phi(e_i \oplus e_j)$ can be written as

$$\phi(e_i \oplus e_j) = \phi(e_\ell) \oplus \phi(e_r),$$

for some ℓ and r. If linearity does not hold for $(e_i \oplus e_j)$ then $(i, j) \neq (\ell, r)$.

If $i = \ell$ (and $j \neq r$), then

$$\begin{aligned} wt(e_j \oplus e_i \oplus e_j) + wt(\phi(e_j) \oplus \phi(e_i \oplus e_j)) &= wt(e_i) + wt(\phi(e_j) \oplus \phi(e_i) \oplus \phi(e_r)) \\ &= 1 + 1 < 4, \end{aligned}$$

a contradiction. The case $j = r$ can be treated similarly.

Next if $\ell, r \notin \{i, j\}$, then

$$\begin{aligned} wt(e_j \oplus e_i \oplus e_j) + wt(\phi(e_j) \oplus \phi(e_i \oplus e_j)) &= wt(e_i) + wt(\phi(e_j) \oplus \phi(e_\ell) \oplus \phi(e_r)) \\ &= 1 + 1 < 4, \end{aligned}$$

which contradicts the fact that $\beta_{\mathtt{d}}(\phi) = 4$. Therefore, for any linear combinations of the form $e_i \oplus e_j$ we must have

$$\phi(e_i \oplus e_j) = \phi(e_i) \oplus \phi(e_j).$$

We now consider linear combinations of the form $e_i \oplus e_j \oplus e_k$. By C4 of Lemma 6, we have $wt(\phi(e_i \oplus e_j \oplus e_k)) = 1$. As $\{\phi(e_0), \phi(e_1), \phi(e_2), \phi(e_3)\}$ forms a basis, so we can write

$$\phi(e_i \oplus e_j \oplus e_k) = \phi(e_\ell) \oplus \phi(e_r) \oplus \phi(e_t).$$

Suppose that linearity does not hold for $e_i \oplus e_j \oplus e_k$, then $(i, j, k) \neq (\ell, r, t)$. Note that we must have $|\{i, j, k\} \cap \{\ell, r, t\}| = 2$. Assume that $i = \ell$ and $j = r$. Then

$$\begin{aligned} &wt(e_i \oplus e_k \oplus e_i \oplus e_j \oplus e_k) + wt(\phi(e_i \oplus e_k) \oplus \phi(e_i \oplus e_j \oplus e_k)) \\ &= wt(e_j) + wt(\phi(e_i) \oplus \phi(e_k) \oplus \phi(e_i) \oplus \phi(e_j) \oplus \phi(e_t)) \\ &= wt(e_j) + wt(\phi(e_k) \oplus \phi(e_j) \oplus \phi(e_t)) \\ &= 1 + 1 < 4, \end{aligned}$$

a contradiction. Therefore, for any linear combinations of the form $e_i \oplus e_j \oplus e_k$ we must have

$$\phi(e_i \oplus e_j \oplus e_k) = \phi(e_i) \oplus \phi(e_j) \oplus \phi(e_k).$$

Thus we conclude that ϕ is linear, and the theorem follows. □

Recall that, by definition an $n \times n$ S-box is a strictly nonlinear permutation of $\mathbb{F}_2^n$. Using Lemma 5 and Theorem 4 we get the following strict upper bound on the differential branch number of 4×4 S-boxes.

Theorem 5. *The maximum possible differential branch number of a* 4×4 *S-box is* 3.

The paper [13] followed the work of [10] to search for optimal 4×4 S-boxes in the affine equivalent classes. The maximum differential branch number in the affine equivalent classes of the 16 optimal 4×4 S-boxes from [10] is 3. As this search did not consider the so-called non-optimal S-boxes, the question of the maximal differential branch number of any 4×4 S-box remained unanswered. Theorem 5 settles this question.

We now give a family of linear permutations $\mathtt{LS}_n$ of $\mathbb{F}_2^n$ with $\beta_{\mathtt{d}}(\mathtt{LS}_n) = 4$. Definition of these permutations varies slightly depending on whether n is even or odd. Since these permutations are linear we specify their action on basis $\mathcal{B}_n = \{e_0, \dots, e_{n-1}\}$ of $\mathbb{F}_2^n$ and the maps extend linearly to other elements of $\mathbb{F}_2^n$.

Example 1. Let n be an even integer. The linear permutation $\mathtt{LS}_n$ of $\mathbb{F}_2^n$, defined on the basis $\mathcal{B}_n$ as

$$\mathtt{LS}_n(e_i) = \bar{e} \oplus e_i \tag{11}$$

has $\beta_{\mathtt{d}}(\mathtt{LS}_n) = 4$ and it is also involution. Further, observe that matrix representing the map $\mathtt{LS}_n$ is symmetric from which it follows that $\beta_{\ell}(\mathtt{LS}_n) = 4$.

Next we give a family of linear permutations with the differential branch number 4 defined over $\mathbb{F}_2^n$ for odd values of n

Example 2. Let n be an odd integer. The linear permutation $\mathtt{LS}_n$ of $\mathbb{F}_2^n$, defined on basis $\mathcal{B}_n$ as

$$\mathtt{LS}_n(e_i) = \begin{cases} \bar{e} \oplus e_i \oplus e_{i+1} & \text{if} \quad 0 \leq i \leq n-2 \\ \\ \bar{e} \oplus e_{n-1} \oplus e_0 & \text{if} \quad i = n-1 \end{cases}$$

has the differential branch number 4.

In both cases it is easy to show that the set $\{\mathtt{LS}_n(e_0), \dots, \mathtt{LS}_n(e_{n-1})\}$ is a basis of $\mathbb{F}_2^n$ asserting that the maps $\mathtt{LS}_n$ indeed are bijections. The fact that $\beta_{\mathtt{d}}(\mathtt{LS}_n) = 4$ can also be easily checked from the Definition 1 of the differential branch number for linear maps. Next we present bounds for permutations of $\mathbb{F}_2^n$, for $n \geq 5$.

4.2 Differential Branch Number of Permutations of $\mathbb{F}_2^n$, for $n \geq 5$

In this section we present bounds on the differential branch number of a general permutation of $\mathbb{F}_2^n$. In the remainder of this paper we assume that $n \geq 5$ unless specified otherwise. We begin with some initial observations.

Suppose that $x \in \mathbb{F}_2^n$ with $wt(x) = n - \delta$ for some $\delta \geq 1$. Then x can be expressed as $x = \bar{e} \oplus e_{x_1} \oplus \dots \oplus e_{x_\delta}$ for unique set of elements $e_{x_1}, \dots e_{x_\delta} \in \mathcal{B}_n$. Using this one can easily see the following fact which we will be using frequently in this paper:

Fact 1 *For $x, x' \in \mathbb{F}_2^m$ with $x \neq x'$, $wt(x) \geq n - \delta$ and $wt(x') \geq n - \delta'$ we have*

$$wt(x \oplus x') \leq \delta + \delta'.$$

Lemma 7. *Let ϕ be a permutation of $\mathbb{F}_2^n$ with $\phi(0) = 0$ and the differential branch number $\beta_{\mathtt{d}}(\phi) = n - \beta + 1$ for some $1 \leq \beta \leq n - 1$. Then we have for $0 \leq i \leq n-1$*

$$n - \beta \leq wt(\phi(e_i)) \leq 2\beta + 1 \tag{12}$$

and for $0 \leq i \neq j \leq n-1$,

$$n - (\beta + 1) \leq wt(\phi(e_i) \oplus \phi(e_j)) \leq 2\beta. \tag{13}$$

Proof. From the definition of the differential branch number it follows that

$$wt(\phi(e_i)) \geq n - \beta, \tag{14}$$

as $\phi(0) = 0$. Then using $x = \phi(e_i), x' = \phi(e_j)$ in Fact 1 we get

$$wt(\phi(e_i) \oplus \phi(e_j)) \leq 2\beta. \tag{15}$$

Again for every pair of indices $i \neq j$

$$wt(\phi(e_i) \oplus \phi(e_j)) \geq n - (\beta + 1). \tag{16}$$

Using (14) and (16) in Fact 1 we get (12). Further combining (15) and (16) we get (13). □

Lemma 8. *Let δ be an integer such that $1 \leq \delta \leq n$. Denote by $\mathcal{W}_\delta^n$ the following set*

$$\mathcal{W}_\delta^n = \{x \in \mathbb{F}_2^n : wt(x) = n - \delta\}. \tag{17}$$

Then for any $x, x' \in \mathcal{W}_\delta^n$ we have $wt(x \oplus x') = 2k$ for some $1 \leq k \leq \delta$. Further suppose $\mathcal{V} \subseteq \mathcal{W}_\delta^n$ defined as

$$\mathcal{V} = \{x \in \mathcal{W}_\delta^n : wt(x \oplus x') = 2\delta \text{ for all } x' \in \mathcal{V}\}$$

then $|\mathcal{V}| \leq \lfloor \frac{n}{\delta} \rfloor$.

Proof. First claim is obvious. To see second part, first observe that given any $x \in \mathcal{W}_\delta^n$ there exist a unique set of elements $\{e_{x_1} \dots, e_{x_\delta}\} \subseteq \mathcal{B}_n$ such that $x = \bar{e} \oplus e_{x_1} \oplus \dots \oplus e_{x_\delta}$.

An element $y \in \mathcal{W}_\delta^n$ is in $\mathcal{V}$ if and only if

$$\{e_{y_1} \dots, e_{y_\delta}\} \cap \{e_{x_1} \dots, e_{x_\delta}\} = \emptyset$$

for every element x already in $\mathcal{V}$. Consequently, we have $|\mathcal{V}| \leq \lfloor \frac{n}{\delta} \rfloor$ as required. □

Using the above observations we prove the following bound on the differential branch number of a permutation of $\mathbb{F}_2^n$.

Theorem 6. *If $n \geq 5$ then for any permutation ϕ of $\mathbb{F}_2^n$ we have*

$$\beta_d(\phi) \leq \left\lceil 2\frac{n}{3} \right\rceil. \tag{18}$$

Proof. First it is easy to see that

$$\left\lceil 2\frac{n}{3} \right\rceil = n - \left\lfloor \frac{n}{3} \right\rfloor,$$

and hence we substitute the bound in (18) by $n - \lfloor \frac{n}{3} \rfloor$ to make the proof easy.

On the contrary to (18) assume that $\beta_{\mathrm{d}}(\phi) \geq n - \lfloor \frac{n}{3} \rfloor + 1$. Using $\beta = \lfloor \frac{n}{3} \rfloor$ in Lemma 7 we get

$$n - \left\lfloor \frac{n}{3} \right\rfloor \leq wt(\phi(e_i)) \leq 2 \left\lfloor \frac{n}{3} \right\rfloor + 1 \tag{19}$$

for $0 \leq i \leq n-1$, and

$$n - (\left\lfloor \frac{n}{3} \right\rfloor + 1) \leq wt(\phi(e_i) \oplus \phi(e_j)) \leq 2 \left\lfloor \frac{n}{3} \right\rfloor \tag{20}$$

for $0 \leq i \neq j \leq n-1$. Now, recall that the integer n can be written as

$$n = 3 \left\lfloor \frac{n}{3} \right\rfloor + r \tag{21}$$

for a unique r such that $0 \leq r \leq 2$. We prove our claim separately for each value of r.

Case 1. $r = 2$. From (19) we have

$$n - \left\lfloor \frac{n}{3} \right\rfloor \leq 2 \left\lfloor \frac{n}{3} \right\rfloor + 1$$

and substituting $n = 3 \lfloor \frac{n}{3} \rfloor + 2$ in this we get $2 \leq 1$ which is a contradiction.

Case 2. $r = 1$. In this case, by substituting $n = 3 \lfloor \frac{n}{3} \rfloor + 1$ the inequalities (19) and (20) become the following equalities

$$\begin{aligned} wt(\phi(e_i)) &= n - \left\lfloor \frac{n}{3} \right\rfloor \\ wt(\phi(e_i) \oplus \phi(e_j)) &= 2 \left\lfloor \frac{n}{3} \right\rfloor \end{aligned} \tag{22}$$

Note that both identities in (22) must be satisfied by all the elements of the set $\{\phi(e_0), \ldots, \phi(e_{n-1})\}$. We show that this is impossible. Since $wt(\phi(e_i)) = n - \lfloor \frac{n}{3} \rfloor$ for all $0 \leq i \leq n-1$, we are in the situation of Lemma 8 with $\phi(e_i) \in \mathcal{W}_\delta^n$ where $\delta = \lfloor \frac{n}{3} \rfloor$. Consequently, we see that there can be at most $\lfloor \frac{n}{\lfloor \frac{n}{3} \rfloor} \rfloor = 3$ elements $\phi(e_r), \phi(e_s), \phi(e_t)$ for which the latter identity in (22) can hold. On the other hand, since $n \geq 5$, there exists at least two basis elements e_u and e_v apart from e_r, e_s, e_t, and by Lemma 8 we will have

$$wt(\phi(e_u) \oplus \phi(e_v)) \leq 2(\delta - 1) < 2 \left\lfloor \frac{n}{3} \right\rfloor$$

which contradicts (22).

Case 3. $r = 0$. In this case we have $n = 3 \lfloor \frac{n}{3} \rfloor$ and the inequalities (19), (20) simplify to

$$wt(\phi(e_i)) = n - \left\lfloor \frac{n}{3} \right\rfloor \text{ or } n - \left\lfloor \frac{n}{3} \right\rfloor + 1 \tag{23}$$

$$wt(\phi(e_i) \oplus \phi(e_j)) = n - \left\lfloor \frac{n}{3} \right\rfloor - 1 \text{ or } n - \left\lfloor \frac{n}{3} \right\rfloor \tag{24}$$

Note that for every element of $\{\phi(e_0), \ldots, \phi(e_{n-1})\}$ there are only two possibilities for $wt(\phi(e_i))$ as in (23). First we show that $wt(\phi(e_i)) = wt(\phi(e_j)) = n - \lfloor \frac{n}{3} \rfloor + 1$ cannot hold, for $i \neq j$, otherwise using $x = \phi(e_i), x' = \phi(e_j)$ and $\delta = \delta' = \lfloor \frac{n}{3} \rfloor - 1$ in Fact 1 we get

$$wt(\phi(e_i) \oplus \phi(e_j)) \leq 2(\left\lfloor \frac{n}{3} \right\rfloor - 1) = n - \left\lfloor \frac{n}{3} \right\rfloor - 2 < n - \left\lfloor \frac{n}{3} \right\rfloor - 1$$

contradicting (24). Thus there can be at most one element $\phi(e_i)$ such that $wt(\phi(e_i) = n - \lfloor \frac{n}{3} \rfloor + 1$. Without loss of generality assume that $wt(\phi(e_0)) = n - \lfloor \frac{n}{3} \rfloor + 1$, then it follows from (23) that for $i = 1, \ldots, n-1$ the weights of $wt(\phi((e_i))$ satisfy

$$wt(\phi(e_i)) = n - \left\lfloor \frac{n}{3} \right\rfloor. \tag{25}$$

Thus, we are in situation of Lemma 8 with $\phi(e_1), \ldots, \phi(e_{n-1}) \in \mathcal{W}_\delta^n$ for $\delta = \lfloor \frac{n}{3} \rfloor$. Hence there can be only three elements $\phi(e_r), \phi(e_s), \phi(e_t)$, $1 \leq r \neq s \neq t \leq n-1$ such that for any two indices $i, j \in \{r, s, t\}$

$$wt(\phi(e_i) \oplus \phi(e_j)) \;=\; 2\,\delta \;=\; 2\left\lfloor \frac{n}{3} \right\rfloor$$

holds. Since $n \geq 5$ there exist at least one element e_k, where $k \neq 0$ and also $k \notin \{r, s, t\}$. Then for any $i \in \{r, s, t\}$ we must have (by Lemma 8) $wt(\phi(e_k) \oplus \phi(e_i)) \leq 2(\delta - 1)$, which means that

$$wt(\phi(e_k) \oplus \phi(e_i)) \;\leq\; 2\left\lfloor \frac{n}{3} \right\rfloor - 2 \;<\; n - \left\lfloor \frac{n}{3} \right\rfloor - 1,$$

contradicting (24). This concludes the proof of Case 3 and also of the theorem. □

4.3 Comparison with Griesmer Bound

Recall that Griesmer bound (Lemma 4) is applicable to linear permutations only. Notably our bound as in (18) works for any permutation. The Table 3 shows different n with corresponding values of Griesmer Bound and our bound (18).

It is noticeable that our bound is very close to Griesmer bound, and in fact matching for some small values of n. The Griesmer bound is not sharp, for example for an $[8, 4]$ binary linear code the maximum possible minimum distance d is 5 (see [1]), whereas the Griesmer bound says $d \leq 6$. Our bound for the differential branch number of permutations of $\mathbb{F}_2^8$ is also 6. At this moment we also do not know the existence of any nonlinear permutation with the differential branch number 6, and in general for $\mathbb{F}_2^n$ with $n \geq 5$, it is not known whether there is any nonlinear permutation for which the bound of the differential branch number is achieved. We suspect that like Griesmer bound our bound is also not sharp in general.

Table 3. Comparison between the differential branch number of linear permutations obtained from Griesmer bound and that of general permutations obtained from our bound (18).

n	Griesmer bound	Our bound
4	4	4
5	4	4
6	4	4
7	5	5
8	6	6
9	6	6
10	7	7
11	8	8
12	8	8
13	8	9
14	8	10
15	9	10
16	10	11
17	10	12
18	11	12
19	12	13

5 Conclusions

In this paper we have analyzed the differential and the linear branch numbers of permutations. We have theoretically proved that 4×4 S-boxes can have the maximum differential branch number 3. This is important for the designers who are aiming to construct lightweight block ciphers following the design like `PRESENT`. We have also presented upper bounds on both the linear and the differential branch number for permutations over $\mathbb{F}_2^n$, for general n. We feel that there is still a scope of improving these bounds. We showed that the maximum differential branch number and the maximum linear branch number of liner permutations match. However, it is not known whether the same happens for nonlinear permutations as well. It will be interesting to pursue the following question.

Question 1. Can an S-box achieve both the maximum linear and differential branch numbers?

As we have seen that the differential branch number is associated with difference distribution table, whereas the linear branch number is associated with the correlation matrix. Therefore, if there is a relation between these two matrices, then probably we have the answer to Question 1. In fact [17] has shown that there is a relationship between the DDT and the correlation matrix (in a

different form). Let $\mathtt{C}_\phi^2$ denote the following matrix which is derived from the correlation matrix of ϕ.
Recall from (1) that the correlation coefficient of ϕ with respect to (α, β) is given by

$$\mathtt{C}_\phi(\alpha, \beta) = \sum_{x \in \mathbb{F}_2^n} (-1)^{\alpha^t \cdot x \oplus \beta^t \cdot \phi(x)}$$

Now define $\mathtt{C}_\phi^2 = [\mathtt{C}_\phi^2(\alpha, \beta)]_{2^n \times 2^n}$ as the matrix whose (α, β)-th element is given by $(\mathtt{C}_\phi(\alpha, \beta))^2$. Then we have the following relation as mentioned in [17, Lemma 2 (iii)]

$$\mathtt{C}_\phi^2 = \mathcal{H}_n \mathcal{D}_\phi \mathcal{H}_n, \tag{26}$$

where $\mathcal{H}_n$ is the Hadamard matrix of order $2^n \times 2^n$.

It will be interesting to explore (26) in order to establish a relationship between the linear and the differential branch numbers.

References

1. Bounds on the minimum distance of linear codes over GF(2). http://www.codetables.de/BKLC/Tables.php?q=2&n0=1&n1=256&k0=1&k1=256. Accessed 25 Aug 2017
2. Banik, S., Pandey, S.K., Peyrin, T., Sasaki, Y., Sim, S.M., Todo, Y.: GIFT: a small present. In: Fischer, W., Homma, N. (eds.) CHES 2017. LNCS, vol. 10529, pp. 321–345. Springer, Cham (2017). https://doi.org/10.1007/978-3-319-66787-4_16
3. Biham, E., Shamir, A.: Differential cryptanalysis of DES-like cryptosystems. In: Menezes, A.J., Vanstone, S.A. (eds.) CRYPTO 1990. LNCS, vol. 537, pp. 2–21. Springer, Heidelberg (1991). https://doi.org/10.1007/3-540-38424-3_1
4. Bogdanov, A., Knudsen, L.R., Leander, G., Paar, C., Poschmann, A., Robshaw, M.J.B., Seurin, Y., Vikkelsoe, C.: PRESENT: an ultra-lightweight block cipher. In: Paillier, P., Verbauwhede, I. (eds.) CHES 2007. LNCS, vol. 4727, pp. 450–466. Springer, Heidelberg (2007). https://doi.org/10.1007/978-3-540-74735-2_31
5. Carlet, C.: Vectorial Boolean functions for cryptography. In: Crama, P.H.Y. (ed.) Boolean Methods and Models. Cambridge University Press, Cambridge (2010)
6. Daemen, J., Rijmen, V.: The wide trail design strategy. In: Honary, B. (ed.) Cryptography and Coding 2001. LNCS, vol. 2260, pp. 222–238. Springer, Heidelberg (2001). https://doi.org/10.1007/3-540-45325-3_20
7. Daemen, J., Rijmen, V.: The Design of Rijndael: AES - The Advanced Encryption Standard. Information Security and Cryptography. Springer, Heidelberg (2002). https://doi.org/10.1007/978-3-662-04722-4
8. Griesmer, J.: A bound for error-correcting codes. IBM J. Res. Dev. **7**, 532–542 (1960)
9. Jean, J.: TikZ for Cryptographers (2016). https://www.iacr.org/authors/tikz/
10. Leander, G., Poschmann, A.: On the classification of 4 bit S-boxes. In: Carlet, C., Sunar, B. (eds.) WAIFI 2007. LNCS, vol. 4547, pp. 159–176. Springer, Heidelberg (2007). https://doi.org/10.1007/978-3-540-73074-3_13
11. Macwilliams, F.J., Sloane, N.J.A.: The Theory of Error-Correcting Codes (North-Holland Mathematical Library). North Holland, January 1983

12. Matsui, M.: Linear Cryptanalysis method for DES cipher. In: Helleseth, T. (ed.) EUROCRYPT 1993. LNCS, vol. 765, pp. 386–397. Springer, Heidelberg (1994). https://doi.org/10.1007/3-540-48285-7_33
13. Saarinen, M.-J.O.: Cryptographic analysis of all 4 × 4-bit s-boxes. In: Miri, A., Vaudenay, S. (eds.) SAC 2011. LNCS, vol. 7118, pp. 118–133. Springer, Heidelberg (2012). https://doi.org/10.1007/978-3-642-28496-0_7
14. Shannon, C.E.: Communication theory of secrecy systems. Bell Syst. Tech. J. **28**, 656–715 (1949)
15. Shirai, T., Shibutani, K., Akishita, T., Moriai, S., Iwata, T.: The 128-bit blockcipher CLEFIA (extended abstract). In: Biryukov, A. (ed.) FSE 2007. LNCS, vol. 4593, pp. 181–195. Springer, Heidelberg (2007). https://doi.org/10.1007/978-3-540-74619-5_12
16. Siegenthaler, T.: Correlation-immunity of nonlinear combining functions for cryptographic applications (corresp.). IEEE Trans. Inf. Theory **30**(5), 776–780 (1984)
17. Zhang, X., Zheng, Y., Imai, H.: Relating differential distribution tables to other properties of of substitution boxes. Des. Codes Crypt. **19**(1), 45–63 (2000)

Keyed Sponge with Prefix-Free Padding: Independence Between Capacity and Online Queries Without the Suffix Key

Yusuke Naito(✉)

Mitsubishi Electric Corporation, Kanagawa, Japan
Naito.Yusuke@ce.MitsubishiElectric.co.jp

Abstract. In this paper, we study the pseudo-random function (PRF) security of keyed sponges. "Capacity" is a parameter of a keyed sponge that usually defines a dominant term in the PRF-security bound. So far, the PRF-security of the "prefix" keyed sponge has mainly been analyzed, where for a key K, a message M and the sponge function $\texttt{Sponge}$, the output is defined as $\texttt{Sponge}(K\|M)$. A tight bound for the capacity term was given by Naito and Yasuda (FSE 2016): $O((qQ+q^2)/2^c)$ for the capacity c, the number of online queries q and the number of offline queries Q. Later, Naito (CANS 2016) showed that using the sandwich method where the output is defined as $\texttt{Sponge}(K\|M\|K)$, the dependence between c and q can be removed, i.e., the capacity term is improved to $O(rQ/2^c)$, where r is the rate. However, unlike the prefix keyed sponge, the sandwich keyed sponge uses the suffix key that requires the memory to keep the suffix key. The additional memory requirement seems not to be appropriate for lightweight settings.

For this problem, we consider a keyed sponge with a prefix-free padding, $\texttt{KSpongePF}$, where for a prefix-free padding function $\textsf{pfpad}$, the output is defined as $\texttt{Sponge}(K\|\textsf{pfpad}(M))$. We show that $\texttt{KSpongePF}$ achieves the same level of PRF-security as the sandwich keyed sponge: the capacity term is $O(rQ/2^c)$. Hence, using $\texttt{KSpongePF}$, the independence between c and q can be ensured without the suffix key.

Keywords: Keyed sponge · Prefix-free padding · PRF-security

1 Introduction

Sponge Function. The sponge function introduced by Bertoni et al. [4] is a state-of-the-art permutation-based mode of operation for cryptographic hash functions. It offers variable-output-length hash functions that are called extendable output functions (XOFs), and is employed in the SHA-3 functions (a.k.a. Keccak) [9,20]. The sponge function has the structure of iterating a permutation, and unlike Merkle-Damgård-type hash functions such as SHA-2 hash functions [19], does not require feed-forward operations, i.e., the memory for this

W. Susilo and G. Yang (Eds.): ACISP 2018, LNCS 10946, pp. 225–242, 2018.
https://doi.org/10.1007/978-3-319-93638-3_14

operation is not required, and thus it has been adopted to the area of lightweight hashing e.g., [2,10,14].

The sponge construction consists of a sequential application of a permutation on an internal state of b bits. The internal state is partitioned into an r-bit part and a c-bit part with $b = r + c$. Here r is called rate and c is called capacity. The internal state is updated, by xor-ing the current message block of r bits with the r-bit part of the previous internal state and then inputting the resultant state into the next permutation call. After the absorbing phase, (r-bit) output blocks are generated, by squeezing the r-bit part of the current internal state and then inputting the internal state into the next permutation. This phase is called "squeezing phase."

Keyed Sponge. Hash functions are mainly used as components of cryptographic algorithms such as message authentication code, key derivation function and pseudo-random bit generator. In these algorithms, a hash function is used in the keyed setting, and in order to securely use the keyed hash function, it is required to become a secure pseudo-random function (PRF).

Bertoni et al. suggested (e.g., [5]) that a keyed sponge should simply occur by prepending a key K to a message M, where the output is defined as $\mathsf{Sponge}(K\|M)$ for sponge function Sponge. We call the keyed sponge "prefix keyed sponge." The PRF-security of the prefix keyed sponge has been analyzed in the random permutation model. The first PRF-security bound of the prefix keyed sponge was derived from the indifferentiability of the sponge construction [5]: the dominant term in the bound is $O((\ell q+Q)^2/2^c)$ against a adversary with parameters q, Q, and ℓ: the number of online queries (queries to the keyed sponge/a random function), the number of offline queries (queries to a random permutation), and the maximum number of permutation calls by an online query, respectively. Their result was generalized by Bertoni et al. [6], where a duplex construction was introduced, which becomes building blocks of keyed sponges and sponge-based authenticated encryptions. However, the indifferentiability-based PRF-security bound is rather loose, and the actual PRF-security bound should be much smaller, as first noticed by Bertoni et al. [7].

Andreeva et al. [1] successfully removed the term $Q^2/2^c$ and obtained a PRF-security bound with the capacity term $O(((\ell q)^2 + \mu Q)/2^c)$. Here, μ is an adversarial parameter called "multiplicity" and lies somewhere between $2\ell q/2^r$ and $2\ell q$. Mennink et al. [16] analyzed the full state keyed sponge (i.e., the donkey sponge [8] is considered) and introduced a duplex construction supporting the full state absorption. Their result can be seen as a generalization of Andreeva et al.'s result. Gaži et al. [13] succeeded in giving a tight PRF-security bound. Their result supports the full-state absorption but considers only single-block outputs. Naito and Yasuda [18] provided a tight PRF-security bound of the prefix keyed sponge with extendable outputs whose capacity term is $O((q^2 + qQ)/2^c)$. Daemen et al. [12] introduced a duplex construction that supports the full state absorption and the multi-user setting, and that can be seen as a generalization of Naito and Yasuda's result.

Keyed Sponge Without the Dependence Between q and c. Regarding the prefix keyed sponge, the previous works attained the tight result regarding the capacity term. From the tight result, it is natural move on to find another type of keyed sponge with a better security bound.

For this motivation, Naito [17] showed that using the sandwich method, i.e., $\texttt{Sponge}(K\|M\|K)$, the online query influence can be removed from the capacity term: the capacity term becomes $O(rQ/2^c)$. However, the disadvantage of the sandwich keyed sponge over the prefix one is that the suffix key K is required after absorbing a message M, i.e., the memory to keep the suffix key K is required. The additional memory requirement seems not to be appropriate for lightweight settings. On the other hand, the capacities of the sponge-based lightweight hash functions are small, and in order to ensure the longevity of the keyed sponge functions, we want to keep the security bound without the dependence between q and c.

Our Result. In this paper, we consider a keyed sponge with a prefix-free padding denoted by KSpongePF. For a message M, the output is defined as $\texttt{Sponge}(K\|\mathsf{pfpad}(M))$, where pfpad is a prefix-free padding function. Hence, the suffix key is not required in KSpongePF. We show that KSpongePF achieves the same level of PRF-security as the sandwich keyed sponge, that is, the capacity term in PRF-bound of KSpongePF is $O(rQ/2^c)$. Note that the prefix-free padding method has been applied to several schemes such as CBC MAC [3,22] and Merkle-Damgård [11] in order for the resultant schemes to be secure, but it has not been applied to keyed sponges. Thus, our result is the first one applying the padding to keyed sponges. Note that as the previous works for keyed sponges such as [8,12,13,16], our result supports the keyed sponge with the full state absorption. To cover the full state absorption, the capacities in the procedures of absorbing input blocks and of squeezing output blocks are distinguished. The capacity c in the PRF-security bound is of the squeezing phase, and the PRF-security bound is independent of the capacity c' in the absorbing phase. Note that if $c' = c$ then the (original) sponge function is considered, and if $c' = 0$ then the full state absorption is considered.

An example of pfpad that does not require the suffix key is that $\mathsf{pfpad}(M) = (0\|M_1)\|\cdots\|(0\|M_{m-1})\|(1\|M_m\|10^*)$, where for the rate r' in the absorbing phase, $M = M_1\|M_2\|\cdots\|M_m$, $|M_i| = r' - 1$ and 10^* is a one-zero padding. Note that KSpongePF can be seen as a generalization of the sandwich keyed sponge, since the padding method in the sandwich keyed sponge, i.e., a message with the suffix key $(M\|K)$, becomes a prefix-free padding if the key K is not revealed (the probability that K is revealed is negligible).

Regarding the security proof, we take a similar approach to Naito-Yasuda's proof for the prefix keyed sponge [18]. The proof makes use of the game-playing technique, introducing just one intermediate game between the real and ideal worlds. This transition between the games heavily relies on the coefficient H technique of Patarin [21]. In this proof, we need to consider "bad" events in which an adversary may distinguish between the real and ideal worlds. The bad events come from collisions for b-bit internal state values, since in the real world the collisions may occur whereas in the ideal world the collisions never occur due to a monolithic random function. Regarding the prefix keyed sponge, an adversary can control the outer part by message blocks and thus the collision probability largely depends on the c-bit hidden part. More precisely, once an adversary finds a collision on the c-bit part (by online queries) or a collision between the c-bit part and offline queries, he can perform the same attack as the plain CBC-MAC, i.e., the real and ideal worlds are distinguished by the message length extension attack. This yields the capacity term $(q^2+qQ)/2^c$. On the other hand, KSpongePF uses a prefix-free padding pfpad, and thus he cannot perform the message length extension attack on KSpongePF. Therefore, the dependence between c and q can be removed.

Table 1. Comparison of PRF-bounds of keyed sponges with extendable output.

Scheme/Construction	Bound	Ref
Prefix keyed sponge $\mathsf{Sponge}(K\|M)$	$O\left(\frac{q^2+qQ}{2^c}+\left(\frac{\ell qQ}{2^b}\right)^{1/2}+\frac{(\ell q)^2}{2^b}\right)$	[18]
Sandwich keyed sponge $\mathsf{Sponge}(K\|M\|K)$	$O\left(\frac{rQ}{2^c}+\left(\frac{\ell qQ}{2^b}\right)^{1/2}+\frac{(\ell q)^2}{2^b}\right)$	[17]
KSpongePF $\mathsf{Sponge}(K\|\mathsf{pfpad}(M))$	$O\left(\frac{rQ}{2^c}+\left(\frac{\ell qQ}{2^b}\right)^{1/2}+\frac{(\ell q)^2}{2^b}\right)$	Ours

Comparison. In Table 1, the PRF-security bounds of the prefix keyed sponge, the sandwich keyed sponge and KSpongePF are summarized, where for simplicity, the k-terms (k is the key size) are omitted. In the following, we compare the bounds of the prefix keyed sponge, the sandwich keyed sponge and KSpongePF. This comparison is quoted from [17].

We first consider the parameters of the SHA-3 functions SHAKE128 and SHAKE256 [20]: $(b,c) = (1600, 128)$ and $(b,c) = (1600, 256)$, respectively. For these parameters, it may safely be assumed that b-terms are negligible compared with the capacity terms. The PRF-security bound of the prefix keyed sponge becomes a constant if $qQ = O(2^c)$, whereas that of KSpongePF becomes a constant if $rQ = O(2^c)$. Therefore, if $r \leq q$, KSpongePF and the sandwich keyed sponge achieve a higher level of PRF-security than the prefix keyed sponge.

We next consider sponge-based lightweight hash functions e.g., [2,10,14] whose parameters satisfy $b/2 < c < b$. The PRF-security bound of the prefix keyed sponge becomes a constant if $qQ = O(2^c)$ or $\ell qQ = O(2^b)$, and those of KSpongePF and the sandwich keyed sponge become a constant if $rQ = O(2^c)$ or

$\ell q Q = O(2^b)$. Therefore, if $2^c < 2^b/\ell$ (i.e., $\ell < 2^r$), then qQ affects the security of the prefix keyed sponge. In this case, KSpongePF and the sandwich keyed sponge have a higher level of security than the prefix keyed sponge. On the other hand, if $2^c \geq 2^b/\ell$ ($\ell \geq 2^r$), then KSpongePF is as secure as the prefix keyed sponge.

2 Preliminaries

Basic Definitions. Let $\{0,1\}^*$ be the set of all bit strings. For an integer $b \geq 0$, let $\{0,1\}^b$ be the set of all b-bit strings, 0^b the bit string of b-bit zeroes, and $(\{0,1\}^b)^*$ the set of all bit strings whose bit lengths are multiples of b. Let λ be an empty string and $\emptyset$ an empty set. For integers $0 \leq i, j$, $[i,j] := \{i, i+1, \ldots, j\}$, if $i = 1$ then i is omitted, i.e., $[j] := [1,j]$, and if $i > j$ then $[i,j] := \emptyset$. For a finite set X, $x \xleftarrow{\$} X$ denotes uniformly random sampling of x from X. For a bit string x resp. a set X, $|x|$ resp. $|X|$ denote the bit length of x resp. the number of elements in X. For integers i, b with $0 \leq i \leq b$ and $x \in \{0,1\}^b$, let $\mathsf{lsb}_i(x)$ resp. $\mathsf{msb}_i(x)$ be the least resp. most significant i bits of x. For integers i and b with $0 \leq i \leq 2^b - 1$, let $\mathsf{str}_b(i)$ be the b-bit binary representation of i. For an integer $b \geq 0$, $\mathsf{Perm}(b)$ denotes the set of all permutations: $\{0,1\}^b \to \{0,1\}^b$, $\mathsf{Func}(b)$ denotes the set of all functions: $\{0,1\}^b \to \{0,1\}^b$, and $\mathsf{Func}(*, b)$ denotes the set of all functions: $\{0,1\}^* \to \{0,1\}^b$. For a permutation $\mathsf{P} \in \mathsf{Perm}(b)$, the inverse permutation is denoted by P^{-1}. For an integer $s > 0$ and a set X, X^s denotes the s-array Cartesian power of X.

Pseudo-Random Function (PRF) Security. For an integer $b > 0$, let $\mathsf{P} \in \mathsf{Perm}(b)$ be a public permutation. For a finite set $\mathcal{M} \subset \{0,1\}^*$ and an integer $\ell > 0$, let $\mathtt{F}[\mathsf{P}] : \mathcal{M} \to \{0,1\}^\ell$ be a function using the permutation P. We focus on the random permutation model, namely, P is a public random permutation that is defined as $\mathsf{P} \xleftarrow{\$} \mathsf{Perm}(b)$. Through this paper, an adversary $\mathcal{A}$ is a computationally unbounded algorithm. It is given query access to the set of oracles $\mathcal{O}$, and the $\mathcal{A}$'s output is denoted by $\mathcal{A}^{\mathcal{O}}$. Its complexity is solely measured by the number of queries made to its oracles.

The PRF-security of $\mathtt{F}[\mathsf{P}]$ is defined in terms of indistinguishability between the real and ideal worlds. In the real world, $\mathcal{A}$ has query access to $\mathtt{F}[\mathsf{P}]$, P, and P^{-1}, where $\mathsf{P} \xleftarrow{\$} \mathsf{Perm}(b)$. In the ideal world, it has query access to a random function R, P, and P^{-1}, where $\mathsf{P} \xleftarrow{\$} \mathsf{Perm}(b)$ and a random function is defined as $\mathsf{R} \xleftarrow{\$} \mathsf{Func}(*, \ell)$ and queries by $\mathcal{A}$ are in $\mathcal{M}$. After interacting with the oracles, $\mathcal{A}$ outputs a decision bit $y \in \{0,1\}$. For the function $\mathtt{F}[\mathsf{P}]$, the advantage function of an adversary $\mathcal{A}$ is defined as

$$\mathbf{Adv}_{\mathsf{F}}^{\mathsf{prf}}(\mathcal{A}) = \Pr\left[\mathsf{P} \xleftarrow{\$} \mathsf{Perm}(b) : \mathcal{A}^{\mathsf{F}[\mathsf{P}],\mathsf{P},\mathsf{P}^{-1}} = 1\right] - \Pr\left[\mathsf{R} \xleftarrow{\$} \mathsf{Func}(*, \ell), \mathsf{P} \xleftarrow{\$} \mathsf{Perm}(b) : \mathcal{A}^{\mathsf{R},\mathsf{P},\mathsf{P}^{-1}} = 1\right],$$

where the probabilities are taken over P, R and $\mathcal{A}$. Though this paper, queries to $\mathtt{F}[\mathsf{P}]/\mathsf{R}$ "online queries," queries to P or P^{-1} "offline queries."

Algorithm 1. Sponge

▶ Main Procedure $\mathsf{Sponge}[\mathsf{P}](M)$

Partition $\mathsf{pad}(M)$ into r'-bit blocks $M_1, \ldots, M_m$

$S \leftarrow 0^b$; **for** $i = 1, \ldots, m$ **do** $S \leftarrow \mathsf{P}(S \oplus (M_i \| 0^{c'}))$ ▷ Absorbing

$Z \leftarrow \mathsf{msb}_r(S)$; **for** $i = 1, \ldots, \ell_{\mathsf{max}} - 1$ **do** $S \leftarrow \mathsf{P}(S)$; $Z \leftarrow Z \| \mathsf{msb}_r(S)$ ▷ Squeezing

Algorithm 2. KSpongePF

▶ Main Procedure $\mathsf{KSpongePF}[\mathsf{P}](K, M)$

Partition $K \| 0^p$ into r'-bit blocks $K_1, \ldots, K_\kappa$ where $p = 0$ if $k \mod r = 0$; $p = r' - (k \mod r')$ otherwise

$V_0 \leftarrow 0^b$; **for** $i = 1, \ldots, \kappa$ **do** $U_i \leftarrow V_{i-1} \oplus (K_i \| 0^{c'})$; $V_i \leftarrow \mathsf{P}(U_i)$

Partition $\mathsf{pfpad}(M)$ into r'-bit blocks $M_1, \ldots, M_m$

$T_0 \leftarrow V_\kappa$; **for** $i = 1, \ldots, m-1$ **do** $S_i \leftarrow T_{i-1} \oplus (M_i \| 0^{c'})$; $T_i \leftarrow \mathsf{P}(S_i)$

$H_0 \leftarrow T_{m-1} \oplus (M_m \| 0^{c'})$; $Z \leftarrow \lambda$;

for $i = 1, \ldots, \ell_{\mathsf{max}}$ **do** $H_i \leftarrow \mathsf{P}(H_{i-1})$; $Z \leftarrow Z \| \mathsf{msb}_r(H_i)$

return Z

3 Keyed Sponge with Prefix-Free Padding

Sponge. Firstly, the sponge function, denoted by Sponge, is defined, which is the underlying function of the keyed sponge function. Sponge accepts a variable-length input $M \in \{0,1\}^*$ and returns a variable-length output $Z \in \{0,1\}^*$. For an integer $b > 0$, let $\mathsf{P} \in \mathsf{Perm}(b)$ be the underlying permutation. Let $r', c' \geq 0$ be integers with $b = r' + c'$, and $r, c \geq 0$ integers with $b = r + c$. Let $\mathsf{pad} : \{0,1\}^* \rightarrow (\{0,1\}^{r'})^*$ be an injective padding function. In this paper, we slightly generalize the sponge function, where the parameters for handling input message blocks are distinguished from those for handling output blocks. In Sponge, the padded message $\mathsf{pad}(M)$ is partitioned into r'-bit message blocks $M_1, \ldots, M_m$. Then for each message block M_i, M_i is absorbed into the most significant r'-bit part of the b-bit internal state S, and then the permutation P is applied. After absorbing all message blocks, an output block is squeezed from the most significant r-bit part of the internal state and then P is applied. This procedure is iterated until an output becomes the desired length. In this paper, for the sake of simplicity, the output length is fixed as the maximum one $\ell_{\mathsf{max}} \times r$ bits (i.e., ℓ_{max} blocks of r bits). Note that shorter outputs can be obtained by truncation. This procedure is defined in Algorithm 1. Note that it becomes the original sponge function, when $c = c'$.

KSpongePF. Next, a keyed sponge with a prefix-free padding is defined. Let $\mathsf{pfpad} : \{0,1\}^* \rightarrow (\{0,1\}^b)^*$ be a prefix-free injective padding function. We say pfpad is prefix-free if for any distinct messages M, M', $\mathsf{pfpad}(M)$ is not a prefix of $\mathsf{pfpad}(M')$, i.e., for any $W \in \{0,1\}^{|\mathsf{pfpad}(M')| - |\mathsf{pfpad}(M)|}$, $\mathsf{pfpad}(M') \neq \mathsf{pfpad}(M) \| W$, where $|\mathsf{pfpad}(M')| \geq |\mathsf{pfpad}(M)|$. Let $k > 0$ be an integer and the key size in bits. In this paper, similar to the previous works [1,13,17,18], for the sake of simplicity, if $k \mod r' \neq 0$, then a zero string is appended to the secret

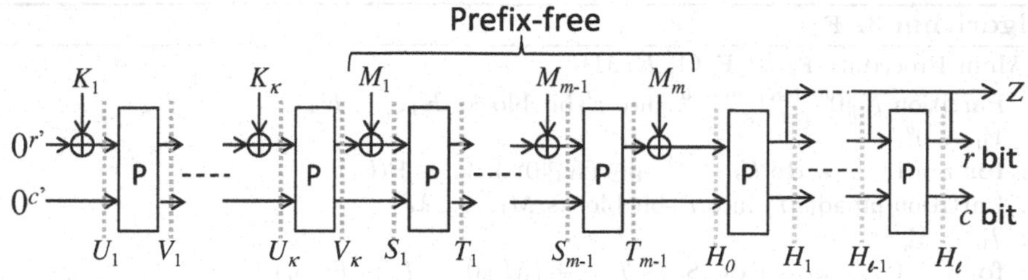

Fig. 1. KSpongePF.

key so that the length becomes a multiple of r'. Let $\kappa = |K\|0^p| \mod r'$ be the block size of the padded key, where $p = 0$ if $k \mod r = 0$; $p = r' - (k \mod r')$ otherwise. Then, for a secret key $K \in \{0,1\}^k$ and a message $M \in \{0,1\}^*$, the keyed sponge is defined as $\texttt{KSpongePF}(K, M) = \texttt{Sponge}(K\|0^p\|M)$, where the padding function in Sponge is defined as pad = pfpad. This procedure is defined in Algorithm 2 and illustrated in Fig. 1.

4 PRF-Security of KSpongePF

The PRF-security bound of KSpongePF is given below, where the underlying permutation is a (public) random permutation.

Theorem 1. *Assume that $\kappa \le 2^{b-1}$. For any adversary $\mathcal{A}$ making q online queries of σ random permutation calls and Q offline queries,*

$$\mathbf{Adv}^{\mathsf{prf}}_{\texttt{KSpongePF}}(\mathcal{A}) \le \frac{2\sigma Q + 2.5\sigma^2}{2^b} + \frac{2r(\kappa+Q)}{2^c} + \left(\frac{44\sigma(\kappa+Q)}{2^b}\right)^{1/2} + \lambda(Q,k,r',b),$$

where $\lambda(Q,k,r',b) = \frac{Q}{2^k}$ *if* $k \le r'$; $\min\left\{\frac{Q^2}{2^{c'+1}} + \frac{Q}{2^k}, \frac{1}{2^b} + \frac{Q}{2^{\left(\frac{1}{2} - \frac{\log_2(3b)}{2r'} - \frac{1}{r'}\right)k}}\right\}$ *otherwise.*

Remark 1. Regarding the parameter c', the terms except for $\lambda(Q,k,r',b)$ are independent from c'. Although $\lambda(Q,k,r',b)$ includes the parameter c', by choosing k properly, one can select any value for c' without sacrificing the PRF-security, e.g., $c' = 0$ (full state absorption).

Remark 2. Regarding the key term $\lambda(Q,k,r',b)$, this term is derived by using the analysis of Gaži *et al.* [13]. From this term, if $k > r'$ and a-bit security is required with respect to the key, then we need to define the key size roughly $k = 2a$. On the other hand, by using the indifferentiability result of the sponge function [5], the key term is $O(Q/2^k)$ (though the capacity term becomes $O((\sigma+Q)^2/2^c)$). Hence, we conjecture that the key term becomes $O(Q/2^k)$, yet deriving the optimal key term without using the birthday term regarding capacity is an open problem from the previous and this papers.

Algorithm 3. F_M

► Main Procedure $F_M[\mathsf{P}, \mathbf{F}, \mathbf{G}](K, M)$
1: Partition $K\|0^{b-(|K| \bmod b)}$ into r'-bit blocks $K_1, \ldots, K_\kappa$
2: $V_0 \leftarrow 0^b$
3: **for** $i = 1, \ldots, \kappa$ **do** $U_i \leftarrow V_{i-1} \oplus (K_i\|0^{c'})$; $V_i \leftarrow \mathsf{P}(U_i)$
4: Partition $\mathsf{pfpad}(M)$ into r'-bit blocks $M_1, \ldots, M$
5: $T_0 \leftarrow V_\kappa$
6: **for** $i = 1, \ldots, m-1$ **do** $S_i \leftarrow T_{i-1} \oplus (M_i\|0^{c'})$; $T_i \leftarrow \mathsf{F}_i(S_i)$
7: $H_0 \leftarrow T_{m-1} \oplus (M_m\|0^{c'})$; $Z \leftarrow \lambda$
8: **for** $i = 1, \ldots, \ell_{\mathsf{max}}$ **do** $H_i \leftarrow \mathsf{G}_i(H_{i-1})$; $Z \leftarrow Z\|\mathsf{msb}_r(H_i)$
9: **return** Z

4.1 Proof of Theorem 1

As the previous proofs of keyed sponges such as [17,18], the security proof uses the multi-collision technique for the r-bit part given in [15] and the coefficient H technique given in [21].

Let $\mathsf{F} = \mathsf{KSpongePF}$. Let m_{max} be the maximum block length of messages, i.e., $m \leq m_{\mathsf{max}}$. The message length m at the α-th query is denoted by m_α, a value x defined at the α-th query is denoted by $x^{(\alpha)}$. For the β-th offline query-response pair is denoted by $(X^{(\beta)}, Y^{(\beta)})$, i.e., $Y^{(\beta)} = \mathsf{P}(X^{(\beta)})$ or $X^{(\beta)} = \mathsf{P}^{-1}(Y^{(\beta)})$. Let $\sigma_{\mathsf{m}} = (m_1 - 1) + (m_2 - 1) + \cdots + (m_q - 1)$ be the total number of message blocks except for the last blocks by online queries, and $\sigma_{\mathsf{z}} = q\ell_{\mathsf{max}}$ the total number of output blocks. Hence, $\sigma = \sigma_{\mathsf{m}} + \sigma_{\mathsf{z}} + \kappa$. In this proof, we consider three worlds, $\mathsf{World}_R, \mathsf{World}_M$ and World_I, where World_R is the real world and World_I is the ideal one.

$$\mathsf{World}_R = \left(\mathsf{P} \xleftarrow{\$} \mathsf{Perm}(b) : \mathcal{A}^{\mathsf{F}[P],\mathsf{P},\mathsf{P}^{-1}} = 1\right).$$

$$\mathsf{World}_M = \left(\mathsf{P} \xleftarrow{\$} \mathsf{Perm}(b), (\mathbf{F}, \mathbf{G}) \xleftarrow{\$} \mathsf{Func}(b)^{m_{\mathsf{max}}-1+\ell_{\mathsf{max}}} : \mathcal{A}^{F_M[\mathsf{P},\mathbf{F},\mathbf{G}],\mathsf{P},\mathsf{P}^{-1}} = 1\right).$$

$$\mathsf{World}_I = \left(\mathsf{R} \xleftarrow{\$} \mathsf{Func}(*, b), \mathsf{P} \xleftarrow{\$} \mathsf{Perm}(b) : \mathcal{A}^{\mathsf{R},\mathsf{P},\mathsf{P}^{-1}} = 1\right).$$

Here, $\mathbf{F} = (\mathsf{F}_1, \ldots, \mathsf{F}_{m_{\mathsf{max}}-1})$ and $\mathbf{G} = (\mathsf{G}_1, \ldots, \mathsf{G}_{\ell_{\mathsf{max}}})$. $F_M[\mathsf{P}, \mathbf{F}, \mathbf{G}]$ is defined in Algorithm 3. In $F_M[\mathsf{P}, \mathbf{F}, \mathbf{G}]$, a random function F_i is used just after absorbing the i-th message block M_i, and a random function G_i is used just before squeezing the i-th output block.

Then, we have

$$\mathbf{Adv}^{\mathsf{prf}}_{\mathsf{F}}(\mathcal{A}) = (\Pr[\mathsf{World}_R] - \Pr[\mathsf{World}_M]) + (\Pr[\mathsf{World}_M] - \Pr[\mathsf{World}_I]).$$

These upper-bounds are given in (12) and (13), and thus we have

$$\mathbf{Adv}^{\mathsf{prf}}_{\mathsf{F}}(\mathcal{A}) \leq \frac{2\sigma Q + 2.5\sigma^2}{2^b} + \frac{2r(\kappa + Q)}{2^c} + \left(\frac{44\sigma(\kappa + Q)}{2^b}\right)^{1/2} + \lambda(Q, k, r', b).$$

4.2 Upper-Bound of Pr[World$_R$] − Pr[World$_M$]

This proof permits an adversary $\mathcal{A}$ to obtain a secret key K and input-output pairs of the underlying primitives defined by online queries, just after finishing all queries. Note that this modification does not reduce the advantage of $\mathcal{A}$. Hence, in World_R and World_M, $\mathcal{A}$ obtains the following transcript τ:

$$\tau = \Big(K, (X^{(1)}, Y^{(1)}), \dots, (X^{(Q)}, Y^{(Q)}), (U_1, V_1), \dots, (U_\kappa, V_\kappa),$$
$$\text{for} \alpha \in [q] : (S_1^{(\alpha)}, T_1^{(\alpha)}), \dots, (S_{m_\alpha-1}^{(\alpha)}, T_{m_\alpha-1}^{(\alpha)}), (H_0^{(\alpha)}, H_1^{(\alpha)}), \dots, (H_{\ell_{\mathsf{max}}-1}^{(\alpha)}, H_{\ell_{\mathsf{max}}}^{(\alpha)})\Big).$$

Note that online query-responses can be obtained from τ, and thus are omitted from τ. Let T_R be the transcript in World_R obtained by sampling $K \xleftarrow{\$} \{0,1\}^k$ and $\mathsf{P} \xleftarrow{\$} \mathsf{Perm}(b)$. Let T_M be the transcript in World_M obtained by sampling $K \xleftarrow{\$} \{0,1\}^k$, $\mathsf{P} \xleftarrow{\$} \mathsf{Perm}(b)$ and $(\mathbf{F}, \mathbf{G}) \xleftarrow{\$} \mathsf{Func}(b)^{m_{\mathsf{max}}-1+\ell_{\mathsf{max}}}$. We call τ *valid* if $\Pr[\mathsf{T}_M = \tau] > 0$. Let $\mathcal{T}$ be the set of all valid transcripts. Then

$$\Pr[\mathsf{World}_R] - \Pr[\mathsf{World}_M] = \mathsf{SD}(\mathsf{T}_R, \mathsf{T}_M) = \frac{1}{2} \sum_{\tau \in \mathcal{T}} |\Pr[\mathsf{T}_R = \tau] - \Pr[\mathsf{T}_M = \tau]|.$$

The statistical distance $\mathsf{SD}(\mathsf{T}_R, \mathsf{T}_M)$ can be upper-bounded by the following lemma (the coefficient H technique [21]). In this technique, $\mathcal{T}$ is partitioned into two sets: good transcripts $\mathcal{T}_{\mathsf{good}}$ and bad transcripts $\mathcal{T}_{\mathsf{bad}}$.

Lemma 1. *Let* $0 \le \varepsilon \le 1$ *be such that for all* $\tau \in \mathcal{T}_{\mathsf{good}}$, $\frac{\Pr[\mathsf{T}_R = \tau]}{\Pr[\mathsf{T}_M = \tau]} \ge 1 - \varepsilon$. *Then,* $\mathsf{SD}(\mathsf{T}_R, \mathsf{T}_M) \le \Pr[\mathsf{T}_M \in \mathcal{T}_{\mathsf{bad}}] + \varepsilon$.

Good and Bad Transcripts

In World_M, for each block in F except for key blocks, a distinct random function is used, whereas in World_R, for any block in F_M (and offline queries), the same random permutation is used. Moreover, for any distinct inputs to P, the outputs are distinct, whereas there exists a collision in outputs of a random function. Hence, $\mathcal{T}_{\mathsf{good}}$ is defined so that input-output pairs with distinct blocks do not overlap with each other, and no collision occurs in outputs of the underlying primitives. More precisely, $\mathcal{T}_{\mathsf{bad}}$ is defined so that one of the following conditions is satisfied, and $\mathcal{T}_{\mathsf{good}} := \mathcal{T} \backslash \mathcal{T}_{\mathsf{bad}}$ (i.e., $\mathcal{T}_{\mathsf{good}}$ is defined so that none of the following conditions are not satisfied). The following conditions deal with the overlap (the first seven conditions) and the collision (the last two conditions).

$$\mathsf{hit}_{\mathsf{st,xy}} : \exists \alpha \in [q], i \in [m_\alpha - 1], \beta \in [Q] \text{ s.t. } S_i^{(\alpha)} = X^{(\beta)} \vee T_i^{(\alpha)} = Y^{(\beta)}$$
$$\mathsf{hit}_{\mathsf{st,uv}} : \exists \alpha \in [q], i \in [m_\alpha - 1], j \in [\kappa] \text{ s.t. } S_i^{(\alpha)} = U_j \vee T_i^{(\alpha)} = V_j$$
$$\mathsf{hit}_{\mathsf{hh,xy}} : \exists \alpha \in [q], i \in [\ell_{\mathsf{max}}], \beta \in [Q] \text{ s.t. } H_{i-1}^{(\alpha)} = X^{(\beta)} \vee H_i^{(\alpha)} = Y^{(\beta)}$$
$$\mathsf{hit}_{\mathsf{hh,uv}} : \exists \alpha \in [q], i \in [\ell_{\mathsf{max}}], j \in [\kappa] \text{ s.t. } H_{i-1}^{(\alpha)} = U_j \vee H_i^{(\alpha)} = V_j$$

$$\begin{aligned}
\mathsf{hit}_{\mathsf{st,hh}} &: \exists \alpha, \beta \in [q], i \in [m_\alpha - 1], j \in [\ell_{\mathsf{max}}] \text{ s.t. } S_i^{(\alpha)} = H_{j-1}^{(\beta)} \vee T_i^{(\alpha)} = H_j^{(\beta)}\\
\mathsf{hit}_{\mathsf{st,st}} &: \exists \alpha, \beta \in [q], i \in [m_\alpha - 1], j \in [m_\beta - 1]\\
&\qquad\qquad \text{s.t. } i \neq j \wedge \left(S_i^{(\alpha)} = S_j^{(\beta)} \vee T_i^{(\alpha)} = T_j^{(\beta)}\right)\\
\mathsf{hit}_{\mathsf{hh,hh}} &: \exists \alpha, \beta \in [q], i, j \in [0, \ell_{\mathsf{max}}] \text{ s.t. } i \neq j \wedge H_i^{(\alpha)} = H_j^{(\beta)}\\
\mathsf{coll}_{\mathsf{t}} &: \exists \alpha, \beta \in [q], i \in [\min\{m_\alpha, m_\beta\} - 1] \text{ s.t. } S_i^{(\alpha)} \neq S_i^{(\beta)} \wedge T_i^{(\alpha)} = T_i^{(\beta)}\\
\mathsf{coll}_{\mathsf{h}} &: \exists \alpha, \beta \in [q], i \in [\ell_{\mathsf{max}}] \text{ s.t. } H_{i-1}^{(\alpha)} \neq H_{i-1}^{(\beta)} \wedge H_i^{(\alpha)} = H_i^{(\beta)}
\end{aligned}$$

Upper-Bound of $\Pr[\mathsf{T}_M \in \mathcal{T}_{\mathsf{bad}}]$

Firstly, we note that this analysis is in World_M. Let $\mathcal{H} := \bigcup_\alpha^q \bigcup_{i=1}^{\ell_\alpha} \{H_i^{(\alpha)}\}$ be the set of all H values except for H_0 values. Then, the following events are defined:

$$\begin{aligned}
\mathsf{hit}_{\mathsf{uv,xy}} &: \exists \beta \in [Q] \text{ s.t. } V_\kappa = Y^{(\beta)}\\
\mathsf{mcoll}_{\mathsf{h}} &: \exists H[1], \ldots, H[\rho] \in \mathcal{H} \text{ s.t. } \mathsf{msb}_r(H[1]) = \cdots = \mathsf{msb}_r(H[\rho]),
\end{aligned}$$

where ρ is a free parameter which will be defined later in this proof. Let $\mathsf{bad} = \mathsf{hit}_{\mathsf{st,xy}} \vee \mathsf{hit}_{\mathsf{st,uv}} \vee \mathsf{hit}_{\mathsf{hh,xy}} \vee \mathsf{hit}_{\mathsf{hh,uv}} \vee \mathsf{hit}_{\mathsf{st,hh}} \vee \mathsf{hit}_{\mathsf{st,st}} \vee \mathsf{hit}_{\mathsf{hh,hh}} \vee \mathsf{coll}_{\mathsf{t}} \vee \mathsf{coll}_{\mathsf{h}}$. Then,

$$\begin{aligned}
&\Pr[\mathsf{T}_M \in \mathcal{T}_{\mathsf{bad}}] = \Pr[\mathsf{bad}] \leq \Pr[\mathsf{bad} | \neg(\mathsf{hit}_{\mathsf{uv,xy}} \vee \mathsf{mcoll}_{\mathsf{h}})] + \Pr[\mathsf{hit}_{\mathsf{uv,xy}}] + \Pr[\mathsf{mcoll}_{\mathsf{h}}]\\
&\leq \Pr[\mathsf{hit}_{\mathsf{st,xy}} | \neg \mathsf{hit}_{\mathsf{uv,xy}}] + \Pr[\mathsf{hit}_{\mathsf{st,uv}} | \neg \mathsf{hit}_{\mathsf{uv,xy}}] + \Pr[\mathsf{hit}_{\mathsf{hh,xy}} | \neg(\mathsf{hit}_{\mathsf{uv,xy}} \vee \mathsf{mcoll}_{\mathsf{h}})]\\
&\quad + \Pr[\mathsf{hit}_{\mathsf{hh,uv}} | \neg(\mathsf{hit}_{\mathsf{uv,xy}} \vee \mathsf{mcoll}_{\mathsf{h}})] + \Pr[\mathsf{hit}_{\mathsf{st,hh}} | \neg \mathsf{hit}_{\mathsf{uv,xy}}] + \Pr[\mathsf{hit}_{\mathsf{st,st}}]\\
&\quad + \Pr[\mathsf{hit}_{\mathsf{hh,hh}}] + \Pr[\mathsf{coll}_{\mathsf{t}}] + \Pr[\mathsf{coll}_{\mathsf{h}}] + \Pr[\mathsf{hit}_{\mathsf{uv,xy}}] + \Pr[\mathsf{mcoll}_{\mathsf{h}}].
\end{aligned}$$

These upper-bounds are given in (1), (2), (3), (4), (5), (6), (7), (8), (9), (10), (11) and thus we have

$$\begin{aligned}
&\Pr[\mathsf{T}_M \in \mathcal{T}_{\mathsf{bad}}]\\
&\leq \frac{2\sigma_{\mathsf{m}} Q}{2^b} + \frac{2\sigma_{\mathsf{m}} \kappa}{2^b} + \left(\frac{2qQ}{2^b} + \frac{2(\rho - 1)Q}{2^c}\right) + \left(\frac{2q\kappa}{2^b} + \frac{2(\rho - 1)\kappa}{2^c}\right) + \frac{3\sigma_{\mathsf{m}}\sigma_{\mathsf{z}}}{2^b}\\
&\quad + \frac{\sigma_{\mathsf{m}}^2}{2^b} + \frac{2\sigma_{\mathsf{z}}^2}{2^b} + \frac{q\sigma_{\mathsf{m}}}{2^b} + \frac{q\sigma_{\mathsf{z}}}{2^b} + \left(\lambda(Q, k, r', c', b) + \frac{2\kappa Q}{2^b}\right) + 2^r \times \left(\frac{e \cdot \sigma_{\mathsf{z}}}{\rho 2^r}\right)^\rho\\
&\leq \frac{2\sigma Q + 2\sigma^2}{2^b} + \frac{2(\rho - 1)(\kappa + Q)}{2^c} + 2^r \times \left(\frac{e \cdot \sigma}{\rho 2^r}\right)^\rho + \lambda(Q, k, r', b).
\end{aligned}$$

Putting $\rho = \max\left\{r, \left(\frac{2^c e\sigma}{2^r(\kappa+Q)}\right)^{1/2}\right\}$ gives

$$\Pr[\mathsf{T}_M \in \mathcal{T}_{\mathsf{bad}}] \leq \frac{2\sigma Q + 2\sigma^2}{2^b} + \frac{2r(\kappa + Q)}{2^c} + \left(\frac{44\sigma(\kappa + Q)}{2^b}\right)^{1/2} + \lambda(Q, k, r', b).$$

• *Upper-Bound of* $\Pr[\mathsf{hit}_{\mathsf{st,xy}} | \neg \mathsf{hit}_{\mathsf{uv,xy}}]$. First, we fix $\alpha \in [q], i \in [m_\alpha - 1], \beta \in [Q]$ and upper-bound the probability that $S_i^{(\alpha)} = X^{(\beta)} \vee T_i^{(\alpha)} = Y^{(\beta)}$. In this analysis, the following cases are considered.

- The first case is that $S_1^{(\alpha)} = X^{(\beta)}$. In this case, $S_1^{(\alpha)} = X^{(\beta)} \Leftrightarrow V_\kappa \oplus (M_1^{(\alpha)} \| 0^{c'}) = X^{(\beta)}$. By $\neg\mathsf{hit}_{\mathsf{uv,xy}}$, V_κ is defined independently of all offline queries. Since V_κ is randomly drawn from at least $2^b - \kappa$ values, the probability that $S_1^{(\alpha)} = X^{(\beta)}$ is satisfied is at most $1/(2^b - \kappa) \le 2/2^b$, assuming $\kappa \le 2^{b-1}$.
- The second case is that $S_i^{(\alpha)} = X^{(\beta)}$ and $i \neq 1$. In this case, $S_i^{(\alpha)} = X^{(\beta)} \Leftrightarrow T_{i-1}^{(\alpha)} \oplus (M_i^{(\alpha)} \| 0^{c'}) = X^{(\beta)}$. Since $T_{i-1}^{(\alpha)}$ is randomly drawn from $\{0,1\}^b$, the probability that $S_i^{(\alpha)} = X^{(\beta)}$ is satisfied is $1/2^b$.
- The third case is that $T_i^{(\alpha)} = Y^{(\beta)}$. Since $T_i^{(\alpha)}$ is randomly drawn from $\{0,1\}^b$, the probability that $T_i^{(\alpha)} = Y^{(\beta)}$ is satisfied is $1/2^b$.

By the above analyses, we have

$$\begin{aligned}\Pr[\mathsf{hit}_{\mathsf{st,xy}} | \neg\mathsf{hit}_{\mathsf{uv,xy}}] &\le \frac{2qQ}{2^b} + \sum_{\alpha=1}^{q}\sum_{i=2}^{m_\alpha - 1} \frac{Q}{2^b} + \sum_{\alpha=1}^{q}\sum_{i=1}^{m_\alpha - 1} \frac{Q}{2^b} \\ &\le \frac{2qQ}{2^b} + \frac{2(\sigma_{\mathsf{m}} - q)Q}{2^b} \le \frac{2\sigma_{\mathsf{m}} Q}{2^b}. \qquad (1)\end{aligned}$$

• *Upper-Bound of* $\mathbf{Pr}[\mathsf{hit}_{\mathsf{st,uv}} | \neg\mathsf{hit}_{\mathsf{uv,xy}}]$. This analysis is the same as that of $\Pr[\mathsf{hit}_{\mathsf{hh,xy}} | \neg(\mathsf{hit}_{\mathsf{uv,xy}} \vee \mathsf{mcoll}_{\mathsf{h}})]$, where in this case, (U_i, V_i) is considered instead of $(X^{(i)}, Y^{(i)})$, and thus the upper-bound can be obtained by replacing Q with κ in (1). Hence, we have

$$\Pr[\mathsf{hit}_{\mathsf{st,uv}} | \neg\mathsf{hit}_{\mathsf{uv,xy}}] \le \frac{2\sigma_{\mathsf{m}}\kappa}{2^b}, \text{ assuming } \kappa \le 2^{b-1}. \qquad (2)$$

• *Upper-Bound of* $\mathbf{Pr}[\mathsf{hit}_{\mathsf{hh,xy}} | \neg(\mathsf{hit}_{\mathsf{uv,xy}} \vee \mathsf{mcoll}_{\mathsf{h}})]$. First, we fix $\alpha \in [q], i \in [\ell_{\mathsf{max}}], \beta \in [Q]$ and upper-bound the probability that $H_{i-1}^{(\alpha)} = X^{(\beta)} \vee H_i^{(\alpha)} = Y^{(\beta)}$ is satisfied. In this analysis, the following cases are considered.

- The first case is that $H_0^{(\alpha)} = X^{(\beta)}$ and $m_\alpha = 1$. In this case, $H_0^{(\alpha)} = X^{(\beta)} \Leftrightarrow V_\kappa \oplus M_1^{(\alpha)} = X^{(\beta)}$. By $\neg\mathsf{hit}_{\mathsf{uv,xy}}$, V_κ is defined independently of all offline queries. Since V_κ is randomly drawn from at least $2^b - \kappa$ values, the probability that $H_0^{(\alpha)} = X^{(\beta)}$ is satisfied is at most $1/(2^b - \kappa) \le 2/2^b$, assuming $\kappa \le 2^{b-1}$.
- The second case is that $H_0^{(\alpha)} = X^{(\beta)}$ and $m_\alpha \neq 1$. In this case, $H_0^{(\alpha)} = X^{(\beta)} \Leftrightarrow T_{m_\alpha - 1}^{(\alpha)} \oplus M_{m_\alpha}^{(\alpha)} = X^{(\beta)}$. Since $T_{m_\alpha - 1}^{(\alpha)}$ is randomly drawn from $\{0,1\}^b$, the probability that $H_0^{(\alpha)} = X^{(\beta)}$ is satisfied is $1/2^b$.
- The third case is that $H_{i-1}^{(\alpha)} = X^{(\beta)}$ and $i \neq 1$. Note that the probability that $H_{i-1}^{(\alpha)} = X^{(\beta)}$ is satisfied is upper-bounded by the one that $\mathsf{lsb}_c(H_{i-1}^{(\alpha)}) = \mathsf{lsb}_c(X^{(\beta)})$. Since $H_{i-1}^{(\alpha)}$ is randomly drawn from $\{0,1\}^b$, the probability that $H_{i-1}^{(\alpha)} = X^{(\beta)}$ is satisfied is at most $1/2^c$.
- The forth case is that $H_i^{(\alpha)} = Y^{(\beta)}$ and $i \neq 0$. By the same analysis as the third case, this probability is at most $1/2^c$.

Then, we have

$$\Pr[\mathsf{hit_{hh,xy}}|\neg(\mathsf{hit_{uv,xy}} \vee \mathsf{mcoll_h})] \le \max\left\{\frac{2qQ}{2^b}, \frac{qQ}{2^b} + \frac{2(\rho-1)Q}{2^c}\right\} \le \frac{2qQ}{2^b} + \frac{2(\rho-1)Q}{2^c}. \quad (3)$$

Note that the term $\frac{2(\rho-1)Q}{2^c}$ comes from the third and fourth cases. By $\neg\mathsf{mcoll_h}$, for each $X^{(\beta)}$ resp. $Y^{(\beta)}$, the number of elements in $\mathcal{H}$ whose first r bits are equal to $\mathsf{msb}_r(X^{(\beta)})$ resp. $\mathsf{msb}_r(Y^{(\beta)})$ is at most $\rho - 1$. Hence, the term is introduced.

- *Upper-Bound of* $\mathbf{Pr}[\mathsf{\mathbf{hit_{hh,uv}}}|\neg(\mathsf{\mathbf{hit_{uv,xy}}} \vee \mathsf{\mathbf{mcoll_h}})]$. This analysis is the same as that of $\Pr[\mathsf{hit_{hh,xy}}|\neg(\mathsf{hit_{uv,xy}} \vee \mathsf{mcoll_h})]$, where in this case, (U_i, V_i) is considered instead of $(X^{(i)}, Y^{(i)})$, and thus the upper-bound can be obtained by replacing Q with κ in (3). Hence, we have

$$\Pr[\mathsf{hit_{hh,uv}}|\neg(\mathsf{hit_{uv,xy}} \vee \mathsf{mcoll_h})] \le \frac{2q\kappa}{2^b} + \frac{2(\rho-1)\kappa}{2^c}, \text{assuming} \kappa \le 2^{b-1}. \quad (4)$$

- *Upper-Bound of* $\mathbf{Pr}[\mathsf{\mathbf{hit_{st,hh}}}|\neg\mathsf{\mathbf{hit_{uv,xy}}}]$. First, we fix $\alpha, \beta \in [q], i \in [m_\alpha - 1], j \in [\ell_{\mathsf{max}}]$ and upper-bound the probability that $S_i^{(\alpha)} = H_{j-1}^{(\beta)} \vee T_i^{(\alpha)} = H_j^{(\beta)}$ is satisfied. Note that in this case, $m_\alpha \ge 2$ (if $m_\alpha = 1$ then $S_i^{(\alpha)}$ cannot be defined). Then the following cases are considered.

  - The first case is that $S_1^{(\alpha)} = H_0^{(\beta)}$ and $m_\beta = 1$. Then $S_1^{(\alpha)} = H_0^{(\beta)} \Leftrightarrow V_\kappa \oplus M_1^{(\alpha)} = V_\kappa \oplus M_1^{(\beta)} \Leftrightarrow M_1^{(\alpha)} = M_1^{(\beta)}$. By $m_\beta = 1$, $\mathsf{pfpad}(M^{(\beta)}) = M_1^{(\beta)}$, and $M_1^{(\alpha)} = M_1^{(\beta)}$ implies that $\mathsf{pfpad}(M^{(\alpha)}) = \mathsf{pfpad}(M^{(\beta)})\|M_2^{(\alpha)}\|\cdots\|M_{m_\alpha}^{(\alpha)}$. However, since pfpad is prefix-free, this case does not occur.
  - The second case is that $S_1^{(\alpha)} = H_0^{(\beta)}$ and $m_\beta \ge 2$. Then $S_1^{(\alpha)} = H_0^{(\beta)} \Leftrightarrow V_\kappa \oplus M_1^{(\alpha)} = T_{m_\beta-1}^{(\beta)} \oplus M_{m_\beta}^{(\beta)}$. Since $T_{m_\beta-1}^{(\beta)}$ is randomly drawn from $\{0,1\}^b$, the probability that $S_1^{(\alpha)} = H_0^{(\beta)}$ is $1/2^b$.
  - The third case is that $S_1^{(\alpha)} = H_j^{(\beta)}$ and $j \ge 1$. Then $S_1^{(\alpha)} = H_j^{(\beta)} \Leftrightarrow V_\kappa \oplus M_1^{(\alpha)} = H_j^{(\beta)}$. By $\neg\mathsf{hit_{uv,xy}}$, V_κ is defined independently of all offline queries and is randomly drawn from at least $2^b - \kappa$ values. Hence, the probability that $S_1^{(\alpha)} = H_j^{(\beta)}$ is at most $1/(2^b - \kappa) \le 2/2^b$, assuming $\kappa \le 2^{b-1}$.
  - The four case is that $S_i^{(\alpha)} = H_0^{(\beta)}$ and $i \ge 2$. Then, $S_i^{(\alpha)} = H_0^{(\beta)} \Leftrightarrow T_{i-1}^{(\alpha)} \oplus M_i^{(\alpha)} = T_{m_\beta-1}^{(\beta)} \oplus M_{m_\beta}^{(\beta)}$.
    - If $i \ne m_\beta$, then $T_{i-1}^{(\alpha)}$ and $T_{m_\beta-1}^{(\beta)}$ are independently drawn by different random functions, thereby the probability that $S_i^{(\alpha)} = H_0^{(\beta)}$ is $1/2^b$.
    - If $i = m_\beta$, then since pfpad is a prefix-free padding, $\mathsf{pfpad}(M^{(\beta)})$ is not a prefix of $\mathsf{pfpad}(M^{(\alpha)})$. Hence, there exists $a \in [0, i]$ such that $M_a^{(\alpha)} \ne M_a^{(\beta)}$, that is, there exists $a \in [i-1]$ such that the a-th block inputs are distinct (i.e., $S_a^{(\alpha)} \ne S_a^{(\beta)}$) but the $(a+1)$-th block inputs are the

same (i.e., $S_{a+1}^{(\alpha)} = S_{a+1}^{(\beta)}$) where $S_{m_\beta}^{(\beta)} := H_0^{(\beta)}$. Fixing $a \in [i-1]$ with $S_a^{(\alpha)} \neq S_a^{(\beta)}$, since the outputs $T_a^{(\alpha)}$ and $T_a^{(\beta)}$ are independently drawn, the probability that $S_{a+1}^{(\alpha)} = S_{a+1}^{(\beta)}$ is satisfied is at most $1/2^b$. Hence, the probability that for some $a \in [i-1], S_a^{(\alpha)} = S_a^{(\beta)}$ is satisfied is at most $(i-1)/2^b = (m_\beta - 1)/2^b$.

- The fifth case is that $S_i^{(\alpha)} = H_{j-1}^{(\beta)}$, $i \geq 2$ and $j \geq 2$. Then $S_i^{(\alpha)} = H_{j-1}^{(\beta)} \Leftrightarrow T_{i-1}^{(\alpha)} \oplus M_i^{(\alpha)} = H_{j-1}^{(\beta)}$, where $T_{i-1}^{(\alpha)}$ and $H_{j-1}^{(\beta)}$ are independently drawn. Hence, the probability that $S_i^{(\alpha)} = H_{j-1}^{(\beta)}$ is satisfied is $1/2^b$.
- The sixth case is that $T_i^{(\alpha)} = H_j^{(\beta)}$. Since $T_i^{(\alpha)}$ and $H_j^{(\beta)}$ are independently drawn by the distinct random functions, the probability that $T_i^{(\alpha)} = H_j^{(\beta)}$ is satisfied is $1/2^b$.

By the above analysis, for $\alpha, \beta \in [q]$, the probability that $\exists i \in [m_\alpha - 1], j \in [\ell_{\mathsf{max}}]$ s.t. $S_i^{(\alpha)} = H_{j-1}^{(\beta)} \vee T_i^{(\alpha)} = H_j^{(\beta)}$ is at most

$$\frac{1}{2^b} + \frac{2\ell_{\mathsf{max}}}{2^b} + \frac{(m_\alpha - 2)(\ell_{\mathsf{max}} - 1)}{2^b} + \frac{(m_\alpha - 2)(\ell_{\mathsf{max}} - 2)}{2^b} + \frac{(m_\alpha - 1)(\ell_{\mathsf{max}} - 1)}{2^b},$$

and thus we have

$$\begin{aligned}\Pr[\mathsf{hit}_{\mathsf{st},\mathsf{hh}} | \neg\mathsf{hit}_{\mathsf{uv},\mathsf{xy}}] &\leq \sum_{\alpha=1}^{q}\sum_{\beta=1}^{q}\left(\frac{1}{2^b} + \frac{2\ell_{\mathsf{max}}}{2^b} + \frac{3(m_\alpha - 1)(\ell_{\mathsf{max}} - 1)}{2^b}\right) \\ &\leq \frac{q^2}{2^b} + \frac{2q\sigma_{\mathsf{z}}}{2^b} + \frac{3\sigma_{\mathsf{m}}\sigma_{\mathsf{z}} - 3q(\sigma_{\mathsf{m}} + \sigma_{\mathsf{z}}) + 3q^2}{2^b} \leq \frac{3\sigma_{\mathsf{m}}\sigma_{\mathsf{z}}}{2^b}. \quad (5)\end{aligned}$$

• *Upper-Bound of* $\Pr[\mathsf{hit}_{\mathsf{st},\mathsf{st}}]$. We fix $\alpha, \beta \in [q], i \in [m_\alpha - 1], j \in [m_\beta - 1]$ with $i \neq j$. First we upper-bound the probability that $S_i^{(\alpha)} = S_j^{(\beta)}$ is satisfied. Without loss of generality, we assume that $j \neq 1$. Then $S_i^{(\alpha)} = S_j^{(\beta)} \Leftrightarrow S_i^{(\alpha)} = T_{j-1}^{(\beta)} \oplus M_j^{(\beta)}$. Since $i \neq j$, $T_{j-1}^{(\beta)}$ is drawn independently of $S_i^{(\alpha)}$. Hence, the probability that $S_i^{(\alpha)} = S_j^{(\beta)}$ is satisfied is $1/2^b$. Next, regarding the probability that $T_i^{(\alpha)} = T_j^{(\beta)}$ is satisfied, since $i \neq j$, $T_i^{(\alpha)}$ and $T_j^{(\beta)}$ are independently drawn, thereby this probability is $1/2^b$.

Finally, we have

$$\Pr[\mathsf{hit}_{\mathsf{st},\mathsf{st}}] \leq \binom{\sigma_{\mathsf{m}}}{2} \cdot \frac{2}{2^b} \leq \frac{\sigma_{\mathsf{m}}^2}{2^b}. \quad (6)$$

• *Upper-Bound of* $\Pr[\mathsf{hit}_{\mathsf{hh},\mathsf{hh}}]$. First, we fix $\alpha, \beta \in [q], i, j \in [0, \ell_{\mathsf{max}}]$ with $i \neq j$, and upper-bound the probability that $H_i^{(\alpha)} = H_j^{(\beta)}$ is satisfied. By $i \neq j$, $H_i^{(\alpha)}$ and $H_j^{(\beta)}$ are independently drawn, and thus this probability is $1/2^b$.

Finally, we have

$$\Pr[\mathsf{hit}_{\mathsf{hh},\mathsf{hh}}] \leq \binom{q(\ell_{\mathsf{max}} + 1)}{2} \cdot \frac{1}{2^b} \leq \frac{0.5(\sigma_{\mathsf{z}} + q)^2}{2^b} \leq \frac{2\sigma_{\mathsf{z}}^2}{2^b}. \quad (7)$$

• *Upper-Bound of* $\mathbf{Pr}[\mathsf{coll_t}]$. Fixing $\alpha, \beta \in [q], i \in [\min\{m_\alpha, m_\beta\} - 1]$ with $S_i^{(\alpha)} \neq S_i^{(\beta)}$, since $T_i^{(\alpha)}$ and $T_i^{(\beta)}$ are independently drawn, the probability that $T_i^{(\alpha)} = T_i^{(\beta)}$ is satisfied is $1/2^b$. Hence, we have

$$\Pr[\mathsf{coll_t}] \leq \sum_{\alpha=1}^{q} \sum_{\substack{\beta=1 \\ \text{s.t. } \alpha \neq \beta}}^{q} \frac{\min\{m_\alpha, m_\beta\} - 1}{2^b} \leq \frac{q\sigma_{\mathsf{m}}}{2^b}. \tag{8}$$

• *Upper-Bound of* $\mathbf{Pr}[\mathsf{coll_h}]$. Fixing $\alpha, \beta \in [q], i \in [\ell_{\mathsf{max}}]$ with $H_{i-1}^{(\alpha)} \neq H_{i-1}^{(\beta)}$, since $H_i^{(\alpha)}$ and $H_i^{(\beta)}$ are independently drawn, the probability that $H_i^{(\alpha)} = H_i^{(\beta)}$ is satisfied is $1/2^b$. Hence, we have

$$\Pr[\mathsf{coll_h}] \leq \sum_{\alpha=1}^{q} \sum_{\substack{\beta=1 \\ \text{s.t. } \alpha \neq \beta}}^{q} \frac{\ell_{\mathsf{max}}}{2^b} \leq \frac{q\sigma_{\mathsf{z}}}{2^b}. \tag{9}$$

• *Upper-Bound of* $\mathbf{Pr}[\mathsf{hit_{uv,xy}}]$. $\mathsf{hit_{uv,xy}}$ means that $\mathcal{A}$ makes an offline query whose query-response pair is (U_κ, V_κ). Since U_κ is defined from the sequence of the previous blocks $(U_1, V_1), \ldots, (U_{\kappa-1}, V_{\kappa-1})$, $\mathsf{hit_{uv,xy}}$ can be split into the two cases: the first case denoted by $\mathsf{hit}^{\rightarrow}_{\mathsf{uv,xy}}$ is that $\mathcal{A}$ has been made queries corresponding with all previous blocks $(U_1, V_1), \ldots, (U_{\kappa-1}, V_{\kappa-1})$, and then makes the query corresponding with (U_κ, V_κ); the second case denoted by $\mathsf{hit}^{\not\rightarrow}_{\mathsf{uv,xy}}$ is that $\mathcal{A}$ has not been made queries corresponding with some of the previous blocks, and then makes the query corresponding with (U_κ, V_κ). More precisely, these two cases are defined as follows. Note that for $i \in \{1, \ldots, \kappa\}$, "$(U_i, V_i)$ is defined" means that $\mathcal{A}$ makes an offline query whose query-response pair is (U_i, V_i).

– $\mathsf{hit}^{\rightarrow}_{\mathsf{uv,xy}} \Leftrightarrow \forall i \in \{2, \ldots, \kappa\} : (U_i, V_i)$ is defined after (U_{i-1}, V_{i-1}) is defined. That is, firstly (U_1, V_1) is defined, secondly (U_2, V_2) is defined, ..., and finally (U_κ, V_κ) is defined.
– $\mathsf{hit}^{\not\rightarrow}_{\mathsf{uv,xy}} \Leftrightarrow \exists i \in \{2, \ldots, \kappa\}$ s.t. (U_i, V_i) is defined before (U_{i-1}, V_{i-1}) is defined.

Since $\mathsf{hit_{uv,xy}} \Rightarrow \mathsf{hit}^{\rightarrow}_{\mathsf{uv,xy}} \vee \mathsf{hit}^{\not\rightarrow}_{\mathsf{uv,xy}}$, we have $\Pr[\mathsf{hit_{uv,xy}}] \leq \Pr[\mathsf{hit}^{\rightarrow}_{\mathsf{uv,xy}}] + \Pr[\mathsf{hit}^{\not\rightarrow}_{\mathsf{uv,xy}}]$.

Regarding the condition $\mathsf{hit}^{\rightarrow}_{\mathsf{uv,xy}}$, this analysis is non-trivial and very complex, and Gaži *et al.* [13] analyzed the non-trivial part, and gave the upper-bound $\Pr[\mathsf{hit}^{\rightarrow}_{\mathsf{uv,xy}}] \leq \lambda(Q, k, r', c', b)$. In this proof, the upper-bound is used.

Regarding the condition $\mathsf{hit}^{\not\rightarrow}_{\mathsf{uv,xy}}$, this condition implies that there exists a maximal index $i \in \{1, \ldots, \kappa - 1\}$ such that (U_{i+1}, V_{i+1}) is defined, yet (U_i, V_i) is not defined. Since $U_{i+1} = K_i \| 0^{c'} \oplus V_i$ where V_i is randomly drawn from at least $2^b - \kappa$ values, we have

$$\Pr[\mathsf{hit}^{\not\rightarrow}_{\mathsf{uv,xy}}] \leq \kappa \times \frac{Q}{2^b - \kappa} \leq \frac{2\kappa Q}{2^b}, \text{ assuming } \kappa \leq 2^{b-1}.$$

Finally, the above upper-bounds give

$$\Pr[\mathsf{hit_{uv,xy}}] \leq \Pr[\mathsf{hit}^{\rightarrow}_{\mathsf{uv,xy}}] + \Pr[\mathsf{hit}^{\not\rightarrow}_{\mathsf{uv,xy}}] \leq \lambda(Q, k, r', b) + \frac{2\kappa Q}{2^b}. \tag{10}$$

• *Upper-Bound of* $\mathbf{Pr}[\mathsf{mcoll_h}]$. Since all elements in $\mathcal{H}$ are randomly drawn from $\{0,1\}^b$, we have

$$\Pr[\mathsf{mcoll_h}] \leq 2^r \times \binom{\sigma_\mathsf{z}}{\rho} \times \left(\frac{1}{2^r}\right)^\rho \leq 2^r \times \left(\frac{e \cdot \sigma_\mathsf{z}}{\rho 2^r}\right)^\rho, \tag{11}$$

using Starling's approximation ($x! \geq (x/e)^x$ for any x, where e is Napier's constant).

Upper-Bound of ε

Let $\tau \in \mathcal{T}_\mathsf{good}$ be a good transcript. For $i = \{R, M\}$, let all_i be the set of instantiations of all oracles in World_i, and let $\mathrm{comp}_i(\tau)$ be the set of instantiations of oracles compatible with τ in World_i. Then

$$\Pr[\mathsf{T}_R = \tau] = |\mathrm{comp}_R(\tau)|/|\mathrm{all}_R| \text{ and } \Pr[\mathsf{T}_M = \tau] = |\mathrm{comp}_M(\tau)|/|\mathrm{all}_M|.$$

In the analyses, the following notations are used.

- $\gamma_i^\mathsf{st} = \bigcup_{\alpha=1}^q \{(S_i^{(\alpha)}, T_i^{(\alpha)})\}$ for $i \in [m_\mathsf{max} - 1]$: the set of input-output pairs just after the i-th message blocks.
- $\gamma^\mathsf{st} = \bigcup_{i=1}^{m_\mathsf{max}-1} \gamma_i^\mathsf{st}$.
- $\gamma_j^\mathsf{hh} = \bigcup_{\alpha=1}^q \{(H_{j-1}^{(\alpha)}, H_j^{(\alpha)})\}$ for $j \in [\ell_\mathsf{max}]$: the set of input-output pairs just before the j-th output blocks.
- $\gamma^\mathsf{hh} = \bigcup_{j=1}^{\ell_\mathsf{max}} \gamma_j^\mathsf{hh}$.
- $\gamma^\mathsf{sthh} = \gamma^\mathsf{st} \cup \gamma^\mathsf{hh}$.
- $\gamma^\mathsf{xyuv} = \bigcup_{\beta=1}^Q \{(X^{(\beta)}, Y^{(\beta)})\} \cup \bigcup_{i=1}^\kappa \{(U_i, V_i)\}$: the set of offline query-response pairs and input-output pairs regarding a secret key K.
- $\gamma = \gamma^\mathsf{sthh} \cup \gamma^\mathsf{xyuv}$.

First, $|\mathrm{all}_R|$, $|\mathrm{all}_M|$, $|\mathrm{comp}_R(\tau)|$ and $|\mathrm{comp}_M(\tau)|$ are counted.

- $|\mathrm{all}_R|$ is counted. Since $K \in \{0,1\}^k$ and $\mathsf{P} \in \mathsf{Perm}(b)$, we have $|\mathrm{all}_R| = 2^k \cdot (2^b!)$.
- $|\mathrm{all}_M|$ is counted. Since $K \in \{0,1\}^k$, $\mathsf{P} \in \mathsf{Perm}(b)$, and $(\mathbf{F}, \mathbf{G}) \in \mathsf{Func}(b)^{m_\mathsf{max}-1+\ell_\mathsf{max}}$ we have $|\mathrm{all}_M| = 2^k \cdot (2^b!) \cdot ((2^b)^{2^b})^{m_\mathsf{max}+\ell_\mathsf{max}-1}$.
- $|\mathrm{comp}_R(\tau)|$ is counted. Since K is uniquely determined, we have $|\mathrm{comp}_R(\tau)| = (2^b - |\gamma|)!$.
- $|\mathrm{comp}_M(\tau)|$ is counted. Since K is uniquely determined, we have

$$|\mathrm{comp}_M(\tau)| = (2^b - |\gamma^\mathsf{xyuv}|)! \cdot \prod_{i=1}^{m_\mathsf{max}-1} (2^b)^{2^b - |\gamma_i^\mathsf{st}|} \cdot \prod_{j=1}^{\ell_\mathsf{max}} (2^b)^{2^b - |\gamma_j^\mathsf{hh}|}.$$

By the definition of $\mathcal{T}_\mathsf{good}$, $\gamma_1^\mathsf{st}, \ldots, \gamma_{m_\mathsf{max}-1}^\mathsf{st}, \gamma_1^\mathsf{hh}, \ldots, \gamma_{\ell_\mathsf{max}}^\mathsf{hh}, \gamma^\mathsf{xyuv}$ do not overlap with each other. Hence, $|\gamma^\mathsf{st}| = |\gamma_1^\mathsf{st}| + \cdots + |\gamma_{m_\mathsf{max}-1}^\mathsf{st}|$, $|\gamma^\mathsf{hh}| = |\gamma_1^\mathsf{hh}| + \cdots + |\gamma_{\ell_\mathsf{max}}^\mathsf{hh}|$ and $|\gamma^\mathsf{sthh}| = |\gamma^\mathsf{st}| + |\gamma^\mathsf{hh}|$ are satisfied, and

$$\begin{aligned}|\mathrm{comp}_M(\tau)| &= (2^b - |\gamma^\mathsf{xyuv}|)! \cdot (2^b)^{(m_\mathsf{max}-1)2^b - |\gamma^\mathsf{st}|} \cdot (2^b)^{\ell_\mathsf{max} 2^b - |\gamma^\mathsf{hh}|} \\ &= (2^b - |\gamma^\mathsf{xyuv}|)! \cdot (2^b)^{(m_\mathsf{max}+\ell_\mathsf{max}-1)2^b - |\gamma^\mathsf{sthh}|}.\end{aligned}$$

Finally, by $|\gamma| = |\gamma^{\mathsf{sthh}}| + |\gamma^{\mathsf{xyuv}}|$ (γ^{sthh} and γ^{xyuv} do not overlap with each other), we have

$$\frac{\Pr[\mathsf{T}_R = \tau]}{\Pr[\mathsf{T}_M = \tau]} = \frac{(2^b - |\gamma|)!}{2^k \cdot (2^b!)} \cdot \frac{2^k \cdot (2^b!) \cdot ((2^b)^{2^b})^{m_{\mathsf{max}}+\ell_{\mathsf{max}}-1}}{(2^b - |\gamma^{\mathsf{xyuv}}|)! \cdot (2^b)^{(m_{\mathsf{max}}+\ell_{\mathsf{max}}-1)2^b - |\gamma^{\mathsf{sthh}}|}}$$
$$= \frac{(2^b - |\gamma|)! \cdot (2^b)^{|\gamma^{\mathsf{sthh}}|}}{(2^b - |\gamma^{\mathsf{xyuv}}|)!} \geq 1,$$

thereby $\varepsilon = 0$.

Upper-Bound of $\Pr[\mathsf{World}_R = 1] - \Pr[\mathsf{World}_M = 1]$

Putting the upper-bounds of $\Pr[\mathsf{T}_2 \in \mathcal{T}_{\mathsf{bad}}]$ and ε into Lemma 1 gives

$$\Pr[\mathsf{World}_R] - \Pr[\mathsf{World}_M]$$
$$\leq \frac{2\sigma Q + 2\sigma^2}{2^b} + \frac{2r(\kappa + Q)}{2^c} + \left(\frac{6\sigma(\kappa + Q)}{2^b}\right)^{1/2} + \lambda(Q, k, r', b). \qquad (12)$$

4.3 Upper Bound of $\Pr[\mathsf{World}_M] - \Pr[\mathsf{World}_I]$

First the following collision event in World_M is defined.

$$\mathsf{coll_h} \Leftrightarrow \exists \alpha, \beta \in \{1, \ldots, q\} \text{ with } \alpha \neq \beta \text{ and } \exists i \in [0, \ell_{\mathsf{max}} - 1] \text{ s.t. } H_i^{(\alpha)} = H_i^{(\beta)}.$$

If $\mathsf{coll_h}$ does not occur, then all H-values are independently drawn. Thus, all outputs of $\mathrm{F}_M[\mathrm{P}, \mathbf{F}, \mathbf{G}]$ are randomly and independently drawn, and $\Pr[\mathsf{World}_M | \neg\mathsf{coll_h}] = \Pr[\mathsf{World}_I]$. Hence, we have

$$\Pr[\mathsf{World}_M] - \Pr[\mathsf{World}_I] \leq \Pr[\mathsf{coll_h}] + \Pr[\mathsf{World}_M | \neg\mathsf{coll_h}] - \Pr[\mathsf{World}_I] \leq \Pr[\mathsf{coll_h}].$$

Hereafter, $\Pr[\mathsf{coll_h}]$ is upper-bounded.

First, we fix $\alpha, \beta \in [q]$ with $\alpha \neq \beta$, and upper-bound the probability that $\exists i \in [0, \ell_{\mathsf{max}} - 1]$ s.t. $H_i^{(\alpha)} = H_i^{(\beta)}$ In this analysis, the following cases are considered.

- $\mathsf{coll_h} \wedge (H_0^{(\alpha)} \neq H_0^{(\beta)})$:
  In this case, there exists $i \in [\ell_{\mathsf{max}} - 1]$ such that $H_{i-1}^{(\alpha)} \neq H_{i-1}^{(\beta)}$ and $H_i^{(\alpha)} = H_i^{(\beta)}$. Since $H_i^{(\alpha)}$ and $H_i^{(\beta)}$ are independently drawn, the probability that $\exists i \in [\ell_{\mathsf{max}} - 1]$ s.t. $H_i^{(\alpha)} = H_i^{(\beta)}$ is at most $(\ell_{\mathsf{max}} - 1)/2^b$.
- $\mathsf{coll_h} \wedge (H_0^{(\alpha)} = H_0^{(\beta)}) \wedge (m_\alpha = m_\beta)$:
  Since $M^{(\alpha)} \neq M^{(\beta)}$, $H_0^{(\alpha)} = H_0^{(\beta)}$ implies that there exists $i \in [m_\alpha - 1]$ such that $S_i^{(\alpha)} \neq S_i^{(\beta)}$ and $S_{i+1}^{(\alpha)} = S_{i+1}^{(\beta)}$, where $S_{m_\delta}^\delta := H_0^{(\delta)}$ for $\delta \in \{\alpha, \beta\}$. Note that
  $$S_{i+1}^{(\alpha)} = S_{i+1}^{(\beta)} \Leftrightarrow T_i^{(\alpha)} \oplus (M_{i+1}^{(\alpha)} \| 0^{c'}) = T_i^{(\beta)} \oplus (M_{i+1}^{(\beta)} \| 0^{c'}),$$
  where $T_i^{(\alpha)}$ and $T_i^{(\beta)}$ are independently drawn if $S_i^{(\alpha)} \neq S_i^{(\beta)}$. Hence, the probability that $\exists i \in [\ell_{\mathsf{max}} - 1]$ s.t. $H_i^{(\alpha)} = H_i^{(\beta)}$ is at most $m_\alpha/2^b$.

– $\mathsf{coll_h} \wedge (H_0^{(\alpha)} = H_0^{(\beta)}) \wedge (m_\alpha \neq m_\beta)$:
In this case,

$$H_0^{\alpha} = H_0^{\beta} \Leftrightarrow T_{m_\alpha-1}^{(\alpha)} \oplus (M_{m_\alpha}^{(\alpha)} \| 0^{c'}) = T_{m_\beta-1}^{(\beta)} \oplus (M_{m_\beta}^{(\beta)} \| 0^{c'}),$$

and by $m_\alpha \neq m_\beta$, $T_{m_\alpha-1}^{(\alpha)}$ and $T_{m_\beta-1}^{(\beta)}$ are independently drawn by distinct random functions. Hence, the probability that $\exists i \in [\ell_{\mathsf{max}}-1]$ s.t. $H_i^{(\alpha)} = H_i^{(\beta)}$ is $1/2^b$.

Finally, the above bounds give

$$\Pr[\mathsf{World}_M] - \Pr[\mathsf{World}_I] \leq \sum_{\substack{\alpha,\beta\in[q] \\ \text{s.t. } \alpha\neq\beta}} \left(\frac{\min\{m_\alpha, m_\beta\} + \ell_{\mathsf{max}} - 1}{2^b} \right) \leq \frac{q\sigma}{2^{b+1}}. \quad (13)$$

5 Conclusion

In this paper, we showed that the keyed sponge with any prefix-free padding `KSpongePF` achieves the same level of PRF-security as the sandwiched keyed sponge. Hence, using `KSpongePF`, the independence between c and q is ensured without the suffix key that is used in the sandwiched keyed sponge.

References

1. Andreeva, E., Daemen, J., Mennink, B., Van Assche, G.: Security of keyed sponge constructions using a modular proof approach. In: Leander, G. (ed.) FSE 2015. LNCS, vol. 9054, pp. 364–384. Springer, Heidelberg (2015). https://doi.org/10.1007/978-3-662-48116-5_18
2. Aumasson, J.-P., Henzen, L., Meier, W., Naya-Plasencia, M.: QUARK: A lightweight hash. In: Mangard, S., Standaert, F.-X. (eds.) CHES 2010. LNCS, vol. 6225, pp. 1–15. Springer, Heidelberg (2010). https://doi.org/10.1007/978-3-642-15031-9_1
3. Bellare, M., Pietrzak, K., Rogaway, P.: Improved security analyses for CBC MACs. In: Shoup, V. (ed.) CRYPTO 2005. LNCS, vol. 3621, pp. 527–545. Springer, Heidelberg (2005). https://doi.org/10.1007/11535218_32
4. Bertoni, G., Daemen, J., Peeters, M., Assche, G.V.: Sponge functions. In: Ecrypt Hash Workshop 2007 (2007)
5. Bertoni, G., Daemen, J., Peeters, M., Van Assche, G.: On the indifferentiability of the sponge construction. In: Smart, N. (ed.) EUROCRYPT 2008. LNCS, vol. 4965, pp. 181–197. Springer, Heidelberg (2008). https://doi.org/10.1007/978-3-540-78967-3_11
6. Bertoni, G., Daemen, J., Peeters, M., Van Assche, G.: Duplexing the sponge: single-pass authenticated encryption and other applications. In: Miri, A., Vaudenay, S. (eds.) SAC 2011. LNCS, vol. 7118, pp. 320–337. Springer, Heidelberg (2012). https://doi.org/10.1007/978-3-642-28496-0_19
7. Bertoni, G., Daemen, J., Peeters, M., Assche, G.V.: On the security of the keyed sponge construction. In: Symmetric Key Encryption Workshop (SKEW) (2011)

8. Bertoni, G., Daemen, J., Peeters, M., Assche, G.V.: Permutation-based encryption, authentication and authenticated encryption. In: DIAC 2012 (2012)
9. Bertoni, G., Daemen, J., Peeters, M., Van Assche, G.: Keccak. In: Johansson, T., Nguyen, P.Q. (eds.) EUROCRYPT 2013. LNCS, vol. 7881, pp. 313–314. Springer, Heidelberg (2013). https://doi.org/10.1007/978-3-642-38348-9_19
10. Bogdanov, A., Knežević, M., Leander, G., Toz, D., Varıcı, K., Verbauwhede, I.: SPONGENT: a lightweight hash function. In: Preneel, B., Takagi, T. (eds.) CHES 2011. LNCS, vol. 6917, pp. 312–325. Springer, Heidelberg (2011). https://doi.org/10.1007/978-3-642-23951-9_21
11. Coron, J.-S., Dodis, Y., Malinaud, C., Puniya, P.: Merkle-Damgård revisited: how to construct a hash function. In: Shoup, V. (ed.) CRYPTO 2005. LNCS, vol. 3621, pp. 430–448. Springer, Heidelberg (2005). https://doi.org/10.1007/11535218_26
12. Daemen, J., Mennink, B., Van Assche, G.: Full-state keyed duplex with built-in multi-user support. In: Takagi, T., Peyrin, T. (eds.) ASIACRYPT 2017. LNCS, vol. 10625, pp. 606–637. Springer, Cham (2017). https://doi.org/10.1007/978-3-319-70697-9_21
13. Gaži, P., Pietrzak, K., Tessaro, S.: The exact PRF security of truncation: tight bounds for keyed sponges and truncated CBC. In: Gennaro, R., Robshaw, M. (eds.) CRYPTO 2015. LNCS, vol. 9215, pp. 368–387. Springer, Heidelberg (2015). https://doi.org/10.1007/978-3-662-47989-6_18
14. Guo, J., Peyrin, T., Poschmann, A.: The PHOTON family of lightweight hash functions. In: Rogaway, P. (ed.) CRYPTO 2011. LNCS, vol. 6841, pp. 222–239. Springer, Heidelberg (2011). https://doi.org/10.1007/978-3-642-22792-9_13
15. Jovanovic, P., Luykx, A., Mennink, B.: Beyond $2^{c/2}$ security in sponge-based authenticated encryption modes. In: Sarkar, P., Iwata, T. (eds.) ASIACRYPT 2014. LNCS, vol. 8873, pp. 85–104. Springer, Heidelberg (2014). https://doi.org/10.1007/978-3-662-45611-8_5
16. Mennink, B., Reyhanitabar, R., Vizár, D.: Security of full-state keyed sponge and duplex: applications to authenticated encryption. In: Iwata, T., Cheon, J.H. (eds.) ASIACRYPT 2015. LNCS, vol. 9453, pp. 465–489. Springer, Heidelberg (2015). https://doi.org/10.1007/978-3-662-48800-3_19
17. Naito, Y.: Sandwich construction for keyed sponges: independence between capacity and online queries. In: Foresti, S., Persiano, G. (eds.) CANS 2016. LNCS, vol. 10052, pp. 245–261. Springer, Cham (2016). https://doi.org/10.1007/978-3-319-48965-0_15
18. Naito, Y., Yasuda, K.: New bounds for keyed sponges with extendable output: independence between capacity and message length. In: Peyrin, T. (ed.) FSE 2016. LNCS, vol. 9783, pp. 3–22. Springer, Heidelberg (2016). https://doi.org/10.1007/978-3-662-52993-5_1
19. NIST: Secure Hash Standard (SHS). FIPS PUB 180–4 (2015)
20. NIST: SHA-3 Standard: Permutation-Based Hash and Extendable-Output Functions. FIPS PUB 202 (2015)
21. Patarin, J.: The "Coefficients H" technique. In: Avanzi, R.M., Keliher, L., Sica, F. (eds.) SAC 2008. LNCS, vol. 5381, pp. 328–345. Springer, Heidelberg (2009). https://doi.org/10.1007/978-3-642-04159-4_21
22. Petrank, E., Rackoff, C.: CBC MAC for Real-Time Data Sources. J. Cryptol. **13**(3), 315–338 (2000)

Public-Key Cryptography

Forward-Secure Linkable Ring Signatures

Xavier Boyen[1] and Thomas Haines[1,2(✉)]

[1] QUT, Brisbane, Australia
xb@boyen.org, t1.haines@qut.edu.au
[2] Polyas GmbH, Berlin, Germany
t.haines@polyas.de

Abstract. We present the first linkable ring signature scheme with both unconditional anonymity and forward-secure key update: a powerful tool which has direct applications in elegantly addressing a number of simultaneous constraints in remote electronic voting. We propose a comprehensive security model, and construct a scheme based on the hardness of finding discrete logarithms, and (for forward security) inverting bilinear or multilinear maps of moderate degree to match the time granularity of forward security. We prove efficient security reductions—which, of independent interest, apply to, and are much tighter than, linkable ring signatures without forward security, thereby vastly improving the provable security of these legacy schemes. If efficient multilinear maps should ever admit a secure realisation, our contribution would elegantly address a number of problems heretofore unsolved in the important application of (multi-election) practical internet voting. Even if multilinear maps never obtain, our minimal two-epoch construction instantiated from bilinear maps can be combinatorially boosted to synthesize a polynomial time granularity, which would be sufficient for internet voting and more.

Keywords: Linkable ring signature · Bilinear map · Multilinear map
Electronic voting · Forward security · Unconditional anonymity

1 Introduction

Ring signatures, and especially linkable ring signatures, garner much interest in the applied cryptographic community for their promise to simplify certain aspects of the notoriously hard problem of remote electronic voting, which has conflicting and sometimes frustrating security requirements. In particular, linkability [18] or the closely related notion of traceability [13] make it easy to detect when the same signer has signed twice on the same matter, thereby preventing double spending in an electronic cash system, double voting in the same election.

However, so far these signatures have not assisted in simultaneously resolving two critical issues in electronic voting. These two issues are: (1) how to register

X. Boyen—Supported as Australian Research Council Future Fellow, ARC grant FT140101145.

W. Susilo and G. Yang (Eds.): ACISP 2018, LNCS 10946, pp. 245–264, 2018.
https://doi.org/10.1007/978-3-319-93638-3_15

voters, and; (2) how to ensure their long term privacy. To address these issues, an offline key update mechanism would allow the potentially costly registration of a voter's public key to happen once, whereafter the corresponding private key can be refreshed or updated multiple times, efficiently and *non-interactively*, for use in subsequent elections. In this context, forward security refers to the notion that the leakage or compromise of an updated private key will not compromise one's privacy in a past election—or let an attacker forge signatures ostensibly in the past, which could be linked to real votes. For practical electoral systems in particular, it is important that the public-key update mechanism be efficient and non-interactive. The ideal public-key update is the identity function, or "no-op." The private-key update serves to provide forward security to protect old elections against future data exposure and compromises.

The related but different notion of unconditional anonymity refers to the inability, even by a computationally unbounded attacker, to identify a signer without knowledge of their private key. This notion is important to protect the voter against future increases in computational power (or cryptanalytic attacks, or quantum computers), once they have destroyed their private key after it is no longer needed. Together with linkability, these features make substantially easier the task of designing a secure and useable remote election protocol. Our forward-secure linkable ring signature scheme, when dropped into a number of existing election protocols, directly results in a straightforward and secure electronic voting solution without the cumbersome and procedurally risky steps that would normally be necessary to manage a dedicated key for each election.

Unfortunately—as often with the contradictory requirements of voting—it is easy to convince oneself that anonymity can only hold unconditionally if no *authentic* private key for the relevant signing ring is ever leaked, not even after having been updated. Indeed, if an adversary knows a voter's authentic private key, he can always trivially deanonymise their current and future votes using the linkability feature. The same is true for past votes if a past private key can be recovered, by brute force or by breaking a hardness assumption, from a current key. In light of this, we deliberately choose to focus on the problem of achieving unconditional anonymity against outsiders, but only computational forward security against insiders in the sense of unforgeability after key update.

1.1 Our Results

We present the first candidate strategy for a linkable ring signature with unconditional anonymity and forward-secure key update. Such tool would enable significantly more simple and secure remote electronic voting, even within the framework of existing electronic voting protocols, and open the door to a number of simplified general anonymous authentication protocols for online systems.

To achieve our result we construct a linkable ring signature from unconditionally hiding commitments, and make sparing use of a multilinear map [14,17] to lift it to multiple time periods or "epochs". Without forward security or key update, our results are inspired by the linkable ring scheme from [18]—which we incidentally vastly improve via much tighter security reductions[1].

To get forward security, we build from an n-multilinear map an n-time one-way private-key update mechanism which requires no public-key update. We prove the scheme information-theoretically anonymous, and its other security properties from Discrete Logarithm and two multilinear-map hardness assumptions—one of which amount to the neo-classic Multilinear Decoding Problem [14] and the other is a natural generalisation of Decisional Diffie-Hellman. Notably, a mere 2-linear map (a.k.a. *bilinear pairing*) already gives us forward security for 2 time periods, which is enough for us to combine n-wise combinatorially to get an n^2-epoch system from uncontroversial assumptions.

1.2 Related Work

Group signatures were introduced by Chaum and van Heyst [7]. They allow the members of a group to generate signatures which can only be verified as emanating from one authorised signer within that group, with the additional property that the signature can be "opened" to reveal the true signer. The ability to open a signature is an important requirement in certain managed applications, but presents an unacceptable privacy loophole in the context of electronic voting.[2]

Ring signatures are a variation of group signatures which do not allow pre-authorisation of keys nor deanonymisation of signatures, and hence, do not have those privacy issues. Ring signatures were first presented by Rivest et al. [24] as a way to leak secrets anonymously. Since then, many variants have been proposed to suit a large number of applications. For elections, double voting is a major issue which vanilla ring signatures are not readily able to rectify. Linkable ring signatures [19] and traceable ring signatures [13] have been proposed as a way to address this issue. Nevertheless, neither of [13,19] or their variants provide forward security; hence in a voting application they would require impractically frequent re-registration of new keys to ensure acceptable levels of privacy.

Subsequent notable results in that area include Liu et al. [18], who presented a linkable ring signature with unconditional anonymity, but still without forward security. Our scheme addresses this shortcoming, by providing an offline (non-interactive) private-key-update mechanism with forward security (as well as much improved security reduction tightness over the previous schemes).

---

1 The original linkable ring signatures of Liu et al. [18,19] had proofs with losses exponential in the number of users, due to nested use of the forking lemma [23] on Pedersen commitments [22] in the random-oracle model. Our updated proofs and reductions are independent of the number of users, thanks to a single consolidated use of the forking lemma; and the same techniques directly apply to their construction.

2 In the UK there is a requirement that a judge be able to order a voter's ballot revealed. Group signatures would be perfect for such subtle voter intimidation, though Continentals would of course disapprove.

Multilinear Maps. Following the blockbuster impact of bilinear maps on cryptography, the question of using multilinear maps for cryptographic applications was first studied at a theoretical level by Boneh and Silverberg [5]. Nearly a decade later, Garg et al. [14] proposed the first practical candidate construction, based on lattice problems. There have since been several additional candidates from lattice- and number-based assumptions, as well as attacks and repair attempts [6,8,10,15,17], with the side of the "offence" presently having the upper hand. Our scheme relies on a multilinear generalisation of the Discrete Logarithm problem, which is a weaker assumption than the myriad of Diffie-Hellman variants and extensions typically found in cryptographic constructions based on bilinear or multilinear maps. However, it should be noted that there are no currently unbroken candidates for multilinear maps, and hence the construction in this work is currently unrealisable. (Our vastly improved security reductions for this class of unconditionally anonymous linkable ring signature scheme with or without forward security still apply, though, providing substantial improvements to the concrete security of [18,19].) We will discuss in Sect. 3.2 the major issues at hand regarding the known multilinear-map candidate constructions.

Voting Systems. In the world of election systems research, the recent Helios [1] protocol is, perhaps, the best known secure internet voting scheme. It has seen a significant variety of expansions and applications [12,25], but one of its shortcomings is that the voters have to place (too) much trust on the election authority. Our linkable ring signature construction would fit nicely within the Helios protocol to enable powerful anonymous authentication and achieve privacy against the election authority, a property which is not achieved by most implementations of Helios[3]. More generally, and beyond election systems, our new signature scheme can be used as a general rate-limited[4] anonymous authentication system with forward secrecy and information-theoretic privacy.

2 Definitions

A *forward secure linkable ring signature* (FS-LRS) scheme is a tuple of seven algorithms (Setup, KeyGen, Sign, Verify, Link, PubKeyUpd, and PriKeyUpd).[5]

- **param** ← **Setup**(λ) on security parameter λ, returns a public setup **param**.
- (sk_i, pk_i) ←**KeyGen(param)** given **param** returns a key pair (sk_i, pk_i).
- σ ← **Sign**($event, n, \boldsymbol{pk}_t, sk, M, t$) given an event-id *event*, a group size n, a set $\boldsymbol{pk}_t$ of n public keys, a private key sk whose corresponding public key is in $\boldsymbol{pk}_t$, a message M and a time t, produces a signature σ.

[3] In its standardasised version [2], Helios relies on a mixnet technique to distribute the election authority's ability to deanonymise. Even for Helios implementations that use this technique, the ability to enforce anonymity in the authentication mechanism itself would provide stronger privacy guarantees.

[4] Rate limitation in the context of authentication refers to an intentional bound on the number of uses, typically one, that can be made of a credential on a given target.

[5] Our definations are fairly direct forward secure variants of Liu et al. [18].

- **accept|reject** $\leftarrow$ **Verify**$(event, n, \boldsymbol{pk}_t, M, \sigma, t)$ given an event-id *event*, a group size n, a set $\boldsymbol{pk}_t$ of n public keys, a message-signature pair (M, σ), and time t, returns **accept** or **reject**. We define a signature σ as valid for $(event, n, \boldsymbol{pk}_t, M, t)$ if **Verify** outputs **accept**.
- **linked|unlinked** $\leftarrow$ **Link**$(event, t, n_1, n_2, \boldsymbol{pk}_{t_1}, \boldsymbol{pk}_{t_2}, M_1, M_2, \sigma_1, \sigma_2)$ given an event-id *event*, time t, two group sizes n_1, n_2, two sets $\boldsymbol{pk}_{t_1}, \boldsymbol{pk}_{t_2}$ of n_1, n_2 public keys respectively, and two valid signature and message pairs $(M_1, \sigma_1, M_2, \sigma_2)$, outputs **linked** or **unlinked**.
- $Z_{t+1} \leftarrow$ **PubKeyUpd**(Z_t) given a public key, Z at time t, produces a public key for time $t+1$.
- $sk_{t+1} \leftarrow$ **PriKeyUpd**(sk_t) given a private key sk at time t, produces the corresponding private key for time $t+1$.

2.1 Correctness Notions

To be functional, an **FS-LRS** scheme must satisfy the following:

- *Verification correctness:* Signatures signed correctly will verify.
- *Updating correctness:* For any time period of the system, the secret key derived from the private-key update function will create a valid signature on a ring, verifiable using the public key derived using the public-key update.
- *Linking correctness:* Two honestly created signatures on the same event and time period will link if and only if they have the same signer. (This is implied by the two security notions of linkability and non-slanderability; see below.)

2.2 Security Model

Security of FS-LRS has six aspects: unforgeability, anonymity, linkability, non-slanderability, forward-secure unforgeability, and forward-secure anonymity. [6] The following oracles model the ability of the adversary to break the scheme:

- $pk_{i,t} \leftarrow \mathcal{JO}(t)$. The *Joining Oracle*, upon request, adds a new user to the system, and returns the public key pk of the new user at the current time t.
- $sk_{i,t} \leftarrow \mathcal{CO}(pk_i, t)$. The *Corruption Oracle*, on input a previously joined public key pk_i, returns the matching secret key sk_i at the current time t.
- $\sigma' \leftarrow \mathcal{SO}(event, n, \boldsymbol{pk}_t, pk_\pi, M, t)$. The *Signing Oracle*, on input an event-id *event*, a group size n, a set $\boldsymbol{pk}_t$ of n public keys, the public key of the signer pk_π, a message M, and a time t, returns a valid signature σ'.

We omit the time and user subscripts t, i when clear from context. In particular, our public key does not undergo updating, so pk_t will be independent of t.

- $h \leftarrow \mathcal{H}(x)$. The *Random Oracle*, on input x, returns h independently and uniformly at random. If an x is repeated, the same h will be returned again.

[6] The last two aspects are generalisations of the first two. We present them all because the standard variants use weaker assumptions than the forward-secure variants.

Unforgeability. FS-LRS unforgeability is defined as a game between a challenger $\mathcal{C}$ and an adversary $\mathcal{A}$ with access to the oracles $\mathcal{JO}$, $\mathcal{CO}$, $\mathcal{SO}$, and $\mathcal{H}$:

1. $\mathcal{C}$ generates and gives $\mathcal{A}$ the system parameters **param**.
2. $\mathcal{A}$ queries the oracles polynomially many times using any adaptive strategy.
3. $\mathcal{A}$ gives $\mathcal{C}$ an event-id *event*, a group size n, a set $\boldsymbol{pk}_t$ of n public keys, a message M, a time t, and a signature σ.

$\mathcal{A}$ wins the game if:

i. $\mathbf{Verify}(event, n, \boldsymbol{pk}_t, M, \sigma, t) = \mathbf{accept}$;
ii. all of the public keys in $\boldsymbol{pk}_t$ are query outputs of $\mathcal{JO}$;
iii. no public keys in $\boldsymbol{pk}_t$ have been input to $\mathcal{CO}$; and
iv. σ is not a query output of $\mathcal{SO}$.

We denote the adversary's advantage as $\mathbf{Adv}_{\mathcal{A}}^{Unf}(\lambda) = Pr[\mathcal{A}$ wins the game$]$.

Definition 1: ***Unforgeability.*** *An* ***LRS*** *scheme is unforgeable if for all PPT adversaries* $\mathcal{A}$*,* $\boldsymbol{Adv}_{\mathcal{A}}^{Unf}(\lambda)$ *is negligible.*

Unconditional Anonymity. It should not be possible for an adversary $\mathcal{A}$ to tell the public key of the signer with a probability larger than $1/n$, where n is the cardinality of the ring, even if the adversary has unlimited computing resources. Specifically, **FS-LRS** unconditional anonymity is defined in a game between a challenger $\mathcal{C}$ and an unbounded adversary $\mathcal{A}$ with access to $\mathcal{JO}$:

1. $\mathcal{C}$ generates and gives $\mathcal{A}$ the system parameters **param**.
2. $\mathcal{A}$ may query $\mathcal{JO}$ according to any adaptive strategy.
3. $\mathcal{A}$ gives $\mathcal{C}$ an event-id e, a time t, a group size n, a set of $\boldsymbol{pk}_t$ of n public keys such that all of the public keys in $\boldsymbol{pk}_t$ are query outputs of $\mathcal{JO}$, a message M, and a time t. Parsing the set $\boldsymbol{pk}_t$ as $\{pk_1, \ldots, pk_n\}$. $\mathcal{C}$ randomly picks $\pi \in \{1, \ldots, n\}$ and computes $\sigma_\pi = \mathbf{Sign}(e, n, \boldsymbol{pk}_t, sk_\pi, M, t)$, where sk_π is a valid private key corresponding to pk_π at time t. The signature σ_π is given to $\mathcal{A}$.
4. $\mathcal{A}$ outputs a guess $\pi' \in \{1, \ldots, n\}$.

We denote the adversary's advantage by $\mathbf{Adv}_{\mathcal{A}}^{Anon}(\lambda) = |Pr[\pi = \pi'] - \frac{1}{n}|$.

Definition 2: ***Unconditional Anonymity.*** *An* ***FS-LRS*** *scheme is unconditionally anonymous if for all unbounded adversaries* $\mathcal{A}$*,* $\boldsymbol{Adv}_{\mathcal{A}}^{Anon}(\lambda)$ *is zero.*

Linkability. It should be infeasible for the same signer to generate two signatures for the same ring and event, such that they are determined to be **unlinked**. Linkability for an **FS-LRS** scheme is defined in a game between a challenger $\mathcal{C}$ and an adversary $\mathcal{A}$ with access to oracles $\mathcal{JO}, \mathcal{CO}, \mathcal{SO}$ and $\mathcal{H}$:

1. $\mathcal{C}$ generates and gives $\mathcal{A}$ the system parameters **param**.
2. $\mathcal{A}$ may query the oracles according to any adaptive strategy.
3. $\mathcal{A}$ gives $\mathcal{C}$ an event-id *event*, a time t, two sets $\boldsymbol{pk}_{t_1}, \boldsymbol{pk}_{t_2}$ of public keys of sizes n_1, n_2, two messages M_1, M_2, and two signatures σ_1, σ_2.

$\mathcal{A}$ wins the game if

i. All of the public keys in $\boldsymbol{pk}_t$ are query outputs of $\mathcal{JO}$;
ii. **Verify**($event, n_i, \boldsymbol{pk}_{t_i}, M_i, \sigma_i$,t) = **accept** for σ_1, σ_2 not outputs of $\mathcal{SO}$;
iii. At most one query has been made to $\mathcal{CO}$; and
iv. **Link**(σ_1, σ_2) = **unlinked**.

We denote the adversary's advantage as $\mathbf{Adv}_{\mathcal{A}}^{Link}(\lambda) = Pr[\mathcal{A}$ wins the game].

Definition 3: ***Linkability.*** *An **FS-LRS** scheme is linkable if for all PPT adversaries $\mathcal{A}$, $\boldsymbol{Adv}_{\mathcal{A}}^{Link}(\lambda)$ is negligible.*

Non-slanderability. Non-slanderability ensures that no signer can generate a signature which is determined to be **linked** with another signature not generated by the signer. **FS-LRS** non-slanderabilty is defined in a game between a challenger $\mathcal{C}$ and an adversary $\mathcal{A}$ with access to the oracles $\mathcal{JO}, \mathcal{CO}, \mathcal{SO}$ and $\mathcal{H}$:

1. $\mathcal{C}$ generates and gives $\mathcal{A}$ the system parameters **param**.
2. $\mathcal{A}$ may query the oracles according to any adaptive strategy.
3. $\mathcal{A}$ gives $\mathcal{C}$ an event-id $event$, a time t, a group size n, a message M, a set of n public keys $\boldsymbol{pk}_t$, and the public key of an insider $pk_\pi \in \boldsymbol{pk}_t$ such that pk_π has neither been queried to $\mathcal{CO}$ nor included as the insider public key of any query to $\mathcal{SO}$. $\mathcal{C}$ uses the private key sk_π corresponding to pk_π to run **Sign**($event, n, \boldsymbol{pk}_t, sk_\pi, M, t$) and to produce a signature σ' given to $\mathcal{A}$.
4. $\mathcal{A}$ queries oracles adaptively, except that pk_π cannot be queried to $\mathcal{CO}$, or included as the insider public key of any query to $\mathcal{SO}$. In particular, $\mathcal{A}$ is allowed to query any public key which is not pk_π to $\mathcal{CO}$.
5. $\mathcal{A}$ outputs n^*, n^* public keys $\boldsymbol{pk}_t^*$, a message M^*, and a signature $\sigma^* \neq \sigma'$.

A wins the game if

- **Verify**($event, n^*, \boldsymbol{pk}_t^*, M^*, \sigma^*$, t) = **accept** on σ^* not an output of $\mathcal{SO}$;
- all of the public keys in $\boldsymbol{pk}_t^*$, $\boldsymbol{pk}_t$ are query outputs of $\mathcal{JO}$;
- pk_π has not been queried to $\mathcal{CO}$; and
- **Link**(σ^*, σ') = **linked**.

We denote the adversary's advantage by $\mathbf{Adv}_{\mathcal{A}}^{NS}(\lambda) = Pr[\mathcal{A}$ wins the game].

Definition 4: ***Non-slanderabilty.*** *An **FS-LRS** scheme is non-slanderable if for any PPT adversaries $\mathcal{A}$, $\boldsymbol{Adv}_{\mathcal{A}}^{NS}(\lambda)$ is negligible.*

Forward-Secure Unforgeability. Forward-secure unforgeability ensures that it is not feasible for an adversary with a private key for a time period strictly greater than t to create valid signatures for any period less than or equal to t. Forward-secure unforgeability is defined in the following game between a challenger $\mathcal{C}$ and an adversary $\mathcal{A}$ given access to the oracles $\mathcal{JO}, \mathcal{CO}, \mathcal{SO}$ and $\mathcal{H}$:

1. $\mathcal{C}$ generates and gives $\mathcal{A}$ the system parameters **param**.
2. $\mathcal{A}$ may query the oracles according to any adaptive strategy.
3. $\mathcal{A}$ gives $\mathcal{C}$ an event-id e, a group size n, a set $\boldsymbol{pk}_t$ of n public keys, a message M, a time t and a signature σ.

A wins the game if

i. $\mathbf{Verify}(e, n, \boldsymbol{pk}_t, M, \sigma, t) = \mathbf{accept}$;
ii. all of the public keys in $\boldsymbol{pk}_t$ are query outputs of $\mathcal{JO}$;
iii. no public keys in $\boldsymbol{pk}_t$ have been input to $\mathcal{CO}$ at time t or earlier; and
iv. σ is not a query output of $\mathcal{SO}$.

We denote the adversary's advantage by $\mathbf{Adv}_{\mathcal{A}}^{FS-Unf}(\lambda) = Pr[\mathcal{A}$ wins the game].

Definition 5: *Forward-Secure Unforgability.* *An* **FS-LRS** *scheme is forward-secure against forgeries if for PPT adversaries* $\mathcal{A}$, $\boldsymbol{Adv}_{\mathcal{A}}^{FS-Unf}(\lambda)$ *is negligible.*

Forward-Secure Anonymity. Forward-secure anonymity ensures that it is not feasible for an adversary with a private key for a time period strictly greater than t to de-anonymise signatures for any time period less than or equal to t. Forward-secure anonymity is defined in a game between a challenger $\mathcal{C}$ and an adversary $\mathcal{A}$ given access to oracles $\mathcal{JO}, \mathcal{CO}, \mathcal{SO}$ and the random oracle:

1. $\mathcal{C}$ generates and gives $\mathcal{A}$ the system parameters **param**.
2. $\mathcal{A}$ may query the oracles according to any adaptive strategy.
3. $\mathcal{A}$ gives $\mathcal{C}$ an event-id e, a time t, a group size n, a set of $\boldsymbol{pk}_t$ of n public keys such that all of the public keys in $\boldsymbol{pk}_t$ are query outputs of $\mathcal{JO}$, and a message M. Parsing the set $\boldsymbol{pk}_t$ as $\{pk_1, \ldots, pk_n\}$. $\mathcal{C}$ randomly picks $\pi \in \{1, \ldots, n\}$, and computes $\sigma_\pi = \mathbf{Sign}(e, n, \boldsymbol{pk}_t, sk_\pi, M, t)$, where sk_π is a valid private key corresponding to pk_π at time t. The signature σ_π is given to $\mathcal{A}$.
4. $\mathcal{A}$ outputs a guess $\pi' \in \{1, \ldots, n\}$.

A wins the game if

i. $\pi = \pi'$;
ii. e and t have never been input together to $\mathcal{SO}$; and
iii no public keys in $\boldsymbol{pk}_t$ have been input to $\mathcal{CO}$ at time t or earlier.

We denote the adversary's advantage by $\mathbf{Adv}_{\mathcal{A}}^{FS-Anon}(\lambda) = Pr[\mathcal{A}$ wins the game].

Definition 6: *Forward-Secure Anonymity.* *An* **FS-LRS** *scheme is forward-secure anonymous if for any PPT adversaries* $\mathcal{A}$, $\boldsymbol{Adv}_{\mathcal{A}}^{FS-Anon}(\lambda)$ *is negligible.*

3 Multilinear Maps

Our notation is similar to that used by Zhandry in [26]. Let $\mathcal{E}$ be an $l-$linear map over additive cyclic groups $[\mathbb{G}]_1, \ldots, [\mathbb{G}]_l$ of prime order p, where $[\mathbb{G}]_0 = \mathbb{Z}_q$ and all $[\mathbb{G}]_i$ for $i = 1, \ldots, l$ are homomorphic to $(\mathbb{Z}_q, +)$. Let $[\alpha]_i$ denote the element $\alpha \in \mathbb{Z}_q$ raised to the level-i group $[\mathbb{G}]_i$, for $i \in (0, \ldots, l)$. Let $\alpha \in_R [\mathbb{G}]_i$ denote the random sampling of an element in $[\mathbb{G}]_i$. We have access to efficient functions:

Addition, **Add** or +: given two elements $[\alpha]_i, [\beta]_i$ returns $[\alpha + \beta]_i$.

Negation, **Neg** or −: given one element $[\alpha]_i$ returns $[-\alpha]_i$.

Cross-level multiplication or multilinear **Map**, denoted $\mathcal{E}$: given two elements $[\alpha]_i, [\beta]_j$, returns $[\alpha * \beta]_{i+j}$. The cryptographic security of multilinear maps requires, among other things, that multiplication *within* any $[\mathbb{G}]_i$ be hard for $i > 0$.

3.1 Multilinear Assumptions

For convenience, we will prove the security of our construction using the following hard problem, which we call Equivalent Decoding Problem, and which we prove to be equivalent to the central Decoding Problem from [14], itself a specific instance of the Generalised Decoding Problem [14]. We define and recall:

Definition 7 ((κ, h)-Equivalent Decoding Problem ((κ, h)-EDP)). *For any PPT $\mathcal{A}$, $Pr[\mathcal{A}([\alpha]_0, [\alpha * x]_h, [x]_\kappa) = [x]_j] = negl$, with $j < \kappa \leq h$ and $\alpha, x \in_R \mathbb{Z}_q$.*

Definition 8 (Multilinear Discrete-log Problem (MDLP) [14]). *For any PPT algorithm $\mathcal{A}$, the probability $Pr[\mathcal{A}([\alpha]_1) = [\alpha]_0]$ is negligible, where $\alpha \in_R \mathbb{Z}_q$.*

Definition 9 (i-Decoding Problem ($i - DP$) [14]). *For any PPT algorithm $\mathcal{A}$, the probability $Pr[\mathcal{A}([\delta]_i) = [\delta]_j]$ is negligible, where $j < i$ and $\delta \in_R \mathbb{Z}_q$.*

For the efficiency and correctness of our scheme we let $h = l$ and $\kappa \in (1, \ldots, l)$, where l is the size or height of the multilinear map. We now prove equivalence.

Theorem 10. *(κ, h)-EDP is equivalent to i-DP, for $i = \kappa$:*

Proof. Given an (κ, h)-EDP instance $([\alpha]_0, [\alpha * x]_h, [x]_\kappa)$ we simulate an i-DP instance $[\delta]_i$ as, $[\delta]_i = [x]_\kappa$. Having obtained the output from a successful DP adversary, $\mathcal{A}([\delta]_i) \to [\delta]_j$ for $j < i$, we return $[\delta]_j$ as answer to the EDP instance.

Conversely, given an i-DP instance $([\delta]_i)$ we simulate a (κ, h)-DP instance $([\alpha]_0, [\alpha * x]_h, [x]_\kappa)$ by sampling $[\alpha]_0 \in_R \mathbb{Z}_q$, setting $[x]_\kappa = [\delta]_i$, and computing $[\alpha * x]_h = \mathcal{E}([x]_\kappa, [\alpha]_{h-\kappa})$. Given a successful EDP adversary's output, $\mathcal{A}([\alpha]_0, [\alpha * x]_h, [x]_\kappa) \to [x]_j$ for $j < \kappa$, we return $[x]_j$ as answer to the EDP instance. □

In the same way that the Discrete Log Problem is generalised to Multilinear Discrete Log Problem (MDLP), the Decisional Diffie-Hellmann problem generalise to Multilinear Decisional Diffie-Hellmann (MDDH) problem. Intuitively, given three group elements it is infeasible to tell if one is the product of the others, provided that the sum of any two levels is greater than maximum allowed.

Definition 11 (Multilinear Decisional Diffie-Hellmann Problem(i, j, κ)-(MDDH)). *For any PPT $\mathcal{A}$, the distinguishing probability $Pr[\mathcal{A}([\alpha]_i, [\beta]_j, [\gamma]_\kappa) =$ "true" $- \mathcal{A}([\alpha]_i, [\beta]_j, [\alpha\beta]_\kappa) =$ "true"$]$ is negligible, where $\alpha, \beta, \gamma \in_R \mathbb{Z}_q$ and all pairwise sums of i, j, κ are greater than the maximum map level l.*

3.2 Is Multilinearity Achievable?

Three major multilinear map candidates have been proposed in [10,14,15]. Since their introduction, they have been the targets of many attacks, patches, and more attacks that remain unpatched.

One powerful class of attacks on multilinear maps are the so-called "zeroising" attacks; they run in polynomial time but require the availability of an encoding of zero in the lower levels of the multilinear ladder [14,16]. There are also sub-exponential and quantum attacks [3,9,11]. Further to this, recently Miles *et al.* introduced a class of "annihilation" attacks on multilinear maps [20].

There are reasons to believe that multilinear maps may be unrealisable. In particular, their near equivalence to indistinguishability obfuscation [21]—an extremely powerful tool which in an even stronger variant is known not to exist [4]—is worrying. Furthermore, Boneh and Silverberg [5] in their original paper on applications of hypothetical multilinear maps, present several results which cast doubt on the likeliness of multilinear maps' existence, and soberingly concluded that "such maps might have to either come from outside the realm of algebraic geometry, or occur as unnatural computable maps arising from geometry."

If multilinear maps fail to be repaired, bilinear maps still give us an efficient 2-period FS-LRS scheme that can be combinatorially boosted to multiple periods.

4 Construction

Intuition. To ensure unconditional anonymity in spite of linkability, a Pederson commitment can provide unconditional hiding with computational binding of the private key in the public key. A multilinear map can then raise and ratchet the private key at each time period, which provides forward security.

In the signature we use two Fiat-Shamir heuristic on two knowledge-of-discrete-logarithm proofs, rolled into one. The signer proves firstly that they know x behind $f = dx$, and secondly that they know x and y such that $gx + hy$ is one of the public keys. Random challenges c_i serve as decoys for the other public keys. Since both the real challenge c and the decoy challenges c_i are uniformly random, an adversary is unable to discern which party signed.

Setup(n): Take as input the number of time periods $\mathcal{T} \geq 1$. Denote by $t \in (0, 1, 2, \ldots, \mathcal{T} - 1)$ the current time period. Run a multilinear map setup algorithm to construct a bounded-level l-multilinear map and obtain its public parameters **mmpp**. We refer to the map's maximum allowed level as l and require $l \geq \mathcal{T} \geq 1$. Let H_i denote the ith element in a family of hash functions H such that H_i: $\{0,1\}^* \rightarrow [\mathbb{G}]_i$. Construct $[g]_0 = H_0$("Generator-g") and $[h]_l = H_l$("Generator-h"). The public **param** are (**mmpp**, $[g]_0, [h]_l, H$, "Generator-g", "Generator-h").

KeyGen: Sample $[x]_0, [y]_0 \in_R [\mathbb{G}]_0$ and let $[Z]_l = \mathcal{E}(\mathcal{E}([g]_0, [x]_0), [1]_l) + \mathcal{E}([h]_l, [y]_0) = [g * x + h * y]_l$. The public key is $pk = [Z]_l$ and initial secret key $sk = ([x]_0, [y]_0)$.

Sign: On input $(event, n, \boldsymbol{pk}_t, sk_\pi, M, t)$, with: *event* some description, n the ring size, $\boldsymbol{pk}_t = \{pk_1, \ldots, pk_n\} = \{[Z_1]_l, \ldots, [Z_n]_l\}$ the ring public keys, sk_π the signer's secret key with public key $pk_\pi \in \boldsymbol{pk}_t$ (w.l.o.g., $\pi \in [1, n]$), M the message, and t the time period; the signer (holder of $sk_\pi = ([x]_t, [y]_0)$) does the following:

1. Hash $[d]_{l-t} = H_{l-t}(t||event)$, and multilinearly map $[f]_l = \mathcal{E}([d]_{l-t}, [x]_t)$;
2. Sample $[r_x]_t \in_R [\mathbb{G}]_t$ and $[c_1]_0, \ldots, [c_{\pi-1}]_0, [c_{\pi+1}]_0, \ldots, [c_n]_0, [r_y]_0 \in_R [\mathbb{G}]_0$;
3. Compute $[K]_l = \mathcal{E}([g]_{l-t}, [r_x]_t) + \mathcal{E}([h]_l, [r_y]_0) + \sum_{i=1, i\neq\pi}^n \mathcal{E}([Z_i]_l, [c_i]_0)$, and $[K']_l = \mathcal{E}([d]_{l-t}, [r_x]_t) + \mathcal{E}([f]_l, \sum_{i=1, i\neq\pi}^n [c_i]_0)$;
4. Find $[c_\pi]_0$ s.t. $[c_\pi]_0 = H_0(\boldsymbol{pk}_t||event||[f]_l||M||[K]_l||[K']_l||t) - \sum_{i=1, i\neq\pi}^n [c_i]_0$;
5. Compute $[\tilde{x}]_t = [r_x]_t - \mathcal{E}([c_\pi]_0, [x]_t)$ and $[\tilde{y}]_0 = [r_y]_0 - \mathcal{E}([c_\pi]_0, [y]_0)$;
6. Output the signature $\sigma = ([f]_l, [\tilde{x}]_t, [\tilde{y}]_0, [c_1]_0, \ldots, [c_n]_0)$.

Verify: On input $(event, n, \boldsymbol{pk}_t, M, \sigma, t)$, first let $[d]_{l-t} = H_{l-t}(t||event)$ and, using the components of $\sigma = ([f]_l, [\tilde{x}]_t, [\tilde{y}]_0, [c_1]_0, \ldots, [c_n]_0)$, compute

$$[K]_l = \mathcal{E}([g]_{l-t}, [\tilde{x}]_t) + \mathcal{E}([h]_l, [\tilde{y}]_0) + \sum\nolimits_{i=1}^n \mathcal{E}([Z_i]_l, [c_i]_0)$$
$$[K']_l = \mathcal{E}([d]_{l-t}, [\tilde{x}]_t) + \mathcal{E}([f]_l, \sum\nolimits_{i=1}^n [c_i]_0)$$
$$\text{and} \quad [c_0]_0 = H_0((\boldsymbol{pk}_t||event||[f]_l||M||[K]_l||[k']_l||t))$$

then check and output whether $\sum_{i=1}^n [c_i]_0 = [c_0]_0$.

Link. On input two signatures $\sigma_1 = ([f_1]_l, *)$ and $\sigma_2 = ([f_2]_l, *)$, two messages M_1 and M_2, an event description *event*, and a time t, first check whether the two signatures are valid. If yes, output **linked** if $[f_1]_l = [f_2]_l$; else output **unlinked**.

Private-Key Update: In a given time period t, to calculate the private key for time $t + 1 < l$, do: $[x]_{t+1} = \mathcal{E}([1]_1, [x]_t)$

Public-Key Update: The public key does not need to be updated in our scheme.

5 Correctness

Verification Correctness. For verification correctness, it suffices to show that the verification values K and K' calculated by each party are the same. For the K: $[K_v]_l = [g * \tilde{x}]_l + [h * \tilde{y}]_l + \sum_{i\in[n]} [Z_i * c_i]_l = [g * r_x]_l + [h * r_y]_l + \sum_{i\in[n]\setminus\{\pi\}} [Z_i * c_i]_l$
$[K_s]_l = [g * r_x]_l + [h * r_y]_l + \sum_{i\in[n]\setminus\{\pi\}} [Z_i * c_i]_l$ hence $[K_s]_l = [K_v]_l$. For the K': $[K'_v]_l = [d * \tilde{x}]_l + [f * \sum_{i\in[n]} c_i]_l = [d * r_x]_l + [f * \sum_{i\in[n]\setminus\{\pi\}} c_i]_l$ and
$[K'_s]_l = [d * r_x]_l + [f * \sum_{i\in[n]\setminus\{\pi\}} c_i]_l$ and therefore also $[K'_s]_l = [K'_v]_l$. □

Linking Correctness. For a given event *event*, time t, and private key $[x]_t$ the linking component, $[d]_{l-t} = H_{l-t}(t||event)$, $[f]_l = \mathcal{E}([d]_{l-t}, [x]_t)$, is completely deterministic. Since the linking component is deterministic, under the above conditions, given any two signatures a simple equality check on the linking component suffices. Conversely, for a given event *event*, time t, and two different private keys $[x]_t$ and $[x']_t$ the linking element will be different.[7]

Update Correctness. Given a time period t, to calculate the updated keys for the next time period using the update function, we observe that the relation between public and private keys is unchanged. Recall that the use of the pairing produces the product of the input values at the level of the sum of the input levels. The only changes to the private keys and public key is $[x]_{t+1} = \mathcal{E}([1]_2, [x]_t)$, which simply "raises" x by two levels without changing the encoded value.

6 Security

Theorem 12. *The FS-LRS scheme is unforgeable in the ROM, if EDP is hard.*

Liu et al. [18,19] reduced unforgeability from discrete log by rewinding and forking the execution, in the worst case, for every $[c]_i$, causing the success of their simulation to shrink exponentially in n, the number of users in the ring. Our proof extracts an EDP solution from the single value $\sum_{i=1}^{n}[c_i]_0$ which means that we merely have to fork and rewind once. Our reduction is thus *independent* of, rather than exponential in, the (user-controlled) parameter n.

Proof. Given an (l, l)-EDP instance $([\alpha]_0, [\alpha * x]_l, [x]_l)$, $\mathcal{B}$ is asked to output some $[x]_j$ where $j < l$. Note that $[x]_t$ in the secret key at any time period $t \leq \mathcal{T} < l$ in our scheme will satisfy this bound. $\mathcal{B}$ gives $\mathcal{A}$ the public key $[h]_l = [\alpha * x]_l$ and $[g]_0 = [\alpha]_0$. $\mathcal{B}$ then simulates the oracles as follows.

- *Random Oracles* H_i: For query input H_0("GENERATOR-g"), $\mathcal{B}$ returns $[g]_0$. For query input H_l("GENERATOR-h"), $\mathcal{B}$ returns $[h]_l$. For other queries, $\mathcal{B}$ randomly picks $[\lambda]_0 \in_R [\mathbb{G}]_0$, sets $[a]_i = \mathcal{E}([\lambda]_0, [1]_i)$ and returns $[a]_i$.
- *Joining Oracle* $\mathcal{JO}$: $\mathcal{B}$ samples $[x']_0, [y']_0 \in_R [\mathbb{G}]_0$, lets $[Z']_l = \mathcal{E}([g\,x']_0, [1]_l) + \mathcal{E}([h]_l, [y']_0)$, stores the tuple $([Z']_l, [x']_0, [y']_0)$, and outputs $[Z']_l$.
- *Corruption Oracle* $\mathcal{CO}$: On input a public key *pk* which is an output from $\mathcal{JO}$, $\mathcal{B}$ outputs the corresponding private key.
- *Signing Oracle* $\mathcal{SO}$: On input a signing query for event *event*, a set of public keys $\boldsymbol{pk}_t = \{[Z_1]_l, \ldots, [Z_n]_l\}$, the public key for the signer $[Z_\pi]_l$, where $\pi \in [1, n]$, and a message M and time t, $\mathcal{B}$ simulates as follows:
  - If no query for $H_{l-t}(t||event)$ has been made yet, carry out the H-query on input $t||event$ as described above. Set $[d]_{l-t}$ to $H_{l-t}(t||event)$.

[7] While it is possible for two different private keys to have the same public key, violating the assertion above, this would also break the Pedersen commitments and reveal the relationship between g and h. It is also possible for the hash function to collide. These events are assumed of negligible probability.

- Since $\mathcal{B}$ knows the private key for all π, it constructs σ as in the scheme.
- $\mathcal{B}$ returns the signature $\sigma = ([f]_l, [\tilde{x}]_t, [\tilde{y}]_0, [c_1]_0, \ldots, [c_n]_0)$. $\mathcal{A}$ cannot distinguish $\mathcal{B}$'s simulation from real life, as they have identical distributions.

For one successful simulation, suppose the forgery given by $\mathcal{A}$ on some event *event*, time t and set of public keys $\boldsymbol{pk}_t''$, is $\sigma^1 = ([f^1]_l, [\tilde{x}^1]_t, [\tilde{y}^1]_0, [c_1^1]_0, \ldots, [c_{n'}^1]_0)$. In the random oracle model, $\mathcal{A}$ must have made a query $H_{l-t}(t||event)$, denoted by $[d]_{l-t}$, and a query $H_0(\boldsymbol{pk}_t||event||[f]_l||M||[K]_l||[K']_l||t)$ where:

$$[K]_l = \mathcal{E}([g]_{l-t}, [\tilde{x}^1]_t) + \mathcal{E}([h]_l, [\tilde{y}^1]_0) + \sum\nolimits_{i=1}^{n} \mathcal{E}([Z_i]_l, [c_i^1]_0) \text{ and}$$

$$[K']_l = \mathcal{E}([d]_{l-t}, [\tilde{x}^1]_t) + \mathcal{E}([f^1]_l, \sum\nolimits_{i=1}^{n} [c_i^1]_0)$$

After rewinding the execution and answering the random-oracle query differently, if successful, we get another signature $\sigma^2 = ([f^1]_l, [\tilde{x}^2]_t, [\tilde{y}^2]_0, [c_1^2]_0, \ldots, [c_{n'}^2]_0)$. Note that $[f^1]_l, [K]_l, [K']_l$ and $\boldsymbol{pk}_t$ must be the same, since we rewind only to the point of the H_0 query. In the rewound execution we force a change in the H_0 oracle output to the query which determines $\sum_{i=1}^{n}[c_i]$; but for $i = [1,2]$, the following equation holds because the signatures accept for the same $[K']_l$:

$$[d * \tilde{x}^1 + f * \sum_{i=1}^{n} c_i^1]_l = [d * \tilde{x}^2 + f * \sum_{i=1}^{n} c_i^2]_l$$

Therefore we have $[\tilde{x}^1] \neq [\tilde{x}^2]$ and find a response $[x]_t$ to the EDP challenge as:

$$[x]_t = \frac{[g\tilde{x}^1 + \sum_{i=1}^{n} gx_i c_i^1]_t - [g\tilde{x}^2 + \sum_{i=1}^{n} gx_i c_i^2]_t}{[\tilde{y}^2 - \tilde{y}^1 - \sum_{i=1}^{n} y_i(c_i^1 - c_i^2)]_0}$$

Note that the above works when the $[\tilde{x}]_t$ and $[\tilde{y}]_0$ encode a tuple $([x']_t, [y']_0) \neq ([x]_t, [y]_0)$, i.e., not one which we already knew. By unconditional anonymity (see Theorem 13), this will be true except with probability $1/n$. By the forking lemma [23], the chance of each successful rewind simulation is at least $\xi/4$, where ξ is the probability that $\mathcal{A}$ successfully forges a signature. Hence the probability that for a given adversary $\mathcal{A}$, we can extract $[x]_t$ is at least $\frac{\xi}{4}\frac{n-1}{n}$. □

The next few proofs (other than the forward security ones) are similar to those of Liu et al. [18] in structure and efficiency. We give them for completeness.

Theorem 13. *The FS-LRS scheme is unconditionally anonymous.*

Proof. The proof of unconditional anonymity is largely unchanged from [18], since both schemes rely on Pederson commitments. For each $\mathcal{JO}$ query, a value $[Z]_l = \mathcal{E}([g]_0, [x]_0) + \mathcal{E}([h]_l, [y]_0)$ is returned for some random pair $([x]_0, [y]_0)$. The challenge signature is created from the key of a random user in the ring.

In what follows, we are going to show that the advantage of the adversary is information-theoretically zero. The proof is divided into three parts. First, we show that given a signature $\sigma = ([f]_l, [\tilde{x}]_t, [\tilde{y}]_0, [c_1]_0, \ldots, [c_\pi]_0)$ for a ring $([Z_1]_l, \ldots, [Z_n]_l)$ on message M, event *event* and time t, there exists a matching private key $([x_\pi]_t, [y_\pi]_0)$ for each possible public key $[Z_\pi]_l$, for any $\pi \in \{1, \ldots, n\}$, that can construct the linking tag $[f]_l$. That is, $[f]_l = \mathcal{E}(H_{l-t}(t||event), [x_\pi]_t) = \mathcal{E}([d]_{l-t}, [x_\pi]_t)$, where $[d]_{l-t} = H_{l-t}(t||event)$. Second, given such a private key $([x_\pi]_t, [y_\pi]_0)$ there exists a tuple $([r_{x_\pi}]_t, [r_{y_\pi}]_0)$ so that σ matches $([x_\pi]_t, [y_\pi]_0)$ using randomness $([r_{x_\pi}]_t, [r_{y_\pi}]_0)$. Finally, for any $\pi \in \{1, \ldots, n\}$, the distribution of the tuple $([x_\pi]_t, [y_\pi]_0, [r_{x_\pi}]_t, [r_{y_\pi}]_0)$ defined in parts one and two is identical.

Therefore, in the view of the adversary, the signature σ is independent to the value π, the index of the actual signer. We conclude that even an unbounded adversary cannot guess the value of π better than at random. In details:

1. *Part I.* Let x, y be so that $[f]_l = \mathcal{E}([d]_{l-t}, [x]_t)$ and $[g]_0 = \mathcal{E}([h]_0, [y]_0)$. Let $[Z_i]_l = \mathcal{E}([h]_0, [z_i]_l)$ for $i = 1$ to n. For each $\pi \in \{1, \ldots, n\}$, consider the values

$$[x_\pi]_t = [x]_t, \qquad \text{and} \qquad [y_\pi]_t = [z_\pi]_t - \mathcal{E}([x_\pi]_t, [y]_0)$$

   Obviously, $([x_\pi]_t, [y_\pi]_t)$ is a private key corresponding to the public key $[Z_\pi]_l$ (since $[Z_\pi]_l = \mathcal{E}([h]_{l-t}, [z_\pi]_t) = \mathcal{E}([h]_{l-t}, \mathcal{E}([x_\pi]_t, [y]_0) + [y_\pi]_t) = \mathcal{E}([g]_{l-t}, [x_\pi]_t) + \mathcal{E}([h]_{l-t}, [y_\pi]_t))$ and $[f]_l = \mathcal{E}([d]_{l-t}, [x]_t]) = \mathcal{E}([d]_{l-t}, [x_\pi]_t)$.
2. *Part II.* For each possible $([x_\pi]_t, [y_\pi]_t)$ defined in Part I, consider the values

$$[r_{x_\pi}]_t := [\tilde{x}]_t + \mathcal{E}([c_\pi]_0, [x_\pi]_t), \qquad \text{and} \qquad [r_{y_\pi}]_t := [\tilde{y}]_t + \mathcal{E}([c_\pi]_0, [y_\pi]_t),$$

   It can be seen that σ can be created by the private key $([x_\pi]_t, [y_\pi]_t)$ using the randomness $([r_{x_\pi}]_t, [y_{y_\pi}]_t)$, for any $\pi \in \{1, \ldots, n\}$.
3. *Part III.* The distribution of $([x_\pi]_t, [y_\pi]_t, [r_{x_\pi}]_t, [y_{y_\pi}]_t)$ for each possible π is identical to that of a signature created by a signer with public key $[Z_\pi]_l$.

In other words, the signatures σ can be created by any signer equipped with private key $([x_\pi]_t, [y_\pi]_t)$ for any $\pi \in \{1, \ldots, n\}$ using randomness $([r_{x_\pi}]_t, [y_{y_\pi}]_t)$. Even if the unbounded adversary can compute $([x_\pi]_t, [y_\pi]_t, [r_{x_\pi}]_t, [y_{y_\pi}]_t)$ for all $\pi \in [n]$, it cannot guess, amongst the n possible choices, who the signer is.

We are using the fact that a public key in our construction corresponds to multiple secret keys. For each public key in the ring of possible signers, there exists a unique corresponding private key that fits the given linking tag. □

Theorem 14. *The FS-LRS scheme is linkable in the ROM, if the EDP is hard.*

Proof. If $\mathcal{A}$ can produce two valid and unlinked signatures from just one private key, we can use this to successfully break EDP. We use the same setting as in the proof in Theorem 12, with the exception that the adversary is given a pair (x, y) valid for $[Z] \in \boldsymbol{pk}_t$ as an output of the corruption oracle.

If given a pair of $\sigma^i = ([f^i]_l, [\tilde{x}^i]_t, [\tilde{y}^i]_0, [c_1^i]_0, \ldots, [c_{n'}^i]_0)$ on an event *event*, time t and a set of public keys $\boldsymbol{pk}_t^{''}$, then, in the random-oracle model, $\mathcal{A}$ must have made two queries $H_{l-t}^i(t||event)$ which are denoted by $[d^i]_{l-t}$, and two queries $H_0^i(\boldsymbol{pk}_t||event||[f^i]_l||M||[K^i]_l||[K'^i]_l||t)$ where

$$[K]_l = \mathcal{E}([g]_{l-t}, [\tilde{x}^1]_t) + \mathcal{E}([h]_l, [\tilde{y}^1]_0) + \sum\nolimits_{i=1}^{n} \mathcal{E}([Z_i]_l, [c_i^1]_0) \text{ and}$$
$$[K']_l = \mathcal{E}([d]_{l-t}, [\tilde{x}^1]_t) + \mathcal{E}([f^1]_l, \sum\nolimits_{i=1}^{n} [c_i^1]_0)$$

Since $\sigma^1 \neq \sigma^2$ and they are unlinked, by definition of linkability we have $[f^1]_l \neq [f^2]_l$. Since, by definition of the game, the σ^i are both valid for the same time and event, $[d^1]_{l-t} = H_{l-t}(t||event) = [d^2]_{l-t}$. Recall that $[f^i]_l = [d^1 x^i]_l$, where we have shown $[d^1]_{l-t} = [d^2]_{l-t}$. Hence, $[x^1]_t \neq [x^2]_t$. Therefore at most one $[f]_l$, and hence σ^i, encodes the pair (x, y) which we gave to the adversary. We use the method from Theorem 12 to extract $[x]_t$ from the other signature σ'.

The probability that, for a given $\mathcal{A}$, we can extract $[x]_l$ is at least $\frac{\xi}{4}\frac{n-1}{n}$. □

Theorem 15. *The FS-LRS is non-slanderable in the ROM, if EDP is hard.*

Proof. We use the setting of Theorem 12. $\mathcal{A}$ can query any oracle other than to submit a chosen public key pk_π to $\mathcal{CO}$. It then gives $\mathcal{B}$: the key pk_π, a list of public keys $\boldsymbol{pk}_t \ni pk_\pi$ (w.l.o.g., we have $|\boldsymbol{pk}_t| = n$), a message M, a description *event*, and a time t. In return, $\mathcal{B}$ generates a signature $\sigma([f]_l, .)$ using the standard method for the joining oracle, and gives it back to $\mathcal{A}$. Since we choose $[f]_l = [dx]_l$ at random for a fixed d we have implicitly defined $[x]_t$ at random. $\mathcal{A}$ continues to query various oracles, expect that it is not allowed to submit pk_π to $\mathcal{CO}$.

Suppose $\mathcal{A}$ produces another valid signature $\sigma^* = ([f']_l, .)$ that was not an output from $\mathcal{SO}$ but is linkable to σ. Since they are linkable, we have $[f']_l = [f]_l$ and hence $\frac{[x]_l}{[d]_0} = \frac{[x]_l}{[d]_0}$. Recall that, by definition of the game, $\sigma^* \neq \sigma'$ which implies that $[\tilde{x}^*] \neq [\tilde{x}]'$ and hence $[\tilde{y}^*] \neq [\tilde{y}']$. We then extract $[x]_t$ from σ^* as outlined in Theorem 12.

The probability that, for a given adversary $\mathcal{A}$, we can extract $[x]_l$ is $\frac{\xi}{4}\frac{n-1}{n}$. □

Theorem 16. *The FS-LRS scheme is forward-secure against forgeries in the random-oracle model, if EDP is hard.*

Proof. We show that the ability of the adversary to make corruption queries at times later than t does not allow it to calculate the private key or forge signatures at time t, without breaking $(\kappa = t+1, l)$-EDP, and hence the system achieves forward security for $\kappa \in [1, l]$. In this proof we start by guessing the break point t for which the adversary's forgery σ will be valid.

Given an (κ, l)-EDP instance $([\alpha]_0, [\alpha * x]_l, [x]_\kappa)$, $\mathcal{B}$ is asked to output some $[x]_j$ where $j < \kappa$. $\mathcal{B}$ picks $[h]_0 \in_R [\mathbb{G}]_0$ and sets $[h]_l = \mathcal{E}([h]_0, [1]_l)$. $\mathcal{B}$ also chooses $[y]_0 \in_R [\mathbb{G}]_0$ and sets $[Z]_l = [\alpha * x]_l + (\mathcal{E}([h]_l, [y]_0)$. $\mathcal{B}$ simulates the oracles thusly:

- *Random Oracles* H_i: For query input H_0("GENERATOR-g"), $\mathcal{B}$ returns $[\alpha]_0$. For query input H_l("GENERATOR-h"), $\mathcal{B}$ returns $[h]_l$. For other queries, $\mathcal{B}$ randomly picks $[\lambda]_0 \in_R [\mathbb{G}]_0$, sets $[a]_i = \mathcal{E}([\lambda]_0, [1]_i)$ and returns $[a]_i$.

- *Joining Oracle* $\mathcal{JO}$: Assume $\mathcal{A}$ can only query $\mathcal{JO}$ for a maximum n' times, where $n' = n+1$. W.l.o.g., $(1,\ldots,n)$ will be the indices for which $\mathcal{B}$ knows the private keys, and n' the challenge index. For the first n indices, $\mathcal{B}$ generates the public/private key pair as in the scheme. For index n', it sets the public key to $[Z]_l$. Upon the jth query, $\mathcal{B}$ returns the matching public key.
- *Corruption Oracle* $\mathcal{CO}$: On input a public key pk_i obtained from $\mathcal{JO}$, and a time t, $\mathcal{B}$ checks whether it is corresponding to $[1,n]$, if yes, then $\mathcal{B}$ returns the private key. Otherwise, if time $t \geq \kappa$, $\mathcal{B}$ returns $sk_i = ([x_i]_t, [y_i]_t)$ at time t, otherwise $\mathcal{B}$ halts.
- *Signing Oracle* $\mathcal{SO}$: On input a signing query for event *event*, a set of public key $\boldsymbol{pk}_t = \{[Z_1]_l, \ldots, [Z_n]_l\}$, the public key for the signer $[Z_\pi]_l$, where $\pi \in [1,n]$, and a message M, and time t, $\mathcal{B}$ simulates as follows:
  - If the query of $H_{l-t}(t||event)$ has not been made, carry out the H-query of $t||event$ as described above. Set $[d]_{l-t}$ to $H_{l-t}(t||event)$. Note that $\mathcal{B}$ knows the $[\lambda]_0$ that corresponds to $[d]_{l-t}$.
  - If $[Z_\pi]_l$ is not corresponding to n', $\mathcal{B}$ knows the private key and computes the signature according to the algorithm. Otherwise, B sets $[f]_l = [dx]_l$.
  - $\mathcal{B}$ randomly chooses $[\tilde{x}]_t \in_R [\mathbb{G}]_t$ and $[c_i]_0, [\tilde{y}]_0 \in_R [\mathbb{G}]_0$ for all $i \in [1,n]$ and sets the H_0 oracle output of

$$H_0\Big(\boldsymbol{pk}_t||event||[f]_l||M||\mathcal{E}([g]_{l-t},[\tilde{x}]_t) + \mathcal{E}([h]_{l-t},[\tilde{y}]_t) + \sum_{i=1}^{n}\mathcal{E}([Z_i]_l,[c_i]_0)||\mathcal{E}([d]_{l-t},[\tilde{x}]_t) + \mathcal{E}([f]_l,\sum_{i=1}^{n}c_i)||t\Big)$$

  - $\mathcal{B}$ returns the signature $\sigma = ([f]_l, [\tilde{x}]_t, [\tilde{y}]_t, [c_1]_0, \ldots, [c_n]_0)$. $\mathcal{A}$ cannot distinguish between $\mathcal{B}$'s simulation and real life.

For one successful simulation, suppose the forgery returned by $\mathcal{A}$, on an event *event*, time t and a set of public keys $\boldsymbol{pk}_t''$, is $\sigma^1 = ([f^1]_l, [\tilde{x}^1]_t, [\tilde{y}^1]_0, [c_1^1]_0, \ldots, [c_{n'}^1]_0)$. In the random-oracle model, $\mathcal{A}$ must have queried $H_{l-t}(t||event)$, denoted by $[d]_{l-t}$, and queried $H_0(\boldsymbol{pk}''||event||[f]_l||M||[K]_l||[K']_l||t)$ where

$$[K]_l = \mathcal{E}([g]_{l-t},[\tilde{x}^1]_t) + \mathcal{E}([h]_l,[\tilde{y}^1]_0) + \textstyle\sum_{i=1}^{n}\mathcal{E}([Z_i]_l,[c_i^1]_0) \text{ and}$$
$$[K']_l = \mathcal{E}([d]_{l-t},[\tilde{x}^1]_t) + \mathcal{E}([f^1]_l,\textstyle\sum_{i=1}^{n}[c_i^1]_0)$$

After a successful rewind we get another $\sigma^2 = ([f^1]_l, [\tilde{x}^2]_t, [\tilde{y}^2]_0, [c_1^2]_0, \cdots, [c_{n'}^2]_0)$. Note that $[f^1]_l$ and the $[K]_l, [K']_l$ must be the same since we rewind only to the point of lth query, and that in the rewind we forced a change in $H_0 = \sum_{i=1}^{n}[c_i]$. Recall that for $i = [1,2]$, by the definitions of $\tilde{x}, H$ and K':

$$[\tilde{x}^i]_t = [r_x^i]_t - [c_\pi^i x']_t = \frac{[K']_l}{[d]_0} - [x'H^i]_l$$

We now have two commitments to $[x']_l$ for a fixed $\frac{[K']_l}{[d]_0}$ which we know, and for different H^i which we also know. We can therefore calculate $[x']_t$ as follows:

$$\frac{[\tilde{x}^1]_t - [\tilde{x}^2]_t}{-[H^1]_0 + [H^2]_0} = \frac{\frac{[K']_l}{[d]_0} - [x'H^1]_l - \frac{[K']_l}{[d]_0} + [x'H^2]_l}{-[H^1]_0 + [H^2]_0}$$

We can find $\sum_{\kappa=1}^{n}[y_\kappa]_t$ as:

$$\sum_{\kappa=1}^{n}[y_\kappa]_t = \frac{([\tilde{y}^1]_0 + \frac{[\tilde{x}]_t}{[h]_0} + \frac{\sum_{\kappa=1}^{n}[gx_\kappa c_\kappa^1]_0}{[h]_0}) - ([\tilde{y}^2]_t + \frac{[\tilde{x}]_t}{[h]_0} + \frac{\sum_{\kappa=1}^{n}[gx_\kappa c_\kappa^2]_0}{[h]_0})}{-[H^1]_0 + [H^2]_0}$$

We can then calculate $[y']_t = \sum_{\kappa=1}^{n}[y_\kappa]_t - \sum_{\kappa=1;\kappa\neq\pi}^{n}[y_\kappa]_t$ since we know $[y]_\kappa$ for all but the target.

We now break the simulation into three cases:

Case 1 $\mathcal{E}([x]'_t, [1]_{\kappa-t}) = [x]_\kappa$, in this case $[x']_t$ is a valid answer to the *EDP* instance and we succeed.

Case 2 We have extracted from the adversary a pair $([x']_t, [y']_t)$ which is a valid solution to the challenge public key $(gx + hy)$ but not the pair $([x]_t, [y]_t)$ which we used to construct it. We now know $([x']_t, [y']_t, [y]_t)$ and wish to find the challenge answer $[x]_t$, which we calculate as $[x]_t = \frac{[gx']_t + [hy']_t - [hy]_t}{[g]_0}$. We then return $[x]_t$ and succeed.

Case 3 The adversary has returned a private key for a public key for which we already knew the private key. In this case we fail to complete the reduction.

By the forking lemma [23], the chance of each successful rewind simulation is at least $\xi/4$, where ξ is the probability that $\mathcal{A}$ successfully forges a signature. Hence, the probability that for a given adversary $\mathcal{A}$ we can extract $[x]_l$ is $\frac{1}{n} * \frac{1}{t} * \frac{\xi}{4} = \frac{\xi}{4nt}$, where n is the number of queries to $\mathcal{JO}$ and t is the number of time periods. □

Theorem 17. *The FS-LRS scheme is forward-secure anonymous in the random-oracle model, if MDDH is hard.*

Proof. We show that the ability of the adversary to make corruption queries at times later than t does not allow it to de-anonymise signatures at time t or earlier, without breaking (t,l-t+1,l)-MDDH, and hence the system achieves forward-secure anonymity. In this proof we start by guessing the break point t at which the adversary's will choose to be challenged.

Given an MDDH instance $([\alpha]_t, [\beta]_{l-t+1}, [\gamma]_l)$, $\mathcal{B}$ is asked to decide whether $[\gamma]_l = [\alpha\beta]_l$. $\mathcal{B}$ picks $[h]_0, [\alpha]_0 \in_R [\mathbb{G}]_0$ and sets $[h]_l = \mathcal{E}([h]_0, [1]_l)$. $\mathcal{B}$ simulates:

- *Random Oracles* H_i: For all queries except those outlined below, $\mathcal{B}$ randomly picks $[\lambda]_0 \in_R [\mathbb{G}]_0$, sets $[a]_i = \mathcal{E}([\lambda]_0, [1]_i)$ and returns $[a]_i$.
- *Joining Oracle* $\mathcal{JO}$: $\mathcal{B}$ generates a public key and private key pair by choosing $[x']_0, [y]_0 \in_R [\mathbb{G}]_0$ and setting $[Z]_l = [g]_0 + \mathcal{E}([x']_0, [\alpha]_t) + \mathcal{E}([h]_l, [y]_0)$.
- *Corruption Oracle* $\mathcal{CO}$: On input a public key pk_i obtained from $\mathcal{JO}$, and a time t', if time $t' \geq t$, $\mathcal{B}$ returns $sk_i = ([\alpha \times x'_i]_t, [y_i]_t)$ at time t; else $\mathcal{B}$ halts.
- *Signing Oracle* $\mathcal{SO}$: On input a signing query for event *event*, a set of public keys $\boldsymbol{pk}_t = \{[Z_1]_l, \ldots, [Z_n]_l\}$, the public key for the signer $[Z_\pi]_l$ where $\pi \in [1, n]$, a message M, and a time t, $\mathcal{B}$ simulates as follows:

- If the query of $H_{l-t}(t||event)$ has not been made, carry out the H-query of $t||event$ as described above. Set $[d]_{l-t}$ to $H_{l-t}(t||event)$. Note that $\mathcal{B}$ knows the $[\lambda]_0$ that corresponds to $[d]_{l-t}$. $\mathcal{B}$ sets $[f]_l = [d * \alpha * x'_\pi]_l$, which it can compute from the challenge $[\alpha]_t$.
- $\mathcal{B}$ randomly chooses $[\tilde{x}]_t \in_R [\mathbb{G}]_t$ and $[c_i]_0, [\tilde{y}]_0 \in_R [\mathbb{G}]_0$ for all $i \in [1, n]$ and sets the H_0 oracle output of

$$H_0\Big(\boldsymbol{pk}_t||event||[f]_l||M||\mathcal{E}([g]_{l-t}, [\tilde{x}]_t) + \mathcal{E}([h]_{l-t}, [\tilde{y}]_t) +$$

$$\textstyle\sum_{i=1}^{n} \mathcal{E}([Z_i]_l, [c_i]_0)||\mathcal{E}([d]_{l-t}, [\tilde{x}]_t) + \mathcal{E}([f]_l, \sum_{i=1}^{n} c_i)||t\Big)$$

- $\mathcal{B}$ returns the signature $\sigma = ([f]_l, [\tilde{x}]_t, [\tilde{y}]_t, [c_1]_0, \ldots, [c_n]_0)$. $\mathcal{A}$ cannot distinguish between $\mathcal{B}$'s simulation and real life.

At some point $\mathcal{A}$ requests to be challenged on $e, t', n, \boldsymbol{pk}'_t, M$ where $t' < t$. W.l.o.g. assume $t' = t - 1$. $\mathcal{B}$ sets $H_{l-t+1}(e||t) = [\beta]_{l-t+1}$, samples $i \in [n]$, sets $[f]_l = [\gamma x'_i]_l$, and then performs the remaining steps of the signing oracle as above. Notice that if $[\gamma]_l$ is equal to $[\alpha\beta]_l$ then this signature is normally formed; but if $[\gamma]_l$ is a random group element than the linking element is random, while the rest of the signature is independent of the signer. If $\mathcal{A}$ successfully guesses i then $\mathcal{B}$ guesses that $[\gamma] = [\alpha\beta]$, otherwise $\mathcal{B}$ guesses that $[\gamma]$ is random. □

7 Generalisations and Bilinear Maps

While the basic scheme can natively support $\mathcal{T}$ time periods given a multilinear linear map with a finite number of levels $l \in [\mathcal{T}, \infty)$, it is rather straightforward to combine multiple instances of the scheme to achieve a greater number of epochs without changing the multilinear map. Several combinations are possibles, to realise a total number of periods polynomial in the time and space complexity of the combination.

This observation is of particular interest for $l = 2$, the case of traditional 2-linear or bilinear maps such as the Weil and Tate pairings, which have been studied extensively and are generally accepted as being cryptographically secure (barring quantum attacks) *without* relying on unproven multilinear hardness assumptions. Details are omitted for lack of space.

References

1. Adida, B.: Helios: web-based open-audit voting. In: USENIX Security (2008)
2. Adida, B.: Helios v3 verification specs. Technical report, Helios Voting (2010)
3. Albrecht, M., Bai, S., Ducas, L.: A subfield lattice attack on overstretched NTRU assumptions. In: Robshaw, M., Katz, J. (eds.) CRYPTO 2016. LNCS, vol. 9814, pp. 153–178. Springer, Heidelberg (2016). https://doi.org/10.1007/978-3-662-53018-4_6
4. Barak, B., Goldreich, O., Impagliazzo, R., Rudich, S., Sahai, A., Vadhan, S.P., Yang, K.: On the (im)possibility of obfuscating programs. J. ACM **59**(2), 6 (2012)

5. Boneh, D., Silverberg, A.: Applications of multilinear forms to cryptography. Contemp. Math. **324**(1), 71–90 (2003)
6. Boneh, D., Wu, D.J., Zimmerman, J.: Immunizing multilinear maps against zeroizing attacks. IACR Cryptol. ePrint Archive **2014**, 930 (2014)
7. Chaum, D., van Heyst, E.: Group signatures. In: Davies, D.W. (ed.) EUROCRYPT 1991. LNCS, vol. 547, pp. 257–265. Springer, Heidelberg (1991). https://doi.org/10.1007/3-540-46416-6_22
8. Cheon, J.H., Han, K., Lee, C., Ryu, H., Stehlé, D.: Cryptanalysis of the multilinear map over the integers. In: Oswald, E., Fischlin, M. (eds.) EUROCRYPT 2015. LNCS, vol. 9056, pp. 3–12. Springer, Heidelberg (2015). https://doi.org/10.1007/978-3-662-46800-5_1
9. Cheon, J.H., Jeong, J., Lee, C.: An algorithm for NTRU problems and cryptanalysis of the GGH multilinear map without a low level encoding of zero. IACR Cryptol. ePrint Archive **19**, 255–266 (2016)
10. Coron, J.-S., Lepoint, T., Tibouchi, M.: Practical multilinear maps over the integers. In: Canetti, R., Garay, J.A. (eds.) CRYPTO 2013. LNCS, vol. 8042, pp. 476–493. Springer, Heidelberg (2013). https://doi.org/10.1007/978-3-642-40041-4_26
11. Cramer, R., Ducas, L., Peikert, C., Regev, O.: Recovering short generators of principal ideals in cyclotomic rings. In: Fischlin, M., Coron, J.-S. (eds.) EUROCRYPT 2016. LNCS, vol. 9666, pp. 559–585. Springer, Heidelberg (2016). https://doi.org/10.1007/978-3-662-49896-5_20
12. Demirel, D., Van De Graaf, J., Araújo, R.: Improving helios with everlasting privacy towards the public. In: Proceedings of eVOTE/Trustworthy Elections. USENIX (2012)
13. Fujisaki, E., Suzuki, K.: Traceable ring signature. In: Okamoto, T., Wang, X. (eds.) PKC 2007. LNCS, vol. 4450, pp. 181–200. Springer, Heidelberg (2007). https://doi.org/10.1007/978-3-540-71677-8_13
14. Garg, S., Gentry, C., Halevi, S.: Candidate multilinear maps from ideal lattices. In: Johansson, T., Nguyen, P.Q. (eds.) EUROCRYPT 2013. LNCS, vol. 7881, pp. 1–17. Springer, Heidelberg (2013). https://doi.org/10.1007/978-3-642-38348-9_1
15. Gentry, C., Gorbunov, S., Halevi, S.: Graph-induced multilinear maps from lattices. In: Dodis, Y., Nielsen, J.B. (eds.) TCC 2015. LNCS, vol. 9015, pp. 498–527. Springer, Heidelberg (2015). https://doi.org/10.1007/978-3-662-46497-7_20
16. Hu, Y., Jia, H.: Cryptanalysis of GGH map. In: Fischlin, M., Coron, J.-S. (eds.) EUROCRYPT 2016. LNCS, vol. 9665, pp. 537–565. Springer, Heidelberg (2016). https://doi.org/10.1007/978-3-662-49890-3_21
17. Langlois, A., Stehlé, D., Steinfeld, R.: GGHLite: more efficient multilinear maps from ideal lattices. In: Nguyen, P.Q., Oswald, E. (eds.) EUROCRYPT 2014. LNCS, vol. 8441, pp. 239–256. Springer, Heidelberg (2014). https://doi.org/10.1007/978-3-642-55220-5_14
18. Liu, J.K., Au, M.H., Susilo, W., Zhou, J.: Linkable ring signature with unconditional anonymity. IEEE Trans. Knowl. Data Eng. **26**(1), 157–165 (2014)
19. Liu, J.K., Wei, V.K., Wong, D.S.: Linkable spontaneous anonymous group signature for Ad Hoc groups. In: Wang, H., Pieprzyk, J., Varadharajan, V. (eds.) ACISP 2004. LNCS, vol. 3108, pp. 325–335. Springer, Heidelberg (2004). https://doi.org/10.1007/978-3-540-27800-9_28
20. Miles, E., Sahai, A., Zhandry, M.: Annihilation attacks for multilinear maps: cryptanalysis of indistinguishability obfuscation over GGH13. In: Robshaw, M., Katz, J. (eds.) CRYPTO 2016. LNCS, vol. 9815, pp. 629–658. Springer, Heidelberg (2016). https://doi.org/10.1007/978-3-662-53008-5_22

21. Paneth, O., Sahai, A.: On the equivalence of obfuscation and multilinear maps. IACR Cryptol. ePrint Archive **2015**, 791 (2015)
22. Pedersen, T.P.: Non-interactive and information-theoretic secure verifiable secret sharing. In: Feigenbaum, J. (ed.) CRYPTO 1991. LNCS, vol. 576, pp. 129–140. Springer, Heidelberg (1992). https://doi.org/10.1007/3-540-46766-1_9
23. Pointcheval, D., Stern, J.: Security proofs for signature schemes. In: Maurer, U. (ed.) EUROCRYPT 1996. LNCS, vol. 1070, pp. 387–398. Springer, Heidelberg (1996). https://doi.org/10.1007/3-540-68339-9_33
24. Rivest, R.L., Shamir, A., Tauman, Y.: How to leak a secret. In: Boyd, C. (ed.) ASIACRYPT 2001. LNCS, vol. 2248, pp. 552–565. Springer, Heidelberg (2001). https://doi.org/10.1007/3-540-45682-1_32
25. Tsoukalas, G., Papadimitriou, K., Louridas, P., Tsanakas, P.: From helios to zeus. USENIX J. Elect. Technol. Syst. (JETS) **1**, 1–17 (2013)
26. Zhandry, M.: Adaptively secure broadcast encryption with small system parameters. IACR Cryptol. ePrint Archive **2014**, 757 (2014)

Revocable Identity-Based Encryption from the Computational Diffie-Hellman Problem

Ziyuan Hu[1,2], Shengli Liu[1,2,3(✉)], Kefei Chen[3,4], and Joseph K. Liu[5,6]

[1] Department of Computer Science and Engineering, Shanghai Jiao Tong University, Shanghai 200240, China
{huziyuan1989,slliu}@sjtu.edu.cn

[2] State Key Laboratory of Cryptology, P.O. Box 5159, Beijing 100878, China

[3] Westone Cryptologic Research Center, Beijing 100070, China

[4] Department of Mathematics, Hangzhou Normal University, Hangzhou 310036, China
kfchen@hznu.edu.cn

[5] Faculty of Information Technology, Monash University, Melbourne, Australia
joseph.liu@monash.edu

[6] ATR Key Laboratory of National Defense Technology, College of Information Engineering, Shenzhen University, Shenzhen, China

Abstract. An Identity-based encryption (IBE) simplifies key management by taking users' identities as public keys. However, how to dynamically revoke users in an IBE scheme is not a trivial problem. To solve this problem, IBE scheme with revocation (namely revocable IBE scheme) has been proposed. Apart from those lattice-based IBE, most of the existing schemes are based on decisional assumptions over pairing-groups. In this paper, we propose a revocable IBE scheme based on a weaker assumption, namely Computational Diffie-Hellman (CDH) assumption over non-pairing groups. Our revocable IBE scheme was inspired by the IBE scheme proposed by Döttling and Garg in Crypto2017. Like Döttling and Garg's IBE scheme, the key authority maintains a complete binary tree where every user is assigned to a leaf node. To adapt such an IBE scheme to a revocable IBE, we update the nodes along the paths of the revoked users in each time slot. Upon this updating, all revoked users are forced to be equipped with new encryption keys but without decryption keys, thus they are unable to perform decryption any more. We proved that our revocable IBE is adaptive IND-ID-CPA secure in the standard model. Our scheme serves as the first revocable IBE scheme from the CDH assumption. Moreover, the size of updating key in each time slot is only related to the number of newly revoked users in the past time slot.

Keywords: Revocable identity-based encryption · CDH assumption

1 Introduction

The concept of Identity-Based Encryption (IBE) was proposed by Shamir [17] in 1984. In an IBE scheme, the public key of a user can simply be the identity id of

W. Susilo and G. Yang (Eds.): ACISP 2018, LNCS 10946, pp. 265–283, 2018.
https://doi.org/10.1007/978-3-319-93638-3_16

the user, like name, email address, etc. An IBE scheme considers three parties: key authority, sender and receiver. The key authority is in charge of generating secret key $\mathsf{sk}_{\mathsf{id}}$ for user id. A sender simply encrypts plaintexts under the receiver's identity id and the receiver uses his own secret key $\mathsf{sk}_{\mathsf{id}}$ for decryption. With IBE, there is no need for senders to ask for authenticated public keys from Public-Key Infrastructures, hence key management is greatly simplified.

Over the years, there have been many IBE schemes proposed from various assumptions in the standard model. Most of the assumptions are decisional ones, like the bilinear Diffie-Hellman assumption [7,13,20] over pairing-groups, or the decisional learning-with-errors (LWE) assumption from lattices [1,4,8]. Most recently, a breakthrough work was done by Döttling and Garg [6], who proposed the first IBE scheme based solely on the Computational Diffie-Hellman (CDH) assumption over groups free of pairings.

Though IBE enjoys the advantage of easy key management, how to revoke users in an IBE system is a non-trivial problem. It was Boneh and Franklin [3] who first proposed revocable IBE (RIBE) to solve the problem. Later, Boldyreva et al. [2] formalized the definition of selective-ID security and constructed a more efficient RIBE scheme based on a fuzzy IBE scheme [15]. Then Libert and Vergnaud proposed the first adaptive-ID secure revocable IBE scheme [11]. In [16], Seo and Emura strengthened the security model by introducing an additional important security notion, called Decryption Key Exposure Resistance (DKER). They also constructed a revocable IBE scheme in the strengthened model, and the security of this scheme is from the Decisional Bilinear Diffie-Hellman (DBDH) assumption. Since then, most of the revocable IBE schemes constructed from pairing groups achieved DKER. For example, in the strengthened security model, Lee et al. [9] constructed a revocable IBE scheme via subset difference methods to reduce the size of key updating based on the DBDH assumption, and Watanabe et al. [19] introduced a new revocable IBE with short public parameters based on both the Decisional Diffie-Hellman (DDH) assumption and the Augmented Decisional Diffie-Hellman (ADDH) assumption over pairing-friendly group. Furthermore, Park et al. [14] constructed a revocable IBE whose key update cost is only $O(1)$, but the scheme relied on multilinear maps. Without pairing, it seems difficult to achieve DKER. In [5], Chen et al. proposed the first selective-ID secure revocable IBE scheme from the LWE assumption over lattices in the traditional security model (without DKER). Later, Takayasu and Watanabe [18] designed a lattice-based revocable IBE with bounded DKER. In fact, revocable property is so important that it is studied not only in IBE but also in Identity-Based Proxy Re-encryption [10], Fine-Grained Encryption of Cloud Data [21,22] and Attribute-Based Encryption [12]. However bilinear pairings are essential techniques in these schemes [10,12,21,22].

Note that all the existing RIBE schemes are based on assumptions over pairing-friendly groups or the LWE assumption over lattices. On the other hand, Döttling and Garg's IBE scheme [6] is based on the CDH assumption over non-pairing group, but it does not consider user revocation. In this paper, we aim to fill the gap by designing RIBE from the CDH assumption without use of pairing.

1.1 Our Contributions

In this paper, we propose the first revocable IBE (RIBE) scheme based on the Computational Diffie-Hellman (CDH) assumption over groups free of pairings. The corner stone of this scheme is the IBE scheme proposed by Döttling and Garg [6]. Our RIBE scheme enjoys the following features.

1. **Weaker security assumption.** The security of our RIBE scheme can be reduced to the CDH assumption. Hence our scheme serves as the first RIBE scheme from the CDH assumption over non-pairing groups.
2. **Smaller size of key updating.** when a time slot begins, the key updating algorithm of our RIBE will issue updating keys whose size is only linear to the number of newly revoked users in the past time slot. In comparison, most of the existing RIBE schemes have to update keys whose number is related to the number of all revoked users across all the previous time slots.

Table 1. Comparison with RIBE schemes (in the standard model). Here n is the total number of users, r is the number of all revoked users and Δr is the number of newly revoked users the past time slot. DKER means decryption key exposure resistance.

IBE	Security assumption	Pairing free	Security model	Key updating size	DKER
[5]	LWE	✓	Selective-IND-ID-CPA	$O(r\log(n/r))$	×
[18]	LWE	✓	Selective-IND-ID-CPA	$O(r\log(n/r))$	Bounded
[2]	DBDH	×	Selective-IND-ID-CPA	$O(r\log(n/r))$	×
[11]	DBDH	×	Adaptive-IND-ID-CPA	$O(r\log(n/r))$	×
[16]	DBDH	×	Adaptive-IND-ID-CPA	$O(r\log(n/r))$	✓
[9]	DBDH	×	Adaptive-IND-ID-CPA	$O(r)$	✓
[19]	DDH and ADDH	×	Adaptive-IND-ID-CPA	$O(r\log(n/r))$	✓
[14]	Multilinear	×	Selective-IND-ID-CPA	$O(1)$	✓
Ours	CDH	✓	Adaptive-IND-ID-CPA	$O(\Delta r(\log n - \log(\Delta r)))$	×

In Table 1, we compare our RIBE scheme with some existing RIBE schemes.

Remark 1. Döttling and Garg's IBE makes use of garbled circuits to implement the underlying cryptographic primitives. Hence it is prohibitive in terms of efficiency. Our RIBE inherits their idea, hence the efficiency of our RIBE scheme is also incomparable to the RIBE schemes from bilinear maps. However, since no RIBE scheme is available from the CDH assumption over non-pairing groups, our scheme serves as a theoretical exploration in the field of RIBE.

Remark 2. As noted before, achieving DKER seems technically difficult without pairing. Our scheme cannot achieve decryption key exposure resistance either. We leave it as an open question how to construct a revocable IBE scheme with DKER from the CDH assumption over non-pairing groups.

1.2 Paper Organization

In Sect. 2, we collect notations and some basic definitions used in the paper and present the framework. We illustrate our idea of RIBE in Sect. 3. In Sect. 4, we construct a revocable IBE scheme based on the computational Diffie-Hellman assumption and present the correctness and security analysis of the scheme. In Sect. 5, we show the complexity analysis of our scheme.

2 Preliminaries

2.1 Notations

The security parameter is λ. "PPT" abbreviates "probabilistic polynomial-time". We denote by $[n]$ the set $\{1, \cdots, n\}$, $[a, b]$ the set $\{a, \cdots b\}$, $\{0,1\}^*$ a bit-string of arbitrary length, $\{0,1\}^{\leq \ell}$ a bit-string of length at most ℓ, ε an empty string, $|v|$ the length of a bit-string v ($|\varepsilon| = 0$), $x||y$ the concatenation of two bit-strings x and y, x_i denotes the i-th bit of x, $x \xleftarrow{\$} \mathcal{S}$ the process of sampling the element x from the set $\mathcal{S}$ uniformly at random, and $a \leftarrow \mathcal{X}$ the process of sampling the element a over the distribution $\mathcal{X}$. By $a \leftarrow f(\cdot)$ we mean that a is the output of a function f. A function $\mathsf{negl} : \mathbb{N} \rightarrow \mathbb{R}$ is negligible if for any polynomial $p(\lambda)$ it holds that $\mathsf{negl}(\lambda) < 1/p(\lambda)$ for all sufficiently large $\lambda \in \mathbb{N}$.

2.2 Pseudorandom Functions

Let PRF: $\mathcal{K} \times \mathcal{X} \rightarrow \mathcal{Y}$ be an efficiently computable function. For an adversary $\mathcal{A}$, define its advantage function as

$$\mathrm{Adv}_{\mathcal{A}}^{\mathrm{PRF}}(1^\lambda) := |\Pr[b = 1 \,|k \xleftarrow{\$} \mathcal{K}; b \leftarrow \mathcal{A}^{\mathsf{PRF}(k,\cdot)}] - \Pr[b = 1 \mid b \leftarrow \mathcal{A}^{\mathsf{RF}(\cdot)}]|,$$

where $\mathsf{RF} : \mathcal{X} \rightarrow \mathcal{Y}$ is a truly random function. PRF is a pseudorandom function (PRF) if the above advantage function $\mathrm{Adv}_{\mathcal{A}}^{\mathrm{PRF}}(1^\lambda)$ is negligible for any PPT $\mathcal{A}$.

2.3 Revocable Identity-Based Encryption

A revocable IBE (RIBE) consists of seven PPT algorithms RIBE = (RIBE.Setup, RIBE.KG, RIBE.KU, RIBE.KU, RIBE.Enc, RIBE.Enc, RIBE.R). Let $\mathcal{M}$ denote the message space, $\mathcal{ID}$ the identity space and $\mathcal{T}$ the space of time slots.

- **Setup:** The setup algorithm RIBE.Setup is run by the key authority. The input of the algorithm is a security parameter λ and a maximal number of users N. The output of this algorithm consists of a pair of key $(\mathsf{mpk}, \mathsf{msk})$, an initial state st=(KL, PL, RL,KU), where KL is the key list, PL is the list of public information, RL is the list of revoked users and KU is the update key list. In formula, $(\mathsf{mpk}, \mathsf{msk}, \mathsf{st}) \leftarrow \mathsf{RIBE.Setup}(1^\lambda, N)$.

- **Private Key Generation**: This algorithm $\mathsf{RIBE.KG}$ is run by the key authority which takes as input the key pair $(\mathsf{mpk}, \mathsf{msk})$, an identity id and the state st. The output of this algorithm is a private key $\mathsf{sk_{id}}$ and an updated state st'. In formula, $(\mathsf{sk_{id}}, \mathsf{st}') \leftarrow \mathsf{RIBE.KG}(\mathsf{mpk}, \mathsf{msk}, \mathsf{id}, \mathsf{st})$.
- **Key Update Generation**: This algorithm $\mathsf{RIBE.KU}$ is run by the authority. Given the key pair $(\mathsf{mpk}, \mathsf{msk})$, an update time t, and a state st, this algorithm updates the update key list KU and the the list of public information PL. In formula, $\mathsf{st}' \leftarrow \mathsf{RIBE.KU}(\mathsf{mpk}, \mathsf{msk}, \mathsf{t}, \mathsf{st})$.
- **Decryption key generation**: This algorithm $\mathsf{RIBE.DK}$ is run by the receiver. Given the master public key mpk, a private key $\mathsf{sk_{id}}$, the update key list KU and the time slot t, this algorithm outputs a decryption key $\mathsf{sk_{id}^{(t)}}$ for time slot t. In formula, $\mathsf{sk_{id}^{(t)}} \leftarrow \mathsf{RIBE.DK}(\mathsf{mpk}, \mathsf{sk_{id}}, \mathsf{KU}, \mathsf{t})$.
- **Encryption**: This algorithm $\mathsf{RIBE.Enc}$ is run by the sender. Given the public key mpk, a public list PL, an identity id, a time slot t and a message m, this algorithm outputs a ciphertext ct. In formula, $\mathsf{ct} \leftarrow \mathsf{RIBE.Enc}(\mathsf{mpk}, \mathsf{id}, \mathsf{t}, m, \mathsf{PL})$.
- **Decryption**: This algorithm $\mathsf{RIBE.Enc}$ is run by the receiver. The algorithm takes as input the master public key mpk, the decryption key $\mathsf{sk_{id}^{(t)}}$ and the ciphertext ct, and outputs a message m or a failure symbol $\perp$. In formula, $m/\perp \leftarrow \mathsf{RIBE.Dec}(\mathsf{mpk}, \mathsf{sk_{id}^{(t)}}, \mathsf{ct})$.
- **Revocation**: This algorithm $\mathsf{RIBE.R}$ is run by the key authority. Given a revoked identity id and the time slot t during which id is revoked and a state $\mathsf{st} = (\mathsf{KL}, \mathsf{PL}, \mathsf{RL}, \mathsf{KU})$, this algorithm updates the revocation list RL with $\mathsf{RL} \leftarrow \mathsf{RL} \cup \{(\mathsf{id}, \mathsf{t})\}$. It outputs a new state $\mathsf{st}' = (\mathsf{KL}, \mathsf{PL}, \mathsf{RL}, \mathsf{KU})$.

Correctness. For all $(\mathsf{mpk}, \mathsf{msk}, \mathsf{st}) \leftarrow \mathsf{RIBE.Setup}(1^\lambda, N)$, all $m \in \mathcal{M}$, all identity $\mathsf{id} \in \mathcal{ID}$, all time slot $\mathsf{t} \in \mathcal{T}$, and revocation list RL, for all $(\mathsf{sk_{id}}, \mathsf{st}') \leftarrow \mathsf{RIBE.KG}(\mathsf{msk}, \mathsf{id}, \mathsf{st})$, $\mathsf{st}'' \leftarrow \mathsf{RIBE.KU}(\mathsf{msk}, \mathsf{t}, \mathsf{st})$, and $\mathsf{sk_{id}^{(t)}} \leftarrow \mathsf{RIBE.DK}(\mathsf{mpk}, \mathsf{sk_{id}}, \mathsf{KU}, \mathsf{t})$, we have $\mathsf{RIBE.Dec}(\mathsf{mpk}, \mathsf{sk_{id}^{(t)}}, \mathsf{RIBE.Enc}(\mathsf{mpk}, \mathsf{id}, \mathsf{t}, m, \mathsf{PL})) = m$ if $(\mathsf{id}, \mathsf{t}) \notin \mathsf{RL}$(i.e., id is not revoked at time t) and $\mathsf{PL} \in \mathsf{st}''$.

Now we explain how a revocable IBE system works. To setup the system, the key authority invokes $\mathsf{RIBE.Setup}$ to generate master public key mpk, master secret key msk and the state st. Then it publishes the public key mpk. When a user registers in the system with identity id, the key authority invokes $\mathsf{RIBE.KG}(\mathsf{msk}, \mathsf{id}, \mathsf{st})$ to generate the private key $\mathsf{sk_{id}}$ for user id. If a user id needs to be revoked during time slot t, the key authority invokes $\mathsf{RIBE.R}(\mathsf{id}, \mathsf{t}, \mathsf{st})$. Next it updates the state st. At the beginning of each time slot t, the key authority might invoke $\mathsf{RIBE.KU}(\mathsf{msk}, \mathsf{t}, \mathsf{st})$ to update keys by updating set KU. Then it publishes some information about the updated set KU. Meanwhile it may also publishes some public information PL. During time slot t, when a user wants to send a message m to another user id, he/she invokes $\mathsf{RIBE.Enc}(\mathsf{mpk}, \mathsf{id}, \mathsf{t}, m, \mathsf{PL})$ to encrypt m to obtain the ciphertext ct, then sends $(\mathsf{t}, \mathsf{ct})$ to user id. To decrypt a ciphertext ct encrypted at time t, the receiver id first invokes $\mathsf{RIBE.DK}(\mathsf{mpk}, \mathsf{sk_{id}}, \mathsf{KU}, \mathsf{t})$ to generate its own decryption key $\mathsf{sk_{id}^{(t)}}$ of time t. The receiver id invokes $\mathsf{RIBE.Dec}(\mathsf{mpk}, \mathsf{sk_{id}^{(t)}}, \mathsf{ct})$ to decrypt the ciphertext and recover the plaintext.

Remark. In the definition of our RIBE, KL is the key list which stores the essential information used to generate the update key. PL is a public information list which is used in the encryption algorithm. In the traditional definition of RIBE in other works, no PL is defined. However, in our construction, PL will serves as an essential input to the encryption algorithm and that is the reason why we define it. Nevertheless, our definition can be regarded as a general one, while the traditional definition of RIBE can be seen as a special case of $\mathsf{PL} = \emptyset$.

Security. Now we formalize the security of a revocable IBE. We first consider three oracles: private key generation oracle $\mathrm{KG}(\cdot)$, key update oracle KU and revocation oracle $\mathrm{RVK}(\cdot,\cdot)$ which are shown in Table 2. The security of IND-ID-CPA defines as follows.

Table 2. Three oracles that the adversary can query.

$\mathrm{KG}(\mathsf{id})$: $(\mathsf{sk}_{\mathsf{id}}, \mathsf{st}') \leftarrow \mathsf{RIBE.KG}(\mathsf{msk}, \mathsf{id}, \mathsf{st})$ Output $\mathsf{sk}_{\mathsf{id}}$.	KU : $\mathsf{st}' \leftarrow \mathsf{RIBE.KU}(\mathsf{msk}, \mathsf{t}, \mathsf{st})$ $\mathsf{st} := \mathsf{st}'$. Parse $\mathsf{st} = (\mathsf{KL}, \mathsf{PL}, \mathsf{RL}, \mathsf{KU})$ Output $(\mathsf{KU}, \mathsf{PL})$.
$\mathrm{RVK}(\mathsf{id}, \mathsf{t})$: $\mathsf{st}' \leftarrow \mathsf{RIBE.R}(\mathsf{id}, \mathsf{t}, \mathsf{st})$ $\mathsf{st}' := (\mathsf{KL}, \mathsf{PL}, \mathsf{RL}, \mathsf{KU})$ Output RL.	

Definition 1. *Let $\mathsf{RIBE} = (\mathsf{RIBE.Setup}, \mathsf{RIBE.KG}, \mathsf{RIBE.KU}, \mathsf{RIBE.DK}, \mathsf{RIBE.Enc}, \mathsf{RIBE.Dec}, \mathsf{RIBE.R})$ be a revocable IBE scheme. Below describes an experiment between a challenger $\mathcal{C}$ and a PPT adversary $\mathcal{A}$.*

$\boldsymbol{EXP}_{\mathcal{A}}^{IND\text{-}ID\text{-}CPA}(\lambda)$:
$(mpk, msk, st) \leftarrow RIBE.Setup(1^{\lambda}, 1^{n})$;
Parse $st = (KL, PL, RL, KU)$;
$(M_0, M_1, id^*, t^*, \overline{st_{\mathcal{A}}}) \leftarrow \mathcal{A}^{\mathrm{KG}(\cdot),\mathrm{KU},\mathrm{RVK}(\cdot,\cdot)}(mpk)$;
$\theta \xleftarrow{\$} \{0,1\}$;
$ct^* \leftarrow RIBE.Enc(mpk, id^*, t^*, M_\theta, PL)$
$\theta' \leftarrow \mathcal{A}^{\mathrm{KG}(\cdot),\mathrm{KU},\mathrm{RVK}(\cdot,\cdot)}(ct^*, \overline{st_{\mathcal{A}}})$
If $\theta = \theta'$ *Return* 1; *If* $\theta \neq \theta'$ *Return* 0.

The experiment has the following requirements for $\mathcal{A}$.

- *The two plaintexts submitted by $\mathcal{A}$ have the same length, i.e., $|M_0| = |M_1|$.*
- *The time slot t submitted to* KU *and* $\mathrm{RVK}(\cdot,\cdot)$ *by $\mathcal{A}$ is in ascending order.*
- *If the challenger has published* KU *at time t, then it is not allowed to query oracle* $\mathrm{RVK}(\cdot, t')$ *with $t' < t$.*
- *If $\mathcal{A}$ has queried id^* to oracle* $\mathrm{KG}(\cdot)$, *then there must be query (id^*, t) to oracle* $\mathrm{RVK}(\cdot)$ *satisfies $t < t^*$, i.e., id^* must has been revoked before time t^*.*

A revocable IBE scheme is IND-ID-CPA secure if for all PPT adversary $\mathcal{A}$, the following advantage is negligible in the security parameter λ, i.e.,

$$\mathbf{Adv}_{RIBE,\mathcal{A}}^{IND\text{-}ID\text{-}CPA}(\lambda) = |\Pr[\boldsymbol{EXP}_{\mathcal{A}}^{IND\text{-}ID\text{-}CPA}(\lambda) = 1] - 1/2| = negl(\lambda).$$

2.4 Garbled Circuits

A garbled circuits scheme consists of two PPT algorithms $(\mathsf{GCircuit}, \mathsf{Eval})$.

- $\mathsf{GCircuit}(\lambda, \mathsf{C}) \rightarrow (\tilde{\mathsf{C}}, \{\mathsf{lab}_{w,b}\}_{w\in \mathsf{inp}(\mathsf{C}), b\in\{0,1\}})$: The algorithm GCircuit takes a security parameter λ and a circuit C as input. This algorithm outputs a garbled circuit $\tilde{\mathsf{C}}$ and labels $\{\mathsf{lab}_{w,b}\}_{w\in \mathsf{inp}(\mathsf{C}), b\in\{0,1\}}$ where each $\mathsf{lab}_{w,b} \in \{0,1\}^\lambda$. Here $\mathsf{inp}(\mathsf{C})$ represents the set $[\ell]$ where ℓ is the bit-length of the input of the circuit C.
- $\mathsf{Eval}(\tilde{\mathsf{C}}, \{\mathsf{lab}_{w,x_w}\}_{w\in \mathsf{inp}(\mathsf{C})}) \rightarrow y$: The algorithm Eval takes as input a garbled circuit $\tilde{\mathsf{C}}$ and a set of label $\{\mathsf{lab}_{w,x_w}\}_{w\in \mathsf{inp}(\mathsf{C})}$, and it outputs y.

Correctness. In a garbled circuit scheme, for any circuit C and an input $x \in \{0,1\}^\ell$, it holds that

$$\Pr[\mathsf{C}(x) = \mathsf{Eval}(\tilde{\mathsf{C}}, \{\mathsf{lab}_{w,x_w}\}_{w\in \mathsf{inp}(\mathsf{C})})] = 1$$

where $(\tilde{\mathsf{C}}, \{\mathsf{lab}_{w,b}\}_{w\in \mathsf{inp}(\mathsf{C}), b\in\{0,1\}}) \leftarrow \mathsf{GCircuit}(1^\lambda, \mathsf{C})$.
Security. In a garbled circuit scheme, the security means that there is a PPT simulator Sim such that for any C, x and for any PPT adversary $\mathcal{A}$, the following advantage of $\mathcal{A}$ is negligible in the security parameter λ:

$$\mathbf{Adv}_{\mathcal{A}}^{GC}(\lambda) = |\Pr[\mathcal{A}(\tilde{\mathsf{C}}, \{\mathsf{lab}_{w,x_w}\}_{w\in \mathsf{inp}(\mathsf{C})}) = 1] - \Pr[\mathcal{A}(\mathsf{Sim}(1^\lambda, \mathsf{C}(\mathsf{x}))) = 1]| = \mathsf{negl}(\lambda),$$

where $(\tilde{\mathsf{C}}, \{\mathsf{lab}_{w,b}\}_{w\in \mathsf{inp}(\mathsf{C}), b\in\{0,1\}}) \leftarrow \mathsf{GCircuit}(1^\lambda, \mathsf{C})$.

2.5 Computational Diffie-Hellman Problem

Let $(\mathbb{G}, g, p) \leftarrow \mathsf{GGen}(1^\lambda)$ be a group generation algorithm which outputs a cyclic group $\mathbb{G}$ of order p and a generator of $\mathbb{G}$.

Definition 2 *[CDH Assumption]. The computational Diffie-Hellman (CDH) assumption holds w.r.t. GGen, if for any PPT algorithm $\mathcal{A}$ its advantage ϵ in solving computational Diffie-Hellman (CDH) problem in $\mathbb{G}$ is negligible. In formula, $Pr\left[\mathcal{A}(g, g^a, g^b) = g^{ab} \mid (\mathbb{G}, g, p) \leftarrow \mathsf{GGen}(1^\lambda); a, b \leftarrow \mathbb{Z}_p\right] = \mathsf{negl}(\lambda)$.*

2.6 Chameleon Encryption

A chameleon encryption scheme has five PPT algorithms $\mathsf{CE} = (\mathsf{HGen}, \mathsf{H}, \mathsf{H}^{-1}, \mathsf{HEnc}, \mathsf{HDec})$.

- HGen: The algorithm HGen takes the security parameter λ and a message-length n as input. This algorithm outputs a key k and a trapdoor t.
- H: The algorithm H takes the key k, a message $x \in \{0,1\}^n$ and a randomness r as input. This algorithm outputs a hash value h and the length of h is λ.
- H^{-1}: The algorithm H^{-1} takes a trapdoor t, a previously used message $x \in \{0,1\}^n$, random coins r and a message $x' \in \{0,1\}^n$ as input. It outputs r'.
- HEnc: The algorithm HEnc takes a key k, a hash value h, an index $i \in [n]$, a bit $b \in \{0,1\}$, and a message $m \in \{0,1\}^*$ as input. It outputs a ciphertext ct.

- HDec: The algorithm HDec takes a key k, a message $x \in \{0,1\}^n$, a randomness r and a ciphertext ct as input. It outputs a value m or $\perp$.

The chameleon encryption scheme enjoys the following properties:

- **Uniformity.** For all $x, x' \in \{0,1\}^n$, if both r and r' are chosen uniformly at random, the two distribution $\mathsf{H}(k, x; r)$ and $\mathsf{H}(k, x'; r')$ are statistically indistinguishable.
- **Trapdoor Collisions.** For any $x, x' \in \{0,1\}^n$ and r, if $(k, t) \leftarrow \mathsf{HGen}(1^\lambda, n)$ and $r' \leftarrow \mathsf{H}^{-1}(t, (x, r), x')$, then it holds that $\mathsf{H}(k, x; r) = \mathsf{H}(k, x'; r')$. Moreover, if r is chosen uniformly and randomly, r' is statistically close to uniform.
- **Correctness.** For all $x \in \{0,1\}^n$, randomness r, index $i \in [n]$ and message m, if $(k, t) \leftarrow \mathsf{HGen}(1^\lambda, n)$, $h \leftarrow \mathsf{H}(k, x; r)$ and $ct \leftarrow \mathsf{HEnc}(k, (h, i, x_i), m)$, then $\mathsf{HDec}(k, ct, (x, r)) = m$
- **Security.** For a PPT adversary $\mathcal{A}$ against a chameleon encryption, consider the following experiment:

EXP$_{\mathcal{A}}^{\text{IND-CE}}(\lambda)$:
$(k, t) \leftarrow \mathsf{HGen}(1^\lambda, n)$.
$(x, r, i, m_0, m_1) \leftarrow \mathcal{A}(k)$.
$b \xleftarrow{\$} \{0,1\}$.
$ct \leftarrow \mathsf{HEnc}(k, (\mathsf{H}(k, x; r), i, 1 - x_i), m_b)$.
$b' \leftarrow \mathcal{A}(k, ct, (x, r))$.
Output 1 if $b = b'$ and 0 otherwise.

The security of a chameleon encryption defines as follows: For any PPT adversary $\mathcal{A}$, the advantage of $\mathcal{A}$ in experiment $\mathbf{EXP}_{\mathcal{A}}^{\text{IND-CE}}(\lambda)$ satisfies $|\Pr[\mathbf{Adv}_{\mathcal{A}}^{\text{IND-CE}}(\lambda) = 1] - 1/2| = \mathsf{negl}$.

In [6], such a chameleon encryption was constructed from the CDH assumption.

3 Idea of Our Revocable IBE Scheme

3.1 Idea of the DG Scheme

In the IBE scheme [6] proposed by Döttling and Garg, say the DG scheme, each id is an n-bit binary string. In other words, each user can be regarded as a leaf of a complete binary tree of depth n, which is the length of a user's identity id. For each level $j \in [n]$ in the tree, the key authority generates a pair of chameleon encryption key and trapdoor (k_j, td_j). As shown in Fig. 1, a leaf v is attached with a key pair $(\mathsf{ek}_v, \mathsf{dk}_v)$, which is the public/secret key of an IND-CPA secure public-key encryption scheme PKE=(G, E, D), i.e., $(\mathsf{ek}_v, \mathsf{dk}_v) \leftarrow \mathsf{G}(1^\lambda)$. In addition, a non-leaf node v in the tree is attached with four values: the hash value h_v of this node, the hash value $h_{v||0}$ of the left child node, the hash value $h_{v||1}$ of the right child node, a randomness r such that $h_v = \mathsf{H}(k_{|v|}, h_{v||0}||h_{v||1}; r_v)$. Specially, for $|v| = n - 1$, $(h_{v||0}, h_{v||1}) := (\mathsf{ek}_{v||0}, \mathsf{ek}_{v||1})$. The master public key of IBE is given by the hash keys $(k_0, \ldots, k_{n-1})$ and the hash value h_ε of the root. The master secret key is the seed of a pseudorandom function to generate r_v and the trapdoors of the chameleon encryption.

Key Generation. Each user is assigned to a leaf in the tree according to id. The secret key is just all the values attached to those nodes on the path from the root to the leaf. For example, in Fig. 1, if id = 010, then the secret key is $\mathsf{sk}_{010} = (\{h_\varepsilon, h_0, h_1, r_\varepsilon\}, \{h_0, h_{00}, h_{01}, r_0\}, \{h_{01}, \mathsf{ek}_{010}, \mathsf{ek}_{011}, r_{01}\}, \mathsf{dk}_{010})$.
Encryption. As for encryption, two kinds of circuits are defined.

(1) $Q[m](\mathsf{ek})$ is a circuit with m hardwired and its input is ek. It computes and outputs the PKE ciphertext of message m under the public-key ek.
(2) $\mathsf{P}[\beta \in \{0,1\}, k, \overline{\mathsf{lab}}](h)$ is a circuit which hardwires bit β, key k and a serial of labels $\overline{\mathsf{lab}}$. It computes and outputs $\{\mathsf{HEnc}(k, (h, j+\beta\cdot\lambda, b), \mathsf{lab}_{j,b})\}_{j\in[\lambda], b\in\{0,1\}}$, where $\overline{\mathsf{lab}}$ is the short for $\{\mathsf{lab}_{j,b}\}_{j\in[\lambda], b\in\{0,1\}}$.

To encrypt a message m under id, the sender generates a series of garbled circuits from the bottom to the top. Specifically, for level n, it generates $\tilde{Q}$, the garbled circuit of $Q[m]$, and the corresponding label $\overline{\mathsf{lab}}$, i.e., $(\tilde{Q}, \overline{\mathsf{lab}}) \leftarrow \mathsf{GCircuit}(1^\lambda, \mathsf{T}[m])$.
Then, id_n, k_{n-1} and $\overline{\mathsf{lab}}$ are hardwired into circuit $P^{n-1}[\mathsf{id}_n, k_{n-1}, \overline{\mathsf{lab}}]$. Next, invoke the garbled circuit $(\tilde{P}^{n-1}, \overline{\mathsf{lab}}') \leftarrow \mathsf{GCircuit}(1^\lambda, P^{n-1}[\mathsf{id}_n, k_{n-1}, \overline{\mathsf{lab}}])$.
Let $\overline{\mathsf{lab}} := \overline{\mathsf{lab}}'$. Invoke $(\tilde{P}^{n-2}, \overline{\mathsf{lab}}') \leftarrow \mathsf{GCircuit}(1^\lambda, P^{n-2}[\mathsf{id}_{n-1}, k_{n-2}, \overline{\mathsf{lab}}])$. Repeat this procedure and we have $(\tilde{P}^0, \overline{\mathsf{lab}}') \leftarrow \mathsf{GCircuit}(1^\lambda, P^0[\mathsf{id}_1, k_0, \overline{\mathsf{lab}}])$. Recall that $\overline{\mathsf{lab}}' = \{\mathsf{lab}_{j,b}\}_{j\in[\lambda], b\in\{0,1\}}$. Choose λ labels from $\overline{\mathsf{lab}}'$ according to the λ bits of h_ϵ.
The final ciphertext is $\mathsf{ct} = (\{\mathsf{lab}_{j,h_{\epsilon j}}\}_{j\in[\lambda]}, \tilde{P}^0, \ldots, \tilde{P}^{n-1}, \tilde{\mathsf{T}})$.

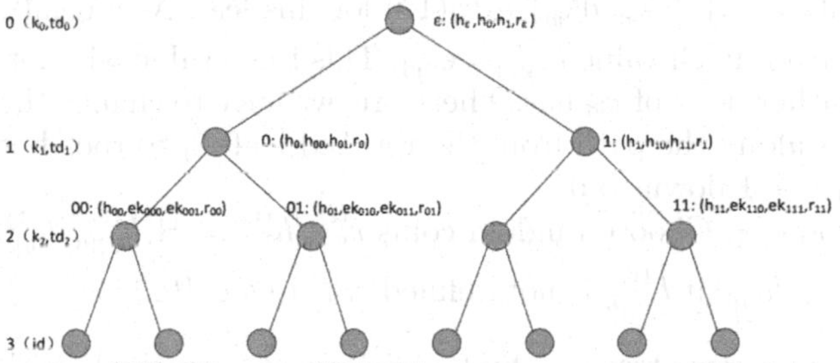

Fig. 1. The IBE tree of depth $n = 3$

Decryption. The decryption goes from the top to bottom. It will invoke the evaluation algorithm Eval of the garbled circuits to obtain chameleon encryption of labels, and uses the secret key of chameleon encryption scheme to recover the corresponding label. For the leaf, it will use the decryption algorithm of PKE to recover the message m.

3.2 Idea of Our Revoked IBE Scheme

Our revoked IBE is based on the original DG scheme. An important observation of the DG scheme is that among all the elements in the secret key

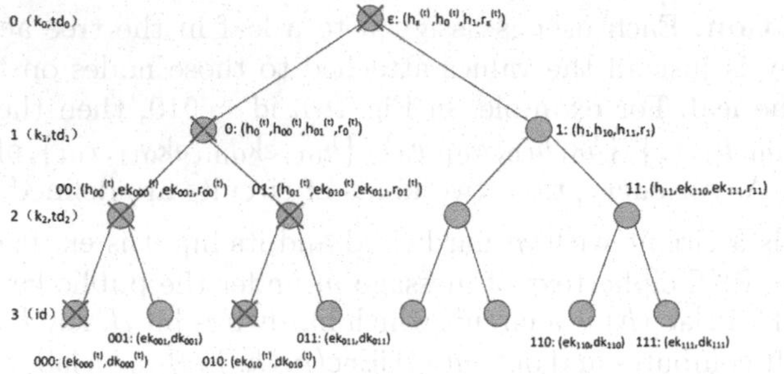

Fig. 2. The IBE tree of depth $n = 3$ when user "000" and "010" has been revoked

$\mathsf{sk}_{\mathsf{id}} = (\{h_{\mathsf{v}}, h_{\mathsf{v}||0}, h_{\mathsf{v}||1}, r_{\mathsf{v}}\}_{v\in\mathcal{V}}, \mathsf{dk}_{\mathsf{id}})$ of user id, $\mathsf{dk}_{\mathsf{id}}$ is the most critical element. Recall that $\mathcal{V} = \{\varepsilon, \mathsf{id}[1], \mathsf{id}[12], \ldots, \mathsf{id}[12\ldots n-1]\}$ and $\mathsf{dk}_{\mathsf{id}}$ is the decryption key of the underlying building block PKE. The sibling of leaf id knows everything about $\mathsf{sk}_{\mathsf{id}}$ except $\mathsf{dk}_{\mathsf{id}}$. This gives us a hint for revocation. To revoke user id, we can change the decryption key $\mathsf{dk}_{\mathsf{id}}$ in $\mathsf{sk}_{\mathsf{id}}$ into a new one $\mathsf{dk}'_{\mathsf{id}}$ and this fresh decryption key will not issued to the revoked user id. As long as the essential element $\mathsf{dk}'_{\mathsf{id}}$ is missing, user id will not be able to decrypt anything. Now we outline how the revocable IBE works.

The tree is updated according to the revoked users.

- If a leaf v_{id} is revoked during time period t, then a new public/secret key pair will generated with $(\mathsf{ek}'_{\mathsf{id}}, \mathsf{dk}'_{\mathsf{id}}) \leftarrow \mathsf{G}(1^\lambda)$ for this leaf. As a result, $h_{v_{\mathsf{id}}} = \mathsf{ek}_{\mathsf{id}}$ is replaced with a fresh value $h^{(\mathsf{t})}_{v_{\mathsf{id}}} := \mathsf{ek}'_{\mathsf{id}}$. This fresh value will not consistent to what the father node of v_{id} has. Therefore, we have to change the attachments of all nodes along the path from the revoked leaf v_{id} to root bottom upward.
- For i from $n-1$ down to 0
  Let $v := v_{\mathsf{id}[12\ldots i]}$. Choose random coins $r^{(\mathsf{t})}_v$; $h^{(\mathsf{t})}_v := \mathsf{H}(h^{(\mathsf{t})}_{v||0}, h^{(\mathsf{t})}_{v||1}, r^{(\mathsf{t})}_v)$;
  Here $h^{(\mathsf{t})}_{v||b} := h_{v||b}$ if $h^{(\mathsf{t})}_{v||b}$ is not defined, where $b \in \{0, 1\}$.

In this way, a new tree is built with root attached with new value $(h^{(\mathsf{t})}_\varepsilon, h^{(\mathsf{t})}_0, h^{(\mathsf{t})}_1, r^{(\mathsf{t})}_\varepsilon)$. Note that the hash keys $(k_0, \ldots, k_{n-1})$ remain unchanged.

When revocation happens, what a sender does is updating the new hash value $h^{(\mathsf{t})}_\varepsilon$, then invoking the encryption algorithm for encryption.

For decryption to go smoothly, the IBE system has to issue updating keys to users. The updating key include all the information of the nodes on the paths from revoked leaves to the root, but the new $\mathsf{dk}^{(\mathsf{t})}_{\mathsf{id}}$ is not issued. In Fig. 2, for example, two users, namely 000 and 010, are revoked and determine two paths. Then all the nodes along the two paths are marked with cross. All the nodes are updated with new attachments, but leaf 000 is only attached with a new $\mathsf{ek}^{(\mathsf{t})}_{000}$ (without $\mathsf{dk}^{(\mathsf{t})}_{000}$) and leaf 010 is only attached with a new $\mathsf{ek}^{(\mathsf{t})}_{010}$ (without $\mathsf{dk}^{(\mathsf{t})}_{010}$). The updating key are $\{\varepsilon, (h_\varepsilon^{(t)}, h_0^{(t)}, h_1^{(t)}, r_\varepsilon^{(t)}),\ 0, (h_0^{(t)}, h_{00}^{(t)}, h_{01}^{(t)}, r_0^{(t)}),\ 00, (h_{00}^{(t)}, h_{000}^{(t)}, h_{001}^{(t)}, r_{00}^{(t)}),$ $01, (h_{01}^{(t)}, h_{010}^{(t)}, h_{011}^{(t)}, r_{01}^{(t)}), 000, (h_{000}^{(t)} = \mathsf{ek}_{000}^{(t)}, \perp), 010, (h_{010}^{(t)} = \mathsf{ek}_{010}^{(t)}, \perp)\}$.

Any legal user is able to update his secret key $\mathsf{sk}_{\mathsf{id}}$ with the new attachments of nodes along the path from his leaf to the root. For example, the updated secret key $\mathsf{sk}_{001}^{(t)}$ of user 001 is now $\{\varepsilon, (h_\varepsilon^{(t)}, h_0^{(t)}, h_1^{(t)}, r_\varepsilon^{(t)}),\ 0, (h_0^{(t)}, h_{00}^{(t)}, h_{01}^{(t)}, r_0^{(t)}),$ $00, (h_{00}^{(t)}, h_{000}^{(t)}, h_{001}^{(t)}, r_{00}^{(t)}), 001, (h_{001} = \mathsf{ek}_{001}, \mathsf{dk}_{001})\}$. The updated secret key $\mathsf{sk}_{111}^{(t)}$ of user 111 is now $\{\varepsilon, (h_\varepsilon^{(t)}, h_0^{(t)}, h_1^{(t)}, r_\varepsilon^{(t)}), 1, (h_1, h_{10}, h_{11}, r_1), 11, (h_{11}, h_{110}, h_{111},$ $r_{11}), 111, (h_{111} = \mathsf{ek}_{001}, \mathsf{dk}_{111})\}$.

In this way, any legal user is able to decrypt ciphertexts since he knows the secret key corresponding to the new tree. Any revoked user id is unable to implement decryption anymore, since the new $\mathsf{dk}_{\mathsf{id}}^{(t)}$ is missing.

4 Revocable IBE Scheme

In this section, we present our construction of revocable IBE scheme from chameleon encryption. Let PRF: $\{0,1\}^\lambda \times \{0,1\}^{\leq \ell+n} \cup \{\varepsilon\} \rightarrow \{0,1\}^\lambda$ be a pseudo-random function. Let $\mathsf{CE} = (\mathsf{HGen}, \mathsf{H}, \mathsf{H}^{-1}, \mathsf{HEnc}, \mathsf{HDec})$ be a chameleon encryption scheme and $\mathsf{PKE} = (\mathsf{G}, \mathsf{E}, \mathsf{D})$ be an IND-CPA secure public-key encryption scheme. We denote by $\mathsf{id}[i]$ the i-th bit of id and by $\mathsf{id}[1 \cdots i]$ the first i bits of id. Define $\mathsf{id}[1 \cdots 0] := \varepsilon$. We first introduce five subroutines which will be used repeatedly in our scheme (as shown in Table 3). All of these five subroutines are run by the key authority. The subroutines NodeGen and LeafGen are invoked by the key authority in setup algorithm, where NodeGen is used to generate non-leaf nodes and LeafGen to generate leaves and their parents. Just like [6], given all chameleon keys, trapdoors, a randomness s, a node v and a length parameter ℓ, the NodeGen subroutine generates four values stored in node v: the hash value of the node h_v, the hash value of it left-child node $h_{v||0}$, the hash value of it right-child node $h_{v||1}$, and the randomness of this node r_v. Given all chameleon keys k_{n-1} and trapdoors td_{n-1} of the $n-1$-th level, a randomness s, a node v in the $n-1$-th level and a length parameter ℓ, the LeafGen subroutine generates two pairs of public/secret keys $(\mathsf{ek}_{v||0}, \mathsf{dk}_{v||0})$, $(\mathsf{ek}_{v||1}, \mathsf{dk}_{v||1})$ of the PKE scheme, and generates the hash value h_v and the randomness r_v of the node v. The children of v are two leaves associated by $\mathsf{ek}_{v||0}$ and $\mathsf{ek}_{v||1}$. Each user can be uniquely represented by a leaf node. The subroutine FindNodes, subroutine NodeChange and subroutine LeafChange are invoked by the key authority in key update algorithm. Given a revocation list RL, a time t and the global key list KL, subroutine FindNodes(RL, t, KL) outputs all leaves which are revoked at time t and all their ancestor nodes. Given a chameleon key, a chameleon trapdoor, a node v, two hash values $(h_{v||0}, h_{v||0})$ of the two children of node v and a randomness s, subroutine NodeChange outputs a new hash value and a new randomness for node v. Given a leaf node v, a time t, a randomness s, subroutine LeafChange outputs a fresh public key by invoking the key generation algorithm G of PKE.
Construction of RIBE. Now we describe our revocable IBE scheme (RIBE.Setup, RIBE.KG, RIBE.KU, RIBE.DK, RIBE.Enc, RIBE.Dec, RIBE.R).

Table 3. Five subroutines run by the key authority.

<table>
<tr>
<td>$\underline{\mathsf{NodeGen}}((k_0, \cdots, k_n), (td_0, \cdots, td_n, s), v \in \{0,1\}^{\leq n-1} \cup \{\varepsilon\}, \ell)$:
Let $i := |v|$
$h_v \leftarrow \mathsf{H}(k_i, 0^{2\lambda}; \mathsf{PRF}(s, 0^{\ell}||v))$,
$h_{v||0} \leftarrow \mathsf{H}(k_{i+1}, 0^{2\lambda}; \mathsf{PRF}(s, 0^{\ell}||v||0))$,
$h_{v||1} \leftarrow \mathsf{H}(k_{i+1}, 0^{2\lambda}; \mathsf{PRF}(s, 0^{\ell}||v||1))$.
$r_v \leftarrow \mathsf{H}^{-1}(td_i, (0^{2\lambda}, \mathsf{PRF}(s, 0^{\ell}||v)), h_{v||0}||h_{v||1})$.
Output $(h_v, h_{v||0}, h_{v||1}, r_v)$.</td>
<td>$\underline{\mathsf{FindNodes}}(\mathsf{RL}, \mathsf{t}, \mathsf{KL})$:
$\mathsf{Y} \leftarrow \emptyset$
$\forall(\mathsf{id}, \mathsf{t}_i) \in \mathsf{RL}$
If t_i=t, then add id to Y.
For $i = n-1$ to 0: \\ find the ancestors of id $\in$ Y.
$\forall(v, \cdot, \cdot) \in \mathsf{KL}$ with $|v| = i$:
If $(v||0 \in \mathsf{Y}) \vee (v||1 \in \mathsf{Y})$, add v to Y.
Output Y.</td>
</tr>
<tr>
<td>$\underline{\mathsf{LeafGen}}(k_{n-1}, (td_{n-1}, s), v \in \{0,1\}^{n-1}, \ell)$:

$h_v \leftarrow \mathsf{H}(k_n, 0^{2\lambda}; \mathsf{PRF}(s, v))$,
$(\mathsf{ek}_{v||0}, \mathsf{dk}_{v||0}) \leftarrow \mathsf{G}(1^{\lambda}, \mathsf{PRF}(s, 0^{\ell}||v||0))$,
$(\mathsf{ek}_{v||1}, \mathsf{dk}_{v||1}) \leftarrow \mathsf{G}(1^{\lambda}, \mathsf{PRF}(s, 0^{\ell}||v||1))$,
$r_v \leftarrow \mathsf{H}^{-1}(td_{n-1}, (0^{2\lambda}, \mathsf{PRF}(s, 0^{\ell}||v)), \mathsf{ek}_{v||0}||\mathsf{ek}_{v||1})$.
Output $((h_v, \mathsf{ek}_{v||0}, \mathsf{ek}_{v||1}, r_v), \mathsf{dk}_{v||0}, \mathsf{dk}_{v||1})$.</td>
<td>$\underline{\mathsf{NodeChange}}(k, td, v \in \{0,1\}^{\leq n-1} \cup \{\varepsilon\}, h_{v||0}, h_{v||1}, \mathsf{t}, s)$:
$h_v^{(\mathsf{t})} \leftarrow \mathsf{H}(k, 0^{2\lambda}; \mathsf{PRF}(s, \mathsf{t}||v))$,
$r_v^{(\mathsf{t})} \leftarrow \mathsf{H}^{-1}(td, (0^{2\lambda}, \mathsf{PRF}(s, \mathsf{t}||v)); h_{v||0}||h_{v||1})$.
Output $(h_v^{(\mathsf{t})}, h_{v||0}, h_{v||1}, r_v^{(\mathsf{t})})$.

$\underline{\mathsf{LeafChange}}(v \in \{0,1\}^n, \mathsf{t}, s)$:
$(\mathsf{ek}_v^{(\mathsf{t})}, \mathsf{dk}_v^{(\mathsf{t})}) \leftarrow \mathsf{G}(1^{\lambda}, \mathsf{PRF}(s, \mathsf{t}||v))$.
Output $(\mathsf{ek}_v^{(\mathsf{t})}, \perp)$.</td>
</tr>
</table>

- **Setup** $\mathsf{RIBE.Setup}(1^{\lambda}, 1^n)$: given a security parameter λ, an integer n where 2^n is the maximal number of users that the scheme supports. Define identity space as $\mathcal{ID} = \{0,1\}^n$ and time space as $\mathcal{T} = \{0,1\}^{\ell}$, and do the following.
  1. Sample $s \xleftarrow{\$} \{0,1\}^{\lambda}$.
  2. For each $i \in [n]$, invoke $(k_i, td_i) \xleftarrow{\$} \mathsf{HGen}(1^{\lambda}, 2\lambda)$.
  3. Initialize key list $\mathsf{KL} := \emptyset$, public list $\mathsf{PL} = \emptyset$, key update list $\mathsf{KU} = \emptyset$ and revocation list $\mathsf{RL} := \emptyset$.
  4. $\mathsf{mpk} := (k_0, \cdots, k_{n-1}, \ell)$; $\mathsf{st} := \{\mathsf{KL}, \mathsf{PL}, \mathsf{RL}, \mathsf{KU}\}$; $\mathsf{msk} := (\mathsf{mpk}, td_0, \cdots, td_{n-1}, s)$.
  5. Output $(\mathsf{mpk}, \mathsf{msk}, \mathsf{st})$.
- **Private Key Generation** $\mathsf{RIBE.KG}(\mathsf{msk}, \mathsf{id} \in \{0,1\}^n, \mathsf{st})$
  1. Parse $\mathsf{msk} = (\mathsf{mpk}, td_0, \cdots, td_{n-1}, s)$ and $\mathsf{mpk} = (k_0, \cdots, k_{n-1}, \ell)$.
  2. $\mathsf{W} := \{\varepsilon, \mathsf{id}[1], \cdots, \mathsf{id}[1 \cdots n-1]\}$, where ε is the empty string.
  3. For all $v \in \mathsf{W} \setminus \{\mathsf{id}[1 \cdots n-1]\}$:
     $(h_v, h_{v||0}, h_{v||1}, r_v) \leftarrow \mathsf{NodeGen}((k_0, \cdots, k_{n-1}), (td_0, \cdots, td_{n-1}, s), v, \ell)$,
     $\mathsf{KL} := \mathsf{KL} \cup \{(v, h_v, h_{v||0}, h_{v||1}, r_v)\}$,
     $\mathsf{lk}_v := (h_v, h_{v||0}, h_{v||1}, r_v)$.
  4. For $v = \mathsf{id}[1 \cdots n-1]$:
     $(h_v, h_{v||0} = \mathsf{ek}_{v||0}, h_{v||1} = \mathsf{ek}_{v||1}, r_v, \mathsf{dk}_{v||0}, \mathsf{dk}_{v||1}) \leftarrow \mathsf{LeafGen}(k_{n-1}, (td_{n-1}, s), v, \ell)$,
     $\mathsf{KL} := \mathsf{KL} \cup \{(v, h_v, \mathsf{ek}_{v||0}, \mathsf{ek}_{v||1}, r_v), (v||0, \mathsf{ek}_{v||0}, \perp), (v||1, \mathsf{ek}_{v||1}, \perp)\}$,
     $\mathsf{lk}_v := (h_v, \mathsf{ek}_{v||0}, \mathsf{ek}_{v||1}, r_v)$.
  5. $\mathsf{st} = \{\mathsf{KL}, \mathsf{PL}, \mathsf{RL}, \mathsf{KU}\}$ and $\mathsf{sk_{id}} := (\mathsf{t} = 0, \mathsf{id}, \{\mathsf{lk}_v\}_{v \in \mathsf{W}}, \mathsf{dk_{id}})$.
  6. Output $(\mathsf{sk_{id}}, \mathsf{st})$.
- **Key Update Generation** $\mathsf{RIBE.KU}(\mathsf{msk}, \mathsf{t}, \mathsf{st})$:
  1. Parse $\mathsf{msk} = (\mathsf{mpk}, td_0, \cdots, td_{n-1}, s)$, $\mathsf{st} = \{\mathsf{KL}, \mathsf{PL}, \mathsf{RL}, \mathsf{KU}\}$ and $\mathsf{mpk} = (k_0, \cdots, k_{n-1}, \ell)$.
  2. $\mathsf{Y} \leftarrow \mathsf{FindNodes}(\mathsf{RL}, \mathsf{t}, \mathsf{KL})$. // Y stores all revoked leaves and their ancestors
  3. If $\mathsf{Y} = \emptyset$, Output$(\mathsf{KU}, \mathsf{PL})$ //stay unchanged.

4. Set key update list $\mathsf{KU}^{(\mathsf{t})} := \emptyset$.
5. For all node $v \in \mathsf{Y}$ such that $|v| = n$: // deal with all leaves in Y
   $(\mathsf{ek}_v^{(\mathsf{t})}, \perp) \leftarrow \mathsf{LeafChange}(v, \mathsf{t}, s)$,
   $\mathsf{KU}^{(\mathsf{t})} := \mathsf{KU}^{(\mathsf{t})} \cup \{(v, \mathsf{ek}_v^{(\mathsf{t})}, \perp)\}$. // new attachments for all leaves in Y
   $h_v^{(\mathsf{t})} := \mathsf{ek}_v^{(\mathsf{t})}$.
6. For $i = n-1$ to 0: // generate new attachments for all non-leaf nodes in Y
   For all node $v \in \mathsf{Y}$ and $|v| = i$:
   Set $j := \mathsf{t}$, $\mathsf{KU}^{(0)} := \mathsf{KL}$.
   While$(j \geq 0)$
   If $\exists v||b$ s.t. $(v||b, h_{v||b}, \cdot, \cdot, \cdot) \in \mathsf{KU}^{(j)}$,
   $h_{v||b}^{(\mathsf{t})} := h_{v||b}$,
   Break;
   $j := j - 1$.
   $(h_v^{(\mathsf{t})}, h_{v||0}^{(\mathsf{t})}, h_{v||1}^{(\mathsf{t})}, r_v^{(\mathsf{t})}) \leftarrow \mathsf{NodeChange}(k_i, td_i, v, h_{v||0}^{(\mathsf{t})}, h_{v||1}^{(\mathsf{t})}, \mathsf{t}, s)$.
   $\mathsf{KU}^{(\mathsf{t})} := \mathsf{KU}^{(\mathsf{t})} \cup \{(v, h_v^{(\mathsf{t})}, h_{v||0}^{(\mathsf{t})}, h_{v||1}^{(\mathsf{t})}, r_v^{(\mathsf{t})})\}$.
7. $\mathsf{KU} := \mathsf{KU} \cup \{(\mathsf{t}, \mathsf{KU}^{(\mathsf{t})})\}$ and $\mathsf{PL} := \mathsf{PL} \cup \{(\mathsf{t}, h_\varepsilon^{(\mathsf{t})})\}$.
8. $\mathsf{st} := \{\mathsf{KL}, \mathsf{PL}, \mathsf{RL}, \mathsf{KU}\}$
9. Output st.

- **Decryption Key Generation** $\mathsf{RIBE.DK}(\mathsf{mpk}, \mathsf{sk}_{\mathsf{id}}, \mathsf{KU}, \mathsf{t})$:
  1. $\mathsf{W} := \{\varepsilon, \mathsf{id}[1], \cdots, \mathsf{id}[1 \cdots n-1]\}$, where ε is the empty string.
  2. Parse $\mathsf{mpk} = (k_0, \cdots, k_{n-1}, \ell)$ and $\mathsf{sk}_{\mathsf{id}} = (0, \mathsf{id}, \{h_v, h_{v||0}, h_{v||1}, r_v\}_{v \in \mathsf{W}}, \mathsf{dk}_{\mathsf{id}})$.
  3. From KU retrieve a set $\Omega := \{(\tilde{\mathsf{t}}, \mathsf{KU}^{(\tilde{\mathsf{t}})}) \mid (\tilde{\mathsf{t}}, \mathsf{KU}^{(\tilde{\mathsf{t}})}) \in \mathsf{KU}, 0 \leq \tilde{\mathsf{t}} < \mathsf{t}\}$.
  4. For each $(\tilde{\mathsf{t}}, \mathsf{KU}^{(\tilde{\mathsf{t}})}) \in \Omega$ with $\tilde{\mathsf{t}}$ in ascending order, does the following:
     For $i = 0$ to $n-1$:
     $v := \mathsf{id}[1 \cdots i]$ (Recall $\mathsf{id}[1 \cdots 0] = \varepsilon$).
     If $\exists (v, h_v^{(\tilde{\mathsf{t}})}, h_{v||0}^{(\tilde{\mathsf{t}})}, h_{v||1}^{(\tilde{\mathsf{t}})}, r_v^{(\tilde{\mathsf{t}})}) \in \mathsf{KU}^{(\tilde{\mathsf{t}})}$:
     $\mathsf{lk}_v^{(\mathsf{t})} := (h_v^{(\tilde{\mathsf{t}})}, h_{v||0}^{(\tilde{\mathsf{t}})}, h_{v||1}^{(\tilde{\mathsf{t}})}, r_v^{(\tilde{\mathsf{t}})})$.
  5. If $\exists (\tilde{\mathsf{t}}, \mathsf{KU}^{(\tilde{\mathsf{t}})}) \in \mathsf{KU}$ s.t. $(\mathsf{id}, \mathsf{ek}_v^{(\tilde{\mathsf{t}})}, \perp) \in \mathsf{KU}^{(\tilde{\mathsf{t}})}$: \\id is revoked at $\tilde{\mathsf{t}}$
     Output $\mathsf{sk}_{\mathsf{id}}^{(\mathsf{t})} := (\mathsf{t}, \mathsf{id}, \{\mathsf{lk}_v^{(\mathsf{t})}\}_{v \in \mathsf{W}}, \perp)$.
  6. Output $\mathsf{sk}_{\mathsf{id}}^{(\mathsf{t})} := (\mathsf{t}, \mathsf{id}, \{\mathsf{lk}_v^{(\mathsf{t})}\}_{v \in \mathsf{W}}, \mathsf{dk}_{\mathsf{id}})$
- **Encryption** $\mathsf{RIBE.Enc}(\mathsf{mpk}, \mathsf{id}, \mathsf{t}, m, \mathsf{PL}))$:
  We describe two circuits that will be garbled during the encryption procedure.
  - $\mathsf{Q}[m](ek)$: Compute and output $\mathsf{E}(ek, m)$.
  - $\mathsf{P}[\beta \in \{0,1\}, k, \overline{\mathsf{lab}}](h)$: Compute and output $\{\mathsf{HEnc}(k, (h, j + \beta \cdot \lambda, b), \mathsf{lab}_{j,b})\}_{j \in [\lambda], b \in \{0,1\}}$, where $\overline{\mathsf{lab}}$ is the short for $\{\mathsf{lab}_{j,b}\}_{j \in [\lambda], b \in \{0,1\}}$.

  Encryption proceeds as follows:
  1. Retrieve the last item $(\bar{\mathsf{t}}, h_\epsilon^{(\bar{\mathsf{t}})})$ from PL. If $\mathsf{t} < \bar{\mathsf{t}}$, output $\perp$; otherwise $h_\epsilon^{(\mathsf{t})} := h_\epsilon^{(\bar{\mathsf{t}})}$.
  2. Parse $\mathsf{mpk} = (k_0, \cdots, k_{n-1}, \ell)$.
  3. $(\tilde{Q}, \overline{\mathsf{lab}}) \xleftarrow{\$} \mathsf{GCircuit}(1^\lambda, \mathsf{Q}[m])$.

4. For $i = n-1$ to 0,
$(\tilde{P}^i, \overline{\mathsf{lab}}') \xleftarrow{\$} \mathsf{GCircuit}(1^\lambda, \mathsf{P}[\mathsf{id}[i+1], k_i, \overline{\mathsf{lab}}])$ and set $\overline{\mathsf{lab}} := \overline{\mathsf{lab}}'$.
5. Output $\mathsf{ct} := \left(\left\{\mathsf{lab}_{j,h^{(\mathsf{t})}_{\varepsilon,j}}\right\}_{j\in[\lambda]}, \{\tilde{P}^0, \cdots, \tilde{P}^{n-1}, \tilde{Q}\}\right)$, where $h^{(\mathsf{t})}_{\varepsilon,j}$ is the jth bit of $h^{(\mathsf{t})}_{\varepsilon}$.

- **Decryption** $\mathsf{RIBE.Dec}(\mathsf{mpk}, \mathsf{sk}^{(\mathsf{t})}_{\mathsf{id}}, \mathsf{ct})$
1. $\mathsf{W} := \{\varepsilon, \mathsf{id}[1], \cdots, \mathsf{id}[1\cdots n-1]\}$, where ε is the empty string.
2. Parse $\mathsf{mpk} = (k_0, \cdots, k_{n-1}, \ell)$ and $\mathsf{sk}^{(\mathsf{t})}_{\mathsf{id}} = (\mathsf{id}, \{\mathsf{lk}^{(\mathsf{t})}_v\}_{v\in\mathsf{W}}, \mathsf{dk}_{\mathsf{id}})$, where $\mathsf{lk}^{(\mathsf{t})}_v = (h^{(\mathsf{t})}_v, h^{(\mathsf{t})}_{v||0}, h^{(\mathsf{t})}_{v||1}, r^{(\mathsf{t})}_v)$.
3. Parse $\mathsf{ct} := \left(\left\{\mathsf{lab}_{j,h^{(\mathsf{t})}_{\varepsilon,j}}\right\}_{j\in[\lambda]}, \{\tilde{P}^0, \cdots, \tilde{P}^{n-1}, \tilde{Q}\}\right)$
4. Set $y := h^{(\mathsf{t})}_{\varepsilon}$.
5. For $i = 0$ to $n-1$:
Set $v := \mathsf{id}[1\cdots i]$ (Recall $\mathsf{id}[1\cdots 0] = \varepsilon$);
$\{c_{j,b}\}_{j\in[\lambda], b\in\{0,1\}} \leftarrow \mathsf{Eval}(\tilde{P}^i, \{\mathsf{lab}_{j,y_j}\}_{j\in[\lambda]})$;
If $i \neq n-1$, set $v' := \mathsf{id}[1\cdots i+1]$ and $y := h^{(\mathsf{t})}_{v'}$, and for each $j \in [\lambda]$,
$$\{\mathsf{lab}_{j,y_j}\}_{j\in[\lambda]} \leftarrow \mathsf{HDec}(k_i, c_{j,y_j}, (h^{(\mathsf{t})}_{v||0}||h^{(\mathsf{t})}_{v||1}), r^{(\mathsf{t})}_v).$$
If $i = n-1$, set $y := \mathsf{ek}_{\mathsf{id}}$ and for each $j \in [\lambda]$, compute
$$\{\mathsf{lab}_{j,y_j}\}_{j\in[\lambda]} \leftarrow \mathsf{HDec}(k_i, c_{j,y_j}, (\mathsf{ek}_{v||0}||\mathsf{ek}_{v||1}) = (h^{(\mathsf{t})}_{v||0}||h^{(\mathsf{t})}_{v||1}), r^{(\mathsf{t})}_v).$$
6. Compute $f \leftarrow \mathsf{Eval}(\tilde{Q}, \{\mathsf{lab}_{j,y_j}\}_{j\in[\lambda]})$.
7. Output $m \leftarrow \mathsf{D}(\mathsf{dk}_{\mathsf{id}}, f)$.

- **Revocation** $\mathsf{RIBE.R}(\mathsf{id}, \mathsf{t}, \mathsf{st})$:
1. Parse $\mathsf{st} := \{\mathsf{KL}, \mathsf{PL}, \mathsf{RL}, \mathsf{KU}\}$.
2. Update the revocation list by $\mathsf{RL} := \mathsf{RL} \cup \{(\mathsf{id}, \mathsf{t})\}$.
3. Parse $\mathsf{ct} := \left(\left\{\mathsf{lab}_{j,h^{(\mathsf{t})}_{\varepsilon,j}}\right\}_{j\in[\lambda]}, \{\tilde{P}^0, \cdots, \tilde{P}^{n-1}, \tilde{Q}\}\right)$.
4. $\mathsf{st} := \{\mathsf{KL}, \mathsf{PL}, \mathsf{RL}, \mathsf{KU}\}$.
5. Output st.

Remark. It is possible for us to reduce the cost of users' key updating in our construction. Now we provide a more efficient variant of decryption key generation algorithm $\mathsf{RIBE.DK'}$. With this variant algorithm, if a user has already generated a key $\mathsf{sk}^{(\mathsf{t}')}_{\mathsf{id}}$ at time period t' where $\mathsf{t}' \leq \mathsf{t}$, he or she can use $\mathsf{sk}^{(\mathsf{t}')}_{\mathsf{id}}$ as the input instead of $\mathsf{sk}_{\mathsf{id}}$ and generates the decryption key with lower computational cost. The algorithm proceeds as follows:
Decryption Key Generation $\mathsf{RIBE.DK'}(\mathsf{mpk}, \mathsf{sk}^{(\mathsf{t}')}_{\mathsf{id}}, \mathsf{KU}, \mathsf{t})$:

1. $\mathsf{W} := \{\varepsilon, \mathsf{id}[1], \cdots, \mathsf{id}[1\cdots n-1]\}$, where ε is the empty string.
2. Parse $\mathsf{mpk} = (k_0, \cdots, k_{n-1}, \ell)$ and $\mathsf{sk}^{(\mathsf{t}')}_{\mathsf{id}} = (\mathsf{t}', \mathsf{id}, \{h_v, h_{v||0}, h_{v||1}, r_v\}_{v\in\mathsf{W}}, \mathsf{dk}_{\mathsf{id}})$.
3. If $\mathsf{t}' > \mathsf{t}$, Output $\perp$.

4. If $t' = t$, Output $\mathsf{sk}_{\mathsf{id}}^{(t')}$.
5. From KU retrieve a set $\Omega := \{(\tilde{t}, \mathsf{KU}^{(\tilde{t})}) \mid (\tilde{t}, \mathsf{KU}^{(\tilde{t})}) \in \mathsf{KU}, t' \leq \tilde{t} < t\}$.
6. For each $(\tilde{t}, \mathsf{KU}^{(\tilde{t})}) \in \Omega$ with $\tilde{t}$ in ascending order, does the following:
   For $i = 0$ to $n - 1$:
   $v := \mathsf{id}[1 \cdots i]$ (Recall $\mathsf{id}[1 \cdots 0] = \varepsilon$).
   If $\exists (v, h_v^{(\tilde{t})}, h_{v||0}^{(\tilde{t})}, h_{v||1}^{(\tilde{t})}, r_v^{(\tilde{t})}) \in \mathsf{KU}^{(\tilde{t})}$:
   $\mathsf{lk}_v^{(t)} := (h_v^{(\tilde{t})}, h_{v||0}^{(\tilde{t})}, h_{v||1}^{(\tilde{t})}, r_v^{(\tilde{t})})$.
7. If $\exists (\tilde{t}, \mathsf{KU}^{(\tilde{t})}) \in \mathsf{KU}$ s.t. $(\mathsf{id}, \mathsf{ek}_v^{(\tilde{t})}, \perp) \in \mathsf{KU}^{(\tilde{t})}$: \\id is revoked at $\tilde{t}$
   Output $\mathsf{sk}_{\mathsf{id}}^{(t)} := (t, \mathsf{id}, \{\mathsf{lk}_v^{(t)}\}_{v \in \mathsf{W}}, \perp)$.
8. Output $\mathsf{sk}_{\mathsf{id}}^{(t)} := (t, \mathsf{id}, \{\mathsf{lk}_v^{(t)}\}_{v \in \mathsf{W}}, \mathsf{dk}_{\mathsf{id}})$.

4.1 Correctness

We first show that our revocable IBE is correct. During the time slot t, the key updating algorithm RIBE.KU (together with the key generation algorithm RIBE.KG) uniquely determines a fresh tree of time t. The root of the fresh tree has attachment $(h_\varepsilon^{(t)}, h_0^{(t)}, h_1^{(t)}, r_\varepsilon^{(t)})$. Set $\mathsf{W} := \{\varepsilon, \mathsf{id}[1], \cdots, \mathsf{id}[1 \cdots n-1]\}$, where ε is the empty string. Note that each id uniquely determines a path (from the root of the tree to the leaf of id). W records all non-leaf nodes on the path. For all nodes $v \in \mathsf{W}$, we have $\mathsf{H}(k_{|v|}, h_{v||0}^{(t)} || h_{v||1}^{(t)}; r_v^{(t)}) = h_v^{(t)}$, and $(h_{v||0}^{(t)}, h_{v||1}^{(t)}) := (\mathsf{ek}_{v||0}, \mathsf{ek}_{v||1})$ if $|v| = n - 1$.

Consider the ciphertext $\mathsf{ct} = \left(\left\{\mathsf{lab}_{\ell, h_{\varepsilon,\ell}^{(t)}}\right\}_{\ell \in [\lambda]}, \{\tilde{P}^0, \cdots, \tilde{P}^n, \tilde{Q}\}\right)$, which is the output of RIBE.Enc(mpk, id, t, m, PL). Consider the secret key $\mathsf{sk}_{\mathsf{id}}^{(t)} :=$ (id, $\{\mathsf{lk}_v^{(t)}\}_{v \in \mathsf{W}}, \mathsf{dk}_{\mathsf{id}}$), which is the output RIBE.DK. Obviously, $\mathsf{sk}_{\mathsf{id}}^{(t)}$ is exactly the the secret key of id in the tree (of time t). As long as the $h_\varepsilon^{(t)}$ used in RIBE.Enc to generate ct is identical to the $h_\varepsilon^{(t)}$ in $\mathsf{lk}_\varepsilon^{(t)} = (h_\varepsilon^{(t)}, h_0^{(t)}, h_1^{(t)}, r_\varepsilon^{(t)})$, the decryption RIBE.Dec can always recover the plaintext due to the correctness of the DG scheme.

Below we show the details of the correctness (this analysis is similar to that in [6]). For all nodes $v \in \mathsf{W}$, we have the following facts.

1. $\{c_{j,b}\}_{j \in [\lambda], b \in \{0,1\}} := \mathsf{Eval}\left(\tilde{P}^{|v|}, \left\{\mathsf{lab}_{j, h_{v,j}^{(t)}}\right\}_{j \in [\lambda]}\right) = P[\mathsf{id}[|v|+1], k_{|v|}, \{\mathsf{lab}'_{j,b}\}_{j \in [\lambda], b}](h_v^{(t)}) = \{\mathsf{HEnc}(k_{|v|}, (h_v^{(t)}, j + \mathsf{id}[|v|+1] \cdot \lambda, b), \mathsf{lab}'_{j,b})\}_{j \in [\lambda], b \in \{0,1\}}$. Recall that $\overline{\mathsf{lab}'} := \{\mathsf{lab}'_{j,b}\}_{j \in [\lambda], b \in \{0,1\}}$ and $(\overline{\mathsf{lab}'}, \tilde{P}^{(|v|+1)})$ are the output of $\mathsf{GCircuit}(1^\lambda, \mathsf{P}[\mathsf{id}[|v|+2], k_{|v|+1}, \overline{\mathsf{lab}''}])$.
2. Due to the correctness of the chameleon encryption, we know that given $(h_{v||0}^{(t)}, h_{v||1}^{(t)}, r_v^{(t)})$ one can recover $\left\{\mathsf{lab}'_{\ell, h_{v||\mathsf{id}[|v|+1],\ell}^{(t)}}\right\}_{\ell \in [\lambda]}$ by decrypting $\{c_{j, h_{v||\mathsf{id}[|v|+1],j}^{(t)}}\}_{j \in [\lambda]}$. And $\left\{\mathsf{lab}'_{\ell, h_{v||\mathsf{id}[|v|+1],\ell}^{(t)}}\right\}_{\ell \in [\lambda]}$ is the label for the next garbled circuit $\tilde{P}^{(|v|+1)}$.

3. When $|v| = n - 1$, we obtain the set of labels $\{\mathsf{lab}_{j,\mathsf{ek}_{\mathsf{id},j}}\}_{j\in[\lambda]}$. Recall that $\{\mathsf{lab}_{j,b}\}_{j\in[\lambda],b\in\{0,1\}}$ and $\tilde{Q}$ are the output of $\mathsf{GCircuit}(1^\lambda, Q[m])$. And $\{\mathsf{lab}_{j,\mathsf{ek}_{\mathsf{id},j}}\}_{j\in[\lambda]}$ is the result of $\{\mathsf{lab}_{j,b}\}_{j\in[\lambda],b\in\{0,1\}}$ selected by $\mathsf{ek}_{\mathsf{id}}$. Thus,

$$f := \mathsf{Eval}\left(\tilde{Q}, \{\mathsf{lab}_{j,\mathsf{ek}_{\mathsf{id},j}}\}_{j\in[\lambda]}\right) = Q[m](\mathsf{ek}_{\mathsf{id}}) = \mathsf{E}(\mathsf{ek}_{\mathsf{id}}, m).$$

Due to the correctness of $\mathsf{PKE} = (\mathsf{G}, \mathsf{E}, \mathsf{D})$, given decryption key $\mathsf{dk}_{\mathsf{id}}$, one can always recover the original message m correctly with $m \leftarrow \mathsf{D}(\mathsf{dk}_{\mathsf{id}}, f)$.

4.2 Security

In this subsection, we prove that our revocable IBE scheme is IND-ID-CPA secure. Assume q is a polynomial upper bound for the running-time of an adversary $\mathcal{A}$, and it is also an upper bound for the number of $\mathcal{A}$'s queries (which contains private key queries, key update queries, and revocation queries).

Theorem 1. *Assume that t_{max} is the size of the time space and 2^n be the maximal number of users. If PRF is a pseudorandom function, the garbled circuit scheme is secure, the chameleon encryption scheme CE is secure and $PKE = (G, E, D)$ is IND-CPA secure, the above proposed revocable IBE scheme is IND-ID-CPA secure. More specifically, for any PPT adversary $\mathcal{A}$ issuing at most q queries, there exist PPT adversaries $\mathcal{B}_1$, $\mathcal{B}_2$, $\mathcal{B}_3$ and $\mathcal{B}_4$ such that*

$$\begin{aligned} \boldsymbol{Adv}_{\mathcal{A}}^{IND\text{-}ID\text{-}CPA}(\lambda) \leq \boldsymbol{Adv}_{\mathcal{B}_1}^{PRF}(\lambda) + (n+1)\cdot \boldsymbol{Adv}_{\mathcal{B}_2}^{GC}(\lambda) + n\cdot\lambda\cdot \boldsymbol{Adv}_{\mathcal{B}_3}^{CE}(\lambda) \\ +(2q+1)\cdot \boldsymbol{Adv}_{\mathcal{B}_4}^{PKE}(\lambda). \end{aligned} \quad (1)$$

Proof. Due to the space limitation, we leave the proof in the full version.

5 Performance Analysis of Key Updating

In this section, we analyze the key updating efficiency of our revocable IBE scheme. Different from an IBE scheme, a revocable IBE scheme has enormous cost on the publishing updating keys at each time slot. In our RIBE, the number of updating keys is linear to the number of updated nodes. Therefore, we focus on the number of updated nodes for the performance. The advantage of our RIBE lies in the fact that the nodes that needs to updated is only related to the number Δr of newly revoked users in the past time slot. More precisely, the number of nodes needs to be updated in each time plot is at most $O(\Delta r(\log n - \log(\Delta r)))$. If there is no new users revoked in the previous time slot, then key updating is not necessary at all.

Recall that in the most of RIBE schemes, the size of updating keys is closely related to the total number r of *all* the revoked users across *all* the past slots. For example, in [2] the size of updated key during each time slot is of order $O(r\log(n/r))$, where n is the number of users.

For simulation, we use Poisson distribution to simulate the number of revoked users at each time period, where α denotes the expected number of revoked users in each time slot. We evaluate the number of nodes needing to be updated in our RIBE and the RIBE in [2]. The simulation results for $n = 15$ and $n = 25$ are shown in Figs. 3 and 4 respectively.

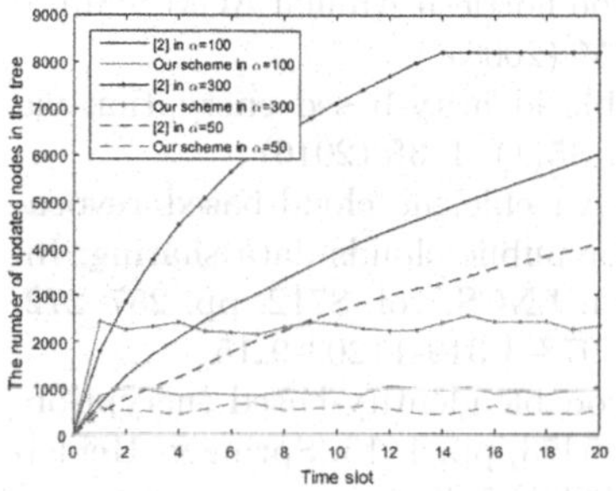

Fig. 3. n=15

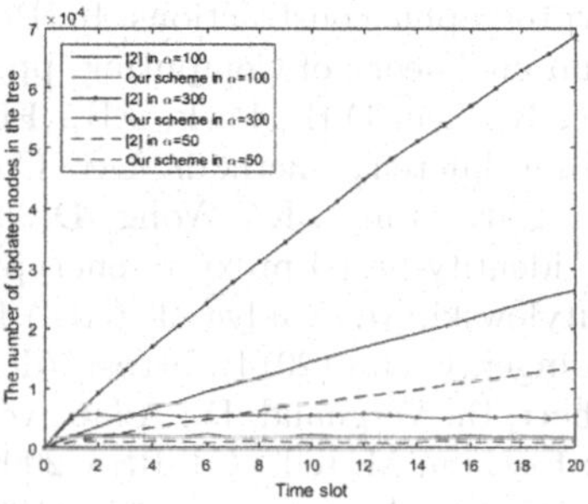

Fig. 4. n=25

Acknowledgements. The authors thank the anonymous reviewers for their helpful comments. Special thanks go to Atsushi Takayasu who helps us to give a better presentation of this paper. This work was supported by the National Natural Science Foundation of China (NSFC Grant No. 61672346). Kefei Chen was supported by National Key R&D Program of China (Grant No. 2017YFB0802000), NSFC (Grant No. U1705264) and (Grant No. 61472114). This work was also supported by NSFC (Grant No. 61702342) and the Science and Technology Innovation Projects of Shenzhen (GJHZ20160226202520268, JCYJ20170302145623566).

References

1. Agrawal, S., Boneh, D., Boyen, X.: Efficient lattice (H)IBE in the standard model. In: Gilbert, H. (ed.) EUROCRYPT 2010. LNCS, vol. 6110, pp. 553–572. Springer, Heidelberg (2010). https://doi.org/10.1007/978-3-642-13190-5_28
2. Boldyreva, A., Goyal, V., Kumar, V.: Identity-based encryption with efficient revocation. In: ACM Conference on Computer and Communications Security, pp. 417–426 (2008)
3. Boneh, D., Franklin, M.: Identity-based encryption from the Weil pairing. SIAM J. Comput. **32**(3), 586–615 (2003)
4. Cash, D., Hofheinz, D., Kiltz, E., Peikert, C.: Bonsai trees, or how to delegate a lattice basis. In: Gilbert, H. (ed.) EUROCRYPT 2010. LNCS, vol. 6110, pp. 523–552. Springer, Heidelberg (2010). https://doi.org/10.1007/978-3-642-13190-5_27
5. Chen, J., Lim, H.W., Ling, S., Wang, H., Nguyen, K.: Revocable identity-based encryption from lattices. In: Susilo, W., Mu, Y., Seberry, J. (eds.) ACISP 2012. LNCS, vol. 7372, pp. 390–403. Springer, Heidelberg (2012). https://doi.org/10.1007/978-3-642-31448-3_29

6. Döttling, N., Garg, S.: Identity-based encryption from the Diffie-Hellman assumption. In: Katz, J., Shacham, H. (eds.) CRYPTO 2017. LNCS, vol. 10401, pp. 537–569. Springer, Cham (2017). https://doi.org/10.1007/978-3-319-63688-7_18
7. Gentry, C.: Practical identity-based encryption without random oracles. In: Vaudenay, S. (ed.) EUROCRYPT 2006. LNCS, vol. 4004, pp. 445–464. Springer, Heidelberg (2006). https://doi.org/10.1007/11761679_27
8. Gentry, C., Peikert, C., Vaikuntanathan, V.: Trapdoors for hard lattices and new cryptographic constructions. In: Proceedings of the Fortieth Annual ACM Symposium on Theory of Computing, pp. 197–206. ACM (2008)
9. Lee, K., Lee, D.H., Park, J.H.: Efficient revocable identity-based encryption via subset difference methods. Des. Codes Cryptogr. **85**(1), 1–38 (2016)
10. Liang, K., Liu, J.K., Wong, D.S., Susilo, W.: An efficient cloud-based revocable identity-based proxy re-encryption scheme for public clouds data sharing. In: Kutyłowski, M., Vaidya, J. (eds.) ESORICS 2014. LNCS, vol. 8712, pp. 257–272. Springer, Cham (2014). https://doi.org/10.1007/978-3-319-11203-9_15
11. Libert, B., Vergnaud, D.: Adaptive-ID secure revocable identity-based encryption. In: Fischlin, M. (ed.) CT-RSA 2009. LNCS, vol. 5473, pp. 1–15. Springer, Heidelberg (2009). https://doi.org/10.1007/978-3-642-00862-7_1
12. Liu, J.K., Yuen, T.H., Zhang, P., Liang, K.: Time-based direct revocable ciphertext-policy attribute-based encryption with short revocation list. Cryptology ePrint Archive, Report 2018/330 (2018)
13. Okamoto, T., Takashima, K.: Fully secure functional encryption with general relations from the decisional linear assumption. In: Rabin, T. (ed.) CRYPTO 2010. LNCS, vol. 6223, pp. 191–208. Springer, Heidelberg (2010). https://doi.org/10.1007/978-3-642-14623-7_11
14. Park, S., Lee, K., Lee, D.H.: New constructions of revocable identity-based encryption from multilinear maps. IEEE Trans. Inf. Forensics Secur. **10**(8), 1564–1577 (2015)
15. Sahai, A., Waters, B.: Fuzzy identity-based encryption. In: Cramer, R. (ed.) EUROCRYPT 2005. LNCS, vol. 3494, pp. 457–473. Springer, Heidelberg (2005). https://doi.org/10.1007/11426639_27
16. Seo, J.H., Emura, K.: Revocable identity-based encryption revisited: security model and construction. In: Kurosawa, K., Hanaoka, G. (eds.) PKC 2013. LNCS, vol. 7778, pp. 216–234. Springer, Heidelberg (2013). https://doi.org/10.1007/978-3-642-36362-7_14
17. Shamir, A.: Identity-based cryptosystems and signature schemes. In: Blakley, G.R., Chaum, D. (eds.) CRYPTO 1984. LNCS, vol. 196, pp. 47–53. Springer, Heidelberg (1985). https://doi.org/10.1007/3-540-39568-7_5
18. Takayasu, A., Watanabe, Y.: Lattice-based revocable identity-based encryption with bounded decryption key exposure resistance. In: Pieprzyk, J., Suriadi, S. (eds.) ACISP 2017. LNCS, vol. 10342, pp. 184–204. Springer, Cham (2017). https://doi.org/10.1007/978-3-319-60055-0_10
19. Watanabe, Y., Emura, K., Seo, J.H.: New revocable IBE in prime-order groups: adaptively secure, decryption key exposure resistant, and with short public parameters. In: Handschuh, H. (ed.) CT-RSA 2017. LNCS, vol. 10159, pp. 432–449. Springer, Cham (2017). https://doi.org/10.1007/978-3-319-52153-4_25
20. Waters, B.: Efficient identity-based encryption without random oracles. In: Cramer, R. (ed.) EUROCRYPT 2005. LNCS, vol. 3494, pp. 114–127. Springer, Heidelberg (2005). https://doi.org/10.1007/11426639_7

21. Yang, Y., Liu, J.K., Liang, K., Choo, K.-K.R., Zhou, J.: Extended proxy-assisted approach: achieving revocable fine-grained encryption of cloud data. In: Pernul, G., Ryan, P.Y.A., Weippl, E. (eds.) ESORICS 2015. LNCS, vol. 9327, pp. 146–166. Springer, Cham (2015). https://doi.org/10.1007/978-3-319-24177-7_8
22. Yang, Y., Liu, J., Wei, Z., Huang, X.: Towards revocable fine-grained encryption of cloud data: reducing trust upon cloud. In: Pieprzyk, J., Suriadi, S. (eds.) ACISP 2017. LNCS, vol. 10342, pp. 127–144. Springer, Cham (2017). https://doi.org/10.1007/978-3-319-60055-0_7

Private Functional Signatures: Definition and Construction

Shimin Li[1,2], Bei Liang[3(✉)], and Rui Xue[1,2]

[1] State Key Laboratory of Information Security, Institute of Information Engineering, Chinese Academy of Sciences, Beijing 100093, China
{lishimin,xuerui}@iie.ac.cn

[2] School of Cyber Security, University of Chinese Academy of Sciences, Beijing 100049, China

[3] Chalmers University of Technology, Gothenburg, Sweden
lbei@chalmers.se

Abstract. In this paper, we introduce a new cryptographic primitive: *private functional signatures*, where functional signing keys sk_f for functions f derived from master signing key msk which can be used to sign any message, allow one to sign any message in the range of the underlying function f. Besides, there is an encryption algorithm which takes as input the master secret key msk to produce a ciphertext c_x for message x. And the signing algorithm applies a signing key sk_f on the ciphertext c_x to produce a signature $\sigma_{f(x)}$ on the result $f(x)$.

We also formalize the security notions of private functional signatures. Furthermore, we provide a general compiler from any (single-key) symmetric-key predicate encryption scheme into a single-key private functional signature scheme. By instantiating our construction with schemes for symmetric-key predicate encryption, we obtain private functional signature schemes based on a variety of assumptions (including the LWE assumption, simple multilinear-maps assumptions, obfuscation assumptions, and even the existence of any one-way function) offering various trade-offs between security and efficiency.

Keywords: Functional signature · Functional encryption
Predicate encryption

1 Introduction

While recent ground breaking work has shown how to sign any message in the range of an arbitrary function by using restricted key that is derived from the master signing key [BGI14] to work on any *plaintext* directly, far less is known about how to achieve such goal when accessing and working on an *encrypted message* together with restricted key.

Informally, the problem of how to sign an image resulted from a pre-image on function f given the encryption of the pre-image and the secondary signing key for function f, is as follows. Consider the scenario in a clinic with a doctor

W. Susilo and G. Yang (Eds.): ACISP 2018, LNCS 10946, pp. 284–303, 2018.
https://doi.org/10.1007/978-3-319-93638-3_17

and a number of lab assistants. The doctor wants to allow his assistants to add "APPROVAL" on the medical reports of his patients and then sign such approved reports on their behalf only for those medical reports with a certain tag, such as "signed by the assistant". Let P be a predicate that outputs 1 on messages with the proper tag, and 0 on all other messages. In order to delegate the signing process of this restricted set of messages, doctor would give the assistants a signing key sk_f for the following function:

$$f(m) := \begin{cases} \text{adding APPROVAL on } m, & P(\mathrm{m}) = 1; \\ \perp, & \text{otherwise.} \end{cases}$$

However, considering that the information of patients' medical reports are sensitive data, it is not allowed the assistants to have access it firsthand. Instead of giving the firsthand medical reports m to assistants to work with, doctor has to encrypt them first and then send the encrypted medical reports c_m to assistants. Now, assistants holding the functional signing key sk_f and an encryption of message m, can generate a signature σ for the message $f(m)$ but cannot learn any additional information about the message m beyond the function value itself. Moreover, the pair (m, σ) can be published and anyone can check that the assistants correctly applied f to the original message by verifying that σ is a signature on the message $f(m)$, which means the signature authenticates the result of applying f to the original message.

As we all know, in *functional signatures* (FS) introduced by Boyle et al. [BGI14] the signing procedure proceeds on the pre-image straightforward while in our case the pre-image is required not to be shown up as a plaintext but to be encoded. Therefore, in order to address our problem in the above scenario, in this paper we define a new primitive called *Private Functional Signatures* (PFS), which is able to generate signature for value $f(x)$ by utilizing a functional signing key sk_f for f to work on the encryption of x. More specifically, in a PFS scheme, the authority firstly generates a master signing key msk that can be used to sign any message, and a public verification key mvk. In addition, there are secondary functional signing keys sk_f for functions f derived from msk, which allow one to sign any message in the range of the underlying function f. Besides, there is an encryption algorithm which takes as input the master secret key msk and a plaintext x, and outputs a ciphertext c_x. The signing algorithm applies a signing key sk_f on the ciphertext c_x to produce a signature $\sigma_{f(x)}$ on the result $f(x)$.

We also consider two new properties – namely, *function privacy for keys* which intuitively requires that functional signing key reveals no unnecessary information on its functionality that the signing key used in the signing process is associated with beyond what is implied by the function value and corresponding signature in one's possession, and *message privacy for ciphertexts* which states that anyone holding the functional signing key sk_f and an encryption of some message m, cannot learn any additional information about the message m other than the value $f(m)$ and its signature.

1.1 Our Contributions

In this paper, we define the syntax of private functional signature schemes and formalize the notions of the security requirement: *unforgeability* as well as the efficiency requirement for signatures: *succinctness*. Besides, we innovatively put forth two new notions for PFS: *function privacy for keys* and *message privacy for ciphertexts* (see Sect. 3.2 for more details). Then, we propose a general construction of single-key private functional signature scheme for any class of functions $\mathcal{F}$ from a (single-key) symmetric-key predicate encryption for a larger class of functions $\mathcal{F}'$, where $\mathcal{F}'$ contains the function computing the i-th bit of the $f \in \mathcal{F}$. Moreover, our scheme can be instantiated using a variety of existing schemes based either on the Learning with Errors assumption, on obfuscation assumptions, on simple multilinear-maps assumptions, and even on the existence of any one-way function.

Theorem 1 (Informal). *Assuming the existence of a (single-key) symmetric-key predicate encryption scheme for a class of predicates $\mathcal{F}'$ (as above), there is a single-key private functional signature scheme for the class of functions $\mathcal{F}$. Note the scheme has succinct signatures: their size is independent of the size of the function size, and of the size of the input to the function.*

Despite that our scheme can only securely provide a *single key*, we can repeat the scheme q times in parallel to obtain a secure scheme against an adversary who receives q *keys*, which merely results in the ciphertext size grows linearly with q. If the single-key PFS is succinct, i.e. the size of the ciphertext is independent of the size of the circuit, the resulting q-keys PFS scheme is also *succinct*. Hence, we mainly focus on the single-key case.

1.2 Related Work

Functional Encryption. *Functional encryption* (FE), which was formalized by Boneh et al. in [BSW11], is motivated to realize decrypting the ciphertext in a more fine-grained manner, allowing tremendous flexibility when accessing encrypted data. More specifically, in a functional encryption scheme, a trusted authority holds a master secret key, which allows authority to generate a functional key sk_f for the function f. Anyone holding the functional key sk_f and an encryption c_m of some message m, can compute $f(m)$ but cannot learn any additional information about the message m.

While in our private functional signature scheme, what we realize is to generate not only the function value $f(m)$ but also the corresponding signature σ using the functional signing key, which can be considered as the combination of a functional encryption scheme with a signature scheme – namely, using the decryption algorithm of FE to obtain the function value first and then signing on such result to get a signature. From this point of view, our new primitive PFS is an even stronger notion that integrates both the functionality of FE and signature in only one building block. On the other hand, by returning back a signature σ for $f(m)$ which can be seen as a proof to convince any verifier the correctness of computation for the result $f(m)$ by verifying that σ is a signature on the message $f(m)$.

Functional Signature. *Functional signatures* (FS) introduced by Boyle et al. [BGI14] is an extension of the classical digital signature, where in addition to a master signing key that can be used to sign any message, there are secondary signing keys for functions f (called sk_f) derived from the master signing key, which allow one to produce a signature for any message in the range of f from the original message. In the literature perspective, our PFS employs an encryption algorithm to compute a ciphertext of original message, which in turn should be taken as input to the signing algorithm rather than the original message that is used in FS.

Besides the unforgeability requirement, Boyle et al. also defined a privacy notion called *function privacy*, which captures the idea that the signature should reveal neither the function f that the secret key used in the signing process corresponds to, nor the message m that f was applied to. In our PFS, we provide even stronger notion of privacy: function privacy for keys and message privacy for ciphertexts respectively, which together imply the so-called function privacy.

1.3 Overview of Our Techniques

In this section, we provide a high-level overview of our techniques. As we point out in the related work, our PFS can be considered as a combination of a functional encryption scheme with a signature scheme. A natural idea to construct a PFS would be to integrate the functional secret key sk_f of FE and the signing key sik of standard signature scheme as the functional signing key of PFS. However, such a simple method of combining two kinds of secret keys will lead to the complete exposure of the real signing key sik. In order to avoid the exposure of sik in the functional signing key of PFS, we employ the garbled circuit which is hardwired with sik and performs the signing algorithm of standard signature scheme.

Concretely, when compute the encryption of a message x, the encrypter firstly generates a garbled circuit for the (deterministic) signature signing algorithm $\mathsf{S.Sign}(\mathsf{sik}, \cdot)$ with the signing key sik hardcoded in it, meanwhile, she obtains a set of garbled circuit labels $\{L_i^0, L_i^1\}_i$. In this setting, in order to compute the signature of $f(x)$, the signer of PFS system who owns the encryption c_x and a signing key sk_f must obtain the input labels corresponding to $f(x)$, namely, the labels $\{L_i^{a_i}\}_i$ where a_i is the i-th bit of $f(x)$.

We can easily find that the functionality of symmetric-key predicate encryption (PE) is almost what we want, but not sufficient. For simplicity, we prefer to consider a variant notion of PE (called PE_2) that can be simply transformed from a standard PE. In symmetric-key PE_2, the encryption algorithm encrypts a value x with two messages m_0, m_1: $\mathsf{c}_x \leftarrow \mathsf{PE}_2(\mathsf{msk}, x, m_0, m_1)$, where msk is the master secret key. Then, the key generation algorithm produces a key for a function f: $\mathsf{sk}_f \leftarrow \mathsf{PE}_2.\mathsf{KeyGen}(\mathsf{msk}, f)$. Finally, the decryption algorithm evaluating on c_x and sk_f outputs m_0 if $f(x) = 0$ or outputs m_1 if $f(x) = 1$.

Now, we describe how the signer gets the label $L_i^{a_i}$ corresponding to the i-th bit of $f(x)$. Firstly, perform $\mathsf{PE}_2.\mathsf{Enc}$ on a pair of messages (L_i^0, L_i^1): $\mathsf{PE}_2(\mathsf{msk}, x, L_i^0, L_i^1)$, then generate the key corresponding to f_i (output the i-th bit of f on some values): $\mathsf{PE}_2.\mathsf{KeyGen}(\mathsf{msk}, f_i)$. Finally, the signer runs $\mathsf{PE}_2.\mathsf{Dec}$ to obtain $L_i^{a_i}$ where $a_i = f_i(x)$. By performing the above process bit by bit, the signer can naturally get the whole labels of $f(x)$. With these labels and the garbled circuit corresponding to the signing algorithm, the signer eventually obtains the signature of $f(x)$.

The security of the PE_2 ensures the signer cannot decrypt any other labels, so she can only obtain the signature of $f(x)$, in addition, the security of the garbling scheme provides a way of producing an encryption oracle without the signing key in security proof. In this way, the security reduction of the above PFS scheme can be easily completed.

1.4 Applications

Privately Search on Encrypted Data with Verifiability. Let us consider a scenario where a user stores her encrypted files on a service. The user can then remotely query her data by providing the service with a functional key sk_f corresponding to any query f. It seems that FE is sufficient to achieve privately searching on encrypted data. However, we observe that only when the service honestly works and returns the corresponding results can the privately searching on encrypted data is achieved. Therefore, we have to provide a verification mechanism for the results returned by service. Fortunately, by performing our PFS system which can verify the validity of a message/signature pair returned by the service via the verification algorithm, the user can be convinced to receive the right result.

Verifiable Delegation Scheme with Function-Privacy and Input-Privacy. Another main application of PFS is for verifiable delegation schemes which need to ensure the privacy of function and input. In this setting, there is a client who wants to allow a more powerful server to compute a function f on inputs x both of which are chosen by the client, and be able to verify the result returned by the server is correct, without revealing function f and input x to the server. By using our PFS scheme, the client sends the cipertext c_x of input x together with the signing key sk_f corresponding to f to the server. To prove $y = f(x)$, the server returns the computation result y as well as the corresponding signature σ, which is a correct result if (y, σ) is verified by the verification process of PFS. We stress that, due to the function privacy and message privacy of PFS scheme, the server cannot obtain any information either of function f or of input x except what the result reveals.

2 Preliminaries

2.1 Garbled Circuits

Definition 1 (Garbling scheme). *A garbling scheme for a family of boolean circuits* $\mathcal{C} = \{C : \{0,1\}^n \to \{0,1\}^k\}$ *is a tuple of PPT algorithms* $\mathsf{Gb} = (\mathsf{Gb.Garble}, \mathsf{Gb.Enc}, \mathsf{Gb.Eval})$ *such that*

- $\mathsf{Gb.Garble}(1^\lambda, C) \to (\Gamma, \mathsf{sk})$: *Takes as input the security parameter* λ *and a circuit* $C \in \mathcal{C}$ *for some* n *and* k, *and outputs the garbled circuit* Γ *and a secret key* sk.
- $\mathsf{Gb.Enc}(\mathsf{sk}, x) \to c$: *Takes as input* $x \in \{0,1\}^*$ *and outputs an encoding* c.
- $\mathsf{Gb.Eval}(\Gamma, c) \to C(x)$: *Takes as input a garbled circuit* Γ, *an encoding* c *and outputs a value* y *which should be* $C(x)$.

Correctness. *For all sufficiently large security parameters* λ, *for* $n = n(\lambda), k = k(\lambda)$, *for all circuits* $C \in \mathcal{C}$ *and all* $x \in \{0,1\}^n$,

$$\Pr[(\Gamma, \mathsf{sk}) \leftarrow \mathsf{Gb.Garble}(1^\lambda, C);\ c \leftarrow \mathsf{Gb.Enc}(\mathsf{sk}, x);\ y \leftarrow \mathsf{Gb.Eval}(\Gamma, c) \colon C(x) = y] = 1 - \mathrm{negl}(\lambda).$$

Input and Circuit Privacy. Regarding the security of one-time garbled circuits, we focus on the *input privacy*, and *circuit privacy*. Note these two properties hold with the limitation of one-time evaluation of the circuit, namely the adversary can receive at most one encoding of an input with regard to a garbled circuit, and could compromise the security if obtaining more than one encoding. Below, We provide the one-time security of garbing circuits.

Definition 2 (Input and circuit privacy). *A garbling scheme* Gb *for a family of boolean circuits* $\mathcal{C} = \{C : \{0,1\}^n \to \{0,1\}^k\}$ *is input and circuit private if there exists a PPT simulator* $\mathsf{Sim}_{\mathsf{Garble}}$, *such that for every PPT adversaries* $\mathcal{A}$ *and* $\mathcal{D}$, *for all sufficiently large security parameters* λ,

$$|\Pr[(x, C, \alpha) \leftarrow \mathcal{A}(1^\lambda); (\Gamma, \mathsf{sk}) \leftarrow \mathsf{Gb.Garble}(1^\lambda, C); c \leftarrow \mathsf{Gb.Enc}(\mathsf{sk}, x) : D(\alpha, x, \Gamma, c) = 1]$$
$$- \Pr[(x, C, \alpha) \leftarrow \mathcal{A}(1^\lambda); (\bar{\Gamma}, \bar{c}) \leftarrow \mathsf{Sim}_{\mathsf{Garble}}(1^\lambda, C(x), 1^{|C|}, 1^{|x|}) : D(\alpha, x, C, \bar{\Gamma}, \bar{c}) = 1]|$$
$$= \mathrm{negl}(\lambda),$$

where $n, k, x \in \{0,1\}^n$ *and* $C \in \mathcal{C}$, *and* α *represents any state information that* $\mathcal{A}$ *wants to convey to* $\mathcal{D}$.

Theorem 2 [Yao82,LP09]. *Assuming one-way functions exist, there exists a Yao (one-time) garbling scheme that is input- and circuit-private for all circuits over GF(2).*

2.2 Symmetric-Key Two-Outcome Predicate Encryption

For our construction, we need to give a slightly modified definition of symmetric-key predicate encryption which we call *symmetric-key two-outcome predicate encryption.* The formal definition of symmetric-key predicate encryption is referred to Appendix 5.2. We formalize the definition of symmetric-key two-outcome predicate encryption and the related security notions as follows.

Definition 3 (Symmetric-Key Two-Outcome Predicate Encryption). *A symmetric-key two-outcome predicate encryption (PE_2) for a class of predicates $\mathcal{F} = \{\mathcal{F}_l\}_{l\in\mathbb{N}}$ represented as boolean circuits with l input bits and one output bit and an associated message space $\mathcal{M}$ is a tuple of algorithms ($\mathsf{PE}_2.\mathsf{Setup}, \mathsf{PE}_2.\mathsf{KeyGen}, \mathsf{PE}_2.\mathsf{Enc}, \mathsf{PE}_2.\mathsf{Dec}$) as follows:*

- $\mathsf{PE}_2.\mathsf{Setup}(1^\lambda) \to \mathsf{pmsk}$: *Takes as input a security parameter λ and outputs a master secret key* pmsk.
- $\mathsf{PE}_2.\mathsf{KeyGen}(\mathsf{pmsk}, f) \to \mathsf{sk}_f$: *Given a master secret key* pmsk *and a predicate $f \in \mathcal{F}$, outputs a secret key sk_f corresponding to f.*
- $\mathsf{PE}_2.\mathsf{Enc}(\mathsf{pmsk}, x, m_0, m_1) \to c$: *Takes as input the master secret key* pmsk, *an attribute $x \in \{0,1\}^l$, for some l, and two messages $m_0, m_1 \in \mathcal{M}$ and outputs a ciphertext c.*
- $\mathsf{PE}_2.\mathsf{Dec}(\mathsf{sk}_f, c) \to m$ *or* $\perp$: *Takes as input a secret key for a predicate and a ciphertext and outputs $m \in \mathcal{M}$ or $\perp$.*

Correctness. *For every sufficiently large security parameter λ, all predicates $f \in \mathcal{F}$, all attributes $x \in \{0,1\}^l$, and all pair of messages $m_0, m_1 \in \mathcal{M}$:*

$$\Pr[\mathsf{pmsk} \leftarrow \mathsf{PE}_2.\mathsf{Setup}(1^\lambda);\ \mathsf{sk}_f \leftarrow \mathsf{PE}_2.\mathsf{KeyGen}(\mathsf{pmsk}, f); c \leftarrow \mathsf{PE}_2.\mathsf{Enc}(\mathsf{pmsk}, x, m_0, m_1);\ m \leftarrow \mathsf{PE}_2.\mathsf{Dec}(\mathsf{sk}_f, c) : m = m_{f(x)}] = 1 - \mathrm{negl}(\lambda).$$

We now define the security for single-key symmetric two-outcome predicate encryption. Throughout the paper we regard a pair of attribute and message as a context. Note we focus on the case that the adversary can only ask a *single key*.

Definition 4 (Context hiding (PE_2)). *Let PE_2 be a symmetric-key two-outcome predicate encryption scheme for the class of predicates $\mathcal{F}$ and an associated message space $\mathcal{M}$. Let $\mathcal{A}$ be a PPT adversary. Consider the following experiment:*

Setup: *The challenger runs* $\mathsf{PE}_2.\mathsf{Setup}(1^\lambda)$ *and keeps* pmsk *to itself.*
Respond the secret key: *$\mathcal{A}$ gives the predicate $f \in \mathcal{F}$, then the challenger responds with* $\mathsf{PE}_2.\mathsf{KeyGen}(\mathsf{pmsk}, f)$.
Ciphertext query 1: *$\mathcal{A}$ can query ciphertexts of some messages at most polynomial times. On the ith ciphertext query, $\mathcal{A}$ outputs a tuple $(x_i \in \{0,1\}^l, m_i^0 \in \mathcal{M}, m_i^1 \in \mathcal{M})$. The challenger responds with* $\mathsf{PE}_2.\mathsf{Enc}(\mathsf{pmsk}, x_i, m_i^0, m_i^1)$.
Challenge: *$\mathcal{A}$ outputs a tuple of (m, m_0, m_1, x_0, x_1). The challenger chooses a random bit $b \in \{0,1\}$ and responds with*

$$c = \begin{cases} \mathsf{PE}_2.\mathsf{Enc}(\mathsf{pmsk}, x_b, m, m_b), & \textit{if } f(x_b) = 0, \\ \mathsf{PE}_2.\mathsf{Enc}(\mathsf{pmsk}, x_b, m_b, m), & \textit{otherwise.} \end{cases}$$

where $f \in \mathcal{F}$ is the predicate queried before.
Ciphertext query 2: *$\mathcal{A}$ adaptively issues additional queries as in Ciphertext query* 1.
Guess: *$\mathcal{A}$ outputs a guess bit b'.*

The advantage of $\mathcal{A}$ is defined as $\mathsf{Adv}_{PE_2,\mathcal{A}} = |\Pr[b' = b] - 1/2|$. *We say the scheme is single-key context hiding if, for all PPT adversaries $\mathcal{A}$, the advantage of $\mathcal{A}$ in winning the above game is negligible in λ.*

Definition 5 (Predicate privacy (PE_2)). *Let PE_2 be a symmetric-key two-outcome predicate encryption scheme for the class of predicates $\mathcal{F}$ and an associated message space $\mathcal{M}$. Let $\mathcal{A}$ be a PPT adversary. Consider the following experiment:*

Setup: *The challenger runs* $\mathsf{PE}_2.\mathsf{Setup}(1^\lambda)$ *and keeps* pmsk *to itself.*
Ciphertext query 1: *$\mathcal{A}$ can query ciphertexts of some messages at most polynomial times. On the ith ciphertext query, $\mathcal{A}$ outputs a tuple $(x_i \in \{0,1\}^l, m_i^0 \in \mathcal{M}, m_i^1 \in \mathcal{M})$. The challenger responds with* $\mathsf{PE}_2.\mathsf{Enc}(\mathsf{pmsk}, x_i, m_i^0, m_i^1)$.
Challenge: *$\mathcal{A}$ outputs two predicates $f_0^*, f_1^* \in \mathcal{F}$ such that, for all previous ciphertext queries x_i, $f_0^*(x_i) = f_1^*(x_i)$. The challenger chooses a random bit $b \in \{0,1\}$ and responds with* $\mathsf{PE}_2.\mathsf{KeyGen}(\mathsf{pmsk}, f_b^*)$.
Ciphertext query 2: *$\mathcal{A}$ adaptively issues additional queries as in Ciphertext query* 1.
Guess: *$\mathcal{A}$ outputs a guess bit b'.*

The advantage of $\mathcal{A}$ is defined as $\mathsf{Adv}_{PE_2,\mathcal{A}} = |\Pr[b' = b] - 1/2|$. *We say the scheme is predicate private if, for all PPT adversaries $\mathcal{A}$, the advantage of $\mathcal{A}$ in winning the above game is negligible in λ.*

Goldwasser et al. [GKP+13] has proven that assuming there is an ABE scheme for a class of predicates closed under negation, there exists a two-outcome ABE scheme for the same class of predicates. We can apply the same transformation to a symmetric-key predicate encryption scheme to obtain a symmetric-key two-outcome predicate encryption. Due to space constraints, we refer the reader to [GKP+13] for the concrete techniques of this transformation, and we here omit the presentation.

3 Private Functional Signatures: Definition and Construction

We now give a formal definition of a private functional signature scheme, and explain in more detail the unforgeability, function privacy and message privacy properties a private functional signature scheme should satisfy.

3.1 Formal Definition

Definition 6 (Private Functional Signature). *A private functional signature scheme (PFS) for a function family $\mathcal{F} = \{f : \{0,1\}^l \to \{0,1\}^n\}$, where $l = l(\lambda), n = n(\lambda)$ consists of algorithms* ($\mathsf{PFS.Setup}, \mathsf{PFS.KeyGen}, \mathsf{PFS.Enc}, \mathsf{PFS.Sign}, \mathsf{PFS.Verify}$):

- $\mathsf{PFS.Setup}(1^\lambda) \to (\mathsf{msk}, \mathsf{mvk})$: *the setup algorithm takes as input a security parameter* λ *and outputs the master secret key* msk *and the master verification key* mvk.
- $\mathsf{PFS.KeyGen}(\mathsf{msk}, f) \to \mathsf{sk}_f$: *the key generation algorithm takes as input the master secret key and a function* $f \in \mathcal{F}$ *(represented as a circuit), and outputs a signing key for* f.
- $\mathsf{PFS.Enc}(\mathsf{msk}, x) \to \mathsf{c}_x$: *the encryption algorithm takes as input the master secret key and a message* $x \in \{0,1\}^l$*, and outputs an encryption of* x.
- $\mathsf{PFS.Sign}(\mathsf{sk}_f, \mathsf{c}_x) \to (f(x), \sigma)$: *the signing algorithm takes as input the signing key for a function* $f \in \mathcal{F}$ *and an encryption of* x*, and outputs* $f(x)$ *and a signature of* $f(x)$.
- $\mathsf{PFS.Verify}(\mathsf{mvk}, x^*, \sigma) \to \{0,1\}$: *the verification algorithm takes as input the master verification key* mvk*, a message* x^* *and a signature* σ*, and outputs 1 if the signature is valid.*

Correctness. *For all* $f \in \mathcal{F}$, $x \in \{0,1\}^l$, $(\mathsf{msk}, \mathsf{mvk}) \leftarrow \mathsf{PFS.Setup}(1^\lambda)$, $\mathsf{sk}_f \leftarrow \mathsf{PFS.KeyGen}(\mathsf{msk}, f)$, $\mathsf{c}_x \leftarrow \mathsf{PFS.Enc}(\mathsf{msk}, x)$, $(x^*, \sigma) \leftarrow \mathsf{PFS.Sign}(\mathsf{sk}_f, \mathsf{c}_x)$, *it holds that* $\mathsf{PFS.Verify}(\mathsf{mvk}, x^*, \sigma) = 1$.

Unforgeability. *The scheme is single-key unforgeable if the advantage of any PPT adversary in the following game is negligible:*

- *The challenger generates* $(\mathsf{msk}, \mathsf{mvk}) \leftarrow \mathsf{PFS.Setup}(1^\lambda)$*, and gives* mvk *to the adversary.*
- *The adversary outputs the function* $f \in \mathcal{F}$*, then the challenger computes* $\mathsf{sk}_f \leftarrow \mathsf{PFS.KeyGen}(\mathsf{msk}, f)$ *and returns* sk_f *to the adversary.*
- *The adversary is allowed to query an encryption oracle* $\mathcal{O}_{\mathsf{Enc}}$ *and a signing oracle* $\mathcal{O}_{\mathsf{Sign}}$ *for at most* $\mathsf{poly}(\lambda)$ *times. The two oracles are defined as follows:*
  - ▷ $\mathcal{O}_{\mathsf{Enc}}(x)$*: compute* $\mathsf{c}_x \leftarrow \mathsf{PFS.Enc}(\mathsf{msk}, x)$ *and output* c_x.
  - ▷ $\mathcal{O}_{\mathsf{Sign}}(f, x)$*: firstly compute an encryption* $\mathsf{c}_x \leftarrow \mathsf{PFS.Enc}(\mathsf{msk}, x)$ *and a signing key* $\mathsf{sk}_f \leftarrow \mathsf{PFS.KeyGen}(\mathsf{msk}, f)$*, then generate a signature on* $f(x)$, $\sigma \leftarrow \mathsf{PFS.Sign}(\mathsf{sk}_f, \mathsf{c}_x)$*, and output* σ.
- *The adversary wins the game if it can produce* $(\hat{x}, \hat{\sigma})$ *such that*
  - $\mathsf{PFS.Verify}(\mathsf{mvk}, \hat{x}, \hat{\sigma}) = 1$.
  - *there exists no a query* x *for the* $\mathcal{O}_{\mathsf{Enc}}$ *oracle such that* $\hat{x} = f(x)$ *for* f *which is the function output by adversary in the second step.*
  - *there exists no a* (f, x) *pair such that* (f, x) *was a query to the* $\mathcal{O}_{\mathsf{Sign}}$ *oracle and* $\hat{x} = f(x)$.

Succinctness. *There exists a polynomial* $p(\cdot)$ *such that for every* $\lambda \in \mathbb{N}, f \in \mathcal{F}, x \in \{0,1\}^l$*, it holds with probability 1 over* $(\mathsf{msk}, \mathsf{mvk}) \leftarrow \mathsf{PFS.Setup}(1^\lambda)$; $\mathsf{sk}_f \leftarrow \mathsf{PFS.Key\ Gen}(\mathsf{msk}, f)$; $\mathsf{c}_x \leftarrow \mathsf{PFS.Enc}(\mathsf{msk}, x)$; $\sigma \leftarrow \mathsf{PFS.Sign}(\mathsf{sk}_f, \mathsf{c}_x)$ *that the resulting signature on* $f(x)$ *has size* $|\sigma| \leq p(\lambda, |f(x)|)$*. In particular, the signature size is independent of the size* $|x|$ *of the input to the function, and of the size* $|f|$ *of a description of the function* f.

3.2 Privacy

In our private functional signature sheme, we discuss two distinct *privacy* properties respectively referring to the function and the message. Intuitively, the first one captures the idea that the signing key sk_f reveals no unnecessary information on the function f, which is *function privacy for keys.* While another property requires that the encryption c_x reveals no information of the underlying message x, which we call *message privacy for ciphertexts.* Formally, the above two properties are captured by the following definitions.

Definition 7 (Function privacy for keys). *The scheme satisfies function privacy for keys if the advantage of any PPT adversary in the following game is negligible:*

- *The challenger firstly generates* $(\mathsf{msk}, \mathsf{mvk}) \leftarrow \mathsf{PFS.Setup}(1^\lambda)$ *and gives* mvk *to the adversary.*
- *The adversary outputs a pair of functions* (f_0, f_1) *for which* $|f_0| = |f_1|$.
- *The adversary queries encryptions on the messages* $(x_1, \ldots, x_k)$ *which satisfy that* $f_0(x_i) = f_1(x_i)$ *for all* $i = 1, \ldots, k$, *and receives the encryptions* $\mathsf{c}_i \leftarrow \mathsf{PFS.Enc}(\mathsf{msk}, x_i)$ *for* $i = 1, \ldots, k$ *from the challenger. Note that the messages* $x_1, \ldots, x_k$ *can be output adaptively.*
- *The challenger chooses a random bit* $b \leftarrow \{0, 1\}$, *then computes* $\mathsf{sk}_f^* \leftarrow \mathsf{PFS.KeyGen}\ (\mathsf{msk}, f_b)$ *and returns* sk_f^* *to the adversary.*
- *The adversary outputs a bit* b', *and wins the game if* $b' = b$.

Definition 8 (Message privacy for ciphertexts). *The scheme satisfies message privacy for ciphertexts if the advantage of any PPT adversary in the following game is negligible:*

- *The challenger firstly generates* $(\mathsf{msk}, \mathsf{mvk}) \leftarrow \mathsf{PFS.Setup}(1^\lambda)$ *and gives* mvk *to the adversary.*
- *The adversary outputs a pair of messages* (x_0, x_1) *for which* $|x_0| = |x_1|$.
- *The adversary queries signing keys on the functions* $(f_1, \ldots, f_k)$ *which satisfy* $f_i(x_0) = f_i(x_1)$ *for all* $i = 1, \ldots, k$, *then receives the related signing keys* $\mathsf{sk}_{f_i} \leftarrow \mathsf{PFS.KeyGen}(\mathsf{msk}, f_i)$ *for* $i = 1, \ldots, k$ *from the challenger. Note that the functions* $f_1, \ldots, f_k$ *can be output adaptively.*
- *The challenger chooses a random bit* $b \leftarrow \{0, 1\}$, *computes* $\mathsf{c}^* \leftarrow \mathsf{PFS.Enc}(\mathsf{msk}, x_b)$ *and sends* c^* *to the adversary.*
- *The adversary outputs a bit* b', *and wins the game if* $b' = b$.

We can easily deduce that if a private functional signature scheme satisfies both the function privacy for keys and the message privacy for ciphertexts, then the signature of this scheme cannot reveal neither the function f whose corresponding signing key was used in the signing process, nor the message m that f was applied to.

4 Construction

In this section, we present our construction of a private functional signature scheme in detail. Our construction relies on the following three building blocks:

- A two-outcome predicate encryption scheme in symmetric-key setting $\mathsf{PE}_2 = (\mathsf{PE}_2.\mathsf{Setup}, \mathsf{PE}_2.\mathsf{KeyGen}, \mathsf{PE}_2.\mathsf{Enc}, \mathsf{PE}_2.\mathsf{Dec})$.
- A Yao garbling scheme $\mathsf{Gb} = (\mathsf{Gb.Garble}, \mathsf{Gb.Enc}, \mathsf{Gb.Eval})$.
- A deterministic signature scheme $\mathsf{S} = (\mathsf{S.Gen}, \mathsf{S.Sign}, \mathsf{S.Verify})$ with signature space $\{0,1\}^{l_{sig}}$.

Let g be any one way function, function family $\mathcal{F} = \{f\colon \{0,1\}^l \rightarrow \{0,1\}^n\}$, where $l = l(\lambda), n = n(\lambda)$. The construction of $\mathsf{PFS} = (\mathsf{PFS.Setup}, \mathsf{PFS.KeyGen}, \mathsf{PFS.Enc}, \mathsf{PFS.Sign}, \mathsf{PFS.Verify})$ proceeds as follows.

- $\mathsf{PFS.Setup}(1^\lambda) \rightarrow (\mathsf{msk}, \mathsf{mvk})$:
  Run the setup algorithm for PE_2 n times: $\mathsf{pmsk}_i \leftarrow \mathsf{PE}_2.\mathsf{Setup}(1^\lambda)$ for $i \in [n]$. Then run the key generation algorithm for signature scheme: $(\mathsf{sik}, \mathsf{vk}) \leftarrow \mathsf{S.Gen}(1^\lambda)$. Output a master secret key $\mathsf{msk} = (\mathsf{pmsk}_1, \ldots, \mathsf{pmsk}_n, \mathsf{sik})$ and a master verification key $\mathsf{mvk} = \mathsf{vk}$.
- $\mathsf{PFS.KeyGen}(\mathsf{msk}, f) \rightarrow \mathsf{sk}_f$:
  Let $f_i(x)$ is the i-th bit of the computation of $f \in \mathcal{F}$ on $x \in \{0,1\}^l$, where $i \in [n]$. Thus, $f_i\colon \{0,1\}^l \rightarrow \{0,1\}$. Run the key generation algorithm of PE_2 with different master secret keys for the function f_i: $\mathsf{sk}_{f_i} \leftarrow \mathsf{PE}_2.\mathsf{KeyGen}(\mathsf{pmsk}_i, f_i)$ for $i \in [n]$. Output $\mathsf{sk}_f = (\mathsf{sk}_{f_1}, \ldots, \mathsf{sk}_{f_n})$ as the signing key for the function f.
- $\mathsf{PFS.Enc}(\mathsf{msk}, x) \rightarrow \mathsf{c}_x$:
  Run the Yao garbled circuit generation algorithm to produce a garbled circuit for S's signing algorithm $\mathsf{S.Sign}(\mathsf{sik}, \cdot)\colon \{0,1\}^n \rightarrow \{0,1\}^{l_{sig}}$: $(\Gamma, \{L_i^0, L_i^1\}_{i=1}^n) \leftarrow \mathsf{Gb.Garble}(1^\lambda, \mathsf{S.Sign}(\mathsf{sik}, \cdot))$, where Γ is the garbled circuit and $\{L_i^0, L_i^1\}_{i=1}^n$ are the input labels.
  Let $vk_i^0 = g(L_i^0)$, $vk_i^1 = g(L_i^1)$ for $i \in [n]$, set $vk := \{vk_i^0, vk_i^1\}_{i=1}^n$.
  Then run encryption algorithm of PE_2 with $\{L_i^0, L_i^1\}_{i=1}^n$ to get ciphertexts $\mathsf{c}_1, \ldots, \mathsf{c}_n$: $\mathsf{c}_i \leftarrow \mathsf{PE}_2.\mathsf{Enc}(\mathsf{pmsk}_i, x, L_i^0, L_i^1)$ for $i \in [n]$. Output the ciphertext $\mathsf{c}_x = (\mathsf{c}_1, \ldots, \mathsf{c}_n, \Gamma, vk)$.
- $\mathsf{PFS.Sign}(\mathsf{sk}_f, \mathsf{c}_x) \rightarrow (f(x), \sigma)$:
  Run the PE_2 decryption algorithm on the ciphertexts $\mathsf{c}_1, \ldots, \mathsf{c}_n$ to recover the corresponding labels: $L_i^{a_i} \leftarrow \mathsf{PE}_2.\mathsf{Dec}(\mathsf{sk}_{f_i}, c_i)$ for $i \in [n]$, where a_i is equal to $f_i(x_1, \ldots, x_n)$. Firstly, for $i \in [n]$, compute $f(x) = a_1 \ldots a_n$:

$$a_i = \begin{cases} 0, & \text{if } g(L_i^{a_i}) = vk_i^0, \\ 1, & \text{if } g(L_i^{a_i}) = vk_i^1. \end{cases}$$

  Then run the garbled circuit evaluation algorithm on the garbled circuit Γ and the labels $L_i^{a_i}$ to compute $\mathsf{Gb.Eval}(\Gamma, L_1^{a_1}, \ldots, L_n^{a_n}) = \mathsf{S.Sign}(\mathsf{sik}, a_1 a_2 \ldots a_n) = \sigma$.
  Output $(f(x), \sigma)$.

– $\mathsf{PFS.Verify}(\mathsf{mvk}, x^*, \sigma) \rightarrow \{0, 1\}$:
  Run S's verification algorithm on the pair of (x^*, σ): $\mathsf{S.Verify}(\mathsf{vk}, x^*, \sigma) \rightarrow \{0, 1\}$.
  Output the value of the above verification algorithm.

Correctness. Correctness of our PFS scheme follows directly from the correctness of the underlying PE_2 scheme, the garbling scheme and the signature scheme.
Succinctness. Succinctness of our private functional signature scheme follows from the fact that $\sigma = \mathsf{S.Sign}(\mathsf{sik}, f(x))$. That is, the signatures of PFS are essentially the classical signatures of a standard signature scheme. Thus, the signature size of our PFS only depends on the size of range of the underlying signature scheme and is independent of the size of the function f and the input x.

4.1 Unforgeability

In this section, we argue our private functional signature scheme holds the essential security requirement, namely unforgeability.

Theorem 3. *If the signature scheme* S *is existentially unforgeable under chosen message attack, and the symmetric-key two-outcome predicate encryption* PE_2 *satisfies context hiding, and the Yao's garbling scheme* Gb *is input- and circuit-private, then* PFS *as specified above satisfies the unforgeability requirement for private functional signatures.*

Proof. Fix a PPT adversary $\mathcal{A}_{\mathsf{PFS}}$, and let $Q(\lambda)$ be a polynomial upper bound on the number of the queries made by $\mathcal{A}_{\mathsf{PFS}}$ to the oracles $\mathcal{O}_{\mathsf{Enc}}$ and $\mathcal{O}_{\mathsf{Sign}}$. Note that $\mathcal{A}_{\mathsf{PFS}}$ can query a *single* signing key during the game.

Game 0. $\mathsf{Exp}^{\mathsf{G_0}}_{\mathsf{PFS},\mathcal{A}}$ is the real unforgeability game between the challenger and $\mathcal{A}_{\mathsf{PFS}}$.
Game 1. $\mathsf{Exp}^{\mathsf{G_1}}_{\mathsf{PFS},\mathcal{A}}$ is the same as Game 0, except that the way that $\mathcal{O}_{\mathsf{Sign}}$ computes signature on the query (f, x) changes. Specifically, the challenger directly runs S.Sign with sik to compute the signature: $\sigma_{f(x)} \leftarrow \mathsf{S.Sign}(\mathsf{sik}, f(x))$, then returns $\sigma_{f(x)}$ to $\mathcal{A}$.
Game 2. $\mathsf{Exp}^{\mathsf{G_2}}_{\mathsf{PFS},\mathcal{A}}$ is the same as Game 1, except that the ciphertexts of PE_2 computed by $\mathcal{O}_{\mathsf{Enc}}$ change, namely: $\bar{c}_i \leftarrow \mathsf{PE}_2.\mathsf{Enc}(\mathsf{pmpk}_i, x, L_i^{a_i}, L_i^{a_i})$ for $i \in [n]$, where $a_i = f_i(x)$, the i-th bit of $f(x)$, and f is the function that $\mathcal{A}_{\mathsf{PFS}}$ queried for the signing key before. Then set $\bar{c}_x := (\bar{c}_1, \ldots, \bar{c}_n, \Gamma, vk)$.
Game 3. Firstly, let $\mathcal{S}^{\mathsf{Gb}} = (\mathcal{S}_1^{\mathsf{Gb}}, \mathcal{S}_2^{\mathsf{Gb}})$ be the simulator for the underlying garbling scheme for the class of circuits corresponding to $\mathsf{S.Sign}(\mathsf{sik}, \cdot)$. $\mathsf{Exp}^{\mathsf{G_3}}_{\mathsf{PFS},\mathcal{A}}$ is the same as Game 2, except that we employ the simulator $\mathcal{S}^{\mathsf{Gb}}$ instead of the real garbling algorithm to produce a simulated circuit $\overline{\Gamma}$ and the simulated labels $\{\overline{L}_i\}_{i=1}^n$ for every encryption query on x. More precisely, in the $\mathcal{O}_{\mathsf{Enc}}$ oracle:

1. We run $\mathcal{S}_1^{\mathsf{Gb}}$ to generate a simulated circuit: $(\overline{\Gamma}, \mathsf{state}_{\mathcal{S}^{\mathsf{Gb}}}) \leftarrow \mathcal{S}_1^{\mathsf{Gb}}(1^\lambda, 1^{|\mathsf{S.Sign}(\mathsf{sik},\cdot)|})$.

2. Then we perform $\mathcal{S}_2^{\mathsf{Gb}}$ to compute the simulated labels. In detail, $\mathcal{O}_{\mathsf{Enc}}$ computes the encryption of the query x below:
   (a) Firstly, compute the signature of $f(x)$: $\sigma_{f(x)} \leftarrow \mathsf{S.Sign}(\mathsf{sik}, f(x))$, where f is the function that $\mathcal{A}_{\mathsf{PFS}}$ queried for the signing key before.
   (b) Then run $\mathcal{S}_2^{\mathsf{Gb}}$ to compute the simulated labels corresponding to $f(x)$: $\{\overline{L}_i\}_{i=1}^n \leftarrow \mathcal{S}_2^{\mathsf{Gb}}(\sigma_{f(x)}, 1^n, \mathsf{state}_{\mathcal{S}^{\mathsf{Gb}}})$.
   (c) Next, for $i \in [n]$, we compute $\overline{vk}_i^{a_i} = g(\overline{L}_i)$, $\overline{vk}_i^{1-a_i} = g(r_i)$, where $a_i = f_i(x)$, and r_i is randomly chosen from $\{0,1\}^{|\overline{L}_i|}$. Set $\overline{vk} := \{\overline{vk}_i^{a_i}, \overline{vk}_i^{1-a_i}\}_{i=1}^n$.
   (d) Now produce the encryption of PE_2 with the above simulated labels $\{\overline{L}_i\}_{i=1}^n$: $\overline{c}_i \leftarrow \mathsf{PE}_2.\mathsf{Enc}(\mathsf{pmpk}_i, x, \overline{L}_i, \overline{L}_i)$ for $i \in [n]$.
3. Finally set $\overline{c}_x := (\overline{c}_1, \ldots, \overline{c}_n, \overline{\Gamma}, \overline{vk})$.

First step: We firstly prove each pair of consecutive games to be computationally indistinguishable in the following three lemmas: Lemmas 1, 2 and 3 in Appendix 5.3.
Second step: Now, we prove the advantage for any PPT adversary that wins in Game 3 is negligible. The proof is given in Appendix 5.4 in detail.
Remark. We stress that if we want a PFS scheme which merely satisfies the unforgeability requirement, then we can directly replace PE_2 with a *more lightweight* tool: a two-outcome attribute-based encryption (ABE_2) scheme defined by [GKP+13]. The security of ABE_2 ensures that an adversary can decrypt one of the two messages encrypted in the ciphertext based on the evaluation of a predicate f on the attribute, but does not learn anything about the other message, which is sufficient for the unforgeability proof of a PFS scheme.

4.2 Privacy

According to the construction of our PFS scheme, the ciphertexts of message x consists of n encryptions of PE_2 and a garbled circuit Γ (which is irrelevant to x). We notice that the message x in our scheme actually acts as the attribute for n ciphertexts of PE_2 scheme. Thus, it is trivial to conclude that context hiding PE_2 certifies the message privacy for ciphertexts of our PFS scheme.

Theorem 4. *If the two-outcome predicate encryption* PE_2 *satisfies context hiding, then the above private functional signature scheme holds the property of message privacy for ciphertexts.*

In our PFS scheme, the signing key sk_f for the function f consists of n related secret keys sk_{f_i} of PE_2, where the value of the function f_i on a message is the i-th output of f over the same message. Thus, we can directly deduce that if the underlying PE_2 satisfies predicate privacy, then the signing key of our PFS scheme holds the function privacy for keys.

Theorem 5. *If the two-outcome predicate encryption* PE_2 *satisfies predicate privacy, then the above private functional signature scheme holds the property of function privacy for keys.*

4.3 Discussions

We here discuss the instantiations of our PFS scheme. Since garbling schemes and signature schemes can be constructed from one-way functions, and the underlying PE_2 can be built from PE which is able to be instantiated from various assumptions, we conclude that our single-key PFS scheme for all functions can be instantiated either from LWE assumptions, from obfuscation assumptions, from simple multilinear-maps assumptions, and even from the existence of any one-way function.

Although the PFS scheme proposed above is single-key, we can extend it to a q-keys PFS scheme for any bounded q where the adversary can obtain signing keys of up to q functions of her choice, by increasing the size of the ciphertexts linearly with q.

Acknowledgment. This work was supported by National Natural Science Foundation of China [grant number 61472414, 61772514, 61602061], and National Key R&D Program of China (2017YFB1400700).

5 Appendix

5.1 Signature Schemes

Definition 9 (Signature Scheme). *A signature scheme* S *for a message space* $\mathcal{M}$ *is a tuple* $(\mathsf{S.Gen}, \mathsf{S.Sign}, \mathsf{S.Verify})$:

- $\mathsf{S.Gen}(1^\lambda) \rightarrow (\mathsf{sik}, \mathsf{vk})$: *Takes as input a security parameter* λ, *and outputs a signing and verification key pair* $(\mathsf{sik}, \mathsf{vk})$.
- $\mathsf{S.Sign}(\mathsf{sik}, m) \rightarrow \sigma$: *Takes as inputs the signing key* sik *and a message* $m \in \mathcal{M}$ *and outputs a string* σ *which we call the signature of* m.
- $\mathsf{S.Verify}(\mathsf{vk}, m, \sigma) \rightarrow \{0, 1\}$: *Given the verification key* vk, *a message* m, *and signature* σ, *returns* 1 *or* 0 *indicating whether the signature is valid.*

Correctness.
$\forall m \in \mathcal{M}, (\mathsf{sik}, \mathsf{vk}) \leftarrow \mathsf{S.Gen}(1^\lambda), \sigma \leftarrow \mathsf{S.Sign}(\mathsf{sik}, m), \mathsf{S.Verify}(\mathsf{vk}, m, \sigma) \rightarrow 1.$

Unforgeability under chosen message attack.
A signature scheme is unforgeable under chosen message attack if the winning probability of any PPT adversary in the following game is negligible in the security parameter:

- *The challenger generates* $(\mathsf{sik}, \mathsf{vk}) \leftarrow \mathsf{S.Gen}(1^\lambda)$ *and gives* vk *to the adversary.*
- *The adversary requests signatures from the challenger for a polynomial number of messages. Once receiving the query* m, *the challenger computes* $\sigma \leftarrow \mathsf{S.Sign}(\mathsf{sik}, m)$ *and returns* σ *to the adversary.*
- *The adversary outputs* $(\hat{m}, \hat{\sigma})$, *and wins if* $\mathsf{S.Verify}(\mathsf{vk}, \hat{m}, \hat{\sigma}) \rightarrow 1$ *and the adversary has not previously queried a signature of* $\hat{m}$ *from the challenger.*

Lemma 1 [Rom90]. *Under the assumption that one-way functions exist, there exists a signature scheme which is secure against existential forgery under adaptive chosen message attacks by polynomial-time algorithms.*

We stress that the definitions of *deterministic* signature schemes are the same as signature schemes except that the signing algorithm is deterministic.

5.2 Symmetric-Key Predicate Encryption

We provide the full-fledged definition of *predicate encryption in symmetric-key setting* based on [SSW09] with some adaptations, and we present the formal notions of security for it.

Definition 10 (Symmetric-Key Predicate Encryption). *A symmetric-key predicate encryption (*PE*) for a class of predicates* $\mathcal{F} = \{\mathcal{F}_l\}_{l \in \mathbb{N}}$ *represented as boolean circuits with* l *input bits and one output bit and an associated message space* $\mathcal{M}$ *is a tuple of algorithms (*$\mathsf{PE.Setup}, \mathsf{PE.KeyGen}, \mathsf{PE.Enc}, \mathsf{PE.Dec}$*) as follows:*

- $\mathsf{PE.Setup}(1^\lambda) \rightarrow \mathsf{pmsk}$: *Takes as input a security parameter* λ *and outputs a master secret key* pmsk.
- $\mathsf{PE.KeyGen}(\mathsf{pmsk}, f) \rightarrow \mathsf{sk}_f$: *Given a master secret key* pmsk *and a predicate* $f \in \mathcal{F}$, *outputs a secret key* sk_f *corresponding to* f.
- $\mathsf{PE.Enc}(\mathsf{pmsk}, x, m) \rightarrow c$: *Takes as input the master secret key* pmsk, *an attribute* $x \in \{0,1\}^l$, *and a message* $m \in \mathcal{M}$ *and outputs a ciphertext* c.
- $\mathsf{PE.Dec}(\mathsf{sk}_f, c) \rightarrow m \text{ or } \bot$: *Takes as input a secret key* sk_f *for a predicate* f *and a ciphertext* c *and outputs either* $m \in \mathcal{M}$ *or* $\bot$.

Correctness.
For every sufficiently large security parameter λ, *all predicates* $f \in \mathcal{F}$, *all attributes* $x \in \{0,1\}^l$, *and all messages* $m \in \mathcal{M}$:

$$\Pr\left[\begin{array}{l} \mathsf{pmsk} \leftarrow \mathsf{PE.Setup}(1^\lambda); \\ \mathsf{sk}_f \leftarrow \mathsf{PE.KeyGen}(\mathsf{pmsk}, f); \\ c \leftarrow \mathsf{PE.Enc}(\mathsf{pmsk}, x, m): \\ \mathsf{PE.Dec}(\mathsf{sk}_f, c) = \begin{cases} m, & \text{if } f(x) = 1, \\ \bot, & \text{otherwise.} \end{cases} \end{array}\right] = 1 - \mathrm{negl}(\lambda).$$

We now give formal definitions of security for symmetric-key predicate encryption. Throughout the paper we regard a pair of attribute and message as a context. Note that we only provide the security definitions for the case when the adversary can ask a *single key* because this is all we need for our results.

Definition 11 (Context hiding (PE)). *Let* PE *be a symmetric-key predicate encryption scheme for the class of predicates* $\mathcal{F}$ *and an associated message space* $\mathcal{M}$. *Let* $\mathcal{A}$ *be a PPT adversary. Consider the following experiment:*

Setup: *The challenger runs* $\mathsf{PE.Setup}(1^\lambda)$ *and keeps* pmsk *to itself.*
Respond the secret key: $\mathcal{A}$ *gives the predicate* $f \in \mathcal{F}$, *then the challenger responds with* $\mathsf{PE.KeyGen}(\mathsf{pmsk}, f)$.

Ciphertext query 1: *$\mathcal{A}$ can query ciphertexts of some messages at most polynomial times. On the ith ciphertext query, $\mathcal{A}$ outputs a context $(x_i \in \{0,1\}^l, m_i \in \mathcal{M})$. The challenger responds with* $\mathsf{PE.Enc}(\mathsf{pmsk}, x_i, m_i)$.
Challenge: *$\mathcal{A}$ outputs two tuples (x_0^*, m_0^*) and (x_1^*, m_1^*) where $x_0^*, x_1^* \in \{0,1\}^l$ and satisfies $f(x_0^*) = f(x_1^*) = 0$ for the previous secret key query f, and $m_0^*, m_1^* \in \mathcal{M}$. The challenger chooses a random bit $b \in \{0,1\}$ and responds with* $\mathsf{PE.Enc}(\mathsf{pmsk}, x_b^*, m_b^*)$.
Ciphertext query 2: *$\mathcal{A}$ adaptively issues additional queries as in Ciphertext query* 1.
Guess: *$\mathcal{A}$ outputs a guess bit b'.*
The advantage of $\mathcal{A}$ is defined as $\mathsf{Adv}_{PE,\mathcal{A}} = |\Pr[b' = b] - 1/2|$.

We say the scheme is single-key context hiding if, for all PPT adversaries $\mathcal{A}$, the advantage of $\mathcal{A}$ in winning the above game is negligible in λ.

Definition 12 (Predicate privacy (PE)). *Let* PE *be a symmetric-key predicate encryption scheme for the class of predicates $\mathcal{F}$ and an associated message space $\mathcal{M}$. Let $\mathcal{A}$ be a PPT adversary. Consider the following experiment:*

Setup: *The challenger runs* $\mathsf{PE.Setup}(1^\lambda)$ *and keeps* pmsk *to itself.*
Ciphertext query 1: *$\mathcal{A}$ can query ciphertexts of some messages at most polynomial times. On the ith ciphertext query, $\mathcal{A}$ outputs a context $(x_i \in \{0,1\}^l, m_i \in \mathcal{M})$. The challenger responds with* $\mathsf{PE.Enc}(\mathsf{pmsk}, x_i, m_i)$.
Challenge: *$\mathcal{A}$ outputs two predicates $f_0^*, f_1^* \in \mathcal{F}$ such that, for all previous ciphertext queries x_i, $f_0^*(x_i) = f_1^*(x_i)$. The challenger chooses a random bit $b \in \{0,1\}$ and responds with* $\mathsf{PE.KeyGen}(\mathsf{pmsk}, f_b^*)$.
Ciphertext query 2: *$\mathcal{A}$ adaptively issues additional queries as in Ciphertext query* 1.
Guess: *$\mathcal{A}$ outputs a guess bit b'.*
The advantage of $\mathcal{A}$ is defined as $\mathsf{Adv}_{PE,\mathcal{A}} = |\Pr[b' = b] - 1/2|$.

We say the scheme is predicate private if, for all PPT adversaries $\mathcal{A}$, the advantage of $\mathcal{A}$ in winning the above game is negligible in λ.

According to the results of [BS15], we conclude that (single-key) symmetric-key predicate encryption schemes for all functions can be obtained either from LWE assumptions, from obfuscation assumptions, from simple multilinear-maps assumptions, and even from the existence of any one-way function (offering various trade-offs between security and efficiency).

5.3 Proofs in the First Step

Lemma 1. *Game* 0 *and Game* 1 *are identical.*

Despite that the processes are different, both the signature oracles $\mathcal{O}_{\mathsf{Sign}}$ in Game 0 and Game 1 output the deterministic signature of $f(x)$ on each query (f, x). Hence, Game 0 and Game 1 are identical.

Lemma 2. *Assuming the underlying PE_2 scheme is context hiding, Game 1 and Game 2 are computationally indistinguishable.*

Proof. In Game 1 and Game 2, there are n PE_2 encryptions, each with a pair of independent PE_2 keys. To prove Game 1 and Game 2 are computationally indistinguishable, we firstly prove that they are computationally indistinguishable with only one of these encryption. In detail, the argument proceeds in a standard way with n hybrids, where the hybrid i has the first i ciphertexts as in Game 1 and the rest $n-i$ as in Game 2, where $i = 0, \ldots, n$. In this setting, hybrid 0 corresponds to Game 2 and Hybrid n corresponds to Game 1. We now firstly prove that the adjacent hybrids are computationally indistinguishable. Suppose a PPT adversary $\mathcal{A}$ can distinguish Hybrid $k-1$ and Hybrid k for $k \in [n]$, then we can use $\mathcal{A}$ to construct a PPT adversary $\mathcal{B}_{\mathsf{PE}_2}$ to break the security of PE_2 as follows.

$\mathcal{B}_{\mathsf{PE}_2}(1^\lambda)$:

Public parameters. PE_2 challenger generates pmsk^*, $\mathcal{B}$ views pmsk^* as pmsk_k (Note $\mathcal{B}$ can not get pmsk^*). For $i \in [n]\backslash\{k\}$, $\mathcal{B}$ firstly generates $\mathsf{pmsk}_i \leftarrow \mathsf{PE}_2.\mathsf{Setup}(1^\lambda)$, then run $\mathsf{S.Gen}(1^\lambda) \rightarrow (\mathsf{sik}, \mathsf{vk})$. Set $\mathsf{msk} := (\mathsf{pmsk}_1, \ldots, \mathsf{pmsk}_{k-1}, \mathsf{pmsk}_{k+1}, \ldots, \mathsf{pmsk}_m)$, $\mathsf{mvk} := \mathsf{vk}$, and give mvk to $\mathcal{A}$.

Private key query. When $\mathcal{A}$ queries the signing key for the function f, $\mathcal{B}$ firstly queries PE_2 challenger for sk_{f_k}, then for $i \in [n]\backslash\{k\}$, generate $\mathsf{sk}_{f_i} \leftarrow \mathsf{PE}_2.\mathsf{KeyGen}(\mathsf{pmsk}_i, f_i)$, finally set $\mathsf{sk}_f := (\mathsf{sk}_{f_1}, \ldots, \mathsf{sk}_{f_n})$, and return sk_f to $\mathcal{A}$.

Encryption queries. $\mathcal{A}$ can adaptively query the encryptions for some messages for $Q(\lambda)$ times. When receiving the query x from $\mathcal{A}$, $\mathcal{B}_{\mathsf{PE}_2}$ proceeds the computations below.

1. Compute $(\Gamma, \{L_i^0, L_i^1\}_{i=1}^n) \leftarrow \mathsf{Gb.Garble}(1^\lambda, \mathsf{S.Sign}(\mathsf{sik}, \cdot))$.
2. Let $vk_i^0 = g(L_i^0)$, $vk_i^1 = g(L_i^1)$ for $i \in [n]$. Set $vk := \{vk_i^0, vk_i^1\}_{i=1}^n$.
3. Let $a_i = f_i(x)$, for $i \in [n]$, where f is the function that $\mathcal{A}$ queried for the signing key before. Then set $m := L_k^{a_k}, m_0 := L_k^{a_k}, m_1 := L_k^{1-a_k}, x_0 := x, x_1 = x$, and give the tuple (m, m_0, m_1, x_0, x_1) to PE_2 challenger.
4. PE_2 challenger returns the challenge ciphertext c^* corresponding to either m_0 or m_1. Firstly set $c_k := c^*$, then for $i \in [1, k-1]$, compute $c_i \leftarrow \mathsf{PE}_2.\mathsf{Enc}.(\mathsf{pmsk}_i, x, L_i^0, L_i^1)$; for $i \in [k+1, n]$, compute $c_i \leftarrow \mathsf{PE}_2.\mathsf{Enc}.(\mathsf{pmsk}_i, x, L_i^{a_i}, L_i^{a_i})$.
5. Set $c_x := (c_1, \ldots, c_{k-1}, c^*, c_{k+1}, \ldots, c_n, \Gamma, vk)$, and return c_x to $\mathcal{A}$.

Signature queries. $\mathcal{A}$ can adaptively query $Q(\lambda)$ numbers of signatures. When $\mathcal{B}$ receives the query (f, x) from $\mathcal{A}$, it firstly computes the value $f(x)$, then generates $\sigma_{f(x)} \leftarrow \mathsf{S.Sign}(\mathsf{sik}, f(x))$, and returns $\sigma_{f(x)}$ to $\mathcal{A}$.

Forge. Finally, $\mathcal{A}$ outputs a signature $(\hat{x}, \hat{\sigma})$. If it is a forge for PFS, outputs 1, and outputs 0 if not.

We notice that when c^* is the encryption corresponding to m_0, the view of $\mathcal{A}$ is as in Hybrid k, when c^* is the encryption corresponding to m_1, the view of $\mathcal{A}$ is as in Hybrid $k-1$. Thus, the advantage of $\mathcal{B}_{\mathsf{PE}_2}$ to break PE_2's security is the same as $\mathcal{A}$'s advantage to distinguish Hybrid $k-1$ and Hybrid k. Since we have assumed the underlying PE_2 scheme is plaintext privacy, $\mathcal{A}$ can distinguish Hybrid $k-1$ and Hybrid k only with a negligible probability $\epsilon(1^\lambda)$. According to the hybrid argument, for any PPT adversary, the maximal probability to successfully distinguish Game 1 (Hybrid n) and Game 2 (Hybrid 0) is $n \cdot \epsilon(1^\lambda)$, which is also a negligible probability. □

Lemma 3. *Assuming the underlying garbling scheme is circuit- and input-private, Game 2 and Game 3 are computationally indistinguishable.*

Proof. Suppose a PPT adversary A can distinguish Game 2 and Game 3, then use $\mathcal{A}$ to construct a PPT adversary $\mathcal{B}$ to break the security of the garbling scheme as follows.

$\mathcal{B}_{\mathsf{Gb}}(1^\lambda)$:

Public parameters. $\mathcal{B}_{\mathsf{Gb}}$ generates the master keys.
$\mathcal{B}$ firstly generates $\mathsf{pmsk}_i \leftarrow \mathsf{PE_2.Setup}(1^\lambda)$ for $i \in [n]$, then generates $(\mathsf{sik}, \mathsf{vk}) \leftarrow \mathsf{S.Gen}(1^\lambda)$. Set $\mathsf{msk} := \mathsf{pmsk}_1, \ldots, \mathsf{pmsk}_n, \mathsf{sik}, \mathsf{mvk} := \mathsf{vk}$, and give mvk to $\mathcal{A}$.

Private key query. When $\mathcal{A}$ queries the signing key for the function f, $\mathcal{B}_{\mathsf{Gb}}$ computes $\mathsf{sk}_{f_i} \leftarrow \mathsf{PE_2.KeyGen}(\mathsf{pmsk}_i, f_i)$ for $i \in [n]$. Set $\mathsf{sk}_f := (\mathsf{sk}_{f_1}, \ldots, \mathsf{sk}_{f_n})$, then return sk_f to $\mathcal{A}$.

Encryption queries. $\mathcal{A}$ can adaptively query the encryptions for some messages for $Q(\lambda)$ times. When $\mathcal{B}_{\mathsf{Gb}}$ receives the query x from $\mathcal{A}$, it proceeds as follows:

1. $\mathcal{B}_{\mathsf{Gb}}$ provides a circuit $C(\cdot) := \mathsf{S.Sign}(\mathsf{sik}, \cdot)$, then receives a garbled circuit Γ^* which could be output either of the real algorithm $\mathsf{Gb.Garble}$ or of simulator $\mathcal{S}_1^{\mathsf{Gb}}$.
2. $\mathcal{B}_{\mathsf{Gb}}$ queries $f(x)$ then receives a set of labels $\{L_i^*\}_{i=1}^n$, which could be the output either of the real algorithm $\mathsf{Gb.Enc}$ or of the simulator $\mathcal{S}_2^{\mathsf{Gb}}$.
3. For $i \in [n]$, let $vk_i^{a_i} = g(L_i^*), vk_i^{1-a_i} = g(r_i^*)$, where r_i^* is randomly chosen from $\{0,1\}^{|L_i^*|}, a_i = f_i(x)$. Set $vk^* := \{vk_i^{a_i}, vk_i^{1-a_i}\}_{i=1}^n$.
4. Compute $c^* = (\{\mathsf{PE_2.Enc}(\mathsf{pmpk}_i, (x, L_i^*, L_i^*))\}_{i=1}^n, \Gamma^*, vk^*)$, then return c^* to $\mathcal{A}$.

Signature queries. $\mathcal{A}$ can adaptively query $Q(\lambda)$ numbers of signatures. When $\mathcal{B}$ receives the query (f, x) from $\mathcal{A}$, it firstly computes the value $f(x)$, then computes $\sigma_{f(x)} \leftarrow \mathsf{S.Sign}(\mathsf{sik}, f(x))$, and returns $\sigma_{f(x)}$ to $\mathcal{A}$.

Forge. Finally, $\mathcal{A}$ outputs a signature $(\hat{x}, \hat{\sigma})$. If it is a forge for PFS, outputs 1, and outputs 0 if not.

We notice that if $(\Gamma^*, \{L_i^*\}_{i=1}^n)$ are outputs of the real garbling scheme, the view of $\mathcal{A}$ is as in Game 2, else if $(\Gamma^*, \{L_i^*\}_{i=1}^n)$ are outputs of the $\mathsf{Sim_{Garble}}$, the view of $\mathcal{A}$ is as in Game 3. Thus, if $\mathcal{A}$ can distinguish Game 2 and Game 3 with non-negligible probability, $\mathcal{B}_{\mathsf{Gb}}$ is able to output the correct decision with non-negligible probability. Since we have assumed the underlying garbling scheme is circuit- and input-private, this is not the case. □

5.4 Proof in the Second Step

We use $\mathcal{A}_{\mathsf{PFS}}$ to construct an adversary $\mathcal{A}_{\mathsf{S}}$ such that, if $\mathcal{A}_{\mathsf{PFS}}$ wins in Game 3 with non-negligible probability, then $\mathcal{A}_{\mathsf{S}}$ breaks the underlying signature scheme S, which is assumed to be secure against chosen message attack.

$\mathcal{B}_{\mathsf{S}}^{\mathsf{unforge}}(1^\lambda)$:

Public parameters. $\mathcal{B}$ firstly gets verification key vk from the challenger of S, then computes $\mathsf{pmsk}_i \leftarrow \mathsf{PE}_2.\mathsf{Setup}(1^\lambda)$ for $i \in [n]$. Set $\mathsf{msk} := \mathsf{pmsk}_1, \ldots, \mathsf{pmsk}_n, \mathsf{mvk} := \mathsf{vk}$, and give mvk to $\mathcal{A}_{\mathsf{S}}$.

Private key query. When $\mathcal{A}_{\mathsf{S}}$ queries the signing key for the function f, $\mathcal{B}$ computes $\mathsf{sk}_{f_i} \leftarrow \mathsf{PE}_2.\mathsf{KeyGen}(\mathsf{pmsk}_i, f_i)$ for $i \in [n]$, then sets $\mathsf{sk}_f := (\mathsf{sk}_{f_1}, \ldots, \mathsf{sk}_{f_n})$ and returns sk_f to $\mathcal{A}_{\mathsf{S}}$.

Encryption queries. $\mathcal{A}$ can adaptively query the encryptions for some messages for $Q(\lambda)$ times. When receiving the query x from $\mathcal{A}_{\mathsf{S}}$, $\mathcal{B}$ proceeds as follows.

1. Use $\mathcal{S}_1^{\mathsf{Gb}}$ to simulate the garbled circuit: $(\overline{\Gamma}, \mathsf{state}_{\mathcal{S}^{\mathsf{Gb}}}) \leftarrow \mathcal{S}_1^{\mathsf{Gb}}(1^\lambda, 1^{|C|})$.
2. Query the challenger of S for the signature on $f(x)$ and receive back $\sigma_{f(x)}$, where f is the function that $\mathcal{A}$ queried for the signing key before, then run the simulator $\mathcal{S}_2^{\mathsf{Gb}}$ to compute the simulated labels: $\{\bar{L}_i\}_{i=1}^n \leftarrow \mathcal{S}_2^{\mathsf{Gb}}(\sigma_{f(x)}, 1^{|f(x)|}, \mathsf{state}_{\mathcal{S}^{\mathsf{Gb}}})$.
3. For $i \in [n]$, compute $\overline{vk}_i^{a_i} = g(\overline{L}_i), \overline{vk}_i^{1-a_i} = g(r_i)$, where r_i is randomly chosen from $\{0,1\}^{|\overline{L}_i|}, a_i = f_i(x)$, then set $\overline{vk} := \{\overline{vk}_i^{a_i}, \overline{vk}_i^{1-a_i}\}_{i=1}^n$.
4. Produce encryptions of PE_2: $\overline{\mathsf{c}}_i \leftarrow \mathsf{PE}_2.\mathsf{Enc}(\mathsf{pmpk}_i, x, \overline{L_i}, \overline{L_i})$ for $i \in [n]$. Set $\overline{\mathsf{c}}_x := (\overline{\mathsf{c}}_1, \ldots, \overline{\mathsf{c}}_n, \overline{\Gamma}, \overline{vk})$ and return $\overline{\mathsf{c}}_x$ to $\mathcal{A}_{\mathsf{S}}$.

Signature queries. $\mathcal{A}$ can adaptively query $Q(\lambda)$ numbers of signatures. When $\mathcal{B}$ receives the query (f, x) from $\mathcal{A}_{\mathsf{S}}$, it firstly computes the value $f(x)$, then queries the challenger of S for signature of $f(x)$. Once receiving back $\sigma_{f(x)}$, $\mathcal{B}$ returns $\sigma_{f(x)}$ to $\mathcal{A}_{\mathsf{S}}$.

Forge. Finally, $\mathcal{A}_{\mathsf{S}}$ outputs a pair $(\hat{x}, \hat{\sigma})$, if it is a forge for PFS, then $\mathcal{B}$ returns $(\hat{x}, \hat{\sigma})$ as a forge for the signature scheme S.

Obviously, $\mathcal{B}$ simulates the same environment for $\mathcal{A}_{\mathsf{S}}$ perfectly as in the Game 3. Thus, if $\mathcal{A}_{\mathsf{S}}$ produces a forgery in the Game 3 with non-negligible probability, then $\mathcal{B}$ successfully forges in the underlying signature scheme with non-negligible probability. But, this is cannot be the case, since we have assumed that S is the existentially unforgeable against chosen-message attack. From the above discussion and Lemmas 1, 2 and 3, we finally draw the conclusion of Theorem 3 thus complete the proof. □

References

[BGI14] Boyle, E., Goldwasser, S., Ivan, I.: Functional signatures and pseudorandom functions. In: Krawczyk, H. (ed.) PKC 2014. LNCS, vol. 8383, pp. 501–519. Springer, Heidelberg (2014). https://doi.org/10.1007/978-3-642-54631-0_29

[BS15] Brakerski, Z., Segev, G.: Function-private functional encryption in the private-key setting. In: Dodis, Y., Nielsen, J.B. (eds.) TCC 2015. LNCS, vol. 9015, pp. 306–324. Springer, Heidelberg (2015). https://doi.org/10.1007/978-3-662-46497-7_12

[BSW11] Boneh, D., Sahai, A., Waters, B.: Functional encryption: definitions and challenges. In: Ishai, Y. (ed.) TCC 2011. LNCS, vol. 6597, pp. 253–273. Springer, Heidelberg (2011). https://doi.org/10.1007/978-3-642-19571-6_16

[GKP+13] Goldwasser, S., Kalai, Y.T., Popa, R.A., Vaikuntanathan, V., Zeldovich, N.: Reusable garbled circuits and succinct functional encryption. In: Symposium on Theory of Computing Conference, STOC 2013, 1–4 June 2013, Palo Alto, CA, USA (2013)

[LP09] Lindell, Y., Pinkas, B.: A proof of security of Yao's protocol for two-party computation. J. Cryptol. **22**(2), 161–188 (2009)

[Rom90] Rompel, J.: One-way functions are necessary and sufficient for secure signatures. In: Proceedings of the 22nd Annual ACM Symposium on Theory of Computing, 13–17 May 1990, Baltimore, Maryland, USA, pp. 387–394 (1990)

[SSW09] Shen, E., Shi, E., Waters, B.: Predicate privacy in encryption systems. In: Reingold, O. (ed.) TCC 2009. LNCS, vol. 5444, pp. 457–473. Springer, Heidelberg (2009). https://doi.org/10.1007/978-3-642-00457-5_27

[Yao82] Yao, A.C.-C.: Protocols for secure computations. In: 23rd Annual Symposium on Foundations of Computer Science, 3–5 November 1982, Chicago, Illinois, USA (1982)

Linkable Group Signature for Auditing Anonymous Communication

Haibin Zheng[1,2], Qianhong Wu[1(✉)], Bo Qin[3,4], Lin Zhong[1], Shuangyu He[1], and Jianwei Liu[1]

[1] School of Cyber Science and Technology, Beihang University, Beijing, China
{zhenghaibin29,qianhong.wu}@buaa.edu.cn
[2] Network and Data Security Key Laboratory of Sichuan Province, University of Electronic Science and Technology of China, Chengdu 610054, China
[3] State Key Laboratory of Information Security, Institute of Information Engineering, Chinese Academy of Sciences, Beijing 100093, China
[4] School of Information, Renmin University of China, Beijing, China
bo.qin@ruc.edu.cn

Abstract. Abusing anonymity has become a severe threat for anonymous communication system. Auditing and further tracing the identity of illegal users become an urgent requirement. Although a large body of anonymous communication mechanisms have been proposed, there is almost no research on auditing and supervising. In this paper, we propose a general construction of linkable group signature to achieve the anonymity, auditing and tracing functions for communication sender simultaneously. The general framework is constructed by using basic cryptography modules of blind signature, public key encryption, trapdoor indicative commitment and signature of knowledge. Furthermore, we first formally define a new concept called trapdoor indicative commitment, which helps to determine whether two given signatures are signed by the same member without opening signatures. Finally, we present an efficient linkable group signature instance. Performance analysis shows that our instance requires less computation and shorter signature length, compared with related works, making it suitable for practical applications.

Keywords: Linkable group signature
Trapdoor indicative commitment · Blind signature
Signature of knowledge

1 Introduction

With the rapid popularity of network applications, more and more people have concerns on their privacy during communication. Being a main tool to protect anonymity, anonymous communication has received extensive attentions. Anonymous communication is a protocol that makes the eavesdropper incapable to

W. Susilo and G. Yang (Eds.): ACISP 2018, LNCS 10946, pp. 304–321, 2018.
https://doi.org/10.1007/978-3-319-93638-3_18

obtain or infer the relationship and content between two communication parties by taking a series of measures to conceal the communication relationship. Anonymous communication technology is widely used in the situation of requiring to protect users' privacy, such as electronic cash, anonymous e-mail, online anonymous voting, electronic auction and many other activities.

The concept of anonymous communication was first proposed by David Chaum in 1981 [11]. He proposed an anonymous communication algorithm based on the Mix-Net. Since then, various anonymous communication systems have been emerged. These systems can be mainly divided into two major types according to the implementation technology: anonymous communication system based on rerouting mechanism (including Anonymizer [5], Onion Routing [23], Crowds [24], Tor [12]) and anonymous communication system based on non-rerouting mechanism (including DC-Net [9], broadcast [14], ring signature [17], group signature [26]). Depending on the information to be hidden, there are three types of anonymous protection: sender anonymity, receiver anonymity, and unlinkability of sender and receiver. The current research in our paper mainly focuses on the sender anonymous service.

Group signature, which was first introduced by Chaum and Van Heyst in 1991 [10], also is a technical method to protect sender anonymity in the anonymous communication system. It allows group members to sign messages on behalf of a group without revealing any identity information about the members except for group manager. As we all know, in some anonymous communication circumstances such as anonymous credential or electronic cash system, a large number of illegal users who abused the network are always existing, and the corresponding illegal behavior needs to be supervised. But how to judge whether an anonymous sender is an illegal user? Clearly, a natural way to realize this requirement can be operated by the group manager using group signature, who can, given two signatures, open their identities and decide whether they are generated by the same signer. But, obviously, it is not the perfect approach to this requirement. Thus, designing a group signature mechanism that possesses the ability of auditing different signatures without opening signers' identities is a meaningful research.

Compared to group signature, linkable group signature (LGS) additionally allows an authority to determine if two given signatures are signed by the same group member without opening the signatures. In 1999, Nakanishi et al. [21] first proposed the concept of linkable group signature, and applied it in secret voting protocol to prevent a single person from casting multiple votes. But this proposed scheme requires no any reliable authority, which couldn't apply to all realistic scenarios, especially when some authorities are required to participate. Besides the authority-free linking approaches, Manulis et al. [20] proposed a linkable democratic group signature scheme based on the idea of democratic group signature to achieve higher group member anonymity. But this proposed scheme needs assigning a unique pseudonym to every group member used for communicating with the non-member verifier, which will be a huge calculation when encountering a large group. Afterward, Hwang et al. [16] and Slamanig et al. [25] separately constructed a group signature scheme supporting so-called controllable linkability. In these proposed schemes, a designated linking authority is added similar to the position of issuer and opener, which is able to decide whether two given signatures have been issued by the same unknown signer using the linking key. But in this new mechanism of controllable linkability, the signing keys of group members are generated by the issuer instead of themselves, which makes the anonymity property become controllable anonymity rather than full anonymity. What's worse, the above proposed schemes only support the construction based on bilinear pairing or in random oracle. It still remains a significant challenge to design a generic contribution of linkable group signature with high security and strong availability.

1.1 Our Contribution

To achieve the auditing and supervising functions for anonymous communication on the basis of preserving sender's anonymity, we propose a generic construction and specific instance of linkable group signature. The contributions of this work can be summarized as follows.

- We formally refine the notion of linkable group signature and its security model. The proposed LGS scheme contains four entities: user, registration manager, auditing manager and supervision manager. It can effectively achieve auditing and supervising functions and solve the centralized power of traditional group manager through separating manager's ability in this LGS scheme. Our scheme achieves the security property of full-anonymity, linkable and full-traceability.
- We present a generic construction of linkable group signature scheme using basic cryptography modules, including blind signature, public key encryption, trapdoor indicative commitment and signature of knowledge. Any cryptography scheme of these building blocks which meets the pre-defined security requirements can be combined into a linkable group signature scheme.
- We construct an efficient linkable group signature instance based on the general framework and underlying building blocks. This new instance possesses high security and strong availability. Meanwhile, this process is also a reference for constructing other LGS instances.
- As a main building block for generic construction, we define a new concept of trapdoor indicative commitment. It operates against two given commitments, allowing only authority with trapdoor key to determine whether the two committed secret values are equal without opening the commitments. The indicative property is reflected on the output result of 1 or 0.

1.2 Related Work

Anonymous communication, while protecting users' anonymity, also provide attackers with the opportunity to use anonymous technology for illegal activities. Therefore, tracking the identity of malicious user is particularly important.

As we all know, there have been many mechanisms to implement the sender anonymity protection. For example, the typical rerouting mechanism represented by Mix-Net [11], Anonymizer [5], Onion Routing [23] and Crowds [24], and the typical cryptographic mechanism represented by ring signature [17], group signature [26], democratic group signature [19] and ad-hoc group signature [13]. Among them, the rerouting mechanism only provides anonymity property without the property of authentication; the ring signature, democratic group signature and ad-hoc group signature could provide both anonymous and authentication functions at the same time, but no tracking function is supported when illegal user exists; the group signature can further implement the operation of anonymity, authentication, and tracking simultaneously. But how to find illegal users through audit operations, and then discover the user's identity to prevent the network abuse? There has not been perfect solution to this problem in existing work at present.

As indicated above, the concept of group signature was introduced by Chaum and van Heyst [10], and they also gave the first realizations. Since then, many other improved schemes were proposed by Pedersen [22] and Camenisch [8]. In 2003, Bellare et al. [2] defined the security requirements of group signature and presented a security model with full traceability and full anonymity properties known as BMW security model. Then they strengthened the security model to include dynamic enrollment of members in 2005 [3]. During that period, Boneh et al. [4] designed a short group signature in the random oracle model, using a variant of the security definition of BMW model. Moreover, Groth [15] constructed a group signature scheme using efficient zero-knowledge proofs for bilinear groups in the standard model, where each group contains a constant number of group members. In addition to these schemes, lattice-based group signature scheme [18] and attribute-based group signature construction [1] were also proposed.

1.3 Paper Organization

The rest of this paper is organized as follows. In Sect. 2, we formalize the definition of trapdoor indicative commitment and the security model. In Sect. 3, we formalize the definition of linkable group signature and the security model. In Sect. 4, we present a generic construction of LGS using basic building blocks and analyze its security. In Sect. 5, we construct a specific LGS instance based on the proposed generic framework. Finally, in Sect. 6, we conclude this paper.

2 Trapdoor Indicative Commitment

Trapdoor indicative commitment is a new concept we first proposed, which also is a main building block for generic construction of linkable group signature. It operates against any two commitments, allowing only user with trapdoor information can determine whether the two committed secret values are equal without opening the commitments. The indicative property of this new concept is reflected on the output result of 1 or 0.

Trapdoor indicative commitment is a special commitment protocol. We give the formal definition of trapdoor indicative commitment according to the first definition of commitment given by Brassard et al. [6].

Definition 1 (Trapdoor Indicative Commitment). *A trapdoor indicative commitment protocol consists of three polynomial time algorithms: key generation TKeyGen, commit TCom, and indicate TIndic.*

$(param_{ic}, sk_{ic}) \leftarrow TKeyGen(1^k)$. On input a security parameter 1^k, outputs public parameter $param_{ic}$ and trapdoor key sk_{ic}.

$C_{ic} \leftarrow TCom(param_{ic}, s)$, $C'_{ic} \leftarrow TCom(param_{ic}, s')$. On input public parameter $param_{ic}$ and committed value s,s', outputs the commitments $C_{ic} = TCom(param_{ic}, s)$, $C'_{ic} = TCom(param_{ic}, s')$.

$1/0 \leftarrow TIndic(sk_{ic}, C_{ic}, C'_{ic})$. On input trapdoor key sk_{ic} and two commitments C_{ic}, C'_{ic}, this algorithm outputs 1 if and only if the corresponding two committed secret values s, s' of C_{ic}, C'_{ic} are equal, otherwise outputs 0.

Refer to the general commitment protocol, trapdoor indicative commitment should satisfy the security property of hiding [6]. In addition to that, it should also satisfy the security property of trapdoor indication.

Hiding. Hiding property means that any malicious recipient can not obtain any information about the committed secret values during the commitment period. Equivalent to say, for any two committed values s, s', and any probabilistic polynomial-time adversary $\mathcal{A}$, C_{ic} generated by the algorithm $C_{ic} \leftarrow TCom(param_{ic}, s)$ and C'_{ic} generated by the algorithm $C'_{ic} \leftarrow TCom(param_{ic}, s')$ are indistinguishable. A trapdoor indicative commitment has the secure property of hiding if for any probabilistic polynomial-time adversary $\mathcal{A}$, its advantage $Adv(\mathcal{A})$ is negligible in the following experiment.

- Setup. Challenger runs $TKeyGen$ algorithm, outputs public parameters $param_{ic}$ to $\mathcal{A}$.
- Challenge. $\mathcal{A}$ chooses two committed values (s_0, s_1) of the same length and sends them to commit oracle machine. The commit oracle machine chooses a bit $b \in \{0,1\}$ randomly, then runs $TCom$ algorithm $C^*_{ic} \leftarrow TCom(param_{ic}, s_b)$, and sends the result C^*_{ic} to $\mathcal{A}$.
- Guess. $\mathcal{A}$ outputs a bit $b' \in \{0,1\}$ as a guess of b.

Adversary $\mathcal{A}$ wins the game if $b' = b$. The advantage of $\mathcal{A}$ is defined as $Adv(\mathcal{A}) = |\Pr[b' = b] - 1/2|$.

Trapdoor Indication. Trapdoor Indication property means that only user with trapdoor information can determine whether the corresponding two committed secret values are equal without opening the commitments. Equivalent to say, for any two committed values s, s', C_{ic}, C'_{ic} generated by the algorithm $TCom$, when owning the trapdoor key sk_{ic}, the following formula holds with overwhelming probability

$$TIndic(sk_{ic}, C_{ic}, C'_{ic}) = \begin{cases} 1, & s = s' \\ 0, & \text{others} \end{cases}$$

A trapdoor indicative commitment has the secure property of trapdoor indication if for any probabilistic polynomial-time adversary $\mathcal{A}$, its advantage $Adv(\mathcal{A})$ is negligible in the following experiment.

- Setup. Challenger runs *TKeyGen* algorithm, outputs public parameters $param_{ic}$ to $\mathcal{A}$.
- Challenge. Challenger chooses two committed values (s^*, s'^*) of the same length and runs *TCom* algorithm $C^*_{ic} \leftarrow TCom(param_{ic}, s^*)$, $C'^*_{ic} \leftarrow TCom(param_{ic}, s'^*)$, and sends commitments C^*_{ic}, C'^*_{ic} to $\mathcal{A}$.
- Query. During this phase, $\mathcal{A}$ makes a polynomial bounded number of queries to indicate oracle machine. After given queried commitments (C_{ic}, C'_{ic}), the indicate oracle machine runs algorithm *TIndic* and sends the result to $\mathcal{A}$. The only restriction is that adversary $\mathcal{A}$ is not allowed to make a indicate query for (C^*_{ic}, C'^*_{ic}) nor $(C^*_{ic}, *)$ nor $(*, C'^*_{ic})$.
- Guess. $\mathcal{A}$ outputs a bit $b \in \{0,1\}$ as a guess of the indicative result.

Adversary $\mathcal{A}$ wins the game if (1) $b = 0$ when $s^* = s'^*$; (2) $b = 1$ when $s^* \neq s'^*$. The advantage of $\mathcal{A}$ is defined as $Adv(\mathcal{A}) = \frac{1}{2}\Pr[b = 0|s^* = s'^*] + \frac{1}{2}\Pr[b = 1|s^* \neq s'^*]$.

3 Linkable Group Signature

This section first refines the formal definition of linkable group signature, and then gives the security model.

3.1 System Model

A linkable group signature scheme contains four entities: user, registration manager, auditing manager and supervision manager. The user first registers with registration manager and then performs an group signature operation. After given signatures, the auditing manager can determine whether these signatures from the same user, the supervision manager can further trace to the user's identity.

Definition 2 (Linkable group signature). *A linkable group signature scheme (LGS) consists of the following six algorithms: setup Setup, join Join, group signature GSig, verify GVer, link Link and trace Trace.*

$(GP, RSK, LSK, TSK) \leftarrow Setup(1^k)$: On input a security parameter 1^k, the registration manager, auditing manager and supervision manager run $\mathcal{G}(1^k)$ respectively, generate the register key pair (RPK, RSK), link key pair (LPK, LSK) and trace key pair (TPK, TSK). The system public parameter $GP = (RPK, LPK, TPK)$.
$Cert \leftarrow Join(< U(USK, GP), RM(RSK) >)$: The *Join* algorithm is an interactive protocol which user U and registration manager RM engaged in.

- Given system public parameters GP, user U generates (UPK, USK) and registration parameters γ, then outputs UPK and γ to registration manager RM;
- Given user's public key UPK and registration parameters γ, registration manager RM generates user's certificate $Cert$, then outputs $Cert$ to the user U. At the same time, record the user identity $(UPK, Cert)$ in the registration list $\mathcal{C}$.

$\sigma \leftarrow GSig(GP, USK, Cert, m)$: Suppose $m \in \{0,1\}^*$. On input the system public parameters GP and user's private key USK, certificate $Cert$ and message m, outputs the group signature σ.

$1/0 \leftarrow GVer(GP, m, \sigma)$: On input the system public parameters GP, message m and group signature σ, outputs 1 if and only if the signature is valid, otherwise outputs 0.

$1/0 \leftarrow Link(GP, LSK, (m,\sigma), (m',\sigma'))$: The auditing manager makes judgment operation using link private key LSK. On input two valid message-signature pairs $(m,\sigma), (m',\sigma')$, outputs 1 if and only if the two signatures come from the same user, otherwise outputs 0.

$(UPK, Cert) \leftarrow Trace(GP, TSK, (m,\sigma))$: The supervision manager makes tracing operation using trace private key TSK. On input the valid message-signature pair (m,σ), outputs the registered user's public key UPK and certificate $Cert$.

3.2 Security Definitions

Since the group signature introduced by Chaum and Van Heyst, some security requirements have been introduced, such as unforgeability, traceability, anonymity, unlinkability, exculpability, coalition resistance and framing resistance. However, these requirements are unformalized and overlapping, where the precise meaning and mutual relationship are not clear. In 2003, Bellare et al. [2] formulated two core requirements of group signature, called full-anonymity and full-traceability, making all the other existing requirements are implied by them. We follow this formal definition of group signature to give a formal definition of the linkable group signature. A secure linkable group signature scheme should satisfy the following properties: correctness, full-anonymity, linkability and full-traceability.

Correctness. An LGS scheme is correct if

(1) $Pr[GP \leftarrow Setup(1^k); \sigma \leftarrow GSig(GP, USK, Cert, m) : GVer(GP, m, \sigma) = 1] = 1 - \epsilon(\lambda)$;

(2) $Pr[GP \leftarrow Setup(1^k); \sigma \leftarrow GSig(GP, USK, Cert, m), \sigma' \leftarrow GSig(GP, USK, Cert', m'), GVer(GP, m, \sigma) = 1, GVer(GP, m', \sigma') = 1 : Link(GP, LSK, (m,\sigma), (m',\sigma') = 1] = 1 - \epsilon(\lambda)$;

(3) $Pr[GP \leftarrow Setup(1^k); \sigma \leftarrow GSig(GP, USK, Cert, m), GVer(GP, m, \sigma) = 1 : Trace(GP, TSK, \sigma) = UPK] = 1 - \epsilon(\lambda)$.

These three checks are respectively regarded as verification correctness, linking correctness and tracing correctness.

Full-Anonymity. Full-Anonymity is an fundamental security property in linkable group signature scheme. The full-anonymity requires that an adversary without supervision manager's trace key couldn't recover the identity of the signer after given a signature of a message. A bit more formally, any polynomially time bounded adversary $\mathcal{A}$ has only negligible advantage in the following attack game played with a challenger.

Here, we define a strong adversary capability that may corrupt all the members of the group, and the adversary can also query the outputs of *Trace* algorithm, which is conducted by the supervision manager on arbitrary signatures of its choice (except the challenge signature).

Setup: Challenger runs *Setup* algorithm and generates registration manager's key (RPK, RSK), auditing manager's key (LPK, LSK) and supervision manager's key (TPK, TSK), then it sends the public parameters $GP = (RPK, LPK, TPK)$ to adversary $\mathcal{A}$.

Query Phase 1: During this phase, adversary $\mathcal{A}$ makes a polynomial bounded number of the following queries to the challenger.

- Join Queries: Adversary $\mathcal{A}$ chooses user's private key USK to request, the challenger performs the *Join* algorithm and returns user's certificate $Cert$ to Adversary $\mathcal{A}$.
- Trace Queries: Adversary $\mathcal{A}$ chooses a signature σ, the challenger answers the query by performing the *Trace* algorithm, and sends the registered user's public key UPK and certificate $Cert$ to $\mathcal{A}$.

Challenge Phase: $\mathcal{A}$ picks two challenge users indicated by their public keys identities UPK_0^*, UPK_1^*, the corresponding private key USK_0^*, USK_1^* and a message m^*. The challenger chooses a bit $b \in \{0, 1\}$ randomly, then computes the user's certificate $Cert^*$ in *Join* algorithm, and generates the challenge signature $\sigma^* = GSig(GP, USK_b^*, Cert^*, m^*)$

Query Phase 2: Adversary $\mathcal{A}$ makes a polynomial bounded queries as in Phase 1. But the adversary is not allowed to make a *Join* query for USK_0^*, USK_1^* and *Trace* query for σ^* to obtain the associated UPK^* and certificate $Cert^*$.

Guess Phase: Eventually, adversary $\mathcal{A}$ outputs a bit b' and it succeeds in this game if $b' = b$.

The advantage of the adversary is defined as $Adv_{LGS,A}^{Full-Anony} = |2\Pr[b' = b] - 1|$.

Definition 3 (Full-Anonymity). *An LGS scheme has full-anonymity if for any polynomial-time adversary $\mathcal{A}$, its advantage $Adv_{LGS,A}^{Full-Anony}$ is negligible in the above game.*

Linkability. In case of signer's malicious behavior, any two signatures (m, σ), (m', σ') should be linked by the auditing manager using link key and judged whether the given signatures came from the same signer. Linkability requires that, no adversary $\mathcal{A}$ can create valid signatures which cannot be linked by the auditing manager. A bit more formally, any polynomially time bounded adversary $\mathcal{A}$ has only negligible advantage in the following attack game played with the challenger.

This game contains the following two attacks: (1) Link algorithm returns 0 under the case of two signatures generated from the same signer; (2) Link algorithm returns 1 under the case of two signatures generated from different signers.

Setup: Challenger runs *Setup* algorithm and generates registration manager's key (RPK, RSK), auditing manager's key (LPK, LSK) and supervision manager's key (TPK, TSK), then it sends the public parameters $GP = (RPK, LPK, TPK)$ to adversary $\mathcal{A}$.

Query Phase: During this phase, the adversary makes a polynomial bounded number of the following queries to the challenger.

- Join Queries: Adversary $\mathcal{A}$ is given access to a Join oracle. Adversary $\mathcal{A}$ chooses user's private key USK to request, the challenger performs the *Join* algorithm and returns user's certificate $Cert$ to adversary $\mathcal{A}$.
- GSig Queries: Adversary $\mathcal{A}$ is given access to a GSig oracle. Adversary $\mathcal{A}$ chooses a user's private key USK, certificate $Cert$ and message m, the challenger answers the query by performing the *GSig* algorithm, and sends signature σ to $\mathcal{A}$.

Challenge Phase: Eventually, adversary $\mathcal{A}$ outputs a challenged message-signature pair (m_i^*, σ_i^*), $i = 1, 2$. The adversary wins if the following any case occurs.

(1) $GVer(GP, m_i^*, \sigma_i^*) = 1$, $i = 1, 2$. $Link(GP, LSK, (m_1^*, \sigma_1^*), (m_2^*, \sigma_2^*)) = 0$: $UPK_1^* = UPK_2^*$;
(2) $GVer(GP, m_i^*, \sigma_i^*) = 1$, $i = 1, 2$. $Link(GP, LSK, (m_1^*, \sigma_1^*), (m_2^*, \sigma_2^*)) = 1$: $UPK_1^* \neq UPK_2^*$;

The advantage of the adversary is defined as $Adv_{LGS,\mathcal{A}}^{Link} = \Pr[\mathcal{A}\ wins]$.

Definition 4 (Linkability). *An LGS scheme has linkability if for any polynomial-time adversary* $\mathcal{A}$*, its advantage* $Adv_{LGS,\mathcal{A}}^{Link}$ *is negligible in the above game.*

Full-Traceability. In case of malicious behavior, signer's identity UPK should also be revealed by a designated third party, i.e., the supervision manager. Full-traceability requires that, no collusion of group members can create a valid signature which cannot be traced by the supervision manager (even corruption consisted of the entire group, and the possession of supervision manager's trace key). A bit more formally, any polynomially time bounded adversary $\mathcal{A}$ has only negligible advantage in the following attack game played with the challenger.

Setup: Challenger runs *Setup* algorithm and generates registration manager's key (RPK, RSK), auditing manager's key (LPK, LSK) and supervision manager's key (TPK, TSK), then it sends the public parameters $GP = (RPK, LPK, TPK)$ to adversary $\mathcal{A}$.

Corruption Phase: Adversary $\mathcal{A}$ chooses user's public key UPK to request, then adds the corrupted group members to list $\mathcal{L}$. Here, $\mathcal{L}$ represents the identity list of corruption group members, and $\mathcal{L} \subset \mathcal{C}$. At the same time, $\mathcal{A}$ can collude with registration manager and auditing manager. Here, the collusion behavior means the situation that $\mathcal{A}$ can only capture their private key, but not command them to do some tampering operation.

Query Phase: During this phase, the adversary makes a polynomial bounded number of the following queries to the challenger.

- Join Queries: Adversary $\mathcal{A}$ is given access to a Join oracle. Adversary $\mathcal{A}$ chooses user's private key USK to request, the challenger performs the *Join* algorithm and returns user's certificate $Cert$ to Adversary $\mathcal{A}$.
- GSig Queries: Adversary $\mathcal{A}$ is given access to a GSig oracle. Adversary $\mathcal{A}$ chooses a private key USK, certificate $Cert$ and message m, the challenger answers the query by performing the *GSig* algorithm, and sends signature σ to $\mathcal{A}$.
- Trace Queries: Adversary $\mathcal{A}$ chooses a signature σ, the challenger answers the query by performing the *Trace* algorithm, and sends the registered user's public key UPK to $\mathcal{A}$.

Challenge Phase: Eventually, adversary $\mathcal{A}$ outputs a challenge signature σ^*. The adversary wins if the following any case occurs.

(1) $GVer(GP, m^*, \sigma^*) = 1$, $Trace(GP, TSK, \sigma^*) = \perp$;
(2) $GVer(GP, m^*, \sigma^*) = 1$, $Trace(GP, TSK, \sigma^*) = UPK^* \notin \mathcal{L}$. Besides, σ^* was not queried for Trace Queries.

The advantage of the adversary is defined as $Adv_{LGS,\mathcal{A}}^{Full-Trace} = \Pr[\mathcal{A}\ wins]$.

Definition 5 (Full-Traceability). *An LGS scheme has full-traceability if for any polynomial-time adversary $\mathcal{A}$, its advantage $Adv_{LGS,\mathcal{A}}^{Full-Trace}$ is negligible in the above game.*

4 Generic Construction of Linkable Group Signature

This section gives a generic construction of linkable group signature using the building blocks of trapdoor indicative commitment and blind signatures, public key encryption, signature of knowledge. Then presents security analysis of the generic structure.

4.1 Generic Construction

Let $\Pi_1 = (BKeyGen, BSign < U_{bs}, S_{bs} >, BVer)$ represents the blind signature scheme, where $BKeyGen$, $BSign < U_{bs}, S_{bs} >$, and $BVer$ are key generation, blind signature and verify algorithms in this scheme.

Let $\Pi_2 = (PKeyGen, Enc, Dec)$ represents the public key encryption scheme, where $PKeyGen$, Enc and Dec are key generation, encrypt and decrypt algorithms in this scheme.

Let $\Pi_3 = (TKeyGen, TCom, TIndic)$ represents the trapdoor indicative commitment protocol, where $TKeyGen$, $TCom$ and $TIndic$ are key generation, commit and indicate algorithms in this scheme.

Let $\Pi_4 = (KSetup, KSign, KVer)$ represents the signature of knowledge scheme $SK\left\{x\middle|L(x)\right\}(m)$, where $KSetup$, $KSign$ and $KVer$ are setup, signature and verify algorithms in this scheme.

Define $\Pi = (Setup, Join, GSig, GVer, Link, Trace)$ is a general structure of linkable group signature scheme, the specific algorithm is as follows.

$\boldsymbol{(GP, RSK, LSK, TSK) \leftarrow Setup(1^k)}$: On input a security parameter 1^k,

- Registration manager runs $BKeyGen$ algorithm of Π_1, generates the register key pair (RPK, RSK), $(RPK, RSK) \leftarrow BKeyGen(1^k)$.
- Auditing manager runs $TKeyGen$ algorithm of Π_3, generates the link key pair (LPK, LSK), $(LPK, LSK) \leftarrow TKeyGen(1^k)$.
- Supervision manager runs $PKeyGen$ algorithm of Π_2, generates the trace key pair (TPK, TSK), $(TPK, TSK) \leftarrow PKeyGen(1^k)$.

Finally, outputs system public parameter $GP = (RPK, LPK, TPK)$.

$\boldsymbol{Cert \leftarrow Join(< U(USK, GP), RM(RSK) >)}$: User U and registration manager RM make interaction to complete registration by running Π_1 and Π_4, and generate user's certificate $Cert$.

1. User chooses private key USK, runs $BSign(< U(USK, GP), RM(RSK) >)$ algorithm of Π_1 to send blind message of USK to registration manager and get certificate $Cert$ from the manager as the blind signature, $Cert \leftarrow BSign(< U(USK, GP), RM(RSK) >)$.
2. Simultaneously, user runs the signature of knowledge $SK\{USK| L(USK)\}(\gamma)$ of Π_4 based on registration parameters γ to prove the correct blind operation of USK was performed.
3. After given $Cert$, user runs $BVer$ algorithm of Π_1 to verify the validity of the certificate.
4. User sends the certificate $Cert$ and public key UPK (identity ID) to registration manager, keeps private key USK. Registration manager adds (UPK, $Cert$) to registration list $\mathcal{C}$.

$\boldsymbol{\sigma \leftarrow GSig(GP, USK, Cert, m)}$: Suppose $m \in \{0,1\}^*$, user's group signature algorithm is divided into the following sections.

1. Encryption for user's certificate. Runs *Enc* algorithm of Π_2, $(a, b) \leftarrow Enc(Cert, TPK)$.
2. Trapdoor indicative commitment for user's private key. Runs *TCom* algorithm of Π_3, $d \leftarrow TCom(LPK, USK)$.
3. Signature of knowledge for message m. Runs *KSign* algorithm of Π_4, $c \leftarrow KSign(USK, GP, m, a, b, c, d)$.

Finally, outputs group signature $\sigma = (a, b, c, d)$.

$\mathbf{1/0 \leftarrow GVer(GP, m, \sigma)}$: Verify the validity of group signature.

Runs *KVer* algorithm of Π_4, $1/0 \leftarrow KVer(GP, m, \sigma)$. The output result 1 expresses the signature is valid.

$\mathbf{1/0 \leftarrow Link(GP, LSK, (m, \sigma), (m', \sigma'))}$: Auditing manager performs the link operation.

1. Given (m, σ), (m', σ'), auditing manager first runs above *GVer* algorithm to verify the validity of given signature. If the signature is invalid, it terminates.
2. Otherwise, for the component d in signature σ and d' in signature σ', auditing manager runs *TIndic* algorithm of Π_3, $1/0 \leftarrow TIndic(LSK, d, d')$. The output result 1 expresses the two signatures are from the same signer.

$\mathbf{(UPK, Cert) \leftarrow Trace(GP, TSK, (m, \sigma))}$: Supervision manager performs the trace operation.

1. Given (m, σ), supervision manager first runs above *GVer* algorithm to verify the validity of given signature. If the signature is invalid, it terminates.
2. Otherwise, for the component (a, b) in signature σ, supervision manager runs *Dec* algorithm of Π_2, $Cert \leftarrow Dec(TSK, (a, b))$. At the same time, he runs the signature of knowledge scheme $SK\left\{TSK \middle| L(TSK)\right\}(\sigma \| m)$ of Π_4 to prove the correct certificate is calculated.
3. According to the registration list C given by registration manager, find the corresponding user identity ID.

4.2 Security Analysis

Theorem 1. *The proposed generic LGS construction has full-anonymity if the public key encryption scheme Π_2 is IND-CCA2 secure, the trapdoor indicative commitment protocol Π_3 satisfies hiding property.*

Theorem 2. *The proposed generic LGS construction has linkability if the blind signature scheme Π_1 satisfies non-forgeability, the trapdoor indicative commitment protocol Π_3 satisfies trapdoor indication property, and the signature of knowledge scheme Π_4 is UnfExt secure.*

Theorem 3. *The proposed generic LGS construction has full-traceability if the blind signature scheme Π_1 satisfies non-forgeability, the signature of knowledge scheme Π_4 is UnfExt secure.*

The proof of these theorems can be found in the full version of this paper.

5 Instantiating Linkable Group Signature

In this section, we construct a specific linkable group signature instance according to the process of general structure and concrete instances of basic building blocks. Then give the security and performance analysis of this instance.

5.1 Linkable Group Signature Implementation

According to the given general framework of linkable group signature, we can combine a specific LGS scheme using the instances of basic building blocks.
(GP, RSK, LSK, TSK) ← Setup(1^k): Let $\epsilon > 1, k, l_g, l_1, l_2, \hat{l}$ be security parameters, which $\hat{l} = \epsilon(l_2 + k) + 1$, $l_1, l_2, \hat{l} < l_g$. $\mathcal{G}(l_g)$ represents a group cluster with large order ($\approx 2^{l_g}$).

- Registration manager runs $\mathcal{G}(l_g)$, generates the register key pair (RPK, RSK). Particularly, registration manager generates a RIPE composite number n, $n = pq, p = 2p' + 1, q = 2q' + 1$. Then chooses a subgroup $G =< g >$ from $\mathbb{Z}_n^*$, $(g|n) = 1$ (i.e.$G \subset QR(n)$), and the order of group G is $p'q'$. Chooses random elements $z, h \in G$. Let $H : \{0,1\}^* \rightarrow \{0,1\}^k$ be a collision-resistant hash function. Outputs the public key $RPK = (n, g, z, h, G, l_g, l_1, l_2, \hat{l}, \epsilon, k, H)$, register key $RSK = (p, q)$.
- Auditing manager runs $\mathcal{G}(l_g)$, generates the link key pair (LPK, LSK). Particularly, auditing manager generates a RIPE composite number N, $N = PQ, P = 2P' + 1, Q = 2Q' + 1$. Then chooses a subgroup $G_0 =< g_1 >$ from $\mathbb{Z}_N^*$, $(g_1|N) = 1$ (i.e.$G_0 \subset QR(N)$), and the order of group G_0 is $P'Q'$. Chooses a subgroup G_1 of G_0, makes the order of group G_1 is P'. Chooses a random element $h_1 \in G_1$, then the order of h_1 is P', the order of g_1 is $P'Q'$. Outputs the public key $LPK = (N, g_1, h_1, G_0, G_1)$, link key $LSK = P'$.
- Supervision manager runs $\mathcal{G}(l_g)$, generates the trace key pair (TPK, TSK). Particularly, supervision manager chooses $x \in \{0, \cdots, 2^{l_g} - 1\}$, computes $y = g^x$. Outputs the public key $TPK = y$, trace key $TSK = x$.

Finally, outputs system public parameter $GP = (RPK, LPK, TPK)$.
Cert ← Join(< U(USK, GP), RM(RSK) >): User U and registration manager RM make interaction to complete registration, and generate user's certificate $Cert$.

1. User randomly chooses $\widehat{e} \in \{2^{\hat{l}-1}, \cdots, 2^{\hat{l}} - 1\}$, $e \in \{2^{l_1}, \cdots, 2^{l_1} + 2^{l_2} - 1\}$, computes $\widetilde{e} = e\widehat{e}$, $\widetilde{z} = z^{\widehat{e}}$. Then sends $\widetilde{e}, \widetilde{z}$ to registration manager, making a non-interactive proof
$$W = SKDL\left\{(\alpha, \beta)\middle|\begin{array}{c} z^{\widetilde{e}} = \widetilde{z}^{\alpha} \wedge \widetilde{z} = z^{\beta} \wedge \\ (2^{\hat{l}} - 2^{\epsilon(l_2+k)+1}) < \alpha < (2^{\hat{l}} + 2^{\epsilon(l_2+k)+1}) \end{array}\right\}(\widetilde{z})$$
to prove that the user correctly generated $\widetilde{e}, \widetilde{z}$.
2. Registration manager computes $u = \widetilde{z}^{1/\widetilde{e}}$, and sends u to User.

3. User verifies $\widetilde{z} = u^{\widetilde{e}}$ (equal to $z = u^e$). Accepting certificate $Cert = u$ if the equation succeeds. Then sends the certificate $Cert$ and public key UPK (identity ID) to registration manager, keep private key $USK = e$.
4. Registration manager adds $(ID, u, \widetilde{e}, \widetilde{z})$ to registration list $\mathcal{C}$.

$\boldsymbol{\sigma \leftarrow GSig(GP, USK, Cert, m)}$: Suppose $m \in \{0,1\}^*$, user constructs a group signature on the message.

1. Randomly chooses $w \leftarrow \{0,1\}^{l_g}$, computes $a = g^w, b = uy^w$, $d = g_1^e h_1^w$
2. Randomly chooses $r_1 \in \{0,1\}^{\epsilon(l_2+k)}, r_2 \in \{0,1\}^{\epsilon(l_g+l_1+k)}, r_3 \in \{0,1\}^{\epsilon(l_g+k)}$, computes

$$t_1 = b^{r_1}(1/y)^{r_2}, t_2 = a^{r_1}(1/g)^{r_2}, t_3 = g^{r_3}, t_4 = g_1^{r_1}h_1^{r_3}$$
$$c = H(g \parallel h \parallel y \parallel z \parallel a \parallel b \parallel d \parallel t_1 \parallel t_2 \parallel t_3 \parallel t_4 \parallel m)$$
$$s_1 = r_1 - c(e - 2^{l_1}), s_2 = r_2 - cew, s_3 = r_3 - cw$$

3. Finally, outputs the group signature $\sigma = (c, s_1, s_2, s_3, a, b, d)$.

The above group signature is equivalent to a signature of knowledge on message m, which can be denoted as

$$SKDL\left\{(\eta, \vartheta, \xi)\middle| \begin{array}{c} z = b^\eta/y^\vartheta \wedge 1 = a^\eta/g^\vartheta \wedge a = g^\xi \wedge d = g^\eta h^\xi \wedge \\ (2^{l_1} - 2^{\epsilon(l_2+k)+1}) < \eta < (2^{l_1} + 2^{\epsilon(l_2+k)+1}) \end{array}\right\}(m)$$

$\boldsymbol{1/0 \leftarrow GVer(GP, m, \sigma)}$: Perform the Verification of group signature.

1. Computes

$$\widetilde{t_1} = z^c b^{s_1 - c2^{l_1}}/y^{s_2}, \widetilde{t_2} = a^{s_1 - c2^{l_1}}/g^{s_2}, \widetilde{t_3} = a^c g^{s_3}, \widetilde{t_4} = d^c g_1^{s_1 - c2^{l_1}} h_1^{s_3}$$
$$c' = H(g \parallel h \parallel y \parallel z \parallel a \parallel b \parallel d \parallel \widetilde{t_1} \parallel \widetilde{t_2} \parallel \widetilde{t_3} \parallel \widetilde{t_4} \parallel m)$$

2. If $c = c'$, accepts the signature, otherwise, rejects it.

$\boldsymbol{1/0 \leftarrow Link(GP, LSK, (m, \sigma), (m', \sigma'))}$: Auditing manager performs the link operation.

1. Given (m, σ), (m', σ'), auditing manager first runs above $GVer$ algorithm to verify the validity of given signature. If the signature is invalid, it terminates.
2. Otherwise, for the component d in signature σ and d' in signature σ', auditing manager judges $(\frac{d}{d'})^{P'} \stackrel{?}{=} 1$ using the link key. If the equation succeeds, it implies the two signatures are from the same signer, outputs 1 in this case. Otherwise, outputs 0.

$\boldsymbol{(UPK, Cert) \leftarrow Trace(GP, TSK, (m, \sigma))}$: Supervision manager performs the trace operation.

1. Given (m, σ), supervision manager first runs above $GVer$ algorithm to verify the validity of given signature. If the signature is invalid, it terminates.

2. Otherwise, for the component (a, b) in signature σ, supervision manager computes $u' = b/a^x$ using the trace key, and makes a non-interactive proof $SKEQDL\left\{(\alpha)\middle| y = g^\alpha \wedge b/u' = a^\alpha\right\}(\sigma \| m)$ to prove that he does own the trace key.
3. After obtaining the certificate u, according to the registration list $\mathcal{C}$ given by registration manager, find the corresponding user's identity ID.

5.2 Security Analysis of Proposed LGS

According to the formal security definition of linkable group signature in Sect. 3 and related theorems in in Sect. 4, the proposed specific LGS instance satisfies the security properties of full-anonymity, linkability and full-traceability. The detailed proof can be found in the full version of this paper.

5.3 Performance Analysis of Proposed LGS

In this section, we analyze the performance of of linkable group signature instance in the view of the public key, secret key and signature size, the multiplication, exponentiation and pairing operations, and the security properties that it possessed. Specifically, we compare these features with existing related work, such as two typical group signature schemes [4,7] and two typical linkable group signature schemes [20,21]. The results are given in Tables 1 and 2.

As we can see in Tables 1 and 2, our proposed scheme has a slightly shorter secret key, signature size and lower computational complexity, but with a slightly

Table 1. Performance comparison with related works.

Scheme	$\|pk\|$	$\|sk\|$	$\|\sigma\|$	*Mult.*	*Exp.*
GS1 [4]	$6\|\mathbb{G}\|$	$2\|\mathbb{Z}_p\|$	$3\|\mathbb{G}\| + 6\|\mathbb{Z}_p\|$	22	30
GS2 [7]	$4\|\mathbb{G}\| + 4l_g + k$	$2l_g$	$3\|\mathbb{G}\| + k + \varepsilon(4l_g + 3k)$	21	29
LGS [21]	$3\|\mathbb{G}\| + \|\mathbb{Z}_p\|$	$\|\mathbb{Z}_p\|$	$n + 2\|\mathbb{G}\|$	$5 + 3n$	$11 + 7n$
LDGS [20]	$2\|\mathbb{Z}_p\| + \|\mathbb{Z}_q\| + 3(n+1)\|\mathbb{G}\|$	$\|\mathbb{Z}_q\| + 3\|\mathbb{G}\|$	$4\|\mathbb{Z}_p\| + 6\|\mathbb{G}\|$	2	$3n + 8$
Our LGS	$4\|\mathbb{G}\| + 2\|\mathbb{Z}_n\| + 4l_g + k$	$2\|\mathbb{Z}_n\|$	$3\|\mathbb{G}\| + k + \varepsilon(4l_g + 3k)$	20	27

Table 2. Functionality comparison with related works.

Scheme	F-Anony/Anony	F-Trace/Trace	Link	Dynamic-G	Ex-Multi
GS1 [4]	F-Anony	F-Trace	×	×	×
GS2 [7]	Anony	Trace	×	✓	×
LGS [21]	Anony	Trace	✓	✓	×
LDGS [20]	Anony	Trace	✓	✓	✓
Our LGS	F-Anony	F-Trace	✓	✓	✓

longer public key size than [4,7,21]. Moreover, it has the security properties of full-anonymity, full-traceability, linkability, and the properties of dynamic group, extend to multi-party, which is better than the other schemes. Here, $|pk|$,$|sk|$,$|\sigma|$ denote the size of public key, secret key and signature; $Mult.$,$Exp.$ denote the operations of multiplication and exponentiation; $|\mathbb{G}|$ is the size of group $\mathbb{G}$; $|\mathbb{Z}_p|$,$|\mathbb{Z}_q|$,$|\mathbb{Z}_n|$ are the size of $\mathbb{Z}_p$,$\mathbb{Z}_q$,$\mathbb{Z}_n$; n is the maximum number of group members; l_g,k,ε are the size of security parameters. F-Anony means Full-Anonymity; Anony means Anonymity; F-Trace means Full-Traceability; Trace means Traceability; Link means Linkability; Dynamic-G means Dynamic Group; Ex-Multi means Extend to Multi-party.

6 Conclusion

In this paper, we proposed a generic construction and a specific instantiation of linkable group signature scheme. The generic framework is constructed by using basic cryptography modules of blind signatures, public key encryption, trapdoor indicative commitment and signature of knowledge. It could achieve the security goals of full-anonymity, linkability and full-traceability. Furthermore, we realized an efficient linkable group signature instantiation based on the process of general construction. Refer to this construction process, any cryptography scheme of these building blocks which meets the pre-defined security requirements can be combined into a linkable group signature instance.

Acknowledgment. This paper is supported by the National Key R&D Program of China through project 2017YFB0802500, the Natural Science Foundation of China through projects 61772538, 61672083, 61370190, 61532021, 61472429, and 61402029, the National Cryptography Development Fund through project MMJJ20170106, and by Beijing Natural Science Foundation 4182033.

References

1. Ali, S.T., Amberker, B.: Attribute-based group signature without random oracles with attribute anonymity. Int. J. Inf. Comput. Secur. **6**(2), 109–132 (2014)
2. Bellare, M., Micciancio, D., Warinschi, B.: Foundations of group signatures: formal definitions, simplified requirements, and a construction based on general assumptions. In: Biham, E. (ed.) EUROCRYPT 2003. LNCS, vol. 2656, pp. 614–629. Springer, Heidelberg (2003). https://doi.org/10.1007/3-540-39200-9_38
3. Bellare, M., Shi, H., Zhang, C.: Foundations of group signatures: the case of dynamic groups. In: Menezes, A. (ed.) CT-RSA 2005. LNCS, vol. 3376, pp. 136–153. Springer, Heidelberg (2005). https://doi.org/10.1007/978-3-540-30574-3_11
4. Boneh, D., Boyen, X., Shacham, H.: Short group signatures. In: Franklin, M. (ed.) CRYPTO 2004. LNCS, vol. 3152, pp. 41–55. Springer, Heidelberg (2004). https://doi.org/10.1007/978-3-540-28628-8_3
5. Boyan, J.: The anonymizer-protecting user privacy on the web. Comput.-Mediat. Commun. Mag. **9**(4), 1–6 (1997)
6. Brassard, G., Chaum, D., Crépeau, C.: Minimum disclosure proofs of knowledge. J. Comput. Syst. Sci. **37**(2), 156–189 (1988)

7. Camenisch, J., Michels, M.: A group signature scheme with improved efficiency (extended abstract). In: Ohta, K., Pei, D. (eds.) ASIACRYPT 1998. LNCS, vol. 1514, pp. 160–174. Springer, Heidelberg (2000). https://doi.org/10.1007/3-540-49649-1_14
8. Camenisch, J.: Efficient and generalized group signatures. In: Fumy, W. (ed.) EUROCRYPT 1997. LNCS, vol. 1233, pp. 465–479. Springer, Heidelberg (1997). https://doi.org/10.1007/3-540-69053-0_32
9. Chaum, D.: The dining cryptographers problem: unconditional sender and recipient untraceability. J. Cryptol. **1**(1), 65–75 (1988)
10. Chaum, D., van Heyst, E.: Group signatures. In: Davies, D.W. (ed.) EUROCRYPT 1991. LNCS, vol. 547, pp. 257–265. Springer, Heidelberg (1991). https://doi.org/10.1007/3-540-46416-6_22
11. Chaum, D.L.: Untraceable electronic mail, return addresses, and digital pseudonyms. Commun. ACM **24**(2), 84–90 (1981)
12. Dingledine, R., Mathewson, N., Syverson, P.: Tor: the second-generation onion router. Technical report, Naval Research Lab Washington DC (2004)
13. Dodis, Y., Kiayias, A., Nicolosi, A., Shoup, V.: Anonymous identification in *ad hoc* groups. In: Cachin, C., Camenisch, J.L. (eds.) EUROCRYPT 2004. LNCS, vol. 3027, pp. 609–626. Springer, Heidelberg (2004). https://doi.org/10.1007/978-3-540-24676-3_36
14. Dolev, S., Ostrobsky, R.: Xor-trees for efficient anonymous multicast and reception. ACM Trans. Inf. Syst. Secur. (TISSEC) **3**(2), 63–84 (2000)
15. Groth, J.: Fully anonymous group signatures without random oracles. In: Kurosawa, K. (ed.) ASIACRYPT 2007. LNCS, vol. 4833, pp. 164–180. Springer, Heidelberg (2007). https://doi.org/10.1007/978-3-540-76900-2_10
16. Hwang, J.Y., Lee, S., Chung, B.H., Cho, H.S., Nyang, D.: Group signatures with controllable linkability for dynamic membership. Inf. Sci. **222**, 761–778 (2013)
17. Jiang, Y., Ji, Y., Liu, T.: An anonymous communication scheme based on ring signature in VANETs. Comput. Sci. (2014)
18. Langlois, A., Ling, S., Nguyen, K., Wang, H.: Lattice-based group signature scheme with verifier-local revocation. In: Krawczyk, H. (ed.) PKC 2014. LNCS, vol. 8383, pp. 345–361. Springer, Heidelberg (2014). https://doi.org/10.1007/978-3-642-54631-0_20
19. Manulis, M.: Democratic group signatures: on an example of joint ventures. In: Proceedings of the 2006 ACM Symposium on Information, computer and communications security, p. 365. ACM (2006)
20. Manulis, M., Sadeghi, A.-R., Schwenk, J.: Linkable democratic group signatures. In: Chen, K., Deng, R., Lai, X., Zhou, J. (eds.) ISPEC 2006. LNCS, vol. 3903, pp. 187–201. Springer, Heidelberg (2006). https://doi.org/10.1007/11689522_18
21. Nakanishi, T., Fujiwara, T., Watanabe, H.: A linkable group signature and its application to secret voting. Trans. Inf. Process. Soc. Jpn. **40**(7), 3085–3096 (1999)
22. Petersen, H.: How to convert any digital signature scheme into a group signature scheme. In: Christianson, B., Crispo, B., Lomas, M., Roe, M. (eds.) Security Protocols 1997. LNCS, vol. 1361, pp. 177–190. Springer, Heidelberg (1998). https://doi.org/10.1007/BFb0028168
23. Reed, M.G., Syverson, P.F., Goldschlag, D.M.: Anonymous connections and onion routing. IEEE J. Sel. Areas Commun. **16**(4), 482–494 (1998)
24. Reiter, M.K., Rubin, A.D.: Crowds: anonymity for web transactions. ACM Trans. Inf. Syst. Secur. (TISSEC) **1**(1), 66–92 (1998)

25. Slamanig, D., Spreitzer, R., Unterluggauer, T.: Adding controllable linkability to pairing-based group signatures for free. In: Chow, S.S.M., Camenisch, J., Hui, L.C.K., Yiu, S.M. (eds.) ISC 2014. LNCS, vol. 8783, pp. 388–400. Springer, Cham (2014). https://doi.org/10.1007/978-3-319-13257-0_23
26. Thakare, M.V.P., Shelke, C.J.: Implementation of anonymous and secure communication system with group signatures: a review. Int. J. Adv. Res. Ideas Innov. Technol. (2016)

Auditable Hierarchy-Private Public-Key Encryption

Lin Zhong[1,2], Qianhong Wu[1(✉)], Bo Qin[3,4], Haibin Zheng[1], and Jianwei Liu[1]

[1] School of Cyber Science and Technology, Beihang University, Beijing, China
{zhonglin,qianhong.wu,zhenghaibin29,liujianwei}@buaa.edu.cn
[2] State Key Laboratory of Cryptology, P.O. Box 5159, Beijing 100878, China
[3] State Key Laboratory of Integrated Services Networks, Xidian University, Xi'an, China
[4] School of Information, Renmin University of China, Beijing, China
bo.qin@ruc.edu.cn

Abstract. A member of an intelligence agency needs to receive messages secretly from outside. Except for authorized officers of the agency, no one knows how the members are organized, even a receiver only knows the organization of his/her subordinates. However, existing primitives cannot implement this typical scenario. In this paper, we propose a primitive, referred to as *auditable hierarchy-private public-key encryption* (AHPE), to address the problem. The system has several important properties: the organization of the members in the agency is hidden from the outside world, but the members can still communicate with the outside secretly; if there exists a suspicious behaviour in one of the members, managers in the system can still discover him/her. Finally, analyses show that the proposed AHPE scheme is efficient and practical.

Keywords: Hierarchy-private encryption · Auditable · Traceability

1 Introduction

Let us consider a scenario: a member of an intelligence agency needs to receive messages secretly from the outside world. Except authorized officers of the agency, no one knows how the receivers are organized, even a receiver can only know the organization of his/her subordinates. Besides, the content of a message sending to a member of the agency can only be known by himself and his superiors; However, if there exists a suspicious behaviour in one of the members, an auditing department of the agency can still discover this behavior; then, a tracing department can trace his/her identity; finally, an authenticating department can open the content of the message received by the member. In this scenario, the system has four concerns: (i) the organization of members in the agency is hidden from outsides; (ii) the receiver of a message is anonymous; (iii) the rights of management are separated into three parts; (iv) the communication auditing takes place on the premise of protecting the privacy of all members.

W. Susilo and G. Yang (Eds.): ACISP 2018, LNCS 10946, pp. 322–340, 2018.
https://doi.org/10.1007/978-3-319-93638-3_19

Let us investigate whether it is possible to implement the above typical scenario by employing existing primitives. The notion of *key-privacy encryption* was proposed in [1] who manifested that an eavesdropper in possession of a ciphertext cannot be able to tell which specific key, out of a set of known public keys, is the one under which the ciphertext was created, meaning the receiver is anonymous from the point of view of the adversary. However, key-privacy encryption achieves only the property of anonymity, but it cannot satisfy the above multifunction system. Then, *group encryption* was introduced in [2] who showed that the identity of a receiver is anonymous within a population of certified members under the control of a group manager. If a sender of a ciphertext needs to send a message to a receiver, then he must provide firstly universally verifiable guarantees that the ciphertext is well-formed, and some registered group member who will be able to decrypt it. Besides, in some necessary case, an opening authority can open suspicious ciphertexts, and determine the identity of the receiver using his private key. Finally, the plaintext should satisfy a certain relationship such as being a witness for some public relation. Based on group encryption, Libert et al. [3] proposed a *traceable group encryption*, which enjoys the properties of group encryption, and adds an extra property, i.e., the opening authority can reveal a user-specific trapdoor which makes it possible to publicly trace all the ciphertexts encrypted for that user without destroying the anonymity of other ciphertexts. However, there are no hierarchical members in either group encryption or traceable group encryption. Finally, The notion of *hierarchical identity-based encryption* (HIBE) was presented in [4] who demonstrated that an identity at level k of the hierarchy tree can issue private keys to its descendant identities, but cannot decrypt messages intended for other identities. But, in the HIBE scheme, the private key shrinks as the identity depth increases which reveal the organization of the hierarchical users. Besides, the receiver of a message is not anonymous. *Anonymous hierarchical identity-based encryption* (AHIBE) was proposed in [5] to show fully anonymous ciphertexts and hierarchical key delegation. However, communication auditing and identity tracing are not considered in AHIBE scheme.

1.1 Our Contribution

In this work, observing the above gaps, we propose an auditable hierarchy-private public-key encryption (AHPE) scheme to solve the above problem scenario to some extent. We first contribute the AHPE system model and its security definitions. We then present a generic construction and a concrete implementation. Finally, we prove the security of the AHPE scheme strictly. An additional contribution of our work is a new cryptographic tool called trapdoor distinguishable commitment.

- *System Model and Security Definitions.* We propose an AHPE system which possesses the properties of correctness, IND-CPA security, anonymity, linkability, traceability, authenticability, and give strict security definitions for them. The correctness of the AHPE scheme demonstrates that if the participants operate honestly, then the system will work correctly. The IND-CPA security manifests that knowledge of the ciphertext (and length) of some unknown message does not reveal any additional information on the message that can be feasibly extracted. The anonymity indicates that the member in the system could receive messages anonymously. The linkability is that a link manager could audit ciphertexts on the premise of protecting the privacy of all users. The traceability means that a trace manager could discover the identity of a receiver from the suspicious ciphertext provided by the link manager. Finally, the authenticability shows that an authenticate manager could extract the content of the suspicious message.

- *Generic Construction and Concrete Implementation.* We construct the AHPE scheme in a modular way. The building blocks of the AHPE scheme include a pseudorandom generator [6], a digital signature with adaptive chosen message security [7], a public key encryption with both CPA security and key-privacy [1], a zero-knowledge proof [8], a trapdoor distinguishable commitment, and an extractable commitment [9]. Then, we give an efficient concrete implementation of the AHPE scheme by using a hash function, an ElGamal digital signature scheme [10], an ElGamal linear encryption scheme [11], a Σ-protocol [12], a trapdoor distinguishable commitment scheme, and an extractable commitment scheme.

- *Proof and Comparison.* According to our security definitions, we prove the properties of the AHPE scheme rigorously. We demonstrate that if the underlying cryptographic primitives, i.e., pseudorandom generator, digital signature with adaptive chosen message security, public key encryption with both CPA security and key-privacy, zero-knowledge proof, trapdoor distinguishable commitment, and extractable commitment, are secure, then the AHPE system has correctness, IND-CPA security, anonymity, link security, trace security, and authentication security. Then, we compare it with related schemes in performance and functionality.

- *Trapdoor Distinguishable Commitment.* As the AHPE scheme needs to audit ciphertexts that sent to users, we introduce a new cryptographic tool, called trapdoor distinguishable commitment, to judge whether the identities of receivers contained in any two ciphertexts are the same. We define the trapdoor distinguishable commitment strictly, present a concrete implementation, and prove its properties strictly.

1.2 Related Work

The notion of privacy for public key encryption schemes was introduced by Bellare et al. [1] and formalized as key-privacy encryption. Intuitively, the key-privacy encryption makes it impossible to pin down the public key of a receiver from the ciphertext. Then, they proved that the ElGamal scheme [13] provides key-privacy under chosen-plaintext attack assuming the Decision Diffie-Hellman problem is hard, and the Cramer-Shoup scheme [14] provides key-privacy under chosen-ciphertext attack under the same assumption. Based on it, Barth et al. [15] proposed a mechanism, called private broadcast encryption, to protect the privacy of users of encrypted file systems and content delivery systems. Similarly, Ateniese et al. [16] proposed Key-Private Proxy Re-encryption to prevent the proxy from learning the private keys or the contents of messages it re-encrypts. Waters et al. [17] described a new method, called Incomparable Public Key (IPK) cryptosystem, to protect the anonymity of message receivers in an untrusted network. However, key-privacy encryption in above schemes can only achieve anonymity in our problem scenario.

Using key-privacy encryption as a component together with zero-knowledge proofs, digital signatures, and commitment schemes, Kiayias et al. [2] constructed a Group Encryption (GE) cryptosystem. Qin et al. [18] presented a group encryption mechanism, called group decryption, with non-interactive proofs and short ciphertexts. In security analysis, their scheme needs random oracles and interactive assumptions. Meanwhile, Cathalo et al. [19] proposed a non-interactive group encryption cryptosystem, and proved its security in the standard model. Based on GE, Libert et al. [3] proposed a Traceable Group Encryption (TGE) which can trace all the ciphertexts encrypted by a specific user without abolishing the anonymity of the others'. Both GE and TGE have the property of managing the member of the system properly, but they do not consider the organization of the member which is an important goal of our scheme.

Finally, Hierarchical Identity-Based Encryption (HIBE) scheme was defined by Horwitz and Lynn [20]. And then, Gentry and Silverberg [21] gave a construction based on the Bilinear Diffie-Hellman (BDH) assumption in the random oracle model. Canetti et al. [22] demonstrated a HIBE scheme with a (selective-ID) security proof without random oracles, but it is an inefficient scheme. A subsequent construction due to Boneh and Boyen [23] gave an efficient (selective-ID secure) HIBE based on BDH without random oracles. Boyen and Waters [5] proposed a provable security HIBE cryptosystem in the standard model, based on the mild Decision Linear complexity assumption in bilinear groups that features fully anonymous ciphertexts and hierarchical key delegation. However, in above schemes, the length of ciphertexts and private keys, as well as the time needed for encryption and decryption, grows linearly in the depth of the hierarchy which reveals the organization of the members. Boneh et al. [4] presented a HIBE system where the ciphertext consists of three group elements and decryption requires two bilinear map computations, regardless of the hierarchy depth. But the anonymity of the receiver is not considered. In short, existing schemes could not implement the problem scenario properly. Thus, a system which has the properties of anonymity, communication auditing, identity tracing, and constant complexity of algorithms still needs to be researched further.

Organization. Section 2 introduces a new concept, called trapdoor distinguishable commitment. Section 3 presents a system model and its security definitions. Section 4 demonstrates a generic construction and a concrete implementation. Section 5 compares the AHPE scheme with related schemes. Finally, Sect. 6 concludes the paper. For lack of space most proofs are omitted. They will appear in the full version.

2 Trapdoor Distinguishable Commitment

As the AHPE scheme needs to audit ciphertexts in auditing stage, we introduce a new cryptographic tool, called trapdoor distinguishable commitment, to achieve this target. Consider a scheme $TDCOM = (KGen, TDCom, Ver, Disting)$ where $KGen$, $TDCom$, Ver, and $Disting$ are probabilistic polynomial-time algorithms and the following experiments:

$\mathbf{Exp}_{TDCOM}^{Completeness}(1^\lambda)$	$\mathbf{Exp}_{\mathcal{A},TDCOM}^{Binding}(1^\lambda)$	$\mathbf{Exp}_{\mathcal{A},TDCOM}^{Hiding}(1^\lambda)$	$\mathbf{Exp}_{TDCOM}^{Disting}(1^\lambda)$
$(pk, sk) \leftarrow KGen(1^\lambda)$;	$(pk, sk) \leftarrow KGen(1^\lambda)$;	$(pk, sk) \leftarrow KGen(1^\lambda)$;	$(pk, sk) \leftarrow KGen(1^\lambda)$;
$(\psi,\rho) \leftarrow TDCom(pk,m)$;	$(\psi, \rho, m) \leftarrow \mathcal{A}(\text{find}, pk)$;	$(m_1,m_2,aux) \leftarrow \mathcal{A}(\text{find},pk)$;	$(\psi,\rho) \leftarrow TDCom(pk,m)$;
$b_1 \leftarrow Verify(pk,\psi,\rho,m)$;	$(\rho', m') \leftarrow \mathcal{A}(\text{find}, pk)$;	$b \xleftarrow{R} \{0,1\}$,	$(\psi',\rho') \leftarrow TDCom(pk,m')$;
Return b_1.	If $m = m' \vee \rho = \rho'$, abort;	$(\psi,\rho) \leftarrow TDCom(pk,m_b)$;	$b_4 \leftarrow Disting(sk,\psi,\psi')$;
	$b_2 \leftarrow Ver(pk, \psi, \rho', m')$;	$b_3 \leftarrow \mathcal{A}(\text{guess},\psi,pk,aux)$;	Return b_4.
	Return b_2.	Return b_3.	

$TDCOM = (KGen, TDCom, Ver, Disting)$ is a trapdoor distinguishable commitment with completeness, binding, hiding, and distinguishing if there exists a negligible function $\mu(\cdot)$ such that $\Pr[b_1 = 1] > 1 - \mu(\lambda)$, $\Pr[b_2 = 1] \leq \mu(\lambda)$, $\Pr[b_3 = b] \leq \mu(\lambda)$, $\Pr[b_4 = true] > 1 - \mu(\lambda)$.

We provide a concrete implementation for the trapdoor distinguishable commitment. Let $\mathbb{G}_1$ and $\mathbb{G}_2$ be cyclic groups of prime order p, $\mathbb{G}_1 \neq \mathbb{G}_2$, with respective generators g and h, with a computable bilinear map $\hat{e} : \mathbb{G}_1 \times \mathbb{G}_2 \rightarrow \mathbb{G}_T$. The scheme comprises the four algorithms described below:

$KGen(p, g, h)$	$TDCom_{pk}(m)$	$Ver_{pk}(\psi, \rho, m)$	$Disting_{sk}(\psi, \psi')$
$x \xleftarrow{R} \mathbb{Z}_p^*$; $X \leftarrow g^x$;	$u, v \xleftarrow{R} \mathbb{Z}_p^*$; $U \leftarrow g^u$;	$\psi' \leftarrow (g^u, h^v, m^v \cdot X^u)$;	$T \leftarrow W \cdot U^{-x}$;
$pk \leftarrow (p, g, h, X)$;	$V \leftarrow h^v$; $W \leftarrow m^v X^u$;	If $\psi' = \psi$,	$T' \leftarrow W' \cdot U'^{-x}$;
$sk \leftarrow (p, g, h, x)$;	$\psi = (U, V, W), \rho = (u, v)$;	return 1;	$\hat{e}(T', V) \stackrel{?}{=} \hat{e}(T, V')$;
Return (pk, sk).	Return (ψ, ρ).	else return 0.	Return b.

Theorem 1. *The above scheme is a trapdoor distinguishable commitment.*

3 Auditable Hierarchy-Private Encryption

In this section, we propose a system model and give several security definitions from different angles that the adversary is likely to attack.

3.1 System Model

The AHPE system has three managers (authentication manager, trace manager, and link manager) and four other participants (hierarchical users, a sender, a verifier and a receiver). Trusted by all parties, the authentication manager generates system parameter, his public key, and a matching main secret key, and manages the members of the system. The trace manager is capable of tracing the identity of anonymous receivers. The link manager is capable of counting the quantity of ciphertexts received by anonymous users without detecting any other things. The hierarchical users are members of the system. The sender who

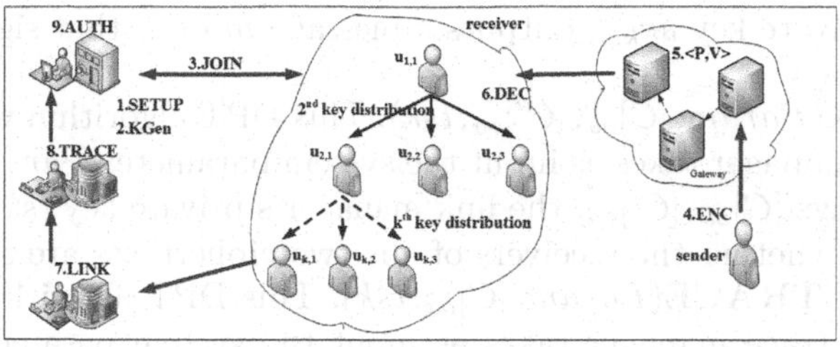

Fig. 1. System model

can be anyone sends messages to legitimate users. The verifier who can be a gateway verifies the validity of ciphertexts, and broadcasts to users if valid, else rejects. The receiver receives messages from outsides anonymously.

Formally, an AHPE scheme (see Fig. 1) is a collection of procedures and protocols that are denoted as **SETUP, KGen, JOIN, ENC, ⟨P,V⟩, DEC, LINK, TRACE, AUTH**. The procedures are as follows:

- $(Param) \leftarrow \mathbf{SETUP}(1^\lambda)$. This Probabilistic Polynomial Time (PPT) algorithm which operated by M_1 takes as input a security parameter λ, outputs the system parameter $Param$.
- $(rpk, rsk) \leftarrow \mathbf{KGen}_{M_1}(Param)$. This PPT algorithm which operated by M_1 takes as input the system parameter $Param$, outputs a register public key and a matching register private key (rpk, rsk).
- $(tpk, tsk) \leftarrow \mathbf{KGen}_{M_2}(Param)$. This PPT algorithm which operated by M_2 takes as input the system parameter $Param$, outputs a trace public key and a matching trace private key (tpk, tsk).
- $(lpk, lsk) \leftarrow \mathbf{KGen}_{M_3}(Param)$. This PPT algorithm which operated by M_3 takes as input the system parameter $Param$, outputs a link public key and a matching link private key (lpk, lsk).
- $(pk_{k,j}, sk_{k,j}, cert_{k,j}) \leftarrow \mathbf{JOIN}(Param, sk_{k-1,j'}, ID_{k,j})$. This protocol which operated between the M_1 and the hierarchical users, takes as input the system parameter $Param$, superior user's private key $sk_{k-1,j'}$, and the identity of register $ID_{k,j}$, outputs a public key, a private key $(pk_{k,j}, sk_{k,j})$, and a certificate $cert_{k,j}$.
- $(C) \leftarrow \mathbf{ENC}(Param, m, pk_{k,j}, rpk, tpk, lpk)$. This PPT algorithm which operated by the sender takes as input the system parameter $Param$, a message m, the intended receiver's public key $pk_{k,j}$, the three managers' public key rpk, tpk, lpk, outputs a ciphertext C in ciphertext space $\mathbb{C}$.
- $\langle done|0/1\rangle \leftarrow \langle \mathbf{P}(m, pk_{k,j}), \mathbf{V}\rangle\ (Param, C, rpk, tpk, lpk)$. This protocol which operated between the sender and the gateway will ensure that the ciphertext is create correctly, and that there exists a member in the system that is capable of decrypting the ciphertext.
- $(m/\perp) \leftarrow \mathbf{DEC}(Param, [C]_{oa}, sk_{k,j})$. This Deterministic Polynomial Time (DPT) algorithm which operated by the anonymous receiver takes as input the system parameter $Param$, a substring of the ciphertext $[C]_{oa}$, the

receiver's private key $sk_{k,j}$, outputs a message m or $\perp$ that signifies an error in decryption.

- $(b) \leftarrow$ **LINK**$(Param, [C]_{oa}, [C']_{oa}, lsk)$. This DPT algorithm which operated by the link manager takes as input the system parameter $Param$, two ciphertext substrings $[C]_{oa}$, $[C']_{oa}$, the link manager's private key lsk, outputs a bit b indicating whether the receivers of any two ciphertexts are the same.
- $(pk_{k,j}/\perp) \leftarrow$ **TRACE**$(Param, [C]_{oa}, tsk)$. This DPT algorithm which operated by the trace manager takes as input the system parameter $Param$, a substring of the ciphertext $[C]_{oa}$, the trace manager's private key tsk, outputs an identity (public key) $pk_{k,j}$ or $\perp$ that signifies an error in trace.
- $(m/\perp) \leftarrow$ **AUTH**$(Param, [C]_{oa}, rsk)$. This DPT algorithm which operated by the authentication manager takes as input the system parameter $Param$, a substring of the ciphertext $[C]_{oa}$, the authentication manager's master key rsk, outputs a message m or $\perp$ that signifies an error in authentication.

In the above AHPE system, **JOIN** $= \langle J_{user}, J_{M_1} \rangle$ is a protocol between a prospective hierarchical member $\mathrm{u}_{k,j}$ (row k, column j) and the M_1. After an execution of a **JOIN** protocol the member will get his public/secret-key pair $(pk_{k,j}, sk_{k,j})$ together with a certificate $cert_{k,j}$. The public key and the certificate will be published in the public directory *database* by the M_1. There are four subprocedures in **ENC** procedure, including a message encryption procedure **ENC**$_1$, i.e., C_1 = **ENC**$_1(Param, pk_{k,j}, m)$, a trapdoor distinguishable commitment procedure **TDCOM**, i.e., C_2 = **TDCOM**$(Param, lpk, pk_{k,j})$, an identity encryption procedure **ENC**$_2$, i.e., C_3 = **ENC**$_2(Param, tpk, pk_{k,j})$, an extractable commitment procedure **ECOM**, i.e., C_4 = **ECOM**$(Param, rpk, m)$. Let $C = (C_1, C_2, C_3, C_4)$. The Prove-Verification protocol $\langle \mathbf{P}, \mathbf{V} \rangle$ is a zero-knowledge proof which proves that the encrypted message in procedure **ENC**$_1$ and the committed message in procedure **ECOM** are identical, and that the public keys used in the message encryption procedure **ENC**$_1$, committed in trapdoor distinguishable commitment procedure **TDCOM**, encrypted in identity encryption procedure **ENC**$_2$ are all the same. Finally, the procedures **DEC, LINK, TRACE, AUTH** operate on different parts (C_1, C_2, C_3, C_4) of the ciphertext C to decrypt, to link, to trace, and to authenticate respectively.

3.2 Security Definitions

In this subsection, we first give three definitions, *correctness*, and the two security related properties of the AHPE, *IND-CPA security*, and *anonymity*. Then, we give three definitions (i.e., *link security*, *trace security*, *authentication security*) for each manager respectively. For simulating a two-party protocol we use the notation: $\langle output_A \mid output_B \rangle \leftarrow \langle A(input_A), B(input_B) \rangle$ (*common–input*). Note that a procedure denotes as bold symbol, such as **ENC**. For simplicity, in this section, we will use $pk, sk, cert, \mathrm{u}$ denotes $pk_{k,j}, sk_{k,j}, cert_{k,j}, \mathrm{u}_{k,j}$; When it needs different key pairs and users, we will use $(pk_0, sk_0, cert_0)$,$(pk_1, sk_1, cert_1)$ denotes $(pk_{k,j}, sk_{k,j}, cert_{k,j}), (pk_{k',j'}, sk_{k',j'}, cert_{k',j'})$, and use u_0, u_1 denotes $\mathrm{u}_{k,j}, \mathrm{u}_{k',j'}$.

Correctness. The AHPE scheme must satisfy the correctness of the following five aspects concurrently. When the non-interaction zero-knowledge protocol ends between the sender (prover) and the verifier (gateway), the prover outputs *done*, and the gateway can judge the validity of a ciphertext correctly. Associated with each public key pk is a message space $MsgSp(pk)$ from which a message m is allowed to be drawn such that $m = Dec(sk, Enc(pk, m))$. The link manager can judge the relation between any two ciphertexts correctly. The trace manager can trace the identity of the anonymous receiver accurately. The authentication manager can authenticate the content of the message correctly. The correctness of the AHPE scheme demonstrates that if the sender operates honestly, then the system will work correctly.

Definition 1 *(Correctness). An AHPE scheme is correct if the following "correctness experiment" return 1 with overwhelming probability.*

$$\begin{aligned}
&\boldsymbol{Exp}^{Correctness}(\lambda) : (Param) \leftarrow \boldsymbol{SETUP}(1^\lambda); (rpk,rsk) \leftarrow \boldsymbol{KGen}_{M_1}(Param);\\
&(tpk, tsk) \leftarrow \boldsymbol{KGen}_{M_2}(Param); (lpk, lsk) \leftarrow \boldsymbol{KGen}_{M_3}(Param);\\
&\langle pk, sk, cert \mid done\rangle \leftarrow \langle \mathrm{u}, M_1(rsk)\rangle\ (Param, rpk);\\
&(C) \leftarrow \boldsymbol{ENC}(Param, m, pk, rpk, tpk, lpk);\\
&if \begin{pmatrix} \langle done \mid b\rangle \leftarrow \langle \boldsymbol{P}(m, pk), \boldsymbol{V}\rangle\ (Param, C, rpk, tpk, lpk) : b = \text{true}\\ \wedge(m = \boldsymbol{DEC}(Param, C_1, sk)) \wedge (d \leftarrow \boldsymbol{LINK}(Param, C_2, C_2', lsk)) : d = \text{true}\\ \wedge(pk = \boldsymbol{TRACE}(Param, C_3, tsk)) \wedge (m = \boldsymbol{AUTH}(Param, C_4, rsk)) \end{pmatrix}\\
&retuen\, 1, else\, return\, 0.
\end{aligned}$$

IND-CPA security. IND-CPA security manifests that knowledge of the ciphertext (and length) of some unknown message does not reveal any additional information on the message that can be feasibly extracted. We think of an adversary running in two stages. In the *find* stage, an adversary $\mathcal{A}$ takes a public key pk, and outputs two messages m_0, m_1 together with some auxiliary information aux. In the *guess* stage, the adversary $\mathcal{A}$ gets a challenge ciphertext C_1 formed by encrypting at random one of the two messages $m_b, b \in \{0,1\}$ under the public key pk, and must say which message was chosen. We said that if an AHPE system satisfies IND-CPA security, then it can work securely.

Definition 2 *(IND-CPA security). An AHPE scheme satisfies IND-CPA security if the function* $\boldsymbol{Adv}^{IND-CPA}_{\mathcal{A},\boldsymbol{ENC}_1}(\cdot)$ *is negligible in the "IND-CPA security experiment" below for any adversary* $\mathcal{A}$ *whose time complexity is polynomial in* λ.

$$\begin{aligned}
&\boldsymbol{EXP}^{IND-CPA}_{\mathcal{A},\boldsymbol{ENC}_1}(1^\lambda) : (Param) \leftarrow \boldsymbol{SETUP}(1^\lambda); (rpk,rsk) \leftarrow \boldsymbol{KGen}_{M_1}(Param);\\
&(tpk, tsk) \leftarrow \boldsymbol{KGen}_{M_2}(Param); (lpk, lsk) \leftarrow \boldsymbol{KGen}_{M_3}(Param);\\
&\langle pk,sk,cert|done\rangle \leftarrow \langle \mathrm{u}, M_1(rsk)\rangle\ (Param, rpk); (m_0,m_1,aux) \leftarrow \mathcal{A}(find,pk);\\
&b \xleftarrow{r} \{0,1\}, C_1 \leftarrow \boldsymbol{ENC}_1(Param, pk, m_b); b' \leftarrow \mathcal{A}(guess, C_1, aux); Return\, b'.
\end{aligned}$$

For chosen plaintext attack, we define the advantages of the adversary via

$$\mathbf{Adv}_{\mathcal{A},\mathbf{ENC}_1}^{IND-CPA}(1^\lambda) = \mathbf{Pr}[\mathbf{EXP}_{\mathcal{A},\mathbf{ENC}_1}^{Attack-1}(1^\lambda) = 1] - \mathbf{Pr}[\mathbf{EXP}_{\mathcal{A},\mathbf{ENC}_1}^{Attack-0}(1^\lambda) = 1]$$

The term $\mathbf{Pr}[\mathbf{EXP}_{\mathcal{A},\mathbf{ENC}_1}^{Attack-1}(1^\lambda) = 1]$ denotes a probability of success. Similarly, the term $\mathbf{Pr}[\mathbf{EXP}_{\mathcal{A},\mathbf{ENC}_1}^{Attack-0}(1^\lambda) = 1]$ means a probability of failure. The success probability subtracting the failure probability is the advantage of the adversary $\mathcal{A}$. In this paper, we define the advantage of the adversary/distinguisher all in this way.

Anonymity. Apart from consistency, the AHPE scheme must satisfy anonymity which indicates that the adversary knows two public keys corresponding to two different entities, and gets a ciphertext formed by encrypting a message under one of these keys. Possession of the ciphertexts should not give the adversary an advantage in determining under which of the two keys was created. We give the notion of anonymity under chosen plaintext attack. An adversary $\mathcal{A}$ running in two stages. In the *find* stage, it takes two public keys pk_0, pk_1, and outputs a message m together with some auxiliary information aux. In the *guess* stage, it gets a challenge ciphertext C_1 formed by encrypting the message m under one of the two public keys $pk_b, b \in \{0,1\}$, and must say which public key was chosen. We said that if an AHPE system satisfies anonymity, then the users in the system can receive messages anonymously.

Definition 3 *(Anonymity). An AHPE scheme satisfies anonymity if the function* $\boldsymbol{Adv}_{\mathcal{A},\boldsymbol{ENC}_1}^{Anonymity}(\cdot)$ *is negligible in the "anonymity experiment" below for any adversary* $\mathcal{A}$ *whose time complexity is polynomial in* λ.

$\boldsymbol{EXP}_{\mathcal{A},\boldsymbol{ENC}_1}^{Anonymity}(1^\lambda)(Param) \leftarrow \boldsymbol{SETUP}(1^\lambda); (rpk, rsk) \leftarrow \boldsymbol{KGen}_{M_1}(Param);$
$(tpk, tsk) \leftarrow \boldsymbol{KGen}_{M_2}(Param); (lpk, lsk) \leftarrow \boldsymbol{KGen}_{M_3}(Param);$
$\langle pk_0, sk_0, cert_0 \mid done\rangle \leftarrow \langle \mathrm{u}_0, M_1(rsk)\rangle\ (Param, rpk);$
$\langle pk_1, sk_1, cert_1 \mid done\rangle \leftarrow \langle \mathrm{u}_1, M_1(rsk)\rangle\ (Param, rpk);$
$(m, aux) \leftarrow \mathcal{A}(find, pk_0, pk_1);$
$b \xleftarrow{r} \{0,1\}, C_1 \leftarrow \boldsymbol{ENC}_1(Param, pk_b, m).b' \leftarrow \mathcal{A}(guess, C_1, aux); Return\, b'.$

For chosen plaintext attack, we define the advantages of the adversary via

$$\mathbf{Adv}_{\mathcal{A},\mathbf{ENC}_1}^{Anonymity}(1^\lambda) = \mathbf{Pr}[\mathbf{EXP}_{\mathcal{A},\mathbf{ENC}_1}^{Attack-1}(1^\lambda) = 1] - \mathbf{Pr}[\mathbf{EXP}_{\mathcal{A},\mathbf{ENC}_1}^{Attack-0}(1^\lambda) = 1]$$

Link Security. Link security manifests that the adversary has a negligible probability of linking any two ciphertexts sent to anonymous receivers correctly. We give the notion of link security under chosen plaintext attack. We think of an adversary running in two stages. In the *find* stage, the adversary $\mathcal{A}$ signs up two accounts u_0, u_1, and obtains two pairs of keys $(pk_0, sk_0), (pk_1, sk_1)$ and two certificates $cert_0, cert_1$ together with some auxiliary information aux. In the *guess* stage, the adversary $\mathcal{A}$ gets two challenge ciphertexts C_2, C_2' formed by committing two public keys in sequence under the link public key lpk, and must say whether the two public keys in ciphertexts C, C' are the same. We said that if AHPE satisfies link security, then the adversary has a negligible probability of linking any two ciphertexts accurately.

Definition 4 *(Link Security). The AHPE scheme satisfies link security if the function $\boldsymbol{Adv}^{Link-Security}_{\mathcal{A},\boldsymbol{TDCOM}}(\cdot)$ is negligible in the "link experiment" below for any adversary $\mathcal{A}$ whose time complexity is polynomial in λ.*

$\boldsymbol{EXP}^{Link-Security}_{\mathcal{A},\boldsymbol{TDCOM}}(1^\lambda)$:$(Param) \leftarrow \boldsymbol{SETUP}(1^\lambda)$;$(rpk, rsk) \leftarrow \boldsymbol{KGen}_{M_1}(Param)$;
$(tpk, tsk) \leftarrow \boldsymbol{KGen}_{M_2}(Param)$; $(lpk, lsk) \leftarrow \boldsymbol{KGen}_{M_3}(Param)$;
$\langle pk_0, sk_0, cert_0, aux \mid done\rangle \leftarrow \langle \mathcal{A}(find, \mathrm{u}_0), M_1(rsk)\rangle\ (Param, rpk)$;
$\langle pk_1, sk_1, cert_1, aux \mid done\rangle \leftarrow \langle \mathcal{A}(find, \mathrm{u}_1), M_1(rsk)\rangle\ (Param, rpk)$;
$b \stackrel{r}{\leftarrow} \{0, 1\}, if\, b = 1,$
$C_2 \leftarrow \boldsymbol{TDCOM}(Param, lpk, pk_0), C_2' \leftarrow \boldsymbol{TDCOM}(Param, lpk, pk_1).$
$else C_2 \leftarrow \boldsymbol{TDCOM}(Param, lpk, pk_0), C_2' \leftarrow \boldsymbol{TDCOM}(Param, lpk, pk_0).$
$b' \leftarrow \mathcal{A}(guess, C_2, C_2', aux).return\, b'.$

For chosen plaintext attack, we define the advantages of the adversary via

$$\mathbf{Adv}^{Link-Security}_{\mathcal{A},\mathbf{TDCOM}}(1^\lambda) = \mathbf{Pr}[\mathbf{EXP}^{Attack-1}_{\mathcal{A},\mathbf{TDCOM}}(1^\lambda) = 1] - \mathbf{Pr}[\mathbf{EXP}^{Attack-0}_{\mathcal{A},\mathbf{TDCOM}}(1^\lambda) = 1]$$

Note that as the sender will select two different nonces in the commitment stage, the commitments C_2, C_2' will be different even the public key pk_0 be committed twice.

Trace Security. Trace security manifests that the adversary has a negligible probability of tracing the identity of anonymous receivers correctly. We give the notion of trace security under chosen plaintext attack. We think of an adversary running in two stages. In the *find* stage, the adversary $\mathcal{A}$ signs up two accounts $\mathrm{u}_0, \mathrm{u}_1$, and obtains two pairs of keys $(pk_0, sk_0), (pk_1, sk_1)$ and two certificates $cert_0, cert_1$ together with some auxiliary information aux. In the *guess* stage, the adversary $\mathcal{A}$ gets a challenge ciphertext C_3 formed by encrypting at random one of the two public keys $pk_b, b \in \{0, 1\}$ under the trace public key tpk, and must say which public key was chosen. We said that if the AHPE scheme satisfies trace security, then the adversary has a negligible probability of tracing the identity of the receiver precisely.

Definition 5 *(Trace Security). The AHPE scheme satisfies trace security if the function $\boldsymbol{Adv}^{Trace-Security}_{\mathcal{A},\boldsymbol{ENC}_2}(\cdot)$ is negligible in the "trace experiment" below for any adversary $\mathcal{A}$ whose time complexity is polynomial in λ.*

$\boldsymbol{EXP}^{Trace-Security}_{\mathcal{A},\boldsymbol{ENC}_2}(1^\lambda): (Param) \leftarrow \boldsymbol{SETUP}(1^\lambda)$;$(rpk, rsk) \leftarrow \boldsymbol{KGen}_{M_1}(Param)$;
$(tpk, tsk) \leftarrow \boldsymbol{KGen}_{M_2}(Param)$; $(lpk, lsk) \leftarrow \boldsymbol{KGen}_{M_3}(Param)$;
$\langle pk_0, sk_0, cert_0, aux \mid done\rangle \leftarrow \langle \mathcal{A}(find, \mathrm{u}_0), M_1(rsk)\rangle\ (Param, rpk)$;
$\langle pk_1, sk_1, cert_1, aux \mid done\rangle \leftarrow \langle \mathcal{A}(find, \mathrm{u}_1), M_1(rsk)\rangle\ (Param, rpk)$;
$b \stackrel{r}{\leftarrow} \{0, 1\}, (C_3) \leftarrow \boldsymbol{ENC}_2(Param, tpk, pk_b); b' \leftarrow \mathcal{A}(guess, C_3, aux); return\, b'.$

For chosen plaintext attack, we define the advantages of the adversary via

$$\mathbf{Adv}_{\mathcal{A},\mathbf{ENC}_2}^{Trace-Security}(1^\lambda)=\mathbf{Pr}[\mathbf{EXP}_{\mathcal{A},\mathbf{ENC}_2}^{Attack-1}(1^\lambda)=1]-\mathbf{Pr}[\mathbf{EXP}_{\mathcal{A},\mathbf{ENC}_2}^{Attack-0}(1^\lambda)=1]$$

Authentication Security. Authentication security manifests that the adversary has a negligible probability of authenticating the content of the message correctly. We give the notion of authentication security under chosen plaintext attack. In the *find* stage, the adversary $\mathcal{A}$ takes the public key of the authentication manager rpk, and outputs two messages m_0, m_1 together with some auxiliary information aux. In the *guess* stage, the adversary $\mathcal{A}$ gets a commitment C_4 formed by committing at random one of the two messages $m_b, b \in \{0,1\}$ under the authentication public key rpk, and must say which message was committed. We said that if the AHPE scheme satisfies authentication security, then the adversary has a negligible probability of authenticating the content of the message precisely.

Definition 6 *(Authentication Security). The AHPE scheme satisfies authentication security if the function* $\boldsymbol{Adv}_{\mathcal{A},\boldsymbol{ECOM}}^{Auth-Security}(\cdot)$ *is negligible in the "authentication security" experiment below for any adversary* $\mathcal{A}$ *whose time complexity is polynomial in* λ.

$\boldsymbol{EXP}_{\mathcal{A},\boldsymbol{ECOM}}^{Auth-Security}(1^\lambda)$: $(Param)\leftarrow \boldsymbol{SETUP}(1^\lambda)$;$(rpk,rsk)\leftarrow \boldsymbol{KGen}_{M_1}(Param)$;
$(tpk, tsk) \leftarrow \boldsymbol{KGen}_{M_2}(Param)$; $(lpk, lsk) \leftarrow \boldsymbol{KGen}_{M_3}(Param)$;
$(m_0, m_1, aux) \leftarrow \mathcal{A}(find, rpk)$; $b \xleftarrow{r} \{0,1\}$, $(C_4) = \boldsymbol{ECOM}(Param, rpk, m_b)$.
$b' \leftarrow \mathcal{A}(guess, C_4, aux).return\, b'$.

We define the advantages of the adversary via

$$\mathbf{Adv}_{\mathcal{A},\mathbf{ECOM}}^{Auth-Security}(1^\lambda)=\mathbf{Pr}[\mathbf{EXP}_{\mathcal{A},\mathbf{ECOM}}^{Attack-1}(1^\lambda)=1]-\mathbf{Pr}[\mathbf{EXP}_{\mathcal{A},\mathbf{ECOM}}^{Attack-0}(1^\lambda)=1]$$

4 Construction

In this section, we first provide a general description of the AHPE scheme. We then give a generic construction and a concrete implementation.

4.1 A Bird View

As the adversary wants to obtain receivers' identity from ciphertexts, the AHPE scheme should prevent the identity of the receiver from being extracted. We will employ a public key encryption $PE_1 = (KGen_1, Enc_1, Dec_1)$ that satisfies both IND-CPA security and Key-privacy to achieve this goal. If anonymous users have suspicious behaviors, the AHPE system can still discover them. In other words, the AHPE scheme is capable of managing the behaviour of users. We will employ (1) a trapdoor distinguishable commitment $TDCOM$ to achieve ciphertexts auditing, (2) a public key encryption algorithm PE_2 that satisfies

IND-CPA security to achieve identity tracing, (3) an extractable commitment $ECOM$ to achieve message authentication.

In order to show that the encrypted message and the committed message are identical, we will couple zero-knowledge proof protocol ZK with public key encryption PE_1 and with the extractable commitment scheme $ECOM$. Besides, in order to show that the public keys used in public key encryption PE_1, committed in trapdoor distinguishable commitment $TDCOM$, encrypted in PE_2 are all the same, we will also couple zero-knowledge proof protocol ZK with public key encryption PE_1 with trapdoor distinguishable commitment $TDCOM$ and with public key encryption PE_2.

4.2 Generic Construction

In generic construction we will employ: (1) pseudorandom generator PRG, (2) digital signature with adaptive chosen message security $SIG = (KGen, Sign, Verify)$, (3) public key encryption with IND-CPA security and key-privacy $PE_1 = (KGen_1, Enc_1, Dec_1)$, and public key encryption with IND-CPA security $PE_2 = (KGen_2, Enc_2, Dec_2)$, (4) zero-knowledge proof protocol $ZK\{w|(x,w) \in R\}$, (5) extractable commitment $ECOM = (KGen, ECom, Verify, Extract)$, (6) a new trapdoor distinguishable commitment $TDCOM = (KGen, TDCom, Verify, Disting)$. The generic construction of the AHPE scheme **SETUP, KGen, JOIN, ENC, ⟨P,V⟩, DEC, LINK, TRACE, AUTH** is as follows:

SETUP. (i) selects a security parameter λ, and performs the extractable commitment initialization algorithm $ECOM.KGen$, output the system parameter $Param$, i.e., $Param \leftarrow ECOM.KGen(1^\lambda)$. (ii) selects two hash functions $\mathcal{H}, \mathcal{H}_1$ from a Universal One-Way Hash (UOWH) family.

KGen. The procedure $\mathbf{KGen}_{M_1}$ will perform the extractable commitment key generation algorithm to get a register private key and a corresponding public key, i.e., $(rsk, rpk) \leftarrow ECOM.KGen(Param)$.

The procedure $\mathbf{KGen}_{M_2}$ will perform the public key encryption key generation algorithm to get a trace private key and a corresponding public key, i.e., $(tsk, tpk) \leftarrow PE_2.KGen_2(Param)$.

The procedure $\mathbf{KGen}_{M_3}$ will perform the trapdoor distinguishable commitment key generation algorithm to get a link private key and a corresponding public key, i.e., $(lsk, lpk) \leftarrow TDCOM.KGen(Param)$.

JOIN. Each prospective user $u_{k,j}$ will get an identity $ID_{k,j}$ from the manager M_1, and then send to his superior who will respond with a secret key $sk_{k,j}$ using the public key encryption key generation algorithm $PE_1.KGen_1$ which invoke the pseudorandom generator PRG, i.e., $sk_{k,j} \leftarrow PE_1.KGen_1(PRG(sk_{k-1,j'}, ID_{k,j}))$. And then, the user will perform the public-key encryption key generation algorithm $PE_1.KGen_1$ to get his public key $pk_{k,j}$, i.e., $pk_{k,j} \leftarrow PE_1.KGen_1(sk_{k,j}, Param)$, and send his public key to the manager M_1. Finally, M_1 will respond with a certificate $cert_{k,j}$ using the signature algorithm $SIG.Sign$, i.e., $cert_{k,j} \leftarrow SIG.Sign(rsk, pk_{k,j})$, and enter the public key $pk_{k,j}$ into the public *database* followed by the signature $cert_{k,j}$.

ENC. *Step 1. Encryption.* The procedure **ENC** will work as follows: (i) perform public key encryption algorithm $PE_1.Enc_1$ to get a message encryption C_1, i.e., $C_1 \leftarrow PE_1.Enc_1(pk_{k,j}, m)$; (ii) perform the trapdoor distinguishable commitment algorithm $TICIOM.TDCom$ to get a trapdoor distinguishable commitment C_2, i.e., $C_2 \leftarrow TICIOM.TDCom(lsk, pk_{k,j})$; (iii) perform the public key encryption algorithm $PE_2.Enc_2$ to get a receriver's public key encryption C_3, i.e., $C_3 \leftarrow PE_2.Enc_2\ (tsk, pk_{k,j})$; (iv) perform the extractable commitment algorithm $ECOM.ECom$ to get a message commitment C_4, i.e., $C_4 \leftarrow ECOM.ECom(rsk, m)$. *Step 2. Zero-knowledge Proof.* The sender will engage in a protocol $\langle \mathbf{P},\mathbf{V} \rangle$ using zero-knowledge Proof ZK to prove that the encrypted message and the committed message are identical, and that the public keys used in the message encryption algorithm Enc_1, committed in trapdoor distinguishable commitment algorithm $TDCom$, encrypted in identity encryption algorithm Enc_2 are all the same. This is the protocol between the sender (prover) and a verifier (gateway).

$$ZK\left\{m,pk_{k,j}\left|\begin{array}{c}C_1{\leftarrow}PE_1.Enc_1(pk_{k,j},m),C_2{\leftarrow}TDCOM.TDCom(lsk,pk_{k,j}),\\C_3{\leftarrow}PE_2.Enc_2(tsk,pk_{k,j}),C_4{\leftarrow}ECOM.ECom(rsk,m)\end{array}\right.\right\}$$

$\langle \mathbf{P},\mathbf{V} \rangle$. The verifier (gateway) will check the validity of the ciphertext using zero-knowledge proof ZK, and broadcast it to users if valid, or else reject.

DEC. The procedure **DEC** will perform the decryption algorithm $PE_1.Dec_1$ to get a plaintext m for the ciphertext C_1, i.e., $m \leftarrow PE_1.Dec_1(sk_{k,j}, C_1)$. Besides, the receiver can also decrypt the ciphertexts of his subordinates for he can calculate the private keys of them.

LINK. It will perform the distinguishing algorithm $TDCOM.Disting$ for any two trapdoor distinguishable commitments C_2, C_2', i.e., $b \leftarrow TDCOM.Disting\ (lsk, C_2, C_2')$.

TRACE. It will perform the decryption algorithm $PE_2.Dec_2$ for the ciphertext C_3, i.e., $pk_{k,j} \leftarrow PE_2.Dec_2(tsk, C_3)$.

AUTH. It will perform the extracting algorithm $ECOM.Extract$ for the extractable commitment C_4, i.e., $m \leftarrow ECOM.Extract(rsk, C_4)$. This ends the generic construction.

Theorem 2 *The AHPE scheme above satisfies (i) Correctness, given that all involved primitives, i.e., SIG, PK_1, PK_2 are correct, and $TDCOM$, $ECOM$, ZK satisfy completeness. (ii) Anonymity, given that PK_1 satisfies key-privacy, ZK satisfies zero-knowledge. (iii) IND-CPA security, given that PK_1 satisfies IND-CPA security, ZK satisfies zero-knowledge. (iv) Link Security, given that $TDCOM$ satisfies hiding, ZK satisfies zero-knowledge. (v) Trace Security, given that PK_2 satisfies IND-CPA security, ZK satisfies zero-knowledge. (vi) Authentication Security, given that $ECOM$ satisfies hiding, ZK satisfies zero-knowledge.*

4.3 Concrete Implementation

A concrete implementation of the AHPE scheme is as follows:

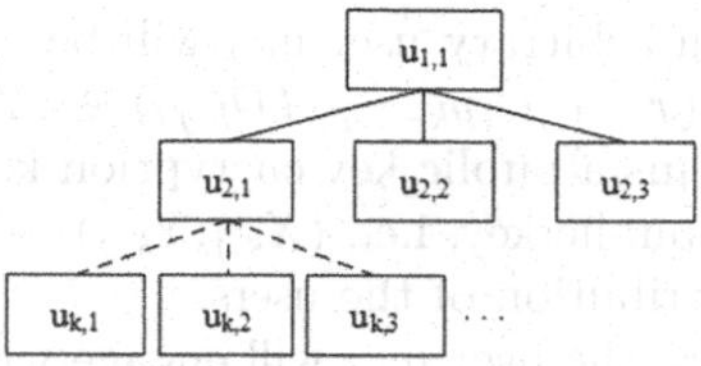

Fig. 2. Hierarchical key distribution

SETUP. (i) selects a security parameter $\lambda \in \mathbb{Z}^+$, and perform the extractable commitment initialization algorithm *ECOM.KGen* which generates two groups $\mathbb{G}_1, \mathbb{G}_2$ of prime order $p, 2^{\lambda-1} < p < 2^\lambda$, i.e., $\mathbb{G}_1, \mathbb{G}_2 \xleftarrow{R} SETUP(1^\lambda)$, $|\mathbb{G}_1| = |\mathbb{G}_2| = p$, such that $\mathbb{G}_1 \neq \mathbb{G}_2$ in which the DDH problem is hard, and $\hat{e}: \mathbb{G}_1 \times \mathbb{G}_2 \to \mathbb{G}_T$ a bilinear map between them. And then selects a generator g of $\mathbb{G}_1$ and a generator h of $\mathbb{G}_2$, thus $\hat{e}(g, h)$ is a generator of $\mathbb{G}_T$; (ii) selects two hash functions $\mathcal{H}, \mathcal{H}_1$ from a Universal One-Way Hash (UOWH) family such that $\mathcal{H}: \{0,1\}^{3p} \to \{0,1\}^{2p}$, $\mathcal{H}_1: \{0,1\}^* \to \{0,1\}^p$; The system parameters are given by $Param = (p, g, h, \hat{e}, \mathcal{H}, \mathcal{H}_1)$.

KGen. The procedure $\mathbf{KGen}_{M_1}$ will perform the extractable commitment key generation *ECOM.KGen* algorithm which selects $rsk = (\alpha_1, \beta_1) \xleftarrow{R} (\mathbb{Z}_p^*, \mathbb{Z}_p^*)$, and sets $rpk = (A_1, B_1) \leftarrow (g^{\alpha_1}, g^{\beta_1})$.

The procedure $\mathbf{KGen}_{M_2}$ will perform the public key encryption key generation algorithm $PE_2.KGen_2$ which selects $tsk = (\alpha_2, \beta_2) \xleftarrow{R} (\mathbb{Z}_p^*, \mathbb{Z}_p^*)$, and sets $tpk = (A_2, B_2) \leftarrow (g^{\alpha_2}, g^{\beta_2})$.

The procedure $\mathbf{KGen}_{M_3}$ will perform the trapdoor distinguishable commitment key generation algorithm *TDCOM.KGen* which selects $lsk = \alpha_3 \xleftarrow{R} \mathbb{Z}_p^*$, and sets $lpk = A_3 \leftarrow g^{\alpha_3}$. Note that the generator h of $\mathbb{G}_2$ is not used in procedures **KGen** and **JOIN**. It is only used in procedures **ENC**, **LINK**.

JOIN. Each prospective user $u_{k,j}$ will get an identity $ID_{k,j} \in \mathbb{Z}_p^*, (1 \leq k \leq l, j \geq 1)$ from the manager M_1.

1. When receiving an identity $ID_{1,1}$ from the root user $u_{1,1}$, the authentication manager M_1 will execute the public key encryption key generation algorithm $PE_1.KGen_1$ which invoke the hash function $\mathcal{H}$, i.e., $r_{1,1} \leftarrow PE_1.KGen_1(\mathcal{H}(\alpha_1, \beta_1, ID_{1,1})) \in \mathbb{Z}_{2p}^*$, and send $r_{1,1}$ to the root user $u_{1,1}$. The root user $u_{1,1}$ will take $r_{1,1}$ as private key, i.e., $(x_{1,1}, y_{1,1}) \leftarrow r_{1,1}$, and perform a public key encryption key generation algorithm $PE_1.KGen_1$ to get his public key, i.e., $(X_{1,1}, Y_{1,1}) \leftarrow (g^{x_{1,1}}, g^{y_{1,1}})$.

2. Similarly, when receiving an identity $ID_{2,i}$ from the user $u_{2,i}$, the root user $u_{1,1}$ will execute the public key encryption key generation algorithm $PE_1.KGen_1$ which invoke the hash function $\mathcal{H}$, i.e., $r_{2,i} \leftarrow KGen_1(\mathcal{H}(x_{1,1}, y_{1,1}, ID_{2,i})) \in \mathbb{Z}_{2p}^*$, and send $r_{2,i}$ to the user $u_{2,i}$. The user $u_{2,i}$ will take $r_{2,i}$ as private key, i.e., $(x_{2,i}, y_{2,i}) \leftarrow r_{2,i}$, and perform a public-key encryption key generation algorithm $PE_1.KGen_1$ to get his public key, i.e., $(X_{2,i}, Y_{2,i}) \leftarrow (g^{x_{2,i}}, g^{y_{2,i}})$.

3. The private key of an arbitrary user $u_{k,j}$ will be $(x_{k,j}, y_{k,j}) \leftarrow r_{k,j}$ where $r_{k,j} \leftarrow PE_1.KGen_1(\mathcal{H}(x_{k-1,j'}, y_{k-1,j'}, ID_{k,j})) \in \mathbb{Z}_{2p}^*$ sent by his superior $u_{k-1,j'}$. Then, he performs a public key encryption key generation algorithm $PE_1.KGen_1$ to get his public key, i.e., $(X_{k,j}, Y_{k,j}) \leftarrow (g^{x_{k,j}}, g^{y_{k,j}})$. See Fig. 2 the hierarchical key distribution of the users.
After getting a key pairs, the user $u_{k,j}$ will engage with the M_1 in a proof of membership for the validity of $(X_{k,j}, Y_{k,j})$. Upon acceptance the M_1 will perform the signature algorithm $SIG.Sign$, i.e., $\tilde{X}_{k,j} \leftarrow (g^u \bmod p, (\mathcal{H}_1(X_{k,j}) - \alpha_1 \cdot g^u \bmod p)u^{-1} \bmod (p-1))$, $\tilde{Y}_{k,j} \leftarrow (g^v \bmod p, (\mathcal{H}_1(Y_{k,j}) - \alpha_1 \cdot g^v \bmod p)v^{-1} \bmod (p-1))$, and return a certificate $cert_{k,j} = (\tilde{X}_{k,j}, \tilde{Y}_{k,j})$. Finally, M_1 will enter $(X_{k,j}, Y_{k,j})$ and $cert_{k,j}$ into the public *database*.

ENC. *Step 1. Encryption.* For reducing the length of ciphertexts, we integrate some common parameters. Given a plaintext $m \in \mathbb{G}_1$ and a public key $pk_{k,j}$ of a user $u_{k,j}$, the procedure **ENC** selects $s_1, s_2, s_3, s_4 \xleftarrow{R} \mathbb{Z}_p^*$, and sets

$$C_{1,1} \leftarrow g^{s_1}, C_{1,2} \leftarrow g^{s_2}, C_{1,3} \leftarrow m \cdot X_{k,j}^{s_1} Y_{k,j}^{s_2},$$
$$C_{2,1} \leftarrow g^{s_3}, C_{2,2} \leftarrow g^{s_4}, C_{2,3} \leftarrow h^{s_3},$$
$$C_{3,1} \leftarrow X_{k,j}^{s_3} \cdot A_3^{s_4}, C_{3,2} \leftarrow X_{k,j} \cdot A_2^{s_3} B_2^{s_4}, C_{3,3} \leftarrow m \cdot A_1^{s_3} B_1^{s_4}.$$

Let $C_0 = (C_{1,1}, C_{1,2}, C_{1,3}, C_{2,1}, C_{2,2}, C_{2,3}, C_{3,1}, C_{3,2}, C_{3,3})$, $C_1 = (C_{1,1}, C_{1,2}, C_{1,3})$, $C_2 = (C_{2,2}, C_{2,3}, C_{3,1})$, $C_3 = (C_{2,1}, C_{2,2}, C_{3,2})$, $C_4 = (C_{2,1}, C_{2,2}, C_{3,3})$. It can be seen that C_1 is a public key encryption output by algorithm $PE_1.Enc_1$, C_2 is a trapdoor distinguishable commitment output by $TICIOM.TDCom$, C_3 is an identity encryption ciphertext output by algorithm $PE_2.Enc_2$, C_4 is a commitment output by algorithm $ECOM.ECom$. Note that among above all ciphertexts, only $C_{2,3} \in \mathbb{G}_2$.

Step 2. Zero-knowledge Proof. The sender will engage in a protocol $\langle \mathbf{P}, \mathbf{V} \rangle$ using zero-knowledge proof ZK to prove that the encrypted message and the committed message are identical, and that the public keys used in public key encryption algorithm Enc_1, committed in trapdoor distinguishable commitment algorithm $TDCom$, encrypted in identity encryption algorithm Enc_2 are all the same. This is the protocol between the sender (prover) and a verifier (gateway). We denote the protocol by

$$ZK\left\{\begin{matrix} m, X_{k,j}, Y_{k,j}, \\ s_1, s_2, s_3, s_4 \end{matrix}\middle| \begin{matrix} C_{1,1} \leftarrow g^{s_1}, C_{1,2} \leftarrow g^{s_2}, C_{1,3} \leftarrow m X_{k,j}^{s_1} Y_{k,j}^{s_2}, \\ C_{2,1} \leftarrow g^{s_3}, C_{2,2} \leftarrow g^{s_4}, C_{2,3} \leftarrow h^{s_3}, \\ C_{3,1} \leftarrow X_{k,j}^{s_3} A_3^{s_4}, C_{3,2} \leftarrow X_{k,j} A_2^{s_3} B_2^{s_4}, C_{3,3} \leftarrow m A_1^{s_3} B_1^{s_4} \end{matrix}\right\}$$

The zero-knowledge proof protocol $\langle \mathbf{P}, \mathbf{V} \rangle$ is as follows.

1. The sender will select $m', X_{k',j'}, Y_{k',j'} \xleftarrow{R} \mathbb{G}_1, s_1', s_2', s_3', s_4' \xleftarrow{R} \mathbb{Z}_p^*$, and compute $C_{1,1}' \leftarrow g^{s_1'}$, $C_{1,2}' \leftarrow g^{s_2'}$, $C_{1,3}' \leftarrow m' \cdot X_{k',j'}^{s_1'} Y_{k',j'}^{s_2'}$, $C_{2,1}' \leftarrow g^{s_3'}$, $C_{2,2}' \leftarrow g^{s_4'}$, $C_{2,3}' \leftarrow h^{s_3'}$, $C_{3,1}' \leftarrow X_{k',j'}^{s_3'} \cdot A_3^{s_4'}$, $C_{3,2}' \leftarrow X_{k',j'} \cdot A_2^{s_3'} B_2^{s_4'}$, $C_{3,3}' \leftarrow m \cdot A_1^{s_3'} B_1^{s_4'}$. Let $C_0' = (C_{1,1}', C_{1,2}', C_{1,3}', C_{2,1}', C_{2,2}', C_{2,3}', C_{3,1}', C_{3,2}', C_{3,3}')$.
2. Then, he will compute $\tau \leftarrow \mathcal{H}_1(C_0, C_0')$.

3. Finally, he will compute $\sigma_1 \leftarrow m' \cdot m^\tau \bmod p$, $\sigma_2 \leftarrow X_{k',j'} \cdot X_{k,j}^\tau \bmod p$, $\sigma_3 \leftarrow Y_{k',j'} \cdot Y_{k,j}^\tau \bmod p$, $\sigma_4 \leftarrow s_1' + \tau \cdot s_1 \bmod p$, $\sigma_5 \leftarrow s_2' + \tau \cdot s_2 \bmod p$, $\sigma_6 \leftarrow s_3' + \tau \cdot s_3 \bmod p$, $\sigma_7 \leftarrow s_4' + \tau \cdot s_4 \bmod p$. Let $\sigma_0 = (\sigma_1, \sigma_2, \sigma_3, \sigma_4, \sigma_5, \sigma_6, \sigma_7)$, and sends$(C_0', \tau, \sigma_0)$ to the verifier (gateway).
4. The verifier will check that $C_{1,1}^\tau \cdot C_{1,1}' \stackrel{?}{=} A_1^{\sigma_4}$, $C_{1,2}^\tau \cdot C_{1,2}' \stackrel{?}{=} B_1^{\sigma_5}$, $C_{1,3}^\tau \cdot C_{1,3}' \stackrel{?}{=} \sigma_1\sigma_2\sigma_3$, $C_{2,1}^\tau \cdot C_{2,1}' \stackrel{?}{=} g^{\sigma_6}$, $C_{2,2}^\tau \cdot C_{2,2}' \stackrel{?}{=} g^{\sigma_7}$, $C_{2,3}^\tau \cdot C_{2,3}' \stackrel{?}{=} h^{\sigma_6}$, $C_{3,1}^\tau \cdot C_{3,1}' \stackrel{?}{=} \sigma_2 \cdot A_3^{\sigma_7}$, $C_{3,2}^\tau \cdot C_{3,2}' \stackrel{?}{=} \sigma_2 \cdot A_2^{\sigma_6} \cdot B_2^{\sigma_7}$, $C_{3,3}^\tau \cdot C_{3,3}' \stackrel{?}{=} \sigma_1 \cdot A_1^{\sigma_6} \cdot B_1^{\sigma_7}$

Thus, the ciphertext sent to an arbitrary user is $\mathrm{u}_{k,j}$ is $C = (C_0, C_0', \tau, \sigma_0)$. In the AHPE system, we consider that a non-interactive zero-knowledge proof is more reasonable for it can even prevent the privacy of a sender from being detected by the verifier (gateway) and the adversary.

⟨P,V⟩. The verifier (gateway) will output 1, and broadcast it to users if all above checks hold, else output 0, and reject.

DEC. The procedure **DEC** will perform the decryption algorithm $PE_1.Dec_1$ to get a plaintext m for the ciphertext C_1, i.e., $m \leftarrow C_{1,3} \cdot C_{1,1}^{-x_{k,j}} \cdot C_{1,2}^{-y_{k,j}}$.

LINK. It will perform the distinguishing algorithm $TDCOM.Disting$ for any two trapdoor distinguishable commitments C_2, C_2', i.e., $C_{tem} \leftarrow C_{3,1} \cdot C_{2,2}^{-\alpha_3}$, $C_{tem}' \leftarrow C_{3,1}' \cdot C_{2,2}'^{-\alpha_3}$, $\hat{e}(C_{tem}', C_{2,3}) \stackrel{?}{=} \hat{e}(C_{tem}, C_{2,3}')$. If the equation holds, then outputs 1, which means that the public keys contained in the ciphertexts are the same, i.e., $X_{k',j'} = X_{k,j}$, else outputs 0.

TRACE. It will perform the decryption algorithm $PE_2.Dec_2$ for the ciphertext C_3, i.e., $X_{k,j} \leftarrow C_{3,2} \cdot C_{2,1}^{-\alpha_2} \cdot C_{2,2}^{-\beta_2}$.

AUTH. It will perform the extracting algorithm $ECOM.Extract$ for the extractable commitment C_4, i.e., $m \leftarrow C_{3,3} \cdot C_{2,1}^{-\alpha_1} \cdot C_{2,2}^{-\beta_1}$. This ends the instance.

Corollary 1. *The AHPE scheme above satisfies (i) Correctness; (iii) Anonymity and (iv) IND-CPA security, both properties under the DLP assumption; (v) Link Security, under the DDH assumption; (vi) Trace Security and (vii) Authentication Security, both properties under the DLP assumption.*

Theorem 3 *The link manager M_3 in above AHPE scheme is unaware of anything, excepts linkability.*

5 Comparison

In Tables 1 and 2 we compare our AHPE scheme with related schemes in [1–5]. In Table 1 the second to the fourth columns show the size of the secret key, the public key and the ciphertext. The fifth and sixth columns show the computation complexity of encryption and decryption algorithms respectively. In Table 2 the second to the seventh columns show the functionalities of the schemes, i.e., hierarchy, anonymity, link, trace, constant ciphertext. The eighth and last columns show the securities of the schemes and the underlying assumptions for guaranteeing the security respectively. It can be learnt from Table 1 that our scheme has a slightly shorter secret key, public key, ciphertext and lower computational complexity than [2–5]. But, it has longer secret key, public key, ciphertext and higher computational complexity than [1] which only has anonymity. From Table 2, it can be seen that our AHPE scheme has the properties of private hierarchy, anonymity, linkability, traceability, authenticability, constant ciphertext which is better than [1–5]. But, it only has IND-CPA security without INC-CCA2 security. However, the AHPE scheme can also achieve IND-CCA2 security based on Cramer-Shoup cryptosystem [14] with the disadvantage that it has a longer secret key, public key, ciphertext than [2,3].

Table 1. Performance comparison with related works

	$\|sk\|$	$\|pk\|$	$\|C\|$	Enc	Dec
KPE [1]	$1\|\mathbb{Z}_p\|/5\|\mathbb{Z}_p\|$	$\|\mathbb{G}\|/5\|\mathbb{G}\|$	$2\|\mathbb{G}\|/4\|\mathbb{G}\|$	2E/5E	1E/3E
GE [2]	$5\|\mathbb{Z}_p\|$	$3\|\mathbb{G}\|$	$25\|\mathbb{G}\|$	37E	5E
TGE [3]	$5\|\mathbb{Z}_p\|$	$4\|\mathbb{G}\|$	$35\|\mathbb{G}\|$	47E	3E + 12P
HIBE [4]	$(2D - L)\|\mathbb{G}\|$	$L\|\mathbb{Z}_p\|$	$3\|G\|$	(L + 2)E + 1P	2P
AHIBE [5]	$(2D + 5)\|\mathbb{G}\|$	$(L + 1)\|\mathbb{Z}_p\|$	$(2D + 7)\|\mathbb{G}\|$	(2L + 6)E	(D + 3)P
AHPE	$2\|\mathbb{Z}_p\|$	$2\|\mathbb{G}\|$	$8\|\mathbb{Z}_p\| + 18\|\mathbb{G}\|$	29E	21E

$|sk|, |pk|, |C|$: the size of the secret key, public key, ciphertext of users; L: the hierarchy's level; D: the hierarchy's maximum depth; P: pairing maps; E: exponent; There are two schemes in [1] with different $|sk|, |pk|, |C|$ etc.

Table 2. Functionality comparison with related works

	Hie	Ano	Link	Trace	Auth	Con	Security	Assumption
KPE [1]	×	✓	×	×	×	✓	CPA/CCA2	DDH
GE [2]	×	✓	×	×	×	✓	CCA2	DDH$_{\text{SQNR}}$
TGE [3]	×	✓	×	✓	×	✓	CCA2	q-SFP,D3DH,DLP
HIBE [4]	✓	×	×	×	×	✓	CPA,CCA1	BDHE
AHIBE [5]	✓	✓	×	×	×	×	CPA	D-BDH,DLP
AHPE	✓	✓	✓	✓	✓	✓	CPA	DDH

Hie: Hierarchy; Ano: Anonymity; Auth: Authentication; Con: Constant Ciphertext; CPA: IND-CPA; CCA1: IND-CCA1; CCA2: IND-CCA2

6 Conclusion

We proposed a new cryptographic primitive, referred to as auditable hierarchy-private public-key encryption (AHPE) which is better than group encryption, hierarchical identity-based encryption, and key-privacy encryption. The AHPE scheme could discovery malicious users on the premise of protecting the anonymity of all of them, and then trace the identities of malicious users, and authenticate the contents of the messages. Thus, it is an multifunctional and practical management system. We gave a generic construction and a concrete implementation, and proved its correctness, IND-CPA security, anonymity, linkability, traceability, and authenticability strictly. The private key, public key, ciphertext, and computation overhead in the AHPE system are constant which hides the hierarchy of all users. Finally, analyses show that the proposed AHPE scheme is efficient and practical.

Acknowledgment. Qianhong Wu is the corresponding author. This paper is supported by the National Key R&D Program of China under grant No. 2017YFB0802400, the Natural Science Foundation of China through projects 61772538, 61672083, 61370190, 61532021, 61472429, and 61402029, by the National Cryptography Development Fund through project MMJJ20170106.

References

1. Bellare, M., Boldyreva, A., Desai, A., Pointcheval, D.: Key-privacy in public-key encryption. In: Boyd, C. (ed.) ASIACRYPT 2001. LNCS, vol. 2248, pp. 566–582. Springer, Heidelberg (2001). https://doi.org/10.1007/3-540-45682-1_33
2. Kiayias, A., Tsiounis, Y., Yung, M.: Group encryption. In: Kurosawa, K. (ed.) ASIACRYPT 2007. LNCS, vol. 4833, pp. 181–199. Springer, Heidelberg (2007). https://doi.org/10.1007/978-3-540-76900-2_11
3. Libert, B., Yung, M., Joye, M., Peters, T.: Traceable group encryption. In: Krawczyk, H. (ed.) PKC 2014. LNCS, vol. 8383, pp. 592–610. Springer, Heidelberg (2014). https://doi.org/10.1007/978-3-642-54631-0_34
4. Boneh, D., Boyen, X., Goh, E. J.: Hierarchical identity based encryption with constant size ciphertext. In: Cramer, R. (ed.) EUROCRYPT 2005. LNCS, vol. 3494, pp. 440–456. Springer, Heidelberg (2005). https://doi.org/10.1007/11426639_26
5. Boyen, X., Waters, B.: Anonymous hierarchical identity-based encryption (without random oracles). In: Dwork, C. (ed.) CRYPTO 2006. LNCS, vol. 4117, pp. 290–307. Springer, Heidelberg (2006). https://doi.org/10.1007/11818175_17
6. Goldreich, O.: Foundations of Cryptography: Basic Tools. Cambridge University Press, pp. 359–364 (2001)
7. Boneh, D., Boyen, X.: Short signatures without random oracles. In: Cachin, C., Camenisch, J.L. (eds.) EUROCRYPT 2004. LNCS, vol. 3027, pp. 56–73. Springer, Heidelberg (2004). https://doi.org/10.1007/978-3-540-24676-3_4
8. Groth, J., Ostrovsky, R., Sahai, A.: Perfect non-interactive zero knowledge for NP. In: Vaudenay, S. (ed.) EUROCRYPT 2006. LNCS, vol. 4004, pp. 339–358. Springer, Heidelberg (2006). https://doi.org/10.1007/11761679_21
9. Abdalla, M., Chevalier, C., Pointcheval, D.: Smooth projective hashing for conditionally extractable commitments. In: Halevi, S. (ed.) CRYPTO 2009. LNCS, vol. 5677, pp. 671–689. Springer, Heidelberg (2009). https://doi.org/10.1007/978-3-642-03356-8_39
10. Pointcheval, D., Stern, J.: Security arguments for digital signatures and blind signatures. J. Cryptol. **13**(3), 361–396 (2000)
11. Boneh, D., Boyen, X., Shacham, H.: Short group signatures. In: Franklin, M. (ed.) CRYPTO 2004. LNCS, vol. 3152, pp. 41–55. Springer, Heidelberg (2004). https://doi.org/10.1007/978-3-540-28628-8_3
12. Damgård, I.: On Σ-protocols. University of Aarhus, Department for Computer Science, Lecture Notes (2002)

13. Tsiounis, Y., Yung, M.: On the security of ElGamal based encryption. In: Imai, H., Zheng, Y. (eds.) PKC 1998. LNCS, vol. 1431, pp. 117–134. Springer, Heidelberg (1998). https://doi.org/10.1007/BFb0054019
14. Cramer, R., Shoup, V.: A practical public key cryptosystem provably secure against adaptive chosen ciphertext attack. In: Krawczyk, H. (ed.) CRYPTO 1998. LNCS, vol. 1462, pp. 13–25. Springer, Heidelberg (1998). https://doi.org/10.1007/BFb0055717
15. Barth, A., Boneh, D., Waters, B.: Privacy in encrypted content distribution using private broadcast encryption. In: Di Crescenzo, G., Rubin, A. (eds.) FC 2006. LNCS, vol. 4107, pp. 52–64. Springer, Heidelberg (2006). https://doi.org/10.1007/11889663_4
16. Ateniese, G., Benson, K., Hohenberger, S.: Key-private proxy re-encryption. In: Fischlin, M. (ed.) CT-RSA 2009. LNCS, vol. 5473, pp. 279–294. Springer, Heidelberg (2009). https://doi.org/10.1007/978-3-642-00862-7_19
17. Waters, B.R., Felten, E.W., Sahai, A.: Receiver anonymity via incomparable public keys. In: Proceedings of the 10th ACM Conference on Computer and Communications Security, pp. 112–121 (2003)
18. Qin, B., Wu, Q., Susilo, W., Mu, Y.: Publicly verifiable privacy-preserving group decryption. In: Yung, M., Liu, P., Lin, D. (eds.) Inscrypt 2008. LNCS, vol. 5487, pp. 72–83. Springer, Heidelberg (2009). https://doi.org/10.1007/978-3-642-01440-6_8
19. Cathalo, J., Libert, B., Yung, M.: Group encryption: non-interactive realization in the standard model. In: Matsui, M. (ed.) ASIACRYPT 2009. LNCS, vol. 5912, pp. 179–196. Springer, Heidelberg (2009). https://doi.org/10.1007/978-3-642-10366-7_11
20. Horwitz, J., Lynn, B.: Toward hierarchical identity-based encryption. In: Knudsen, L.R. (ed.) EUROCRYPT 2002. LNCS, vol. 2332, pp. 466–481. Springer, Heidelberg (2002). https://doi.org/10.1007/3-540-46035-7_31
21. Gentry, C., Silverberg, A.: Hierarchical ID-based cryptography. In: Zheng, Y. (ed.) ASIACRYPT 2002. LNCS, vol. 2501, pp. 548–566. Springer, Heidelberg (2002). https://doi.org/10.1007/3-540-36178-2_34
22. Canetti, R., Halevi, S., Katz, J.: A forward-secure public-key encryption scheme. In: Biham, E. (ed.) EUROCRYPT 2003. LNCS, vol. 2656, pp. 255–271. Springer, Heidelberg (2003). https://doi.org/10.1007/3-540-39200-9_16
23. Boneh, D., Boyen, X.: Efficient selective-ID secure identity-based encryption without random oracles. In: Cachin, C., Camenisch, J.L. (eds.) EUROCRYPT 2004. LNCS, vol. 3027, pp. 223–238. Springer, Heidelberg (2004). https://doi.org/10.1007/978-3-540-24676-3_14

Key-Updatable Public-Key Encryption with Keyword Search: Models and Generic Constructions

Hiroaki Anada[1], Akira Kanaoka[2], Natsume Matsuzaki[1], and Yohei Watanabe[3,4](✉)

[1] University of Nagasaki, Nagasaki, Japan
{anada,matsuzaki}@sun.ac.jp
[2] Toho-University, Chiba, Japan
akira.kanaoka@is.sci.toho-u.ac.jp
[3] The University of Electro-Communications, Tokyo, Japan
[4] AIST, Tokyo, Japan
watanabe@uec.ac.jp

Abstract. *Public-key encryption with keyword search* (PEKS) enables us to search over encrypted data, and is expected to be used between a cloud server and users' devices such as laptops or smartphones. However, those devices might be lost accidentally or be stolen. In this paper, we deal with such a key-exposure problem on PEKS, and introduce a concept of PEKS with key-updating functionality, which we call *key-updatable PEKS* (KU-PEKS). Specifically, we propose two models of KU-PEKS: The key-evolution model and the key-insulation model. In the key-evolution model, a pair of public and secret keys can be updated if needed (e.g., the secret key is exposed). In the key-insulation model, a public key remains fixed while a secret key can be updated if needed. The former model makes a construction simple and more efficient than the latter model. On the other hand, the latter model is preferable for practical use since a user never updates his/her public key. We show constructions of a KU-PEKS scheme in each model in a black-box manner. We also give an experimental result for the most efficient instantiation, and show our proposal is practical.

Keywords: Searchable encryption
Public-key encryption with keyword search
Key-updating functionality

1 Introduction

Public-key encryption with keyword search (PEKS), proposed by Boneh et al. [5], enables a user to search over encrypted data by keywords in a privacy-preserving way. PEKS is one of the efficient solutions to the problem of constructing a private information retrieval (PIR) system [11]; for example, PEKS can be applied

W. Susilo and G. Yang (Eds.): ACISP 2018, LNCS 10946, pp. 341–359, 2018.
https://doi.org/10.1007/978-3-319-93638-3_20

in a searching system on an e-mail server. E-mails and keywords related to each e-mail such as "urgent" are encrypted by S/MIME and PEKS, respectively, and both are stored in a database connected to the server. A user who wants to search for a keyword generates *a trapdoor* of the keyword, and the server can check whether or not each stored e-mail contains the keyword while the server can get only negligible information on the e-mails and the keyword.

The Internet of things (IoT), where secure environments are not necessarily assured, is more and more becoming a reality. In particular, small devices such as smartphones in the IoT are becoming popular communication tools. It is quite convenient, however, such devices might be accidentally lost or be stolen. Besides, side-channel attacks (e.g., [20]) are ones of the powerful attacks that directly leaks secret information such as secret keys. We are interested in such a key exposure problem, and tackle the problem on PEKS in this paper. In fact, according to the NIST guideline SP800-57 [23], "re-keying", which we call "key update" in this paper, is one of the important factors affecting the length of a cryptoperiod.[1] Therefore, it is important to investigate the key-updating functionality for PEKS, however, to the best of our knowledge, there are only a few researches on it thus far. Abdalla et al. [1] considered public-key encryption with temporary keyword search (PETKS), which the server can search over ciphertexts encrypted at a time period by using a trapdoor generated at the same time period. Namely, the trapdoor is available during only the time period, and therefore it reduces information leaked to the server. However, PETKS does not have key-updating functionality. Tang [24] proposed a PEKS scheme secure against the key exposure problem in the sense of forward security (not a PEKS scheme with certain key-updating functionality). The security relies on non-standard assumptions in composite-order groups, and therefore the resulting scheme is inefficient.

1.1 Our Contribution

In this paper, we introduce *key-updatable public-key encryption with keyword search* (KU-PEKS), which is the first PEKS with key-updating functionality. We require that: (1) Secret keys can be updated and it is hard to derive updated keys from exposed secret keys; (2) trapdoors generated from updated keys can be used to search over ciphertexts even if they are encrypted before the update; and (3) trapdoors generated from exposed keys are useless to search for keywords encrypted after the keys are update. Specifically, we propose two models of KU-PEKS: *a key-evolution model* and *a key-insulation model*. The former model is one of the most likely models of KU-PEKS, and the latter model is based on key-insulated cryptography introduced by Dodis et al. [13]. Whereas we realize (2) and (3) by (unidirectionally) updating ciphertexts in both models, we take different approaches to achieving (1) in the two models. We elaborate the difference as follows.

[1] A cryptoperiod [23] means that the time span during which a specific key is authorized for use or in which the keys for a given system or application may remain in effect.

In the key-evolution model, a pair of a public and secret key can be updated if the secret key is exposed. This model makes a construction simple and efficient while not only the secret key but the public key have to be updated. Actually, we construct a KU-PEKS scheme in this model from any public-key encryption (PKE) scheme and any PEKS scheme in a black-box manner, and show that its instantiation (secure in the random oracle model) employing the ElGamal PKE [15] and a PEKS scheme from the Boneh-Franklin identity-based encryption (IBE) [6], is efficient in the sense of both theory and practical use (see Sect. 5). By employing existing anonymous IBE schemes secure in the standard model (e.g., [19,21]) instead of the Boneh-Franklin IBE, we also obtain an instantiation of the generic construction without random oracles.

In the key-insulation model, a public key remains fixed while a secret key can be updated if it is exposed. Namely, this model is more practical than the key-evolution model in the sense of practical use. To give a generic construction of a KU-PEKS scheme, we introduce a new key-insulated cryptographic protocol, *a key-insulated identity-based encryption for master keys (MIKE)*, which has similar key-insulated functionality to key-insulated IBE [18,26]. MIKE realizes *the key-insulated functionality for master keys.* A master key at a time period i generates users' decryption key at i, which can be used to decrypt ciphertexts encrypted at i. Even if a master key at a time period i is exposed, it does not affect master keys at other time periods (i.e., no information on master and decryption keys at other time periods is leaked from the exposed master key). We construct an anonymous MIKE scheme from symmetric external Diffie-Hellman (SXDH) assumption. We believe this new primitive is of independent interest. Then, we show a generic construction of a KU-PEKS scheme in this model from any key-insulated PKE (KI-PKE) [13,26] and any anonymous MIKE scheme.

The Difficulty to Update Ciphertexts and Our Approach. In Abdalla et al.'s transformation, an encryption algorithm is realized by executing an encryption algorithm of IBE with a keyword w, which is regarded as an identity, and the test algorithm is realized by decrypting the ciphertext with a decryption key for the identity w. Therefore, one of the promising approaches to constructing a KU-PEKS scheme without revealing w itself is to use a 2-level anonymous hierarchical IBE (HIBE) scheme. Namely, we use the encryption algorithm of the IBE scheme with an identity vector (w, i) to realize the encryption algorithm for a keyword w at a time period i. Ciphertexts generated in such a way can be decrypted with a decryption key for (w, i), and therefore we can realize $\mathsf{KE.Test}$ in the same way as Abdalla et al.'s transformation. However, it is generally difficult to change an identity vector (w, i) of any IBE ciphertext with (w, i') (unless decrypting it). Actually, if there exists such an algorithm, the security of IBE is immediately broken.

We resolve this problem by re-encrypting w when updating ciphertexts, i.e., we allow the server to decrypt old ciphertexts and re-encrypt them with the current time period when updating them. In fact, this construction methodology does not violate our security definitions since the strongest adversary also obtains all the keywords encrypted before the target time period. In other words, the adversary has all the exposed secret keys, and therefore can decrypt all the old ciphertexts. Hence, taking into account the server that has the maximum information, we can say that the proposed re-encryption algorithm does not reveal information more than necessary. Note that the adversary cannot decrypt the latest (or newest) ciphertexts, and thus our construction provides security at the same level as ordinary PEKS [1,5] even if the adversary gets as much information as possible. Namely, the latest ciphertexts do not reveal any information on the underlying keywords. Nonetheless, it is better to realize the re-encryption algorithm without revealing w itself. We leave this obstacle as an open problem.

1.2 Related Works

The privacy of keywords have been mainly discussed as the security requirement of PEKS (e.g., [1,5]). Namely, a basic security requirement of PEKS is that the encrypted keyword in the database does not reveal any information about the keyword unless a trapdoor of the keyword is available. In addition, various functionalities/security notions such as removing secure channels [2] and security against keyword guessing attacks [7] have been considered. In particular, Emura et al. [16] considered revocation functionality for trapdoors. However, their scheme support neither revocation nor key-updating functionalities for users' secret keys.

In the context of other cryptographic protocols such as PKE and IBE, a lot of researchers have tackled various kinds of researches related to key-updating functionality. Canetti et al. [8] introduced forward-secure PKE. In forward-secure PKE, the exposure of a secret key in period i does not affect on the secrecy of secret keys before the period i. Dodis et al. [13] introduced KI-PKE, which was mentioned above. In KI-PKE, a receiver has two kinds of secret keys, a decryption key and a helper key, which are stored in a different devices, e.g., a smartphone and USB pen drive. The decryption key is updated by the help of the helper key, and if the decryption key at time period i is exposed, no information on decryption keys at other time periods is leaked. Dodis et al. [12] proposed intrusion-resilient PKE, which realizes the both functionalities of forward-secure PKE and KI-PKE at the cost of efficiency.

We remark that proxy re-encryption (PRE) [3], especially, identity-based PRE (IB-PRE) [17] also has similar re-encrypting functionality. It might be possible to construct KU-PEKS from IB-PRE by regarding users as time periods. Namely, we might realize the functionality by re-encrypting ciphertexts for a time period j to that for a time period i. However, we need a multi-hop and unidirectional anonymous IB-PRE scheme to satisfy our requirements, and unfortunately, no such scheme is known.

2 Preliminaries

In this section, we define some notations and cryptographic primitive except for public-key encryption (PKE), since we believe readers are familiar with it.

$\mathsf{Exp}^{\mathsf{CKA}}_{\mathcal{PEKS},\mathcal{A}}(1^\lambda)$

$\mathsf{par}_{\text{PEKS}} \leftarrow \mathsf{Setup}_{\text{PEKS}}(1^\lambda)$
$(\mathsf{msk}, \mathsf{mpk}) \leftarrow \mathsf{KeyGen}_{\text{PEKS}}(\mathsf{par}_{\text{PEKS}})$
$(w_0^*, w_1^*, \mathit{state}) \leftarrow \mathcal{A}^{\mathcal{O}_{\text{TD}}}(\mathsf{par}_{\text{PEKS}}, \mathsf{mpk})$
$b \xleftarrow{\$} \{0,1\}, \quad \mathsf{ct}^*_{w_b^*} \leftarrow \mathsf{Enc}_{\text{PEKS}}(\mathsf{mpk}, w_b^*)$
$b' \leftarrow \mathcal{A}^{\mathcal{O}_{\text{TD}}}(\mathit{state}, \mathsf{ct}^*_{w_b^*})$
If $b' = b$ return 1 else return 0

Fig. 1. The IND-CKA game for PEKS. The adversary $\mathcal{A}$ can access an oracle $\mathcal{O}_{\text{TD}}$ which receives $w(\notin \{w_0^*, w_1^*\})$, and returns $\mathsf{Trapdoor}_{\text{PEKS}}(\mathsf{msk}, w)$.

$\mathsf{Exp}^{\mathsf{Cons}}_{\mathcal{PEKS},\mathcal{A}}(1^\lambda)$

$\mathsf{par}_{\text{PEKS}} \leftarrow \mathsf{Setup}_{\text{PEKS}}(1^\lambda)$
$(\mathsf{msk}, \mathsf{mpk}) \leftarrow \mathsf{KeyGen}_{\text{PEKS}}(\mathsf{par}_{\text{PEKS}})$
$(w_0^*, w_1^*) \leftarrow \mathcal{A}(\mathsf{par}_{\text{PEKS}}, \mathsf{mpk})$
$\mathsf{ct}^*_{w_0^*} \leftarrow \mathsf{Enc}_{\text{PEKS}}(\mathsf{mpk}, w_0^*)$
$\mathsf{t}_{w_1^*} \leftarrow \mathsf{Trapdoor}_{\text{PEKS}}(\mathsf{msk}, w_1^*)$
If $\left\{ \begin{array}{l} \mathsf{Test}_{\text{PEKS}}(\mathsf{t}_{w_1^*}, \mathsf{ct}_{w_0^*}) = 1 \\ \wedge\ w_0^* \neq w_1^* \end{array} \right\}$ return 1
else return 0

Fig. 2. The Computational Consistency game for PEKS.

Notation. If $\mathcal{A}$ is a probabilistic polynomial time (PPT) algorithm, $x \leftarrow \mathcal{A}(y)$ denotes assigning y to the input $\mathcal{A}$ on an output x. Also, $x \leftarrow \mathcal{A}^{\mathcal{O}}(y)$ denotes the $\mathcal{A}$ uses oracle $\mathcal{O}$ to output x. If S is a finite set, $x \xleftarrow{\$} S$ denotes that x is chosen uniformly at random from S. Throughout of this paper, let $\mathcal{T}$ be a set of *time periods*, and we write $\mathcal{T} := \{1, 2, \ldots, \text{poly}(\lambda)\}$ for simplicity.

2.1 Public-Key Encryption with Keyword Search

Public-key encryption with keyword search (PEKS) $\mathcal{PEKS} = (\mathsf{Setup}_{\text{PEKS}}, \mathsf{KeyGen}_{\text{PEKS}}, \mathsf{Enc}_{\text{PEKS}}, \mathsf{Trapdoor}_{\text{PEKS}}, \mathsf{Test}_{\text{PEKS}})$ is defined as follows.

- $\mathsf{Setup}_{\text{PEKS}}(1^\lambda) \rightarrow \mathsf{par}_{\text{PEKS}}$: $\mathsf{Setup}_{\text{PEKS}}$ takes a security parameter 1^λ as input, and outputs a public parameter $\mathsf{par}_{\text{PEKS}}$.
- $\mathsf{KeyGen}_{\text{PEKS}}(\mathsf{par}_{\text{PEKS}}) \rightarrow (\mathsf{mpk}, \mathsf{msk})$: $\mathsf{KeyGen}_{\text{PEKS}}$ takes $\mathsf{par}_{\text{PEKS}}$ as input, and outputs a public key mpk and a secret key msk.
- $\mathsf{Enc}_{\text{PEKS}}(\mathsf{mpk}, w) \rightarrow \mathsf{ct}_w$: $\mathsf{Enc}_{\text{PEKS}}$ takes mpk and a keyword $w \in \mathcal{W}$ as input, and outputs a ciphertext ct_w, where $\mathcal{W}$ is a keyword space determined by security parameters.
- $\mathsf{Trapdoor}_{\text{PEKS}}(\mathsf{mpk}, \mathsf{msk}, w') \rightarrow \mathsf{t}_{w'}$: $\mathsf{Trapdoor}_{\text{PEKS}}$ takes mpk, msk, and a keyword $w' \in \mathcal{W}$ as input, and outputs a trapdoor $\mathsf{t}_{w'}$.
- $\mathsf{Test}_{\text{PEKS}}(\mathsf{mpk}, \mathsf{t}_{w'}, \mathsf{ct}_w) \rightarrow 1$ or 0: $\mathsf{Test}_{\text{PEKS}}$ takes mpk, $\mathsf{t}_{w'}$, and ct_w as input, and outputs 1, which indicates "keyword match", or 0.

$\mathcal{PEKS}$ requires the following correctness: For all $\lambda \in \mathbb{N}$, all $w \in \mathcal{W}$, $\mathsf{par}_{\text{PEKS}} \leftarrow \mathsf{Setup}_{\text{PEKS}}(1^\lambda)$, all $(\mathsf{msk}, \mathsf{mpk}) \leftarrow \mathsf{KeyGen}_{\text{PEKS}}(\mathsf{par}_{\text{PEKS}})$, it holds $\mathsf{Test}_{\text{PEKS}}(\mathsf{mpk}, \mathsf{t}_w, \mathsf{Enc}_{\text{PEKS}}(\mathsf{mpk}, w)) \rightarrow 1$, where $\mathsf{t}_w \leftarrow \mathsf{Trapdoor}_{\text{PEKS}}(\mathsf{mpk}, \mathsf{msk}, w)$.

Figures 1 and 2 show security games of $\mathcal{PEKS}$, indistinguishability against chosen keyword attacks (IND-CKA) and Computational Consistency, respectively. In both games, $\mathcal{A}$ is required to output (w_0^*, w_1^*) such that $|w_0^*| = |w_1^*|$.

$\mathsf{Exp}^{\mathsf{KI\text{-}CPA}}_{\mathcal{KIE},\mathcal{A}}(1^\lambda)$

$(\mathsf{EK}, \mathsf{DK}_0, \mathsf{HK}) \leftarrow \mathsf{KIKG}(1^\lambda)$, $(m_0^*, m_1^*, i^*, state) \leftarrow \mathcal{A}^{\mathcal{O}}(\mathsf{EK})$ s.t. $|m_0^*| = |m_1^*|$

$b \xleftarrow{\$} \{0,1\}$, $\mathsf{C}^*_{i^*,b} \leftarrow \mathsf{KIE}(\mathsf{EK}, m_b^*, i^*)$, $b' \leftarrow \mathcal{A}^{\mathcal{O}}(state, \mathsf{C}^*_{i^*,b})$

If $b' = b$ return 1 else return 0

Fig. 3. The IND-KI-CPA game.

Definition 1 (IND-CKA [1]). *$\mathcal{PEKS}$ is said to be* IND-CKA *secure if for all PPT adversaries $\mathcal{A}$, $\mathsf{Adv}^{\mathsf{CKA}}_{\mathcal{PEKS},\mathcal{A}}(1^\lambda) := |\Pr[\mathsf{Exp}^{\mathsf{CKA}}_{\mathcal{PEKS},\mathcal{A}}(1^\lambda) = 1] - 1/2|$ is negligible in λ.*

Definition 2 (Computational Consistency [1]). *$\mathcal{PEKS}$ is said to meet* Computational Consistency *if for all PPT adversaries $\mathcal{A}$, its advantage defined by $\mathsf{Adv}^{\mathsf{Cons}}_{\mathcal{PEKS},\mathcal{A}}(1^\lambda) := \Pr[\mathsf{Exp}^{\mathsf{Cons}}_{\mathcal{PEKS},\mathcal{A}}(1^\lambda) = 1]$ is negligible in λ.*

2.2 Key-Insulated Public-Key Encryption

Key-insulated public-key encryption (KI-PKE) $\mathcal{KIE} = (\mathsf{KIKG}, \mathsf{KIUG}, \mathsf{KIU}, \mathsf{KIE}, \mathsf{KID})$ is defined as follows.

- $\mathsf{KIKG}(1^\lambda) \rightarrow (\mathsf{EK}, \mathsf{DK}_0, \mathsf{HK})$: KIKG takes a security parameter 1^λ as input, and outputs an encryption key EK, an initial decryption key DK_0, and a helper key HK.
- $\mathsf{KIUG}(\mathsf{HK}, i) \rightarrow \mathsf{UP}_i$: KIUG takes HK and a time period $i \in \mathcal{T}$ as input, and outputs update information UP_i.
- $\mathsf{KIU}(\mathsf{DK}_{i'}, \mathsf{UP}_i) \rightarrow \mathsf{DK}_i$: KIU takes $\mathsf{DK}_{i'}$ at a time period $i' \in \mathcal{T}$ and UP_i as input, and outputs an updated decryption key DK_i at a time period $i \in \mathcal{T}$.
- $\mathsf{KIE}(\mathsf{EK}, m, i) \rightarrow \mathsf{C}_i$: KIE takes EK, a plaintext $m \in \mathcal{M}$, and a current time period $i \in \mathcal{T}$ as input, and outputs a ciphertext C_i at i, where $\mathcal{M}$ is a plaintext space determined by λ.
- $\mathsf{KID}(\mathsf{DK}_i, \mathsf{C}_i) \rightarrow m$ or $\perp$: KID takes DK_i at a time period $i \in \mathcal{T}$ and C_i at the same time period as input, and outputs m or $\perp$, where $\perp$ indicates decryption failure.

$\mathcal{KIE}$ requires the following correctness: For all $\lambda \in \mathbb{N}$, all $m \in \mathcal{M}$, all $(\mathsf{EK}, \mathsf{DK}_0, \mathsf{HK}) \leftarrow \mathsf{KIKG}(1^\lambda)$, and all $i \in \mathcal{T}$, it holds that $\mathsf{KID}(\mathsf{DK}_i, \mathsf{KIE}(\mathsf{EK}, m, i)) = m$, where DK_i is any decryption key at i correctly generated by KIUG and KIU.

We describe a security notion of indistinguishability against chosen plaintext attacks for KI-PKE (IND-KI-CPA). Let $\mathcal{A}$ be a PPT adversary, and we consider an experiment $\mathsf{Exp}^{\mathsf{KI\text{-}CPA}}_{\mathcal{KIE},\mathcal{A}}(1^\lambda)$ in Fig. 3. $\mathcal{A}$ can access an oracle $\mathcal{O}$: Let $\mathcal{L} := \emptyset$. For a query $i \in \mathcal{T} \cup \{\star\}$, $\mathcal{O}$ returns DK_i by computing $\mathsf{KIU}(\mathsf{DK}_0, \mathsf{KIUG}(\mathsf{HK}, i))$ if $i \notin \mathcal{T} \setminus \{i^*\}$ and $\star \notin \mathcal{L}$ and adds i to $\mathcal{L}$. Else if $i = \star$ and $\mathcal{L} = \emptyset$, it returns HK and adds $\star$ to $\mathcal{L}$. Otherwise, it returns $\perp$. It means that $\mathcal{A}$ can obtain either (a number of) decryption keys or the helper key (not both).

Definition 3 (IND-KI-CPA [13]). *$\mathcal{KIE}$ is said to be* IND-KI-CPA *secure if for all PPT adversaries $\mathcal{A}$,* $\mathsf{Adv}^{\mathsf{KI\text{-}CPA}}_{\mathcal{KIE},\mathcal{A}}(1^\lambda) := |\Pr[\mathsf{Exp}^{\mathsf{KI\text{-}CPA}}_{\mathcal{KIE},\mathcal{A}}(1^\lambda) = 1] - 1/2|$ *is negligible in λ.*

3 KU-PEKS in the Key-Evolution Model

We introduce the first framework of KU-PEKS, which is called *a key-evolution model.* Roughly speaking, in this model, both of a public key and secret key are updated periodically. We believe that this is one of the most likely models that ones naturally come up with "PEKS with key-updating functionality".

3.1 Model

KU-PEKS in the key-evolution model is executed as follows. A user first runs $\mathsf{KE.Setup}$ to generate a public key pk_1 and a secret key sk_1. An i-th key pair $(\mathsf{pk}_i, \mathsf{sk}_i)$ can be updated by $\mathsf{KE.Upd}$ if sk_i is exposed, and the user gets an updated key pair $(\mathsf{pk}_{i+1}, \mathsf{sk}_{i+1})$ and a re-encryption key $\mathsf{rk}_{i\to i+1}$. The re-encryption key is sent to the server via a secure channel (we will explain how to use $\mathsf{rk}_{i\to i+1}$ later). Suppose that the current time-period is i. As in PEKS, another user who wants to store an encrypted keyword in a server executes $\mathsf{KE.Enc}$ with i-th public key pk_i and a keyword w, and gets a ciphertext (or, an encrypted keyword) $\mathsf{c}^{(0)}_{w,i}$, which is stored in the server. To search a keyword w', the user runs $\mathsf{KE.Trapdoor}$ with sk_i and w' and gets a trapdoor $\mathsf{t}_{w',i}$, which is sent to the server via the secure channel. The server uses $\mathsf{t}_{w',i}$ to search the stored ciphertexts by the keyword w'. Specifically, it runs $\mathsf{KE.Test}$ with $\mathsf{t}_{w',i}$ and $\mathsf{c}^{(k)}_{w,j}$ such that $j + k = i$, where j indicates a time period when it is generated and k indicates the number of updates. $\mathsf{KE.Test}$ outputs 1 if $w' = w$ holds (i.e., the search keyword matches the encrypted keyword), or outputs 0 otherwise. Note that the server only gets correct search results if and only if $j + k = i$. In other words, $\mathsf{KE.Test}$ never outputs 1 if a trapdoor input to $\mathsf{KE.Test}$ is old, i.e., $j+k > i$. The server returns the search result to the user. The server can update ciphertexts encrypted in the previous time period by using re-encryption keys. More specifically, the server updates a ciphertext $\mathsf{c}^{(k)}_{w,j}$ such that $j + k = i$, by running $\mathsf{KE.ReEnc}$ with $\mathsf{rk}_{i\to i+1}$, and gets an updated ciphertext $\mathsf{c}^{(k+1)}_{w,j}$. We formally define KU-PEKS in the key-evolution model $\Pi_{\mathrm{KE}} = (\mathsf{KE.Setup}, \mathsf{KE.Upd}, \mathsf{KE.Enc}, \mathsf{KE.ReEnc}, \mathsf{KE.Trapdoor}, \mathsf{KE.Test})$.

- $\mathsf{KE.Setup}(1^\lambda) \to (\mathsf{pk}_1, \mathsf{sk}_1)$: $\mathsf{KE.Setup}$ takes security parameter 1^λ as input, and outputs an initial key pair $(\mathsf{pk}_1, \mathsf{sk}_1)$.
- $\mathsf{KE.Upd}(\mathsf{pk}_i, \mathsf{sk}_i) \to (\mathsf{pk}_{i+1}, \mathsf{sk}_{i+1}, \mathsf{rk}_{i\to i+1})$: $\mathsf{KE.Upd}$ takes a key pair $(\mathsf{sk}_i, \mathsf{pk}_i)$ at a time period $i \in \mathcal{T}$ as input, and outputs an updated key pair $(\mathsf{pk}_{i+1}, \mathsf{sk}_{i+1})$ at a next time period $i + 1 \in \mathcal{T}$ and a re-encryption key $\mathsf{rk}_{i\to i+1}$.
- $\mathsf{KE.Enc}(\mathsf{pk}_i, w) \to \mathsf{c}^{(0)}_{w,i}$: $\mathsf{KE.Enc}$ takes pk_i and a keyword $w \in \mathcal{W}$ as input, and outputs a ciphertext $\mathsf{c}^{(0)}_{w,i}$. The superscript of the ciphertext indicates the number of updates. Namely, at this point it is 0.

$\mathsf{Exp}^{\mathsf{KE\text{-}CKA}}_{\Pi_{\mathrm{KE}},\mathcal{A}}(1^\lambda)$

$\mathsf{ctr} := 1,\ (\mathsf{pk}_1, \mathsf{sk}_1) \leftarrow \mathsf{KE.Setup}(1^\lambda)$

$(w_0^*, w_1^*, state) \leftarrow \mathcal{A}^{\mathcal{O}_{\mathrm{KG}},\mathcal{O}_{\mathrm{KL}},\mathcal{O}_{\mathrm{TD}}}(\mathsf{pk}_1)$

$b \xleftarrow{\$} \{0,1\},\ \mathsf{c}^{(0)}_{w_b^*,\mathsf{ctr}} \leftarrow \mathsf{KE.Enc}(\mathsf{pk}_{\mathsf{ctr}}, w_b^*)$

$b' \leftarrow \mathcal{A}^{\mathcal{O}_{\mathrm{KL}},\mathcal{O}_{\mathrm{TD}}}(state, \mathsf{c}^{(0)}_{w_b^*,\mathsf{ctr}})$

If $b' = b$ return 1 else return 0

Fig. 4. The IND-KE-CKA game. $\mathcal{A}$ is required to output (w_0^*, w_1^*) such that $|w_0^*| = |w_1^*|$.

$\mathsf{Exp}^{\mathsf{KE\text{-}Cons}}_{\Pi_{\mathrm{KE}},\mathcal{A}}(1^\lambda)$

$\mathsf{ctr} := 1,\ (\mathsf{pk}_1, \mathsf{sk}_1) \leftarrow \mathsf{KE.Setup}(1^\lambda)$

$(w_0^*, w_1^*, i^*\ state) \leftarrow \mathcal{A}^{\mathcal{O}_{\mathrm{KG}},\mathcal{O}_{\mathrm{KL}}}(\mathsf{pk}_1)$

$\mathsf{c}^{(0)}_{w_0^*,\mathsf{ctr}} \leftarrow \mathsf{KE.Enc}(\mathsf{pk}_{\mathsf{ctr}}, w_0^*)$

$\mathsf{td}_{w_1^*,i^*} \leftarrow \mathsf{KE.Trapdoor}(\mathsf{pk}_{i^*}, \mathsf{sk}_{i^*}, w_1^*)$

If $\left\{ \begin{array}{l} \mathsf{KE.Test}(\mathsf{td}_{w_1^*,i^*}, \mathsf{c}_{w_0^*,\mathsf{ctr}}) = 1 \\ w_0^* \neq w_1^* \end{array} \right\}$

return 1 else return 0

Fig. 5. The KE-Computational Consistency game. $\mathcal{A}$ is required to output (w_0^*, w_1^*, i^*) such that $|w_0^*| = |w_1^*|$, and $i^* \leq \mathsf{ctr}$.

- $\mathsf{KE.ReEnc}(\mathsf{pk}_{i+1}, \mathsf{rk}_{i\to i+1}, \mathsf{c}^{(k)}_{w,j}) \to \mathsf{c}^{(k+1)}_{w,j}$ or $\perp$: KE.ReEnc takes pk_{i+1}, $\mathsf{rk}_{i\to i+1}$ and $\mathsf{c}^{(k)}_{w,j}$ as input, and outputs an updated ciphertext $\mathsf{c}^{(k+1)}_{w,j}$ if $j + k = i$ holds.[2] Otherwise, it outputs $\perp$.
- $\mathsf{KE.Trapdoor}(\mathsf{pk}_i, \mathsf{sk}_i, w') \to \mathsf{t}_{w',i}$: KE.Trapdoor takes pk_i, sk_i, and a keyword $w' \in \mathcal{W}$ as input, and outputs a trapdoor $\mathsf{t}_{w',i}$ (at time period $i \in \mathcal{T}$).
- $\mathsf{KE.Test}(\mathsf{pk}_i, \mathsf{t}_{w',i}, \mathsf{c}^{(k)}_{w,j}) \to 1$ or 0: KE.Test takes pk_i, $\mathsf{t}_{w',i}$, and $\mathsf{c}^{(k)}_{w,j}$ as input, and if $w = w'$ and $j + k = i$, it returns 1. Otherwise, it returns 0.

Π_{KE} requires the following correctness. For all $\lambda \in \mathbb{N}$, all $i \in \mathcal{T}$, all $j \in \{1, \ldots, i-1\}$, all $(\mathsf{pk}_1, \mathsf{sk}_1) \leftarrow \mathsf{KE.Setup}(1^\lambda)$, all $(\mathsf{pk}_\ell, \mathsf{sk}_\ell, \mathsf{rk}_{\ell-1\to\ell}) \leftarrow \mathsf{KE.Upd}(\mathsf{pk}_{\ell-1}, \mathsf{sk}_{\ell-1})$ with $2 \leq \ell \leq i$, and all $w \in \mathcal{W}$, it holds $\mathsf{KE.Test}(\mathsf{pk}_i, \mathsf{KE.Trapdoor}(\mathsf{pk}_i, \mathsf{sk}_i, w), \mathsf{c}^{(i-j)}_{w,j}) \to 1$, where $\mathsf{c}^{(i-j)}_{w,j} \leftarrow \mathsf{KE.ReEnc}(\mathsf{pk}_i, \mathsf{rk}_{i-1\to i}, \mathsf{KE.ReEnc}(\cdots \mathsf{KE.ReEnc}(\mathsf{pk}_{j+1}, \mathsf{rk}_{j\to j+1}, \mathsf{KE.Enc}(\mathsf{pk}_j, w))\cdots))$. It means that KE.Test always outputs 1 if the search keyword matches the encrypted keyword and the ciphertext is generated at j and updated $i - j$ times when the version of the secret key is i.

We next define security of KU-PEKS in the key-evolution model. We consider security against an honest-but-curious server that obtains all leaked secret keys and re-encryption keys. As in traditional PEKS, we consider notions of indistinguishability against chosen keyword attacks in the key-evolution model (IND-KE-CKA) and computational consistency in the key-evolution model (KE-Computational Consistency).

Let $\mathcal{A}$ be a PPT adversary. First, we define experiments of those notions in Figs. 4 and 5, respectively. $\mathcal{A}$ can access a set of the following oracles $\{\mathcal{O}_{\mathrm{KG}}, \mathcal{O}_{\mathrm{KL}}, \mathcal{O}_{\mathrm{TD}}\}$.

[2] For simplicity, we assume that the information of i, j, and k is attached to $\mathsf{t}_{w',i}$ and $\mathsf{c}^{(k)}_{w,j}$.

$\mathcal{O}_{\text{KG}}$: Initially, it sets $\mathcal{SK} := \emptyset$. For a query from $\mathcal{A}$, it computes $(\mathsf{pk}_{\mathsf{ctr}+1}, \mathsf{sk}_{\mathsf{ctr}+1}, \mathsf{rk}_{\mathsf{ctr}\to\mathsf{ctr}+1}) \leftarrow \mathsf{KE.Upd}(\mathsf{pk}_{\mathsf{ctr}}, \mathsf{sk}_{\mathsf{ctr}})$, and returns $(\mathsf{pk}_{\mathsf{ctr}+1}, \mathsf{rk}_{\mathsf{ctr}\to\mathsf{ctr}+1})$ to $\mathcal{A}$. It adds $\mathsf{sk}_{\mathsf{ctr}+1}$ to $\mathcal{SK}$, and finally sets $\mathsf{ctr} := \mathsf{ctr} + 1$.

$\mathcal{O}_{\text{KL}}$: For a query $i \in \mathcal{T}$, it returns $\mathsf{sk}_i \in \mathcal{SK}$ if $i < \mathsf{ctr}$. Otherwise, it returns $\perp$. Note that this oracle captures key leakage.

$\mathcal{O}_{\text{TD}}$: For a query $(w, i) \in \mathcal{W} \times \mathcal{T}$, it returns $\mathsf{KE.Trapdoor}(\mathsf{sk}_i, w)$ if $i \le \mathsf{ctr}$ and $(w, i) \notin \{(w_0^*, \mathsf{ctr}), (w_1^*, \mathsf{ctr})\}$. Otherwise, it returns $\perp$.

Definition 4 (IND-KE-CKA). *Π_{KE} is said to be* IND-KE-CKA *secure if for all PPT adversaries $\mathcal{A}$, $\mathsf{Adv}_{\Pi_{\text{KE}},\mathcal{A}}^{\mathsf{KE\text{-}CKA}}(1^\lambda) := |\Pr[\mathsf{Exp}_{\Pi_{\text{KE}},\mathcal{A}}^{\mathsf{KE\text{-}CKA}}(1^\lambda) = 1] - 1/2|$ is negligible in λ.*

Definition 5 (KE-Computational Consistency). *Π_{KE} is said to meet* KE-Computational Consistency *if for all PPT adversaries $\mathcal{A}$, $\mathsf{Adv}_{\Pi_{\text{KE}},\mathcal{A}}^{\mathsf{KE\text{-}Cons}}(1^\lambda) := \Pr[\mathsf{Exp}_{\Pi_{\text{KE}},\mathcal{A}}^{\mathsf{KE\text{-}Cons}}(1^\lambda) = 1]$ is negligible in λ.*

3.2 Generic Construction from PKE and PEKS

In this section, we show a generic construction of a KU-PEKS scheme Π_{KE} in the key-evolution model from any PKE scheme $\mathcal{PKE}$ and any traditional PEKS scheme $\mathcal{PEKS}$. Let $\mathcal{PKE} = (\mathsf{PG}, \mathsf{G}, \mathsf{E}, \mathsf{D})$ and $\mathcal{PEKS} = (\mathsf{Setup}_{\text{PEKS}}, \mathsf{KeyGen}_{\text{PEKS}}, \mathsf{Enc}_{\text{PEKS}}, \mathsf{Trapdoor}_{\text{PEKS}}, \mathsf{Test}_{\text{PEKS}})$ be a PKE scheme and a PEKS scheme, respectively. Our construction of $\Pi_{\text{KE}} = (\mathsf{KE.Setup}, \mathsf{KE.Upd}, \mathsf{KE.Enc}, \mathsf{KE.ReEnc}, \mathsf{KE.Trapdoor}, \mathsf{KE.Test})$ is given in Fig. 6. The security of Π_{KE} can be proved, however we omit the proof due to the page limitation.

Theorem 1. *If $\mathcal{PKE}$ is* IND-CPA *secure and $\mathcal{PEKS}$ is* IND-CKA *secure and meets Computational Consistency, the construction given in Fig. 6 is* IND-KE-CKA *secure and meets* KE-Computational Consistency.

4 KU-PEKS in the Key-Insulation Model

Taking into account practical use, it is desirable to keep the same public key while secret keys are updated. In this section, we adopt a concept of *key-insulated cryptography* [13,14], which is one of the well-known cryptographic solutions to the key exposure problem, and propose *a key-insulation model* as another model of KU-PEKS. The key-insulation model achieves the property that a public key remains the same while a secret key is updated.

4.1 Model

A key-insulated protocol is said to have *random access key updates* [10] if one can update any old secret key to the latest version, more generally, if one can update a secret key from any time period $j \in \mathcal{T}$ to any time period $i \in \mathcal{T}$. Since

$\underline{\mathsf{KE.Setup}(1^\lambda)}$:
$\mathsf{par}_{\text{PKE}} \leftarrow \mathsf{PG}(1^\lambda)$
$\mathsf{par}_{\text{PEKS}} \leftarrow \mathsf{Setup}_{\text{PEKS}}(1^\lambda)$
$(\mathsf{ek}_1, \mathsf{dk}_1) \leftarrow \mathsf{G}(\mathsf{par}_{\text{PKE}})$
$(\mathsf{mpk}_1, \mathsf{msk}_1) \leftarrow \mathsf{KeyGen}_{\text{PEKS}}(\mathsf{par}_{\text{PEKS}})$
$\mathsf{pk}_1 := (\mathsf{par}_{\text{PKE}}, \mathsf{par}_{\text{PEKS}}, \mathsf{ek}_1, \mathsf{mpk}_1)$
$\mathsf{sk}_1 := (\mathsf{dk}_1, \mathsf{msk}_1)$
return $(\mathsf{pk}_1, \mathsf{sk}_1)$

$\underline{\mathsf{KE.Upd}(\mathsf{pk}_i, \mathsf{sk}_i)}$:
parse $\mathsf{pk}_i = (\mathsf{par}_{\text{PKE}}, \mathsf{par}_{\text{PEKS}}, \mathsf{ek}_i, \mathsf{mpk}_i)$
parse $\mathsf{sk}_i = (\mathsf{dk}_i, \mathsf{msk}_i)$
$(\mathsf{ek}_{i+1}, \mathsf{dk}_{i+1}) \leftarrow \mathsf{G}(\mathsf{par}_{\text{PKE}})$
$(\mathsf{mpk}_{i+1}, \mathsf{msk}_{i+1}) \leftarrow \mathsf{KeyGen}_{\text{PEKS}}(\mathsf{par}_{\text{PEKS}})$
$\mathsf{pk}_{i+1} := (\mathsf{par}_{\text{PKE}}, \mathsf{par}_{\text{PEKS}}, \mathsf{ek}_{i+1}, \mathsf{mpk}_{i+1})$
$\mathsf{sk}_{i+1} := (\mathsf{dk}_{i+1}, \mathsf{msk}_{i+1})$
$\mathsf{rk}_{i \to i+1} := \mathsf{dk}_i$
return $(\mathsf{pk}_{i+1}, \mathsf{sk}_{i+1}, \mathsf{rk}_{i \to i+1})$

$\underline{\mathsf{KE.Enc}(\mathsf{pk}_i, w)}$:
parse $\mathsf{pk}_i = (\mathsf{par}_{\text{PKE}}, \mathsf{par}_{\text{PEKS}}, \mathsf{ek}_i, \mathsf{mpk}_i)$
$\mathsf{ct}_i \leftarrow \mathsf{E}(\mathsf{ek}_i, w)$
// $\mathcal{M}$ (of $\mathcal{PKE}$) $:= \mathcal{W}$ (of $\mathcal{PEKS}$)
$\mathsf{ct}_{w,i} \leftarrow \mathsf{Enc}_{\text{PEKS}}(\mathsf{mpk}_i, w)$
$\mathsf{c}_{w,i}^{(0)} := (\mathsf{ct}_i, \mathsf{ct}_{w,i})$
return $\mathsf{c}_{w,i}^{(0)}$

$\underline{\mathsf{KE.ReEnc}(\mathsf{pk}_{i+1}, \mathsf{rk}_{i \to i+1}, \mathsf{c}_{w,j}^{(k)})}$:
parse $\mathsf{rk}_{i \to i+1} = (\mathsf{ek}_{i+1}, \mathsf{mpk}_{i+1}, \mathsf{dk}_i)$
parse $\mathsf{c}_{w,i}^{(0)} = (\mathsf{ct}_i, \mathsf{ct}_{w,i})$
if $i \neq j + k$
  return $\perp$
else
  $w \leftarrow \mathsf{D}(\mathsf{dk}_i, \mathsf{ct}_i)$
  $\mathsf{c}_{w,j}^{(k+1)} \leftarrow \mathsf{KE.Enc}(\mathsf{pk}_{i+1}, w)$
  // Run KE.Enc constructed as above
return $\mathsf{c}_{w,j}^{(k+1)}$

$\underline{\mathsf{KE.Trapdoor}(\mathsf{pk}_i, \mathsf{sk}_i, w')}$:
parse $\mathsf{sk}_i = (\mathsf{dk}_i, \mathsf{msk}_i)$
$\mathsf{t}_{w',i} \leftarrow \mathsf{Trapdoor}_{\text{PEKS}}(\mathsf{mpk}_i, \mathsf{msk}_i, w')$
return $\mathsf{t}_{w',i}$

$\underline{\mathsf{KE.Test}(\mathsf{pk}_i, \mathsf{t}_{w',i}, \mathsf{c}_{w,j}^{(k)})}$:
parse $\mathsf{c}_{w,j}^{(k)} = (\mathsf{ct}_{j+k}, \mathsf{ct}_{w,j+k})$
if $i \neq j + k$
  return 0
else if $1 \leftarrow \mathsf{Test}_{\text{PEKS}}(\mathsf{mpk}_i, \mathsf{t}_{w',i}, \mathsf{ct}_{w,i})$
  return 1
else if $0 \leftarrow \mathsf{Test}_{\text{PEKS}}(\mathsf{mpk}_i, \mathsf{t}_{w',i}, \mathsf{ct}_{w,i})$
  return 0

Fig. 6. A generic construction of Π_{KE} from $\mathcal{PKE}$ and $\mathcal{PEKS}$.

the functionality of random access key updates is a basic requirement in key-insulated cryptography, we also consider it in this paper. Therefore, it eliminates the need for sequentially updating keys (i.e., $\mathsf{sk}_{i-1} \to \mathsf{sk}_i$), and therefore allows the server to manage only one "global" time-period set $\mathcal{T}$ among all users (e.g., $t_1 := 11/7/2018, t_2 := 12/7/2018, \ldots$), whereas in the key-evolution model, the server has to manage different time-period sets per each user (i.e., a time period set is a counter of updates for each user). We also model re-encryption keys so that it updates ciphertexts from any time period to any time period since secret keys are not sequentially updated.

KU-PEKS in the key-insulation model is executed as follows. A user first runs KI.Setup to generate a public key pk, an initial secret key sk_0, and a helper key hk. sk_0 is stored in a powerful but insecure device such as smartphones, and hk is stored in a physically-secure but computationally-limited device such as USB pen drives. A secret key $\mathsf{sk}_{i'}$ at a time period $i' \in \mathcal{T}$ is periodically updated by Δ-Gen and KI.Upd. Specifically, the user uses the physically-secure devise and runs Δ-Gen with hk to get update information δ_i. The user then executes KI.Upd with δ_i, and updates $\mathsf{sk}_{i'}$ to sk_i. KI.Upd also outputs a re-encryption key rk_i at the same time, and rk_i is sent to the server via a secure channel. Since an adversary cannot get both of the helper key hk and (a number of) decryption keys $\{\mathsf{sk}_{i_1}, \mathsf{sk}_{i_2}, \ldots, \mathsf{sk}_{i_q}\}$, $\mathcal{A}$ can execute neither Δ-Gen nor $\mathsf{KI.Upd}$ (see security definition for details). The flows of encryption, trapdoor generation, test, and re-encryption are almost the same as KU-PEKS in the key-evolution model (Note that any old ciphertext $\mathsf{ct}_{w,j}$ ($j < i$) can be updated by rk_i in this model). We formally define KU-PEKS in the key-insulation model $\Pi_{\mathrm{KI}} = (\mathsf{KI.Setup}, \Delta\text{-}\mathsf{Gen}, \mathsf{KI.Upd}, \mathsf{KI.Enc}, \mathsf{KI.ReEnc}, \mathsf{KI.Trapdoor}, \mathsf{KI.Test})$.

- $\mathsf{KI.Setup}(1^\lambda) \rightarrow (\mathsf{pk}, \mathsf{sk}_0, \mathsf{hk})$: $\mathsf{KI.Setup}$ takes security parameter 1^λ as input, and outputs a public key pk, an initial secret key sk_0, and a helper key hk.
- $\Delta\text{-}\mathsf{Gen}(\mathsf{pk}, \mathsf{hk}, i) \rightarrow \delta_i$: Δ-Gen takes pk, hk, and a time period $i \in \mathcal{T}$ as input, and outputs update information δ_i at i.
- $\mathsf{KI.Upd}(\mathsf{pk}, \mathsf{sk}_{i'}, \delta_i) \rightarrow (\mathsf{sk}_i, \mathsf{rk}_i)$: $\mathsf{KI.Upd}$ takes pk, $\mathsf{sk}_{i'}$ at a time period $i' \in \mathcal{T}$ and δ_i at $i \in \mathcal{T}$ as input, and outputs an updated secret key sk_i and a re-encryption key rk_i.
- $\mathsf{KI.Enc}(\mathsf{pk}, w, i) \rightarrow \mathsf{c}_{w,i}$: $\mathsf{KI.Enc}$ takes pk, a keyword $w \in \mathcal{W}$, and a current time period $i \in \mathcal{T}$ as input, and outputs a ciphertext $\mathsf{c}_{w,i}$.
- $\mathsf{KI.ReEnc}(\mathsf{pk}, \mathsf{rk}_i, \mathsf{c}_{w,j}) \rightarrow \mathsf{c}_{w,i}$ or $\perp$: $\mathsf{KI.ReEnc}$ takes pk, rk_i at $i \in \mathcal{T}$, and a ciphertext $\mathsf{c}_{w,j}$ encrypted at $j \in \mathcal{T}$ as input, and outputs an updated ciphertext $\mathsf{c}_{w,i}$ at i.
- $\mathsf{KI.Trapdoor}(\mathsf{pk}, \mathsf{sk}_i, w') \rightarrow \mathsf{td}_{w',i}$: $\mathsf{KI.Trapdoor}$ takes pk, sk_i at $i \in \mathcal{T}$, and a keyword $w' \in \mathcal{W}$ as input, and outputs a trapdoor $\mathsf{td}_{w',i}$ at i.
- $\mathsf{KI.Test}(\mathsf{pk}, \mathsf{td}_{w',i}, \mathsf{c}_{w,i}) \rightarrow 1$ or 0: $\mathsf{KI.Test}$ takes pk, $\mathsf{td}_{w',i}$, and $\mathsf{c}_{w,i}$ as input, and if $w = w'$, it returns 1. Otherwise, it returns 0.

Π_{KI} requires the following correctness. For all $\lambda \in \mathbb{N}$, all $i, j \in \mathcal{T}$, all $(\mathsf{pk}, \mathsf{sk}_0, \mathsf{hk}) \leftarrow \mathsf{KI.Setup}(1^\lambda)$, and all $w \in \mathcal{W}$, it holds $\mathsf{KI.Test}(\mathsf{pk}, \mathsf{KI.Trapdoor}(\mathsf{pk}, \mathsf{sk}_i, w), \mathsf{c}_{w,i}) \rightarrow 1$, where sk_i is any secret key correctly updated from sk_0, and $\mathsf{c}_{w,i}$ is: (i) if $j = i$, $\mathsf{c}_{w,i} \leftarrow \mathsf{KI.Enc}(\mathsf{pk}, w, i)$; (ii) if $j \neq i$, $\mathsf{c}_{w,i} \leftarrow \mathsf{KI.ReEnc}(\mathsf{pk}, \mathsf{rk}_i, \mathsf{KI.ReEnc}(\cdots \mathsf{KI.Enc}(\mathsf{pk}, w, j) \cdots))$. It means that $\mathsf{KI.Test}$ always outputs 1 if the search keyword matches the encrypted keyword and the ciphertext is (correctly updated to) the same version of the secret key.

We next define security of KU-PEKS in the key-insulation model. As in the key-evolution model, we consider security against an honest-but-curious server that obtains all leaked secret keys and re-encryption keys, that is, we define notions of indistinguishability against chosen keyword attacks in the key-insulation model (IND-KI-CKA) and computational consistency in the key-insulation model (KI-Computational Consistency). Let $\mathcal{A}$ be a PPT adversary. First, we define experiments of those notions in Figs. 7 and 8, respectively. In both games, $\mathcal{A}$ is required to output (w_0^*, w_1^*) such that $|w_0^*| = |w_1^*|$. $\mathcal{A}$ can access sets of the following oracles $\mathcal{O}_{\mathrm{KL}}, \mathcal{O}_{\mathrm{RK}}, \mathcal{O}_{\mathrm{TD}}$. Initially, let $\mathcal{L} := \emptyset$ and $\mathcal{RK} := \emptyset$.

$\mathcal{O}_{\mathrm{KL}}$: For a query $i \in \mathcal{T} \cup \{\star\}$, if $i \notin \mathcal{T} \setminus \{i^*\}$ and $\star \notin \mathcal{L}$, it computes $(\mathsf{sk}_i, \mathsf{rk}_i) \leftarrow \mathsf{KI.Upd}(\mathsf{pk}, \mathsf{sk}_0, \Delta\text{-}\mathsf{Gen}(\mathsf{pk}, \mathsf{hk}, i))$, returns sk_i, and adds i and rk_i to $\mathcal{L}$ and $\mathcal{RK}$, respectively. Else if $i = \star$ and $\mathcal{L} = \emptyset$, it then returns hk and adds $\star$ to $\mathcal{L}$. Otherwise, it returns $\perp$. Note that this oracle captures key leakage, and $\mathcal{A}$ obtains either (a number of) decryption keys or the helper key during the game.

$$\boxed{\begin{array}{l}\textsf{Exp}^{\textsf{KI-CKA}}_{\Pi_{\text{KI}},\mathcal{A}}(1^\lambda)\\ (\textsf{pk},\textsf{sk}_0,\textsf{hk}) \leftarrow \textsf{KI.Setup}(1^\lambda)\\ (w_0^*, w_1^*, i^*, \textit{state}) \leftarrow \mathcal{A}^{\mathcal{O}_{\text{KL}},\mathcal{O}_{\text{RK}},\mathcal{O}_{\text{TD}}}(\textsf{pk})\\ b \xleftarrow{\$} \{0,1\}\\ \textsf{c}_{w_b^*,i^*} \leftarrow \textsf{KI.Enc}(\textsf{pk}, w_b^*, i^*)\\ b' \leftarrow \mathcal{A}^{\mathcal{O}_{\text{KL}},\mathcal{O}_{\text{RK}},\mathcal{O}_{\text{TD}}}(\textit{state}, \textsf{c}_{w_b^*,i^*})\\ \text{If } b' = b \text{ return 1 else return 0}\end{array}}$$

Fig. 7. The IND-KI-CKA game.

$$\boxed{\begin{array}{l}\textsf{Exp}^{\textsf{KI-Cons}}_{\Pi_{\text{KI}},\mathcal{A}}(1^\lambda)\\ (\textsf{pk},\textsf{sk}_0,\textsf{hk}) \leftarrow \textsf{KI.Setup}(1^\lambda)\\ (w_0^*, w_1^*, i^*, j^*, \textit{state}) \leftarrow \mathcal{A}^{\mathcal{O}_{\text{KL}},\mathcal{O}_{\text{RK}}}(\textsf{pk})\\ \textsf{c}_{w_0^*,i^*} \leftarrow \textsf{KI.Enc}(\textsf{pk}, w_0^*, i^*),\\ \delta_{j^*} \leftarrow \Delta\text{-}\textsf{Gen}(\textsf{pk},\textsf{hk}, j^*)\\ (\textsf{sk}_{j^*}, \textsf{rk}_{j^*}) \leftarrow \textsf{KI.Upd}(\textsf{sk}_0, \delta_{j^*})\\ \textsf{td}_{w_1^*,j^*} \leftarrow \textsf{KI.Trapdoor}(\textsf{pk}, \textsf{sk}_{j^*}, w_1^*)\\ \text{If } \left\{ \begin{array}{l} \textsf{KE.Test}(\textsf{td}_{w_1^*,j^*}, \textsf{c}_{w_0^*,i^*}) = 1\\ w_0^* \neq w_1^* \end{array}\right\}\\ \text{return 1 else return 0}\end{array}}$$

Fig. 8. The KI-Computational Consistency game.

$\mathcal{O}_{\text{RK}}$: For a query $i \in \mathcal{T}$, it returns $\textsf{rk}_i \in \mathcal{RK}$ if $i \in \mathcal{L}$.[3]
$\mathcal{O}_{\text{TD}}$: For a query $(w, i) \in \mathcal{W} \times \mathcal{T}$, it returns $\textsf{KI.Trapdoor}(\textsf{pk}, \textsf{sk}_i, w)$ if $(w, i) \notin \{(w_0^*, i^*), (w_1^*, i^*)\}$. Otherwise, it returns $\perp$.

Definition 6 (IND-KI-CKA). *Π_{KI} is said to be IND-KI-CKA secure if for all PPT adversaries $\mathcal{A}$, $\textsf{Adv}^{\textsf{KI-CKA}}_{\Pi_{\text{KI}},\mathcal{A}}(1^\lambda) := |\Pr[\textsf{Exp}^{\textsf{KI-CKA}}_{\Pi_{\text{KI}},\mathcal{A}}(1^\lambda) = 1] - 1/2|$ is negligible in λ.*

Definition 7 (KI-Computational Consistency). *Π_{KI} is said to meet KI-Computational Consistency if for all PPT adversaries $\mathcal{A}$, $\textsf{Adv}^{\textsf{KI-Cons}}_{\Pi_{\text{KI}},\mathcal{A}}(1^\lambda) := \Pr[\textsf{Exp}^{\textsf{KI-Cons}}_{\Pi_{\text{KI}},\mathcal{A}}(1^\lambda) = 1]$ is negligible in λ.*

4.2 Building Block: Anonymous Key-Insulated IBE for Master Keys

Abdalla et al. [1] showed the transformation from an anonymous IBE scheme to a PEKS scheme. We take a similar strategy to the key-evolution model. Namely, we consider a transformation from an anonymous IBE scheme with certain key-insulated functionality to a KU-PEKS scheme (in the key-insulation model). Key-insulated IBE (KI-IBE, or IKE for short) [18,26] is a promising candidate, however, the existing scheme is (i) not anonymous, and (ii) the key-insulated functionality is insufficient to realize key-insulated functionality of KU-PEKS. Let us elaborate (ii). In the Abdalla et al. transformation, a master key of an IBE scheme turns to be a secret key of the resulting PEKS scheme, and secret keys of the IBE scheme are used as trapdoors of the PEKS scheme. However, the existing KI-IBE schemes [18,26] have key-insulated functionality for *users' secret keys*. Therefore, if we apply the the Abdalla et al. transformation to IKE, then we get

[3] For simplicity, we assume $\mathcal{A}$ issues $i \in \mathcal{T}$ to $\mathcal{O}_{\text{RK}}$ after $\mathcal{A}$ issues i to $\mathcal{O}_{\text{KL}}$ except $\text{Ł} = \{\star\}$ (i.e., $\mathcal{A}$ obtains $\textsf{hk}$ from $\mathcal{O}_{\text{KL}}$).

$\mathsf{Exp}^{\mathsf{ID\text{-}KI\text{-}CPA}}_{\mathcal{MIKE},\mathcal{A}}(1^\lambda)$

$(\mathsf{prms}, \mathsf{mk}_0, \mathsf{mhk}) \leftarrow \mathsf{Init}(1^\lambda)$

$(m_0^*, m_1^*, \mathtt{T}^*, \mathtt{I}^*, \mathit{state}) \leftarrow \mathcal{A}^{\mathcal{O}}(\mathsf{prms})$

$b \xleftarrow{\$} \{0,1\}$

$\mathsf{ct}_{\mathtt{T}^*,\mathtt{I}^*} \leftarrow \mathsf{IBEnc}(\mathsf{prms}, m_b^*, \mathtt{T}^*, \mathtt{I}^*)$

$b' \leftarrow \mathcal{A}^{\mathcal{O}_{\mathrm{EXT}},\mathcal{O}_{\mathrm{LEAK}}}(\mathit{state}, \mathsf{ct}_{\mathtt{T}^*,\mathtt{I}^*})$

If $b' = b$ return 1 else return 0

Fig. 9. The IND-ID-KI-CPA game. $\mathcal{A}$ is required to output (m_0^*, m_1^*) such that $|m_0^*| = |m_1^*|$.

$\mathsf{Exp}^{\mathsf{ANO\text{-}KI\text{-}CPA}}_{\mathcal{MIKE},\mathcal{A}}(1^\lambda)$

$(\mathsf{prms}, \mathsf{mk}_0, \mathsf{mhk}) \leftarrow \mathsf{Init}(1^\lambda)$

$(m^*, \mathtt{T}^*, \mathtt{I}_0^*, \mathtt{I}_1^*, \mathit{state}) \leftarrow \mathcal{A}^{\mathcal{O}}(\mathsf{prms})$

$b \xleftarrow{\$} \{0,1\}$

$\mathsf{ct}_{\mathtt{T}^*,\mathtt{I}_b^*} \leftarrow \mathsf{IBEnc}(\mathsf{prms}, m^*, \mathtt{T}^*, \mathtt{I}_b^*)$

$b' \leftarrow \mathcal{A}^{\mathcal{O}_{\mathrm{EXT}},\mathcal{O}_{\mathrm{LEAK}}}(\mathit{state}, \mathsf{ct}_{\mathtt{T}^*,\mathtt{I}_b^*})$

If $b' = b$ return 1 else return 0

Fig. 10. The ANO-ID-KI-CPA game.

PEKS with key-insulated functionality for *trapdoors*. Actually, Emura et al. [16] applied the Abdalla et al. transformation from a revocable IBE scheme [4], which is an IBE enabling ones to revoke secret keys, to a PEKS scheme with revocation functionality for trapdoors. Therefore, we introduce a new key-insulated cryptographic primitive, *IKE for master keys* (MIKE for short). Roughly speaking, MIKE captures leakage of a master key, whereas IKE focuses on leakage of users' secret keys. This primitive may be of independent interest. We also consider the anonymity of MIKE. We can give a concrete construction of this new primitive from the symmetric external Diffie-Hellman (SXDH) assumption (without random oracles), however, due to page limitation we will give it in the full version.

A MIKE scheme $\mathcal{MIKE}$ consists of six-tuple algorithms (Setup, UpdGen, MKUpd, KG, IBEnc, IBDec) defined as follows.

- $\mathsf{Init}(1^\lambda) \rightarrow (\mathsf{prms}, \mathsf{mk}_0, \mathsf{mhk})$: Init takes a security parameter 1^λ as input, and outputs a public parameter prms, an initial master secret key mk_0, and a master helper key mhk.
- $\mathsf{UpdGen}(\mathsf{prms}, \mathsf{mhk}, \mathtt{T}) \rightarrow \mathsf{up}_\mathtt{T}$: UpdGen takes prms, mhk, and a time period $\mathtt{T} \in \mathcal{T}$ as input, and outputs update information $\mathsf{up}_\mathtt{T}$ for T.
- $\mathsf{MKUpd}(\mathsf{prms}, \mathsf{mk}_{\mathtt{T}'}, \mathsf{up}_\mathtt{T}) \rightarrow \mathsf{mk}_\mathtt{T}$: MKUpd takes prms, $\mathsf{mk}_{\mathtt{T}'}$, and $\mathsf{up}_\mathtt{T}$ as input, and outputs an updated master key $\mathsf{mk}_\mathtt{T}$.
- $\mathsf{KG}(\mathsf{prms}, \mathsf{mk}_\mathtt{T}, \mathtt{I}) \rightarrow \mathsf{dk}_{\mathtt{T},\mathtt{I}}$: KG takes prms, $\mathsf{mk}_\mathtt{T}$, and an identity $\mathtt{I} \in \mathcal{I}$ as input, and outputs a decryption key $\mathsf{dk}_{\mathtt{T},\mathtt{I}}$ for I at the time period T.
- $\mathsf{IBEnc}(\mathsf{prms}, m, \mathtt{T}, \mathtt{I}) \rightarrow \mathsf{ct}_{\mathtt{T},\mathtt{I}}$: IBEnc takes prms, a plaintext $m \in \mathcal{M}$, a current time period T, $\mathtt{I} \in \mathcal{I}$ as input, and then outputs a ciphertext $\mathsf{ct}_{\mathtt{T},\mathtt{I}}$.
- $\mathsf{IBDec}(\mathsf{prms}, \mathsf{dk}_{\mathtt{T},\mathtt{I}}, \mathsf{ct}_{\mathtt{T},\mathtt{I}}) \rightarrow m$ or $\perp$: IBDec takes prms, $\mathsf{dk}_{\mathtt{T},\mathtt{I}}$, and $\mathsf{ct}_{\mathtt{T},\mathtt{I}}$ as input and then outputs m or $\perp$.

$\mathcal{MIKE}$ requires the following correctness: For all $\lambda \in \mathbb{N}$, all $(\mathsf{prms}, \mathsf{mk}_0, \mathsf{mhk}) \leftarrow \mathsf{Init}(\lambda)$, all $M \in \mathcal{M}$, all $\mathtt{I} \in \mathcal{I}$, all $\mathtt{T}, \mathtt{T}' \in \mathcal{T}$, it holds that $M \leftarrow \mathsf{IBDec}(\mathsf{prms}, \mathsf{KG}(\mathsf{prms}, \mathsf{MKUpd}(\mathsf{prms}, \mathsf{mk}_{\mathtt{T}'}, \mathsf{UpdGen}(\mathsf{prms}, \mathsf{mhk}, \mathtt{T})), \mathtt{I}), \mathsf{IBEnc}(\mathsf{prms}, M, \mathtt{T}, \mathtt{I}))$.

We consider two kinds of security notions of MIKE, indistinguishability against key exposure and chosen plaintext attacks for MIKE (IND-ID-KI-CPA) and anonymity for MIKE (ANO-ID-KI-CPA). Let $\mathcal{A}$ be a PPT adversary. First, we define experiments of those notions in Figs. 9 and 10, respectively. $\mathcal{A}$ can access the following set of two oracles $\mathcal{O} := \{\mathcal{O}_{\text{EXT}}, \mathcal{O}_{\text{LEAK}}\}$, which is defined as follows.

$\mathcal{O}_{\text{EXT}}$: For a query $(\mathtt{T}, \mathtt{I}) \in \mathcal{T} \times \mathcal{I}$ from $\mathcal{A}$, it recalls $\mathsf{mk}_\mathtt{T}$ if it is already generated. Otherwise, it computes $\mathsf{mk}_\mathtt{T} \leftarrow \mathsf{MKUpd}(\mathsf{mk}_0, \mathsf{UpdGen}(\mathsf{mhk}, \mathtt{T}))$, and stores it. It then returns $\mathsf{KG}(\mathsf{mk}_\mathtt{T}, \mathtt{I})$ if $(\mathtt{T}, \mathtt{I}) \neq (\mathtt{T}^*, \mathtt{I}^*)$ in $\mathsf{Exp}^{\mathsf{ID\text{-}KI\text{-}CPA}}_{\mathcal{MIKE},\mathcal{A}}(1^\lambda)$ (if $(\mathtt{T}, \mathtt{I}) \in \{(\mathtt{T}^*, \mathtt{I}^*_0), (\mathtt{T}^*, \mathtt{I}^*_1)\}$ in $\mathsf{Exp}^{\mathsf{ANO\text{-}KI\text{-}CPA}}_{\mathcal{MIKE},\mathcal{A}}(1^\lambda)$).

$\mathcal{O}_{\text{LEAK}}$: Let $\mathcal{L} := \emptyset$ be an initial list. For a query $\mathtt{T} \in \mathcal{T} \cup \{\star\}$, it returns $\mathsf{mk}_\mathtt{T}$ if $\mathtt{T} \notin \mathcal{T} \setminus \{\mathtt{T}^*\}$ and $\star \notin \mathcal{L}$, and adds $\mathtt{T}$ to $\mathcal{L}$.[4] Else if $\mathtt{T} = \star$ and $\mathcal{L} = \emptyset$, it returns mhk, and adds $\star$ to $\mathcal{L}$. Otherwise, it returns $\perp$.

Definition 8 (IND-ID-KI-CPA). *$\mathcal{MIKE}$ is said to be IND-ID-KI-CPA secure if for all PPT adversaries $\mathcal{A}$, $\mathsf{Adv}^{\mathsf{ID\text{-}KI\text{-}CPA}}_{\mathcal{MIKE},\mathcal{A}}(1^\lambda) := |\Pr[\mathsf{Exp}^{\mathsf{ID\text{-}KI\text{-}CPA}}_{\mathcal{MIKE},\mathcal{A}}(1^\lambda) = 1] - 1/2|$ is negligible in λ.*

Definition 9 (ANO-ID-KI-CPA). *$\mathcal{MIKE}$ is said to be ANO-ID-KI-CPA secure if for all PPT adversaries $\mathcal{A}$, $\mathsf{Adv}^{\mathsf{ANO\text{-}KI\text{-}CPA}}_{\mathcal{MIKE},\mathcal{A}}(1^\lambda) := |\Pr[\mathsf{Exp}^{\mathsf{ANO\text{-}KI\text{-}CPA}}_{\mathcal{MIKE},\mathcal{A}}(1^\lambda) = 1] - 1/2|$ is negligible in λ.*

4.3 Generic Construction from KI-PKE and MIKE

In this section, we show a generic construction of a KU-PEKS scheme Π_{KI} in the key-insulation model from any KI-PKE scheme $\mathcal{KIE}$ and any MIKE scheme $\mathcal{MIKE}$. Basically, we can construct Π_{KI} in a similar way to the generic construction of Π_{KE} in Sect. 3.2. However, the construction only achieves *sequential key updates*, that is, a re-encryption key rk_i at $i \in \mathcal{T}$ can be used for only updating a ciphertext $\mathsf{c}_{w,i-1}$ encrypted in the previous period $i - 1 \in \mathcal{T}$. To achieve random access updates, i.e., to realize update a ciphertext $\mathsf{c}_{w,j}$ at any time period $j \in \mathcal{T}$ to $\mathsf{c}_{w,i}$ at any time period $i \in \mathcal{T}$, we adopt *the KUNode algorithm* (or, *the complete subtree (CS) method*), which was used for broadcast encryption [22], revocable IBE [4], and so forth. The KUNode algorithm is usually used for efficiently revoking malicious users, whereas we would like to use it to efficiently realize random access updates. Therefore, we modify the KUNode algorithm to fit our purpose as follows (see [4,22] for the original KUNode algorithm).
The Modified KUNode Algorithm. Let BTGen be an algorithm that takes N as input, and outputs a binary tree BT with N leaves, where N is a power of two for simplicity. Each time period $i \in \mathcal{T}$ is assigned to a leaf node, and the corresponding i-th leaf node is denoted by η_i. For the sake of simplicity, we assume $N = |\mathcal{T}|$. Now the depth of BT is $\log |\mathcal{T}| + 1$, and the number of all

[4] If $\mathsf{mk}_\mathtt{T}$ is not stored, the oracle generates it by $\mathsf{MKUpd}(\mathsf{mk}_0, \mathsf{UpdGen}(\mathsf{mhk}, \mathtt{T}))$ and stored it.

$\underline{\mathsf{KI.Setup}(1^\lambda)}$:
$\mathsf{BT} \leftarrow \mathsf{BTGen}(|\mathcal{T}|)$
$(\mathsf{EK}, \mathsf{DK}_0, \mathsf{HK}) \leftarrow \mathsf{KIKG}(1^\lambda)$
$(\mathsf{prms}, \mathsf{mk}_0, \mathsf{mhk}) \leftarrow \mathsf{Init}(1^\lambda)$
$\mathsf{pk} := (\mathsf{BT}, \mathsf{EK}, \mathsf{prms})$
$\mathsf{sk}_0 := (\mathsf{DK}_0, \mathsf{mk}_0)$
$\mathsf{hk} := (\mathsf{HK}, \mathsf{mhk})$
return $(\mathsf{pk}, \mathsf{sk}_0, \mathsf{hk})$

$\underline{\Delta\text{-}\mathsf{Gen}(\mathsf{pk}, \mathsf{hk}, i)}$:
parse $\mathsf{pk} = (\mathsf{BT}, \mathsf{EK}, \mathsf{prms})$
parse $\mathsf{hk} = (\mathsf{HK}, \mathsf{mhk})$
$\forall \ell \in \mathsf{KUNode}(\mathsf{BT}, i)$
  $\mathsf{UP}_\ell \leftarrow \mathsf{KIUG}(\mathsf{HK}, \ell)$
$\mathsf{up}_i \leftarrow \mathsf{UpdGen}(\mathsf{prms}, \mathsf{mhk}, i)$
$\delta_i := (\{\mathsf{UP}_\ell\}_{\ell \in \mathsf{KUNode}(\mathsf{BT}, i)}, \mathsf{up}_i)$
return δ_i

$\underline{\mathsf{KI.Upd}(\mathsf{pk}, \mathsf{sk}_{i'}, \delta_i)}$:
parse $\mathsf{pk} = (\mathsf{BT}, \mathsf{EK}, \mathsf{prms})$
parse $\mathsf{sk}_{i'} = (\mathsf{DK}_0, \mathsf{mk}_{i'})$
parse $\delta_i = (\{\mathsf{UP}_\ell\}_{\ell \in \mathsf{KUNode}(\mathsf{BT}, i)}, \mathsf{up}_i)$
$\forall \ell \in \mathsf{KUNode}(\mathsf{BT}, i)$
  $\mathsf{DK}_\ell \leftarrow \mathsf{KIUG}(\mathsf{DK}_0, \mathsf{UP}_\ell)$
$\mathsf{mk}_i \leftarrow \mathsf{MKUpd}(\mathsf{prms}, \mathsf{mk}_{i'}, \mathsf{up}_i)$
$\mathsf{sk}_i := (\mathsf{DK}_0, \mathsf{mk}_i)$
$\mathsf{rk}_i := (\{\mathsf{DK}_\ell\}_{\ell \in \mathsf{KUNode}(\mathsf{BT}, i)})$
return $(\mathsf{sk}_i, \mathsf{rk}_i)$

$\underline{\mathsf{KI.Enc}(\mathsf{pk}, w, i)}$:
parse $\mathsf{pk} = (\mathsf{BT}, \mathsf{EK}, \mathsf{prms})$
$\forall \ell \in \mathsf{Path}(\mathsf{BT}, \theta_{\mathsf{Lab}(i)}) \setminus \{1\}$
  $\mathsf{ct}_\ell \leftarrow \mathsf{KIE}(\mathsf{EK}, w, \ell)$
$R \xleftarrow{\$} \mathcal{M}$
// $\mathcal{M}$: the plaintext space of $\mathcal{MIKE}$
$\mathsf{ct}_{i,w} \leftarrow \mathsf{IBEnc}(\mathsf{prms}, R, i, w)$
$\mathsf{c}_{w,i} := (R, \{\mathsf{ct}_\ell\}_{\ell \in \mathsf{Path}(\mathsf{BT}, \theta_{\mathsf{Lab}(i)})}, \mathsf{ct}_{i,w})$
return $\mathsf{c}_{w,i}$

$\underline{\mathsf{KI.ReEnc}(\mathsf{pk}, \mathsf{rk}_i, \mathsf{c}_{w,j})}$:
parse $\mathsf{rk}_i = (\{\mathsf{DK}_\ell\}_{\ell \in \Theta_i})$
// $\Theta_i = \mathsf{KUNode}(\mathsf{BT}, i)$
parse $\mathsf{c}_{w,j} = (R, \{\mathsf{ct}_\ell\}_{\ell \in \Theta_j}, \mathsf{ct}_{j,w})$
// $\Theta_j = \mathsf{Path}(\mathsf{BT}, \theta_{\mathsf{Lab}(j)})$
if $\Theta_i \cap \Theta_j = \emptyset$
// It occurs if and only if $i \leq j$
  return $\perp$
else
  $\{\ell^*\} := \Theta_i \cap \Theta_j$
  // It contains exactly one element
  $w \leftarrow \mathsf{KID}(\mathsf{DK}_{\ell^*}, \mathsf{ct}_{\ell^*})$
  $\mathsf{c}_{w,i} \leftarrow \mathsf{KI.Enc}(\mathsf{pk}, w, i)$
  // Run KI.Enc constructed as above
return $\mathsf{c}_{w,i}$

$\underline{\mathsf{KI.Trapdoor}(\mathsf{pk}, \mathsf{sk}_i, w')}$:
parse $\mathsf{pk} = (\mathsf{BT}, \mathsf{EK}, \mathsf{prms})$
parse $\mathsf{sk}_i = (\mathsf{DK}_0, \{\mathsf{DK}_\ell\}_{\ell \in \Theta_i}, \mathsf{mk}_i)$
$\mathsf{dk}_{i,w'} \leftarrow \mathsf{KG}(\mathsf{prms}, \mathsf{mk}_i, w')$
$\mathsf{t}_{w',i} := \mathsf{dk}_{i,w'}$
return $\mathsf{t}_{w',i}$

$\underline{\mathsf{KI.Test}(\mathsf{pk}, \mathsf{t}_{w',i}, \mathsf{c}_{w,j})}$:
parse $\mathsf{pk} = (\mathsf{BT}, \mathsf{EK}, \mathsf{prms})$
parse $\mathsf{c}_{w,j} = (\{R, \mathsf{ct}_\ell\}_{\ell \in \Theta_j}, \mathsf{ct}_{j,w})$
if $i \neq j$
  return 0
else if $R = \mathsf{IBDec}(\mathsf{prms}, \mathsf{t}_{w',i}, \mathsf{ct}_{j,w})$
  return 1
else if $R \neq \mathsf{IBDec}(\mathsf{prms}, \mathsf{t}_{w',i}, \mathsf{ct}_{j,w})$
  return 0

Fig. 11. A generic construction of Π_{KI} from $\mathcal{KIE}$ and $\mathcal{MIKE}$.

nodes is $2^{\log|\mathcal{T}|+1} - 1 = 2|\mathcal{T}| - 1$. $\mathsf{Path}(\mathsf{BT}, \eta_i)$ denotes a set of nodes on the path from a root node to η_i. Note that it includes the root node and η_i. The modified $\mathsf{KUNode}(\mathsf{BT}, i)$ algorithm takes as input a binary tree BT and a time period $i \in \mathcal{T}$, and outputs a set of nodes. The modified $\mathsf{KUNode}(\mathsf{BT}, i)$ algorithm is executed as follows. It sets $\mathcal{X} := \emptyset$. For each non-leaf node $\theta \in \mathsf{Path}(\mathsf{BT}, \eta_i)$, it

Table 1. Efficiency comparison among instantiations of the proposed schemes. #pk, #sk, #rk, #td, and #c denote the sizes of public keys, secret keys, re-encryption keys, trapdoors, and ciphertexts, respectively, and Asmp. stands for assumptions. $[a, b, c, d]$ means that the parameter contains a elements of $\mathbb{Z}_p$, b elements of $\mathbb{G}_1$, c elements of $\mathbb{G}_2$, and d elements of $\mathbb{G}_T$. We set $t := \log|\mathcal{T}|$. We assume the plaintext space of the underlying Bone-Franklin IBE in $\Pi_{\mathrm{KE}}^{\mathsf{rom}}$ is $\mathbb{Z}_p$.

	pk is fixed?	#pk	#sk	#rk	#td	#c	Asmp.
$\Pi_{\mathrm{KE}}^{\mathsf{rom}}$	No	$[0, 4, 0, 0]$	$[2, 0, 0, 0]$	$[1, 0, 0, 0]$	$[0, 1, 0, 0]$	$[2, 3, 0, 0]$	DDH1, DBDH
$\Pi_{\mathrm{KE}}^{\mathsf{std}}$	No	$[0, 7, 0, 1]$	$[9, 0, 1, 0]$	$[1, 0, 0, 0]$	$[0, 0, 5, 0]$	$[1, 5, 0, 1]$	SXDH
$\Pi_{\mathrm{KI}}^{\mathsf{std}}$	Yes	$[0, 13, 7, 1]$	$[8, 0, 17, 0]$	$[0, 0, O(t), 0]$	$[0, 0, 5, 0]$	$[2t+1, 3t+3, 0, t+1]$	SXDH

Table 2. Running time of core algorithms of $\Pi_{\mathrm{KE}}^{\mathrm{ROM}}$ (unit: msec). Processor: 3.40 GHz Intel Core i7-3770, Memory: 31 GB, OS: Linux (Ubuntu 15.04, kernel 3.19.0-15-generic).

KE.Enc	KE.Trapdoor	KE.Test
11.20	1.04	4.71

adds the left child θ_L of θ to $\mathcal{X}$ if $\theta_L \notin \mathsf{Path}(\mathsf{BT}, \eta_i)$. Finally, it outputs $\mathcal{X}$. Note that the size of $\mathcal{X}$ is $O(\log|\mathcal{T}|)$.

We are ready to show our construction. Let $\mathcal{KIE}$ = (KIKG, KIUG, KIU, KIE, KID) and $\mathcal{MIKE}$ = (Init, UpdGen, MKUpd, KG, IBEnc, IBDec) be a KI-PKE scheme with a set of time periods $\widehat{\mathcal{T}}$ such that $|\widehat{\mathcal{T}}| = 2|\mathcal{T}| - 1$ and a MIKE scheme with $\mathcal{T}$, respectively. Our construction of Π_{KI} = (KI.Setup, Δ-Gen, KI.Upd, KI.Enc, KI.ReEnc, KI.Trapdoor, KI.Test) is given in Fig. 11. In this construction, we consider the following function $\mathsf{Lab} : i \in \mathcal{T} \mapsto i + |\mathcal{T}| - 1 \in \mathbb{Z}$ for the modified KUNode algorithm. First, we label each node of BT as θ_i $(1 \le i \le 2|\mathcal{T}|-1)$ from the root node. Hence, the root node is θ_1 and leaf nodes are $\theta_{|\mathcal{T}|}, \dots, \theta_{2|\mathcal{T}|-1}$. Then, each time period $i \in \mathcal{T}$ is stored in a leaf node $\theta_{\mathsf{Lab}(i)}$, and we write $\eta_i := \theta_{\mathsf{Lab}(i)}$. Moreover, in the construction, $\mathsf{Path}(\mathsf{BT}, \eta_i)$ and $\mathsf{KUNode}(\mathsf{BT}, i)$ are regarded as a set of indices of the corresponding nodes for readability. Namely, we write $\{1, j_1, j_2, \dots, \mathsf{Lab}(i)\} = \mathsf{Path}(\mathsf{BT}, \eta_i)$ and $\{h_1, h_2, \dots, h_k\} = \mathsf{KUNode}(\mathsf{BT}, i)$, instead of $\{\theta_1, \theta_{j_1}, \theta_{j_2}, \dots, \theta_{\mathsf{Lab}(i)} (= \eta_i)\} = \mathsf{Path}(\mathsf{BT}, \eta_i)$ and $\{\theta_{h_1}, \theta_{h_2}, \dots, \theta_{h_k}\} = \mathsf{KUNode}(\mathsf{BT}, i)$, respectively. We obtain the following theorem, and omit the proof since it can be proved in a way similar to Theorem 1.

Theorem 2. *If $\mathcal{KIE}$ is* IND-KI-CPA *secure and $\mathcal{MIKE}$ is* IND-ID-KI-CPA *secure and* ANO-ID-KI-CPA *secure, the proposed construction given in Fig. 11 is* IND-KI-CKA *secure and meets* KI-Computational Consistency.

5 Efficiency Comparison and Implementation

Table 1 shows efficiency comparisons among three instantiations of our schemes, called $\Pi_{\mathrm{KE}}^{\mathsf{rom}}$, $\Pi_{\mathrm{KE}}^{\mathsf{std}}$, and $\Pi_{\mathrm{KI}}^{\mathsf{std}}$, respectively. $\Pi_{\mathrm{KE}}^{\mathsf{rom}}$, which is an instantiation with the

ElGamal PKE [15] on $\mathbb{G}_1$ and the Boneh-Franklin IBE [6], is secure in the key-evolution model with random oracles. $\Pi_{\mathrm{KE}}^{\mathsf{std}}$ is an instantiation with the ElGamal PKE on $\mathbb{G}_1$ and the Jutla-Roy IBE [19], and hence is secure in the key-evolution model without random oracles. $\Pi_{\mathrm{KI}}^{\mathsf{std}}$ is an instantiation in the key-insulation model with the Watanabe-Shikata KI-PKE [26], which is the most efficient KI-PKE scheme, and a direct construction of an anonymous MIKE scheme, which will appear in the full version. All the instantiations are secure under the simple assumptions such as the DDH1 (DDH on $\mathbb{G}_1$), DBDH, and SXDH assumptions. The first one achieves the most efficient parameters, though the security relies on random oracles. The third one is less efficient than the other two, however it does not require to update public keys. Furthermore, the server only manage *global* $\mathcal{T}$, whereas $\mathcal{T}$ is regarded as just "updating counter" in the key-evolution model. Namely, considering the multi-user setting, the server has to manage each $\mathcal{T}$ per user in the key-evolution model.

Table 2 shows an experimental result for the most efficient scheme, i.e., $\Pi_{\mathrm{KE}}^{\mathsf{rom}}$, using the software library TEPLA [25]. We use the Enron Email Dataset [9], which contains 517,401 e-mails and the average size of them is 2.68 Kbytes, as test data. We here give only *core* algorithms of KU-PEKS in the key-evolution model, KE.Enc, KE.Trapdoor, and KE.Test, since key generation/updating algorithms are not relatively frequently executed, and KE.ReEnc is almost the same as KE.Enc. Note that usual libraries for a pairing cryptosystem like TEPLA [25] are not designed for parallel processing, hence the running time directly depends on the clock frequency of processors. Therefore, for instance, Cortex-M7 CPU by ARM, which is suitable for an embedded device on IoT, is 300 MHz, and hence the running time of KE.Enc and KE.Trapdoor can be estimated as 127.0 and 11.8 msec, respectively, which seem acceptable in our scenario (i.e., PEKS with key-updating functionality for IoT devices).

Acknowledgments. We would like to thank the anonymous reviewers for useful comments. The first author was supported by The Telecommunications Advancement Foundation. The second and third authors were supported by Grant-in-Aid for JSPS Fellows Grant Number JP17K00189. The last author was supported by JSPS Research Fellowship for Young Scientists and Grant-in-Aid for JSPS Fellows Grant Number JP16J10532 and JP17K12697.

References

1. Abdalla, M., Bellare, M., Catalano, D., Kiltz, E., Kohno, T., Lange, T., Malone-Lee, J., Neven, G., Paillier, P., Shi, H.: Searchable encryption revisited: consistency properties, relation to anonymous IBE, and extensions. J. Cryptol. **21**(3), 350–391 (2008)
2. Baek, J., Safavi-Naini, R., Susilo, W.: Public key encryption with keyword search revisited. In: Gervasi, O., Murgante, B., Laganà, A., Taniar, D., Mun, Y., Gavrilova, M.L. (eds.) ICCSA 2008. LNCS, vol. 5072, pp. 1249–1259. Springer, Heidelberg (2008). https://doi.org/10.1007/978-3-540-69839-5_96

3. Blaze, M., Bleumer, G., Strauss, M.: Divertible protocols and atomic proxy cryptography. In: Nyberg, K. (ed.) EUROCRYPT 1998. LNCS, vol. 1403, pp. 127–144. Springer, Heidelberg (1998). https://doi.org/10.1007/BFb0054122
4. Boldyreva, A., Goyal, V., Kumar, V.: Identity-based encryption with efficient revocation. In: Proceedings of CCS 2008, pp. 417–426. ACM, New York (2008)
5. Boneh, D., Di Crescenzo, G., Ostrovsky, R., Persiano, G.: Public key encryption with keyword search. In: Cachin, C., Camenisch, J.L. (eds.) EUROCRYPT 2004. LNCS, vol. 3027, pp. 506–522. Springer, Heidelberg (2004). https://doi.org/10.1007/978-3-540-24676-3_30
6. Boneh, D., Franklin, M.: Identity-based encryption from the Weil pairing. In: Kilian, J. (ed.) CRYPTO 2001. LNCS, vol. 2139, pp. 213–229. Springer, Heidelberg (2001). https://doi.org/10.1007/3-540-44647-8_13
7. Byun, J.W., Rhee, H.S., Park, H.-A., Lee, D.H.: Off-line keyword guessing attacks on recent keyword search schemes over encrypted data. In: Jonker, W., Petković, M. (eds.) SDM 2006. LNCS, vol. 4165, pp. 75–83. Springer, Heidelberg (2006). https://doi.org/10.1007/11844662_6
8. Canetti, R., Halevi, S., Katz, J.: A forward-secure public-key encryption scheme. In: Biham, E. (ed.) EUROCRYPT 2003. LNCS, vol. 2656, pp. 255–271. Springer, Heidelberg (2003). https://doi.org/10.1007/3-540-39200-9_16
9. Carnegie Mellon University: Enron email dataset, 7 May 2015. http://www.cs.cmu.edu/ enron/
10. Cheon, J.H., Hopper, N., Kim, Y., Osipkov, I.: Provably secure timed-release public key encryption. ACM Trans. Inf. Syst. Secur. **11**(2), 4:1–4:44 (2008)
11. Chor, B., Goldreich, O., Kushilevitz, E., Sudan, M.: Private information retrieval. In: FOCS 1995, pp. 41–50 (1995)
12. Dodis, Y., Franklin, M., Katz, J., Miyaji, A., Yung, M.: A generic construction for intrusion-resilient public-key encryption. In: Okamoto, T. (ed.) CT-RSA 2004. LNCS, vol. 2964, pp. 81–98. Springer, Heidelberg (2004). https://doi.org/10.1007/978-3-540-24660-2_7
13. Dodis, Y., Katz, J., Xu, S., Yung, M.: Key-insulated public key cryptosystems. In: Knudsen, L.R. (ed.) EUROCRYPT 2002. LNCS, vol. 2332, pp. 65–82. Springer, Heidelberg (2002). https://doi.org/10.1007/3-540-46035-7_5
14. Dodis, Y., Katz, J., Xu, S., Yung, M.: Strong key-insulated signature schemes. In: Desmedt, Y.G. (ed.) PKC 2003. LNCS, vol. 2567, pp. 130–144. Springer, Heidelberg (2003). https://doi.org/10.1007/3-540-36288-6_10
15. ElGamal, T.: A public key cryptosystem and a signature scheme based on discrete logarithms. In: Blakley, G.R., Chaum, D. (eds.) CRYPTO 1984. LNCS, vol. 196, pp. 10–18. Springer, Heidelberg (1985). https://doi.org/10.1007/3-540-39568-7_2
16. Emura, K., Phong, L.T., Watanabe, Y.: Keyword revocable searchable encryption with trapdoor exposure resistance and re-generateability. In: 2015 IEEE Trustcom/BigDataSE/ISPA, vol. 1, pp. 167–174, August 2015
17. Green, M., Ateniese, G.: Identity-based proxy re-encryption. In: Katz, J., Yung, M. (eds.) ACNS 2007. LNCS, vol. 4521, pp. 288–306. Springer, Heidelberg (2007). https://doi.org/10.1007/978-3-540-72738-5_19
18. Hanaoka, Y., Hanaoka, G., Shikata, J., Imai, H.: Identity-based hierarchical strongly key-insulated encryption and its application. In: Roy, B. (ed.) ASIACRYPT 2005. LNCS, vol. 3788, pp. 495–514. Springer, Heidelberg (2005). https://doi.org/10.1007/11593447_27
19. Jutla, C.S., Roy, A.: Shorter quasi-adaptive NIZK proofs for linear subspaces. In: Sako, K., Sarkar, P. (eds.) ASIACRYPT 2013. LNCS, vol. 8269, pp. 1–20. Springer, Heidelberg (2013). https://doi.org/10.1007/978-3-642-42033-7_1

20. Kocher, P.C.: Timing attacks on implementations of Diffie-Hellman, RSA, DSS, and other systems. In: Koblitz, N. (ed.) CRYPTO 1996. LNCS, vol. 1109, pp. 104–113. Springer, Heidelberg (1996). https://doi.org/10.1007/3-540-68697-5_9
21. Lewko, A.: Tools for simulating features of composite order bilinear groups in the prime order setting. In: Pointcheval, D., Johansson, T. (eds.) EUROCRYPT 2012. LNCS, vol. 7237, pp. 318–335. Springer, Heidelberg (2012). https://doi.org/10.1007/978-3-642-29011-4_20
22. Naor, D., Naor, M., Lotspiech, J.: Revocation and tracing schemes for stateless receivers. In: Kilian, J. (ed.) CRYPTO 2001. LNCS, vol. 2139, pp. 41–62. Springer, Heidelberg (2001). https://doi.org/10.1007/3-540-44647-8_3
23. National Institute of Standards and Technology: Nist special publication 800–57 part 1, revision 4, recommendation for key management part 1: General (2013). http://nvlpubs.nist.gov/nistpubs/SpecialPublications/NIST.SP.800-57pt1r4.pdf
24. Tang, Q.: Towards forward security properties for PEKS and IBE. In: Foo, E., Stebila, D. (eds.) ACISP 2015. LNCS, vol. 9144, pp. 127–144. Springer, Cham (2015). https://doi.org/10.1007/978-3-319-19962-7_8
25. University of Tsukuba: TEPLA: University of Tsukuba Elliptic curve and Pairing Libraary (Jan2013 Released TEPLA 10, Dec-2015 Released TEPLA 20). http://www.cipher.risk.tsukuba.ac.jp/tepla/
26. Watanabe, Y., Shikata, J.: Identity-based hierarchical key-insulated encryption without random oracles. In: Cheng, C.-M., Chung, K.-M., Persiano, G., Yang, B.-Y. (eds.) PKC 2016. LNCS, vol. 9614, pp. 255–279. Springer, Heidelberg (2016). https://doi.org/10.1007/978-3-662-49384-7_10

Anonymous Identity-Based Encryption with Identity Recovery

Xuecheng Ma[1,2], Xin Wang[1,2], and Dongdai Lin[1(✉)]

[1] State Key Laboratory of Information Security, Institute of Information Engineering, Chinese Academy of Sciences, Beijing 100093, China
{maxuecheng,wangxin9076,ddlin}@iie.ac.cn

[2] School of Cyber Security, University of Chinese Academy of Sciences, Beijing 100049, China

Abstract. Anonymous Identity-Based Encryption can protect privacy of the receiver. However, there are some situations that we need to recover the identity of the receiver, for example a dispute occurs or the privacy mechanism is abused. In this paper, we propose a new concept, referred to as Anonymous Identity-Based Encryption with Identity Recovery (AIBEIR), which is an anonymous IBE with identity recovery property. There is a party called the Identity Recovery Manager (IRM) who has a secret key to recover the identity from the ciphertext in our scheme. We construct it with an anonymous IBE and a special IBE which we call it testable IBE. In order to ensure the semantic security in the case where the identity recovery manager is an adversary, we define a stronger semantic security model in which the adversary is given the secret key of the identity recovery manager. To our knowledge, we propose the first AIBEIR scheme and prove the security in our defined model.

Keywords: IBE · Anonymous · Identity recovery · Testable

1 Introduction

Public key encryption is one of the most important primitives in cryptography, which was presented in the great paper titled "New Directions in Cryptograph" in 1976 [DH76]. Public key encryption solves the problem that the sender and the receiver should share a common secret key which is not known to the adversary before communicating. One of the disadvantages in public key encryption is using certificate to bind the public key to the identity of its owner. The issue of management of certificates is complex and cumbersome.

In 1984, Shamir [Sha84] introduced the concept of Identity-Based Encryption (IBE) which solved the problem. IBE is a generalization of public key encryption where the public key of a user can be arbitrary string such as an e-mail address. The first realizations of IBE are given by [SOK00,BF01] using groups equipped with bilinear maps. Since then, realizations from bilinear maps

W. Susilo and G. Yang (Eds.): ACISP 2018, LNCS 10946, pp. 360–375, 2018.
https://doi.org/10.1007/978-3-319-93638-3_21

[BB04a,BB04b,Wat05,Gen06,Wat09], from quadratic residues modulo composite [Coc01,BGH07], from lattices [GPV08,CHKP10,ABB10,Boy10] and from the computational Diffie-Hellman assumption [DG17] have been proposed.

In order to protect the privacy of the receiver, Boyen [Boy03] first explicitly stated the concept of anonymous IBE[1], where the ciphertext does not leak the identity of the recipient. In fact, [BF01] is the first anonymous IBE scheme although they did not state it explicitly. Since then, there are some follow-up works realized from bilinear maps, from quadratic residues modulo composite [AG09], from lattices [GPV08,ABB10] and from the computational Diffie-Hellman assumption [BLSV17].

Anonymous IBE protects the privacy of the message and the receiver's identity in the meantime, but we can only recover the message. However, there are some situations where we need to recover the identity of the receiver, for example a dispute occurs or the privacy mechanism is abused. In a mail system, there is a need to keep the receiver anonymous for everyone except the mail sever who will forward the mail to the receiver. *So can we extract the identity from an anonymous IBE ciphertext with some secret information?* In this paper, we present a new primitive called *anonymous identity-based encryption with identity recovery* (AIBEIR) which can solve this problem. AIBEIR is a special anonymous IBE which has an additional property that the identity recovery manager can recover the identity with a secret key. But the identity recovery manager can not get any information of the message from the ciphertext. Formally, AIBEIR is semantic secure even when the identity recovery manager is the adversary.

1.1 Our Contributions

We propose a new cryptographic primitive called *anonymous IBE with identity recovery*. We first define the model and security notions of AIBEIR. We then present a method to convert an anonymous IBE into AIBEIR with the help of testable IBE and prove that the new scheme satisfies the security we defined. A testable IBE is an IBE which can test whether ciphertext c is a ciphertext under identity id given c and id. It is obvious that a testable IBE is not anonymous. We will show that [BB04a,Wat05] and their variations are testable IBEs. AIBEIR consists of four parties, a Private Key Generator (PKG), an Identity Recovery Manager (IRM), a sender, and a receiver. There are five procedures in an AIBEIR scheme. They are setup procedure, extract procedure, encrypt procedure, decrypt procedure and recover procedure.

Besides correctness and anonymity, we introduce two new security notions in AIBEIR. The first is a stronger semantic security, where the identity recovery manager is the adversary. The second is recovery, which ensures that the recovery is reliable and no adversary can fool the identity recovery manager. Finally, We prove the security of our concrete AIBEIR scheme according to our security

[1] In fact, Boyen gave an ID-based signcryption with a formalization of sender and recipient anonymity.

notions. To the best of our knowledge, our construction is the first anonymous IBE scheme with the identity recovery property.

To construct an AIBEIR scheme, we first encrypt the plaintext by a testable IBE and encrypt the testable IBE ciphertext using an anonymous IBE. Moreover, we encrypt the receiver's identity under the recovery manager's identity. The anonymity is guaranteed by the anonymous IBE and the stronger CPA security is guaranteed by the security of the testable IBE. Given the master secret key of the anonymous IBE, identity recovery manager obtains the identity and the testable IBE ciphertext by decrypting corresponding ciphertext, respectively. Then, check whether the testable IBE ciphertext is under the identity and output the identity if the test algorithm outputs 1.

1.2 Related Work

Identity-based cryptosystems were introduced by Shamir [Sha84]. The first realizations of IBE were given by Boneh and Franklin [BF01] and Sakai *et al.* [SOK00]. Boneh and Franklin gave the security model and their proposal is the first anonymous IBE. The anonymity was first noticed by Boyen [Boy03]. Another view of Anonymous IBE is as a combination of identity-based encryption with the property of key privacy, which was introduced by Bellare *et al.* [BBDP01]. A similar concept called Identity-Based Group Encryption (IBGE) was presented by Luo *et al.* [LRL+16]. Traceability in their scheme is similar to recovery in ours. But there are some differences between IBGE and AIBEIR. On the one hand, we do not have Verify algorithm which is used to verify whether the ciphertext belongs to the group. On the other hand, our construction is implemented by IBEs while they utilized PKE, IBE and ZKP (*Zero-Knowledge Proofs*) to construct their scheme. We do not think their scheme is a "pure" IBE because of the use of PKE. Recently, [GSRD17] pointed that the zero-knowledge proof used in [LRL+16] leaks much more information, due to which the verifier who is honest but curious will be able to identify the designated recipient. They proposed a construction with six random oracles.

2 Preliminaries and Definitions

We denote $s \xleftarrow{\$} \mathcal{S}$ as the operation of assigning to s an element selected uniformly at random from set $\mathcal{S}$. The notation $x \leftarrow \mathsf{A}(\cdot)$ denotes the operation of running an algorithm A with some given input and assigning the output to x. A function $\mathsf{negl}\colon \mathbb{N} \rightarrow \mathbb{R}$ is *negligible* if for every positive polynomial poly and sufficiently large λ, it holds that $\mathsf{negl}(\lambda) < 1/\mathsf{poly}(\lambda)$. We use $\mathbf{0}$ to denote the zero vector whose length is dependent on the context.

2.1 Bilinear Groups

Let $\mathbb{G}_1$, $\mathbb{G}_2$ and $\mathbb{G}_T$ be multiplicative cyclic groups of prime order p. Let g_1, g_2 be generators of groups $\mathbb{G}_1$ and $\mathbb{G}_2$, respectively, and $e : \mathbb{G}_1 \times \mathbb{G}_2 \rightarrow \mathbb{G}_T$ be a bilinear map that holds the following features:

- Bilinearity: $e(u^a, v^b) = e(u, v)^{ab}$ for all $u \in \mathbb{G}_1$, $v \in \mathbb{G}_2$ and $a, b \in \mathbb{Z}_p$.
- Non-degeneracy: $e(g_1, g_2) \neq 1_{\mathbb{G}_T}$.
- Computability: there exists an efficient algorithm to compute $e(u, v)$ for any input pair $u \in \mathbb{G}_1$, $v \in \mathbb{G}_2$.

We assume a symmetric bilinear map such that $\mathbb{G}_1 = \mathbb{G}_2 = \mathbb{G}$ and $g_1 = g_2 = g$.

2.2 Identity-Based Encryption

Let 1^λ be a security parameter. An identity-based encryption is a tuple of algorithms Π_{IBE} = (IBE.Setup, IBE.Extract, IBE.Encrypt, IBE.Decrypt) with the following properties:

- Setup(1^λ): This is a polynomial time algorithm which takes as input 1^λ and outputs the system parameter mpk and a master secret key msk.
- Extract(id, msk): This is a polynomial time algorithm which takes as input user's identity id and master secret key msk, and outputs the user's corresponding private key sk_{id}.
- Encrypt(m, id, mpk): This is a polynomial time algorithm which takes as input a message m in the message space, system parameter mpk, the receiver's identity id and outputs a ciphertext c in the ciphertext space.
- Decrypt(mpk, c, sk_{id}): This is a polynomial time algorithm which takes as input system parameter mpk, ciphertext c, user's private key sk_{id}, outputs the message m in the message space.

Correctness. We require correctness of decryption: that is, for all λ, all identity id in the identity space, all m in the specified message space, $Pr[\mathsf{Decrypt}(mpk, sk_{id}, \mathsf{Encrypt}(m, id, mpk)) = m] = 1 - \mathsf{negl}(\lambda)$ holds, where the probability is taken over the randomness of the algorithms.

Anonymity and Semantic Security. When the ciphertext can not reveal information of the message, we say that the cryptosystem is chosen-plaintext secure. We say that the cryptosystem is anonymous if the ciphertext can not reveal information of the identity of the receiver. We combine these two notions.

Definition 1. *An IBE scheme is anonymous against chosen-identity and chosen-plaintext attacks if there does not exist any polynomial adversary $\mathcal{A}$ who has non-negligible advantage in the following game:*

Setup: The challenger takes as input a security parameter 1^λ and runs the Setup algorithm of the IBE. It provides $\mathcal{A}$ with the system parameters mpk while keeping the master secret key msk to itself.

Phase 1: The adversary $\mathcal{A}$ can make any polynomial key-extraction queries defined as follows: key-extraction query (id): The adversary $\mathcal{A}$ can choose an identity id and sends it to the challenger. The challenger generates a secret key sk_{id} of id and returns it to $\mathcal{A}$.

Challenge: When $\mathcal{A}$ decides that Phase 1 is complete, it chooses two equal-length plaintexts m_0, m_1 and two identities id_0, id_1 under the constraint that they have not been asked for the private keys. The challenger chooses uniformly at random two bits $b \in \{0,1\}, \gamma \in \{0,1\}$ and sends a ciphertext c^* of m_b as the challenge ciphertext under id_γ to $\mathcal{A}$.

Phase 2: The adversary $\mathcal{A}$ can also make queries just like Phase 1 except that it cannot make a key-extraction query of either id_0 or id_1.

Guess: $\mathcal{A}$ outputs a guess (b', γ') of (b, γ).

We define the advantage of the adversary $\mathcal{A}$ as $Adv_\mathcal{A} = |Pr[b = b' \wedge \gamma = \gamma'] - \frac{1}{4}|$.

2.3 Testable Identity-Based Encryption

Definition 2. *An Identity-Based Encryption is testable if the ciphertext c can be partitioned into two parts c_0 and c_1 where c_0 contains information of the identity but no information of the message while c_1 contains information of the message but no information of the identity. Additionally, there exists an algorithm Test$(\cdot,\cdot)$ which takes as input c_0 and an identity id and returns 1 if c_0 is a part of a valid cipertext under id and 0 otherwise.*

Some realizations of IBE from bilinear maps such as [BB04a, Wat05] satisfy the definition of testable IBE. We will prove that the scheme in [Wat05] is a testable IBE.

Let $\mathbb{G}$ be a group of prime order, p, for which there exists an efficiently computable bilinear map into $\mathbb{G}_1$. Additionally, let $e : \mathbb{G} \times \mathbb{G} \to \mathbb{G}_1$ denote the bilinear map and g be the corresponding generator. The size of the group is determined by the security parameter. Identities will be represented as bit strings of length n, a separate parameter unrelated to p. The construction follows.

Setup. The system parameters are generated as follows. We choose a random generator, $g \in \mathbb{G}$ and g_2 randomly in $\mathbb{G}$. We choose a secret $\alpha \in \mathbb{Z}_p$ and set $g_1 = g^\alpha$. Further, choose a random value $u' \in \mathbb{G}$ and a random $n-$length vector $U = (u_i)$, whose elements are chosen at random from $\mathbb{G}$. The published public parameters are g, g_1, g_2, u', and U. The master secret key is g_2^α.

Key Generation. Let v be a n-bit string representing an identity, v_i denote the ith bit of v, and $\mathcal{V} \subseteq \{1, \ldots, n\}$ be the set of all i for which $v_i = 1$. (That is $\mathcal{V}$ is the set of indices for which the bit string v is set to 1.) A private key for identity v is generated as follows. First, a random $r \in \mathbb{Z}_p$ is chosen. Then the private key is constructed as:

$$d_v = (g_2^\alpha (u' \prod_{i \in \mathcal{V}} u_i)^r, g^r)$$

Encryption. A message $M \in \mathbb{G}_1$ is encrypted for an identity v as follows. A value $t \in \mathbb{Z}_p$ is chosen at random. The ciphertext is then constructed as:

$$C = (e(g_1, g_2)^t M, g^t, (u' \prod_{i \in \mathcal{V}} u_i)^t)$$

Decryption. Let $C = (C_1, C_2, C_3)$ be a valid encryption of M under the identity v. Then C can be decrypted by $d_v = (d_1, d_2)$ as:

$$C_1 \frac{e(d_2, C_3)}{e(d_1, C_2)} = (e(g_1, g_2)^t M) \frac{e(g^r, (u' \prod_{i \in \mathcal{V}} u_i)^t)}{e(g_2^\alpha (u' \prod_{i \in \mathcal{V}} u_i)^r), g^t}) = (e(g_1, g_2)^t M) \frac{e(g, (u' \prod_{i \in \mathcal{V}} u_i)^{rt}))}{e(g_1, g_2)^t e((u' \prod_{i \in \mathcal{V}} u_i)^{rt}, g)} = M$$

We can also define a Test algorithm as follows:

Test. Let $C = (C_1, C_2, C_3)$ be a valid encryption under the identity v. Let v' be a n bit string representing an identity, v_i' denote the ith bit of v', and $\mathcal{V}' \subseteq \{1, \ldots, n\}$ be the set of all i for which $v_i' = 1$. Output 1 if $e(g, C_3) = e(C_2, (u' \prod_{i \in \mathcal{V}'} u_i))$ and $\perp$ otherwise. In fact, (C_1, C_2) contain the information of the message and no information of the identity. C_3 contains information of the identity but no information of the message. So it is a testable IBE.

3 Anonymous Identity-Based Encryption with Identity Recovery

Let λ be a security parameter. An anonymous identity-based encryption with recovery is a tuple of algorithms Π_{AIBEIR} = (AIBEIR.Setup, AIBEIR.Extract, AIBEIR.ncrypt, AIBEIR.Decrypt, AIBEIR.Recover) with the following properties:

- Setup(1^λ): This is a polynomial time algorithm which takes as input 1^λ and outputs the system parameter mpk, a master secret key msk and secret key of the identity recovery manager sk_{IRM}. Then PKG sends sk_{IRM} to the identity recovery manager in a secret channel. It is operated by PKG.
- Extract(id, msk): This is a polynomial time algorithm which takes as input a user's identity id and msk, outputs the user's corresponding private key sk_{id}.
- Encrypt(m, mpk, id): This is a polynomial time algorithm which takes as input a message m in a specified message space, system parameter mpk, the receiver's identity id and outputs a ciphertext c in the ciphertext space. It is operated by the sender.
- Decrypt(mpk, c, sk_{id}): This is a polynomial time algorithm which takes as input system parameter mpk, ciphertext c, user's private key sk_{id}, outputs the message m in the message space. It is operated by the receiver.
- Recover(c, sk_{IRM}): The identity recovery manager outputs an identity id if c is a valid cipertext under id and $\perp$ otherwise. It is operated by the identity recovery manager.

Correctness. We say that Π_{AIBEIR} is correct if it satisfies the following two properties:

- **Decryption correctness:** For any id in identity space and m in a specified message space, $Pr[\mathsf{AIBEIR.Decrypt}(sk_{id}, \mathsf{AIBEIR.Encrypt}(m, id, mpk)) = m] = 1 - \mathsf{negl}(\lambda)$.
- **Recovery correctness:** For any valid ciphertext $c = \mathsf{AIBEIR.Encrypt}(m, id, mpk)$, $Pr[\mathsf{Recover}(sk_{IRM}, c) = id] = 1 - \mathsf{negl}(\lambda)$.

Anonymity. The anonymity of AIBEIR is the same as Definition 1.

Stronger Semantic Security. In the semantic security model of IBE, adversary has no information about the master secret key msk. But in the definition of our AIBEIR scheme, the identity recovery manager holds sk_{IRM} which makes it more powerful. So if the identity recovery manager is the adversary, the semantic security model of IBE is not feasible. We define a stronger semantic security as follows:

Definition 3. *An AIBEIR scheme is strongly semantic secure against chosen-identity and chosen-plaintext attacks if there does not exist any polynomial adversary $\mathcal{A}$ who have non-negligible advantage in the game below:*

Setup: The challenger takes as input a security parameter 1^{λ} and runs the Setup algorithm of the AIBEIR. It provides $\mathcal{A}$ with the system parameters mpk and sk_{IRM} while keeping the master secret key msk to itself.

Phase 1: The adversary $\mathcal{A}$ can make any polynomial key-extraction queries defined as follows: key-extraction query (id): $\mathcal{A}$ can choose an identity id and send it to the challenger. The challenger generates secret key sk_{id} and returns it to $\mathcal{A}$.

Challenge: When $\mathcal{A}$ decides that Phase 1 is complete, it chooses two equal-length plaintexts m_0, m_1 and an identity id^* under the constraint that it has not asked for the private key and sends them to the challenger. The challenger chooses uniformly at random a bit $b \in \{0,1\}$ and sends a ciphertext $c^* = \mathsf{Encrypt}(m_b, id^*, mpk)$ as the challenge ciphertext to $\mathcal{A}$.

Phase 2: $\mathcal{A}$ can also make queries just like Phase 1 except that it cannot make a key-extraction query of id^*.

Guess: $\mathcal{A}$ outputs a guess b' of b.

We define the advantage of adversary $\mathcal{A}$ as $Adv_{\mathcal{A}} = |Pr[b = b'] - \frac{1}{2}|$.

Recovery. An AIBEIR scheme is recoverable if Recover algorithm can always extract the right identity from a valid ciphertext and output $\perp$ when the input is an invalid ciphertext.

Definition 4. *An AIBEIR scheme is recoverable if there does not exist any PPT adversary $\mathcal{A}$ who wins the following game with non-negligible probability.*

Setup: The challenger takes as input a security parameter 1^{λ} and runs the Setup algorithm of the AIBEIR. It provides $\mathcal{A}$ with the system parameters mpk while keeping the master secret key msk and sk_{IRM} to itself.

Monitor Phase: The adversary $\mathcal{A}$ can query recover oracle and key-extraction oracle.

Challenge: When $\mathcal{A}$ decides that Monitor Phase is complete, the adversary sends c^* to the challenger. The challenger sends the output of Recover algorithm to $\mathcal{A}$.

Output: $\mathcal{A}$ wins the game if the output of $\mathsf{Recover}(c^*, sk_{IRM})$ is $\perp$ or id while c^* is a valid ciphertext under $id^{'}$ where $id \neq id^{'}$ or the output of $\mathsf{Recover}(c^*, sk_{IRM})$ is id while c^* is not a valid ciphertext. Here we require id has not been asked as a key-extraction query for the need to prove the security.

4 A Construction from Anonymous IBE and Testable IBE

In this section, we present our construction of AIBEIR from anonymous IBE and testable IBE. Let $\Pi_1 =$ (A-IBE.Setup, A-IBE.Enc, A-IBE.Dec, A-IBE.Extract) be an anonymous IBE scheme, $\Pi_2 =$ (T-IBE.Setup, T-IBE.Enc, T-IBE.Dec, T-IBE.Extract, T-IBE.Test) be a testable IBE scheme. Let id_ϵ denote the identity of the identity recovery manager in scheme Π_2. Then, we can construct an AIBEIR scheme Π as follows:

4.1 The Construction

We describe our AIBEIR scheme (AIBEIR.Setup, AIBEIR.Extract, AIBEIR.Enc -rypt, AIBEIR.Decrypt, AIBEIR.Recover) as follows:

- $\mathsf{Setup}(1^\lambda)$: Run the Setup algorithms of A-IBE and T-IBE and obtain $(MPK_A, MSK_A) \leftarrow \mathsf{A\text{-}IBE.Setup}(1^\lambda)$, $(MPK_T, MSK_T) \leftarrow \mathsf{T\text{-}IBE.Setup}(1^\lambda)$, respectively. Compute $SK_{T,id_\epsilon} = \mathsf{T\text{-}IBE.Extract}(MSK_T, id_\epsilon)$. $(mpk, msk) = ((MPK_A, MPK_T), (MSK_A, MSK_T))$, $sk_{IRM} = (MSK_A, SK_{T,id_\epsilon})$.
- $\mathsf{Extract}(id, msk)$: Run the Extract algorithms of A-IBE and T-IBE and obtain $SK_{A,id} = \mathsf{A\text{-}IBE.Extract}(id, MSK_A)$ and $SK_{T,id} = \mathsf{T\text{-}IBE.Extract}(id, MSK_T)$, respectively. Output $sk_{id} = (SK_{A,id}, SK_{T,id})$.
- $\mathsf{Encrypt}(m, id, mpk)$: Run the Encrypt algorithms of A-IBE and T-IBE and obtain $(c_0, c_1) = \mathsf{T\text{-}IBE.Enc}(m, id, MPK_T)$, $c_2 = \mathsf{A\text{-}IBE.Enc}(c_0, id, MPK_A)$ and $c_3 = \mathsf{T\text{-}IBE.Enc}(id, id_\epsilon, MPK_T)$. Output $c = (c_1, c_2, c_3)$.
- $\mathsf{Decrypt}(mpk, c, sk_{id})$: Parse c as c_1, c_2 and c_3. Then compute $c_0 = \mathsf{A\text{-}IBE.Dec}(c_2, SK_{A,id})$, $m = \mathsf{T\text{-}IBE.Dec}(c_0||c_1, SK_{T,id})$.
- $\mathsf{Recover}(c, sk_{IRM})$: Parse c as c_1, c_2 and c_3. Parse sk_{IRM} as MSK_A and SK_{T,id_ϵ}. Then compute $id = \mathsf{T\text{-}IBE.Dec}(c_3, SK_{T,id_\epsilon})$ and $SK_{A,id} = \mathsf{A\text{-}IBE.Extract}(id, MSK_A)$. Take as input $SK_{A,id}$ and c_2, obtain the cipertext c_0 by running the Decrypt algorithm of $\mathsf{A\text{-}IBE.Dec}(SK_{A,id}, c_2)$. Finally, output id if $\mathsf{T\text{-}IBE.Test}(id, c_0) = 1$, and $\perp$ otherwise.

Remark 1. *Here the message space of Π_1 includes the ciphertext space of Π_2. We set the intersection of identity space of Π_1 and Π_2 as the identity space of Π.*

4.2 Correctness

Theorem 1. *If Π_1 is a correct anonymous IBE scheme and Π_2 is a correct testable IBE scheme then Π is a correct AIBEIR scheme.*

- **Decryption correctness:** The decryption correctness is guaranteed by the decryption correctness of Π_1 and Π_2.
- **Recovery correctness:** The recovery correctness is guaranteed by the decryption correctness of Π_1, Π_2 and test correctness of Π_2.

4.3 Anonymity

Theorem 2. *If Π_1 is an IBE scheme which is anonymous against adaptively chosen-identity and chosen-plaintext attacks and Π_2 is a testable IBE scheme which is fully secure against chosen-identity and chosen-plaintext attacks, then Π is an AIBEIR scheme which is anonymous against adaptively chosen-identity and chosen-plaintext attacks.*[2]

Proof. We prove the above theorem by hybrid arguments.

$\mathcal{H}_0$: This hybrid is the real experiment in the Definition 1. The logic of the challenger is shown as follows:
initialization:

$$(MPK_A, MSK_A) \leftarrow \text{A-IBE.Setup}(1^\lambda),\ (MPK_T, MSK_T) \leftarrow \text{T-IBE.Setup}(1^\lambda)$$
$$(mpk, msk) = ((MPK_A, MPK_T), (MSK_A, MSK_T))$$
$$SK_{T,id_\epsilon} = \text{T-IBE.Extract}(MSK_T, id_\epsilon),\ sk_{IRM} = (MSK_A, SK_{T,id_\epsilon})$$

send mpk to $\mathcal{A}$

upon receiving a secret key query(id):

$$SK_{A,id} = \text{A-IBE.Extract}(id, MSK_A) \text{ and } SK_{T,id} = \text{T-IBE.Extract}(id, MSK_T)$$

send $sk_{id} = (SK_{A,id}, SK_{T,id})$ to $\mathcal{A}$

upon receiving the challenge query (m_0, m_1, id_0, id_1):

$b \xleftarrow{\$} \{0,1\}$, $\gamma \xleftarrow{\$} \{0,1\}$,

(1) $(c_0, c_1) = \text{T-IBE.Enc}(m_b, id_\gamma, MPK_T)$
(2) $c_2 = \text{A-IBE.Enc}(c_0, id_\gamma, MPK_A)$
(3) $c_3 = \text{T-IBE.Enc}(id_\gamma, id_\epsilon, MPK_T)$
send $c = (c_1, c_2, c_3)$ to $\mathcal{A}$.

$\mathcal{H}_1$: In this hybrid, it is identical to $\mathcal{H}_0$ except that we just change how the challenge ciphertext is generated. We replace the lines marked (1) in $\mathcal{H}_0$ as follows:

$$c_0, c_1 = \text{T-IBE.Enc}(\mathbf{0}, id_\gamma, MPK_T)^3.$$

[2] Here the adversary can not be the identity recovery manager and has PPT power.
[3] Here $\mathbf{0}$ has the same length with m_0 and m_1.

$\mathcal{H}_2$: Compared to $\mathcal{H}_1$, we replace the lines marked (2) in $\mathcal{H}_0$ as follows:

$c_2 = \text{A-IBE.Enc}(\mathbf{0}, id_\gamma, MPK_A)^4$.

$\mathcal{H}_3$: Same as $\mathcal{H}_2$, except we replace the lines marked (2) in $\mathcal{H}_0$ as follows:

We just randomly choose id from identity space except id_0 and id_1. We then set $c_2 = \text{A-IBE.Enc}(\mathbf{0}, id, MPK_A)$.

$\mathcal{H}_4$: Identical to $\mathcal{H}_3$, except we replace the lines marked (3) in $\mathcal{H}_0$ as follows:

We just set c_3 as $\text{T-IBE.Enc}(\mathbf{0}, id_\epsilon, MPK_T)^5$.

It is easy to know that the challenge ciphertext in $\mathcal{H}_4$ contains no information about b and γ. So the advantage of $\mathcal{A}$ in $\mathcal{H}_4$ is $\frac{1}{4}$. We prove the above theorem by showing that $\mathcal{H}_0 \approx \mathcal{H}_1 \approx \mathcal{H}_2 \approx \mathcal{H}_3 \approx \mathcal{H}_4$ through the following lemmas.

Lemma 1. *Any PPT adversary cannot distinguish $\mathcal{H}_0$ and $\mathcal{H}_1$, if scheme Π_2 is fully secure against adaptively chosen-identity and chosen-plaintext attacks.*

Proof. We can construct a simulator $\mathcal{B}$ to break the full security against chosen-identity and chosen-plaintext attacks of scheme Π_2, if there is an adversary $\mathcal{A}$ who can distinguish $\mathcal{H}_0$ and $\mathcal{H}_1$.

Setup: The challenger takes as input a security parameter 1^λ and runs the Setup algorithm of Π_2. It provides $\mathcal{B}$ with the system parameters MPK_T while keeping the master secret key MSK_T to itself. $\mathcal{B}$ computes $(MPK_A, MSK_A) \leftarrow \text{A-IBE.Setup}(1^\lambda)$, and sends $MPK = (MPK_A, MPK_T)$ to $\mathcal{A}$.

Phase 1: When the adversary $\mathcal{A}$ makes key-extraction query and sends an identity id to $\mathcal{B}$, $\mathcal{B}$ just forwards it as the key-extraction query to the challenger. The challenger sends $SK_{T,id}$ to $\mathcal{B}$. $\mathcal{B}$ computes $SK_{A,id} = \text{A-IBE.Extract}(id, MSK_A)$ and sends $sk_{id} = (SK_{A,id}, SK_{T,id})$ to $\mathcal{A}$.

Challenge: $\mathcal{A}$ chooses id_0 and id_1 under the constraint that they have not been asked for the private keys and two equal-length messages m_0, m_1 and sends them to $\mathcal{B}$. $\mathcal{B}$ just chooses randomly two bits b and γ and sends $(m_b, \mathbf{0}, id_\gamma)$ to the challenger. The challenger chooses uniformly at random a bit b' and sends $c_0, c_1 = \text{T-IBE.Enc}(m, id_\gamma, MPK_T)$ to $\mathcal{B}$. If $b' = 0$, $m = m_b$. If $b' = 1$, $m = \mathbf{0}$. $\mathcal{B}$ obtains c_2, c_3 by running $\text{A-IBE.Enc}(c_0, id_\gamma, MPK_A)$ and $\text{T-IBE.Enc}(id_\gamma, id_\epsilon, MPK_T)$ respectively. $\mathcal{B}$ just sends $c^* = (c_1, c_2, c_3)$ to $\mathcal{A}$.

Phase 2: $\mathcal{A}$ makes key-extraction queries except id_0, id_1. $\mathcal{B}$ answers queries just like Phase 1.

Guess: $\mathcal{A}$ sends a bit $\bar{b}$ as a guess of $\mathcal{H}_{\bar{b}}$ to $\mathcal{B}$. $\mathcal{B}$ just forwards it to the challenger.

The view of $\mathcal{A}$ is identical to $\mathcal{H}_0$ if $b' = 0$ and to $\mathcal{H}_1$ if $b' = 1$. Thus, by the semantic security of scheme Π_2, we can conclude that $\mathcal{H}_0 \approx \mathcal{H}_1$.

[4] Here $\mathbf{0}$ has the same length with c_0.

[5] Here $\mathbf{0}$ has the same length with id_γ.

Lemma 2. *Any PPT adversary cannot distinguish $\mathcal{H}_1$ and $\mathcal{H}_2$, if scheme Π_1 is anonymous against adaptive-identity, chosen-plaintext attacks.*

Proof. Given a PPT adversary $\mathcal{A}$ who can distinguish $\mathcal{H}_1$ and $\mathcal{H}_2$, we can construct a simulator $\mathcal{B}$ attacking the anonymous security of Π_1 against adaptive-identity, chosen-plaintext attacks.

Setup: The challenger takes as input a security parameter 1^λ and runs the Setup algorithm of Π_1. It provides $\mathcal{B}$ with the system parameters MPK_A while keeping the master secret key MSK_A to itself. $\mathcal{B}$ computes $(MPK_T, MSK_T) \leftarrow$ T-IBE.Setup(1^λ), and sends $MPK = (MPK_A, MPK_T)$ to $\mathcal{A}$.

Phase 1: When $\mathcal{A}$ makes key-extraction query and sends an identity id to $\mathcal{B}$, $\mathcal{B}$ just forwards id as the key-extraction query to the challenger. The challenger sends $SK_{A,id}$ to $\mathcal{B}$. $\mathcal{B}$ runs $SK_{T,id} = \text{T-IBE.Extract}(id, MSK_T)$ and sends $sk_{id} = (SK_{A,id}, SK_{T,id})$ to $\mathcal{A}$.

Challenge: $\mathcal{A}$ chooses two equal-length plaintexts m_0, m_1 and two identities id_0, id_1 under the constraint that they have not been asked for the private keys and sends them to $\mathcal{B}$. $\mathcal{B}$ chooses uniformly at random a bit $\gamma' \in \{0,1\}$ and computes $c_0, c_1 = \text{T-IBE.Enc}(\mathbf{0}, id_{\gamma'}, MPK_T), c_3 = \text{T-IBE.Enc}(id_{\gamma'}, id_\epsilon, MPK_T)$. $\mathcal{B}$ sends $(c_0, \mathbf{0}, id_{\gamma'}, id_{\gamma'})$ to the challenger. The challenger chooses uniformly at random a bit γ and a bit b. If $b = 0$, the challenger sends $c_2 = \text{A-IBE.Enc}(c_0, id_{\gamma'}, MPK_A)$ to $\mathcal{B}$. If $b = 1$, the challenger sends $c_2 = \text{A-IBE.Enc}(\mathbf{0}, id_{\gamma'}, MPK_A)$ to $\mathcal{B}$. $\mathcal{B}$ sends (c_1, c_2, c_3) to $\mathcal{A}$.

Phase 2: $\mathcal{B}$ answers queries just like Phase 1, but id_0 and id_1 cannot be queried.

Guess: $\mathcal{A}$ sends a bit $\bar{b}$ as a guess of $\mathcal{H}_{\bar{b}+1}$ to $\mathcal{B}$. $\mathcal{B}$ randomly choose a bit γ and sends $\bar{b}$ and γ to the challenger.

If $b = 0$, the view of $\mathcal{A}$ is identical to $\mathcal{H}_1$. If $b = 1$, the view of $\mathcal{A}$ is identical to $\mathcal{H}_2$. We can see that $\mathcal{H}_1 \approx \mathcal{H}_2$ by the anonymity of Π_1.

Lemma 3. *Any PPT adversary cannot distinguish $\mathcal{H}_2$ and $\mathcal{H}_3$, if scheme Π_1 is anonymous secure against adaptively chosen-identity, chosen-plaintext attacks.*

Proof. Given a PPT adversary $\mathcal{A}$ who can distinguish $\mathcal{H}_2$ and $\mathcal{H}_3$, we can construct a simulator $\mathcal{B}$ attacking the anonymous security of Π_1 against adaptively chosen-identity, chosen-plaintext attacks.

Setup: The challenger takes as input a security parameter 1^λ and runs the Setup algorithm of Π_1. It provides $\mathcal{B}$ with the system parameters MPK_A while keeping the master secret key MSK_A to itself. $\mathcal{B}$ computes $(MPK_T, MSK_T) \leftarrow$ T-IBE.Setup(1^λ), and sends $mpk = (MPK_A, MPK_T)$ to $\mathcal{A}$.

Phase 1: When the adversary $\mathcal{A}$ makes key-extraction query and sends an identity id to $\mathcal{B}$, $\mathcal{B}$ just forwards id as the key-extraction query to the challenger. The challenger sends $SK_{A,id}$ to $\mathcal{B}$. $\mathcal{B}$ obtains $SK_{T,id} = \text{T-IBE.Extract}(id, MSK_T)$ and sends $sk_{id} = (SK_{A,id}, SK_{T,id})$ to $\mathcal{A}$.

Challenge: $\mathcal{A}$ chooses two equal-length plaintexts m_0, m_1 and two identities id_0, id_1 under the constraint that they have not been asked for the private keys and sends them to $\mathcal{B}$. $\mathcal{B}$ chooses uniformly at random a bit $\gamma' \in \{0,1\}$ and computes $c_0, c_1 = \mathsf{T\text{-}IBE.Enc}(\mathbf{0}, id_{\gamma'}, MPK_T)$, $c_3 = \mathsf{T\text{-}IBE.Enc}(id_{\gamma'}, id_\epsilon, MPK_T)$. $\mathcal{B}$ randomly chooses an identity id from identity space except id_0, id_1 and sends $(\mathbf{0}, \mathbf{0}, id_{\gamma'}, id)$ to the challenger. The challenger chooses uniformly at random a bit γ and a bit b. If $\gamma = 0$, the challenger sends $c_2 = \mathsf{A\text{-}IBE.Enc}(\mathbf{0}, id_{\gamma'}, MPK_A)$ to$\mathcal{B}$. If $\gamma = 1$, the challenger sends $c_2 = \mathsf{A\text{-}IBE.Enc}(\mathbf{0}, id, MPK_A)$ to $\mathcal{B}$. $\mathcal{B}$ sends (c_1, c_2, c_3) to $\mathcal{A}$.

Phase 2: $\mathcal{B}$ answers queries just like Phase 1, but id_0 and id_1 cannot be asked.
Guess: $\mathcal{A}$ sends a bit $\bar{\gamma}$ as a guess of $\mathcal{H}_{\bar{\gamma}+2}$ to $\mathcal{B}$. $\mathcal{B}$ randomly choose a bit $\bar{b}$ and sends $\bar{\gamma}$ and $\bar{b}$ to the challenger.

If $\gamma = 0$, the view of $\mathcal{A}$ is identical in $\mathcal{H}_2$. If $\gamma = 1$, the view of $\mathcal{A}$ is identical in $\mathcal{H}_3$. The probability that $\mathcal{A}$ can distinguish $\mathcal{H}_2$ and $\mathcal{H}_3$ equals $|Pr[\bar{\gamma} = \gamma] - \frac{1}{2}| = |2(\frac{1}{4} + \mathsf{negl(n)} - \frac{1}{2}|) = \mathsf{negl(n)}$ because of the anonymity of Π_1. So the conclusion is that $\mathcal{H}_2 \approx \mathcal{H}_3$.

Lemma 4. *Any PPT adversary cannot distinguish $\mathcal{H}_3$ and $\mathcal{H}_4$, if scheme Π_2 is secure against chosen-identity and chosen-plaintext attacks.*

Proof. Given a PPT adversary $\mathcal{A}$ which can distinguish $\mathcal{H}_3$ and $\mathcal{H}_4$, we can construct a simulator $\mathcal{B}$ attacking the semantic security of Π_2 against chosen-identity and chosen-plaintext attacks.

Setup: The challenger takes as input a security parameter 1^λ and runs the Setup algorithm of Π_2 and obtains (MPK_T, MSK_T). It sends MPK_T to $\mathcal{B}$ and keeps MSK_T to itself. $\mathcal{B}$ computes $(MPK_A, MSK_A) \leftarrow \mathsf{A\text{-}IBE.Setup}(1^\lambda)$ and sends $mpk = (MPK_A, MPK_T)$ to $\mathcal{A}$.

Phase 1: When the adversary $\mathcal{A}$ makes key-extraction query and sends an identity id to $\mathcal{B}$, $\mathcal{B}$ just forwards it as the key-extraction query to the challenger. The challenger sends $MSK_{T,id}$ to $\mathcal{B}$. $\mathcal{B}$ computes $SK_{A,id} = \mathsf{A\text{-}IBE.Extract}(id, MSK_A)$ and sends $sk_{id} = (SK_{A,id}, SK_{T,id})$ to $\mathcal{A}$.

Challenge: $\mathcal{A}$ chooses two equal-length plaintexts m_0, m_1 and two identities id_0, id_1 under the constraint that they have not been asked for the private keys and sends them to $\mathcal{B}$. $\mathcal{B}$ chooses uniformly at random a bit $\gamma \in \{0,1\}$ and computes $c_0, c_1 = \mathsf{T\text{-}IBE.Enc}(\mathbf{0}, id_\gamma, MPK_T)$. $\mathcal{B}$ randomly chooses an identity id from the identity space except id_0, id_1 and computes $c_2 = \mathsf{A\text{-}IBE.Enc}(\mathbf{0}, id, MPK_A)$. $\mathcal{B}$ sends $(id_\gamma, \mathbf{0}, id_\epsilon)$to the challenger. The challenger chooses uniformly at random a bit b and sends c_3 to $\mathcal{B}$. $c_3 = \mathsf{T\text{-}IBE.Enc}(id_\gamma, id_\epsilon, MPK_T)$, if $b = 0$. $c_3 = \text{T-IBE.Enc}(\mathbf{0}, id_\epsilon, MPK_T)$, if $b = 1$. $\mathcal{B}$ just sends $c^* = (c_1, c_2, c_3)$ to $\mathcal{A}$.

Phase 2: $\mathcal{A}$ makes key-extraction queries except id_0, id_1. $\mathcal{B}$ answers queries just like Phase 1.

The view of $\mathcal{A}$ is identical to $\mathcal{H}_3$ if $b = 0$, and $\mathcal{H}_4$ otherwise. The probability that the adversary can distinguish $\mathcal{H}_3$ and $\mathcal{H}_4$ equals the advantage of $\mathcal{B}$ breaking the semantic security of Π_2. So we can draw the conclusion that $\mathcal{H}_3 \approx \mathcal{H}_4$.

Having proved the above lemmas, we have completed the proof of Theorem 2.

4.4 Stronger Semantic Security

Theorem 3. *The AIBEIR scheme Π is strongly semantic secure if Π_2 is semantic secure against chosen-identity and chosen-plaintext attack.*

Proof. We can construct a simulator $\mathcal{B}$ breaking semantic security of Π_2 if there exists an adversary $\mathcal{A}$ breaking the stronger semantic security of Π.

Setup: The challenger takes as input a security parameter 1^λ and runs the Setup algorithm of Π_2 and obtains (MPK_T, MSK_T). It sends MPK_T to $\mathcal{B}$ and keeps MSK_T to itself. $\mathcal{B}$ computes $(MPK_A, MSK_A) \leftarrow \mathsf{A\text{-}IBE.Setup}(1^\lambda)$. $\mathcal{B}$ obtains SK_{T,id_ϵ} by making the secret key query of id_ϵ to the challenger and sends $mpk = (MPK_A, MPK_T)$ and $sk_{IRM} = (MSK_A, SK_{T,id_\epsilon})$ to $\mathcal{A}$.
Phase 1: When the adversary $\mathcal{A}$ makes key-extraction query and sends an identity id to $\mathcal{B}$, $\mathcal{B}$ just forwards it as the key-extraction query to the challenger. The challenger sends $MSK_{T,id}$ to $\mathcal{B}$. $\mathcal{B}$ computes $SK_{A,id} = \mathsf{A\text{-}IBE.Extract}(id, MSK_A)$ and sends $sk_{id} = (SK_{A,id}, SK_{T,id})$ to $\mathcal{A}$.

Challenge: $\mathcal{A}$ chooses two equal-length plaintexts m_0, m_1 and an identity id^* under the constraint that it has not been asked for the private key and sends them to $\mathcal{B}$. $\mathcal{B}$ just forwards (m_0, m_1, id^*) to the challenger. The challenger randomly chooses a bit b and sends $(c_0^*, c_1^*) = \mathsf{T\text{-}IBE.Enc}(m_b, id^*, MPK_T)$. $\mathcal{B}$ computes $c_2^* = \mathsf{A\text{-}IBE.Enc}(c_0^*, id^*, MPK_A)$, $c_3^* = \mathsf{T\text{-}IBE.Enc}(id^*, id_\epsilon, MPK_T)$ and sends $c^* = (c_1^*, c_2^*, c_3^*)$ to $\mathcal{A}$.
Phase 2: $\mathcal{A}$ makes key-extraction queries except id^*. $\mathcal{B}$ answers queries just like Phase 1.
Guess: $\mathcal{B}$ just forwards the output of $\mathcal{A}$ to the challenger.

If $\mathcal{A}$ wins, we can see $\mathcal{A}$ as a distinguish oracle. When $\mathcal{B}$ obtains the challenge ciphertext from challenger, $\mathcal{B}$ just encrypts it by the Encrypt algorithm of A-IBE and sends it to $\mathcal{A}$. We can see that the probability that $\mathcal{A}$ breaks the stronger semantic security equals the probability that $\mathcal{B}$ breaks the semantic security of Π_2.

4.5 Recovery

Theorem 4. *If the testable IBE scheme Π_2 is fully secure against adaptive-identity and chosen ciphertext attack, then the AIBEIR scheme Π satisfies recovery.*

Proof. If the adversary wins in the recovery experiment, there are two conditions: (1) the adversary outputs a valid AIBEIR ciphertext but the challenger output $\perp$ or a wrong identity. This will not happen, which is guaranteed by the correctness of Recover algorithm. (2) the adversary outputs an invalid AIBEIR ciphertext but the challenger does not output $\perp$. We just consider the case where (c_1, c_2, c_3) is a valid ciphertxt. In fact, if (c_1, c_2) is not a valid ciphertext, the receiver cannot decrypt correctly using its secret key. And if c_3 is not a valid T-IBE ciphertext under id_ϵ, challenger will output $\perp$.

If (c_1, c_2) is a valid ciphertext under id and c_3 is a testable IBE ciphertext of a different identity $\widehat{id}$ under id_ϵ, we can show that the identity recovery manager will return $\perp$ with overwhelming probability. In fact, if there exists a PPT adversary $\mathcal{A}$ who can fool the identity recovery manager in the recovery game, we can construct a simulator $\mathcal{S}$ attacking Π_2 in adaptive-identity, chosen-plaintext attack.

Setup: The challenger takes as input a security parameter 1^λ and runs the Setup algorithm of Π_2. It provides $\mathcal{B}$ with the system parameters MPK_T while keeping the master secret key MSK_T to itself. $\mathcal{B}$ computes $(MPK_A, MSK_A) \leftarrow$ A-IBE.Setup(1^λ) and sends $mpk = (MPK_A, MPK_T)$ to $\mathcal{A}$.

Phase 1: When the adversary $\mathcal{A}$ makes the key-extraction queries, $\mathcal{B}$ just forwards the identity queried by $\mathcal{A}$ to the challenger and obtains $SK_{T,id}$ from the challenger. $\mathcal{B}$ obtains $SK_{A,id} =$ A-IBE.Extract(id, MSK_A) and sends $sk_{id} = (SK_{A,id}, SK_{T,id})$ to $\mathcal{A}$. When $\mathcal{A}$ makes recover query, $\mathcal{B}$ gets SK_{T,id_ϵ} by making secret key query of id_ϵ to the challenger and obtains id by decrypting c_3 using SK_{T,id_ϵ}. $\mathcal{B}$ computes $SK_{A,id} =$ A-IBE.Extract(id, MSK_A) and then obtains c_0 by running Dec algorithm of A-IBE. $\mathcal{B}$ computes $h =$ T-IBE.Test(c_0, id), and sends id to $\mathcal{A}$ if $h = 1$, and $\perp$ otherwise. We say $\mathcal{A}$ wins if it outputs a valid "double encrypt" IBE ciphertext(*i.e.* c_1, c_2) under id_1 and a valid testable IBE ciphertext(*i.e.* c_3) of id_2 which pass the recover algorithm[6]($\mathcal{A}$ can output the randomness used in the encrypt algorithm to show it). Here we constrain that id_1 has not been queried the private key before. $\mathcal{B}$ obtains SK_{T,id_2} by making the secret key query of id_2.

Challenge: $\mathcal{B}$ randomly chooses two equal-length message m_0, m_1 and sends m_0, m_1 and id_1 to challenger. Challenger randomly chooses a bit $b \in \{0, 1\}$ and obtains $(c_0, c_1) =$ T-IBE.Enc(m_b, id_1, MPK_T).

Phase 2: $\mathcal{B}$ makes some queries to key-extraction oracle. In fact, $\mathcal{B}$ does not need to query now.

Guess: $\mathcal{B}$ computes $c_2 =$ A-IBE.Enc(c_0, id_1, MPK_A) and obtains c_0' which is a part of ciphertext under id_2 by decrypting c_2 using SK_{A,id_2}. Then $\mathcal{B}$ obtains m by decrypting c_0', c_1 using SK_{T,id_2}. $\mathcal{B}$ outputs 0 if $m = m_0$ and 1 otherwise.

5 Conclusion

We define a new primitive called AIBEIR and construct it using double encryption with an anonymous IBE and a testable IBE. AIBEIR is anonymous for all

[6] This means we can obtain a T-IBE ciphertext under id_2 by decrypting the "double-encrypt" ciphertext under id_1 using SK_{A,id_2}.

users except the identity recovery manager who can recover the identity from the ciphertext. But the identity recovery manager can not obtain information about plaintext from ciphertext even holding an identity recover secret key. To our knowledge, [BB04a, Wat05] and their variations satisfy our testable IBE definition. We leave as an open problem the question of constructing testable IBE from other standard assumptions, such as lattice. Another interesting area of research is to construct more practical AIBEIR schemes.

Acknowledgements. We would like to thank the anonymous reviewers of ACISP 2018 for their advice. Xuecheng Ma and Dongdai Lin are supported by the National Natural Science Foundation of China under Grant No. 61379139.

References

[ABB10] Agrawal, S., Boneh, D., Boyen, X.: Efficient lattice (H)IBE in the standard model. In: Gilbert, H. (ed.) EUROCRYPT 2010. LNCS, vol. 6110, pp. 553–572. Springer, Heidelberg (2010). https://doi.org/10.1007/978-3-642-13190-5_28

[AG09] Ateniese, G., Gasti, P.: Universally anonymous IBE based on the quadratic residuosity assumption. In: Fischlin, M. (ed.) CT-RSA 2009. LNCS, vol. 5473, pp. 32–47. Springer, Heidelberg (2009). https://doi.org/10.1007/978-3-642-00862-7_3

[BB04a] Boneh, D., Boyen, X.: Efficient selective-ID secure identity-based encryption without random oracles. In: Cachin, C., Camenisch, J.L. (eds.) EUROCRYPT 2004. LNCS, vol. 3027, pp. 223–238. Springer, Heidelberg (2004). https://doi.org/10.1007/978-3-540-24676-3_14

[BB04b] Boneh, D., Boyen, X.: Secure identity based encryption without random oracles. In: Franklin, M. (ed.) CRYPTO 2004. LNCS, vol. 3152, pp. 443–459. Springer, Heidelberg (2004). https://doi.org/10.1007/978-3-540-28628-8_27

[BBDP01] Bellare, M., Boldyreva, A., Desai, A., Pointcheval, D.: Key-privacy in public-key encryption. In: Boyd, C. (ed.) ASIACRYPT 2001. LNCS, vol. 2248, pp. 566–582. Springer, Heidelberg (2001). https://doi.org/10.1007/3-540-45682-1_33

[BF01] Boneh, D., Franklin, M.: Identity-based encryption from the Weil pairing. In: Kilian, J. (ed.) CRYPTO 2001. LNCS, vol. 2139, pp. 213–229. Springer, Heidelberg (2001). https://doi.org/10.1007/3-540-44647-8_13

[BGH07] Boneh, D., Gentry, C., Hamburg, M.: Space-efficient identity based encryption without pairings. IACR Cryptology ePrint Archive 2007, 177 (2007)

[BLSV17] Brakerski, Z., Lombardi, A., Segev, G., Vaikuntanathan, V.: Anonymous IBE, leakage resilience and circular security from new assumptions. IACR Cryptology ePrint Archive 2017, 967 (2017)

[Boy03] Boyen, X.: Multipurpose identity-based signcryption. In: Boneh, D. (ed.) CRYPTO 2003. LNCS, vol. 2729, pp. 383–399. Springer, Heidelberg (2003). https://doi.org/10.1007/978-3-540-45146-4_23

[Boy10] Boyen, X.: Lattice mixing and vanishing trapdoors: a framework for fully secure short signatures and more. In: Nguyen, P.Q., Pointcheval, D. (eds.) PKC 2010. LNCS, vol. 6056, pp. 499–517. Springer, Heidelberg (2010). https://doi.org/10.1007/978-3-642-13013-7_29

[CHKP10] Cash, D., Hofheinz, D., Kiltz, E., Peikert, C.: Bonsai trees, or how to delegate a lattice basis. In: Gilbert, H. (ed.) EUROCRYPT 2010. LNCS, vol. 6110, pp. 523–552. Springer, Heidelberg (2010). https://doi.org/10.1007/978-3-642-13190-5_27

[Coc01] Cocks, C.: An identity based encryption scheme based on quadratic residues. In: Honary, B. (ed.) Cryptography and Coding 2001. LNCS, vol. 2260, pp. 360–363. Springer, Heidelberg (2001). https://doi.org/10.1007/3-540-45325-3_32

[DG17] Döttling, N., Garg, S.: Identity-based encryption from the Diffie-Hellman assumption. In: Katz, J., Shacham, H. (eds.) CRYPTO 2017. LNCS, vol. 10401, pp. 537–569. Springer, Cham (2017). https://doi.org/10.1007/978-3-319-63688-7_18

[DH76] Diffie, W., Hellman, M.E.: New directions in cryptography. IEEE Trans. Inf. Theory **22**(6), 644–654 (1976)

[Gen06] Gentry, C.: Practical identity-based encryption without random oracles. In: Vaudenay, S. (ed.) EUROCRYPT 2006. LNCS, vol. 4004, pp. 445–464. Springer, Heidelberg (2006). https://doi.org/10.1007/11761679_27

[GPV08] Gentry, C., Peikert, C., Vaikuntanathan, V.: Trapdoors for hard lattices and new cryptographic constructions. In: Proceedings of the 40th Annual ACM Symposium on Theory of Computing, Victoria, British Columbia, Canada, 17–20 May 2008, pp. 197–206 (2008)

[GSRD17] Gupta, K., Selvi, S.S.D., Rangan, C.P., Dighe, S.S.: Identity-based group encryption revisited. In: Qing, S., Mitchell, C., Chen, L., Liu, D. (eds.) ICICS 2017. LNCS, vol. 10631, pp. 205–209. Springer, Cham (2018). https://doi.org/10.1007/978-3-319-89500-0_18

[LRL+16] Luo, X., Ren, Y., Liu, J., Hu, J., Liu, W., Wang, Z., Xu, W., Wu, Q.: Identity-based group encryption. In: Liu, J.K., Steinfeld, R. (eds.) ACISP 2016. LNCS, vol. 9723, pp. 87–102. Springer, Cham (2016). https://doi.org/10.1007/978-3-319-40367-0_6

[Sha84] Shamir, A.: Identity-based cryptosystems and signature schemes. In: Blakley, G.R., Chaum, D. (eds.) CRYPTO 1984. LNCS, vol. 196, pp. 47–53. Springer, Heidelberg (1985). https://doi.org/10.1007/3-540-39568-7_5

[SOK00] Sakai, R., Ohgishi, K., Kasahara, M.: Cryptosystem based on pairings, January 2000

[Wat05] Waters, B.: Efficient identity-based encryption without random oracles. In: Cramer, R. (ed.) EUROCRYPT 2005. LNCS, vol. 3494, pp. 114–127. Springer, Heidelberg (2005). https://doi.org/10.1007/11426639_7

[Wat09] Waters, B.: Dual system encryption: realizing fully secure IBE and HIBE under simple assumptions. In: Halevi, S. (ed.) CRYPTO 2009. LNCS, vol. 5677, pp. 619–636. Springer, Heidelberg (2009). https://doi.org/10.1007/978-3-642-03356-8_36

Asymmetric Subversion Attacks on Signature Schemes

Chi Liu, Rongmao Chen(✉), Yi Wang, and Yongjun Wang(✉)

College of Computer, National University of Defense Technology, Changsha, China
{liuchi16,chromao,wangyi14,wangyongjun}@nudt.edu.cn

Abstract. Subversion attacks against cryptosystems have already received wide attentions since several decades ago, while the Snowden revelations in 2013 reemphasized the need to further exploring potential avenues for undermining the cryptography in practice. In this work, inspired by the kleptographic attacks introduced by Young and Yung in 1990s [Crypto'96], we initiate a formal study of asymmetric subversion attacks against signature schemes. Our contributions can be summarized as follows.

- We provide a formal definition of asymmetric subversion model for signature schemes. Our asymmetric model improves the existing symmetric subversion model proposed by Ateniese, Magri and Venturi [CCS'15] in the sense that the undetectability is strengthened and the signing key recoverability is defined as a strong subversion attack goal.
- We introduce a special type of signature schemes that are splittable and show how to universally mount the subversion attack against such signature schemes in the asymmetric subversion model. Compared with the symmetric attacks introduced by Ateniese, Magri and Venturi [CCS'15], our proposed attack enables much more efficient key recovery that is independent of the signing key size.

Our asymmetric subversion framework is somewhat conceptually simple but well demonstrates that subversion attacks against signature schemes could be quite practical, and thus increases awareness and spurs the search for deterrents.

Keywords: Asymmetric subversion attacks · Splittable signature
Undetectability · Key recovery

1 Introduction

Cryptography has been widely considered as a useful tool to modern information security. However, the revelations of Edward Snowden demonstrated [1–3] that this is not always the case. Precisely, cryptography in practice may be surreptitiously weakened by inserting backdoors into the security system. As these backdoors could make the system far less secure as thought and even completely

W. Susilo and G. Yang (Eds.): ACISP 2018, LNCS 10946, pp. 376–395, 2018.
https://doi.org/10.1007/978-3-319-93638-3_22

broken, the system user's secret communications may become accessible to the attacker who inserts the backdoor. What is worse, due to the extreme complexity of modern cryptographic implementation, these backdoors are difficult to be detected for even cryptographic experts and thus distinctly transparent to the typical user. Inspired by this issue, a new research direction known as Post-Snowden cryptography has arisen in recent years with the aim of safeguarding user privacy in face of possibly subverted cryptographic systems in the real world.

Subversion attacks against the cryptographic systems have already received wide attentions since several decades ago [4–9], while the Snowden revelations in 2013 reemphasized the need to further exploring potential avenues for, and defenses against, undermining the cryptography in practice. In particular, subversion attacks have been formally studied in the context of various cryptographic primitives. In 2013, Bellare *et al.* initiated the study of algorithm substitution attack (ASA) against symmetric encryption where the backdoor is embedded in a symmetric manner [10]. A stateful subversion attack namely biased ciphertext attack is proposed against all randomized encryption schemes that are coin-injective. As a countermeasure, they showed how to construct unique ciphertext schemes that are deterministic and thus subversion-resilient. To make the previous subversion attack stateless and applicable to all randomized schemes, Bellare *et al.* presented a stateless ASA that breaks all randomized symmetric encryption [11].

Regarding digital signature schemes, Ateniese *et al.* provided a formal treatment to the security of signatures against subversion attacks [12]. They showed how to mount symmetric subversion attacks on coin-injective schemes and coin-extractable schemes respectively. To defend such attacks, unique signature schemes are proposed and shown secure against certain subversion attacks that are of verifiability condition. They also illustrated that any re-randomizable signature scheme equipped with an un-tramperable cryptographic reverse firewall of self-destruct capability [20] is resilient against arbitrary subversion attacks. As depicted by Ateniese *et al.* [12], the central idea of their biased-randomness attack against coin-injective signature schemes essentially shares the spirit of the work by Bellare *et al.* [10]. That is, an attacker embeds a trapdoor key of a pseudorandom function in the subverted signing algorithm so that upon signing a message, the randomness is biased in a way that the produced signature under the signing key *sk* leaks one bit of *sk* to the attacker. Precisely, the one-bit output of the keyed pseudorandom function that takes the *i*-th signature as input is exactly the *i*-th bit of the signing key *sk*. Therefore, after obtaining signatures of number $|sk|$, the attacker is able to recover the whole signing key and thus breaks the signature scheme.

Motivations of This Work. One can note that the aforementioned subversion attack is stateful as the subverted signature algorithm needs to maintain a state of logarithmic size to represent which bit of the signing key is to be exfiltrated when signing a new message. Moreover, the subversion attack is symmetric, which means that anyone who knows the embedded trapdoor key could recover the signing key after obtaining enough number of signatures. We insist that such a stateful symmetric subversion attack may be undesirable or less attractive to attackers in the real world due to the following reasons.

- As already indicated by the authors [12], maintaining state might be a strong assumption, since original signature scheme is typically stateless. Moreover, a state reset (e.g., a system reboot) would render the attack detectable [11].
- In order to recover the whole signing key correctly, the attacker needs to successfully capture all sequential signatures (of number $|sk|$) in the correct order. This seems impractical, since collecting all signatures sequentially is quite a strong requirement. In particular, the recovered signing key would be incorrect once the state maintained by the attacker is not fully consistent with the subverted algorithm.
- Another drawback of the aforementioned attack in our view is that obtaining the symmetric subversion key would enable anyone, not only the attacker, to break the signature scheme that are embedded with the same subversion key. In fact, a code inverse analyst can easily recover the trapdoor key and thereafter becomes able to break all subverted signature schemes in the same way as the attacker does. In another aspect, such a code inverse analyse also renders the attack detectable.

Motivated by the aforementioned limitations of the state-of-the-art subversion attacks on signature schemes, we ask the following question in this work.

How to mount subversion attacks on signature schemes in such a way that, (1) the subverted signing algorithm is stateless, (2) the required signature number for recovering the whole signing key is constant, and (3) the attack is undetectable even with the subversion key?

We believe that subversion attacks meeting such three properties are more practical and attractive in the reality. The property (2) means that the number of sequential signatures required to recover the whole signing key is independent of the signing key size, and the property (3) says that the subversion attack is asymmetric so that obtaining the embedded trapdoor key does not help detect the attack in any way. We claim that our intention is to further demonstrate the power of subversion attack in the reality and thus increase awareness and spur the search for effective countermeasures.

Remark. It is worth noting that in the work [12], the authors mentioned that their proposed biased-randomness attack could be made completely stateless under the assumption that the message space is polynomial and that the adversary can control the input messages, as in this case the input message could be meanwhile interpreted as the counter. However, such an assumption may be not reasonable in practice as the subverted signing algorithm is usually out of the attacker's control after it is deployed. Moreover, even the attacker can control the input message, it still remains unknown how to achieve the property (2) and (3). One may wonder that the work [11] by Bellare *et al.* may also provide a potential solution to achieve stateless attack. Indeed, the subversion attack could be made stateless by adapting the pseudorandom function defined in the work [11]. However, such a subversion attack still exfiltrates the signing key bit by bit and thus does not meet property (2). Property (3) does not hold either as the attack is still in a symmetric manner. We notice that Bellare *et al.* proposed the definition of asymmetric subversion attack in the work [10] but they did not show how to mount such an attack on the encryption schemes. In fact, they mentioned that it is an interesting open problem to extend their attacks to break randomized, stateless schemes in the asymmetric setting.

1.1 Overview of Our Contributions

In this work, we address the aforementioned problem via formally demonstrating that subversion attacks on signature schemes could be done better in some sense. Our central idea is essentially inspired by the kleptographic attacks proposed by Young and Yung [7] in 1990s. Following the line of recent works on subversion attacks against various cryptographic primitives [10–12], our work could be also viewed as a modern taken of Young and Yung's kleptographic attacks against signature schemes in the context of subversion attacks.

Particularly, we propose a strong asymmetric subversion attack (AS-SA) against signature schemes that are of a certain form and rigorously prove that it is stateless and could effectively recover the whole signing key from only two successive signatures regardless of the signing key size. Before we describe our results, we briefly introduce the asymmetric subversion model for signatures.

Asymmetric Subversion Model for Signatures. Our first contribution is to introduce and formalize the asymmetric subversion model for signature schemes. It is worth mentioning that Ateniese *et al.* defined a symmetric subversion attack for signature schemes [12]. However, as discussed by Bellare *et al.* in [10], such a symmetric subversion model may not be desirable to the attacker as any reverse engineer who discovers the subversion key from a deployed subverted cryptosystem will has the same cryptographic ability as the attacker. To eliminate such a limitation, an asymmetric subversion model for symmetric encryption scheme was defined in [10]. In this work, we explore the asymmetric subversion model for signature schemes.

Our defined AS-SA model for signatures has the following features.

- *Asymmetric Subversion.* Unlike the existing symmetric subversion model for signatures where only a symmetric subversion key is involved [12], our defined AS-SA model considers a different attack where the attacker adopts a subversion key pair $(psk_{\mathcal{M}}, ssk_{\mathcal{M}})$. Particularly, the *public* subversion key $psk_{\mathcal{M}}$ is embedded in the subverted cryptosystem while the *secret* subversion key $ssk_{\mathcal{M}}$ is required for mounting a successful subversion attack. As mentioned above, such a subversion attack may be more desirable to the attacker in the real world as obtaining the embedded subversion key $psk_{\mathcal{M}}$ only does not provides others with the same cryptographic capabilities as the attacker.
- *Strong Secret Undetectability.* By undetectability, we mean that a normal user with the algorithm output cannot tell whether it is produced by the

subverted or the honest algorithm[1]. The work by Ateniese *et al.* [12] considers the notion of *secret undetectability* which means that the undetectability still holds for a strong detector who knows the underlying signing key. In this work, we consider a stronger detector who may has the knowledge of the public subversion key. Precisely, we further strengthen the model [12] via defining a stronger notion called *strong secret undetectability* which indicates that the subversion is undetectable to a strong detector who not only knows the underlying signing key but also reveals the public subversion key. We insist such a stronger notion is meaningful as in reality a detector could indeed possibly obtain the public subversion key (e.g., via code analysis).

- *Signing Key Recoverability.* The subversion model by Ateniese *et al.* [12] mainly considered two security notions namely *indistinguishability* and *impersonation under chosen-message attacks* for two different adversarial goals respectively. However, as mentioned by Bellare *et al.* in [10], such a notion is a strong measure for security but a weak one for attacks as achieving it provides high security, but violating it entails little loss. Therefore, similar to the work [11] which defined key recover for subversion against encryption, we also target and formalize key recovery in our proposed model for signature. Particularly, the key recovery notion is a strong goal of our defined AS-SA which means that a successful subversion attack should final recover the whole signing key.

Mounting AS-SA on Splittable Signatures. Our second contribution is to present a universal AS-SA on signatures of certain structure. We formally show that the proposed asymmetric subversion attack could be of both strong secret undetectability and effective key recovery as long as the signature structure falls within the framework of so-called *splittable* signature. Before describing the AS-SA, we briefly introduce the concept of splittable signature.

Splittable Signature. Roughly speaking, a signature σ is splittable if the signature consists of two separated components, i.e., $\sigma = (\sigma_R, \sigma_M)$ where σ_R is the *randomness-binded* component that is usually an encrypted form of the randomness (not necessarily decryptable) and σ_M is the message-binded component that contains the randomness, signing key and the message. Besides, a splittable signature scheme should meet the following properties.

- *Randomness Exchangeability.* This is mainly related to the randomness-binded component of the signature. Precisely, by randomness exchangeability, we mean that there exists an efficient randomness derivation algorithm namely RanDer that the output of RanDer taking as input σ_{R_1} (randomness-binded component of r_1) and another randomness r_2 equals to the output of RanDer taking as input σ_{R_2} (randomness-binded component of r_2) and r_1. However, given $(\sigma_{R_1}, \sigma_{R_2})$ only, one cannot compute the above value. We remark that such a property essentially implies a non-interactive key exchange where each party picks a randomness, exchanges its encrypted form, and finally derives a common secret key.

[1] In this work, *honest* algorithms are referred to as algorithms that are not subverted.

- *Secret Recoverability.* This is mainly related to the message-binded component of the signature. A signature is called secret recoverability if given the underlying randomness involved in randomness-binded component, one can derive the signing key from the corresponding message-binded component of the signature. As will be shown later, such a property is essential to the subversion attack proposed in this work. Particularly, the way to leak the signing key in our subversion attack is by revealing the randomness. More details will follow.

A Universal AS-SA on Splittable Signatures. We then present a universal AS-SA on splittable signature. Compared to the existing subversion attack against signatures [12], our attack is stateless[2] and only two signatures generated from two successive sessions are required for recovering the whole signing key regardless of its size. Below is an overview of our central idea.

As stated above, due to the *secret recoverability* of the splittable signature, one could easily recover the signing key if he knows the randomness involved in the message-binded component of the signature. In our attack, we propose an approach to enable the subverted signing algorithm to undetectably reveal the randomness used for the signature generation to the outside attacker. The main idea of our approach is to utilize the property of *randomness exchangeability*. Precisely, the attacker picks a randomness as the secret subversion key $ssk_{\mathcal{M}}$, and compute its randomness-binded component as the public subversion key $psk_{\mathcal{M}}$. The attacker inserts $psk_{\mathcal{M}}$ into the subverted algorithm and keeps $ssk_{\mathcal{M}}$ secretly. Suppose that r_i is the randomness used for the i-th subverted signing session ($i \geq 2$). The only difference between the subverted algorithm and the normal algorithm is the generation of the randomness when signing a new message. Instead of choosing the randomness randomly, the randomness r_i in the subverted algorithm is actually the hash value of the output of RanDer that takes $psk_{\mathcal{M}}$ and the randomness r_{i-1} as input. Due to the randomness exchangeability of the splittable signature, the attacker is able to recover r_i in a asymmetric way by running RanDer that takes the randomness-binded component of the i-1-th signature and $ssk_{\mathcal{M}}$as input, and outputs the hash value of the corresponding output.

One could note that our proposed attack admits very efficient key recovery as the attacker can derive the signing key with probability of almost 1 from two successive signatures. One may wonder whether storing the previous session's randomness is practical or not in the reality. We insist that the randomness r_{i-1} could be copied and stored in the machine's volatile memory and erased after i-th session execution completes. We also formally prove that such an attack is of strong secret undetectability in the random oracle model. That is, even with the public subversion key $psk_{\mathcal{M}}$ and the normal signing/verification key pair, the detector is still unable to figure out which algorithm is chosen as he does not

---

[2] Although the subverted algorithm needs to take as input the randomness used in the previous session, we insist that it is typically not an internal state that should be always maintained by the algorithm.

know either the randomness of the previous session or the secret subversion key $ssk_{\mathcal{M}}$ and thus the randomness of the current session is random from his view point.

Instantiations. To illustrate the feasibility of our universal framework of AS-SA on signatures, we demonstrate that many existing signature schemes indeed fall within our defined splittable structure. Particularly, all ElGamal-like signature schemes [13–16] and Waters signature scheme [17] belong to this type. Moreover, we also show that identity-based signatures such as Schnorr IBS [13], Paterson IBS [18], and Zhang's ID-Based Blind Signature (Schnorr type) [19] are also of splittable structure and thus are subject to our proposed attack.

Comparisons with Kleptographic Attacks Against Signatures [7]. The idea of asymmetric backdoor originally appeared in the filed of kleptography which was proposed by Young and Yung in the 1990s [7]. Particularly, they introduced the concept of secretly embedded tradpdoor with universal protection (SETUP) attack and mainly explored how to use public-key technique to launch such strong kleptographic attacks against various cryptographic primitives, such as RSA key generation, public-key encryption, Diffie-Hellman key exchange, signature schemes, and other cryptographic algorithms and protocols [7–9]. In this work, we purely focus on subversion attacks against signature schemes. To provide a more formal asymmetric subversion model for signature schemes, we explicitly define strong secret undetectability and signing key recoverability as two key properties of asymmetric attacks against signature schemes. These also form the basis of formal analysis of our proposed subversion attack framework. Additionally, our definition of splittable signature well illustrates the structure feature of signatures that inherently suffer from asymmetric subversion attacks, and thus provides a general principle for checking whether a signature scheme is subject to our proposed strong asymmetric subversion attack. In fact, instead of only focusing on typical signature schemes as in [9], in this work we additionally show that our proposed attack also works for identity-based signature schemes as long as they are of splittable structure.

Organization. Section 2 is about preliminaries, including notations, definitions about signature schemes. Then we introduce the model of AS-SA for signature schemes in Sect. 3. Definitions about splittable signature schemes are put forward and a universal AS-SA is also introduced with instantiations in Sect. 4. We discuss several countermeasures to achieve subversion resilience in Sect. 5, and draw a conclusion in Sect. 6.

2 Preliminaries

2.1 Notations

Here are some explanations of notations all over the paper. If $\mathcal{S}$ is a sample space then $x \xleftarrow{\$} \mathcal{S}$ denotes selecting a random element x from $\mathcal{S}$.

2.2 Cryptographic Hardness Assumptions

Computational Diffie-Hellman (CDH) Assumption. Let $\mathbb{G}$ be a group with prime order p and g is the generator. Given $g^a, g^b \in \mathbb{G}$ where $a, b \in \mathbb{Z}_p$, there is no polynomial time algorithm can compute g^{ab} with non-negligible probability.

Bilinear Diffie-Hellman (BDH) Assumption. Let $\mathbb{G}_1, \mathbb{G}_2$ be two groups of prime order p. Let $e : \mathbb{G}_1 \times \mathbb{G}_1 \rightarrow \mathbb{G}_2$ be an admissible bilinear map and let P be a generator of $\mathbb{G}_1$. Given P, aP, bP, cP for some $a, b, c \in \mathbb{Z}_p$, there is no polynomial time algorithm can compute $W = e(P, P)^{abc} \in \mathbb{G}_2$ with non-negligible probability.

2.3 Signature Schemes

A signature scheme Π includes a tuple of PPT (probabilistic polynomial-time) algorithms (KeyGen, Sign, Vrfy), which are defined as follows:

- KeyGen: takes as input a security parameter k and outputs a key pair (vk, sk), where vk is the verification key, and sk is the signing key.
- Sign: takes as input a signing key sk, and a message m, outputs a signature $\sigma \leftarrow \mathsf{Sign}(sk, m)$.
- Vrfy: takes as input a verification key vk, a message m and a signature σ. It outputs a bit b. If σ is a valid signature, b is equal to 1. On the contrary, b is equal to 0.

A signature scheme should satisfy the correctness condition which is defined as follows.

Definition 1 (Correctness). Let $\Pi = (\mathsf{KeyGen}, \mathsf{Sign}, \mathsf{Vrfy})$ be a signature scheme. We say that Π satisfies v_c*-correctness* if for all m:

$$\Pr[\mathsf{Vrfy}(vk, (m, \mathsf{Sign}(sk, m))) = 1 : (vk, sk) \leftarrow \mathsf{KeyGen}(1^k)] \geqslant 1 - v_c$$

where v_c is negligible.

A signature scheme is secure if there is no adversary who can forge the signature on a new message.

Definition 2 (Existential Unforgeability). Let $\Pi = (\mathsf{KeyGen}, \mathsf{Sign}, \mathsf{Vrfy})$ be a signature scheme. We say that Π is (t, q, ε)-existential unforgeable under chosen-message attacks (EUF-CMA) if for all PPT malicious adversaries $\mathcal{A}$ running in time t it holds:

$$\Pr[\mathsf{Vrfy}(vk, (m^*, \sigma^*)) = 1 \wedge m^* \notin \mathcal{T} : (vk, sk) \leftarrow \mathsf{KeyGen}(1^n);$$

$$(m^*, \sigma^*) \leftarrow \mathcal{A}^{\mathsf{Sign}(sk, \cdot)}(vk)] \leqslant \varepsilon$$

where $\mathcal{T} = \{m_1, \cdots, m_t\}$ denotes the set of queries to the signing oracle. ε is negligible, then we say Π is EUF-CMA.

3 Asymmetric Subversion Model for Signature Schemes

In this section, we formalize the concept of asymmetric subversion attack (AS-SA) and the asymmetric subversion model for signature schemes. We will first give an overview of the AS-SA and then formally describe its two key properties, namely *strong secret undetectability* and *signing key recoverability.*

3.1 An Overview

An asymmetric subversion attack (AS-SA) against signature schemes requires a public/private subversion key pair. Particularly, the public subversion key is embedded in the signing algorithms and the secret subversion key is hold by the attacker for recovering the signing key. Formally, via running $(vk_{\mathcal{V}}, sk_{\mathcal{V}}) \xleftarrow{\$}$ KeyGen, the user $\mathcal{V}$ gets his own verification key $vk_{\mathcal{V}}$ and signing key $sk_{\mathcal{V}}$. The subversion attacker $\mathcal{M}$ runs the subversion key generation algorithm $\widetilde{\mathsf{KeyGen}}$ and obtains the subversion key pair $(psk_{\mathcal{M}}, ssk_{\mathcal{M}})$. When signing a message m, the subverted signing algorithm $\widetilde{\mathsf{Sign}}$, takes the signing key $sk_{\mathcal{V}}$, the public subversion key $psk_{\mathcal{M}}$, and the message m as input and outputs a signature σ. Given the signature σ, the underlying message m and the secret subversion key $ssk_{\mathcal{M}}$, the goal of the attacker $\mathcal{M}$ is to recover the signing key $sk_{\mathcal{V}}$ via running algorithm Recv. The signature verification algorithm is the same as a normal one.

3.2 Strong Secret Undetectability

Let $\Pi = (\mathsf{KeyGen}, \mathsf{Sign}, \mathsf{Vrfy})$ be a signature scheme, and consider the following experiment $\mathsf{AS\text{-}SA}^{\mathsf{IND}}_{\mathcal{A},\Pi}(k)$ for a detector $\mathcal{A}$ (a normal user).

- Setup: $\mathsf{KeyGen}(1^k)$ is run to obtain keys $(vk_{\mathcal{V}}, sk_{\mathcal{V}})$ and $\widetilde{\mathsf{KeyGen}}(1^k)$ is run to obtain AS-SA attacker $\mathcal{M}$'s subversion key pair $(psk_{\mathcal{M}}, ssk_{\mathcal{M}})$. Then $(vk_{\mathcal{V}}, sk_{\mathcal{V}}, psk_{\mathcal{M}})$ are given to $\mathcal{A}$.
- Challenge: $\mathcal{M}$ chooses a random bit $b \in \{0,1\}$. If $b = 1$ then signature query oracle $\mathsf{SignProc}(m)$ returns $\sigma \leftarrow \mathsf{Sign}(sk_{\mathcal{V}}, m)$. Otherwise, $\mathsf{SignProc}(m)$ returns $\sigma \leftarrow \widetilde{\mathsf{Sign}}(psk_{\mathcal{M}}, sk_{\mathcal{V}}, m)$.
- Query: $\mathcal{A}$ is given access to the signing oracle $\mathsf{SignProc}(\cdot)$.
- Guess: Once the adversary $\mathcal{A}$ decides that Query is over, it outputs a bit b'. The output of the experiment is defined to be 1 if $b' = b$, and 0 otherwise.

Definition 3 (Strong Secret Undetectability (SSU)). The AS-SA on signature scheme $\Pi = (\mathsf{KeyGen}, \mathsf{Sign}, \mathsf{Vrfy})$ is of $\epsilon(k)$-SSU under chosen-message attacks if for all PPT distinguisher $\mathcal{A}$, there exists a function $\epsilon(k)$ such that:

$$\Pr[\mathsf{AS\text{-}SA}^{\mathsf{IND}}_{\mathcal{A},\Pi}(k) = 1] \leq \frac{1}{2} + \epsilon(k)$$

In particular, we say that AS-SA on Π is of strong secret undetectability if $\epsilon(k)$ is a negligible function.

One can note that compared with symmetric subversion attack, our defined AS-SA captures stronger undetectability. Precisely, even if a reverse analyst manages to get the embedded public subversion key $psk_{\mathcal{M}}$, he is still unable to detect other subverted system embedded with the same subversion key in a black-box manner, let alone breaking the signature scheme security. Unfortunately, for symmetric subversion attack, anyone (not only the attacker) could easily break those subverted signature schemes once he obtains the subversion key. We insist that such a difference make our proposed AS-SA more meaningful as in the real life a simple code analysis could reveal the embedded subversion key. Therefore, a subversion attack of strong secret undetectability could be more desirable to the attacker in the reality.

3.3 Signing Key Recoverability

Let $\Pi = (\mathsf{KeyGen}, \mathsf{Sign}, \mathsf{Vrfy})$ be a signature scheme, and consider the following experiment $\mathsf{AS\text{-}SA}^{\mathsf{KR}}_{\mathcal{M},\Pi}(k)$ for an AS-SA attacker $\mathcal{M}$.

- Setup: $\mathsf{KeyGen}(1^k)$ is run to obtain user $\mathcal{V}$'s keys $(vk_{\mathcal{V}}, sk_{\mathcal{V}})$ and $\widetilde{\mathsf{KeyGen}}(1^k)$ is run to obtain the subversion key pair of the adversary $\mathcal{M}$ as $(psk_{\mathcal{M}}, ssk_{\mathcal{M}})$. Then $(psk_{\mathcal{M}}, ssk_{\mathcal{M}}, vk_{\mathcal{V}})$ are given to the adversary $\mathcal{M}$.
- Challenge: The adversary $\mathcal{M}$ could query the subverted signing key oracle $\widetilde{\mathsf{Sign}}$. Upon each query, the algorithm $\widetilde{\mathsf{Sign}}$ returns a message/signature pair (m, σ_m) to $\mathcal{M}$. $\mathcal{M}$ could repeat this phase for many times.
- Recovery: Finally, $\mathcal{M}$ recovers the secret key k. The output of the experiment is defined to be 1 if $sk_{\mathcal{V}} = k$, and 0 otherwise.

Definition 4 (Signing Key Recoverability). An AS-SA on signature scheme $\Pi = (\mathsf{KeyGen}, \mathsf{Sign}, \mathsf{Vrfy})$ is 1-$v(k)$-recoverable if for all PPT subversion attacker adversaries $\mathcal{M}$, there exists a function $v(k)$ such that:

$$\Pr[\mathsf{AS\text{-}SA}^{\mathsf{KR}}_{\mathcal{M},\Pi}(k) = 1] \geqslant 1 - v(k)$$

In particular, we say that the AS-SA on Π is key recoverable if $v(k)$ is negligible.

We remark that the success of our AS-SA does not rely on the fact that the attacker picks or controls the input message of the subverted signing algorithm. That is, our AS-SA will succeed for all message distribution. As indicated by Bellare *et al.* [11], such an attack is more powerful in reality.

4 Mounting AS-SA on Signature Schemes

In this section, we introduce a new notion of splittable signature schemes and then show how to mount AS-SA on splittable signatures.

4.1 Definitions of Splittable Signatures

The *splittable* signature scheme is a special type of signature schemes and also consists of algorithms (KeyGen, Sign, Vrfy) which are defined as follows.

- KeyGen: takes as input a security parameter k and outputs a pair of keys (vk, sk), where vk is the verification key and sk is the signing key.
- Sign: consists of two sub-algorithms that generate different components of the signature.
  - Sign_R: takes as input a randomness r and outputs the *randomness-binded component* $\sigma_R \leftarrow \mathsf{Sign}_R(r)$.
  - Sign_M: takes as input the random r and the message m, outputs the *message-binded component* $\sigma_M \leftarrow \mathsf{Sign}_M(sk, m, r)$.
- Vrfy: takes as input a verification key vk, a message m and a signature $\sigma = (\sigma_R, \sigma_M)$, and outputs a bit b, with $b = 1$ meaning signature pair VALID and $b = 0$ INVALID.

A splittable signature scheme should also satisfy the following two properties.

Definition 5 (Randomness Exchangeability). Let Π = (KeyGen, Sign, Vrfy) be a splittable signature scheme. We say that Π is $(\varepsilon_1(k), \varepsilon_2(k))$-randomness exchangeable if there exists a randomness derivation algorithm RanDer so that for any two randomness r_1, r_2, and $\sigma_{R_1} \leftarrow \mathsf{Sign}_R(r_1)$, $\sigma_{R_2} \leftarrow \mathsf{Sign}_R(r_2)$,

$$\Pr[\mathsf{RanDer}(\sigma_{R_2}, r_1) \neq \mathsf{RanDer}(\sigma_{R_1}, r_2)] \leqslant \varepsilon_1(k),$$

and for any PPT algorithm $\mathcal{A}$,

$$\mathsf{Adv}_{\mathcal{A},\Pi}(k) \triangleq \Pr[\mathcal{A}(\sigma_{R_1}, \sigma_{R_2}) = \mathsf{RanDer}(\sigma_{R_2}, r_1)] \leqslant \varepsilon_2(k).$$

Here we implicitly assume that the public parameters are part of the input of algorithm RanDer and $\mathcal{A}$.

Another property of splittable signature is called *secret recoverability* which is defined as follow.

Definition 6 (Secret Recoverability). Let Π = (KeyGen, Sign, Vrfy) be a splittable signature scheme and $(vk, sk) \leftarrow \mathsf{KeyGen}(1^k)$. We say that Π is v_z-secret recoverable if for all message m, and $\sigma_M \leftarrow \mathsf{Sign}_M(sk, m, r)$,

$$\Pr[k \leftarrow \mathsf{Recv}(\sigma_M, \sigma_R, r, m) : k = sk] \geqslant 1 - v_z$$

where the probability is taken over the randomness of Sign in Π.

4.2 A Universal AS-SA on Splittable Signature Schemes

We then propose a universal AS-SA on splittable signature scheme. The procedure is depicted in Fig. 1. Below we show that such a universal AS-SA is of both strong secret undetectability and signing key recoverability.

Let $\Pi = (\mathsf{KeyGen}, \mathsf{Sign}, \mathsf{Vrfy})$ be a splittable signature scheme and $\mathsf{H} : \{0,1\}^* \rightarrow \mathcal{R}$ where $\mathcal{R}$ is the randomness space for the sub-algorithm Sign_R. AS-SA on Π consists of a set of algorithms, where each algorithm behaves as follows:

- Setup : KeyGen generates the signing/verification key pair (sk, vk), and $\widetilde{\mathsf{KeyGen}}$ executes by picking $ssk_{\mathcal{M}} \xleftarrow{\$} \mathcal{R}$ and computing $psk_{\mathcal{M}} = \mathsf{Sign}_R(ssk_{\mathcal{M}})$, and then sets the subversion key pair as $(psk_{\mathcal{M}}, ssk_{\mathcal{M}})$.
- $\widetilde{\mathsf{Sign}}$: consists of two sub-algorithms, i.e., $\widetilde{\mathsf{Sign}}_R$ and $\widetilde{\mathsf{Sign}}_M$ working as follows.
  - $\widetilde{\mathsf{Sign}}_R$: Given the number $r_{i-1}, psk_{\mathcal{M}}$, computes the randomness r_i as

$$t_i = \mathsf{RanDer}(psk_{\mathcal{M}}, r_{i-1}), r_i = \mathsf{H}(t_i)$$

    Then computes $\sigma_{R_i} \leftarrow \mathsf{Sign}_R(r_{i-1})$.
  - $\widetilde{\mathsf{Sign}}_M$: Given r_i, sk, and a message m_i, computes $\sigma_{M_i} \leftarrow \mathsf{Sign}_M(sk, m_i, r_i)$.

  Then the signature $\sigma = (\sigma_{R_i}, \sigma_{M_i})$.

Signing Key Recovery. The attacker recovers the signing key of the user using the algorithm RanDer and Recv as follows.

$$t_i = \mathsf{RanDer}(\sigma_{R_{i-1}}, ssk_{\mathcal{M}}), r_i = \mathsf{H}(t_i)$$
$$sk \leftarrow \mathsf{Recv}(\sigma_{M_i}, r_i, m_i).$$

Fig. 1. A universal AS-SA on splittable signature scheme

GAMES G_0-G_2

1: $(vk_{\mathcal{V}}, sk_{\mathcal{V}}) \leftarrow \mathsf{KeyGen}(1^k)$;
2: $(psk_{\mathcal{M}}, ssk_{\mathcal{M}}) \leftarrow \widetilde{\mathsf{KeyGen}}(1^k)$;
3: $r_0 \xleftarrow{\$} \mathbb{Z}_p$;
4: $b \xleftarrow{\$} \{0,1\}$;
5: $b' \leftarrow \mathcal{A}^{\mathsf{H},\mathsf{SignProc}}(vk_{\mathcal{V}}, sk_{\mathcal{V}}, psk_{\mathcal{M}})$;
6: **return** $b \stackrel{?}{=} b'$;

$\mathsf{H}(t)$ ············ G_1-G_2(line 7-10)

7: **if** $\exists r$ s.t. $(t, r) \in \mathcal{L}_{\mathsf{H}}$
8: **return** r;
9: $r \xleftarrow{\$} \mathbb{Z}_p$;
10: $\mathcal{L}_{\mathsf{H}} := \mathcal{L}_{\mathsf{H}} \cup \{(t, r)\}$;

$\mathsf{SignProc}(m_i)$

11: **if** $b = 1$
12: $r \xleftarrow{\$} \mathbb{Z}_p$;
13: $\sigma_{Ri} \leftarrow \mathsf{Sign}_R(r)$;
14: $\sigma_{Mi} \leftarrow \mathsf{Sign}_M(r, sk_{\mathcal{V}}, m_i)$;
15: **else if** $i = 0$ ····· G_0-G_1(line 15-24)
16: $\sigma_{Ri} \leftarrow \mathsf{Sign}_R(r_i)$;
17: $\sigma_{Mi} \leftarrow \mathsf{Sign}_M(r_i, sk_{\mathcal{V}}, m_i)$;
18: **else if** $i = 1$
19: $\sigma_{Ri} \leftarrow \widetilde{\mathsf{Sign}}_R(psk_{\mathcal{M}}, r_{i-1})$;
20: $\sigma_{Mi} \leftarrow \widetilde{\mathsf{Sign}}_M(psk_{\mathcal{M}}, r_{i-1}, sk_{\mathcal{V}}, m_i)$;
21: **else**
22: $r_{i-1} \leftarrow \mathsf{H}(\mathsf{RanDer}(psk_{\mathcal{M}}, r_{i-2}))$;
23: $\sigma_{Ri} \leftarrow \widetilde{\mathsf{Sign}}_R(psk_{\mathcal{M}}, r_{i-1})$;
24: $\sigma_{Mi} \leftarrow \widetilde{\mathsf{Sign}}_M(psk_{\mathcal{M}}, r_{i-1}, sk_{\mathcal{V}}, m_i)$;
25: **else** ··············· G_2(line 25-28)
26: $r' \xleftarrow{\$} \mathbb{Z}_p$;
27: $\sigma_{Ri} \leftarrow \mathsf{Sign}_R(r')$;
28: $\sigma_{Mi} = R$;
29: **return** $\sigma_i = (\sigma_{Ri}, \sigma_{Mi})$;

Fig. 2. The description of game G_0–G_2

Theorem 1. Let Π be a $(\varepsilon_1(k), \varepsilon_2(k))$-randomness exchangeable splittable signature scheme, and $\mathcal{A}$ is a detector that makes q signature queries and has advantage ϵ_{IND} in detecting AS-SA on splittable signature scheme Π. Then we have

$$\epsilon_{\mathsf{IND}} \leq (q-1)\varepsilon_2(k).$$

Proof. We now give a proof of the undetectability of AS-SA on splittable signature scheme using a sequence of games. We define S_i to be the event that $b = b'$ in Game i.

Fix a distinguishing adversary $\mathcal{A}$, the game G_0–G_2 is described in Fig. 2.

In game G_0, the adversary $\mathcal{A}$'s advantage $\epsilon_{\mathsf{IND}} = |\Pr[S_0] - 1/2|$.

We make a change in game G_1. Challenger in game G_1 responds to $\mathcal{A}$'s hash query t by finding the corresponding tuple $\langle t, r\rangle$ in H-list $\mathcal{L}_{\mathsf{H}}$ and returning r. If tuple $\langle t, \cdot\rangle$ doesn't exist, a random $r \leftarrow_R \mathbb{Z}_p$ is returned to $\mathcal{A}$ and tuple $\langle t, r\rangle$ is recorded in H-list. This change is only conceptual. So, $\Pr[S_0] - \Pr[S_1] = 0$.

Game G_2 is the same game as Game G_1, except that we replace part of SignProc. In game G_2, $\sigma_{Ri} \leftarrow \mathsf{Sign}_R(r)$ has the same distribution with $\sigma_{Ri} \leftarrow \mathsf{Sign}_R(r')$. Similarly, since R is a random element of range of Sign_M, it is computationally hard to distinguish $\sigma_{Mi} \leftarrow \mathsf{Sign}_M(r, sk_{\mathcal{V}}, m_i)$ from $\sigma_{Mi} = R$. So, adversary $\mathcal{A}$ in game G_2 will not note the difference of σ in both cases, then $\Pr[S_2] = 1/2$.

Game G_1 and G_2 proceed identically until $\mathcal{A}$ queries t, where $\mathsf{H}(t) \in \{r_i | i = 1, 2, \ldots, q-1\}$ and q is the times of signature queries made by $\mathcal{A}$. Let QUERY_1 and QUERY_2 be the events that above case occurs in game G_1 and G_2. Since $\mathsf{QUERY}_1 = \mathsf{QUERY}_2$ and $S_1 \wedge \neg\mathsf{QUERY}_1 = S_2 \wedge \neg\mathsf{QUERY}_2$, by difference lemma, we have $|\Pr[S_1] - \Pr[S_2]| \leq \Pr[\mathsf{QUERY}_1]$.

Next, we argue that $\Pr[\mathsf{QUERY}_1] \leq (q-1)\varepsilon_2(k)$. We show how to construct an algorithm $\mathcal{B}$ that breaks the randomness exchangeability of Π and perfectly simulates Game G_1 for $\mathcal{A}$. Pick two randomness $r_1^*, r_2^* \xleftarrow{\$} \mathbb{Z}_p$, and compute $\sigma_{R_1^*} \leftarrow \mathsf{Sign}_R(r_1^*), \sigma_{R_2^*} \leftarrow \mathsf{Sign}_R(r_2^*)$. Algorithm $\mathcal{B}$ is given $\sigma_{R_1^*}$ and $\sigma_{R_2^*}$. Its goal is to output $\mathsf{RanDer}(\sigma_{R_1^*}, r_2^*)$ (or $\mathsf{RanDer}(\sigma_{R_2^*}, r_1^*)$). $\mathcal{B}$ simulates the challenger and interacts with $\mathcal{A}$ as shown in Fig. 3.

Let $\mathsf{QUERY}[r_i]$ be the event that $\mathcal{A}$ queries t_i, where $r_i = \mathsf{H}(t_i)$. Once $\mathsf{QUERY}[r_i]$ happened in game G_1, $t_{i+1}, \ldots, t_{q-1}$ are known to $\mathcal{A}$. So, without loss of generality, we focus on the t_i with the smallest index i queried by $\mathcal{A}$ in event QUERY_1. Since the distribution of t_i, $i \in \{1, \ldots, q-1\}$, is independent to each other, then we have $\Pr[\mathsf{QUERY}_1] = (q-1)\Pr[\mathsf{QUERY}[r_i]]$.

If $\mathsf{QUERY}[r_1]$ happened in game G_1, then there exists an entry $\langle \cdot, r_1\rangle$ satisfying $\sigma_R = \mathsf{Sign}_R(r_1)$ and $\mathcal{B}$ returns the correct $\mathsf{RanDer}(psk_{\mathcal{M}}, r_1) = \mathsf{RanDer}(\sigma_{R_1^*}, r_2^*)$ with probability 1. So,

$$\Pr[\mathsf{QUERY}[r_1]] \leq \varepsilon_2(k).$$

Combining equations above, we have $\epsilon_{\mathsf{IND}} \leq (q-1)\varepsilon_2(k)$.

Theorem 2. Let Π be a $(\varepsilon_1(k), \varepsilon_2(k))$-randomness exchangeable and $v_z(k)$-secret recoverable splittable signature scheme. An attacker who mounts an AS-SA described in Fig. 1 on Π will recover the signing key with probability at least $1 - (\varepsilon_1(k) + v_z(k))$.

The above theorem could be straightforwardly obtained and thus we omit the analysis details here.

$\underline{\mathcal{B}(\sigma_{R_1^*}, \sigma_{R_2^*})}$

$(vk_\mathcal{V}, sk_\mathcal{V}) \leftarrow \mathsf{KeyGen}(1^k)$;
$psk_\mathcal{M} = \sigma_{R_1^*}$;
$r_0 \xleftarrow{\$} \mathbb{Z}_p$;
$b \xleftarrow{\$} \{0,1\}$;
$b' \leftarrow \mathcal{A}^{\mathsf{H},\mathsf{SignProc}}(vk_\mathcal{V}, sk_\mathcal{V}, psk_\mathcal{M})$;
$\langle t, r\rangle \leftarrow \mathcal{L}_\mathsf{H}$;
return $\mathsf{RanDer}(\sigma_{R_1^*}, r)$;

$\underline{\mathsf{H}(t)}$

if $\exists r$ s.t. $(t, r) \in \mathcal{L}_\mathsf{H}$
  return r;
$r \xleftarrow{\$} \mathbb{Z}_p$;
$\mathcal{L}_\mathsf{H} := \mathcal{L}_\mathsf{H} \cup \{(t, r)\}$;

$\underline{\mathsf{SignProc}(m_i)}$

if $b = 1$
  $r \xleftarrow{\$} \mathbb{Z}_p$;
  $\sigma_{Ri} \leftarrow \mathsf{Sign}_R(r)$;
  $\sigma_{Mi} \leftarrow \mathsf{Sign}_M(r, sk_\mathcal{V}, m_i)$;
else if $i = 0$
  $\sigma_{Ri} \leftarrow \mathsf{Sign}_R(r_i)$;
  $\sigma_{Mi} \leftarrow \mathsf{Sign}_M(r_i, sk_\mathcal{V}, m_i)$;
else if $i = 1$
  $\sigma_{Ri} = \sigma_R$;
  $\sigma_{Mi} = R$;
else
  $r_{i-1} \leftarrow \mathsf{H}(\mathsf{RanDer}(psk_\mathcal{M}, r_{i-2}))$;
  $\sigma_{Ri} \leftarrow \widetilde{\mathsf{Sign}}_R(psk_\mathcal{M}, r_{i-1})$;
  $\sigma_{Mi} \leftarrow \widetilde{\mathsf{Sign}}_M(psk_\mathcal{M}, r_{i-1}, sk_\mathcal{V}, m_i)$;
return $\sigma_i = (\sigma_{Ri}, \sigma_{Mi})$;

Fig. 3. Algorithm $\mathcal{B}$ that breaks the randomness exchangeability of Π

REMARK. It is worth noting that in Fig. 1, i in r_{i-1} should be greater than 1, and r_1 is randomly chosen as a normal algorithm does. Moreover, as shown later, for some other signature schemes, such as identity-based signature schemes, there are subtle differences in the above attack steps due to the slight difference in the scheme algorithms.

4.3 Instantiations

In this subsection, we instantiate the AS-SA framework with concrete splittable signature schemes. We find that the following signature schemes satisfy the splittable structure.

- All ElGamal-like signature schemes. For examples, Schnorr described in Fig. 4 [13], DSA [14], all modified ElGlmal signature schemes [15,16].
- Waters signature scheme depicted in Fig. 5 [17].

Schnorr signature scheme

- KeyGen: Let $\mathbb{G}$ be a cyclic group of prime order p and g be its generator. Let $\mathsf{H} : \{0,1\}* \rightarrow \mathbb{Z}_p$ be a collision-resilient hash function. Choose a secret $\alpha \in \mathbb{Z}_p^*$ as the signing key sk, then compute the verification key $vk = u = g^{\alpha}$.
- Sign:
  - Sign_R : Choose a random $r \in \mathbb{Z}_p^*$, then the signature related to r is $\sigma_R = g^r$.
  - Sign_M : Take as input a message m, then compute $e = \mathsf{H}(\sigma_R \parallel m)$. The signature related to the message is $\sigma_M = r - \alpha e$.
- Vrfy: Compute $e = \mathsf{H}(\sigma_R \parallel m)$. And verify whether $\sigma_R = g^{\sigma_M} u^e$ or not.

Fig. 4. Schnorr signature scheme [13]

Waters signature scheme

- KeyGen: Let $\mathbb{G}$ be a cyclic group of prime order p and g be its generator. Choose a secret $\alpha \in \mathbb{Z}_p^*$ randomly, choose $g_2, u', g_1 = g^{\alpha}$ in $\mathbb{G}$. Choose a random n-length vector $U = (u_i)$ whose elements are chosen at $\mathbb{G}$ randomly. The verification key is g, g_1, g_2, u', U, and the signing key is g_2^{α}.
- Sign:
  - Sign_R : Choose a random $r \in \mathbb{Z}_p^*$, then the signature related to r is $\sigma_R = g^r$.
  - Sign_M : m is an n-bit message and m_i denotes the i-th bit of m, and $\mathcal{M} \subseteq \{1, \cdots, n\}$ be the set of all i for which $m_i = 1$. Then the signature related to the message $\sigma_M = g_2^{\alpha}(u' \prod_{i \in \mathcal{M}} u_i)^r$.
- Vrfy: Verify whether $e(\sigma_1, g)/e(\sigma_2, u' \quad {}_{i \in \mathcal{M}} u_i) = e(g_1, g_2)$ or not.

Fig. 5. Waters signature scheme [17]

Paterson's signature scheme

- Setup: Let $\mathbb{G}$ be a cyclic group of prime order p and P be its generator. Let $\mathsf{H}_1 : \{0,1\}^* \rightarrow \mathbb{G}$, $\mathsf{H}_2 : \{0,1\}^* \rightarrow \mathbb{Z}_p^*$ and $\mathsf{H}_3 : \{0,1\}^* \rightarrow \mathbb{Z}_p^*$ be cryptographic hash functions. Choose a secret $s \in \mathbb{Z}_p^*$ randomly, and set $P_{pub} = sP$. P_{pub} is the master public key and s is the master secret key.
- Extract: For the given public identity $\mathsf{ID} \in \{0,1\}^*$ of the signer, compute the signer's verification key $Q_{\mathsf{ID}} = \mathsf{H}_1(\mathsf{ID})$, and signing key $S_{\mathsf{ID}} = sQ_{\mathsf{ID}}$.
- Sign:
  - Sign_R : Choose a random $r \in \mathbb{Z}_p^*$, then the signature related to r is $\sigma_R = rP$.
  - Sign_M : Take as input a message m, then compute the signature related to the message is $\sigma_M = r^{-1}(\mathsf{H}_2(m)P + \mathsf{H}_3(\sigma_R)S_{\mathsf{ID}})$.
- Vrfy: Verify whether $e(\sigma_R, \sigma_M) = e(P, P)^{\mathsf{H}_2(m)} e(P_{pub}, Q_{\mathsf{ID}})^{\mathsf{H}_3(\sigma_R)}$ or not.

Fig. 6. Paterson signature scheme [18]

ID-Based Blind Signature Scheme (Schnorr type)

- Setup: Let $\mathbb{G}$ be a cyclic group of prime order p and P be its generator. Let $\mathsf{H} : \{0,1\}^* \rightarrow \mathbb{Z}_p^*$ and $\mathsf{H}_1 : \{0,1\}^* \rightarrow \mathbb{G}$ be two cryptographic hash functions. Choose a secret $s \in \mathbb{Z}_p^*$ randomly as the master secret key, and computes $P_{pub} = sP$ as the master public key.
- Extract: For the given public identity $\mathsf{ID} \in \{0,1\}^*$ of the signer, compute the signer's verification key $Q_{\mathsf{ID}} = \mathsf{H}_1(\mathsf{ID})$, and signing key $S_{\mathsf{ID}} = sQ_{\mathsf{ID}}$.
- Sign:

User		**Signer**
	$\xleftarrow{R}$	$R = rP, r \in \mathbb{Z}_q$
$a, b \xleftarrow{\$} \mathbb{Z}_p^*$		
$t = e(bQ_{\mathsf{ID}} + R + aP, P_{pub})$		
$c = \mathsf{H}(m,t) + b$	$\xrightarrow{c}$	
	$\xleftarrow{S}$	$S = cS_{\mathsf{ID}} + rP_{pub}$
$c' = c - b, S' = S + aP_{pub}$		

The signature of message m is (c', S').
- Vrfy: Verify whether $c' = \mathsf{H}(m, e(S', P)e(Q_{\mathsf{ID}}, P_{pub})^{-c'})$ or not.

Fig. 7. ID-based blind signature scheme (Schnorr type) [19]

Table 1. Instantiations of splittable signatures

Signature schemes	$\mathsf{RanDer}(\sigma_R, r')$	$\mathsf{Recv}(\sigma_M, \sigma_R, r, m)$
ElGamal-like [13–16]	$(\sigma_R)^{r'}$	$(r - \sigma_M) \cdot (\mathsf{H}(\sigma_R \parallel m))^{-1} = \alpha = sk$
Waters [17]		$\sigma_M^{-1} \cdot (u' \prod_{i \in \mathcal{M}} u_i)^r = g_2^\alpha = sk$
Paterson's IBS [18]	$e(P_{pub}, \sigma_R)^{r'}$	$(r \cdot \sigma_M - \mathsf{H}_2(m) \cdot P) \cdot (\mathsf{H}_3(\sigma_R))^{-1} = S_{\mathsf{ID}}$
ID-based blind signature [19]		$(S - r \cdot P_{pub}) \cdot c^{-1} = S_{\mathsf{ID}}$

– We remark that some identity-based signature schemes also belong to the splittable structure. Concretely, Schnorr IBS [13], Paterson's signature scheme in Fig. 6 [18], ID-Based Blind Signature Scheme (Schnorr type) in Fig. 7 [19]. Since identity-based signature scheme consists of four algorithms (Setup, Extract, Sign, Vrfy), one can regard the first two algorithms (Setup, Extract) as the algorithm KeyGen of splittable signature.

Details of algorithms RanDer and Recv on different signature schemes listed above are described in Table 1. We point out that for the ID-based blind signature scheme [19], we consider $\sigma_R = R, \sigma_M = (c, S)$ so that it is consistent with the splittable structure. In particular, the algorithm Recv takes S, c and r as inputs instead of S' and c', as S and c are transformed on public channel and thus are accessible to the attacker. Also, we remark that for the above two identity-based signature schemes [18,19], the algorithm RanDer also takes the system master public key as input. One could verify that all signatures schemes are of randomness exchangeability. Particularly, typical signature schemes [13–17] rely on the CDH assumption while identity-based signature schemes [13,18,19] rely on the BDH assumption.

5 Subversion-Resilient Signatures

In this section, we discuss some potential countermeasures to defend the aforementioned subversion attacks against signatures. Essentially, similar to existing subversion attacks against signatures, our proposed subversion framework also mainly relies on the biased choice of randomness involved in the signing algorithm. Therefore, existing approaches (e.g., [12,20–22]) for constructing subversion-resilient signatures could also be adopted to prevent the asymmetric subversion attacks proposed in this work. Below we briefly review the main progress on the line of constructing subversion-resilient signatures. More details are please referred to the related literature.

Unique Signature. To resist subversion attacks against signature schemes, Atenises et al. [12] showed that fully deterministic schemes with unique signatures could achieve meaningful security against randomness-based subversion attacks of so-called (relaxed) verifiability condition. A signature scheme is unique if for each message, there exists only a single corresponding signature valid under a honestly generated verification key. Intuitively, since the unique signature scheme does not involve the randomness for signing message, all aforementioned subversion attacks will not work any more.

Signature Schemes with Reverse Firewalls. Atenises et al. [12] also considered security of signature schemes against strong subversion attack which may arbitrarily tamper the signing algorithm and thus the verifiability condition does not necessarily hold. Particularly, they showed that by using the so-called cryptographic reverse firewall [20,23,24], one can achieve the ambitious goal of protecting signature schemes against arbitrary subversion attacks. Roughly speaking, a reverse firewall for a signature scheme is an online external party that intercepts and modifies the signature produced by the signing algorithm before it is sent out to the outside. Atenises et al. [12] proved that every re-randomizable signature scheme [25] admits such a reverse firewall that preserves unforgeability against arbitrary subversion attacks if the reverse firewall is of self-destruct capability. It is worth noting that the Waters signature [17] is re-randomizable and thus one could build a reverse firewall to preserve its security against subversion attacks.

Self-Guarding Signature Schemes. Motivated by removing the external parties, Fischlin and Mazaheri [21] provided an alternative approach to reverse firewalls. Instead of relying on the ability of reverse firewall to randomize subverted signatures, a self-guarding signature scheme could use information gathered from the secure initial phase when the algorithm is still not subverted to do the re-randomization. They proposed a self-guarding signature scheme which was built upon any deterministic signature scheme and showed that it self-guards against stateless subversion attacks.

Split-Program Based Signature Schemes. In recent works by Russell et al. [22,26,27], a split-program approach is proposed to prevent instance rejection-sampling attacks. The central idea is to split the algorithm into deterministic and probabilistic blocks that could be individually tested by the so-called watchdog. Precisely, they considered the complete subversion against the signature scheme where the key generation and verification algorithms may be also subverted. To deal with this issue, they showed how to construct a subversion-resilient signature with an online watchdog in the split-program model.

6 Conclusions

In this work, we explored strong subversion attacks against signature schemes. We formalized the asymmetric subversion model for signature schemes and proposed a universal subversion attack on signature schemes of so-called splittable structure. We then proved that our presented subversion attack is strong undetectable and more effective than that proposed in the literature.

Acknowledgment. The work of Rongmao Chen is supported by the National Natural Science Foundation of China (Grant No. 61702541), the Young Elite Scientists Sponsorship Program by CAST (Grant No. 2017QNRC001), and the Science Research Plan Program by NUDT (Grant No. ZK17-03-46). The work of Yongjun Wang is supported by the National Natural Science Foundation of China under Grant No. 61472439.

References

1. Ball, J., Borger, J., Greenwald, G., et al.: Revealed: how US and UK spy agencies defeat internet privacy and security. The Guardian, 6 September 2013
2. Perlroth, N., Larson, J., Shane, S.: NSA able to foil basic safeguards of privacy on web. The New York Times, 5 September 2013
3. Greenwald, G.: No Place to Hide: Edward Snowden, the NSA, and the US Surveillance State. Macmillan, New York (2014)
4. Simmons, G.J.: Message authentication without secrecy. In: AAAS Selected Symposia Series, vol. 69, pp. 105–139 (1982)
5. Simmons, G.J.: Verification of treaty compliance-revisited. In: 1983 IEEE Symposium on Security and Privacy, p. 61. IEEE (1983)
6. Simmons, G.J.: The subliminal channel and digital signatures. In: Beth, T., Cot, N., Ingemarsson, I. (eds.) EUROCRYPT 1984. LNCS, vol. 209, pp. 364–378. Springer, Heidelberg (1985). https://doi.org/10.1007/3-540-39757-4_25
7. Young, A., Yung, M.: Kleptography: using cryptography against cryptography. In: Fumy, W. (ed.) EUROCRYPT 1997. LNCS, vol. 1233, pp. 62–74. Springer, Heidelberg (1997). https://doi.org/10.1007/3-540-69053-0_6
8. Young, A., Yung, M.: The dark side of "Black-Box" cryptography or: should we trust capstone? In: Koblitz, N. (ed.) CRYPTO 1996. LNCS, vol. 1109, pp. 89–103. Springer, Heidelberg (1996). https://doi.org/10.1007/3-540-68697-5_8

9. Young, A., Yung, M.: The prevalence of kleptographic attacks on discrete-log based cryptosystems. In: Kaliski, B.S. (ed.) CRYPTO 1997. LNCS, vol. 1294, pp. 264–276. Springer, Heidelberg (1997). https://doi.org/10.1007/BFb0052241
10. Bellare, M., Paterson, K.G., Rogaway, P.: Security of symmetric encryption against mass surveillance. In: Garay, J.A., Gennaro, R. (eds.) CRYPTO 2014. LNCS, vol. 8616, pp. 1–19. Springer, Heidelberg (2014). https://doi.org/10.1007/978-3-662-44371-2_1
11. Bellare, M., Jaeger, J., Kane, D.: Mass-surveillance without the state: strongly undetectable algorithm-substitution attacks. In: ACM CCS, pp. 1431–1440. ACM (2015)
12. Ateniese, G., Magri, B., Venturi, D.: Subversion-resilient signature schemes. In: ACM CCS, pp. 364–375. ACM (2015)
13. Schnorr, C.P.: Efficient identification and signatures for smart cards. In: Brassard, G. (ed.) CRYPTO 1989. LNCS, vol. 435, pp. 239–252. Springer, New York (1990). https://doi.org/10.1007/0-387-34805-0_22
14. Boneh, D.: Digital signature standard. In: van Tilborg, H.C.A., Jajodia, S. (eds.) Encyclopedia of Cryptography and Security, 2nd edn, p. 347. Springer, Boston (2011). https://doi.org/10.1007/978-1-4419-5906-5_145
15. Menezes, A.J., Van Oorschot, P.C., Vanstone, S.A.: Handbook of Applied Cryptography. CRC Press, Boca Raton (1996)
16. ElGamal, T.: A public key cryptosystem and a signature scheme based on discrete logarithms. IEEE Trans. Inf. Theory **31**(4), 469–472 (1985)
17. Waters, B.: Efficient identity-based encryption without random oracles. In: Cramer, R. (ed.) EUROCRYPT 2005. LNCS, vol. 3494, pp. 114–127. Springer, Heidelberg (2005). https://doi.org/10.1007/11426639_7
18. Paterson, K.G.: ID-based signatures from pairings on elliptic curves. Electron. Lett. **38**(18), 1025–1026 (2002)
19. Zhang, F., Kim, K.: ID-based blind signature and ring signature from pairings. In: Zheng, Y. (ed.) ASIACRYPT 2002. LNCS, vol. 2501, pp. 533–547. Springer, Heidelberg (2002). https://doi.org/10.1007/3-540-36178-2_33
20. Mironov, I., Stephens-Davidowitz, N.: Cryptographic reverse firewalls. In: Oswald, E., Fischlin, M. (eds.) EUROCRYPT 2015. LNCS, vol. 9057, pp. 657–686. Springer, Heidelberg (2015). https://doi.org/10.1007/978-3-662-46803-6_22
21. Fischlin, M., Mazaheri, S.: Self-guarding cryptographic protocols against algorithm substitution attacks. IACR Cryptology ePrint Archive 2017, 984 (2017)
22. Russell, A., Tang, Q., Yung, M., Zhou, H.-S.: Cliptography: clipping the power of kleptographic attacks. In: Cheon, J.H., Takagi, T. (eds.) ASIACRYPT 2016. LNCS, vol. 10032, pp. 34–64. Springer, Heidelberg (2016). https://doi.org/10.1007/978-3-662-53890-6_2
23. Dodis, Y., Mironov, I., Stephens-Davidowitz, N.: Message transmission with reverse firewalls—secure communication on corrupted machines. In: Robshaw, M., Katz, J. (eds.) CRYPTO 2016. LNCS, vol. 9814, pp. 341–372. Springer, Heidelberg (2016). https://doi.org/10.1007/978-3-662-53018-4_13
24. Chen, R., Mu, Y., Yang, G., Susilo, W., Guo, F., Zhang, M.: Cryptographic reverse firewall via malleable smooth projective hash functions. In: Cheon, J.H., Takagi, T. (eds.) ASIACRYPT 2016. LNCS, vol. 10031, pp. 844–876. Springer, Heidelberg (2016). https://doi.org/10.1007/978-3-662-53887-6_31
25. Hofheinz, D., Jager, T., Knapp, E.: Waters signatures with optimal security reduction. In: Fischlin, M., Buchmann, J., Manulis, M. (eds.) PKC 2012. LNCS, vol. 7293, pp. 66–83. Springer, Heidelberg (2012). https://doi.org/10.1007/978-3-642-30057-8_5

26. Russell, A., Tang, Q., Yung, M., Zhou, H.: Destroying steganography via amalgamation: kleptographically CPA secure public key encryption. IACR Cryptology ePrint Archive 2016, 530 (2016)
27. Russell, A., Tang, Q., Yung, M., Zhou, H.: Generic semantic security against a kleptographic adversary. In: ACM CCS, pp. 907–922 (2017)

Cloud Security

Intrusion-Resilient Public Auditing Protocol for Data Storage in Cloud Computing

Yan Xu, Ran Ding, Jie Cui, and Hong Zhong(✉)

School of Computer Science and Technology, Anhui University, Hefei, China
{xuyan,cuijie,zhongh}@ahu.edu.cn, e16201008@stu.ahu.edu.cn

Abstract. Cloud storage auditing is a crucial service that provides integrity checking for clients' data in the cloud server. However, if the client's auditing secret key is exposed, the malicious cloud server can tamper even throw away the client's data without being detected. In this paper, we propose an intrusion-resilient public auditing protocol that can reduce the damage caused by key exposure. In our protocol, the auditing secret key is managed by the client with the help of a third party auditor (TPA), who cannot compute the client's auditing secret key. Our protocol divides the lifetime of file stored on cloud into several time periods, and each time period is further divided into several refreshing periods. We show that our protocol is secure (i.e., backward security and forward security) against the adversary as long as the client and TPA are compromised in different refreshing period. Our protocol still captures the forward security when the client and TPA are compromised in the same refreshing period.

Keywords: Key exposure · Intrusion-resilient · Cloud computing
Cloud storage auditing

1 Introduction

Cloud storage attracts many individuals and enterprises putting their data on the cloud server. However, after uploading their data to the cloud server, the clients usually delete locally stored data. Therefore, whether the data on the cloud server is under well preservation is a significant security problems, i.e., the problem of data's integrity.

In 2007, Ateniese *et al.* firstly put forward PDP (Provable Data Possession), which intended to ensure the data possession stored on untrusted servers [1]. Using the method of random sample and homomorphic linear authenticators (HLA), this scheme can verify integrity of outsourced data. Juels et al. proposed Proof of Retrievability (PoR) [8]. With the technologies of spot checking and error correcting codes, PoR can ensure not only the data's possession but also the data's retrievability. Shacham and Waters [10] gave an improved PoR, which

W. Susilo and G. Yang (Eds.): ACISP 2018, LNCS 10946, pp. 399–416, 2018.
https://doi.org/10.1007/978-3-319-93638-3_23

is able to support stateless verification. During the past few years, different fields about auditing has been researched, such as data dynamic problem [13,21], privacy protection problem of clients' data [12,14], the data sharing [11,20], and cloud data's multi-copies [2,4]. Recently, several key-exposure resilient cloud storage auditing protocols have been proposed in last few years [15–17]. If a malicious cloud server has the secret key of the client, it can conceal loss of a client's data to maintain its fame, even deliberately delete the data that are rarely accessed for the sake of storage saving. It's necessary to study key-exposure resilient cloud storage auditing protocol.

Yu *et al.* [16] firstly investigate the key-exposure resilient cloud storage auditing protocol which divided the lifetime of the file stored on cloud server into discrete time periods. The client's auditing secret key, which is used to generate files' auditing authenticators, will be updated during each time period, and the forward security of auditing secret key is preserved [16]. In 2016, a protocol to outsource key update to TPA was proposed, which reduced the client's computation overhead [15]. However, in [15,16] the client updates its auditing secret key by itself. If the client is compromised, the adversary could update the auditing secret key and then forge the file authenticators after the key-exposed time period, i.e., these protocols [15,16] cannot realize the backward security of the auditing secret key.

In 2017, Yu and Wang [17] proposed a strong key-exposure resilient auditing protocol, which preserved not only the forward security but also the backward security of the auditing secret key. In their protocol, the secret value to update auditing secret keys is split into two parts, one is given to TPA, and the other one is kept by the client itself. So TPA has a new task that is helping the client update its auditing secret keys, besides providing auditing service that is similar to [16]. It should be noted that TPA is incapable of computing the auditing secret key for it does not know the client's secret part. If only the client is compromised, the adversary cannot compute auditing secret key for it is unable get the update token generated by TPA's secret part. However, each part of the secret value that TPA and the client hold are unchangeable in the protocol. Therefore, as long as the adversary compromises the client and TPA during the lifetime of the auditing protocol, the adversary can update the auditing secret key of every time periods without being disclosed.

1.1 Our Contributions

We found that if the adversary can compromise both the client and TPA, no auditing protocol proposed in the literature is secure. Therefore, in this paper, we propose an intrusion-resilient public auditing protocol to address this security problem. This protocol can preserve the auditing security if the client and TPA are compromised in different refreshing periods. The proposed protocol divides each time period into several refreshing periods. During each time period, TPA and the client perform one time key update algorithm to update the auditing secret key which is used to compute file's auditing authenticator of the next time period. Different from the protocol [17], TPA and the client perform one time key refresh algorithm during each refreshing period to update TPA and the client's secret parts which is used to update the auditing secret key. The key refresh algorithm makes our protocol avoid the problem in [17]. The major contributions of this paper are as shown below:

1. We propose an intrusion-resilient public auditing protocol, where the secret value to update auditing secret keys is also split into two parts, one is given to TPA, and the other is kept by the client itself. In each refresh period, we choose a random number, and then TPA and client accordingly refresh their secret parts using the random number. One multiples its secret part by the random number, while the other divides its secret part by the random number. The secret value can be recovered jointly from the secret parts of the client and TPA in the same refreshing period. If the adversary compromises client and TPA respectively during different refreshing periods, it can't obtain other auditing secret keys except the refreshing period that the client is compromised. Therefore, the proposed protocol further alleviates the harm of key exposure on cloud storage auditing.
2. We give a formalized definition and security model for proposed protocol. In security model, adversary can query key update tokens, key refresh tokens, secret keys of the client and TPA for all time periods, except an unexposed time period. The computation overhead and communication overhead are analyzed through numerical analysis.

The remaining part of this paper is organized as follows: we give the model of our system, definition of the protocol, the security model and preliminaries in Sect. 2. A concrete protocol is elaborated in Sect. 3. Security proof and performance analysis are respectively shown in Sects. 4 and 5. Ultimately, paper's conclusion is Sect. 6.

2 Definitions and Preliminaries

2.1 System Model

The intrusion-resilient cloud storage auditing system in Fig. 1 includes three parties: the cloud server, the client, and TPA. The cloud server provides storage service and data access for clients. The client can compute authenticators of files, upload authenticators and files to the cloud server and delete corresponding data from its own storage space. TPA, a trusted organization, that is governed by the government, plays two roles in this system. One role is to provide impartial auditing service for clients. The other is to correctly assist clients to update their auditing secret keys. Similar with previous works, TPA is honest for auditing service for clients. Besides, we assume that TPA is trustworthy for assisting clients to update secret keys.

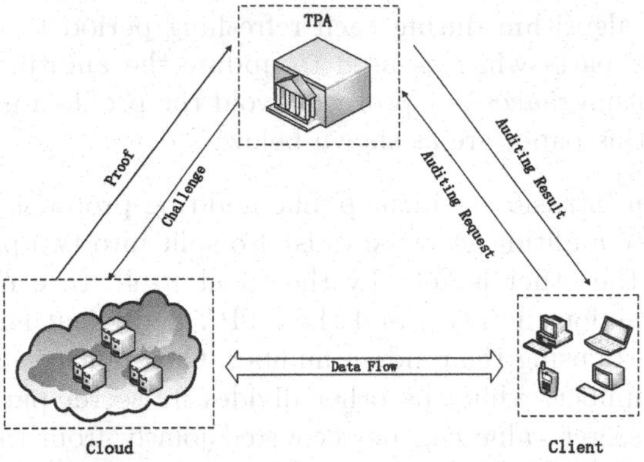

Fig. 1. System model

2.2 Definition of Intrusion-Resilient Public Auditing Protocol

In this proposed protocol, each time period t is divided into $RN(t)$ refreshing periods that are marked with r, i.e. $r \in [0, RN(t)-1]$. Following the prior work [5], key update algorithm is executed promptly after key generates, as well as key refresh algorithm promptly after key updates, so as to the keys with $t=0$ or $r=0$ are never used. The proposed protocol is composed of the following six algorithms:

(1) $\mathsf{SysSetup}(1^k, T) \rightarrow (SKC_{0.0}, SKT_{0.0}, PK)$: the system setup algorithm is probabilistic and the client runs this algorithm. The input is security parameter 1^k and the number of periods T. The output is the client's initial secret key $SKC_{0.0}$, TPA's preliminary secret key $SKT_{0.0}$, as well as public key PK.

(2) $\mathsf{KeyUpd}(SKT_{t.r}, SKC_{t.r}, PK, t) \rightarrow (SKT_{t+1.0}, SKC_{t+1.0})$: the key update algorithm is probabilistic. TPA and the client interactively run this algorithm. The input is TPA's secret key $SKT_{t.r}$, the client's secret key $SKC_{t.r}$, public key PK and time period t. Specifically, TPA generates key update token TU_t to help the client update its secret key. The outputs is TPA's secret key $SKT_{t+1.0}$ and the client's secret key $SKC_{t+1.0}$ for the next time period.

(3) $\mathsf{KeyRef}(SKT_{t.r}, SKC_{t.r}, PK, t) \rightarrow (SKT_{t.r+1}, SKC_{t.r+1})$: the key refresh algorithm is probabilistic. TPA and the client interactively run this algorithm. The input is TPA's secret key $SKT_{t.r}$, the client's secret key $SKC_{t.r}$, public key PK, and time period t. Specifically, TPA generates key refresh token $TR_{t.r}$ to help the client refresh its secret key. The output is TPA's secret key $SKT_{t.r+1}$ and the client's secret key $SKC_{t.r+1}$ for the next refresh period.

(4) $\mathsf{AuthGen}(SKC_{t.r}, PK, F, t) \rightarrow (\Phi)$: the authenticator generation algorithm is probabilistic and the client runs this algorithm. The input is the client's secret key $SKC_{t.r}$, a file F that will be stored on cloud server, public key

PK, and time period t. The output is authenticator set Φ of file F in time period t.

(5) $\mathsf{ProofGen}(Chal, F, \Phi, PK, t) \rightarrow (P)$: the storage proof generation algorithm is probabilistic and the cloud server runs this algorithm. The input is the challenge $Chal$ issued by TPA, the file F, authenticator set Φ, public key PK, and time period t. The output is proof P of possession of file F.

(6) $\mathsf{ProofVerify}(P, Chal, PK, t) \rightarrow (''T''or''F'')$: TPA runs this deterministic proof verifying algorithm. The input is proof P, challenge $Chal$, public key PK, and time period t. The output is "Ture" or "False".

2.3 Definition of Security

Similar with [5]. We use SKC^*, SKT^*, TU^*, TR^* to denote the client's secret keys, TPA's secret keys, key update tokens, and key refresh tokens in all time periods respectively. File F stored in the cloud server is divided into n blocks $m_i(i = 1, \cdots, n)$. The probabilistic polynomial-time adversary can steal these messages, so the oracles are as shown below.

- Authenticator oracle. Inputting some block m_i of file F in time period t, this oracle outputs the authenticator of block m_i.
- Osec. This is a key exposure oracle, which is based on SKC^*, SKT^*, TU^*, TR^*. The adversary inputs $(''s'', t.r)$, $(''b'', t.r)$, $(''u'', t)$, $(''r'', t.r)$, then obtains $SKC_{t.r}$, $SKT_{t.r}$, TU_t and $TR_{t+1.0}$, $TR_{t.r}$ respectively, which are shown below.

1. Inputting $(''s'', t.r)$, obtains $SKC_{t.r}$;
2. Inputting $(''b'', t.r)$, obtains $SKT_{t.r}$;
3. Inputting $(''u'', t)$, obtains TU_t and $TR_{t+1.0}$;
4. Inputting $(''r'', t.r)$, obtains $TR_{t.r}$.

Compromising of the client or TPA and obtaining key update or refresh tokens are included in this oracle's queries.

Assume Q is a set of secret key queries, we define $SKC_{t.r}$ is $Q - exposed$ when at least one of these cases happens:

(1) $(''s'', t.r) \in Q$
(2) $r > 1, (''r'', t.(r-1)) \in Q$, and $SKC_{t.r-1}$ is $Q - exposed$
(3) $r = 1, (''u'', t-1) \in Q$, and $SKC_{(t-1).RN(t-1)}$ is $Q - exposed$

If $SKC_{t.r}$ is $Q - exposed$, authenticators of file F in period t can be forged. When $SKT_{t.r}$ and $SKC_{t.r}$ are simultaneously $Q - exposed$, the adversary can execute key update and key refresh algorithms itself and forge authenticators of file F in every time period $t' > t$. Therefore, we say proposed protocol is $(t, Q) - compromised$ when $SKC_{t.r}$ is $Q - exposed$ or $SKT_{t'.r}$ and $SKC_{t'.r}$ are simultaneously $Q - exposed$ of which $t' < t$.

The following game describes an adversary against the security of intrusion-resilient cloud storage auditing protocol. If the adversary can forge authenticators of some block $m_i (i = 1, \cdots, n)$ of file F in t^*, and neither the protocol is $(t^*, Q) - compromised$ nor the adversary executes the authenticator query of m_i, we say the adversary succeeds. The game includes these phases:

(1) Setup phase. The challenger sets $t = 0$ and executes SysSetup algorithm to obtain client's secret key $SKC_{0.0}$, TPA's key $SKT_{0.0}$, as well as PK. Challenger sends the adversary the public key PK.
(2) Query phase. We allow adversary to query TU^*, SKT^*, SKC^*, TR^* and authenticators adaptively. Set current time period is t.
   (a) Osec queries. The adversary can adaptively query secret key of client, secret key of TPA, key update tokens, key refresh tokens in time period t and query Osec. The challenger sends the corresponding secret messages to the adversary.
   (b) Authenticator queries. The adversary can select a series of blocks of $m_1, m_2, \cdots, m_n$ and send them to the challenger. The challenger computes authenticators of these blocks in time period t and sends these authenticators to the adversary. The adversary stores all blocks of file $F = (m_1, m_2, \cdots, m_n)$ and their authenticators.
   Subsequently, let current time period $t := t+1$. Before every time period ends, adversary is permitted to continue this query phase or enter the next phase.
(3) Challenge phase. The challenger picks period t^*, the proposed protocol is not $(t^*, Q) - compromised$ in t^* and $Chal = \{i, v_i\}_{i \in I} (I = \{s_1, s_2, \cdots, s_c\}, 1 \leq s_l \leq n, 1 \leq l \leq c, 1 \leq c \leq n)$. The challenger sends $Chal$ to adversary and asks for providing possession proof P for file $F = (m_1, m_2, \cdots, m_n)$ under $Chal$ for blocks $m_{s_1}, m_{s_2}, \cdots, m_{s_c}$ in time period t^*.
4) Forgery phase. A possession proof P is generated by the adversary in time period t^*, which is for the blocks in $Chal$. The adversary sends P to the challenger, which is then verified by the challenger. If ProofVerify$(P, Chal, PK, t^*)$ outputs "True", we say the adversary wins.

Without owing all blocks indicated by $Chal$, adversary can't forge a valid possession proof in time period t as long as the proposed protocol is not $(t, Q) - compromised$, except that it puzzles out all missing blocks. We allow adversary to query all blocks' authenticators of file F in all time periods. Besides, the adversary can adaptively query secret messages of set SKC^*, SKT^*, TU^*, TR^* for all time periods so long as not making the proposed protocol $(t^*, Q) - compromised$. The adversary's goal is forging a valid possession proof P in time period t^* for blocks in $Chal$. The following definition shows that if an adversary's proof is valid in time period t^*, then we can use a knowledge extractor to extract the challenged file blocks.

Definition 1 (Intrusion-resilient Auditing). *We say an auditing protocol for cloud storage is intrusion-resilient when these conditions are met: whenever the challenger accepts the adversary's proof in above game with probability that* *is non-negligible, then except possibly with negligible probability, we are able to find a knowledge extractor which is able to extract all the file blocks that are challenged.*

The following definition shows detectability of the proposed auditing protocol. It ensures that the cloud stores the unchallenged blocks with a high probability.

Definition 2 (Detectability). *The intrusion-resilient auditing protocol is* (q, p) *detectable* $(0 < q, p < 1)$, *if bad blocks are checked with probability that is at least* p, *given a fraction* q *of bad blocks.*

2.4 Preliminaries

(1) Bilinear Map: G_1 and G_2 are two multiplicative cyclic groups with prime order q. If $\hat{e}: G_1 \times G_1 \rightarrow G_2$ meets these conditions, we call it bilinear map:
   (a) Bilinearity: $\forall g_1, g_2 \in G_1$ and $\forall a, b \in Z_q^*$, $\hat{e}(g_1^a, g_2^b) = \hat{e}(g_1, g_2)^{ab}$.
   (b) Non-degeneracy: g_1, g_2 are generators in G_1, $\hat{e}(g_1, g_2) \neq 1$.
   (c) Computability: $\hat{e}(g_1, g_2)$ can be computed using an efficient algorithm.

(2) CDH Problem: Given (g, g^a, g^b), compute g^{ab}, where $a, b \in Z_q^*$ and g is a generator in multiplicative group G_1 with order q .

3 The Proposed Protocol

3.1 Technique Explanation

In this section, we give the representation of time period firstly, explain symbols about time periods and secret keys secondly, and describe the procedure of key update between TPA and the client finally.

Time Period Representation. Similar with [3,6,7,18,19], we take advantage of a full binary tree structure with depth $l+1$, and divide the lifetime of file F stored on cloud server into $T = 2^l$ discrete time periods, from 0 to $T-1$. Each time period t is further divided into $RN(t)$ refreshing periods that are marked with r. We set $t_1.r_1 = t_2.r_2$ when $t_1 = t_2$ and $r_1 = r_2$, $t_1.r_1 < t_2.r_2$ when $t_1 < t_2$ or when $t_1 = t_2$ and $r_1 < r_2$, which is shown in Fig. 2. Time periods are matched with the tree's leaf nodes from the most left to the most right. The node of the binary tree is labelled with binary string ω, and we call the node with label ω as "node ω" for simplification. A non-leaf node ω's left child and right child are represented by binary string $\omega 0$ and $\omega 1$ respectively. Node $\langle t \rangle$ is the leaf node corresponding to time period t, and $\langle t \rangle$ is a binary string with length l.

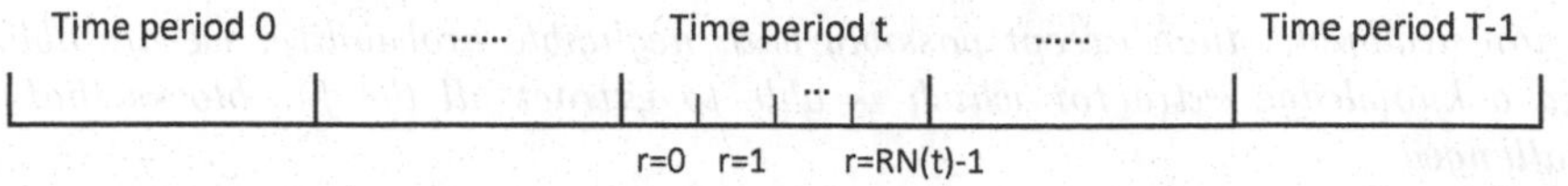

Fig. 2. Time period and refreshing period

Symbol Explanation. In the binary tree, each leaf node $\langle t\rangle$ has one secret value $S_{\langle t\rangle} \in G_1$, and $S_{\langle t\rangle}$ is the client's auditing secret key in time period t. Each non-leaf node ω has two values $R_\omega, S_\omega \in G_1$. R_ω is a verification value to verify file authenticators, and S_ω is a secret value to compute its children's secret value. When node ω is the root node which is labelled with an empty string ϵ, we have $S_\epsilon = 1$. For each node ω, we define three sets $\theta(\beta,\omega)$, $\varphi(\omega)$ and $\Omega_{\beta,\omega}$. Set $\theta(\beta,\omega)$ contains node ω's ancestor on the route from node β to ω, and set $\varphi(\omega)$ contains the right siblings of nodes on the route from root to node ω. Set $\Omega_{\beta,\omega} = \{R_\pi | \pi \in \theta(\beta,\omega)\}$ contains verification value of each node in the set $\theta(\beta,\omega)$. If β is the root node, $\theta(\beta,\omega)$ and $\Omega_{\beta,\omega}$ are taken as $\theta(\omega)$ and Ω_ω respectively. For every leaf node $\langle t\rangle$, we additionally define a set $\mathrm{Sec}_{\langle t\rangle} = \{S_\omega | \omega \in \varphi(\langle t\rangle)\}$, that contains the secret value of each node in the set $\varphi(\langle t\rangle)$. Set $\mathrm{Sec}_{\langle t\rangle}$ is used to compute auditing secret key $S_{\langle t+1\rangle}$ for the next time period. Every value S_ω in $\mathrm{Sec}_{\langle t\rangle}$ is divided into two parts, i.e. $S_\omega = S_\omega^{'} \cdot S_\omega^{''}$, and $\mathrm{Sec}^{'}_{\langle t\rangle} = \{S_\omega^{'} | \omega \in \varphi(\langle t\rangle)\}$, $\mathrm{Sec}^{''}_{\langle t\rangle} = \{S_\omega^{''} | \omega \in \varphi(\langle t\rangle)\}$. TPA's secret key in time period t is $SKT_{t.r} = \mathrm{Sec}^{'}_{\langle t\rangle}$, and the client's secret key in time period t is $SKC_{t.r} = \{S_{\langle t\rangle}, \Omega_{\langle t\rangle}, \mathrm{Sec}^{''}_{\langle t\rangle}\}$. These symbols are concluded in Table 1.

Figure 3 gives an example to explain some symbols. In this example, the depth of binary tree is 4, and $l = 3$, thus the number of time periods T is 8, from 0 to 7. We label the left child of root with binary string $\omega = 0$, node 0's left child with $\omega 0 = 00$ and right child with $\omega 1 = 01$. Node 0 has two values R_0, S_0, and S_0 is used to compute secret values S_{00} and S_{01}.

The leaf node 000 has value S_{000}, which is the client's auditing secret key for the time period 0. At the same time, node 000 has four sets $\theta(\beta,000)$, $\Omega_{\beta,000}$, $\varphi(000)$, Sec_{000}. We have $\varphi(000) = \{\mathrm{node}\,1, \mathrm{node}\,01, \mathrm{node}\,001\}$, $\mathrm{Sec}_{000} = \{S_1, S_{01}, S_{001}\}$. If node β is root ϵ, sets $\theta(\beta,000) = \theta(000) = \{\mathrm{node}\,\epsilon, \mathrm{node}\,0, \mathrm{node}\,00\}$ and $\Omega_{\beta,000} = \Omega_{000} = \{R_\epsilon, R_0, R_{00}\}$. In time period 0, the secret key of the client is $SKC_{0.r} = \{S_{000}, \Omega_{000}, \mathrm{Sec}^{''}_{000}\}$, in which $\mathrm{Sec}^{''}_{\langle 0\rangle} = \{S_1^{''}, S_{01}^{''}, S_{001}^{''}\}$ and TPA's secret key is $SKT_{0.r} = \mathrm{Sec}^{'}_{000}$, in which $\mathrm{Sec}^{'}_{000} = \{S_1^{'}, S_{01}^{'}, S_{001}^{'}\}$. Secret values S_1, S_{01}, S_{001} in Sec_{000} is respectively product of corresponding factors in $\mathrm{Sec}^{'}_{000}$ and $\mathrm{Sec}^{''}_{000}$, i.e. $S_1 = S_1^{'} \cdot S_1^{''}$, $S_{01} = S_{01}^{'} \cdot S_{01}^{''}$, $S_{001} = S_{001}^{'} \cdot S_{001}^{''}$.

Key Update. The key update at the end of time period t can be describe as following. Assume the client's secret key is $SKC_{t.r} = \{S_{\langle t\rangle}, \Omega_{\langle t\rangle}, \mathrm{Sec}^{''}_{\langle t\rangle}\}$, and TPA's secret key is $SKT_{t.r} = \mathrm{Sec}^{'}_{\langle t\rangle}$. We have $\langle t\rangle = t_1 t_2 \cdots t_l$, and the key update is executed according to the value of binary bit t_l.

Table 1. Symbol explanation

Symbol	Meaning
$SKT_{t.r}$	The secret key of TPA at time period t after r times refreshes
$SKC_{t.r}$	The secret value of the client at time period t after r times refreshes
TU_t	Key update token generated by TPA at the end of time period t
$TR_{t.r}$	Key refresh token generated by TPA after the $(r+1)-th$ refreshing
T	The total time periods
ω	The binary string remarks a node of the binary tree
$\omega 0$	The binary string remarks left child of node ω
$\omega 1$	The binary string remarks right child of node ω
$\langle t \rangle$	The binary string of leaf node corresponding to time period t
R_ω	The verification value of tree node whose binary string is ω
S_ω	The secret value of tree node ω
$\Omega_{\langle t \rangle}$	The verification value set of tree nodes in the route from root to leaf node $\langle t \rangle$
$\varphi(\langle t \rangle)$	The set of right siblings of nodes on the route from root to leaf node $\langle t \rangle$
$\mathsf{Sec}_{\langle t \rangle}$	The set of secret values of nodes in $\varphi(\langle t \rangle)$
$\theta(\beta, \omega)$	The set of node ω's ancestors on the route from node β to ω

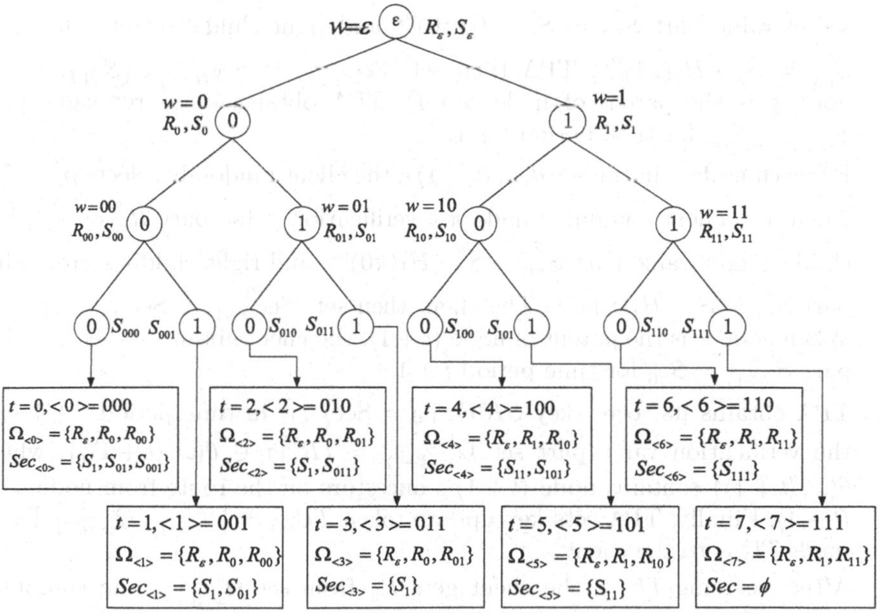

Fig. 3. An example of key construction with $l = 3$

In the case $t_l = 0$. Node $\langle t \rangle$ is a left leaf node and node $\langle t+1 \rangle$ is the right sibling of node $\langle t \rangle$, i.e. $\langle t+1 \rangle = t_1 t_2 \cdots t_{l-1} 1$. Therefore, TPA can find $S'_{\langle t+1 \rangle}$ in set $\mathrm{Sec}'_{\langle t \rangle}$, and the client can find $S''_{\langle t+1 \rangle}$ in set $\mathrm{Sec}''_{\langle t \rangle}$. TPA sets the key update token $TU_{\langle t \rangle} = \{S'_{\langle t+1 \rangle}\}$ and sends $TU_{\langle t \rangle}$ to the client. After receiving $TU_{\langle t \rangle}$, the client computes $S_{\langle t+1 \rangle} = S'_{\langle t+1 \rangle} \cdot S''_{\langle t+1 \rangle}$, that is the auditing secret key in time period $t+1$. In time period $t+1$, TPA's secret key is $SKT_{t+1.0} = \mathrm{Sec}'_{\langle t+1 \rangle}$, and the client's secret key is $SKC_{t+1.0} = \{S_{\langle t+1 \rangle}, \Omega_{\langle t+1 \rangle}, \mathrm{Sec}''_{\langle t+1 \rangle}\}$, where $\mathrm{Sec}'_{\langle t+1 \rangle} = \mathrm{Sec}'_{\langle t \rangle} \setminus \{S'_{\langle t+1 \rangle}\}$ and $\mathrm{Sec}''_{\langle t+1 \rangle} = \mathrm{Sec}''_{\langle t \rangle} \setminus \{S''_{\langle t+1 \rangle}\}$. Because node $\langle t+1 \rangle$ is the right sibling of node $\langle t \rangle$, the verification value set in time period $t+1$ does not change, i.e. $\Omega_{\langle t+1 \rangle} = \Omega_{\langle t \rangle}$.

In the case $t_l = 1$. Node $\langle t \rangle$ is a right leaf node and node $\langle t+1 \rangle$ is a left leaf node. TPA gets i that is the largest value satisfying $t_i = 0$, then the nearest common ancestor of node $\langle t \rangle$ and $\langle t+1 \rangle$ is node $t_1 t_2 \cdots t_{i-1}$. Node $\beta = t_1 t_2 \cdots t_{i-1} 0$ is the left child of node $t_1 t_2 \cdots t_{i-1}$, while node $\omega = t_1 t_2 \cdots t_{i-1} 1$ is the right child. Therefore, TPA and the client can find $S'_\omega \in \mathrm{Sec}'_{\langle t \rangle}$, $S''_\omega \in \mathrm{Sec}''_{\langle t \rangle}$ respectively. TPA sets its secret key $\mathrm{Sec}'_{\langle t+1 \rangle} = \mathrm{Sec}'_{\langle t \rangle} \setminus \{S'_\omega\}$ for time period $t+1$, and the client sets $\mathrm{Sec}''_{\langle t+1 \rangle} = \mathrm{Sec}''_{\langle t \rangle} \setminus \{S''_\omega\}$. Then, the client cooperates with TPA to compute secrets for time period $t+1$ according to the following three steps.

(a). For each node π in the set $\theta(\omega, \langle t+1 \rangle)$, TPA randomly selects $\rho'_\pi \in Z_q^*$. Then, TPA computes node π's verification value part $R'_\pi = g^{\rho'_\pi}$, left child's secret value part $S'_{\pi 0} = S'_\pi \cdot H_1(\pi 0)^{\rho'_\pi}$ and right child's secret value part $S'_{\pi 1} = S'_\pi \cdot H_1(\pi 1)^{\rho'_\pi}$. TPA then sets $\mathrm{Sec}'_{\langle t+1 \rangle} = \mathrm{Sec}'_{\langle t+1 \rangle} \cup \{S'_{\pi 1}\}$. When node π is the parent of node $\langle t+1 \rangle$, TPA obtains its secret value part $S'_{\langle t+1 \rangle} = S'_{\pi 0}$ for time period $t+1$.
For each node π in the set $\theta(\omega, \langle t+1 \rangle)$, the client randomly selects $\rho''_\pi \in Z_q^*$. Then, the client computes node π's verification value part $R''_\pi = g^{\rho''_\pi}$, left child's secret value part $S''_{\pi 0} = S''_\pi \cdot H_1(\pi 0)^{\rho''_\pi}$ and right child's secret value part $S''_{\pi 1} = S''_\pi \cdot H_1(\pi 1)^{\rho''_\pi}$. The client then sets $\mathrm{Sec}''_{\langle t+1 \rangle} = \mathrm{Sec}''_{\langle t+1 \rangle} \cup \{S''_{\pi 1}\}$. When node π is the parent of node $\langle t+1 \rangle$, the client obtains its secret value part $S''_{\langle t+1 \rangle} = S''_{\pi 0}$ for time period $t+1$.

(b). TPA obtains its secret key $SKT_{t+1.0} = \mathrm{Sec}'_{\langle t+1 \rangle}$ in time period $t+1$ and the verification value part set $\Omega'_{\omega,\langle t+1 \rangle} = \{R'_\pi | \pi \in \theta(\omega, \langle t+1 \rangle)\}$, where $\theta(\omega, \langle t+1 \rangle)$ contains node $\langle t+1 \rangle$'s ancestors on the route from node ω to $\langle t+1 \rangle$. Finally, TPA sets key update token $TU_{\langle t \rangle} = \{S'_{\langle t+1 \rangle}, \Omega'_{\omega,\langle t+1 \rangle}\}$ and sends $TU_{\langle t \rangle}$ to the client.
After receiving $TU_{\langle t \rangle}$, the client gets R'_π from set $\Omega'_{\omega,\langle t+1 \rangle}$ and computes verification value $R_\pi = R'_\pi \cdot R''_\pi$ for $\pi \in \theta(\omega, \langle t+1 \rangle)$. The client then sets verification value set $\Omega_{\langle t \rangle} = \Omega_{\langle t \rangle} \cup \{R_\pi\}$. Because $\theta(\beta, \langle t \rangle)$ is not used during the time period $t+1$, the verification value set $\Omega_{\beta,\langle t \rangle}$ should be removed,

where node β is the left sibling of node ω. Finally, the client gets $\Omega_{\langle t+1\rangle} = \Omega_{\langle t\rangle} \setminus \Omega_{\beta,\langle t\rangle}$, where $\Omega_{\langle t+1\rangle}$ is the set of verification values of nodes on the route from root to node $\langle t+1\rangle$.

(c). The client computes auditing secret key $S_{\langle t+1\rangle} = S'_{\langle t+1\rangle} \cdot S''_{\langle t+1\rangle}$ of leaf node $\langle t+1\rangle$. Thus the client's secret key in time period $t+1$ is $SKC_{t+1.0} = \{S_{\langle t+1\rangle}, \Omega_{\langle t+1\rangle}, \mathrm{Sec}''_{\langle t+1\rangle}\}$.

Finally, TPA and the client delete key update token $TU_{\langle t+1\rangle}$, all random values and secret value parts of left child generated in step b.

3.2 Description of the Proposed Protocol

Similar with previous auditing protocols [15–17], we adopt a digital signature $SSig$ to compute the file tag for file F's unique identifier $name$, verification value set $\Omega_{\langle t\rangle}$, and time period t. The client divides file F into blocks $m_1, \cdots, m_n \in Z_q^*$. The proposed protocol contains six algorithms as follows:

(1) SysSetup. The input is the number of time periods T and security parameter k.

(a) The client obtains two cycle groups G_1, G_2 whose orders are both prime q and bilinear pairing $\hat{e}: G_1 \times G_1 \rightarrow G_2$. Then it chooses generators $g, u \in G_1$ and two cryptographic hash functions $H_1: \{0,1\}^* \rightarrow G_1$, $H_2: \{0,1\}^* \times G_1 \rightarrow G_1$. The client sets public key $PK = (G_1, G_2, H_1, H_2, \hat{e}, g, u)$.

(b) For each node π in the set $\theta(\langle 0\rangle)$, the client randomly selects $\rho_\pi \in Z_q^*$. Then, the client computes node π's verification value $R_\pi = g^{\rho_\pi}$, left child's secret value $S_{\pi 0} = S_\pi \cdot H_1(\pi 0)^{\rho_\pi}$ and right child's secret value $S_{\pi 1} = S_\pi \cdot H_1(\pi 1)^{\rho_\pi}$. It's noticed that $S_\pi = 1$, when node π is root node. When node π is the parent of node $\langle 0\rangle$, the client obtains auditing secret key $S_{\langle 0\rangle} = S_{\pi 0}$ for time period 0.

(c) The client obtains its verification value set $\Omega_{\langle 0\rangle} = \{R_\pi | \pi \in \theta(\langle 0\rangle)\}$, where $\theta(\langle 0\rangle)$ contains node $\langle 0\rangle$'s ancestors until root. The client then sets $\mathrm{Sec}_{\langle 0\rangle} = \{S_\pi | \pi \in \varphi(\langle 0\rangle)\}$, which is used to compute secret values for next time period. $\varphi(\langle 0\rangle)$ includes right sibling of each node in the path from root to node $\langle 0\rangle$.

(d) For each node ω in the set $\varphi(\langle 0\rangle)$, the client randomly chooses S'_ω and S''_ω that satisfie $\mathrm{S}_\omega = \mathrm{S}'_\omega \cdot \mathrm{S}''_\omega$, and then sets $\mathrm{Sec}'_{\langle 0\rangle} = \{S'_\omega | \omega \in \varphi(\langle 0\rangle)\}$ and $\mathrm{Sec}''_{\langle 0\rangle} = \{S''_\omega | \omega \in \varphi(\langle 0\rangle)\}$. In time period 0, TPA's secret key is $SKT_{0.0} = \mathrm{Sec}'_{\langle 0\rangle}$, and the client's secret key is $SKC_{0.0} = \{S_{\langle 0\rangle}, \Omega_{\langle 0\rangle}, \mathrm{Sec}''_{\langle 0\rangle}\}$. $S_{\langle 0\rangle}$ is current time period's auditing secret key to generate file auditing authenticator in AuthGen algorithm. Set $\Omega_{\langle 0\rangle}$ is used to verify the file authenticators in ProofVerify algorithm. Sets $\mathrm{Sec}'_{\langle 0\rangle}$ and $\mathrm{Sec}''_{\langle 0\rangle}$ are used to compute secret value to update auditing secret key for next time period. The client sends $SKT_{0.0}$ to TPA secretly, and then deletes any values except $SKC_{0.0}$.

(2) KeyUpd. The input is secret key $SKT_{t.(RN(t)-1)}, SKC_{t.(RN(t)-1)}$, public key PK and time period t. $t.(RN(t)-1)$ represents that the secret keys of client and TPA are in the last refreshing period of time period t. The key update procedure is the same as Key Update described in Sect. 3.1.

(3) KeyRef. Input secret keys $SKT_{t.r}, SKC_{t.r}$ that have been refreshed r times in time period t, public key PK and time period t. $SKT_{t.r} = \mathrm{Sec}'_{\langle t\rangle} = \{S'_\omega | \omega \in \varphi(\langle t\rangle)\}$ is TPA's secret key. The client's secret key is $SKC_{t.r} = \{S_{\langle t\rangle}, \Omega_{\langle t\rangle}, \mathrm{Sec}''_{\langle t\rangle}\}$, where $\mathrm{Sec}''_{\langle t\rangle} = \{S''_\omega | \omega \in \varphi(\langle t\rangle)\}$.
   (a) For every node $\omega \in \varphi(\langle t\rangle)$, TPA randomly selects $X_\omega \in G_1$ and sets $S'_\omega := S'_\omega \cdot X_\omega$. Then TPA's secret key is $SKT_{t.r+1} = \{S'_\omega | \omega \in \varphi(\langle t\rangle)\}$, and key refresh token is $TR_{t.r} = \{X_\omega | \omega \in \varphi(t)\}$. TPA then sends $TR_{t.r}$ to the client.
   After receiving key refreshing token $TR_{t.r}$, the client computes $S''_\omega := S''_\omega \cdot X_\omega^{-1}$ for every node $\omega \in \varphi(\langle t\rangle)$. The client's new secret key for next refresh period is $SKC_{t.r+1} = \{S_{\langle t\rangle}, \Omega_{\langle t\rangle}, \mathrm{Sec}''_{\langle t\rangle}\}$, where the secret value set is $\mathrm{Sec}''_{\langle t\rangle} = \{S''_\omega | \omega \in \varphi(\langle t\rangle)\}$.
   (b) TPA and the client deletes $TR_{t.r}$ from local.

(4) AuthGen. The input is current time period t, client's secret key $SKC_{t.r} = \{S_{\langle t\rangle}, \Omega_{\langle t\rangle}, \mathrm{Sec}''_{\langle t\rangle}\}$, a file $F = \{m_1, m_2, \cdots, m_n\}$ that will be uploaded to the cloud in time period t, and public key PK.
   (a) The client randomly selects $name \in Z_q^*$ as the unique identifier of F, and uses signature algorithm SSig to compute a file tag $\sigma = \mathsf{SSig}(\Omega_{\langle t\rangle}, name, t)$. The client selects a random number $r \in Z_q^*$, and then computes $U = g^r$ and F's auditing authenticator $\delta_i = H_2(name||i||t, U)^r \cdot S_{\langle t\rangle} \cdot u^{rm_i}$ for every block $m_i, i \in [1, n]$.
   (b) The authenticator set of file F in time period t is $\Phi = \{t, U, \{\delta_i\}_{1 \le i \le n}, \Omega_{\langle t\rangle}\}$. The client sends file F, file tag σ, and authenticator set Φ to the cloud server.

(5) ProofGen. TPA issues a challenge $Chal = \{(i, v_i)\}_{i \in I}$ to the cloud server, where $v_i \in Z_q^*$, and $I = \{s_1, \cdots, s_c\}$ is a subset of $[1, n]$, c is the number of challenged blocks of file F.
   After inputting challenge $Chal$, file F, F's authenticator set $\Phi = (t, U, \{\delta_i\}_{1 \le i \le n}, \Omega_{\langle t\rangle})$, the cloud server computes $\delta = \prod_{i \in I} \delta_i^{v_i}$, $\mu = \sum_{i \in I} v_i m_i$. The cloud server sets proof $P = \{t, U, \delta, \mu, \Omega_{\langle t\rangle}\}$, and sends (P, σ) to TPA as the response of TPA's challenge.

(6) ProofVerify. The input is proof P, file tag σ, a challenge $Chal$, public key PK and time period t.
   TPA firstly checks the file tag σ to verify whether $name, t, \Omega_{\langle t\rangle}$ is integrated. If $name, t, \Omega_{\langle t\rangle}$ is integrated, TPA checks whether the following equation holds:

$$\hat{e}(U, u^\mu \prod_{i \in I} H_2(name||i||t, U)^{v_i}) \cdot \prod_{\substack{\pi, \beta \in \theta(\langle t\rangle) \\ \beta\ is\ \pi's\ child}} \hat{e}(R_\pi, H_1(\beta)^{\sum_{i \in I} v_i}) = \hat{e}(g, \delta)$$

TPA sends "True" to the client if the equation holds. Otherwise, TPA sends "False" to the client.

4 Security Analysis

Theorem 1 (Correctness). *The* ProofVerify *algorithm must outputs* "True" *for a valid proof P and corresponding challenge Chal.*

Proof: The proposed protocol is correct because the following equation holds:

$$\hat{e}(U, u^{\mu}\prod_{i\in I} H_2(name||i||t, U)^{v_i}) \cdot \prod_{\substack{\pi\in\theta(\langle t\rangle)\\ \beta \text{ is } \pi\text{'s child}}} \hat{e}(R_\pi, H_1(\beta)^{\sum_{i\in I} v_i})$$

$$= \hat{e}(g, u^{r\mu}\prod_{i\in I} H_2(name||i||t, U)^{rv_i}) \cdot \hat{e}(g, \prod_{\substack{\pi\in\theta(\langle t\rangle)\\ \beta \text{ is } \pi\text{'s child}}} H_1(\beta)^{\rho_\pi\cdot\sum_{i\in I} v_i})$$

$$= \hat{e}(g, u^{r\sum_{i\in I} v_i m_i}\prod_{i\in I} H_2(name||i||t, U)^{rv_i}) \cdot \hat{e}(g, S_{\langle t\rangle}{}^{\sum_{i\in I} v_i})$$

$$= \hat{e}(g, \prod_{i\in I} u^{rm_i v_i} \cdot H_2(name||i||t, U)^{rv_i} \cdot S_{\langle t\rangle}{}^{v_i})$$

$$= \hat{e}(g, \prod_{i\in I} u^{rm_i} \cdot H_2(name||i||t, U)^{r} \cdot S_{\langle t\rangle})^{v_i}$$

$$= \hat{e}(g, \prod_{i\in I} \delta_i^{v_i}) = \hat{e}(g, \delta)$$

Theorem 2 (Intrusion-resilience). *The proposed protocol is intrusion-resilient, provided digital signature* SSig *is existentially unforgeable and CDH problem in G_1 is hard.*

Proof: We define five games, and prove that the difference of adversary's success probabilities in these games is negligible.

Game0: Game0 is the same as the game defined in Sect. 2.

Game1: Apart from one difference, Game1 is analogous to Game0. The challenger maintains the list that contains file tags included in the authenticator set. If adversary generates a valid file tag that isn't generated by challenger but by signature scheme SSig, the challenger aborts.

Analysis: Analysis of this game is analogous to the analysis in [10]. Clearly, if the probability that the challenger aborts is non-negligible, taking advantage of the adversary, we can find a forger that can break SSig. Therefore, *name*, t and each value of $\Omega_{\langle t\rangle}$ are all issued by the challenger.

Game2: Apart from one difference, Game2 is analogous to Game1. The challenger maintains the list that contains response to the adversary's queries for authenticators. If adversary wins in Game2, but U that the adversary computed does not equal to the U in the list of $\Phi = (t, U, \{\delta_i\}_{1\leq i\leq n}, \Omega_{\langle t\rangle})$ that the challenger stores, then the challenger aborts.

Analysis: If the challenger aborts, there exists a simulator that can work out CDH problem with a non-negligible probability. The action of the simulator is similar with the action of the challenger in Game1. Thus U in $P = (t^*, U, \delta, \mu, \Omega_{\langle t^* \rangle})$ must be correct. This implies that there exists negligible difference between probabilities of adversary's success in Game1 and Game2.

Game3: Apart from one difference, Game3 is analogous to Game2. A list is maintained by the challenger, which contains answers to authenticator queries. The challenger watches each interaction. If in one interaction adversary succeeds in Game3 but the δ in its proof isn't equal to $\delta = \prod_{i \in I} \delta_i^{v_i}$, then the challenger aborts.

Analysis: Assume the challenger aborts at time period t^* under the file F named *name* that contains blocks $m_1, \cdots, m_n$, the authenticator set generated by the challenger is $\Phi = (t^*, U, \{\delta_i\}_{1 \le i \le n}, \Omega_{\langle t^* \rangle})$. Assume the challenge which forces the challenger to abort is $(t^*, Chal = \{i, v_i\}_{i \in I})$, and the proof responded by adversary is $P = (t^*, U, \delta', \mu', \Omega_{\langle t^* \rangle})$. Assume $P = (t^*, U, \delta, \mu, \Omega_{\langle t^* \rangle})$ is responded by honest party. For the honest party's proof P, the following equation holds

$$\hat{e}(U, u^{\mu} \prod_{i \in I} H_2(name||i||t, U)^{v_i}) \cdot \prod_{\substack{\pi, \beta \in \theta(\langle t \rangle) \\ \beta \text{ is } \pi\text{'s child}}} \hat{e}(R_\pi, H_1(\beta)^{\sum_{i \in I} v_i}) = \hat{e}(g, \delta)$$

For the adversary's proof that makes the challenger abort, we have $\delta \neq \delta'$, but the following equation holds:

$$\hat{e}(U, u^{\mu'} \prod_{i \in I} H_2(name||i||t, U)^{v_i}) \cdot \prod_{\substack{\pi, \beta \in \theta(\langle t \rangle) \\ \beta \text{ is } \pi\text{'s child}}} \hat{e}(R_\pi, H_1(\beta)^{\sum_{i \in I} v_i}) = \hat{e}(g, \delta')$$

Compared with equation in Theorem 1, we have $\mu \neq \mu'$, otherwise, it implies that $\delta = \delta'$. Let $\Delta\mu = \mu' - \mu$. If the challenger aborts, there exists a simulator that can work out CDH problem with a non-negligible probability.

Therefore, there exists negligible difference between probabilities of adversary's success in Game2 and Game3.

Game4: Game4 is analogous to Game3, except with one difference. In Game4, the challenger watches each interaction. If adversary succeeds in one interaction but μ in its proof is not the same as $\mu = \sum_{i \in I} v_i m_i$, then the challenger aborts.

Analysis: Assume the challenger's abort happens in time period t^* and the file named *name* contains blocks $m_1, \cdots, m_n$, and the authenticator set generated by the challenger is $\Phi = (t^*, U, \{\delta_i\}_{1 \le i \le n}, \Omega_{\langle t^* \rangle})$. Assume the challenge that forces the challenger to abort is $(t^*, Chal = \{i, v_i\}_{i \in I})$, and the adversary's proof is $P = (t^*, U, \delta', \mu', \Omega_{\langle t^* \rangle})$. Let the response generated by an honest party be $P = (t^*, U, \delta, \mu, \Omega_{\langle t^* \rangle})$. From Game3, we can know $\delta = \delta'$. Let $\Delta\mu = \mu' - \mu$, and $\Delta\mu \neq 0$. If the challenger aborts, there exists a simulator that can work out discrete logarithm problem with a non-negligible probability.

Therefore, there exists negligible difference between probabilities of adversary's success in Game3 and Game4. In conclusion, there are only negligible differences of the probabilities of adversary's success in above five games.

Because CDH problem can be reduced to discrete logarithm problem, TPA will reject unless the cloud server responds correct values in $P = (t, U, \delta, \mu, \Omega_{\langle t \rangle})$ as long as digital signature $SSig$ is existentially unforgeable and CDH problem in G_1 is hard.

If the cloud server passes the verification with correct $P = (t, U, \delta, \mu, \Omega_{\langle t \rangle})$, we are able to find a knowledge extractor which is able to extract all the file blocks $m_{s_1}, \cdots, m_{s_c}$ that are challenged. The method is the same as that in [3]. Executing the proposed protocol's auditing challenge on the same blocks $m_{s_1}, \cdots, m_{s_c}$ for c times by selecting independent coefficients $v_1, \cdots, v_c$, c linear equations that are independent will be obtained by the extractor in variables $m_{s_1}, \cdots, m_{s_c}$. The extractor can extract $m_{s_1}, \cdots, m_{s_c}$ by solving these equations. Thus, we finish the proof of Theorem 2.

Theorem 3 (Detectability). *The proposed protocol is* $(\frac{b}{a}, 1-(\frac{a-b}{a})^c)$ *detectable if the file stored on the cloud server is divided into* a *blocks and has* b *bad blocks, which are modified or deleted by the adversary, and* c *blocks are challenged.*

Proof: Assume a file divided into a blocks is stored on the cloud server, which has b bad blocks that are modified or deleted by the adversary, and c blocks are challenged. Bad blocks are found out if and only if at least one bad block is included in challenged blocks. Assume challenged blocks contains Y bad blocks. Challenged blocks contains more than one bad block with probability P_Y. So

$$\begin{aligned} P_Y &= P\{Y \geq 1\} \\ &= 1 - P\{Y = 0\} \\ &= 1 - \frac{a-b}{a} \cdot \frac{a+1-b}{a-1} \cdot \dots \cdot \frac{a-c+1-b}{a-c+1} \end{aligned}$$

We can get $P_Y \geq 1 - \left(\frac{a-b}{a}\right)^c$. Thus, this cloud storage auditing protocol is $\left(\frac{b}{n}, 1 - \left(\frac{a-b}{a}\right)^c\right)$ detectable.

5 Performance Analysis

We show comparison of computation overhead in Table 2. The overhead of AuthenGen and ProofGen algorithm of our protocol is the same as protocols in [16,17], while the overhead of SysSetup, KeyUpdate, KeyRefresh, ProofVerify algorithms are a little higher. However, previous protocols cannot remain secure when both TPA and the client are compromised. Our protocol can remain secure as long as the client and TPA are not be compromised in the same refreshing period. Therefore, it's acceptable for our protocol to have more computation overhead to attain higher security. In Table 2, Exp represents one exponentiation operation in G_1, Pair represents one bilinear pairing from G_1 to G_2, and Mul represents one multiplication operation in G_1.

Other operations such as the operations on Z_q^* and G_2, set operations, and hashing operations are ignored because the overhead of these operations is negligible. As shown in Table 2, the overhead of SysSetup algorithm is logarithmic in T and a little bit higher than the other three protocols, but SysSetup algorithm will be executed only once in the whole lifetime of our protocol. The overhead of KeyUpdate algorithm is logarithmic in T, but this is the worst-case computation overhead. In half of time periods, it only requires some set operations. The KeyRefresh algorithm only requires some multiplication operations in G_1. ProofVerify algorithm of our protocol executes more pairing computation than other protocols.

Table 2. Computation overhead

Protocols	Sys-Steup	Key-Update	Key-Refresh	Auth-Gen	Proof-Gen	Proof-Verify
The proposed protocol	$(logT)\cdot 3\cdot$ Exp	$(logT)\cdot 3\cdot$ Exp	$(logT)\cdot$ Mul	$3\cdot$ Exp	$c\cdot$ Exp	$(c+1+logT)\cdot$ Exp+$(2+logT)\cdot$ Pair
Protocol in[16]	$2\cdot$ Exp	$4\cdot$ Exp	–	$3\cdot$ Exp	$c\cdot$ Exp	$(c+1+log(T+2))\cdot$Exp+$3\cdot$Pair
Protocol in [17]	$2\cdot$ Exp	Exp	–	$3\cdot$ Exp	$c\cdot$ Exp	$(c+2)\cdot$ Exp+$3\cdot$ Pair

In Table 3, $|G_1|$ represents the length of on element in group G_1, $|Z_q^*|$ represents the length of one element in Z_q^*. The communication overhead of KeyUpdate and KeyRefresh are logarithmic in T. The challenge overhead is the same as protocols in [16,17]. The proof overhead is the same as [16], and is logarithmic in T.

Table 3. Communication overhead

Protocols	KeyUpdate	KeyRefresh	Challenge	Proof
The proposed protocol	$(logT)\cdot\|G_1\|$	$(logT)\cdot\|G_1\|$	$c\cdot\|Z_q^*\|$	$(logT+2)\cdot\|G_1\|+\|Z_q^*\|$
Protocol in [16]	–	–	$c\cdot\|Z_q^*\|$	$(logT+2)\cdot\|G_1\|+\|Z_q^*\|$
Protocol in [17]	$\|G_1\|$	–	$c\cdot\|Z_q^*\|$	$2\cdot\|G_1\|+\|Z_q^*\|$

6 Conclusion

We proposed an intrusion-resilient cloud storage auditing protocol that reduces the damage caused by key exposure. As long as the client and TPA are not compromised in the same refreshing period, the adversary is unable to compute the client's auditing secret keys. The security of the proposed protocol is also be proved through formal security proof. The performance of the proposed protocol is evaluated through numerical analysis.

Acknowledgment. The work was supported by the National Natural Science Foundation of China (No. 61502008, No. 61572001), The Natural Science Foundation of Anhui Province (No. 1708085QF136, No. 1508085QF132), Doctorial Research Start-up Foundation of Anhui University. The authors are very grateful to the anonymous referees for their detailed comments and suggestions regarding this paper.

References

1. Ateniese, G., Burns, R., Curtmola, R., Herring, J., Kissner, L., Peterson, Z., Song, D.: Provable data possession at untrusted stores. In: Proceedings of the 14th ACM Conference on Computer and Communications Security, CCS 2007, pp. 598–609. ACM, New York (2007). https://doi.org/10.1145/1315245.1315318
2. Barsoum, A.F., Hasan, M.A.: Provable multicopy dynamic data possession in cloud computing systems. IEEE Trans. Inf. Forensics Secur. **10**(3), 485–497 (2015). https://doi.org/10.1109/TIFS.2014.2384391
3. Canetti, R., Halevi, S., Katz, J.: A forward-secure public-key encryption scheme. In: Biham, E. (ed.) EUROCRYPT 2003. LNCS, vol. 2656, pp. 255–271. Springer, Heidelberg (2003). https://doi.org/10.1007/3-540-39200-9_16
4. Curtmola, R., Khan, O., Burns, R., Ateniese, G.: MR-PDP: multiple-replica provable data possession. In: Proceedings of the 28th International Conference on Distributed Computing Systems, pp. 411–420 (2008). https://doi.org/10.1109/ICDCS.2008.68
5. Dodis, Y., Franklin, M., Katz, J., Miyaji, A., Yung, M.: Intrusion-resilient public-key encryption. In: Joye, M. (ed.) CT-RSA 2003. LNCS, vol. 2612, pp. 19–32. Springer, Heidelberg (2003). https://doi.org/10.1007/3-540-36563-X_2
6. Gentry, C., Silverberg, A.: Hierarchical ID-based cryptography. In: Zheng, Y. (ed.) ASIACRYPT 2002. LNCS, vol. 2501, pp. 548–566. Springer, Heidelberg (2002). https://doi.org/10.1007/3-540-36178-2_34
7. Hu, F., Wu, C.H., Irwin, J.D.: A new forward secure signature scheme using bilinear maps. IACR Cryptology Eprint Archive 2003 (2003)
8. Juels, A., Kaliski Jr., B.S.: PORs: proofs of retrievability for large files. In: Proceedings of CCS 2007, pp. 584–597 (2007). https://doi.org/10.1145/1315245.1315317
9. Kang, B.G., Park, J.H., Hahn, S.G.: A new forward secure signature scheme. IACR Cryptol. Eprint Archive **13**(5), 821–825 (2008)
10. Shacham, H., Waters, B.: Compact proofs of retrievability. In: Pieprzyk, J. (ed.) ASIACRYPT 2008. LNCS, vol. 5350, pp. 90–107. Springer, Heidelberg (2008). https://doi.org/10.1007/978-3-540-89255-7_7
11. Wang, B., Li, B., Li, H.: Public auditing for shared data with efficient user revocation in the cloud. Proc. IEEE INFOCOM **2013**, 2904–2912 (2013). https://doi.org/10.1109/INFCOM.2013.6567101
12. Wang, C., Chow, S.S.M., Wang, Q., Ren, K., Lou, W.: Privacy-preserving public auditing for secure cloud storage. IEEE Trans. Comput. **62**, 362–375 (2013). https://doi.org/10.1109/TC.2011.245

13. Wang, Q., Wang, C., Ren, K., Lou, W., Li, J.: Enabling public auditability and data dynamics for storage security in cloud computing. IEEE Trans. Parallel Distrib. Syst. **22**, 847–859 (2010). https://doi.org/10.1109/TPDS.2010.183
14. Yang, K., Jia, X.: An efficient and secure dynamic auditing protocol for data storage in cloud computing. IEEE Trans. Parallel Distrib. Syst. **24**(9), 1717–1726 (2013). https://doi.org/10.1109/TPDS.2012.278
15. Yu, J., Ren, K., Wang, C.: Enabling cloud storage auditing with verifiable outsourcing of key updates. IEEE Trans. Inf. Forensics Secur. **11**(6), 1362–1375 (2016). https://doi.org/10.1109/TIFS.2016.2528500
16. Yu, J., Ren, K., Wang, C., Varadharajan, V.: Enabling cloud storage auditing with key-exposure resistance. IEEE Trans. Inf. Forensics Secur. **10**(6), 1167–1179 (2015). https://doi.org/10.1109/TIFS.2015.2400425
17. Yu, J., Wang, H.: Strong key-exposure resilient auditing for secure cloud storage. IEEE Trans. Inf. Forensics Secur. **12**(8), 1931–1940 (2017). https://doi.org/10.1109/TIFS.2017.2695449
18. Yu, J., Hao, R., Kong, F., Cheng, X., Fan, J., Chen, Y.: Forward-secure identity-based signature: security notions and construction. Inf. Sci. **181**(3), 648–660 (2011). https://doi.org/10.1016/j.ins.2010.09.034
19. Yu, J., Kong, F., Cheng, X., Hao, R., Li, G.: One forward-secure signature scheme using bilinear maps and its applications. Inf. Sci. **279**, 60–76 (2014). https://doi.org/10.1016/j.ins.2014.03.082
20. Yuan, J., Yu, S.: Public integrity auditing for dynamic data sharing with multiuser modification. IEEE Trans. Inf. Forensics Secur. **10**(8), 1717–1726 (2015). https://doi.org/10.1109/TIFS.2015.2423264
21. Zhu, Y., Ahn, G.J., Hu, H., Yau, S.S., An, H.G., Hu, C.J.: Dynamic audit services for outsourced storages in clouds. IEEE Trans. Serv. Comput. **6**(2), 227–238 (2013). https://doi.org/10.1109/TSC.2011.51

Secure Publicly Verifiable Computation with Polynomial Commitment in Cloud Computing

Jian Shen[1], Dengzhi Liu[1], Xiaofeng Chen[2], Xinyi Huang[3,4], Jiageng Chen[5], and Mingwu Zhang[6](✉)

[1] Jiangsu Engineering Center of Network Monitoring, Nanjing University of Information Science and Technology, Nanjing, China
s_shenjian@126.com, liudzdh@126.com

[2] State Key Laboratory of Integrated Service Networks, Xidian University, Xi'an, China
xfchen@xidian.edu.cn

[3] School of Mathematics and Computer Science, Fujian Normal University, Fuzhou, China
xyhuang81@gmail.com

[4] HIFIVE Lennon Laboratory, Chengdu HiFive Technology Co., Ltd., Chengdu, China

[5] School of Computer Science, Central China Normal University, Wuhan, China
chinkako@gmail.com

[6] School of Computer Science, Hubei University of Technology, Wuhan, China
scauzhang@gmail.com

Abstract. Computation outsourcing is a vital cloud service that can be provided for users. Using the cloud to address complex computations is crucial to users with lightweight devices. However, computations may not be correctly executed by the cloud due to monetary reasons. In this paper, we propose a secure publicly verifiable computation scheme in cloud computing, which is designed based on the polynomial commitment. Owing to the public key de-commitment of the polynomial commitment, our scheme can provide public verifiability for computation results. Security analysis shows that the proposed scheme is correct and can support public verifiability. Comparison and simulation results reveal that our scheme can be performed with low computational cost compared to previous schemes.

Keywords: Computation outsourcing · Verifiable computation
Polynomial commitment · Public verifiability

1 Introduction

Cloud computing is an Internet-based technology, which has been developed with computer techniques [3,20]. The cloud consists of many distributed servers that

W. Susilo and G. Yang (Eds.): ACISP 2018, LNCS 10946, pp. 417–430, 2018.
https://doi.org/10.1007/978-3-319-93638-3_24

can provide various consumer services [8,24,36], such as multimedia entertainment, real-time information sharing and remote medical treatment [10,11,16,19]. Cloud consumers can enjoy cloud services via the Internet anywhere and anytime [5,17,21,30,33], and cloud servers are managed by a cloud service provider (CSP) [20,22]. Clients must pay for their usage in a pay-as-you-use manner [12,28]. Although it is not free to use the cloud, the charge for cloud usage is not expensive compared to traditional storage and computing devices. According to the latest price on the Amazon web site, the price for a general solid state drive (SSD) is \$ 0.10/GB[1]. More importantly, exploiting the cloud to store data and execute computations can reduce hardware and software investments [7,14,23,25,29,35], which brings great economic benefits to individuals, companies, and organizations.

With the development of the Internet and cloud computing, numerous cloud-based remote services have been generated. Computation outsourcing is an important cloud service. Resource-limited users can delegate the cloud to execute complex computations for themselves [4,6,14,32,37,38]. Many fields rely on the cloud to execute computations based on the stored data [15,18]. For example, the weather bureau uses statistical rainfall, snowfall or disastrous climate data for years past to infer the probability of corresponding abnormal weather in each season of the next year. Doctors use the cloud to assess patient disease data and evaluate the seasonality of common diseases.

The particularity of cloud computing determines that the design of computation outsourcing schemes faces many security issues [9,27,31]. On the one hand, the cloud may attack the stored data, which will result in wrong outputs for outsourced computations. On the other hand, the cloud may discard infrequently used data in order to save storage resources. When one user wants to use the corresponding data for computation, the cloud randomly selects a result or uses a previous computational result to cheat the user. Hence, designing a computation outsourcing scheme with verifiability is necessary [2,26]. In recent years, many researchers have devoted themselves to the research of verifiable computation [18,34,37,38]. To enhance the security of the system, some researchers designed verifiable computation schemes with public verifiability [1,26,32], which is more practical in real-world computation outsourcing systems. However, the existing verifiable schemes mainly focus on the study of homomorphic encryption, which brings great computational cost to the system. Moreover, users also need to participate in the verification process, which affects the security and efficiency of the system. Therefore, it is necessary to design a novel secure publicly verifiable computation system with high efficiency for cloud computing.

In this paper, by taking advantage of the polynomial commitment, we propose a secure publicly verifiable computation scheme for cloud computing. The main contributions of this paper are as follows:

- Due to the utilization of the polynomial commitment, computational results of the cloud in the proposed scheme can be securely verified by the trusted agency (TA) on behalf of users.

[1] https://aws.amazon.com/cn/pricing/.

- The proposed scheme can provide public verifiability for computational results. In other words, any entity can delegate the TA to verify the correctness of the computational results using the public key.
- The input and computation polynomial are independent of the system efficiency; the data size and computation polynomial degree do not introduce additional burdens into the system.

The remainder of this paper is organized as follows. Section 2 presents work related to the proposed scheme. Section 3 lists some preliminaries used in the proposed scheme. Section 4 describes the system model of the proposed scheme as well as the threat model and the design goals. Section 5 introduces the proposed scheme in detail, and Sect. 6 provides the security and performance analyses. The conclusion of this paper is given in Sect. 7.

2 Related Work

In verifiable computation research, many related schemes have been proposed [18,34,37,38]. In [37], Zhou *et al.* proposed a secure and verifiable outsourcing of exponentiation operations in cloud computing. In the outsourcing phase, the scheme only needed a very limited number of modular multiplications at the local side, which is very efficient such that the scheme can be performed on lightweight mobile devices. Moreover, the scheme by Zhou *et al.* can provide a verification mechanism for users to check the validity of computational results. To solve the problem of privacy leakage, Zhuo *et al.* in [38] proposed a privacy-preserving verifiable set operation in big data. In Zhuo *et al.*'s scheme, users can verify the correctness of the operation result with privacy preservation. Meanwhile, Zhuo *et al.* extended their scheme to support the data preprocess and the batch verification, which greatly reduces the computational cost of the system. In [18], Liu *et al.* proposed an efficient privacy-preserving outsourced computation scheme over public data, which allows users to outsource complex computations over public data to the cloud. Note that this scheme is designed based on switchable homomorphic encryption, and the privacy of the computational function and its outputs can be preserved during the computation outsourcing. To address the problem of key updates in cloud auditing, Yu *et al.* in [34] used verifiable computation outsourcing in the design of cloud storage auditing with verifiable outsourcing of key updates. The tasks of key updating are safely outsourced to a third-party auditor (TPA). The secret key in the TPA is stored in an encrypted form, so when one user wants to upload data to the cloud, he/she needs to download the encrypted key and then decrypt it. In addition, the user can verify whether the secret key has been updated by the TPA.

To meet practical requirements and enhance system security, some researchers proposed outsourced computation schemes with public verifiability [1,26,32]. Alderman *et al.* in [1] proposed a revocable publicly verifiable computation scheme, which can revoke a cheating server from the system. To process key generation and key distribution, Alderman *et al.* introduced a key distribution center (KDC) in their scheme. The KDC can verify the correctness of results from the cloud; furthermore, the KDC is a trusted entity that can execute server revocation in the system. In [32], Wang *et al.* proposed a secure collaborative publicly verifiable computation scheme to strengthen the flexibility of the computation outsourcing system. By taking advantage of an algebraic operation structure, the scheme by Wang *et al.* can construct a target function based on previous functions and the function of the private cloud. Moreover, this scheme allows the private cloud to verify the integrity of the target function and allows users check the correctness of the results. In [26], Song *et al.* proposed a verification scheme for polynomial evaluation based on the homomorphic verifiable computation tag structure, which can be used in multiple data sources with public verifiability. In addition, the scheme is more efficient, and the computational cost of the client side is independent of the input and polynomial sizes, making it very suitable for the mobile environment.

3 Preliminaries

In this section, the preliminaries of the proposed scheme are introduced. First, the bilinear pairing used to construct the proposed scheme is presented. Then, the technology of the polynomial commitment is briefly introduced.

3.1 Bilinear Pairing

Let $\mathbb{G}_1$ and $\mathbb{G}_2$ be two multiplicative groups of prime order q. The bilinear pairing can be denoted as $\widehat{e}$: $\mathbb{G}_1 \times \mathbb{G}_1 \rightarrow \mathbb{G}_2$. Suppose that $\mathcal{P}$, $\mathcal{Q} \in \mathbb{G}_1$, x, $y \in \mathbb{Z}_q^*$ and $\mathcal{G}$ is the generator of $\mathbb{G}_1$. Three properties of the bilinear pairing are shown in the following:

- Bilinear: $\widehat{e}(\mathcal{P}^x, \mathcal{Q}^y) = \widehat{e}(\mathcal{P}, \mathcal{Q})^{xy}$.
- Non-degenerate: $\widehat{e}(\mathcal{G}, \mathcal{G}) \neq 1$.
- Computable: $\widehat{e}(\mathcal{P}, \mathcal{Q})$ can be computed by an algorithm.

3.2 Polynomial Commitment

The technology of the polynomial commitment [13] can be used in the design of verifiable schemes. Here, the process of the polynomial commitment is briefly introduced as follows:

- Setup(1^θ, t): This process generates the secret key and the public key, supposing that a trusted entity in the system executes this process. Here, t is the degree of the polynomial.
- Commit(PK, $\phi(x)$): This process has two functionalities. First, this process computes a commitment for polynomial $\phi(x)$. Second, this process generates a de-commitment key dk for the system.
- Open(PK, C, dk): This process uses dk to de-commitment commitment C.
- VerifyPoly(PK, C, $\phi(x)$, i, dk): The verifier verifies the correctness of commitment C according to PK, $\phi(x)$, i and dk.
- VerifyEval(PK, C, i, $\phi(x)$, w_i): This process verifies whether $\phi(x)$ is the evaluation of the polynomial committed in commitment C.

4 Problem Statement

The system model and the threat model are formalized in this section. In addition, the design goals of the proposed scheme are introduced.

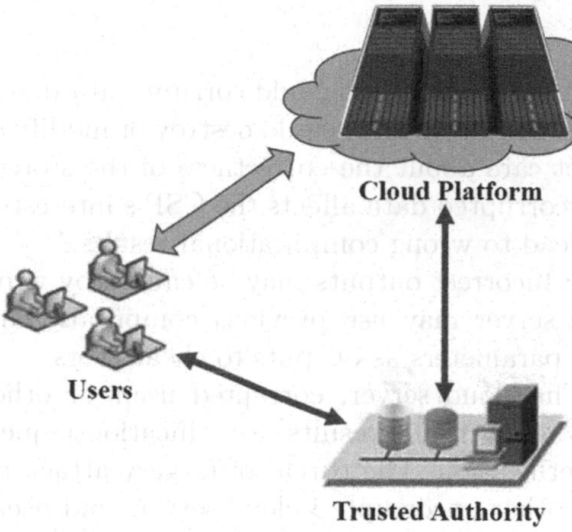

Fig. 1. The system model

4.1 The System Model

Three types of entities are included in our verifiable computation system, which are the *Trusted Agency* (TA), *Users* and *Cloud Platform*. The system model is shown in Fig. 1. A detailed introduction of these entities is given below:

- Trusted Agency (TA): The TA is a fully trusted entity in the system. The main task of the TA is to assist the user in verifying computational results from the cloud. Moreover, the TA is responsible for generating polynomials, security parameters and the computation polynomial for the system. In addition, the TA can also verify the correctness of computational results on behalf of users.
- Users: Users are cloud consumers who use cloud services via the Internet. In the proposed scheme, users upload their data to the cloud server and delegate computation tasks to the cloud. Users use computation services, paid for in a pay-per-use manner. Note that the computing capability and the storage resources of users are limited.
- Cloud Platform: The cloud platform consists of many distributed servers. These servers are connected through the network. The cloud platform provides various services for cloud users. Compared to the TA, the cloud platform is semi-trusted. The cloud platform has powerful computing capability, and it can execute computation tasks for users using the corresponding data and the computation polynomial.

4.2 Threat Model

In the proposed system, the cloud is responsible for storing user data and helping users process the data. However, the cloud is curious-but-honest. Moreover, some corrupted users or external adversaries may collaborate with the cloud to attack a system [26]. In this paper, three potential threats are considered, as listed below.

- Data Corruption: The cloud server could corrupt data due to monetary reasons. Moreover, outside adversaries could destroy or modify data in the cloud. The cloud does not care about the correctness of the stored data unless the appearance of the corrupted data affects the CSP's interests. Corrupted data in the cloud may lead to wrong computational results.
- Incorrect Outputs: Incorrect outputs may be caused by wrong or incomplete inputs. The cloud server may use previous computational results or other randomly selected parameters as outputs to cheat users.
- Forgery Attack: The cloud server, corrupted users or other outside adversaries may forge computational results or verification requests for the TA to attempt to pass verification. The threat of forgery attack may influence the trustworthiness of other uncorrupted cloud servers and users in the system.

4.3 Design Goals

In this paper, we propose a secure verifiable computation scheme for cloud computing. The design goals of our scheme are as follows:

- Correctness: The TA can verify the correctness of computational results under the security threats mentioned above. In other words, regardless of whether the current computational result is correct or not, the TA can verify the result.
- Public Verifiability: The verifiable computation scheme should support public verifiability. That is, any user or entity in the system can request the TA to verify the correctness of computational results from the cloud using public parameters or keys.
- Efficiency: The verifiable computation scheme can be executed with a low computational cost. Note that most computing tasks are delegated to the cloud and the TA. The user side only needs to generate the necessary security parameters and keys after his/her data are outsourced to the cloud. Moreover, the computation polynomial and the system input are independent of the system efficiency.

5 The Proposed Scheme

In this section, the proposed scheme is described in detail. The process of the proposed scheme can be found in Fig. 2. A detailed introduction of our scheme is given below:

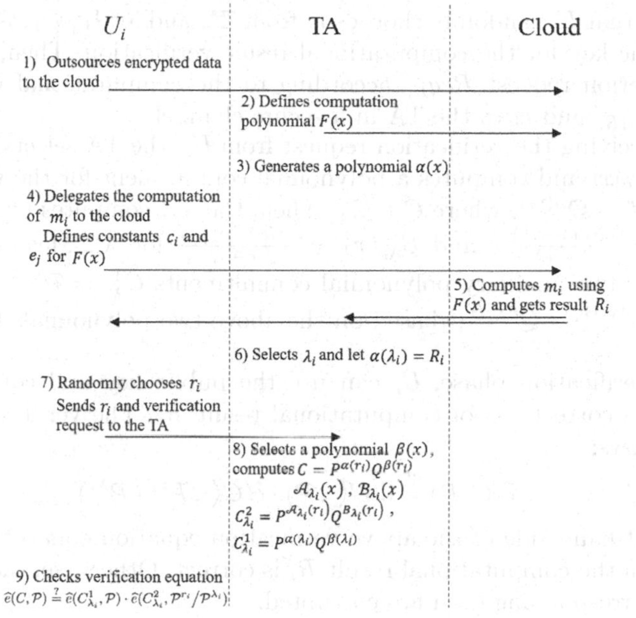

Fig. 2. The process of the proposed scheme

(1) Users rely on the cloud to store and compute their data. In general, the data are encrypted by users and then uploaded to the cloud. Suppose that one user U_i uploads his/her data M to the cloud. The data of M are divided into n blocks, and the corresponding block indexes are $I_1, I_2, \cdots, I_n$.

(2) The TA defines a polynomial $F(x) = \sum_{i,j=1}^{n} c_i \cdot x^{e_j}$, which is used to execute computations with the data for users. Note that c_i and e_j are constants defined by users. The polynomial of $F(x)$ is sent to the cloud. Meanwhile, the TA generates a polynomial $\alpha(x) \in \mathbb{Z}_q[x]$ for further computational result verification, where q is a big prime order. Suppose that the degree of $\alpha(x)$ is t. Accordingly, coefficients of $\alpha(x)$ can be denoted as α_i, where $0 \leq i \leq t$.

(3) If U_i wants to compute m_i, he/she needs to define constants c_i and e_j according to his/her computation demands. Meanwhile, U_i needs to generate a computation request that contains the corresponding index information of the data block. The constants and the computation request are sent to the cloud. After the cloud receives the computation request, the cloud computes m_i using computation polynomial $F(x)$. Assuming that the computational result of m_i is R_i, the computational result R_i is sent to U_i and the TA. Upon receiving R_i, the TA generates a security parameter $\lambda_i \in \mathbb{Z}_q$ based on the data block information and $\alpha(\lambda_i) = R_i$. The parameter of λ_i is saved locally by the TA for further computational result verification.

(4) If U_i wants to check the correctness of the computational result R_i, he/she needs to generate a request for the TA to setup the verification mechanism.

Suppose that U_i randomly chooses r_i from $\mathbb{Z}_q^*$, and let $\{\hat{e}, \mathbb{G}_1, \mathbb{G}_2, \mathcal{P}, \mathcal{P}^{r_i}\}$ be the public key for the computational result verification. Then, U_i generates a verification request Req_{R_i} according to the computational result R_i and sends Req_{R_i} and r_i to the TA in a secure channel.

(5) Upon receiving the verification request from U_i, the TA selects a polynomial $\beta(x) \in \mathbb{Z}_q[x]$ and computes a polynomial commitment for the verification as $C = \mathcal{P}^{\alpha(r_i)} \cdot \mathcal{Q}^{\beta(r_i)}$, where $C \in \mathbb{G}_1$. Then, the TA computes two polynomials $\mathcal{A}_{\lambda_i}(x) = \frac{\alpha(x)-\alpha(\lambda_i)}{x-\lambda_i}$ and $\mathcal{B}_{\lambda_i}(x) = \frac{\beta(x)-\beta(\lambda_i)}{x-\lambda_i}$ for λ_i. Meanwhile, the TA computes two auxiliary polynomial commitments $C^1_{\lambda_i} = \mathcal{P}^{\alpha(\lambda_i)} \cdot \mathcal{Q}^{\beta(\lambda_i)}$ and $C^2_{\lambda_i} = \mathcal{P}^{\mathcal{A}_{\lambda_i}(r_i)} \cdot \mathcal{Q}^{\mathcal{B}_{\lambda_i}(r_i)}$ based on the above two polynomials for parameter λ_i.

(6) In the verification phase, U_i can use the public key and commitments to verify the correctness of computational result R_i. The verification equation is as follows:

$$\hat{e}(C, \mathcal{P}) \stackrel{?}{=} \hat{e}(C^1_{\lambda_i}, \mathcal{P}) \cdot \hat{e}(C^2_{\lambda_i}, \mathcal{P}^{r_i}/\mathcal{P}^{\lambda_i})$$

If the left-hand side of the above verification equation equals the right-hand side, then the computational result R_i is correct. Otherwise, the cloud server or the corresponding data are corrupted.

6 Security Analysis and Performance Analysis

The security analysis and performance analysis are introduced in this section. In the security analysis, the correctness and public verifiability of the proposed scheme are proved. In the performance analysis, the simulation of our scheme and its comparison with previous schemes are given.

6.1 Security Analysis

Theorem 1. *The proposed scheme is correct in verifying the correctness of computational results.*

Proof. Per the description of the scheme in Sect. 5, U_i can determine that the verification of this scheme is correct if the verification equation holds. The right-hand side of the verification equation can be computed as $\hat{e}(C^1_{\lambda_i}, \mathcal{P}) \cdot \hat{e}(C^2_{\lambda_i}, \mathcal{P}^{r_i}/\mathcal{P}^{\lambda_i}) = \hat{e}(\mathcal{P}^{\alpha(\lambda_i)}\mathcal{Q}^{\beta(\lambda_i)}, \mathcal{P}) \cdot \hat{e}(\mathcal{P}^{\mathcal{A}_{\lambda_i}(r_i)}\mathcal{Q}^{\mathcal{B}_{\lambda_i}(r_i)}, \mathcal{P}^{r_i-\lambda_i})$. Assuming that $Q = \mathcal{P}^{\kappa}$, we can obtain

$$\begin{aligned}
&\hat{e}(\mathcal{P}^{\alpha(\lambda_i)}\mathcal{P}^{\kappa\cdot\beta(\lambda_i)}, \mathcal{P}) \cdot \hat{e}(\mathcal{P}^{\mathcal{A}_{\lambda_i}(r_i)}\mathcal{P}^{\kappa\cdot\mathcal{B}_{\lambda_i}(r_i)}, \mathcal{P}^{r_i-\lambda_i})\\
&= \hat{e}(\mathcal{P}^{\alpha(\lambda_i)+\kappa\cdot\beta(\lambda_i)}, \mathcal{P}) \cdot \hat{e}(\mathcal{P}^{\mathcal{A}_{\lambda_i}(r_i)+\kappa\cdot\mathcal{B}_{\lambda_i}(r_i)}, \mathcal{P}^{r_i-\lambda_i})\\
&= \hat{e}(\mathcal{P}, \mathcal{P})^{(\alpha(\lambda_i)+\kappa\cdot\beta(\lambda_i))+(\mathcal{A}_{\lambda_i}(r_i)+\kappa\cdot\mathcal{B}_{\lambda_i}(r_i))\cdot(r_i-\lambda_i)}
\end{aligned}$$

Note that $\mathcal{A}_{\lambda_i}(r_i) + \kappa \cdot B_{\lambda_i}(r_i) = \frac{\alpha(r_i)-\alpha(\lambda_i)}{r_i-\lambda_i} + \kappa \cdot \frac{\beta(r_i)-\beta(\lambda_i)}{r_i-\lambda_i}$. Then, $(\mathcal{A}_{\lambda_i}(\lambda_i) + \kappa \cdot B_{\lambda_i}(\lambda_i)) \cdot (r_i - \lambda_i)$ can be computed as follows:

$$\begin{aligned}
&(\mathcal{A}_{\lambda_i}(\lambda_i) + \kappa \cdot B_{\lambda_i}(\lambda_i)) \cdot (r_i - \lambda_i)\\
&= (\tfrac{\alpha(r_i)-\alpha(\lambda_i)}{r_i-\lambda_i} + \kappa \cdot \tfrac{\beta(r_i)-\beta(\lambda_i)}{r_i-\lambda_i}) \cdot (r_i - \lambda_i)\\
&= \alpha(r_i) - \alpha(\lambda_i) + \kappa \cdot (\beta(r_i) - \beta(\lambda_i))
\end{aligned}$$

According to the computational result of $(\mathcal{A}_{\lambda_i}(\lambda_i) + \kappa \cdot B_{\lambda_i}(\lambda_i)) \cdot (r_i - \lambda_i)$, we can obtain

$$\begin{aligned}&(\alpha(\lambda_i) + \kappa \cdot \beta(\lambda_i)) + (\mathcal{A}_{\lambda_i}(\lambda_i) + \kappa \cdot B_{\lambda_i}(\lambda_i)) \cdot (r_i - \lambda_i)\\ &= (\alpha(\lambda_i) + \kappa \cdot \beta(\lambda_i)) + \alpha(r_i) - \alpha(\lambda_i) + \kappa \cdot (\beta(r_i) - \beta(\lambda_i))\\ &= \alpha(r_i) + \kappa \cdot \beta(r_i)\end{aligned}$$

The result of the right-hand side of the verification equation can be computed as $\widehat{e}(\mathcal{P}, \mathcal{P})^{\alpha(r_i)+\kappa\cdot\beta(r_i)} = \widehat{e}(\mathcal{P}^{\alpha(r_i)+\kappa\cdot\beta(r_i)}, \mathcal{P}) = \widehat{e}(\mathcal{P}^{\alpha(r_i)}\mathcal{Q}^{\beta(r_i)}, \mathcal{P})$. As mentioned above, we have $C = \mathcal{P}^{\alpha(r_i)} \cdot \mathcal{Q}^{\beta(r_i)}$. That is, the verification equation holds. Hence, it can be determined that the verification process of this paper is correct. □

Theorem 2. *The proposed scheme supports public verifiability for computational results.*

Proof. In the phase of computational result verification, U_i can check the correctness of computational result R_i using public key $\mathcal{P}$, $\mathcal{P}^{r_i}$ and commitments C, $C^1_{\lambda_i}$ and $C^2_{\lambda_i}$. That is, any entity can use the public key to delegate the TA to verify the correctness of computational results. Thus, the proposed scheme supports public verifiability. □

6.2 Performance Analysis

The performance of the proposed scheme is analyzed in this subsection. We compare our scheme with two previous schemes [18,26] in terms of comparison analysis and simulation analysis.

(1) Comparison Analysis
For convenience of the performance comparison, we use the symbols $P.$, $M.$, $E.$, $A.$ and $H.$ to denote the operations of pairing, multiplication, exponentiation, addition and hash. The comparison result is shown in Table 1. From the comparison result, we can find that the computational cost of our scheme is $3P.+(6+n)E.+(10+n)M.+(4+n)A.$. Note that symbol n is the degree of the computation polynomial. Table 1 shows that our scheme and the scheme of Song *et al.* have relatively the same computational cost for exponentiation, multiplication and addition if n is large enough. However, the cost of pairing in the scheme by Song *et al.* is higher than that in our scheme. More importantly, Song *et al.*'s scheme has hash operations that greatly increase the computational cost of the system, so our scheme is more efficient than their scheme. Compared to the computational cost of the scheme by Liu *et al.* [18], it is obvious that our scheme has less cost for exponentiation, multiplication and addition. The computational cost of pairing in our scheme is negligible because n is very large in practical verifiable computation systems,

Table 1. Comparison of computational cost

Scheme	Computational cost	Public verifiability
Song *et al.*'s scheme [26]	$4P.+(7+n)E.+2H.+(4+n)M.+(7+n)A.$	Y
Liu *et al.*'s scheme [18]	$(14+3n)E.+(18+4n)M.+(8+n)A.$	N
Our scheme	$3P.+(6+n)E.+(10+n)M.+(4+n)A.$	Y

*P.: Pairing; M.: Multiplication; n.: Degree of the computation polynomial
*E.: Exponentiation; A: Addition; H.: Hash.

which determines that Liu *et al.*'s scheme has much higher computational cost than our scheme. In addition, the support for public verifiability in the two schemes and our scheme is also listed in Table 1. From the comparison result, it can be summarized that our scheme can be performed with public verifiability and less computational cost compared to the schemes of Song *et al.* and Liu *et al.*

(2) Simulation Analysis
The proposed scheme and the two similar schemes [18,26] are simulated in an experimental platform configured by the GMP Library (GMP-6.1.2) and the PBC Library (pbc-0.5.14). The experimental platform is constructed on a Linux system with 8 GB RAM and 2.6 GHz CPU. To simulate our scheme and the two similar schemes on the experimental platform, we set the degree number of the computation polynomial to 100. Because the computation tasks are executed by the cloud using the computation polynomial, the input size does not affect the system efficiency. We use different data sizes as the input for computation polynomial $F(x)$. The simulation results of the computation polynomial under different data sizes are shown in Fig. 3, from which we determine that the computational time difference under various data sizes is very small. That is, the computational time is relatively constant when the system inputs data of different sizes. Hence, the simulation results of the computation polynomial under different input sizes meet the efficiency design goal.

Figure 4 shows the simulation result of the proposed scheme and the two similar schemes [18,26]. Note that the x-axis of Fig. 4 is computing counts. From Fig. 4, we find that the computational times of our scheme and the two similar schemes increase linearly with the increase of computing counts. However, for the same counts, the computational time of our scheme is always less than those of the two similar schemes. Hence, our scheme is more efficient than those by Liu *et al.* [18] and Song *et al.* [26].

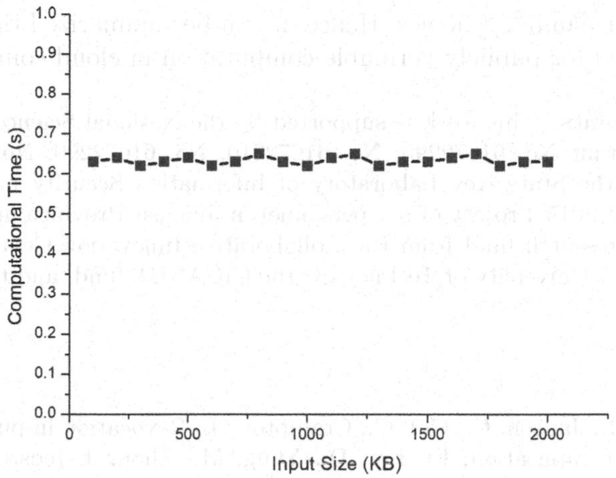

Fig. 3. Simulation result of the computation polynomial

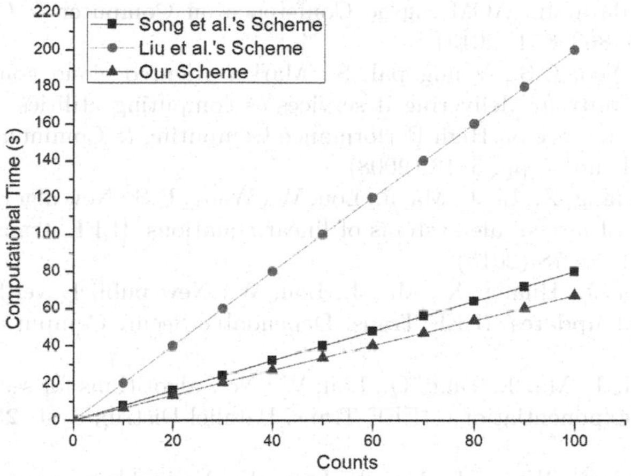

Fig. 4. Simulation results of our scheme and the two similar schemes

7 Conclusion

In this paper, we propose a secure publicly verifiable computation scheme based on the polynomial commitment in cloud computing. In our scheme, the public key can be used to verify computation results from the cloud. In other words, our scheme supports public verifiability. The correctness and public verifiability are proved in the security analysis, which meets the design goals of the proposed scheme. In the performance analysis, we compare our scheme with those by Liu *et al.* [18] and Song *et al.* [26]. From the comparison result, it can be determined that our scheme is more efficient than the similar schemes. In addition, the simulation result shows that our scheme indeed uses less computational time compared to the similar schemes. Hence, it can be summarized that our scheme can be well used for publicly verifiable computation in cloud computing.

Acknowledgments. This work is supported by the National Science Foundation of China under Grant No. 61672295, No. 61672010, No. 61672290, No. 61772280 and No. U1405254, the State Key Laboratory of Information Security under Grant No. 2017-MS-10, the 2015 Project of six personnel in Jiangsu Province under Grant No. R2015L06, the research fund from the Collaborative Innovation Center of Industrial Bigdata in Hubei University of Technology, the CICAEET fund, and the PAPD fund.

References

1. Alderman, J., Janson, C., Cid, C., Crampton, J.: Revocation in publicly verifiable outsourced computation. In: Lin, D., Yung, M., Zhou, J. (eds.) Inscrypt 2014. LNCS, vol. 8957, pp. 51–71. Springer, Cham (2015). https://doi.org/10.1007/978-3-319-16745-9_4
2. Backes, M., Fiore, D., Reischuk, R.M.: Verifiable delegation of computation on outsourced data. In: ACM Sigsac Conference on Computer & Communications Security, pp. 863–874 (2013)
3. Buyya, R., Yeo, C.S., Venugopal, S.: Market-oriented cloud computing: vision, hype, and reality for delivering it services as computing utilities. In: IEEE International Conference on High Performance Computing & Communications, HPCC 2008, vol. 11, no. 4, pp. 5–13 (2008)
4. Chen, X., Huang, X., Li, J., Ma, J., Lou, W., Wong, D.S.: New algorithms for secure outsourcing of large-scale systems of linear equations. IEEE Trans. Inf. Forensics Secur. **10**(1), 69–78 (2015)
5. Chen, X., Li, J., Huang, X., Ma, J., Lou, W.: New publicly verifiable databases with efficient updates. IEEE Trans. Dependable Secur. Comput. **12**(5), 546–556 (2015)
6. Chen, X., Li, J., Ma, J., Tang, Q., Lou, W.: New algorithms for secure outsourcing of modular exponentiations. IEEE Trans. Parallel Distrib. Syst. **25**(9), 2386–2396 (2012)
7. Chen, X., Li, J., Weng, J., Ma, J., Lou, W.: Verifiable computation over large database with incremental updates. IEEE Trans. Comput. **65**(10), 3184–3195 (2016)
8. Dikaiakos, M.D., Katsaros, D., Mehra, P., Pallis, G., Vakali, A.: Cloud computing: distributed internet computing for IT and scientific research. IEEE Internet Comput. **13**(5), 10–13 (2009)
9. Dillon, T., Wu, C., Chang, E.: Cloud computing: issues and challenges. In: Proceedings of the International Conference on Advanced Information Networking and Applications, pp. 27–33 (2010)
10. He, D., Zeadally, S., Wu, L.: Certificateless public auditing scheme for cloud-assisted wireless body area networks. IEEE Syst. J. **12**(1), 64–73 (2018)
11. Jiang, Q., Ma, J., Wei, F.: On the security of a privacy-aware authentication scheme for distributed mobile cloud computing services. IEEE Syst. J. **12**(2), 2039–2042 (2018)
12. Jiang, T., Chen, X., Wu, Q., Ma, J., Susilo, W., Lou, W.: Secure and efficient cloud data deduplication with randomized tag. IEEE Trans. Inf. Forensics Secur. **12**(3), 532–543 (2017)

13. Kate, A., Zaverucha, G.M., Goldberg, I.: Constant-size commitments to polynomials and their applications. In: Abe, M. (ed.) ASIACRYPT 2010. LNCS, vol. 6477, pp. 177–194. Springer, Heidelberg (2010). https://doi.org/10.1007/978-3-642-17373-8_11
14. Li, J., Chen, X., Huang, X., Tang, S., Xiang, Y., Hassan, M.M., Alelaiwi, A.: Secure distributed deduplication systems with improved reliability. IEEE Trans. Comput. **64**(12), 3569–3579 (2015)
15. Li, J., Li, Y., Chen, X., Lee, P., Lou, W.: A hybrid cloud approach for secure authorized deduplication. IEEE Trans. Parallel Distrib. Syst. **26**(5), 1206–1216 (2015)
16. Li, X., Ibrahim, M.H., Kumari, S., Sangaiah, A.K., Gupta, V., Choo, K.K.R.: Anonymous mutual authentication and key agreement scheme for wearable sensors in wireless body area networks. Comput. Netw. **129**(2), 429–443 (2017)
17. Lin, W., Wu, Z., Lin, L., Wen, A., Li, J.: An ensemble random forest algorithm for insurance big data analysis. IEEE Access **5**, 16568–16575 (2017)
18. Liu, X., Qin, B., Deng, R.H., Li, Y.: An efficient privacy-preserving outsourced computation over public data. IEEE Trans. Serv. Comput. **10**(5), 756–770 (2017)
19. Marston, S., Li, Z., Bandyopadhyay, S., Zhang, J., Ghalsasi, A.: Cloud computing-the business perspective. Decis. Support Syst. **51**(1), 176–189 (2011)
20. Mell, P., Grance, T.: The NIST definition of cloud computing. Commun. ACM **53**(6), 50 (2011)
21. Shen, J., Liu, D., Shen, J., Liu, Q., Sun, X.: A secure cloud-assisted urban data sharing framework for ubiquitous-cities. Pervasive Mob. Comput. **2017**(41), 219–230 (2017)
22. Shen, J., Shen, J., Chen, X., Huang, X., Susilo, W.: An efficient public auditing protocol with novel dynamic structure for cloud data. IEEE Trans. Inf. Forensics Secur. **12**(10), 2402–2415 (2017)
23. Shen, J., Zhou, T., Chen, X., Li, J., Susilo, W.: Anonymous and traceable group data sharing in cloud computing. IEEE Trans. Inf. Forensics Secur. **13**(4), 912–925 (2018)
24. Shen, J., Zhou, T., He, D., Zhang, Y., Sun, X., Xiang, Y.: Block design-based key agreement for group data sharing in cloud computing. IEEE Trans. Dependable Secur. Comput. (2017). https://doi.org/10.1109/TDSC.2017.2725953
25. Shi, J., Li, H., Zhou, L.: The technical security issues in cloud computing. Int. J. Inf. Commun. Technol. **5**(3–4), 109–116 (2013)
26. Song, W., Wang, B., Wang, Q., Shi, C., Lou, W., Peng, Z.: Publicly verifiable computation of polynomials over outsourced data with multiple sources. IEEE Trans. Inf. Forensics Secur. **12**(10), 2334–2347 (2017)
27. Subashini, S., Kavitha, V.: A survey on security issues in service delivery models of cloud computing. J. Netw. Comput. Appl. **34**(1), 1–11 (2011)
28. Wang, C., Wang, Q., Ren, K., Cao, N., Lou, W.: Toward secure and dependable storage services in cloud computing. IEEE Trans. Serv. Comput. **5**(2), 220–232 (2012)
29. Wang, J., Chen, X., Li, J., Zhao, J., Shen, J.: Towards achieving flexible and verifiable search for outsourced database in cloud computing. Future Gener. Comput. Syst. **67**, 266–275 (2017)
30. Wang, L., Laszewski, G.V., Younge, A., He, X., Kunze, M., Tao, J., Fu, C.: Cloud computing: a perspective study. New Gener. Comput. **28**(2), 137–146 (2010)
31. Wang, Q., Wang, C., Li, J., Ren, K., Lou, W.: Enabling public verifiability and data dynamics for storage security in cloud computing. In: European Conference on Research in Computer Security, pp. 355–370 (2009)

32. Wang, Q., Zhou, F., Chen, C., Xuan, P., Wu, Q.: Secure collaborative publicly verifiable computation. IEEE Access **5**(99), 2479–2488 (2017)
33. Xu, X.: From cloud computing to cloud manufacturing. Robot. Comput. Integr. Manuf. **28**(1), 75–86 (2012)
34. Yu, J., Ren, K., Wang, C.: Enabling cloud storage auditing with verifiable outsourcing of key updates. IEEE Trans. Inf. Forensics Secur. **11**(6), 1362–1375 (2016)
35. Zhang, Q., Cheng, L., Boutaba, R.: Cloud computing: state-of-the-art and research challenges. J. Internet Serv. Appl. **1**(1), 7–18 (2010)
36. Zhang, Y., Chen, X., Li, J., Wong, D.S., Li, H., You, I.: Ensuring attribute privacy protection and fast decryption for outsourced data security in mobile cloud computing. Inf. Sci. **379**, 42–61 (2016)
37. Zhou, K., Afifi, H.M., Ren, J.: ExpSOS: secure and verifiable outsourcing of exponentiation operations for mobile cloud computing. IEEE Trans. Inf. Forensics Secur. **20**(11), 2518–2531 (2017)
38. Zhuo, G., Jia, Q., Guo, L., Li, M., Li, P.: Privacy-preserving verifiable set operation in big data for cloud-assisted mobile crowdsourcing. IEEE Internet Things J. **4**(2), 572–582 (2017)

Privacy-Preserving Mining of Association Rule on Outsourced Cloud Data from Multiple Parties

Lin Liu[1], Jinshu Su[1,2(✉)], Rongmao Chen[1(✉)], Ximeng Liu[3,4], Xiaofeng Wang[1], Shuhui Chen[1], and Hofung Leung[5]

[1] School of Computer, National University of Defense Technology, Changsha, China
{liulin16,sjs,chromao,xf_wang,shchen}@nudt.edu.cn
[2] National Key Laboratory for Parallel and Distributed Processing, National University of Defense Technology, Changsha, China
[3] School of Information Systems, Singapore Management University, Singapore, Singapore
snbnix@gmail.com
[4] College of Mathematics and Computer Science, Fuzhou University, Fuzhou, China
[5] Department of Computer Science and Engineering, Chinese University of Hong Kong, Shatin, Hong Kong
lhf@cuhk.edu.hk

Abstract. It has been widely recognized as a challenge to carry out data analysis and meanwhile preserve its privacy in the cloud. In this work, we mainly focus on a well-known data analysis approach namely association rule mining. We found that the data privacy in this mining approach have not been well considered so far. To address this problem, we propose a scheme for privacy-preserving association rule mining on outsourced cloud data which are uploaded from multiple parties in a twin-cloud architecture. In particular, we mainly consider the scenario where the data owners and miners have different encryption keys that are kept secret from each other and also from the cloud server. Our scheme is constructed by a set of well-designed two-party secure computation algorithms, which not only preserve the data confidentiality and query privacy but also allow the data owner to be offline during the data mining. Compared with the state-of-art works, our scheme not only achieves higher level privacy but also reduces the computation cost of data owners.

Keywords: Association rule mining · Frequent itemset mining
Privacy preserving outsourcing · Cloud computing

1 Introduction

Cloud computing has attracted more and more attentions due to its capability of supporting real-time and massive data storing and processing. For a long time, it

W. Susilo and G. Yang (Eds.): ACISP 2018, LNCS 10946, pp. 431–451, 2018.
https://doi.org/10.1007/978-3-319-93638-3_25

has been a growing interest in the paradigm of data mining as a service in cloud computing [1–5]. Since internet giants such as Google and Amazon can collect large-scale data from millions of users and devices, mining on cloud data can also dramatically improve the accuracy and effectiveness of mining. However, when uploading data to cloud service provider, users lose control of their data. Therefore, even though outsourcing data storage and data mining benefit from the scale of economy, it comes with the privacy and security issues.

In this work, we mainly consider the security and privacy problems existing in mining association rule on the outsourced cloud data. Frequent itemset mining, key of association rule, is a popular data mining approach, which is usually employed to discover frequently co-occurring data items and relationships between data items in large transaction databases. These techniques have been widely used in market prediction, intrusion detection, network traffic management and so on. For instance, if customers are buying bread, how likely are they going to buy beer (and what kind of beer) on the same trip to the supermarket? Such information can help retailers do selective marketing and arrange their shelf space for increasing sales. Kantarcioglu and Clifton [6] and Vaidya and Clifton [7] first identified and addressed privacy issues in horizontally and vertically partitioned databases. Due to the increase of data security and privacy demanding, researchers have proposed various methods on privacy-preserving association rule mining. These works can be roughly divided into randomization-based schemes and cryptography-based schemes. Despite the high efficiency in randomization-based schemes, they suffer from the inaccuracy of mining result for adding random noise to the raw data. Compared with the randomization-based scheme, the cryptography-based scheme can apply stronger security level and accurate mining result. Recently, Yi *et al.* [4] have proposed a privacy-preserving association rule mining scheme on the outsourced cloud data encrypted by using ElGamal homomorphic encryption scheme [8]. However, the communication cost was huge due to the fact that their scheme needs n cloud servers to cooperate with each other. Qiu *et al.* [1] proposed a framework for privacy-preserving frequent itemset mining on encrypted cloud data in the twin-cloud architecture. Both of Yi *et al.* [4] and Qiu *et al.* [1] designed three different privacy level protocols, which achieved item privacy, transaction privacy and database privacy respectively. However, even in the highest security level, the mining result was still in plaintext form to the cloud server. Li *et al.* [9] proposed a privacy-preserving association rules mining system on vertically partitioned databases via a symmetric homomorphic encryption scheme. Their scheme achieved high efficiency, but the data owners in that scheme need to stay online during the mining process and some information about the raw data may be revealed.

Motivating Scenario. In this paper, we mainly consider a scenario where a higher privacy level is required. In most cases, the mining result is miner's personal property, which should be kept secret to any other entities including the untrusted cloud server. For example, if the mining result from business data is enterprise's market prediction, leaking this information to competitors will damage this enterprise's profits. In our scenario, it is required that both the raw data outsourced by the data owners and the mining result for the miner are confidential to the cloud server. Moreover, we consider a large number of data owners and miners in our system, and hence supporting offline users is desirable for improving the system's scalability. In addition, we insist that the frequent itemset mining is the cornerstone for association rule mining. Only mining frequent itemset is not enough to get the strong association rule, which is the key to find the relationship among itemsets. Overall speaking, in this work, we aim at designing a secure scheme, which supports that, (1) the raw data and the mining result are protected from other entities; (2) offline users and; (3) mining both the frequent itemset and association rule simultaneously.

Our Contributions. In this paper, we propose a privacy-preserving association rule mining scheme in the twin-cloud architecture. The contributions of this paper are four-fold, namely:

- To our best knowledge, this is the first work that studies privacy-preserving association rule mining on encrypted data under different keys. Our proposed scheme allows different data owners to outsource their data with different encryption keys to the cloud server for secure storage and processing.
- We build a set of cryptographic blocks for privacy-preserving association rule mining based on BCP cryptosystem [10], which play the cornerstone of our system.
- Based on the cryptographic blocks proposed, we construct a privacy-preserving association rule scheme with multiple keys. And we also prove that our scheme is secure under the semi-honest model.
- We show that our scheme can indeed achieve higher privacy level than most of the recent works [1,4,9]. And also, we fully prove the security of our scheme under the semi-honest mode.

We make a comparison between our work and the most recent works [1,4,9], which is shown in Table 1. In Qiu *et al.*'s work [1] and Yi *et al.*'s work [4], they proposed three different privacy level protocols. Here, we just compare their highest privacy level protocol with ours. Yi *et al.*'s work [4] and Qiu *et al.*'s work [1] can only support frequent itemset mining. Both of their works cannot protect the miner's mining result privacy. Moreover, the data owners' computation cost is highest. Li *et al.*'s [9] algorithm is the most efficient but cannot support the offline data owners. More importantly, their work can only achieve partial data privacy.

Related Work. Data perturbation is widely used to protect sensitive information when outsourcing data mining of association rule. This randomization-based approach can be used to protect the raw data but cannot protect the mining results. Randomization-based approach [3,5] may have unpredictable impacts on data mining precision, due to the random noise added to the raw data. Differential privacy is used to protect privacy mining the association rule. However, the key limitation of such solutions is that the mining results are not accurate with 100%.

Table 1. Comparison summary

Algorithm	Support FIM[a]	Support ARM[b]	Support Offline	D. Privacy[c]	M.R. Privacy[d]	DO Cost[e]	Support multi-key
[4]	Yes	No	Yes	Yes	No	Medium	No
[9]	Yes	Yes	No	Partial	Yes	Low	No
[1]	Yes	No	Yes	Yes	No	High	No
Ours	Yes	Yes	Yes	Yes	Yes	Medium	Yes

[a]FIM means Frequent Itemset Mining.
[b]ARM means Association Rule Mining.
[c]D.Privacy means Data Privacy.
[d]M.R.Privacy means Mining Result Privacy.
[e]DO Cost means Data owner's computation cost.

Compared with randomization-based approaches, cryptography-based approaches usually provide a well-defined security model and an exact mining result for privacy-preserving data mining. Earlier works [6,7] are not efficient enough for the practical requirement facing the prevalent of large scale datasets. Dong and Chen [11] employed an efficient inner product protocol [12] for evaluating association rule mining. But this solution is a two-party protocol, which involves extensive interactions. Lai *et al.* [13] first proposed a semantically secure solution for outsourcing association rule mining with both privacy and mining privacy, but the efficiency is still undesirable for the practice. Yi *et al.* [4] proposed a privacy-preserving association rule mining in cloud computing. To mine association rule from its data, the user outsources the task to $n(\geq 2)$ "semi-honest" servers, which cooperate to perform mining algorithm on encrypted data and return encrypted association rules to the user. In his work $n(\geq 2)$ servers are needed which cause huge communication cost. Li *et al.* [9] proposed a privacy-preserving outsourced association rule mining on vertically partitioned databases. However, their solution still leaks information about the raw data. Most recently, Qiu *et al.* [1] proposed a privacy-preserving frequent itemset mining scheme on outsourced encrypted cloud data. In their work, they proposed three different privacy level protocols. In their privacy level I protocol, only the transaction database in the cloud is encrypted while the miner's query is in plaintext. This protocol work quite efficiently but without protecting the query's privacy. In their protocol II and protocol III, the miner's query is protected or partial protected, but the mining result is known to cloud. For adopting time consuming homomorphic cryptosystem BGN [14], the computation cost of data owners is quite large in protocol II.

2 Preliminaries

In this section, we introduce essential preliminary concepts which serve as the basis of our scheme. Table 2 lists the key notations used throughout this paper.

2.1 Frequent Itemset Mining and Association Rule Mining

Frequent itemset mining, the key of association rule mining, is first proposed by Agrawal *et al.* [15]. Given a set of items, and a transaction databases over these items, frequent itemsets are items which appear with frequency more than a given number. In the following, we give the specific definition of this concept.

Table 2. Notation used

Notations	Definition
pk_{DO_i}/sk_{DO_i}	Public/private key of data owner i
pk_M/sk_M	Public/private key of miner
pk_Σ	The product of all the data owners and miner's public key
$[\![x]\!]_{pk}$	Encrypted data x under pk
MK	Master key of BCP cryptosystem
$\mathbf{mDec}_{(pk,\mathbf{MK})}(X)$	Decrypt X with the master key
$\|x\|$	Bit length of x
$supp(X)$	Support of X
$conf(X)$	Confidence of X
SMAD	Secure multiplication across domain
SCAD	Secure comparison across domain
SC	Secure comparison
SIP	Secure inner product
SFIM	Secure frequent itemset mining

Definition 1 (Frequent Itemset). *Let $I = \{i_1, \cdots, i_m\}$ be a set of items. A transaction T is a set of items. A transaction database is denoted as $T = \{t_1, \cdots, t_m\}$, where m is the total number of transactions. An itemset $X \subseteq I$ is a set of items from I. If $X \subseteq t_i$, X is contained by a transaction t_i. The support of itemset X, is the number of transactions containing X in T, which is referred as $supp(X)$. $supp_{min}$ is the user-defined minimum threshold. If $supp(X) \geq supp_{min}$, X is the frequent itemset.*

The purpose of the frequent itemset mining is to discover the frequency of the item/itemsets, which will further be used to find the relationship of two items. Generally, the relationship between two items are measured by *support* and *confidence*. An association rule is of the form $X \Rightarrow Y$ where $X, Y \subset I$ and $X \cap Y = \emptyset$. The $supp(X \Rightarrow Y)$, support of the rule $X \Rightarrow Y$, is the number of the transactions containing $X \cup Y$. The *confidence* of rule $X \Rightarrow Y$ is a measure of the relation between two items, denoted by $conf(X \Rightarrow Y) = supp(X \Rightarrow Y)/supp(X)$.

Definition 2 (Strong Association Rule). *Assume a minimum support threshold $supp_{min}$ and a minimum confidence threshold $conf_{min}$ are given. The rule $X \Rightarrow Y$ is strong iff $supp(X \Rightarrow Y) \geq supp_{min}$ and $conf(X \Rightarrow Y) \geq conf_{min}$.*

Here, we illustrate the above two definition by the following example. A transaction dataset T is given in Table 3. All the items are presented as boolean types, i.e., an item is described as absent by 0, otherwise by 1. Suppose that, if $X = \{Coke\}$, and $Y = \{Milk\}$, we can represent $X \cup Y$ as $\boldsymbol{q} = (0, 1, 1, 0)$. We want to find out that whether $Coke \Rightarrow Milk$ is a strong association rule or not. First, we make an inner product $v_i = \boldsymbol{q} \cdot \boldsymbol{t_i}$, where $\boldsymbol{t_i}, i \in (1, \cdots, 5)$ is the row in the table. It can be easily got that only v_1 and v_3 are equal to 2. Therefore, $supp(X \Rightarrow Y) = 2$. If $supp(X \Rightarrow Y) < supp_{min}$, we can conclude that $X \Rightarrow Y$ is not the strong rule, because $X \cup Y$ is not a frequent itemset. Here, assume that $supp_{min} = 2$, thus $X \cup Y$ is a frequent itemset. Next, we can calculate $supp(X)$ in the same way. In Table 3, it can be easily calculated that $supp(X \Rightarrow Y) = 2$ and $supp(X) = 3$. Therefore, we can easily get $conf(X \Rightarrow Y) = 2/3$. If the $conf(X \Rightarrow Y) \geq conf_{min}$, $X \Rightarrow Y$ is the strong association rule. Otherwise, it's not.

Table 3. Market-basket transaction dataset T

ID	Bread	Coke	Milk	Beer
1	1	1	1	0
2	1	0	0	1
3	0	1	1	1
4	1	1	0	1
5	0	0	1	0

2.2 BCP Cryptosystem

BCP Cryptosystem is an additively homomorphic cryptosystem, proposed by Bresson et al. [10]. BCP is a double decryption mechanism, meaning that it offers two independent decryption mechanisms. The most prominent characteristic of such scheme is that if given the master key of this cryptosystem, any given ciphertext can be successfully decrypted. The BCP cryptosystem works as follows:

Setup(κ): Given a security parameter κ, choose a safe-prime RSA-modulus $N = pq$ (i.e., $p = 2p' + 1$ and $q = 2q' + 1$ for distinct primes p' and q', respectively) of bitlength κ. In the following, we use $|N|$ to denote the length of N. Then a random element $g \in \mathbb{Z}^*_{N^2}$ with order $pp'qq'$ is picked, such that $g^{p'q'} \bmod N^2 = 1 + \lambda N$ for $\lambda \in [1, N-1]$. Thus, the algorithm outputs the public parameter **PP** and the master key **MK** as follows, $\mathbf{PP} = (N, \lambda, g)$ and $\mathbf{MK} = (p', q')$.

KeyGen(PP): Randomly pick $a \in \mathbb{Z}_{N^2}^*$ and compute $h = g^a \bmod N^2$. Then, output the public key $\mathbf{pk} = h$ and secret key $\mathbf{sk} = a$.

$\mathbf{Enc}_{(\mathbf{PP},pk)}(m)$: For a given plaintext $m \in \mathbb{Z}_N$, randomly pick $r \in \mathbb{Z}_{N^2}$, then output the ciphtext (A, B) as $A = g^r \bmod N^2$, $B = h^r(1 + mN) \bmod N^2$.

$\mathbf{Dec}_{(\mathbf{PP},sk)}(A, B)$: The plaintext of the given ciphtext (A, B) and secret key $\mathbf{sk} = a$, can be calculated as $m = (B/(A^a) - 1 \bmod N^2)/N$.

$\mathbf{mDec}_{(\mathbf{PP},pk,\mathbf{MK})}(A, B)$: Using the master secret key **MK** of this cryptosystem, the plaintext of the above ciphtertext (A, B) can be calculated as follows. First compute $a \bmod N$ as $a \bmod N = (h^{p'q'} - 1 \bmod N^2)/N \cdot k^{-1} \bmod N$, where k^{-1} denotes the inverse of k modulo N. Then $r \bmod N$ can be computed as $r \bmod N = (A^{p'q'} - 1 \bmod N^2)/N \cdot k^{-1} \bmod N$. Therefore, the when a and r is obtained, the plaintext can be easily get by the following equation, $m = ((B/g^{ar})^{p'q'} - 1 \bmod N^2)/N \cdot (p'q')^{-1} \bmod N$, where $(p'q')^{-1}$ is the inverse of $p'q'$ modulo N.

The BCP cryptosystem is additively homomorphic, which can be verified as $\mathbf{Dec}_{sk}$ $(\llbracket m_1 \rrbracket_{pk} \cdot \llbracket m_2 \rrbracket_{pk}) = m_1 + m_2$. Note that for any given $m, k \in \mathbb{Z}_N$, we can easily get $(\llbracket m \rrbracket_{pk})^k = \llbracket k \cdot m \rrbracket_{pk}$. Moreover, if $k = N - 1$, we can get $(\llbracket m \rrbracket_{pk})^{N-1} = \llbracket -m \rrbracket_{pk}$. In this paper, for simplicity we use $\llbracket m \rrbracket_{pk}$ instead of $\mathbf{Enc}_{(\mathbf{PP},pk)}(m)$. More proofs of the correctness and semantic security of the BCP cryptosystem can be found in [10].

3 System Model and Design Goal

3.1 Problem Statement

Suppose that the cloud service provider has collected a large set of encrypted transactions from data owners. A miner, who has limited transactions, wants to mine the frequent itemsets. If mining from his own transaction database, the mining results may not be accurate. Therefore, he need make some queries to cloud to find out whether the itemsets in his own database are frequent or not in cloud's database which is much larger. We follow the same assumption in previous sections that each transaction is represented as a binary vector, and a mining query is represented as another binary vector.

3.2 System Model

In our system, we focus on preserving privacy association rule mining on the cloud. Specifically, we define the system model by dividing this system into five parties: Key Generation Center (KGC), Evaluator, Cloud Service Provider (CSP), Data Owners (DO) and Miner. The overall system model of our preserving privacy association rule mining system can be found in Fig. 1.

(1) **Key Generation Center:** The trusted KGC is responsible for generating and managing both public and private keys for every party in our system (See ①).

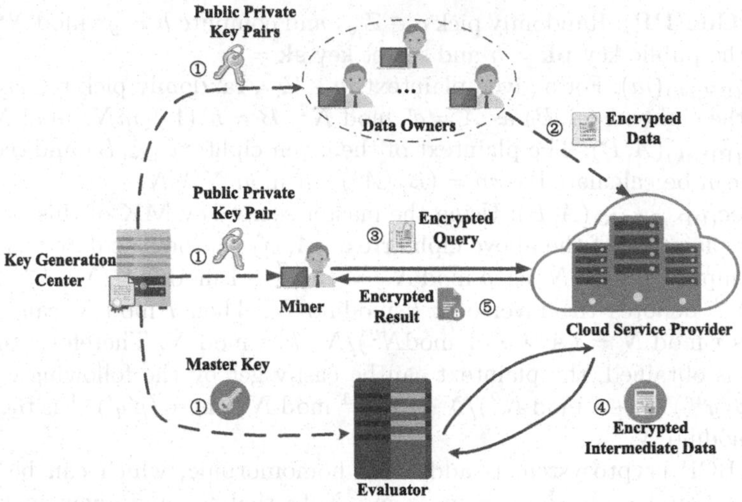

Fig. 1. System model

(2) **Data Owners:** Generally, the DOs use their public key to encrypt their sensitive data, before uploading them to the CSP (See ②).
(3) **Cloud Service Provider:** CSP has massive storage space. It could store and manage data outsourced from all the DOs (See ②). In addition, CSP has some computation abilities to perform some calculations over the outsourced data. In our system, the CSP provides the service of association rule mining for the miners through cooperating with Evaluator (See ④).
(4) **Evaluator:** Evaluator provides online computation in our system. It has the master key of the BCP cryptosystem. In our system, the CSP need cooperate with the Evaluator to mine the frequent itemsets and association rules (See ④).
(5) **Miner:** In our system, Miner is the data mining service user. Data owner can also be a miner. The miner has some transaction itemsets. The goal of the miner is to find the frequent itemsets and strong association rules for his limited dataset. To achieve this purpose, he sends the encrypted itemsets to the CSP to find out whether they are frequent or not (See ③). The mining results obtained from the CSP can only be decrypted by miner himself (See ⑤).

Note that the Evaluator is an essential part in our system. On one hand, since BCP cryptosystem is not fully homomorphic, a CSP alone cannot perform various compute operations. On the other hand, this twin-cloud architecture composed by CSP and Evaluator, can minimize the interactions between the request users and the cloud servers while the one cloud cannot [16]. In this scheme, the Miner only sends encrypted queries and then remains offline until receiving the encrypted mining results.

3.3 Threat Model

In our threat model, we assume the KGC is fully trusted by all the entities. On the other hand, CSP, Evaluator, DOs and Miner are *curious-but-honest* entities, which means that these entities intend to follow the protocols strictly and return correct computation results, but may try to infer the private information of other parties according to the data received and held. In addition, we also assume that the CSP and Evaluator don't conclude with each other. Now, we introduce an active adversary $\mathcal{A}$ in this model. The goal of $\mathcal{A}$ is to get the original data from the DOs and the Miner. What's more, $\mathcal{A}$ also wants to know the Miner's final mining results. Such an adversary has the following capabilities:

(1) $\mathcal{A}$ may eavesdrop all communication to obtain the encrypted data.
(2) $\mathcal{A}$ may compromise CSP and try to obtain all the plaintext value of the ciphertext uploaded by the DOs and all the intermediate results sent by Evaluator during the executing an interactive protocol.
(3) $\mathcal{A}$ may compromise one or more DOs to obtain their decryption abilities.

The adversary $\mathcal{A}$ is restricted from comprising (1) Evaluator, (2) all the DOs and (3) the Miner. Here we remark that such restrictions are typical and widely used in adversary model used in cryptographic protocols [1,16,17].

3.4 Design Goals

Under the aforementioned system model and attack model, our design goal is the following four objects.

(1) *The security and privacy should be guaranteed.* The data uploaded by the DOs, the query information from the Miner and the mining result from the encrypted data contains sensitive data of themselves which could not be disclosed to the CSP, Evaluator or $\mathcal{A}$. Meanwhile, the access pattern shouldn't be revealed and inferred by CSP, Evaluator or $\mathcal{A}$ either. Access pattern is defined as the original encrypted input corresponding to the computed value, e.g., the comparison result, the most frequent class label, etc.
(2) *Data query result's accuracy should be guaranteed.* It is also really important that the mining accuracy must be guaranteed when applying the privacy-preserving strategy. Therefore, the proposed system should achieve same accuracy compared with the non-privacy-preserving data mining system.
(3) *Low communication overhead and efficiency of computation should be guaranteed.* Consider the real-time requirements of online service and the diversity of terminals, the proposed scheme should have low overhead in terms of communication and computation. Especially, the DOs and the Miners in our system are usually resource-constrained users, their computation and communication cost should be as small as possible.
(4) *Offline DOs and miners should be supported.* After outsourcing the encrypted data, the DOs should be offline. There are many miners involved in our system. Therefore, supporting offline DOs and miners is rather necessary in terms of the system's scalability.

4 Privacy-Preserving Frequent Itemset Mining and Association Rule Mining

4.1 Setup

Recall that in Sect. 3 we have stated that the CSP holds a set of encrypted transactions from multiple DOs. Suppose we have η DOs in our system. The KGC generates pairs of the public and private keys (pk_{DO_i}, sk_{DO_i}), $i = 1, 2, \cdots, \eta$ and pk_M, sk_M. Then, KGC distributes the individual public-private key pair (pk_{DO_i}, sk_{DO_i}) to the DO i and (pk_M, sk_M) to the miner, respectively. Meanwhile, the strong private key is sent to the Evaluator. Moreover, all the entities' public keys are known to the others.

After receiving the public-private key pair from the KGC, the DOs encrypt every record $\boldsymbol{p_i}$ in his own database, and outsource these encrypted data to the CSP. So far, the work of the DOs' is over, meaning that all the DOs can remain offline from now on.

4.2 Privacy-Preserving Building Blocks

In this section, we propose a set of privacy-preserving building blocks, including secure multiplication accross domains algorithm, secure inner product calculation algorithm, secure comparison accross domains algorithm and secure comparison. In Andreas *et al* 's work [18], they have proposed **KeyProd** and **TransDec** algorithm in the similiar system model based on BCP. **KeyProd** and **TransDec** can be used to transform the encryptions under pk_{DO_i} or pk_M into encryption under $pk_{\Sigma} = \prod_{i=1}^{m} pk_{DO_i} pk_M$ or vice verse. For more details of these algorithms, please see [18]. These cryptographic blocks, proposed in this paper and Andreas *et al.*'s work [18], serve as the basic constructions of our privacy-preserving association rule mining system.

Secure Multiplication Across Domains. Note that Andreas *et al.* [18] have proposed a secure multiple protocol (i.e., **Mult.**) based on BCP cryptosystem. Here, we present the secure multiplication across different encryption domains with the similar idea. For simplicity and readability, we use $[\![x]\!]_{pk_{DO}}$ instead of $[\![x]\!]_{pk_{DO_i}}$ in the following context. Suppose that CSP has encrypted data $[\![x]\!]_{pk_{DO}}$ and $[\![y]\!]_{pk_M}$. The goal of secure multiplication across domains (**SMAD**) algorithm is to calculate $[\![xy]\!]_{pk_{\Sigma}}$. We introduce the details of our **SMAD** algorithm as follows.

Step 1 (CSP): (1) $a, b, c, d \xleftarrow{R} \mathbb{Z}_N$.
(2) $X_0 = [\![x]\!]_{pk_{DO}} \cdot [\![a]\!]_{pk_{DO}}$, $Y_0 = [\![y]\!]_{pk_M} \cdot [\![b]\!]_{pk_M}$, $X_1 = [\![x]\!]^{b}_{pk_{DO}} \cdot [\![c]\!]_{pk_{DO}}$, $Y_1 = [\![y]\!]^{a}_{pk_M} \cdot [\![d]\!]_{pk_M}$.
(3) Send X_0, Y_0, X_1 and Y_1 to Evaluator.
Step
2 (Evaluator): (1) $z_0 \leftarrow$ $\mathbf{mDec}_{(pk_{DO},MK)}(X_0)$, $z_1 \leftarrow$ $\mathbf{mDec}_{(pk_M,MK)}(Y_0)$, $z_2 \leftarrow$ $\mathbf{mDec}_{(pk_{DO},MK)}(X_1)$, $z_3 \leftarrow$ $\mathbf{mDec}_{(pk_M,MK)}(Y_1)$.

(2) $Z_1 \leftarrow [\![z_0 \cdot z_1]\!]_{pk_\Sigma}$, $Z_2 \leftarrow [\![z_2]\!]_{pk_\Sigma}^{N-1}$, $Z_3 \leftarrow [\![z_3]\!]_{pk_\Sigma}^{N-1}$.
(3) Send Z_1, Z_2, Z_3 to CSP.
Step 3 (CSP): (1) $S_1 \leftarrow ([\![a \cdot b]\!]_{pk_\Sigma})^{N-1}$, $S_2 \leftarrow [\![c]\!]_{pk_\Sigma}$, $S_3 \leftarrow [\![d]\!]_{pk_\Sigma}$.
(2) $[\![xy]\!]_{pk_\Sigma} \leftarrow Z_1 \cdot Z_2 \cdot Z_3 \cdot S_1 \cdot S_2 \cdot S_3$.

REMARK. The basic idea of **SMAD** is based on the following equation, i.e., $xy = (x + a)(y + b) - (bx + c) - (ay + d) - ab + (c + d)$.

Secure Inner Product. Suppose that CSP has an encrypted data vector $[\![\boldsymbol{x}]\!]_{pk_{DO}} = ([\![x_1]\!]_{pk_{DO}}, \cdots, [\![x_n]\!]_{pk_{DO}})$ and an encrypted data vector $[\![\boldsymbol{y}]\!]_{pk_M} = ([\![y_1]\!]_{pk_M}, \cdots, [\![y_n]\!]_{pk_M})$. For every $[\![x_i]\!]_{pk_{DO}}$ and $[\![y_i]\!]_{pk_M}$, CSP and Evaluator run **SMAD** algorithm to get $[\![x_i y_i]\!]_{pk_\Sigma}$. Then, CSP multiplies all the encrypted data. Thus, CSP can obtain $[\![\boldsymbol{x} \cdot \boldsymbol{y}]\!]_{pk_\Sigma} = (x_1 y_1 + \cdots + x_n y_n)_{pk_\Sigma}$.

Secure Comparison Across Domains. Suppose that CSP has two encrypted data $[\![x]\!]_{pk_M}$ and $[\![y]\!]_{pk_\Sigma}$, where where $x, y \leq 2^l$, $l < |N|/2 - 1$. The purpose of CSP is to find out whether $[\![x]\!]_{pk_M}$ is larger than $[\![y]\!]_{pk_\Sigma}$ or not, without leaking the original value of x and y to Evaluator.

Step 1 (CSP): (1) $A \leftarrow ([\![x]\!]_{pk_M})^2 \cdot [\![1]\!]_{pk_M}$, $B \leftarrow ([\![y]\!]_{pk_\Sigma})^2$.
(2) Randomly pick $a \xleftarrow{R} \{0, 1\}$, $C \leftarrow A^{a(N-1)}$, $D \leftarrow B^{(1-a)(N-1)}$.
(3) Randomly choose $r_a, r_b \xleftarrow{R} \mathbb{Z}_N$, and calculate $C' \leftarrow C \cdot [\![r_a]\!]_{pk_M}$, $D' \leftarrow D \cdot [\![r_b]\!]_{pk_\Sigma}$. Send C' and D' to Evaluator.
Step 2 (Evaluator): (1) $c' \leftarrow \mathbf{mDec}_{(pk_M, MK)}(C')$, $d' \leftarrow \mathbf{mDec}_{(pk_\Sigma, MK)}(D')$.
(2) Calculate $E \leftarrow [\![c' + d']\!]_{pk_\Sigma}$, then send E to CSP.
Step 3 (CSP): (1) $F \leftarrow E \cdot ([\![r_a + r_b]\!]_{pk_\Sigma})^{N-1}$.
(2) Randomly choose r_1, r_2, where $r_1, r_2 \xleftarrow{R} \{1, \cdots, 2^l\}$, $r_2 \ll r_1$, and calculate $F' \leftarrow F^{r_1} \cdot [\![r_2]\!]_{pk_\Sigma}$. Send F' to Evaluator.
Step 4 (Evaluator): (1) $z \leftarrow \mathbf{mDec}_{(pk_\Sigma, MK)}(F')$.
(2) If $z < N/2$, $\delta \leftarrow 1$ else $\delta \leftarrow 0$. Send $[\![\delta]\!]_{pk_\Sigma}$.
Step 5 (CSP): If $a = 0$, $[\![t]\!]_{pk_\Sigma} = [\![\delta]\!]_{pk_\Sigma}$. Else, $[\![t]\!]_{pk_\Sigma} \leftarrow [\![1]\!]_{pk_\Sigma} \cdot ([\![\delta]\!]_{pk_\Sigma})^{N-1}$.

Finally, CSP gets the encrypted comparison result $[\![t]\!]_{pk_M}$. If $t = 1$, it means $x \geq y$. Otherwise, it shows $x < y$.

Discussion. In the secure comparison algorithm of Qiu *et al* 's work [1], the CSP sends $[\![r(x-y)]\!]$ directly to Evaluator ($[\![x]\!]$ means the encryption of x under paillier [19]). There are several problems. First, if the decryption is 0, Evaluator could easily know $x = y$. Second, according to the decryption is smaller than $N/2$, the evaluator can infer whether x is smaller than y or not. Thus, we can conclude that, the comparison result is leaked to Evaluator in the secure comparison algorithm in Qiu *et al*'s work [1]. Moreover, if $x - y$ is a small number, the adversary $\mathcal{A}$ may infer the relationship of x and y according to the factoring result of $r(x - y)$, i.e., one large prime and a small number. Therefore, we can conclude the comparison algorithm in Qiu *et al.*'s work [1] is not secure to the adversary either. On one hand, in order to avoid showing the relationship of x and y, CSP should send $[\![r_1(x' - y')]\!]_{pk_\Sigma}$ or $[\![r_1(y' - x')]\!]_{pk_\Sigma}$ randomly, where

$x' = 2x + 1$ and $y' = 2y$. If $x > y$, it is obvious that $x' > y'$ or vice verse. On the other hand, to keep the comparison result from the factoring of $r_1(x' - y')$, CSP also blinds $r_1(x' - y')$ with a small random number r_2, i.e., $r_1(x' - y') + r_2$ before sending it to Evaluator. Since $r_2 \ll r_1$, blinding such a number dose not influence the comparison result of x and y.

Secure Comparison. We follow the same idea of **SCAD** to design the **SC** algorithm. Suppose that CSP has two encrypted data $[\![x]\!]_{pk_\Sigma}$ and $[\![y]\!]_{pk_\Sigma}$, where $x, y \leq 2^l$, $l < |N|/2 - 1$. The purpose of CSP is to find out whether $[\![x]\!]_{pk_\Sigma}$ is larger than $[\![y]\!]_{pk_\Sigma}$ or not, without leaking the original value of x and y to Evaluator. The details of the **SC** is as follows.

Step 1 (CSP): (1) Calculate $A \leftarrow ([\![x]\!]_{pk_\Sigma})^2 \cdot [\![1]\!]_{pk_\Sigma}$, $B \leftarrow ([\![y]\!]_{pk_\Sigma})^2$.
(2)Randomly pick $a \xleftarrow{R} \{0, 1\}$, $C \leftarrow A^{a(N-1)} \cdot B^{(1-a)(N-1)}$.
(3) Randomly choose r_1, r_2, where $r_1, r_2 \xleftarrow{R} \{1, \cdots, 2^l\}$, $r_2 \ll r_1$, and calculate $D \leftarrow C^{r_1} \cdot [\![r_2]\!]_{pk_\Sigma}$. Send D to Evaluator.
Step 2 (Evaluator): (1) $z \leftarrow \mathbf{mDec}_{(pk_\Sigma, MK)}(D)$.
(2) If $z < N/2$, $\delta \leftarrow 1$ else $\delta \leftarrow 0$. Send $[\![\delta]\!]_{pk_\Sigma}$.
Step 3 (CSP): If $a = 0$, $[\![t]\!]_{pk_\Sigma} \leftarrow [\![\delta]\!]_{pk_\Sigma}$. Else, $[\![t]\!]_{pk_\Sigma} \leftarrow [\![1]\!]_{pk_\Sigma} \cdot ([\![\delta]\!]_{pk_\Sigma})^{N-1}$.

At the end of the algorithm, CSP gets the encrypted comparison result, i.e., $[\![t]\!]_{pk_\Sigma}$. If $t = 1$, it means $x \geq y$. Otherwise, we can conclude $x < y$.

4.3 Secure Frequent Itemset Mining

CSP, Evaluator and Miner together run this secure frequent itemset mining algorithm. At the end of the algorithm, Miner gets the encrypted mining results. If the decrypted data is 1, it means that the query itemset is frequent. Otherwise, it is not. Assume that CSP holds m encrypted transactions data $\mathbf{C} = \{\boldsymbol{C}_1, \cdots, \boldsymbol{C}_m\}$, where $\boldsymbol{C}_j = ([\![c_{j,1}]\!]_{pk_{DO_i}}, \cdots, [\![c_{j,n}]\!]_{pk_{DO_i}})$, $i \in (1, \cdots, \eta)$, $j \in (1, \cdots, m)$. Miner has the encrypted mining request $\boldsymbol{Q}$ and $[\![z]\!]_{pk_M}$ as well as the encrypted minimum support $[\![supp_{min}]\!]_{pk_M}$, where $\boldsymbol{Q} = ([\![q_1]\!]_{pk_M}, \cdots, [\![q_n]\!]_{pk_M})$, z is the number of the 1s in $\boldsymbol{Q}$. Evaluator has the master key **MK**.

Step 1 (DO): Each DO encrypts his transactions with his own public key and sends the encrypted data to CSP. Thus, CSP gets m encrypted transactions data $\mathbf{C} = \{\boldsymbol{C}_1, \cdots, \boldsymbol{C}_m\}$, where $\boldsymbol{C}_j = ([\![c_{j,1}]\!]_{pk_{DO_i}}, \cdots, [\![c_{j,n}]\!]_{pk_{DO_i}})$, $i \in (1, \cdots, \eta)$, $j \in (1, \cdots, m)$.
Step 2 (Miner): The miner uses pk_M to encrypt his mining quest and minimum support, thus obtaining $\boldsymbol{Q}$, $[\![z]\!]_{pk_M}$ and $[\![supp_{min}]\!]_{pk_M}$, where $\boldsymbol{Q} = ([\![q_1]\!]_{pk_M}, \cdots, [\![q_n]\!]_{pk_M})$, z is the number of the 1s in $\boldsymbol{Q}$. Miner sends $\{\boldsymbol{Q}, [\![z]\!]_{pk_M}, [\![supp_{min}]\!]_{pk_M}\}$ to CSP.
Step 3 (CSP): CSP selects a *dummy* transactions set $\mathbf{D} = \{\boldsymbol{D}_1, \cdots, \boldsymbol{D}_k\}$, where $\boldsymbol{D}_l = (d_{l,1}, \cdots, d_{l,n})$, $d_{l,t} \in \{0, 1\}$, $l \in \{1, \cdots, k\}$ and $t \in \{1, \cdots, n\}$. CSP randomly chooses a DO's public key pk_{DO_i} to encrypt every D_l. Then, CSP

combines the transactions **C** uploaded by DOs with the dummy transaction set **D**, which can be denoted as $\mathbf{E} = \mathbf{C} \bigcup \mathbf{D}$, and $E = \{\boldsymbol{E}_1, \cdots, \boldsymbol{E}_k\}$. Finally, CSP runs a secret permutation function on E, $E' = \pi(E)$.

Step 4 (CSP and Evaluator): CSP and Evaluator run **Keyprod** together on $[\![z]\!]_{pk_M}$ to get $[\![z]\!]_{pk_\Sigma}$. After that, CSP and Evaluator run **SIP** together on every transaction in the permuted database and miner's query. Thus, CSP gets $[\![x_i]\!]_{pk_\Sigma}, i \in (1, \cdots, m+k)$ at the end of every round of **SIP**.

Step 5 (CSP): For every $[\![x_i]\!]_{pk_\Sigma}$, CSP randomly chooses an α_i from $\mathbb{Z}_n$, and calculates $[\![w_i]\!]_{pk_\Sigma} \leftarrow \alpha_i([\![x_i]\!]_{pk_\Sigma} \cdot ([\![z]\!]_{pk_\Sigma})^{(N-1)})$. Then, CSP sends $\boldsymbol{W} = \{[\![w_1]\!]_{pk_\Sigma}, \cdots, [\![w_{m+k}]\!]_{pk_\Sigma}\}$ it to Evaluator.

Step 6 (Evaluator): Given $\boldsymbol{W}$, the Evaluator uses **MK** to decrypt every $[\![w_i]\!]_{pk_\Sigma}$. If $w_i = 0$, set $v_i = 1$, else $v_i = 0$. Then, he encrypts every v_i, before sending $\boldsymbol{V} = ([\![v_1]\!]_{pk_\Sigma}, \cdots, [\![v_{m+k}]\!]_{pk_\Sigma})$ to CSP.

Step 7 (CSP): On receiving $\boldsymbol{V}'$, CSP computes $\boldsymbol{V} = \pi^{-1}(\boldsymbol{V})$, then he removes the dummy results and calculates $[\![u]\!]_{pk_\Sigma} = \prod_{i=1}^{m} v_i'$.

Step 8 (CSP and Evaluator): CSP and Evaluator run **SCAD** together on $[\![supp_{min}]\!]_{pk_M}$ and $[\![u]\!]_{pk_\Sigma}$ and obtain the encrypted comparison result $[\![t]\!]_{pk_\Sigma}$. After that, CSP gets $[\![t]\!]_{pk_M}$ through running **TransDec** with Evaluator. CSP sends it to Miner.

Step 9 (Miner): Miner decrypts the $[\![t]\!]_{pk_M}$. If $t = 1$, the query itemset is frequent, else it is not.

REMARK. In our **SFIM**, the dummy transactions are needed. Without the dummy transactions, Evaluator can deduce the support of q by counting the number of 0s in $\boldsymbol{W}$. With these dummy transactions, the support of q will be covered. Since, CSP knows the inverse of the permutation function, he can use it to remove the dummy results thus getting the original support of q.

Discussion. In Step 6 of our **SFIM**, Evaluator encrypts v_i by pk_Σ rather than pk_M. If using pk_M, in Step 8, CSP and Evaluator run **SC** instead of **SCAD**. However, the miner in our system is "honest-but-curious". If v_i is encrypted by pk_M, it could be leaked to Miner, which shouldn't be known to him. To protect DOs' data privacy, all the intermediate data should be encrypted by pk_Σ. For the reason that no one has private key of pk_Σ, only Evaluator is capable of decrypting the data encrypted by pk_Σ.

4.4 Secure Association Rule Mining

Getting frequent itemsets is not enough for Miner to figure out the relationship between the itemset. In the following context, we will describe how to securely mine association rule from the frequent itemsets. In our algorithm, the Miner is supposed to have the threshold of confidence, i.e., $conf_{min}$. If the Miner expects to know whether $X \Rightarrow Y$ is strong or not, CSP just needs to give him *supp*(X) and *supp*($X \cup Y$). Assume that CSP has m encrypted transactions data $\mathbf{C} = \{\boldsymbol{C}_1, \cdots, \boldsymbol{C}_m\}$, where $\boldsymbol{C}_j = ([\![c_{j,1}]\!]_{pk_{DO_i}}, \cdots, [\![c_{j,n}]\!]_{pk_{DO_i}})$, $i \in (1, \cdots, \eta)$, $j \in$

$(1, \cdots, m)$. The CSP also has the support of query $[\![u]\!]_{pk_\Sigma}$ from **SFIM**. Miner has the frequent itemset $\boldsymbol{f}$ and the threshold of confidence α/β, where $\boldsymbol{f} = ([\![f_1]\!]_{pk_M}, \cdots, [\![f_n]\!]_{pk_M})$. Please note that, for the easiness and convenience of comparison, we denote the threshold of confidence as α/β. Evaluator has the master key **MK**. The details of our **SARM** is given as follows.

Step 1 (Miner): (1) Get the sets of $\boldsymbol{f}$'s nonvoid proper subset H, where $H = \{\boldsymbol{h}_1, \cdots, \boldsymbol{h}_{2^z-2}\}$ [1]. Suppose that the number of 1s in $\boldsymbol{h}_i$ is k_i.
(2) Encrypt every $\boldsymbol{h}_i$, k_i, α and β, where $i \in (1, \cdots, 2^z - 2)$. Send them to CSP.
Step 2: For each $i = 1$ to $2^z - 2$,
(CSP and Evaluator): (1) The same procedure as in **SFIM** from Step 3 to Step 7. At the end, CSP gets $[\![u_i]\!]_{pk_\Sigma}$.
(2) $[\![\tau_i]\!]_{pk_\Sigma} \leftarrow$ **SMAD**$([\![\beta]\!]_{pk_M}, [\![u]\!]_{pk_\Sigma})$, $[\![\varepsilon_i]\!]_{pk_\Sigma} \leftarrow$ **SMAD**$([\![\alpha]\!]_{pk_M}, [\![u_i]\!]_{pk_\Sigma})$.
(3) $[\![\gamma_i]\!]_{pk_M} \leftarrow$ **SC**$([\![\tau_i]\!]_{pk_\Sigma}, [\![\varepsilon_i]\!]_{pk_\Sigma})$. Send $[\![\gamma_i]\!]_{pk_M}$ to the miner.
Miner: (1) $\gamma_i \leftarrow$ **Dec**$_{sk_M}([\![\gamma_i]\!]_{pk_M})$.
(2) If $\gamma_i = 1$, If $\gamma_i = 1$, $\boldsymbol{h}_i \Rightarrow (\boldsymbol{f} - \boldsymbol{h}_i)$ is a strong association rule. Else, it is not.

5 Security Analysis

5.1 Security of Cryptographic Blocks

In this section, we prove the security of **SMAD**, **SIP**, **SCAD**, and **SC**. First, we give the definition of security in the semi-honest model in [16,20].

Definition 3 (Security in the Semi-Honest Model [20]**).** *Let a_i be the input of party P_i, $\Pi_i(\pi)$ be P_i's execution image of the protocol π and b_i be the output for party P_i computed from π. Then π is secure if $\Pi_i(\pi)$ can be simulated from a_i and b_i such that distribution of the simulated image is computationally indistinguishable from $\Pi_i(\pi)$ (More details can be found in [20]).*

From **Definition** 3, we can conclude that the simulated execution image and the actual execution image should be computational indistinguishable when proving the security of these cryptographic blocks. In our scheme, the execution image generally includes the data exchanged and the information computed from these data.

Theorem 1. *The **SMAD** proposed is secure under semi-honest model.*

Proof. Here, let the execution image of Evaluator be denoted by $\Pi_{Evaluator}(SMAD)$ which is given by $\Pi_{Evaluator}(SMAD) = \{(X_0, z_0), (X_1, z_1), (Y_0, z_2), (Y_1, z_3)\}$ where $z_0 = x + a$, $z_1 = y + b$, $z_2 = bx + c$ and $z_3 = ay + d$

[1] For example, if $\boldsymbol{f} = \{1, 1, 1, 0\}$ which means $\{X, Y, Z\}$. The sets of $\boldsymbol{f}$'s nonvoid proper subset is $H = \{\{X\}, \{Y\}\{Z\}, \{X, Y\}, \{X, Z\}, \{Y, Z\}\}$, which can be represent as

$$H = \{\{1,0,0,0\}, \{0,1,0,0\}, \{0,0,0,1\}, \{1,1,0,0\}, \{1,0,1,0\}, \{0,1,1,0\}\}.$$

are derived by decrypting X_0, X_1, X_2 and X_3 respectively. Note that a, b, c, d are random numbers in $\mathbb{Z}_N$. We assume that $\Pi^S_{Evaluator}(SMAD) = \{(X'_0, z'_0), (X'_1, z'_1), (Y'_0, z'_2), (Y'_1, z'_3)\}$ where all the elements are randomly generated from $\mathbb{Z}_N$. Since BCP is a semantic secure encryption scheme, (X_i, z_i) is computationally indistinguishable from (X'_i, z'_i), $i \in (0, 1, 2, 3)$. Meanwhile, as every z'_i is randomly chosen from $\mathbb{Z}_N$, z_i is computationally indistinguishable from z_i. Based on the above analysis, we can draw a conclusion that $\Pi_{Evaluator}(SMAD)$ is indistinguishable from $\Pi^S_{Evaluator}(SMAD)$.

The proof of CSP is analogous to Evaluator. Combining the above analysis, we can confirm that **SMAD** is secure under the semi-honest model.

Theorem 2. *The **SIP** is secure under semi-honest model.*

Proof. Our **SIP** is based on **SMAD**. Since we have proven the security of **SMAD**, we can conclude that **SIP** is secure too.

Theorem 3. *The **SCAD** proposed is secure under semi-honest model.*

Proof. According to **SCAD**, the execution image of **SCAD** for Evaluator can be denoted by $\Pi_{Evaluator}(SCAD)$, which is $\Pi_{Evaluator}(SCAD) = \{(C', c'), (D', d'), (F', z), \delta\}$ where $c' = (-1)^a \cdot (2x + 1) + r_a$, $d' = (-1)^{1-a} \cdot (2y) + r_b$, $z = r_1((-1)^a \cdot (2x + 1) + (-1)^{1-a} \cdot (2y)) + r_2$ are separately derived from the decryption of C', D', F. Note that a is a random number from $(0, 1)$, r_a, r_b are random numbers form $\mathbb{Z}_N$, and r_1, r_2 is a random number from $\{1, \cdots, 2^l\}, 2^{2l+1} < N/2, r_1 \ll r_2$. In addition, δ is the comparison result from z. We assume $\Pi^S_{Evaluator}(SCAD) = \{(C'', c''), (D'', d''), (F'', z'), \delta'\}$ where (C'', c''), (D'', d''), (F'', z') are randomly generated from $\mathbb{Z}_N$, and δ' is set to 1 or 0 according to the randomly tossed coin. Since BCP is a semantically secure encryption scheme, (C', c'), (D', d'), (F', z) are computationally indistinguishable from (C'', c''), (D'', d''), (F'', z'). Furthermore, because the element a is randomly chosen from $\{0, 1\}$, δ is either 0 or 1 with equal probability. Thus, δ is computationally indistinguishable from δ'. Combining the above results, we can claim that $\Pi_{Evaluator}(SCAD)$ is computationally indistinguishable from $\Pi^S_{Evaluator}(SCAD)$.

On the other hand, the execution image of CSP, denoted by $\Pi_{CSP}(SCAD)$, is given by $\Pi_{Evaluator}(SCAD) = \{E, [\![\delta]\!]_{pk_\Sigma}\}$. Let the simulated image of CSP be given by $\Pi^S_{Evaluator}(SCAD) = \{E', \alpha\}$, where E', α are random numbers from $\mathbb{Z}_N$. Since BCP is semantically secure encryption scheme, E, and $[\![\delta]\!]_{pk_\Sigma}$ are computationally indistinguishable from E', and α. Thus, we can conclude that $\Pi_{CSP}(SCAD)$ is computationally indistinguishable from $\Pi^S_{CSP}(SCAD)$.

Based on the above analysis, we can claim that **SCAD** is secure under the semi-honest model.

Theorem 4. *The **SC** described is secure under semi-honest model.*

Proof. Since **SC** is designed by the similar idea of **SCAD**, we can easily get the proof from Theorem 3.

5.2 Security of SFIM and SARM

Theorem 5. *The **SFIM** proposed is secure under semi-honest model and also can preserve the data confidentiality and query privacy against active adversary.*

Proof. In the similar maner we can prove that our **SFIM** is secure under the semi-honest model firstly. In Step 1 to Step 2, DOs and Miner send C and Q, $[\![z]\!]_{pk_M}$, $[\![supp_{min}]\!]_{pk_M}$ to CSP. Due to the semantic security of BCP, the semi-honest CSP has no advantage to distinguish them from random numbers from $\mathbb{Z}_N$. In Step 3, the CSP randomly chooses a dummy transactions set and encrypts it with a random public key from DOs. Then, he mixes it with the original dataset uploaded from DOs. After that, CSP and Evaluator run the **SIP**. Since the Evaluator cannot distinguish the original dataset and the dummy data and the security proof of **SIP**, we can confirm the protocol is secure in Step 3 and Step 4. Furthermore, the data operation in Step 5 to Step 7 is similar to the process of **SMAD**, all the exchanged messages are in encrypted format, and each value deduced by CSP and Evaluator is blinded by random numbers. In Step 8, the **SCAD**, **TransDec** are adopted as the fundamental building blocks, which has been proved secure in previous section and [18]. In Step 9, CSP and Miner just deal with encrypted data, the security is from the semantic security of BCP. As a result, we can easily conclude that our **SFIM** is secure under the semi-honest model.

Next, we discuss the data confidentiality and query privacy against an active adversary $\mathcal{A}$. Assume that $\mathcal{A}$ eavesdrops the transmission link between DOs and CSP, the encrypted database and all the intermediate data is got by $\mathcal{A}$. Because all the data is encrypted by BCP, $\mathcal{A}$ cannot get the original data. If $\mathcal{A}$ comprises some DOs and gets their private keys, they still cannot decrypt the Miner's query since the encryption key is different. As long as the evaluator is not comprised all the data confidentiality and query privacy defined is satisfied.

As a result, we can claim that our **SFIM** is secure under semi-honest model and also can preserve the data confidentiality and query privacy against active adversary.

Theorem 6. *The **SARM** described in Sect. 4.4 is secure under semi-honest model and also can preserve the data confidentiality and query privacy against active adversary.*

It is worth noting that the proofs are similar to Theorem 5 and hence we omit it due to the space limitation.

6 Performance Analysis

In this section, we evaluate the performance of our scheme. In [10], the author also proposed a variant of the original BCP cryptosystem, where the randomness r is chosen in a smaller set, namely in $\mathbb{Z}_N$ rather than $\mathbb{Z}_{N^2}$. The variant of the original BCP cryptosystem is secure based on the *Small Decisional Diffie-Hellman Assumption* (S-DDH) over a squared composite modulus of the form

$N = pq$. (More details of S-DDH and the security analysis can be found in [10]) In this section, we will analyse the performance of our system based on BCP and the variant of BCP.

6.1 Experiment Analysis

The performance evaluations of the proposed system are tested on five laptop computers running Windows 8.1 with Intel Core I5-5200U 2.20 GHz CPU and 4 GB RAM. We implement BCP and its variant cryptosystem by BigInteger Class in Java development kit, and using this to implement our computation protocols. Specially, two of them are acted as the DOs, which encrypt the data and upload them to CSP; one is used as the Miner, and the rest of them are leveraged as the CSP and Evaluator respectively. In our experiment, we first test the efficiency of our cryptographic blocks. Then, we make an efficiency comparison with the most recent work [1] over the same chess database[2] as our transaction dataset, which totally has 3196 transactions and 75 attributes. Moreover, we analyse the performance of the schemes by varying parameters.

Table 4. Performance of cryptographic blocks (100-times for average, 80-bits security level)

Algorithm	CSP Compute.	Evaluator Compute.	CSP Commu.	Evaluator Commu.
SMAD	0.391 s	0.368 s	1.998 KB	1.499 KB
SCAD	0.398	0.214 s	1.498 KB	0.999 KB
SC	0.137	0.098 s	0.498 KB	0.499 KB
SIP (10 bits Vector)	3.951 s	3.822 s	19.991 KB	14.991 KB

Efficiency of Cryptographic Blocks. We first evaluate the performance of the basic cryptographic blocks, which can be seen in Table 4. For the BCP algorithm, we denote N as 1024 bits to achieve 80-bit security [21] levels. We can observe from Table 4 that in the **SMAD** algorithm the computation of CSP costs 0.391 s and he sends 1.998 KB data when communicating with Evaluator, while Evaluator needs 0.368 s to complete the computation and the communication will cost 1.499 KB. Moreover, in the **SCAD** algorithm, the CSP needs 0.398 s to compute and send 1.498 KB data to Evaluator, while the Evaluator needs 0.214 s to compute and send 0.999 KB data. In the **SC** algorithm, the CSP costs 0.137 s for computing and sends 0.498 KB data to Evaluator, while the Evaluator needs 0.098 s to compute and send 0.499 KB data. We also test **SIP** over two 10-bit vectors, we can see from Table 4, the cost of CSP and Evaluator is almost ten times of single **SMAD**.

We also test our scheme based on the variant of the BCP cryptosystem. The running result can be found in Table 5.

[2] http://fimi.ua.ac.be/data/.

Table 5. Performance of cryptographic blocks based on the variant BCP (100-times for average, 80-bits security level)

Algorithm	CSP Compute.	Evaluator Compute.	CSP Commu.	Evaluator Commu.
SMAD	0.297 s	0.251 s	1.998 KB	1.498 KB
SCAD	0.254	0.171 s	1.499 KB	0.999 KB
SC	0.083	0.063 s	0.499 KB	0.499 KB
SIP (10 bits Vector)	2.301 s	3.102 s	19.981 KB	14.989 KB

Efficiency Comparison. For a fair comparison, we also implement Qiu *et al.*'s work [1] in Java by BigInteger Class in Java development kit and JPBC library[3]. We choose $\mid p \mid = 160$ bits with at least 80-bit security with Type A pairing in BGN and N as 1024 bits in Paillier [19]. We first make a comparison about the data encryption and uploading and then the frequent itemset mining protocol is compared.

Performance of Data Encryption and Uploading. Note that the data encryption is done in off-line by the DOs. In most conditions, the DOs are resource-constrained users. The performance of data encryption is shown in Fig. 2(a) and the uploading communication costs are shown Fig. 2(b).

As shown in Fig. 2, the running time of data encryption by BCP is much less than BGN, and the BCP variant's is more less, while both of them are higher than the Paillier's running time. The communication cost of BCP and BCP varinat is almost same which is larger than Paillier and BGN. Since most of the DOs are resource-constrained, our scheme extensively reduce the DOs' computation cost than [1]'s protocol 2, but with slight higher communication cost.

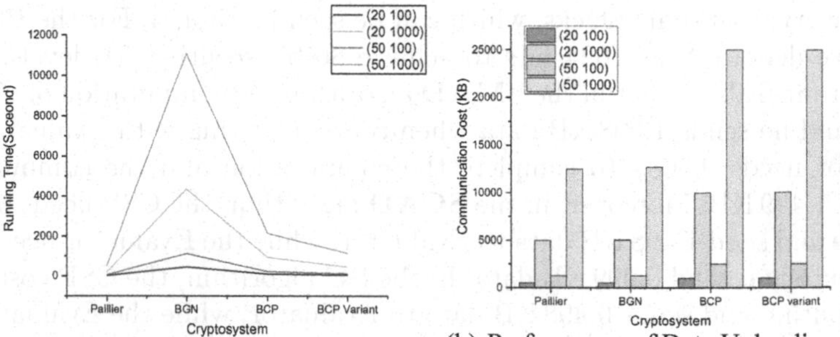

(a) Performance of Data Encryption

(b) Performance of Data Uploading

Fig. 2. Performance of data owner

[3] http://gas.unisa.it/projects/jpbc.

Table 6. Cloud computation time (in minutes) of frequent itemset mining

Protocol 2	Our protocol based on BCP	Our protocol based on BCP variant
1354.021	4321.612	2930.398

Performance of Frequent Itemset Mining. We test the cloud's (including CSP and Evaluator) running time in our scheme and [1]'s protocol on the Chess dataset. The overall running time is shown in Table 6. In our experiment, the size of dummy transactions in all of the protocols is $m/2$. From Table 6, we can conclude that our protocol is slower than [1]'s protocol 2. Since our protocol achieves higher privacy level, we think it is reasonable. In addition, if we use the BCP variant as the basic cryptosystem in our scheme, the running time can be largely reduced. What's more, the cloud is usually has "unlimited" computing resource and power, the running time of our scheme can be dramatically reduced in real cloud system.

7 Conclusions

In this paper, we propose a practical privacy-preserving frequent itemset mining and association rule mining protocol on encrypted cloud data. Compared with the state-of-art works, our scheme achieves higher privacy level, and also reduces the data owners' computation cost. The computation cost in cloud is higher than Qiu *et al.*'s work [1]. Since the cloud has massive computation resource, the computation time in real cloud service will be quite small. In our future work, we will focus on further improving the efficiency of our scheme.

Acknowledgement. The authors would like to thank Dr. Shuo Qiu for her generous feedback. The work is supported by the National Natural Science Foundation of China (No. 61702541, No. 61702105), the Young Elite Scientists Sponsorship Program by CAST (2017QNRC001), the Science and Technology Research Plan Program by NUDT (Grant No. ZK17-03-46), the national key research and development program under grant 2017YFB0802301, and Guangxi cloud computing and large data Collaborative Innovation Center Project.

References

1. Qiu, S., Wang, B., Li, M., Liu, J., Shi, Y.: Toward practical privacy-preserving frequent itemset mining on encrypted cloud data. IEEE Trans. Cloud Comput. (2017)
2. Sarawagi, S., Nagaralu, S.H.: Data mining models as services on the internet. ACM SIGKDD Explor. Newslett. **2**(1), 24–28 (2000)
3. Giannotti, F., Lakshmanan, L.V.S., Monreale, A., Pedreschi, D., Wang, H.: Privacy-preserving mining of association rules from outsourced transaction databases. IEEE Syst. J. **7**(3), 385–395 (2013)

4. Yi, X., Rao, F.Y., Bertino, E., Bouguettaya, A.: Privacy-preserving association rule mining in cloud computing. In: ACM Symposium on Information, Computer and Communications Security, pp. 439–450 (2015)
5. Tai, C.-H., Yu, P.S., Chen, M.-S.: k-Support anonymity based on pseudo taxonomy for outsourcing of frequent itemset mining. In: Proceedings of the 16th ACM SIGKDD International Conference on Knowledge Discovery and Data Mining, pp. 473–482. ACM (2010)
6. Kantarcioglu, M., Clifton, C.: Privacy-preserving distributed mining of association rules on horizontally partitioned data. IEEE Trans. Knowl. Data Eng. **16**(9), 1026–1037 (2004)
7. Vaidya, J., Clifton, C.: Privacy preserving association rule mining in vertically partitioned data. In: Proceedings of the Eighth ACM SIGKDD International Conference on Knowledge Discovery and Data Mining, pp. 639–644. ACM (2002)
8. ElGamal, T.: A public key cryptosystem and a signature scheme based on discrete logarithms. IEEE Trans. Inf. Theory **31**(4), 469–472 (1985)
9. Li, L., Lu, R., Choo, K.-K.R., Datta, A., Shao, J.: Privacy-preserving-outsourced association rule mining on vertically partitioned databases. IEEE Trans. Inf. Forensics Secur. **11**(8), 1847–1861 (2016)
10. Bresson, E., Catalano, D., Pointcheval, D.: A simple public-key cryptosystem with a double trapdoor decryption mechanism and its applications. In: Laih, C.-S. (ed.) ASIACRYPT 2003. LNCS, vol. 2894, pp. 37–54. Springer, Heidelberg (2003). https://doi.org/10.1007/978-3-540-40061-5_3
11. Dong, C., Chen, L.: A fast secure dot product protocol with application to privacy preserving association rule mining. In: Tseng, V.S., Ho, T.B., Zhou, Z.-H., Chen, A.L.P., Kao, H.-Y. (eds.) PAKDD 2014. LNCS (LNAI), vol. 8443, pp. 606–617. Springer, Cham (2014). https://doi.org/10.1007/978-3-319-06608-0_50
12. Dong, C., Chen, L., Wen, Z.: When private set intersection meets big data: an efficient and scalable protocol. In: Proceedings of the 2013 ACM SIGSAC Conference on Computer & Communications Security, pp. 789–800. ACM (2013)
13. Lai, J., Li, Y., Deng, R.H., Weng, J., Guan, C., Yan, Q.: Towards semantically secure outsourcing of association rule mining on categorical data. Inf. Sci. **267**(2), 267–286 (2014)
14. Boneh, D., Goh, E.-J., Nissim, K.: Evaluating 2-DNF formulas on ciphertexts. In: Kilian, J. (ed.) TCC 2005. LNCS, vol. 3378, pp. 325–341. Springer, Heidelberg (2005). https://doi.org/10.1007/978-3-540-30576-7_18
15. Agrawal, R., Imieliński, T., Swami, A.: Mining association rules between sets of items in large databases. In: ACM SIGMOD Record, vol. 22, pp. 207–216. ACM (1993)
16. Cheng, K., Wang, L., Shen, Y., Wang, H., Wang, Y., Jiang, X., Zhong, H.: Secure k-NN query on encrypted cloud data with multiple keys. IEEE Trans. Big Data (2017)
17. Liu, X., Deng, R.H., Choo, K.-K.R., Weng, J.: An efficient privacy-preserving outsourced calculation toolkit with multiple keys. IEEE Trans. Inf. Forensics Secur. **11**(11), 2401–2414 (2016)
18. Peter, A., Tews, E., Katzenbeisser, S.: Efficiently outsourcing multiparty computation under multiple keys. IEEE Trans. Inf. Forensics Secur. **8**(12), 2046–2058 (2013)

19. Paillier, P.: Public-key cryptosystems based on composite degree residuosity classes. In: Stern, J. (ed.) EUROCRYPT 1999. LNCS, vol. 1592, pp. 223–238. Springer, Heidelberg (1999). https://doi.org/10.1007/3-540-48910-X_16
20. Goldreich, O.: Foundations of Cryptography: Volume 2, Basic Applications. Cambridge University Press, Cambridge (2009)
21. Barker, E., Barker, W., Burr, W., Polk, W., Smid, M.: NIST special publication 800–57. NIST Spec. Publ. **800**(57), 1–142 (2007)

Post-quantum Cryptography

Cryptanalysis of the Randomized Version of a Lattice-Based Signature Scheme from PKC'08

Haoyu Li[1,2], Renzhang Liu[3], Abderrahmane Nitaj[4], and Yanbin Pan[1(✉)]

[1] Key Laboratory of Mathematics Mechanization, NCMIS, Academy of Mathematics and Systems Science, Chinese Academy of Sciences, Beijing 100190, China
lihaoyu14@mails.ucas.ac.cn, panyanbin@amss.ac.cn

[2] School of Mathematical Sciences, University of Chinese Academy of Sciences, Beijing 100049, China

[3] State Key Laboratory of Information Security, Institute of Information Engineering, Chinese Academy of Sciences, Beijing 100093, China
liurenzhang@iie.ac.cn

[4] Département de Mathématiques, Université de Caen, Caen, France
abderrahmane.nitaj@unicaen.fr

Abstract. In PKC'08, Plantard, Susilo and Win proposed a lattice-based signature scheme, whose security is based on the hardness of the closest vector problem with the infinity norm (CVP_∞). This signature scheme was proposed as a countermeasure against the Nguyen-Regev attack, which improves the security and the efficiency of the Goldreich, Goldwasser and Halevi scheme (GGH). Furthermore, to resist potential side channel attacks, the authors suggested modifying the deterministic signing algorithm to be randomized. In this paper, we propose a chosen message attack against the randomized version. Note that the randomized signing algorithm will generate different signature vectors in a relatively small cube for the same message, so the difference of any two signature vectors will be relatively short lattice vector. Once collecting enough such short difference vectors, we can recover the whole or the partial secret key by lattice reduction algorithms, which implies that the randomized version is insecure under the chosen message attack.

Keywords: Lattice-based cryptography · Signature schemes
Lattice reduction

1 Introduction

It is well known that classical cryptography is vulnerable to quantum computers since Shor's algorithm [21] will solve the integer factorization and the

This work was supported in part by the NNSF of China (No. 61572490 and No. 11471314), and in part by the National Center for Mathematics and Interdisciplinary Sciences, CAS.

W. Susilo and G. Yang (Eds.): ACISP 2018, LNCS 10946, pp. 455–466, 2018.
https://doi.org/10.1007/978-3-319-93638-3_26

logarithm discrete problems efficiently. This has motivated the development of post-quantum cryptography, especially lattice-based cryptosystems. In general, the security of lattice-based cryptosystems is always related to some hard computational problems in lattices, such as the Shortest Vector Problem (SVP) and the Closest Vector Problem (CVP).

As important cryptographic primitives, several lattice-based digital signature schemes have been proposed in recent years, such as [5,8–10,19]. In 1997, Goldreich et al. [9] proposed the GGH signature scheme based on lattices, whose security is related to the hardness of approximate CVP. In fact, GGH is not only a concrete signature scheme, but also a general framework to construct lattice-based digital signature schemes. The GGH framework consists of a good lattice basis $\boldsymbol{G}$, a bad basis $\boldsymbol{B}$ for the same lattice and a reduction algorithm as the signing algorithm. Usually, the good basis is used as the secret key, with which the reduction algorithm can efficiently output an approximation for the closest vector of a target vector corresponding to the message. Such approximation is the signature of the message. The bad basis is published as the public key, with which one can check if the signature is in the lattice and close enough to the target vector. In GGH scheme, they used a nearly orthogonal basis $\boldsymbol{G}$ as the good basis, a random basis as the bad basis $\boldsymbol{B}$, and Babai's rounding-off algorithm [2] as the reduction algorithm.

Based on GGH framework, Hoffstein et al. [11] presented the NTRUSign as a more efficient lattice-based signature scheme. They used some special short basis as a good basis, a "random" basis as the bad basis $\boldsymbol{B}$, and Babai's rounding-off algorithm as the reduction algorithm.

However, Nguyen and Regev [18] proposed a clever method to recover the secret key of the GGH signature scheme and NTRUSign by studying the parallelepiped of the lattice. More precisely, by collecting enough message-signature pairs, they can obtain many samples uniformly distributed in the parallelepiped due to Babai's rounding-off algorithm employed as reduction algorithm in this two signature schemes. Then with these samples, they can finally recover the parallelepiped which leaks the good basis. They also pointed out that even taking Babai's nearest plane algorithm [2] as the signing algorithm, these two schemes are still insecure. Later, Ducas and Nguyen [7] proposed some method to analyze some countermeasures against the Nguyen-Regev attack.

By the Nguyen-Regev attack, it seems that the security of GGH type signature schemes depends heavily on the reduction algorithms. To resist such attack, at least two different reduction algorithms have been proposed. In 2008, Gentry et al. [8] presented a Gaussian sample algorithm similar to [12]. Based on such a random vector-sampling algorithm, Gentry, Peikert and Vaikuntanathan constructed a signature scheme, with a short trap-door basis as the private key and a long basis as the public key. Since the lattice vectors outputted by the new sampling algorithm do not reveal the trap-door, the signature scheme of Gentry, Peikert and Vaikuntanathan can be proved to be secure under the chosen message attack (CMA).

In 2008, Plantard et al. [19] proposed another signature scheme at PKC'08 to resist the Nguyen-Regev attack. They employed a special type of lattices as the good basis which has a basis that can be written into the sum of a diagonal matrix and a ternary random matrix. With such a basis, they proposed a reduction algorithm to reduce any vector into a small cube. Since the cube is public and it seems hard to recover the private basis from the cube, the authors claimed that their scheme can resist the Nguyen-Regev attack well.

As pointed out by Plantard, Susilo, and Win, since their reduction algorithm is deterministic, the scheme may suffer some potential side channel attacks. To make the scheme more secure, they modified their reduction algorithm to be randomized.

In this paper, we show that the randomized version of the PSW signature scheme is insecure under the CMA model. Simply speaking, note that when we query the signing oracle with the single message $\boldsymbol{m}$ for many times, we will usually obtain different signature vectors $\boldsymbol{w}_1, \boldsymbol{w}_2, \cdots, \boldsymbol{w}_k$ with $k \geq 2$. Denote by $\mathcal{H}(\boldsymbol{m})$ the hash vector of the message $\boldsymbol{m}$. Note that, in the PSW scheme, the difference $\boldsymbol{w}_i - \mathcal{H}(\boldsymbol{m})$, $1 \leq i \leq k$ are all in the given lattice. It is easy to see that $\boldsymbol{w}_i - \boldsymbol{w}_j$, $1 \leq i < j \leq k$ are all in the lattice. Note that each signature $\boldsymbol{w}_i$ is contained in a relatively small cube, then their difference vectors $\boldsymbol{w}_i - \boldsymbol{w}_j$ are relatively short. Once we obtain many such difference vectors, the $\mathbb{Z}$-linear combinations of these vectors will span the given lattice with high probability. By using the lattice reduction algorithms such as LLL [13] and BKZ [4,20] to these short difference vectors, we could obtain a much shorter basis, which may leak the good basis in this signature scheme. In fact, we find that for dimension less than 400, BKZ-20 will recover all or partial rows of the good basis in our experiments.

To fix the randomized version of the PSW signature scheme, we will give two methods as presented in [8]. The first method is to store the message-signature pairs locally. When signing a message, we first check whether the message is in storage or not. If the message is in storage, we output the stored corresponding signature, otherwise, we apply the randomized reduction algorithm to generate a signature. The second method is using the randomized reduction algorithm to generate the signature for the hash value of a message and some additional random number instead of the hash value of just the message.

Roadmap. The remainder of the paper is organized as follows. First we present some notations and preliminaries on lattices and hard problems in Sect. 2. Then we describe the Plantard, Susilo, and Win signature scheme in Sect. 3. Finally we describe our attacks and some experimental results in detail in Sect. 4, and some strategies to fix the randomized version of PSW signature scheme are discussed in Sect. 5.

2 Preliminaries

Denote by $\mathbb{R}$, $\mathbb{Z}$ the real number field and the integer ring respectively. For a vector $\boldsymbol{v} = (v_1, v_2, \cdots, v_n) \in \mathbb{R}^n$, denote by v_i its i-th component and denote by $\|\boldsymbol{v}\| = \sqrt{v_1^2 + v_2^2 + \cdots + v_n^2}$ its length.

2.1 Lattices

A lattice Λ is a discrete subgroup of $\mathbb{R}^n$. Equivalently, a lattice is a $\mathbb{Z}$-linear combinations of m linearly independent vectors in $\mathbb{R}^n$. The set of these linearly independent vectors is called a basis of Λ. Given a matrix $\boldsymbol{B} \in \mathbb{Z}^{m\times n}$, we denote by $\Lambda(\boldsymbol{B})$ the lattice spanned by the row vectors of $\boldsymbol{B}$. That is,

$$\Lambda(\boldsymbol{B}) = \Big\{\sum_{i=1}^{m} x_i \boldsymbol{b}_i | x_i \in \mathbb{Z}, 1 \leq i \leq m\Big\},$$

where $\boldsymbol{b}_i$ is the i-th row of $\boldsymbol{B}$. If the rows of $\boldsymbol{B}$ are linearly independent, we call $\boldsymbol{B}$ a basis of $\Lambda(\boldsymbol{B})$. For a basis $\boldsymbol{B}$, we denote by $\det(\Lambda(\boldsymbol{B}))$ the determinant of the lattice $\Lambda(\boldsymbol{B})$ as $\sqrt{\det(\boldsymbol{B}\boldsymbol{B}^T)}$.

A lattice $\Lambda(\boldsymbol{B})$ may have many bases. If $\boldsymbol{B}$ is a nonsingular square matrix with all entries in $\mathbb{Z}$, then $\Lambda(\boldsymbol{B})$ has a special basis in Hermite Normal Form. In general, a nonsingular square matrix $\boldsymbol{H} = (h_{ij}) \in \mathbb{Z}^{n\times n}$ is in Hermite Normal Form if

(1) $h_{ij} = 0$ for $1 \leq j < i \leq n$;
(2) $h_{ii} > 0$ for $1 \leq i \leq n$;
(3) $0 \leq h_{ij} < h_{jj}$ for $1 \leq i < j \leq n$.

Hermite Normal Form of any integer matrix can be computed in polynomial time, and Micciancio [15] suggested publishing the Hermite Normal Form as the public key which will improve the security of some lattice-based cryptosystems.

2.2 Lattice Problems and Algorithms

In lattice theory, the Shortest Vector Problem (SVP) and the Closest Vector Problem (CVP) are two famous computational problems which have been proved to be NP-hard [1,3]. Given a lattice basis $\boldsymbol{B} \in \mathbb{Z}^{m\times n}$, the shortest vector problem aims to find a nonzero shortest vector in $\Lambda(\boldsymbol{B})$, and the closest vector problem aims to find the closest vector to a target vector $\boldsymbol{t} \in \mathbb{Z}^n$. We denote by $\lambda_1(\Lambda(\boldsymbol{B}))$ the length of the shortest nonzero lattice vectors in the lattice $\Lambda(\boldsymbol{B})$.

The approximation versions of SVP and CVP are usually used to evaluate the security for lattice-based schemes. For the approximation of SVP, we need to find a lattice vector $\boldsymbol{v}$ such that $\|\boldsymbol{v}\| \leq \gamma\lambda_1$, and for the approximation of CVP, our aim is to find a lattice vector $\boldsymbol{w}$ satisfying $\|\boldsymbol{w} - \boldsymbol{t}\| \leq \gamma \min_{\boldsymbol{v}\in\Lambda(\boldsymbol{B})} \|\boldsymbol{v} - \boldsymbol{t}\|$ with $\gamma \geq 1$.

Some polynomial-time algorithms have been presented to solve approximate SVP and approximate CVP with exponentially large factor γ, such as LLL [13],

BKZ [4,20] for the approximate SVP and Babai's nearest plane algorithm [2] for approximate CVP.

LLL algorithm is a polynomial-time lattice reduction algorithm which was presented in [13]. An important property of this algorithm is the output vectors are relatively short. Furthermore, in practice, the output of LLL algorithm is much better than the theoretical analysis.

Blockwise Korkine-Zolotarev (BKZ) algorithm [4,20] is also a widely used lattice reduction algorithm in the analysis for lattice-based cryptosystems. In general, BKZ algorithm has an additional parameter $\beta \geq 2$ as the block size. In the process of BKZ algorithm, a subalgorithm which finds the shortest vector of the projective lattice with dimension β is called at each iteration. Generally speaking, BKZ algorithm will cost more time than LLL, but the output will be much shorter than that of LLL when β becomes larger.

3 The PSW Digital Signature Scheme

In PKC'08, Plantard et al. [19] proposed a new digital signature based on CVP_∞, which was claimed to be a countermeasure against the Nguyen-Regev attack.

3.1 The Original Signature Scheme

The original PSW signature scheme consists of three main steps as the following:

Setup

1. Choose an integer n.
2. Compute a random matrix $\boldsymbol{M} \in \{-1, 0, 1\}^{n \times n}$.
3. Compute $d = \lfloor 2\rho(\boldsymbol{M}) + 1 \rfloor$ and $\boldsymbol{D} = dI_n$, where $\rho(\boldsymbol{M})$ is the maximum of the absolute value of the eigenvalues of $\boldsymbol{M}$.
4. Compute the Hermite Normal Form $\boldsymbol{H}$ of the basis $\boldsymbol{D} - \boldsymbol{M}$.
5. The public key is $(\boldsymbol{D}, \boldsymbol{H})$, and the secret key is $\boldsymbol{M}$.

To sign a message $\boldsymbol{m} \in \{0, 1\}^*$, one does the following.

Sign

1. Compute the vector $\boldsymbol{v} = \mathcal{H}(\boldsymbol{m}) \in \mathbb{Z}^n$ where $\mathcal{H}$ is a hash function which maps $\boldsymbol{m}$ to $\{\boldsymbol{x} \in \mathbb{Z}^n \| x_i| < d^2, 1 \leq i \leq n\}$.
2. By Algorithm 1, compute $\boldsymbol{w}$ as the signature of $\boldsymbol{m}$.

To verify a message-signature pair $(\boldsymbol{m}, \boldsymbol{w})$, one does the following.

Verify

1. Check if $|w_i| < d, 1 \leq i \leq n$.
2. Compute the vector $\mathcal{H}(\boldsymbol{m}) \in \mathbb{Z}^n$.
3. Check if the vector $\mathcal{H}(\boldsymbol{m}) - \boldsymbol{w}$ is in the lattice of basis $\boldsymbol{H}$.

Algorithm 1. Signing algorithm

Input: A vector $\boldsymbol{v} \in \mathbb{Z}^n$, the matrix $\boldsymbol{D}$ and $\boldsymbol{M}$ obtained in the Setup step.

Output: A vector $\boldsymbol{w} \in \mathbb{Z}^n$ such that $\boldsymbol{w} \equiv \boldsymbol{v} \pmod{\Lambda(\boldsymbol{D} - \boldsymbol{M})}$ and $|w_i| < d$ for all $i = 1, 2, \cdots, n$.

$\boldsymbol{w} \leftarrow \boldsymbol{v}$
$i \leftarrow 1$
$k \leftarrow 0$
while $k < n$ **do**
  $k \leftarrow 0$
  $q \leftarrow \lceil \frac{w_i}{d} \rfloor$;
  $w_i \leftarrow w_i - qd$
  for $j \leftarrow 1$ to n **do**
    $w_{i+j \bmod n} \leftarrow w_{i+j \bmod n} + q\boldsymbol{M}_{i,i+j \bmod n}$
    if $|w_{i+j \bmod n}| < d$ **then**
      $k \leftarrow k + 1$
    end if
  end for
  $i \leftarrow i + 1 \bmod n$
end while
return $\boldsymbol{w}$

Algorithm 2. Randomized signing algorithm

Input: A vector $\boldsymbol{v} \in \mathbb{Z}^n$, the matrix $\boldsymbol{D}$ and $\boldsymbol{M}$ obtained in the Setup step.

Output: A vector $\boldsymbol{w} \in \mathbb{Z}^n$ such that $\boldsymbol{w} \equiv \boldsymbol{v} \pmod{\Lambda(\boldsymbol{D} - \boldsymbol{M})}$ and $|w_i| < d$ for all $i = 1, 2, \cdots, n$.

$\boldsymbol{w} \leftarrow \boldsymbol{v}$
$i \xleftarrow{\$} \{1, 2, \cdots, n\}$
$k \leftarrow 0$
while $k < n$ **do**
  $k \leftarrow 0$
  $q \leftarrow \lceil \frac{w_i}{d} \rfloor$;
  $w_i \leftarrow w_i - qd$
  for $j \leftarrow 1$ to n **do**
    $w_{i+j \bmod n} \leftarrow w_{i+j \bmod n} + q\boldsymbol{M}_{i,i+j \bmod n}$
    if $|w_{i+j \bmod n}| < d$ **then**
      $k \leftarrow k + 1$
    end if
  end for
  $i \leftarrow i + 1 \bmod n$
end while
return $\boldsymbol{w}$

3.2 The Randomized Version of PSW Signature Scheme

As pointed out by Plantard, Susilo, and Win, since the reduction algorithm is deterministic, the original PSW scheme may suffer some potential side channel attacks. To resist the potential side channel attacks, they suggest using the following randomized algorithm (Algorithm 2) as the signing algorithm.

4 The Chosen Message Attack Against the Randomized Version of PSW Scheme

4.1 Key Idea of Our Chosen Message Attack

As we can see, in the randomized version of the PSW signature scheme, the signature vectors for the same message may not be unique. Therefore, in the CMA model, if we query the randomized signing oracle with the same message $\boldsymbol{m}$, we may obtain different signature vectors $\boldsymbol{w}_1, \boldsymbol{w}_2, \cdots, \boldsymbol{w}_k$ where $k \geq 2$. Note that $\boldsymbol{w}_i - \mathcal{H}(\boldsymbol{m})$, $1 \leq i \leq k$ are all in the lattice, and so are their difference vectors

$$(\boldsymbol{w}_i - \mathcal{H}(\boldsymbol{m})) - (\boldsymbol{w}_j - \mathcal{H}(\boldsymbol{m})) = \boldsymbol{w}_i - \boldsymbol{w}_j,$$

where $1 \leq i \leq j \leq k$.

Since each component of $\boldsymbol{w}_i$ is in $(-d, d)$, we know that each component of $\boldsymbol{w}_i - \boldsymbol{w}_j$ is in $(-2d, 2d)$. Since $d \in \Theta(\sqrt{n})$ as stated in [19], the lattice vectors $\boldsymbol{w}_i - \boldsymbol{w}_j$'s are very short.

Once we obtain many such short difference vectors, the $\mathbb{Z}$-linear combinations of these vectors will span the lattice $\Lambda(\boldsymbol{D} - \boldsymbol{M})$. By using the lattice reduction algorithms such as LLL and BKZ to the set of short generators, we expect to obtain a much shorter basis, which may leak the private key.

We present the framework of our attack as the following:

1. Generate some messages $\boldsymbol{m}_1, \boldsymbol{m}_2, \cdots$ randomly;
2. For any message $\boldsymbol{m}_j \in \{\boldsymbol{m}_1, \boldsymbol{m}_2, \cdots\}$, querying the signing oracle for several times to obtain many different signatures $\{\boldsymbol{w}_{j1}, \boldsymbol{w}_{j2}, \cdots, \boldsymbol{w}_{jk}\}$ with $k \geq 2$;
3. Collect enough difference vectors $\boldsymbol{w}_{ji} - \boldsymbol{w}_{j1}$'s such that they can span the lattice $\Lambda(\boldsymbol{D} - \boldsymbol{M})$. Denote by $\boldsymbol{L}$ the set of these $\boldsymbol{w}_{ji} - \boldsymbol{w}_{j1}$'s;
4. Use lattice basis reduction algorithm to $\boldsymbol{L}$ to output a square matrix $\boldsymbol{LL}$, and expect to obtain some information about the private key.

4.2 Our Strategy to Collect the Difference Vectors

To collect the difference vectors, we have to decide how many messages we will choose in Step 1 and how many signatures for one message we will query with the oracle in Step 2. Below we give a very simple but efficient strategy, that is, for one message we query as many different signatures as possible and we choose as few messages as possible to satisfy Step 3.

Note that for every message, the signing algorithm (Algorithm 2) will generate at most n different signatures since there are n choices for the index i. Assume there were exactly n different signatures, then it is natural to ask how many times we query the signing oracle to collect all these signatures. Since every signature is uniformly randomly returned by the oracle, by the classical result for Coupon Collector's Problem [16,17], it can be easily concluded that the expectation of this number is

$$n(1 + \frac{1}{2} + \cdots + \frac{1}{n}) = n \ln n + \gamma n + \frac{1}{2} + O(\frac{1}{n}),$$

where $\gamma \approx 0.5772156649$ is the Euler's constant. Hence, we can query one message for $\lceil n \log n \rceil$ times, and then we know that the probability of collecting all the n signatures is greater than $1 - n^{-\frac{1}{\ln 2}+1}$ [16,17]. When $n \geq 100$, this value is greater than 0.85, which is acceptable.

Therefore, in our attack we query $\lceil n \log n \rceil$ signatures for each message, and choose random messages until we collect enough difference vectors, then applying LLL and BKZ to obtain a short basis for the lattice.

We present the attack as Algorithm 3.

Algorithm 3. Chosen message attack against the randomized version of PSW scheme

---

Input: The public key $\boldsymbol{H}$, the randomized signing oracle $\mathcal{O}$ and a message generator $\mathcal{G}$ to generate the messages randomly.
Output: A set of short basis for $\Lambda(\boldsymbol{H})$.

```
Let LL be a zero matrix of n × n
while det LL/ det H != 1 and det LL/ det H != −1 do
    W = {}
    m ← G
    for i ← 1 to ⌈n log n⌉ do
        w ← O(m)
        If w is not in W, append w to W
    end for
    Collect all w_1 − w_i, 1 ≤ i ≤ |W| to append to the matrix LL
    LL ← the last n rows of LLL(LL) (since LLL algorithm puts linearly independent vectors in the last rows)
end while
B ← LatticeReduction(LL)
Check whether B leaks the private key or not.
```

4.3 Experimental Results

In our experiments, we used SageMath 7.5.1 [23] to implement our attacks, and the LLL's parameter is set to the default value. For BKZ algorithm, we set the parameter "algorithm" as "NTL" to call the NTL library [22] to implement this algorithm. All experiments were run on a machine with Intel(R) Xeon(R) CPU E5-2620 v4 @2.1 GHz.

We chose the dimension n to be 200, 300, 400, and for any dimension we chose 5 randomized generated instances. For the lattice reduction algorithms, we used LLL algorithm, BKZ-10, and BKZ-20 respectively. The results are listed in Table 1.

We would like to point out a natural attempt to recover the rows of $\boldsymbol{D} - \boldsymbol{M}$ is by applying lattice basis reduction algorithm on the public key $\boldsymbol{H}$ directly, since every row of $\boldsymbol{D} - \boldsymbol{M}$ is very short. However, for just dimension $n = 165$ in

Table 1. Experimental results for our attack

dim	200					300					400				
#msg	3	2	3	2	3	3	2	2	2	2	3	4	3	2	3
#sig	4587	3058	4587	3058	4587	7407	4938	4938	4938	4938	10374	13832	10374	6916	10374
LLL	A	P(22)	A	A	P(32)	N	N	N	N	N	N	N	N	N	N
BKZ10	A	A	A	A	A	N	N	P(3)	N	N	N	N	N	N	N
BKZ20	A	A	A	A	A	A	N	A	P(4)	P(22)	N	P(2)	N	N	N

[a] dim: The dimension of the lattice $\Lambda(\boldsymbol{D}-\boldsymbol{M})$;
[b] #msg: The number of messages we need to span the lattice $\Lambda(\boldsymbol{D}-\boldsymbol{M})$;
[c] #sig: The number of signatures we need;
[d] N: The lattice reduction algorithm can not recover any rows of the matrix $\boldsymbol{D}-\boldsymbol{M}$;
[e] A: The lattice reduction algorithm can recover all rows of the matrix $\boldsymbol{D}-\boldsymbol{M}$;
[f] P: The lattice reduction algorithm can recover partial rows of the matrix $\boldsymbol{D}-\boldsymbol{M}$, and the number in the bracket is the number of rows we recovered.

our experiments, we could not recover any row of $\boldsymbol{D}-\boldsymbol{M}$ when we even applied BKZ-20 on the public key $\boldsymbol{H}$ directly.

In contrast, with our attack, for the dimension $n=200$, LLL algorithm could recover all (or partial) rows of $\boldsymbol{D}-\boldsymbol{M}$, and BKZ-10 could recover all the rows of $\boldsymbol{D}-\boldsymbol{M}$ for our instances. For the dimension $n=300$, we could recover all rows of $\boldsymbol{D}-\boldsymbol{M}$ in 2 instances and partial rows in 2 instances when BKZ-20 was used.

For the dimension $n=400$, we just obtain partial rows in $\boldsymbol{D}-\boldsymbol{M}$ for only one instance with BKZ-20 algorithm. Employing BKZ algorithm with bigger blocksize, we may obtain more rows.

However, we would like to point out that even only partial rows are recovered, the randomized version of the PSW signature scheme is not secure. Since the messages are all generated randomly, we may expect to recover all the rows of the matrix $\boldsymbol{D}-\boldsymbol{M}$ by repeating our attack several times.

Remark 1. Once obtaining a short basis, we can also recover the matrix $\boldsymbol{M}$ by finding some lattice vector close to $(0,\cdots,d,\cdots,0)$. Using some strategies in [14] to solve the Bounded Distance Decoding (BDD) problem may improve our results.

Remark 2. We would like to point out that the strategy to collect the difference vectors also plays an important role in our attack. Another natural strategy is to query the signing oracle just twice for each message and collect enough difference vectors to mount the attack. However, the new strategy did not work so well as Algorithm 3. For dimension $n=180$ and larger dimensions, we could never recover any rows of the matrix $\boldsymbol{D}-\boldsymbol{M}$ by using this strategy in our experiments.

5 Possible Ways to Fix the Randomized Version

There are two possible ways to fix the randomized version similar to the strategies in [8].

The first way is to store the message-signature pairs locally, which seems a bit impractical. In detail, once given a message $\boldsymbol{m}$, we will modify the Sign step as the following:

Sign

1. Check whether $\boldsymbol{m}$ has been signed or not.
2. If $\boldsymbol{m}$ is stored locally, return the locally stored signature $\boldsymbol{w}$ corresponding to $\boldsymbol{m}$.
3. Otherwise, use Algorithm 2 to output a signature $\boldsymbol{w}$ and store $(\boldsymbol{m}, \boldsymbol{w})$ locally.

The second way is to add some random number to the hash function. This strategy is usually used in the hash-then-sign schemes. Since the original PSW scheme has no security proof and we do not know the exact hardness of CVP_∞ over the PSW instances, we can not present some formal security proof for this fixed version, but just present it as the following:

Sign

1. Choose $\boldsymbol{r} \leftarrow \{0,1\}^n$ at random.
2. Compute the vector $\boldsymbol{v} = \mathcal{H}(\boldsymbol{m}||\boldsymbol{r})$, where $\mathcal{H}$ maps $(\boldsymbol{m}||\boldsymbol{r})$ to the area $(-d^2, d^2)^n$.
3. Applying Algorithm 2, compute the signature $\boldsymbol{w}$.

Once given the signature $(\boldsymbol{m}, \boldsymbol{r}, \boldsymbol{w})$, we will modify the Verify step as below.

Verify

1. Check if $|w_i| < d$ for $1 \leq i \leq n$.
2. Compute the vector $\mathcal{H}(\boldsymbol{m}||\boldsymbol{r})$.
3. Check whether the vector $\mathcal{H}(\boldsymbol{m}||\boldsymbol{r}) - \boldsymbol{w} \in \Lambda(\boldsymbol{H})$ or not.

6 Conclusions and Open Problems

In this paper, we show that the randomized PSW signature scheme is not secure under the chosen message attack at least for dimension less than or equal to 400. However, for the scheme with bigger dimension which becomes less efficient apparently, it seems that we need the BKZ algorithm with bigger blocksize to recover the private key. In fact, our attack reveals that the storage of previous signature or the use of random nonce employed in the randomized signature scheme is crucial.

However, there are still some unsolved theoretical problems, such as presenting a theoretical reason why the strategy in Remark 2 does not work as well as Algorithm 3. The lattice vectors we collected by the two strategies have almost the same length. However, Algorithm 3 usually succeeded, whereas the strategy in Remark 2 always failed when the dimension is between 200 and 400. It seems a bit strange. We conjecture the reason may relate to the fact that the lattice vectors collected with the strategy in Remark 2 seems more "independent" and "random", but we can not present a rigorous analysis.

Moreover, we tried to apply our attack to analyze the security of some signature schemes with GPV algorithm [8] as the signing algorithm, such as [6]. However, we could only recover the private key with dimension 128 for [6], but failed for larger dimensions such as 256. This phenomenon also lacks theoretical explanation.

Hence, the theory about how the lattice basis reduction algorithm behaves with shorter input should be further studied. Usually, we measure the quality of the output for the lattice basis reduction algorithm with the determinant of the input lattice (such as Gauss heuristic), but it can be expected that with shorter input, we can have shorter output, although the determinant keeps the same. A natural problem is if there is some tight relation between the length of output and input on average, with which we can describe the attack more rigorously in theory.

References

1. Ajtai, M.: The shortest vector problem in L2 is NP-hard for randomized reductions (extended abstract). In: Proceedings of the Thirtieth Annual ACM Symposium on Theory of Computing, STOC 1998, pp. 10–19. ACM, New York (1998). https://doi.org/10.1145/276698.276705
2. Babai, L.: On Lovász' lattice reduction and the nearest lattice point problem. Combinatorica **6**(1), 1–13 (1986). https://doi.org/10.1007/BF02579403
3. Boas, P.V.E.: Another NP-complete problem and the complexity of computing short vectors in lattices. Mathematics Department Report 81–04. University of Amsterdam (1981)
4. Chen, Y., Nguyen, P.Q.: BKZ 2.0: better lattice security estimates. In: Lee, D.H., Wang, X. (eds.) ASIACRYPT 2011. LNCS, vol. 7073, pp. 1–20. Springer, Heidelberg (2011). https://doi.org/10.1007/978-3-642-25385-0_1
5. Ducas, L., Durmus, A., Lepoint, T., Lyubashevsky, V.: Lattice signatures and bimodal Gaussians. In: Canetti, R., Garay, J.A. (eds.) CRYPTO 2013. LNCS, vol. 8042, pp. 40–56. Springer, Heidelberg (2013). https://doi.org/10.1007/978-3-642-40041-4_3
6. Ducas, L., Lyubashevsky, V., Prest, T.: Efficient identity-based encryption over NTRU lattices. In: Sarkar, P., Iwata, T. (eds.) ASIACRYPT 2014. LNCS, vol. 8874, pp. 22–41. Springer, Heidelberg (2014). https://doi.org/10.1007/978-3-662-45608-8_2
7. Ducas, L., Nguyen, P.Q.: Learning a zonotope and more: cryptanalysis of NTRUSign countermeasures. In: Wang, X., Sako, K. (eds.) ASIACRYPT 2012. LNCS, vol. 7658, pp. 433–450. Springer, Heidelberg (2012). https://doi.org/10.1007/978-3-642-34961-4_27
8. Gentry, C., Peikert, C., Vaikuntanathan, V.: Trapdoors for hard lattices and new cryptographic constructions. In: Proceedings of the Fortieth Annual ACM Symposium on Theory of Computing, STOC 2008, pp. 197–206. ACM, New York (2008). https://doi.org/10.1145/1374376.1374407
9. Goldreich, O., Goldwasser, S., Halevi, S.: Public-key cryptosystems from lattice reduction problems. In: Kaliski, B.S. (ed.) CRYPTO 1997. LNCS, vol. 1294, pp. 112–131. Springer, Heidelberg (1997). https://doi.org/10.1007/BFb0052231
10. Hoffstein, J., Howgrave-Graham, N., Pipher, J., Silverman, J.H., Whyte, W.: NTRUSign: digital signatures using the NTRU lattice. In: Joye, M. (ed.) CT-RSA 2003. LNCS, vol. 2612, pp. 122–140. Springer, Heidelberg (2003). https://doi.org/10.1007/3-540-36563-X_9
11. Hoffstein, J., Pipher, J., Silverman, J.H.: NTRU: a ring-based public key cryptosystem. In: Buhler, J.P. (ed.) ANTS 1998. LNCS, vol. 1423, pp. 267–288. Springer, Heidelberg (1998). https://doi.org/10.1007/BFb0054868

12. Klein, P.: Finding the closest lattice vector when it's unusually close. In: Proceedings of the Eleventh Annual ACM-SIAM Symposium on Discrete Algorithms, SODA 2000, pp. 937–941. Society for Industrial and Applied Mathematics, Philadelphia (2000). http://dl.acm.org/citation.cfm?id=338219.338661
13. Lenstra, A.K., Lenstra, H.W., Lovász, L.: Factoring polynomials with rational coefficients. Mathematische Annalen **261**(4), 515–534 (1982). https://doi.org/10.1007/BF01457454
14. Liu, M., Nguyen, P.Q.: Solving BDD by enumeration: an update. In: Dawson, E. (ed.) CT-RSA 2013. LNCS, vol. 7779, pp. 293–309. Springer, Heidelberg (2013). https://doi.org/10.1007/978-3-642-36095-4_19
15. Micciancio, D.: Improving lattice based cryptosystems using the Hermite normal form. In: Silverman, J.H. (ed.) CaLC 2001. LNCS, vol. 2146, pp. 126–145. Springer, Heidelberg (2001). https://doi.org/10.1007/3-540-44670-2_11
16. Mitzenmacher, M., Upfal, E.: Probability and Computing: Randomized Algorithms and Probabilistic Analysis. Cambridge University Press, New York (2005)
17. Motwani, R., Raghavan, P.: Randomized Algorithms. Cambridge University Press, Cambridge (1995). https://doi.org/10.1145/211542.606546
18. Nguyen, P.Q., Regev, O.: Learning a parallelepiped: cryptanalysis of GGH and NTRU signatures. In: Vaudenay, S. (ed.) EUROCRYPT 2006. LNCS, vol. 4004, pp. 271–288. Springer, Heidelberg (2006). https://doi.org/10.1007/11761679_17
19. Plantard, T., Susilo, W., Win, K.T.: A digital signature scheme based on CVP_∞. In: Cramer, R. (ed.) PKC 2008. LNCS, vol. 4939, pp. 288–307. Springer, Heidelberg (2008). https://doi.org/10.1007/978-3-540-78440-1_17
20. Schnorr, C.P., Euchner, M.: Lattice basis reduction: improved practical algorithms and solving subset sum problems. Math. Program. **66**(1–3), 181–199 (1994). https://doi.org/10.1007/BF01581144
21. Shor, P.W.: Algorithms for quantum computation: discrete logarithms and factoring. In: Proceedings 35th Annual Symposium on Foundations of Computer Science, pp. 124–134. IEEE, Santa Fe, November 1994. https://doi.org/10.1109/SFCS.1994.365700
22. Shoup, V.: NTL: A library for doing number theory (2001). http://www.shoup.net/ntl
23. Stein, W., et al.: Sage Mathematics Software Version 7.5.1. The Sage Development Team (2017). http://www.sagemath.org

Complete Attack on RLWE Key Exchange with Reused Keys, Without Signal Leakage

Jintai Ding[1], Scott Fluhrer[2], and Saraswathy Rv[1(✉)]

[1] University of Cincinnati, Cincinnati, USA
jintai.ding@gmail.com, ramanasy@mail.uc.edu
[2] Cisco Systems, San Jose, USA

Abstract. Key Exchange (KE) from RLWE (Ring-Learning with Errors) is a potential alternative to Diffie-Hellman (DH) in a post quantum setting. Key leakage with RLWE key exchange protocols in the context of key reuse has already been pointed out in previous work. The initial attack described by Fluhrer is designed in such a way that it only works on Peikert's KE protocol and its variants that derives the shared secret from the most significant bits of the approximately equal keys computed by both parties. It does not work on Ding's key exchange that uses the least significant bits to derive a shared key. The Signal leakage attack relies on changes in the signal sent by the responder reusing his key, in a sequence of key exchange sessions initiated by an attacker with a malformed key. A possible defense against this attack would be to require the initiator of a key exchange to send the signal, which is the one pass case of the KE protocol. In this work, we describe a new attack on Ding's one pass case without relying on the signal function output but using only the information of whether the final key of both parties agree. We also use LLL reduction to create the adversary's keys in such a way that the party being compromised cannot identify the attack in trivial ways. This completes the series of attacks on RLWE key exchange with key reuse for all variants in both cases of the initiator and responder sending the signal. Moreover, we show that the previous Signal leakage attack can be made more efficient with fewer queries and how it can be extended to Peikert's key exchange, which was used in the BCNS implementation and integrated with TLS and a variant used in the New Hope implementation.

Keywords: RLWE · Key exchange · Post quantum · Key reuse
Active attacks

1 Introduction

Post-quantum cryptography refers to cryptographic algorithms (usually public key algorithms) that are thought to be secure against an attack by a quantum

W. Susilo and G. Yang (Eds.): ACISP 2018, LNCS 10946, pp. 467–486, 2018.
https://doi.org/10.1007/978-3-319-93638-3_27

computer. According to studies, a sufficiently large quantum computer can efficiently break most widely used public-key algorithms such as RSA and ECDSA. In 1994, Shor devised a quantum algorithm [24] that can be used to solve the Discrete Log Problem (the hardness of which the security of different variants of Diffie-Hellman (DH) key exchange algorithms are based on) in polynomial time with quantum computers [24]. This led to the search for quantum resistant cryptographic protocols. Cryptographic primitives that are believed to be resistant to quantum computer attacks include Multivariate, Hash based, Code based and Lattice based, that have their security based on mathematical problems that are hard to solve with currently known efficient quantum algorithms. In the recent years, lattice based cryptographic primitives have proven to have versatile applications in Key Exchange, Signature, FHE (Fully Homomorphic Encryption) and more. Key Exchange protocols allow two or more participants to derive a shared cryptographic key, often used for authenticated encryption. RLWE (Ring-Learning With Errors) key exchange is a lattice based variant of DH type protocol that also has properties like quantum resistance, forward and provable security that makes it a desirable replacement for currently used DH protocols. In RLWE key exchange, the two parties in a key exchange initially compute approximately equal values, after which one of the parties sends information about the interval in which its computation of the key value lies, to the other party. Then, both the parties use this information to derive a final shared secret. This additional information, referred to as the signal was exploited by active adversaries to retrieve the secret of a reused key as shown in [9] and applies to the RLWE based key exchange protocol in [14] and all its variants [3,5,22]. The signal function attack works when the responder (party that reuses its key) sends the signal and can be defended against by requiring the initiator to send the signal. In this work, we explore a new and more sophisticated attack to recover the secret without using the signal function output by querying the party with reused key for mismatch of the final shared key. The attack is set up for the one pass case of the protocol, when the initiator (instead of the responder) performing the key exchange sends the signal to the other party. The other details of the KE protocol remains the same as the two pass case. This work is an attack description on the KE protocol in [14] which uses the least significant bits of the computed keys to derive a shared secret key. The work in [10] focuses on an attack on KE protocol in [22] and its variants [3,5] that uses the most significant bits to derive the shared key. With this attack description, we show that all RLWE based KE protocols are vulnerable to attacks when keys are reused, excluding the ones designed as IND-CCA KEMs (Key Encapsulation Mechanism).

1.1 Previous Work

Key leakage in RLWE based key exchange with key reuse was pointed out in [15] but without any concrete description of an attack to exploit the leakage. An attack was described by Fluhrer in [10] with the attack strategy that tries to use the agreement of final shared key to derive information about the secret but does not work in the case of [14] where the final shared key is derived from the least significant bits.

Another attack presented in [13] is executed on the one pass case of the Authenticated Key Exchange protocol from RLWE in [25] and exploits properties of the CRT (Chinese Remainder Theorem) basis of R_q. It recovers every CRT coefficient of the secret s of a key $p = as + 2e$ in order to recover s, with an attack complexity of $\frac{q-1}{2}(\delta.q^{\delta} + q - \frac{\delta.q}{n})$, where δ is a moderately large constant.

The signal function attack is used to recover information about the secret of a reused key in an attack description in [9]. It works by looking at the number of times the signal value of the key computation k_B changes when varying k across all values in $\mathbb{Z}_q$ in the adversary's public key of $p_A = as_A + ke_A$. The number of signal changes is expected to be exactly 2 times the secret value by the choice of s_A, e_A and the definition of the signal region. The secret is recovered with $2q$ queries to the party with the reused key.

1.2 Our Contributions

We present a new attack on RLWE based key exchange in the context of key reuse. We focus on the one pass case of the KE protocol since the other case can already be attacked with previous work. Thus, having the initiator send the signal is not a possible defense against attacks with key reuse and unsuccessful key exchange sessions can be used to reveal information about the secret. We carefully work through the details of the adversary's queries and perform an attack with query complexity $O(n^2\alpha)$. The query complexity is independent of q, making it more efficient than the signal function attack. Here, α is the standard deviation of the error distribution. The goal of the work is to show that RLWE keys when reused in key exchange can always be exploited and broken. The success of such attacks comes from the hardness of distinguishing RLWE samples from uniform. Section 3 reviews definitions and results that are relevant to indistinguishability of RLWE samples. We have verified the success of our attacks with experiments.

This attack does not rely on the leakage of the signal and can still be applied to protocols in the case that the initiator is required to send the signal to avoid the signal function attack. Although the attack approach is similar to [10] in using key mismatch to compromise the secret, we use a different strategy for the attack. In [10], the attack focuses on key exchange protocols that derive the most significant bits of the approximately equal key computed. The approach is to query for the boundary between 0 and 1, corresponding to the signal quadrants defined in the protocol. But this does not work in the case of key exchange protocols that use the least significant bit to derive the final shared key. In our attack, the attacker forces the other party to reveal information about the secret from the final key mismatch. In practice, this is possible because a key mismatch results in an unsuccessful key exchange. So, if the attacker uses his computation of the key, he cannot decrypt a message from the other party or does not get a desired response from the other party. The attacker creates his public key in such a way that mismatch in the final shared key is linked with a change in sign of a particular coefficient of the intermediate (approximately equal) key computed.

We choose a secret $s_{\mathcal{A}}$ for the adversary such that the $n-1$-th coordinate of the key computation is small, by solving linear equations involving the reused public key $p_B = as_B + 2e_B$. Here, p_B is an RLWE public key with secrets s_B, e_B sampled from an error distribution and a uniform randomly sampled from the ring. To recover useful information using success or failure of a session, the attacker's secret needs to be small. This is because the attacker only checks for match or mismatch of final key in one coordinate to recover the secret s_B but with a key exchange session failure, the attacker cannot know which coordinates of the key did not match. So, keeping $s_{\mathcal{A}}$ small ensures that the other coordinates are computed following the protocol and matches for both parties, implying that a key exchange session success or failure relies on match or mismatch of the specific coordinate of the final key. To ensure that $s_{\mathcal{A}}$ is small, we apply the LLL reduction algorithm on the solution space of the system of linear equations solved. We refer to this work as a complete attack since it fills the gap on available attacks for all variants of RLWE based KE protocols and both cases where the initiator and responder sends the signal. We also discuss the signal function attack to make it more efficient in terms of the query complexity. Later, we discuss about extending the signal attack to the key exchange in [22] which follows the same approach as in [14] and uses a slightly different signal function, referred to as the cross rounding function. The BCNS implementation uses the key exchange in [22]. The New Hope implementation uses a modified version with a different error distribution and error reconciliation, and was tested in Google Chrome Canary browser for its post quantum experiment [1].

2 Organization

In Sect. 3, We discuss some background on RLWE and the functions used in the key exchange protocol. The protocol being attacked is reviewed in Sect. 4. The attack is described in Sect. 5, which is divided into two parts - simplified and improved. The simplified attack aims at providing a basic understanding of the attack assuming that the attacker's secret is 0. The improved attack further builds on the simplified case to describe the actual attack strategy. Other subsections of this attack section discusses query complexity and experiments we performed to verify the attack. Section 6 reviews the signal function attack and describes how it can be applied to the KE protocol in [22]. Section 7 discusses about reducing the query complexity of the signal function attack.

3 Preliminaries

3.1 Notation

Let n be an integer and a power of 2. Define $f(x) = x^n + 1$ and consider the ring $R := \mathbb{Z}[x]/\langle f(x)\rangle$. For any positive integer q, we define the ring $R_q =$

$\mathbb{Z}_q[x]/\langle f(x)\rangle$ analogously, where the ring of polynomials over $\mathbb{Z}$ (respectively $\mathbb{Z}_q = \mathbb{Z}/q\mathbb{Z}$) we denote by $\mathbb{Z}[x]$ (respectively $\mathbb{Z}_q[x]$). Let χ_α denote the Discrete Gaussian distribution on R_q, naturally induced by that over $\mathbb{Z}^n$ with standard deviation α. A polynomial $p \in R$ (or R_q) can be alternatively represented in vector form $(p_0, \ldots, p_{n-1})$ corresponding to its coefficients and $p[i] = p_i$ denotes the i-th coefficient of the polynomial. Let the norm $||p||$ of a polynomial $p \in R$ (or R_q) be defined as the norm of the corresponding coefficient vector in $\mathbb{Z}$ (or $\mathbb{Z}_q$). For a vector $v = (v_0, \ldots, v_{n-1})$ in $\mathbb{R}^n$ or $\mathbb{C}^n$ and $p \in [1, \infty)$, we define the ℓ_p norm as $||v||_p = (\sum_{i=0}^{n-1} |v_i|^p)^{1/p}$ and the ℓ_∞ norm as $||v||_\infty = max_{i\in[n]}|v_i|$. The ℓ_2 norm corresponds to the ℓ_p norm with $p = 2$ and is denoted as $||.||$ in this paper. In applying the norms, we assume the coefficient embedding of elements from R to $\mathbb{R}^n$. For any element $s = \sum_{i=0}^{n-1} s_i x^i$ of R, we can embed this element into $\mathbb{R}^n$ as the vector $(s_0, \ldots s_{n-1})$.

3.2 Learning with Errors and RLWE

A Lattice $L(b_1, \ldots, b_n) = \{\sum_{i=1}^n x_i b_i | x_i \in \mathbb{Z}\}$ is formed by integer linear combinations of n linearly independent vectors $b_1, \ldots, b_n \in \mathbb{R}^n$ called the "Lattice Basis". In 1996, Ajtai's seminal result [2] heralded the use of lattices for constructing cryptographic systems, with the security based on hardness of problems such as the Shortest Vector Problem (SVP) and Closest Vector Problem (CVP). The Learning with Errors (LWE) problem introduced by Oded Regev in 2005 [23] is a generalization of the parity-learning problem. The reduction from solving hard problems in lattices in the worst case to solving LWE in the average case provides strong security guarantees for LWE based cryptosystems, yet it is not efficient enough for practical applications due to its large key sizes of $O(n^2)$. Ring-Learning with Errors (RLWE) is the version of LWE in the ring setting, that overcomes the efficiency disadvantages of LWE. Similar to LWE, there is a quantum reduction from solving worst case lattice problems in ideal lattices to solving the RLWE problem in average case. The search version of RLWE is to find a secret s in R_q given $(a, as+e)$ for polynomial number of samples, where a is sampled uniform from R_q and e is sampled according to the error distribution χ_α. An equivalent problem of the search version is the decision version which is commonly used for security proof of cryptographic algorithms based on RLWE. Let A_{s,χ_α} denote the distribution of the pair $(a, as + e)$, where a, s is sampled uniformly from R_q and e is sampled according to the error distribution χ_α. The decision version of the RLWE problem is to distinguish A_{s,χ_α} from the uniform distribution on $R_q \times R_q$ with polynomial number of samples. We provide the definition of the Discrete Gaussian distribution (error distribution) here:

Discrete Gaussian Distribution

Definition 1. *[25] For any positive real $\alpha \in \mathbb{R}$, and vectors $c \in \mathbb{R}^n$, the continuous Gaussian distribution over $\mathbb{R}^n$ with standard deviation α centered at c is defined by the probability function $\rho_{\alpha,c}(x) = (\frac{1}{\sqrt{2\pi}\alpha})^n exp(\frac{-||x-c||^2}{2\alpha^2})$. For integer vectors $c \in \mathbb{R}^n$, let $\rho_{\alpha,c}(\mathbb{Z}^n) = \sum_{x\in\mathbb{Z}^n} \rho_{\alpha,c}(x)$. Then, we define the Discrete*

Gaussian distribution over $\mathbb{Z}^n$ *as* $D_{\mathbb{Z}^n,\alpha,c}(x) = \frac{\rho_{\alpha,c}(x)}{\rho_{\alpha,c}(\mathbb{Z}^n)}$, *where* $x \in \mathbb{Z}^n$. *The subscripts* α *and* c *are taken to be* 1 *and* 0 *(respectively) when omitted.*

In practice, we use a Spherical Gaussian distribution where each coordinate is sampled independently from a one dimensional Discrete Gaussian distribution $D_{\mathbb{Z},\alpha}$.

We recall two useful lemmas here:

Lemma 1 ([25]). *Let* $f(x)$ *and* R *be defined as above. Then, for any* $s, t \in R$, *we have* $\|s \cdot t\| \leq \sqrt{n} \cdot \|s\| \cdot \|t\|$ *and* $\|s \cdot t\|_\infty \leq n \cdot \|s\|_\infty \cdot \|t\|_\infty$.

Lemma 2 ([12,19]). *For any real number* $\alpha = \omega(\sqrt{\log n})$, *we have* $\Pr_{\mathbf{x} \leftarrow \chi_\alpha}[\|\mathbf{x}\| > \alpha\sqrt{n}] \leq 2^{-n+1}$.

The *normal form* [6,7] of the RLWE problem is by modifying the above definition by choosing s from the error distribution χ_α rather than uniformly. It has been proven that the ring-LWE assumption still holds even with this variant [4,18].

Proposition 1 ([18]). *Let* n *be a power of* 2, *let* α *be a real number in* $(0,1)$, *and* q *a prime such that* $q \bmod 2n = 1$ *and* $\alpha q > \omega(\sqrt{\log n})$. *Define* $R = \mathbb{Z}[x]/\langle x^n + 1\rangle$ *as above. Then there exists a polynomial time quantum reduction from* $\tilde{O}(\sqrt{n}/\alpha)$*-SIVP (Short Independent Vectors Problem) in the worst case to average-case* $RLWE_{q,\beta}$ *with* ℓ *samples, where* $\beta = \alpha q \cdot (n\ell/\log(n\ell))^{1/4}$.

For the Key Exchange from RLWE presented in [14], the signal function is required for the two parties in the key exchange to derive a final shared key. The signal function is usually sent by the responding party to the initiator of the key exchange, which gives additional information about whether the respondent's key computed lies in a specific region. The case when the initiator sends the signal is the One pass protocol. It is formally defined as follows:

Definition 2. *Signal function: Given* $\mathbb{Z}_q = \{-\frac{q-1}{2}, \dots, \frac{q-1}{2}\}$ *and the middle subset* $E := \{-\lfloor\frac{q}{4}\rfloor, \dots, \lfloor\frac{q}{4}\rceil\}$, *we define Sig as the characteristic function of the* complement *of* E: $Sig(v) = 0$ *if* $v \in E$ *and* 1 *otherwise.*

Definition 3. *The final key is derived using the* Mod_2 *function (Reconciliation) defined as below:* $\mathsf{Mod}_2\colon \mathbb{Z}_q \times \{0,1\} \to \{0,1\}$: $\mathsf{Mod}_2(v,w) = (v + w \cdot \frac{q-1}{2}) \bmod q \bmod 2$.

To discuss the key exchange in [22], we recall the following definitions: Let $I_0 := \{0, 1, \dots \lfloor\frac{q}{4}\rceil - 1\}$, $I_1 := \{-\lfloor\frac{q}{4}\rfloor, \dots -1\}$ and $E' := [-\frac{q}{8}, \frac{q}{8}) \cap \mathbb{Z}$. Let $I_0' = \frac{q}{2} + I_0$ and $I_1' = \frac{q}{2} + I_1$.

Definition 4. *The cross rounding function,* $< \cdot >_2\colon \mathbb{Z}_q \to \mathbb{Z}_2$ *is defined as* $< v >_2 := \lfloor\frac{4}{q} \cdot v\rfloor \bmod 2$.

Definition 5. *The randomization function* $dbl : \mathbb{Z}_q \to \mathbb{Z}_{2q}$, *which is used in the case of an odd modulus* q *is defined as* $dbl(v) = 2v - \bar{e}$, *where* $\bar{e}$ *is uniformly random modulo* 2. *In practice,* $\bar{e}$ *is chosen such that* $Pr(\bar{e} = 0) = \frac{1}{2}$ *and* $Pr(\bar{e} = \pm 1) = \frac{1}{4}$.

Definition 6. *The final key derivation of the initiator of the key exchange uses the reconciliation function,* $rec : \mathbb{Z}_q \times \mathbb{Z}_2 \rightarrow \mathbb{Z}_2$ *which is defined as*

$$rec(w, b) = \begin{cases} 0 & w \in I_b + E \,(mod\, q), \\ 1 & otherwise. \end{cases}$$

Definition 7. *The Modular rounding function* $\lfloor \cdot \rceil_2 : \mathbb{Z}_q \rightarrow \mathbb{Z}_2$*, is defined as* $\lfloor x \rceil_2 = \lfloor \frac{2}{q} \cdot x \rceil \bmod 2$.

4 The Protocol

Let the notations be as defined in Sect. 3. Generate the parameters q, n, α for the protocol and choose public $a \leftarrow R_q$ uniformly. We recall the key exchange protocol in [14] in the Figs. 1 and 2.

Party A		Party B
Sample $s_A, e_A \leftarrow \chi_\alpha$ Secret Key: $s_A \in R_q$ Public Key: $a, p_A = as_A + 2e_A \in R_q$	$\xrightarrow{p_A}$	Sample $s_B, e_B \leftarrow \chi_\alpha$ Secret Key: $s_B \in R_q$ Public Key: $a, p_B = as_B + 2e_B \in R_q$
	$\xleftarrow{p_B, w_B}$	Sample $g_B \leftarrow \chi_\alpha$ Set $k_B = p_A s_B + 2g_B$ Find $w_B = Sig(k_B) \in \{0,1\}^n$
Sample $g_A \leftarrow \chi_\alpha$ Set $k_A = p_B s_A + 2g_A$		
$sk_A = \mathsf{Mod}_2(k_A, w_B) \in \{0,1\}^n$		$sk_B = \mathsf{Mod}_2(k_B, w_B) \in \{0,1\}^n$

Fig. 1. Protocol from [14]

5 New Attack Using Key Mismatch - One Pass Case

Suppose that party B reuses its public key p_B and $\mathcal{A}$ is an active adversary with the knowledge of p_B and with the ability to initiate multiple key exchange sessions to query party B. We present an attack in the one pass case of the KE protocol, in which the adversary can initiate multiple key exchange sessions with party B and use key mismatch in each session to retrieve the secret s_B. We use the notation $p_{\mathcal{A}}$ for the public key of the adversary and $s_{\mathcal{A}}, e_{\mathcal{A}}$ for the corresponding secret and error respectively.

Party A		Party B
Sample $s_A, e_A \leftarrow \chi_\alpha$ Secret Key: $s_A \in R_q$ Public Key: $a, p_A = as_A + 2e_A \in R_q$		Sample $s_B, e_B \leftarrow \chi_\alpha$ Secret Key: $s_B \in R_q$ Public Key: $a, p_B = as_B + 2e_B \in R_q$
	$\xrightarrow{p_A, w_A}$	Sample $g_B \leftarrow \chi_\alpha$ Set $k_B = p_A s_B + 2g_B$
Sample $g_A \leftarrow \chi_\alpha$ Set $k_A = p_B s_A + 2g_A$ Compute $w_A = Sig(k_A) \in \{0,1\}^n$		
$sk_A = \mathsf{Mod}_2(k_A, w_A) \in \{0,1\}^n$		$sk_B = \mathsf{Mod}_2(k_B, w_A) \in \{0,1\}^n$

Fig. 2. Protocol from [14] - One pass case

5.1 Simplified Attack

We first consider the simpler case when party B does not add the error term g_B to its key computation k_B, to explain the attack strategy and then extend to the case of adding the noise.

Choice of $s_{\mathcal{A}}$ *and* $e_{\mathcal{A}}$: The attacker chooses $s_{\mathcal{A}}$ to be 0 in R_q (This is later improved by choosing $s_{\mathcal{A}}$ to be non-zero so that party B cannot verify that $p_{\mathcal{A}}$ is malformed trivially). For recovering the i-th coefficient $s_B[i]$, the attacker $\mathcal{A}$ chooses an $e_{\mathcal{A}}$ with coefficient vector that consists of all zeros, except for the coordinate $n-1-i$, for which it is 1, and coordinate $n-1-j$, which is a small integer k. So, we have $e_{\mathcal{A}}[i] = 0$ for all $i = 0, \dots n-1$ except $i = n-1-i, n-1-j$ and $e_{\mathcal{A}}[n-1-i] = 1$, $e_{\mathcal{A}}[n-1-j] = k$. He then performs the protocol honestly, except that he deliberately flips bit $n-1$ of the signal vector $w_{\mathcal{A}}$ that he sends. The index j is chosen such that $s_B[j] = \pm 1$. Thus, the attacker first needs to identify such a j. This is explained in Sect. 5.4.

Remark 1. The attacker can actually flip any bit of the signal $w_{\mathcal{A}}$ and use the corresponding index of the final shared key to look for mismatch to recover the secret; we use the bit $n-1$ because that allows us to ignore the complications with signs during polynomial multiplication in the ring, simplifying the attack. For example, if we want to use the 0-th coefficient of the final shared key to recover value of $s_B[i]$, we can choose the $(n-i)$-th coordinate of the coefficient vector of $e_{\mathcal{A}}$ to be -1 and $(n-j)$-th coordinate to be $-k$ and flip the 0-th bit of the signal $w_{\mathcal{A}}$ that he sends.

If we look at party B's computation of the key k_B, we have $k_B = s_B p_{\mathcal{A}}$ which results in $k_B[n-1] = 2s_B[i] + 2ks_B[j] = 2s_B[i] + 2k$ by the choice of $s_{\mathcal{A}}, e_{\mathcal{A}}$ of the attacker. Since the $(n-1)$-th coordinate of the signal $w_{\mathcal{A}}$ received from the attacker is flipped to be 1, we have $sk_B[n-1] = k_B[n-1] + \frac{q-1}{2} \bmod q \bmod 2$. Also, the attacker's final shared key is $sk_{\mathcal{A}} = 0$ since $s_{\mathcal{A}} = 0$.

Constructing Oracle $\mathcal{B}$: We build an oracle $\mathcal{B}$ that performs the action of party B and the adversary $\mathcal{A}$ has access to this oracle to make multiple queries. $\mathcal{B}$ takes

$(p_{\mathcal{A}}, w_{\mathcal{A}}, sk_{\mathcal{A}})$ as input where $p_{\mathcal{A}}, sk_{\mathcal{A}}$ corresponds to the public key and the final shared key respectively of $\mathcal{A}$. $w_{\mathcal{A}}$ corresponds to the signal sent by $\mathcal{A}$ with the $n-1$ bit flipped to 1. The oracle computes $k_B = p_{\mathcal{A}} s_B$ and $sk_B = \mathsf{Mod}_2(k_B, w_{\mathcal{A}})$. $\mathcal{B}$ then outputs 1 if $sk_B = sk_{\mathcal{A}}$ and 0 otherwise.

From the construction of the oracle, it is clear that the oracle indicates if a key exchange session is successful or not. Then the attacker can invoke the oracle $\mathcal{B}$ with $p_{\mathcal{A}}$ corresponding to different values of k to check for key mismatch. Because the attacker performs the protocol mostly honestly (and both $s_{\mathcal{A}}$ and $e_{\mathcal{A}}$ qualify as small vectors until k remains small), the attacker can compute the value sk_B, except for index $n-1$, for which he flips the signal bit. The attacker can then determine the value of that bit by guessing a sk_B that has a 0 in that position and the computed values elsewhere (In the case of $s_{\mathcal{A}} = 0$, all other index values are also 0 but this is not the case when $s_{\mathcal{A}}$ is not 0), and checking with the oracle $\mathcal{B}$ to see if his guess was correct.

Flipping the signal bit allows the attacker to force party B to change the parity of the final $sk_B[n-1]$ before the mod 2 operation, in every instantiation of a session with the attacker. This is useful in associating a change in output of $\mathcal{B}$ with a change from positive to negative values of $k_B[n-1]$ or vice versa as explained here:

Notice that the terms $2s_B[i] + 2k$ of $sk_B[n-1]$ are even and also from the usual choice of parameters for RLWE (following from Lemma 1) such that $q = 1 \bmod 2n$, we have $\frac{q-1}{2}$ to be even. Thus, if $s_B[i]$ is negative, we have $sk_B[n-1] = 0$ as long as $2s_B[i] + 2k$ is negative and there is no change in the parity. So, a query to $\mathcal{B}$ with these values of $(p_{\mathcal{A}}, w_{\mathcal{A}}, sk_{\mathcal{A}})$ results in an output of 1. As k increases in value, we can see that $k_B[n-1]$ changes from negative to positive values. As this happens, we have $sk_B[n-1] = 1$ since the addition of $\frac{q-1}{2}$ to a positive value changes its parity by the representation of $\mathbb{Z}_q$ to be $\{-\frac{q-1}{2} \dots \frac{q-1}{2}\}$ and the output of $\mathcal{B}$ becomes 0. So, a change from negative to positive values of $k_B[n-1]$ results in a change of output from 1 to 0 of $\mathcal{B}$.

Also, if $s_B[i]$ is negative, then as k varies, $k_B[n-1]$ changes from negative to positive values at the point when $2k$ is greater than the absolute value of $2s_B[i]$ i.e, $k > |s_B[i]|$. Thus, the k value when there is a change in output of $\mathcal{B}$ reveals the value of $s_B[i]$.

But if $s_B[i]$ is positive, sk_B does not change parity until k takes on larger values (change only occurs when $2s_B[i]+2k > q$ by the representation of $\mathbb{Z}_q$). As k becomes large, the output of $\mathcal{B}$ is no longer reliable to indicate the difference in the $n-1$-th index since the errors amplify and other indexes of sk_B are not guaranteed to match with that of $sk_{\mathcal{A}}$. To handle this, the query that the attacker sends modifies the $e_{\mathcal{A}}$ chosen above so that $e_{\mathcal{A}}[n-1-j] = -k$, when $s_B[i]$ is positive.

So if $s_B[i]$ is positive, then we have $k_B[n-1] = 2s_B[i] - 2k$ and this value changes from positive to negative as k increases when $k > s_B[i]$. Also, $sk_B[n-1] = 1$ as long as $k_B[n-1]$ is positive because of the change in parity of $sk_B[n-1]$ caused by adding $\frac{q-1}{2}$ and results in the output of $\mathcal{B}$ to be 0. As the value changes to negative, the output of $\mathcal{B}$ changes to 1.

The attack can be summarized with the following steps for every coefficient i of the secret s_B, i from 0 to $n-1$:

Step 1: The first step is to create an $e_\mathcal{A}$ as described above and thus involves identifying a j such that $s_B[j] = \pm 1$. This is discussed in detail in Sect. 5.4. The consequent steps here assume that the attacker succeeds in finding such a j.

Step 2: Now, the attacker needs to resolve the sign of $s_B[i]$ to create queries accordingly. The attacker queries $\mathcal{B}$ with $p_\mathcal{A}, w_\mathcal{A}, sk_\mathcal{A}$. Here, $p_\mathcal{A} = 2e_\mathcal{A}$ corresponds to $e_\mathcal{A}[n-1-j] = k = 0$ and will result in $k_B[n-1] = 2s_B[i]$. $w_\mathcal{A}$ and $sk_\mathcal{A}$ correspond to the signal with the last bit flipped to 1 and final shared key of the attacker with the guess for the $n-1$ coefficient to be 0, respectively. This can be used by the attacker to determine the sign of $s_B[i]$ since the sign of $k_B[n-1]$ and $s_B[i]$ are the same. If the output is 1 (i.e, the final keys match), the attacker concludes that the sign of $s_B[i]$ is negative and if the output is 0, then the sign is positive. One problem here is that if the coefficient value is 0, the output of $\mathcal{B}$ would still be 1. So, to identify 0 values, the attacker can query again corresponding to $k = 0$ but with $e_\mathcal{A}[n-1-i] = -1$ which results in $k_B[n-1] = -2s_B[i]$. If the output of $\mathcal{B}$ remains the same for both queries for a coefficient, then the coefficient value has to be 0.

Step 3: If $s_B[i]$ is negative, as inferred from the previous step, the attacker creates e_B with $e_\mathcal{A}[n-1-j] = k$ and varies k over values from 0 until there is a change in the output of $\mathcal{B}$. If s_B is positive, e_B is created with $e_\mathcal{A}[n-1-j] = -k$.

Step 4: Looking for the k value when the output of $\mathcal{B}$ changes from 0 to 1 reveals the exact value of a negative $s_B[i]$ and a change from 1 to 0 reveals the value of a positive $s_B[i]$.
Note here that the output of $\mathcal{B}$ only gives information about whether the final shared key of both parties agree or not. It is not possible for the attacker to know which coordinates of the final key match and which ones don't. But the attack works since a change in the output bit of $\mathcal{B}$ for smaller values of k would mean that it is caused by the $n-1$-th index by the bit flip in the signal as $s_\mathcal{A}$ and $e_\mathcal{A}$ remain small. As k becomes larger, there is no assurance for the keys to match in the other indexes.

Step 5: The recovered secret s_B can be verified by checking the distribution of $p_B - as_B$.

Remark 2. Consider the case $s_\mathcal{A}[j] = -1$; by following the above logic, the attacker can flip the sign of k in $e_\mathcal{A}$ to recover $s_B[i]$.

As we can repeat the above process for all i, this means we can read party B's secret key directly. The attack for one query is shown in Fig. 3 to recover a negative $s_B[i]$. Here, the adversary computes $sk_\mathcal{A} = 0$ and B computes $sk_B = 0$ until $k_B[n-1]$ is negative.

Adversary $\mathcal{A}$		Party B
Choose $s_{\mathcal{A}} = 0, e_{\mathcal{A}} = 0$ Set $e_{\mathcal{A}}[n-1-i] = 1$, $e_{\mathcal{A}}[n-1-j] = k$ Public Key: $a, p_{\mathcal{A}} = as_{\mathcal{A}} + 2e_{\mathcal{A}} \in R_q$		Reused Public Key: $a, p_B = as_B + 2e_B \in R_q$
Set $k_{\mathcal{A}} = p_B s_{\mathcal{A}}$ Compute $w_{\mathcal{A}} = Sig(k_{\mathcal{A}}) \in \{0,1\}^n$ Flip $w_{\mathcal{A}}[n-1] = 1$		
	$\xrightarrow{p_{\mathcal{A}}, w_{\mathcal{A}}}$	Compute $k_B = p_{\mathcal{A}} s_B$
$sk_{\mathcal{A}} = \mathsf{Mod}_2(k_{\mathcal{A}}, w_{\mathcal{A}}) \in \{0,1\}^n$		$sk_B = \mathsf{Mod}_2(k_B, w_{\mathcal{A}}) \in \{0,1\}^n$

Fig. 3. One instance of the attack in the simplified case choosing Adversary's secret $s_{\mathcal{A}} = 0$, when error g_B is not added to the key computation k_B

5.2 Extending the Attack When Adding the Error g_B

In this case, the number of queries required to recover $s_B[i]$ increases compared to the steps above, due to the complexity involved in eliminating the effect of the noise $g_B[n-1]$. The strategy here is to look at the distribution of k values when there is a change in the output of $\mathcal{B}$, while running the attack on the same coefficient of s_B multiple times. The error $g_B[n-1]$ fluctuates k_B but the k value when k_B changes from positive to negative or vice versa is centered around the actual value of $s_B[i]$ since $g_B[n-1]$ values are sampled from an error distribution (Discrete Gaussian) centered at 0. The oracle $\mathcal{B}$ can be modified to be contructed as follows:

Constructing Oracle $\mathcal{B}$: $\mathcal{B}$ takes p, w, sk as input where p, sk corresponds to the public key and the final shared key respectively of $\mathcal{A}$. The oracle computes $k_B = ps_B + 2g_B$, where $g_B \leftarrow \chi_\alpha$ and $sk_B = \mathsf{Mod}_2(k_B, w)$. $\mathcal{B}$ then outputs 1 if $sk_B = sk$ and 0 otherwise.

Thus, the steps for the attack in this case are the same as above except that step 3 is repeated a constant number of times and the distribution of k values reveal the exact value of $s_B[i]$ for every coefficient i. For step 2, the attacker queries by modifying $(n-1-i)$-th coordinate to be 2 so that $k_B[n-1] = 4s_B[i] \pm 2k + 2g_B[n-1]$ to override the effect of $g_B[n-1]$ on the sign.

In our experiments, we queried for the same $s_B[i]$ coefficient 1000 times and derived the value from the distribution of k values corresponding to a change in output of $\mathcal{B}$, obtained from each run. The number of runs 1000 is chosen to derive a reasonable number of samples for analyzing the distribution of k with a certain confidence level and is independent of the choice of parameters n, q, α for the protocol. For a confidence level of 95%, we estimated the number of samples to be ≈ 1000 with margin of error 3%. From the description of the attack, the distribution of k obtained for a coefficient value of 7 (on the top) and -3 (on the bottom) are shown in Fig. 4.

The attacker can generate the distribution of k corresponding to different values of a coefficient by running an initial attack, choosing a p_B himself and then perform the actual attack on party B.

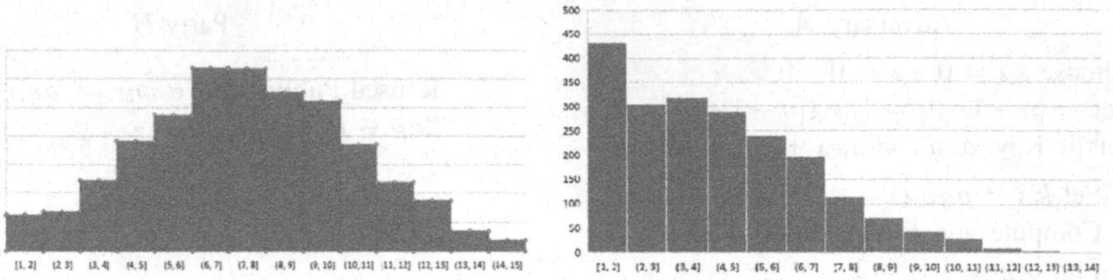

Fig. 4. Comparison of distribution of k while recovering coefficients 7 and -3 respectively

5.3 Improved Attack

Finally, a simple randomness check at party B's end could protect B from this attack, as the public key is just all 0s and non-zero in 2 coordinates. To avoid this, we perform the attack when the attacker's public key is of the form $as_{\mathcal{A}} + 2e_{\mathcal{A}}$ with $s_{\mathcal{A}}$ chosen as follows. We believe that this makes it more difficult for party B to identify the attack.

We choose $s_{\mathcal{A}}$ to be such that $p_B s_{\mathcal{A}}[n-1] = 0$. This way we can obtain an $s_{\mathcal{A}}$ such that for the index $n-1$, the value of $as_B s_{\mathcal{A}}$ is small since $p_B s_{\mathcal{A}} = as_B s_{\mathcal{A}} + 2e_B s_{\mathcal{A}}$, where $e_B s_{\mathcal{A}}$ is small. We require such a $s_{\mathcal{A}}$ so that the $as_B s_{\mathcal{A}}[n-1]$ term in $k_B[n-1]$ cannot override $2s_B[i]+2k$ and the attack strategy can still be used. Since p_B is known to the adversary, he can solve the polynomial equation to find $s_{\mathcal{A}}$ such that $p_B s_{\mathcal{A}}[n-1] = 0$. However, such an $s_{\mathcal{A}}$ is not necessarily small. If $s_{\mathcal{A}}$ is not small, the errors amplify in the final key computed by the adversary and party B and the two final keys need not necessarily match. Thus, the adversary can no longer guess the final key computation of party B. To handle this, we use LLL reduction on the solution space of the equation $p_B s_{\mathcal{A}}[n-1] = 0$ to derive a small $s_{\mathcal{A}}$ that satisfies the equation. We achieved this in our implementation using Magma.

$\mathcal{B}$'s computation of k_B yields $k_B[n-1] = as_B s_{\mathcal{A}}[n-1]+2(s_B[i]+k+g_B[n-1])$. Then, the attacker can perform the following process to recover the secret $s_B[i]$:

Step 1: To determine the sign of $s_B[i]$, the attacker queries with $e_{\mathcal{A}}$ such that $e_{\mathcal{A}}[n-1-i] = 4$ and $e_{\mathcal{A}}[n-1-j] = k = 0$, so that the key k_B can override the effect of $as_B s_{\mathcal{A}}[n-1]$ and $g_B[n-1]$ on the sign of $s_B[i]$. This is possible since we know that $as_B s_{\mathcal{A}}[n-1]$ is small, by the choice of $s_{\mathcal{A}}$. Querying $\mathcal{B}$ a constant number of times, further counters the effect of $g_B[n-1]$ and reveals the sign of $s_B[i]$. If the output of $\mathcal{B}$ is 1, then $s_B[i]$ is negative and if $\mathcal{B}$ output is 0, then $s_B[i]$ is positive. Querying again with $e_{\mathcal{A}}[n-1-i] = -4$ resolves the 0 value coordinates of s_B.

Step 2: Run the attack to obtain k value, denote k_1 that recovers the value of $as_B s_{\mathcal{A}}[n-1] + s_B[i]$.

Step 3: Repeat the attack by modifying $e_{\mathcal{A}}$ such that $e_{\mathcal{A}}[n-1-i] = 2$, which results in party B's computation of $k_B[n-1] = as_B s_{\mathcal{A}}[n-1]+2(2s_B[i]+$

$k + g_B[n-1]$). Recover k (denote k_2) value corresponding to change in output of $\mathcal{B}$, hence recovering $as_B s_\mathcal{A}[n-1] + 2s_B[i]$.

Step 4: Compute $k_2 - k_1$ to recover the value $s_B[i]$.

There is one possibility in the above attack that $as_\mathcal{A} s_B[n-1] = -2s_B[i]$ in which case $k_B[n-1] = 2k + 2g_B[n-1]$. In this case, as we increase k, the mismatch of final keys does not reveal the value of $s_B[i]$. This case can be identified by querying with $k = -1$ and checking if the output of $\mathcal{B}$ is different from the output corresponding to $k = 0$. Recovering every coefficient of s_B by running the attack recovers the secret. With this section, we show that there are other possible ways to improve the attack and it seems to be very difficult to prevent it by just checking the randomness.

5.4 Determining Index j Such that $s_B[j] = 1$

If $s_B[j] = 0$, then modifying k doesn't affect index $n-1$ at all and thus can be easily identified. Also, this case is already identified while determining the sign of the coefficients.

We repeat for each coefficient j of s_B, the following procedure until a j such that $s_B[j] = 1$ is identified, starting with the first positive coefficient, denote j_1. Since we can already determine the signs of every coefficient, it is enough to check through only the positive coefficients for value 1.

Step 1: Start with $j = j_1$. Assuming $s_B[j_1] = 1$, perform the attack on other coefficients of s_B.

If $s_B[j_1] = 1$, then running the attack would yield the correct secret s_B. We can verify that this value of s_B recovered is actually the secret by verifying the distribution of $p_B - as_B$. This is possible since a, p_B are known and as_B can be computed using the recovered s_B. Now, suppose $s_B[j_1] > 1$, the key k_B of party B recovers very small values since $k_B = as_\mathcal{A} s_B[n-1] + 2s_B[i] + 2ks_B[j_1] + 2g_B[n-1]$ changes from negative to positive faster when $s_B[j_1]$ is greater than 1 and $s_B[i]$ is negative. The same logic applies for $s_B[i]$ positive. Thus, all the coefficients recovered are very small and $p_B - as_B$ computed with this recovered s_B does not follow the error distribution.

Step 2: Repeat Step 1 through all positive coefficients until a j such that $s_B[j] = 1$ is found.

If none of the positive coefficients are 1, then we can follow the same process with a different $e_\mathcal{A}$ (sign of k flipped) to check through the negative coefficients to find a j such that $s_B[j] = -1$.

Remark 3. There exists an index j such that $s[j] = \pm 1$ with high probability when $s \leftarrow \chi_\alpha$.

Since the error distribution χ_α used is the Discrete Gaussian distribution and we use the polynomial representation with two power cyclotomics, sampling an element $s \in R_q$ is equivalent to sampling each coordinate of its coefficient vector as a one dimensional Discrete Gaussian. The probability density function of the continuous one dimensional Gaussian distribution with mean 0 and standard deviation α is given by $\phi_\alpha(x) = \frac{1}{\sqrt{2\pi}\alpha}e^{-x^2/2\alpha^2}$.

For the parameter choice used in the experiments with $q = 12289, \alpha = 2.828, n = 1024$, we have the probability of a coefficient $s[i]$ of $s \leftarrow \chi_\alpha$ to be ± 1 given by

$$Pr(s[i] = \pm 1) = \frac{\sum_{z=1 \; mod \; q} \rho_\alpha(z)}{\sum_{y\in\mathbb{Z}} \rho_\alpha(y)} + \frac{\sum_{z=-1 \; mod \; q} \rho_\alpha(z)}{\sum_{y\in\mathbb{Z}} \rho_\alpha(y)}$$

$$= \frac{\sum_{k=-\infty}^{\infty} \frac{1}{\sqrt{2\pi}(2.828)} e^{-\frac{(12289*k+1)^2}{2(2.828)^2}}}{\sum_{y=-\infty}^{\infty} \frac{1}{\sqrt{2\pi}(2.828)} e^{-\frac{y^2}{2(2.828)^2}}} + \frac{\sum_{k=-\infty}^{\infty} \frac{1}{\sqrt{2\pi}(2.828)} e^{-\frac{(12289*k-1)^2}{2(2.828)^2}}}{\sum_{y=-\infty}^{\infty} \frac{1}{\sqrt{2\pi}(2.828)} e^{-\frac{y^2}{2(2.828)^2}}} \approx 0.265038$$

So, the failure probability of the vector s sampled from the error distribution not having a coefficient ± 1 is given by $(1 - 0.265038)^{1024} \approxeq 0$. This can also be verified in general when n is large and α is small.

In the extreme case that there does not exist an index j for which $s[j] = 1$, the attack can still be performed by choosing 2 indexes j_1, j_2 such that $s_B[j_1] + s_B[j_2] = 1$. In this case, the public key of the attacker would be $p_\mathcal{A} = as_\mathcal{A} + e_\mathcal{A}$ where the vector $e_\mathcal{A}$ has k in the $n-1-j_1$ and $n-1-j_2$ coordinates and 1 in the $(n-1-i)$ coordinate. Thus, we have $p_\mathcal{A}s_B[n-1] = as_\mathcal{A}s_B[n-1] + 2s_B[i] + 2k(s_B[j_1] + s_B[j_2]) = 2s_B[i] + 2k$.

5.5 Adversary Query Complexity

To compute the query complexity of the attack, we compute the query complexity of each phase of the attack: (1) Determining the sign of each coefficient, (2) Determining index j such that $s_B[j] = \pm 1$, (3) Determining a coefficient value $s_B[i]$ when the error term g_B is added to the key k_B of party B when the attacker's secret $s_\mathcal{A} = 0$, (4) Recovering (using query complexity of 1, 2 and 3) the secret s_B with $s_\mathcal{A}$ non-zero.

(1) The sign is determined by querying with $p_\mathcal{A}$ corresponding to $k = 0$ a small constant number of times (in our experiments, 10 queries were sufficient). Thus, the query complexity here is constant for each coefficient, so the query complexity to recover the signs of all the coefficients of s_B is $2c'n \approx 20n$, where c' is a constant.
(2) s_B is sampled from the error distribution that has standard deviation α. So, to determine each coefficient, we need at most $t\alpha$ queries, where t is a constant. Thus, to recover complete s_B, we need $nt\alpha$ queries. Since the error distribution we consider is the Discrete Gaussian and 99% of the values lie within 3 standard deviations of the mean, in our experiments with $\alpha = 2.828$, we run 16 queries for each coefficient, allowing for fluctuations

when error g_B is added. Also, this is run at least 1000 times to get the distribution of k, as described in Sect. 5.1 in attack extension. Thus, the attack complexity in this case would be $1000nt\alpha = Cn\alpha$, where C is the constant $= 1000t$.

(3) Recovering the secret with $s_{\mathcal{A}}$ of attacker non-zero: This is the actual attack performed. In this case, the complete attack is run twice with different $e_{\mathcal{A}}$. So, the number of queries required is $2Cn\alpha$.

(4) Determining index j such that $s_B[j] = 1$: This requires running the attack for every coefficient i assuming that $s_B[j] = 1$ starting with the first positive coefficient until such a j is found. So, the best case query complexity is $2Cn\alpha$, when the first positive coefficient turns out to be the required index with $s_B[j] = 1$ The same applies for searching -1. The worst case query complexity is $2Cn^2\alpha$.

Thus the query complexity of the complete attack would be $2c'n + 2Cn^2\alpha \approx O(n^2\alpha)$ in the worst case and $2c'n + 2Cn\alpha \approx O(n\alpha)$ in the best case.

5.6 Experiments

We have run experiments to verify the attack strategy. We use parameters $n = 1024, q = 12289, \alpha = 2.828$, used in [3] implementation. We used C++ with NTL and p_B value hard coded to be fixed for the experiments on a Windows 10, 64 bit system equipped with a 2.40 GHz Intel(R) Core(TM) i7-4700MQ CPU and 8 GB RAM. The LLL reduction to find an appropriate short secret $s_{\mathcal{A}}$ of the attacker was executed using Magma[1]. In our preliminary experiments, with the attacker's key of the form $p = as_{\mathcal{A}} + 2e_{\mathcal{A}}$, $s_{\mathcal{A}}$ non-zero chosen as described above, the time taken for running 1000 queries for one coefficient value to get the distribution of k is 35.1 mins with FFT for polynomial multiplication without any optimization. This time taken is to run 16000 queries to party B with queries varying k from 0 to 15 are run 1000 times to get the distribution of k for one coefficient.

6 Extending Signal Function Attack

Protocol Review: We note that the signal function attack can also be extended to the key exchange by Peikert [22] that was implemented in [5]. We review the key exchange protocol in [22] that uses the cross rounding function (Signal) for sending the additional information to compute the final shared key. Please refer to Sect. 3 for notations and definitions of the functions used in the protocol. The key exchange is as described below:

Party A: Set $p_A = as_A + e_A$, where $s_A, e_A \leftarrow \chi_\alpha$ and publish p_A.

Party B: On receiving p_A, choose $s_B, e_B, g_B \leftarrow \chi_\alpha$ and compute $p_B = as_B + e_B$. Then to obtain the shared key, compute $k_B = p_A s_B + g_B$. Let $\bar{k}_B = dbl(k_B)$, $w_B = <\bar{k}_B>_2$ and output p_B, w_B to party A. The final shared key is $sk_B = \lfloor \bar{k}_B \rceil_2$.

[1] https://github.com/Saras16/PaperMagmaCode.

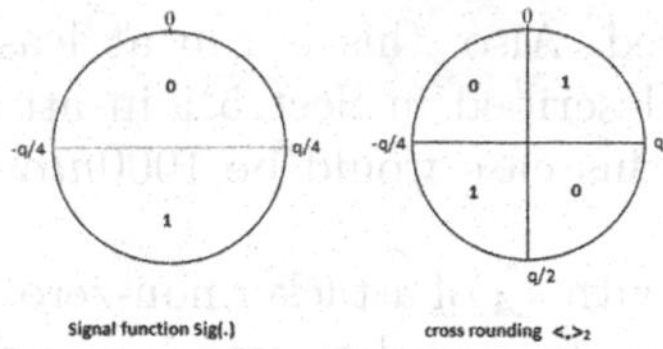

Fig. 5. Comparison of signal in the two RLWE based key exchange protocols in [14,22].

Party A: To finish the key exchange, compute $k_A = p_B s_A$ and the final shared key $sk_A = rec(2k_A, w_B)$ (Fig. 5).

The Attack: The attack here is very similar to the attack using the signal function in [9]. In this case, the additional information required for agreeing on the final shared key sk_A, sk_B is achieved by party B sending the value of the cross rounding function $< . >_2$. By definition, $<v>_2$ returns 0 when $v \in I_0, I'_0$ and 1 when $v \in I_1, I'_1$, where the sets I_0, I'_0, I_1 and I'_1 are as defined in Sect. 3. Thus, we refer to the output w_B of the cross rounding function $<\bar{k}_B>_2$ as the signal. The variation here, compared to the signal function in [14] is that the signal regions are defined as quadrants as opposed to E, E^c in Definition 2 and the signal function is applied on $dbl(k_B)$. The dbl function is applied on k_B in the protocol to remove bias when q is odd, which is usually the case in RLWE instantiations.

The strategy behind the initial signal function attack is that when the attacker's key is chosen in such a way that party B's computation of $k_B = ks_B$ for k values ranging over all values in $\mathbb{Z}_q$, $k_B[i]$ value varies in multiples of $s_B[i]$ and the number of signal changes is exactly $2s_B[i]$ for every coefficient i. This is because there are 2 boundary points (from the way the signal regions E, E^c are defined) where the signal bit flips.

In the key exchange described above, the cross rounding function divides $\mathbb{Z}_q$ into quadrants resulting in 4 boundary points where the value of the signal flips. Thus, following the same approach as the signal function attack in [9], the number of signal changes while using the cross rounding function is exactly $4s_B[i]$, for every coefficient i. So, the secret can be compromised in $2q$ queries to the honest party reusing the key. Essentially we get the signal values of party B's secret with the error $2g_B - \bar{e}$ causing fluctuations in the signal changes with this protocol as well. This can be handled by not counting the fluctuations as signal changes. The fluctuations are easier to identify since the changes are within a smaller interval.

7 Signal Function Attack with Reduced Query Complexity

The signal function attack works by counting the number of times the signal bit $Sig(k_B)$ changes for each coefficient of k_B, for k across all values of $\mathbb{Z}_q$ in the public key $p_{\mathcal{A}} = as_{\mathcal{A}} + ke_{\mathcal{A}}$ of the adversary. The adversary specifically chooses $s_{\mathcal{A}}$ to be 0 and $e_{\mathcal{A}}$ to be 1 in R_q in the simplified form of the attack. $\mathcal{A}$ then queries with his public key as $(1+x)p_{\mathcal{A}}$ to eliminate the ambiguity of the $\pm$ sign of the coefficients recovered from previous queries and determine the exact values. The attack is also then extended to the case when $s_{\mathcal{A}}$ is sampled from the error distribution χ_α so that the adversary's public key $p_{\mathcal{A}}$ is an RLWE sample indistinguishable from uniform. This attack requires $2q$ queries to party B to extract the exact value of the secret s_B. For a detailed description of the attack, refer to [9].

We now show that the attack can be more efficient with fewer queries. This comes from the observation that it is not necessary to vary k through all the values of $\mathbb{Z}_q$ to determine the value of s_B accurately. For each coefficient of the secret $s_B[i]$, as k varies from 0 to $q-1$, the key value $k_B[i]$ changes in multiples of $s_B[i]$. Thus, depending on the value of $s_B[i]$, the period of signal change varies and this can be used to perform the attack more efficiently. We consider the different cases of the protocol here to see how fewer queries can still successfully recover the secret.

Case 1: First, we consider the simplified case when the error term g_B is not added to the key computation k_B and the secret of the adversary $s_{\mathcal{A}}$ is 0, with public key $p_{\mathcal{A}} = k$. It is then clear that determining the first k value when the signal changes gives the value of $s_B[i]$ upto $\pm$ sign since the first flip of the signal bit happens when k changes from $\lfloor \frac{q}{4s_B[i]} \rceil$ to $\lfloor \frac{q}{4s_B[i]} \rceil + 1$ by the definition of the signal region E, E^c. Also, instead of querying for each coefficient separately, we can query for all coefficients at once varying k from 0 to $q/4+2$. This is because the smaller $s_B[i]$ values need more number of queries for counting the first signal change. For example, $s_B[i] = \pm 1$ needs $q/4+2$ queries, $s_B[i] = \pm 2$ needs $q/4+1$ queries and so on. Again using $q/4+2$ queries to party B with public key of adversary $p_{\mathcal{A}} = (1+x)k$, the ambiguity of $\pm$ sign is resolved. Thus, the adversary can recover s_B with $2(q/4+2) = q/2+4$ queries thus reducing the query complexity by a factor of 1/4 compared to previous complexity of $2q$ described above.

Case 2: This is the case of the original protocol where the adversary only slightly deviates from the protocol by choosing $e_{\mathcal{A}} = 1$, $s_{\mathcal{A}}$ is chosen according to the error distribution χ_α and $p_{\mathcal{A}} = as_{\mathcal{A}} + ke_{\mathcal{A}} = as_{\mathcal{A}} + k$ so that an attacker's public key cannot be distinguished from uniform. In this case, we cannot use the first k where the signal flips to determine the value of s_B since $k_B = as_{\mathcal{A}}s_B + ks_B + 2g_B$; For every coefficient i, we have $as_{\mathcal{A}}s_B[i]$ as a constant value that is unknown to the adversary along with the noise g_B, added to $ks_B[i]$. In order to count the number of signal changes here, the attacker varies k starting with $k=0$ and records the first signal change at $k = k_1$. Then he can vary k for negative values and record the first signal change in this direction at $k = k_2$. Now, $k_1 - k_2$ is the span of the region E or E^c in multiples of $s_B[i]$. Thus, $\lfloor \frac{q}{2(k_1-k_2)} \rceil$ reveals the value of $s_B[i]$ upto $\pm$ sign since the period of the signal change is $k_1 - k_2$. When the error g_B is added to the key computation k_B, the signal change does not happen in specific intervals due to the fluctuations. Here, we can query a small constant number of times more than $q/2$ until the signal stabilizes after a change. Thus, with $\frac{q}{2}+c$ queries where c is a small constant, we can recover $s_B[i]$ upto sign. c is small since the values stabilize when k increases and $ks_B[i]$ is away from the boundary points. So, to recover the exact value of the secret requires $q + c$ queries.

This is further illustrated with the help of an example in the full version of paper.

8 Conclusion

In this work, we have presented a new attack on the RLWE key exchange showing that even an unsuccessful key exchange session, when the final computed keys of both parties do not match can be used to recover the secret of a fixed public key. We also extend a previous attack based on the signal function to the KE protocol described in [22]. This shows that reuse of keys should always be avoided while replacing a key exchange protocol based on RLWE as a potential post-quantum alternative. This does not apply to the case of IND-CCA KEMs using the Fujisaki-Okamoto transformation. We also note that in the New Hope implementation, the public a is chosen at random for every new key exchange session. However, the active attacks on the KE protocols rely on the fact that the public key is reused in certain Internet protocols. So, even if the New Hope implementation is integrated into such protocols, a new a might not be chosen for every key exchange session as suggested in the work and hence is vulnerable to such attacks. The security risk associated with key reuse is acknowledged in the works of New Hope and [22].

Acknowledgements. Jintai Ding and Saraswathy RV would like to thank NSF and US Air Force for its partial support.

References

1. Experimenting with post-quantum cryptography, July 2016. https://security.googleblog.com/2016/07/experimenting-with-post-quantum.html
2. Ajtai, M.: Generating hard instances of lattice problems (extended abstract). In: Proceedings of the Twenty-Eighth Annual ACM Symposium on Theory of Computing, STOC 1996, pp. 99–108. ACM, New York (1996)
3. Alkim, E., Ducas, L., Pöppelmann, T., Schwabe, P.: Post-quantum key exchange—a new hope. In: 25th USENIX Security Symposium (USENIX Security 2016), pp. 327–343. USENIX Association, Austin (2016)
4. Applebaum, B., Cash, D., Peikert, C., Sahai, A.: Fast cryptographic primitives and circular-secure encryption based on hard learning problems. In: Halevi, S. (ed.) CRYPTO 2009. LNCS, vol. 5677, pp. 595–618. Springer, Heidelberg (2009). https://doi.org/10.1007/978-3-642-03356-8_35

5. Bos, J.W., Costello, C., Naehrig, M., Stebila, D.: Post-quantum key exchange for the TLS protocol from the ring learning with errors problem. In: 2015 IEEE Symposium on Security and Privacy, pp. 553–570, May 2015
6. Brakerski, Z., Gentry, C., Vaikuntanathan, V.: (Leveled) fully homomorphic encryption without bootstrapping. In: Proceedings of the 3rd Innovations in Theoretical Computer Science Conference, pp. 309–325. ACM (2012)
7. Brakerski, Z., Vaikuntanathan, V.: Fully homomorphic encryption from ring-LWE and security for key dependent messages. In: Rogaway, P. (ed.) CRYPTO 2011. LNCS, vol. 6841, pp. 505–524. Springer, Heidelberg (2011). https://doi.org/10.1007/978-3-642-22792-9_29
8. Diffie, W., Hellman, M.: New directions in cryptography. IEEE Trans. Inf. Theor. **22**(6), 644–654 (2006)
9. Ding, J., Alsayigh, S., Saraswathy, R.V., Fluhrer, S., Lin, X.: Leakage of signal function with reused keys in RLWE key exchange. In: 2017 IEEE International Conference on Communications (ICC), pp. 1–6, May 2017
10. Fluhrer, S.: Cryptanalysis of ring-lwe based key exchange with key share reuse. Cryptology ePrint Archive, Report 2016/085 (2016). http://eprint.iacr.org/2016/085
11. Fujioka, A., Suzuki, K., Xagawa, K., Yoneyama, K.: Strongly secure authenticated key exchange from factoring, codes, and lattices. In: Fischlin, M., Buchmann, J., Manulis, M. (eds.) PKC 2012. LNCS, vol. 7293, pp. 467–484. Springer, Heidelberg (2012). https://doi.org/10.1007/978-3-642-30057-8_28
12. Gentry, C., Peikert, C., Vaikuntanathan, V.: Trapdoors for hard lattices and new cryptographic constructions. In: Proceedings of the 40th Annual ACM Symposium on Theory of Computing, STOC 2008, pp. 197–206. ACM, New York (2008)
13. Gong, B., Zhao, Y.: Cryptanalysis of RLWE-based one-pass authenticated key exchange. In: Lange, T., Takagi, T. (eds.) PQCrypto 2017. LNCS, vol. 10346, pp. 163–183. Springer, Cham (2017). https://doi.org/10.1007/978-3-319-59879-6_10
14. Ding, J., Xie, X., Lin, X.: A simple provably secure key exchange scheme based on the learning with errors problem. Cryptology ePrint Archive, Report 2012/688 (2012). http://eprint.iacr.org/
15. Kirkwood, D., Lackey, B.C., McVey, J., Motley, M., Solinas, J.A., Tuller, D.: Failure is not an option: standardization issues for post-quantum key agreement (2016). http://csrc.nist.gov/groups/ST/post-quantum-2015/presentations/session7-motley-mark.pdf
16. Lyubashevsky, V.: Lattice-based identification schemes secure under active attacks. In: Cramer, R. (ed.) PKC 2008. LNCS, vol. 4939, pp. 162–179. Springer, Heidelberg (2008). https://doi.org/10.1007/978-3-540-78440-1_10
17. Lyubashevsky, V.: Fiat-Shamir with aborts: applications to lattice and factoring-based signatures. In: Matsui, M. (ed.) ASIACRYPT 2009. LNCS, vol. 5912, pp. 598–616. Springer, Heidelberg (2009). https://doi.org/10.1007/978-3-642-10366-7_35
18. Lyubashevsky, V., Peikert, C., Regev, O.: On ideal lattices and learning with errors over rings. In: Gilbert, H. (ed.) EUROCRYPT 2010. LNCS, vol. 6110, pp. 1–23. Springer, Heidelberg (2010). https://doi.org/10.1007/978-3-642-13190-5_1
19. Micciancio, D., Regev, O.: Worst-case to average-case reductions based on Gaussian measures. SIAM J. Comput. **37**, 267–302 (2007)
20. NIST: Post quantum cryptography: Nist's plan for the future (2016). http://csrc.nist.gov/groups/ST/post-quantum-crypto/documents/pqcrypto-2016-presentation.pdf

21. Peikert, C.: Public-key cryptosystems from the worst-case shortest vector problem: extended abstract. In: Proceedings of the 41st Annual ACM Symposium on Theory of Computing, STOC 2009, pp. 333–342. ACM, New York (2009)
22. Peikert, C.: Lattice cryptography for the internet. In: Mosca, M. (ed.) PQCrypto 2014. LNCS, vol. 8772, pp. 197–219. Springer, Cham (2014). https://doi.org/10.1007/978-3-319-11659-4_12
23. Regev, O.: On lattices, learning with errors, random linear codes, and cryptography. In: Proceedings of the Thirty-Seventh Annual ACM Symposium on Theory of Computing, STOC 2005, pp. 84–93. ACM, New York (2005)
24. Shor, P.W.: Polynomial-time algorithms for prime factorization and discrete logarithms on a quantum computer. SIAM J. Comput. **26**(5), 1484–1509 (1997)
25. Zhang, J., Zhang, Z., Ding, J., Snook, M., Dagdelen, Ö.: Authenticated key exchange from ideal lattices. In: Oswald, E., Fischlin, M. (eds.) EUROCRYPT 2015. LNCS, vol. 9057, pp. 719–751. Springer, Heidelberg (2015). https://doi.org/10.1007/978-3-662-46803-6_24

Efficient Decryption Algorithms for Extension Field Cancellation Type Encryption Schemes

Yacheng Wang[1(✉)], Yasuhiko Ikematsu[1], Dung Hoang Duong[2], and Tsuyoshi Takagi[1]

[1] Department of Mathematical Informatics, University of Tokyo, Hongo 7-3-1, Bunkyo-ku, Tokyo 113-8656, Japan
{yacheng_wang,ikematsu,takagi}@mist.i.u-tokyo.ac.jp

[2] Institute of Mathematics for Industry, Kyushu University, 744 Motooka, Nishi-ku, Fukuoka 819-0395, Japan
duong@imi.kyushu-u.ac.jp

Abstract. Extension Field Cancellation (EFC) was proposed by Alan et al. at PQCrypto 2016 as a new trapdoor for constructing secure multivariate encryption cryptographic schemes. Along with this trapdoor, two schemes EFC_p^- and $\mathrm{EFC}_{pt^2}^-$ that apply this trapdoor and some modifiers were proposed. Though their security seems to be high enough, their decryption efficiency has room for improvement. In this paper, we introduce a new and more efficient decryption approach for EFC_p^- and $\mathrm{EFC}_{pt^2}^-$, which manages to avoid all redundant computation involved in the original decryption algorithms, and theoretically speed up the decryption process of EFC_p^- and $\mathrm{EFC}_{pt^2}^-$ by around 3.4 and 8.5 times, respectively, under 128-bit security parameters with our new designed private keys for them. Meanwhile, our approach does not interfere with the public key, so the security remains the same. The implementation results of both decryption algorithms for EFC_p^- and $\mathrm{EFC}_{pt^2}^-$ are also provided.

Keywords: Multivariate cryptography · Extension field cancellation Decryption algorithm · Minus

1 Introduction

In 1994, Shor [17] introduced an algorithm that can solve the integer factorization problem and the discrete logarithm problem in polynomial time on a quantum computer. Hence once large-scale quantum computers are put into use, the currently used public key cryptosystems such as RSA [16] and ECC [9] will be totally broken. The cryptology research community is seeking for alternative cryptosystems that are secure in the quantum era. Specially, the National Institute of Standards and Technology (NIST) [11] in the United States is calling for post-quantum cryptosystems (PQC) proposals to be standardized. It has also

W. Susilo and G. Yang (Eds.): ACISP 2018, LNCS 10946, pp. 487–501, 2018.
https://doi.org/10.1007/978-3-319-93638-3_28

been emphasized by the National Security Agency (NSA) [6] on their plan for switching to quantum resistant algorithms in the future.

According to NIST [11], multivariate cryptography is one of the main candidates for PQC. Multivariate cryptography is in general very fast and requires only modest computational resources, which makes it attractive for its use on low cost devices such as smart cards and RFID chips [1,2]. One traditional method for building a multivariate scheme is to construct an easy-to-invert quadratic polynomial map $\mathcal{F} \in \mathbb{F}[x_1, \ldots, x_n]^m$ over a finite field $\mathbb{F}$ as the *central map*. One can also construct the central map $\mathcal{F}$ by first choosing a map from an extension field $\mathbb{E}$ of $\mathbb{F}$ and then mapping down to $\mathbb{F}$. The *public key* $\mathcal{P}$ is generated by hiding the central map $\mathcal{F}$ with two secret invertible linear or affine maps $\mathcal{S}$ and $\mathcal{T}$, i.e., $\mathcal{P} = \mathcal{T} \circ \mathcal{F} \circ \mathcal{S}$. Therefore, the public key consists of quadratic polynomials. The security basis of multivariate cryptographic systems is the *$\mathcal{MQ}$-Problem,* which aims to solve a given system of multivariate quadratic polynomials over a certain finite field, and this problem (for $m \approx n$) is generally considered to be an NP-hard problem [15]. To investigate the hardness of the $\mathcal{MQ}$-problem, the MQ challenge is currently being held [21].

Since the first multivariate cryptosystem MI [10] was proposed, many multivariate cryptosystems inheriting its construction have been proposed. As multivariate signature schemes, UOV [8] and Rainbow [5] have drawn great attention in cryptography community. UOV has been standing secure for almost 20 years, and as its improved version, Rainbow is considered as a very promising signature scheme for post-quantum cryptography. Moreover, in order to put UOV and Rainbow into practical use, many efficient implementation on IoT devices of UOV [1,4] and Rainbow [2,19] have been devised. On the other hand, many attempts of constructing secure multivariate encryption schemes have also been made, such as HFE [13], ABC [20], ZHFE [14], SRP [22] and EFC [18]. Most of them were proven to be insecure by many different attacks, such as MinRank [7], HighRank [3], Linearization [12]. Nevertheless, ABC and EFC are still standing secure.

At PQCrypto 2016, Szepieniec et al. [18] proposed a new type of trapdoor called Extension Field Cancellation (EFC), and two encryption schemes EFC_p^- and $\mathrm{EFC}_{pt^2}^-$. They use both matrix multiplications as in the ABC [20] scheme and extension field structure as in MI [10], HFE [13] and ZHFE [14]. By utilizing the commutativity property in the extension field, the decryption process of EFC_p^- and $\mathrm{EFC}_{pt^2}^-$ can be done by solving linear systems. This combination makes EFC secure against all current attacks and become one of the main candidates for multivariate encryption systems at the moment.

In this paper, we break down the operations involved in the key generation and decryption processes, and introduce a more efficient decryption approach for EFC_p^- and $\mathrm{EFC}_{pt^2}^-$. The decryption algorithms for EFC_p^- and $\mathrm{EFC}_{pt^2}^-$ rely on the bilinear relation between the plaintext and an augmented ciphertext, that is the concatenation of ciphertext and the values of the removed polynomials by the minus modifier. This bilinear relation is used for constructing linear systems in the decryption process of EFC_p^- and $\mathrm{EFC}_{pt^2}^-$. The values of the removed polynomials have to be exhaustively searched until the correct values are found. For each guess, the linear system derived from the bilinear relation has to be reconstructed, which indicates redundant computations. Our proposed decryption algorithms aim to separate the computation of constructing the linear system into two kinds of computations. One is the computation involving the plaintext and the ciphertext. The other one is computation involving the plaintext and the guessed values. Therefore, the repetitive computation involving the plaintext and the ciphertext can be avoided.

This paper is structured as follows. In Sect. 2, we recall the construction of EFC_p^- and $\text{EFC}_{pt^2}^-$, and their decryption algorithms in [18]. In Sect. 3, we introduce our proposed new decryption algorithms for EFC_p^- and $\text{EFC}_{pt^2}^-$, and end it with a comparison between the original decryption approach and our proposed new one. Finally, We conclude the paper in Sect. 4.

2 Extension Field Cancellation (EFC)

EFC is one of the few multivariate cryptographic trapdoors that still remain secure. Although this trapdoor is exposed under bilinear attack, MinRank attack and differential attack, its modified versions, EFC_p^- and $\text{EFC}_{pt^2}^-$, manage to avoid all of those threats. EFC_p^- is constructed by applying minus and projection modifiers to EFC. Minus modifier increases the rank of the quadratic forms associated with the central map polynomials over the extension field, which makes MinRank attack and direct algebraic attack more difficult to practice. Projection modifier is used to avoid the potential differential attack. The minus modifier affects the performance of decryption process drastically when the number of removed polynomials from the public key is large. Under this circumstances, $\text{EFC}_{pt^2}^-$ was proposed, which is basically EFC_p^- with frobenius tail. It increases the rank of the quadratic forms associated with the central map polynomials over the extension field, that enables us to use a smaller number of removed polynomials. Therefore, it results in a significant speedup on the decryption algorithm. More cryptanalysis of EFC_p^- and $\text{EFC}_{pt^2}^-$ can be found in [18].

In this section, we recall the constructions of EFC_p^- and $\text{EFC}_{pt^2}^-$ [18], and the original decryption algorithms designed for them.

2.1 Notations

Let $\mathbb{F}$ be a finite field of q elements. Given a positive integer n, $x_1, \ldots, x_n$ are n variables over $\mathbb{F}$, and define $\mathbf{x} = (x_1, \ldots, x_n)$. $\mathbb{E}$ denotes a degree n extension field of $\mathbb{F}$. Denote the set of all $n \times m$ matrices by $\mathbb{F}^{n\times m}$. Matrices are denoted by capital letters, vectors are denoted by bold lowercase letters, and all vectors are treated as row vectors. The i-th entry of a vector $\mathbf{v}$ is denoted by v_i, the i-th row of a matrix M is denoted by M_i. For a matrix M, $M_{[i,j;k,s]}$ denotes a submatrix of M formed by i-th to j-th rows, and k-th to s-th columns.

Choose $\{\theta_1, \ldots, \theta_n\}$ as a basis for $\mathbb{E}/\mathbb{F}$, let $\mathbf{b} = (\theta_1, \ldots, \theta_n) \in \mathbb{E}^n$, and define an isomorphism $\varphi : \mathbb{F}^n \ni \mathbf{v} \mapsto \mathbf{v}\mathbf{b}^\top \in \mathbb{E}$. For $A \in \mathbb{F}^{n\times n}$, and $\mathbf{v} = (v_1, \ldots, v_n) \in \mathbb{F}^n$, define $\alpha(\mathbf{v}) = \varphi(\mathbf{v}A) \in \mathbb{E}$. The multiplication by $\alpha(\mathbf{v})$ is an $\mathbb{F}$-endomorphism on $\mathbb{E}$. This endomorphism is identified with an endomorphism on $\mathbb{F}^n$ by the isomorphism φ. The matrix corresponding to this endomorphism is denoted by $\alpha_m(\mathbf{v}) \in \mathbb{F}^{n\times n}$. For a matrix $B \in \mathbb{F}^{n\times n}$ and $\mathbf{v} \in \mathbb{F}^n$, we define $\beta(\mathbf{v})$ and $\beta_m(\mathbf{v})$ in the same way as $\alpha(\mathbf{v})$ and $\alpha_m(\mathbf{v})$. For a positive integer a, π_a stands for the following map:

$$\pi_a : \mathbb{F}^{2n} \ni (v_1, \cdots, v_{2n}) \mapsto (v_1, \cdots, v_{2n-a}) \in \mathbb{F}^{2n-a}.$$

2.2 Construction of the $\mathrm{EFC}_\mathrm{p}^-$ Schemes

– **Key Generation**

Given a prime number n, randomly choose $A, B \in \mathbb{F}^{n\times n}$ of rank $n-1$ such that the intersection of the kernel spaces of A and B is the zero subspace. Randomly choose two invertible linear maps $\mathcal{S} : \mathbb{F}^n \to \mathbb{F}^n$ and $\mathcal{T} : \mathbb{F}^{2n} \to \mathbb{F}^{2n}$, we denote the matrices associated to these linear maps by $S \in \mathbb{F}^{n\times n}$, $T \in \mathbb{F}^{2n\times 2n}$, i.e. $\mathcal{S}(\mathbf{x}) = \mathbf{x}S$. The central map $\mathcal{F}$ for EFC_p^- is

$$\mathcal{F} : \mathbb{F}^n \ni \mathbf{x} \mapsto (\mathbf{x} \cdot \alpha_m(\mathbf{x}),\ \mathbf{x} \cdot \beta_m(\mathbf{x})) \in \mathbb{F}^{2n}.$$

The public key for EFC_p^- is given by

$$\mathcal{P} = (p_1, \cdots, p_{2n-a}) = \pi_a \circ \mathcal{T} \circ \mathcal{F} \circ \mathcal{S} : \mathbb{F}^n \to \mathbb{F}^{2n-a},$$

where p_i $(1 \le i \le 2n - a)$ are quadratic polynomials in $x_1, \ldots, x_n$ over $\mathbb{F}$.

Next we take a look at the explicit form of the central map $\mathcal{F}$. Since $\alpha(\mathbf{x}) \in \mathbb{E}$, it can be represented with basis $\{\theta_1, \ldots, \theta_n\}$, i.e. $\alpha(\mathbf{x}) = \mathbf{x}A\mathbf{b}^\top$. Let $\alpha_i = A_i\mathbf{b}^\top \in \mathbb{E}$ for $1 \le i \le n$, then we have $\alpha(\mathbf{x}) = \sum_{i=1}^n x_i\alpha_i$. Define matrices $C^{(i)} \in \mathbb{F}^{n\times n}$ by $(C^{(i)})_j^\top = \varphi^{-1}(\alpha_i\theta_j)$ for $1 \le i, j \le n$. It is easy to check that $C^{(i)}$ satisfies $\mathbf{b}C^{(i)} = \alpha_i\mathbf{b}$ for $1 \le i \le n$, which indicates $\alpha_m(\mathbf{x}) = \sum_{i=1}^n x_iC^{(i)}$. Similarly, we define matrices $D^{(i)} \in \mathbb{F}^{n\times n}$ for $1 \le i \le n$ and they satisfy $\beta_m(\mathbf{x}) = \sum_{i=1}^n x_iD^{(i)}$. Therefore, the explicit form of $\mathcal{F}$ is

$$\mathcal{F} : \mathbb{F}^n \ni \mathbf{x} \mapsto \left(\mathbf{x} \cdot \left(\sum_{i=1}^n C^{(i)}x_i\right),\ \mathbf{x} \cdot \left(\sum_{i=1}^n D^{(i)}x_i\right)\right) \in \mathbb{F}^{2n}.$$

– **Encryption**

Given the public key $\mathcal{P}$ and a plaintext $\mathbf{z} \in \mathbb{F}^n$, its ciphertext is $\mathbf{c} = \mathcal{P}(\mathbf{z}) \in \mathbb{F}^{2n}$.

– **Decryption**

Given the private key $\{A, B, \mathcal{S}, \mathcal{T}\}$ and a ciphertext $\mathbf{c} \in \mathbb{F}^{2n-a}$, we find the plaintext $\mathbf{z} \in \mathbb{F}^n$ such that $\mathcal{P}(\mathbf{z}) = \mathbf{c}$. First, we need to guess the value $\mathbf{v}$ from

$\mathbb{F}^a$ for the deleted polynomials by π_a. Second, we compute $\mathbb{F}^n \times \mathbb{F}^n \ni (\mathbf{d}_1, \mathbf{d}_2) = \mathbf{d} = \mathcal{T}^{-1}(\mathbf{c}, \mathbf{v})$. Next we invert the map $\mathcal{F}$ by solving the linear system

$$\mathbf{d}_2 \alpha_m(\mathbf{x}) = \mathbf{d}_1 \beta_m(\mathbf{x}), \tag{1}$$

and obtain a solution $\mathbf{h} \in \mathbb{F}^n$. Finally, if $\mathcal{F}(\mathbf{h}) = (\mathbf{d}_1, \mathbf{d}_2)$, then we obtain the plaintext by $\mathbf{z} = \mathcal{S}^{-1}(\mathbf{h})$. The loop of guessing the value $\mathbf{v}$ from $\mathbb{F}^a$ terminates when the correct plaintext $\mathbf{z}$ is found. The details are shown in Algorithm 1.

Algorithm 1. Decryption algorithm for EFC_p^-

Input : A ciphertext $\mathbf{c} \in \mathbb{F}^{2n-a}$,
The private key $A, B, S \in \mathbb{F}^{n\times n}$ and $T \in \mathbb{F}^{2n\times 2n}$.
Output: The plaintext $\mathbf{z} \in \mathbb{F}^n$.

- $S_{inv} \leftarrow S^{-1}, T_{inv} \leftarrow T^{-1}$
- Generate $\alpha_m(\mathbf{x}), \beta_m(\mathbf{x})$ and $\mathcal{F}$ from A, B
- **for** $\mathbf{v} \in \mathbb{F}^a$ **do**
  - $\mathbb{F}^n \times \mathbb{F}^n \ni (\mathbf{d}_1, \mathbf{d}_2) = \mathbf{d} \leftarrow (\mathbf{c}, \mathbf{v}) \cdot T_{inv}$
  - construct a linear system $\mathbf{d}_2 \cdot \alpha_m(\mathbf{x}) - \mathbf{d}_2 \cdot \beta_m(\mathbf{x}) = 0$
  - solve $\mathbf{d}_2 \cdot \alpha_m(\mathbf{x}) - \mathbf{d}_2 \cdot \beta_m(\mathbf{x}) = 0$, and choose a solution $\mathbf{h} \in \mathbb{F}^n$
  - **if** $\mathcal{F}(\mathbf{h}) = \mathbf{d}$ **then**
    - break
- $\mathbb{F}^n \ni \mathbf{z} \leftarrow \mathbf{h} \cdot S_{inv}$
- **Return z.**

Regrading the complexity of this decryption algorithm, we have the following proposition:

Proposition 1. *The number of* $\mathbb{F}$*-additions and* $\mathbb{F}$*-multiplications involved in the decryption algorithm for* EFC_p^- *are*

$$\begin{aligned} &4n^4 + \frac{3}{2}n^3 - \frac{5}{2}n + \frac{q^a}{2}\left(\frac{13}{3}n^3 + \frac{7}{2}n^2 - \frac{29}{6}n\right), \text{ and} \\ &4n^4 + \frac{15}{2}n^3 + \frac{1}{2}n^2 - n + \frac{q^a}{2}\left(\frac{13}{3}n^3 + 7n^2 - \frac{1}{3}n\right), \end{aligned} \tag{2}$$

respectively.

Proof. Let $[+]_{\mathbb{F}}$ denotes $\mathbb{F}$-addition, and $[\times]_{\mathbb{F}}$ denotes $\mathbb{F}$-multiplication of $\mathbb{F}$. We recall the complexity of Gaussian Elimination, and multiplication in $\mathbb{E}$. For an input of $n \times m$ $(m \geq n)$ matrix over $\mathbb{F}$, Gaussian Elimination requires $\sum_{i=1}^{n-1}(n-i)(m-i)$ $[+]_{\mathbb{F}}$ and $\sum_{i=1}^{n-1}(n-i)(m-i) + \sum_{i=1}^{n-1}(n-i)$ $[\times]_{\mathbb{F}}$. For any $a, b \in \mathbb{E}$, represented in basis $\{\theta_1, \ldots, \theta_n\}$, $a \cdot b$ requires $(n-1)(2n-1)$ $[+]_{\mathbb{F}}$ and $2n^2$ $[\times]_{\mathbb{F}}$.

Now we analyze the complexity based on the Algorithm 1.

In step 1, computing T^{-1} requires $\frac{n(20n^2-12n+1)}{3}$ $[+]_{\mathbb{F}}$ and $\frac{2n(10n^2-3n-1)}{3}$ $[\times]_{\mathbb{F}}$, and computing S^{-1} requires $\frac{n(5n^2-6n+1)}{6}$ $[+]_{\mathbb{F}}$ and $\frac{n(5n^2-3n-2)}{6}$ $[\times]_{\mathbb{F}}$. In step 2, to obtain $\alpha_m(\mathbf{x})$, we need to compute $\alpha(\mathbf{x}) = \sum_{i=1}^{n} x_i \alpha_i$, where $\alpha_i = A_i \mathbf{b}^\top$ $(1 \leq i \leq n)$, and this requires $n(n-1)$ $[+]_{\mathbb{F}}$ and n^2 $[\times]_{\mathbb{F}}$. Then we need to compute $\alpha_i \mathbf{b}$ for $1 \leq i \leq n$, which indicates n^2 $[\times]_{\mathbb{E}}$, and it requires $n^2(n-1)(2n-1)$ $[+]_{\mathbb{F}}$ and $2n^4$ $[\times]_{\mathbb{F}}$. Same complexity holds for obtaining $\beta_m(\mathbf{x})$.

From step 3 to step 8, we enter a loop of size q^a. In step 4, $(\mathbf{c}, \mathbf{v}) \cdot T_{inv}$ requires $2n(2n-1)$ $[+]_{\mathbb{F}}$ and $4n^2$ $[\times]_{\mathbb{F}}$. In step 5, constructing the linear system needs $2n^3 - n^2$ $[+]_{\mathbb{F}}$ and $2n^3$ $[\times]_{\mathbb{F}}$. In step 6, solving the linear system with Gaussian Elimination requires $\frac{n(n-1)(2n+5)}{6}$ $[+]_{\mathbb{F}}$ and $\frac{n(n^2+3n-1)}{3}$ $[\times]_{\mathbb{F}}$. In step 7, verifying whether $\mathcal{F}(\mathbf{h}) = \mathbf{d}$ holds costs $2n(n^2-1)$ $[+]_{\mathbb{F}}$ and $2n^2(n+1)$ $[\times]_{\mathbb{F}}$. The loop terminates in step 8 after an average of $\frac{q^a}{2}$ times. Therefore, the loop costs $\frac{q^a}{2}(\frac{13}{3}n^3 + \frac{7}{2}n^2 - \frac{29}{6}n)$ $[+]_{\mathbb{F}}$ and $\frac{q^a}{2}(\frac{13}{3}n^3 + 7n^2 - \frac{1}{3}n)$ $[\times]_{\mathbb{F}}$ in average.

In step 9, computing $\mathbf{h} \cdot S_{inv}$ needs $n(n-1)$ $[+]_{\mathbb{F}}$ and n^2 $[\times]_{\mathbb{F}}$.

Since step 1, step 2 and step 9 together costs $4n^2 + \frac{3}{2}n^3 - \frac{5}{2}n$ $[+]_{\mathbb{F}}$ and $4n^2 + \frac{15}{2}n^3 + \frac{1}{2}n^2 - n$ $[\times]_{\mathbb{F}}$, the total cost of this decryption algorithm is Eq. (2). This completes the proof. □

2.3 Construction of the $\mathrm{EFC}_{pt^2}^-$ Scheme

- **Key Generation**

Choose the secret key A, B and $\mathcal{S}, \mathcal{T}$ as in EFC_p^-. The central map $\mathcal{F}$ for $\mathrm{EFC}_{pt^2}^-$ is

$$\mathcal{F} : \mathbb{F}^n \ni \mathbf{x} \mapsto \left(\mathbf{x}\alpha_m(\mathbf{x}) + \varphi^{-1}(\beta(\mathbf{x})^3),\ \mathbf{x}\beta_m(\mathbf{x}) + \varphi^{-1}(\alpha(\mathbf{x})^3)\right) \in \mathbb{F}^{2n}. \quad (3)$$

The public key for $\mathrm{EFC}_{pt^2}^-$ is $\mathcal{P} = (p_1, \ldots, p_{2n-a}) = \pi_a \circ \mathcal{T} \circ \mathcal{F} \circ \mathcal{S} : \mathbb{F}^n \to \mathbb{F}^{2n-a}$. The private key consists of A, B and $\mathcal{S}, \mathcal{T}$.

Remark 1. Let q be the cardinality of $\mathbb{F}$, then $\mathbb{E} \ni x \mapsto x^{q^i} \in \mathbb{E}$ is a linear map over $\mathbb{F}$ for any $i \in \mathbb{N}$. In order to let $\varphi^{-1}(\alpha(\mathbf{x})^3)$ and $\varphi^{-1}(\beta(\mathbf{x})^3)$ become quadratic polynomials, we need to let $\mathbb{F}$ be the finite field of 2 elements.

We take a look at the explicit structure of (3) using $\mathbf{b} = (\theta_1, \ldots, \theta_n)$. Since $\mathbf{x} \cdot \alpha_m(\mathbf{x})$ and $\mathbf{x} \cdot \beta_m(\mathbf{x})$ can be represented in the same way as in Sect. 2.2, we show the explicit form of $\varphi^{-1}(\alpha(\mathbf{x}))$ and $\varphi^{-1}(\beta(\mathbf{x}))$ here. Let $\Theta = \mathbf{b}^\top \mathbf{b} \in \mathbb{E}^{n \times n}$ and $\varphi^{-1}(\Theta) = (\Theta_1, \ldots, \Theta_n) \in (\mathbb{F}^{n \times n})^n$. Define a matrix $\Delta \in \mathbb{F}^{n \times n}$ by $\Delta_i = \varphi^{-1}(\theta_i^2)$. Then $\alpha(\mathbf{x})^3$ can be represented as

$$\alpha(\mathbf{x})^3 = \alpha(\mathbf{x})^2 \cdot \alpha(\mathbf{x}) = \mathbf{x}A \begin{pmatrix} \theta_1^2 \\ \vdots \\ \theta_n^2 \end{pmatrix} \cdot \mathbf{b}(\mathbf{x}A)^\top$$

$$= \mathbf{x}A\Delta\Theta(\mathbf{x}A)^\top = \sum_{i=1}^{n} \theta_i \cdot \mathbf{x}A\Delta\Theta_i(\mathbf{x}A)^\top.$$

$\beta(\mathbf{x})^3$ can be represented in the same way. Therefore, we have

$$\varphi^{-1}(\alpha(\mathbf{x})^3) = (\mathbf{x}A\Delta\Theta_1(\mathbf{x}A)^\top, \ldots, \mathbf{x}A\Delta\Theta_n(\mathbf{x}A)^\top),$$
$$\varphi^{-1}(\beta(\mathbf{x})^3) = (\mathbf{x}B\Delta\Theta_1(\mathbf{x}B)^\top, \ldots, \mathbf{x}B\Delta\Theta_n(\mathbf{x}B)^\top).$$

– **Encryption**

Given the public key $\mathcal{P}$ and a plaintext $\mathbf{z} \in \mathbb{F}^n$, the ciphertext is $\mathbf{c} = \mathcal{P}(\mathbf{z}) \in \mathbb{F}^{2n-a}$.

– **Decryption**

Before showing the decryption process for $\mathrm{EFC}^-_{pt^2}$, we take a look at how to invert the central map $\mathcal{F}$. Which requires solving the system $\mathcal{F}(\mathbf{x}) = \mathbf{d} \in \mathbb{F}^{2n}$, i.e.

$$\begin{aligned} \mathbf{x} \cdot \alpha_m(\mathbf{x}) + \varphi^{-1}(\beta(\mathbf{x})^3) &= \mathbf{d}_1, \\ \mathbf{x} \cdot \beta_m(\mathbf{x}) + \varphi^{-1}(\alpha(\mathbf{x})^3) &= \mathbf{d}_2, \end{aligned} \tag{4}$$

where $\mathbf{d} = (\mathbf{d}_1, \mathbf{d}_2) \in \mathbb{F}^n \times \mathbb{F}^n$. By definition of $\alpha_m(\mathbf{x})$ in Sect. 2.1, the equation $\varphi(\mathbf{x} \cdot \alpha_m(\mathbf{x})) = \varphi(\mathbf{x})\alpha(\mathbf{x})$ holds. Thus (4) is equivalent to

$$\varphi(\mathbf{x})\alpha(\mathbf{x}) + \beta(\mathbf{x})^3 = \varphi(\mathbf{d}_1),$$
$$\varphi(\mathbf{x})\beta(\mathbf{x}) + \alpha(\mathbf{x})^3 = \varphi(\mathbf{d}_2),$$

from which the following system can be constructed:

$$\mathbf{d}_2\alpha_m(\mathbf{x}) - \mathbf{d}_1\beta_m(\mathbf{x}) = \varphi^{-1}(\alpha(\mathbf{x})^4 - \beta(\mathbf{x})^4). \tag{5}$$

Define a matrix $\Lambda \in \mathbb{F}^{n\times n}$ by $\Lambda_i = \varphi^{-1}(\theta_i^4)$ for $1 \leq i \leq n$, and apply it to (5). Then (5) turns into

$$\mathbf{d}_2\alpha_m(\mathbf{x}) - \mathbf{d}_1\beta_m(\mathbf{x}) = \mathbf{x}(A - B)\Lambda, \tag{6}$$

which is a linear system in $\mathbf{x}$.

Now we explain the decryption process of $\mathrm{EFC}^-_{pt^2}$. Given the private key $\{A, B, \mathcal{S}, \mathcal{T}\}$ and a ciphertext $\mathbf{c} \in \mathbb{F}^{2n-a}$, we find the plaintext $\mathbf{z} \in \mathbb{F}^n$, such that $\mathcal{P}(\mathbf{z}) = \mathbf{c}$. First, we need to guess the value $\mathbf{v}$ from $\mathbb{F}^a$ for the deleted polynomials by π_a. Second, we compute $\mathbb{F}^n \times \mathbb{F}^n \ni (\mathbf{d}_1, \mathbf{d}_2) = \mathbf{d} = \mathcal{T}^{-1}(\mathbf{c}, \mathbf{v})$. Next we invert the map $\mathcal{F}$ by solving the linear system (6), and obtain a solution $\mathbf{h} \in \mathbb{F}^n$. Finally, if $\mathcal{F}(\mathbf{h}) = \mathbf{d}$, then we obtain the plaintext by $\mathbf{z} = \mathcal{S}^{-1}(\mathbf{h})$. The guessing of $\mathbf{v}$ from $\mathbb{F}^a$ terminates when the correct plaintext $\mathbf{z}$ is found. The details are shown in Algorithm 2.

We analyze the complexity of the decryption algorithm for $\mathrm{EFC}^-_{pt^2}$ adopting the same approach as in the proof of Proposition 1, and obtain the number of $\mathbb{F}$-additions and $\mathbb{F}$-multiplications involved in the decryption algorithm for $\mathrm{EFC}^-_{pt^2}$ as

$$\begin{aligned} &4n^4 + \frac{11}{2}n^3 - 6n^2 - \frac{1}{2}n + \frac{q^a}{2}(\frac{16}{3}n^3 + \frac{5}{2}n^2 - \frac{29}{6}n) \text{ and} \\ &4n^4 + \frac{23}{2}n^3 + \frac{1}{2}n^2 - n + \frac{q^a}{2}(\frac{16}{3}n^3 + 7n^2 - \frac{1}{3}n), \end{aligned} \tag{7}$$

respectively.

Algorithm 2. Decryption algorithm for $\mathrm{EFC}_{pt^2}^{-}$

Input : $\mathbf{b} = (\theta_1, \ldots, \theta_n) \in \mathbb{E}^n$. A ciphertext $\mathbf{c} \in \mathbb{F}^{2n-a}$,
The private key $A, B, S \in \mathbb{F}^{n\times n}$ and $T \in \mathbb{F}^{2n\times 2n}$.
Output: The plaintext $\mathbf{z} \in \mathbb{F}^n$.

$S_{inv} \leftarrow S^{-1}, T_{inv} \leftarrow T^{-1}$
Define $\Lambda \in \mathbb{F}^{n\times n}$ by $\Lambda_i = \varphi^{-1}(\theta_i^4)$
Generate $\alpha_m(\mathbf{x}), \beta_m(\mathbf{x})$ and $\mathcal{F}$ from A, B
for $\mathbf{v} \in \mathbb{F}^a$ **do**
  $\mathbb{F}^n \times \mathbb{F}^n \ni (\mathbf{d}_1, \mathbf{d}_2) = \mathbf{d} \leftarrow (\mathbf{c}, \mathbf{v}) \cdot T_{inv}$
  construct a linear system $\mathbf{d}_2\alpha_m(\mathbf{x}) - \mathbf{d}_1\beta_m(\mathbf{x}) = \mathbf{x}(A - B)\Lambda$
  solve $\mathbf{d}_2\alpha_m(\mathbf{x}) - \mathbf{d}_1\beta_m(\mathbf{x}) = \mathbf{x}(A - B)\Lambda$ and choose a solution $\mathbf{h} \in \mathbb{F}^n$
  if $\mathcal{F}(\mathbf{h}) = \mathbf{d}$ **then**
    break
$\mathbb{F}^n \ni \mathbf{z} \leftarrow \mathbf{h} \cdot S_{inv}$
Return z.

3 Our Proposed Efficient Decryption Algorithms for EFC_p^- and $\mathrm{EFC}_{pt^2}^-$

In this section, we introduce our new decryption algorithms for EFC_p^- and $\mathrm{EFC}_{pt^2}^-$.

3.1 New Decryption Algorithm for EFC_p^-

The new decryption algorithm is derived from linearization equations, which represent a relation between the plaintext and ciphertext. We start with developing a new decryption algorithm for EFC_p^- without applying the minus modifier, i.e. EFC_p.

Recall the linear system (1) for inverting the central map of EFC_p^-

$$\mathbf{d}_2\alpha_m(\mathbf{x}) - \mathbf{d}_1\beta_m(\mathbf{x}) = 0,$$

which is equivalent to

$$\begin{aligned} &\alpha(\mathbf{x})\varphi(\mathbf{d}_2) - \beta(\mathbf{x})\varphi(\mathbf{d}_1) \\ &= \mathbf{x}A\mathbf{b}^\top \cdot \mathbf{b}\mathbf{d}_2^\top - \mathbf{x}B\mathbf{b}^\top \cdot \mathbf{b}\mathbf{d}_1^\top = 0. \end{aligned}$$

Let $\Theta = \mathbf{b}^\top\mathbf{b}$ and $(\Theta_1, \ldots, \Theta_n) = \varphi^{-1}(\Theta)$, then from this equation, we can obtain linearization equations corresponding to the central map of EFC_p^- as follows:

$$\mathbf{x}A\Theta_i(0_n, I_n)\mathbf{d}^\top - \mathbf{x}B\Theta_i(I_n, 0_n)\mathbf{d}^\top = 0, \ (1 \le i \le n), \tag{8}$$

where $\mathbf{d} = (\mathbf{d}_1, \mathbf{d}_2)$. Let $\mathbf{c} \in \mathbb{F}^{2n}$ be a ciphertext of EFC_p, then $\mathbf{c} = \mathcal{T}(\mathbf{d})$. Apply the linear maps $\mathcal{S}$ and $\mathcal{T}$ to Eq. (8), we obtain the linearization equations between a plaintext $\mathbf{x}$ and $\mathbf{c}$ as

$$\mathbf{x}SA\Theta_i(0_n, I_n)(\mathbf{c}T^{-1})^\top - \mathbf{x}SB\Theta_i(I_n, 0_n)(\mathbf{c}T^{-1})^\top = 0. \tag{9}$$

For a ciphertext $\mathbf{c}$ of EFC_p, its corresponding plaintext can be found by solving Eq. (9).

Next we show how to represent Eq. (9) into one simple equation. Let $T_1 = (T^{-1}_{[1,2n;1,n]})^\top \in \mathbb{F}^{n\times 2n}$, and $T_2 = (T^{-1}_{[1,2n;n+1,2n]})^\top \in \mathbb{F}^{n\times 2n}$. Apply T_1, T_2 to Eq. (9), we have

$$\mathbf{x}(SA\Theta_i T_2 - SB\Theta_i T_1)\mathbf{c}^\top = 0, \ (1 \le i \le n). \tag{10}$$

Let $N^{(i)} = (SA\Theta_i T_2 - SB\Theta_i T_1)^\top \in \mathbb{F}^{2n\times n}$, and define matrices $U^{(j)}$ by $U^{(j)}_i = N^{(i)}_j$ for $1 \le j \le 2n$ and $1 \le i \le n$. Then Eq. (10) turns into one simple equation

$$(c_1 U^{(1)} + \cdots + c_{2n} U^{(2n)}) \cdot \mathbf{x}^\top = 0. \tag{11}$$

This equation indicates that as long as we have the set $\Psi = (U^{(1)}, \ldots, U^{(2n)})$, the decryption process of EFC_p can be reduced into the computation of the right kernel space of $c_1 U^{(1)} + \ldots + c_{2n} U^{(2n)}$.

Remark 2. Since in our new decryption algorithm, only the ciphertext $\mathbf{c}$ and $U^{(1)}, \ldots, U^{(2n)}$ are necessary, we intend to save $\Psi = (U^{(1)}, \ldots, U^{(2n)})$ as the new private key for EFC_p^-, which is $2n/7$ times larger than the original private key. The details for generating Ψ is shown in Algorithm 3.

Algorithm 3. New private key generation for EFC_p^-

Input : $\mathbf{b} = (\theta_1, \cdots, \theta_n)$, the private key $A, B, S \in \mathbb{F}^{n\times n}$ and $T \in \mathbb{F}^{2n\times 2n}$.
Output: New private key $\Psi = (U^{(i)}, \cdots, U^{(2n)}) \in (\mathbb{F}^{n\times n})^{2n}$.

$\Theta \leftarrow \mathbf{b}^\top \cdot \mathbf{b}$, $(\Theta_1, \ldots, \Theta_n) \leftarrow \varphi^{-1}(\Theta)$
$T_1 \leftarrow (T^{-1}_{[1,2n;1,n]})^\top \in \mathbb{F}^{n\times 2n}$, $T_2 \leftarrow (T^{-1}_{[1,2n;n+1,2n]})^\top \in \mathbb{F}^{n\times 2n}$
for $i \leftarrow 1$ **to** n **do**
  $N^{(i)} \leftarrow (SA\Theta_i T_2 - SB\Theta_i T_1)^\top \in \mathbb{F}^{2n\times n}$
for $j \leftarrow 1$ **to** $2n$ *and* $i \leftarrow 1$ **to** n **do**
  $U^{(j)}_i \leftarrow N^{(i)}_j$
Return $\Psi = (U^{(1)}, \ldots, U^{(2n)})$.

Now we explain our proposed decryption algorithm for EFC_p^-. First, we compute $L = \sum_{i=1}^{2n-a} c_i U^{(i)}$. Second, we guess the values for the deleted polynomials by π_a from $\mathbb{F}^a$, and denote these values by $\mathbf{v} = (v_1, \cdots, v_a)$. Next, we compute the right kernel space $\mathbf{ker} = \ker(L + \sum_{i=1}^{a} v_i U^{(2n-a+i)})$. Finally, we check if

Algorithm 4. Proposed decryption algorithm for EFC_p^-

Input : The new private key $\Psi = (U^{(1)}, \cdots, U^{(2n)}) \in (\mathbb{F}^{n \times n})^{2n}$, the public key $\mathcal{P}$, a ciphertext $\mathbf{c} = (c_1, \cdots, c_{2n-a}) \in \mathbb{F}^{2n-a}$.
Output: The plaintext $\mathbf{z} \in \mathbb{F}^n$ s.t. $\mathcal{P}(\mathbf{z}) = \mathbf{c}$.

1 $L \leftarrow \sum_{i=1}^{2n-a} c_i U^{(i)}$
2 **for** $\mathbf{v} = (v_1, \ldots, v_a) \in \mathbb{F}^a$ **do**
3 $\quad H \leftarrow L + \sum_{i=1}^{a} v_i U^{(2n-a+i)}$
4 $\quad$ **ker** $\leftarrow$ RightKer(H)
5 $\quad$ **for** $\mathbf{z} \in$ **ker do**
6 $\quad\quad$ **if** $\mathcal{P}(\mathbf{z}) = \mathbf{c}$ **then**
7 $\quad\quad\quad$ **Return z**
8 $\quad\quad\quad$ break

there exists $\mathbf{z} \in \mathbf{ker}$, such that $\mathcal{P}(\mathbf{z}) = \mathbf{c}$ holds. If so, then $\mathbf{z}$ is the plaintext, otherwise, go back to the guessing step and start over. The details of this decryption process is shown in Algorithm 4.

Regarding the complexity of the new decryption algorithm for EFC_p^-, we have the following proposition.

Proposition 2. *The number of field additions and multiplications involved in the new decryption for EFC_p^- are*

$$\begin{aligned} &2n^3 - (a+1)n^2 + \frac{q^a}{2}\left(\frac{7}{3}n^3 + \frac{1}{2}n^2 - \frac{17}{6}n\right) \text{ and} \\ &2n^3 - an^2 + \frac{q^a}{2}\left(\frac{7}{3}n^3 + 3n^2 - \left(a + \frac{1}{3}\right)n\right), \end{aligned} \tag{12}$$

respectively.

Proof. Let $[+]_{\mathbb{F}}$ denote $\mathbb{F}$-addition, and $[\times]_{\mathbb{F}}$ denote the $\mathbb{F}$-multiplication. We analyze the complexity based on Algorithm 4.

In step 1, $\sum_{i=1}^{2n-a} c_i U^{(i)}$ requires $n^2(2n-a-1)$ $[+]_{\mathbb{F}}$ and $n^2(2n-a)$ $[\times]_{\mathbb{F}}$.

From step 2 to 8, we enter a loop of size q^a. In step 3, $L + \sum_{i=1}^{a} v_i U^{(2n-a+i)}$ costs an^2 $[+]_{\mathbb{F}}$ and an^2 $[\times]_{\mathbb{F}}$. In step 4, finding the right kernel of H requires $\frac{n(n-1)(2n+5)}{6}$ $[+]_{\mathbb{F}}$ and $\frac{n(n^2+3n-1)}{3}$ $[\times]_{\mathbb{F}}$. In step 6, verifying the solution requires $(2n-a)(n^2-1)$ $[+]_{\mathbb{F}}$ and $(2n-a)(n^2+n)$ $[\times]_{\mathbb{F}}$. In step 8, the loop terminates after an average of $\frac{q^a}{2}$ times. Therefore, the loop requires $\frac{q^a}{2}(\frac{7}{3}n^3 + \frac{1}{2}n^2 - \frac{17}{6}n)$ $[+]_{\mathbb{F}}$ and $\frac{q^a}{2}(\frac{7}{3}n^3 + 3n^2 - (a+\frac{1}{3})n)$ $[\times]_{\mathbb{F}}$ in average.

Therefore, the total cost of this decryption algorithm is Eq. (12). This completes the proof. □

3.2 New Decryption Algorithm for $\text{EFC}_{pt^2}^-$

Same as EFC_p^-, the new decryption algorithm for $\text{EFC}_{pt^2}^-$ also derives from linearization equations. We first consider the new decryption algorithm for $\text{EFC}_{pt^2}^-$

without applying the minus modifier, i.e. EFC_{pt^2}. Recall in Sect. 2.3, inverting the central map of $\mathrm{EFC}_{pt^2}^-$ requires solving the linear system

$$\mathbf{d}_2\alpha_m(\mathbf{x}) - \mathbf{d}_1\beta_m(\mathbf{x}) = \mathbf{x}(A-B)\Lambda, \tag{13}$$

where $\Lambda \in \mathbb{F}^{n\times n}, \Lambda_i = \varphi^{-1}(\theta_i^4)$ for $1 \le i \le n$. Apply isomorphism φ to the both sides of Eq. (13), we have

$$\varphi(\mathbf{d}_2)\alpha(\mathbf{x}) - \varphi(\mathbf{d}_1)\beta(\mathbf{x}) = \varphi(\mathbf{x}(A-B)\Lambda). \tag{14}$$

Let $\Theta = \mathbf{b}^\top\mathbf{b}, (\Theta_1, \dots, \Theta_n) = \varphi^{-1}(\Theta)$, and apply φ^{-1} on both sides of Eq. (14). Then we have

$$\mathbf{x}A\Theta_i(0_n\ I_n)\mathbf{d}^\top - \mathbf{x}B\Theta_i(I_n\ 0_n)\mathbf{d}^\top - (\mathbf{x}(A-B)\Lambda)_i = 0,\ (1 \le i \le n), \tag{15}$$

which are the linearization equations for the central map of EFC_{pt^2}. Let $\mathbf{c} \in \mathbb{F}^{2n}$ be a ciphertext of EFC_{t^2}, then $\mathbf{c} = \mathcal{T}(\mathbf{d})$. Applying linear maps $\mathcal{S}$ and $\mathcal{T}$ on (15) gives us the linearization equations of a plaintext $\mathbf{x}$ and a ciphertext $\mathbf{c}$ for EFC_{pt^2},

$$\mathbf{x}SA\Theta_i(0_n\ I_n)(\mathbf{c}T^{-1})^\top - \mathbf{x}SB\Theta_i(I_n\ 0_n)(\mathbf{c}T^{-1})^\top - (\mathbf{x}S(A-B)\Lambda)_i = 0. \tag{16}$$

Next we show how to represent Eq. (16) into one simple equation. Let $T_1 = (T^{-1}_{[1,2n;1,n]})^\top \in \mathbb{F}^{n\times 2n}$, and $T_2 = (T^{-1}_{[1,2n;n+1,2n]})^\top \in \mathbb{F}^{n\times 2n}$. Applying T_1, T_2 on Eq. (16) yields

$$\mathbf{x}(SA\Theta_iT_2 - SB\Theta_iT_1)\mathbf{c}^\top - (\mathbf{x}S(A-B)\Lambda)_i,\ (1 \le i \le n). \tag{17}$$

Let $M = S(A-B)\Lambda \in \mathbb{F}^{n\times n}$, $N^{(i)} = (SA\Theta_iT_2 - SB\Theta_iT_1) \in \mathbb{F}^{n\times 2n}$, and define matrices $U^{(j)}$ by $U_i^{(j)} = N_j^{(i)}$ for $1 \le j \le 2n$ and $1 \le i \le n$. Then (17) can be rearranged into

$$(c_1U^{(1)} + \cdots + c_{2n}U^{(2n)} - M^\top)\cdot\mathbf{x}^\top = 0. \tag{18}$$

This equation indicates that the decryption of EFC_{pt^2} can be reduced to the computation of the right kernel space of $c_1U^{(1)} + \cdots + c_{2n}U^{(2n)} - M^\top$.

Remark 3. Similar to EFC_p^-, we save $\Psi = (U^{(1)}, \dots, U^{(2n)}, M)$ as the new private key for $\mathrm{EFC}_{pt^2}^-$, which is $(2n+1)/7$ times larger than the original private key. The details for generating Ψ is shown in Algorithm 5.

Now we explain the new decryption algorithm for $\mathrm{EFC}_{pt^2}^-$. First, we compute $L = (\sum_{i=1}^{2n-a} c_iU^{(i)} - M^\top) \in \mathbb{F}^{n\times n}$. Second, we guess the values of the deleted polynomials by π_a, denote them by $\mathbf{v} = (v_1, \dots, v_a) \in \mathbb{F}^a$. Then we compute the right kernel $\mathbf{ker} = \ker(L + \sum_{i=1}^{a} v_iU^{(2n-a+i)})$. Finally, we check if there exists $\mathbf{z} \in \mathbf{ker}$, such that $\mathcal{P}(\mathbf{z}) = \mathbf{c}$ holds. If so, then $\mathbf{z}$ is the plaintext. Otherwise, go back to the guessing step and start over. The details of this algorithm is shown in Algorithm 6.

Algorithm 5. New private key generation for $\text{EFC}^-_{pt^2}$

Input : $\mathbf{b} = (\theta_1, \cdots, \theta_n)$, the private key $A, B, S \in \mathbb{F}^{n\times n}$ and $T \in \mathbb{F}^{2n\times 2n}$.
Output: New private key $\Psi = (U^{(i)}, \cdots, U^{(2n)}, M) \in (\mathbb{F}^{n\times n})^{2n+1}$.

```
Θ ← b^⊤ · b, (Θ_1, ..., Θ_n) ← φ^{-1}(Θ)
T_1 ← (T^{-1}_{[1,2n;1,n]})^⊤ ∈ F^{n×2n}, T_2 ← (T^{-1}_{[1,2n;n+1,2n]})^⊤ ∈ F^{n×2n}
Define Λ ∈ F^{n×n}, where Λ_i = φ^{-1}(θ_i^4)
M ← S(A − B)Λ
for i ← 1 to n do
    N^{(i)} ← (SAΘ_i T_2 − SBΘ_i T_1)^⊤ ∈ F^{2n×n}
for j ← 1 to 2n and i ← 1 to n do
    U_i^{(j)} ← N_j^{(i)}
Return Ψ = (U^{(1)}, ..., U^{(2n)}, M)
```

Algorithm 6. New decryption algorithm for $\text{EFC}^-_{pt^2}$

Input : The new private key $\Psi = (U^{(1)}, \cdots, U^{(2n)}, M) \in (\mathbb{F}^{n\times n})^{2n+1}$, the public key $\mathcal{P}$, a ciphertext $\mathbf{c} = (c_1, \cdots, c_{2n-a}) \in \mathbb{F}^{2n-a}$.
Output: The plaintext $\mathbf{z} \in \mathbb{F}^n$ s.t. $\mathcal{P}(\mathbf{z}) = \mathbf{c}$.

```
L ← Σ_{i=1}^{2n−a} c_i U^{(i)} − M^⊤
for v = (v_1, ..., v_a) ∈ F^a do
    H ← L + Σ_{i=1}^{a} v_i U^{(2n−a+i)};
    ker ← RightKer(H)
    for z ∈ ker do
        if P(z) = c then
            Return z
            break
```

We can analyze the complexity of the decryption algorithm for EFC_{pt^2} using the same approach as in the proof of Proposition 2. The number of $\mathbb{F}$-additions and $\mathbb{F}$-multiplications involved in the new decryption algorithm for $\text{EFC}^-_{pt^2}$ are

$$\begin{aligned} &2n^3 - an^2 + \frac{q^a}{2}(\frac{7}{3}n^3 + \frac{1}{2}n^2 - \frac{17}{6}n) \text{ and} \\ &2n^3 - an^2 + \frac{q^a}{2}(\frac{7}{3}n^3 + 3n^2 - (a + \frac{1}{3})n), \end{aligned} \tag{19}$$

respectively.

3.3 Implementation and Comparison

We compare the new and the original decryption algorithms under estimated 128-bit security parameter for EFC^-_p and $\text{EFC}^-_{pt^2}$. We counted the number of field additions ($[+]_\mathbb{F}$) and multiplications ($[\times]_\mathbb{F}$) involved in EFC^-_p and $\text{EFC}^-_{pt^2}$

for both original and our new decryption algorithms in (2), (7), (12) and (19). Since for $q = 2$, $[+]_{\mathbb{F}}$ is equivalent to one logical XOR operation, and $[\times]_{\mathbb{F}}$ is equivalent to one logical AND operation, we can regard the complexity of all decryption algorithms as the summation of number of $\mathbb{F}$-additions and $\mathbb{F}$-multiplications. Therefore, under 128-bit security parameter, we conclude that theoretically our new decryption algorithms are 3.4 times faster for EFC_p^- and 8.5 times faster for $\text{EFC}_{pt^2}^-$ than the original decryption algorithms. In practice, shown by our implementation on a 2.6 GHz Intel® Core™ i5-4300U CPU with Magma (version 2.22-7) (see Table 1), our decryption algorithms are 6.0 and 5.3 times faster than the original ones for EFC_p^- and $\text{EFC}_{pt^2}^-$, respectively.

Since the public keys for EFC_p^- and $\text{EFC}_{pt^2}^-$ remain the same using our proposed decryption algorithms, their security also remains the same. As for the private key, to match with our proposed decryption algorithms, we use new private keys, which is $2n/7$ times larger for EFC_p^-, and $(2n+1)/7$ times larger for $\text{EFC}_{pt^2}^-$ compared to the original private keys.

Table 1. Timing comparison between original EFC_p^-, $\text{EFC}_{pt^2}^-$ with new EFC_p^-, $\text{EFC}_{pt^2}^-$ under 128-bit security parameter

	Scheme (q, n, a)	KeyGen.(s)	Enc.(s)	Dec.(s)	$\#[+]_{\mathbb{F}} + \#[\times]_{\mathbb{F}}$[a] in decryption
Original	$\text{EFC}_p^-(2, 467, 10)$	6.200	0.007	4.769	8.34×10^{11}
	$\text{EFC}_{pt^2}^-(2, 467, 8)$	6.860	0.007	1.180	5.22×10^{11}
New	$\text{EFC}_p^-(2, 467, 10)$	6.140	0.007	0.789	2.44×10^{11}
	$\text{EFC}_{pt^2}^-(2, 467, 8)$	6.660	0.007	0.223	0.61×10^{11}

[a]Summation of number of $\mathbb{F}$-additions and $\mathbb{F}$-multiplications

4 Conclusion

Extension Field Cancellation, as a new type of trapdoor for constructing multivariate encryption schemes, is one of the few trapdoors that remains secure. Two encryption schemes, EFC_p^- and $\text{EFC}_{pt^2}^-$ were proposed along with this trapdoor. We focus on their efficiency in this paper, and propose new decryption algorithms for them, that manage to theoretically speed up the decryption processes of EFC_p^- and $\text{EFC}_{pt^2}^-$ by 3.4 and 8.5 times, respectively, under our estimated 128-bit security parameters. Our implementation of EFC_p^- and $\text{EFC}_{pt^2}^-$ under 128-bit parameter approximately matches this estimation. Meanwhile, our algorithms do not change their public keys, which indicates their security remain the same. In addition, our decryption algorithms are used coupling with our new designed private keys for EFC_p^- and $\text{EFC}_{pt^2}^-$. The new private keys are $2n/7$ and $(2n+1)/7$ times larger for EFC_p^- and $\text{EFC}_{pt^2}^-$ than their original private keys respectively. Considering the size of the private key is not a crucial factor for the performance of public key cryptography, and the combination of our new algorithms and new private keys simplifies the decryption processes of EFC_p^-

and $EFC^{-}_{pt^2}$ drastically, our proposed decryption algorithms are indeed more efficient.

Acknowledgments. The second and fourth authors were supported by JST CREST (Grant Number JPMJCR14D6). The third author thanks the Japanese Society for the Promotion of Science (JSPS) for financial support under grant KAKENHI 16K17644 and KAKENHI 15H03613.

References

1. Bogdanov, A., Eisenbarth, T., Rupp, A., Wolf, C.: Time-area optimized public-key engines: $\mathcal{MQ}$-cryptosystems as replacement for elliptic curves? In: Oswald, E., Rohatgi, P. (eds.) CHES 2008. LNCS, vol. 5154, pp. 45–61. Springer, Heidelberg (2008). https://doi.org/10.1007/978-3-540-85053-3_4
2. Chen, A.I.-T., Chen, M.-S., Chen, T.-R., Cheng, C.-M., Ding, J., Kuo, E.L.-H., Lee, F.Y.-S., Yang, B.-Y.: SSE implementation of multivariate PKCs on modern x86 CPUs. In: Clavier, C., Gaj, K. (eds.) CHES 2009. LNCS, vol. 5747, pp. 33–48. Springer, Heidelberg (2009). https://doi.org/10.1007/978-3-642-04138-9_3
3. Coppersmith, D., Stern, J., Vaudenay, S.: Attacks on the birational permutation signature schemes. In: Stinson, D.R. (ed.) CRYPTO 1993. LNCS, vol. 773, pp. 435–443. Springer, Heidelberg (1994). https://doi.org/10.1007/3-540-48329-2_37
4. Czypek, P., Heyse, S., Thomae, E.: Efficient implementations of MQPKS on constrained devices. In: Prouff, E., Schaumont, P. (eds.) CHES 2012. LNCS, vol. 7428, pp. 374–389. Springer, Heidelberg (2012). https://doi.org/10.1007/978-3-642-33027-8_22
5. Ding, J., Schmidt, D.: Rainbow, a new multivariable polynomial signature scheme. In: Ioannidis, J., Keromytis, A., Yung, M. (eds.) ACNS 2005. LNCS, vol. 3531, pp. 164–175. Springer, Heidelberg (2005). https://doi.org/10.1007/11496137_12
6. Goodn, D.: NSA preps quantum-resistant algorithms to head off cryptoapocalypse (2015)
7. Goubin, L., Courtois, N.T.: Cryptanalysis of the TTM cryptosystem. In: Okamoto, T. (ed.) ASIACRYPT 2000. LNCS, vol. 1976, pp. 44–57. Springer, Heidelberg (2000). https://doi.org/10.1007/3-540-44448-3_4
8. Kipnis, A., Patarin, J., Goubin, L.: Unbalanced oil and vinegar signature schemes. In: Stern, J. (ed.) EUROCRYPT 1999. LNCS, vol. 1592, pp. 206–222. Springer, Heidelberg (1999). https://doi.org/10.1007/3-540-48910-X_15
9. Koblitz, N.: Elliptic curve cryptosystems. Math. Comput. **48**, 203–209 (1987)
10. Matsumoto, T., Imai, H.: Public quadratic polynomial-tuples for efficient signature-verification and message-encryption. In: Barstow, D., et al. (eds.) EUROCRYPT 1988. LNCS, vol. 330, pp. 419–453. Springer, Heidelberg (1988). https://doi.org/10.1007/3-540-45961-8_39
11. National Institute of Standards and Technology. Call for proposals (2017). https://csrc.nist.gov/projects/post-quantum-cryptography. Accessed 18 Apr 2018
12. Patarin, J.: Cryptanalysis of the matsumoto and imai public key scheme of Eurocrypt'88. In: Coppersmith, D. (ed.) CRYPTO 1995. LNCS, vol. 963, pp. 248–261. Springer, Heidelberg (1995). https://doi.org/10.1007/3-540-44750-4_20
13. Patarin, J.: Hidden fields equations (HFE) and isomorphisms of polynomials (IP): two new families of asymmetric algorithms. In: Maurer, U. (ed.) EUROCRYPT 1996. LNCS, vol. 1070, pp. 33–48. Springer, Heidelberg (1996). https://doi.org/10.1007/3-540-68339-9_4

14. Porras, J., Baena, J., Ding, J.: ZHFE, a new multivariate public key encryption scheme. In: Mosca, M. (ed.) PQCrypto 2014. LNCS, vol. 8772, pp. 229–245. Springer, Cham (2014). https://doi.org/10.1007/978-3-319-11659-4_14
15. Garey, M.R., Johnson, D.S.: Computers and Intractability: A Guide to the Theory of NP-Completeness. W. H. Freeman, New York (1979)
16. Rivest, R.L., Shamir, A., Adleman, L.: A method for obtaining digital signatures and public-key cryptosystems. Commun. ACM **21**(2), 120–126 (1978)
17. Shor, P.: Polynomial-time algorithms for prime factorization and discrete logarithms on a quantum computer. SIAM J. Comput. **26**(5), 1484–1509 (1997)
18. Szepieniec, A., Ding, J., Preneel, B.: Extension field cancellation: a new central trapdoor for multivariate quadratic systems. In: Takagi, T. (ed.) PQCrypto 2016. LNCS, vol. 9606, pp. 182–196. Springer, Cham (2016). https://doi.org/10.1007/978-3-319-29360-8_12
19. Tang, S., Yi, H., Ding, J., Chen, H., Chen, G.: High-speed hardware implementation of rainbow signature on FPGAs. In: Yang, B.-Y. (ed.) PQCrypto 2011. LNCS, vol. 7071, pp. 228–243. Springer, Heidelberg (2011). https://doi.org/10.1007/978-3-642-25405-5_15
20. Tao, C., Diene, A., Tang, S., Ding, J.: Simple matrix scheme for encryption. In: Gaborit, P. (ed.) PQCrypto 2013. LNCS, vol. 7932, pp. 231–242. Springer, Heidelberg (2013). https://doi.org/10.1007/978-3-642-38616-9_16
21. Yasuda, T., Dahan, X., Huang, Y.J., Takagi, T., Sakurai, K.: MQ challenge: hardness evaluation of solving multivariate quadratic problems. Cryptology ePrint Archive: Report 2015/275 (2015)
22. Yasuda, T., Sakurai, K.: A multivariate encryption scheme with rainbow. In: Qing, S., Okamoto, E., Kim, K., Liu, D. (eds.) ICICS 2015. LNCS, vol. 9543, pp. 236–251. Springer, Cham (2016). https://doi.org/10.1007/978-3-319-29814-6_19

Lattice-Based Universal Accumulator with Nonmembership Arguments

Zuoxia Yu[1], Man Ho Au[1(✉)], Rupeng Yang[1,2], Junzuo Lai[3,4], and Qiuliang Xu[2]

[1] Department of Computing, The Hong Kong Polytechnic University, Hong Kong, China
zuoxia.yu@gmail.com, csallen@comp.polyu.edu.hk

[2] School of Computer Science and Technology, Shandong University, Jinan, China
orbbyrp@gmail.com, xql@sdu.edu.cn

[3] College of Information Science and Technology, Jinan University, Guangzhou, China
laijunzuo@gmail.com

[4] State Key Laboratory of Cryptology, Beijing, China

Abstract. Universal accumulator provides a way to accumulate a set of elements into one. For each element accumulated, it can provide a short membership (resp. nonmembership) witness to attest the fact that the element has been (resp. has not been) accumulated. When combined with a suitable zero-knowledge proof system, it can be used to construct many privacy-preserving applications. However, existing universal accumulators are usually based on non-standard assumptions, e.g., the Strong RSA assumption and the Strong Diffie-Hellman assumptions, and are not secure against quantum attacks. In this paper, we propose the first lattice-based universal accumulator from standard lattice-based assumptions. The starting point of our work is the lattice-based accumulator with Merkle-tree structure proposed by Libert et al. (Eurocrypt'16). We present a novel method to generate short witnesses for non-accumulated members in a Merkle-tree, and give the construction of universal accumulator. Besides, we also propose the first zero-knowledge arguments to prove the possession of the nonmembership witness of a non-accumulated value in the lattice-based setting via the abstract Stern's protocol of Libert et al. (Asiacrypt'17). Moreover, our proposed universal accumulator can be used to construct many privacy-preserving cryptographic primitives, such as group signature and anonymous credential.

Keywords: Lattice-based universal accumulator
Zero-knowledge arguments of nonmembership
Abstract stern-like protocol

1 Introduction

Introduced by Benaloh and de Mare [6], cryptographic accumulator provides a way to combine a set of values into one, and simultaneously offers a short

W. Susilo and G. Yang (Eds.): ACISP 2018, LNCS 10946, pp. 502–519, 2018.
https://doi.org/10.1007/978-3-319-93638-3_29

witness for a given value which is accumulated. Since its introduction, accumulator has found many applications, including time-stamping [6], membership testing [6,22], anonymous credential [1,10,11,22,27], group signature [22,25,37], ring signature [25], fail-stop signature [4], anonymous authentication [15], digital cash [3,12,33,35], anonymous attestation [22], certificate revocation [19], etc.

Subsequently, many extensions have been introduced. Among them, Camenisch and Lysyanskaya [11] introduce the notion of dynamic accumulator which allows one to dynamically add and delete a value to and from the accumulator in a way that witnesses of existing elements can be updated efficiently. Later, Li et al. [22] propose universal accumulator which can also provide nonmembership proof for an element which is not accumulated. Compared with dynamic accumulator presented in [11], universal accumulator additionally provides efficient nonmembership proof, but it does not allow values to be added to and deleted from the accumulator dynamically. Despite lacking the functionality of dynamical update, universal accumulator is preferable in cases where nonmembership witness is desirable, as in the following example.

Suppose there is an online forum, where only legitimate users can post messages. Once a current legitimate user misbehaves, the forum manager can flag this user with a label "malicious" and forbid his or her right to post for a while, such as one day. To do this, the forum manager can maintain a list of malicious users, and update it every day. Certainly, registration before the first access of each user is needed. Then for any user who wish to post a message on this forum, besides proof of membership, he or she also needs to provide proof that he/she is not on the list of malicious users.

However, until now, the realizations of universal accumulator are mainly based on two types of non-standard number theoretic assumptions. The first type [22] relies on the group of hidden order, such as Strong RSA assumption. The schemes based on this assumption usually have short public parameter but only permit primes to be accumulated. The second type [2,13] bases on bilinear map assumptions, including Strong Diffie-Hellman assumption. While there exists some hash-based constructions of universal accumulator [7–9], the adoption of hash tree structure made them hardly compatible with efficient zero-knowledge proof. Without a suitable zero-knowledge proof for proving various facts about the accumulated values, they would not be as useful as the aforementioned accumulators.

To the best of our knowledge, there is no construction of lattice-based universal accumulator. As lattice-based cryptography is promising in the post-quantum era due to its attractive properties including strong security from the worst-case hard problem, presumed resistance to quantum attacks [34], we design a lattice-based construction of universal accumulator with compatible zero-knowledge proofs.

1.1 Our Contribution

The contribution of this work can be summarized as follows:

- *The first construction of lattice-based universal accumulator.* We propose the first lattice-based universal accumulator, which can provide a short witness for an accumulated value and a short witness for a non-accumulated value.
- *The first zero-knowledge arguments of nonmembership in the lattice-based setting.* We introduce zero-knowledge arguments of knowledge (ZKAoK) for proving the possession of the nonmembership witness of a non-accumulated value.

Overview of Our Idea. Our Merkle-tree based accumulator considered accumulated set which is sorted. Then for any value not in the accumulated set, it must belong to an open interval formed by two adjacent values in the set. Then we pick the sibling paths of the two sibling leaves (denoting the two interval boundary values) to the root in the tree to be witness. In order to show that a given value is not accumulated, we need to prove two things in zero-knowledge: (1) the given value is between two sibling leaves in the witness; (2) the knowledge of a hash chain (via the method introduced in [25]). While the above approach appears to be very similar to the lattice-based Merkle-tree accumulator [25], the construction of the Merkle-tree in our paper is different to prevent revealing relationships between the given nonmember value and member values.

1.2 Related Work

Lattice-Based Cryptographic Accumulator. Libert et al. [25] propose the first Merkle-tree based accumulator with efficient zero-knowledge argument of membership from standard lattice assumption. Recently, Ling et al. [30] introduce a lattice-based dynamic accumulator on Merkle-tree structure.

Lattice-Based Zero-Knowledge Proofs. Many zero-knowledge proofs systems suitable for the lattice-related language have been designed based on Schnorr-like approach [31,32] and Stern-like approach [23,25,28].

Despite being less efficient, the Stern-like approach results in protocol featuring perfect completeness and allows extraction of witnesses satisfying the original constraints. It is originally presented in [36] and first introduced into the lattice-based setting by Kawachi et al. in [20]. The original version can only give proofs for the binary vectors with fixed hamming weight. This restriction is later loosened by Ling et al. [28] who construct a statistical zero-knowledge proof of knowledge for any vector $\mathbf{x}$ whose infinity norm is less than β and satisfies the form $\mathbf{P} \cdot \mathbf{x} = \mathbf{v} \bmod p$ via the proposed decomposition-extension technique. To support more advanced relations, extensive works have been done [21,23–25,29]. In particular, Libert et al. [25] introduce a method to prove the knowledge of a hash chain in a tree from the secret leaf to the public root in a zero-knowledge way. Some works [23,26] are also done for the utilization of the Stern's protocol in an abstract and generalized manner.

1.3 Organization of This Work

In Sect. 2, we give the preliminaries needed in this paper. Our construction of universal accumulator as well as the corresponding ZKAoK are given in Sect. 3.

In Sect. 4, we introduce an application of our universal accumulator, namely, a fully dynamic group signature scheme.

2 Preliminaries

Notations. Throughout this paper, we will use bold lower-case letters (e.g. $\mathbf{v}$) to denote vectors, and use bold upper-case letters (e.g. $\mathbf{A}$) to denote matrices. All vectors in this paper are column vectors. All elements in vectors and matrices are integers unless otherwise stated. For a vector $\mathbf{v}$ of length n, we use $\|\mathbf{v}\|_1$ to denote the 1 norm of $\mathbf{v}$, and we use $\mathbf{v}[i]$ to denote the ith element of $\mathbf{v}$ where $i \in [0, n-1]$. For a bit b, we use $\bar{b}$ to denote the negation of b. Let $\mathcal{S}$ be a finite set, then we use $s \xleftarrow{\$} \mathcal{S}$ to denote sampling element s uniformly from set $\mathcal{S}$. Also, for a distribution $\mathcal{D}$, we use $d \leftarrow \mathcal{D}$ to denote sampling d according to $\mathcal{D}$. We write $negl(\cdot)$ to denote a negligible function. Let $\mathcal{R}$ be a binary relation, we use $\mathcal{L}_{\mathcal{R}}$ to denote the language characterized by $\mathcal{R}$.

2.1 Cryptographic Assumption

Definition 1 (SIS [17]). *The* $\mathsf{SIS}^{\infty}_{n,m,q,\beta}$ *problem is defined as follows: given uniformly random matrix* $\mathbf{A} \in Z_q^{n \times m}$, *find a non-zero vector* $\mathbf{x} \in Z^m$ *such that* $||\mathbf{x}||_\infty \leq \beta$ *and* $\mathbf{A} \cdot \mathbf{x} = 0 \bmod q$.

If $m, \beta = poly(n)$, and $q \geq \beta \cdot \tilde{\mathcal{O}}(\sqrt{n})$, then $\mathsf{SIS}^{\infty}_{n,m,q,\beta}$ problem is at least as hard as the worst-case lattice problem SIVP_γ for some $\gamma = \beta \cdot \tilde{\mathcal{O}}(\sqrt{nm})$ [17]. In particular, the $\mathsf{SIS}^{\infty}_{n,m,q,1}$ problem is at least as hard as $\mathsf{SIVP}_{\tilde{\mathcal{O}}(n)}$, when $\beta = 1$, $q = \tilde{\mathcal{O}}(n)$, $m = 2n\lceil \log q \rceil$ [25].

2.2 Universal Accumulator

Universal accumulator is first proposed in [22] and formalized by [14]. In this paper, we recall the scheme without trapdoor, and use $\mathsf{type} \in \{0,1\}$ to indicate whether the given witness is a membership ($\mathsf{type} = 0$) or nonmembership ($\mathsf{type} = 1$) witness. The universal accumulator is defined as follows:

$\mathsf{Setup}(n) \rightarrow pp$. The algorithm takes as input a security parameter n, outputs the public parameter pp.

$\mathsf{Acc}_{pp}(R) \rightarrow \mathbf{u}$. On input an accumulated set $R = \{\mathbf{d}_0, \mathbf{d}_1, \ldots, \mathbf{d}_{N-1}\}$ with size N, the algorithm outputs the accumulator value $\mathbf{u}$.

$\mathsf{Witness}_{pp}(\mathbf{d}, R, \mathsf{type}) \rightarrow w$ or $\perp$. The algorithm outputs a type of witness w for $\mathbf{d}$ according to the value of type. It outputs $\perp$ if $\mathbf{d} \notin R \wedge \mathsf{type} = 0$ or $\mathbf{d} \in R \wedge \mathsf{type} = 1$.

$\mathsf{Verify}_{pp}(\mathbf{d}, \mathbf{u}, w, \mathsf{type}) \rightarrow 0$ or 1. The algorithm outputs 1 if the following two cases happen:

1. If $\mathsf{type} = 0$, and w is a witness for $\mathbf{d} \in R$;
2. If $\mathsf{type} = 1$, and w is a witness for $\mathbf{d} \notin R$.

Otherwise, output 0.

Correctness. The correctness requires that for all $pp \leftarrow \textsf{NM-Setup}(n)$, the following equations hold:

1. for all $\mathbf{d} \in R$, $\textsf{Verify}_{pp}(\mathbf{d}, \textsf{Acc}_{pp}(R), \textsf{Witness}_{pp}(\mathbf{d}, R, 0), 0) = 1$;
2. for all $\mathbf{d} \notin R$, $\textsf{Verify}_{pp}(\mathbf{d}, \textsf{Acc}_{pp}(R), \textsf{Witness}_{pp}(\mathbf{d}, R, 1), 1) = 1$.

Security Definition. A universal accumulator scheme defined above is secure if for all probabilistic polynomial-time adversary $\mathcal{A}$, the following equation hold:

$$Pr\left[\begin{array}{c} pp \leftarrow \textsf{NM-Setup}(n); (R, \mathbf{d}^*, \mathbf{w}^*, \textsf{type}) \leftarrow \mathcal{A}(pp): \\ \mathbf{d}^* \in R \wedge \textsf{Verify}_{pp}(\mathbf{d}^*, \textsf{Acc}_{pp}(R), \mathbf{w}^*, \textsf{type} = 1) = 1 \\ or \\ \mathbf{d}^* \notin R \wedge \textsf{Verify}_{pp}(\mathbf{d}^*, \textsf{Acc}_{pp}(R), \mathbf{w}^*, \textsf{type} = 0) = 1 \end{array}\right] = negl(n),$$

where $negl(n)$ is a negligible function about n. In other words, the security says that it is computationally infeasible to prove that a value d^* is not accumulated in the value $\mathbf{u}$ if it is or a value d^* is accumulated in the value $\mathbf{u}$ if it is not.

2.3 Abstract Stern's Protocol

Abstract Stern's protocol [26] is a type of ZKAoK system (description given in Appendix A) capturing the following relations. Let n_i and $d_i \geq n_i$ be positive integers. For public matrices $\{\mathbf{P}_i \in Z_{q_i}^{n_i \times d_i}\}_{i \in [1,n]}$, and vectors $\mathbf{v}_i \in Z_{q_i}^{n_i}$, the prover argues in zero-knowledge the possession of mutually related integer vectors $\{\mathbf{x}_i \in \{-1,0,1\}^{d_i}\}_{i \in [1,n]}$ such that:

$$\forall i \in [1,n] : \mathbf{P}_i \cdot \mathbf{x}_i = \mathbf{v}_i \bmod q_i.$$

Let $d = d_1 + d_2 + \ldots + d_n$, and $\mathbf{x} = (\mathbf{x}_1 || \mathbf{x}_2 || \ldots || \mathbf{x}_n)$. Assume VALID is a subset of $\{-1,0,1\}^d$, and S be a finite set such that one can associate every $\pi \in S$ with a permutation T_π of d elements which satisfies the conditions (1), then we can get Lemma 1.

$$\begin{cases} \mathbf{x} \in \textsf{VALID} \Longleftrightarrow T_\pi(\mathbf{x}) \in \textsf{VALID}; \\ \textit{If } \mathbf{x} \in \textsf{VALID} \textit{ and } \pi \textit{ is uniform in } S, \textit{ then } T_\pi(\mathbf{x}) \textit{ is uniform in } \textsf{VALID}. \end{cases} \quad (1)$$

Lemma 1 (Theorem 1 in [26]). *The constructed abstract Stern's protocol shown in Fig. 1 is a statistical* ZKAoK *with perfect completeness, soundness error* 2/3*, and communication cost* $\mathcal{O}(\Sigma_{i=1}^n d_i \cdot \log q_i)$*. In particular:*

- *There exists an efficient simulator that, on input* $\{\mathbf{P}_i, \mathbf{v}_i\}_{i \in [1,n]}$*, outputs an accepted transcript which is statistically close to that produced by the real prover.*
- *There exists an efficient knowledge extractor that, on input a commitment CMT and 3 valid response (*RSP_1*,* RSP_2*,* RSP_3*) to all 3 possible values of the challenger Ch, outputs* $\mathbf{x}' = (\mathbf{x}'_1, \cdots, \mathbf{x}'_n) \in \textsf{VALID}$ *such that* $\mathbf{P}_i \cdot \mathbf{x}'_i = \mathbf{v}_i \bmod q_i$ *for all* $i \in [1,n]$.

1. **Commitment:** Prover P sample $\pi \xleftarrow{\$} S$, $\mathbf{r}_1 \xleftarrow{\$} Z_{q_1}^{d_1}, \ldots, \mathbf{r}_n \xleftarrow{\$} Z_{q_n}^{d_n}$, and computes $\mathbf{r} = (\mathbf{r}_1 \| \ldots \| \mathbf{r}_n)$, $\mathbf{z} = \mathbf{x} \boxplus \mathbf{r}$. Then P samples ρ_1, ρ_2, ρ_3 for commitment COM, then computes and sends $\mathsf{CMT} = \{C_1, C_2, C_3\}$ to verifier V, where

$$C_1 = \mathsf{COM}(\pi, \{\mathbf{P}_i \cdot \mathbf{r}_i \bmod q_i\}_{i\in[1,n]}; \rho_1)$$
$$C_2 = \mathsf{COM}(T_\pi(\mathbf{r}); \rho_2)$$
$$C_3 = \mathsf{COM}(T_\pi(\mathbf{z}); \rho_3).$$

2. **Challenge:** Verifier V picks a uniformly random challenge $Ch \xleftarrow{\$} \{1, 2, 3\}$, and sends it to P.
3. **Response:** According to the Ch, P reveals different commitments via sending RSP in the following way:
   - $Ch = 1$: let $t_x = T_\pi(\mathbf{x})$, $t_r = T_\pi(\mathbf{r})$, RSP $= (t_x, t_r, \rho_2, \rho_3)$.
   - $Ch = 2$: let $\pi_2 = \pi$, $\mathbf{w} = \mathbf{z}$, RSP $= (\pi_2, \mathbf{w}, \rho_1, \rho_3)$.
   - $Ch = 3$: let $\pi_3 = \pi$, RSP $= (\pi_3, \mathbf{r}, \rho_1, \rho_2)$.

Verification: Once receiving RSP, verifier V checks as follows:

- $Ch = 1$: check that t_x is VALID, $C_2 = \mathsf{COM}(t_r; \rho_2)$, $C_3 = \mathsf{COM}(t_x \boxplus t_r; \rho_3)$.
- $Ch = 2$: parse $\mathbf{w} = (\mathbf{w}_1 \| \ldots \| \mathbf{w}_n)$, where $\mathbf{w}_i \in Z_{q_i}^{d_i}$ for all $i \in [1, n]$, then check that $C_1 = \mathsf{COM}(\pi_2, \{\mathbf{P}_i \cdot \mathbf{w}_i - \mathbf{v}_i \bmod q_i\}_{i\in[1,n]}; \rho_1)$, and $C_3 = \mathsf{COM}(T_{\pi_2}(\mathbf{w}); \rho_3)$.
- $Ch = 3$: parse $\mathbf{r} = (\mathbf{r}_1 \| \ldots \| \mathbf{r}_n)$, then check that $C_1 = \mathsf{COM}(\pi_3, \{\mathbf{P}_i \cdot \mathbf{r}_i \bmod q_i\}_{i\in[1,n]}; \rho_1)$, and $C_2 = \mathsf{COM}(T_{\pi_3}(\mathbf{r}); \rho_2)$.

In each case, V outputs 1 if and only if all conditions hold.

Fig. 1. Abstract Stern's protocol. COM denotes the statistically hiding and computationally binding string commitment scheme in [20]. '$\boxplus$' is the modular addition operator, such that $\mathbf{z} = ((\mathbf{x}_1 \boxplus \mathbf{r}_1) \bmod q_1) \| \ldots \| (\mathbf{x}_n \boxplus \mathbf{r}_n) \bmod q_n))$.

Therefore, to employ the abstract Stern's protocol to prove a statement, one needs to first transform the statement into the form of $\mathbf{P}_i \cdot \mathbf{x}_i = \mathbf{v}_i \bmod q_i$ with a specifically designed witness set VALID, then specify the set S and permutations of d elements $\{T_\pi, \pi \in S\}$ which can make conditions (1) hold. In this way, a ZKAoK can be constructed via the framework of abstract Stern's protocol.

3 Lattice-Based Universal Accumulator

In this section, we present our construction of a universal accumulator, that is, an accumulator with membership and nonmemberhship proof. Our starting point is the accumulator from Libert et al. [25]. Here we show how to create nonmembership proof. For completeness, we separate the part of accumulator for nonmembership from universal accumulator, and give its definition in Appendix B.

Throughout this section, we work with these positive integers, n, q, k, and m, where n is used as security parameter, q is $\tilde{\mathcal{O}}(n^{1.5})$, $k = \lceil \log q \rceil$, and $m = 2nk$.

Besides, for any vector $\mathbf{v} \in Z_q^n$, and its **binary representation** $\mathsf{bin}(\mathbf{v}) \in \{0,1\}^{nk}$, we have $\mathbf{G} \cdot \mathsf{bin}(\mathbf{v}) = \mathbf{v}$, where matrix $\mathbf{G}$ is defined as follows:

$$\mathbf{G} = \begin{Bmatrix} 1\ 2\ 2^2 \ldots\ 2^{k-1} & & & \\ & 1\ 2\ 2^2 \ldots\ 2^{k-1} & & \\ & & \ddots & \\ & & & 1\ 2\ 2^2 \ldots 2^{k-1} \end{Bmatrix} \in Z_q^{n \times nk}.$$

In order to assign a unique value for each binary vector with length nk, we define the notion of **integer value**. The **integer value** $\mathsf{Int}(\mathbf{v})$ of a binary vector $\mathsf{bin}(\mathbf{v}) \in \{0,1\}^{nk}$ is computed as

$$\mathsf{Int}(\mathbf{v}) = (1\ 2\ 2^2\ 2^3\ \ldots 2^{(nk-1)}) \cdot \mathsf{bin}(\mathbf{v}),$$

where we label $(1\ 2\ 2^2\ 2^3\ \ \ldots 2^{(nk-1)})$ as $\mathbf{G}'$ in the following contents.

3.1 Our Construction of Accumulator for Nonmembership

In this section, we give our solution for nonmembership via constructing a Merkle-tree with $2^{\ell+1}$ leaves, where ℓ is a positive integer. Similar to [25], our Merkle-tree is based on a family of lattice-based collision-resilient hash function $\mathcal{H} = \{h_{\mathbf{A}} | \mathbf{A} = [\mathbf{A}_0 || \mathbf{A}_1], \mathbf{A}_0, \mathbf{A}_1 \in Z_q^{n \times nk}\}$, mapping from $\{0,1\}^{nk} \times \{0,1\}^{nk}$ to $\{0,1\}^{nk}$. For any $(\mathbf{u}_0, \mathbf{u}_1) \in \{0,1\}^{nk} \times \{0,1\}^{nk}$, $h_{\mathbf{A}}(\mathbf{u}_0, \mathbf{u}_1) = \mathsf{bin}(\mathbf{A}_0 \cdot \mathbf{u}_0 + \mathbf{A}_1 \cdot \mathbf{u}_1 \bmod q) \in \{0,1\}^{nk}$.

Our construction of accumulator for nonmembership consists of four algorithms. Besides, for any input accumulated set S with size $N = 2^\ell - 1$, two auxiliary nodes are additionally chosen, denoted as $\mathbf{F}_{irst}$ and $\mathbf{L}_{ast}$.

NM-Setup(n). Pick $\mathbf{A} \xleftarrow{\$} Z_q^{n \times m}$, $\mathbf{F}_{irst} = \mathbf{0}^{nk}$, and $\mathbf{L}_{ast} = \mathbf{1}^{nk}$. Then output $pp = \{\mathbf{A}, \mathbf{F}_{irst}, \mathbf{L}_{ast}\}$.

NM-Acc$_{pp}$(S). The algorithm takes input an accumulated set $S = \{\mathbf{x}_1, \ldots, \mathbf{x}_N\}$, where each element $\mathbf{x}_i \in \{0,1\}^{nk} \setminus \{\mathbf{0}^{nk}, \mathbf{1}^{nk}\}$ ($i \in [1, N]$), and proceeds as follows:

1. **Sort Inputs**. First sort S in ascending order via the corresponding integer value $\mathsf{Int}(\mathbf{x}_j)$ (within 2^{nk}) of each element $\mathbf{x}_j$, and let $(\mathbf{x}'_1, \ldots, \mathbf{x}'_N)$ be the sorting result.
2. **Assign Values**. Let $(\mathbf{u}_0, \mathbf{u}_1, \mathbf{u}_2, \ldots, \mathbf{u}_{2^{\ell+1}-1})$ be $2N+2 = 2^{\ell+1}$ variables. Then we assign value for each variable as follows:
   - $\mathbf{u}_0 = \mathbf{F}_{irst}$;
   - for $j = 1$ to N, $\mathbf{u}_j = \mathbf{x}'_j$;
   - for $j = N+1$ to $2N$, $\mathbf{u}_j = \mathbf{x}'_{j-N}$;
   - $\mathbf{u}_{2^{\ell+1}-1} = \mathbf{L}_{ast}$.

   In addition, for each $j \in [0, (2^{\ell+1} - 1)]$, let $(j_1, j_2, \ldots, j_{\ell+1})$ be its binary representation string, then $\mathbf{u}_j = \mathbf{u}_{j_1, j_2, \ldots, j_{\ell+1}}$.
3. **Construct Tree**. Then construct a tree with depth $(\ell + 1)$ based on the leaves $(\mathbf{u}_0, \mathbf{u}_1, \mathbf{u}_2, \ldots, \mathbf{u}_{2^{\ell+1}-1})$.

– At any depth $i \in [1, \ell]$, for each $(b_1, b_2, \ldots, b_i) \in \{0,1\}^i$, each node $\mathbf{u}_{b_1,b_2,\ldots,b_i}$ is defined as

$$u_{b_1,b_2,\ldots,b_i} = h_{\mathbf{A}}(\mathbf{u}_{b_1,b_2,\ldots,b_i,0}, \mathbf{u}_{b_1,b_2,\ldots,b_i,1});$$

– At depth 0, the root node is $\mathbf{u} = h_{\mathbf{A}}(\mathbf{u}_0, \mathbf{u}_1)$.

The algorithm outputs the nonmembership accumulator value $\mathbf{u}$.

$\mathsf{NM\text{-}Witness}_{pp}(S, \mathbf{d})$, where $\mathbf{d} \notin S$.

Let $\mathsf{Int}(\mathbf{d})$ be the integer value of $\mathbf{d}$. First find two **sibling** leaves $(\mathbf{u}_{b_1,\ldots,b_\ell,0}, \mathbf{u}_{b_1,\ldots,b_\ell,1})$ in the tree such that

$$\mathsf{Int}(\mathbf{u}_{b_1,b_2,\ldots,b_\ell,0}) < \mathsf{Int}(\mathbf{d}) < \mathsf{Int}(\mathbf{u}_{b_1,b_2,\ldots,b_\ell,1}).$$

Then return the witness for $\mathbf{d}$ as follows.

$$w = ((b_1, b_2, \ldots, b_\ell), (\mathbf{u}_{b_1,b_2,\ldots,b_\ell,0}, \mathbf{u}_{b_1,b_2,\ldots,b_\ell,1}, \mathbf{u}_{b_1,b_2,\ldots,\bar{b}_\ell}, \ldots, \mathbf{u}_{b_1,\bar{b}_2}, \mathbf{u}_{\bar{b}_1})) \in \{0,1\}^\ell \times (\{0,1\}^{nk})^{\ell+2}.$$

$\mathsf{NM\text{-}Verify}_{pp}(\mathbf{u}, \mathbf{d}, w)$. Assume the witness w is of the form $w = ((b_1, b_2, \ldots, b_\ell), (\mathbf{w}_{\ell,1}, \mathbf{w}_{\ell,2}, \mathbf{w}_\ell, \mathbf{w}_{\ell-1}, \ldots, \mathbf{w}_1))$.

- First check whether $\mathsf{Int}(\mathbf{w}_{\ell,1}) < \mathsf{Int}(\mathbf{d}) < \mathsf{Int}(\mathbf{w}_{\ell,2})$.
- If yes, then compute $\mathbf{v}_\ell = h_{\mathbf{A}}(\mathbf{w}_{\ell,1}, \mathbf{w}_{\ell,2})$, and

$$\forall i \in \{\ell-1, \ell-2, \ldots, 1, 0\} : \mathbf{v}_i = \begin{cases} h_{\mathbf{A}}(\mathbf{v}_{i+1}, \mathbf{w}_{i+1}) \; if \; b_{i+1} = 0 \\ h_{\mathbf{A}}(\mathbf{w}_{i+1}, \mathbf{v}_{i+1}) \; if \; b_{i+1} = 1 \end{cases}.$$

Finally, the algorithm returns 1 if $\mathbf{v}_0$ equals $\mathbf{u}$. Otherwise, returns 0.

Then we give an example of a tree with 2^3 leaves, where the size of the accumulated set is 3, and denote the set as $S = \{\mathbf{x}_1, \mathbf{x}_2, \mathbf{x}_3\}$. For simplicity, we assume that elements in S are in ascending order. Then the tree is shown in Fig. 2.

Correctness. The correctness of the above construction requires that for any binary string $\mathbf{d} \in \{0,1\}^{nk} \backslash \{0\ldots0, 1\ldots1\}$, $\mathbf{d} \notin S$, and $\mathbf{u} \leftarrow \mathsf{NM\text{-}Acc}_{pp}(S)$, computes witness $w \leftarrow \mathsf{NM\text{-}Witness}_{pp}(S, \mathbf{d})$, $\mathsf{NM\text{-}Verify}_{pp}(\mathbf{u}, \mathbf{d}, w) = 1$. We also argue that for any $\mathbf{d}$, its witness w is unique in the above Merkle-tree.

Since set S is sorted via the integer value of each element in $\mathsf{NM\text{-}Acc}_{pp}$ algorithm, here we directly assume that $S = \{\mathbf{x}_1, \ldots, \mathbf{x}_N\}$ be a sorted binary string set, and each element inside is different. We use interval $\mathbf{I}_i$ to denote the open interval $(\mathsf{Int}(\mathbf{x}_{i-1}), \mathsf{Int}(\mathbf{x}_i))$, which is illustrated in Fig. 3. Observe that value $\mathsf{Int}(\mathbf{d})$ must fall into one and only one interval $\mathcal{I}_i$ in Fig. 3 since $\mathbf{d} \notin S$. Then the corresponding elements in S, namely $\mathbf{x}_i$ and $\mathbf{x}_{i+1}$, constitute the first two nodes (sibling leaves) in the witness. Since we require them to be sibling leaves in the tree T, then we choose the corresponding sibling leaves $\mathbf{u}_j$ and $\mathbf{u}_{j+1}$ based on $\mathcal{I}_i$. If i is even, then choose $\mathbf{u}_{N+i-1}$ and $\mathbf{u}_{N+i}$, and the siblings of each node in the path from them to root to be witness. Otherwise, picks $\mathbf{u}_{i-1}$ and $\mathbf{u}_i$, and the siblings of each node in the path from them to root.

Regarding the security of our construction, we have the following theorem.

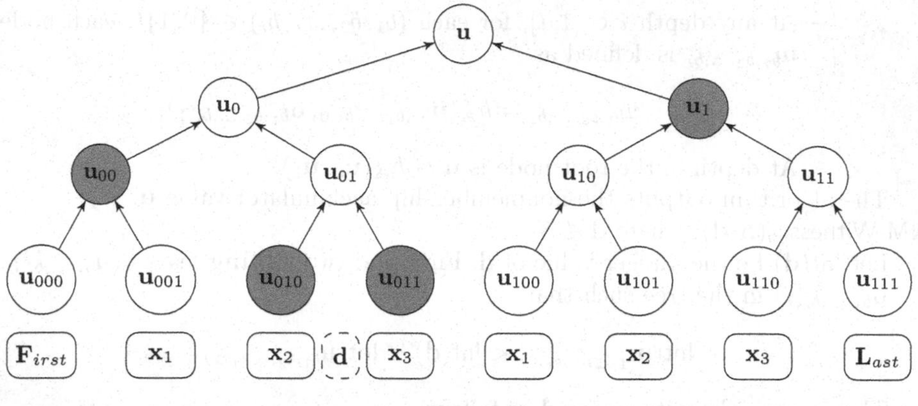

Fig. 2. A Merkle-tree with 2^3 leaves, which accumulates the data blocks in the set $S = \{\mathbf{x}_1, \mathbf{x}_2, \mathbf{x}_3\}$ with ascending integer values, into an accumulator value $\mathbf{u}$. In addition, the bit string (01) and the gray nodes consist the witness for a node $\mathbf{d}$, which is not accumulated in $\mathbf{u}$, and $\mathsf{Int}(\mathbf{x}_2) < \mathsf{Int}(\mathbf{d}) < \mathsf{Int}(\mathbf{x}_3)$.

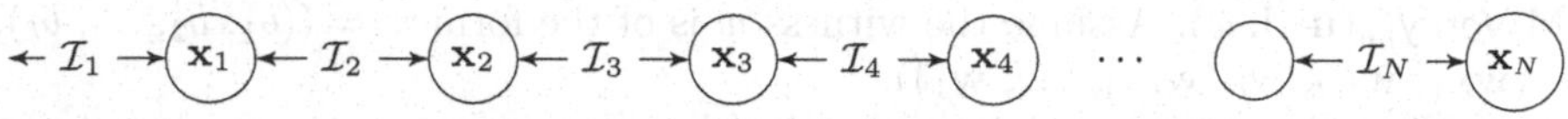

Fig. 3. Illustration of correctness.

Theorem 1. *Under the hardness of* SIS *problem, the construction for nonmembership witness presented above is secure.*

Proof. Assume that there exists an adversary $\mathcal{B}$ who can break the security of the above accumulator scheme. Then we can construct another algorithm which can break the collision-resilient property of the hash function h used in the scheme, whose hardness is based on the SIS problem.

Given the public parameter $pp = (\mathbf{A}, \mathbf{F}_{irst}, \mathbf{L}_{ast})$ output by NM-Setup(n), $\mathcal{B}$ outputs $(S^*, \mathbf{d}^*, w^*)$ such that $\mathbf{d}^* \in S^*$, and algorithm NM-Verify$_{pp}$(NM-Acc$_{pp}(S^*)$, $\mathbf{d}^*$, w^*) $= 1$, where w^* is in the form $((b_1^*, b_2^*, \ldots, b_\ell^*), (w_{\ell,1}^*, w_{\ell,2}^*, w_\ell^*, w_{\ell-1}^*, \ldots, w_1^*))$.

Since NM-Verify$_{pp}$(NM-Acc$_{pp}(S^*)$, d^*, w^*) $= 1$, hence $\mathsf{Int}(w_{\ell,1}^*) < \mathsf{Int}(\mathbf{d}^*) < \mathsf{Int}\,(w_{\ell,2}^*)$, which implies that $d^* \neq \mathbf{w}_{\ell,1}^*$ and $d^* \neq \mathbf{w}_{\ell,2}^*$. Let $\mathbf{v}_\ell^*, \mathbf{v}_{\ell-1}^*, \mathbf{v}_{\ell-2}^*, \ldots, \mathbf{v}_0^*$ be the path computed by algorithm NM-Verify$_{pp}$. We also set $\mathbf{v}_{\ell,0}^* = w_{\ell,1}^*$, and $\mathbf{v}_{\ell,1}^* = w_{\ell,2}^*$. Then $\mathbf{v}_0^*$ must be equal to $\mathbf{u}$.

Next we construct the Merkle-tree T^* based on the sorted set S^*,$\mathbf{F}_{rist}$, and $\mathbf{L}_{ast}$. Notably, each node in T^* is represented via $\mathbf{u}_i$. Recall that $(b_1^*, b_2^*, \ldots, b_\ell^*)$ is the bit string contained in w^*. Let $\mathbf{u}_{b_1^*,b_2^*,\ldots,b_\ell^*,0}$, $\mathbf{u}_{b_1^*,b_2^*,\ldots,b_\ell^*,1}$, $\mathbf{u}_{b_1^*,b_2^*,\ldots,b_\ell^*}$, $\mathbf{u}_{b_1^*,b_2^*,\ldots,b_{\ell-1}^*}$, $\ldots$, $\mathbf{u}_{b_1^*}$, $\mathbf{u}$ be the path from leaves $\mathbf{u}_{b_1^*,b_2^*,\ldots,b_\ell^*,0}$ and $\mathbf{u}_{b_1^*,b_2^*,\ldots,b_\ell^*,1}$ to root $\mathbf{u}$. Notably, $\mathbf{d}^*$ must be equal to either $\mathbf{u}_{b_1^*,b_2^*,\ldots,b_\ell^*,0}$ or

$\mathbf{u}_{b_1^*,b_2^*,\ldots,b_\ell^*,1}$ since $\mathbf{d}^* \in S^*$. In this way, we get two paths, they are

$$Path1: \mathbf{v}_{\ell,0}^*, \mathbf{v}_{\ell,1}^*, \mathbf{v}_{\ell}^*, \mathbf{v}_{\ell-1}^*, \mathbf{v}_{\ell-2}^*, \ldots, \mathbf{v}_1^*, \mathbf{v}_0^*$$

$$Path2: \mathbf{u}_{b_1^*,b_2^*,\ldots,b_\ell^*,0}, \mathbf{u}_{b_1^*,b_2^*,\ldots,b_\ell^*,1}, \mathbf{u}_{b_1^*,b_2^*,\ldots,b_\ell^*}, \mathbf{u}_{b_1^*,b_2^*,\ldots,b_{\ell-1}^*}, \ldots, \mathbf{u}_{b_1^*}, \mathbf{u}$$

Comparing *Path1* and *Path2*, we can find the smallest integer $k \in [1, \ell+1]$ such that $\mathbf{v}_k^* \neq \mathbf{u}_{b_1^*,b_2^*,\ldots,b_k^*}$. Notably, in the case $k = \ell+1$, we mean either $\mathbf{v}_{\ell,0} \neq \mathbf{u}_{b_1^*,b_2^*,\ldots,b_\ell^*,0}$ or $\mathbf{v}_{\ell,1} \neq \mathbf{u}_{b_1^*,b_2^*,\ldots,b_\ell^*,1}$ or both. In this way, we find a collision for $h_{\mathbf{A}}$ for $\mathbf{v}_{k-1}^*$.

3.2 Zero-Knowledge Argument of Knowledge of Nonmembership Witness

In this section, we give a ZKAoK to prove the possession of the nonmembership witness of a non-accumulated value. More specifically, given common inputs ($pp = (\mathbf{A}, \mathbf{F}_{irst}, \mathbf{L}_{ast})$, $\mathbf{u}$), prover $\mathcal{P}$ convinces verifier $\mathcal{V}$ that he has ($\mathbf{d}$, w) such that $\mathsf{NM\text{-}Verify}_{pp}$ ($\mathbf{u}$, $\mathbf{d}$, w) = 1. The relevant relation is defined as $\mathcal{R}_{nm}$:

$$\mathcal{R}_{nm} = \left\{ \begin{array}{r} ((pp, \mathbf{u}) \in (Z_q^{n\times m} \times 0^{nk} \times 1^{nk} \times \{0,1\}^{nk}); \\ \mathbf{d} \in \{0,1\}^{nk}, w \in \{0,1\}^{\ell} \times (\{0,1\}^{nk})^{\ell+2}) : \\ \mathsf{NM\text{-}Verify}_{pp}(\mathbf{u}, \mathbf{d}, w) = 1 \end{array} \right\}.$$

Overview of Our Argument. Assume w is of the form ((b_1, b_2, ..., b_ℓ), ($\mathbf{w}_{\ell,1}$, $\mathbf{w}_{\ell,2}$, $\mathbf{w}_\ell$, $\mathbf{w}_{\ell-1}$, ..., $\mathbf{w}_1$)). Observe that for any ($\mathbf{d}$, w), algorithm $\mathsf{NM\text{-}Verify}_{pp}$($\mathbf{u}$, $\mathbf{d}$, w) = 1 if and only if the following two requirements being satisfied:

1. The integer value of $\mathbf{d}$ belongs to the open interval ($\mathsf{Int}(\mathbf{w}_{\ell,1})$, $\mathsf{Int}(\mathbf{w}_{\ell,2})$), namely
$$\mathsf{Int}(\mathbf{w}_{\ell,1}) < \mathsf{Int}(\mathbf{d}) < \mathsf{Int}(\mathbf{w}_{\ell,2}). \quad (2)$$
2. The path computed by $\mathsf{NM\text{-}Verify}_{pp}$($\mathbf{u}$, $\mathbf{d}$, w) satisfies $\mathbf{v}_0 = \mathbf{u}$, and

$$\mathbf{v}_\ell = h_{\mathbf{A}}(\mathbf{w}_{\ell,1}, \mathbf{w}_{\ell,2}),$$
$$\forall i \in \{\ell-1, \ell-2, \ldots, 1, 0\} : \mathbf{v}_i = \begin{cases} h_{\mathbf{A}}(\mathbf{v}_{i+1}, \mathbf{w}_{i+1}) & if \ \ b_{i+1} = 0 \\ h_{\mathbf{A}}(\mathbf{w}_{i+1}, \mathbf{v}_{i+1}) & if \ \ b_{i+1} = 1 \end{cases}. \quad (3)$$

Roughly speaking, our proof can be reduced to proving the above two requirements in zero-knowledge. Before going into details, we first give a brief sketch about the techniques used in our proof. Based on the observation that if we can adjust each requirement into the form of $\mathbf{P}_i \cdot \mathbf{x}_i = \mathbf{v}_i \bmod q_i$, and define the valid set and permutation set for the two requirements satisfying the condition (1), then we can use the abstract Stern's protocol [26] to get the zero-knowledge arguments protocol. For the first requirement, we observe that for any vector $\mathbf{u}$, $\mathbf{v} \in \{0,1\}^{nk}$, if $\mathsf{Int}(\mathbf{u}) < \mathsf{Int}(\mathbf{v})$, then there is one and only one binary vector $\mathbf{diff} \in \{0,1\}^{nk}$, such that $\mathsf{Int}(\mathbf{v})$ - $\mathsf{Int}(\mathbf{u}) - \mathsf{Int}(\mathbf{diff}) = 1 \mod (2q^n)$. This part can also be used as range proof of integer values. For the second requirement, we need to provide membership proof to sibling leaves $\mathbf{w}_{\ell,1}$ and $\mathbf{w}_{\ell,2}$, which can utilize the technique of membership proof presented by Libert et al. in [25] based on modulus q.

In the following contents, we first transform the above requirements into the linear form $\mathbf{P} \cdot \mathbf{x} = \mathbf{v} \bmod q$, then define the corresponding valid set and permutation set for the abstract Stern's protocol.

Transformation of Requirement **(2).** Observe that for any vector $\mathbf{v} \in \{0,1\}^{nk}$, its integer value is within the set $\{0, 1, 2, 3, \ldots, 2^{nk}\text{-}1\}$. Then for any three vectors $\mathbf{v}_1, \mathbf{v}_2, \mathbf{v}_3 \in \{0,1\}^{nk}$, if $\mathsf{Int}(\mathbf{v}_1) - \mathsf{Int}(\mathbf{v}_2) - \mathsf{Int}(\mathbf{v}_3) = 1 \bmod (2q^n)$, then we can get that $\mathsf{Int}(\mathbf{v}_1) > \mathsf{Int}(\mathbf{v}_2) \bmod q^n$. According to this observation, we can equivalently rewrite condition (2) to be

$$\begin{cases} \mathsf{Int}(\mathbf{w}_{\ell,1}) < \mathsf{Int}(\mathbf{d}) \mod q^n \\ \quad \Leftrightarrow \mathsf{Int}(\mathbf{d}) - \mathsf{Int}(\mathbf{w}_{\ell,1}) - 1 = \mathsf{Int}(\mathbf{diff}_1) \mod 2q^n; \\ \mathsf{Int}(\mathbf{d}) < \mathsf{Int}(\mathbf{w}_{\ell,2}) \mod q^n \\ \quad \Leftrightarrow \mathsf{Int}(w_{\ell,2}) - \mathsf{Int}(\mathbf{d}) - 1 = \mathsf{Int}(\mathbf{diff}_2) \mod 2q^n, \end{cases} \tag{4}$$

where vectors $\mathbf{diff}_1, \mathbf{diff}_2 \in \{0,1\}^{nk}$ are binary vectors of the differences.

Since for any binary vector $\mathbf{v}$, we have $\mathsf{Int}(\mathbf{v}) = \mathbf{G}' \cdot \mathbf{v}$, then requirement (2) can be equivalently rewritten as

$$\begin{cases} \mathbf{G}' \cdot \mathbf{d} - \mathbf{G}' \cdot \mathbf{w}_{\ell,1} - \mathbf{G}' \cdot \mathbf{diff}_1 = 1 \mod 2q^n; \\ \mathbf{G}' \cdot \mathbf{w}_{\ell,2} - \mathbf{G}' \cdot \mathbf{d} - \mathbf{G}' \cdot \mathbf{diff}_2 = 1 \mod 2q^n. \end{cases} \tag{5}$$

Transformation of Requirement (3)**.** Before going into details, we first recall some notations and techniques introduced in [25].

- B_m^{nk} is used to denote the set of all vectors in $\{0,1\}^m$ with hamming weight nk. Besides, we denote S_m the set of all permutations of all m elements.
- Let $\mathsf{ext}(b, \mathbf{v})$ denote the vector $\mathbf{z} \in \{0,1\}^{2i}$ of the form $\mathbf{z} = \begin{pmatrix} \bar{b} \cdot \mathbf{v} \\ b \cdot \mathbf{v} \end{pmatrix}$, where $\mathbf{v} \in \{0,1\}^i$ $(i \in \{nk, m\})$, and $b \in \{0,1\}$.
- For any $b \in \{0,1\}$, and for any $\pi \in S_m$, let $F_{b,\pi}$ be the permutation on vector $\mathbf{z} = \begin{pmatrix} \mathbf{z}_0 \\ \mathbf{z}_1 \end{pmatrix} \in \{0,1\}^{2m}$ with two blocks of size m, which is defined as $F_{b,\pi} = \begin{pmatrix} \pi(\mathbf{z}_b) \\ \pi(\mathbf{z}_{\bar{b}}) \end{pmatrix}$.

Next, via the same transformation strategy presented in [25], the second requirement (3) can be equivalently rewritten to be

$$\begin{cases} \mathbf{A} \cdot \begin{pmatrix} \mathbf{w}_{\ell,1} \\ \mathbf{w}_{\ell,2} \end{pmatrix} - \mathbf{G} \cdot \mathbf{v}_\ell = \mathbf{0} \bmod q; \\ \forall i \in [1, \ell] : \mathbf{z}_i = \mathsf{ext}(b_i, \mathbf{v}_i), \mathbf{y}_i = \mathsf{ext}(\bar{b}_i, \mathbf{w}_i); \\ \forall i \in [1, \ell - 1] : \mathbf{A} \cdot \mathbf{z}_{i+1} + \mathbf{A} \cdot \mathbf{y}_{i+1} - \mathbf{G} \cdot \mathbf{v}_i = \mathbf{0} \bmod q; \\ \mathbf{A} \cdot \mathbf{z}_1 + \mathbf{A} \cdot \mathbf{y}_1 = \mathbf{G} \cdot \mathbf{u} \bmod q. \end{cases} \tag{6}$$

Until now, NM-Verify$(\mathbf{u}, \mathbf{d}, w)$ =1 equals the Eqs. (5) and (6) hold. Beside the above transformations, extension technique presented in [28] is also needed, which does the follows:

- Matrix extension: $\mathbf{A} = [\mathbf{A}_0||\mathbf{A}_1]$ is modified to be $\mathbf{A}^* = [\mathbf{A}_0||\mathbf{0}^{n\times nk}||\mathbf{A}_1||\mathbf{0}^{n\times nk}]$, $\mathbf{G}$ is modified to be $\mathbf{G}^* = [\mathbf{G}||\mathbf{0}^{n\times nk}]$, and $\mathbf{G}'$ is modified to be $\mathbf{G}'' = [\mathbf{G}'||\mathbf{0}^{1\times nk}]$.
- Vector extension: all $\mathbf{w}_{\ell,0}, \mathbf{w}_{\ell,1}, \ldots, \mathbf{w}_1, \mathbf{v}_\ell, \mathbf{v}_{\ell-1}, \ldots, \mathbf{v}_1$, $\mathbf{d}$, $\mathbf{diff}_1$, $\mathbf{diff}_2$ are extended into $\mathbf{w}^*_{\ell,0}$, $\mathbf{w}^*_{\ell,1}$, ..., $\mathbf{w}^*_1$, $\mathbf{v}^*_\ell$, $\mathbf{v}^*_{\ell-1}$, ..., $\mathbf{v}^*_1$, $\mathbf{d}^*$, $\mathbf{diff}^*_1$, $\mathbf{diff}^*_2 \in \mathsf{B}^{nk}_m$ respectively. For each vector, this is done by appending it with a binary vector of length nk with the restriction that the resulted vector's Hamming weight is nk.

Then Eqs. (5) and (6) can be equivalently written as follows:

$$\begin{cases} \mathbf{G}''\cdot\mathbf{d}^* - \mathbf{G}''\cdot\mathbf{w}^*_{\ell,1} - \mathbf{G}''\cdot\mathbf{diff}^*_1 = 1 \mod 2q^n, \\ \mathbf{G}''\cdot\mathbf{w}^*_{\ell,2} - \mathbf{G}''\cdot\mathbf{d}^* - \mathbf{G}''\cdot\mathbf{diff}^*_2 = 1 \mod 2q^n, \\ \mathbf{A}^*\cdot\begin{pmatrix}\mathbf{w}^*_{\ell,1}\\ \mathbf{w}^*_{\ell,2}\end{pmatrix} - \mathbf{G}^*\cdot\mathbf{v}^*_\ell = \mathbf{0} \mod q, \\ \forall i\in[1,\ell] : \mathbf{z}_i = \mathsf{ext}(b_i, \mathbf{v}^*_i), \mathbf{y}_i = \mathsf{ext}(\bar{b}_i, \mathbf{w}^*_i), \\ \forall i\in[1,\ell-1] : \mathbf{A}^*\cdot\mathbf{z}_{i+1} + \mathbf{A}^*\cdot\mathbf{y}_{i+1} - \mathbf{G}^*\cdot\mathbf{v}^*_i = \mathbf{0} \mod q; \\ \mathbf{A}^*\cdot\mathbf{z}_1 + \mathbf{A}^*\cdot\mathbf{y}_1 = \mathbf{G}\cdot\mathbf{u} \bmod q. \end{cases} \tag{7}$$

Upon the above preparation, the interactive protocol can be summarized as follows.

Common inputs: Matrices $\mathbf{G}''$, $\mathbf{A}^*$, $\mathbf{G}^*$, $\mathbf{G}$, and vector $\mathbf{u}$.
Prover's inputs: $(\mathbf{diff}^*_1, \mathbf{diff}^*_2, \mathbf{d}^*)$, $(b_1, \ldots, b_\ell)$,$(\mathbf{w}^*_{\ell,1}, \mathbf{w}^*_{\ell,2}, \mathbf{w}^*_\ell, \ldots, \mathbf{w}^*_1)$, $(\mathbf{v}^*_\ell, \ldots, \mathbf{v}^*_1)$, $(\mathbf{z}_\ell, \ldots, \mathbf{z}_1)$, $(\mathbf{y}_\ell, \ldots, \mathbf{y}_1)$
Prover's goal: prove the following things in a zero-knowledge manner. (1) $\mathbf{w}^*_{\ell,1}$, $\mathbf{w}^*_{\ell,2} \in \mathsf{B}^{nk}_m$; (2) for all $i \in [1,\ell]$, $\mathbf{v}^*_i$, $\mathbf{w}^*_i \in \mathsf{B}^{nk}_m$, and $\mathbf{z}_i = \mathsf{ext}(b_i, \mathbf{v}^*_i)$, $\mathbf{y}_i = \mathsf{ext}(\bar{b}_i, \mathbf{w}^*_i)$; (3) Eq. (7) hold.

Let $\mathbf{x} = (\mathbf{diff}^*_1 \parallel \mathbf{diff}^*_2 \parallel \mathbf{d}^* \parallel \mathbf{w}^*_{\ell,1} \parallel \mathbf{w}^*_{\ell,2} \parallel \mathbf{v}^*_\ell \parallel \mathbf{z}_\ell \parallel \mathbf{y}_\ell \parallel \ldots \parallel \mathbf{v}^*_1 \parallel \mathbf{z}_1 \parallel \mathbf{y}_1)$. Next, we specify the definition of set VALID, set S and the associated permutation T_π for $\mathbf{x}$ which satisfy conditions (1).

Let VALID be the set of all vectors in $\{0,1\}^{5m+5m\ell}$ with the same form of vector $\mathbf{x}$, where

- $\mathbf{diff}^*_1, \mathbf{diff}^*_2, \mathbf{d}^*, \mathbf{w}^*_{\ell,1}, \mathbf{w}^*_{\ell,2}, \mathbf{v}^*_\ell, \mathbf{v}^*_{\ell-1} \ldots, \mathbf{v}^*_1 \in \mathsf{B}^{nk}_m$;
- for all $j \in [1,\ell]$ $(\mathbf{z}_i \in (\mathsf{B}^{nk}_m \times \mathbf{0}^m) \wedge \mathbf{y}_i \in (\mathbf{0}^m \times \mathsf{B}^{nk}_m))$ or $(\mathbf{z}_i \in (\mathbf{0}^m \times \mathsf{B}^{nk}_m) \wedge \mathbf{y}_i \in (\mathsf{B}^{nk}_m \times \mathbf{0}^m))$.

The set S as well as the permutation $\{T_\pi : \pi \in S\}$ is defined as follows:

- $S = \overbrace{S_m \times S_m \times \ldots \times S_m}^{(5+2\ell)}$, where S_m is the set of all permutations for m elements.

- For each $\pi = (\pi_1, \pi_2, \pi_3, \pi_4, \pi_5, \ldots, \pi_{5+2\ell}) \in S$, where each $\pi_i \in S_m$ ($i \in [1, 5+2\ell]$), and for each $\mathbf{x} = (\,\mathbf{diff}_1, \mathbf{diff}_1, \mathbf{d}, \mathbf{w}_{\ell,1}, \mathbf{w}_{\ell,2}, \mathbf{v}_\ell, \mathbf{z}_\ell, \mathbf{y}_\ell, \mathbf{v}_{\ell-1}, \ldots, \mathbf{z}_1, \mathbf{y}_1)$, where $\mathbf{diff}_1$, $\mathbf{diff}_1$, $\mathbf{d}$, $\mathbf{w}_{\ell,1}$, $\mathbf{w}_{\ell,2}$, $\mathbf{v}_\ell$, $\mathbf{v}_{\ell-1}$, ..., $\mathbf{v}_1$ are with length m, and each other vector has length $2m$. For $\mathbf{z}_i \in \mathbf{x}$, we denote it as $\mathbf{z}_i = \begin{pmatrix} \mathbf{z}_{i,1} \\ \mathbf{z}_{i,2} \end{pmatrix}$, where $\mathbf{z}_{i,1}$ and $\mathbf{z}_{i,2}$ have m elements respectively. We denote $\mathbf{y}_i = \begin{pmatrix} \mathbf{y}_{i,1} \\ \mathbf{y}_{i,2} \end{pmatrix}$ similarly. The main technique used in the follows is that each pair of $\mathbf{v}_i$ and $\mathbf{z}_i$ shares an identical permutation. Pick $b_\ell, b_{\ell-1}, \ldots, b_1 \xleftarrow{\$} \{0,1\}$.

$$T_\pi(\mathbf{x}) = \pi_1(\mathbf{diff}_1) \parallel \pi_2(\mathbf{diff}_2) \parallel \pi_3(\mathbf{d}) \parallel \pi_4(\mathbf{w}_{\ell,1}) \| \pi_5(\mathbf{w}_{\ell,2}) \parallel \pi_6(\mathbf{v}_\ell) \parallel$$
$$\begin{pmatrix} \pi_6(\mathbf{z}_{\ell,(1+b_\ell)}) \\ \pi_6(\mathbf{z}_{\ell,(2-b_\ell)}) \end{pmatrix} \parallel \begin{pmatrix} \pi_7(\mathbf{y}_{\ell,(1+b_\ell)}) \\ \pi_7(\mathbf{y}_{\ell,(2-b_\ell)}) \end{pmatrix} \parallel \pi_8(\mathbf{v}_{\ell-1}) \parallel \begin{pmatrix} \pi_8(\mathbf{z}_{\ell-1,(1+b_{\ell-1})}) \\ \pi_8(\mathbf{z}_{\ell-1,(2-b_{\ell-1})}) \end{pmatrix} \parallel$$
$$\begin{pmatrix} \pi_9(\mathbf{y}_{\ell-1,(1+b_{\ell-1})}) \\ \pi_9(\mathbf{y}_{\ell-1,(2-b_{\ell-1})}) \end{pmatrix} \parallel \ldots\ldots \parallel \begin{pmatrix} \pi_{5+2\ell}(\mathbf{y}_{1,1+b_1}) \\ \pi_{5+2\ell}(\mathbf{y}_{1,2-b_1}) \end{pmatrix}.$$

Thanks to the useful equivalences introduced in [25], which state that

- For any vector $\mathbf{v} \in \{0,1\}^m$, and $\pi \in S_m$, we have

$$\mathbf{v} \in B_m^{nk} \iff \pi(\mathbf{v}) \in B_m^{nk};$$

- For any vector $\mathbf{v}, \mathbf{w} \in \{0,1\}^m$, $c, b \in \{0,1\}$, $\pi, \phi \in S_m$, we have

$$\mathbf{z} = \mathsf{ext}(c, \mathbf{v}) \wedge \mathbf{v} \in B_m^{nk} \iff F_{b,\pi}(\mathbf{z}) = \mathsf{ext}(c \oplus b, \pi(\mathbf{v})) \wedge \pi(\mathbf{v}) \in B_m^{nk}$$
$$\mathbf{y} = \mathsf{ext}(\bar{c}, \mathbf{w}) \wedge \mathbf{w} \in B_m^{nk} \iff F_{\bar{b},\phi}(\mathbf{y}) = \mathsf{ext}(c \oplus b, \phi(\mathbf{w})) \wedge \phi(\mathbf{w}) \in B_m^{nk}.$$

We can get that $\mathbf{x} \in \mathsf{VALID}$ if and only if $T_\pi(\mathbf{x}) \in \mathsf{VALID}$. Besides, if π is uniformly chosen from S, then $T_\pi(\mathbf{x})$ is uniformly distributed in VALID. In this way, we can run the abstract Stern's protocol [26] to prove the knowledge of $\mathbf{x}$ satisfying all requirements stated in Prover's goal.

4 Application of Our Accumulator

As an independent interest, we give a brief introduction about one potential application of our above proposed accumulator, i.e. fully dynamic group signature. Unlike a static group signature, a fully dynamic group signature should enable the users dynamical joining and user revocation. Our idea is that we construct two Merkle-trees in our constructed dynamic group signature scheme, one is for membership proof and another one is for non-membership proof. In the following, we call the Merkle-tree used for membership proof as T_1, and the Merkle-tree used for nonmembership proof as T_2.

Firstly, group manager computes enough number of chameleon hash values, and use them as the leaves to construct the Merkle-tree T_1. Once a user is joining, group manager opens a non-designed chameleon hash values to be the user's public key. Notably, in our scheme, the joining operation of a user won't affect the root value of T_1, and once a chameleon hash value is open, it won't change forever.

As mentioned before, T_2 is the tree whose leaves are all users who have been revoked, which is constructed via the method presented in **Sect.** 3. When group manger wants to revoke a user at some time, he can just add this user to be a leaf in T_2, and this process needs to reconstruct T_2.

Then any member wants to produce a group signature, he needs to give two types of proofs. The first one is to prove that he is a member in T_1, this can be done via utilizing the technique presented in [25]. The second type of proof is to prove that he is not a member in the second tree T_2 via our technique. Then if these two parts are both valid, we say the signature is valid.

Recently, Ling et al. [30] present a fully dynamic group signature from updatable Merkle-tree accumulator where the cost of adding and deleting element is logarithmic size in the number of group member. In our scheme, via the help of the chameleon hash function, the complexity of adding a node is $\mathcal{O}(1)$, which needs to utilize a trapdoor of the chameleon hash function. While every time the group manager issue a new revoked list, he needs to reconstruct the second accumulator (based on revoked members) for nonmembership proof. Hence the cost of deleting is the cost for constructing a Merkle-tree for the revoked set, which is worse than [30]. Besides, the signature size of our scheme is not as compact as [30]. However, we argue that our fully dynamic group signature fits for the scenario that user's status frequently changes (either be valid or revoked) in different time period, and the revoked list periodically updates.

Acknowledgement. We appreciate the anonymous reviewers for their valuable suggestions. Part of this work was supported by the National Natural Science Foundation of China (Grant No. 61602396, U1636205, 61572294, 61632020), the MonashU-PolyU-Collinstar Capital Joint Lab on Blockchain and Cryptocurrency Technologies, and from the Research Grants Council of Hong Kong (Grant No. 25206317). The work of Junzuo Lai was supported by the National Natural Science Foundation of China (Grant No. 61572235), and Guangdong Natural Science Funds for Distinguished Young Scholar (No. 2015A030306045).

A Zero-Knowledge Arguments of Knowledge

Zero-knowledge arguments of knowledge [18] (ZKAoK) is an interactive protocol where a prover can convince the verifier that he possesses the witness for a statement in a NP relation without revealing any information about the witness. Moreover, we require it to have the following security properties [18]:

Completeness. The prover can convince the verifier if he knows a witness testifying to the truth of the statement.

Soundness. A malicious prover cannot convince the verifier if the statement is false.

Zero-knowledege. A malicious verifier can know nothing but the statement is true from the proof.

Extractability. A probabilistic polynomial time extractor can extract the witness for a true statement from a convincing argument made by prover.

In addition, as mentioned in [16], also known as Fiat-Shamir heuristic, a three round public-coin interactive ZKAoK can be transformed into a non-interactive one in the random oracle model. We refer reader to [5] for the security analysis Fiat-Shamir heuristic.

B Accumulator for Nonmembership

Observe that a universal accumulator concerns two types of witness, one is the witness for membership and another is the witness for nonmembership, where the first part is the original definition of accumulator. We refer the reader to Definition 1 in [14] for the formal definition of accumulator (for membership). For the part about nonmembership, we separate the scheme for it as follows:

Accumulator for Nonmembership. An accumulator for nonmembership is consisted of a tuple algorithms (NM-Setup, NM-Acc, NM-Witness, NM-Verify) given below:

NM-Setup(n) $\rightarrow pp$. The algorithm takes as input a security parameter n, outputs the public parameter pp.

NM-Acc$_{pp}(R) \rightarrow \mathbf{u}$. On input a set $R = \{\mathbf{d}_0, \mathbf{d}_1, \ldots, \mathbf{d}_{N-1}\}$ with size N, the algorithm outputs the accumulator value $\mathbf{u}$.

NM-Witness$_{pp}(\mathbf{d}, R) \rightarrow w$. On input a set R and a value $\mathbf{d}$, if $\mathbf{d} \in R$, then outputs $\perp$. Otherwise, outputs a witness w for the fact that $\mathbf{d}$ is not accumulated in the output of NM-Acc$_{pp}(R)$.

NM-Verify$_{pp}(\mathbf{u}, \mathbf{d}, w) \rightarrow \{0, 1\}$. The algorithm outputs 1 if witness w can prove that $\mathbf{d}$ is not accumulated into $\mathbf{u}$. Otherwise, outputs 0.

Correctness. The correctness requires that for all $pp \leftarrow$ NM-Setup(n), the following equation holds for all $\mathbf{d} \notin R$:

$$\mathsf{NM\text{-}Verify}_{pp}(\mathsf{NM\text{-}Acc}_{pp}(R), \mathbf{d}, \mathsf{NM\text{-}Witness}_{pp}(\mathbf{d}, R)) = 1.$$

Security Definition. An accumulator for non-membership is secure if for all probabilistic polynomial-time adversary $\mathcal{A}$,

$$Pr[pp \leftarrow \mathsf{NM\text{-}Setup}(n); (L, d^*, \mathbf{w}^*) \leftarrow \mathcal{A}(pp) : d^* \in L \wedge \mathsf{NM\text{-}Verify}_{pp}(\mathsf{NM\text{-}Acc}_{pp}(L), d^*, \mathbf{w}^*) = 1] = negl(n),$$

where $negl(n)$ is a negligible function about n. In other words, the security says that it is computationally infeasible to prove that a value d^* is not accumulated in the value $\mathbf{u}$ if it is.

It is obviously that if we run the algorithms of accumulator and accumulator for nonmembership independently, then the combination of these two parts can give a universal accumulator. More precisely, let (M-Setup, M-Acc, M-Witness,

M-Verify) be an accumulator scheme, and (NM-Setup, NM-Acc, NM-Witness, NM-Verify) be an accumulator for nonmembership scheme, then a universal accumulator scheme (Setup, Acc,Witness,Verify) can be constructed as follows:

Setup(n). Run $pp_m \leftarrow$M-Setup(n), $pp_{nm} \leftarrow$NM-Setup(n). Output $pp = (pp_m, pp_{nm})$.

Acc$_{pp}(R)$. Run $\mathbf{u}_m \leftarrow$M-Acc$_{pp_m}(R)$, $\mathbf{u}_{nm} \leftarrow$NM-Acc$_{pp_{nm}}(R)$. Return $(\mathbf{u}_m, \mathbf{u}_{nm})$.

Witness$_{pp}(\mathbf{d}, R, \text{type})$. If type $= 0$, run $w_m \leftarrow$ M-Witness$_{pp_m}(\mathbf{d}, R)$, and return w_m. Otherwise, run $w_{nm} \leftarrow$NM-Witness$_{pp_{nm}}(\mathbf{d}, R)$, and return the output.

Verify$_{pp}(\mathbf{d}, \mathbf{u}, w, \text{type})$. If type $= 0$, then recall M-Verify$_{pp_m}(\mathbf{u}, \mathbf{d}, w)$, and return the output. Otherwise, run NM-Verify$_{pp_{nm}}(\mathbf{u}, \mathbf{d}, w)$ and return the output.

Both the correctness and the security can be reduced to underlying primitives (accumulator and accumulator for nonmembership) straightforwardly, and we just omit the details here.

References

1. Acar, T., Nguyen, L.: Revocation for delegatable anonymous credentials. In: Catalano, D., Fazio, N., Gennaro, R., Nicolosi, A. (eds.) PKC 2011. LNCS, vol. 6571, pp. 423–440. Springer, Heidelberg (2011). https://doi.org/10.1007/978-3-642-19379-8_26
2. Au, M.H., Tsang, P.P., Susilo, W., Mu, Y.: Dynamic universal accumulators for DDH groups and their application to attribute-based anonymous credential systems. In: Fischlin, M. (ed.) CT-RSA 2009. LNCS, vol. 5473, pp. 295–308. Springer, Heidelberg (2009). https://doi.org/10.1007/978-3-642-00862-7_20
3. Au, M.H., Wu, Q., Susilo, W., Mu, Y.: Compact E-cash from bounded accumulator. In: Abe, M. (ed.) CT-RSA 2007. LNCS, vol. 4377, pp. 178–195. Springer, Heidelberg (2006). https://doi.org/10.1007/11967668_12
4. Barić, N., Pfitzmann, B.: Collision-free accumulators and fail-stop signature schemes without trees. In: Fumy, W. (ed.) EUROCRYPT 1997. LNCS, vol. 1233, pp. 480–494. Springer, Heidelberg (1997). https://doi.org/10.1007/3-540-69053-0_33
5. Bellare, M., Rogaway, P.: Random oracles are practical: a paradigm for designing efficient protocols. In: Proceedings of the 1st ACM Conference on Computer and Communications Security, pp. 62–73. ACM (1993)
6. Benaloh, J., de Mare, M.: One-way accumulators: a decentralized alternative to digital signatures. In: Helleseth, T. (ed.) EUROCRYPT 1993. LNCS, vol. 765, pp. 274–285. Springer, Heidelberg (1994). https://doi.org/10.1007/3-540-48285-7_24
7. Buldas, A., Laud, P., Lipmaa, H.: Accountable certificate management using undeniable attestations. In: Proceedings of the 7th ACM Conference on Computer and Communications Security, pp. 9–17. ACM (2000)
8. Buldas, A., Laud, P., Lipmaa, H.: Eliminating counterevidence with applications to accountable certificate management. J. Comput. Secur. **10**(3), 273–296 (2002)
9. Camacho, P., Hevia, A., Kiwi, M., Opazo, R.: Strong accumulators from collision-resistant hashing. In: Wu, T.-C., Lei, C.-L., Rijmen, V., Lee, D.-T. (eds.) ISC 2008. LNCS, vol. 5222, pp. 471–486. Springer, Heidelberg (2008). https://doi.org/10.1007/978-3-540-85886-7_32

10. Camenisch, J., Kohlweiss, M., Soriente, C.: An accumulator based on bilinear maps and efficient revocation for anonymous credentials. In: Jarecki, S., Tsudik, G. (eds.) PKC 2009. LNCS, vol. 5443, pp. 481–500. Springer, Heidelberg (2009). https://doi.org/10.1007/978-3-642-00468-1_27
11. Camenisch, J., Lysyanskaya, A.: Dynamic accumulators and application to efficient revocation of anonymous credentials. In: Yung, M. (ed.) CRYPTO 2002. LNCS, vol. 2442, pp. 61–76. Springer, Heidelberg (2002). https://doi.org/10.1007/3-540-45708-9_5
12. Canard, S., Gouget, A.: Multiple denominations in E-cash with compact transaction data. In: Sion, R. (ed.) FC 2010. LNCS, vol. 6052, pp. 82–97. Springer, Heidelberg (2010). https://doi.org/10.1007/978-3-642-14577-3_9
13. Damgård, I., Triandopoulos, N.: Supporting non-membership proofs with bilinear-map accumulators. IACR Cryptology ePrint Archive 2008:538 (2008)
14. Derler, D., Hanser, C., Slamanig, D.: Revisiting cryptographic accumulators, additional properties and relations to other primitives. In: Nyberg, K. (ed.) CT-RSA 2015. LNCS, vol. 9048, pp. 127–144. Springer, Cham (2015). https://doi.org/10.1007/978-3-319-16715-2_7
15. Dodis, Y., Kiayias, A., Nicolosi, A., Shoup, V.: Anonymous identification in *Ad Hoc* groups. In: Cachin, C., Camenisch, J.L. (eds.) EUROCRYPT 2004. LNCS, vol. 3027, pp. 609–626. Springer, Heidelberg (2004). https://doi.org/10.1007/978-3-540-24676-3_36
16. Fiat, A., Shamir, A.: How to prove yourself: practical solutions to identification and signature problems. In: Odlyzko, A.M. (ed.) CRYPTO 1986. LNCS, vol. 263, pp. 186–194. Springer, Heidelberg (1987). https://doi.org/10.1007/3-540-47721-7_12
17. Gentry, C., Peikert, C., Vaikuntanathan, V.: Trapdoors for hard lattices and new cryptographic constructions. In: Proceedings of the Fortieth Annual ACM Symposium on Theory of Computing, pp. 197–206. ACM (2008)
18. Goldwasser, S., Micali, S., Rackoff, C.: The knowledge complexity of interactive proof systems. SIAM J. Comput. **18**(1), 186–208 (1989)
19. Goodrich, M.T., Tamassia, R., Hasić, J.: An efficient dynamic and distributed cryptographic accumulator*. In: Chan, A.H., Gligor, V. (eds.) ISC 2002. LNCS, vol. 2433, pp. 372–388. Springer, Heidelberg (2002). https://doi.org/10.1007/3-540-45811-5_29
20. Kawachi, A., Tanaka, K., Xagawa, K.: Concurrently secure identification schemes based on the worst-case hardness of lattice problems. In: Pieprzyk, J. (ed.) ASIACRYPT 2008. LNCS, vol. 5350, pp. 372–389. Springer, Heidelberg (2008). https://doi.org/10.1007/978-3-540-89255-7_23
21. Langlois, A., Ling, S., Nguyen, K., Wang, H.: Lattice-based group signature scheme with verifier-local revocation. In: Krawczyk, H. (ed.) PKC 2014. LNCS, vol. 8383, pp. 345–361. Springer, Heidelberg (2014). https://doi.org/10.1007/978-3-642-54631-0_20
22. Li, J., Li, N., Xue, R.: Universal accumulators with efficient nonmembership proofs. In: Katz, J., Yung, M. (eds.) ACNS 2007. LNCS, vol. 4521, pp. 253–269. Springer, Heidelberg (2007). https://doi.org/10.1007/978-3-540-72738-5_17
23. Libert, B., Ling, S., Mouhartem, F., Nguyen, K., Wang, H.: Signature schemes with efficient protocols and dynamic group signatures from lattice assumptions. In: Cheon, J.H., Takagi, T. (eds.) ASIACRYPT 2016. LNCS, vol. 10032, pp. 373–403. Springer, Heidelberg (2016). https://doi.org/10.1007/978-3-662-53890-6_13
24. Libert, B., Ling, S., Mouhartem, F., Nguyen, K., Wang, H.: Zero-knowledge arguments for matrix-vector relations and lattice-based group encryption. In:

Cheon, J.H., Takagi, T. (eds.) ASIACRYPT 2016. LNCS, vol. 10032, pp. 101–131. Springer, Heidelberg (2016). https://doi.org/10.1007/978-3-662-53890-6_4
25. Libert, B., Ling, S., Nguyen, K., Wang, H.: Zero-knowledge arguments for lattice-based accumulators: logarithmic-size ring signatures and group signatures without trapdoors. In: Fischlin, M., Coron, J.-S. (eds.) EUROCRYPT 2016. LNCS, vol. 9666, pp. 1–31. Springer, Heidelberg (2016). https://doi.org/10.1007/978-3-662-49896-5_1
26. Libert, B., Ling, S., Nguyen, K., Wang, H.: Zero-knowledge arguments for lattice-based PRFs and applications to E-Cash. In: Takagi, T., Peyrin, T. (eds.) ASIACRYPT 2017. LNCS, vol. 10626, pp. 304–335. Springer, Cham (2017). https://doi.org/10.1007/978-3-319-70700-6_11
27. Lin, Z., Hopper, N.: Jack: Scalable accumulator-based Nymble system. In: Proceedings of the 9th Annual ACM Workshop on Privacy in the Electronic Society, pp. 53–62. ACM (2010)
28. Ling, S., Nguyen, K., Stehlé, D., Wang, H.: Improved zero-knowledge proofs of knowledge for the ISIS problem, and applications. In: Kurosawa, K., Hanaoka, G. (eds.) PKC 2013. LNCS, vol. 7778, pp. 107–124. Springer, Heidelberg (2013). https://doi.org/10.1007/978-3-642-36362-7_8
29. Ling, S., Nguyen, K., Wang, H.: Group signatures from lattices: simpler, tighter, shorter, ring-based. In: Katz, J. (ed.) PKC 2015. LNCS, vol. 9020, pp. 427–449. Springer, Heidelberg (2015). https://doi.org/10.1007/978-3-662-46447-2_19
30. Ling, S., Nguyen, K., Wang, H., Xu, Y.: Lattice-based group signatures: achieving full dynamicity with ease. In: Gollmann, D., Miyaji, A., Kikuchi, H. (eds.) ACNS 2017. LNCS, vol. 10355, pp. 293–312. Springer, Cham (2017). https://doi.org/10.1007/978-3-319-61204-1_15
31. Lyubashevsky, V.: Fiat-shamir with aborts: applications to lattice and factoring-based signatures. In: Matsui, M. (ed.) ASIACRYPT 2009. LNCS, vol. 5912, pp. 598–616. Springer, Heidelberg (2009). https://doi.org/10.1007/978-3-642-10366-7_35
32. Lyubashevsky, V.: Lattice signatures without trapdoors. In: Pointcheval, D., Johansson, T. (eds.) EUROCRYPT 2012. LNCS, vol. 7237, pp. 738–755. Springer, Heidelberg (2012). https://doi.org/10.1007/978-3-642-29011-4_43
33. Miers, I., Garman, C., Green, M., Rubin, A.D.: Zerocoin: anonymous distributed e-cash from bitcoin. In: 2013 IEEE Symposium on Security and Privacy (SP), pp. 397–411. IEEE (2013)
34. Peikert, C., et al.: A decade of lattice cryptography. Found. Trends® Theoret. Comput. Sci. **10**(4), 283–424 (2016)
35. Sasson, E.B., Chiesa, A., Garman, C., Green, M., Miers, I., Tromer, E., Virza, M.: Zerocash: decentralized anonymous payments from bitcoin. In: 2014 IEEE Symposium on Security and Privacy (SP), pp. 459–474. IEEE (2014)
36. Stern, J.: A new paradigm for public key identification. IEEE Trans. Inf. Theory **42**(6), 1757–1768 (1996)
37. Tsudik, G., Xu, S.: Accumulating composites and improved group signing. In: Laih, C.-S. (ed.) ASIACRYPT 2003. LNCS, vol. 2894, pp. 269–286. Springer, Heidelberg (2003). https://doi.org/10.1007/978-3-540-40061-5_16

Lattice-Based Dual Receiver Encryption and More

Daode Zhang[1,2], Kai Zhang[3(✉)], Bao Li[1,2], Xianhui Lu[1,2], Haiyang Xue[1,2], and Jie Li[1,2]

[1] School of Cyber Security, University of Chinese Academy of Sciences, Beijing, China
{zhangdaode,libao,luxianhui,xuehaiyang,lijie}@iie.ac.cn

[2] Data Assurances and Communications Security, Institute of Information Engineering, Chinese Academy of Sciences, Beijing, China

[3] Department of Information Security, Shanghai University of Electric Power, Shanghai, China

Abstract. Dual receiver encryption (DRE), proposed by Diament et al. at ACM CCS 2004, is a special extension notion of public-key encryption, which enables two independent receivers to decrypt a ciphertext into a same plaintext. This primitive is quite useful in designing combined public key cryptosystems and denial of service attack-resilient protocols. Up till now, a series of DRE schemes are constructed with bilinear pairing groups. In this work, we introduce the first construction of lattice-based DRE. Our scheme is secure against chosen-ciphertext attacks from the standard Learning with Errors (LWE) assumption with a public key of bit-size about $2nm \log q$, where m and q are small polynomials in n. Additionally, for the DRE notion in the identity-based setting, identity-based DRE (ID-DRE), we also give a lattice-based ID-DRE scheme that achieves chosen-plaintext and adaptively chosen identity security based on the LWE assumption with public parameter size about $(2\ell + 1)nm \log q$, where ℓ is the bit-size of the identity in the scheme.

Keywords: Lattices · Dual receiver encryption
Identity-based dual receiver encryption · Learning with errors

1 Introduction

The notion of dual receiver encryption (DRE), formlized by Diament et al. [8] at ACM CCS 2004, is an extension version of public key encryption, in which a ciphertext can be decrypted into the same plaintext by two independent users. More precisely, in a DRE scheme, the encryption algorithm takes as input a message M and two receivers' independently generated public keys pk_1 and pk_2 and produces a ciphertext c. Once the receivers receive the ciphertext c, either of them can decrypt c and obtain the message M using their respective secret

W. Susilo and G. Yang (Eds.): ACISP 2018, LNCS 10946, pp. 520–538, 2018.
https://doi.org/10.1007/978-3-319-93638-3_30

key. With such a DRE primitive, one can obtain a combined public key cryptosystem or design a denial of service attack-resilient protocol [8]. A decade later, in CT-RSA 2014, Chow et al. [6] refined the syntax of DRE and appended some appealing features for DRE. Recently, to simplify the difficulty of certificate management in traditional certificate-based DRE schemes, Zhang et al. [21] extended the DRE concept into the identity-based setting by introducing the identity-based dual receiver encryption (ID-DRE) notion.

In [8], Diament et al. presented the first DRE scheme by transforming the three-party one-round Diffie-Hellman key exchange scheme by Joux [11], and also proved that it is indistinguishable secure against chosen ciphertext attacks (CCA). However, their scheme relied on the existence of random oracle heuristic (RO), where a DRE that proven to be secure in the RO model may turn into insecure one when the RO is instantiated by an actual hash function in practice. Hence, Youn and Smith [20] began with attempting to give a provably secure DRE scheme in the standard model by combining a adaptively CCA secure encryption scheme and a non-interactive zero-knowledge protocol, while suffered low efficiency due to the prohibitively huge proof size. Later on, Chow et al. [6] proposed a CCA secure DRE scheme via combining a selective-tag weakly CCA-secure tag-based DRE (based on the tag-based encryption scheme in [13]) and a strong one-time signature scheme, as well as other DRE instantiations for non-malleable and other properties[1]. Recently, Zhang et al. [21] constructed two provably secure ID-DRE schemes against adaptively chosen plaintext or ciphertext and chosen identity attacks based on an identity-based encryption scheme in [19].

However, it is worth noticing that all the existing concrete (ID-)DRE schemes are constructed over bilinear pairing groups. Moreover, recent advances in quantum computing have triggered widespread interest in developing post-quantum cryptographic schemes. Therefore in this work, inspired by the appealing potentials of DRE, we consider (identity-based) dual receiver encryption notion in the context of lattice-based cryptography due to its conjectured resistance against quantum adversaries.

1.1 Our Contributions

We introduce the first construction of DRE and ID-DRE from lattices. Our two schemes are constructed in the standard model and satisfy chosen-ciphertext or chosen-plaintext security, which are both based on the hardness of the Learning With Errors (LWE) problem. Specifically, based on the beautiful work of Agrawal et al. [1], our works are stated as follows.

- We construct a secure DRE scheme against chosen-ciphertext attacks from the standard Learning with Errors assumption with a public key of bit-size about

[1] Note that Chow et al. [6] also gave two generic DRE constructions: one is combining Naor-Yung "two-key" paradigm [14] with Groth-Sahai proof system [10], the other is from lossy trapdoor functions [15].

$2nm \log q$, where m and q are small polynomials in n. In order to encrypt a n-bit message, the ciphertext consists of two parts: one is a $(n+4m)\log q$-bit ciphertext which is an encryption of the message, the other is a one-time signature of the first part.

- Additionally, we construct a secure ID-DRE scheme against chosen-plaintext and adaptively chosen-identity attacks from the same assumption. As a result, the public parameter of our ID-DRE achieves $(2\ell+1)nm\log q$ bit-size, where ℓ is the bit-size of the identity. In order to encrypt a n-bit message, the bit-size of ciphertext will become $(n+3m)\log q$. Note that one can still get two ID-DRE schemes with more compact public parameters via relying on other lattice-based IBE works that achieved short public parameter sizes, which is formally discussed in Sect. 4.3.

Organization. The rest of this paper is organized as follows. In Appendix A and Sect. 2, we recall some lattice background, dual-receiver encryption and identity-based dual-receiver encryption. Our DRE construction and its proof are presented in Sect. 3, and ID-DRE construction along with its proof are described in Sect. 4. In Sect. 5, we give a conclusion.

2 Preliminaries

Notations. Let λ be the security parameter, and all other quantities are implicitly dependent on λ. Let $\mathsf{negl}(\lambda)$ denote a negligible function and $\mathsf{poly}(\lambda)$ denote unspecified function $f(\lambda) = \mathcal{O}(\lambda^c)$ for a constant c. For $n \in \mathbb{N}$, we use $[n]$ to denote a set $\{1, \cdots, n\}$. And for integer $q \geq 2$, $\mathbb{Z}_q$ denotes the quotient ring of integer modulo q. We use bold capital letters to denote matrices, such as $\mathbf{A}, \mathbf{B}$, and bold lowercase letters to denote column vectors, such as $\mathbf{x}, \mathbf{y}$. The notations $\mathbf{A}^\top$ and $[\mathbf{A}|\mathbf{B}]$ denote the transpose of the matrix $\mathbf{A}$ and the matrix of concatenating $\mathbf{A}$ and $\mathbf{B}$, respectively. Additionally, we use $(\mathbf{a})_i$, $(\mathbf{A})_i$ to denote the i-th element, column of $\mathbf{a}$, $\mathbf{A}$. $\mathbf{I}_n$ denotes the $n \times n$ identity matrix and $\mathbf{Inv}_n$ denotes the set of invertible matrices in $\mathbb{Z}_q^{n\times n}$.

2.1 Encoding Vectors into Matrices

In [7], Cramer and Damgård described an encoding function $\mathcal{H}_{t,\mathbb{F}}$ that maps a domain $\mathbb{F}^t$ to matrices in $\mathbb{F}^{t\times t}$ with certain, strongly injective properties, where $\mathbb{F}$ is a field. For a polynomial $g \in \mathbb{F}[X]$ of degree less than $t-1$, $\mathsf{coeff}(g) \in \mathbb{F}^t$ is the t- vector of coefficients of g. Let f be a polynomial of degree t in $\mathbb{F}[X]$ that is irreducible. Then for $g \in \mathbb{F}[X]$, the polynomial $g \mod f$ has degree at most $t-1$, so $\mathsf{coeff}(g \mod f) \in \mathbb{F}^t$. Now, for an input $\mathbf{h} = (h_0, h_1, \cdots, h_{t-1})^\top \in \mathbb{F}^t$ define the polynomial $g_{\mathbf{h}}(X) = \sum_{i=0}^{t-1} h_i x^i \in \mathbb{F}[X]$. Define $\mathcal{H}_{t,\mathbb{F}}(\mathbf{h})$ as

$$\mathcal{H}_{t,\mathbb{F}}(\mathbf{h}) := \begin{pmatrix} \mathsf{coeff}(g_{\mathbf{h}} \mod f)^\top \\ \mathsf{coeff}(x \cdot g_{\mathbf{h}} \mod f)^\top \\ \vdots \\ \mathsf{coeff}(x^{t-1} \cdot g_{\mathbf{h}} \mod f)^\top \end{pmatrix} \in \mathbb{F}^{t\times t}.$$

From here on, we take $\mathbb{F} := \mathbb{Z}_q$ for a prime q. As stated in [4], it is easy to verify that $\mathcal{H}_{t,q} : \mathbb{Z}_q^t \to \mathbb{Z}_q^{t\times t}$ obeys the following properties:

- $\mathcal{H}_{t,q}(a\mathbf{h}_1 + b\mathbf{h}_2) = a \cdot \mathcal{H}_{t,q}(\mathbf{h}_1) + b \cdot \mathcal{H}_{t,q}(\mathbf{h}_2)$ for any $a, b \in \mathbb{Z}_q, \mathbf{h}_1, \mathbf{h}_2 \in \mathbf{Z}_q^t$.
- For any vector $\mathbf{h} \neq \mathbf{0}$, $\mathcal{H}_{t,q}(\mathbf{h})$ is invertible, and $\mathcal{H}_{t,q}(\mathbf{0}) = \mathbf{0}$.

In [1], according to function $\mathcal{H}_{t,q}$, Agrawal et al. defined the following equation $\mathcal{H}_{\mathrm{ABB}} : \mathbb{Z}_q^\ell \to \mathbb{Z}^{n\times n}$: For $\mathbf{x} = (x_1, \cdots, x_\ell)^\top \in \mathbb{Z}_q^\ell$,

$$\mathcal{H}_{\mathrm{ABB}}(\mathbf{x}) = \mathbf{I}_n + \sum_{i=1}^{\ell} x_i \cdot \mathcal{H}_{t,q}(\mathbf{h}_i) \otimes \mathbf{I}_{n/t},$$

where $\mathbf{h}_i \xleftarrow{\$} \mathbf{Z}_q^t$ for $i \in \{1, \cdots, \ell\}$, and assume that n is a multiple of t. Then, they implicitly presented the following lemma. However, they did not give a complete proof.

Lemma 1. *For any integers ℓ, t, n, and a prime q, let $\mathcal{H}_{\mathrm{ABB}}$ be the hash function family defined as above. Then for any fixed set $\mathcal{S} \subseteq \mathbb{Z}_q^\ell, |\mathcal{S}| \leq Q$, and any $\mathbf{x} \in \mathbb{Z}_q^\ell \backslash \mathcal{S}$, we have*

$$\Pr\left[\mathcal{H}_{\mathrm{ABB}}(\mathbf{x}) = \mathbf{0} \wedge (\forall \mathbf{x}' \in \mathcal{S}, \mathcal{H}_{\mathrm{ABB}}(\mathbf{x}') \in \mathbf{Inv}_n)\right] \in \left(\frac{1}{q^t}(1 - \frac{Q}{q^t}), \frac{1}{q^t}\right).$$

Proof. For a vector $\mathbf{e}_1 = (1, 0, \cdots, 0)^\top \in \mathbb{Z}_q^t$, we have $\mathcal{H}_{t,q}(\mathbf{e}_1) = \mathbf{I}_t$. For $\mathbf{x} = (x_1, \cdots, x_\ell)^\top \in \mathbb{Z}_q^\ell$, let $\mathcal{S}_0$ be the set of functions in $\mathcal{H}_{\mathrm{ABB}}$ such that $\mathcal{H}_{\mathrm{ABB}}(\mathbf{x}) = \mathbf{0}$. It is straightforward to verify that the following equation holds:

$$\begin{aligned}\mathcal{H}_{\mathrm{ABB}}(\mathbf{x}) &= \mathbf{I}_n + \sum_{i=1}^{\ell} x_i \cdot \mathcal{H}_{t,q}(\mathbf{h}_i) \otimes \mathbf{I}_{n/t} = \left(\mathbf{I}_t + \sum_{i=1}^{\ell} x_i \cdot \mathcal{H}_{t,q}(\mathbf{h}_i)\right) \otimes \mathbf{I}_{n/t} \\ &= \left(\mathcal{H}_{t,q}(\mathbf{e}_1) + \sum_{i=1}^{\ell} x_i \cdot \mathcal{H}_{t,q}(\mathbf{h}_i)\right) \otimes \mathbf{I}_{n/t} = \mathcal{H}_{t,q}\left(\mathbf{e}_1 + \sum_{i=1}^{\ell} x_i \mathbf{h}_i\right) \otimes \mathbf{I}_{n/t}.\end{aligned}$$

By a simple observation, we have $\mathcal{H}_{\mathrm{ABB}}(\mathbf{x}) = \mathbf{0}$ if and only if $\sum_{i=1}^{\ell} x_i \mathbf{h}_i = -\mathbf{e}_1$. As a result, we can get $|\mathcal{S}_0| = q^{(\ell-1)t}$. In the same way, we can get $|\mathcal{S}_i'| = q^{(\ell-1)t}$, where $\mathcal{S}_i'$ is the set of functions $\mathcal{H}_{\mathrm{ABB}}$ such that $\mathcal{H}_{\mathrm{ABB}}(\mathbf{x}_i') = \mathbf{0}$ for $\mathbf{x}_i' \in \mathcal{S} = \{\mathbf{x}_1', \cdots, \mathbf{x}_{|\mathcal{S}|}'\}$. Moreover, $|\mathcal{S}_0 \cap \mathcal{S}_i'| \leq q^{(\ell-2)t}$ for $i \in \{1, \cdots, |\mathcal{S}|\}$. The set of functions in $\mathcal{H}_{\mathrm{ABB}}$ such that $\mathcal{H}_{\mathrm{ABB}}(\mathbf{x}) = \mathbf{0}$ and $\forall \mathbf{x}' \in \mathcal{S}, \mathcal{H}_{\mathrm{ABB}}(\mathbf{x}') \in \mathbf{Inv}_n$ is exactly $\widetilde{\mathcal{S}} = \mathcal{S}_0 \setminus \{\mathcal{S}_1' \cup \cdots \cup \mathcal{S}_{|\mathcal{S}|}'\}$. Now, we have

$$\left|\widetilde{\mathcal{S}}\right| = \left|\mathcal{S}_0 \setminus \{\mathcal{S}_1' \cup \cdots \cup \mathcal{S}_{|\mathcal{S}|}'\}\right| \geq |\mathcal{S}_0| - \sum_{i=1}^{|\mathcal{S}|} |\mathcal{S}_0 \cap \mathcal{S}_i'| \geq q^{(\ell-1)t} - Qq^{(\ell-2)t}.$$

Therefore the above probability holds with $|\widetilde{\mathcal{S}}|/q^{t\ell}$ is at least $\frac{1}{q^t}(1 - \frac{Q}{q^t})$. And the probability is at most $\frac{1}{q^t}$ since $|\widetilde{\mathcal{S}}| \leq |\mathcal{S}_0| = q^{(\ell-1)t}$. □

2.2 (Identity-Based) Dual Receiver Encryption

Dual Receiver Encryption [8]. A DRE scheme consists of the following four algorithms:

- $\mathsf{CGen}_{\mathsf{DRE}}(1^\lambda) \rightarrow \mathsf{crs}$: The randomized common reference string (CRS) generation algorithm takes as input a security parameter λ and outputs a CRS crs.
- $\mathsf{Gen}_{\mathsf{DRE}}(\mathsf{crs}) \rightarrow (pk, sk)$: The randomized key generation algorithm takes as input crs and outputs a public/secret key pair (pk, sk). We regard (pk_1, sk_1) and (pk_2, sk_2) as the key pairs of two independent users. Without loss of generality, we assume $pk_1 <^d pk_2$, where $<^d$ is a "less-than" operator based on lexicographic order throughout this paper.
- $\mathsf{Enc}_{\mathsf{DRE}}(\mathsf{crs}, pk_1, pk_2, M) \rightarrow c$: The randomized encryption algorithm takes as input crs, two public keys pk_1 and pk_2 (such that $pk_1 <^d pk_2$) and a message M, and outputs a ciphertext c.
- $\mathsf{Dec}_{\mathsf{DRE}}(\mathsf{crs}, pk_1, pk_2, sk_j, c) \rightarrow M$: The deterministic decryption algorithm takes two public keys pk_1 and pk_2 (such that $pk_1 <^d pk_2$), one of the secret keys sk_j ($j \in \{1, 2\}$), and a ciphertext c as input, and outputs a message M (which may be the special symbol $\perp$).

Correctness. For consistency, we require that, if $\mathsf{crs} \leftarrow \mathsf{CGen}_{\mathsf{DRE}}(1^\lambda)$, $(pk_1, sk_1) \leftarrow \mathsf{Gen}_{\mathsf{DRE}}(\mathsf{crs})$ and $(pk_2, sk_2) \leftarrow \mathsf{Gen}_{\mathsf{DRE}}(\mathsf{crs})$, and $c \leftarrow \mathsf{Enc}_{\mathsf{DRE}}(\mathsf{crs}, pk_1, pk_2, M)$, then we have the probability

$$\Pr\left[\mathsf{Dec}_{\mathsf{DRE}}(\mathsf{crs}, pk_1, pk_2, sk_1, c) = \mathsf{Dec}_{\mathsf{DRE}}(\mathsf{crs}, pk_1, pk_2, sk_2, c) = M\right] = 1 - \mathsf{negl}(\lambda).$$

Security. A DRE scheme is said to be indistinguishable against chosen-ciphertext attacks (IND-CCA) if for any PPT adversary $\mathcal{A}$,

$$\mathbf{Adv}^{\mathsf{ind-cca}}_{\mathcal{DRE},\mathcal{A}}(1^\lambda) = \left|\Pr\left[\mathsf{Exp}^{\mathsf{ind-cca}}_{\mathcal{DRE},\mathcal{A}}(1^\lambda) = 1\right] - \frac{1}{2}\right|$$

is negligible in λ.

Identity-Based Dual Receiver Encryption [21]. An ID-DRE scheme consists of the following four algorithms:

- $\mathsf{Setup}_{\mathsf{ID}}(1^\lambda) \rightarrow (PP, Msk)$. The setup algorithm takes in a security parameter 1^λ as input. It outputs public parameters PP and a master secret key Msk.
- $\mathsf{KeyGen}_{\mathsf{ID}}(PP, Msk, id_{1st}, id_{2nd} \in ID) \rightarrow sk_{id_{1st}}, sk_{id_{2nd}}$. The key generation algorithm takes public parameters PP, master secret key Msk, and two identities id_{1st}, id_{2nd} as input. It outputs $sk_{id_{1st}}$ as the secret key for the first receiver id_{1st}, and $sk_{id_{2nd}}$ for the second receiver id_{2nd}.
- $\mathsf{Enc}_{\mathsf{ID}}(PP, id_{1st}, id_{2nd}, M) \rightarrow c$. The encryption algorithm takes in public parameters PP, two identities id_{1st} and id_{2nd}, and a message M as input. It outputs a ciphertext c.
- $\mathsf{Dec}_{\mathsf{ID}}(PP, c, sk_{id_j}) \rightarrow M$. The decryption algorithm takes in public parameters PP, a ciphertext c, and one secret key sk_{id_j} as input, where $j \in \{1st, 2nd\}$. It outputs a message M.

Experiment $\mathsf{Exp}^{\mathsf{ind-cca}}_{\mathcal{DRE},\mathcal{A}}(1^\lambda)$: $\mathsf{crs} \xleftarrow{\$} \mathsf{CGen}_{\mathsf{DRE}}(1^\lambda)$; $(pk_j, sk_j) \xleftarrow{\$} \mathsf{Gen}_{\mathsf{DRE}}(\mathsf{crs})$ for $j \in 1, 2$; $(M_0, M_1, s) \xleftarrow{\$} \mathcal{A}^{\mathsf{Dec}_{\mathsf{DRE}}(sk_j, c)}(\mathsf{crs}, pk_1, pk_2)$; $b \xleftarrow{\$} \{0,1\}$, $c^\star \xleftarrow{\$} \mathsf{Enc}_{\mathsf{DRE}}(\mathsf{crs}, pk_1, pk_2, M_b)$; $b' \xleftarrow{\$} \mathcal{A}^{\mathsf{Dec}_{\mathsf{DRE}}(sk_j, c) \wedge c \neq c^\star}(c^\star, s)$; if $b' = b$ then return 1 else return 0.
Experiment $\mathsf{Exp}^{\mathsf{ind-id-cpa}}_{\mathcal{ID-DRE},\mathcal{A}}(1^\lambda)$: $(PP, Msk) \xleftarrow{\$} \mathsf{Setup}_{\mathsf{ID}}(1^\lambda)$ $(id^\star_{1st}, id^\star_{2nd}, M_0, M_1, s) \xleftarrow{\$} \mathcal{A}^{\mathsf{KeyGen}_{\mathsf{ID}}(PP, Msk, id_{1st}, id_{2nd})}(PP)$; $b \xleftarrow{\$} \{0,1\}$,$c^\star \xleftarrow{\$} \mathsf{Enc}_{\mathsf{ID}}(PP, id^\star_{1st}, id^\star_{2nd}, M_b)$; $b' \xleftarrow{\$} \mathcal{A}^{\mathsf{KeyGen}_{\mathsf{ID}}(PP, Msk, id_{1st}, id_{2nd}) \wedge id_j \neq id^\star_{j, j=1st,2nd}}(c^\star, s)$; if $b' = b$ then return 1 else return 0.

Fig. 1. IND-CCA security for DRE and IND-ID-CPA security for ID-DRE

Correctness. For all $(PP, Msk) \xleftarrow{\$} \mathsf{Setup}_{\mathsf{ID}}(1^\lambda)$, all identities $id_j \in \mathcal{ID}$, all messages M, all $sk_{id_j} \leftarrow \mathsf{KeyGen}_{\mathsf{ID}}(PP, Msk, id_j)$, all $c \leftarrow \mathsf{Enc}_{\mathsf{ID}}(PP, id_{1st}, id_{2nd}, M)$, we have

$$\Pr[\mathsf{Dec}_{\mathsf{ID}}(PP, sk_{id_{1st}}, c) = \mathsf{Dec}_{\mathsf{ID}}(PP, sk_{id_{2nd}}, c) = M] = 1 - \mathsf{negl}(\lambda).$$

Security. An ID-DRE scheme is said to be indistinguishable against chosen-plaintext and adaptively chosen-identity attacks (IND-ID-CPA) if for any PPT adversary $\mathcal{A}$,

$$\mathbf{Adv}^{\mathsf{ind-id-cpa}}_{\mathcal{ID-DRE},\mathcal{A}}(1^\lambda) = \left| \Pr\left[\mathsf{Exp}^{\mathsf{ind-id-cpa}}_{\mathcal{ID-DRE},\mathcal{A}}(1^\lambda) = 1\right] - \frac{1}{2} \right|$$

is negligible in λ.

The Relation Between DRE and Broadcast Encryption. As studied in [6,21], the (ID-) DRE can be viewed as a special instance of a dynamic (ID-) broadcast encryption primitive that supports multiple recipients in an encryption system. Different from (ID-) broadcast encryption schemes usually relying on strong security assumptions or/and random oracle heuristic [18], (ID-) DRE aims to give a more straightforward understanding and direct construction under simple assumptions in the standard model. In general, broadcast encryption is more expensive than dual-receiver encryption.

3 Dual Receiver Encryption Construction

Our scheme relies upon a strongly unforgeable one-time signature scheme $\mathcal{OTS} = (\mathsf{Gen}_{\mathsf{OTS}}, \mathsf{Sig}_{\mathsf{OTS}}, \mathsf{Vrf}_{\mathsf{OTS}})$ whose verification key is exactly λ bits long. The description of our DRE scheme $\mathcal{DRE}$ is as follows.

- $\mathsf{CGen}_{\mathsf{DRE}}(1^\lambda)$. On input a security parameter λ, algorithm $\mathsf{CGen}_{\mathsf{DRE}}$ sets the parameters n, m, q as specified in Fig. 2. Then it selects a uniformly random matrix $\mathbf{U} \in \mathbb{Z}_q^{n \times n}$. Finally it outputs a CRS $\mathsf{crs} = (n, m, q, \mathbf{U})$.
- $\mathsf{Gen}_{\mathsf{DRE}}(\mathsf{crs})$. For user $j \in \{1, 2\}$, this algorithm generates a pair matrices $(\mathbf{A}_j, \mathbf{T}_{\mathbf{A}_j}) \in \mathbb{Z}_q^{n \times m} \times \mathbb{Z}_q^{m \times m}$ by running $\mathsf{TrapGen}(1^n, 1^m, q)$ and selects a random matrix $\mathbf{B}_j \xleftarrow{\$} \mathbb{Z}_q^{n \times m}$. Finally, it outputs

$$pk_j = (\mathbf{A}_j, \mathbf{B}_j) \qquad \text{and} \qquad sk_j = \mathbf{T}_{\mathbf{A}_j}.$$

- $\mathsf{Enc}_{\mathsf{DRE}}(\mathsf{crs}, pk_1, pk_2, \mathbf{m} \in \{0,1\}^n)$. It first obtains a pair $(\mathsf{vk}, \mathsf{sk})$ by running $\mathsf{Gen}_{\mathsf{OTS}}(1^\lambda)$ and computes $\mathbf{C}_1 = [\mathbf{A}_1 | \mathbf{B}_1 + \mathcal{H}_{n,q}(\mathsf{vk}) \cdot \mathbf{G}] \in \mathbb{Z}_q^{n \times 2m}$, $\mathbf{C}_2 = [\mathbf{A}_2 | \mathbf{B}_2 + \mathcal{H}_{n,q}(\mathsf{vk}) \cdot \mathbf{G}] \in \mathbb{Z}_q^{n \times 2m}$. Then, it picks $\mathbf{s} \xleftarrow{\$} \mathbb{Z}_q^n$, $\widetilde{\mathbf{e}}_0 \xleftarrow{\$} \mathcal{D}_{\mathbb{Z}^n, \alpha q}$, and $\mathbf{e}_{1,1}, \mathbf{e}_{2,1}, \mathbf{e}_{1,2}, \mathbf{e}_{2,2} \xleftarrow{\$} \mathcal{D}_{\mathbb{Z}^m, \alpha' q}$. Finally, it computes and returns the ciphertext $\mathbf{c} = (\mathsf{vk}, \mathbf{c}_0, \mathbf{c}_1, \mathbf{c}_2, \delta)$, where $\delta = \mathsf{Sig}_{\mathsf{OTS}}(\mathsf{sk}, (\mathbf{c}_0, \mathbf{c}_1, \mathbf{c}_2))$ and

$$\mathbf{c}_0 = \mathbf{U}^\top \mathbf{s} + \widetilde{\mathbf{e}}_0 + \left\lceil \frac{q}{2} \right\rceil \cdot \mathbf{m} \in \mathbb{Z}_q^n,$$

$$\mathbf{c}_1 = \mathbf{C}_1^\top \mathbf{s} + \begin{bmatrix} \mathbf{e}_{1,1} \\ \mathbf{e}_{1,2} \end{bmatrix} \in \mathbb{Z}_q^{2m}, \mathbf{c}_2 = \mathbf{C}_2^\top \mathbf{s} + \begin{bmatrix} \mathbf{e}_{2,1} \\ \mathbf{e}_{2,2} \end{bmatrix} \in \mathbb{Z}_q^{2m}.$$

- $\mathsf{Dec}_{\mathsf{DRE}}(\mathsf{crs}, pk_1, pk_2, sk_1, \mathbf{c})$. To decrypt a ciphertext $\mathbf{c} = (\mathsf{vk}, \mathbf{c}_0, \mathbf{c}_1, \mathbf{c}_2, \delta)$ with a private key $sk_1 = \mathbf{T}_{\mathbf{A}_1}$, the algorithm $\mathsf{Dec}_{\mathsf{DRE}}$ performs each of the following steps:
  (1) it runs $\mathsf{Vrf}_{\mathsf{OTS}}(\mathsf{vk}, (\mathbf{c}_0, \mathbf{c}_1, \mathbf{c}_2), \delta)$, outputs $\perp$ if $\mathsf{Vrf}_{\mathsf{OTS}}$ rejects;
  (2) for $i \in \{1, \cdots, n\}$, it runs $\mathsf{SampleLeft}(\mathbf{A}_1, \mathbf{B}_1 + \mathcal{H}_{n,q}(\mathsf{vk}) \cdot \mathbf{G}, (\mathbf{U})_i, \mathbf{T}_{\mathbf{A}_1}, \sigma)$ to obtain $(\mathbf{E}_1)_i$, i.e., it obtains $\mathbf{E}_1 \in \mathbb{Z}_q^{2m \times n}$ such that $\mathbf{C}_1 \cdot \mathbf{E}_1 = \mathbf{U}$;
  (3) it computes $\mathbf{b} = \mathbf{c}_0 - \mathbf{E}_1^\top \mathbf{c}_1$ and treats each element of $\mathbf{b} = [(\mathbf{b})_1, \cdots, (\mathbf{b})_n]^\top$ as an integer in $\mathbb{Z}$, and sets $(\mathbf{m})_i = 1$ if $\left|(\mathbf{b})_i - \lceil \frac{q}{2} \rceil\right| < \lceil \frac{q}{4} \rceil$, else $(\mathbf{m})_i = 0$, where $i \in \{1, \cdots, n\}$.
  (4) finally, it returns the plaintext $\mathbf{m} = [(\mathbf{m})_1, \cdots, (\mathbf{m})_n]^\top$.

3.1 Correctness and Parameter Selection

In order to satisfy the correctness requirement and make the security proof work, we need that

- for $i \in \{1, \cdots, n\}$, the error term is bounded by

$$\left| (\widetilde{\mathbf{e}}_0)_i - (\mathbf{E})_i^\top \begin{bmatrix} \mathbf{e}_{1,1} \\ \mathbf{e}_{1,2} \end{bmatrix} \right| \le \alpha q \sqrt{m} + (\sigma \sqrt{2m}) \cdot (\alpha' q \sqrt{2m}) < q/4.$$

- $\mathsf{TrapGen}$ in Lemma 12 (Item 1) can work ($m \ge 6n \lceil \log q \rceil$), and it returns $\mathbf{T}_{\mathbf{A}}$ satisfying $\|\widetilde{\mathbf{T}_{\mathbf{A}}}\| \ge \mathcal{O}(\sqrt{n \log q})$.
- the Leftover Hash Lemma in Lemma 12 (Item 4) can be applied to the security proof ($m > (n+1) \log q + \omega(\log n)$).

- SampleLeft in Lemma 12 (Item 2) can operate ($\sigma \geq \|\widetilde{\mathbf{T}_{\mathbf{A}}}\| \cdot \omega(\sqrt{\log m}) = \mathcal{O}(\sqrt{n \log q}) \cdot \omega(\sqrt{\log m})$).
- SampleRight in Lemma 12 (Item 3) can operate ($\sigma \geq \|\widetilde{\mathbf{T}_{\mathbf{G}}}\| \cdot s_1(\mathbf{R}_j) \cdot \omega(\sqrt{\log m})$, for $j = 1, 2$).
- ReRand (Lemma 13) in the security proof can operate ($\alpha q > \omega(\sqrt{\log m})$, and $\alpha' q/(2\alpha q) > s_1([\mathbf{I}_m|\mathbf{R}_j]^\top)$, where $s_1([\mathbf{I}_m|\mathbf{R}_j]^\top) \leq (1 + s_1(\mathbf{R}_j)) \leq (1 + 12\sqrt{2m})$, for $j = 1, 2$.

To satisfy the above requirements, we set the parameters in Fig. 2.

Parameters	Description	Setting
λ	security parameter	
n	PK-matrix row number	$n = \lambda$
m	PK-matrix column number	$6n \log q$
σ	SampleLeft,SampleRight width	$12\sqrt{10m} \cdot \omega(\sqrt{\log n})$
q	modulus	$96\sqrt{5}m^{3/2}n\omega(\sqrt{\log n})$
αq	error width	$2\sqrt{2n}$
$\alpha' q$	error width	$96\sqrt{mn}$

Fig. 2. Parameter selection of DRE construction

3.2 Security Proof

Theorem 1. *If $\mathcal{OTS}$ is a strongly existential unforgeable one-time signature scheme and the* $\mathrm{DLWE}_{q,n,n+2m,\alpha}$ *assumption holds, then the above scheme $\mathcal{DRE}$ is a secure DRE against chosen-ciphertext attacks.*

Proof (of Theorem 1). Assume $\mathcal{A}$ is a probabilistic polonomial time (PPT) adversary attacks $\mathcal{DRE}$ in a chosen-ciphertext attack. If $\mathsf{Vrf}_{\mathsf{OTS}}(\mathsf{vk}, (\mathbf{c}_0, \mathbf{c}_1, \mathbf{c}_2), \delta) = 1$, we say the ciphertext $\mathbf{c} = (\mathsf{vk}, (\mathbf{c}_0, \mathbf{c}_1, \mathbf{c}_2), \delta)$ is valid. Let $\mathbf{c}^\star$ denote the challenge ciphertext $(\mathsf{vk}^\star, (\mathbf{c}_0^\star, \mathbf{c}_1^\star, \mathbf{c}_2^\star), \delta^\star)$ received by $\mathcal{A}$ during a particular run of the experiment, and let Forge denote the event that $\mathcal{A}$ submits a valid ciphertext $(\mathsf{vk}^\star, (\mathbf{c}_0, \mathbf{c}_1, \mathbf{c}_2), \delta)$ to the decryption oracle (we assume that $\mathsf{vk}^\star$ is chosen at the outer of the experiment so this well-defined even before $\mathcal{A}$ is given $\mathbf{c}^\star$.) According to the security of $\mathcal{OTS}$, Pr [Forge] is negligible. We then prove the following lemma:

Lemma 2. $\left|\Pr\left[\mathsf{Exp}^{\mathrm{ind-cca}}_{\mathcal{DRE},\mathcal{A}}(1^\lambda) = 1 \wedge \overline{\mathsf{Forge}}\right] + \frac{1}{2}\Pr\left[\mathsf{Forge}\right] - \frac{1}{2}\right|$ *is negligible, if assuming that the* $\mathrm{DLWE}_{q,n,n+2m,\alpha}$ *assumption holds.*

To see that this implies the theorem, note that

$$\begin{aligned}\mathsf{Adv}^{\mathsf{ind-cca}}_{\mathcal{DRE},\mathcal{A}}(1^\lambda) &= \left|\Pr\left[\mathsf{Exp}^{\mathsf{ind-cca}}_{\mathcal{DRE},\mathcal{A}}(1^\lambda)=1\right]-\frac{1}{2}\right| \\ &\leq \left|\Pr\left[\mathsf{Exp}^{\mathsf{ind-cca}}_{\mathcal{DRE},\mathcal{A}}(1^\lambda)=1\wedge \mathsf{Forge}\right]-\frac{1}{2}\Pr\left[\mathsf{Forge}\right]\right| \\ &\quad + \left|\Pr\left[\mathsf{Exp}^{\mathsf{ind-cca}}_{\mathcal{DRE},\mathcal{A}}(1^\lambda)=1\wedge \overline{\mathsf{Forge}}\right]+\frac{1}{2}\Pr\left[\mathsf{Forge}\right]-\frac{1}{2}\right| \\ &\leq \frac{1}{2}\Pr\left[\mathsf{Forge}\right]+\left|\Pr\left[\mathsf{Exp}^{\mathsf{ind-cca}}_{\mathcal{DRE},\mathcal{A}}(1^\lambda)=1\wedge \overline{\mathsf{Forge}}\right]+\frac{1}{2}\Pr\left[\mathsf{Forge}\right]-\frac{1}{2}\right|.\end{aligned}$$

Proof (of Lemma 2)**.** We sketch the proof via a sequence of games. The games involve the challenger and an adversary $\mathcal{A}$. In the following, we define X_κ as the event that the challenger outputs 1 in $\mathbf{Game}_\kappa$, for $\kappa \in \{1,2,3,4,5\}$.

Game₁: This game is the original experiment $\mathsf{Exp}^{\mathsf{ind-cca}}_{\mathcal{DRE},\mathcal{A}}(1^\lambda)$ except that when the adversary $\mathcal{A}$ submits a valid ciphertext $(\mathsf{vk}^\star, (\mathbf{c}_0, \mathbf{c}_1, \mathbf{c}_2), \delta)$ to the decryption oracle, the challenger outputs a random bit. It is easy to see that

$$\left|\Pr\left[X_1\right]-\frac{1}{2}\right| = \left|\Pr\left[\mathsf{Exp}^{\mathsf{ind-cca}}_{\mathcal{DRE},\mathcal{A}}(1^\lambda)=1\wedge \overline{\mathsf{Forge}}\right]+\frac{1}{2}\Pr\left[\mathsf{Forge}\right]-\frac{1}{2}\right|.$$

Game₂: This game is identical to **Game₁** except that the challenger changes (1) the generation of public keys pk_1, pk_2: the challenger selects random matrices $\mathbf{A}_1, \mathbf{A}_2 \in \mathbb{Z}_q^{n\times m}$ instead of running $\mathsf{TrapGen}$, and random matrices $\mathbf{R}_1, \mathbf{R}_2 \in \{-1,1\}^{m\times m}$; then, the challenger computes $\mathbf{B}_1 = \mathbf{A}_1\mathbf{R}_1 - \mathcal{H}_{n,q}(\mathsf{vk}^\star)\mathbf{G}, \mathbf{B}_2 = \mathbf{A}_2\mathbf{R}_2 - \mathcal{H}_{n,q}(\mathsf{vk}^\star)\mathbf{G} \in \mathbb{Z}_q^{n\times m}$. (2) the decryption oracle: when $\mathcal{A}$ submits a valid ciphertext $(\mathsf{vk} \neq \mathsf{vk}^\star, (\mathbf{c}_0, \mathbf{c}_1, \mathbf{c}_2), \delta)$, the challenger generates $\mathbf{E}_1$ by running $\mathsf{SampleRight}(\mathbf{A}_1, \mathbf{G}, \mathbf{R}_1, \mathcal{H}_{n,q}(\mathsf{vk}-\mathsf{vk}^\star), (\mathbf{U})_i, \mathbf{T}_\mathbf{G}, \sigma)$ (In the similar way, the challenger can obtain $\mathbf{E}_2$ by running the algorithm $\mathsf{SampleRight}(\mathbf{A}_1, \mathbf{G}, \mathbf{R}_2, \mathcal{H}_{n,q}(\mathsf{vk}-\mathsf{vk}^\star), (\mathbf{U})_i, \mathbf{T}_\mathbf{G}, \sigma)$) instead of $\mathsf{SampleLeft}$, for $i \in \{1, \cdots, n\}$. Note that the following equation holds:

$$\mathbf{c}_0^\star = \mathbf{U}^\top\mathbf{s} + \widetilde{\mathbf{e}}_0 + \left\lceil\frac{q}{2}\right\rceil\cdot\mathbf{m}_b,$$

$$\mathbf{c}_1^\star = \begin{bmatrix}(\mathbf{A}_1)^\top\mathbf{s}+\mathbf{e}_{1,1}\\ (\mathbf{R}_1)^\top(\mathbf{A}_1)^\top\mathbf{s}+\mathbf{e}_{1,2}\end{bmatrix}, \mathbf{c}_2^\star = \begin{bmatrix}(\mathbf{A}_2)^\top\mathbf{s}+\mathbf{e}_{2,1}\\ (\mathbf{R}_2)^\top(\mathbf{A}_2)^\top\mathbf{s}+\mathbf{e}_{2,2}\end{bmatrix},$$

where $\widetilde{\mathbf{e}}_0 \xleftarrow{\$} \mathcal{D}_{\mathbb{Z}^n,\alpha q}$ and $\mathbf{e}_{1,1}, \mathbf{e}_{1,2}, \mathbf{e}_{2,1}, \mathbf{e}_{2,2} \xleftarrow{\$} \mathcal{D}_{\mathbb{Z}^m,\alpha' q}$.

Game₃: In this game, the challenger changes the way that the challenge ciphertext $\mathbf{c}^\star$ is created: the challenger first picks $\mathbf{s} \xleftarrow{\$} \mathbb{Z}_q^n, \widetilde{\mathbf{e}}_0 \xleftarrow{\$} \mathcal{D}_{\mathbb{Z}^n,\alpha q}, \widetilde{\mathbf{e}}_{1,1}, \widetilde{\mathbf{e}}_{2,1} \xleftarrow{\$} \mathcal{D}_{\mathbb{Z}^m,\alpha q}$ and sets $\mathbf{w} = \mathbf{U}^\top\mathbf{s} + \widetilde{\mathbf{e}}_0, \mathbf{b}_1 = (\mathbf{A}_1)^\top\mathbf{s} + \widetilde{\mathbf{e}}_{1,1}, \mathbf{b}_2 = (\mathbf{A}_2)^\top\mathbf{s} + \widetilde{\mathbf{e}}_{2,1}$. Then, it computes

$$\mathbf{c}_0^\star = \mathbf{w} + \left\lceil\frac{q}{2}\right\rceil\cdot\mathbf{m}_b,$$

$$\mathbf{c}_1^\star = \mathsf{ReRand}\left(\begin{bmatrix}\mathbf{I}_m\\ (\mathbf{R}_1)^\top\end{bmatrix}, \mathbf{b}_1, \alpha q, \frac{\alpha' q}{2\alpha q}\right), \mathbf{c}_2^\star = \mathsf{ReRand}\left(\begin{bmatrix}\mathbf{I}_m\\ (\mathbf{R}_2)^\top\end{bmatrix}, \mathbf{b}_2, \alpha q, \frac{\alpha' q}{2\alpha q}\right).$$

Game$_4$: In this game, the challenger changes the way that the challenge ciphertext $\mathbf{c}^\star$ is created: the challenger first picks random vectors $\mathbf{w} \xleftarrow{\$} \mathbb{Z}_q^n, \widetilde{\mathbf{b}}_1 \xleftarrow{\$} \mathbb{Z}_q^m, \widetilde{\mathbf{b}}_2 \xleftarrow{\$} \mathbb{Z}_q^m, \widetilde{\mathbf{e}}_{1,1}, \widetilde{\mathbf{e}}_{2,1} \xleftarrow{\$} \mathcal{D}_{\mathbb{Z}^m,\alpha q}$ and sets $\mathbf{b}_1 = \widetilde{\mathbf{b}}_1 + \widetilde{\mathbf{e}}_{1,1}, \mathbf{b}_2 = \widetilde{\mathbf{b}}_2 + \widetilde{\mathbf{e}}_{2,1}$. Then, it computes

$$\mathbf{c}_0^\star = \mathbf{w} + \left\lceil \frac{q}{2} \right\rceil \cdot \mathbf{m}_b,$$

$$\mathbf{c}_1^\star = \mathsf{ReRand}\left(\begin{bmatrix} \mathbf{I}_m \\ (\mathbf{R}_1)^\top \end{bmatrix}, \mathbf{b}_1, \alpha q, \frac{\alpha' q}{2\alpha q} \right), \mathbf{c}_2^\star = \mathsf{ReRand}\left(\begin{bmatrix} \mathbf{I}_m \\ (\mathbf{R}_2)^\top \end{bmatrix}, \mathbf{b}_2, \alpha q, \frac{\alpha' q}{2\alpha q} \right).$$

Game$_5$: In this game, the challenger changes the way that the challenge ciphertext $\mathbf{c}^\star$ is created: the challenger first picks $\mathbf{w} \xleftarrow{\$} \mathbb{Z}_q^n, \widetilde{\mathbf{b}}_1 \xleftarrow{\$} \mathbb{Z}_q^m, \widetilde{\mathbf{b}}_2 \xleftarrow{\$} \mathbb{Z}_q^m, \mathbf{e}_{1,1}, \mathbf{e}_{1,2}, \mathbf{e}_{2,1}, \mathbf{e}_{2,2} \xleftarrow{\$} \mathcal{D}_{\mathbb{Z}^m,\alpha' q}$ and computes

$$\mathbf{c}_0^\star = \mathbf{w} + \left\lceil \frac{q}{2} \right\rceil \cdot \mathbf{m}_b,$$

$$\mathbf{c}_1^\star = \begin{bmatrix} \widetilde{\mathbf{b}}_1 + \mathbf{e}_{1,1} \\ (\mathbf{R}_1)^\top \widetilde{\mathbf{b}}_1 + \mathbf{e}_{1,2} \end{bmatrix}, \mathbf{c}_2^\star = \begin{bmatrix} \widetilde{\mathbf{b}}_2 + \mathbf{e}_{2,1} \\ (\mathbf{R}_2)^\top \widetilde{\mathbf{b}}_2 + \mathbf{e}_{2,2} \end{bmatrix}.$$

Analysis of Games. We use the following lemmas to give a analysis between each adjacent games.

Lemma 3. **Game$_1$** *and* **Game$_2$** *are statistically indistinguishable.*

Lemma 4. **Game$_2$** *and* **Game$_3$** *are identically distributed, and* **Game$_4$** *and* **Game$_5$** *are identically distributed.*

Lemma 5. *Assume the* $\text{DLWE}_{q,n,n+2m,\alpha}$ *assumption holds,* **Game$_3$** *and* **Game$_4$** *are computationally indistinguishable.*

***Complete the Proof of Theorem* 1.** It is obvious that $\Pr[X_5] = \frac{1}{2}$, this is because the challenge bit b is independent of the $\mathcal{A}$'s view. From Lemmas 3 to 5, we know that

$$\Pr[X_1] \approx \Pr[X_2], \Pr[X_2] = \Pr[X_3], \Pr[X_4] = \Pr[X_5].$$

From Lemma 5, we know that

$$|\Pr[X_3] - \Pr[X_4]| = \left| \Pr[X_4] - \frac{1}{2} \right| \leq \text{DLWE}_{q,n,n+2m,\alpha},$$

which implies $\left|\Pr\left[X_1\right] - \frac{1}{2}\right| \leq \text{DLWE}_{q,n,n+2m,\alpha} - \mathsf{negl}(\lambda)$. □□

4 Identity-Based Dual Receiver Encryption Construction from Lattice

Assume an identity space $\mathcal{ID} = \{-1, 1\}^\ell$ (In general, ID-DRE needs to support n-bit length identity, i.e., $\ell = n$) and a message space $\mathcal{M} = \{0, 1\}^n$, our ID-DRE scheme $\mathcal{ID} - \mathcal{DRE}$ consists of the following four algorithms:

- $\mathsf{Setup_{ID}}(1^\lambda) \to (PP, Msk)$: On input a security parameter λ, it sets the parameters n, m, q as specified in Fig. 3. Then it obtains a pair matrices $(\mathbf{A}, \mathbf{T_A}) \in \mathbb{Z}_q^{n\times m} \times \mathbb{Z}_q^{m\times m}$ by running $\mathsf{TrapGen}(1^n, 1^m, q)$ and selects a uniformly random matrix $\mathbf{U} \in \mathbb{Z}_q^{n\times n}, \mathbf{A}_i^1, \mathbf{A}_i^2 \in \mathbb{Z}_q^{n\times m}$, where $i \in \{1, \cdots, n\}$. Finally it outputs $PP = (n, m, q, \mathbf{A}, \mathbf{A}_i^1, \mathbf{A}_i^2, \mathbf{U})$ and $Msk = \mathbf{T_A}$.
- $\mathsf{KeyGen_{ID}}(PP, Msk, \mathbf{id}_{1st}, \mathbf{id}_{2nd} \in \mathcal{ID}) \to sk_{\mathbf{id}_{1st}}, sk_{\mathbf{id}_{2nd}}$: On input public parameters PP, a master key Msk, and identities $\mathbf{id}_{1st}, \mathbf{id}_{2nd}$, it first computes $\mathbf{A}_{\mathbf{id}_1} = \sum_{i=1}^n (\mathbf{id}_{1st})_i \cdot \mathbf{A}_i^1 + \mathbf{G}, \mathbf{A}_{\mathbf{id}_2} = \sum_{i=1}^n (\mathbf{id}_{2nd})_i \cdot \mathbf{A}_i^2 + \mathbf{G}$. Then for $i \in \{1, \cdots, n\}$, it runs $\mathsf{SampleLeft}(\mathbf{A}, \mathbf{A}_{\mathbf{id}_1}, (\mathbf{U})_i, \mathbf{T_A}, \sigma)$ to obtain $(\mathbf{E}_{\mathbf{id}_1})_i$ and sets $sk_{\mathbf{id}_{1st}} = \mathbf{E}_{\mathbf{id}_1} \in \mathbb{Z}_q^{2m\times n}$. Similarly, it can obtain $sk_{\mathbf{id}_{2nd}} = \mathbf{E}_{\mathbf{id}_2}$ such that $[\mathbf{A}|\mathbf{A}_{\mathbf{id}_2}] \cdot \mathbf{E}_{\mathbf{id}_2} = \mathbf{U}$.
- $\mathsf{Enc_{ID}}(PP, \mathbf{id}_{1st}, \mathbf{id}_{2nd}, \mathbf{m}) \to \mathbf{c}$. It computes $\mathbf{A}_{\mathbf{id}_1}, \mathbf{A}_{\mathbf{id}_2}$ as above. Then, it picks $\mathbf{s} \xleftarrow{\$} \mathbb{Z}_q^n$, $\widetilde{\mathbf{e}}_0 \xleftarrow{\$} \mathcal{D}_{\mathbb{Z}^n,\alpha q}$, and $\mathbf{e}_{1,1}, \mathbf{e}_{2,1}, \mathbf{e}_{1,2}, \mathbf{e}_{2,2} \xleftarrow{\$} \mathcal{D}_{\mathbb{Z}^m,\alpha' q}$. Finally, it computes and returns the ciphertext $\mathbf{c} = (\mathbf{c}_0, \mathbf{c}_1)$, where

$$\mathbf{c}_0 = \mathbf{U}^\top \mathbf{s} + \mathbf{e}_0 + \left\lceil \frac{q}{2} \right\rceil \cdot \mathbf{m} \in \mathbb{Z}_q^n,$$

$$\mathbf{c}_1 = \begin{bmatrix} \mathbf{c}_{1,1} \\ \mathbf{c}_{1,2} \\ \mathbf{c}_{1,3} \end{bmatrix} = \begin{bmatrix} \mathbf{A}^\top \\ (\mathbf{A}_{\mathbf{id}_1})^\top \\ (\mathbf{A}_{\mathbf{id}_2})^\top \end{bmatrix} \mathbf{s} + \begin{bmatrix} \mathbf{e}_{1,1} \\ \mathbf{e}_{1,2} \\ \mathbf{e}_{1,3} \end{bmatrix} \in \mathbb{Z}_q^{3m},$$

- $\mathsf{Dec_{ID}}(PP, sk_{\mathbf{id}_j}, \mathbf{c}) \to \mathbf{m}$. To decrypt a ciphertext $\mathbf{c} = (\mathbf{c}_0, \mathbf{c}_1)$ with a private key $sk_{\mathbf{id}_{1st}} = \mathbf{E}_{\mathbf{id}_1}$, it computes $\mathbf{b} = \mathbf{c}_0 - \mathbf{E}_{\mathbf{id}_1}^\top \cdot \begin{bmatrix} \mathbf{c}_{1,1} \\ \mathbf{c}_{1,2} \end{bmatrix}$ and regards each coordinate of $\mathbf{b} = [(\mathbf{b})_1, \cdots, (\mathbf{b})_n]^\top$ as an integer in $\mathbb{Z}$, and sets $(\mathbf{m})_i = 1$ if $\left|(\mathbf{b})_i - \lceil \frac{q}{2} \rceil\right| < \lceil \frac{q}{4} \rceil$; otherwise sets $(\mathbf{m})_i = 0$ where $i \in \{1, \cdots, n\}$. Finally, it returns a plaintext $\mathbf{m} = [(\mathbf{m})_1, \cdots, (\mathbf{m})_n]^\top$.

4.1 Correctness and Parameter Selection

In order to satisfy the correctness requirement and make the security proof work (which is very similar to Subsect. 3.1), we set the parameters in Fig. 3.

Parameters	Description	Setting
λ	security parameter	
n	PK-matrix row number	$n = \lambda$
m	PK-matrix column number	$6n \log q$
ℓ	length of identity	n
σ	SampleLeft,SampleRight width	$12\sqrt{10mn} \cdot \omega(\sqrt{\log n})$
q	modulus	$\mathcal{O}(m^2 n^{5/2} \omega(\sqrt{\log n}))$
αq	error width	$2\sqrt{2n}$
$\alpha' q$	error width	$192 n^{3/2} \sqrt{m}$

Fig. 3. Parameter selection of ID-DRE construction

4.2 Security Proof

Theorem 2. *If the* $\mathrm{DLWE}_{q,n,n+m,\alpha}$ *assumption holds, then the above scheme* $\mathcal{ID}$-$\mathcal{DRE}$ *is a secure ID-DRE scheme against chosen-plaintext and adaptively chosen-identity attacks.*

Proof (of Theorem 2). We prove the theorem with showing that if a PPT adversary $\mathcal{A}$ can break our $\mathcal{ID}$-$\mathcal{DRE}$ scheme with a non-negligible advantage ϵ (i.e., success probability $\frac{1}{2}+\epsilon$), then there exists a reduction that can break the $\mathrm{DLWE}_{q,n,n+m,\alpha}$ assumption with an advantage $\mathrm{poly}(\epsilon)-\mathrm{negl}(1^\lambda)$. Let $Q=Q(\lambda)$ be the upper bound of the number of $\mathsf{KeyGen}_{\mathsf{ID}}$ queries and $I^*=\{(\mathbf{id}^*_{1st},\mathbf{id}^*_{2nd}),(\mathbf{id}^\jmath_{1st},\mathbf{id}^\jmath_{2nd})_{\jmath\in[Q]}\}$ be the challenge ID along with the queried ID's.

We formally give the proof via a sequence of games and define X_κ as the event that the challenger outputs 1 in $\mathbf{Game}_\kappa$, for $\kappa\in\{0,1,2,3,4,5,6\}$.

$\mathbf{Game_0}$: This game is the original experiment $\mathsf{Exp}^{\mathrm{ind-id-cpa}}_{\mathcal{ID}-\mathcal{DRE},\mathcal{A}}(1^\lambda)$ in Fig. 1. It is easy to see that

$$\epsilon=\left|\Pr[X_0]-\frac{1}{2}\right|=\left|\Pr\left[\mathsf{Exp}^{\mathrm{ind-id-cpa}}_{\mathcal{ID}-\mathcal{DRE},\mathcal{A}}(1^\lambda)=1\right]-\frac{1}{2}\right|.$$

$\mathbf{Game_1}$: This game is as same as $\mathbf{Game_0}$ except that we add an abort event that is independent of the adversary's view. Let n,ℓ,q be the parameters as in the scheme's setup algorithm and the challenger selects $t=\lceil\log_q(2Q/\epsilon)\rceil$, hence we have $q^t\geq 2Q/\epsilon\geq q^{t-1}$. Then the challenger chooses $2n$ random integer vectors $\mathbf{h}^1_i,\mathbf{h}^2_i\in\mathbb{Z}^t_q$ and defines two functions $\mathcal{H}^1_{\mathrm{ABB}},\mathcal{H}^2_{\mathrm{ABB}}:\mathcal{ID}\to\mathbb{Z}_q^{n\times n}$ as follows: $\forall\mathbf{id}\in\mathcal{ID}$,

$$\mathcal{H}^1_{\mathrm{ABB}}(\mathbf{id})=\mathbf{I}_n+\sum_{i=1}^{n}(\mathbf{id})_i\cdot\mathcal{H}(\mathbf{h}^1_i)\otimes\mathbf{I}_{n/t},\mathcal{H}^2_{\mathrm{ABB}}(\mathbf{id})=\mathbf{I}_n+\sum_{i=1}^{n}(\mathbf{id})_i\cdot\mathcal{H}(\mathbf{h}^2_i)\otimes\mathbf{I}_{n/t}.$$

We then describe how the challenger behaves in $\mathbf{Game_1}$ as follows:

- **Setup:** The same as $\mathbf{Game_0}$ except that the challenger keeps the hash functions $\mathcal{H}^1_{\mathrm{ABB}}$ and $\mathcal{H}^2_{\mathrm{ABB}}$ passed from the experiment.
- **Secret key and ciphertext query:** The challenger responds to secret key queries for identities and challenge ciphertext query (with a random bit $b\in\{0,1\}$) as same as that in $\mathbf{Game_0}$.
- **Gauss:** When the adversary returns a bit b', the challenger checks if

$$\mathcal{H}^2_{\mathrm{ABB}}(\mathbf{id}^\star_{1st})=\mathbf{0},\mathcal{H}^2_{\mathrm{ABB}}(\mathbf{id}^\jmath_{1st})\in\mathbf{Inv}_n$$

$$\mathcal{H}^2_{\mathrm{ABB}}(\mathbf{id}^\star_{2nd})=\mathbf{0},\mathcal{H}^2_{\mathrm{ABB}}(\mathbf{id}^\jmath_{2nd})\in\mathbf{Inv}_n$$

for $\jmath\in\{1,\cdots,Q\}$ where $\mathbf{Inv}_n$ denotes invertible matrices in $\mathbf{Z}_q^{n\times n}$. If the condition does not hold, the challenger outputs a random bit $\tilde{b}\in\{0,1\}$, namely we say the challenger aborts the game.

Note that $\mathcal{A}$ never sees the random hash functions $\mathcal{H}^1_{\text{ABB}}$ and $\mathcal{H}^2_{\text{ABB}}$, and has no idea if an abort event took place. While it is convenient to describe the abort action at the end of the game, nothing would change if the challenger aborts the game as soon as the abort condition becomes true.

Game$_2$: This game is as same as **Game$_1$** except that we slightly change the way that the challenger generates the matrices $\mathbf{A}^1_i, \mathbf{A}^1_i$ for $i \in \{1, \cdots, n\}$. Taking t as $t = \lceil \log_q 2Q/\epsilon \rceil$, we thus have $q^t \geq 2Q/\epsilon \geq q^{t-1}$. Assume n is a multiple of t. For $i = 1, \cdots, n$, the challenger chooses $2n$ random integer vectors $\mathbf{h}^1_i, \mathbf{h}^2_i \in \mathbb{Z}^t_q$ and random matrices $\mathbf{R}^1_i, \mathbf{R}^2_i \in \{-1, 1\}^{m \times m}$. Then it sets $\mathbf{A}^1_i = \mathbf{A}\mathbf{R}^1_i + (\mathcal{H}_{t,q}(\mathbf{h}^1_i) \otimes \mathbf{I}_{n/t}) \cdot \mathbf{G}, \mathbf{A}^2_i = \mathbf{A}\mathbf{R}^2_i + (\mathcal{H}_{t,q}(\mathbf{h}^2_i) \otimes \mathbf{I}_{n/t}) \cdot \mathbf{G}$.

Game$_3$: This game is identical to **Game$_2$** except that the challenger chooses a random matrix $\mathbf{A}$ instead of running TrapGen and responds to private key queries by involving the algorithm SampleRight instead of SampleLeft. To respond to a private key query for $\mathbf{id}_{1st}, \mathbf{id}_{2nd}$, the challenger needs short vectors $(\mathbf{E}_{\mathbf{id}_1})_i \in \Lambda_q^{(\mathbf{U})_i}([\mathbf{A}|\mathbf{A}_{\mathbf{id}_1}])$ and $(\mathbf{E}_{\mathbf{id}_2})_i \in \Lambda_q^{(\mathbf{U})_i}([\mathbf{A}|\mathbf{A}_{\mathbf{id}_2}])$, where

$$\mathbf{A}_{\mathbf{id}_1} = \sum_{i=1}^{n} (\mathbf{id}_{1st})_i \cdot \mathbf{A}^1_i + \mathbf{G} = \mathbf{A}\left(\sum_{i=1}^{n} (\mathbf{id}_{1st})_i \cdot \mathbf{R}^1_i\right) + \mathcal{H}^1_{\text{ABB}}(\mathbf{id}_{1st}) \cdot \mathbf{G};$$

$$\mathbf{A}_{\mathbf{id}_2} = \sum_{i=1}^{n} (\mathbf{id}_{2nd})_i \cdot \mathbf{A}^2_i + \mathbf{G} = \mathbf{A}\left(\sum_{i=1}^{n} (\mathbf{id}_{2nd})_i \cdot \mathbf{R}^2_i\right) + \mathcal{H}^2_{\text{ABB}}(\mathbf{id}_{2nd}) \cdot \mathbf{G}.$$

If $\mathcal{H}^1_{\text{ABB}}(\mathbf{id}_{1st}) \notin \mathbf{Inv}_n$ or $\mathcal{H}^2_{\text{ABB}}(\mathbf{id}_{2nd}) \notin \mathbf{Inv}_n$, the challenger aborts this game and returns a random bit. Otherwise, the challenger responds the private key query by running

$$\mathsf{SampleRight}(\mathbf{A}, \mathbf{G}, \sum_{i=1}^{n} (\mathbf{id}_{1st})_i \mathbf{R}^1_i, \mathcal{H}^1_{\text{ABB}}(\mathbf{id}_{1st}), (\mathbf{U})_i, \mathbf{T}_{\mathbf{G}}, \sigma), \text{ to get } \mathbf{E}_{\mathbf{id}_1},$$

$$\mathsf{SampleRight}(\mathbf{A}, \mathbf{G}, \sum_{i=1}^{n} (\mathbf{id}_{2nd})_i \mathbf{R}^2_i, \mathcal{H}^2_{\text{ABB}}(\mathbf{id}_{2nd}), (\mathbf{U})_i, \mathbf{T}_{\mathbf{G}}, \sigma), \text{ to get } \mathbf{E}_{\mathbf{id}_2},$$

for $i \in \{1, \cdots, n\}$. Since $\mathcal{H}^1_{\text{ABB}}(\mathbf{id}^\star_{1st}) = \mathbf{0}, \mathcal{H}^2_{\text{ABB}}(\mathbf{id}^\star_{2nd}) = \mathbf{0}$, it holds:

$$\mathbf{c}^\star_0 = \mathbf{U}^\top \mathbf{s} + \widetilde{\mathbf{e}}_0 + \left\lceil \frac{q}{2} \right\rceil \cdot \mathbf{m}_b, \mathbf{c}^\star_1 = \begin{bmatrix} \mathbf{A}^\top \mathbf{s} + \mathbf{e_{1,1}} \\ \left(\sum_{i=1}^n (\mathbf{id}^\star_{1st})_i \cdot \mathbf{R}^1_i\right)^\top \mathbf{A}^\top \mathbf{s} + \mathbf{e_{1,2}} \\ \left(\sum_{i=1}^n (\mathbf{id}^\star_{2nd})_i \cdot \mathbf{R}^2_i\right)^\top \mathbf{A}^\top \mathbf{s} + \mathbf{e_{1,2}} \end{bmatrix},$$

where $\widetilde{\mathbf{e}}_0 \xleftarrow{\$} \mathcal{D}_{\mathbb{Z}^n, \alpha q}, \mathbf{e_{1,1}}, \mathbf{e_{1,2}}, \mathbf{e_{1,3}} \xleftarrow{\$} \mathcal{D}_{\mathbb{Z}^m, \alpha' q}$.

Game$_4$: In this game, the challenge ciphertext is generated as follows: it chooses $\mathbf{s} \xleftarrow{\$} \mathbb{Z}^n_q, \widetilde{\mathbf{e}}_0 \xleftarrow{\$} \mathcal{D}_{\mathbb{Z}^n, \alpha q}, \widetilde{\mathbf{e}}_1 \xleftarrow{\$} \mathcal{D}_{\mathbb{Z}^m, \alpha q}$ and sets $\mathbf{w} = \mathbf{U}^\top \mathbf{s} + \widetilde{\mathbf{e}}_0, \mathbf{b} = \mathbf{A}^\top \mathbf{s} + \widetilde{\mathbf{e}}_1$. Then, it computes

$$\mathbf{c}^\star_0 = \mathbf{w} + \left\lceil \frac{q}{2} \right\rceil \cdot \mathbf{m}_b, \mathbf{c}^\star_1 = \mathsf{ReRand}\left(\begin{bmatrix} \mathbf{I}_m \\ \left(\sum_{i=1}^n (\mathbf{id}^\star_{1st})_i \cdot \mathbf{R}^1_i\right)^\top \\ \left(\sum_{i=1}^n (\mathbf{id}^\star_{2nd})_i \cdot \mathbf{R}^2_i\right)^\top \end{bmatrix}, \mathbf{b}, \alpha q, \frac{\alpha' q}{2\alpha q} \right).$$

Game₅: In this game, the challenge ciphertext is generated as follows: it first picks random vectors $\mathbf{w} \xleftarrow{\$} \mathbb{Z}_q^n, \widetilde{\mathbf{b}} \xleftarrow{\$} \mathbb{Z}_q^m, \widetilde{\mathbf{e}}_1 \xleftarrow{\$} \mathcal{D}_{\mathbb{Z}^m,\alpha q}$ and sets $\mathbf{b} = \widetilde{\mathbf{b}} + \widetilde{\mathbf{e}}_1$. Then, it computes

$$\mathbf{c}_0^\star = \mathbf{w} + \left\lceil \frac{q}{2} \right\rceil \cdot \mathbf{m}_b, \mathbf{c}_1^\star = \mathsf{ReRand}\left(\begin{bmatrix} \mathbf{I}_m \\ \left(\sum_{i=1}^n (\mathbf{id}_{1st}^\star)_i \cdot \mathbf{R}_i^1\right)^\top \\ \left(\sum_{i=1}^n (\mathbf{id}_{2nd}^\star)_i \cdot \mathbf{R}_i^2\right)^\top \end{bmatrix}, \mathbf{b}, \alpha q, \frac{\alpha' q}{2\alpha q} \right).$$

Game₆: In this game, the challenge ciphertext is generated as follows: it first picks $\mathbf{w} \xleftarrow{\$} \mathbb{Z}_q^n, \widetilde{\mathbf{b}} \xleftarrow{\$} \mathbb{Z}_q^m$ and $\mathbf{e}_{1,1}, \mathbf{e}_{1,2}, \mathbf{e}_{1,3} \xleftarrow{\$} \mathcal{D}_{\mathbb{Z}^m,\alpha' q}$ and computes

$$\mathbf{c}_0^\star = \mathbf{w} + \left\lceil \frac{q}{2} \right\rceil \cdot \mathbf{m}_b, \mathbf{c}_1^\star = \begin{bmatrix} \widetilde{\mathbf{b}} + \mathbf{e}_{1,1} \\ \left(\sum_{i=1}^n (\mathbf{id}_{1st}^\star)_i \cdot \mathbf{R}_i^1\right)^\top \widetilde{\mathbf{b}} + \mathbf{e}_{1,2} \\ \left(\sum_{i=1}^n (\mathbf{id}_{2nd}^\star)_i \cdot \mathbf{R}_i^2\right)^\top \widetilde{\mathbf{b}} + \mathbf{e}_{1,3} \end{bmatrix}.$$

Analysis of Games. We use the following lemmas to give a analysis between each adjacent games.

The only difference between **Game₁** and **Game₀** is the abort event. We use Lemma 28 in [1] to argue that the adversary still has a non-negligible advantage in **Game₁** even though the abort event happens.

Lemma 6 ([1]). *Let I^* be a $(Q+1)$-ID tuple $\{\mathbf{id}^*, \{\mathbf{id}^\jmath\}^{\jmath \in [Q]}\}$ denoted the challenge ID along with the queried ID's, and $\eta(I^*)$ be the probability that an abort event does not happen in* **Game₁**. *Let $\eta_{max} = \max \eta(I^*)$ and $\eta_{min} = \min \eta(I^*)$. For $\kappa = 0, 1$, we let X_κ be the event that the challenger returns 1 as the output of* **Game**$_\kappa$. *Then, we have $\left|\Pr[X_1] - \frac{1}{2}\right| \geq \eta_{min} \left|\Pr[X_0] - \frac{1}{2}\right| - \frac{1}{2}(\eta_{max} - \eta_{min})$.*

Lemma 7. *Let $\epsilon = \left|\Pr[X_0] - \frac{1}{2}\right|$, then $\left|\Pr[X_1] - \frac{1}{2}\right| \geq \frac{\epsilon^3}{64 q^2 Q^2}$.*

Lemma 8. **Game₁** *and* **Game₂** *are statistically indistinguishable.*

Lemma 9. **Game₂** *and* **Game₃** *are statistically indistinguishable.*

Lemma 10. **Game₃** *and* **Game₄** *are identically distributed, and* **Game₅** *and* **Game₆** *are identically distributed.*

Lemma 11. *Assume the* $\mathrm{DLWE}_{q,n,n+m,\alpha}$ *assumption holds,* **Game₄** *and* **Game₅** *are computationally indistinguishable.*

***Complete the Proof of Theorem* 2.** It is obvious that $\Pr[X_6] = \frac{1}{2}$, this is because the challenge bit b is independent of the $\mathcal{A}$'s view. From Lemmas 7 to 10, we know that

$$\Pr[X_1] \approx \Pr[X_2], \Pr[X_2] \approx \Pr[X_3], \Pr[X_3] = \Pr[X_4], \Pr[X_5] = \Pr[X_6]. \quad (1)$$

From Lemma 11, we know that

$$|\Pr[X_4] - \Pr[X_5]| = \left|\Pr[X_4] - \frac{1}{2}\right| \leq \mathrm{DLWE}_{q,n,n+m,\alpha},$$

which implies $\mathrm{DLWE}_{q,n,n+m,\alpha} \geq \frac{\epsilon^3}{64q^2Q^2} - \mathsf{negl}(\lambda)$, according to Lemma 7 and Eq. 1. □□

4.3 Extension: ID-DRE with More Compact Parameters

As mentioned above, our ID-DRE scheme is based on the beautiful work of Agrawal et al. [1], i.e., an adaptively secure identity-based encryption (IBE) scheme. However, one drawback of Agarwal et al.'s adaptive secure IBE scheme [1] is the large public parameter sizes: namely, the public parameters contain $\ell + 1$ matrices composed of $n \times m$ elements, where ℓ is the size of the bit-string representing identities. As a result, the public parameters in our ID-DRE scheme contain $2 \cdot \ell + 1$ matrices composed of $n \times m$ elements.

In [17], Singh et al. considered identities as one chunk rather than bit-by-bit. In fact, the maximum of the above chunk is a number in $\mathbb{Z}_q$, so that they can reduce the number of the matrices in the scheme by a factor at most $\log q$, while encryption and decryption are almost as efficient as that in [1]. Applying their technique (they called "Blocking Technique") to our construction, we can get an ID-DRE scheme with more compact public parameter sizes. More precisely, we can get a more efficient ID-DRE scheme in which there exist only $2 \cdot \frac{\ell}{\log q} + 1$ matrices composed of $n \times m$ elements, or about $\mathcal{O}(\frac{n}{\log n})$ matrices (since $l = n$ and q is a polynomial of n).

Based the IBE schemes in [1,17], Apon et al. [4] proposed an identity-based encryption scheme which only needs $\mathcal{O}(\frac{n}{\log^2 n})$ public matrices to support n-bit length identity. The reason why the number of the matrices in their scheme is less about $\log n$ times than that of the IBE scheme in [17] is that they used a different gadget matrix $\widehat{\mathbf{G}}$ and flattening function $\widehat{\mathbf{G}}^{-1}$ in logarithmic ($\log n$) base instead of the usual gadget matrix $\mathbf{G}$ and flattening function $\mathbf{G}^{-1}$ in 2 base. Note that the encryption and decryption of the IBE scheme in [4] are less efficient than that in [1,17], this is because the flattening function $\widehat{\mathbf{G}}^{-1}$ is much slower than $\mathbf{G}^{-1}$. Applying their technique to our construction, we can get a more efficient ID-DRE scheme in which there exist about $\mathcal{O}(\frac{n}{\log^2 n})$ matrices.

Overall, we can further obtain more compact ID-DRE schemes from the IBE schemes in [4,17].

5 Conclusion

The learning with errors (LWE) problem is a promising cryptographic primitive that is believed to be resistant to attacks by quantum computers. Under this assumption, we construct a dual-receiver encryption scheme with a CCA security. Additionally, for the DRE notion in the identity-based setting, namely ID-DRE, we also give a lattice-based ID-DRE scheme that achieves IND-ID-CPA security.

Acknowledgments. We thank the anonymous ACISP'2018 reviewers for their helpful comments. This work is supported by the National Natural Science Foundation of China (No.61772515, No.61602473, No.61571191), the National Basic Research Program of China (973 project, No.2014CB340603), the National Cryptography Development Fund (No. MMJJ20170116), the Dawn Program of Shanghai Education Commission (No. 16SG21) and the Open Foundation of Co-Innovation Center for Information Supply & Assurance Technology (No. ADXXBZ201701).

Appendix A: Lattice Background

For positive integers q, n, m, and a matrix $\mathbf{A} \in \mathbb{Z}_q^{n\times m}$, the m-dimensional integer lattices are defined as: $\Lambda_q(\mathbf{A}) = \{\mathbf{y} : \mathbf{y} = \mathbf{A}^\top\mathbf{s} \text{ for some } \mathbf{s} \in \mathbb{Z}^n\}$ and $\Lambda_q^\perp(\mathbf{A}) = \{\mathbf{y} : \mathbf{A}\mathbf{y} = \mathbf{0} \mod q\}$.

Let $\mathbf{S}$ be a set of vectors $\mathbf{S} = \{\mathbf{s}_1, \cdots, \mathbf{s}_n\}$ in $\mathbb{R}^m$. We use $\widetilde{\mathbf{S}} = \{\widetilde{\mathbf{s}}_1, \cdots, \widetilde{\mathbf{s}}_n\}$ to denote the Gram-Schmidt orthogonalization of the vectors $\mathbf{s}_1, \cdots, \mathbf{s}_n$ in that order, and $\|\mathbf{S}\|$ to denote the length of the longest vector in $\mathbf{S}$. For a real-valued matrix $\mathbf{R}$, let $s_1(\mathbf{R}) = \max_{\|\mathbf{u}\|=1} \|\mathbf{R}\mathbf{u}\|$ (respectively, $\|\mathbf{R}\|_\infty = \max \|\mathbf{r}_i\|_\infty$) denote the operator norm (respectively, infinity norm) of $\mathbf{R}$.

For $\mathbf{x} \in \Lambda$, define the Gaussian function $\rho_{s,\mathbf{c}}(\mathbf{x})$ over $\Lambda \subseteq \mathbb{Z}^m$ centered at $\mathbf{c} \in \mathbb{R}^m$ with parameter $s > 0$ as $\rho_{s,\mathbf{c}}(\mathbf{x}) = \exp(-\pi\|\mathbf{x} - \mathbf{c}\|/s^2)$. Let $\rho_{s,\mathbf{c}}(\Lambda) = \sum_{\mathbf{x}\in\Lambda} \rho_{s,\mathbf{c}}(\mathbf{x})$, and define the discrete Gaussian distribution over Λ as $\mathcal{D}_{\Lambda,s,\mathbf{c}}(\mathbf{x}) = \frac{\rho_{s,\mathbf{c}}(\mathbf{x})}{\rho_{s,\mathbf{c}}(\Lambda)}$, where $\mathbf{x} \in \Lambda$. For simplicity, $\rho_{s,\mathbf{0}}$ and $\mathcal{D}_{\Lambda,s,\mathbf{0}}$ are abbreviated as ρ_s and $\mathcal{D}_{\Lambda,s}$, respectively.

Learning with Errors Assumption. The learning with errors problem, denoted by $\mathrm{LWE}_{q,n,m,\alpha}$, was first proposed by Regev [16]. For integer $n, m = m(n)$, a prime integer $q > 2$, an error rate $\alpha \in (0, 1)$, the LWE problem $\mathrm{LWE}_{q,n,m,\alpha}$ is to distinguish the following pairs of distributions: $\{\mathbf{A}, \mathbf{A}^\top\mathbf{s} + \mathbf{e}\}$ and $\{\mathbf{A}, \mathbf{u}\}$, where $\mathbf{A} \xleftarrow{\$} \mathbb{Z}_q^{n\times m}, \mathbf{s} \xleftarrow{\$} \mathbb{Z}_q^n, \mathbf{u} \xleftarrow{\$} \mathbb{Z}_q^m$ and $\mathbf{e} \xleftarrow{\$} \mathcal{D}_{\mathbb{Z}^m,\alpha q}$. Regev [16] showed that solving decisional $\mathrm{LWE}_{q,n,m,\alpha}$ (denoted by $\mathrm{DLWE}_{q,n,m,\alpha}$) for $\alpha q > 2\sqrt{2n}$ is (quantumly) as hard as approximating the SIVP and GapSVP problems to within $\widetilde{\mathcal{O}}(n/\alpha)$ factors in the worst case.

Lemma 12. *Let p, q, n, m be positive integers with $q \geq p \geq 2$ and q prime. There exists PPT algorithms such that*

- *([2, 3]):* $\mathsf{TrapGen}(1^n, 1^m, q)$ *a randomized algorithm that, when $m \geq 6n\lceil\log q\rceil$, outputs a pair $(\mathbf{A}, \mathbf{T_A}) \in \mathbb{Z}_q^{n\times m} \times \mathbb{Z}^{m\times m}$ such that $\mathbf{A}$ is statistically close to uniform in $\mathbb{Z}_q^{n\times m}$ and $\mathbf{T_A}$ is a basis of $\Lambda_q^\perp(\mathbf{A})$, satisfying $\|\widetilde{\mathbf{T_A}}\| \leq \mathcal{O}(\sqrt{n\log q})$ with overwhelming probability.*
- *([5]):* $\mathsf{SampleLeft}(\mathbf{A}, \mathbf{B}, \mathbf{u}, \mathbf{T_A}, \sigma)$ *a randomized algorithm that, given a full rank matrix $\mathbf{A} \in \mathbb{Z}_q^{n\times m}$, a matrix $\mathbf{B} \in \mathbb{Z}_q^{n\times m}$, a basis $\mathbf{T_A}$ of $\Lambda_q^\perp(\mathbf{A})$, a vector $\mathbf{u} \in \mathbb{Z}_q^n$ and $\sigma \geq \|\widetilde{\mathbf{T_A}}\| \cdot \omega(\sqrt{\log m})$, then outputs a vector $\mathbf{r} \in \mathbb{Z}_q^{2m}$ distributed statistically close to $\mathcal{D}_{\Lambda_q^{\mathbf{u}}(\mathbf{F}),\sigma}$ where $\mathbf{F} = [\mathbf{A}|\mathbf{B}]$.*

- *([1]):* SampleRight$(\mathbf{A}, \mathbf{G}, \mathbf{R}, \mathbf{S}, \mathbf{u}, \mathbf{T_G}, \sigma)$ *a randomized algorithm that, given a full rank matrix* $\mathbf{A} \in \mathbb{Z}_q^{n\times m}$*, a matrix* $\mathbf{R} \in \mathbb{Z}_q^{m\times m}$*, an invertible matrix* $\mathbf{S} \in \mathbb{Z}_q^{n\times n}$*, a vector* $\mathbf{u} \in \mathbb{Z}_q^n$ *and* $\sigma \geq \|\widetilde{\mathbf{T_G}}\| \cdot s_1(\mathbf{R}) \cdot \omega(\sqrt{\log m})$*, then it outputs a vector* $\mathbf{r} \in \mathbb{Z}_q^{2m}$ *statistically close to* $\mathcal{D}_{\Lambda_q^{\mathbf{u}}(\mathbf{F}),\sigma}$ *where* $\mathbf{F} = [\mathbf{A}|\mathbf{AR} + \mathbf{SG}]$.
- *(Generalized Leftover Hash Lemma [1, 9]): For* $m > (n+1)\log q + \omega(\log n)$ *and prime* $q > 2$*, let* $\mathbf{R} \xleftarrow{\$} \{-1, 1\}^{m\times k}$ *and* $\mathbf{A} \xleftarrow{\$} \mathbb{Z}_q^{n\times m}, \mathbf{B} \xleftarrow{\$} \mathbb{Z}_q^{n\times k}$ *be uniformly random matrices. Then the distribution* $(\mathbf{A}, \mathbf{AR}, \mathbf{R}^\top \mathbf{w})$ *is* $\mathsf{negl}(n)$*-close to the distribution* $(\mathbf{A}, \mathbf{B}, \mathbf{R}^\top \mathbf{w})$ *for all vector* $\mathbf{w} \in \mathbb{Z}_q^m$*. When* $\mathbf{w}$ *is always* $\mathbf{0}$*, this lemma is called Leftover Hash Lemma.*

In [12], Katsuamta and Yamada introduced the "Noise Rerandomization" lemma which plays an important role in the security proof because of creating a well distributed challenge ciphertext.

Lemma 13 (Noise Rerandomization [12]**).** *Let* q, w, m *be positive integers and* r *a positive real number with* $r > \max\{\omega(\sqrt{\log m}), \omega(\sqrt{\log w})\}$*. For arbitrary column vector* $\mathbf{b} \in \mathbb{Z}_q^m$*, vector* $\mathbf{e}$ *chosen from* $\mathcal{D}_{\mathbb{Z}^m,r}$*, any matrix* $\mathbf{V} \in \mathbb{Z}^{w\times m}$ *and positive real number* $\sigma > s_1(\mathbf{V})$*, there exists a PPT algorithm* ReRand$(\mathbf{V}, \mathbf{b} + \mathbf{e}, r, \sigma)$ *that outputs* $\mathbf{b}' = \mathbf{Vb} + \mathbf{e}' \in \mathbb{Z}^w$ *where* $\mathbf{e}'$ *is distributed statistically close to* $\mathcal{D}_{\mathbb{Z}^w,2r\sigma}$*.*

Appendix B: Signature

Definition 1 (Signature Scheme). *A signature scheme is a triple of probabilistic polynomial-time algorithms as follows:*

- Gen(1^λ) *outputs a verification key* vk *and a signing key* sk*.*
- Sign(sk, μ)*, given* sk *and a message* $\mu \in \{0, 1\}^\star$*, outputs a signature* $\sigma \in \{0, 1\}^\star$*.*
- Ver(vk, μ, σ) *either accepts or rejects the signature* σ *for message* μ*.*

The correctness requirement is: for any message $\mu \in \mathcal{M}$, and for $(vk, sk) \xleftarrow{\$}$ Gen(1^λ), $\sigma \xleftarrow{\$}$ Sign$(sk; \mu)$, Ver(vk, μ, σ) should accept with overwhelming probability (over all the randomness of the experiment).

The notion of security that we require for our IND-CCA DRE construction is strong existential unforgeability under a one-time chosen-message attack. The attack is defined as follows: generate $(vk, sk) \xleftarrow{\$}$ Gen(1^λ) and give vk to the adversary $\mathcal{A}$, then $\mathcal{A}$ outputs a message μ. Generate $\sigma \xleftarrow{\$}$ Sign(sk, μ) and give σ to $\mathcal{A}$. The advantage of $\mathcal{A}$ in the attack is the probability that it outputs some $(\mu^\star, \sigma^\star) \neq (\mu, \sigma)$ such that Ver$(vk, \mu^\star, \sigma^\star)$ accepts. We say that the signature scheme is secure if for every PPT adversary $\mathcal{A}$, its advantage in the attack is $\mathsf{negl}(\lambda)$.

References

1. Agrawal, S., Boneh, D., Boyen, X.: Efficient lattice (H)IBE in the standard model. In: Gilbert, H. (ed.) EUROCRYPT 2010. LNCS, vol. 6110, pp. 553–572. Springer, Heidelberg (2010). https://doi.org/10.1007/978-3-642-13190-5_28
2. Ajtai, M.: Generating hard instances of the short basis problem. In: Wiedermann, J., van Emde Boas, P., Nielsen, M. (eds.) ICALP 1999. LNCS, vol. 1644, pp. 1–9. Springer, Heidelberg (1999). https://doi.org/10.1007/3-540-48523-6_1
3. Alwen, J., Peikert, C.: Generating shorter bases for hard random lattices. In: STACS 2009, pp. 75–86 (2009)
4. Apon, D., Fan, X., Liu, F.: Compact identity based encryption from LWE. IACR Cryptology ePrint Archive 2016:125 (2016)
5. Cash, D., Hofheinz, D., Kiltz, E., Peikert, C.: Bonsai trees, or how to delegate a lattice basis. In: Gilbert, H. (ed.) EUROCRYPT 2010. LNCS, vol. 6110, pp. 523–552. Springer, Heidelberg (2010). https://doi.org/10.1007/978-3-642-13190-5_27
6. Chow, S.S.M., Franklin, M., Zhang, H.: Practical dual-receiver encryption. In: Benaloh, J. (ed.) CT-RSA 2014. LNCS, vol. 8366, pp. 85–105. Springer, Cham (2014). https://doi.org/10.1007/978-3-319-04852-9_5
7. Cramer, R., Damgård, I.: On the amortized complexity of zero-knowledge protocols. In: Halevi, S. (ed.) CRYPTO 2009. LNCS, vol. 5677, pp. 177–191. Springer, Heidelberg (2009). https://doi.org/10.1007/978-3-642-03356-8_11
8. Diament, T., Lee, H.K., Keromytis, A.D., Yung, M.: The dual receiver cryptosystem and its applications. In: CCS 2004, pp. 330–343 (2004)
9. Dodis, Y., Ostrovsky, R., Reyzin, L., Smith, A.D.: Fuzzy extractors: how to generate strong keys from biometrics and other noisy data. SIAM J. Comput. **38**(1), 97–139 (2008)
10. Groth, J., Sahai, A.: Efficient non-interactive proof systems for bilinear groups. In: Smart, N. (ed.) EUROCRYPT 2008. LNCS, vol. 4965, pp. 415–432. Springer, Heidelberg (2008). https://doi.org/10.1007/978-3-540-78967-3_24
11. Joux, A.: A one round protocol for tripartite Diffie-Hellman. In: Proceedings of the 4th International Symposium Algorithmic Number Theory, ANTS-IV, Leiden, The Netherlands, 2–7 July 2000, pp. 385–394 (2000)
12. Katsumata, S., Yamada, S.: Partitioning via non-linear polynomial functions: more compact IBEs from ideal lattices and bilinear maps. In: Cheon, J.H., Takagi, T. (eds.) ASIACRYPT 2016. LNCS, vol. 10032, pp. 682–712. Springer, Heidelberg (2016). https://doi.org/10.1007/978-3-662-53890-6_23
13. Kiltz, E.: Chosen-ciphertext security from tag-based encryption. In: Halevi, S., Rabin, T. (eds.) TCC 2006. LNCS, vol. 3876, pp. 581–600. Springer, Heidelberg (2006). https://doi.org/10.1007/11681878_30
14. Naor, M., Yung, M.: Public-key cryptosystems provably secure against chosen ciphertext attacks. In: STOC 1990, pp. 427–437 (1990)
15. Peikert, C., Waters, B.: Lossy trapdoor functions and their applications. In: STOC 2008, pp. 187–196 (2008)
16. Regev, O.: On lattices, learning with errors, random linear codes, and cryptography. In: STOC 2005, pp. 84–93 (2005)
17. Singh, K., Pandurangan, C., Banerjee, A.K.: Adaptively secure efficient lattice (H)IBE in standard model with short public parameters. In: Bogdanov, A., Sanadhya, S. (eds.) SPACE 2012. LNCS, pp. 153–172. Springer, Heidelberg (2012). https://doi.org/10.1007/978-3-642-34416-9_11

18. Wang, J., Bi, J.: Lattice-based identity-based broadcast encryption scheme. IACR Cryptology ePrint Archive 2010:288 (2010)
19. Waters, B.: Efficient identity-based encryption without random oracles. In: Cramer, R. (ed.) EUROCRYPT 2005. LNCS, vol. 3494, pp. 114–127. Springer, Heidelberg (2005). https://doi.org/10.1007/11426639_7
20. Youn, Y., Smith, A.: An efficient construction of dual-receiver encryption (2008, unpublished)
21. Zhang, K., Chen, W., Li, X., Chen, J., Qian, H.: New application of partitioning methodology: identity-based dual receiver encryption. Secur. Commun. Netw. **9**(18), 5789–5802 (2016)

Anonymous Identity-Based Hash Proof System from Lattices in the Standard Model

Qiqi Lai[1,2], Bo Yang[1,2(✉)], Yong Yu[1(✉)], Yuan Chen[3], and Liju Dong[4,5]

[1] School of Computer Science, Shaanxi Normal University, Xi'an 710119, People's Republic of China
{laiqq,byang,yuyong}@snnu.edu.cn

[2] State Key Laboratory of Information Security, Institute of Information Engineering, Chinese Academy of Sciences, Beijing 100093, People's Republic of China

[3] State Key Laboratory of Integrated Services Networks, Xidian University, Xi'an 710071, People's Republic of China
yuanchen@xidian.edu.cn

[4] Faculty of Engineering and Information Sciences, University of Wollongong, Wollongong, NSW 2522, Australia
liju@uow.edu.au

[5] School of Information Science and Engineering, Shenyang University, Shenyang 110044, People's Republic of China

Abstract. An Identity-Based Hash Proof System (IB-HPS) is a fundamental and important primitive, which is widely adapted to construct a number of cryptographic schemes and protocols, especially for leakage-resilient ones. Therefore it is significant to instantiate IB-HPSs from various assumptions. However, all existing IB-HPSs based on lattices are set only in the random oracle model. Thus, proposing an IB-HPS from lattices in the standard model is an essential and interesting work.

In this paper, we introduce a much more compact definition for an anonymous IB-HPS, defining computational indistinguishability of valid/invalid ciphertexts and anonymity of identity simultaneously. Then, through utilizing the technique for delegating a short lattice basis due to Agrawal *et al.* in CRYPTO 2010 and the property of the smoothing parameter over random lattices, we present a new construction of IB-HPS in the standard model. Furthermore, we show that our new construction is selectively secure and anonymous based on the standard learning with errors (LWE) assumption in the standard model.

Keywords: Identity-Based Hash Proof System · Smooth Anonymous · Selective · Lattice · Standard model

1 Introduction

Since first presented by Boneh *et al.* in FOCS 2007 [7] and formally defined by Alwen *et al.* in Eurocrypt 2010 [3], an Identity-Based Hash Proof System

W. Susilo and G. Yang (Eds.): ACISP 2018, LNCS 10946, pp. 539–557, 2018.
https://doi.org/10.1007/978-3-319-93638-3_31

(IB-HPS) has become a widely used primitive in the field of cryptography, which is a generalization of the concept of hash proof system due to [21] to the identity-based setting. Besides its usage for leakage-resistant public-key encryption schemes in the bounded-retrieval model, an IB-HPS has also found many other cryptographic applications, such as identity-based encryption (IBE) schemes secure against chosen plaintext attacks (CPA) [3], IBE schemes secure against adaptive chosen ciphertext attacks (CCA2) [6,7], CCA2-secure identity-based key encapsulation mechanisms (IB-KEM) based on search assumptions [16] and practical leakage-resilient IBE schemes [20].

Similar to the description of hash proof systems (HPS) in [21,24,27], an IB-HPS consists of two basic components: a subset membership problem and a projective hash family. And it is convenient to view an IB-HPS as an IB-KEM[1], except that an IB-HPS has two different encapsulation algorithms: Encap generates a valid ciphertext c together with the corresponding encapsulated key k while the other Encap* generates only an invalid ciphertext c'. In this case, subset membership problem can also be renamed as indistinguishability between valid and invalid ciphertexts. More specifically, given a finite ciphertext set C and a valid ciphertext subset $V \subseteq C$, it is computationally hard to distinguish a random valid ciphertext $c \in V$ from a random invalid ciphertext $c' \in V' \subseteq C$, where $V \cap V' = \emptyset$.

A projective hash family in an IB-HPS is denoted by decapsulation functions $\mathsf{Decap}_{sk_{id}}$ mapping C to some set K, which has two important properties: correctness and smoothness. Here, id is an identity for a user, and sk_{id} is extracted from id through using the master secret key of this identity-based setting. When evaluated on a valid ciphertext $c \in V$, $\mathsf{Decap}_{sk_{id}}(c)$ will output the same encapsulated key k as Encap does with overwhelming probability, which is always called as correctness. For an invalid ciphertext $c' \in V'$, the smoothness property states that $\mathsf{Decap}_{sk_{id}}(c')$ is independent of id. More precisely, the value $\mathsf{Decap}_{sk_{id}}(c')$ is statistically uniform even with id and c'.

As a powerful primitive for cryptographic researches, the construction of IB-HPSs has already attracted a lot of attentions. As known, many previous works succeeded in constructing IB-HPSs based on various classical assumptions, such as truncated augmented bilinear Diffie-Hellman exponent (q-TABDHE) assumption [3], Quadratic Residuosity assumption [3,7], decisional bilinear Diffie-Hellman assumption [20], subgroup decision assumption in composite order bilinear group [20] and decisional square bilinear Diffie-Hellman assumption [17]. In contrast, only a handful of hash proof systems are known based on post-quantum assumptions, for instance lattice-based assumptions. Compared with

[1] In order to understand the difference between the concepts of an IB-HPS and an IB-KEM, one can refer to the similar relationship between a HPS and a KEM in the public-key setting. A HPS can always be viewed as a KEM in the modular construction of public-key encryption schemes. Besides, a HPS is a basic cryptographic primitive, which can be furthermore construct many protocols in different applications [9–15]. However, a KEM can be utilized only in the encryption schemes for message transmission.

other assumptions, lattice-based ones enjoy several advantages: worst-case to average-case hardness reduction, much higher asymptotic efficiency and resistance so far to quantum attacks.

The first IB-HPS from lattice-based assumptions was given by Alwen *et al.* in [3], which was a slight variant of the IBE scheme presented in [23]. To do this, they used vectors close to certain random lattice $\Lambda(\mathbf{A})$ and randomly chosen vectors in $\mathbb{Z}_q^m$ as one part of valid ciphertexts and invalid ciphertexts respectively, where $\mathbf{A}$ is a random matrix in $\mathbb{Z}_q^{m\times n}$. According to the basic lattice theory, the intersection of valid and invalid ciphertext sets can be set to be empty with overwhelming probability. Similarly, several IB-HPSs based on the LWE assumption have also be described in [16,17].

Notice that all existing IB-HPSs based on lattices are set only in the random oracle model and have to use a subexponential modulus q to ensure both correctness and smoothness properties. We should also remark that there is no straightforward transformation from an IBE to an IB-HPS, although both concepts have certain similarities and an IB-HPS essentially implies an IBE scheme. One of main reasons for this case is that the security model of an IBE scheme only allow the adversary to query identity secret key for non-challenge identities, but an IB-HPS allows to query all identities even including the adaptive challenge identities.

As known, polynomial moduli, standard model and adaptive security are always the much more popular settings in the field of cryptographic researches. Therefore it should be a significant work to propose such an adaptive IB-HPS with a polynomial modulus in the standard model. Unfortunately, no one know how to give such a construction based on lattices. In particular, existing lattice-based adaptive simulation technologies for IBE schemes in [1,8] and their followups can not be used to simulate the secret key of the challenge identity in the adaptive way. To approach this significant target more closely, we propose a new selective IB-HPS based on lattices in the standard model but still with subexponential moduli for correctness and smoothness.

1.1 Our Contributions

In this paper, our main contribution is a selective IB-HPS with anonymity based on the LWE assumption in the standard model but still with a subexponential modulus. Along the way, we develop the much more compact definition for an anonymous IB-HPS. More formally, our contributions in this paper can be listed in the following way.

First, we introduce a much more compact definition for an anonymous IB-HPS, defining computational indistinguishability of valid/invalid ciphertexts and anonymity of identity simultaneously. This explicitly implies that anonymity does not need an individual proof again.

Second, we propose a selectively secure IB-HPS in the standard model. As we know, it should be the first construction in the standard model, even it is just selectively secure and still have to use a subexponential modulus, and the

Table 1. Rough Comparison with other Identity-Based Hash Proof Systems based on LWE (Although there are many different IB-HPSs from different assumptions in [3,16,17], here we only focus on their lattice-based constructions. Here we use [3,16,17] to denote their constructions from the LWE assumption. And use $|mpk|$ to denote the bit-size of the master public key. $|msk|$ and $|sk_{id}|$ are the bit-sizes of the master secret key and the identity secret key, respectively. Two columns in Encap and Decap are the related computation overheads. n is the main security parameter, and m is a function of n. We let the subexponential modulus to be 2^{n^c} with certain constant $0 < c < 1$. Hence its bit-length is denoted as n^c. Similarly, the bit-length of the polynomial modulus is denoted as $O(\log n)$.)

	$\lvert mpk\rvert$	$\lvert msk\rvert$	$\lvert sk_{id}\rvert$	Encap	Decap	Ciphertext size	Security	Model
[3]	mn^{1+c}	m^2n^c	mn^c	$O((m+1)n^{2c+1})$	$O(mn^{2c})$	$(m+1)n^c$	Adaptive	Random oracle
[16]	mn^{1+c}	m^2n^c	mn^c	$O((m+1)n^{2c+1})$	$O(mn^{2c})$	$(m+1)n^c$	Adaptive	Random oracle
[17]	mn^{1+c}	m^2n^c	mn^c	$O((m+1)n^{2c+1})$	$O(mn^{2c})$	$(m+1)n^c$	Adaptive	Random oracle
Our IB-HPS in Sect. 3	$mn^{1+c}(2m+1)+n^{1+c}$	m^2n^c	mn^c	$(O(m^3n)+O(m^2n^2))\cdot O(\log^2 n)$	$O(mn^{2c})$	$(m+1)n^c$	Selective	Standard model

size of master public key becomes much larger than others in the random oracle model. In Table 1, we give a rough comparison of IB-HPSs based on the LWE assumption.

1.2 Our Technologies

In this section, we present the detailed technologies used for our new IB-HPS based on the LWE assumption.

For the IB-HPS from lattices in the standard model, we need to show the computational indistinguishability of valid/invalid ciphertexts in the standard model. Here, we use several core technologies introduced in [2] to establish a reduction from the LWE problem. More specifically, all identities are denoted by bit strings of length d. And every bit in different positions is corresponding to a different $\mathbb{Z}_q$-invertible matrix with low norm columns. We also use two algorithms *BasisDel* and *SampleRwithBasis* to simulate the trapdoors for arbitrary identities except the challenge identity, and answer the corresponding identity secret key queries.

Besides these, we utilize the algorithm *SampleGaussian* and the property of the smoothing parameter over random lattices to generate the public vector in the master public key, which are further used to answer the secret key query for the challenge identity.

Moreover, for our new construction in the standard model, we try to view this decapsulation function as an universal hash function, and use random extractors to show the smoothness property.

1.3 Other Related Work

Until now, there exists other variants of IB-HPS. Chen *et al.* introduce the concept of identity-based extractable hash proof system, which is an extension of extractable hash proof system proposed by Wee in CRYPTO 2010. This primitive can be used to build and interpret CCA-secure IBE schemes and IB-KEMs based on search assumptions [18,19].

1.4 Paper Organization

This paper is organized as follows. In Sect. 2, we present several useful notations, definitions and lemmas. We then describe our new anonymous IB-HPS based on lattices in the standard model in Sect. 3. Due to the limited space, the detailed definition on an anonymous IB-HPS is presented in Appendix.

2 Preliminaries

2.1 Notations

We write $\mathbb{N}$ as the set of integers and $\mathbb{R}$ as real numbers. In this paper, $n \in \mathbb{N}$ is treated as the main security parameter. We denote log as the logarithm to the base 2. Use $O(f(n))$ to denote the set of functions growing equivalent to $cf(n)$ for certain hidden parameter $c > 0$, and $\omega(f(n))$ grows faster than $cf(n)$ for any constant parameter $c > 0$. If $f(n) = O(g(n) \cdot \log^c n)$ for certain parameter $c > 0$, we can write $f(n) = \tilde{O}(n)$. A negligible function, denoted by $negl(n)$, is a function $f(n) > 0$ such that $f(n) < 1/n^c$ for any $c > 0$ and all sufficiently large n. We call a probability to be overwhelming if it is $1 - negl(n)$.

For any real number $x \in \mathbb{R}$, $\lfloor x \rfloor$ denotes the largest integer not greater than x, $\lceil x \rceil$ denote the smallest integer not less than x, and $\lfloor x \rceil$ denotes a nearest integer to $\lfloor x + 1/2 \rfloor$. We use bold lower case letter (e.g., $\mathbf{x}$) to denote column vectors, and bold upper case letters (e.g., $\mathbf{A}$) to denote matrices. For a vector $\mathbf{x}$, its Euclidean norm (also known as the ℓ_2 norm) is defined to be $\|\mathbf{x}\| = (\sum_i x_i^2)^{1/2}$. For a matrix $\mathbf{A}$, its ith column vector is denoted by $\mathbf{a}_i$ and its transposition is denoted by $\mathbf{A}^T$. The Euclidean norm of a matrix is the norm of its longest column: $\|\mathbf{A}\| = max_i \|\mathbf{a}_i\|$.

For a set D, we denote by $u \leftarrow D$ the operation of sampling a uniformly random element u from the set D, and represent $|u|$ as the bit length of u. For an integer $v \in \mathbb{N}$, we use U_v to denote the uniform distribution over $\{0, 1\}^v$. Given a algorithm or function $f(\cdot)$, we use $y \leftarrow f(x)$ to denote y as the output of f and

x as input. For a distribution X, we denote by $x \leftarrow X$ the operation of sampling a random u according to the distribution X. Given two different distributions X and Y over a countable domain D, we can define their statistical distance to be $\mathrm{SD}(X, Y) = \frac{1}{2}\sum_{d\in D}|X(d) - Y(d)|$. Moreover, if $\mathrm{SD}(X, Y)$ is negligible in n, we say that both distributions are statistically close. For a random variable $x \in X$, its min-entropy is $H_\infty(x) = -\log(\max_{x_0\in X}\Pr[x = x_0])$.

2.2 Extractors and Leftover-Hash Lemma

Definition 1 ([3], Definition 2.1). *An efficient randomized function Ext:*$\{0,1\}^u \times \{0,1\}^t \to \{0,1\}^v$ *is called to be an* (m, ε)*-extractor if for all* $x \in \{0,1\}^u$ *such that* $H_\infty(x) \geq m$*, it holds that* $\mathrm{SD}((h, \mathrm{Ext}(x; h)), (h, u_0)) \leq \varepsilon$*, where* $h \leftarrow \{0,1\}^t$ *and* $u_0 \leftarrow U_v$.

Definition 2 ([3], Definition 2.2). *A family* $H : \{0,1\}^u \to \{0,1\}^v$ *is called to be a* ρ*-universal hash family if for any* $m_1 \neq m_2 \in \{0,1\}^u$*, it holds that* $\Pr_{h\leftarrow H}[h(m_1) = h(m_2)] \leq \rho$.

Lemma 1 ([3], Lemma 2.2). *Given a* ρ*-universal hash family* $H : \{0,1\}^u \to \{0,1\}^v$*, the randomized extractor* $\mathrm{Ext}(x; h)$ *with* $h \leftarrow H$ *is an* (m, ε)*-extractor as long as* $m \geq v + 2\log(1/\varepsilon) - 1$ *and* $\rho \leq \frac{1}{2^v}(1 + \varepsilon^2)$.

2.3 Lattices

Let $\mathbf{B} = (\mathbf{b}_1, \ldots, \mathbf{b}_m) \subset \mathbb{R}^m$ consist of m linearly independent vectors. The m-dimensional lattice Λ generated by the basis $\mathbf{B}$ is $\Lambda = \mathcal{L}(\mathbf{B}) = \{\mathbf{Bc} = \sum_{i\in[m]} c_i \cdot \mathbf{b}_i : \mathbf{c} \in \mathbb{Z}^m\}$. We let $\widetilde{\mathbf{B}}$ denote the Gram-Schmidt orthogonalization of $\mathbf{B}$, and $\|\widetilde{\mathbf{B}}\|$ is the length of the longest vector in it.

The minimum distance $\lambda_1(\Lambda)$ of a lattice Λ is the length in the Euclidean ℓ_2 norm of the shortest nonzero vector: $\lambda_1(\Lambda) = \min_{0\neq\mathbf{x}\in\Lambda}\|\mathbf{x}\|$. For an approximation factor $\gamma = \gamma(n) > 1$, we define the problem of GapSVP_γ as follows: given a basis $\mathbf{B}$ of an m-dimensional lattice $\Lambda = \mathcal{L}(\mathbf{B})$ and a positive number d, distinguish between the case where $\lambda_1(\Lambda) \leq d$ and the case where $\lambda_1(\Lambda) \geq \gamma d$.

Let $\mathbf{A} \in \mathbb{Z}_q^{m\times n}$ for three positive integers m, n, q, where m and q are functions of n. Then we consider the following two kinds of full-rank m-dimensional q-ary integer lattices defined by $\mathbf{A}$: $\Lambda_q^\perp(\mathbf{A}) = \{\mathbf{e} \in \mathbb{Z}^m : \mathbf{A}^T\mathbf{e} = 0 \bmod q\}$ and $\Lambda_q(\mathbf{A}) = \{\mathbf{y} \in \mathbb{Z}^m : \exists \mathbf{s} \in \mathbb{Z}_q^n \text{ s.t. } \mathbf{y} = \mathbf{As} \bmod q\}$.

According to their definitions, it can be seen that $\Lambda^\perp(\mathbf{A})$ and $\Lambda(\mathbf{A})$ are dual lattices, up to a q scaling factor: $\Lambda^\perp(\mathbf{A}) = q\Lambda(\mathbf{A})^*$ and vice-versa.

We need the following two basic lemmas for our construction.

Lemma 2 ([23], implicit in Lemma 5.3). *For any integers* $n \geq 1$*, prime* $q \geq 2$*, let* $m \geq 2n\log q$*. Then for all but an at most* q^{-n} *fraction of* $\mathbf{A} \in \mathbb{Z}_q^{m\times n}$*, we have* $\lambda_1(\Lambda(\mathbf{A})) \geq q/4$.

Lemma 3 ([4,5,23]). *For any integers $n \geq 1$, $q \geq 2$, and sufficiently large $m = \lceil 6n \log q \rceil$, there is a probabilistic polynomial-time algorithm* TrapGen(q, n) *outputting* $(\mathbf{A} \in \mathbb{Z}_q^{m \times n}, \mathbf{T_A} \in \mathbb{Z}^{m \times m})$ *such that the distribution of* $\mathbf{A}$ *is statistically close to the uniform distribution over* $\mathbb{Z}_q^{m \times n}$ *and* $\mathbf{T_A}$ *is a short basis for* $\Lambda_q^{\perp}(\mathbf{A})$ *satisfying* $\|\widetilde{\mathbf{T_A}}\| \leq O(\sqrt{n \log q})$ *and* $\|\mathbf{T_A}\| \leq O(n \log q)$ *with overwhelming probability in* n.

2.4 Gaussians on Lattices

For any real number $r > 0$, we define the Gaussian function on $\mathbb{R}^n$ centered at $\mathbf{c}$ with parameter r to be: $\forall \mathbf{x} \in \mathbb{R}^n, \rho_{r,\mathbf{c}}(\mathbf{x}) = \exp(-\pi \|\mathbf{x} - \mathbf{c}\|^2 / r^2)$. Usually, subscript r and $\mathbf{c}$ are omitted, when both of them are taken to be 1 and 0, respectively. For any discrete set $A \subseteq \mathbb{R}^n$, this definition can be extended to be $\rho_{r,\mathbf{c}}(A) = \sum_{\mathbf{x} \in A} \rho_{r,\mathbf{c}}(\mathbf{x})$. For any $c \in \mathbb{R}^n$, $r > 0$, and n-dimensional lattice Λ, the discrete Gaussian distribution over Λ is defined as: $\forall \mathbf{x} \in \Lambda, D_{\Lambda,r,\mathbf{c}}(\mathbf{x}) = \frac{\rho_{r,\mathbf{c}}(\mathbf{x})}{\rho_{r,\mathbf{c}}(\Lambda)}$.

Lemma 4 ([2], **Lemma 7**). *Let* $\mathbf{A}$ *and* $\mathbf{T_A}$ *be a pair of matrices output by* TrapGen(q, n), *and* $r \geqslant \|\widetilde{\mathbf{T_A}}\| \cdot \omega(\sqrt{\log m})$. *Then for* $\mathbf{c} \in \mathbb{R}^m$ *and* $\mathbf{u} \in \mathbb{Z}_q^n$, *we have:*

1. $\Pr[\mathbf{x} \leftarrow D_{\Lambda_q^{\mathbf{u}}(\mathbf{A}),r} : \|\mathbf{x}\| > r\sqrt{m}] \leq negl(n)$.
2. *There exists a probabilistic polynomial-time algorithm* SampleGaussian $(\mathbf{A}, \mathbf{T_A}, r, \mathbf{c})$ *that outputs a sample from a distribution statistically close to* $D_{\Lambda,r,\mathbf{c}}$.
3. *There exists a probabilistic polynomial-time algorithm* SamplePre $(\mathbf{A}, \mathbf{T_A}, \mathbf{u}, r)$ *that outputs a sample from a distribution statistically close to* $D_{\Lambda_q^{\mathbf{u}}(\mathbf{A}),r}$.

We also need use the following min-entropy on the output of *SamplePre*.

Lemma 5 ([3], **Lemma D.2**). *Given a pair matrices* $(\mathbf{A}, \mathbf{T_A})$ *output by* Trap -Gen(q, n) *and a vector* $\mathbf{u} \in \mathbb{Z}_q^n$, *for constant* $c > 0$ *and* $r > \|\widetilde{\mathbf{T_A}}\|\omega(\sqrt{\log m})$, *let* $\mathbf{e} \leftarrow$Sample -Pre$(\mathbf{A}, \mathbf{T_A}, \mathbf{u}, r)$, *it holds that* $H_\infty(\mathbf{e}) \geq m(\log(r) - \log(m^c))$.

We also recall the notion of the smoothing parameter in [26].

Definition 3 ([26], **Definition 3.1**). *For any lattice* Λ *and real number* $\epsilon > 0$, *the smoothing parameter* $\eta_\epsilon(\Lambda)$ *is defined to be the smallest positive real number* $s > 0$ *such that* $\rho_{1/s}(\Lambda^* \setminus 0) \leq \epsilon$.

We will use a bound on the smoothing parameter due to [29], which is relevant to the minimum distance of the dual lattice in the ℓ_2 norm.

Lemma 6 ([29], **implicit in Lemma 3.5**). *For any lattice* Λ *of dimension* m *and any real* $\epsilon > 0$, $\eta_\epsilon(\Lambda) \leq \frac{\sqrt{m \log(2m(1+1/\epsilon))/\pi}}{\lambda_1(\Lambda^*)}$. *Then for any function* $\omega(\sqrt{\log m})$, *there exists a negligible* $\epsilon(m)$ *such that* $\eta_\epsilon(\Lambda) \leq \omega(\sqrt{\log m})/\lambda_1(\Lambda^*)$.

We now recall an important facts on q-ary random lattices that will be used to prove the anonymous indistinguishability for our new construction.

Lemma 7 ([23], Lemma 5.2). *Let $\epsilon \in (0, 1/2)$ and $r \geq \eta_\epsilon(\Lambda^\perp(\mathbf{A}))$ and assume the columns of $\mathbf{A}^T$ generate $\mathbb{Z}_q^n$. Then for $\mathbf{e} \leftarrow D_{\mathbb{Z}^m,r}$, the distance between $\mathbf{u} = \mathbf{A}^T\mathbf{e} \bmod q$ and uniform over $\mathbb{Z}_q^n$ is less than 2ϵ.*

A matrix $\mathbf{R} \in \mathbb{Z}^{m\times m}$ is said to be $\mathbb{Z}_q$-invertible if $\mathbf{R} \bmod q$ is invertible in $\mathbb{Z}_q^{m\times m}$. Similar to [2], our new constructions make use of $\mathbb{Z}_q$-invertible matrices $\mathbf{R} \in \mathbb{Z}^{m\times m}$ where all the columns of $\mathbf{R}$ are low norm. Let $\sigma_R := \sqrt{n\log q}\cdot\omega(\sqrt{\log m})$. We define $D_{m\times m}$ as $(D_{\mathbb{Z}^m,\sigma_R})^{m\times m}$ with the restriction on the resulting matrix being $\mathbb{Z}_q$-invertible. In fact, $D_{m\times m}$ can be sampled by an efficient algorithm.

Lemma 8 ([2], in Sect. 4). *There is a probabilistic polynomial-time algorithm* SampleR(1^m) *that samples matrices from a distribution statistically close to $D_{m\times m}$.*

We also need use two efficient algorithms *BasisDel* and *SampleRwithBasis* to generate identity secret key and prove the anonymous indistinguishability for our new construction in the standard model.

Lemma 9 ([2], Theorem 14). *Let $\mathbf{A} \in \mathbb{Z}_q^{m\times n}$ and $\mathbf{T_A} \in \mathbb{Z}^{m\times m}$ be a pair of matrices output by* TrapGen(q, n)*, let $\mathbf{R}$ be a $\mathbb{Z}_q$-invertible matrix sampled from $D_{m\times m}$ (or a product of such matrix), and r satisfy $r > \|\widetilde{\mathbf{T_A}}\|\cdot\sigma_R\sqrt{m}\omega(\sqrt{\log^{3/2} m})$. There is a probabilistic polynomial-time algorithm* BasisDel$(\mathbf{A}, \mathbf{R}, \mathbf{T_A}, r)$ *that outputs a basis $\mathbf{T_B}$ of $\Lambda_q^\perp(\mathbf{B})$ where $\mathbf{B} = \mathbf{AR}^{-1}$ such that $\|\widetilde{\mathbf{T_B}}\| \leq r\sqrt{m}$.*

If $\mathbf{R}$ is a product of ℓ matrices sampled from $D_{m\times m}$, then the bound on σ degrades to $r > \|\widetilde{\mathbf{T_A}}\|\cdot(\sigma_R\sqrt{m}\omega(\log^{1/2} m))^\ell\cdot\omega(\sqrt{\log m})$.

Lemma 10 ([2], Theorem 15). *Let $m > 2n\log q$, and let $q > 2$ be a prime. Then for all but at most q^{-n} fraction of $\mathbf{A} \in \mathbb{Z}_q^{m\times n}$, there is a probabilistic polynomial-time algorithm* SampleRwithBasis$(\mathbf{A})$ *that outputs a matrix $R \in \mathbb{Z}^{m\times m}$ sampled from a distribution statistically close to $D_{m\times m}$ and a basis $\mathbf{T_B}$ of $\Lambda_q^\perp(\mathbf{AR}^{-1})$ satisfies $\|\widetilde{\mathbf{T_B}}\| \leq \sigma_R/\omega(\sqrt{\log m})$ with overwhelming probability.*

2.5 Learning with Errors (LWE)

Given an integer $q \geq 2$ and a probability distribution χ over $\mathbb{Z}_q$, an integer dimension $n > 0$ and a vector $s \in \mathbb{Z}_q^n$, define $A_{\mathbf{s},\chi}$ as the distribution obtained by sampling $\mathbf{a} \in \mathbb{Z}_q^n$ uniformly at random and $x \leftarrow \chi$, and then outputting $(\mathbf{a}, \mathbf{a}^T\cdot\mathbf{s} + x) \in \mathbb{Z}_q^n \times \mathbb{Z}_q$.

Definition 4 (LWE). *Given an integer $q = q(n)$ and an error distribution $\chi = \chi(n)$ on $\mathbb{Z}_q$, the decisional version of the LWE problem, denoted by $DLWE_{n,q,\chi}$, is to distinguish (with a non-negligible advantage) between an oracle returning independent samples from $A_{\mathbf{s},\chi}$ for a uniformly random $\mathbf{s} \in \mathbb{Z}_q^n$ and an oracle returning independent samples from the uniform distribution on $\mathbb{Z}_q^n \times \mathbb{Z}_q$.*

The decisional version of the LWE problem can also be described as the following matrix forms: for a uniformly random matrix $\mathbf{A} \in \mathbb{Z}_q^{m\times n}$ with $m = \text{poly}(n)$, an LWE secret vector $\mathbf{s} \leftarrow \mathbb{Z}_q^n$ and an error vector $\mathbf{e} \leftarrow \chi^m$, the $\text{DLWE}_{m,n,q,\chi}$ problem is to distinguish between $(\mathbf{A}, \mathbf{A}\mathbf{s} + \mathbf{e})$ and $(\mathbf{A}, \mathbf{u})$, where $\mathbf{u}$ is a uniformly random vector in $\mathbb{Z}_q^m$.

Gaussian Error Distribution $\bar{\psi}_\beta$. In this paper, we treat the error distribution $\chi = \chi(n)$ on $\mathbb{Z}_q$ as a variant of Gaussian. For any $r > 0$, a one-dimensional Gaussian distribution over $\mathbb{R}$ has density function $D_r(x) = 1/r \cdot \exp(-\pi(x/r)^2)$. For $\beta > 0$, define ψ_β to be the Gaussian distribution with mean 0 and standard deviation $\beta/\sqrt{2\pi}$. The distribution of $\bar{\psi}_\beta$ is the discretization of ψ_β over $\mathbb{Z}_q$, that is obtained by choosing $y \leftarrow D_\beta$ and outputting $\lfloor q \cdot y \rceil (\text{mod} q)$.

The hardness of the DLWE problem with certain parameters can be based on standard worst-case lattice problem, which can be described in detail as follows.

Lemma 11 (**[28], Theorem 1.1**). *Let $n, q \geq 1$ be integers and $\beta \in (0, 1)$ be a real number such that $\beta q \geq 2\sqrt{n}$. Then there exists a quantum reduction from the n-dimensional $\text{GapSVP}_{\tilde{O}(n/\beta)}$ problem in the worst-case to the $\text{DLWE}_{n,q,\chi}$ problem in the average case.*

Here we recall a basic fact on Gaussian error distribution $\bar{\psi}_\beta$.

Lemma 12 (**[22], Lemma B.1**). *Let $\beta > 0$ and $q \in \mathbb{Z}$, and let $\mathbf{x} \in \mathbb{Z}^n$ be an arbitrary vector and $\mathbf{y} \leftarrow \bar{\psi}_\beta^n$, then with overwhelming probability over the choice of $\mathbf{y}$, it holds $|\langle \mathbf{x}, \mathbf{y}\rangle| \leqslant \|\mathbf{x}\| \cdot \beta q \cdot \omega(\sqrt{\log n})$.*

Notice that for any $\mathbf{y} \leftarrow \bar{\psi}_\beta^n$, there always exists a unit vector $\mathbf{x} \in \mathbb{Z}^n$ with the same direction as $\mathbf{y}$. Hence, this lemma shows that for $\mathbf{y} \leftarrow \bar{\psi}_\beta^n$, $\|\mathbf{y}\| \leq \beta q \cdot \omega(\sqrt{\log n})$ holds with all but negligible probability in n.

Note that for $\mathbf{A} \in \mathbb{Z}_q^{m\times n}$ with $m \geq 2n \log q$, the lattice $\Lambda(\mathbf{A})$ is very sparse.

Lemma 13 (**[25], implicit in Lemma 1**). *For all but a negligible fraction of matrices $\mathbf{A} \in \mathbb{Z}_q^{m\times n}$ with $m \geq 2n \log q$, we have* $\Pr_{\mathbf{x} \leftarrow \mathbb{Z}_q^m}[\text{dist}(\mathbf{x}, \Lambda(\mathbf{A})) \leqslant \sqrt{q}/4] \leqslant \frac{1}{q^{(n+m)/2}}$.

3 Selectively Secure Construction in the Standard Model

Our new selectively secure construction is similar to the selective secure hierarchical IBE scheme due to Agrawal *et al.* in [2]. However, in order to prove it correctly, we make one main modification: sample a short vector as the identity secret key rather than a short basis.

3.1 Construction

This construction uses several parameters which will be described in detail in Sect. 3.2. Besides the security parameter n, the bit-length d of an identity is also a basic parameter, which means all other parameters are functions of n and d.

Setup(1^n)**:** For an identity set ID composed of length d bit strings[2], run the algorithm $TrapGen(q, n)$ to generate a random matrix $\mathbf{A} \in \mathbb{Z}_q^{m\times n}$ together with a short basis $\mathbf{T_A} \in \mathbb{Z}^{m\times m}$ for $\Lambda_q^{\perp}(\mathbf{A})$. Choose $2d$ matrices $\mathbf{R}_{1,0}, \mathbf{R}_{1,1}, \ldots, \mathbf{R}_{d,0}, \mathbf{R}_{d,1}$ from the distribution $D_{m\times m}$ using the algorithm $SampleR(1^m)$ in Lemma 8. Given a random vector $\mathbf{u}_0 \in \mathbb{Z}_q^n$, output $mpk = (\mathbf{A}, \mathbf{u}_0, \mathbf{R}_{1,0}, \mathbf{R}_{1,1}, \ldots, \mathbf{R}_{d,0}, \mathbf{R}_{d,1})$, $msk = (\mathbf{T_A})$.

KeyGen(id, msk)**:** For any identity $id = (id_1, \ldots, id_d) \in \{0,1\}^d$, compute $\mathbf{F}_{id} = \mathbf{A}^T(\mathbf{R}_{1,id_1})^{-1}(\mathbf{R}_{2,id_2})^{-1}\cdots(\mathbf{R}_{d,id_d})^{-1} \in \mathbb{Z}_q^{n\times m}$, and run the basis delegation algorithm $BasisDel(\mathbf{A}, \mathbf{R}, \mathbf{T_A}, \sigma)$ to output a short random basis $\mathbf{T_B}$ of $\Lambda_q^{\perp}(\mathbf{F}_{id})$, where $\mathbf{R} = \mathbf{R}_{d,id_d}\mathbf{R}_{d-1,id_{d-1}}\cdots\mathbf{R}_{2,id_2}\mathbf{R}_{1,id_1}$. Furthermore, choose a gaussian parameter τ, and run $SamplePre(\mathbf{F}_{id}, \mathbf{T_B}, \mathbf{u}_0, \tau)$ to sample $\mathbf{v} \leftarrow D_{\Lambda_q^{\mathbf{u}_0}(\mathbf{F}_{id}),\tau}$ such that $\mathbf{F}_{id}\cdot\mathbf{v} = \mathbf{u}_0 \bmod q$. Finally, set the identity secret key sk_{id} to be the vector $\mathbf{v}$.

Encap(id)**:** For an identity $id = (id_1, \ldots, id_d) \in \{0,1\}^d$, compute the matrix $\mathbf{F}_{id}$ just as the above key generation algorithm. Sample $\mathbf{s} \leftarrow \mathbb{Z}_q^n$, error vector $\mathbf{e} \leftarrow \bar{\psi}_\beta^m$ and integer $v \leftarrow \mathbb{Z}_q$. Compute $\mathbf{x} = \mathbf{F}_{id}^T\cdot\mathbf{s}+\mathbf{e} \bmod q \in \mathbb{Z}_q^m$. If $|v - \mathbf{u}_0^T\cdot\mathbf{s}| \le \frac{q-1}{4}$, set $k = 1$ else set $k = 0$. Output $c := (\mathbf{x}, v)$ and the decapsulated key k simultaneously.

Encap*(id)**:** Sample $\mathbf{x} \leftarrow \mathbb{Z}_q^m$ and integer $v \leftarrow \mathbb{Z}_q$. Output $c := (\mathbf{x}, v)$.

Decap(c, sk_{id})**:** Given $c := (\mathbf{x}, v)$ and $sk_{id} := \mathbf{v} \in \mathbb{Z}_q^m$, compute $\langle\mathbf{v}, \mathbf{x}\rangle \bmod q$. If $|v - \mathbf{v}^T\cdot\mathbf{x}| \le \frac{q-1}{4}$, then output $k = 1$. Otherwise output $k = 0$.

Similar to prior existing lattice-based hash proof systems presented in [3, 16, 17], we let q to be a subexponential function in n and $K = \{0,1\}$. In fact, the above set $K = \{0,1\}$ can be easily extended to $\mathbf{k} = \{0,1\}^l$ by choosing as the random vectors in master public key l vectors $(\mathbf{u}_0^1, \ldots, \mathbf{u}_0^l)$ unifromly and independently from $\mathbb{Z}_q^n$, and outputing as the identity secret key $\mathbf{v}_i \leftarrow D_{\Lambda_q^{\mathbf{u}_0^i}(\mathbf{F}_{id}),\tau}$ for $1 \le i \le l$.

3.2 Parameter Setting

Notice that for the system to work correctly, we need that:

- The algorithm $TrapGen$ can work, which means $m > 6n\log q$ and results in $\|\widetilde{\mathbf{T_A}}\| \le O(\sqrt{n\log q})$ by Lemma 3.

[2] More strictly, we need first choose a collision-resilient hash function $h : \{0,1\}^* \rightarrow \{0,1\}^d$, then map arbitrary identity, such as email address, phone number and passport number, to the bit strings of length d.

- The algorithm *BasisDel* used in KeyGen can work, which means $\sigma > \|\widetilde{\mathbf{T_A}}\| \cdot (\sigma_R\sqrt{m}\omega(\log^{1/2} m))^d \omega(\log m)$, and results in $\|\widetilde{\mathbf{T_B}}\| \leq \sigma\sqrt{m}$ by Lemma 9.
- The algorithm *SamplePre* used in KeyGen can work, which means $\tau \geq \sigma\sqrt{m}\omega(\sqrt{\log m})(\geq \|\widetilde{\mathbf{T_B}}\|\omega(\sqrt{\log m}))$ and results in $\mathbf{v} \leftarrow D_{\Lambda_q^{\mathbf{u}_0}(\mathbf{F}_{id}),\tau}$ by Lemma 4. Hence, we have $\|\mathbf{v}\| \leq \sqrt{m}\tau$ except with a negligible probability.
- The reduction for the LWE problem can work, which means $\beta q > 2\sqrt{n}$ by Lemma 11.
- The intersection of valid and invalid ciphertext sets should be empty with overwhelming probability, which means the norm of error vector $\mathbf{e} \leftarrow \bar{\psi}_\beta^m$ should less than $\sqrt{q}/4$ with overwhelming probability by Lemma 13. It suffices to set $\beta q\omega(\sqrt{\log m}) < \sqrt{q}/4$ according to Lemma 12.

To satisfy all above requirements, for instance, we can set the parameters as follows:

$$\begin{aligned} &m = O(dn\log n), \quad q = 2^{\omega(\log n)}, \quad \sigma = m^{\frac{3}{2}d+\frac{1}{2}} \cdot \omega(\log^{2d} n), \\ &\tau = \sigma\sqrt{2\pi m} \cdot \omega(\sqrt{\log m}), \quad \beta = [\sigma m\sqrt{2n} \cdot \omega(\log m)]^{-1} \end{aligned} \tag{1}$$

3.3 Proof for IB-HPS in Sect. 3

Theorem 1. *Let n be the security parameter, d denote the bit length of any $id \in ID$, and all parameters are set as above Eq. (1). Then the above HPS is smooth under the DLWE assumption.*

Proof. The whole proof can be divided into three parts: correctness, indistinguishability, and smoothness.

Lemma 14 (Correctness). *For the above parameters in IB-HPS, the construction is correct.*

We defer the proof of the above lemma for correctness to Appendix B due to the limited space.

Lemma 15 (Anonymous Indistinguishability). *For the above parameters in IB-HPS, the corresponding valid/invalid ciphertexts are computationally indistinguishable.*

Proof. According to the definition of anonymous indistinguishability of valid/inv-alid ciphertexts in Appendix A, we prove this lemma by using a reduction from the DLWE assumption. This means if there exists an efficient algorithm $\mathcal{A}$ distinguishing a valid ciphertext regarding to certain *id* and a random invalid ciphertext with a non-negligible advantage, we can construct another algorithm $\mathcal{B}$ solving the DLWE problem with almost the same advantage.

Suppose $\mathcal{B}$ is given an oracle $\mathcal{O}$ which returns the LWE challenge $(\mathbf{a}, b) \in \mathbb{Z}_q^n \times \mathbb{Z}_q$. After making m queries to $\mathcal{O}$, it receives $\{(\mathbf{a}_i, b_i)\}_{i\in[m]}$, and then constructs a matrix $\mathbf{A}_0 \in \mathbb{Z}_q^{m\times n}$ whose i-th column is set to be $\mathbf{a}_i$ and the challenge vector

$\mathbf{b} = (b_1, \ldots, b_m) \in \mathbb{Z}_q^m$. As we only consider the selective security here, an identity $id^* = (id_1, \ldots, id_d)$ will be sent in advance to $\mathcal{B}$ as the challenge identity.

For setup, $\mathcal{B}$ first samples random matrices $\mathbf{R}_{1,id_1}, \mathbf{R}_{2,id_2}, \cdots, \mathbf{R}_{d,id_d} \leftarrow \mathcal{D}_{m\times m}$ by using the algorithm *SampleR*(1^m) and sets $\mathbf{A}^T = \mathbf{A}_0^T \mathbf{R}_{d,id_d} \cdots \mathbf{R}_{2,id_2} \mathbf{R}_{1,id_1} \in \mathbb{Z}_q^{n\times m}$. In fact, the matrix $\mathbf{A}$ should be uniform over $\mathbb{Z}_q^{m\times n}$ since $\mathbf{A}_0$ is uniform and all the $\mathbf{R}_{i,id_i}$ mod q are invertible.

$\mathcal{B}$ then samples a vector $\mathbf{v}_0 \leftarrow D_{\mathbb{Z}^m,\tau}$ by using the algorithm *SampleGaussian* with the canonical basis of $\mathbb{Z}^{m\times m}$ as the trapdoor basis. Note that for our parameter setting $\tau = \sigma\sqrt{2\pi m}\omega(\log m) \geq \omega(\sqrt{\log m})$ in (1), the above sample for $\mathbf{v}_0$ could be implemented efficiently. Furthermore, $\mathcal{B}$ sets $\mathbf{u}_0 = \mathbf{A}_0^T \cdot \mathbf{v}_0 \bmod q$. According to Lemmas 2, 6 and 7 together with our parameter setting for τ in (1), the distribution of $\mathbf{u}_0$ should be statistically close to uniform over $\mathbb{Z}_q^n$.

Next, $\mathcal{B}$ set d new matrices as $\mathbf{F}_i = \mathbf{A}^T \mathbf{R}_{1,id_1}^{-1} \cdots \mathbf{R}_{i,id_i}^{-1}$ for $i = 0, \ldots, (d-1)$. Given each matrix $\mathbf{F}_i$, $\mathcal{B}$ can invoke the algorithm *SampleRwithBasis*$(\mathbf{F}_i)$ in Lemma 10 to get a matrix $\mathbf{R}_{i,1-id_i}$ and a corresponding short basis $\mathbf{T}_i$ for $\Lambda_q^\perp(\mathbf{F}_i \cdot (\mathbf{R}_{i,1-id_i}^{-1}))$.

Finally, $\mathcal{B}$ sends to the adversary $\mathcal{A}$ the following parameters PP $= (\mathbf{A}, \mathbf{u}_0, \mathbf{R}_{1,0}, \mathbf{R}_{1,1}, \ldots, \mathbf{R}_{d,0}, \mathbf{R}_{d,1})$. It is also clear that the distribution of PP is statistically close to that of real master public key *mpk*. Hence, this simulation for setup is completely legitimate.

For test stage 1, $\mathcal{B}$ needs to compute identity secret keys sk_{id} for any $id \in ID$, which can be divided into two parts. First, for queries on $id \neq id^*$, without loss of generality, assume $j \in \{1, \ldots, d\}$ to be the minimum index such that the corresponding bits of id and id^* are different, and denote $(id'_{j+1}, \ldots, id'_d)$ as the latter $(d-j)$ bits of id. As we have analyzed above for setup, the known matrix $\mathbf{T}_j$ should be a short basis for $\Lambda_q^\perp(\mathbf{F}_j \cdot (\mathbf{R}_{j,1-id_j}^{-1}))$. Then according to the Lemma 9, $\mathcal{B}$ invokes the algorithm *BasisDel*$(\mathbf{F}_j \cdot (\mathbf{R}_{j,1-id_j}^{-1}), \mathbf{R}, \mathbf{T}_j, \sigma_j)$ with $\mathbf{R} = \mathbf{R}_{d,id'_d} \mathbf{R}_{d-1,id'_{d-1}} \cdots \mathbf{R}_{j+1,id'_{j+1}}$ and $\sigma_j = m^{\frac{3}{2}j+\frac{1}{2}} \cdot \omega(\log^{2j} n)$, and attain a short basis $\mathbf{T}_{id}$ for $\mathbf{F}_{id} = \mathbf{F}_j \cdot (\mathbf{R}_{j,1-id_j}^{-1})\mathbf{R}^{-1} = \mathbf{A}\mathbf{R}_{1,id_1}^{-1} \cdots \mathbf{R}_{j-1,id_{j-1}}^{-1} \mathbf{R}_{j,1-id_j}^{-1} \mathbf{R}_{j+1,id'_{j+1}}^{-1} \mathbf{R}_{j+2,id'_{j+2}}^{-1} \cdots \mathbf{R}_{d,id'_d}^{-1}$. Finally, $\mathcal{B}$ runs the algorithm *SamplePre*$(\mathbf{F}_{id}, \mathbf{T}_{id}, \mathbf{u}_0, \tau)$ to sample $\mathbf{v}$ such that $\mathbf{F}_{id} \cdot \mathbf{v} = \mathbf{u}_0 \bmod q$, and responds with $sk_{id} = \mathbf{v}$. Notice that for our parameters setting in (1), all these computations could be efficiently completed. As a result, this response for query on $id \neq id^*$ should be completely legitimate according to Lemmas 4 and 9.

Second, for the query on $id^* = (id_1, \ldots, id_d)$, $\mathcal{B}$ computes $\mathbf{F}_{id^*} = \mathbf{A}^T \mathbf{R}_{1,id_1}^{-1} \mathbf{R}_{2,id_2}^{-1} \cdots \mathbf{R}_{d,id_d}^{-1} = \mathbf{A}_0^T$. Clearly, we do not know any short basis for $\Lambda_q^\perp(\mathbf{A}_0)$, and it can not be simulated as above since id^* is just the challenge identity. Fortunately, however, $\mathcal{B}$ can respond directly with the above $\mathbf{v}_0 \in D_{\mathbb{Z}^m,\tau}$. Since $\mathbf{u}_0 = \mathbf{A}_0^T \cdot \mathbf{v}_0 = \mathbf{F}_{id^*} \cdot \mathbf{v}_0 \bmod q$, this response for query on id^* should be completely legitimate.

For challenge, $\mathcal{B}$ first choose $v \leftarrow \mathbb{Z}_q$ returns $c = (\mathbf{b}, v)$ where $\mathbf{b}$ is the LWE challenge vector for $\mathcal{B}$.

For test stage 2, $\mathcal{B}$ answers the queries as he did in the above test stage 1. Finally, $\mathcal{B}$ outputs the same guess bit as $\mathcal{A}$ does.

It is easy to see that if $\mathcal{O}$ is a LWE oracle, then the challenge ciphertext returned by $\mathcal{B}$ should be a valid ciphertext for the challenge identity id^*. Otherwise, the challenge ciphertext should be a random invalid ciphertext. As a result, the advantage of $\mathcal{B}$ in breaking the LWE assumption is almost the same to the advantage of $\mathcal{A}$ in distinguishing valid and invalid ciphertexts in the above selective identity game.

Lemma 16 (Smoothness). *For the above parameters in IB-HPS, the construction is smooth.*

We defer the proof of the above lemma for smoothness to Appendix C due to the limited space.

At last, the above three lemmas conclude the proof of Theorem 1.

4 Conclusion

In this paper, we present an anonymous and selective IB-HPS based on the LWE assumption in the standard model but still with a subexponential modulus. And the master public key consists of many matrixes, resulting in too many overheads in storage and computation. It should be an interesting work to construct more efficient adaptive IB-HPS from lattices in the standard model.

Acknowledgments. We would like to thank anonymous reviewers for their creative comments on this paper. This work is supported by the National Key R&D Program of China(No. 2017YFB0802000), the National Natural Science Foundation of China (61772326, 61572303, 61602290), NSFC Research Fund for International Young Scientists (61750110528), National Cryptography Development Fund during the 13th Five-year Plan Period (MMJJ20170216), the Foundation of State Key Laboratory of Information Security (2017-MS-03) and the Fundamental Research Funds for the Central Universities (GK201603084, GK201603092, GK201603093, GK201702004, GK201703062).

Appendix

A Anonymous Identity-Based Hash Proof Systems

Formally, an anonymous IB-HPS consists of five probabilistic polynomial-time algorithms (Setup, KeyGen, Encap, Encap*, Decap) as follows.

- Setup(1^n): given security parameter n as an input, output a pair of the master public key mpk and master secret key msk. The master public key mpk also defines an identity set ID, a symmetric key set K, and two ciphertext sets C and V.

- KeyGen(id, msk, mpk): for any identity $id \in ID$, sample an identity secret key sk_{id}.
- Encap(id, mpk): for any identity $id \in ID$, this valid encapsulation algorithm outputs a pair (c, k) where $c \in V$ is a valid ciphertext, and $k \in K$ is the encapsulated-key.
- Encap*(id, mpk): for any identity $id \in ID$, this alternative invalid encapsulation algorithm samples an invalid ciphertext $c \in V'$.
- Decap(sk_{id}, c, mpk): take as input a secret key $sk_{id} \in SK$ and a ciphertext $c \in C$, then output the encapsulated symmetric key k.

We remark that an anonymous IB-HPS should have the following three properties.

I. **Correctness of decapsulation.** For any (mpk, msk) output by Setup(1^n), any $id \in ID$, it holds

$$\Pr[k \neq k' | sk_{id} \leftarrow \text{KeyGen}(id, msk, mpk), (c, k) \leftarrow \text{Encap}(id, mpk), \\ k' = \text{Decap}(sk_{id}, c, mpk)] \leq negl(n).$$

II. **Anonymous indistinguishability of valid/invalid ciphertext.** This means that the two random ciphertexts $c_0 \in V$ and $c_1 \in V'$ are computationally indistinguishable, where C, V and V' are defined by the master public-key mpk. More formally, this indistinguishability is always described by the following game between an adversary $\mathcal{A}$ and a challenger $\mathcal{C}$.

- Setup: The challenger $\mathcal{C}$ gets a pair of (mpk, msk) by running Setup(1^n), and sends mpk to $\mathcal{A}$.
- Test Stage 1: $\mathcal{A}$ adaptively queries the challenger $\mathcal{C}$ with $id \in ID$. Then $\mathcal{C}$ responds with sk_{id}.
- Challenge Stage: $\mathcal{A}$ chooses an arbitrary challenge identity $id^* \in ID$. Then $\mathcal{C}$ selects $b \leftarrow \{0, 1\}$. If $b = 0$, $\mathcal{C}$ gets $c \leftarrow$Encap(id^*, mpk). Otherwise, $\mathcal{C}$ choose a random $c \leftarrow C \backslash V$. Finally, $\mathcal{C}$ returns c to $\mathcal{V}$.
- Test Stage 2: $\mathcal{A}$ adaptively queries the challenger $\mathcal{C}$ with $id \in ID$. And then $\mathcal{C}$ responds with sk_{id}.
- Output: The adversary $\mathcal{A}$ outputs a bit $b' \in \{0, 1\}$ as the output of the game.

The adversary $\mathcal{A}$ wins the game if $b = b'$.

Notice that in test stages the challenger computes sk_{id} for the first time that id is queried, then returns the same sk_{id} for the latter queries on the same $id \in ID$. And the challenge identity id^* might also be queried in Test Stage 1 and Test Stage 2. We define the advantage of $\mathcal{A}$ in distinguishing valid/invalid ciphertexts to be $Adv(\text{IB}-\text{HPS}, \mathcal{A}) = |\Pr[\mathcal{A}\ wins] - 1/2|$. We require that $Adv(\text{IB}-\text{HPS}, \mathcal{A}) \leq negl(n)$.

III. **Smoothness.** Besides the above two properties, we also need one information theoretic property. This ensures that for any one only with public parameters the decapsulation of invalid ciphertext $c \in V'$ under sk_{id} will be statistically uniform. More formally, we define the smoothness as follows.

Definition 5 (Smooth IB-HPS). *We say an anonymous IB-HPS is smooth if, for any fixed values of mpk,msk output by Setup*(1^n)*, any* $id \in ID$*, it holds* $\mathrm{SD}((c,k),(c,k')) \leq negl(n)$*, where* $c \leftarrow \mathrm{Encap}^*(id, mpk)$*,* $k' \leftarrow U_{|k|}$ *and k is output by first choosing* $sk_{id} \leftarrow \mathrm{KeyGen}(id, msk, mpk)$ *and then computing* $k = \mathrm{Decap}(c, sk_{id}, mpk)$*.*

Similar to identity-based encryption schemes, IB-HPSs can also be divided into two types: selectively secure ones and adaptively secure ones. We call it to be selectively secure, if the challenge identity in the above indistinguishability game has to be sent to the challenger $\mathcal{C}$ in advance. Adaptive security implies that the adversary can adaptively choose arbitrary challenge identity in the above game.

B Proof of Lemma 13

Given a matrix $\mathbf{F}_{id} \leftarrow \mathbb{Z}_q^{n\times m}$, and a vector $\mathbf{x} \in \mathbb{Z}_q^m$ output by Encap, there exists one vector $\mathbf{s} \in \mathbb{Z}_q^n$ and some error vector $\mathbf{e} \leftarrow \bar{\psi}_\beta^m$ such that $\mathbf{x} = \mathbf{F}_{id}^T\mathbf{s} + \mathbf{e} \bmod q$. Therefore,

$$\begin{aligned} <\mathbf{v},\mathbf{x}> \bmod q &= <\mathbf{v},\mathbf{x} = \mathbf{A}\mathbf{s}+\mathbf{e}> \bmod q = (<\mathbf{v},\mathbf{A}\mathbf{s}> + <\mathbf{v},\mathbf{e}>) \bmod q \\ &= (<\mathbf{v}^T\mathbf{A},\mathbf{s}> + <\mathbf{v},\mathbf{e}>) \bmod q = (<\mathbf{y},\mathbf{s}> + <\mathbf{v},\mathbf{e}>) \bmod q \end{aligned}$$

Then since $\mathbf{v} \leftarrow D_{\Lambda_q^{\mathbf{u}_0}(\mathbf{F}_{id}),\tau}$, it holds that $\|\mathbf{v}\| \leqslant \tau\sqrt{m}$. According to the definition of $\bar{\psi}_\beta$, $c_i = q \cdot t_i \bmod q$, where t_i are independent normal variables with mean 0 and variance $\beta^2/2\pi$. Then $\|\mathbf{e} - \mathbf{t}\| \leqslant \sqrt{m}/2$, and by Cauchy-Schwarz inequality, $\langle \mathbf{v}, \mathbf{e}\rangle$ is at most $\tau m/2$ away from $\langle \mathbf{v}, \mathbf{t}\rangle$. Furthermore, since t_i are independent, $\langle \mathbf{v}, \mathbf{t}\rangle$ is distributed as a normal variable with mean 0 and standard deviation $\|\mathbf{v}\|\cdot\beta/\sqrt{2\pi} \leqslant \tau\sqrt{m}\cdot\beta/\sqrt{2\pi} \leqslant 1/\sqrt{2n}$. Therefore by the tail inequality on normal variables, the probability that $|\langle \mathbf{v}, \mathbf{t}\rangle| > 1$ is negligible. Thus the probability that $|\langle \mathbf{v}, \mathbf{e}\rangle| > \tau m/2 + 1$ is negligible as well.

For correctness it is sufficient to show that Decap will output the wrong bit with at most negligible probability. This happens if and only if one of $\langle \mathbf{v}, \mathbf{x}\rangle$ and $\langle \mathbf{u}_0, \mathbf{s}\rangle$ is further than $\frac{q-1}{4}$ from v. Let $\ell = |\tau m/2 + 1|$, then there are 2ℓ values of v such that the wrong bit is output. According to our parameter setting, ℓ is a polynomial in n. And since $q = 2^{\omega(\log n)}$, $2\ell/q$ is negligible in n. As a result, for any $(\mathbf{x}, v)$ output by Encap both related bits b output by Encap and Decap are equivalent with overwhelming probability.

C Proof of Lemma 15

According to the corresponding definition, we need to prove that for any $c \leftarrow \mathrm{Encap}^*(id, mpk)$, it holds

$$\mathrm{SD}((c,k),(c,k')) \leq negl(n), \tag{2}$$

where k is a decapsulation of c, i.e., $k = \text{Decap}(sk_{id}, c)^3$ and $k' \leftarrow U_{|k|}$. Hence, the above Eq. (2) can be rewritten as

$$\text{SD}((c, \text{Decap}(sk_{id}, c)), (c, k')) \leq negl(n), \tag{3}$$

Notice that as an output of the algorithm *SamplePre*, $sk_{id} := \mathbf{v}$ has a lower bound on its min-entropy by Lemma 5. In this case, if Decap can also be treated as an universal hash family indexed by c with low collision probability, it is possible to prove the above (3) through Lemma 1. Hence, let us further analyze the two conditions for Lemma 1: min-entropy and collision probability. Details follow.

Firstly, according to the Lemma 5, it holds $H_\infty(\mathbf{v}) \geq m(\log(\tau) - \log(m^c))$ for a constant $c > 0$. Considering the above parameter setting in (1), we can get

$$\begin{aligned} H_\infty(\mathbf{v}) &\geq m \log(\frac{\tau}{m^c}) \\ &= m \log(m^{\frac{3}{2}d+\frac{1}{2}-c}\sqrt{2\pi m} \cdot \omega(\log^{2d} n) \cdot \omega(\sqrt{\log m})) \\ &\geq m \log(m \cdot \omega(\log^{2d} n)) \\ &\geq \omega(\log n). \end{aligned} \tag{4}$$

Secondly, for any fixed $id \in ID$ and different $\mathbf{v} \neq \mathbf{v}'$ such that $\mathbf{F}_{id}\mathbf{v} = \mathbf{F}_{id}\mathbf{v}' \bmod q$, we compute

$$\rho = \Pr_{c \leftarrow \text{Encap}^*(id)}[\text{Decap}(c, \mathbf{v}) = \text{Decap}(c, \mathbf{v}')]. \tag{5}$$

Note also that for any invalid ciphertext $c := (\mathbf{x}, v)$ with $\mathbf{x} = (x_1, \ldots, x_m) \in \mathbb{Z}_q^m$, the output of $\text{Decap}(c, \mathbf{v})$ depends on the value $\langle \mathbf{v}, \mathbf{x} \rangle$. As a result, the computation in (5) can be divided into two steps. We first determine the distribution of the value $\ell = |\langle \mathbf{v}, \mathbf{x} \rangle - \langle \mathbf{v}', \mathbf{x} \rangle| = |\langle \mathbf{v} - \mathbf{v}', \mathbf{x} \rangle|$. Then calculate the collision probability conditioned on each ℓ.

For two different vector $\mathbf{v} = (v_1, \ldots, v_m)$ and $\mathbf{v}' = (v_1', \ldots, v_m')$, we denote $i \in [m]$ as the indexes where $v_i \neq v_i'$. Then we have $\ell = |\sum_i (v_i - v_i')x_i|$. Since q is a prime, there should be a bijection between x_i and ℓ, which implies that ℓ should also be uniform over $\mathbb{Z}_q$.

Then we try to compute ρ conditioned on each value of ℓ. According to the above analysis for correctness, collision could be viewed as a complement event for decapsulation fail. Thus, for $\ell_0 \in [(q-1)/2]$ the corresponding collision probability ρ_{ℓ_0} should be $1 - (2\ell_0)/q$. Thus for Eq. (5) we have:

$$\begin{aligned} \rho = \sum_{\ell_0=0}^{q-1} \rho_{\ell_0} \cdot \Pr[\ell = \ell_0] &= \frac{1}{q} + 2 \sum_{\ell_0=0}^{(q-1)/2} \rho_{\ell_0} \cdot \Pr[\ell = \ell_0] = \frac{1}{q} + \frac{2}{q} \sum_{\ell_0=0}^{(q-1)/2} \rho_{\ell_0} \\ &= \frac{1}{q} + \frac{2}{q} \sum_{\ell_0=0}^{(q-1)/2} (1 - \frac{2d}{q}) = \frac{1}{2} + \frac{1}{2q^2}. \end{aligned} \tag{6}$$

[3] Here it is more convenient for us to view *mpk* as an implicit parameter. This is because all different decapsulation algorithms have the same *mpk* as input.

Thus, it is reasonable to see Decap as a ρ-universal hash family according to the Definition 2.

We also notice that the above Eqs. (4) and (6) can be used to prove Eq. (3) directly through Lemma 1, where the corresponding parameters v and ε should be set to be 1 and $1/q$, respectively. As a result, our IB-HPS is smooth.

References

1. Agrawal, S., Boneh, D., Boyen, X.: Efficient lattice (H)IBE in the standard model. In: Gilbert, H. (ed.) EUROCRYPT 2010. LNCS, vol. 6110, pp. 553–572. Springer, Heidelberg (2010). https://doi.org/10.1007/978-3-642-13190-5_28
2. Agrawal, S., Boneh, D., Boyen, X.: Lattice basis delegation in fixed dimension and shorter-ciphertext hierarchical IBE. In: Rabin, T. (ed.) CRYPTO 2010. LNCS, vol. 6223, pp. 98–115. Springer, Heidelberg (2010). https://doi.org/10.1007/978-3-642-14623-7_6
3. Alwen, J., Dodis, Y., Naor, M., Segev, G., Walfish, S., Wichs, D.: Public-key encryption in the bounded-retrieval model. In: Gilbert, H. (ed.) EUROCRYPT 2010. LNCS, vol. 6110, pp. 113–134. Springer, Heidelberg (2010). https://doi.org/10.1007/978-3-642-13190-5_6
4. Alwen, J., Peikert, C.: Generating shorter bases for hard random lattices. In: Proceedings of STACS 2009, Freiburg, Germany, pp. 75–86 (2009)
5. Ajtai, M.: Generating hard instances of the short basis problem. In: Wiedermann, J., van Emde Boas, P., Nielsen, M. (eds.) ICALP 1999. LNCS, vol. 1644, pp. 1–9. Springer, Heidelberg (1999). https://doi.org/10.1007/3-540-48523-6_1
6. Baek, J., Duncan, S., Li, J., Au, M.H.: Efficient generic construction of CCA-secure identity-based encryption from randomness extraction. Comput. J. **59**(4), 508–521 (2016)
7. Boneh, D., Gentry, C., Hamburg M.: Space-efficient identity based encryption without pairings. In: Proceedings of FOCS 2007, Providence, RI, USA, pp. 647–657 (2007)
8. Cash, D., Hofheinz, D., Kiltz, E., Peikert, C.: Bonsai trees, or how to delegate a lattice basis. In: Gilbert, H. (ed.) EUROCRYPT 2010. LNCS, vol. 6110, pp. 523–552. Springer, Heidelberg (2010). https://doi.org/10.1007/978-3-642-13190-5_27
9. Chen, R., Mu, Y., Yang, G., Susilo, W., Guo, F., Zhang, M.: Cryptographic reverse firewall via malleable smooth projective hash functions. In: Cheon, J.H., Takagi, T. (eds.) ASIACRYPT 2016. LNCS, vol. 10031, pp. 844–876. Springer, Heidelberg (2016). https://doi.org/10.1007/978-3-662-53887-6_31
10. Chen, R., Mu, Y., Yang, G., Susilo, W., Guo, F.: Strong authenticated key exchange with auxiliary inputs. Des. Codes Cryptogr. **85**(1), 145–173 (2017)
11. Chen, R., Mu, Y., Yang, G., Susilo, W., Guo, F.: Strongly leakage-resilient authenticated key exchange. In: Sako, K. (ed.) CT-RSA 2016. LNCS, vol. 9610, pp. 19–36. Springer, Cham (2016). https://doi.org/10.1007/978-3-319-29485-8_2
12. Chen, R., Mu, Y., Yang, G., Susilo, W., Guo, F., Zheng, Y.: A note on the strong authenticated key exchange with auxiliary inputs. Des. Codes Cryptogr. **85**(1), 175–178 (2017)

13. Chen, R., Mu, Y., Yang, G., Guo, F., Wang, X.: Dual-server public-key encryption with keyword search for secure cloud storage. IEEE Trans. Inf. Forensics Secur. **11**(4), 789–798 (2016)
14. Chen, R., Mu, Y., Susilo, W., Yang, G., Guo, F., Zhang, M.: One-round strong oblivious signature-based envelope. In: Liu, J.K., Steinfeld, R. (eds.) ACISP 2016. LNCS, vol. 9723, pp. 3–20. Springer, Cham (2016). https://doi.org/10.1007/978-3-319-40367-0_1
15. Chen, R., Mu, Y., Yang, G., Guo, F., Wang, X.: A new general framework for secure public key encryption with keyword search. In: Foo, E., Stebila, D. (eds.) ACISP 2015. LNCS, vol. 9144, pp. 59–76. Springer, Cham (2015). https://doi.org/10.1007/978-3-319-19962-7_4
16. Chen, Y., Zhang, Z., Lin, D., Cao, Z.: Anonymous identity-based hash proof system and its applications. In: Takagi, T., Wang, G., Qin, Z., Jiang, S., Yu, Y. (eds.) ProvSec 2012. LNCS, vol. 7496, pp. 143–160. Springer, Heidelberg (2012). https://doi.org/10.1007/978-3-642-33272-2_10
17. Chen, Y., Zhang, Z., Lin, D., Cao, Z.: Generalized (identity-based) hash proof system and its applications. Secur. Commun. Netw. **9**(12), 1698–1716 (2016)
18. Chen, Y., Zhang, Z., Lin, D., Cao, Z.: Identity-based extractable hash proofs and their applications. In: Bao, F., Samarati, P., Zhou, J. (eds.) ACNS 2012. LNCS, vol. 7341, pp. 153–170. Springer, Heidelberg (2012). https://doi.org/10.1007/978-3-642-31284-7_10
19. Chen, Y., Zhang, Z., Lin, D., Cao, Z.: CCA-secure IB-KEM from identity-based extractable hash proof system. Comput. J. **57**(10), 1537–1556 (2014)
20. Chow, S.M., Dodis, Y., Rouselakis, Y., Waters, B.: Practical leakage-resilient identity-based encryption from simple assumptions. In: Proceedings of the 17th ACM Conference on Computer and Communications Security–CCS 2010, Chicago, Illinois, USA, pp. 152–161 (2010)
21. Cramer, R., Shoup, V.: Universal hash proofs and a paradigm for adaptive chosen ciphertext secure public-key encryption. In: Knudsen, L.R. (ed.) EUROCRYPT 2002. LNCS, vol. 2332, pp. 45–64. Springer, Heidelberg (2002). https://doi.org/10.1007/3-540-46035-7_4
22. Dodis, Y., Goldwasser, S., Tauman Kalai, Y., Peikert, C., Vaikuntanathan, V.: Public-key encryption schemes with auxiliary inputs. In: Micciancio, D. (ed.) TCC 2010. LNCS, vol. 5978, pp. 361–381. Springer, Heidelberg (2010). https://doi.org/10.1007/978-3-642-11799-2_22
23. Gentry, C., Peikert, C., Vaikuntanathan, V.: Trapdoors for hard lattices and new cryptographic constructions. In: Proceedings of the 40th Annual ACM Symposium on Theory of Computing–STOC 2008, Victoria, British Columbia, Canada, pp. 197–206 (2008)
24. Hofheinz, D., Kiltz, E.: Secure hybrid encryption from weakened key encapsulation. In: Menezes, A. (ed.) CRYPTO 2007. LNCS, vol. 4622, pp. 553–571. Springer, Heidelberg (2007). https://doi.org/10.1007/978-3-540-74143-5_31
25. Katz, J., Vaikuntanathan, V.: Smooth projective hashing and password-based authenticated key exchange from lattices. In: Matsui, M. (ed.) ASIACRYPT 2009. LNCS, vol. 5912, pp. 636–652. Springer, Heidelberg (2009). https://doi.org/10.1007/978-3-642-10366-7_37
26. Micciancio, D., Regev, O.: Worst-case to average-case reductions based on Gaussian measures. SIAM J. Comput. **37**(1), 267–302 (2007)

27. Naor, M., Segev, G.: Public-key cryptosystems resilient to key leakage. In: Halevi, S. (ed.) CRYPTO 2009. LNCS, vol. 5677, pp. 18–35. Springer, Heidelberg (2009). https://doi.org/10.1007/978-3-642-03356-8_2
28. Regev, O.: On lattices, learning with errors, random linear codes, and cryptography. J. ACM **56**(6), 1–40 (2009)
29. Peikert, C.: Limits on the hardness of lattice problems in ℓ_p norms. Comput. Complex. **17**(2), 300–351 (2008)

Post-Quantum One-Time Linkable Ring Signature and Application to Ring Confidential Transactions in Blockchain (Lattice RingCT v1.0)

Wilson Abel Alberto Torres[1(✉)], Ron Steinfeld[1(✉)], Amin Sakzad[1(✉)], Joseph K. Liu[1(✉)], Veronika Kuchta[1], Nandita Bhattacharjee[1], Man Ho Au[2], and Jacob Cheng[3]

[1] Faculty of IT, Monash University, Melbourne, Australia
{Wilson.Torres,Ron.Steinfeld,Amin.Sakzad,Joseph.Liu,Veronika.Kuchta, Nandita.Bhattacharjee}@monash.edu

[2] Hong Kong Polytechnic University, Hung Hom, Hong Kong
csallen@comp.polyu.edu.hk

[3] Collinstar Capital, Melbourne, Australia
jacob@collinstar.com

Abstract. In this paper, we construct a Lattice-based one-time Linkable Ring Signature (L2RS) scheme, which enables the public to verify if two or more signatures were generated by same signatory, whilst still preserving the anonymity of the signatory. The L2RS provides unconditional anonymity and security guarantees under the Ring Short Integer Solution (Ring-SIS) lattice hardness assumption. The proposed L2RS scheme is extended to be applied in a protocol that we called *Lattice Ring Confidential transaction (Lattice RingCT) v1.0*, which forms the foundation of the privacy-preserving protocol in any post-quantum secure cryptocurrency such as Hcash.

Keywords: Linkable ring signature · Lattice-based cryptography
Post-quantum cryptography · Cryptocurrencies

1 Introduction

The notion of a *Ring Signature* scheme was initially formalised in [1]. This scheme allows signing a message on behalf of a spontaneous group of signers, while preserving the anonymity of the signer. The creation of a ring signature does not require members of a group to cooperate, meaning that this scheme will not longer have a manager who eventually can reveal the identity of the signer, and thus the anonymity will be unconditionally preserved. This approach was a remarkable security improvement when compared with the group signature scheme [2] where a group manager was part of its construction. Later, an extended property called *Linkability* was introduced in a ring signature scheme,

W. Susilo and G. Yang (Eds.): ACISP 2018, LNCS 10946, pp. 558–576, 2018.
https://doi.org/10.1007/978-3-319-93638-3_32

under the name of *Linkable Spontaneous Anonymous Group* but is now known as *Linkable Ring Signature* [3]. The linkability property of ring signatures allows one to detect if two signatures were generated by the same signer (using the same private-key) whilst still preserving their anonymity. This scheme was proved to be secure under the discrete logarithm assumption and in Random Oracle Model (ROM). In comparison with previous unlinkable ring signature schemes, this scheme adds an efficient algorithm to verify the linkability property. Each signature (σ) is accompanied by a label (or tag), which is computed based on the signer's private key and a hash function modelled as a random oracle in a deterministic manner. The label can be used by the linking algorithm the check whether two signatures are created by the same signer. Specifically, if the labels accompanying two signatures are the same, it means that the two signatures are created by the same signer. This particular feature opens the possibility of many practical scenarios [4], such as, cryptocurrency, in particular the RingCT confidential transaction protocol adapted in Monero cryptocurrency [5], and e-voting applications.

Nevertheless, the above ring signature schemes are based on classical number-theory mathematical assumptions, for instance, the hardness of discrete logarithm [6] and factoring large numbers [7]. As a consequence, they are believed to be vulnerable with the onset of powerful quantum computers [8]. This situation has sparked the primarily motivation of researchers in the area of post-quantum cryptography to construct secure approaches against these type of computers. Among the alternatives, lattice-based cryptography has attracted the attention of this field due to its distinguishing features and new applications. Algorithms based on lattices tend to be efficient, simple, highly parallelisable and provide strong provable security guarantees [9].

1.1 Contribution

- We construct a Lattice-based one-time Linkable Ring Signature (**L2RS**) scheme. Our L2RS is a generalisation of the BLISS [10] scheme which is currently one of the practical lattice digital signatures. L2RS provides unconditional anonymity as well as unforgeability security guarantees under the hardness of standard lattice assumptions.
- We devise a new cryptocurrency privacy-preserving protocol that we call **Lattice RingCT v1.0**. This protocol employs our proposed post-quantum L2RS as a fundamental building block along with a homomorphic commitment primitive to provide post-quantum secure confidential transactions which forms the foundation of the privacy-preserving protocol for blockchain cryptocurrencies, such as Hcash.

This paper is organised in eight parts, including the introduction. Section 2 gives a brief background of the current linkable ring signature approaches. After describing the technical description used in Sect. 3 and the security model in Sect. 4, this research shows the construction of the L2RS scheme in Sect. 5 along with the security analysis in Sect. 6. In Sect. 7, we present an application of this

L2RS in a cryptocurrency protocol that we called Lattice RingCT v1.0. Finally, a performance analysis of these proposals is presented in Sect. 8.

2 Related Work

Linkable Ring Signature (LRS) primitive is receiving attention thanks to its distinguishing capabilities of anonymously detecting if two linkable ring signatures are being signed by same signatory. Most of the current linkable ring signature schemes along with different variants [3,11–18] rely on the hardness assumptions of classical cryptography. Technically, this primitive uses a linkability tag that has a secure relationship with the signer's publick-key, then the LRS uses this tag to verify whether or not a singer signs two signatures. Monero, a cryptocurrency application, exploits this property to prevent double spending while keeping the user's anonymity [5].

However, this primitive and its variants will be vulnerable to quantum attacks [8]. This situation has led to a new area in the field of cryptography called *Post-Quantum Cryptography*, aimed at constructing new cryptographic algorithms that are intractable even in the presence of powerful quantum computers. Among the current post-quantum cryptographic proposals [19], lattice-based cryptography has attracted the attention of cryptographers. It is a candidate to be standardised as a post-quantum cryptography solution due to its efficiency, parallelism, uniqueness and strong security assurances under the *worst-case hardness* of lattice problems, which is significantly better than the *average-case hardness* of other cryptographic constructions [9].

Digital signatures which are constructed based on lattice-based cryptography can be categorised into GGH/NTRUSign [20,21], Hash-and-sign [22] and Fiat-Shamir signatures [23]. Fiat-Shamir transformation [24] is used by the Bimodal Lattice Signature Scheme (BLISS) [10], which is currently one of the most practical lattice-based digital signature schemes. BLISS has been constructed using the following well known lattice-based cryptography problems, the Short Integer Solution (SIS) [25], Ring-SIS [26] and the Ring-LWE (Learning With Errors) [27] problems[1]. The Ring-SIS version of BLISS offers practical runtime and key sizes. Moreover, this scheme uses a probabilistic test based on rejection sampling technique to make the distribution of the private-key independent, an important property that completely hides the private-key from any adversary.

Several lattice-based ring signatures schemes have been proposed in [28–30] and there were recently three LRS proposals based on lattice-based cryptography. The first of these constructions [31], is based on the development of a lattice-based weak Pseudo Random Function (wPRF), an accumulator scheme (Acc) and a framework named as Zero-Knowledge Arguments of Knowledge (ZKAoK). These techniques are used to construct LRS schemes where the security guarantees for the LRS properties' *unforgeability, anonymity, linkability and non-slanderability* rely on the lattice problems. The second lattice LRS scheme

[1] The *Ring*-SIS and *Ring*-LWE refer to the *Ring* mathematical structure and differ from the *Ring* in the *Ring Signature* scheme.

[32], uses ideal lattices along with a lattice-based homomorphic commitment in its construction. The security properties are based on the hardness of lattices; however, there is no discussion as to how to secure the scheme in terms of *non-slanderability.* This scheme is shown to be used in a cryptocurrency application. The last lattice LRS proposal [33], is devised using lattice-based variants named Module-SIS and Module-LWE problems and its security properties rely on the lattice assumptions.

Our (L2RS) scheme was designed independently and concurrently with [33]. The schemes share similar features, but our scheme offers unconditional anonymity. The construction of this work, which we call Lattice-based one-time Linkable Ring Signature (L2RS), is an extension of BLISS, a demonstrated practical lattice-based digital signature [10]. It is secure in terms of *unforgeability, linkability and non-slanderability* under the lattice hardness of the Ring-SIS problem and unlike the above Lattice-based LRS schemes [31–33], the L2RS scheme achieves *unconditional anonymity,* meaning that this scheme will be secure even if an adversary has unlimited computational resources and time. As an application of this construction, we designed the Lattice RingCT v1.0, a cryptocurrency protocol that provides confidential transactions and which its security guarantees rely on our post-quantum cryptographic L2RS scheme.

3 Preliminaries

The ring $\mathcal{R} = \mathbb{Z}[x]/f(x)$ is a degree-n polynomial ring, where $f(x)$ is a polynomial of degree of n. The ring $\mathcal{R}_q$ is then defined to be the quotient ring $\mathcal{R}_q = \mathcal{R}/(q\mathcal{R}) = \mathbb{Z}_q[x]/f(x)$, where $\mathbb{Z}_q$ denotes the set of all positive integers modulo q (a prime number $q = 1 \bmod 2n$) in the interval $[-q/2, q/2]$ and $f(x) = x^n + 1$ where n is a power of 2. The challenge $\mathcal{S}_{n,\kappa}$, is the set of all binary vectors of length n and weight κ. Two hash functions modeled as Random Oracle Model (ROM), H_1 with range $\mathcal{S}_{n,\kappa} \subseteq \mathcal{R}_{2q}$, and H_2 with range $\mathcal{R}_q^{1\times(m-1)}$. When we use $x \leftarrow D$, it means that x is chosen from the distribution D, and $y \leftarrow \mathcal{R}_q$ means that y is chosen uniformly at random according to $\mathcal{R}_q$. Matrices are written in bold upper case letters whereas vectors are represented in bold lower case letters, where vectors are column vectors and $\mathbf{v}^T$ is the transpose of the vector $\mathbf{v}$. The hardness assumption of this work is the Ring-SIS (Short Integer Solution) problem and this is defined as follows.

Definition 1 ($\mathcal{R}$-SIS$^{\mathcal{K}}_{q,n,m,\beta}$ problem). (Based on [10], Definition 2.3). *Let denote $\mathcal{K}$ some uniform distribution over the ring $\mathcal{R}_q^{n\times m}$. Given a random matrix $\mathbf{A} \in \mathcal{R}_q^{n\times m}$ sampled from $\mathcal{K}$ distribution, find a non-zero vector $\mathbf{v} \in \mathcal{R}_q^m$ such that $\mathbf{Av} = \mathbf{0}$ and $\|\mathbf{v}\|_2 \leq \beta$, where $\|\cdot\|_2$ denotes the Euclidean norm.*

Lemma 1 (Leftover Hash Lemma (LHL)). (Based on [10], Lemma B.1). *Let $\mathcal{H}$ be a universal hash family of hash functions from X to Y. If $h \leftarrow \mathcal{H}$ and $x \leftarrow X$ are chosen uniformly and independently, then the statistical distance between (h,h(x)) and the uniform distribution on $\mathcal{H} \times Y$ is at most $\frac{1}{2}\sqrt{|Y|/|X|}$.*

Remark 1. We use this lemma for a SIS family of hash function $H(\mathbf{S}_0) = \mathbf{A}'_0 \cdot \mathbf{S}_0 \in \mathcal{R}_q$, with $\mathbf{S}_0 \in \mathsf{Dom}_{\mathbf{S}_0}$, where each function is indexed by $\mathbf{A}'_0 \in \mathcal{R}_q^{1\times(m-1)}$. The $\mathsf{Dom}_{\mathbf{S}_0} \subseteq \mathcal{R}_q^{1\times(m-1)}$ consists of a vector of $\mathcal{R}_q$ elements with coefficients in set $\Gamma \stackrel{\text{def}}{=} (-2^\gamma, 2^\gamma)$. This is a universal hash family if $s - s'$ is invertible in $\mathcal{R}_q$ for all distinct pairs s, s' in $\Gamma^n \subseteq \mathcal{R}_q$. This can be guaranteed by appropriate choice q of $\mathcal{R}_q$, e.g. as shown in ([34], Corollary 1.2), it is sufficient to use q such that $f(x) = x^n + 1$ factors into k irreducible factors $\mod q$ and $2^\gamma < \frac{1}{\sqrt{k}} \cdot q^{1/k}$. We assume that $\mathcal{R}_q$ is chosen to satisfy this condition.

Lemma 2 (Rejection Sampling). (Based on [10], Lemma 2.1). *Let V be an arbitrary set, and $h : V \to \mathbb{R}$ and $f : \mathbb{Z}^m \to R$ be probability distributions. If $g_v : \mathbb{Z}^m \to R$ is a family of probability distributions indexed by $v \in V$ with the property that there exists a $M \in \mathbb{R}$ such that $\forall v \in V, \forall \mathbf{v} \in \mathbb{Z}^m, M \cdot g_v(\mathbf{z}) \geq f(\mathbf{z})$. Then the output distributions of the following two algorithms are identical:*

1. *$v \leftarrow h, z \leftarrow g_v$, output$(\mathbf{z}, v)$ with probability $f(\mathbf{z})/(M \cdot g_v(\mathbf{z}))$.*
2. *$v \leftarrow h, z \leftarrow f$, output$(\mathbf{z}, v)$ with probability $1/M$.*

Definition 2 (Gaussian Distribution). *The discrete Gaussian distribution over $\mathbb{Z}^m$ with standard deviation $\sigma \in \mathbb{R}$ and center at zero, is defined by $D_\sigma^m(\boldsymbol{x}) = \rho_\sigma(\boldsymbol{x})/\rho_\sigma(\mathbb{Z}^m)$, where ρ_σ is m dimensional Gaussian function $\rho_\sigma(\boldsymbol{x}) = \exp\left(\frac{-\|\boldsymbol{x}\|^2}{2\sigma^2}\right)$.*

4 Security Model

4.1 Structure of Lattice-Based One-Time Linkable Ring Signature (L2RS)

A L2RS scheme has five PPT algorithms (Setup, KeyGen, SigGen, SigVer, SigLink). In addition, the correctness of this scheme is satisfied by the Signature correctness SigGen Correctness and the Linkability correctness SigLink Correctness. These algorithms are defined as follows:

- Setup: a PPT algorithm that takes the security parameter λ and produces the Public Parameters (Pub-Params).
- KeyGen: a PPT algorithm that by taking the Pub-Params, it produces a pair of keys: the public-key and the private-key.
- SigGen: a PPT algorithm that receives a singer π's private-key, a message μ and the list of users' public-keys in the ring signature L, and outputs a signature $\sigma_L(\mu)$.
- SigVer: a PPT algorithm that takes a signature $\sigma_L(\mu)$, a list of public-keys L and the message μ, and it verifies if this signature was legitimately created, this algorithm outputs either: **Accept** or **Reject**.
- SigLink: a PPT algorithm that inputs two valid signatures $\sigma_L(\mu_1)$ and $\sigma_L(\mu_2)$ and it anonymously determines if these signatures were produced by same signer π. Thus, this algorithm has a deterministic output: **Linked** or **Unlinked**.

CORRECTNESS REQUIREMENTS:

- SigGen Correctness: this guarantees that valid signatures signed by honest signers will be accepted with overwhelming probability by a verifier.
- SigLink Correctness: this ensures that if two signatures $\sigma_L(\mu_1)$ and $\sigma_L(\mu_2)$ are signed by an honest signer π, SigLink will output **Linked** with overwhelming probability.

4.2 Oracles for Adversaries

The following oracles will be available to any adversary who tries to break the security of an L2RS scheme:

1. $\mathbf{A}_i \leftarrow \mathcal{JO}(\perp)$. The *Joining Oracle*, on request, adds a new user to the system. It returns the public-key $\mathbf{A} \in \mathcal{R}_{2q}^{1\times m}$ of the new user.
2. $\mathbf{S}_i \leftarrow \mathcal{CO}(\mathbf{A}_i)$. The *Corruption Oracle*, on input a public-key $\mathbf{A}_i \in \mathcal{R}_{2q}^{1\times m}$ that is a query output of $\mathcal{JO}$, returns the corresponding private-key $\mathbf{S}_i \in \mathcal{R}_q^{m\times 1}$.
3. $\sigma'_L(\mu) \leftarrow \mathcal{SO}(w, L, \mathbf{A}_\pi, \mu)$. The *Signing Oracle*, a group size w, a set L of w public-keys, the public-key of the signer $\mathbf{A}_\pi$, and a message μ, returns a valid signature $\sigma'_L(\mu)$.

4.3 Threat Model

- ONE-TIME UNFORGEABILITY. One time unforgeability for the L2RS scheme is defined in the following game between a simulator $\mathcal{S}$ and an adversary $\mathcal{A}$ who has access to the oracles $\mathcal{JO}$, $\mathcal{CO}$, $\mathcal{SO}$ and the random oracle:
  1. $\mathcal{S}$ generates and gives the list of public-keys L to $\mathcal{A}$.
  2. $\mathcal{A}$ may query the oracles according to any adaptive strategy.
  3. $\mathcal{A}$ gives $\mathcal{S}$ a ring signature size w, a set L of w public-keys, a message μ and a signature $\sigma_L(\mu)$.

$\mathcal{A}$ wins the game if:

- $\mathsf{Verify}(w, L, \mu, \sigma_L(\mu)) = \mathsf{accept}$.
- All of the public-keys in L are query outputs of $\mathcal{JO}$.
- No public-key in L have been input to $\mathcal{CO}$.
- $\sigma_L(\mu)$ is not a query output of $\mathcal{SO}$.
- No signing key $\mathbf{A}_\pi$ was queried more than once to $\mathcal{SO}$.

The advantage of the one-time unforgeability in the L2RS scheme is denoted by

$$\mathbf{Advantage}_{\mathcal{A}}^{ot-unf}(\lambda) = \Pr[\mathcal{A} \text{ wins the game }]$$

Definition 3 (One-Time Unforgeability). *The L2RS scheme is one-time unforgeable if for all PPT adversary $\mathcal{A}$, $\mathbf{Advantage}_{\mathcal{A}}^{ot-unf}(\lambda)$ is negligible.*

- Unconditional Anonymity. It should not be possible for an adversary $\mathcal{A}$ to tell the public-key of the signer with a probability larger than $1/w$, where w is the cardinality of the ring signature, even assuming that the adversary has unlimited computing resources.
Unconditional anonymity for L2RS schemes is defined in the following game between a simulator $\mathcal{S}$ and an unbounded adversary $\mathcal{A}$ who has access to the oracle $\mathcal{JO}$.
  1. $\mathcal{S}$ generates and gives the list of public-keys L to $\mathcal{A}$.
  2. $\mathcal{A}$ may query $\mathcal{JO}$ according to any adaptive strategy.
  3. $\mathcal{A}$ gives $\mathcal{S}$, a group size w, a set L of w public-keys which are the outputs of $\mathcal{JO}$, a message μ. Parse the set L as $\{\mathbf{A}_1, \ldots, \mathbf{A}_w\}$. $\mathcal{S}$ randomly picks $\pi \in \{1, \ldots, w\}$ and computes $\sigma_\pi = \mathsf{Sign}(w, L, \mathbf{S}_\pi, \mu)$, where $\mathbf{S}_\pi$ is a corresponding private-key of $\mathbf{A}_\pi$. Then, σ_π is given to $\mathcal{A}$.
  4. $\mathcal{A}$ outputs a guess $\pi' \in \{1, \ldots, w\}$.

  The anonymity advantage of the L2RS scheme is denoted by

$$\mathbf{Advantage}_{\mathcal{A}}^{Anon}(\lambda) = \left| \Pr[\pi' = \pi] - \frac{1}{w} \right|$$

Definition 4 (Unconditional Anonymity). *The L2RS scheme is unconditional anonymous if for any unbounded adversary $\mathcal{A}$,* $\mathbf{Advantage}_{\mathcal{A}}^{Anon}(\lambda)$ *is zero.*

- Linkability. It should be infeasible for a signer to generate two signatures such that they are determined **unlinked** using the SigLink algorithm. In this scenario, the adversary attempts to generate two signatures, using only one private-key $\mathbf{S}_\pi$. To describe this, we use the interaction between a simulator $\mathcal{S}$ and an adversary $\mathcal{A}$:
  1. The $\mathcal{A}$ queries the $\mathcal{JO}$ multiple times and $\mathcal{CO}$ only once to get the private-key $\mathbf{S}_\pi$, corresponding to the public-key $\mathbf{A}_\pi$.
  2. The $\mathcal{A}$ outputs two signatures $\sigma_L(\mu)$ and $\sigma'_{L'}(\mu')$ and two lists of public-keys L and L'.

  the $\mathcal{A}$ wins the game if:
  - The public-keys in L and L' are outputs of $\mathcal{JO}$.
  - By calling SigVer on input $\sigma_L(\mu)$ and $\sigma'_{L'}(\mu')$, it outputs **Accept** on both inputs.
  - Finally, it gets **Unlinked**, when calling SigLink on input $\sigma_L(\mu)$ and $\sigma'_{L'}(\mu')$.

  Thus the advantage of the linkability in the L2RS scheme is denoted by

$$\mathbf{Advantage}_{\mathcal{A}}^{Link}(\lambda) = \Pr[\mathcal{A} \text{ wins the game}].$$

Definition 5 (Linkability). *The L2RS scheme is linkable if for all PPT adversary $\mathcal{A}$,* $\mathbf{Advantage}_{\mathcal{A}}^{Link}$ *is negligible.*

- Non-slanderability. It should be infeasible for an adversary to generate a valid signature that is **linked** with respect to a signature created by an honest user. This means that an adversary can frame an honest user for signing a valid signature so the adversary can produce another valid signature such that the SigLink algorithm outputs **Linked**. To describe this, we use the interaction between a simulator $\mathcal{S}$ and an adversary $\mathcal{A}$:

1. The $\mathcal{S}$ generates and gives the list of public-keys L to $\mathcal{A}$.
2. The $\mathcal{A}$ queries the $\mathcal{JO}$ and $\mathcal{CO}$ to obtain $\mathbf{A}_\pi$ and $\mathbf{S}_\pi$, respectively.
3. $\mathcal{A}$ gives the generated parameters to $\mathcal{S}$.
4. $\mathcal{S}$ uses the private-key $\mathbf{S}_\pi$ and calls the $\mathcal{SO}$ to output a valid signature $\sigma_L(\mu)$, which is given to $\mathcal{A}$.
5. The $\mathcal{A}$ uses the remaining keys of the ring signature $(w-1)$ to create a second signature $\sigma'_L(\mu)$ by calling the $\mathcal{SO}$ algorithm.

the $\mathcal{A}$ wins the game if:

- The verification algorithm SigVer, on input $\sigma_L(\mu)$ and $\sigma'_L(\mu)$, outputs **Accept**.
- The keys $\mathbf{A}_\pi$ and $\mathbf{S}_\pi$ were not used to generated the second signature $\sigma'_L(\mu)$.
- When calling the SigLink on input $\sigma_L(\mu)$ and $\sigma'_L(\mu)$, it outputs **Linked**.

Thus the advantage of the non-slanderability in the L2RS scheme is denoted by

$$\mathbf{Advantage}_{\mathcal{A}}^{NS}(\lambda) = \Pr[\mathcal{A} \text{ wins the game}].$$

Definition 6 (Non-Slanderability). *The L2RS scheme is* non-slanderable *if for all PPT adversary $\mathcal{A}$, $\mathbf{Advantage}_{\mathcal{A}}^{NS}$ is negligible.*

5 Our Proposed L2RS Scheme

5.1 Setup

By receiving the security parameter λ, this L2RS.Setup algorithm randomly chooses $\mathbf{A}'_0 = (\mathbf{a}_{0,1}, \ldots, \mathbf{a}_{0,m-1}) \leftarrow \mathcal{R}_q^{1\times(m-1)}$ and $\mathbf{H}'_0 = (\mathbf{h}_{0,1}, \ldots, \mathbf{h}_{0,m-1}) \leftarrow \mathcal{R}_q^{1\times(m-1)}$. This outputs the public parameters (Pub-Params): $\mathbf{A}'_0$ and $\mathbf{H}'_0$.

Remark 2. To prevent malicious attack, L2RS.Setup incorporates a trapdoor in $\mathbf{A}'_0$ or $\mathbf{H}'_0$, in practice L2RS.Setup would generate $\mathbf{A}'_0$ and $\mathbf{H}'_0$ based on the cryptographic Hash function H_2 evaluated of two distinct and fixed constants.

Definition 7 (Function L2RS.Lift). *This function maps $\mathcal{R}_q^{1\times m}$ to $\mathcal{R}_{2q}^{1\times m}$ with respect to a public parameter $\mathbf{A}'_0 \in \mathcal{R}_q^{1\times(m-1)}$. Given $\mathbf{a}'_1 \in \mathcal{R}_q$, we let L2RS.Lift$(\mathbf{A}'_0, \mathbf{a}'_1) \triangleq (2\cdot \mathbf{A}'_0, -2\cdot \mathbf{a}'_1 + q \bmod 2q) \in \mathcal{R}_{2q}^{1\times m}$.*

5.2 Key Generation - KeyGen

This algorithm receives the public parameters Pub-Params: $\mathbf{A}'_0$ and $\mathbf{H}'_0$.

1. To generate a key pair in $\mathcal{R}_q$, we:
   - Pick $(\mathbf{s}_{0,1}, \ldots, \mathbf{s}_{0,m-1})$, where every component is chosen uniformly and independently with coefficients in $(-2^\gamma, 2^\gamma)$.
   - Define $\mathbf{S}_0^T = (\mathbf{s}_{0,1}, \ldots, \mathbf{s}_{0,m-1}) \in \mathcal{R}_q^{1\times(m-1)}$, and let $\mathbf{S}^T = (\mathbf{S}_0^T, 1) \in \mathcal{R}_q^{1\times m}$.

- Compute $\mathbf{a}_1' = \mathbf{A}_0' \cdot \mathbf{S}_0 \bmod q \in \mathcal{R}_q$.
- Return $(\mathbf{A}_0', \mathbf{a}_1') \in \mathcal{R}_q^{1\times m}$, $(\mathbf{S}_0^T, 1) \in \mathcal{R}_{2q}^{1\times m}$.

2. The L2RS.Lift function is used to compute and return: $\mathbf{A} = (\mathbf{A}_0, \mathbf{a}_1) = \mathsf{L2RS.Lift}(\mathbf{A}_0', \mathbf{a}_1') = (2 \cdot \mathbf{A}_0', -2 \cdot \mathbf{a}_1' + q \bmod 2q) \in \mathcal{R}_{2q}^{1\times m}$.
3. In the private-key $\mathbf{S}^T = (\mathbf{S}_0^T, 1) \in \mathcal{R}_q^{1\times m}$, we consider $\mathbf{S}_0$ an element in $\mathcal{R}_{2q}$, so that this returns the private-key $\mathbf{S} \in \mathcal{R}_{2q}^{m\times 1}$.

Note that $\mathbf{A} \cdot \mathbf{S} = q \in \mathcal{R}_{2q}$. The list of the users' public-keys is defined as $L = \{\mathbf{A}_1, \ldots, \mathbf{A}_w\}$, where w is the number of users in the ring signature scheme. This KeyGen algorithm is described in the following Algorithm 1:

Algorithm 1. L2RS Algorithm - Key pair generation $(\mathbf{A}, \mathbf{S})$

Input: The public parameters Pub-Params: $\mathbf{A}_0'$ and $\mathbf{H}_0'$.
Output: $(\mathbf{A}, \mathbf{S})$, where $\mathbf{A}$ is the public-key and $\mathbf{S}$ is the private-key.

procedure L2RS.KeyGen(Pub-Params)
  Let $\mathbf{S}_0^T = (\mathbf{s}_{0,1}, \ldots, \mathbf{s}_{0,m-1}) \in \mathcal{R}_q^{1\times(m-1)}$, where $\mathbf{s}_{0,i} \leftarrow (-2^\gamma, 2^\gamma)^n$, for $1 \le i \le m-1$
  Let $\mathbf{S}^T = (\mathbf{S}_0^T, 1) \in \mathcal{R}_q^{1\times m}$.
  Compute $\mathbf{a}_1' = \mathbf{A}_0' \cdot \mathbf{S}_0 \bmod q \in \mathcal{R}_q$.
  Call function $\mathsf{L2RS.Lift}(\mathbf{A}_0', \mathbf{a}_1')$, and it returns $\mathbf{A} = (\mathbf{A}_0, \mathbf{a}_1) = (2 \cdot \mathbf{A}_0', -2 \cdot \mathbf{a}_1' + q \bmod 2q) \in \mathcal{R}_{2q}^{1\times m}$
  Remark: $\mathbf{A} \cdot \mathbf{S} = q \in \mathcal{R}_{2q}$, where $\mathbf{S} \in \mathcal{R}_{2q}^{m\times 1}$.
  return $(\mathbf{A}, \mathbf{S})$.

5.3 Signature Generation - SigGen

The SigGen algorithm inputs the user's private-key $\mathbf{S}_\pi$, the message μ, the list of user's public-keys L, and will output the signature $\sigma_L(\mu)$. We call π the index in $\{1, \ldots, w\}$ of the user or signatory who wants to sign a message μ. For a message $\mu \in \{0,1\}^*$, the fixed list of public-keys L and the private-key $\mathbf{S}_\pi$ which corresponds to $\mathbf{A}_\pi$ with $1 \le \pi \le w$; the following computations are performed:

1. We define the linkability tag as $\mathbf{H} = \big(\mathbf{H}_0, \mathbf{h}_1\big)$, where $\mathbf{H}_0$ is a fixed public parameter for all users: $\mathbf{H}_0 = 2 \cdot \mathbf{H}_0' \in \mathcal{R}_{2q}^{1\times(m-1)}$, and $\mathbf{h}_1 = -\mathbf{H}_0 \cdot \mathbf{S}_{\pi,0} + q \in \mathcal{R}_{2q}$, where $\mathbf{S}_\pi^T = \big(\mathbf{S}_{\pi,0}^T, 1\big) \in \mathcal{R}_{2q}^{1\times m}$, such that $\mathbf{H} \cdot \mathbf{S}_\pi = q \in \mathcal{R}_{2q}$.
2. By choosing a random vector $\mathbf{u}_\pi = (u_1, \ldots, u_m)^T$, where $u_i \leftarrow D_\sigma^n$, for $1 \le i \le m$, we calculate $\mathbf{c}_{\pi+1} = H_1\Big(L, \mathbf{H}, \mu, \mathbf{A}_\pi \cdot \mathbf{u}_\pi, \mathbf{H} \cdot \mathbf{u}_\pi\Big)$.
3. We choose random vector $\mathbf{t}_i = (t_{i,1}, \ldots, t_{i,m})^T$, where $t_{i,j} \leftarrow D_\sigma^n$, for $1 \le j \le m$, then for $(i = \pi+1, \ldots, w, 1, 2, \ldots, \pi-1)$, we compute $\mathbf{c}_{i+1} = H_1\Big(L, \mathbf{H}, \mu, \mathbf{A}_i \cdot \mathbf{t}_i + q \cdot \mathbf{c}_i, \mathbf{H} \cdot \mathbf{t}_i + q \cdot \mathbf{c}_i\Big)$.
4. Select a random bit $b \in \{0,1\}$ and finally compute $\mathbf{t}_\pi = \mathbf{u} + \mathbf{S}_\pi \cdot \mathbf{c}_\pi \cdot (-1)^b$ using rejection sampling (Definition 2).

5. Output the signature $\sigma_L(\mu) = \Big(\mathbf{c}_1, \mathbf{t}_1, \ldots, \mathbf{t}_w, \mathbf{H}\Big)$.

A formal description of this algorithm is shown in Algorithm 2.

Algorithm 2. L2RS Algorithm - Signature Generation $\sigma_L(\mu)$

Input: $\mathbf{S}_\pi, \mu, L$, where $L = \{\mathbf{A}_1, \ldots, \mathbf{A}_w\}$.
Output: $\sigma_L(\mu) = \Big(\mathbf{c}_1, \mathbf{t}_1, \ldots, \mathbf{t}_w, \mathbf{H}\Big)$

procedure L2RS.SigGen($\mathbf{S}_\pi, \mu, L$)
  Set $\mathbf{H} = (\mathbf{H}_0, \mathbf{h}_1)$, where $\mathbf{H}_0 = 2 \cdot \mathbf{H}_0'$ and $\mathbf{h}_1 = -\mathbf{H}_0 \cdot \mathbf{S}_{\pi,0} + q \bmod 2q$
  Let $\mathbf{u} = (u_1, \ldots, u_m)^T$, where $u_i \leftarrow D_\sigma^n$, for $1 \le i \le m$.
  Compute $\mathbf{c}_{\pi+1} = H_1\Big(L, \mathbf{H}, \mu, \mathbf{A}_\pi \cdot \mathbf{u}, \mathbf{H} \cdot \mathbf{u}\Big)$.
  for $(i = \pi+1, \pi+2, \ldots, w, 1, 2, \ldots, \pi-1)$ **do**
    Let $\mathbf{t}_i = (t_{i,1}, \ldots, t_{i,m})^T$, where $t_{i,j} \leftarrow D_\sigma^n$, for $1 \le j \le m$.
    Compute $\mathbf{c}_{i+1} = H_1\Big(L, \mathbf{H}, \mu, \mathbf{A}_i \cdot \mathbf{t}_i + q \cdot \mathbf{c}_i, \mathbf{H} \cdot \mathbf{t}_i + q \cdot \mathbf{c}_i\Big)$.
  Choose $b \leftarrow \{0, 1\}$.
  Let $\mathbf{t}_\pi \leftarrow \mathbf{u} + \mathbf{S}_\pi \cdot \mathbf{c}_\pi \cdot (-1)^b$.
  Continue with prob. $\dfrac{1}{M \exp\left(-\dfrac{\|\mathbf{S}_\pi \cdot \mathbf{c}_\pi\|^2}{2\sigma^2}\right) \cosh\left(\dfrac{\langle \mathbf{t}_\pi, \mathbf{S}_\pi \cdot \mathbf{c}_\pi\rangle}{\sigma^2}\right)}$ otherwise **Restart**.
  return $\sigma_L(\mu) = \Big(\mathbf{c}_1, \mathbf{t}_1, \ldots, \mathbf{t}_w, \mathbf{H}\Big)$.

5.4 Signature Verification - SigVer

The SigVer algorithm receives the signature $\sigma_L(\mu)$ along with the message μ and the fixed list L, and will output a decisional verification answer: whether accept or reject the signature (see **Algorithm 3**). The signature $\sigma_L(\mu)$ can be publicly validated by computing $\mathbf{H} = (\mathbf{H}_0, \mathbf{h}_1)$ in $\mathbf{c}_{i+1}$ for $(i = 1, \ldots, w)$, and it is verified and only accepted under the following four conditions: $\|\mathbf{t}_i\|_2 \le B_2$ for $1 \le i \le w$, $\|\mathbf{t}_i\|_\infty < q/4$ for $1 \le i \le w$, $\mathbf{c}_1 = H_1\Big(L, \mathbf{H}, \mu, \mathbf{A}_w \cdot \mathbf{t}_w + q \cdot \mathbf{c}_w, \mathbf{H} \cdot \mathbf{t}_w + q \cdot \mathbf{c}_w\Big)$ and $\mathbf{H}_0 = 2 \cdot \mathbf{H}_0'$.

Theorem 1. *Let $q > 2\eta\sqrt{m}\sigma$ and $\sigma_L(\mu) = \Big(\mathbf{c}_1, \mathbf{t}_1, \ldots, \mathbf{t}_w, \boldsymbol{H}\Big)$ be generated based on Algorithm 2 such that $\|\mathbf{t}_i\|_\infty \le q/4$, for $1 \le i \le m$. Then the output of Algorithm 3 on input $\sigma_L(\mu)$ is* ***Accept*** *with probability $1 - 2^{-\lambda}$.*

Note that η is chosen such that $\|\mathbf{t}_i\| \le q/2$ is verified with probability $1 - 2^{-\lambda}$ for all $1 \le i \le w$. The proof of this theorem will be given in the full version.

Algorithm 3. L2RS Algorithm - Signature Verification

Input: $\sigma_L(\mu) = \left(\mathbf{c}_1, \mathbf{t}_1, \ldots, \mathbf{t}_w, \mathbf{H}\right)$, L, μ
Output: Accept or Reject

```
procedure L2RS.SigVer(σ_L(μ))
    if H = (H_0, h_1) and H_0 = 2 · H'_0 then Continue
        for (i = 1, ..., w) do
            if c_{i+1} = H_1(L, H, μ, A_i · t_i + q · c_i, H · t_i + q · c_i) then Continue
            else if ||t_i||_2 ≤ B_2 then Continue
            else if ||t_i||_∞ < q/4 then Continue
    else if c_1 = H_1(L, H, μ, A_w · t_w + q · c_w, H · t_w + q · c_w) then Accept
    else Reject
    return Accept or Reject
```

5.5 Signature Linkability - SigLink

The SigLink algorithm, illustrated in Algorithm 4, takes two signatures as its input $\sigma_L(\mu_1)$ and $\sigma_L(\mu_2)$ and it outputs **Linked** if these signatures were generated by same signatory, it will output **Unlinked** otherwise. For a fixed list of public-keys L and given two signatures: $\sigma_L(\mu_1)$ and $\sigma_L(\mu_2)$, with the list L which can be described as: $\sigma_L(\mu_1) = \left(\mathbf{c}_{1,\mu_1}, \mathbf{t}_{1,\mu_1}, \ldots, \mathbf{t}_{w,\mu_1}, \mathbf{H}_{\mu_1}\right)$ and $\sigma_L(\mu_2) = \left(\mathbf{c}_{1,\mu_2}, \mathbf{t}_{1,\mu_2}, \ldots, \mathbf{t}_{w,\mu_2}, \mathbf{H}_{\mu_2}\right)$.

These two signatures must be successfully accepted by the SigVer algorithm, then one can verify that the linkability property can be achieved if the linkability tags ($\mathbf{H}_{\mu_1}$ and $\mathbf{H}_{\mu_2}$) of the above signatures $\sigma_L(\mu_1)$ and $\sigma_L(\mu_2)$ are equal. The correctness proofs of L2RS.SigGen and L2RS.SigLink are given in [35].

6 Security Analysis

Theorem 2 (One-Time Unforgeability). *Suppose* $\sqrt{\frac{q^{2n}}{2^{(\gamma+1)\cdot(m-1)\cdot n}}}$ *is negligible in* n *and* $\frac{1}{|\mathcal{S}_{n,\kappa}|}$ *is negligible and* $y = h$ *is polynomial in* n*, where* h *denotes*

Algorithm 4. L2RS Algorithm - Signature Linkability

Input: $\sigma_L(\mu_1)$ and $\sigma_L(\mu_2)$
Output: Linked or Unlinked

```
procedure L2RS.SigLink(σ_L(μ1), σ_L(μ2))
    if (L2RS.SigVer(σ_L(μ1)) = Accept and L2RS.SigVer(σ_L(μ2)) = Accept) then
  Continue [
    else if H_{μ1} = H_{μ2} then Linked
    else Unlinked ]
    return Linked or Unlinked
```

the number of queries to the random oracle H_1. If there is a PPT algorithm against one-time unforgeability of L2RS with non-negligible probability δ, then there exist a PPT algorithm that can extract a solution to the $\mathcal{R}$-$\mathbf{SIS}^{\mathcal{K}}_{q,n,m,\beta}$ problem (for $\beta = 2B_2$) with non-negligible probability $\left(\delta - \frac{1}{|\mathcal{S}_{n,\kappa}|}\right) \cdot \left(\frac{\delta - \frac{1}{|\mathcal{S}_{n,\kappa}|}}{y} - \frac{1}{|\mathcal{S}_{n,\kappa}|}\right) - \sqrt{\frac{q^{2n}}{2^{(\gamma+1)\cdot(m-1)\cdot n}}}$.

Proof. The proof is given in the full version [35].

Theorem 3 (Anonymity). *Suppose $\sqrt{\frac{q^{2n}}{2^{(\gamma+1)\cdot(m-1)\cdot n}}}$ is negligible in n with an attack against the unconditional anonymity that makes h queries to the random oracle H_1, where h, w are polynomial in n, then the L2RS scheme is unconditionally secure as defined in Definition 4.*

Proof. The proof is given in the full version [35].

Theorem 4 (Linkability). *The L2RS scheme is linkable in the random oracle model if the $\mathcal{R}$-$\mathbf{SIS}^{\mathcal{K}}_{q,n,m,\beta}$ problem is hard.*

Proof The proof is given in the full version [35].

Theorem 5 (Non-Slanderability). *For any linkable ring signature, if it satisfies unforgeability and unlinkability, then it satisfies non-slanderability.*

Proof. The proof is given in the full version [35].

Corollary 1 (Non-Slanderability). *The L2RS scheme is non-slanderable under the assumptions of Theorems 2 and 4.*

7 Lattice RingCT v1.0 Protocol

This protocol can be regarded as the lattice analogy of the original Ring CT protocol [5], and is constructed based on our L2RS scheme described in Sect. 5. Its algorithms are defined as follows (we follow the definition given in [36]):

- Setup: this PPT algorithm uses L2RS.Setup where it takes the security parameter λ and outputs the public parameters.
- KeyGen: this PPT algorithm uses L2RS.KeyGen, it receives the public parameters and produces a pair of keys, the public-key and the private-key.
- Mint: a PPT algorithm that is used to generate new coins. This algorithm receives the public-key $\mathbf{A}$ and the amount a, and it outputs a coin $\mathbf{cn}$ along with its associated coin-key $\mathbf{ck}$. An account is formed using the public-key $\mathbf{A}$ and the coin $\mathbf{cn}$. Likewise, the private-key $\mathbf{S}$ along with the coin-key $\mathbf{ck}$ is used for the spending authorization.

- Spend: a PPT algorithm, which is used to generate the linkable ring signature, receives the fixed list of users' public-keys in the ring signature L, the Output Wallet OW and some transaction string $m \in \{0,1\}^*$, these three parameter constitute the transaction TX. This algorithm outputs the signature $\sigma_L(\mu)$ along with the TX.
- Verify: a deterministic PPT algorithm that takes as input the signature $\sigma_L(\mu)$ and the TX, it outputs either: **Accept** or **Reject**.

7.1 Scheme Construction

Our Lattice RingCT scheme requires homomorphic commitment (Com) as an additional primitive. It is a cryptographic technique used to provide confidential transactions, in particular cryptocurrencies [5]. This primitive allows one party to commit to a chosen value while keeping it secret to other parties, then this committed value can be revealed later. This model is restricted to have one Input Wallet (IW) that will be spent into one Output Wallet (OW) only. We use the structure of the L2RS.KeyGen scheme Algorithm 1, where the public parameter $\mathbf{A}'_0 \in \mathcal{R}_q^{1\times(m-1)}$ is used to commit to a scalar message $\mathrm{m} \in \mathsf{Dom}_\mathrm{m} \subseteq \mathcal{R}_q$ with $\mathsf{Dom}_\mathrm{m} = [0,\ldots,2^{\ell-1}] \subseteq \mathbb{Z}$. This property is defined as $\mathsf{Com}_{\mathbf{A}'_0}(\mathrm{m},\mathbf{S}_0) = \mathbf{A}'_0 \cdot \mathbf{S}_0 + \mathrm{m}$, where $\mathbf{S}_0 \in \mathsf{Dom}_{\mathbf{S}_0} \subseteq \mathcal{R}_q^{(m-1)\times 1}$ is the randomness. The properties of the homomorphic operations are also defined as:

$$\begin{aligned}\mathsf{Com}_{\mathbf{A}'_0}(\mathrm{m}_1,\mathbf{S}_0) \oplus \mathsf{Com}_{\mathbf{A}'_0}(\mathrm{m}_2,\mathbf{S}'_0) &\triangleq \mathsf{Com}_{\mathbf{A}'_0}(\mathrm{m}_1,\mathbf{S}_0) + \mathsf{Com}_{\mathbf{A}'_0}(\mathrm{m}_2,\mathbf{S}'_0) \bmod q\\ &= \mathsf{Com}_{\mathbf{A}'_0}(\mathrm{m}_1+\mathrm{m}_2,\mathbf{S}_0+\mathbf{S}'_0) \bmod q, \quad (1)\end{aligned}$$

$$\begin{aligned}\mathsf{Com}_{\mathbf{A}'_0}(\mathrm{m}_1,\mathbf{S}_0) \ominus \mathsf{Com}_{\mathbf{A}'_0}(\mathrm{m}_2,\mathbf{S}'_0) &\triangleq \mathsf{Com}_{\mathbf{A}'_0}(\mathrm{m}_1,\mathbf{S}_0) - \mathsf{Com}_{\mathbf{A}'_0}(\mathrm{m}_2,\mathbf{S}'_0) \bmod q\\ &= \mathsf{Com}_{\mathbf{A}'_0}(\mathrm{m}_1-\mathrm{m}_2,\mathbf{S}_0-\mathbf{S}'_0) \bmod q, \quad (2)\end{aligned}$$

where $\mathrm{m}_1,\mathrm{m}_2 \in \mathcal{R}_q$; and $\mathbf{S}_0,\mathbf{S}'_0 \in \mathcal{R}_q^{(m-1)\times 1}$. The integers $\mathrm{m}_1,\mathrm{m}_2 \in \mathbb{Z}$ are encoded in binary as coefficient vectors $\mathbf{m}_1 = (\mathrm{m}_{1,0},\ldots,\mathrm{m}_{1,\ell-1},0,\ldots,0) \in \{0,1\}^n$ and $\mathbf{m}_2 = (\mathrm{m}_{2,0},\ldots,\mathrm{m}_{2,\ell-1},0,\ldots,0) \in \{0,1\}^n$ where $\mathbf{m}_j = \sum_{i=0}^{\ell-1}(\mathrm{m}_{j,i}\cdot 2^i)$, with $\mathrm{m}_{j,i} \in \{0,1\}$ and $j \in \{0,1\}$, and $\mathbf{m} = \mathbf{m}_1 - \mathbf{m}_2 = (\mathrm{m}_{1,0} - \mathrm{m}_{2,0},\ldots,\mathrm{m}_{1,\ell-1} - \mathrm{m}_{2,\ell-1},0,\ldots,0) \in \{-1,0,1\}^n$. The difference between these vectors is zero $\in \mathcal{R}_q$ if $\mathbf{m}_1 = \mathbf{m}_2$, non-zero otherwise. Hence the commitment is done to bits.

The construction of the Lattice RingCT v1.0 algorithm has the following steps:

1. (Pub-Params) $\leftarrow$ Setup(λ): On input security parameter λ, this algorithm calls L2RS.Setup and outputs the public parameters, $\mathbf{A}'_0$ and $\mathbf{H}'_0$.
2. $(\mathbf{A}_{in},\mathbf{S}_{in}) \leftarrow$ KeyGen(Pub-Params): Given the public parameters, we call L2RS.KeyGen to generate the pair of keys. Thus it outputs the IW pair of keys $(\mathbf{A}_{in},\mathbf{S}_{in})$, where $\mathbf{A}_{in} \in \mathcal{R}_{2q}^{1\times m}$ is the public-key (or one-time address) and $\mathbf{S}_{in} = (\mathbf{S}_0,1) \in \mathsf{Dom}_{\mathbf{S}_0} \subseteq \mathcal{R}_{2q}^{m\times 1}$ is the private-key. The commitment of the KeyGen is defined as $\mathbf{a}'_{1(in)} = \mathbf{A}'_0 \cdot \mathbf{S}_{0(in)} \bmod q \in \mathcal{R}_q = \mathsf{Com}_{\mathbf{A}'_0}(0,\mathbf{S}_{0(in)})$.

3. $(\mathbf{cn}', \mathbf{ck}') \leftarrow \mathsf{Mint}(\mathbf{A}_{in}, a_{in})$: It receives a valid one-time address $\mathbf{A}_{in}$ as well as an input amount $a_{in} \in \mathbb{B}_w^n$, where $\mathbb{B} = \{0, 1\}$. Then, to create a coin $\mathbf{cn}'_{in}$, this algorithm chooses a coin-key $\mathbf{ck}'_{in} \in \mathsf{Dom}_{\mathbf{S}_0}$, where every component is chosen uniformly and independently with coefficients in $(-2^\gamma, 2^\gamma)$. Then, the commitment is computed as $\mathbf{cn}'_{in} = \mathsf{Com}_{\mathbf{A}'_0}(a_{in}, \mathbf{ck}'_{in})$ and it returns $(\mathbf{cn}'_{in}, \mathbf{ck}'_{in})$. An account constitutes $(\mathbf{a}'_{1(in)}, \mathbf{cn}'_{in}) \in \mathcal{R}_q \times \mathcal{R}_q$.
4. $(TX, \sigma_{L'}(\mu)) \leftarrow \mathsf{Spend}(\mu, OW)$: This algorithm follows the steps:
   (a) A new coin for the OW is created by the spender. It generates $\mathbf{ck}'_{out} \in \mathsf{Dom}_{\mathbf{S}_0}$, where every component is chosen uniformly and independently with coefficients in $(-2^\gamma, 2^\gamma)$, then it is computed $\mathbf{cn}'_{out} = Com_{\mathbf{A}'_0}(a_{out}, \mathbf{ck}'_{out})$. The new OW is set as $(\mathbf{a}'_{1(out)}, \mathbf{cn}'_{out}) \in \mathcal{R}_q \times \mathcal{R}_q$.
   (b) A transaction string $\mu \in \{0, 1\}^*$ defines the ring signature message.
   (c) The list of the ring signature is constructed as $L' = \left\{\left(\widehat{\mathbf{a}}'_{1(in),i}, \mathbf{cn}'_{in,i}\right)\right\} \in \mathcal{R}_q \times \mathcal{R}_q$ for $1 \le i \le w$ with w being the size of the ring signature, its components are produced as:
      - $\widehat{\mathbf{a}}'_{1(in),i} = \mathbf{a}'_{1(in),i} + \mathbf{cn}'_{in,i} - \mathbf{cn}'_{out,i} = \mathsf{Com}_{\mathbf{A}'_0}\left(a_{in,i} - a_{out}, \mathbf{S}_{0(in),i} + \mathbf{ck}'_{in,i} - \mathbf{ck}'_{out}\right)$.
      - $\mathbf{cn}'_{in,i} = \mathsf{Com}_{\mathbf{A}'_0}\left(a_{in,i}, \mathbf{ck}'_{in,i}\right)$.
   (d) We call the L2RS.Lift() function (Definition 7) to lift L' from $\mathcal{R}_q^{1\times m}$ to $\mathcal{R}_{2q}^{1\times m}$:
      - $L' = \left\{\left(\mathsf{L2RS.Lift}(\mathbf{A}'_0, \widehat{\mathbf{a}}'_{1(in),i}), \mathsf{L2RS.Lift}(\mathbf{A}'_0, \mathbf{cn}'_{in,i})\right)\right\} = \left\{\left(\widehat{\mathbf{A}}_{1(in),i}, \mathbf{CN}_{in,i}\right)\right\} \in \mathcal{R}_{2q}^{1\times m} \times \mathcal{R}_{2q}^{1\times m}$, for $1 \le i \le w$.
      - The private-key of π is in the form of $\mathbf{S}''_{in,\pi} = (\mathbf{S}_{in,\pi}, \mathbf{CK}_{in,\pi}) \in \mathcal{R}_{2q}^{m\times 1} \times \mathcal{R}_{2q}^{m\times 1}$, where:
         - $\mathbf{S}_{in,\pi} = \left(\mathbf{S}_{0(in,\pi)} + \mathbf{ck}'_{in,\pi} - \mathbf{ck}'_{out,\pi}\right) \in \mathcal{R}_{2q}^{m\times 1}$.
         - $\mathbf{CK}_{in,\pi} = \left(\mathbf{ck}'_{in,\pi}, 1\right) \in \mathcal{R}_{2q}^{m\times 1}$.
   (e) By calling the $\mathsf{L2RS\text{-}DoubleSignGen}\left(\mathbf{S}''_{in,\pi}, L', \mu\right)$, Algorithm 5, we create the ring signature $\sigma_{L'}(\mu) = \left(\mathbf{c}_1, \begin{pmatrix} \mathbf{t}_1, \ldots, \mathbf{t}_w \\ \mathbf{t}'_1, \ldots, \mathbf{t}'_w \end{pmatrix}, \mathbf{H}\right)$.
   (f) We set the transaction $TX = (\mu, L', OW)$.
   (g) This algorithm ultimately outputs TX and $\sigma_{L'}(\mu)$.
5. $(\textbf{Accept/Reject}) \leftarrow \mathsf{Verify}(TX, \sigma_{L'}(\mu))$: This algorithm calls $\mathsf{L2RS\text{-}DoubleSigVer}(\sigma_{L'}(\mu))$, using Algorithm 6 and will return either **Accept** or **Reject**.

This construction as stated supports one-IW to one-OW and thus in this case the range proof [5] is not needed. In the full version of this work [35], we will provide more details for the correctness and the security analysis of the hiding and binding property. The full version will also extend the Lattice RingCT v1.0 scheme to support Multiple-Inputs to Multiple-Outputs (MIMO) wallets, and therefore a range proof will be given.

Algorithm 5. L2RS-DoubleSignGen Algorithm - Signature Generation $\sigma_{L'}(\mu)$

Input: $\mathbf{S}''_{in,\pi}, \mu, L'$, where $\mathbf{S}''_{in,\pi} = (\mathbf{S}_{in,\pi}, \mathbf{CK}_{in,\pi})$ and $L' = \left\{(\widehat{\mathbf{A}}_{1(in),i}, \mathbf{CN}_{in,i})\right\}_{i=1}^{w}$

Output: $\sigma_{L'}(\mu) = \left(\mathbf{c}_1, \begin{pmatrix} \mathbf{t}_1, \ldots, \mathbf{t}_w \\ \mathbf{t}'_1, \ldots, \mathbf{t}'_w \end{pmatrix}, \mathbf{H}\right)$

procedure L2RS.DoubleSignGen($\mathbf{S}''_{in,\pi}, \mu, L'$)
- Set $\mathbf{H} = (\mathbf{H}_0, \mathbf{h}_1)$, where $\mathbf{H}_0 = 2 \cdot \mathbf{H}'_0$ and $\mathbf{h}_1 = -\mathbf{H}_0 \cdot \mathbf{S}_{\pi,0} + q \bmod 2q$
- **for** $(1 \le i \le m)$ **do**
  - Let $\mathbf{u} = (u_1, \ldots, u_m)^T$, where $u_i \leftarrow D_\sigma^n$.
  - Let $\mathbf{u}' = (u'_1, \ldots, u'_m)^T$, where $u'_i \leftarrow D_\sigma^n$.
- Compute $\mathbf{c}_{\pi+1} = H_1\left(L, \mathbf{H}, \mu, \widehat{\mathbf{A}}_{1(in),\pi} \cdot \mathbf{u}, \mathbf{CN}_{in,\pi} \cdot \mathbf{u}', \mathbf{H} \cdot \mathbf{u}\right)$.
- **for** $(i = \pi+1, \pi+2, \ldots, w, 1, 2, \ldots, \pi-1)$ **do**
  - **for** $(1 \le j \le m)$ **do**
    - Let $\mathbf{t}_i = (t_{i,1}, \ldots, t_{i,m})^T$, where $t_{i,j} \leftarrow D_\sigma^n$.
    - Let $\mathbf{t}'_i = (t'_{i,1}, \ldots, t'_{i,m})^T$, where $t'_{i,j} \leftarrow D_\sigma^n$.
  - Compute $\mathbf{c}_{i+1} = H_1\left(L, \mathbf{H}, \mu, \widehat{\mathbf{A}}_{1(in),i} \cdot \mathbf{t}_i + q \cdot \mathbf{c}_i, \mathbf{CN}_{in,i} \cdot \mathbf{t}'_i + q \cdot \mathbf{c}_i, \mathbf{H} \cdot \mathbf{t}_i + q \cdot \mathbf{c}_i\right)$.
- Choose $b \leftarrow \{0,1\}$ and $b' \leftarrow \{0,1\}$.
- Let $\mathbf{t}_\pi \leftarrow \mathbf{u} + \mathbf{S}_{in,\pi} \cdot \mathbf{c}_\pi \cdot (-1)^b$.
- **Continue** with prob. $\dfrac{1}{M \exp\left(-\dfrac{\|\mathbf{S}_{in,\pi} \cdot \mathbf{c}_\pi\|^2}{2\sigma^2}\right) \cosh\left(\dfrac{\langle \mathbf{t}_\pi, \mathbf{S}_{in,\pi} \cdot \mathbf{c}_\pi \rangle}{\sigma^2}\right)}$ otherwise **Restart**.
- Let $\mathbf{t}'_\pi \leftarrow \mathbf{u}' + \mathbf{CK}_{in,\pi} \cdot \mathbf{c}_\pi \cdot (-1)^{b'}$.
- **Continue** with prob. $\dfrac{1}{M \exp\left(-\dfrac{\|\mathbf{CK}_{in,\pi} \cdot \mathbf{c}_\pi\|^2}{2\sigma^2}\right) \cosh\left(\dfrac{\langle \mathbf{t}'_\pi, \mathbf{CK}_{in,\pi} \cdot \mathbf{c}_\pi \rangle}{\sigma^2}\right)}$ otherwise **Restart**.
- **return** $\sigma_{L'}(\mu) = \left(\mathbf{c}_1, \begin{pmatrix} \mathbf{t}_1, \ldots, \mathbf{t}_w \\ \mathbf{t}'_1, \ldots, \mathbf{t}'_w \end{pmatrix}, \mathbf{H}\right)$.

8 Performance Analysis

We proposed a set of parameters (Table 1) to implement the L2RS and Lattice RingCT v1.0 schemes. They are secure against direct lattice attacks in terms of the BKZ algorithm Hermite factor δ, using the value of $\delta = 1.007$, based on the BKZ 2.0 complexity estimates with pruning enumeration-based Shortest Vector Problem (SVP) [37], this might give 90–100 bits of security. We use the conditions stated in the L2RS.SigVer algorithm and in the security analysis (Sect. 6) with $\gamma = 0$ and $\alpha = 0.5$. This analysis turns out signatures sizes of 53 KB and 60 KB for L2RS and Lattice RingCT v1.0, respectively, when the number of signers in a ring signature (w) is 1. The size of the pair of keys in L2RS is 0.592 KB (private-key) and 1.252 KB (public-key), whereas this size in Lattice RingCT v1.0 is 1.184 KB (private-key) and 1.12 KB (public-key).

Algorithm 6. L2RS-DoubleSigVer Algorithm - Signature Verification

Input: $TX = (\mu, L', OW), \sigma_{L'}(\mu) = \left(\mathbf{c}_1, \begin{pmatrix}\mathbf{t}_1, \ldots, \mathbf{t}_w \\ \mathbf{t}'_1, \ldots, \mathbf{t}'_w\end{pmatrix}, \mathbf{H}\right)$, where $L' = \{(\widehat{\mathbf{A}}_{1(in),i}, \mathbf{CN}_{in,i})\}_{i=1}^{w}$

Output: Accept or Reject

1: **procedure** L2RS.DoubleSigVer($\sigma_{L'}(\mu)$)

2: **if** $\mathbf{H} = (\mathbf{H}_0, \mathbf{h}_1)$ and $\mathbf{H}_0 = 2 \cdot \mathbf{H}'_0$ **then** Continue

3: **for** $(i = 1, \ldots, w)$ **do**

4: **if** $\mathbf{c}_{i+1} = H_1\left(L, \mathbf{H}, \mu, \widehat{\mathbf{A}}_{1(in),i} \cdot \mathbf{t}_i + q \cdot \mathbf{c}_i, \mathbf{CN}_{in,i} \cdot \mathbf{t}'_i + q \cdot \mathbf{c}_i, \mathbf{H} \cdot \mathbf{t}_i + q \cdot \mathbf{c}_i\right)$ **then** Continue

5: **else if** $\|\mathbf{t}_i\|_2 \le B_2$ and $\|\mathbf{t}'_i\|_2 \le B_2$ **then** Continue

6: **else if** $\|\mathbf{t}_i\|_\infty < q/4$ and $\|\mathbf{t}'_i\|_\infty < q/4$ **then** Continue

7: **else if** $\mathbf{c}_1 = H_1\left(L, \mathbf{H}, \mu, \widehat{\mathbf{A}}_{1(in),i} \cdot \mathbf{t}_w + q \cdot \mathbf{c}_w, \mathbf{CN}_{in,w} \cdot \mathbf{t}'_w + q \cdot \mathbf{c}_w, \mathbf{H} \cdot \mathbf{t}_w + q \cdot \mathbf{c}_w\right)$ **then** Accept

8: **else** Reject

9: **return** Accept or Reject

Table 1. Selected parameters for L2RS and Lattice RingCT v1.0

Name of the scheme	L2RS	Lattice-RingCT v1.0
Security parameter (λ)	100	100
n	128	128
κ	32	32
m	73	73
η	2.1	2.1
$\|\mathbf{Sc}\|$	546.8	546.8
σ	273.4	273.4
$\log(\beta)$	13.429	13.429
$\log(q)$	35	35
Signature size ($w = 1$)	51 KB	60 KB
Signature size ($w = 5$)	89 KB	136 KB
Signature size ($w = 10$)	136 KB	231 KB
Signature size ($w = 15$)	183 KB	325 KB
Private-key size	0.592 KB	1.184 KB
Public-key size	1.152 KB	1.12 KB

Acknowledgement. The work of Ron Steinfeld and Amin Sakzad was supported in part by ARC Discovery Project grant DP150100285. This work was also supported by the Monash-HKPU-Collinstar Blockchain Research Lab.

References

1. Rivest, R.L., Shamir, A., Tauman, Y.: How to leak a secret. In: Boyd, C. (ed.) ASIACRYPT 2001. LNCS, vol. 2248, pp. 552–565. Springer, Heidelberg (2001). https://doi.org/10.1007/3-540-45682-1_32
2. Chaum, D., van Heyst, E.: Group signatures. In: Davies, D.W. (ed.) EUROCRYPT 1991. LNCS, vol. 547, pp. 257–265. Springer, Heidelberg (1991). https://doi.org/10.1007/3-540-46416-6_22
3. Liu, J.K., Wei, V.K., Wong, D.S.: Linkable spontaneous anonymous group signature for ad hoc groups. In: Wang, H., Pieprzyk, J., Varadharajan, V. (eds.) ACISP 2004. LNCS, vol. 3108, pp. 325–335. Springer, Heidelberg (2004). https://doi.org/10.1007/978-3-540-27800-9_28
4. Liu, J.K., Au, M.H., Huang, X., Susilo, W., Zhou, J., Yu, Y.: New insight to preserve online survey accuracy and privacy in big data era. In: Kutyłowski, M., Vaidya, J. (eds.) ESORICS 2014. LNCS, vol. 8713, pp. 182–199. Springer, Cham (2014). https://doi.org/10.1007/978-3-319-11212-1_11
5. Noether, S.: Ring signature confidential transactions for monero. IACR Cryptology ePrint Archive, vol. 2015, p. 1098 (2015)
6. Elgamal, T.: A public key cryptosystem and a signature scheme based on discrete logarithms. IEEE Trans. Inf. Theory **31**, 469–472 (1985)
7. Rivest, R.L., Shamir, A., Adleman, L.: A method for obtaining digital signatures and public-key cryptosystems. Commun. ACM **21**(2), 120–126 (1978)
8. Shor, P.W.: Polynomial-time algorithms for prime factorization and discrete logarithms on a quantum computer. SIAM Rev. **41**(2), 303–332 (1999)
9. Micciancio, D., Regev, O.: Lattice-based cryptography. In: Bernstein, D.J., Buchmann, J., Dahmen, E. (eds.) Post-Quantum Cryptography, pp. 147–191. Springer, Heidelberg (2009). https://doi.org/10.1007/978-3-540-88702-7_5
10. Ducas, L., Durmus, A., Lepoint, T., Lyubashevsky, V.: Lattice signatures and bimodal Gaussians. In: Canetti, R., Garay, J.A. (eds.) CRYPTO 2013. LNCS, vol. 8042, pp. 40–56. Springer, Heidelberg (2013). https://doi.org/10.1007/978-3-642-40041-4_3
11. Au, M.H., Liu, J.K., Susilo, W., Yuen, T.H.: Secure ID-based linkable and revocable-iff-linked ring signature with constant-size construction. Theor. Comput. Sci. **469**, 1–14 (2013)
12. Liu, J.K., Wong, D.S.: Enhanced security models and a generic construction approach for linkable ring signature. Int. J. Found. Comput. Sci. **17**(6), 1403–1422 (2006)
13. Au, M.H., Liu, J.K., Susilo, W., Yuen, T.H.: Constant-size ID-based linkable and revocable-iff-linked ring signature. In: Barua, R., Lange, T. (eds.) INDOCRYPT 2006. LNCS, vol. 4329, pp. 364–378. Springer, Heidelberg (2006). https://doi.org/10.1007/11941378_26
14. Liu, J.K., Susilo, W., Wong, D.S.: Ring signature with designated linkability. In: Yoshiura, H., Sakurai, K., Rannenberg, K., Murayama, Y., Kawamura, S. (eds.) IWSEC 2006. LNCS, vol. 4266, pp. 104–119. Springer, Heidelberg (2006). https://doi.org/10.1007/11908739_8
15. Fujisaki, E., Suzuki, K.: Traceable ring signature. In: Okamoto, T., Wang, X. (eds.) PKC 2007. LNCS, vol. 4450, pp. 181–200. Springer, Heidelberg (2007). https://doi.org/10.1007/978-3-540-71677-8_13
16. Tsang, P.P., Au, M.H., Liu, J.K., Susilo, W., Wong, D.S.: A suite of non-pairing ID-based threshold ring signature schemes with different levels of anonymity (extended

abstract). In: Heng, S.-H., Kurosawa, K. (eds.) ProvSec 2010. LNCS, vol. 6402, pp. 166–183. Springer, Heidelberg (2010). https://doi.org/10.1007/978-3-642-16280-0_11

17. Liu, J.K., Au, M.H., Susilo, W., Zhou, J.: Linkable ring signature with unconditional anonymity. IEEE Trans. Knowl. Data Eng. **26**(1), 157–165 (2014)
18. Yuen, T.H., Liu, J.K., Au, M.H., Susilo, W., Zhou, J.: Efficient linkable and/or threshold ring signature without random oracles. Comput. J. **56**, 407–421 (2013)
19. Bernstein, D.J., Lange, T.: Post-quantum cryptography. Nature **549**, 188–194 (2017)
20. Goldreich, O., Goldwasser, S., Halevi, S.: Public-key cryptosystems from lattice reduction problems. In: Kaliski, B.S. (ed.) CRYPTO 1997. LNCS, vol. 1294, pp. 112–131. Springer, Heidelberg (1997). https://doi.org/10.1007/BFb0052231
21. Hoffstein, J., Pipher, J., Silverman, J.H.: NSS: an NTRU lattice-based signature scheme. In: Pfitzmann, B. (ed.) EUROCRYPT 2001. LNCS, vol. 2045, pp. 211–228. Springer, Heidelberg (2001). https://doi.org/10.1007/3-540-44987-6_14
22. Gentry, C., Peikert, C., Vaikuntanathan, V.: Trapdoors for hard lattices and new cryptographic constructions. In: Symposium on Theory of Computing - STOC 2008, pp. 197–206. ACM Press (2008)
23. Lyubashevsky, V.: Fiat-shamir with aborts: applications to lattice and factoring-based signatures. In: Matsui, M. (ed.) ASIACRYPT 2009. LNCS, vol. 5912, pp. 598–616. Springer, Heidelberg (2009). https://doi.org/10.1007/978-3-642-10366-7_35
24. Fiat, A., Shamir, A.: How to prove yourself: practical solutions to identification and signature problems. In: Odlyzko, A.M. (ed.) CRYPTO 1986. LNCS, vol. 263, pp. 186–194. Springer, Heidelberg (1987). https://doi.org/10.1007/3-540-47721-7_12
25. Ajtai, M.: Generating hard instances of lattice problems. In: ACM Symposium on Theory of Computing, pp. 99–108. ACM (1996)
26. Micciancio, D.: Generalized compact knapsacks, cyclic lattices, and efficient one-way functions. Comput. Complex. **16**(4), 365–411 (2007)
27. Lyubashevsky, V., Peikert, C., Regev, O.: On ideal lattices and learning with errors over rings. In: Gilbert, H. (ed.) EUROCRYPT 2010. LNCS, vol. 6110, pp. 1–23. Springer, Heidelberg (2010). https://doi.org/10.1007/978-3-642-13190-5_1
28. Brakerski, Z., Kalai, Y.T.: A Framework for Efficient Signatures, Ring Signatures and Identity Based Encryption in the Standard Model (2010). https://eprint.iacr.org/2010/086/
29. Aguilar Melchor, C., Bettaieb, S., Boyen, X., Fousse, L., Gaborit, P.: Adapting lyubashevsky's signature schemes to the ring signature setting. In: Youssef, A., Nitaj, A., Hassanien, A.E. (eds.) AFRICACRYPT 2013. LNCS, vol. 7918, pp. 1–25. Springer, Heidelberg (2013). https://doi.org/10.1007/978-3-642-38553-7_1
30. Libert, B., Ling, S., Nguyen, K., Wang, H.: Zero-knowledge arguments for lattice-based accumulators: logarithmic-size ring signatures and group signatures without trapdoors. In: Fischlin, M., Coron, J.-S. (eds.) EUROCRYPT 2016. LNCS, vol. 9666, pp. 1–31. Springer, Heidelberg (2016). https://doi.org/10.1007/978-3-662-49896-5_1
31. Yang, R., Ho Au, R., Lai, J., Xu, Q., Yu, Z.: Lattice-Based Techniques for Accountable Anonymity: Composition of Abstract Stern's Protocols and Weak PRF with Efficient Protocols from LWR. https://eprint.iacr.org/2017/781/
32. Zhang, H., Zhang, F., Tian, H., Au, M.H.: Anonymous Post-Quantum Cryptocash (Full Version). https://eprint.iacr.org/2017/716/
33. Baum, C., Huang, L., Sabine, O.: Towards Practical Lattice-Based One-Time Linkable Ring Signatures (2018). https://eprint.iacr.org/2018/107/

34. Lyubashevsky, V., Seiler, G.: Short, invertible elements in partially splitting cyclotomic rings and applications to lattice-based zero-knowledge proofs. In: Nielsen, J.B., Rijmen, V. (eds.) EUROCRYPT 2018. LNCS, vol. 10820, pp. 204–224. Springer, Cham (2018). https://doi.org/10.1007/978-3-319-78381-9_8
35. Alberto Torres, W., Steinfeld, R., Sakzad, A., Liu, J.K., Kuchta, V., Bhattacharjee, N., Au, M.H., Cheng, J.: Post-Quantum One-Time Linkable Ring Signature and Application to Ring Confidential Transactions in Blockchain (Lattice RingCT v1.0). https://eprint.iacr.org/2018/379
36. Sun, S.-F., Au, M.H., Liu, J.K., Yuen, T.H.: RingCT 2.0: a compact accumulator-based (linkable ring signature) protocol for blockchain cryptocurrency monero. In: Foley, S.N., Gollmann, D., Snekkenes, E. (eds.) ESORICS 2017. LNCS, vol. 10493, pp. 456–474. Springer, Cham (2017). https://doi.org/10.1007/978-3-319-66399-9_25
37. Chen, Y., Nguyen, P.Q.: BKZ 2.0: better lattice security estimates. In: Lee, D.H., Wang, X. (eds.) ASIACRYPT 2011. LNCS, vol. 7073, pp. 1–20. Springer, Heidelberg (2011). https://doi.org/10.1007/978-3-642-25385-0_1

Security Protocol

Secure Contactless Payment

Handan Kılınç(✉) and Serge Vaudenay

EPFL, Lausanne, Switzerland
handan.kilinc@epfl.ch

Abstract. A contactless payment lets a card holder execute payment without any interaction (e.g., entering PIN or signing) between the terminal and the card holder. Even though the security is the first priority in a payment system, the formal security model of contactless payment does not exist. Therefore, in this paper, we design an adversarial model and define formally the contactless-payment security against malicious cards and malicious terminals including relay attacks. Accordingly, we design a contactless-payment protocol and show its security in our security model. At the end, we analyze EMV-contactless which is a commonly used specification by most of the mobile contactless-payment systems and credit cards in Europe. We find that it is not secure against malicious cards. We also prove its security against malicious terminals in our model. This type of cryptographic proof has not been done before for the EMV specification.

1 Introduction

A contactless payment (CP) system is a payment method using a card or a device, that allows a user to pay at a point of sale by holding the card/device near a contactless terminal. There are two main ways of performing a contactless transaction: with a card or with a smartphone.

CP technologies advanced quickly in recent years. Therefore, the CP market size is expected to grow from USD 6.70 Billion in 2016 to USD 17.56 Billion by 2021 [1]. One of the reasons of this development is based on the convenience of the payment process (e.g., users do not need to type a PIN code (or sign a bill) and wait for the verification process of the PIN). The first CP was implemented in 1995 by Seoul Bus Transport and since then many leading companies (Apple, Google, Samsung) started to integrate a CP process into smartphones. The first (contactless) payment system launched by a leading company is Google Wallet in 2011. Then, Apple Pay and Samsung Pay followed suit in 2014 and 2015, respectively. Also in 2015, Google announced a new contactless system, Android Pay. Classic CP systems use cards. A majority of them now follow EMV contactless specifications, written by EMVCo [3], a consortium created by payment companies, like Visa and Mastercard. The USA has migrated from old magnetic reader terminals to new EMV compliant ones, already used in Europe.

Despite the big developments in this technology, we realize that some important functionalities such as secure processing of payments have not been considered formally. No standard security model was provided for CP. Some pre-play

W. Susilo and G. Yang (Eds.): ACISP 2018, LNCS 10946, pp. 579–597, 2018.
https://doi.org/10.1007/978-3-319-93638-3_33

attacks were detected for EMV because of poor random generation [7,8]. Roland and Langer [23] discovered a cloning attack for EMV contactless payment cards since the contactless payment permits an attacker to learn the necessary data for cloning. The cloned cards can then be used to perform EMV Mag-Stripe transactions at any EMV contactless payment terminal. Another type of preplay attack [8] was discovered which relies on the fact that EMV do not impose any encryption between merchant and acquirer, or between acquirer and issuer.

The most important attack specific for EMV-contactless (and also most of the contactless applications) is relay attack which has shown up for a while ago [17–19,22,28]. A relay attack in an EMV-contactless payment can be run as follows: the man-in-the-middle (MiM) adversary makes payment by relaying messages from a card to a terminal and vice versa, while terminal and the card think that they communicate with each other. Chothia et al. [14] remark that the first version of EMVco is vulnerable to relay attacks and provide a solution for this. The current EMVco [3], therefore, take precaution partly against relay attacks using the solution proposed by Chothia et al. [14]. It is "partly" because the solution they use is software based where the terminal does not require a specific hardware. So, it protects against relatively trivial adversaries but does not protect against the adversaries using a sophisticated hardware [15,18]. To defend this level of security that they provide against relay attacks, Chothia et al. [14] say that "Considering that contactless payments are limited to small amounts, the cost of the hardware would be a disincentive for criminals". However, limiting to small amounts does not necessarily mean that the relay attack outcome will be also a small amount. An attacker in a crowded area (e.g., metro, concert, museum) can execute many numbers of relay attacks and increase its outcome. In addition, some cards are limited to some small amounts in their issued country currency, but when they are abroad this limit is removed because the conversion from the issued country currency to currency in the current country cannot be computed. Besides this, the solution provided by Chothia et al. [14] for EMV-contactless does not protect against malicious cards who can execute relay attacks in a different way than MiM-adversaries such as:

Distance Fraud (DF): A malicious far-away card tries to prove that he is close enough to the terminal to make the verifier accept the payment.

Distance Hijacking (DH) [16]*:* A far-away malicious prover takes advantage of some honest and active provers who are close to the verifier to make the verifier grant privileges to the far-away prover.

Preventing against DF and DH in payment protocols is important as well. For example, a DF or DH attack can be harmful to a bank in the following case: A credit card holder makes a payment while he is far-away from a POS machine. Then, he asks for a reimbursement of the payment from his bank by claiming that he did not make the payment and he was probably exposed to relay attack or cloning attack. While doing this, he can prove that he was not at the place where the payment has been executed (e.g., showing that he was in another city).

The most promising solution against MiM, DH or DF is distance bounding (DB) [11]. In DB, a verifier determines the distance of a prover who wants to authenticate. If the distance of a prover is close enough, the verifier will be sure of the nonexistence of relay attack during the protocol execution. Apparently, it is necessary to utilize a secure distance bounding [6,9,10,12,20,24–27] in contactless payment.

Our Contributions: Considering all these attacks and the missing formalism, we design a new security model for CP protocols and design a secure contactless-payment protocol. In more detail, our contributions are as follows:

- We formally define CP between parties: an issuer, a terminal, a card. Then, we give two security definitions for malicious cards and for malicious terminals in the adversarial and communication model that we define.
- We construct a secure CP protocol (ClessPay) against malicious cards and malicious terminals. ClessPay uses a distance bounding protocol to protect against relay attacks by malicious cards and MiM-adversaries. We proved formally the security of ClessPay in our security model.
- We analyze EMV-contactless protocol in our model. We give some vulnerabilities on this against malicious cards. We prove the security of EMV-contactless protocol against malicious terminal formally. This type of formal cryptographic analysis is the first for EMV-contactless protocol.

2 Definitions

2.1 Contactless Payment

According to the EMV specifications [2], a (contactless) payment system consists of a card holder, a merchant, an acquirer, an issuer, a payment system, a card and a terminal. Our definitions do not include certification by the payment system, communication between merchant-acquirer and terminal-acquirer. We assume that the setup between payment components has been established. For the sake of simplicity, we assume the terminal represents both the terminal and the acquirer in the payment system and all cards are issued by one issuer.

The Issuer: It issues a personalized card to the card holder. The cards may contact with the issuer during the payment process (in online transactions) for the verification of the payment data. It also gives reimbursements of completed transactions to the acquirer. Each issuer has its policy function Policy to approve or disapprove a transaction. We assume that the issuer has a database *DataB* which stores the card information. *DataB* consists of tuples (Public Key, Card Information) of each card. Card information (CI) may consist of transaction list, the balance or the card limit.

Cards: They have a technology (e.g. NFC, Bluetooth) to communicate with a payment terminal without any contact. In CP, cards are the components which interact with a payment terminal to execute a payment with a certain amount. They include a unique card number. They also store a secret/public key pair in their tamper-resistant module and the issuer's public key. In this paper, we exclude card numbers in our definitions for simplicity. In our definitions, cards are identified with their public keys.

Terminals: Terminals interact with both cards and their issuers via acquirers. They receive an order of payment from a card and validate the payment together with the issuer of the card.

Definition 1 (Contactless Payment (CP)). *A CP consists of algorithms for cards, terminals and issuers. They respectively run the algorithms* $C(\mathsf{sk}_C, \mathsf{pk}_C, \mathsf{pk}_I)$, $T(\mathsf{pk}_I, \tau_T)$ *and* $I(\mathsf{sk}_I, \mathsf{pk}_I, DataB)$. *Here,* $(\mathsf{sk}_C, \mathsf{pk}_C)$ *and* $(\mathsf{sk}_I, \mathsf{pk}_I)$ *are the secret/public key pair of* C *and* I, *respectively. They are generated by the algorithms* $\mathcal{G}_C(1^n)$ *and* $\mathcal{G}_I(1^n)$ *where* n *is a security parameter.* $DataB$ *is the database for cards' information.* I *includes a subroutine* $\mathsf{Policy}(\mathsf{pk}_C, CI, \tau_I)$ *where* CI *represents the card information of a card with* pk_C. *In the end,* I *outputs* $\mathsf{Out}_I \in \{0,1\}$ *and privately outputs* $\mathsf{POut}_I = (\mathsf{pk}_C, id_I, \tau_I)$. *Similarly,* T *outputs* $\mathsf{Out}_T \in \{0,1\}$[1] *and private output* $\mathsf{POut}_T = (\mathsf{pk}_C, id_T, \tau_T)$ *and* C *privately outputs* $\mathsf{POut}_C = (id_C, \tau_C)$. *Here,* τ *is the transaction (*τ_T, τ_I *and* τ_C *are the values seen by the terminal, the issuer and the card),* id *is the identifier of the transaction (*id_T, id_I *and* id_C *are similarly defined) and* $\phi \in \{0,1\}$ *shows the approval or disapproval of the transaction.*

The algorithm Policy depends on the policy of the transaction approval by the issuer. So, we can consider it as an algorithm which decides if a transaction τ_I is possible for the card with pk_C and CI.

We note that Out_I and $\mathsf{Policy}(\mathsf{pk}_C, CI, \tau_I)$ can be different. Out_I (similarly Out_T) shows the result of the CP which can be either accepting or canceling the payment. However, $\mathsf{Policy}(\mathsf{pk}_C, CI, \tau_I)$ shows only if the card with pk_C is able to do the payment. For example, even though the payment is canceled ($\mathsf{Out}_I = 0$) by the issuer, the issuer can approve the payment ($\mathsf{Policy}(\mathsf{pk}_C, CI, \tau_I) = 1$). It means that the card is able to this payment but the payment process is canceled (e.g., because of malicious behaviors).

Definition 2 (Correctness of CP)). *A contactless payment is correct for all* B, *transactions* τ, *database* $DataB$, CI, *and generated key pairs* $(\mathsf{sk}_C, \mathsf{pk}_C)$ *and* $(\mathsf{sk}_I, \mathsf{pk}_I)$ *if*

- *the algorithms* C, T *and* I *are run,*
- T *starts a transaction* τ,
- *there exists a* C *whose distance from* T *is at most* B,
- (pk_C, CI) *is in* $DataB$ *of an issuer* I,

[1] $\mathsf{Out}_I = 0$ or $\mathsf{Out}_T = 0$ mean canceling and $\mathsf{Out}_I = 1$ or $\mathsf{Out}_T = 1$ mean accepting.

then there exists id such that probability of $(\mathsf{Out}_T = \mathsf{Out}_I = \mathsf{Policy}(\mathsf{pk}_C, CI, \tau)) \wedge (\mathsf{POut}_T = \mathsf{POut}_I = (\mathsf{pk}_C, id, \tau)) \wedge (\mathsf{POut}_C = (id, \tau))$ *is 1.*

The output of T has to depend on the output of I because actually I is in the position to decide if the transaction is possible with the card (in fact an honest card cannot know if the transaction is possible).

Adversarial and Communication Model: In contactless payment, we consider the similar adversarial and communication model with the access control (AC) security model by Kılınç and Vaudenay [21]. The parties in AC: a controller, a reader, a tag correspond to the parties contactless payment: an issuer, a terminal, a card, respectively. Differently than AC, in the contactless-payment adversarial model, terminals can be malicious. In a nutshell, the model is as follows:

- The communication between T and I is secure and authenticated. The adversary cannot attack this part of the communication.
- The communication between the parties is limited by the speed of light.
- All parties have polynomially many instances. An instance of a party is an execution of its corresponding algorithm at a given location. Instances of honest parties cannot be run in parallel.
- The adversaries can change the location of honest instances (but they move at a limited speed) or can activate them (See [21] for details).
- Adversaries can create the database.
- Adversaries can change the destination of messages.

Definition 3 (Security in Contactless Payment with Malicious Cards). *The security game is as follows:*

- *Run* $\mathcal{G}_I(1^n) \rightarrow (\mathsf{sk}_I, \mathsf{pk}_I)$ *and* $\mathcal{G}_C(1^n) \rightarrow (\mathsf{sk}_{C_i}, \mathsf{pk}_{C_i})$ *for the issuer and each card* C_i *and give the public keys to the adversary.*
- *The adversary creates instances of cards (*C_i*'s) and the terminals at some locations of his choice. There is a distinguished terminal* T *(*T *is honest).*
- *The adversary sets a database DataB of the issuer. The issuer instance* I *which communicates with* T *is the distinguished issuer.*
- *The adversary creates the instances of himself (malicious cards or terminals) which can run independently and communicate together.*

We denote $\mathsf{POut}_I = (\mathsf{pk}'_C, id_I, \tau_I)$ *and* $\mathsf{POut}_T = (\mathsf{pk}''_C, id_T, \tau_T)$ *the private outputs of* I *and* T*. Following our communication model, the game ends when* T *outputs* Out_T*. A contactless payment is secure, if the adversary wins this game with negligible probability. The adversary wins the game if* $\mathsf{Out}_T = 1$ *and at least one of the following conditions are satisfied:*

1. $(\mathsf{pk}'_C, .) \notin DataB$,
2. $\mathsf{pk}'_C \in \{\mathsf{pk}_{C_i}\}$ *and the distance between any* C *holding* pk *and* T *is more than* B *during the execution of the protocol with* id_T,
3. $\mathsf{pk}'_C \notin \{\mathsf{pk}_{C_i}\}$ *and no instance of the adversary is close to* T *during the execution of the contactless payment protocol with* T *and* I.

4. $(\mathsf{pk}'_C, id_I, \tau_I) \neq (\mathsf{pk}'_C, id_T, \tau_T)$,
5. $\mathsf{pk}'_C \in \{\mathsf{pk}_{C_i}\}$ *and there exists no card with* pk'_C *and* $\mathsf{POut}_C = (id_I, \tau_I)$.

Remarks: The first winning condition shows that a card which does not belong *DataB* should not authenticate. The second and the third conditions are to protect against MiM and DH (DF as well), respectively. Finally, the last two conditions are to be sure that the transaction that I and T approve and complete, and the transaction that I and an honest C approve and complete are the same.

Definition 4 (Security in Contactless Payment with Malicious Terminals). *The security game is as follows:*

- *Run the key generation algorithms* $\mathcal{G}_I(1^n) \to (\mathsf{sk}_I, \mathsf{pk}_I)$ *and* $\mathcal{G}_C(1^n) \to (\mathsf{sk}_{C_i}, \mathsf{pk}_{C_i})$ *for the issuer* I *and each card* C_i *and give away public keys.*
- *The adversary creates instances of* C_i *and the terminals at some locations of his choice. There is a distinguished instance* I.
- *The adversary sets a database DataB.*
- *The adversary creates the instances of himself which can run independently and communicate together (as malicious cards or malicious terminals).*

At the end of the game I *outputs* Out_I *and* $\mathsf{POut}_I = (\mathsf{pk}'_C, id_I, \tau_I)$. *A contactless payment is secure, if the adversary wins this game with negligible probability. The adversary wins the game:*

1. if $\mathsf{Out}_I = 1$ *and if at least one of the following conditions are satisfied:*
   (a) $(\mathsf{pk}'_C, .) \notin DataB$,
   (b) $\mathsf{pk}'_C \in \{\mathsf{pk}_{C_i}\}$ *and there exists no card with* pk'_C *which outputs* (id_I, τ_I),
   (c) $\mathsf{pk}'_C \in \{\mathsf{pk}_{C_i}\}$ *and the instance of this card with* pk'_C *having* (id_I, τ_I) *has distance from the adversary and any honest terminal more than* B.
2. or if there exists an honest card instance with $\mathsf{pk}_C \in \{\mathsf{pk}_{C_i}\}$ *which privately outputs* $\mathsf{POut}_C = (id_C, \tau_C)$ *and there exists an issuer instance which has* $\mathsf{Policy}(\mathsf{pk}_C, CI, \tau_C) = 0$ *and* id_C.

The proximity condition ($1c$) has not been considered by any of the payment systems before. Actually, even though we make sure that the payment can be approved only when the terminal is close to the card, we still cannot prevent a malicious terminal to execute a payment unbeknown to a card holder. For example, a malicious terminal can be moved close to a card while the card is not at the shop. This means $1c$ does not prevent the malicious intention of the terminals. If we can be sure that the terminals can be run in a certain location, then we can guarantee the security against malicious terminals with the proximity condition. This can be possible by using position-based cryptography [13], but current terminals do not support this. Therefore, in our protocol, we eliminate $1c$. We call **almost-secure against malicious terminals** if a protocol is secure without the condition $1c$ in Definition 4. The condition 2 is to prevent honest cards to make payment even though the issuer does not approve it. For example, this condition prevents attacks where malicious terminals make a card pay (maybe without the knowledge of the honest card) for a big amount of money where normally the issuer would not let this amount of payment.

2.2 Preliminaries About Public Key Distance Bounding

We give security definitions (MiM, DF, DH) of public-key distance bounding. In CP, the terminal represents the verifier in DB because the issuer is not at the position to determine the distance of cards and the card represents the prover.

Definition 5 (Public key DB Protocol [20,26]**).** *A public key DB protocol is a two-party probabilistic polynomial-time (PPT) protocol and it consists of a tuple* $(\mathcal{K}_P, \mathcal{K}_V, V, P, B)$. *Here,* $\mathcal{K}_P$ *is the key generation algorithm of the prover algorithm P and outputs secret/public key pair* $(\mathsf{sk}_P, \mathsf{pk}_P)$. $\mathcal{K}_V$ *is the key generation algorithm of the verifier algorithm V and outputs secret/public key pair* $(\mathsf{sk}_V, \mathsf{pk}_V)$. *B is the distance bound.* $P(\mathsf{sk}_P, \mathsf{pk}_P, \mathsf{pk}_V)$ *and* $V(\mathsf{sk}_V, \mathsf{pk}_V)$ *are interactive algorithms. At the end of the protocol,* $V(\mathsf{sk}_V, \mathsf{pk}_V)$ *outputs* Out_V *and privately outputs* $\mathsf{POut}_V = \mathsf{pk}_P$. *If* $\mathsf{Out}_V = 1$, *then V accepts. If* $\mathsf{Out}_V = 0$, *then V rejects. A public-key DB protocol is correct if and only if under honest execution, whenever a verifier V and a close (to V) prover P run the distance bounding protocol, then* $\mathcal{V}$ *outputs* $\mathsf{Out}_V = 1$ *and* $\mathsf{POut}_V = \mathsf{pk}_P$.

We use the same adversarial and communication model as in contactless-payment where the provers are cards and the verifiers are terminals.

Definition 6 (MiM security [26]**).** *The game begins by running the key generations algorithms* $\mathcal{K}_V$ *and* $\mathcal{K}_P$. *They output* $(\mathsf{sk}_V, \mathsf{pk}_V)$ *and* $(\mathsf{sk}_P, \mathsf{pk}_P)$, *respectively. The public keys* pk_V *and* pk_P *are given to the adversary. In the game, we have polynomially many verifier instances where one of them is the distinguished one* $\mathcal{V}$ *and polynomially many honest prover instances which are far away from* $\mathcal{V}$. *The adversary with its instances can be at any location. The adversary wins if* $\mathcal{V}$ *outputs* $\mathsf{Out}_V = 1$ *and* $\mathsf{POut}_V = \mathsf{pk}_P$. *A DB protocol is MiM-secure if for any such game, the probability of an adversary to win is negligible.*

Definition 7 (Distance fraud [26]**).** *The game begins by running the key generation algorithm* $\mathcal{K}_V$. *It outputs* $(\mathsf{sk}_V, \mathsf{pk}_V)$. *The public key* pk_V *is given to the adversary. The adversary generates its secret/public key pair* $(\mathsf{sk}_P, \mathsf{pk}_P)$ *with using an arbitrary algorithm* $\mathcal{K}_P^*$. *In the game, we have polynomially many verifier instances including the distinguished one* $\mathcal{V}$ *and instances of an adversary (prover instances). The adversary wins if* $\mathcal{V}$ *outputs* $\mathsf{Out}_V = 1$ *and* $\mathsf{POut}_V = \mathsf{pk}_P$ *when there is no close party to* $\mathcal{V}$. *A DB protocol is DF-secure, if for any such game, the adversary wins with negligible probability.*

Definition 8 (Distance hijacking [26]**).** *The game includes polynomially many verifier instances* $\mathcal{V}, V_1, V_2, \ldots$, *a far away adversary* P, *and honest prover instances* $\mathsf{P}', \mathsf{P}'_1, \mathsf{P}'_2 \ldots$. *In this game, we consider a DB protocol* $(\mathcal{K}_P, \mathcal{K}_V, V, P, B)$ *with phases: initialization, a challenge and a verification phases. A DB protocol is DH-secure if for all PPT algorithms* $\mathcal{K}_P^*$ *and* $\mathcal{A}$, *the probability of* P *to win the following game is negligible.*

- *The game runs* $\mathcal{K}_V \rightarrow (\mathsf{sk}_V, \mathsf{pk}_V)$ *for the verifier and* $\mathcal{K}_{P'} \rightarrow (\mathsf{sk}_{P'}, \mathsf{pk}_{P'})$ *for the honest prover.*

- *The adversary runs* $\mathcal{K}_P^*(\mathsf{pk}_{P'}, \mathsf{pk}_V) \rightarrow (\mathsf{sk}_P, \mathsf{pk}_P)$.
- *The game aborts, if* $\mathsf{pk}_P = \mathsf{pk}_{P'}$. *Otherwise, instances of* P *run the adversarial algorithm* $\mathcal{A}$*, the honest prover instances* $\mathsf{P}', \mathsf{P}'_1, \mathsf{P}'_2, \ldots$ *run* $P(\mathsf{sk}_{p'}, \mathsf{pk}_V)$*, the verifier instances* $\mathcal{V}, \mathcal{V}_1, \mathcal{V}_2, \ldots$ *run* $V(\mathsf{sk}_V, \mathsf{pk}_V)$.
- P *interacts with* $\mathsf{P}', \mathsf{P}'_1, \mathsf{P}'_2, \ldots$ *and* $\mathcal{V}, \mathcal{V}_1, \mathcal{V}_2, \ldots$ *during the initialization phase of* $\mathcal{V}$ *and* P' *concurrently.*
- P' *and* $\mathcal{V}$ *continue interacting with each other in their challenge phase and* P *remains passive but it sees the exchanged messages.*
- P *interacts with* $\mathsf{P}', \mathsf{P}'_1, \mathsf{P}'_2, \ldots$ *and* $\mathcal{V}, \mathcal{V}_1, \mathcal{V}_2, \ldots$ *in the verification phase.*

The adversary wins if $\mathcal{V}$ *outputs* $\mathsf{Out}_V = 1$ *and* $\mathsf{POut}_V = \mathsf{pk}_P$.

The initialization and verification phase do not have any specific definition but the challenge phase corresponds to the phase where the challenge/response exchanges occur. It is the time critical phase meaning that the verifier determines the proximity of the responses by checking the response time (i.e., If the responses arrived on time, the prover is accepted. Otherwise, it is rejected.).

3 Contactless Payment Protocol

In this section, we construct a secure CP protocol from a public-key distance bounding $DB = (\mathcal{K}_P, \mathcal{K}_V, V, P, B)$, an encryption scheme $(\mathsf{Enc}, \mathsf{Dec})$ and a signature scheme $(\mathsf{Sign}, \mathsf{Verify})$.

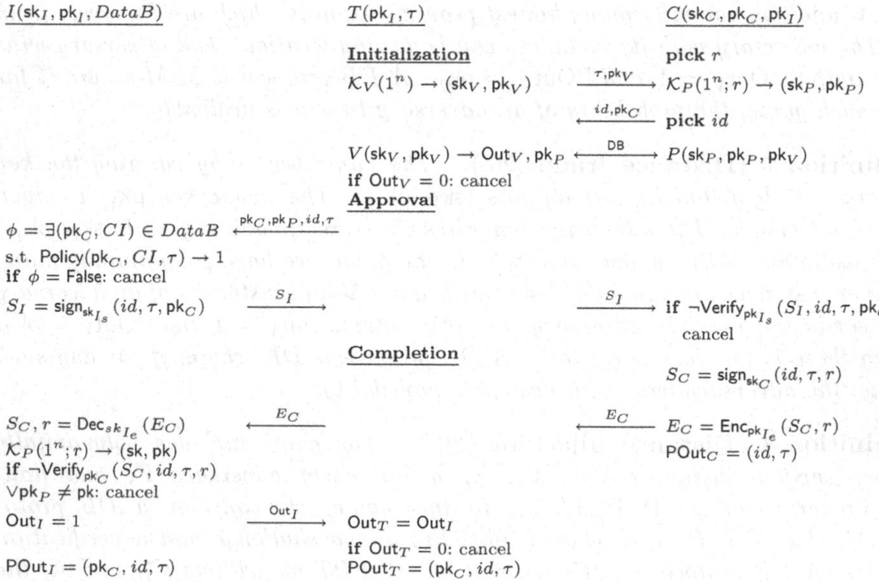

Fig. 1. The ClessPay protocol.

3.1 ClessPay

The protocol ClessPay (See Fig. 1) starts after the terminal T creates a transaction τ and connects with a card C. We do not give the details of τ since it depends on the payment system.

In our protocol, we use signature schemes and an encryption scheme. Therefore, some secret/public key pairs are generated by using their key generation algorithms. More specifically, the key generation algorithm $\mathcal{G}_I$ generates a secret/public key pair $(\mathsf{sk}_I, \mathsf{pk}_I) = ((\mathsf{sk}_{I_s}, \mathsf{sk}_{I_e}), (\mathsf{pk}_{I_s}, \mathsf{pk}_{I_e}))$ where $(\mathsf{sk}_{I_s}, \mathsf{pk}_{I_s})$ is generated by the key generation algorithm of the signature scheme used by issuers and $(\mathsf{sk}_{I_e}, \mathsf{pk}_{I_e})$ is generated by the key generation algorithm of the encryption scheme. The key generation algorithm $\mathcal{G}_C$ generates a secret/public key pair $(\mathsf{sk}_C, \mathsf{pk}_C)$ using the key generation algorithm of the signature scheme used by cards. ClessPay consists of the following phases:

Initialization Phase: This phase is executed by T and C. If this phase cannot be completed successfully, then T cancels the transaction.

T and C generate ephemeral secret/public key pairs for the distance bounding protocol $DB = (\mathcal{K}_P, \mathcal{K}_V, V, P, B)$. So, C first picks the random coins r and runs the deterministic algorithm $\mathcal{K}_P(1^n; r)$ to generate $(\mathsf{sk}_P, \mathsf{pk}_P)$. Here, what C does is equivalent to running $\mathcal{K}_P(1^n)$. C needs to generate the random coins used in $\mathcal{K}_P(1^n)$ because they will be needed in the last phase as a one-time proof for having generated pk_P. Then, T runs $\mathcal{K}_V(1^n)$ to obtain $(\mathsf{sk}_V, \mathsf{pk}_V)$ used for DB. T sends τ and pk_V to C. After receiving them, C picks an identifier id and replies with id and pk_C to introduce itself.

T and C start the distance bounding protocol so that T determines the distance of C. Therefore, T runs the verifier algorithm $V(\mathsf{sk}_V, \mathsf{pk}_V)$ of DB and C runs the prover algorithm $P(\mathsf{sk}_P, \mathsf{pk}_P, \mathsf{pk}_V)$ of DB. At the end, V outputs Out_V which shows if C is close or not and private output $\mathsf{POut}_P = \mathsf{pk}_P$. If $\mathsf{Out}_V = 0$, then T cancels the transaction. Otherwise, they continue with the next phase. Remark that, T still does not know if the card whose distance is determined is an authorized card because C has not authenticated itself with its (static) public key pk_C yet.

Approval Phase: This phase aims to check with the issuer whether the card can execute the transaction. T first sends $\mathsf{pk}_C, \mathsf{pk}_P, id, \tau$ to I. I checks if the card with pk_C is in $DataB$. If it is in $DataB$, it retrieves the card information of the card (CI) and runs the algorithm $\mathsf{Policy}(\mathsf{pk}_C, CI, \tau)$ which outputs 1 if the card has the privilege to execute τ[2]. If this algorithm returns 0, the transaction is canceled. Otherwise, I approves the transaction.

If it is approved, I signs with sk_{I_s} the message $(id, \tau, \mathsf{pk}_C)$. This signature is necessary for cards to be sure that they are approved for the payment. Then, it sends this signature S_I to T and T relays it to C. C runs the verification

[2] The Policy checks the execution right of a card depending on the bank policy. So, we do not discuss about how this verification happens.

algorithm of the signature scheme $\mathsf{Verify}_{\mathsf{pk}_{I_s}}(S_I, id, \tau, \mathsf{pk}_C)$ to be sure that C and I have the same id, τ, pk_C. If C verifies S_I, then the next phase begins. Otherwise, C cancels.

Completion Phase: In this phase, the execution of the transaction τ with id is completed by I, T and C. First, C signs the message id, τ, r with sk_C as a proof of execution of the payment. The reason of signing r is showing that C took part in the DB protocol. Then, it encrypts the signature S_C and r by using the key pk_{I_e}. The reason of the encryption is to hide r. At the end, C sends the encryption (E_C) to T. T relays it to I. At this point, the transaction is completed for C and it privately outputs (id, τ).

In order to obtain S_C and r, I first decrypts E_C with sk_{I_e}. I verifies that r generates pk_P by running $\mathcal{K}_P(1^n; r)$. If it is verified, it also verifies S_C with $\mathsf{Verify}_{\mathsf{pk}_C}(S_C, id, \tau, r)$. If the signature is valid, then it sends $\mathsf{Out}_I = 1$ to T and privately outputs $(\mathsf{pk}_C, id, \tau)$. Otherwise, I cancels the transaction.

Cancel the Transaction: As it can be seen in the protocol, the cancellation can be done by I, T or C. In the case of timeout, parties cancel as well. When I cancels, it sets $\mathsf{Out}_I = 0$ and sends Out_I to T. Then, T cancels as well. When T cancels, it sets $\mathsf{Out}_T = 0$ and terminates. When C cancels, it sends a cancel message to T and terminates with $\mathsf{POut}_C = \perp$.

3.2 Security

Theorem 1. *Assuming that $DB = (\mathcal{K}_P, \mathcal{K}_V, V, P, B)$ is DF secure (Definition 7), DH-secure (Definition 8) and MiM-secure (Definition 6), the encryption scheme is IND-CCA secure and the signature scheme used by cards is secure against the existential forgery under no message attacks (EF-0MA), ClessPay is secure against malicious cards (Definition 3).*

Proof. We define a sequence of games Γ_i where we denote p_i as a success probability of winning Γ_i. We assume that we have honest cards $\{C_1, C_2, \ldots, C_k\}$ and their public keys are in a set $\{pk_{C_i}\}$.

Γ_0 : The instances of the issuer, terminals and cards play the game in Definition 3. There is a distinguished terminal instance $\mathcal{T}$ which privately outputs $\mathsf{POut}_T = (\mathsf{pk}''_C, id_T, \tau_T)$ and in which the V protocol outputs $\mathsf{POut}_V = \mathsf{pk}'_P$, and a distinguished issuer $\mathcal{I}$ which communicates with $\mathcal{T}$ and privately outputs $\mathsf{POut}_I = (\mathsf{pk}'_C, id_I, \tau_I)$. In Γ_0, the adversary cannot win with **the first condition** in Definition 3 because I always cancels the transaction if $(\mathsf{pk}'_C, .) \notin DataB$.

Γ_1 : It is the same game as Γ_0 except that $(\mathsf{pk}'_C, id_I, \tau_I)$ is always equal $(\mathsf{pk}''_C, id_T, \tau_T)$. Because of our secure and authenticated channel assumption between T and I and because of the honesty of T, they have the same public-key, identifier and the transaction. Besides, T outputs 1, if I outputs 1. So, $p_1 = p_0$. In Γ_1, the adversary cannot win with **the fourth condition** in Definition 3.

Γ_2 : It is the same game as in Γ_1 except that instances of honest cards do not sign and they encrypt a random message. Basically, each stores the ciphertext together with the identifier, transaction and static/ephemeral public keys to a table. $\mathcal{I}$ does not decrypt such random ciphertexts and retrieves their data from the table. More specifically, we simulate them as follows:

$C(\mathsf{sk}_C, \mathsf{pk}_C, \mathsf{pk}_I)$	$\mathcal{I}(\mathsf{sk}_I, \mathsf{pk}_I, DataB)$
... (unchanged until sign)	... (unchanged until the reception of E_C)
pick R	**if** $(E_C, id, \tau, \mathsf{pk}_C, .) \in$ TableE:
$E_C = \mathsf{Enc}_{\mathsf{pk}_{I_e}}(R)$	**retrieve** pk **s.t.** $(E_C, id, \tau, \mathsf{pk}_C, \mathsf{pk}) \in$ TableE
store $(E_C, id, \tau, \mathsf{pk}_C, \mathsf{pk}_P)$ **in** TableE	**if** $\mathsf{pk} \neq \mathsf{pk}_P$: cancel
send E_C	$\mathsf{Out}_I = 1, \mathsf{POut}_I = (\mathsf{pk}_C, id, \tau)$
$\mathsf{POut}_C = (id, \tau)$	**else:** the same as after receiving E_C

We can easily show Γ_1 and Γ_2 are indistinguishable by using the IND-CCA security of the encryption scheme. So, $|p_2 - p_1|$ is negligible. Remark that the random coins of the honest cards are not used in Γ_2.

Γ_3 : It is the same game as Γ_2 except that $\mathsf{Out}_V = 0$ after the execution of $V(\mathsf{sk}_V, \mathsf{pk}_V)$ if one of the situations happens:

1. no party is close to $\mathcal{T}$,
2. pk'_P is generated by no honest card and there is no adversary close to $\mathcal{T}$,
3. pk'_P is generated by an honest card but it has no instance close to $\mathcal{T}$.

Γ_3 and Γ_2 are indistinguishable because the probability that $\mathsf{Out}_V = 1$ if one of the situations above happens is negligible. $\mathsf{Out}_V = 1$ when the 1st situation happens with negligible probability due to the DF-security of DB. $\mathsf{Out}_V = 1$ when the 2nd situation happens with negligible probability due to the DH-security of DB. $\mathsf{Out}_V = 1$ when the 3rd situation happens with negligible probability due to the MiM-security of DB. Note that we can simulate an honest card instance in Γ_3 by using a prover instance in the MiM-game because r is not used by honest card instances. Therefore, $|p_3 - p_2|$ is negligible.

Γ_4 : It is the same game as in Γ_3 except that $\mathcal{I}$ cancels after decrypting and obtaining the random coins r where $\mathcal{K}_P(1^n; r) \to (\mathsf{sk}_P, \mathsf{pk}_P)$ and $(\mathsf{sk}_P, \mathsf{pk}_P)$ is generated by an honest card instance.

$\mathcal{I}(\mathsf{sk}_I, \mathsf{pk}_I, DataB)$

... (unchanged until the reception of E_C)
if $(E_C, id, \tau, \mathsf{pk}_C, .) \in$ TableE: **retrieve** pk **s.t.** $(E_C, id, \tau, \mathsf{pk}_C, \mathsf{pk}) \in$ TableE
    if $\mathsf{pk} \neq \mathsf{pk}_P$: cancel
    $\mathsf{Out}_I = 1, \mathsf{POut}_I = (\mathsf{pk}_C, id_T, \tau_T)$
else: $S_C, r = \mathsf{Dec}_{\mathsf{sk}_I}(E_C)$, $\mathcal{K}_P(1^n; r) \to (\mathsf{sk}, \mathsf{pk})$
    if (sk, pk) is generated by an honest instance: cancel
    else if $\neg\mathsf{Verify}(S_C, id, \tau, r) \vee \mathsf{pk}_P \neq \mathsf{pk}$: cancel
    $\mathsf{Out}_I = 1, \mathsf{POut}_I = (\mathsf{pk}_C, id, \tau)$

We can easily prove that if there exists an adversary with pk_C in Γ_3 which obtains a randomness r generating the secret/public key pair used by an honest instance, then we can construct another adversary which breaks the MiM-security of DB. Clearly, during the simulation of Γ_3, if I gets r, then it generates the corresponding secret key of the prover in MiM-game and breaks the MiM-security. Since receiving such r in Γ_4 is negligible, $|p_4 - p_3|$ is negligible.

Now, we show that the adversary cannot win with **the third condition** in Γ_4. If the adversary wins with this in Γ_4, it means that $\mathsf{pk}'_C \notin \{\mathsf{pk}_{C_i}\}$ and no instance of the adversary is close to $\mathcal{T}$ during the execution of the CP protocol with $\mathcal{T}$ and $\mathcal{I}$. Due to the condition 2 in the reduction of Γ_3, pk_P must be generated by an honest card (otherwise, $\mathcal{T}$ cancels). However, in Γ_4, it is not possible to have $\mathsf{Out}_\mathcal{I} = 1$ while $\mathsf{pk}_C \notin \{\mathsf{pk}_{C_i}\}$ and pk_P is generated by an honest card instance (check the dashed underlined parts in the simulation of $\mathcal{I}$). So, it is not possible that $\mathsf{Out}_\mathcal{I} = 1$, if the game is in the third condition.

Since only condition 2 and 5 of Definition 3 remain to win in Γ_3, we can assume that $\mathsf{pk}_C \in \{\mathsf{pk}_{C_i}\}$.

Γ_5 : It is the same game as Γ_4 except we simulate Verify algorithm with Verify$'$ such that it only accepts the signature of malicious cards. It does not accept the signatures of honest cards' instances.

The only difference in Verify and Verify$'$ is in the case of $\mathsf{pk}_C \in \{\mathsf{pk}_{C_i}\}$. In this case, while Verify returns the output of the verification of the signature, Verify$'$ returns 0. In Γ_5 and Γ_4, no honest cards' instances generate a signature. So, the only difference between Γ_4 and Γ_5 happens when $\mathcal{I}$ obtains a forged signature of an honest card instance.

Thanks to EF-0MA security of the signature, we can easily show that forging a signature of any honest cards happens with a negligible probability to prove that Γ_5 and Γ_4 are indistinguishable.

Remark that in Γ_5, $\mathcal{I}$ have $\mathsf{Out}_\mathcal{I} = 1$, if and only if $(E_C, id_T, \tau_T, \mathsf{pk}'_C, \mathsf{pk}'_P)$ is in TableE. So, we can assume that $(E_C, id_T, \tau_T, \mathsf{pk}'_C, \mathsf{pk}'_P) \in$ TableE.

If the adversary wins with the condition 2 in Γ_5, then $\mathsf{pk}'_C \in \{\mathsf{pk}_{C_i}\}$ and the distance between any C holding pk'_C and T is more than B during the execution of the protocol with id_T. Due to condition 3 in Γ_3, pk'_P must not been generated by C. So, $(E_C, id_T, \tau_T, \mathsf{pk}'_C, \mathsf{pk}'_P, .)$ cannot be in TableE which contradicts with our assumption. Hence, the adversary cannot win with **the second** condition.

If the adversary wins with the fifth condition, then it means that $\mathsf{pk}'_C \in \{\mathsf{pk}_{C_i}\}$ and there exists no card with pk'_C which privately outputs id_I, τ_I. Then, it means that $(E_C, id_T, \tau_T, \mathsf{pk}'_C, \mathsf{pk}'_P, .) \notin$ TableE since no honest card instance has (id_T, τ_T). This contradicts with our assumption. Therefore, the adversary cannot win with **the fifth condition.** Remark that in Γ_5, the adversary cannot win the game So, p_5 is negligible meaning that p_0 is negligible. □

Theorem 2. *Assuming that the signature schemes used are existential forgery chosen message attack (EF-CMA) secure then ClessPay is* ***almost-secure*** *against malicious terminal (Definition 4).*

Proof. We recall that in almost-security, we do not need to consider condition 1c of Definition 4 .

Γ_0 : The instances of the issuer, terminals and cards play the game in Definition 4. We have a distinguished issuer instance $\mathcal{I}$ which outputs $(\mathsf{pk}'_C, id_I, \tau_I)$. Remark that in Γ_0, the adversary cannot win **with condition 1*a*** $((\mathsf{pk}'_C, .) \notin$ *DataB*) because $\mathcal{I}$ rejects the cards which are not in *DataB*.

Γ_1 : It is the same game as Γ_2 except that no *id* selected by an honest card instance repeats. Clearly, $|p_1 - p_0|$ is negligible.

Γ_2 : It is the same game as Γ_1 except that we simulate $\mathcal{I}$ and its instances while generating the signature and honest cards' instances in the verification of this signature as follows:

$I(\mathsf{sk}_I, \mathsf{pk}_I, DataB)$	$\mathsf{Verify'}_{\mathsf{pk}_{I_s}}(S, id, \tau, \mathsf{pk}_C)$
$S_I = \mathsf{sign}_{\mathsf{sk}_{I_s}}(id, \tau, \mathsf{pk}_C)$	**if** $(S, id, \tau, \mathsf{pk}_C)$ **in** Table1
store $(S_I, id, \tau, \mathsf{pk}_C)$ **in** Table1	**return** 1
send S_I	**else: return** 0

$|p_2 - p_1|$ is negligible.

The output of issuer instance is the same as issuer instances in Γ_1. Therefore, we have a perfect simulation for it. The only difference happens when honest cards' instances in Γ_1 receive a valid signature verified by pk_{I_s} and not in Table 1. In this case, honest cards in Γ_1 verify the signature but they do not in Γ_2. Otherwise, the simulations of them are perfect. We can easily show that the probability of generating a valid signature which is not in the Table 1 is negligible in Γ_2 thanks to EF-CMA security of the signature scheme. We can use the public key received from the signing game as a public key of the issuer and simulate signatures of issuer instances by using the signing game. Note that sk_{I_s} is not used in the simulation but the signature generation, so we can simulate the rest of the protocol perfectly. Therefore, $|p_2 - p_1|$ is negligible.

The adversary cannot win the game **with condition 2** in Definition 4. Assume that the adversary wins with this. It implies that $(., id_C, \tau_C, \mathsf{pk}_C) \notin$ Table 1 since id_C is unique. So, no honest card instance outputs (id_C, τ_C) in this case.

Γ_3 : It is the same game as Γ_2 except we simulate honest cards' instances while generating the signature and $\mathcal{I}$ in the verification of it as follows:

$C(\mathsf{sk}_C, \mathsf{pk}_C, DataB)$	$\mathsf{Verify''}_{\mathsf{pk}_C}(S, id_I, \tau_I, \mathsf{pk}_C, r)$
$S_C = \mathsf{sign}_{\mathsf{sk}_C}(id, \tau, r)$	**if** $(S, \mathsf{pk}_C, id, \tau, r)$ **in** Table2
store $(S_C, \mathsf{pk}_C, id, \tau, r)$ **in** Table2	**return** 1
$E_C = \mathsf{Enc}_{\mathsf{pk}_{I_e}}(S_C, r)$	**else: return** 0
send E_C	

The only difference is the output of Verify″ and Verify when a forged signature received. To show the indistinguishability of Γ_2 and Γ_3, we can EF-CMA security of the signature scheme. So, $|p_3 - p_2|$ is negligible.

Remark that in this game, the adversary cannot win with **the condition 1*b***. If $\mathcal{I}$ outputs $(\mathsf{pk}'_C, id_I, \tau_I)$, it means that an honest card instance with pk'_C added $(S, \mathsf{pk}'_C, id_I, \tau_I, .)$ in Table2 and outputted (id_I, τ_I). Hence, in Γ_3, the adversary cannot win. So, p_0 is negligible. □

We recommend using Eff-pkDB [20] as a public-key DB in ClessPay since it is shown that it is the most efficient public-key DB protocol having the necessary security requirements for ClessPay. It requires one exponentiation and hashing.

The assumption on the signature scheme used by cards differ in Theorem 1 (EF-0MA) and Theorem 2 (EF-CMA). Hence, it looks like to have security against both terminals and cards we need DF, DH, MiM-secure DB protocol, IND-CCA secure encryption scheme, and EF-CMA secure signature schemes. However, we could have the almost security against malicious terminal if we have the following assumptions in Theorem 2: the encryption scheme is IND-CCA secure and the signature scheme used by cards is EF-0MA secure. In this case, the proof of Theorem 2 would need the same games Γ_2 and Γ_5 in the proof of Theorem 1 instead of Γ_3 in the proof of Theorem 2. So, actually, to have full security in ClessPay, we need DF, DH, MiM-secure DB protocol, IND-CCA secure encryption scheme, EF-CMA secure signature for issuers, and EF-0MA secure signature for cards.

4 EMV Analysis

EMV key setting is different than our contactless payment key setting because it has a symmetric key shared between the card and its issuer as well as asymmetric keys. An issuer I has secret/public key pair S_I/P_I. It also has a master symmetric key MK_{AC}. A card C shares MK_{AC} with its issuer I. It has public/secret key pair P_{IC} and S_{IC}. P_{IC} is signed by I's private key S_I. C stores certified P_I. We assume that the terminal T knows the public key of the certificate authority (CA) to verify P_I and so P_{IC}. We also assume that the channel between I and T is authenticated.

For the sake of simplicity, in our description, we assume that C knows all terminal related information and the authentication method. T also knows the card related information.

EMV contactless session consists of four phases without card holder (user) verification method:

Contact Establishment with NFC Card: T detects C.

Transaction Initialization: T sends the transaction τ to C. Then, C responds with its public key P_{IC} and card information such as PAN and expiration date (ED). If T verifies P_{IC}, it continues.

Relay Resistance Protocol [3]*:* This protocol is executed if C and T support it. Here, we assume that they support this feature. T picks a random number R_1 and sends this to C. C responses with another random number R_2. It also sends timing estimates (*timings*): Min and Max Time For Processing, Device Estimated Transmission Time. Then, T checks if the total time passed after sending R_1 exceeds the limit (let's call it B). If the total time does not exceed B, then the next phase begins. Otherwise, the transaction is canceled.

Data Authentication: There are three type of authentication methods in EMV: Static Data Authentication (SDA), Dynamic Data Authentication (DDA) and Combined Data Authentication (CDA). Because of some weaknesses in SDA and DDA (replay attacks and wedge attacks), we consider CDA which is combined with the next phase.

Transaction: T sends a random number UN_T to request a cryptogram generation from C. In EMV, three type of cryptograms exist: Transaction Certificate (TC), Authorization Request Cryptogram (ARQC), Application Authentication Cryptogram (AAC). Here, we consider the online verification where T requests ARQC. TC is used for the offline verification by the issuer and AAC is used to cancel the transaction.

Online Verification: C increases its counter ATC and generates a secret key SK_{AC} by using ATC and MK_{AC}. Then, it generates the cryptogram $ARQC$: a MAC of UN_T, ATC, τ with using SK_{AC}. C sends the cryptogram AC to T and T relays it to I with the card information. I verifies $ARQC$ and possibly validate the information of C. If $ARQC$ passes verification and card is validated for the transaction, then $ARC = 1$ and I generates a MAC of $ARQC$ and ARC with the secret key SK_{AC}. This MAC is called as $ARPC$. I sends $ARPC$ with the message to T and T relays it to C if $ARC = 1$. Otherwise, it cancels. C verifies $ARPC$. If the verification and ARC is 1 then C generates the second cryptogram TC. TC is a MAC of CDOL2's objects with SK_{AC} (See [4], Table 26)

to show transaction is complete. Also, it picks a random number UN_C and signs UN_C, UN_T, ATC, TC, *timings*, R_1, R_2 with S_{IC}. C At the end, C sends the signature and TC to T.

Terminal checks if the signature and the data signed are valid. Later, the terminal contacts with the issuer to receive the reimbursement and gives TC as a proof of transaction completion by the card. In this case, the issuer verifies TC to execute the reimbursement.

EMV in Our Model: The EMV protocol can have the following maps to have the same structure as in Definition 1: $(\mathsf{sk}_C, \mathsf{pk}_C) = ((MK_{AC}, S_{IC}), P_{IC}), (\mathsf{sk}_I, \mathsf{pk}_I) = ((MK_{AC}, S_I), P_I)$, $id = ATC$, $\mathsf{Policy}(\mathsf{pk}_C, CI, id, \tau) = ARC$, $\mathsf{Out}_T =$ approval/ decline, $\mathsf{Out}_I = \mathsf{Verify}(TC, UN_T, ATC, \tau)$, $\mathsf{POut}_I = (P_{IC}, ATC, \tau)$, $\mathsf{POut}_T = (P_{IC}, ATC, \tau)$ and $\mathsf{POut}_C = (ATC, \tau)$.

Security Against Malicious Terminal in EMV: Clearly, the EMV protocol is not secure according to Definition 4 since the malicious terminal can approve relay resistance protocol without considering the distance of C. However, it is almost-secure against malicious terminals. We prove this as follows:

Theorem 3. *Assuming that* MAC *is EF-CMA secure and* Gen *is a pseudo-random permutation, then EMV protocol is almost-secure against malicious terminals (Definition 4).*

Proof. Γ_0 : The instances of the issuer, terminals and cards play the game in Definition 4. We have a distinguished issuer instance $\mathcal{I}$ which outputs (P_{IC}, ATC, τ_I). In Γ_0, there exists at most one card instance with P_{IC} seeing ATC as ATC is a counter and incremented by each new instance. Let's call this instance as $\mathcal{C}$.

Γ_1 : It is the same game as Γ_0 except that the honest card instances picks a random SK'_{AC} instead of generating it with $\mathsf{Gen}(MK', ATC)$ and stores the random SK'_{AC} in Table 1 as (MK', ATC', SK'_{AC}). If an issuer instance receives card information belongs to an honest card then it retrieves SK'_{AC} from Table 1. Since Gen is pseudo-random permutation, $|p_1 - p_0|$ is negligible.

Γ_2 : It is the same game as Γ_1 except that we simulate MAC generation of honest cards and verification of MACs of honest cards' instances by the issuer as follows:

$\underline{I(P'_{IC}, S'_{IC}, P'_I, MK'_{AC})}$

$ATC' = ATC' + 1$
pick SK'_{AC}
store $(MK'_{AC}, ATC', SK'_{AC})$
$ARQC = \mathsf{MAC}_{SK'_{AC}}(UN_T, ATC', \tau)$
store $(SK'_{AC}, UN'_T, ATC', \tau', ARQC)$ **in** Table_{ARQC}
rest is the same until TC/AAC **generation**
if ARC = 1 **and** Verify$(ARPC', SK'_{AC})$:
  $TC = \mathsf{MAC}_{SK'_{AC}}(UN_T, ATC', \tau)$
  store $(SK'_{AC}, UN'_T, ATC', \tau', TC)$ **in** Table_{TC}
else:
  $AAC = \mathsf{MAC}_{SK'_{AC}}(UN_T, ATC', \tau)$
  store $(SK'_{AC}, UN'_T, ATC', \tau', AAC)$ **in** Table_{AAC}

$\underline{\mathsf{Verify}'(AC, SK_{AC})}$

if $(SK_{AC}, UN_T, ATC, \tau, AC) \in \mathsf{Table}_{AC}$
  return 1
else: return 0

Γ_2 is indistinguishable from Γ_1 because of the security of MAC. The similar reduction in the proof of Theorem 1 from Γ_4 to Γ_5 can be used to prove the indistinguishably. So, $|p_2 - p_1|$ is negligible.

Γ_3 : It is the same game with Γ_2 except that $\mathcal{I}$ generates $ARPC$ and then stores it to Table_{ARPC} (similar storing as in Γ_2). Then, the honest cards verify $ARPC$ by checking if it is in the Table_{ARPC}. Γ_3 is indistinguishable from Γ_2 because of the security of MAC. So, $|p_3 - p_2|$ is negligible.

Clearly, in Γ_3, the adversary cannot win with the condition 1b because $\mathcal{I}$ privately outputs (P_{IC}, ATC, τ) if and only if the card with P_{IC} outputs ATC, τ. In addition, it cannot win with the condition 2 because if $ARC \neq 1$, then no honest card outputs ATC, τ and if an honest card receives a valid $ARPC$ having $ARC = 1$, then it means that $ARPC$ is in Table_{ARPC}. So, $\mathcal{I}$ has (P_{IC}, ATC, τ). Since the adversary cannot win in Γ_3, p_0 is negligible. □

However, there exists another problem in EMV related to ATC which is not considered in our model. It can be explained as follows: ATC is 16-bit number and incremented at the beginning of each session. If ATC reaches the limit which 65535, then the card is not valid anymore because EMV specification does not let rotating the counter due to the security reasons. According to EMV specification [4] if cards are used normally, it will approach the limit (65,535) transaction limit not so fast (60 per day every day for a 3-year card). However, an attacker who does not aim to make a payment but aims to invalidate the card can trigger the card at most 65,535 times. Then, the card cannot be used anymore.

Security Against Malicious Card in EMV: Unfortunately, EMV is not secure against malicious cards. In the followings, we show that an adversary can win with the second, third and fourth condition in Definition 3.

Fake Transaction Attack: This attack comes from the fact that T cannot validate TC in the signature $SDAD$ because it does not have SK_{AC}. Therefore, a malicious card can generate an invalid TC' in the last cryptogram generation process and use this cryptogram while generating this signature. Then, the terminal will approve the payment because the signature is correct. However, TC' is not valid. So, when T contacts with I, I cannot validate TC'. In this case, the malicious card succeeds to break the security of EMV with breaking **the fourth condition** of Definition 3 because I cancels while T does not.

Distance Fraud Attack: A malicious card can initiate a payment process with T, while it is not close T. In this case, it can send R_2 before seeing R_1 in order to reply early enough. In this case, T thinks that the card is close. Here, the malicious card succeeds to break the security of EMV with breaking **the third condition** of Definition 3. This type of attack is dangerous for an EMV payment because the malicious card can claim later that it does not do the payment by showing that it was in somewhere else.

MiM Attack: The relay resistance protocol in EMV constructed to prevent relay attacks by a MiM-adversary. In this attack scenario, a MiM-adversary relays the messages between the card and the terminal to do the payment without the card's consent. The relay resistance protocol aims to prevent it by checking the distance of the card. The assumption on its security based on the fact that the adversary cannot relay the messages faster than the speed of light. Therefore, the adversary cannot succeed to pass the relay resistance protocol because it cannot guess R_2 before R_2 is picked by the card. However, it has been shown that with guessing attacks [15] the security against relay attacks is breakable for the protocols with single challenge/response bit strings exchanges. In addition, Chothia et al. [14] have already explained this vulnerability.

5 Conclusion

In this paper, we concentrated on formalism of CP system. In this direction, we formally define contactless payment by defining the inputs and outputs of the algorithms of issuers, terminals and cards. Based on this definition, we gave two security definitions against malicious cards and malicious terminals. We also considered relay attacks which are very common attacks in CP.

We also designed a contactless-payment protocol ClessPay in our model. In this protocol, the terminal determines the distance of the card by using a secure public-key distance bounding protocol to prevent the relay attack and then the rest of the protocol continues with the authentication of the card and the issuer. We proved the security of ClessPay against malicious cards and malicious terminals formally.

Finally, we analyzed current EMV-contactless protocol [5] in our model. We realized that it is not secure against malicious cards because MiM-attack and DF-attack which are based on relay attacks. In addition to this, we formally proved that EMV-contactless protocol is secure against malicious terminals. Our analysis is the first formal cryptographic analysis of EMV-contactless protocol.

If we compare ClessPay and EMVCo in regard to cryptographic computations executed by the cards, we see that EMVCo is slightly more efficient since public-key operations are less in EMVCo. A card in EMVCo has to compute two MAC, verify one MAC and generate one signature. While a card in ClessPay has to compute one public-key encryption, generate one signature and verify one signature. However, to have the highest level of the security, it is the price to pay and with a dedicated hardware on smart cards, this price is not so high. As a future work, assuming that changing completely EMV specification is very hard, we can recommend some adaptations on EMVCo to have full security without not so much change in the basic structure of the protocol.

References

1. Contactless payment market by solution (payment terminal, mobile payment, transaction and data management, security and fraud management), service (professional, managed), payment mode (mobile handsets, smart cards), vertical - global forecast to 2021. https://www.marketsandmarkets.com/Market-Reports/contactless-payments-market-1313.html
2. EMV Acquirer and Terminal Security Guidelines
3. EMV Contactless Specifications for Payment Systems, Book C-2: Kernel 2 Specification
4. EMV Integrated Circuit Card Specifications for Payment Systems, Book 2: Security and Key Management
5. EMVCo: EMV Contactless Specifications for Payment Systems, Version 2.4 (2014)
6. Avoine, G., Bultel, X., Gambs, S., Gérault, D., Lafourcade, P., Onete, C., Robert, J.-M.: A terrorist-fraud resistant and extractor-free anonymous distance-bounding protocol. In: Proceedings of the 2017 ACM on Asia Conference on Computer and Communications Security, pp. 800–814. ACM (2017)
7. Bond, M., Choudary, M.O., Murdoch, S.J., Skorobogatov, S., Anderson, R.: Be prepared: the EMV preplay attack. IEEE Secur. Priv. **13**(2), 56–64 (2015)
8. Bond, M., Choudary, O., Murdoch, S.J., Skorobogatov, S., Anderson, R.: Chip and skim: cloning EMV cards with the pre-play attack. In: 2014 IEEE Symposium on Security and Privacy (SP), pp. 49–64. IEEE (2014)
9. Boureanu, I., Mitrokotsa, A., Vaudenay, S.: Secure and lightweight distance-bounding. In: Avoine, G., Kara, O. (eds.) LightSec 2013. LNCS, vol. 8162, pp. 97–113. Springer, Heidelberg (2013). https://doi.org/10.1007/978-3-642-40392-7_8
10. Boureanu, I., Vaudenay, S.: Optimal proximity proofs. In: Lin, D., Yung, M., Zhou, J. (eds.) Inscrypt 2014. LNCS, vol. 8957, pp. 170–190. Springer, Cham (2015). https://doi.org/10.1007/978-3-319-16745-9_10
11. Brands, S., Chaum, D.: Distance-bounding protocols (extended abstract). In: Helleseth, T. (ed.) EUROCRYPT 1993. LNCS, vol. 765, pp. 344–359. Springer, Heidelberg (1994). https://doi.org/10.1007/3-540-48285-7_30
12. Bultel, X., Gambs, S., Gérault, D., Lafourcade, P., Onete, C., Robert, J.-M.: A prover-anonymous and terrorist-fraud resistant distance-bounding protocol. In: Proceedings of the 9th ACM Conference on Security & Privacy in Wireless and Mobile Networks, pp. 121–133. ACM (2016)
13. Chandran, N., Goyal, V., Moriarty, R., Ostrovsky, R.: Position based cryptography. In: Halevi, S. (ed.) CRYPTO 2009. LNCS, vol. 5677, pp. 391–407. Springer, Heidelberg (2009). https://doi.org/10.1007/978-3-642-03356-8_23
14. Chothia, T., Garcia, F.D., de Ruiter, J., van den Breekel, J., Thompson, M.: Relay cost bounding for contactless EMV payments. In: Böhme, R., Okamoto, T. (eds.) FC 2015. LNCS, vol. 8975, pp. 189–206. Springer, Heidelberg (2015). https://doi.org/10.1007/978-3-662-47854-7_11
15. Clulow, J., Hancke, G.P., Kuhn, M.G., Moore, T.: So near and yet so far: distance-bounding attacks in wireless networks. In: Buttyán, L., Gligor, V.D., Westhoff, D. (eds.) ESAS 2006. LNCS, vol. 4357, pp. 83–97. Springer, Heidelberg (2006). https://doi.org/10.1007/11964254_9

16. Cremers, C., Rasmussen, K.B., Schmidt, B., Capkun, S.: Distance hijacking attacks on distance bounding protocols. In: 2012 IEEE Symposium on Security and Privacy (SP), pp. 113–127. IEEE (2012)
17. Drimer, S., Murdoch, S.J., et al.: Keep your enemies close: distance bounding against smartcard relay attacks. In: USENIX security symposium, vol. 312 (2007)
18. Francillon, A., Danev, B., Capkun, S.: Relay attacks on passive keyless entry and start systems in modern cars. In: NDSS (2011)
19. Francis, L., Hancke, G., Mayes, K., Markantonakis, K.: Practical NFC peer-to-peer relay attack using mobile phones. In: Ors Yalcin, S.B. (ed.) RFIDSec 2010. LNCS, vol. 6370, pp. 35–49. Springer, Heidelberg (2010). https://doi.org/10.1007/978-3-642-16822-2_4
20. Kılınç, H., Vaudenay, S.: Efficient public-key distance bounding protocol. In: Cheon, J.H., Takagi, T. (eds.) ASIACRYPT 2016. LNCS, vol. 10032, pp. 873–901. Springer, Heidelberg (2016). https://doi.org/10.1007/978-3-662-53890-6_29
21. Kılınç, H., Vaudenay, S.: Contactless access control based on distance bounding. In: Nguyen, P., Zhou, J. (eds.) ISC 2017. LNCS, vol. 10599, pp. 195–213. Springer, Cham (2017). https://doi.org/10.1007/978-3-319-69659-1_11
22. Markantonakis, K., Francis, L., Hancke, G., Mayes, K.: Practical relay attack on contactless transactions by using NFC mobile phones. In: Radio Frequency Identification System Security: RFIDsec, vol. 12, p. 21 (2012)
23. Roland, M., Langer, J.: Cloning credit cards: a combined pre-play and downgrade attack on EMV contactless. In: WOOT (2013)
24. Vaudenay, S.: On modeling terrorist frauds. In: Susilo, W., Reyhanitabar, R. (eds.) ProvSec 2013. LNCS, vol. 8209, pp. 1–20. Springer, Heidelberg (2013). https://doi.org/10.1007/978-3-642-41227-1_1
25. Vaudenay, S.: On privacy for RFID. In: Au, M.-H., Miyaji, A. (eds.) ProvSec 2015. LNCS, vol. 9451, pp. 3–20. Springer, Cham (2015). https://doi.org/10.1007/978-3-319-26059-4_1
26. Vaudenay, S.: Private and secure public-key distance bounding: application to NFC payment. In: Böhme, R., Okamoto, T. (eds.) FC 2015. LNCS, vol. 8975, pp. 207–216. Springer, Heidelberg (2015). https://doi.org/10.1007/978-3-662-47854-7_12
27. Vaudenay, S.: Sound proof of proximity of knowledge. In: Au, M.-H., Miyaji, A. (eds.) ProvSec 2015. LNCS, vol. 9451, pp. 105–126. Springer, Cham (2015). https://doi.org/10.1007/978-3-319-26059-4_6
28. Weiß, M.: Performing relay attacks on ISO 14443 contactless smart cards using NFC mobile equipment. Master's thesis in Computer Science, University of Munich (2010)

New Attacks and Secure Design for Anonymous Distance-Bounding

Ahmad Ahmadi(✉), Reihaneh Safavi-Naini, and Mamunur Akand

University of Calgary, Calgary, Canada
ahmadi@ucalgary.ca

Abstract. Anonymous Distance-Bounding (DB) protocols allow a prover to convince a verifier that they are within a distance bound from the verifier, without revealing their identity. This is an attractive property that enables the prover to enjoy proximity based services while preserving their privacy. Combination of anonymity and distance-bounding however introduces new security challenges. We show two new realistic attacks, using *directional antenna* and the *collusion of multiple users*, that breaks all existing anonymous DB protocols, and propose a new security model that captures these new attacks. We construct a protocol with provable security in this new model and discuss directions for future research.

1 Introduction

Distance upper bounding (DB) protocols were first proposed in [16] to provide security against Man-in- the-Middle (MiM) attack in authentication protocols, and later found wide applications in location and proximity based services [9,13, 17,22]. Early DB protocols use a symmetric key shared by the prover and the verifier, and so the prover's identity is always known to the verifier.

To alleviate the prover's identifiability by the verifier, public key DB and anonymous public key DB protocols have been proposed [4,25]. The focus of this paper is on anonymous DB protocols. In these protocols there are three types of *participants*: *provers* that represent the *registered users* of the system and have registered secret keys, an honest *verifier* who knows the public keys of the provers, and *actors* who are unregistered participants of the system, but try to be accepted by the verifier, or help a dishonest prover to get accepted. A secure DB protocol estimates the distance between the prover and the verifier using a *fast challenge-response phase*, during which the round trip time of a sequence of challenges and their corresponding responses is measured to estimate the distance of the prover to the verifier. The prover's claim is accepted if the estimated distance is below a distance bound $\mathcal{D}$. The prover must immediately respond to a received challenge, otherwise their distance estimation will be enlarged. To allow timely response, the prover pre-computes a *challenge-response table* using their secret key and nonces that are exchanged during the initialization phase of the protocol. This reduces the response calculation to a simple table lookup. Participants closer than $\mathcal{D}$ to the verifier are called *close-by* participants, and those

W. Susilo and G. Yang (Eds.): ACISP 2018, LNCS 10946, pp. 598–616, 2018.
https://doi.org/10.1007/978-3-319-93638-3_34

who are farther than $\mathcal{D}$, are called as *far-away* participants. Widely considered attacks against public key DB protocols are;

(A1) *Distance-Fraud* [10]*;* where a dishonest far-away prover tries to be accepted in the protocol.

(A2) *Mafia-Fraud (MF)* [16]*;* a close-by actor tries to use the communications of a far-away honest prover to succeed in the protocol. A special case of this attack where the far-away prover is not active, is impersonation attack [5].

(A3) *Terrorist-Fraud (TF)* [16]*;* a dishonest far-away prover colludes with a close-by actor, in order to succeed in the protocol. In *original TF-resistance* definition, it is assumed that the prover does not leak their secret key to the actor. In *recent TF-resistance* [24] however, the key leakage is allowed, but success of the TF attack requires negligible improvement in future impersonation attacks by the actor.

Anonymous DB protocols prove that the distance of a registered user is less than the prescribed bound without revealing the prover's identity. Security of anonymous DB protocols has been formalized [4,6,11] against DF, MF and TF. These models have subtle differences in defining TF attack which is the strongest attack against DB protocols. In all these models, that we call *single-user* model, an attack involves at most a single corrupted registered user (MF attack involves outsiders only), possibly helped by an actor (non-registered user).

Our Contributions: We introduce two new attacks, propose a model that captures these attacks and construct a protocol with provable security in this model.

Attacks. In the first attack a malicious prover uses a *directional antenna* with a narrow beam to aim messages towards the verifier. In Sect. 3.1 we show that using directional antennas by malicious provers can break all existing anonymous DB protocols. The use of directional antennas in consumer devices has grown tremendously in recent years [1] and so the attack poses a realistic threat to these systems.

The second attack considers collusion of multiple registered users. These attacks are not applicable to protocols in which users secret keys are independent of each other and a protocol transcript can be linked to the corresponding user's secret key. In such settings combining protocol transcripts of multiple users would not be helpful to the attackers. In anonymous DB protocols however, users' private keys are generated using a master key and depending on the protocol design, combining protocol transcripts of multiple users help in generating a new valid transcript and so a successful attack. In Sect. 3.2 we show that collusion TF attack can be used to subvert traceability function of an anonymous DB protocol. Traceability is an integral part of anonymous DB protocols that ensures user accountability by allowing to "open" a transcript and identify the user, if required. In this attack, a close-by user can interact with the verifier to get accepted, while using credentials of a far-away user, and so during the opening phase a far-away user (who can reject the opening results) be identified.

Model. We propose a formal model that captures the above two new classes of attacks. Our formalization uses a cryptographic approach and models an anonymous DB protocol as a cryptographic identification protocol [15] where the prover, in addition to proving their cryptographic credentials, prove that they are within a distance bound from the verifier. We formalize anonymity in terms of the prover's indistinguishability from protocol transcript.

Construction. We construct an anonymous DB protocol and prove its security in our proposed model. This scheme is a modular construction that adds anonymity and security in the new model to a public-key DB protocol with provable security in the single-user DBID model (See Sect. 5), by using an anonymous group identification with revocable anonymity. The public key DB protocol in our construction is `ProProx` [25], whose security in the single-user `DBID` model was proven in [2]. The group identification uses Goldwasser-Micali cryptosystem [19] to hide the user's identity information

Paper Organization. Section 2 presents preliminaries. Section 3.1 proposes a new directional TF attack that breaks all existing anonymous DB protocols. Section 3.2 proposes collusion DB attacks that extend traditional DB attacks to include multiple users. Section 4 presents our model, Sect. 5 gives the construction and Sect. 6 concludes the paper.

2 Preliminaries

In this section we introduce the primitives that are used in our model and constructions.

A **Σ-protocol** is a 3-message cryptographic protocol between a prover P and a verifier V, that allows P to prove validity of a statement to V. The two parties have a common input y, and P has a private input x for which the relation $\mathcal{R}(x, y)$ holds. `Σ-protocol` is used in many important cryptographic systems [14,18,20,21,23].

Definition 1 (`Σ-protocol`)**.** *Prover P and verifier V execute three algorithms* (`Commit`, `Response`, `Check`) *using inputs (x, y) and (y), respectively. x is private and y is public.*

Let $\mathbb{C}$, $\mathbb{H}$ and $\mathbb{R}$ denote three sets: $\mathbb{C}$ is the set of possible inputs that is chosen by the prover; $\mathbb{H}$ is the set of possible challenges chosen by the verifier; and $\mathbb{R}$ is the set of possible responses of the prover. The steps of the protocol are as follows:

1. *P randomly chooses $a \in \mathbb{C}$ and computes the commitment $A = \texttt{Commit}(a)$. P sends A to V.*
2. *Challenge/Response is a pair of messages:*
   (a) V randomly chooses a challenge $c \in \mathbb{H}$ and sends it to P,
   (b) P computes $r = \texttt{Response}(x, a, c) \in \mathbb{R}$, and sends it to V,
3. *V calculates $ret = \texttt{Check}(y, c, r, A)$, where $ret \in \{accept, reject\}$.*

At the end of the protocol, V outputs $Out_V = 1$ *if* $ret = accept$, *and* $Out_V = 0$ *if* $ret = reject$.

Here we define a more general form of Σ-`protocols`, called Σ*-`protocols`, in which the verifier consecutively sends multiple challenges, each after (except for the first challenge) receiving the response to the previous challenges.

Definition 2 **(Σ*-`protocol`).** *A prover P and verifier V run the following*

Let $\mathbb{C}$, $\mathbb{H}$ *and* $\mathbb{R}$ *denote three sets defined as follows.* $\mathbb{C}$ *is the set of possible input that is chosen by the prover;* $\mathbb{H}$ *is the set of possible challenges chosen by the verifier; and* $\mathbb{R}$ *is the set of possible responses of the prover. The steps of the protocol are as follows:*

1. *P randomly chooses* $a \in \mathbb{C}$, *computes the commitment* $A = \texttt{Commit}(a)$, *and sends A to V.*
2. *Challenge and Response messages that are defined as follows:*
   (a) *V randomly chooses a challenge* $c \in \mathbb{H}$ *and sends it to P,*
   (b) *P computes* $r = \texttt{Response}(x, a, c, \overline{c}) \in \mathbb{R}$, *where* $\overline{c}$ *is the list of previous challenges before c, and sends it to V,*

   Steps 2(a) and 2(b) may be repeated a number of times.
3. *V calculates* $ret = \texttt{Check}(y, [c], [r], A)$, *where* $ret \in \{accept, reject\}$ *and* $[c]$ *and* $[r]$ *are lists of all challenges and responses, respectively.*

At the end of the protocol, V outputs $Out_V = 1$ *if* $ret = accept$, *and* $Out_V = 0$ *otherwise.*

In a cryptographic **identification scheme** (`ID`), a prover $\mathcal{P}$ convinces a verifier $\mathcal{V}$ that they know a *witness* x related to a public value y. A *witness* satisfies a relation $\mathcal{R}(x, y)$ with the public value y.

The scheme is specified by the tuple $\texttt{ID} = (\texttt{KeyGen}, \Pi)$. The key generation algorithm $(x, y) \leftarrow \texttt{KetGen}(1^\lambda)$ is a PPT (probabilistic polynomial time) algorithm that takes the security parameter λ and generates a key pair (x, y). Π is an interactive protocol between the prover and the verifier, each an interactive PPT algorithm. The prover $P(x, y)$ and the verifier $V(y)$ take the values (x, y) and y respectively, as input. At the end of the protocol, the verifier returns *accept* or *reject*. The protocol $\Pi = (\texttt{Commit}, \texttt{Response}, \texttt{Check})$ consists of two PPT algorithms `Commit` and `Response`, and a function `Check`, as defined in Definition 1.

An `ID` scheme is correct if the `Check` function outputs *accept* if $\mathcal{R}(x, y)$ holds, and *reject* otherwise. An `ID` scheme is secure if an adversary with access to a set of valid transcripts $\mathcal{T} = \{(A, [c], [r])\}$, cannot generate a valid transcript $(A', [c'], [r'])$ for a c' that has not appeared in $\mathcal{T}$. Note that a transcript $(A, [c], [r])$ is valid according to public-key y, if the function $\texttt{Check}(y, [c], [r], A)$ returns *accept*.

2.1 DBID

`DBID` model [2] is a security model for public-key DB protocols, that is based on cryptographic identification schemes.

Definition 3 (DBID). *Let* $\lambda \in \mathbb{N}$ *denote the security parameter. A distance-bounding identification (*DBID*) is a tuple* $(\mathbb{X}, \mathbb{Y}, \mathbb{S}, \mathbb{P}, \mathcal{D}, p_{noise}, \texttt{Init}, \texttt{KeyGen}, \Pi, \texttt{Revoke})$, *where;*

(I) $\mathbb{X}$ *and* $\mathbb{Y}$ *are sets of possible master and public keys of the system, chosen based on the security parameter* λ*. The system's master key* $msk \in \mathbb{X}$*, and the public key* $gpk \in \mathbb{Y}$ *are generated using* $(msk, gpk) \leftarrow \texttt{Init}(1^\lambda)$ *algorithm;*
(II) $\mathbb{S}$ *and* $\mathbb{P}$ *are sets of possible (private, public) key pairs of users, with their sizes chosen according to the security parameter* λ*. A (private, public) key pair is generated using* $(sk, pk) \leftarrow \texttt{KeyGen}(1^\lambda, msk, gpk)$ *algorithm;*
(III) Π *is a* Σ^**-protocol (Definition 2) between a prover* $P(sk, pk)$ *and the verifier* $V(pk)$*, that convinces the verifier that the prover is located within the distance bound* $\mathcal{D} \in \mathbb{R}$ *of the verifier.*
(IV) The transmitted bits of a fast challenge and response round in Π *protocol are affected by noise, where* $p_{noise} \in [0, 1]$ *is the probability of a bit flip on each fast challenge-response message.*
(V) $\texttt{Revoke}(msk, gpk, i)$ *is an algorithm that removes the corresponding user* u_i *from the system and updates the group public key accordingly.*

At the end of the protocol Π*,* V *outputs* $Out_V = 1$ *if they accept, or 0 if they reject.*

In this model, the initialization (Init) and key generation (KeyGen) are run by a trusted party. The *distance bounding protocol* of a DBID scheme is denoted by DBID.Π, and in each run involves a single active user that is represented by multiple provers, sharing the same secret key. For honest users, only a single prover is active in a protocol run. For corrupted users, no restriction on the number of active provers exists.

In our construction we consider DBID schemes for which public and private keys of the users are generated using Goldwasser-Micali (probabilistic) [19] encryption system. We refer to DBID schemes with this property as DBID$^{\texttt{GM}}$. An example of DBID$^{\texttt{GM}}$ scheme is ProProx [25].

Security properties of DBID schemes are:

- **Completeness:** in the absence of an adversary, the verifier accepts an execution of Π with high probability when the prover is within the distance bound.
- **Soundness:** the success chance of a close-by adversary who is trying to take advantage of sessions of a far-away honest prover or a close-by inactive prover, is negligible.
- **DF resistance:** the verifier rejects an execution of Π with high probability if there is no close-by prover.
- **TF resistance:** if a dishonest far-away prover and a close-by helper succeeds in an execution of Π, then the helper can impersonate the prover in future Π executions with high probability.

We omit the formal definition of these properties (that have appeared in [2]) and present them in an expanded form in the formalization of anonymous DB in Sect. 4.

3 New Attacks on Anonymous DB Protocols

Here two new classes of attacks on anonymous DB protocols are presented.

3.1 Directional TF Attack on Anonymous DB

DB protocols consist of two *slow phases*, one during protocol initialization and one during the final verification, and a *fast challenge-response phase* that is used for time (and so distance) measurement. By using a directional antenna, a malicious prover can target the messages such that the initialization messages are only received by the verifier and not the helper. This strategy allows the prover to send the whole challenge and response table of a protocol run to the helper, and so take advantage of the helper's location, without leaking their complete long term key. Thus the prover can succeed in TF attack. Note that the prover is not leaking its identity to the helper. Figure 1 shows a directional TF, where the helper $\mathcal{H}$ does not receive the initialization phase messages that are sent by a malicious prover P^* to V because of the use of a directional antenna (orange ribbon in Fig. 1). Before starting of the fast-phase, P^* sends the fast challenge-response table to $\mathcal{H}$, and make $\mathcal{H}$ in-charge of responding to the fast-phase challenges.

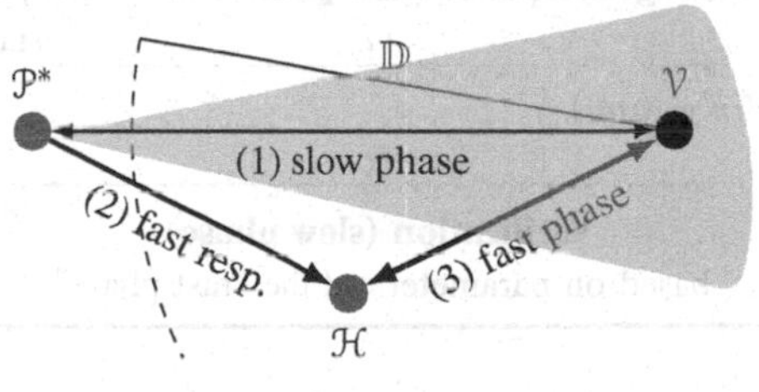

Fig. 1. Directional TF (Color figure online)

Now we show a specific directional TF attack against SPADE [11] in this section, and propose similar attacks against PDB [4] and TREAD [6] in the full version paper [3]. SPADE [11] is an anonymous DB system that use a group signature $GSign_{sk_p}()$ to register users in an authorized group. A registered user can use their credentials to participate in the protocol without leaking their identity, hence ensuring anonymity. Figure 2 presents a summary of the Π distance bounding protocol of SPADE scheme.

Attack. P sends to V the slow phase message e to V using directional antenna. Before starting the fast phase, P sends the fast challenge-response table, $\forall i \in \{1, ..., \lambda\} : (a_i, a_i \oplus N_{\mathcal{P}i} \oplus m_i)$, to $\mathcal{H}$ in order to make it capable of responding V's challenges correctly. The collusion of P and $\mathcal{H}$ makes V to accept (*i.e.*, $Out_V = 1$) and this is without P sending to $\mathcal{H}$ any information that is dependent on the secret key of P (*i.e.*, $sk_{\mathcal{P}}$). The secret key of P is required for generation of correct message e, which will not be known by $\mathcal{H}$.

[3, Lemma 2] shows that the fast challenge-response table does not leak any information about the prover's long-term secret $sk_{\mathcal{P}}$. (Intuitively this is because the table is generated using random values that are independent of $sk_{\mathcal{P}}$.) Since the long term key is not leaked, the helper's success chance in a future impersonation attack will not improve, which is required for a successful TF attack (See Property 4).

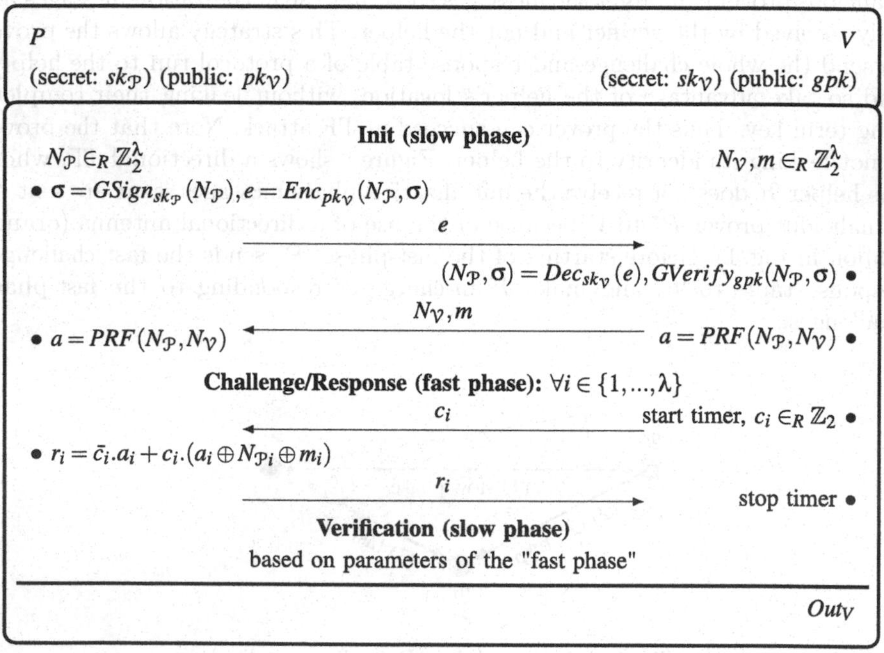

Fig. 2. Π protocol of SPADE scheme. $(GSign_{sk}, GVerify_{pk})$ is a group signature scheme. (Enc_{pk}, Dec_{sk}) is a secure public-key encryption scheme. $PRF : \mathbb{Z}_2^{\lambda} \times \mathbb{Z}_2^{\lambda} \to \mathbb{Z}_2^{\lambda}$ is a pseudo-random function. λ is the security parameter. $N_{\mathcal{P}}$ and $(N_{\mathcal{V}}, m)$ are nonce values of prover and verifier, (c_i, r_i) is a pair of challenge and response.

In all existing anonymous DB protocols, the fast challenge-response table does not determine the prover's credential with overwhelming probability. Directional TF attack allows the prover to limit the view of helper to the fast challenge-response table and so TF succeeds because the leaked information to the helper, does not allow the helper to succeed in a future attack individually, as required by the definition of TF attacks (see Property 4).

3.2 Collusion TF on Anonymous DB

In the following, it will be shown that in anonymous DB protocols collusion of multiple registered users must be considered also. In traditional DB protocol attacks, only the collusion of a single registered user and an actor (non-registered user) is considered. There is no need to consider collusion of multiple users in traditional DB as their secret keys are assumed to be independent and protocol transcript are linkable to a user.

We consider two types of *collusion TF* shown in Fig. 3a and b. In *collusion TF* type 1 attack, both colluding users are outside the bound and use a helper that is inside the bound. In *collusion TF* type 2, the helper can be a prover of a user, that tries to help the far-away provers of another user. Note that in type 2 attack there is a close-by prover $\mathcal{P}_2^*$ who can succeed in the protocol by themselves. However by colluding with $\mathcal{P}_1^*$, can succeed without being traced! (This attack also works in public-key DB protocols such as [12], where users choose their own private-keys, and so can collude and choose related keys that leads to the success of the above attack.)

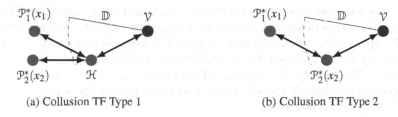

(a) Collusion TF Type 1 (b) Collusion TF Type 2

Fig. 3. Collusion TF attacks

Both collusions can be used to increase the success chance of the attacker. Here we show how Collusion TF Type 2 (Fig. 3b) can break a protocol that is secure against TF in a single-user security model. As noted in Sect. 3.1, all existing anonymous DB protocols are vulnerable to single-user TF attack (directional TF) and so to show that protection against single-user TF attack does not imply security against collusion TF attack, we first modify SPADE protocol to make it (intuitively) secure against single-user TF attacks (given in Sect. 3.1), and then describe how a multi-user collusion TF attack succeeds against the modified protocol.

SPADE* *(modified* SPADE*).* We modify the challenge-response table of SPADE protocol to the following: $r_i = \begin{cases} a_i & \text{if } c_i = 0 \\ a_i \oplus x_i & \text{if } c_i = 1 \end{cases}$, where x is part of the prover secret-key that is chosen independent of $sk_{\mathcal{P}}$, and $|x| = \lambda$. The verification phase will also be revised to accommodate this change and allow the verifier can check if the correct parameters are used in the challenge-response table.

The challenge-response table of SPADE* contains the secret-key of the prover, which makes the protocol intuitively secure against single-user TF attacks (let's assume that). Here if the whole table is leaked to the helper, the helper can learn the secret key of the (malicious) prover by XORing the two response bits of each challenge. Now we propose a collusion TF Type 2 (Fig. 3b) against SPADE*;

Collusion TF Type 2 Attack : First, $\mathcal{P}_1^*(x_1)$ runs the "Initialization" phase of SPADE* with the verifier from outside the distance bound, and sends a to $\mathcal{P}_2^*(x_2)$. Then $\mathcal{P}_2^*(x_2)$ runs the challenge-response and verification phase with the verifier from inside the distance bound with its own credentials (x_2).

The intuition for the attack is that the challenge-response table is not linked to the long-term secret key of the user (group signature key). The verifier sees σ which is the group signature of the far-away prover $\mathcal{P}_1^*$, but runs the distance bounding phase using a key that is not related to group signature key. Thus the tracing authority will link the session to x_1, which is a violation of TF-resistance (Property 4).

4 Anonymous DB Model

Firstly the settings of the system are defined, *i.e.*, entities and how they communicate, protocol and view of an entity, adversary and their capability. Then we provide a definition of anonymous distance-bounding (AnonDB) and also describe AnonDB experiment, which captures an AnonDB scheme in execution. Finally, we formalize six security properties (*Completeness*, *MiM-resistance*, *DF-resistance*, *Soundness*, *Traceability*, *Anonymity*) of anonymous distance-bounding systems based on a game (AnonDB game), which is an AnonDB experiment played between a challenger and an adversary.

Entities. There are m users in the system $\mathcal{U} = \{u_1, \ldots, u_m\}$. Each user in the system can have multiple provers, which captures the practical scenario of a single person having multiple devices. We denote the list of provers for a user u_i as $\mathcal{P}^i$. Thus, there are m lists of provers forming the prover set $\mathcal{P} = \{\mathcal{P}^1, \ldots, \mathcal{P}^m\}$.

A trusted group manger generates the public parameters of the system, registers users and issues a unique group membership certificate to each user. A user u_i $(1 \leq i \leq m)$ is identifiable by their certificate. The certificate, that must be kept secret, forms the secret input of the user in proving their membership in the group. The certificate of user u_i is shared by all provers of the list $\mathcal{P}^i$.

There are three types of *participants* in the system: provers ($\mathcal{P}$), verifiers ($\mathcal{V}$) (a singleton set), and actors ($\mathcal{H}$), called *helpers in TF attack.* $\mathcal{V}$ and $\mathcal{H}$ have access to only the public parameters of the system. Each participant has a location $loc = (x, y) \in \mathbb{R} \times \mathbb{R}$, that is an element of a metric space equipped with Euclidean distance, and is fixed during the protocol. The distance function $d(loc_1, loc_2)$ returns the distance between any two locations. Message travel time between locations loc_1 and loc_2 is $\frac{d(loc_1, loc_2)}{\mathcal{L}}$, where $\mathcal{L}$ is the speed of light. A bit sent over the channel may flip with probability p_{noise} $(0 \leq p_{noise} \leq 1)$. Participants, if located within a predefined distance bound $\mathcal{D}$ from $\mathcal{V}$, are called *close-by* participants, otherwise they are called *far-away* participants.

Communication Structure. Each participant is equipped with a directional and an omni-directional antennas. Having directional antennas enables them to choose the angle of the transmission beam such that only the intended participants receive them.

View. The view of an entity at any point (in time) of a protocol consists of: all the inputs of the entity (including random coin tosses) and the set of messages received by that entity up to that point. Any instance of receiving message is called an *event*. $View_x^\Gamma(e)$ is a random variable that denotes the view of an entity x right after the event e in protocol Γ. $View_x^\Gamma$ denotes the view of x at the end of the protocol Γ, *i.e.*, $View_x^\Gamma = View_x^\Gamma(e_{last})$ where e_{last} is the last event in Γ.

Adversary. An adversary can corrupt any subset of participants $\mathcal{X}^* \subset \mathcal{P} \cup \mathcal{V} \cup \mathcal{H}$. Corrupting one prover from a prover subset (*e.g.*, $x \in \mathcal{P}^j$) effectively corrupts the whole subset, since all members of that subset share the same certificate (of user u_j). Provers of uncorrupted subset follow the protocol, and only one prover from the subset executes the protocol at a time. Provers of corrupted subset are not restricted to do this. For each security property, the adversary has certain goals, which is reflected as restrictions of $\mathcal{X}^*$; in *Completeness* $\mathcal{X}^* = \emptyset$, in *Soundness* $\mathcal{X}^* \subseteq \mathcal{H}$, in *DF-resistance* $\mathcal{X}^* \subseteq \mathcal{P}$, in *TF-resistance* and *Traceability* $\mathcal{X}^* \subseteq \mathcal{P} \cup \mathcal{H}$, and in *Anonymity* $\mathcal{X}^* \subseteq \mathcal{V} \cup \mathcal{H}$. Below the approach of [2] is used to define AnonDB scheme.

Definition 4 (Anonymous Distance-Bounding Scheme). *For a security parameter λ, an anonymous distance-bounding (*AnonDB*) scheme is defined by a tuple $(\mathbb{X}, \mathbb{Y}, \mathbb{S}, \mathcal{D}, p_{noise}, \texttt{Init}, \texttt{CertGen}, \texttt{CertVer}, \Pi, \texttt{Open})$, where; $\mathbb{X}$, $\mathbb{Y}$ and $\mathbb{S}$ are sets of possible system master keys, group public-keys and user membership certificates, respectively. $\texttt{Init}(1^\lambda)$ is the function that the group manager uses to generate the system master key msk, and the group public-key gpk. $\texttt{CertGen}(1^\lambda, msk, gpk, i)$ function generates a user membership certificate s_i, and $\texttt{CertVer}(s_i, gpk)$ validates a user's certificate with respect to the group public-key. Π is a DB protocol between prover $P(s_i, gpk)$ and verifier $V(gpk)$, in which V verifies that a group member is located within the distance bound $\mathcal{D}$ to the verifier. The transmitted bits of a fast challenge-response round is affected by noise where $p_{noise} \in [0, 1]$ is the probability of a bit flip on each fast challenge-response message. $\texttt{Open}(msk, View_V^\Pi)$ is an algorithm that identifies the user that is involved in the Π protocol, using view of the verifier.*

Adversary's capability is modeled as their access to queries presented to the challenger. The security properties of an anonymous DB protocol are based on a game (AnonDB Game) between a challenger and an adversary. Note that provers have access to directional antenna (to captures the directional attack introduced in Sect. 3.1), and presence of multiple, possibly colluding users (with different secret keys) in the system (to capture multiple user collusion attack introduced in Sect. 3.2). We assume the existence of a system clock that assigns time to events. $exLen(\Gamma)$ denotes the execution length of a protocol Γ.

Definition 5 (AnonDB Game). *An* AnonDB *game between a challenger and adversary is an* AnonDB *experiment that is defined by a tuple* (AnonDB, $\mathcal{U}, \mathcal{P}, \mathcal{V}, \mathcal{H}$, CorruptParties) *where* AnonDB *is an anonymous distance-bounding scheme as defined in Definition 4.* $\mathcal{U}, \mathcal{P}, \mathcal{V}$ *and* $\mathcal{H}$ *are the sets of users, provers, verifiers and actors, that are determined through interaction of the challenger and the adversary.* CorruptParties(Q) *is a query that allows the adversary to plan their attack. Q is a set of participants, that may exist in the system or be introduced by the adversary. In more details:*

Initialize: *Challenger runs* (msk/gpk) $\leftarrow$ AnonDB.Init(1^λ) *and publishes gpk. Note that the execution codes of honest prover and verifier are known by the challenger and the adversary at this point, and referred as* AnonDB.$\Pi.P$ *and* AnonDB.$\Pi.V$ *respectively.*

Generate Players: *The sets* ($\mathcal{U}, \mathcal{V}, \mathcal{P}, \mathcal{H}$) *are formed through the interaction of the challenger and the adversary:*

(1) $\mathcal{V} = \{v\}$, *where* $v.Loc = loc_0$, $v.Code =$ AnonDB.$\Pi.V$, $v.St = 0$, *and* $v.Corr = false$.
$\mathcal{U} = \{u_j\}_{j=\{1,\ldots,m\}}$, *where* $u_j.Cert$ *is generated by* AnonDB.CertGen ($1^\lambda, msk, gpk, j$) *function.*
$\mathcal{P} = \cup_{j=1}^{m} \mathcal{P}^j$, *where* $\mathcal{P}^j$ *is created as the prover subset of* $u_j \in \mathcal{U}$. *For all* $p \in \mathcal{P}^j_{\{j=1\ldots m\}}$ *assigns their attributes: p.Loc is set arbitrarily,* $p.Code =$ AnonDB.$\Pi.P$, *p.St is set arbitrarily such that there is no overlap in the execution time of the provers in* $\mathcal{P}^j$, $p.Corr = false$, *and secret-key* $p.Key = u_j.Cert$.
$\mathcal{H} = \emptyset$.

(2) *The challenger sends the attributes* ($x.Loc, x.Code, x.St$) *for all* $x \in \mathcal{X} = \mathcal{P} \cup \mathcal{V} \cup \mathcal{H}$, *along with all prover subsets* $\mathcal{P}^j \in \mathcal{P}$ *to the adversary. The size of the set* $\mathcal{X}$ *is n.*

(3) *The adversary generates* CorruptParties(Q) *query and sends to the challenger. The challenger sends the secret information of the corrupted participants in Q to the adversary and their behavior (Code, Location and Start Time) is assigned according to the adversary instruction and their corruption flag is set to True. For all values of* $j = 1 \ldots m$, *if any prover* $p \in \mathcal{P}^j$ *gets corrupted, then all provers in* $\mathcal{P}^j$ *get corrupted too.*

Run: *Challenger activates all participants* $x \in \mathcal{X} = \mathcal{P} \cup \mathcal{V} \cup \mathcal{H}$ *at time x.St for execution of x.Code. The game ends when the last participant's code completes its execution.*

The properties for anonymous distance-bounding protocols are defined based on the AnonDB Game. Conditions to win the game however varies for property.

Property 1 (AnonDB **Completeness**). *Consider an* AnonDB *scheme and an* AnonDB *game when* $Q = \emptyset$ *in the* CorruptParties(Q) *query and the set* $\mathcal{P}$ *is not empty.*

The AnonDB *scheme is (τ, δ)-complete for $0 \leq \tau, \delta \leq 1$, if the verifier returns $Out_V = 1$ with probability at least $1 - \delta$, under the following assumptions: the fast challenge-response rounds are independently affected by noise and at least τ portion of them are noiseless, and $\tau > 1 - p_{noise} - \varepsilon$ for some constant $\varepsilon > 0$.*

Property 2 (**AnonDB Soundness**). *Consider an* AnonDB *scheme and an* AnonDB *game with the following restrictions: $\forall p$ in the nonempty set $\mathcal{P}$, and v as the only member of $\mathcal{V}$, we have $d(p.Loc, v.Loc) >$* AnonDB.$\mathcal{D}$*, and in the* CorruptParties(Q) *query we have $q_i.type = actor$ for all $q_i \in Q$. The* AnonDB *scheme is γ-sound if the probability of the verifier outputting $Out_V = 1$ is at most γ.*

This general definition captures *relay attack* [10], *mafia-fraud* [16], *impersonation attack* [5], and *strong-impersonation* [2].

- *relay attack* [10] happens when the MiM attacker only relays the messages between the honest verifier and a far-away honest prover. The MiM attacker tries to convince the verifier that the prover is located close to the verifier. This attack is achieved by adding extra restrictions on the adversary of Property 2 as follows:
  $\Rightarrow \forall q_i \in Q$ we have $q_i.code =$ "relay messages".
- *mafia-fraud* [16] is when there is an honest verifier, an honest far-away prover, and a close-by MiM attacker who tries to convince the verifier that the prover is located close to the verifier. The attacker listens to the legitimate communications for a while, before running the attack as the learning phase. This attack corresponds to adding extra restrictions on the adversary in Property 2 as follows:
  $\Rightarrow$ the set of provers consists of only one prover subset, *i.e.*, $\mathcal{P} = \mathcal{P}^1$, and
  $\Rightarrow \forall q_i \in Q$ we have $d(q_i.location, v.Loc) \leq$ AnonDB.$\mathcal{D}$ for $v \in \mathcal{V}$.
- *impersonation attack* [5] happens when there is an honest verifier and a single close-by attacker who tries to convince the verifier that the prover is located close to the verifier. The attacker can have a learning phase before running the attack. This attack can be achieved by adding extra restrictions on the adversary of Property 2 as follows:
  $\Rightarrow \mathcal{P}$ is nonempty, and
  $\Rightarrow \forall q_i \in Q$ we have $d(q_i.location, v.Loc) \leq$ AnonDB.$\mathcal{D}$ for $v \in \mathcal{V}$, and
  $\Rightarrow$ among all the successful AnonDB.Π protocols (Π^{succ} set) during the game, $\exists \pi \in \Pi^{succ}, \forall p \in \mathcal{P} : t = fshTime(\pi), t \notin [p.St, p.St + exLen(p.Code))$.
- *multi-user MF*: there is an honest verifier, multiple honest far-away provers, and a close-by MiM attacker who tries to convince the verifier that one of the provers is located close to the verifier. The attacker can have a learning phase before running the attack. The extra restrictions on the adversary in Property 2 is as follows:
  $\Rightarrow$ the set of provers consists of a least two prover subsets, *i.e.*, $\exists p_1, p_2 \in \mathcal{P} : p_1.Key \neq p_2.Key$, and
  $\Rightarrow \forall q_i \in Q$ we have $d(q_i.location, v.Loc) \leq$ AnonDB.$\mathcal{D}$ for $v \in \mathcal{V}$.

– *strong-impersonation* [2] happens when either *mafia-fraud* or *impersonation* happens. This attack can be achieved by adding extra restrictions on the adversary of Property 2 as follows:
  $\Rightarrow$ the set of provers consists of one prover subset, *i.e.*, $\mathcal{P} = \mathcal{P}^1$,
  $\Rightarrow$ $\forall q_i \in Q$ we have $d(q_i.location, v.Loc) \leq \texttt{AnonDB}.\mathcal{D}$ for $v \in \mathcal{V}$, and
  $\Rightarrow$ among all the successful $\texttt{AnonDB}.\Pi$ protocols (Π^{succ} set) during the game, at least one of the following conditions hold:
  (i) $\exists \pi \in \Pi^{succ}, \forall p \in \mathcal{P} : t = fshTime(\pi), t \notin [p.St, p.St + exLen(p.Code)]$
  (ii) $\exists p \in \mathcal{P}, \exists \pi \in \Pi^{succ}, v \in \mathcal{V} : t = fshTime(\pi), t \in [p.St, p.St + exLen(p.Code)] \wedge d(p.Loc, v.Loc) > \texttt{AnonDB}.\mathcal{D}$.

We consider two types of attacks by a dishonest prover: multi-user far-away dishonest provers (Property 3), and multi-user far-away dishonest provers with close-by helpers (Property 4).

Property 3 (AnonDB **Distance-Fraud**). *Consider an* AnonDB *scheme and an* AnonDB *game with the following restrictions:* $\forall p$ *in the nonempty set* $\mathcal{P}$, *and* v *as the only member of* $\mathcal{V}$, *we have* $d(p.Loc, v.Loc) > \texttt{AnonDB}.\mathcal{D}$, *and in the* CorruptParties(Q) *query,* $q_i.type = prover$ *and* $d(q_i.location, v.Loc) > \texttt{AnonDB}.\mathcal{D}$ *for all* $q_i \in Q$. *The* AnonDB *scheme is* α*-DF-resistant if, for any* $\texttt{AnonDB}.\Pi$ *protocol in such game, we have* $\Pr[Out_{\mathcal{V}} = 1] \leq \alpha$.

In the following TF-resistance of anonymous DB protocols is defined.

Property 4 (AnonDB **Terrorist-Fraud**). *Consider an* AnonDB *scheme and an* AnonDB *game with the following restrictions:* $\forall p$ *in the nonempty set* $\mathcal{P}$, *and* v *as the only member of* $\mathcal{V}$, *we have* $d(p.Loc, v.Loc) > \texttt{AnonDB}.\mathcal{D}$. *The corrupted parties are either prover or actor* $\forall q_i \in Q : q_i.type \in \{prover, actor\}$. *And at least for one value of* $j \in \{1 \ldots m\}$ *we have* $d(q_i.location, v.Loc) > \texttt{AnonDB}.\mathcal{D}$ *for all* $q_i \in Q \cap \mathcal{P}^j$.

The AnonDB *scheme is* μ*-TF-resistant, if the following holds about the above game: if the verifier returns* $Out_{\mathcal{V}} = 1$ *in the* Π *protocol of game* Γ *with non-negligible probability* κ *that is not traceable to any user with close-by provers (Property 6), then there is an impersonation attack (as an* AnonDB *game* Γ' *with honest verifier, no prover and one close-by actor) that takes the view of close-by participants of game* Γ *– excluding the verifier – as input, and makes the verifier return* $Out_{\mathcal{V}} = 1$ *with probability at least* $\kappa - \mu$ *in the* Π *protocol of* Γ' *game.*

Any directional message that is sent to the verifier from outside the distance bound, is not included in the input of the impersonator. Therefore any protocol that is secure in this property, is also secure against directional TF attacks. Note that this definition captures collusion TF (Fig. 3a and b). In anonymous DB, breaking traceability is the only target of the adversary in collusion TF Type 2.

The above attacks define security of the DB game. Now *anonymity* will be defined in terms of distinguishing advantage of adversary between two protocol sessions of two users.

Property 5 (AnonDB **Anonymity**). *Consider an* AnonDB *scheme and an* AnonDB *game with the following restrictions:* $\mathcal{P} = \{\mathcal{P}^1, \mathcal{P}^2\}$ *where the size of each of the sets* $\mathcal{P}^1$ *and* $\mathcal{P}^2$ *is equal to* $l > 0$*, and in the* CorruptParties(Q) *query,* $q_i.type \in \{verifier, actor\}$ *for all* $q_i \in Q$*. In this game, there are two subsets of honest provers of the same size, the adversary corrupts the verifier and adds a set of actors and sets their locations. Before activating the participants, the challenger randomly chooses* $b \in_R \{0,1\}^l$*, and deactivates the* i^{th} *prover in* $\mathcal{P}^{b[i]}$*, i.e.,* $\forall 1 \le i \le l : \mathcal{P}_i^{b[i]}.Code = \varnothing$*. At the end of game,* $\mathcal{A}$ *returns* $b' \in \{0,1\}^l$*. A protocol is* α*-anonymous if for any such experiment, for all values of* $i \in \{1,\dots,l\}$ *we have* $|\Pr[b[i] = b'[i]] - \frac{1}{2}| \le \alpha$*.*

Traceability is defined as a guarantee for the group manager to be able to identify the users from their protocol transcripts.

Property 6 (AnonDB **Traceability**). *Consider an* AnonDB *scheme and an* AnonDB *game with the following restrictions:* $\mathcal{P}$ *is nonempty, and in the* CorruptParties(Q) *query,* $q_i.type \in \{prover, actor\}$ *for all* $q_i \in Q$*. A protocol is called* γ*-traceable, if the success chance of the* AnonDB.*Open algorithm in identifying a user that has a prover in* AnonDB.Π *protocol, from the transcript that is seen by the verifier, is a least as high as the chance of verifier outputting* $Out_V = 1$ *in the* AnonDB.Π *protocol plus* γ*. i.e.,* $\Pr[identify\ user] \ge \gamma + \Pr[Out_V = 1]$*.*

5 AnonDB Construction: dbid2an$^{\mathtt{GM}}$

DBID [2] models security of a public-key DB protocol as a cryptographic identification protocol with the additional distance-bounding properties. Definition 3 formally describes DBID scheme. In our construction we consider DBID schemes for which public and private key of users are generated using Goldwasser-Micali (probabilistic) encryption [19] system, denoted as DBID$^{\mathtt{GM}}$. An example of such schemes is ProProx [25], which is proven secure in the model of DBID schemes (directional antenna and single user attacks) [2].

We refer to our AnonDB scheme as dbid2an$^{\mathtt{GM}}$ to emphasize conversion of a DBID scheme to an *anonymous* DBID. The DBID scheme has to use Goldwasser-Micali encryption system [19] for key generation. In dbid2an$^{\mathtt{GM}}$, a user is first enrolled in the system and is provided with a verifiable "membership" certificate. In addition to verifying the membership of a user, the certificate is used to generate a temporary public-key, which is later used in a public-key DBID protocol. At the end of a successful execution, verifier is convinced that a valid member of the group is within the given distance bound.

Recall (Definition 4) that for a security parameter λ, an anonymous distance-bounding (AnonDB) scheme is defined by a tuple $(\mathbb{X}, \mathbb{Y}, \mathbb{S}, \mathcal{D}, p_{noise}, \mathtt{Init}, \mathtt{CertGen}, \mathtt{CertVer}, \Pi, \mathtt{Revoke}, \mathtt{Open})$. For our proposed (AnonDB) scheme dbid2an$^{\mathtt{GM}}$, these operations are named as dbid2an$^{\mathtt{GM}}$.Init, dbid2an$^{\mathtt{GM}}$.CertGen, dbid2an$^{\mathtt{GM}}$.CertVer, dbid2an$^{\mathtt{GM}}$.Π, dbid2an$^{\mathtt{GM}}$.Revoke and dbid2an$^{\mathtt{GM}}$.Open.

In $\texttt{dbid2an}^{\texttt{GM}}.\texttt{CertGen}$, the group manager generates a membership certificate for a new user, and accumulates the certificates of all users to form a public commitment on them. Then the $\texttt{dbid2an}^{\texttt{GM}}.\Pi$ protocol takes place as below:

(i) a prover of the user u_l, $l = 1..m$, anonymously proves that it owns one of the accumulated certificates (according to the public accumulated commitment).
(ii) a temporary public-key is generated for the prover. The temporary public-key is generated using Goldwasser-Micali encryption, *i.e.*, we have $C[j] = Enc^{GM}(x_l[j], v_l[j])$ where for the $j = 1 \ldots \lambda$: $x_l[j]$ is certificate of the user, $v_l[j]$ is a random value chosen by the prover, and $C[j]$ is temporary public-key. In this paper $Enc^{GM}(.,.)$ is refereed as $\texttt{Commit}^{\texttt{GM}}(.,.)$ function. This temporary public-key generation is equivalent to the $\texttt{DBID}^{\texttt{GM}}.\texttt{KeyGen}$ function. After establishing the temporary public-key, the prover and the verifier run a $\texttt{DBID}^{\texttt{GM}}.\Pi$ protocol, where the prover uses (x_l, v_l) as input, and the verifier uses C as input.

In this scheme, a hash function H is used to make coins for $\texttt{Commit}^{\texttt{GM}}$. A deterministic commitment is defined by $Com_{H_e}(x, v) = (\texttt{Commit}^{\texttt{GM}}(x_1, H(x, 1).H(v, 1)^e), \ldots, \texttt{Commit}^{\texttt{GM}}(x_\lambda, H(x, \lambda).H(v, \lambda)^e), \texttt{Commit}^{\texttt{GM}}(v_1, H(v, 1)), \ldots, \texttt{Commit}^{\texttt{GM}}(v_\lambda, H(v, \lambda)))$ for $x, v \in \mathbb{Z}_2^\lambda$ and $\texttt{Commit}^{\texttt{GM}}(.,.)$ being Goldwasser-Micali encryption function. We assume $H(0, i) = 1$ for all values of i, and also assume that Com_{H_e} is a one-way function. The details of operations is as follows:

$\texttt{dbid2an}^{\texttt{GM}}.\texttt{Init}$: $(msk, gpk) \leftarrow \texttt{Init}(1^\lambda)$. The group manager initiates the system as follows:

- Initialize Goldwasser-Micali cryptosystem: $(p, q, N, \theta) \leftarrow \texttt{DBID}^{\texttt{GM}}.\texttt{Init}(1^\lambda)$ for λ bit security choose $N = p.q$ and θ as a quadratic residue modulo N. Private: (p, q) and Public: (N, θ).
- Initialize RSA cryptosystem for the same N: generate (d, e) such that $gcd(e, \phi(N)) = 1$ and $d = e^{-1}(\bmod \phi(N))$. d is private and e is public.

The group master key is $msk = (p, q, d, U)$ where U is the list of all user private-keys, initialized to $U = \emptyset$. The group public-key is $gpk = (e, N, \theta, \hat{y}, \tilde{y}, \Xi)$ where $\hat{y}$ is commitment accumulation vector of user private-keys, $\tilde{y}$ is signature vector of group manager on $\hat{y}$ and Ξ is the list of all user membership signatures. These are initialized to $\hat{y} = \tilde{y} = [0]_\lambda$ and $\Xi = \emptyset$.

$\texttt{dbid2an}^{\texttt{GM}}.\texttt{CertGen}$: $(s, msk', gpk') \leftarrow \texttt{CertGen}(msk, gpk)$. The group manager first generates a certificate $s = (x_l, \sigma_l)$ and sends it to a new user (x_l is called user private-key, and σ_l is called user membership signatures). And second, the system master key and public-key get updated accordingly, i.e., $msk \leftarrow msk'$ and $gpk \leftarrow gpk'$. The details is as follows, assuming $l - 1$ users have already joined the group: (a) randomly choose $x_l \in \mathbb{Z}_2^\lambda$, (b) $y_l = Com_{H_e}(x_l, 0)$, which is $\forall j \in \{1, \ldots, \lambda\} : y_l[j] = \texttt{Commit}^{\texttt{GM}}(x_l[j], H(x_l, j)) = \theta^{x_l[j]}.H(x_l, j)^2 \bmod N$ and $y_l[\lambda + j] = 1$. (c) Sign $\sigma_l[j] = (y_l[j])^d$. (d) $\forall j \in \{1, \ldots, \lambda\}$: (i) accumulate j^{th} bit of all user private-keys into a single bit $\hat{x}[j] = x_1[j] \oplus \ldots \oplus x_l[j]$, (ii) accumulate hash values $\hat{v}[j] = \prod_{1 \le i \le l} H(x_i, j)$, and (iii) commit to accumulated values

$\hat{y}[j] = \texttt{Commit}^{\text{GM}}(\hat{x}[j], \hat{v}[j]) = \theta^{\hat{x}[j]}\hat{v}[j]^2 \bmod N$. (e) Sign accumulated values $\tilde{y} = [\hat{y}[1]^{-d}, ..., \hat{y}[\lambda]^{-d}]$.

The updated group master key is $msk' = (p, q, d, U)$ where $U = \{x_1, ..., x_l\}$, and the updated group public-key is $gpk' = (e, N, \theta, \hat{y}, \tilde{y}, \Xi)$ where $\Xi = \{\sigma_1, ..., \sigma_l\}$. The certificate $s = (x_l, \sigma_l)$ is securely sent to the new user.

$\texttt{dbid2an}^{\text{GM}}$.$\texttt{CertVer}$: *accept*/*reject* $\leftarrow$ $\texttt{CertVer}(s, gpk)$. Upon receiving a certificate $s = (x, \sigma)$, the user can check its validity. By reading the group public-key $gpk = (e, N, \theta, \hat{y}, \tilde{y}, \Xi)$, the user calculates $y = Com_{H_e}(x, 0)$ and checks $y[j] \stackrel{?}{=} (\sigma[j])^e \bmod N$, for $j = \{1 \dots \lambda\}$.

$\texttt{dbid2an}^{\text{GM}}$.$\Pi$: *accept*/*reject* $\leftarrow \Pi\{P(s, gpk) \leftrightarrow V(gpk)\}$. When a prover ($\mathcal{P}_l$) of a registered user wants to run the $\texttt{AnonDB}$.Π protocol with the verifier, they will follow the protocol described in Fig. 4. The protocol consists of two main steps. The first step is a message from the prover to the verifier (y', π) that generates a temporary public-key (C), and then provides a non-interactive zero-knowledge (NIZK), which proves that the prover knows the privates related to the temporary public-key C. Note that in the non-interactive zero-knowledge proof, the verifier does not send any message to the prover [7,8]. The second step is running the $\texttt{DBID}^{\text{GM}}$.$\Pi$ protocol.

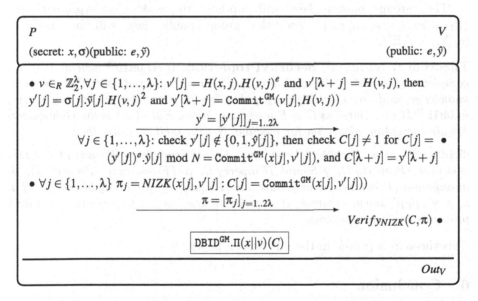

P	V
(secret: x, σ)(public: $e, \tilde{y}$)	(public: $e, \hat{y}$)

• $v \in_R \mathbb{Z}_2^{\lambda}, \forall j \in \{1, \dots, \lambda\}$: $v'[j] = H(x, j).H(v, j)^e$ and $v'[\lambda + j] = H(v, j)$, then $y'[j] = \sigma[j].\tilde{y}[j].H(v, j)^2$ and $y'[\lambda + j] = \texttt{Commit}^{\text{GM}}(v[j], H(v, j))$

$$\xrightarrow{y' = [y'[j]]_{j=1..2\lambda}}$$

$\forall j \in \{1, \dots, \lambda\}$: check $y'[j] \notin \{0, 1, \hat{y}[j]\}$, then check $C[j] \neq 1$ for $C[j] = (y'[j])^e.\hat{y}[j] \bmod N = \texttt{Commit}^{\text{GM}}(x[j], v'[j])$, and $C[\lambda + j] = y'[\lambda + j]$ •

• $\forall j \in \{1, \dots, \lambda\}$ $\pi_j = NIZK(x[j], v'[j] : C[j] = \texttt{Commit}^{\text{GM}}(x[j], v'[j]))$

$$\xrightarrow{\pi = [\pi_j]_{j=1..2\lambda}}$$

$Verify_{NIZK}(C, \pi)$ •

$\texttt{DBID}^{\text{GM}}.\Pi(x||v)(C)$

Out_V

Fig. 4. Π protocol in $\texttt{dbid2an}^{\text{GM}}$ scheme for the lth user. $C = Com_{H_e}(x, v)$.

$\texttt{dbid2an}^{\text{GM}}$.$\texttt{Open}$: $(l) \leftarrow \texttt{Open}(msk, transcript)$. The tracing authority who holds the group master key msk, uses the verifier's view of a successful run of Π with the prover $\mathcal{P}_l$, and returns index of the corresponding user in $\mathcal{U}$. The algorithm runs as follows, knowing that the group master key is $msk = (p, q, d, U = \{x_1, \dots, x_m\})$:

(1) Determine inverse of 2 as $\hat{2} = 2^{-1} (\bmod \phi(N))$, *i.e.*, $\hat{2}$ is the multiplicative inverse of 2 (mod $\phi(N)$). (2) $\hat{y}^d = [\hat{y}[1]^d, \ldots, \hat{y}[\lambda]^d]$. (3) Parse verifier's view of the protocol to obtain y' and C. (4) Return the first $i \in \{1, \ldots, m\}$ that all the following holds: $\forall j \in \{1, \ldots, \lambda\}$: $C[j] \stackrel{?}{=} \mathtt{Commit}^{\mathtt{GM}}(x_i[j], v[j])$, where $v[j] = H(x_i, j).v_j'^e$ for $v_j' = (v_j'^2)^{\hat{2}} \bmod N$ and $v_j'^2 = y'[j].\hat{y}[j]^d.(y_i[j])^{-d}$.

$\mathtt{dbid2an^{GM}.Revoke}$: $(msk', gpk') \leftarrow \mathtt{Revoke}(msk, gpk, l)$. In this operation, the entity holding the group master key msk, updates the group master key and the group public key such that the provers of lth user ($l \in \{1 \ldots m\}$) cannot succeed in any Π protocol anymore. The algorithm runs as follows, knowing that the group master key is $msk = (p, q, d, U = \{x_1, \ldots, x_m\})$ and the group public key is $gpk = (e, N, \theta, \hat{y}, \tilde{y}, \Xi)$ where $\Xi = \{\sigma_1, \ldots, \sigma_m\}$;
$\forall j \in \{1, \ldots, \lambda\}$:

- $\hat{x}[j] = x_1[j] \oplus \ldots x_{l-1}[j] \oplus x_{l+1}[j] \oplus \ldots \oplus x_m[j]$,
- $\hat{v}[j] = \prod_{i \in \{1,\ldots,m\} \setminus l} H(x_i, j)$,
- $\hat{y}'[j] = \mathtt{Commit}^{\mathtt{GM}}(\hat{x}[j]; \hat{v}[j]) = \theta^{\hat{x}[j]} \hat{v}[j]^2 \bmod N$, and
- $\tilde{y}'[j] = \hat{y}'[j]^{-d}$.

$\Xi' = \Xi \setminus \{\sigma_l\}$.

The group master key will update to $msk' = (p, q, d, U = \{x_1, \ldots, x_{l-1}, x_{l+1}, \ldots, x_m\})$ and the group public key will be $gpk' = (e, N, \hat{y}', \tilde{y}', \Xi')$.

Theorem 1. ($\mathtt{dbid2an^{GM}}$ **SecurityProperties**). *If (i)* $\mathtt{DBID^{GM}}$ *scheme is* (τ, δ)*-complete,* γ'*-sound,* θ*-DF-resistant,* μ'*-TF-resistant and* $\mathtt{DBID^{GM}}.\Pi$ *is zero-knowledge, and (ii) the temporary public-key* (C) *and the private key* (x_l, v_l) *of* $\mathtt{DBID^{GM}}.\Pi$ *are related as* $C = Enc_N(x_l, v_l)$ *where* $Enc_N(.,.)$ *is the Goldwasser-Micali encryption algorithm for modulus* N *with* λ*-bit security, then*

$\mathtt{dbid2an^{GM}}$ *is an* $\mathtt{AnonDB}$ *scheme that is* (τ, δ)*-complete (Property 1),* θ*-DF-resistant (Property 3),* γ*-Sound (Property 2),* μ*-TF-resistant (Property 4),* α*-anonymous (Property 5) and* γ*-traceable (Property 6), for negligible values of* α*,* δ*,* γ*,* γ'*,* μ*,* μ' *and* θ*, assuming that quadratic residuosity, factorization and RSA problems are hard problems.*

This theorem is proven in the full version paper [3].

6 Conclusion

We showed the security challenges that arise when identity information is not directly used in DB protocols, and proposed a new model that captures all known attacks, and a construction with provable security in this model. We introduced two attacks; directional attack that uses the capability of an attacker at the physical layer of communication, and collusion attack where multiple user collude to deceive the verifier. We showed that all existing anonymous DB schemes are vulnerable against the new attacks.

We proposed a construction that converts special types of DBID protocols to anonymous ones and gave an instance of this construction. The resulting protocol is the first anonymous DB that is resistant against all distance-bounding attacks, including the new ones proposed in this paper. Considering attackers that use physical layer properties of the communication system to compromise security of DB protocols is an interesting direction for future research.

References

1. Agiwal, M., Roy, A., Saxena, N.: Next generation 5G wireless networks: a comprehensive survey. IEEE Commun. Surv. Tutor. **18**, 1617–1655 (2016)
2. Ahmadi, A., Safavi-Naini, R.: Distance-bounding identification. In: Proceedings of the 3rd International Conference on Information Systems Security and Privacy: ICISSP, INSTICC, vol. 1, pp. 202–212. SciTePress (2017)
3. Ahmadi, A., Safavi-Naini, R., Akand, M.: Anonymous distance-bounding identification. Cryptology ePrint Archive, Report 2018/365 (2018). https://eprint.iacr.org/2018/365
4. Ahmadi, A., Safavi-Naini, R.: Privacy-preserving distance-bounding proof-of-knowledge. In: 16th ICICS (2014)
5. Avoine, G., Bingöl, M.A., Kardaş, S., Lauradoux, C., Martin, B.: A framework for analyzing RFID distance bounding protocols. J. Comput. Secur. **19**, 289–317 (2011)
6. Avoine, G., Bultel, X., Gambs, S., Gérault, D., Lafourcade, P., Onete, C., Robert, J.-M.: A terrorist-fraud resistant and extractor-free anonymous distance-bounding protocol. In: Proceedings of the 2017 ACM on Asia Conference on Computer and Communications Security, pp. 800–814. ACM (2017)
7. Bellare, M., Goldwasser, S.: New paradigms for digital signatures and message authentication based on non-interactive zero knowledge proofs. In: Brassard, G. (ed.) CRYPTO 1989. LNCS, vol. 435, pp. 194–211. Springer, New York (1990). https://doi.org/10.1007/0-387-34805-0_19
8. Blum, M., Feldman, P., Micali, S.: Non-interactive zero-knowledge and its applications. In: Proceedings of the Twentieth Annual ACM Symposium on Theory of Computing (1988)
9. Boureanu, I., Mitrokotsa, A., Vaudenay, S.: Secure and lightweight distance-bounding. In: Avoine, G., Kara, O. (eds.) LightSec 2013. LNCS, vol. 8162, pp. 97–113. Springer, Heidelberg (2013). https://doi.org/10.1007/978-3-642-40392-7_8
10. Brands, S., Chaum, D.: Distance-bounding protocols. In: Helleseth, T. (ed.) EUROCRYPT 1993. LNCS, vol. 765, pp. 344–359. Springer, Heidelberg (1994). https://doi.org/10.1007/3-540-48285-7_30
11. Bultel, X., Gambs, S., Gérault, D., Lafourcade, P., Onete, C., Robert, J.-M.: A prover-anonymous and terrorist-fraud resistant distance-bounding protocol. In: WiSec 2016 (2016)
12. Bussard, L., Bagga, W.: Distance-bounding proof of knowledge protocols to avoid terrorist fraud attacks. Technical report, Institut Eurecom, France (2004)
13. Cremers, C., Rasmussen, K.B., Schmidt, B., Capkun, S.: Distance hijacking attacks on distance bounding protocols. In: Security and Privacy (2012)
14. Damgård, I.: On Σ-protocols. Lecture Notes, Department for Computer Science, University of Aarhus (2002)

15. Damgård, I., Dupont, K., Pedersen, M.Ø.: Unclonable group identification. In: Vaudenay, S. (ed.) EUROCRYPT 2006. LNCS, vol. 4004, pp. 555–572. Springer, Heidelberg (2006). https://doi.org/10.1007/11761679_33
16. Desmedt, Y.: Major security problems with the ünforgeable(feige-)fiat-Shamir proofs of identity and how to overcome them. In: SECURICOM 1988 (1988)
17. Francillon, A., Danev, B., Capkun, S.: Relay attacks on passive keyless entry and start systems in modern cars. In: NDSS (2011)
18. Gennaro, R.: Multi-trapdoor commitments and their applications to proofs of knowledge secure under concurrent man-in-the-middle attacks. In: Franklin, M. (ed.) CRYPTO 2004. LNCS, vol. 3152, pp. 220–236. Springer, Heidelberg (2004). https://doi.org/10.1007/978-3-540-28628-8_14
19. Goldwasser, S., Micali, S.: Probabilistic encryption. J. Comput. Syst. Sci. **28**(2), 270–299 (1984)
20. Guillou, L.C., Quisquater, J.-J.: A practical zero-knowledge protocol fitted to security microprocessor minimizing both transmission and memory. In: Barstow, D., et al. (eds.) EUROCRYPT 1988. LNCS, vol. 330, pp. 123–128. Springer, Heidelberg (1988). https://doi.org/10.1007/3-540-45961-8_11
21. Kurosawa, K., Heng, S.-H.: The power of identification schemes. In: Yung, M., Dodis, Y., Kiayias, A., Malkin, T. (eds.) PKC 2006. LNCS, vol. 3958, pp. 364–377. Springer, Heidelberg (2006). https://doi.org/10.1007/11745853_24
22. Rasmussen, K.B., Capkun, S.: Realization of RF distance bounding. In: USENIX Security Symposium, pp. 389–402 (2010)
23. Schnorr, C.P.: Efficient signature generation by smart cards. J. Cryptol. **4**, 161–174 (1991)
24. Vaudenay, S.: On modeling terrorist frauds. In: Susilo, W., Reyhanitabar, R. (eds.) ProvSec 2013. LNCS, vol. 8209, pp. 1–20. Springer, Heidelberg (2013). https://doi.org/10.1007/978-3-642-41227-1_1
25. Vaudenay, S.: Proof of proximity of knowledge. IACR eprint, 695 (2014)

System and Network Security

Automatically Identifying Security Bug Reports via Multitype Features Analysis

Deqing Zou[1,2], Zhijun Deng[1], Zhen Li[1,3](✉), and Hai Jin[1]

[1] Services Computing Technology and System Lab,
Big Data Technology and System Lab, Cluster and Grid Computing Lab,
School of Computer Science and Technology,
Huazhong University of Science and Technology, Wuhan 430074, China
{deqingzou,elaine,lizhen_hust,hjin}@hust.edu.cn

[2] Shenzhen Huazhong University of Science and Technology Research Institute,
Shenzhen, China

[3] School of Cyber Security and Computer, Hebei University, Baoding, China

Abstract. Bug-tracking systems are widely used by software developers to manage bug reports. Since it is time-consuming and costly to fix all the bugs, developers usually pay more attention to the bugs with higher impact, such as security bugs (i.e., vulnerabilities) which can be exploited by malicious users to launch attacks and cause great damages. However, manually identifying security bug reports from millions of reports in bug-tracking systems is difficult and error-prone. Furthermore, existing automated identification approaches to security bug reports often incur many false negatives, causing a hidden danger to the computer system. To address this important problem, we present an automatic security bug reports identification model via multitype features analysis, dubbed Security Bug Report Identifier (SBRer). Specifically, we make use of multiple kinds of information contained in a bug report, including *meta features* and *textual features*, to automatically identify the security bug reports via natural language processing and machine learning techniques. The experimental results show that SBRer with imbalanced data processing can successfully identify the security bug reports with a much higher precision of 99.4% and recall of 79.9% compared to existing work.

Keywords: Security bug identification · Bug report
Natural language processing · Machine learning

1 Introduction

At present, bug-tracking systems, such as Bugzilla [3] and Jira [15], are widely used by software developers to manage bug reports which are submitted by different persons, including developers, test teams, and end-users. These bug reports are related to all aspects of software quality, such as performance, compatibility, stability, and security. Particularly, security bugs (i.e., vulnerabilities) are bugs which can be exploited by malicious users to launch attacks against the software

W. Susilo and G. Yang (Eds.): ACISP 2018, LNCS 10946, pp. 619–633, 2018.
https://doi.org/10.1007/978-3-319-93638-3_35

systems. These security bugs are conceptually different from non-security bugs which represent wrong or insufficient functionality rather than abusive functionality [4]. Since it is time-consuming and costly to fix all the bugs, developers usually devote more efforts to handle the bugs with higher impact, such as security bugs. However, existing bug-tracking systems, such as Bugzilla [3], cannot provide the ability to identify whether a bug report is related to a security bug or not (i.e., *Security Bug Reports* (SBRs) or *Non-Security Bug Reports* (NSBRs)). The bug reporters may fail to correctly identify the dangerous security bugs due to the lack of knowledge in the field of security. As a consequence, the majority of security bugs can not be disclosed to public, causing a hidden danger to the computer system.

A natural way to identify SBRs is to review bug reports manually. For example, Mozilla, the famous free software community, has established a special security bug group to handle Mozilla SBRs [21]. However, manually reviewing bug reports (usually tens of thousands) in a bug-tracking system requires a lot of professional knowledge, and it is very time-consuming and costly. Therefore, an alternate solution is to automatically identify SBRs in bug-tracking systems. There have been a lot of research focused on this problem [2,10,36,39,40]. However, existing solutions often miss many SBRs (i.e., incurring many false negatives). For example, the model proposed by Yang *et al.* [39] only correctly identified 39% to 56% of the high impact bug reports (e.g., SBRs) with four imbalanced learning strategies (based on 2,845 bug reports). One possible reason is that they only considered the limited features (e.g., some *textual features*), ignoring other rich information in a bug report.

In this paper, we address the following research problem: *Given a bug report, how can we automatically identify whether the report is related to a security bug or not (i.e., SBR or NSBR)?* This problem should be solved with high precision and high recall.

Our Contributions. The present paper makes the following contributions.

First, we propose an automatic security bug reports identification model via multitype features analysis, dubbed <u>S</u>ecurity <u>B</u>ug <u>R</u>eport Identifi<u>er</u> (SBRer). Specifically, we make use of multiple kinds of information contained in a bug report which involve the non-textual fields of a bug report (*meta features*, e.g., time, severity, and priority) and the textual content of a bug report (*textual features*, i.e., the text in summary fields). Based on these features, we build an identification model to automatically identify the SBRs via natural language processing and machine learning techniques.

Second, we construct a dataset with 23,608 bug reports in Bugzilla which are collected from three popular open source products (i.e., Firefox, Seamonkey, and Thunderbird), including 3,346 SBRs and 20,262 NSBRs submitted from April 1999 to July 2017.

Third, we conduct a series of experiments based on the dataset to evaluate the performance of SBRer. The experimental results show that SBRer with imbalanced data processing can successfully identify the SBRs with the precision of 99.4% and the recall of 79.9%. Specifically, compared to existing automated identification models, SBRer improves the recall by 22.9% while maintaining a high precision.

The rest of the paper is organized as follows. Section 2 reviews the related prior work. Section 3 describes the design of SBRer. Section 4 discusses the experimental evaluation of SBRer and the results. Section 5 concludes the present study with a discussion on future work.

2 Related Work

We first review the previous research on the identification of security bugs (i.e., vulnerabilities).

Identification of Security Bugs. At present, the existing SBRs identification approaches mainly make use of the textual content of reports. The text-based identification approaches include the following three steps. First, they need to obtain the textual content of the bug reports, including the summary, descriptions, and comments. Second, a feature space is generated based on the most important syntactical information extracted from the textual content via text mining techniques. Finally, feature vectors in the feature space are used to perform the final identification. Behl *et al.* [2] claimed to use *Term Frequency-Inverse Document Frequency* (TF-IDF) to identify and analyze SBRs with Naive Bayes. Gegick *et al.* [10] used an industrial text mining tool called SAS Text Miner [28] to create feature vectors and trained a statistical model to identify SBRs in the form of *Singular Value Decomposition* (SVD). Wijayasekara *et al.* [36] also used the text mining techniques to generate the feature vector of each bug report based on the frequent words to identify the *Hidden Impact Bugs* (HIBs). HIBs refer to the software bugs that have the security impact but have not yet been classified as vulnerabilities, similar to security bugs of this paper. Yang *et al.* [39] claimed to identify high impact bug reports (e.g., SBRs) with the help of *Term Frequency* (TF) and Naive Bayes. Furthermore, they compared the effectiveness of four imbalanced learning strategies on the datasets provided by Ohira *et al.* [23]. Zhou and Sharma [40] used commit messages and bug reports to automatically identify security issues via a series of classification algorithms.

Our work and the aforesaid research mainly focus on the identification of security bugs (i.e., vulnerabilities). However, the precision and recall of the above methods are far from ideal. On the one hand, the majority of these approaches do not consider the imbalanced phenomenon which has a strong impact on the classification [33]. On the other hand, only small part of the features of bug reports are involved in these methods, limiting the performance of classifiers.

There are a lot of other remotely related work which can be further divided to the following two aspects.

Discovery of New Vulnerabilities. This work mainly focuses on the identification of security bugs (i.e., vulnerabilities). There are many other approaches to discover new vulnerabilities, mainly including two categories, i.e., static analysis and dynamic analysis. Static analysis is an approach to find vulnerabilities by scanning source code without actually executing it [13,16,24,38]. Much work has been used in practice, such as Coverity [7], Flawfinder [9], and RATS [26]. However, these approaches are generally language-specific and usually incur many false positives in practice. Dynamic analysis aims to detect vulnerabilities by executing the source code with real inputs, such as dynamic taint tracking [8,29] and fuzz testing [11,31,34]. Dynamic analysis can address the deficiencies of static analysis (less false positives) by trying a wide range of possible inputs. However, it means more cost and leads to the path explosion problem.

Compared with these studies, SBRer takes advantage of information available in bug reports and performs the identification via machine learning techniques. It means SBRer is applicable to all programming languages and less costly.

Bug Reports Analysis. Our work aims to identify SBRs via analyzing bug reports. There are many other studies focus on solving problems in the whole bug life cycle via the analysis of information contained in bug reports. These problems mainly involve four aspects, i.e., bug triage [1,14], bug-fix time prediction [6,17], bug reports priority prediction [19,20,32], and duplicate bug reports detection [25,27,35].

Compared with these studies, the goal of SBRer focuses more on the identification of security bugs (i.e., vulnerabilities), so that experienced security experts can fix the security bugs timely and professionally.

3 Design of SBRer

Recall that we want to design a tool that can automatically identify whether the bug report is related to a security bug or not (i.e., SBR or NSBR), and explore what types of features can be used for effective identification. This should be achieved without manually inspecting each bug reports in a bug-tracking system and with high precision and high recall. In this section, we start with an overview of SBRer, and then elaborate its components in the following subsections.

3.1 Overview of SBRer

As highlighted in Fig. 1, SBRer has two phases: the learning (i.e., training) phase and the identification phase. In the learning phase, SBRer takes a set of labeled bug reports collected from bug-tracking systems as the input. Some of these bug reports are related to security bugs (i.e., SBRs), and the others are not (i.e., NSBRs). The output of the learning phase is the security bug reports identification model. In the identification phase, SBRer identifies the type of the target bug reports and outputs the identified SBRs.

The Learning Phase. As shown in Fig. 1, the learning phase has three steps.

- **Step 1: Feature extraction from training bug reports.** Features are multiple quantifiable signatures that can be used to distinguish the type of a bug report. Two types of features, i.e., *meta features* and *textual features*, are extracted from training bug reports.

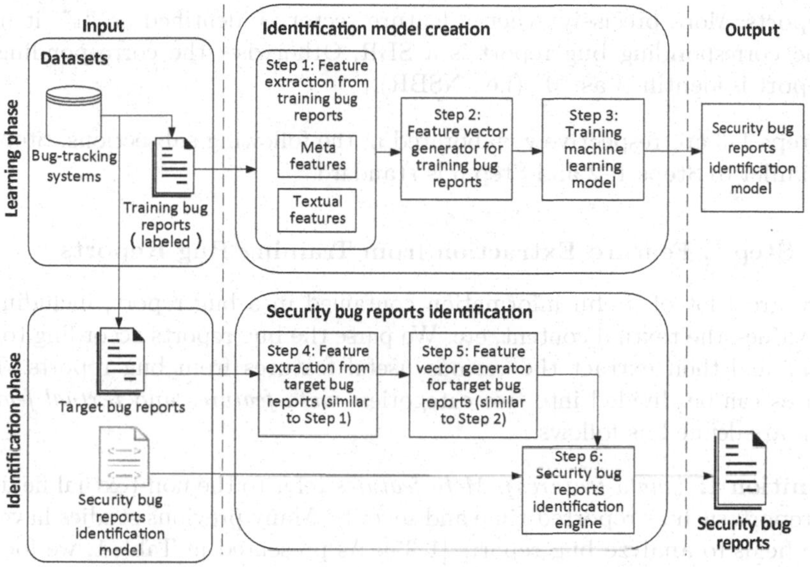

Fig. 1. Overview of SBRer. The learning phase aims to build a security bug reports identification model via the multitype features analysis, and the identification model is in turn used to identify whether a target bug report is a security one or not in the identification phase.

- **Step 2: Feature vector generator for training bug reports.** The extracted features are used to generate a feature vector for each bug report. Each feature vector has a corresponding label ("1" for SBR, and "0" for NSBR), meaning the type of bug report (security or non-security).
- **Step 3: Training machine learning model.** The security bug reports identification model is trained based on the labeled bug report feature vectors in the training set. The identification model is a machine learning model whose training process is standard.

The Identification Phase. Given one or multiple target bug reports, we extract the corresponding multitype features from them. The multitype features are transformed into vector representations, which are used as the input of the trained machine learning model. The model identifies whether the vectors (i.e., bug reports) are related to security bugs ("1") or not ("0") and outputs the identified SBRs. As highlighted in Fig. 1, this phase has three steps.

- **Step 4: Feature extraction from target bug reports.** Two types of features are extracted from the target bug reports (similar to Step 1).
- **Step 5: Feature vector generator for target bug reports.** The features are transformed into the vector representations (similar to Step 2).
- **Step 6: Identification.** This step uses the learned machine learning model to identify the types of the vectors which correspond to the features of bug

reports. More precisely, when a feature vector is identified as "1", it means the corresponding bug report is a SBR. Otherwise, the corresponding bug report is identified as "0" (i.e., NSBR).

Steps 1–3 are respectively elaborated in the following subsections. Steps 4–5 are similar to Steps 1–2 and Step 6 is standard.

3.2 Step 1: Feature Extraction from Training Bug Reports

There are a lot of useful information contained in a bug report, including the field values, the textual content, etc. We parse the bug reports according to their format and then extract the various useful features from bug reports. These features can be divided into two categories: *meta features* and *textual features*, which are defined as follows.

Definition 1: (*meta features*). *Meta features* refer to the non-textual fields of a bug report, such as reported-time and severity. Many previous studies have used these fields to analyze bug reports [1,35]. As presented in Table 1, we focus on the following 9 fields: *reported time, severity, priority, created time, last time, #bugs submitted, #comments, #bugs assigned, and #patches submitted*, as these fields are usually available in most of the bug reports. Besides, they can provide potential signals for SBRs. On the one hand, the *reported time, severity, and priority* reflect the attributes of bug report itself. On the other hand, *created time, last time, #bugs submitted, #comments, #bugs assigned, #patches submitted* reflect the profile of bug reporters. Since bugs are contributed by people specializing in one area (e.g., security), the profile of bug reporters may differ from each other and heavily impact the identification of SBRs [12].

Definition 2: (*textual features*). *Textual features* refer to the textual content of a bug report which have been used to identify SBRs [2,39,40]. In this paper, it refers to the summary field, which is a sentence provided by the reporter in the length of around 5–10 words. These words give a summarized description of the bug and may contain potential semantic information for the identification of SBRs.

3.3 Step 2: Feature Vector Generator for Training Bug Reports

The goal of the feature vector generation module is to transform the features extracted in Step 1 into vector representations, which is necessary for training a machine learning model. The training set consists of a set of input samples, each of which comprises an input object (i.e., feature vector) and its label (i.e., "1" for SBR, and "0" for NSBR). As described above, the feature vector should characterize a bug report in two dimensions: *meta* and *textual.* For each dimension, a set of features is extracted. Thus a vector of the features for a bug report can be represented as:

$$V_{report} = \{v_{meta}, v_{text}\} \tag{1}$$

Table 1. Fields of bug reports related to *meta features*

No.	Field	Description	Example (Bug 1292443)
1	Reported time	The time when a bug is reported	2016-08-04 22:40
2	Severity	The possible impact of a bug estimated by the reporter	Critical
3	Priority	The order of a bug in which a bug should be fixed	–
4	Created time	The time when the bug reporter creates the account	2010-10-24 22:46:28
5	Last time	The last time when the reporter is active	2017-08-08 21:30:46
6	#Bugs submitted	The number of bug reports submitted by the reporter in the past	221
7	#Comments	The number of comments made by the reporter in the past	528
8	#Bugs assigned	The number of bugs assigned to the reporter in the past	1
9	#Patches submitted	The number of patches submitted by the reporter in the past	0

where, v_{meta} is transformed from a set of *meta features*, and v_{text} is transformed from a set of *textual features*.

For *meta features*, we extract 9 fields of bug reports listed in Table 1. These fields are transformed into the vector, represented as:

$$v_{meta} = \{v_{m_1}, v_{m_2}, \cdots, v_{m_8}\} \tag{2}$$

where, v_{m_1} refers to the reported time of a bug report. v_{m_2} refers to the bug severity. Its value ranges from 0 to 6, corresponding to 6 different severity labels (i.e., blocker, critical, major, normal, minor, and trivial), where "0" indicates that the severity field is empty. v_{m_3} refers to the bug priority. Its value ranges from 0 to 5, corresponding to 5 different priority labels (i.e., P1, P2, P3, P4, and P5), where "0" indicates that the priority field is empty. $v_{m_i} (4 \leq i \leq 8)$ correspond to the remaining features in Table 1 in turn. Particularly, v_{m_4} refers to the active time of the bug reporter, which can be calculated by the difference between the created time and the last-active time of a bug reporter, corresponding to the feature of *No.* 4 and 5 in Table 1.

For *textual features*, we focus on the summary field of a bug report, which is a sentence giving the summarized description of a bug. We convert the sentence into a vector via natural language processing, including the following three steps:

- First, *tokenization*. Tokenization is a process to split the sentence into a set of tokens according to the delimiters, such as spaces and punctuation marks, via lexical analysis. While tokenizing, the tokens also should be transformed to the lower case and the special characters should be removed.

- Second, *stop words removal.* Many words are frequently used in the text but might not carry plenty of useful information. These words are called as *stop words*, such as pronouns (e.g., "I", "he", and "she"), articles (e.g., "a", "an", and "the"), and conjunctions (e.g., "and", "but", and "then"). It is necessary to remove these stop words from the set of tokens generated in the previous step, because they might impact on the performance of the identification model due to their skewed distributions.
- Third, *vector generation.* After stop words removal, we get a large corpus of tokens. In order to map these tokens into vectors, we use the *word2vec* tool [37], which is widely used in text mining. It can convert a token into a vector whose dimension is fixed, named as *word embedding.* Finally, the sentence vector (i.e., v_{text} represented in (3)) is a summation of the *word embeddings* of all the tokens that make up the sentence. Since the *word embedding* can be trained as different fixed dimensions (e.g., 5, 10, and 15), the corresponding sentence vector may have different dimensions. The dimension of sentence vector can be tuned to improve the effectiveness of security bug identification (see Sect. 4.3).

$$v_{text} = \{v_{t_1}, v_{t_2}, \ldots, v_{t_n}\} \tag{3}$$

3.4 Step 3: Training Machine Learning Model

Having generated the feature vectors, we utilize the *Support Vector Machine* (SVM) to build an identification model in this step. SVM is a popular supervised machine learning method, which maximizes the distance between the decision line (the line separating the two classes) and each of the two classes. Although it is a linear model, it can realize the non-linear classification effectively via a kernel function which could map the input into a higher dimensionality feature space. Based on the training set (i.e., labeled feature vectors), we adopt grid-search and 10-fold cross validation to select the best parameter values according to the effectiveness for the identification of SBRs.

As we noted, the number of SBRs is much smaller than the number of NSBRs, i.e., the class imbalanced phenomenon is observed. In order to identify the small class (i.e., SBRs), we increase the weight of small samples to make the classifier focus more on the small class (i.e., SBRs) during the training process. As a result, we get a machine learning model with fine-tuned model parameters which can be used to identify the type of a bug report.

4 Experiments and Results

4.1 Evaluation Metrics

The effectiveness of SBRer can be evaluated by standard metrics, such as *accuracy*, *precision*, *recall*, and *F1-measure*, which are widely used to evaluate the performance of classification. Let *True Positive* (TP) be the number of SBRs identified correctly, *False Positive* (FP) be the number of SBRs identified incorrectly, *False Negative* (FN) be the number of true SBRs unidentified, and *True Negative* (TN) be the number of true NSBRs identified. The metric $accuracy = (TP + TN)/(TP + TN + FP + FN)$ reflects the total number of correctly identified bug reports with respect to all bug reports. The metric $precision = TP/(TP + FP)$ reflects the total number of correctly identified SBRs out of all bug reports identified to be SBRs. The metric $recall = TP/(TP + FN)$ reflects the completeness of identifying SBRs. It refers to the ratio of the number of SBRs identified correctly to the entire true SBRs. The metric $F1\text{-}measure = 2 * precision * recall/(precision + recall)$ reflects the overall identification effectiveness.

4.2 Datasets

In this paper, the bug reports we experiment on are mainly collected from the Mozilla bug database, Bugzilla [3]. There are mainly three reasons why the Bugzilla is selected. First, Bugzilla is widely used as a bug-tracking system to manage bug reports. Second, all bug reports from Bugzilla generally follow the same format. Third, the SBRs in Bugzilla usually have the corresponding *Common Vulnerabilities and Exposures IDentifiers* (CVE-IDs) and the links to *Mozilla Foundation Security Advisory* (MFSA) [21], which has reported security problems for each version of Mozilla's products since 2005. With the help of MFSA, we can distinguish the type of each bug report and build the datasets with ground truth. More specifically, for the bug reports collected from Bugzilla, we label the bug reports issued in the MFSA as "1" (i.e., SBRs), and other bug reports as "0" (i.e., NSBRs).

In the present study, we mainly focus on Mozilla's three open source products: Firefox, Seamonkey, and Thunderbird. Security is one of the main quality requirements for such open source products and their bug reports are common so that we can collect enough data for using machine learning techniques.

Table 2. Datasets of the experiments

Product	Time		Versions		#SBRs	#NSBRs
	From	To	From	To		
Firefox	2002-09-29	2017-07-28	Firefox 0.8	Firefox 56.0	1,338	8,503
Seamonkey	1999-04-07	2017-07-09	Seamonkey M11	SeaMonkey 2.48	909	6,301
Thunderbird	2000-04-12	2017-07-12	Thunderbird 3.0b4	Thunderbird 52.0	1,099	5,458
All	1999-04-07	2017-07-28	—	—	3,346	20,262

Table 2 shows the statistics of three products we experiment on. In Table 2, columns *Time* and *Versions* refer to the submitted time of bug reports and the versions that the bug reports impact on, respectively. In the end, we have collected 23,608 bug reports, including 3,346 SBRs and 20,262 NSBRs submitted from April 1999 to July 2017.

4.3 Experiments and Discussion

In this paper, the experiments are conducted on a machine with AMD A10-7300 Radeon R6 1.90 GHz CPU, 8 GB RAM and Windows 7 (64-bit) operating system.

Experimental Settings. To implement an automatical model to identify whether a bug report is related to a security bug (i.e., SBR) via machine learning techniques, we use the open-source tool LibSVM [5]. We randomly select 70% of the bug reports we collect as training set and the remaining 30% as target bug reports to evaluate the effectiveness. This is applied equally when dealing with other approaches.

For our purpose, the *Radial Basis Function* (RBF) kernel is a reasonable choice, because it can deal with the non-linear relationship between the class labels and the attributes. After choosing RBF function as the kernel, the SVM model has two very important parameters, i.e., c and g, corresponding to the cost and kernel parameters.

As shown in Table 2, only 14.2% of the collected bug reports are related to security bugs. In order to make the SVM model work well in the imbalanced data (i.e., having much less SBRs than NSBRs), we also take another important parameter into account, i.e., w_i. The parameter w_i can increase the cost (i.e., parameter c) of failing to correctly identify the small class samples. The extra cost can make the classifier "care" more about small class samples (i.e., SBRs). To search the global optimal parameters combination of c, g, and w_i, we perform the grid-search and 10-fold cross-validation on the training set.

Selection of Sentence Vector Dimension for Textual Features. To select a suitable sentence vector dimension for *textual features*, we choose seven values of sentence vector dimension (from 2 to 50) to observe the influence on the evaluation metrics mentioned above. Table 3 shows the metrics concerning different sentence vector dimensions.

Table 3. Experimental results of SVM models with different sentence vector dimensions

Dimension	Accuracy (%)	Precision (%)	Recall (%)	F1-measure (%)
2	88.4	65.6	37.5	47.7
5	92.6	83.1	60.2	69.8
10	94.7	89.7	71.1	79.3
20	**95.1**	**90.9**	**72.7**	**80.8**
30	94.9	90.5	71.8	80.1
40	94.9	90.9	71.5	80.0
50	94.8	90.3	70.6	79.2

We observe that the F1-measure of the SVM model reaches the maximum (i.e., 80.8%) when the sentence vector dimension is set to 20, which is less than the general word vector dimensions (e.g., 50) [18]. This can be explained by the fact that the size of corpus extracted from the summary field is much smaller (i.e., 2M), compared to the corpus for general natural language processing tasks (e.g., 100M) [18]. We further observe that with the increase of the sentence vector dimension, there is an increasing trend of the evaluation metrics of the SVM model, and finally falls slightly after reaching the maximum. We speculate this is caused by the following reason: as the sentence vector dimension increases, the more information the vector can express, which contributes to the identification of the SBRs. However, when the dimension increases to a certain threshold (in our case, 20), bigger dimension will not increase the information it conveys, even cause a decline in the effectiveness of identification. These observations lead to the following preliminary understanding:

Insight 1: The sentence vector representation of the summary field in a bug report can be used to identify the security bug report, but the effectiveness is sensitive to the sentence vector dimension which is related to the size of corpus extracted from the summary field.

Comparison and Discussion Among Identification Models. After selecting a suitable sentence vector dimension for *textual features* (i.e., 20), we perform grid-search and 10-fold cross validation and then get the SVM classifier with fine-tuned model parameters (i.e., SBRer). Considering that we have multitype features, i.e., *meta features* and *textual features*, we also retrain two different machine learning models built on single feature to explore which type feature makes more contributions to the identification with higher precision or recall. We refer them as Meta-ML and Text-ML (dimension = 20).

In order to estimate how effective SBRer is when compared with other identification approaches of SBRs, we compare the effectiveness of SBRer with the methods proposed by Behl *et al.* [2] and Yang *et al.* [39] on the same datasets described in Table 2. We implement their algorithms based on *Natural Language Toolkit* (NLTK) [22], which is one of the most commonly used Python library in the field of NLP, together with Scikit-learn [30], an efficient open source framework specifically for data mining and machine learning.

Table 4. Experimental results of SBRer compared with two single models (i.e., Meta-ML, Text-ML with dimension = 20), and identification models proposed by Behl *et al.* [2] and Yang *et al.* [39].

Model		Accuracy (%)	Precision (%)	Recall (%)	F1-measure (%)
Meta	Meta-ML	93.9	83.9	70.5	76.6
Textual	Text-ML (dimension = 20)	95.1	90.9	72.7	80.8
	Behl's [2]	90.0	97.6	29.0	44.7
	Yang's [39]	94.9	98.0	65.0	78.2
Multitype	**SBRer**	**97.1**	**99.4**	**79.9**	**88.6**

Table 4 summarizes the experimental results of SBRer compared with two single models (i.e., Meta-ML, Text-ML with dimension = 20), and identification models proposed by Behl *et al.* [2] and Yang *et al.* [39]. We make the following observations.

First, we observe that the Text-ML outperforms the Meta-ML in four metrics. That is to say, *textual features* give a better performance in the identification of SBRs among the two kinds of features. Furthermore, the evaluation metrics of SBRer are improved by 2.1%, 9.4%, 9.9%, and 9.7% for accuracy, precision, recall, and F1-measure respectively, compared to the Text-ML. On the whole, SBRer is more effective than the other two single models, i.e., Meta-ML, and Text-ML. These observations lead to the following explanation of the SBRer identification results:

Insight 2: We can achieve a better performance for the identification of SBRs by considering the two kinds of features (i.e., *meta* and *textual*) together. If the multitype features are incomplete or unavailable, the machine learning model based on textual features (Text-ML) is a good alternative for SBRer.

Second, the experimental results between the three textual models (i.e., Text-ML, Behl's [2], and Yang's [39]) show that Text-ML significantly improves the recall (by 150.7% to Behl's, 11.8% to Yang's) while maintaining a high precision rate. This can be explained by the fact that the sentence vector can represent the semantic information of textual description better, compared to the frequency of words (i.e., term frequency).

Third, we improve the performance of Behl *et al.*'s method by 7.9%, 1.8%, 175.5%, and 98.2% for accuracy, precision, recall, and F1-measure, respectively. The improvement of SBRer over Yang *et al.*'s method mainly reflect in the recall and F1-measure (by 22.9% and 13.3% respectively). It can be explained by the following facts: first, Behl *et al.*'s method does not take the imbalanced phenomenon into account which seriously impacts the performance of classification; second, SBRer takes more features into account which can result in a better performance. These observations lead to:

Insight 3: SBRer can be more effective via multitype features analysis, compared to other identification approaches which just consider the textual features. Besides, the sentence vector can better represent the semantic information of textual description and imbalanced phenomenon should also be taken into account to make the classifier "care" more about small class samples (i.e., SBRs).

5 Conclusion

We have presented SBRer, an automatic security bug reports identification model via multitype features analysis, which aims to relieve human experts from the tedious work and reduce the false negatives that incurred by other existing security bug reports identification approaches. We present two types of features, i.e., *meta features* and *textual features*, and train the machine learning model to automatically identify SBRs. We have collected a bug report dataset for evaluating the performance of SBRer. Experimental results show that SBRer with imbalanced data processing can successfully identify the SBRs with the precision of 99.4% and the recall of 79.9%, which are higher than those of the existing models, especially the recall.

For future work, we intend to try more classification algorithms, software systems, and bug-tracking systems. In particular, how to identify more key features contributed to the identification of the SBRs is an interesting research problem.

Acknowledgments. The paper is supported by the National Basic Research Program of China (973 Program) under grant No. 2014CB340600, the National Science Foundation of China under grant No. 61672249, the Shenzhen Fundamental Research Program under grant No. JCYJ20170413114215614, and the Youth Foundation of Hebei Educational Committee under grant No. QN2016149.

References

1. Anvik, J., Hiew, L., Murphy, G.C.: Who should fix this bug? In: Proceedings of the 28th International Conference on Software engineering (ICSE), pp. 361–370 (2006)
2. Behl, D., Handa, S., Arora, A.: A bug mining tool to identify and analyze security bugs using Naive Bayes and TF-IDF. In: Proceedings of the 2014 International Conference on Optimization, Reliabilty, and Information Technology (ICROIT), pp. 294–299 (2014)
3. Bugzilla. https://www.bugzilla.org/. Accessed 18 Apr 2018
4. Camilo, F., Meneely, A., Nagappan, M.: Do bugs foreshadow vulnerabilities? A study of the chromium project. In: Proceedings of the 12th IEEE/ACM Working Conference on Mining Software Repositories (MSR), pp. 269–279 (2015)
5. Chang, C.C., Lin, C.J.: LIBSVM: a library for support vector machines. ACM Trans. Intell. Syst. Technol. (TIST) **2**(3), 27:1–27:27 (2011)
6. da Costa, D.A., McIntosh, S., Kulesza, U., Hassan, A.E., Abebe, S.L.: An empirical study of the integration time of fixed issues. Empir. Softw. Eng. (ESE) **23**(1), 334–383 (2018). https://doi.org/10.1007/s10664-017-9520-6
7. Coverity. https://www.synopsys.com/software-integrity.html. Accessed 18 Apr 2018
8. Enck, W., Gilbert, P., Han, S., Tendulkar, V., Chun, B.G., Cox, L.P., Jung, J., McDaniel, P., Sheth, A.N.: TaintDroid: an information-flow tracking system for realtime privacy monitoring on smartphones. ACM Trans. Comput. Syst. (TOCS) **32**(2), 5:1–5:29 (2014)
9. Flawfinder. https://www.dwheeler.com/flawfinder/. Accessed 18 Apr 2018
10. Gegick, M., Rotella, P., Xie, T.: Identifying security bug reports via text mining: an industrial case study. In: Proceedings of the 7th IEEE/ACM Working Conference on Mining Software Repositories (MSR), pp. 11–20 (2010)
11. Haller, I., Slowinska, A., Neugschwandtner, M., Bos, H.: Dowsing for overflows: a guided fuzzer to find buffer boundary violations. In: Proceedings of the 22nd USENIX Security Symposium, pp. 49–64 (2013)
12. He, J., Zhang, J., Ma, H., Nazar, N., Ren, Z.: Mining authorship characteristics in bug repositories. Sci. China Inf. Sci. (SCIS) **60**(1), 1–16 (2017)
13. Jang, J., Brumley, D., Agrawal, A.: ReDeBug: finding unpatched code clones in entire OS distributions. In: Proceedings of the 33rd IEEE Symposium on Security and Privacy (S&P), pp. 48–62 (2012)

14. Jeong, G., Kim, S., Zimmermann, T.: Improving bug triage with bug tossing graphs. In: Proceedings of the 7th Joint Meeting of the European Software Engineering Conference and the ACM Joint European Software Engineering Conference and Symposium on the Foundations of Software Engineering (ESEC/FSE), pp. 111–120 (2009)
15. Jira. https://www.atlassian.com/software/jira. Accessed 18 Apr 2018
16. Kim, S., Woo, S., Lee, H., Oh, H.: VUDDY: a scalable approach for vulnerable code clone discovery. In: Proceedings of the 38th IEEE Symposium on Security and Privacy (S&P), pp. 595–614 (2017)
17. Kim, S., Whitehead Jr., E.J.: How long did it take to fix bugs? In: Proceedings of the 3rd IEEE/ACM International Workshop on Mining Software Repositories (MSR), pp. 173–174 (2006). https://doi.org/10.1145/1137983.1138027
18. Lai, S., Liu, K., He, S., Zhao, J.: How to generate a good word embedding. IEEE Intell. Syst. **31**(6), 5–14 (2016)
19. Lamkanfi, A., Demeyer, S., Giger, E., Goethals, B.: Predicting the severity of a reported bug. In: Proceedings of the 7th IEEE/ACM Working Conference on Mining Software Repositories (MSR), pp. 1–10 (2010)
20. Lamkanfi, A., Demeyer, S., Soetens, Q.D., Verdonck, T.: Comparing mining algorithms for predicting the severity of a reported bug. In: Proceedings of the 15th European Conference on Software Maintenance and Reengineering (CSMR), pp. 249–258 (2011)
21. Mozilla Foundation Security Advisories (MFSA). https://www.mozilla.org/en-US/security/advisories/. Accessed 18 Apr 2018
22. Natural Language Toolkit. http://www.nltk.org/. Accessed 18 Apr 2018
23. Ohira, M., Kashiwa, Y., Yamatani, Y., Yoshiyuki, H.: A dataset of high impact bugs: manually-classified issue reports. In: Proceedings of the 12th IEEE/ACM Working Conference on Mining Software Repositories (MSR), pp. 518–521 (2015)
24. Pham, N.H., Nguyen, T.T., Nguyen, H.A., Nguyen, T.N.: Detection of recurring software vulnerabilities. In: Proceedings of the IEEE/ACM International Conference on Automated Software Engineering (ASE), pp. 447–456. ACM (2010)
25. Prifti, T., Banerjee, S., Cukic, B.: Detecting bug duplicate reports through local references. In: Proceedings of the 7th International Conference on Predictive Models in Software Engineering (PROMISE), pp. 1–9 (2011)
26. Rough Auditing Tool for Security (RATS). https://code.google.com/archive/p/rough-auditing-tool-for-security/. Accessed 18 Apr 2018
27. Runeson, P., Alexandersson, M., Nyholm, O.: Detection of duplicate defect reports using natural language processing. In: Proceedings of the 29th International Conference on Software Engineering (ICSE), pp. 499–510 (2007)
28. SAS Text Miner. http://support.sas.com/software/products/txtminer/. Accessed 18 Apr 2018
29. Schwartz, E.J., Avgerinos, T., Brumley, D.: All you ever wanted to know about dynamic taint analysis and forward symbolic execution (but might have been afraid to ask). In: Proceedings of the 31st IEEE Symposium on Security and Privacy (S&P), pp. 317–331 (2010). https://doi.org/10.1109/SP.2010.26
30. Scikit-learn. http://scikit-learn.org/stable/. Accessed 18 Apr 2018
31. Stephens, N., Grosen, J., Salls, C., Dutcher, A., Wang, R., Corbetta, J., Shoshitaishvili, Y., Kruegel, C., Vigna, G.: Driller: augmenting fuzzing through selective symbolic execution. In: Proceedings of the 23rd Network and Distributed Systems Security Symposium (NDSS), vol. 16, pp. 1–16 (2016)
32. Tian, Y., Lo, D., Xia, X., Sun, C.: Automated prediction of bug report priority using multi-factor analysis. Empir. Softw. Eng. (ESE) **20**(5), 1354–1383 (2015)

33. Wang, S., Yao, X.: Using class imbalance learning for software defect prediction. IEEE Trans. Reliab. **62**(2), 434–443 (2013). https://doi.org/10.1109/TR.2013.2259203
34. Wang, T., Wei, T., Gu, G., Zou, W.: TaintScope: a checksum-aware directed fuzzing tool for automatic software vulnerability detection. In: Proceedings of the 31st IEEE Symposium on Security and Privacy (S&P), pp. 497–512. IEEE (2010)
35. Wang, X., Zhang, L., Xie, T., Anvik, J., Sun, J.: An approach to detecting duplicate bug reports using natural language and execution information. In: Proceedings of the 30th ACM/IEEE International Conference on Software Engineering (ICSE), pp. 461–470 (2008)
36. Wijayasekara, D., Manic, M., Mcqueen, M.: Vulnerability identification and classification via text mining bug databases. In: Proceedings of the 40th Annual Conference of the IEEE Industrial Electronics Society (IECON), pp. 3612–3618 (2014)
37. Word2vec. http://radimrehurek.com/gensim/models/word2vec.html. Accessed 18 Apr 2018
38. Yamaguchi, F., Golde, N., Arp, D., Rieck, K.: Modeling and discovering vulnerabilities with code property graphs. In: Proceedings of the 35th IEEE Symposium on Security and Privacy (S&P), pp. 590–604. IEEE (2014)
39. Yang, X., Lo, D., Huang, Q., Xia, X., Sun, J.: Automated identification of high impact bug reports leveraging imbalanced learning strategies. In: Proceedings of the 40th IEEE Computer Software and Applications Conference (COMPSAC), pp. 227–232 (2016)
40. Zhou, Y., Sharma, A.: Automated identification of security issues from commit messages and bug reports. In: Proceedings of the 11th ACM Joint European Software Engineering Conference and Symposium on the Foundations of Software Engineering (ESEC/FSE), pp. 914–919 (2017)

A Practical Privacy Preserving Protocol in Database-Driven Cognitive Radio Networks

Yali Zeng[1], Xu Li[1(✉)], Xu Yang[2], Qikui Xu[3], and Dongcheng Wang[1]

[1] Fujian Provincial Key Laboratory of Network Security and Cryptology, School of Mathematics and Informatics, Fujian Normal University, Fuzhou, China
xuli@fjnu.edu.cn
[2] School of Science, RMIT University, Melbourne, Australia
[3] Faculty of Science, University of Sydney, Sydney, Australia

Abstract. Cognitive radio technique is regarded as a promising way for allowing secondary users (SUs) to access available channels without introducing the interference to the primary users (PUs). However, database-driven cognitive radio networks (CRNs) are facing a series of security and privacy threats, especially the privacy breaches of SUs. To address this issue, this paper proposes a practical privacy-preserving protocol for database-driven CRNs that allows SUs to get the available channels in their vicinity efficiently while protecting their privacy. Our protocol takes advantage of modular square root technique to verify the identity of a SU and enables a legitimate SU to obtain the available channel without leaking its privacy. By prefetching channels, our protocol reduces the latency of obtaining available channels for SUs. Besides, the proposed protocol provides strong privacy preservation that the database cannot trace any SUs and get nothing about location or identity information of SUs, even the database colludes with all base stations. The results of security analysis and performance evaluation indicate the feasibility and practicality of the proposed privacy-preserving protocol.

Keywords: Cognitive Radio Networks · Privacy-preserving Authentication · Prediction · Modular square root

1 Introduction

Cognitive radio is emerging as a potential candidate for alleviating spectrum scarcity and improving spectrum utilization by allowing spectrum sharing among users [1,2]. In cognitive radio networks (CRNs), primary users (PUs) are the owners of the licensed channels, while secondary users (SUs) are only allowed to operate on the vacant parts of the channels allocated to PUs [3]. In database-driven CRNs [4,5], a SU needs to send a request to the database (DB) with its specific location in order to obtain the available channels. Then the DB returns a response to the SU that contains a list of available channels at the SU's location,

W. Susilo and G. Yang (Eds.): ACISP 2018, LNCS 10946, pp. 634–648, 2018.
https://doi.org/10.1007/978-3-319-93638-3_36

among which the SU chooses one channel for transmission. The DB may require a SU to send back a channel-usage notification message. In the message, the SU notifies the DB which channel it intends to use.

Though the database-driven CRNs have advantages of simplicity and easy operation, they suffer from serious security and privacy threats, especially the privacy breaches of SUs. This is simply because SUs have to provide their location information to the DB to learn about channel availability. The administrators of the DB such as Google and Microsoft [6] may be honest but are curious about the location-identity binding or association information of SUs. That is, the DB (refers to the administrators of the DB hereinafter) is curious about what the real identity of the SU is and where this SU has been. Moreover, the DB may require SUs to report the selected channels, from which the DB can also geolocate a SU [7]. Through the location-identity binding information, the DB can receive clues about private information such as political affiliations, habits, or medical problems [8]. Being aware of such potential privacy threats, SUs would be reluctant to access the DB to obtain the available channel information, and the original intention to the CRNs is lost. Therefore, a privacy preserving protocol is necessary to prevent the DB from inferring the identity and location information of each SU.

On the other hand, authentication is a critical security property in CRNs, wherein the identity of a SU is verified before obtaining service. In CRNs, each SU needs to register itself in the certificate authority (CA) before it can get the available channels. An illegal SU cannot obtain any channel when it uses a false identity in order to avoid charges for usage. Hence, a privacy preserving protocol should authenticate the SUs to ensure that only the legitimate SUs can use the channels.

To meet the aforementioned demands, we propose a practical privacy preserving protocol (*PraPP*) for database-driven CRNs. *PraPP* aims at allocating channels efficiently with the capability of authenticating the identity and protecting the privacy of SUs against the DB. The contributions of this paper are summarized as below.

- We propose a protection protocol named *PraPP* that can verify the identity and protect the privacy of SUs in database-driven CRNs, as well as improve the efficiency of channel allocation. Taking advantage of the Markov model, *PraPP* predicts the number of channels and pre-fetches channels to reduce the latency of obtaining available channels for SUs. Moreover, *PraPP* authenticates SUs while protect their privacy by utilizing the modular square root technique.
- We analyze the security and evaluate the performance of *PraPP*. The results show that *PraPP* authenticates the identity of SUs and prevents the DB from inferring the identity and location information of SUs. *PraPP* also can resist various security attacks as well as provide user anonymity and collusion resistance. The analysis results demonstrate the feasibility and practicality of *PraPP*.

The rest of this paper is organized as follows. Related works are presented in Sect. 2. Section 3 introduces the preliminaries. Section 4 presents the proposed protocol. Section 5 analyzes the security and evaluates the performance of the proposed protocol. Finally, Sect. 6 concludes the paper.

2 Related Works

Security and privacy issues in CRNs have raised more and more attention recently. In this section, we give an overview of the related literature. We summarize the comparison between these schemes and our proposed protocol in Table 1.

Table 1. Comparison of existing privacy-preserving protocols in database-driven CRNs

Protocol	Technique	Privacy protection	Identity authentication	Channel prefetching
Gao et al. [7]	PIR	✓	×	×
Troja and Bakiras [9]	PIR	✓	×	×
Xin et al. [10]	PIR	✓	×	×
Grissa et al. [11]	Cuckoo filter	✓	×	×
Zhang et al. [12]	k-anonymity	✓	×	×
Li et al. [13]	Public key encryption	✓	✓	×
Our protocol	Modular square root	✓	✓	✓

As required by the FCC rule, SUs should provide their locations to the DB to obtain channel availability information, which may breach SUs' privacy. To address this issue, the straightforward approach is to send the whole database to SUs and let SUs search the database themselves to choose the available channels, which will provide the ideal privacy. Obviously, this is costly and unpractical. To reduce the communication cost, Grissa et al. [11] compact the DB by using the cuckoo filter technique and then send the filter to SUs. Upon receiving the filter, SUs keep constructing the query to match items in the compact DB until they find the available channels or until they try all channels. Obviously, This approach incurs high communication overhead.

Private Information Retrieval (PIR) [14] is a more efficient technique to protect the privacy of SUs than the straightforward approach. PIR allows SUs to retrieve available channels from the DB while maintaining their query private. Gao et al. [7] identify a new attack that the DB can locate a target SU when the DB has the knowledge of the used channels of the SU. They propose a privacy preserving spectrum retrieval and utilization scheme, which enables a SU to query the DB without leaking SU's location. Troja and Bakiras [9] propose a privacy-preserving protocol based on the Hilbert space filling curve so as to reduce the number of PIR queries. Xin et al. [10] propose a privacy-preserving scheme based on PIR techniques, which allows the DB to find out the available channels regarding a querying SU's location without learning its detail. Although PIR-based approaches do protect the privacy of SUs, these approaches incur high computation or communication overhead.

k-anonymity [15] is another privacy-preserving technique in database-driven CRNs. Zhang et al. [12] exploit the k-anonymity technique to enhance SUs' privacy, which makes SUs send square cloak region that includes SUs' real location to the DB. Their approach makes a tradeoff between providing high location privacy and maximizing some utility, that is, their approach obtains higher location privacy level with sacrifice of spectrum utility.

Another focus of this paper is on the authentication of SUs. In CRNs, the identity of each SU needs to be verified before it can get the available channel so as to protect the right of legitimate SUs. Li et al. [13] propose a location privacy-preserving channel allocation scheme, which authenticates the identity of a SU, as well as protects the privacy of a SU. However, the DB should execute the authentication and channel allocation for all SUs, which may be inefficient.

From the above discussion, it can be seen that there needs a more satisfactory privacy preservation protocol for SUs in database-driven CRNs.

3 Preliminaries

This section briefly introduces the system model, security requirements and modular square root technique.

3.1 System Model

In database-driven CRNs, SUs send requests to the DB with their locations such that they can obtain the available channels. Figure 1 shows the network model in database-driven CRNs, which consists of four parities: the DB, BSs, SUs and the certificate authority (CA). SUs can be mobile devices with limited power and computation capabilities. The DB stores available channel information of the whole network. Before a SU communicates with others, it sends an available-channel request message with its location information to the nearest BS, and then the BS forwards the request to the DB. Upon receiving the request, the DB lookups the available channels at SU's location and returns a channel list to the SU through BSs. Each SU needs to register itself in the CA before using channels. BSs verify the legitimacy of each SU and let channels are only accessed by legal SUs.

3.2 Security Requirements

We assume that the DB has the knowledge of the complete communication content between BS and the DB as well as between BS and SUs. We also assume that the DB is honest-but-curious. The honest-but-curious means that the DB will

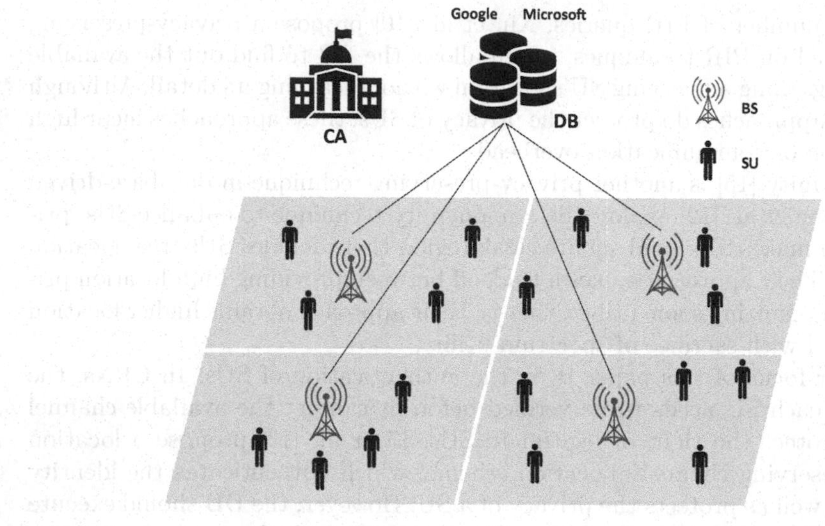

Fig. 1. Network model

follow the protocol honestly, and correctly process and respond to messages, but are curious about the SUs identity-location binding or association information. That is, the DB is curious about the real identity of a SU and the places this SU has been. Therefore, the first goal of this paper is to avoid the DB obtaining anything about identity-location binding or association information of SUs. Besides, it is assumed that BSs are also honest-but-curious. However, BSs have the knowledge of the location information of SUs when SUs communicate with a BS. The second goal of this paper is to protect the real identity of each SU from the tracing of BSs. Assumed that BSs will not collude with illegal SUs. SUs want to receive channels for their locations while keeping their identity-location binding or association information secret.

A practical privacy-preserving protocol in database-driven CRNs should have the following desirable properties:

- **Privacy Preservation.** The proposed protocol should achieve privacy requirements of SUs. In particular, the proposed protocol should prevent the DB from inferring the identity and location information of SUs. Except the CA, SUs are anonymous to anyone including the DB and BSs, and nobody can trace SUs' locations. Moreover, even the DB collude with all BSs, the identity and location information of SUs still cannot be inferred by the DB.
- **Identity Authentication.** The identity of a SU should be authenticated to ensure that an illegal SU using a false identity cannot obtain available channels.
- **Attack Resistance.** Under various types of attacks (such as eavesdropping, replaying and so on), the security of the proposed protocol will not be compromised.

All these properties are considered in the design of our protocol.

3.3 Modular Square Root Technique

The modular square root technique is built on quadratic residues and their properties [16]. Let y be any integer and n a natural number, such that $gcd(y, n) = 1$. Then y is called *quadratic residue* modulo n if there exists an x with $x^2 = y \ mod \ n$. x is called a *modular square root* of y.

Euler's Criterion: Let p be an odd prime and $gcd(y, p) = 1$. Then y is a quadratic residue modulo p if and only if

$$y^{\frac{p-1}{2}} = 1 \ (mod \ p) \tag{1}$$

if $p = 3 \ (mod \ 4)$ and y is a quadratic residue modulo p, the modular square roots of y modulo p can be computed as follow:

$$r_{1,2} = \pm y^{\frac{p+1}{4}} \ (mod \ p) \tag{2}$$

Based on Euler's Criterion, we have the following property.

Property 1. Let $n = p \cdot q$ and $gcd(y, n) = 1$, where p and q are two distinct odd primes and $p = q = 3 \ (mod \ 4)$. Then y is a quadratic residue modulo n if and only if

$$y^{\frac{p-1}{2}} = 1 \ (mod \ p) \ and \ y^{\frac{q-1}{2}} = 1 \ (mod \ q) \tag{3}$$

Using the Chinese reminder theorem, the four modular square roots of y modulo n can be computed as follow:

$$r_{1,2,3,4} = \pm(y^{\frac{p+1}{4}} \ (mod \ p))uq \pm (y^{\frac{q+1}{4}} \ (mod \ q))vp \ (mod \ n) \tag{4}$$

where $uq = 1 \ (mod \ p)$, $vp = 1 \ (mod \ q)$.

The security of the modular square root technique is based on the difficulty of extraction modular square roots of a quadratic residue modulo $n = p \cdot q$, when the large distinct primes p and q are unknown.

4 Proposed Scheme

In this section, we present our practical privacy-preserving protocol (*PraPP*) in detail. Specially, *PraPP* consists of two phases, the channel prediction phase and the channel allocation phase. The channel prediction phase predicts the number of channels needed in the next period, while the channel allocation phase deals with the privacy query and authentication of SUs.

4.1 Channel Prediction

In this phase, BSs try to predict the number of channels which will be requested by SUs in the next period. Assume that the update period of available channel information in the DB is T. BSs will predict the number of channels before the DB updates and prefetch the certain number of channels after the DB updates. It is worthwhile to note that the DB can also predict the number of channels for each BS. Consider a Markov chain of three states s_1, s_2 and s_3, with the probability of transition from state s_i to state s_j being denoted p_{ij} $(i, j \in \{1, 2, 3\})$. The arrivals of SUs in state s_1, s_2 and s_3 are $[0, \eta)$, $[\eta, 2\eta)$, and $[2\eta, \infty)$, respectively, where η is a positive integer and can be different values according to different scenarios. It is assumed that the arrivals of SUs follow a Poisson process with average arrival rate λ [17]. The probability that the arrivals of SUs are s_1 during T is

$$p_1 = \sum_{s_1=0}^{s_1=\eta-1} e^{-\lambda T} \frac{(\lambda T)^{s_1}}{s_1!}. \tag{5}$$

The probability that the arrivals is s_2 during T is

$$p_2 = \sum_{s_2=\eta}^{s_2=2\eta-1} e^{-\lambda T} \frac{(\lambda T)^{s_2}}{s_2!}. \tag{6}$$

The probability that the arrival number is s_3 during T is

$$p_3 = 1 - \sum_{s_1=0}^{s_1=\eta-1} e^{-\lambda T} \frac{(\lambda T)^{s_1}}{s_1!} - \sum_{s_2=\eta}^{s_2=2\eta-1} e^{-\lambda T} \frac{(\lambda T)^{s_2}}{s_2!}. \tag{7}$$

According to the historical data, BSs can obtain the state transition probability among three states as follows:

$$P = \begin{bmatrix} p_{11} \; p_{12} \; p_{13} \\ p_{21} \; p_{22} \; p_{23} \\ p_{31} \; p_{32} \; p_{33} \end{bmatrix} \tag{8}$$

where p_{ij} means the transition probability from state s_i to state s_j, $i, j \in \{1, 2, 3\}$.

Suppose that probability of the current state of a BS in s_i $(i \in \{1, 2, 3\})$ is p_i, then the BS computes $[p_1 \; p_2 \; p_3] \cdot P$ and obtains three probability values corresponding to three states. The largest one is the most possible state that the BS will be in the next period. Then the BS prefetches the corresponding number of channels denoted as χ. For example, if the most possible state is s_1, the BS will prefetch η channels.

4.2 Channel Allocation

In this phase, the legitimate SUs will obtain the available channels. Consider a database-driven CRN composed of M_{SU} SUs and M_{BS} BSs. If a SU can communication directly with a BS, we consider the SU and the BS at the same location. Therefore, SUs can use the channels prefetched by BSs in the channel prediction phase.

System Initialization. The CA executes the following operations:

(1) Chooses two large distinct odd primes p_{CA} and q_{CA} such that $p_{CA} = q_{CA} = 3\ (mod\ 4)$ and computes $n_{CA} = p_{CA} \cdot q_{CA}$.
(2) Chooses two large distinct odd primes p_{BS_i} and q_{BS_i} for BS_i whose identity information is ID_{BS_i} and computes $n_{BS_i} = p_{BS_i} \cdot q_{BS_i}$, then sends $\{n_{BS_i}, p_{BS_i}, q_{BS_i}\}$ to BS_i, $i \in M_{BS}$.
(3) Chooses a secure hash function H.
(4) Publishes n_{CA} and n_{BS_i}.

In the rest of the paper, we use BS instead of BS_i for simplicity.

For each SU_j whose real identity is ID_j ($j \in M_{SU}$), the CA issues K triples $(R_{j,k}, s_{j,k}, r_{j,k})$ ($k \in K$) to SU_j, where $(R_{j,k}, s_{j,k}, r_{j,k})$ is generated as follows:

(1) Let $s_{j,k} = 0$ and selects a unique random number $R_{j,k}$ for SU_j. Then computes $y = H(R_{j,k}||s_{j,k})$.
(2) Checks if
$y^{\frac{p_{CA}-1}{2}} = 1\ (mod\ p_{CA})$ and $y^{\frac{q_{CA}-1}{2}} = 1\ (mod\ q_{CA})$.
if not, $s_{j,k} = s_{j,k} + 1$ and go to 2).
(3) Computes four modular square roots $x_{1,2,3,4}$ of $x^2 = y\ mod\ n_{CA}$ and chooses the smallest square root as $r_{j,k}$.
(4) Outputs $(R_{j,k}, s_{j,k}, r_{j,k})$ and halt.

The CA sends $(R_{j,k}, s_{j,k}, r_{j,k})$ to SU_j in a secure control channel, where $(R_{j,k}, s_{j,k}, r_{j,k})$ satisfies $r_{j,k}^2 = H(R_{j,k}||s_{j,k})\ (mod\ n_{CA})$. $(R_{j,k}, s_{j,k}, r_{j,k})$ serves as one of SU_j's pseudo-IDs, that is, each SU_j has K pseudo-IDs.

In the rest of the paper, we use SU instead of SU_j for simplicity.

Channel Prefetching Request. BS sends the predicted number of channels χ, the location of BS and ID_{BS} to the DB. When receiving the channel prefetching request, the DB lookups the available channels at the location of BS and sends back the channel list as BS requests via a secure channel. After BS receives the channel list, it saves this list in its buffer and waits for SUs' requests.

Identity Authentication and Channel Allocation. When SU wants to transmit data, it sends a channel request to BS who is within its communication range. If there are multiple BSs, SU chooses the one with the strongest signal strength. Since only the legitimate SUs can use channels, there is a need for BS to verify SU's identity.

Let $\beta = 2^l$ and $2^{l-1} < n_{BS} < 2^l$. (Note that β is used to eliminate the need for division in the modular step [18].) SU executes the following operations:

(1) Chooses a random value α such that $\sqrt{n_{BS}} \leq \alpha \leq \frac{n_{BS}}{2}$.
(2) Computes $U_{j,k} = \alpha^2 \cdot \beta^{-1}\ (mod\ n_{BS})$.
(3) Computes $sk = H(\alpha)$ and $V_{j,k} = MAC_{sk}(ID_{BS})$.
(4) Encrypts $(R_{j,k},\ s_{j,k},\ r_{j,k})$, time stamp ts_1 and msg as $W_{j,k} = E_{sk}(R_{j,k}||s_{j,k}||r_{j,k}||ts_1||msg)$, where msg is the specific demands for channels, such as power, QoS, available time, etc.

SU sends $\{U_{j,k},\ V_{j,k},\ W_{j,k}\}$ to BS. BS verifies the legality of SU as follows:

(1) Computes four modular square roots $\alpha_{1,2,3,4}$ of $\alpha^2 = U_{j,k} \cdot \beta\ (mod\ n_{BS})$ with the knowledge of p_{BS} and q_{BS}.
(2) Computes the hash and MAC values of the four roots $\alpha_{1,2,3,4}$, namely, $sk_{1,2,3,4} = H(\alpha_{1,2,3,4})$, $V_{j,k} = MAC_{sk_{1,2,3,4}}(ID_{BS})$. Then picks up the right sk.
(3) Decrypts $W_{j,k}$ with sk and gets $\{R_{j,k},\ s_{j,k},\ r_{j,k},\ ts_1,\ msg\}$.
(4) Checks the validity of time stamp ts_1, and checks whether $r_{j,k}^2 = H(R_{j,k}||s_{j,k})\ (mod\ n_{CA})$ holds. If holds, then it means that SU is legal, go to 5); otherwise, go to 6).
(5) Chooses a channel from the channel list in its buffer to meet demands as msg requests and encrypts this channel with sk as $e = E_{sk}(channel||ts_2)$, where ts_2 is a new time stamp. Then sends e to SU.
(6) Sends $e = E_{sk}(\phi||ts_2)$ to SU, where ϕ is the empty set.

On receiving the data from BS, SU checks the validity of the time stamp ts_2 and uses sk to decrypt e and obtains the channel. If SU is illegal, it will get nothing.

5 Security Analysis and Performance Evaluation

In this section, we analyze the security and evaluate the performance of the proposed protocol.

5.1 Security Analysis

We analyze the required security properties of the proposed protocol with respect to the security requirements given in Sect. 3. It is worthwhile to note that the primary object of our protocol is to prevent the DB from inferring the identity and location information of SU when the DB observes the communication messages between SUs and BSs or between BSs and the DB. The second object of our protocol is to protect the real identity of SU from BSs' or the DB's tracing.

- **Identity Privacy of SU.** In our protocol, the CA chooses K triples for each SU, and each SU's real identity is converted into K pseudo-IDs $(R_{j,k},\ s_{j,k},\ r_{j,k})$ before a SU sends the channel request to a BS. Then these pseudo-IDs are used in identity authentication without disclosing any private information. Only the CA has the knowledge of the relationship between a pseudo-ID and the real identity. From the pseudo-IDs, the DB and BSs know nothing about the real identity of SUs. Even all BSs conclude with the DB, both the DB and BSs get nothing about the real identity of the SU.

- **Location Privacy of SU.** In our protocol, SUs do not provide their locations to the DB, so the DB has no knowledge about where a SU has been. Moreover, each SU uses pseudo-IDs to request the available channel, and both the DB and BSs cannot infer the identity-location binding or association information of SUs. Since there is no location or identity information related to SUs stored in DB, even though the DB is compromised by the attacker, the attacker cannot get anything about SUs' privacy. Besides, since there is no linkage between pseudo-IDs, everyone (expect the CA and SU) is unable to link two sessions initiated by the same SU. Hence, no one can trace a SU's activities.
- **Identity Authentication.** The BSs should authenticate all SUs to ensure that a SU cannot obtain available channels using a false identity. In our protocol, SU_j is authenticated through the triple $(R_{j,k},\ s_{j,k},\ r_{j,k})$ such that $r_{j,k}^2 = H(R_{j,k}||s_{j,k})\ (mod\ n_{CA})$. Forging such a triple requires a forger to correctly compute the modular square roots of a quadratic residue $H(R_{j,k}||s_{j,k})(mod\ n_{CA})$ to determine corresponding $r_{j,k}$. However, it is difficult for the forger to do so without knowing p_{CA} and q_{CA}. With the assumption that BSs will not collude with the illegal SUs, that is, BSs will not reveal $(R_{j,k},\ s_{j,k},\ r_{j,k})$ to illegal SUs, only the legitimate SU_j can provide the triple $(R_{j,k},\ s_{j,k},\ r_{j,k})$ to BSs. In other words, nobody can impersonate SU_j.
  In our protocol, only the BS with the knowledge of p_{BS} and q_{BS} can extract the sk from SU_j by computing modular square roots of the quadratic residue $U_{j,k} \cdot \beta\ (mod\ n_{BS})$. Without p_{BS} and q_{BS}, an attacker cannot obtain sk and hence cannot encrypt channels correctly. Therefore, by decrypting e correctly, a SU can authenticate a BS in an indirect way.
- **Prevention of Collusion Attack.** As the real identity of a SU is stored as pseudo-ID in a BS, even though the DB is in collusion with a BS, both the DB and BS only have the knowledge about that someone with a pseudo-ID has been in the BS's communication range. They can get nothing else about a SU. Therefore, if the DB collude with a BS, they cannot infer the identity-location binding or association information of SUs. If the DB collude with all BSs, the DB and BSs still cannot trace a SU as they cannot know which pseudo-IDs are mapping to the same SU. Hence, our protocol can prevent the collusion attack.
- **Prevention of Eavesdropping Attack.** Although the data transmits in the wireless environment can be captured by attackers, the attackers cannot acquire the content of packets. This is because the contents of packets are encrypted and protected by sk. Without knowing p_{BS} and q_{BS}, an attacker cannot obtain the secret key sk to decrypt the messages.
- **Prevention of Replaying Attack.** An efficient measure against a replaying attack is inserting a time stamp ts into transmitted messages and setting an expected legal interval for transmission delay Δt. Replaying attack is infeasible in our protocol as two time stamps ts_1 and ts_2 are used to prevent replaying attack, so that any relaying messages must beyond the service expiration time. For example, in our protocol, a SU transmits a channel request containing time stamp ts_1 to a BS. On receiving the request, the BS determines the validity of the request by checking if $t - ts_1 < \Delta t$, where t is the current time.

If the inequation holds, the message is valid; otherwise, the BS treats it as a replaying message and rejects this request. As all messages in our protocol contain time stamp, the replaying attack can be prevented.

5.2 Performance Evaluation

In CRNs, SUs are always the devices with low power and limited computing capability. It is impractical for such devices to execute the operations with high computational and communication complexity. In this section, we evaluate the performance of our protocol and compare it with other closely related ones [10, 11]. Since the public key encryption algorithm in [13] has not been specified, we do not include it in our analysis. We consider that the DB covered region is divided into $m \times m$ cells and there are c channels in total.

Communication Overhead. Table 2 provides the analytical communication overhead comparison. We assume that the modulus n_{CA} and n_{BS} are 1024 bits, respectively; p_{CA}, q_{CA}, p_{BS} and q_{BS} have 512 bits, respectively; the time stamp ts_i ($i \in \{1, 2\}$) is denoted with 32 bits [16]; the output of the MAC function, ID_{BS}, msg, $R_{i,j}$ are 64 bits, respectively; the location of a BS is denoted with 32 bits [19] and the number of channels is denoted with 32 bits [11]. In our protocol, the communication overhead for a SU to send $\{U_{j,k}, V_{j,k}, W_{j,k}\}$ to a BS is about $1024 + 64 + 64 + 1024 + 32 + 64 = 2272$ bits. The communication overhead for a BS to send the predicted number of channels χ, the location and ID_{BS} to the DB is about $32 + 32 + 64 = 128$ bits. However, a BS sends the message once per period, so the communication overhead is about $128/\chi$ bits. The available channel lists returned by the DB is denoted with 32 bits. The ciphertext e that a BS replies to a SU is about 128 bits. The system communication overhead is about $2272 + 128 + (128 + 32)/\chi = 2400 + 160/\chi$ bits.

Table 2. Communication overhead

Protocol	Communication overhead
Xin et al. [10]	$2c \cdot ((4m + 1) \cdot \lvert n\rvert + \lvert ts\rvert + \lvert\sigma\rvert)$
Grissa et al. [11]	$\lvert k\rvert + \lvert char\rvert + \lvert ts\rvert + \rho \cdot c \cdot m^2 \cdot (log_2(1/\epsilon) + log_2(2\delta))/\xi + c \cdot \lvert\zeta_{HMAC}\rvert$
Our protocol	$2\lvert n\rvert + \lvert\zeta_{MAC}\rvert + 2\lvert ts\rvert + \lvert msg\rvert + \vartheta^\sharp$

Variables: $|ts|$ is the size of time stamp, $|n|$ is size of n, $|\zeta_x|$ is the output size of x function. $|k|$ and $|char|$ are the size of secret key and characteristics in [11], respectively. ρ is the percentage of entries with available channels, ϵ is the false positive rate of the cuckoo filter, δ is the number of entries in a bucket of the cuckoo filter, ξ is the load factor in [11]. $|\sigma|$ is the size of ring signature in [10]. $\vartheta^\sharp$ is the size of the message transmitted between a BS and the DB.

For illustration purpose, we simulate the communication overhead of different protocols in Fig. 2. From Fig. 2(a) we can know that the communication overhead of our protocol remains unchanged with increasing number of cells. This is because the communication overhead of ours is independent of the number of cells as analysed in Table 2. Moreover, the communication overheads of Grissa et al. and Xin et al. become higher with increasing number of cells. We reduce the range of cell number and plot Fig. 2(b) to elaborate our advantage. As shown in Fig. 2(b), the communication overhead of Grissa et al. is smaller than ours when the number of cells is less than 15. However, the number of cells is large in reality and the communication overhead of Grissa et al. is higher than ours. Hence, our protocol has a lower communication overhead and a better scalability as the communication overhead is independent of the number of cells.

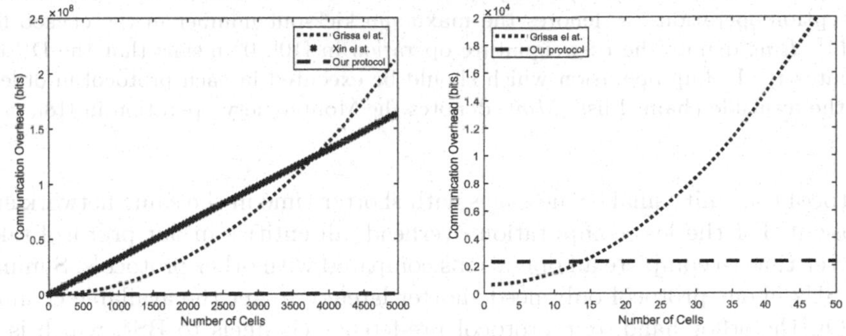

(a) (b)

Fig. 2. Communication overhead

Computation Overhead. Table 3 provides the analytical computation overhead comparison. In our protocol, SUs only need to execute a hashing, a MAC, an encrypting and a decrypting operations, which are all low computation complexity. Besides, SU needs to compute $\alpha^2 \cdot \beta^{-1}\ (mod\ n_{BS})$, as shown in Table 3. Utilizing the Montgomery method [18] can eliminate the need for division in the modular step. With the Montgomery method, the complexity of computing $\alpha^2 \cdot \beta^{-1}\ (mod\ n_{BS})$ is only one Montgomery operation, i.e.,

$$M(\alpha_j, \alpha_j) = \alpha^2 \cdot \beta^{-1}. \tag{9}$$

Therefore, the critical operations required in SUs in our protocol have been minimized to only a single Montgomery operation [16].

From Table 3, we can know that the computation cost of our protocol is less than that of Xin et al. on each entity. The total computation overhead of our protocol is less than that of Xin et al. and Grissa et al. as their protocols have to execute a high number of operations on DB when m is large.

Latency Reduction. As discussed in communication and computation overheads, our protocol has less communication and computation overheads compared with other protocols. The less communication overhead means that our

Table 3. Computation overhead

	Computation overhead		
	SU	BS	DB
Xin et al. [10]	$c \cdot (2m \cdot Sqr + Exp)$	$Ring + 2c \cdot Sqr + E$	$c \cdot (m^2 \cdot Sqr + 2m \cdot (m+1) \cdot Mulp + D)$
Grissa et al. [11]	$c \cdot HMAC$	$3c \cdot Hash$	$\rho \cdot c \cdot m^2 \cdot (3+\kappa) Hash$
Our protocol	$Mont + Hash + MAC + E + D$	$2Exp + 3Mulp + 3Hash + 2MAC + D + E$	0^a

Variables: $Mulp$, Exp and Sqr denote a modular multiplication, a modular exponentiation and a modular squaring operations. E and D denote the encryption and decryption operations. κ denotes the maximum kick-out number in the cuckoo filter in [11]. *Ring* denote the ring signature operation in [10]. 0^a means that the DB only executes the lookup operation which should be executed in each protocol in order to get the available channel list. *Mont* denotes the Montgomery operation in [18].

protocol transmits smaller messages with shorter time in the same network environment. For the less computation overhead, all entities in our protocol take a shorter time to complete all operations compared with other protocols. Summing up, SUs in our protocol only need shorter latency to get the available channels.

On the other hand, our protocol pre-fetches channels to BSs, which is not considered in other protocols. All BSs in our protocol authenticate the legitimacy of SUs and allocate channels to SUs locally and concurrently, which also reduces the latency of obtaining channels for SUs.

6 Conclusion

In this paper, we propose a practical privacy preserving protocol for database-driven CRNs that allows SUs to get the available channels in their vicinity efficiently while protecting their privacy. The proposed protocol efficiently reduces the latency of obtaining available channels for SUs and protects the right of the legitimate SU by making the illegal SU get nothing. We also analyze the security and performance of the proposed protocol to demonstrate its feasibility and practicality. In our future work, we will work on providing the formal security proof and more implementations and simulations on performance evaluation.

Acknowledgment. The authors would like to thank the National Natural Science Foundation of China (Grant No. 61771140, No. 61572010 and No. U1405255), Natural Science Foundation of Fujian Province (Grant No. 2013J01222 and No. 2016J01287), Fujian Normal University Innovative Research Team (Grant No. IRTL1207), Fujian Province Department of Education Project (Grant No. JAT160123), Fuzhou Science and Technology Bureau Project (Grant No. 2015-G-59), Fujian Province University industry Cooperation of Major Science and Technology Project (Grant No. 2017H6005).

References

1. Haykin, S.: Cognitive radio: brain-empowered wireless communications. IEEE J. Sel. Areas Commun. **23**(2), 201–220 (2005)
2. Sharma, S.K., Bogale, T.E., Chatzinotas, S., Ottersten, B.E., Le, L.B., Wang, X.: Cognitive radio techniques under practical imperfections: a survey. IEEE Commun. Surv. Tutor. **17**(4), 1858–1884 (2015)
3. Li, J., Zhao, H., Wei, J., Ma, D., Zhou, L.: Sender-jump receiver-wait: a simple blind rendezvous algorithm for distributed cognitive radio networks. IEEE Trans. Mob. Comput. **17**(1), 183–196 (2018)
4. Gao, Z., Zhu, H., Liu, Y., Li, M., Cao, Z.: Location privacy leaking from spectrum utilization information in database-driven cognitive radio network. In: ACM Conference on Computer and Communications Security, CCS 2012, 16–18 October 2012, Raleigh, NC, USA, pp. 1025–1027 (2012)
5. Al-Ali, A.K., Sun, Y., Di Felice, M., Paavola, J., Chowdhury, K.R.: Accessing spectrum databases using interference alignment in vehicular cognitive radio networks. IEEE Trans. Veh. Technol. **64**(1), 263–272 (2015)
6. Federal communications commission, third memorandum opinion and order http://hraunfoss.fcc.gov/edocs~public/attachmatch/fcc-12-36a1.pdf
7. Gao, Z., Zhu, H., Liu, Y., Li, M., Cao, Z.: Location privacy in database-driven cognitive radio networks: attacks and countermeasures. In: Proceedings of the IEEE INFOCOM 2013, 14–19 April 2013, Turin, Italy, pp. 2751–2759 (2013)
8. Wicker, S.B.: The loss of location privacy in the cellular age. Commun. ACM **55**(8), 60–68 (2012)
9. Troja, E., Bakiras, S.: Optimizing privacy-preserving DSA for mobile clients. Ad Hoc Netw. **59**, 71–85 (2017)
10. Xin, J., Li, M., Luo, C., Li, P.: Privacy-preserving spectrum query with location proofs in database-driven CRNs. In: 2016 IEEE Global Communications Conference, GLOBECOM 2016, 4–8 December 2016, Washington, DC, USA, pp. 1–6 (2016)
11. Grissa, M., Yavuz, A.A., Hamdaoui, B.: Location privacy preservation in database-driven wireless cognitive networks through encrypted probabilistic data structures. IEEE Trans. Cogn. Commun. Netw. **3**(2), 255–266 (2017)
12. Zhang, L., Fang, C., Li, Y., Zhu, H., Dong, M.: Optimal strategies for defending location inference attack in database-driven CRNs. In: 2015 IEEE International Conference on Communications, ICC 2015, 8–12 June 2015, London, United Kingdom, pp. 7640–7645 (2015)
13. Li, H., Pei, Q., Zhang, W.: Location privacy-preserving channel allocation scheme in cognitive radio networks. Int. J. Distrib. Sens. Netw. **12**(7), 3794582–3794582 (2016)
14. Sun, H., Jafar, S.A.: The capacity of private information retrieval. IEEE Trans. Inf. Theory **63**(7), 4075–4088 (2017)
15. Sweeney, L.: k-anonymity: A model for protecting privacy. Int. J. Uncertain. Fuzziness Knowl.-Based Syst. **10**(5), 557–570 (2002)
16. Yi, X., Siew, C.K., Tan, C.H.: A secure and efficient conference scheme for mobile communications. IEEE Trans. Veh. Technol. **52**(4), 784–793 (2003)
17. Zhu, Z., Cao, G.: APPLAUS: a privacy-preserving location proof updating system for location-based services. In: Proceedings of the IEEE INFOCOM 2011, 10–15 April 2011, Shanghai, China, pp. 1889–1897 (2011)

18. Montgomery, P.L.: Modular multiplication without trial division. Math. Comput. **44**(170), 519–521 (1985)
19. Yi, X., Paulet, R., Bertino, E., Varadharajan, V.: Practical approximate k nearest neighbor queries with location and query privacy. IEEE Trans. Knowl. Data Eng. **28**(6), 1546–1559 (2016)

TDDAD: Time-Based Detection and Defense Scheme Against DDoS Attack on SDN Controller

Jie Cui[1,2], Jiantao He[1,2], Yan Xu[1,2], and Hong Zhong[1,2(✉)]

[1] School of Computer Science and Technology, Anhui University, Hefei 230039, China
cuijie@mail.ustc.edu.cn, Hjt_1994@outlook.com, {xuyan,zhong}@ahu.edu.cn
[2] Anhui Engineering Laboratory of IoT Security Technologies, Anhui University, Hefei 230039, China

Abstract. Software defined network (SDN) is the key part of the next generation networks. Its central controller enables the high programmability and flexibility. However, SDN can be easily disrupted by a new DDoS attack which triggers enormous Packet_IN messages. Since the existing solutions focus on checking current network states with content feature to detect the attack, they can possibly be misled. In this paper, we propose a detection and defense scheme against the DDoS attack based on the time feature. Specifically, the time feature is the hit rate gradient of the flow table. We first extract the temporal behavior of an attack. A back propagation neural network is trained to extract an attack pattern and used to recognize an attack. Then either a defense or recovery action will be taken. We test our scheme with the DARPA 1999 intrusion detection data set and compare our scheme with another method using sequential probability ratio test (SPRT). The experiment and evaluation show that our scheme enables the real-time detection, effective defense and quick recovery from DDoS attacks.

Keywords: DDoS · SDN · BPNN · Time feature · Dynamic recovery

1 Introduction

Software defined network (SDN) is a new network architecture that separates the control and data planes. A central control plane enables the global view of the network, which makes SDN programmable and more flexible than a traditional network. Using SDN can drastically increase the throughput and forwarding speed in IoT [3] or DCN [1]. However, there are a variety of security concerns in SDN [2]. One problem is that the central data plane of SDN may lead to the single point failure, especially when a DDoS attack happens [9].

Especially, there exists an SDN-specific DDoS attack against SDN controller. Different from the traditional DDoS attack, an attack against the controller aims to overload the controller and disrupt the entire network. It utilizes the operations defined by the OpenFlow protocol [11] to launch an attack. In SDN,

W. Susilo and G. Yang (Eds.): ACISP 2018, LNCS 10946, pp. 649–665, 2018.
https://doi.org/10.1007/978-3-319-93638-3_37

the OpenFlow (OF for short) switch encapsulates the packet that matches no flow entry into a Packet_IN message and sends it to the controller. The controller decapsulates the Packet_IN message, then calculates the route and finally pushes a flow entry to the OF switch. To launch a DDoS attack, an attacker only need to send enormous fake packets to the OF switch. Since the packets are fake, they match no existing flow entry and trigger enormous Packet_IN messages. Finally, the controller resources for handling the Packet_IN messages will be exhausted [15].

Normally, the attacker sends random packets to the OF switch as long as each packet has a different IP address or port from others. Because the attacker can combine different attacks, such as SYN Flooding, ICMP Flooding, and UDP Flooding [19], to confuse us, the traditional detection method may be unsuitable for the hybrid attack. Meanwhile, the attacker uses the OF switch to attack the controller instead of attacking the controller directly. Therefore, the packets can be divided and sent to serval switches, but the Packet_IN messages shall still be sent to the controller automatically. Thus, it may not work to detect the attack against the controller with the traditional method in a single switch.

1.1 Related Work

As SDN is likely to become the heart of the next generation networks, security issues in SDN become very important. There are many studies on securing SDN with a focus on detecting DDoS attacks in SDN.

In 2010, Rodrigo Braga et al. [4] proposed a method for detecting a DDoS attack using OpenFlow. They combined the statistics from an OF switch with a self-organized map (SOM) to detect a DDoS attack. By using this method, they detected the DDoS attack without the specific middleware and got a good accuracy. However, this method was designed for detecting a traditional DDoS attack but not a DDoS attack against the controller. It is unknown to us whether this method work to detect a DDoS attack against the controller.

Though studies on the traditional DDoS detection are still active [5,17,20], many researchers realize that the detection of the DDoS attacks against a controller is more important. Thus, plentiful methods for detecting a DDoS attack against controller have been proposed [7,8,14,16,18].

Mousavi and St-Hilaire [13] proposed an entropy-based detection of the DDoS attacks against SDN controllers in 2015. They used the entropy of IP addresses to detect an attack. When an attack occurs, the attacker sends enormous fake packets to the OF switch. Consequently, the entropy of incoming packets increases sharply, which can be used to detect the attack. This method shows a great promptness, but it may make a misjudgment when the attacker tries to confuse it [6]. It is not a universal method though it shows a great promptness.

The hit rate of a flow entry can be simply represented by the amount of the packets that match the flow entry in a fixed time. For example, if a flow entry is hit 20 times in 1 second, then its hit rate is 20. One primary characteristic of the attack is that almost every packet has different IP address from another, which causes the low rate of the flow table. Ping Dong et al. [6] proposed a detection method with SPRT. They defined a flow entry with an extremely low hit rate as "low-traffic flow". First, they used SPRT to analyze the DARPA 1999 intrusion detection data set. Then, they used SPRT with the experienced parameters to detect an attack. This method reduces the possibility of misjudgment since the normal flows are always continuous but the low-traffic flows are not. It is a universal method to detect the attack against controller, but they still ignored the temporal characteristics of a DDoS attack, which could have achieved a faster detection.

In all methods mentioned before, the feature used to detect an attack is always a content feature, such as the entropy and the statistics from OF switch. Thus, the attacker can confuse these detection systems by changing the contents of malicious packets, such as the distribution of the IP addresses [6]. We notice that the principle of the attack is to trigger massive Packet_IN messages, thus the attack must cause a sharp decrease in the hit rates. This change is an inherent behavior feature of the attack. Therefore, we can use the gradients of hit rate as the time feature to detect the attack.

1.2 Our Contributions

In this paper, we propose a method to detect and defend the DDoS attack against controller based on time feature. It relies on the detection of the attacking behavior according to the time feature. First, we collect statistics from the OF switch, such as the count and duration of each flow entry. Then we calculate the hit rate with the count and duration of flow entry. The hit rate gradient is the gradient between two successive hit rates and it shows the changing rate of the hit rates. For example, if the hit rate changes from 2 to 3, the hit rate gradient is 1.5. With the multiple successive hit rates, we can calculate hit rate gradients as the time feature. Then we use the time feature to train a BPNN. Finally, a DDoS attack can be detected with the BPNN, and the appropriate response will be taken. In the comparison with the methods mentioned before, [6,13] particularly, our method has the following advantages:

- First, we use the temporal feature to predict the next state of the network in some respects. By contrast, the methods mentioned before use the current network state to detect a DDoS attack. For example, method [6] use low-traffic flow, which is a current state of flow table, to detect the attack. Thus, our method can detect the attack earlier.
- Second, the temporal feature is also the inherent behavior feature of the attack and we use it to detect the attack. It reduces the false positive (FP) rate caused by attacker's strategy. The method [13], for example, can be confused by the attacker and make a misjudgment.
- Finally, we implement a defense method and a dynamic port recovery mechanism, which makes our scheme more complete than method [13] and method [6]. The defense method interdicts attack flows effectively, while the port recovery mechanism decreases the negative effect on the legitimate services.

We have to admit that there are still shortages in our scheme. BPNN is a classical machine learning algorithm. Compared with other algorithms, it shows some limitations due to its simple structure. Though our defense method can effectively protect the controller, it causes the unavailability of the legitimate services sometimes. The time to recover a victim port is hard to predict and control. Fortunately, the experiment and evaluation show that our scheme is still feasible.

The rest of this paper is organized as follows. In Sect. 2, we are going to introduce the OpenFlow protocol and the BPNN. Details of the method and experiment are shown in Sects. 3 and 4. Finally, we will present conclusions in Sect. 5.

2 Background

The OpenFlow protocol is the key protocol of SDN while BPNN is a useful algorithm in the field of pattern recognition. Attacker utilizes the principle of OpenFlow to launch an attack and we use the BPNN to detect this attack, so it is necessary to introduce the OpenFlow and BPNN first.

2.1 OpenFlow

The OpenFlow protocol was proposed by professor N. McKeown in 2008. It suggests separating a network into the control plane and the data plane independently, communicating via a secure channel. The overview of OpenFlow architecture is shown in Fig. 1.

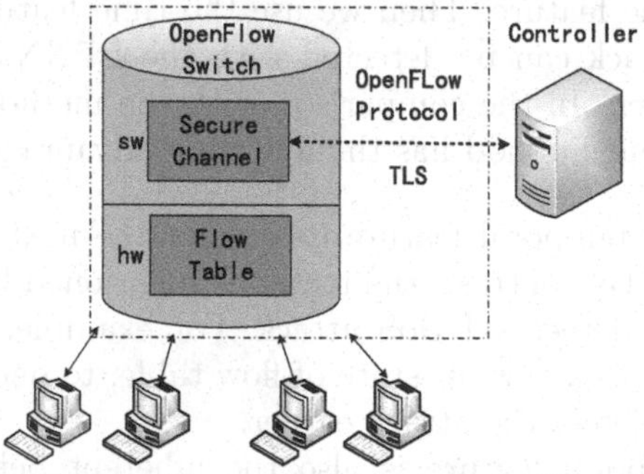

Fig. 1. OpenFlow architecture

In an OF switch, packets are always handled as the "flows". When a packet arrives at an OF switch, the switch tries to match the packet with the flow table which contains many flow entries. If the packet matches any flow entry, the switch will handle the packet as the instruction and update the counter of the flow entry. The packet that matches no flow entry should be encapsulated into Packet_IN message and sent to the controller. Controller makes a decision, then pushes a flow entry to the OF switch. The process of handling a packet in the OF switch is shown in Fig. 2.

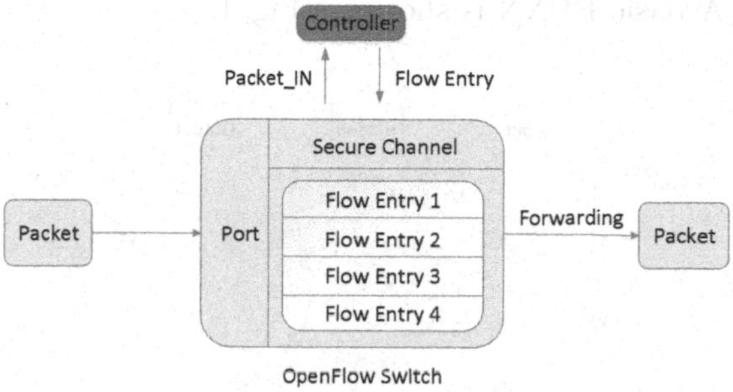

Fig. 2. Handle process of packet in SDN

According to the OpenFlow 1.0, a flow entry is mainly divided into three parts: match field, counter, and instructions. The match field consists of many segments from a packet, such as IP address, MAC address, port, type of protocol etc. The match field is used to match packet and determine which instruction should be chosen. The counter stores statistics of the packets matching this flow entry. As for the instructions, they tell the switch what kind of action should be taken, such as dropping, queuing or forwarding. Three main parts of a flow entry are shown in Fig. 3.

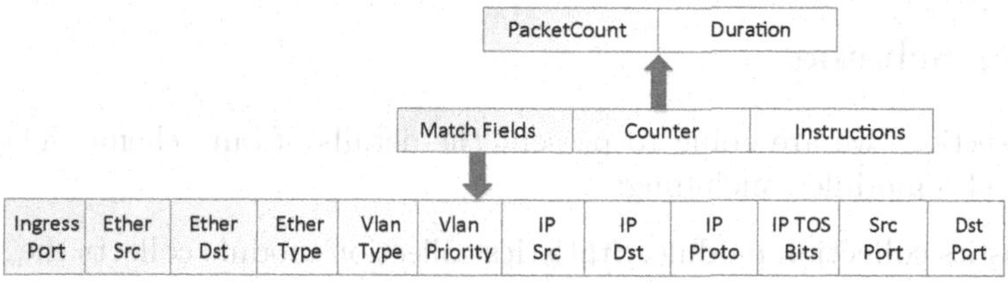

Fig. 3. Flow entry

From Fig. 3 we can see two important segments: "PacketCount" and "Duration". Once we get these two statistics from the OF switch, we calculate the hit rate of the flow table. Furthermore, we can calculate the gradient of hit rate with successive hit rates.

2.2 BPNN

Back propagation neural network(BPNN) [10] is one of the most useful artificial neural networks. It is a supervised neural network. A BPNN commonly consists of three layers: input layer, hidden layer, and output layer. The input layer and the output layer are single-layer structure, but the hidden layer can be a multi-layer structure. A basic BPNN is shown in Fig. 4.

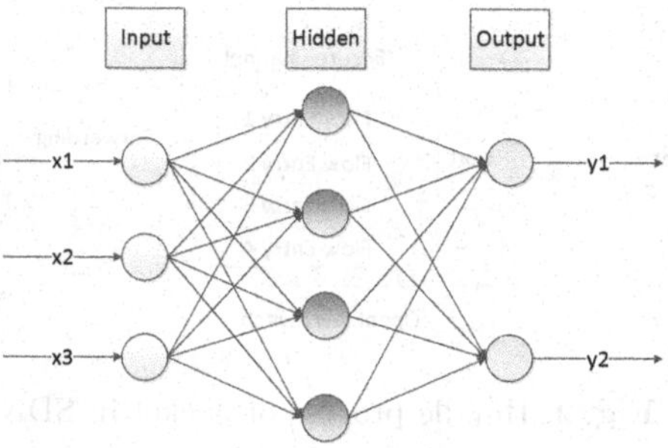

Fig. 4. Back propagation neural network

We choose BPNN to recognize the patterns of the attack since it makes our method adaptive to the hybrid attacks. Though attacker can confuse a detection system by combining different types of DDoS attacks, the behavior characteristics of the attack are still unchanged. BPNN needs a long time to train while little time to calculate, which helps us save a significant time and resource. The structure of BPNN may seem to be too simple, but it is already sufficient for an effective detection.

3 Our Scheme

In this section, we are going to present the details of our scheme. The scheme consists of 5 modules, including:

- Statistics collection module. Statistics collection module collects the statistics for port P in period T_1. The statistics that collected include the duration of each flow entry, the packet count of each flow entry and the number of flow entry for port P, represented by *Duration*, *FlowCount*, *Num* respectively.
- Feature extraction module. Feature extraction module calculates the average hit rate e of flow table in period T_1, then calculates the gradient of average hit rate in T_1, finally arranges n the gradients orderly in period $T_2 = n \cdot T_1 (n = 2, 3, \ldots)$.
- Attack detection module. Attack detection module mainly consists of a well-trained BPNN. The BPNN was trained with massive historical samples offline. With a well-trained BPNN, attack detection module can recognize the DDoS attack patterns in real time.

- Attack defense module. Attack defense module defends the attack in real time. It pushes a flow entry to the corresponding OF switch, then the switch drops all packets arriving at victim port P. The result is that malicious packets from the attacker are entirely intercepted.
- Port recovery module. Port recovery module helps to recover the victim port automatically. We implement this module with the help of the flow entry pushed by attack defense module.

The whole working process of our scheme is shown in Fig. 5. And in the following sections, we will explain how every module works in details.

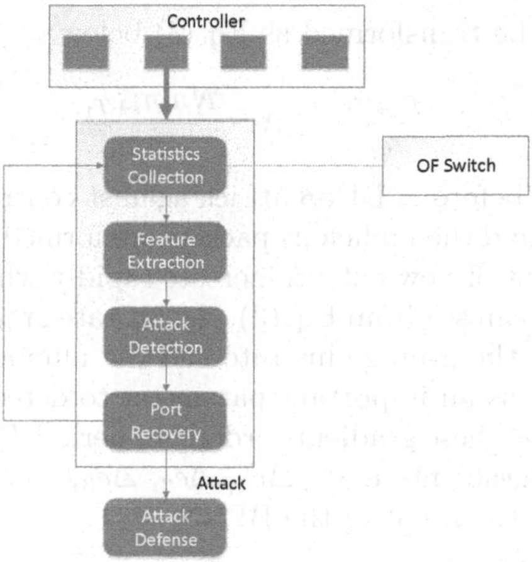

Fig. 5. Working process

3.1 Statistics Collection Module

Statistics collection module is embedded in the controller. It asks the controller for the statistics of port P in period T_1. The statistics that collected at time t include the duration of each flow entry, the packet count of each flow entry and the number of flow entry for port P. We order these statistics as a vector (P, *Duration, FlowCount, Num*).

3.2 Feature Extraction Module

Feature extraction module is also embedded in the controller. We get the time feature by calculating flow table's hit rate gradients in this module. First, we calculate the average hit rate of flow table for port P at time t. The equation we used is shown as Eq. (1) below.

$$e_t = \frac{\sum_{f \in F_P} FlowCount}{Num \cdot \sum_{f \in F_P} Duration} \tag{1}$$

The f is an existing flow entry in the flow table of the OF switch, and F_P is the set of flow entries in the flow table for port P.

We use Eq. (1) to calculate the average hit rates at time t and $t + T_1$, then calculate the gradient of average hit rates Δe between t and $t + T_1$ as Eq. (2) below.

$$\Delta e = \frac{e_{t+T_1}/Num_{t+T_1}}{e_t/Num_t} \tag{2}$$

Equation (2) can be transformed as Eq. (3) below.

$$\frac{e_{t+T_1}}{e_t} = \Delta e \cdot \frac{Num_{t+T_1}}{Num_t} \tag{3}$$

As we mentioned before, a DDoS attack against controller triggers enormous Packet_IN messages and the malicious packets are formed with a spoofed header. Therefore, the amount of flow entries increase rapidly while the average hit rate decrease rapidly. We can see from Eq. (3), the hit rate gradient Δe represents the relationship between the average hit rate and the number of flow entries. That is why we choose Δe as an important parameter to detect the DDoS attack.

Finally, we arrange these gradients orderly in period $T_2 = n \cdot T_1 (n = 2, 3, \ldots)$ and get a vector of gradients $\boldsymbol{e} = (\Delta e_1, \Delta e_2, \Delta e_3, \ldots, \Delta e_n)$. The vector $\boldsymbol{e}$ is the time feature and the input of the BPNN.

3.3 Attack Detection Module

After we get the inputs from feature extraction module, the next step is to train the BPNN. Since the BPNN is supervised, we have to label the inputs before training. After labeling, we get the training samples ($\boldsymbol{e}$, *Abnormal*, *Normal*). The first dimension is a gradients vector, the second and the third dimension are traffic patterns representing the DDoS attack and the normal traffic respectively.

In the detection phase, we use the well-trained BPNN to detect an attack in real time. First, we activate the statistic collection module and the feature extraction module to get a new $\boldsymbol{e}$, then put it into the BPNN without labeling, finally the BPNN judges which class this $\boldsymbol{e}$ belongs to. And we take the corresponding action according to the result.

We should point out that BPNN can be continuous updated online, even it has already been employed. The matter is the design of a correction strategy. Though a single mislabeled sample make little influence on BPNN, multiple mislabeled samples may lead to a totally wrong result due to the snowball effect. A correction strategy is necessary. But it involves the optimizing of a machine learning algorithm and is pretty complex. So we choose a static BPNN instead until we can design an effective correction strategy.

3.4 Attack Defense Module

Once a DDoS attack has been detected, this module is going to be activated. Attack defense module will push a special flow entry to the OF switch. The flow entry is shown in Table 1.

Table 1. Defense flow entry

Priority	Match field	Counter	Instructions
Minimal	In_Port = P	···	Action = *Drop*

The function of this flow entry is to directly drop all packets arriving at port P. It cuts off the way from attacker to the controller so that the controller can be well protected. First, the new coming packets trigger no Packet_IN message but update the "Counter" of the flow entry. Meanwhile, the existing flow entries for legitimate services can still match their packets, since they have a higher priority. As a result, existing services will not be interdicted, but new services need a longer time to establish a link.

3.5 Port Recovery Module

Since the attack defense module has shut down port P for new flows, the new legitimate services can be shut down, too. In order to decrease the negative influence due to the defense method, we design a port recovery module to recover the victim ports dynamically. The main idea of this method is contrary to the detection method. In the detection method, we regard a low hit rate as a symbol of the attack. As for recovery method, we can expect that there will still exist massive packets arriving at the port P if the attack still goes on. Thus, the defense flow entry must show an extremely high hit rate since each unknown packet hits this flow entry. By calculating the hit rate of defense flow entry and comparing it with other flow entries representing legitimate flows, we can judge whether port P is still under attack or not. The complete recovery process is shown as below.

1. We traverse the flow entries of all the legitimate flow entries and calculate the average hit rate of them as Eq. (4). If there is no or very few legitimate flow entries for P, we turn to other ports. F_{normal} is the set of flow entries that belongs to all normal ports.

$$\bar{e} = \frac{\sum_{f \in F_{normal}} FlowCount}{\sum_{f \in F_{normal}} Duration} \tag{4}$$

2. Then, we calculate the hit rate of the flow entry as Eq. (5).

$$e = \frac{FlowCount}{Duration} \tag{5}$$

3. Finally, we compare these two hit rates. If the result satisfies Eq. (6), we judge that the victim port is out of the attack and remove the flow entry.

$$\frac{e}{\bar{e}} < \lambda \tag{6}$$

If we make assumptions that (1) attacker sends packets in a speed p_1 (2) attack lasted for time t_1 (3) legitimate users send packets in an average speed p_2 (4) it takes time t_2 to recover the victim port since the attack ended. Consequently, we can somehow transfer Eq. (6) into Eq. (7).

$$\frac{p_1 \cdot t_1 + p_2 \cdot t_2}{p_2 \cdot t_2} < \lambda \tag{7}$$

Furthermore, Eq. (7) can be transformed into Eq. (8).

$$\frac{p_1 \cdot t_1}{p_2 \cdot (\lambda - 1)} < t_2 \tag{8}$$

From Eq. (8), we can see that the time needed to recover the victim port depends on the attack scale and the λ we set. The larger attack scale is and the smaller value of λ we set, the longer time it needs to recover the victim. Normally, a port that had suffered from a large-scale attack is more likely to be attacked again, thus it will be better to set a longer recovery time for it. However, a long recovery time makes legitimate services unavailable sometimes. The existence of λ makes the time controllable. We can set a suitable value of λ to achieve the effective defense and reduce the recovery time, which will be shown in the experiment. In general, if the network is time-sensitive, we set a larger λ; if the network is security-sensitive, we set a smaller λ. In our concern, the set of a suitable λ requires an experienced administrator, and it is better if we can enable adaptive λ.

4 Experiment and Evaluation

In the experiment, we trained BPNN with the DARPA 1999 Intrusion Detection Data Set [12]. In this way, we used the DARPA 1999 Intrusion Detection Data Set as the source of network flow, then programmed to simulated the controller and switch instead of the real one. We used a computer with 2.6 GHz Intel Core i7-6700HQ CPU and 8G RAM to perform the experiment, also, the OS of the computer is Windows 10 × 64.

4.1 Experiment Parameter

The parameters of experiment include: the period of statistics collection T_1, the period of feature extraction T_2, the parameters of BPNN, a number threshold of flow entries and the threshold 4λ. We set these parameters as Table 2 shows.

We set the T_1 as 100 packets time, which means statistics collection module collects statistics when 100 packets arrive at port P every time. The reasons

Table 2. Experiment parameters

Parameter	Value
T_1	100 packets
T_2	$5 \cdot T_1$
Input layer nodes	5
Hidden layer nodes	40
Output layer nodes	2
Learning rate	0.25
Positive (attack) samples	500
Negative (normal) samples	1500
Number threshold	30
λ	9

are to decrease the time of detection and lessen the burden of the controller. Actually, we also collect the statistics when the time changes. This operation causes that the time of detecting an attack is not always an integer. The T_2 decides dimension of the input vector. With a smaller dimension, we can make a judgment earlier, but it increases the FP value. Through several experiments, we find it suitable to set the T_2 as 5 times of the T_1. The number threshold is a check parameter to decrease FP value. Only when the BPNN gives a positive result and the number of flow entries exceeds this threshold will we judge that port P is under attack. Finally, we performed several times experiments to determine the value of λ.

4.2 Accuracy and Recall

In the detection of the attack, the accuracy and recall are two of the most important measurements. The DARPA 1999 Intrusion Detection Data Set includes the training data and testing data and contains 56 types of attack, 201 attack instances. After training BPNN with this data set, we begin to test it. Figure 6 shows the attack instances actually occurred on April 5th, 1999.

As we mentioned before, we simulated the controller and switch to test our scheme with the data. But, it did not decrease the accuracy and recall, since the statistics supposed to be got from controller and switch can be extracted directly from the data set.

Theoretically, there are 4 types of attacks that trigger massive Packet_IN messages. The attack principles of 4 kinds of attacks are shown in Table 3.

Since ipsweep attack did not occur, we evaluate our method by detecting 3 attacks.

Figure 7 shows the attack instances detected by [6]. We can see that 3 attack instances have been detected. Figure 8 shows the attack instances we detected. Our method detected smurf and neptune, but we did not detect portsweep.

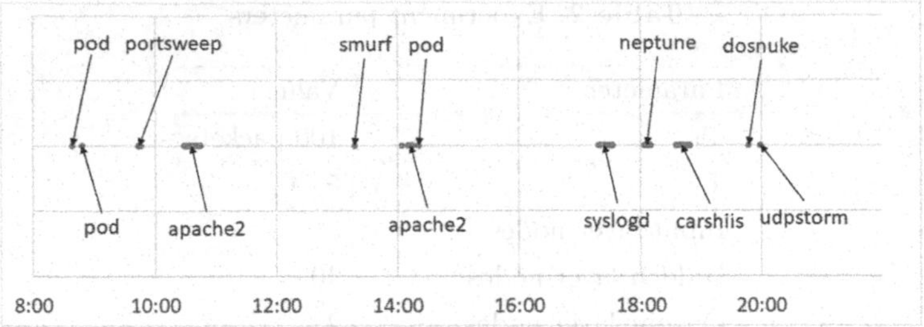

Fig. 6. Attack instances actually occurred

Table 3. Attack types

Attack	Principle
portsweep	Attacker sends a few packets, normally, 1 packet to every port of the target host to determine which port is available to attack
ipsweep	Attacker sends a few packets, normally, 1 packet to every host of the target network to determine which host is available to attack
smurf	Attacker sends massive ICMP packets with forged source IP address to the target host, then the target host replies to all nonexistent source hosts, and become too busy to handle other legitimate packets
neptune	Attacker sends massive SYN packets with different ports to target host, then the target host replies every SYN packet and waits, finally all the ports of target host are occupied

However, the portsweep attack detected by [6] triggers only 1 Packet_IN message per second. In fact, portsweep is not quite similar to the attack we try to detect. Though we did not detect portsweep, we detected another hidden attack and called it "burst". It represents a burst of TCP flow with random ports. Compared with portsweep, it is more likely to be a DDoS attack against controller, since it triggers massive Packet_IN messages. The "burst" is not defined as an attack in the DARPA 1999 Intrusion Detection Data Set, because the data set is used for the traditional network intrusions. Also, this flow is not considered as an attack instance in [6], either.

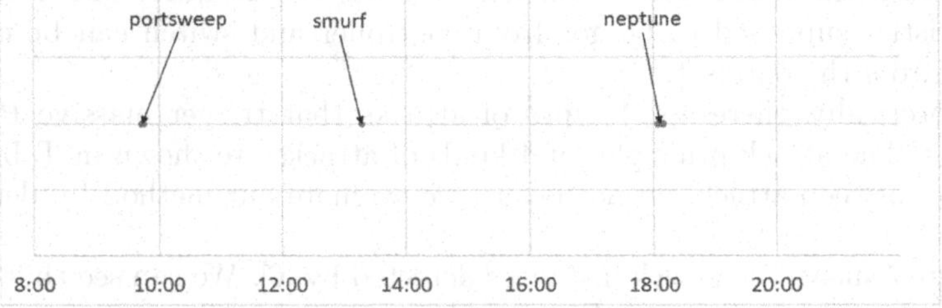

Fig. 7. Attack instances detected by method [6]

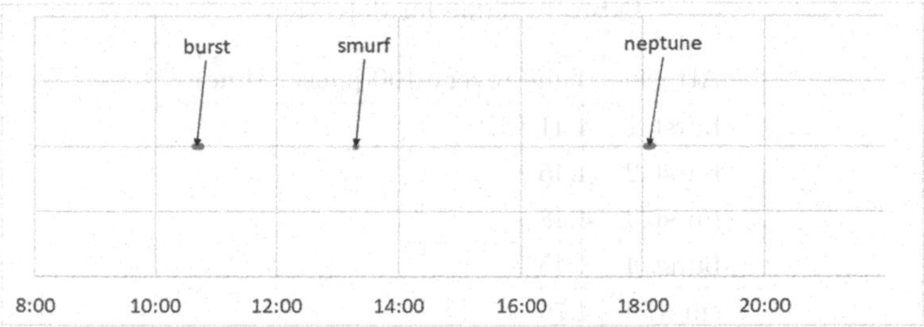

Fig. 8. Attack instances detected by our method

In fact, the value of the number threshold can be one of the factors that decide the detecting accuracy. The value of number threshold is the amount of the flow entries in the flow table. The accuracy is shown in Table 4.

Table 4. Threshold test

Number threshold	Actual attacks	Detected attacks	Misjudgment	Error rate
5	6	50	44	0.89
10	6	18	12	0.67
15	6	9	3	0.33
20	6	6	0	0

The 6 attack instances actually occurred are 4 "burst" instances, 1 smurf instance and 1 neptune instances. From Table 4 we can see, when number threshold increases, the number of misjudgment decreases. For this dataset, it is enough to set number threshold as 20. Since we set number threshold as 30 to ensure the accuracy, the attacks we detected in the experiment can be confirmed to be the real attack. However, the increase of number threshold may decrease the recall. For example, portsweep triggered only 1 Packet_IN message per second, therefore the amount of the flow entries did not exceed the number threshold and we did not detect it.

4.3 Promptness

Benefiting from using the gradients of hit rates rather than the hit rate itself, our method detected attack earlier, since we are detecting a tendency of the attack. The time it takes to detect 6 attack instances are shown in Table 5.

Table 5. Time for detection

Attack	Time (every 100 packet time)
burst 1	4.41
burst 2	4.45
burst 3	4.48
burst 4	4.45
smurf	4.76
neptune	4.75

As we mentioned before, we also collect statistics when time changes, such as 4.41 shown in Table 5. The average time our method takes to detect an attack is 4.55 times of period T_1, in another word, we detect a DDoS attack through the first 455 packets. Method [6] shows that they detect a DDoS attack by observing 6 successive "low-traffic flows", which means that it takes at least 6 periods of observation to detect an attack. Obviously, our method can detect the attack with fewer observations. It can be expected that an advanced machine learning algorithm shall help our scheme show a better performance.

4.4 Versatility

The time feature is extracted from the statistics in OF switch. It does not involve the content characteristics of flows, such as the IP address and protocol, but involves the behavior characteristics. The time feature can be used to detect all attacks aiming at disabling controller with massive Packet_IN message since their attack principles are the same. Consequently, our method can detect hybrid attacks in different scales or protocols.

4.5 Recovery

We have detected 3 kinds of attack and 6 attack instances, then activate the attack defense module 6 times. All the recovery time are shown in Table 6. The time is represented as seconds it passed from 08:00:00, for example, 08:00:05 is represented as "5 s".

From Table 6 we can see that the average time needed to recover a victim port is 31 seconds. Moreover, if we set a larger λ, we may even defend 4 "burst" attack instances with a single flow entry, then the controller only suffered from 441 packets. In our opinion, a time-sensitive network needs a smaller λ while security-sensitive network needs a larger λ. Since it need an experienced administrator to set a suitable λ, we may have to find a way to determine the value of λ automatically.

Table 6. Time for recovery

Attack	Start	End	Recover	Time
burst 1	9609 s	9611 s	9657 s	46 s
burst 2	9729 s	9731 s	9737 s	6 s
burst 3	9849 s	9851 s	9866 s	15 s
burst 4	9969 s	9971 s	9998 s	27 s
smurf	19088 s	19090 s	19127 s	37 s
neptune	36241 s	36651 s	39760 s	55 s

5 Conclusion

In this paper, we proposed a detection and defense method based on the temporal features of the DDoS attack against the controller. We calculated the gradients of the average hit rate with the statistics collected from OF switch. Then we used the gradients as the inputs of a BPNN. A well-trained BPNN can successfully detect a DDoS attack against a controller, then we defend against the attack effectively. Furthermore, we designed a method to dynamically recover the victim port. Our method was evaluated using the DARPA 1999 intrusion detection data set and compared with [6]. The results show that our method can detect an attack with greater speed and accuracy.

Acknowledgments. The work was supported by the National Natural Science Foundation of China (No. 61572001, No. 61502008, No. 61702005), The Natural Science Foundation of Anhui Province (No. 1508085QF132, No. 1708085QF136), and the Excellent Talent Project of Anhui University. The authors are very grateful to the anonymous referees for their detailed comments and suggestions regarding this paper.

References

1. Abdelmoniem, A.M., Bensaou, B., Abu, A.J.: SICC: SDN-based incast congestion control for data centers. In: IEEE International Conference on Communications, ICC 2017, Paris, France, 21–25 May 2017, pp. 1–6 (2017). https://doi.org/10.1109/ICC.2017.7996826
2. Akhunzada, A., Ahmed, E., Gani, A., Khan, M.K., Razzak, M.I., Guizani, S.: Securing software defined networks: taxonomy, requirements, and open issues. IEEE Commun. Mag. **53**(4), 36–44 (2015). https://doi.org/10.1109/MCOM.2015.7081073
3. Bizanis, N., Kuipers, F.A.: SDN and virtualization solutions for the internet of things: a survey. IEEE Access **4**, 5591–5606 (2016). https://doi.org/10.1109/ACCESS.2016.2607786
4. Braga, R., de Souza Mota, E., Passito, A.: Lightweight DDOS flooding attack detection using NOX/OpenFlow. In: Proceedings of the 35th Annual IEEE Conference on Local Computer Networks, LCN 2010, 10–14 October 2010, Denver, Colorado, USA, pp. 408–415 (2010). https://doi.org/10.1109/LCN.2010.5735752

5. Dayal, N., Srivastava, S.: Analyzing behavior of DDOS attacks to identify DDOS detection features in SDN. In: 9th International Conference on Communication Systems and Networks, COMSNETS 2017, 4–8 January 2017, Bengaluru, India, pp. 274–281 (2017). https://doi.org/10.1109/COMSNETS.2017.7945387
6. Dong, P., Du, X., Zhang, H., Xu, T.: A detection method for a novel DDOS attack against SDN controllers by vast new low-traffic flows. In: 2016 IEEE International Conference on Communications, ICC 2016, 22–27 May 2016, Kuala Lumpur, Malaysia, pp. 1–6 (2016). https://doi.org/10.1109/ICC.2016.7510992
7. Huang, X., Du, X., Song, B.: An effective DDOS defense scheme for SDN. In: IEEE International Conference on Communications, ICC 2017, 21–25 May 2017, Paris, France, pp. 1–6 (2017). https://doi.org/10.1109/ICC.2017.7997187
8. Kotani, D., Okabe, Y.: A packet-in message filtering mechanism for protection of control plane in OpenFlow networks. In: Proceedings of the 10th ACM/IEEE Symposium on Architectures for Networking and Communications Systems, ANCS 2014, 20–21 October 2014, Los Angeles, CA, USA, pp. 29–40 (2014). https://doi.org/10.1145/2658260.2658276
9. Kreutz, D., Bessani, A.N., Feitosa, E., Cunha, H.: Towards secure and dependable authentication and authorization infrastructures. In: 20th IEEE Pacific Rim International Symposium on Dependable Computing, PRDC 2014, 18–21 November 2014, Singapore, pp. 43–52 (2014). https://doi.org/10.1109/PRDC.2014.14
10. LeCun, Y., Bengio, Y., Hinton, G.E.: Deep learning. Nature **521**(7553), 436–444 (2015). https://doi.org/10.1038/nature14539
11. McKeown, N., Anderson, T., Balakrishnan, H., Parulkar, G.M., Peterson, L.L., Rexford, J., Shenker, S., Turner, J.S.: OpenFlow: enabling innovation in campus networks. Comput. Commun. Rev. **38**(2), 69–74 (2008). https://doi.org/10.1145/1355734.1355746
12. MITLincolnLaboratory: DARPA 1999 Intrusion Detection Data Set. https://www.ll.mit.edu/ideval/docs/attackDB.html
13. Mousavi, S.M., St-Hilaire, M.: Early detection of DDOS attacks against SDN controllers. In: International Conference on Computing, Networking and Communications, ICNC 2015, 16–19 February 2015, Garden Grove, CA, USA, pp. 77–81 (2015). https://doi.org/10.1109/ICCNC.2015.7069319
14. Kokila, R.T., Selvi, S.T., Govindarajan, K.: DDOS detection and analysis in SDN-based environment using support vector machine classifier. In: 2014 6th International Conference on Advanced Computing (ICoAC), pp. 205–210, December 2014
15. Shin, S., Gu, G.: Attacking software-defined networks: a first feasibility study. In: Proceedings of the 2nd ACM SIGCOMM Workshop on Hot Topics in Software Defined Networking, HotSDN 2013, Friday, 16 August 2013, pp. 165–166. The Chinese University of Hong Kong, Hong Kong (2013). https://doi.org/10.1145/2491185.2491220
16. Wang, R., Jia, Z., Ju, L.: An entropy-based distributed DDOS detection mechanism in software-defined networking. In: 2015 IEEE TrustCom/BigDataSE/ISPA, 20–22 August 2015, Helsinki, Finland, vol. 1, pp. 310–317 (2015). https://doi.org/10.1109/Trustcom.2015.389
17. Xu, Y., Liu, Y.: DDOS attack detection under SDN context. In: 35th Annual IEEE International Conference on Computer Communications, INFOCOM 2016, 10–14 April 2016, San Francisco, CA, USA, pp. 1–9 (2016). https://doi.org/10.1109/INFOCOM.2016.7524500

18. Yan, Q., Gong, Q., Deng, F.: Detection of DDOS attacks against wireless SDN controllers based on the fuzzy synthetic evaluation decision-making model. Ad Hoc Sens. Wirel. Netw. **33**(1–4), 275–299 (2016). http://www.oldcitypublishing.com/journals/ahswn-home/ahswn-issue-contents/ahswn-volume-33-number-1-4-2016/ahswn-33-1-4-p-275-299/
19. Zargar, S.T., Joshi, J., Tipper, D.: A survey of defense mechanisms against distributed denial of service (DDOS) flooding attacks. IEEE Commun. Surv. Tutor. **15**(4), 2046–2069 (2013). https://doi.org/10.1109/SURV.2013.031413.00127
20. Zhang, Y.: An adaptive flow counting method for anomaly detection in SDN. In: Conference on Emerging Networking Experiments and Technologies, CoNEXT 2013, 9–12 December 2013, Santa Barbara, CA, USA, pp. 25–30 (2013). https://doi.org/10.1145/2535372.2535411

Blockchain and Cryptocurrency

Fast Lottery-Based Micropayments for Decentralized Currencies

Kexin Hu[1,2(✉)] and Zhenfeng Zhang[1,2]

[1] Laboratory of Trusted Computing and Information Assurance, Institute of Software, Chinese Academy of Sciences, Beijing, China
[2] University of Chinese Academy of Sciences, Beijing, China
{hukexin,zfzhang}@tca.iscas.ac.cn

Abstract. Transactions using the Bitcoin system, which is built atop a novel blockchain technology where miners run distributed consensus to ensure the security, will cause relatively high transaction costs to incentivize miners to behave honestly. Besides, a transaction should wait a quite long time (about 10 min on average) before being confirmed on the blockchain, which makes micropayments not cost-effective. In CCS'15, Pass and shelat proposed three novel micropayment schemes for any ledger-based transaction system, using the idea of *probabilistic payments* suggested by Wheeler (1996) and Rivest (1997), which are called as the "Lottery-based Micropayments". However, the one among the three schemes, which is fully compatible with the current Bitcoin system and only requires an "invisible" verifiable third party, needs two on-chain transactions during each execution, even if both the user and the merchant are honest. To reduce the transaction costs and increase efficiency, this paper proposes a fast lottery-based micropayment scheme to improve their work. By setting up a time-locked deposit, whose secure utilization is assured by the security of a primitive called accountable assertions under the discrete logarithm assumption, our scheme reduces the number of on-chain transactions to one, and yet maintains the original scheme's advantages.

Keywords: Lottery-based micropayments · Decentralized currencies · High efficiency · Accountable assertions

1 Introduction

Decentralized cryptocurrency systems based on and led by Bitcoin [1,7,12] have gained rapid popularity in recent years, and are often quoted as "a peek into the future financial and payment infrastructure". Although it is striking using the idea of maintaining a distributed ledger known as the *blockchain* to provide a decentralized and open platform, the blockchain is in its childhood and there's still room for improvement.

The original version of this chapter was revised: The *University of Chinese Academy of Sciences* has been added as second affiliation for both authors. The correction to this chapter is available at https://doi.org/10.1007/978-3-319-93638-3_52

W. Susilo and G. Yang (Eds.): ACISP 2018, LNCS 10946, pp. 669–686, 2018.
https://doi.org/10.1007/978-3-319-93638-3_38

Since Satashi Nakamoto proposed Bitcoin [12] in 2008, plenty of work and debates about the Bitcoin system and the corresponding blockchain technology are springing up in various aspects, such as enhancing and analyzing their security [13,17,20], increasing the efficiency [5,23], etc. We believe that besides the security, a currency system's durability also relies on the its efficiency and convenient level.

However, the inherent scalability insufficiency derived from Bitcoin blockchain protocol is still one of the main reasons that limit the widely adoption of Bitcoin-like currency systems. Bitcoin currently bears less than ten transactions per second, compared to the credit card that deals with 10,000 transactions per second, especially where Visa can achieve 47,000 peak transactions per second [24], Bitcoin's throughput capacity cannot bear real-world demand. As for the transaction latency, Bitcoin costs 10 min to create a new valid block on average. In general, only if a block has been backed up by at least six blocks, the transactions contained can be fully confirmed. This totally costs about one hour which makes the latency too long to suite for many practical payment scenarios, such as supermarkets, vending machines, and take-away stores. Another drawback of Bitcoin is the transaction size. On average, the size of a transaction is 500 bytes. A turnover of 500 transactions per second would require 10 TB of additional disk space per year, which is at the limit of a consumer's storage capacity [9].

Micropayments, i.e. payments of small amounts like cents or fractions of a cent, have relatively high transaction costs. Besides what we have discussed above, the transaction fee for a Bitcoin payment costs at least 0.0001 bitcoin corresponding to between 2.5 and 10 cents in the year of 2013 and 2014 [14], which would be higher considering the rise in value of Bitcoin in recent years [6]. The relative high transaction cost makes micropayments not cost-effective, where the transferred value is just a few cents. Unfortunately, micropayments have many practical applications. Imagine Alice wants to use wireless service that Bob provides. For every minute Alice used, she should pay Bob a relative small amount of money, and this payment happens in every few minutes. Other streaming services such as a user pays for every music he downloaded, every video he watched are all micropayment instances, and some of them can happen *very frequently*. This shows that, how to increase efficiency and reduce transaction costs are central issues when designing micropayment schemes for decentralized cryptocurrencies like Bitcoin.

One idea to overcome this problem is to reduce transaction volume arriving at the blockchain by batching multiple transactions into a larger one. The leading proposals are the micropayment channels [5] and its following work - the Lightning Network [16]. However, the approach of micropayment channels limits in the number of payment recipients to a *single predetermined* one for each channel. Although the Lightning Network can mitigate this restriction, there are several other drawbacks such AS THE Worsening of Bitcoin's privacy weakness, the high bandwidth consumption and the massive storage needed.

Compared to the micropayment channels and the Lightning Network, another interesting proposal, proposed by Pass and shelat at CCS'15 [14], targeting at non-channel based peer-to-peer micropayments has a better performance in the number of payment recipients, meanwhile avoids the drawbacks of the Lightning Network. Their work is based on the idea of *probabilistic payments* suggested by Wheeler [25] and Rivest [18]. The key idea of probabilistic payments is to batch several small transactions into a large transaction, and this process employs probabilistic "lottery-based" payments that instead of sending a transaction of value v, one can also send a lottery ticket whose *expected payout* is v. That is, between every η transactions (e.g., $\eta = 100$), only one transaction will actually happen on average, and this transaction will pay η times the amount of a transaction should pay. For every payment, it's just like issuing a "lottery ticket", which has a winning probability of $1/\eta$, from a user to a merchant. The advantage of this approach is that only the winning lottery ticket yields in a recorded transaction, but every (unopened) lottery ticket is a transfer of value.

Pass and shelat presented three micropayment schemes in their paper, and all of them can support making payments to *arbitrary* recipients. Compared with the first scheme whose implementation needs a modification to the existing Bitcoin script, the second scheme is Bitcoin-compatible by introducing a *verifiable* third party $\mathcal{T}$ to overcomes this barrier. All of $\mathcal{T}$'s operations can be publicly verified by irrefutable evidences (i.e., unforgeable signatures) and it can be legally punished or replaced if anyone catches $\mathcal{T}$'s cheating. In reality, this party $\mathcal{T}$ can be instantiated by a currency Exchange [10] in which clients deposit their money for a better user experience, or any company/organization that regards its reputation as a central concern. For a currency Exchange, its reputation is the key factor for gaining clients' trust and collecting money from clients. Hence, no such company/organization will risk of losing its reputation. Therefore, we believe that the usage of $\mathcal{T}$ is feasible.

The third scheme inherits the advantages of the former two, furthermore, it only requires the intervention of an "invisible" verifiable third party $\mathcal{T}$. Namely, $\mathcal{T}$ is not involved in payment executions when both sides of payments are honest. However, to prevent a user's cheating by refusing to pay for the services/goods he has enjoyed, which can break the financial fairness to the merchant, the third scheme needs two on-chain transactions during each payment execution *even if both sides of a payment are honest.* Considering the scalability limit of Bitcoin blockchain and the frequent uses of micropayments, we believe that every on-chain transaction's cutting down is meaningful.

It's not trivial to design a *secure* lottery-based micropayment scheme *for decentralized currencies* to achieve this goal, meanwhile maintain the prior scheme's advantages. The basic security requirement is to prevent double spending, where users gain additional utilities by issuing the same lottery ticket to several merchants that multiple of them might win but only one will be able to cash in his ticket. Another security property, which is important for people to adopt the scheme in reality, is the financial fairness. It says, neither side of a payment will loss more than it deserves due to a malicious behavior of the other side.

Contributions. In this paper we propose a fast lottery-based micropayment scheme for decentralized currencies like Bitcoin. Our scheme uses a set of technologies as well as some primitives to construct a micropayment scheme focusing on enhancing the third scheme in [14], in reducing transaction costs and increasing efficiency. By use of a deposit mechanism which is supported by a primitive called the accountable assertions, our scheme only requires one on-chain transaction during each execution when both sides of payments are honest, compared to the two on-chain transactions needed in the prior scheme, and our scheme can still ensure financial fairness. The secure utilization of the deposit is assured by the security of the accountable assertions which can prevent double-spending attack as well as limit the value needed in the deposit. We define two security properties that should at least be satisfied by a lottery-based micropayment scheme for decentralized currencies, called *double-spending determent* and *financial fairness*, and we prove our scheme can achieve these properties. Furthermore, we give a performance comparison among some related micropayment schemes. More specifically, our micropayment scheme has the following advantages:

- It reduces the number of on-chain transactions during a payment's execution into one without breaking the security of micropayments. Compared to the prior scheme, our proposal increases efficiency, decreases the latency by half and reduces the average micropayment transaction fees, which we believe it's meaningful especially when micropayments are conducted frequently.
- It only requires an "invisible" verifiable third party $\mathcal{T}$ in the process of payments. When both participants honestly follow their instructions, $\mathcal{T}$ is not involved in a payment.
- It can support for making micropayments to *arbitrary* recipients.
- It attains financial fairness, especially to merchants, i.e., merchants can get what he deserves even if users has cheat.
- Our scheme is Bitcoin-compatible. It needs no modification to the existing Bitcoin script when adopting this scheme to make micropayments.

Paper Organization. We start with the preliminary on the fundamental of the Bitcoin system and a description of the accountable assertions, also the security assumptions and standard cryptographic building blocks are concerned in this section. In Sect. 3, we define some security requirements and briefly review the third scheme at CCS'15, then we present our proposal with a security analysis. Section 4 shows a performance comparison. Section 5 concludes the paper.

2 Preliminary

2.1 Background on Bitcoin

Like most cryptocurrencies, Bitcoin is a digital cryptographic currency built atop a decentralized peer-to-peer network, the blockchain. Every transaction published to the Bitcoin network can be verified according to some rules called *release conditions*, which are realized by the Bitcoin script. Transactions are posted to the blockchain within a block after solving a Proof-of-Work (PoW) puzzle. This work is done by nodes from the Bitcoin network called *miners*. The block-contained transactions are publicly readable and verifiable. Once a block is added into the blockchain, especially backed up by a few blocks, like six, as its successors, it is very hard to be modified or deleted. We normally regard blockchain as an append-only decentralized public ledger.

Transaction. Before making transactions in the Bitcoin network, a user generates at least one Bitcoin account with a ECDSA key pair (pk, sk) and an (pseudonymous) address. Every user is identified by his addresses[1]. Informally, a Bitcoin transaction is to transfer bitcoins from input addresses to output addresses using valid signatures, w.r.t. input addresses public keys respectively, to satisfy the predefined release condition. In the following, we use a triple (a, a', v) to indicate a transaction transferring v bitcoins from address a to address a', which is simplified as (a, a') to indicate transferring all bitcoins in a to a'.

We denote a Bitcoin address as $a = (pk, \sqcap)$, where pk is a's public key, and $\sqcap$ is a's release condition. A release condition can be simply seen as a script that contains a sequence of instructions, which limits the redemption of an account. We regard $\sqcap$ as a predicate function that returns 0/1. If a user wants to withdraw v bitcoins in address a to some other address a', he should present a witness x to satisfy a's release condition, such that $\sqcap(x, (a, a', v)) = 1$. In most cases, x is a signature on the transaction (a, a', v) w.r.t. a's public key.

Bitcoin Script. The Bitcoin scripting language ("Bitcoin script" for short) is not Turing-complete. To support the basic functionalities a transaction needed, Bitcoin includes a list of script instructions [4]. Besides some fundamental ones, one of the most popular and practical instructions is `OP_CHECKLOCKTIMEVERIFY` [3], which is used for locking an address until some predetermined point in the future. We explain the idea behind this instruction.

Lock Time. The lock time mechanism is to allow a transaction output to be made unspendable until some predetermined time T in the future. For a time-locked account, if the current time $t < T$, then the evaluation fails and a transaction with this account as input is consequently invalid. Only when $t \geq T$, the transactions involved can pass the verification and the funds covered are spendable.

A time-locked account usually serves as a deposit to prevent malicious behaviour. For example, before the locked time T, an account a can only be redeemed by a witness generated by some specific parties, such as someone trusted by both sides of a payment. However, after T, a is free and the money inside can be transferred using a signature w.r.t. a's public key. This can be very helpful to a scheme to realize financial fairness.

1 In this paper, we use the terms "address" and "account" interchangeably.

2.2 Accountable Assertions

Our construction uses a cryptographic primitive called accountable assertions. This primitive was first proposed by Ruffing et al. [19]. Intuitively, it allows users to assert statements to contexts for no more than a fixed number. Whenever a user asserts two distinct statements $st_1 \neq st_2$ to the same context ct, the private key of the user can be extracted *publicly*.

The authors gave out a concrete construction built upon the idea of chameleon authentication trees [11,21,22]. We describe the accountable assertions using the following algorithms:

- $\texttt{Setup}(\lambda) \rightarrow params$. This algorithm chooses a secure elliptic curve and a base point g of prime order q ($|q| \geq 2\lambda$ bites), where λ is a security parameter. Let l and n be positive integers defining the depth of a tree and its branching factor. It outputs (g, q, l, n) as $params$.
- $\texttt{KeyGen}(params) \rightarrow (pk, sk, auxsk)$. The key generation algorithm chooses a key $k \leftarrow \{0,1\}^\lambda$ for a pseudo-random function F_k, and a random integer $\alpha \in \mathrm{Z}_q^*$ to generate a key pair $(pk', sk') = (X, \alpha)$ with $X = g^\alpha$. Compute the root node as $x_i^1 = \mathsf{F}_k(p, i, 0), r_i^1 = \mathsf{F}_k(p, i, 1)$, where p is a unique identifier for the position of the root node, and $y_i^1 = g^{x_i^1} X^{r_i^1}$ for $i \in \{1, ..., n\}$ and set $z = \mathsf{H}(y_1^1, ..., y_n^1)$, where H is a collision-resistant hash function. Finally, it sets $pk := (pk', z), sk := sk', auxsk := k$.
- $\texttt{Assert}(sk, auxsk, ct, st) \rightarrow \tau$. Each node $Y_j = (y_1^j, ..., y_n^j)$ stores n entries, and $a_j \in \{1, ..., n\}$ defines the position in the node. Let Y_l represents the leaf stores the entry with the number ct, where $ct \in \{1, ..., n^l\}$, counted across all leaves from left to right, and a_l is the position of this entry within Y_l. In the following, let $x_i^j = \mathsf{F}_k(p_j, i, 0), r_i^j = \mathsf{F}_k(p_j, i, 1)$, where p_j is a unique identifier of the position of the node Y_j.
  - Compute Y_l: Assert statement st to ct by computing $r'^l_{a_l} = \alpha^{-1}(x^l_{a_l} - \mathsf{S}(st)) + r^l_{a_l} \pmod q$, where S is a hash function modeled as a random oracle. Observe that $g^{x^l_{a_l}} X^{r^l_{a_l}} = y^l_{a_l} = g^{\mathsf{S}(st)} X^{r}$. For $i \in \{1, ..., n\} \backslash \{a_l\}$, $y_i^l = g^{x_i^l} X^{r_i^l}$. Let $z_{l-1} = \mathsf{H}(y_1^l, ..., y_n^l)$ and let further $f_l = (y_1^l, ..., y^l_{a_l - 1}, y^l_{a_l+1}, ..., y_n^l)$.
  - Compute the nodes up to the root for $h = l-1, ..., 1$: Assert z_h with respect to Y_h by computing $r'^h_{a_h} = \alpha^{-1}(x^h_{a_h} - z_h) + r^h_{a_h} \pmod q$. Observe that $g^{x^h_{a_h}} X^{r^h_{a_h}} = y^h_{a_h} = g^{z_h} X^{r'^h_{a_h}}$. For $i \in \{1, ..., n\} \backslash \{a_h\}$, $y_i^h = g^{x_i^h} X^{r_i^h}$. Let $z_{h-1} = \mathsf{H}(y_1^h, ..., y_n^h)$ and let further $f_h = (y_1^h, ..., y^h_{a_h-1}, y^h_{a_h+1}, ..., y_n^h)$.

  Finally, it outputs the assertion $\tau := (r'^l_{a_l}, f_l, a_l, ..., r'^1_1, f_1, a_1)$.
- $\texttt{Verify}(pk, ct, st, \tau) \rightarrow b$. The verification algorithm parses pk as (pk', z), and τ as $(r'^l_{a_l}, f_l, a_l, ..., r'^1_1, f_1, a_1)$. It first verifies that pk' is a valid public key, then it checks the validity of a statement st in a context ct by reconstructing a path including nodes $(Y_l, Y_{l-1}, ..., Y_1)$ from a leaf Y_l to the root Y_1, and verifies whether $H(y_1^1, ..., y_n^1) = z$. If any of the above verifications fails, this algorithm outputs 0. Otherwise, it outputs 1.

- $\texttt{Extract}(pk, ct, st_1, \tau_1, st_2, \tau_2) \to sk/\bot$. The extraction algorithm computes, like the verification algorithm, the assertion paths for both st_1 and st_2 from the bottom up to the root until a position in the tree is found where the two paths form a collision, i.e., a position in the tree where values (x_1, r_1) are used in the assertion path of st_1 and values (x_2, r_2) are used in the assertion path of st_2 such that $g^{x_1}X^{r_1} = g^{x_2}X^{r_2}$. Then this algorithm outputs $sk = (x_1 - x_2)/(r_2 - r_1) \pmod q$. If no such position is found, it fails.

We illustrate with Fig. 1. Assume the context ct we would like to assert a statement maps to the node entry y_2^3. Node entries written in gray background constitute an assertion path for statement st from a leaf to the root. In this example, the assertion is $\tau = (r'^3_2, f_3, 2, r'^2_3, f_2, 3, r'^1_2, f_1, 2)$.

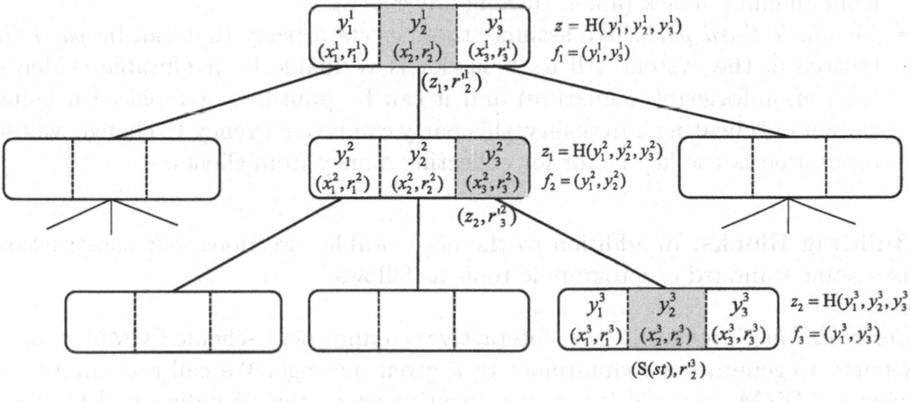

Fig. 1. A tree with a specific assertion path, where $l = 3$ and $n = 3$.

Ruffing, Kate and Schröder showed that the accountable assertions satisfy completeness, and security properties of extractability and secrecy under the discrete logarithm assumption. Informally, *extractability* states whenever two different statements have been asserted to the same context, the unique private key can be extracted except for a negligible probability. Opposed to extractability, *secrecy* states if no equivocation happens, i.e., there is a unique statement st for each context ct, the private key cannot be extracted except for a negligible probability.

2.3 Assumptions and Building Blocks

In this part, we present assumptions and a few more building blocks involved in our scheme.

Assumptions. In this paper, we regard the blockchain as a public transaction ledger who runs a consensus protocol among miners to agree on a global state. We make the following assumptions:

- *Correctness and availability.* We assume the blockchain will compute correctly following the predefined instructions, and the blockchain is always available.
- *Public state.* All nodes can see the state of the blockchain at any time, i.e., transactions in the blockchain is public. The blockchain can be seen as a public transaction ledger.
- *Time.* The blockchain embodies a discrete clock. Time increases in rounds. The lock time mechanism, described in Sect. 2.1, relies on this discrete clock to make a decision on the validity of a transaction. Time can be aware by all nodes in the system.
- *Message delivery.* Messages will arrive at the blockchain at the beginning of the next round. This makes the confirmation of any transaction costs a period of time. An adversary has the ability to arbitrarily reorder messages sent to the blockchain within a round, which makes the adversary may attempt a front-running attack (a.k.a. rushing adversary).
- *Verifiable third party.* We assume, there exists a party that can be *partially* trusted in the system. All its behavior is verifiable by irrefutable evidence (i.e., an unforgeable signature) and it can be punished or replaced if being caught of "cheating". In reality, this party can be a currency Exchange, whose reputation is the key factor for collecting money from clients.

Building Blocks. In addition to the accountable assertions, our construction uses some standard cryptographic tools as follows.

Commitment Schemes. A (non-interactive) commitment scheme COMM enables a party to generate a commitment to a given message. We call a commitment scheme COMM secure if it satisfies security properties of hiding and binding. Informally, *hiding* states a commitment does not reveal the committed value, and *binding* states a commitment cannot be opened to two different values, i.e., it is computationally (or statistically) infeasible to find (r, s, r', s'), such that, $r \neq r'$ but $\mathsf{COMM}_s(r) = \mathsf{COMM}_{s'}(r')$.

Signature Schemes. Our protocol uses signature scheme (`Gen,Sig,Vrf`) that is existentially unforgeable under adaptively chosen-message attacks (EUF-CMA) for all PPT adversaries. Informally, it states that any PPT adversary that is given the public key of the signature scheme and can query to the signing oracle for signatures of polynomial-time messages, the adversary still cannot output a valid pair of signature and the signed message that hasn't be queried before.

3 Fast Lottery-Based Micropayments

In this section, we provide our fast lottery-based micropayment protocol based on the prior scheme proposed by Pass and shelat in CCS'15 [14]. First, we define two important security requirements for lottery-based micropayments for decentralized currencies. Second, we briefly review the prior scheme. Finally, we present our protocol and give a security analysis.

3.1 Security Definitions

We define the following security definitions that we believe should at least be satisfied by lottery-based payments between users and merchants for decentralized currencies.

Definition 1 (Double-Spending Determent). *This property requires that a malicious user cannot produce two valid spending evidences for different payments that share the same serial number without being detected or punished.*

Definition 2 (Financial Fairness). *This property requires that in a lottery-based payment between a user and a merchant, the user should pay exactly the same amount of money according to the result of the lottery ticket and his behavior, i.e., whether he cheats, and the merchant can get what he deserves from the user.*

3.2 A Brief Review of the Scheme in CCS'15

In the third scheme of [14], the user U and the merchant M jointly generate a lottery ticket used to decide whether the merchant should be paid in this payment by invoking a coin-tossing protocol. Only if the lottery ticket wins, U should pay η times the amount of every transaction should pay (suppose the winning probability of the lottery ticket is $1/\eta$). To prevent a malicious U's cheating by withdrawing the money in the account that are supposed to be used to pay M, or using the same account to conduct payments with someone else (i.e., double spending), which both can lead to M's loss, this scheme was designed to send M a credential before M tells U the ticket result. With this credential, M can transfer bitcoins from U's account a to a special account a'. The specialty of a' relies on its release condition. It limits the recipient account to be either a^U, which is fully controlled by U, or a^M that belongs to M. Furthermore, the release condition of a' demands a 2-of-3 multi-signature from the set $\{\sigma_U, \sigma_M, \sigma_\mathcal{T}\}$ which are signed by $U, M, \mathcal{T}$ respectively. Therefore, U cannot withdraw/transfer the money in account a' without the help of M or $\mathcal{T}$. If U and M are honest, they can complete a payment by themselves. However, if U cheats, M will not help U otherwise he will suffer a loss, and $\mathcal{T}$ will not help U if he suspects U's honesty. In this case, M can ask $\mathcal{T}$'s help to get the money he deserves from account a'. If M cheats about his winning and maliciously locks U's money into account a', U can still withdraw his money with the help of $\mathcal{T}$ by providing a multi-signature of $(\sigma_U, \sigma_\mathcal{T})$ to satisfy the release condition of a'. Thus, this scheme can ensure financial fairness both for the user and the merchant as well as preventing double-spending attack.

3.3 Our Protocol

We proceed to present the construction of our protocol, shown in Fig. 2. Similar to the prior scheme, our protocol requires the intervention of an "invisible" verifiable third party $\mathcal{T}$, which is involved in an execution only when participants deviate from their prescribed instructions. All transaction-related instructions described in our protocol can be conducted using the existing Bitcoin script, thus, our protocol is Bitcoin-compatible.

We adopt two accounts to prevent potential attacks from U. If U and M are honest, an execution only involves the first account to transfer an amount of money when the lottery ticket wins. If, however, a malicious U refuses to pay, M can be compensated using the second account with $\mathcal{T}$'s help before a expiry time T. The second account is a locked deposit of U with a expiry time T. If M can present a valid evidence showing U has cheated before time T, $\mathcal{T}$ will transfer the same amount of value the merchant deserves from the second account, together with a public verifiable evidence showing that $\mathcal{T}$'s computation is correct.

Next, we concern more details. The front-running attack should be prevented where a malicious user wants to avoid losses by withdrawing his deposit before M being compensated. We set a period of time T' as a safety margin to enable a successful transfer on the blockchain, e.g., $T' = 10$ min. Thus, when M receives a ticket from U, he should check whether the current time satisfies $t < T - T'$. If it fails, M should reject and abort. Also, to prevent U's double-spending attack by conducting multiple payments concurrently which makes a deposit insufficient to pay all victims, we adopt the accountable assertions to limit the number of payments a deposit can be linked. A malicious user will lose all his money in the deposit if he ever initiates even one double-spending payment. Moreover, we set a period of time $\bar{T}$ as a safety margin to protect U's asset when M is malicious and wants to double his income by showing an evidence to $\mathcal{T}$ that U has not published a transaction, and after that telling U that he wins the lottery. U will not do any operation if the current time goes out of scope as defined. Finally, we expect the protocol can be conducted without the intervention of $\mathcal{T}$ when U and M are honest, thus, U should have the ability to withdraw his deposit (i.e., money in the second account) by himself after time T.

Money in the first account $a = (pk_a, \sqcap^a)$ gets released if U agrees to a transaction to M. Money in the second account $a^{dep} = (pk_d, \sqcap^d)$ can only be released if either (a) both U and $\mathcal{T}$ agree to a transaction before a certain time T, or (b) U agrees to a transaction after time T. We implement it using the lock time mechanism. Let $\sqcap^a(x, (a, a')) = 1$ if and only if $x = \sigma_1$ is a signature of the transaction (a, a') w.r.t. pk_a. This can be implemented with a standard release condition. Define $\sqcap^d(x', (a^{dep}, a'', v)) = 1$ if and only if either (a) before time T, x' contains a signature $\sigma_{\mathcal{T}}$ of the transaction (a^{dep}, a'', v) w.r.t. $pk_{\mathcal{T}}$, where v denotes the value being transferred, or (b) after time T, x' is a signature σ'_U of the transaction (a^{dep}, a'', v) w.r.t. pk_d. In the optimistic case when U and M honestly follow their instructions, $\mathcal{T}$ will not involve into an execution. If M finds out that U deviates from his instructions before time T, i.e., U refuses to transfer the money to M, M and $\mathcal{T}$ can present a valid witness to release the same amount of money from a^{dep}, and showing an evidence of $\mathcal{T}$'s honesty.

Let "[·]" be an operation when inputting a random string, it outputs 1 with a probability of $1/\eta$, or 0 otherwise. For example, if the last two digits of the input random string are 00, it outputs 1 and this happens with probability 1/100.

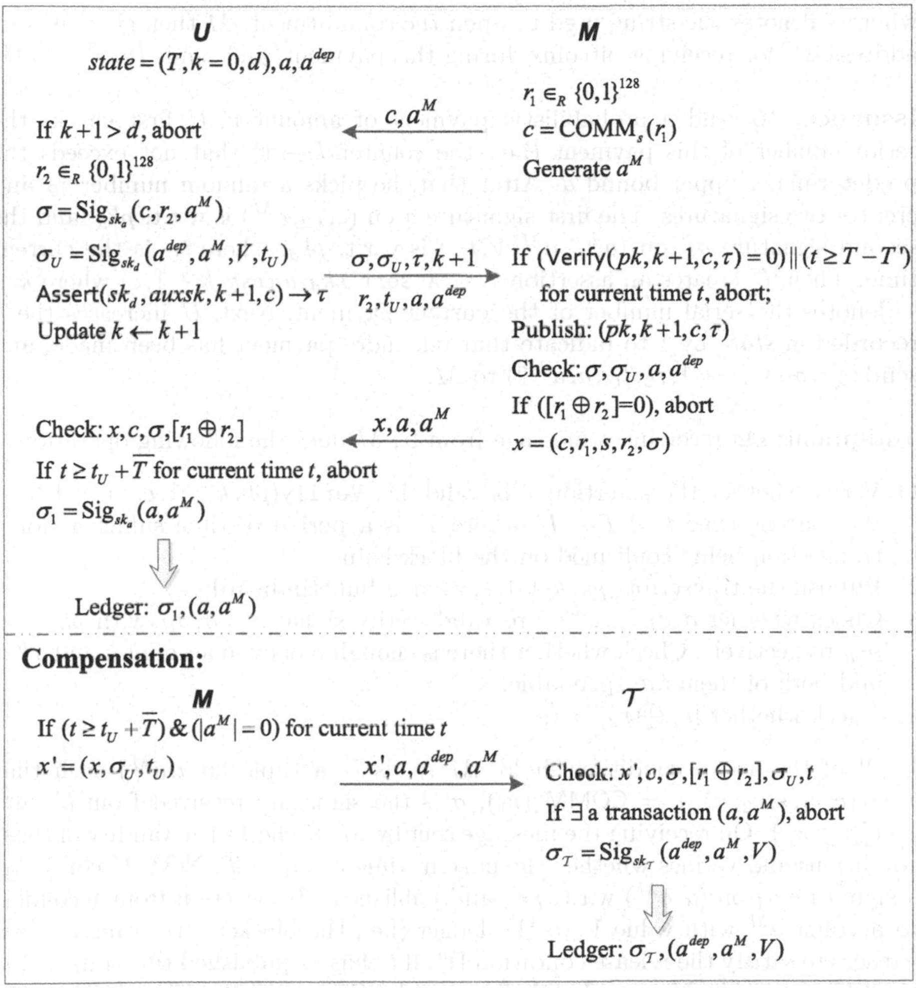

Fig. 2. Fast "Lottery-based" micropayments.

Set Up: A user U generates a Bitcoin key pair (pk_a, sk_a) and transfers $V = \eta \cdot v$ bitcoins to an address $a = (pk_a, \Pi^a)$. U generates another Bitcoin key pair (pk_d, sk_d) together with accountable assertions keys $(pk, sk = sk_d, auxsk)$, and transfers $(dV + p)$ bitcoins to an address $a^{dep} = (pk_d, \Pi^d)$ with a expiry time T, where p is the penalty if U double spends. U keeps an initial deposit state

state := $(T, k = 0, d)$, where k is a counter and d is the number of payments this deposit can be involved.

Request: Whenever M wants to request a payment of v bitcoins from U, he picks a random number $r_1 \leftarrow \{0,1\}^{128}$, generates a commitment $c = \mathsf{COMM}_s(r_1)$ where s denotes the string used to open the commitment. M then generates an address a^M for receiving bitcoins during this payment, and sends (c, a^M) to U.

Issuance: To send a probabilistic payment of amount v, U first checks the serial number of this payment (i.e., the counter $k+1$) that not exceeds the predetermined upper bound d. After that, he picks a random number r_2 and creates two signatures. The first signature σ on (c, r_2, a^M) is w.r.t. pk_a, and the second signature σ_U on (a^{dep}, a^M, V, t_U) is w.r.t. pk_d, where t_U is the current time. Then, U creates an assertion $\tau \leftarrow \mathtt{Assert}(sk_d, auxsk, k+1, c)$ where $k+1$ denotes the serial number of the current payment. Next, U increases the k recorded in *state* by 1 to indicate that one more payment has been made, and sends $(\sigma, \sigma_U, \tau, k+1, r_2, t_U, a, a^{dep})$ to M.

Judgment: On receiving a message from U, M does the following operations:

1) Verify whether the assertion τ is valid, i.e. $\mathtt{Verify}(pk, k+1, c, \tau) = 1$, and the current time $t < T - T'$ where T' is a period of time sufficient for a transaction being confirmed on the blockchain;
2) Publish the transcript $(pk, k+1, c, \tau)$ on a bulletin board;
3) Check whether $\sigma, \sigma_U, a, a^{dep}$ are valid: verify signatures σ, σ_U with pk_a and pk_d respectively. Check whether there is enough money in account a and a^{dep}, and both of them are spendable;
4) Check whether $[r_1 \bigoplus r_2] = 1$.

If all of the above conditions hold, M sends U a tuple (x, a, a^M) such that $x = (c, r_1, s, r_2, \sigma)$, $c = \mathsf{COMM}_s(r_1)$, σ is the signature received from U, and $[r_1 \bigoplus r_2] = 1$. On receiving the message sent by M, U checks the validity of these conditions and verifies whether the current time $t < t_U + \bar{T}$. Next, U computes a signature σ_1 on (a, a^M) w.r.t. pk_a and publishes a transaction from account a to account a^M with value V to the ledger (i.e., the blockchain), using σ_1 as a witness to satisfy the release condition $\sqcap^a$. If U hasn't published this transaction until time $t_U + \bar{T}$, M immediately invokes the Compensation procedure.

Compensation: When $\mathcal{T}$ receives a tuple (x', a, a^{dep}, a^M) such that $x' = (x, \sigma_U, t_U)$, $c = \mathsf{COMM}_s(r_1)$, σ is a valid signature on (c, r_2, a^M) w.r.t. pk_a, $[r_1 \bigoplus r_2] = 1$, σ_U is a valid signature on (a^{dep}, a^M, V, t_U) w.r.t. pk_d, and the current time t satisfies $t_U + \bar{T} \leq t < T$, $\mathcal{T}$ checks if there is a transaction from address a to a^M in the Bitcoin network or on the ledger. If not, $\mathcal{T}$ signs (a^{dep}, a^M, V) w.r.t. $pk_{\mathcal{T}}$, and publishes a transaction from account a^{dep} to account a^M with value V to the ledger, using $\sigma_{\mathcal{T}}$ as the witness to satisfy the release condition

Π^d before time T. $\mathcal{T}$ also publishes an evidence related to this payment showing its honesty.

Penalty: If there exists two assertions (c, τ) and (c', τ') that corresponding to the same (pk, k), anyone, including $\mathcal{T}$, can *immediately* extract $sk(= sk_d)$. Before U can withdraw the money in a^{dep}, which is only allowed after time T, $\mathcal{T}$ can take out all bitcoins in a^{dep} by publishing a signature w.r.t. pk_d as an evidence that U has cheated.

After the expiry time T, U is free to withdraw the remaining money in the account a^{dep} with a signature w.r.t. pk_d. Even if there are several merchants contacting $\mathcal{T}$ during the period of T, as long as $\mathcal{T}$ has settled these disputes *before time* T, the honest merchants can be compensated. It is convenient for $\mathcal{T}$ to merge all honest requests into one larger transaction and only release this transaction to the ledger.

3.4 Security Analysis

We present three theorems to state that our lottery-based micropayment protocol can achieve the security properties defined in Sect. 3.1, and we defer the proofs to Appendix A.

Theorem 1. *If COMM is a secure commitment scheme, and the signature scheme* (Gen,Sig,Vrf) *is existentially unforgeable under adaptively chosen-message attacks (EUF-CMA), then the probability that an execution of the proposed lottery-based micropayment protocol results in an transaction on the blockchain is exactly* $1/\eta$.

Theorem 2. *If accountable assertions* (Setup, KeyGen, Assert, Verify, Extract) *is extractable, and COMM is a secure commitment scheme, then the proposed lottery-based micropayment protocol is double-spending deterrable.*

Theorem 3. *If COMM is a secure commitment scheme, signature scheme* (Gen,Sig,Vrf) *is EUF-CMA, and accountable assertions* (Setup, KeyGen, Assert, Verify, Extract) *satisfy extractability and secrecy, then the proposed lottery-based micropayment protocol can achieve financial fairness.*

4 Performance Comparison

In this section, we give a brief comparison of the performances among our protocol, Pass and shelat's scheme (i.e., the third one) presented at CCS'15 [14], the full version [15] of CCS'15, and a lottery-based micropayment protocol on Zerocash [20]. In Table 1, we measure the performances of the four schemes with the transaction number needed, the financial fairness property, and the communication and computation costs both on the user and the merchant sides.

Table 1. Performance comparison

Ref.	Transaction number[a]	Financial fairness	Communication (in rounds)[a]	User[b]	Merchant[b]
CCS'15	1 off-line[c] 2 on-chain	Yes	4	6·exp	5·exp
The full version [15]	2 off-line 1 on-chain	No	3	7·exp	6·exp
DAM	2 off-line 1 on-chain	No	3	10·exp+△[d]	10·exp+⊙[d]
Ours	2 off-line 1 on-chain	Yes	3	6·exp	10·exp

[a] We only measure the number of transactions (in the 2rd column) and the rounds (in the 4th column) that a *winning* payment needed between *honest* parties.
[b] In comparison of computation cost, we only take into account of the expensive operations that a *winning* payment needed between *honest* parties, where "exp" denotes an exponentiation operation in group $\mathbb{G}$.
[c] We divide the transactions involved in a protocol into two categories: off-line and on-chain, where "off-line" indicates a transaction that can be computed on the fly before an execution of payments.
[d] "△": a Zerocash Pour operation + a NIZK prove operation + 4 (non-)membership prove operation. "⊙": a NIZK verify operation.

Our protocol requires 1 on-chain transaction during each winning micropayment for transferring money from U to M directly. Besides, U creates another 2 off-line transactions, which can be conducted on the fly, to transfer money to U's paying account a and deposit account a^{dep} separately.

In the version of Pass and shelat's third scheme at CCS'15, it requires 1 off-line transaction, which transfers money to U's paying account (i.e. account a in Sect. 3.2), and 2 on-chain transactions. The first on-chain transaction transfers money from account a to a frozen account a', and the second one transfers money from a' to M. Compared to ours, the total number of transactions seems to remain unchanged, however, one of our off-line transactions, related to a^{dep}, can support for several payments. Considering micropayments can happen frequently, our protocol reduces the average micropayment transaction fees.

The full version [15] improves the third scheme to involve only 1 on-chain transaction using the multi-signature [2]. Besides 1 off-line transaction for transferring money to U's paying account, it needs an extra deposit account that uniquely binds to a lottery ticket (i.e. a paying account) and burns on an evidence of double-spending to deal with the front-running/parallel attack. The size of the deposit requires to be large enough but is unspecified in the paper, and the uniquely binding limits the number of tickets a user can validly create due to the requirement of the size of a binding deposit, thus narrows the number of services a user can enjoy concurrently. Our protocol enables concurrent micropayments with a same deposit by the use of accountable assertions. This is a practical extension for applications of micropayments.

The DAM (Decentralized Anonymous Micropayment) scheme [8], proposed at EUROCRYPT'17, is a lottery-based micropayment scheme based on Zerocash [20]. To resolve the tension between the anonymity and double-spending determent, the DAM scheme involves a deposit account like ours and [15], and introduces plenty of primitives such as NIZK. However, similar to [15], the deposit burns on an evidence of double-spending. This makes a payment not financial fair, i.e., M cannot be compensated if U cheats. The computation cost of the DAM scheme is obviously higher than the other three schemes, and in Table 1 we only take out some very expensive operations in the DAM scheme as a whole in "$\triangle$" and "$\odot$".

5 Conclusion

Bitcoin, as well as many crypto-currencies based on the novel blockchain technology, has inherent scalability limits such as low capacity in transaction throughput, long transaction latency, large transaction size and relatively high transaction costs, which makes micropayments not cost-effective. This paper proposed a fast lottery-based micropayment scheme for decentralized currencies, especially for Bitcoin. It adopted the idea of probabilistic "lottery-based" micropayments, but further reduced transaction costs and increased efficiency of a prior scheme at CCS'15 by establishing a time-locked deposit account with the accountable assertions. As long as both sides of payments are honest, our scheme can be conducted without any third party's involvement and require at most one "on-chain" transaction during each execution. However, if a user or a merchant is malicious, our scheme can protect the counterparty's fund security with the help of a verifiable third party.

Acknowledgements. We thank the anonymous reviewers for their comments which helped to improve the paper. This work was supported by the National Key R&D Program of China (Nos. 2017YFB0802500, 2017YFB0802000), and the National Natural Science Foundation of China (No. U1536205).

A Proofs for Theorems

Theorem 1. *If COMM is a secure commitment scheme, and signature scheme* (`Gen`,`Sig`,`Vrf`) *is existentially unforgeable under adaptively chosen-message attacks (EUF-CMA), then the probability that an execution of the proposed lottery-based micropayment protocol results in an transaction on the blockchain is exactly* $1/\eta$.

Proof. Suppose the user can bias the result and spend less than he ought to be, which means that after he receiving a commitment c from the merchant, the user can select a r_2 satisfying $[r_1 \bigoplus r_2] = 0$. This equals to that the user can know r_2, the committed value of the commitment c, before the merchant opens c. This will break the hiding property of the commitment scheme.

Suppose the merchant can bias the result and earn more money, which means that he can either present a new $r_1'(\neq r_1)$ satisfying $([r_1' \bigoplus r_2] = 1) \wedge (c = \mathsf{COMM}_{s'}(r_1'))$ which breaks the binding property of the commitment scheme where c is the commitment of r_1, or he can succeed by presenting a new pair (r_2', σ') satisfying $([r_1 \bigoplus r_2'] = 1) \wedge (\mathtt{Vrf}_{pk_a}(\sigma', (c, r_2', a^M)) = 1)$, and this will break the existentially unforgeable of the signature scheme. □

Theorem 2. *If accountable assertions* (Setup, KeyGen, Assert, Verify, Extr – act) *is extractable, and COMM is a secure commitment scheme, then the proposed lottery-based micropayment protocol is double-spending deterrable.*

Proof. Suppose an adversary $\mathcal{A}$ can break the double-spending determent of our lottery-based micropayment protocol, then he can produce at least two assertions τ and τ' with $\tau \leftarrow \mathtt{Assert}(sk_d, auxsk, k, c)$, $\tau' \leftarrow \mathtt{Assert}(sk_d, auxsk, k, c')$ and finish the corresponding payments without being caught, where c and c' belong to two different payments generated by the corresponding merchants, and k denotes a serial number. When $c \neq c'$, this means that $\mathcal{A}$ can break the extractability of the accountable assertions. When $c = c'$, where $c = \mathsf{COMM}_s(r_1)$ and $c = \mathsf{COMM}_{s'}(r_1')$, according to the binding property of the commitment scheme, $(r_1, s) = (r_1', s')$. However, this happens with only a negligible probability when two merchants randomly choose the same pair (r_1, s) which is used to ensure the merchants asset security. □

Theorem 3. *If COMM is a secure commitment scheme, signature scheme* (Gen, Sig, Vrf) *is EUF-CMA, and accountable assertions* (Setup, KeyGen, Assert, Verify, Extract) *satisfy extractability and secrecy, then the proposed lottery-based micropayment protocol can achieve financial fairness.*

Proof. Suppose a malicious merchant can break the financial fairness of the user by receiving more money than the user should pay for the payment. This means that the merchant can either (1) bias the result of the lottery ticket, or (2) transfer the money from a to his account a^M even if he loses the lottery ticket by forging a signature $\sigma = \mathtt{Sig}_{sk_a}(a, a^M)$, or (3) collect all published assertions related to the user and extract the private key of a^{dep} then generate a valid signature, or (4) transfer the money from a^{dep} to his account a^M by forging a signature $\sigma = \mathtt{Sig}_{sk_{\mathcal{T}}}(a^{dep}, a^M, V)$ before time T, or (5) publish a signature $\sigma = \mathtt{Sig}_{sk_d}(a^{dep}, a^M, V)$ to withdraw the money in a^{dep} after time T.

The condition (1) is infeasible due to our proof for Theorem 1. For the condition (2), (4) and (5), any one of them can break the existentially unforgeable of the signature scheme. The condition (3) is conflicting with the secrecy of the accountable assertions. Besides, a transaction published by the user in order to transfer money from a and a transaction published by $\mathcal{T}$ in order to transfer money from a^{dep} will not coexistent, due to the assumptions that the blockchain is available and public, and the discrete clock blockchain embodies makes the time in the system is synchronous.

Suppose a malicious user can break the financial fairness of the merchant by refusing to pay the merchant even the lottery ticket has won. The user may refuse to publish a transaction from a to a^M, and M cannot obtain the money he deserves from the deposit account a^{dep} by himself. Remember that there exist a verifiable third party $\mathcal{T}$ whose operations should follow the instructions of the scheme. Thus, a merchant can ask $\mathcal{T}$'s help to obtain the money from the deposit account a^{dep} when facing a malicious user. The user cannot withdraw the money in the locked account a^{dep} before time T, otherwise it violates the assumption of the correctness of the blockchain. Although the deposit is unlocked after the time T and the user can freely withdraw the money, the protocol limits that every request received by M should be before the time $T - T'$ where it leaves a period of time T' for $\mathcal{T}$ to handle a dispute.

It remains one more case that should be considered, i.e., the money in the deposit account a^{dep} may be insufficient to compensate M. In this case, the user has conducted multiple (more than d) payments by issuing n assertions $\{\tau_i\}_{i=1}^n$, where n ($n > d$) is the number of payments the user conducts hoping that the deposit cannot afford all merchants compensation requests. As a result, there must be at least two assertions satisfying $(\tau_i \leftarrow \texttt{Assert}(sk_d, auxsk, k_i, c_i)) \wedge (\tau_j \leftarrow \texttt{Assert}(sk_d, auxsk, k_j, c_j)) \wedge (\texttt{Verify}(pk, k_i, c_i, \tau_i) = 1) \wedge (\texttt{Verify}(pk, k_j, c_j, \tau_j) = 1) \wedge (k_i = k_j)$. According the proof of Theorem 2, this can either break the extractability of the accountable assertions, or the binding property of the commitment scheme. □

References

1. Barber, S., Boyen, X., Shi, E., Uzun, E.: Bitter to better—how to make bitcoin a better currency. In: Keromytis, A.D. (ed.) FC 2012. LNCS, vol. 7397, pp. 399–414. Springer, Heidelberg (2012). https://doi.org/10.1007/978-3-642-32946-3_29
2. Bitcoin Wiki. BIP 0010. https://en.bitcoin.it/wiki/Multisignature
3. Bitcoin Wiki. BIP 0065. https://en.bitcoin.it/wiki/BIP_0065
4. Bitcoin Wiki. Script. https://en.bitcoin.it/wiki/Script
5. Bitcoinj Project. Working with micropayment channels. https://bitcoinj.github.io/working-with-micropayments
6. BLOCKCHAIN. Blockchain Charts. https://blockchain.info/charts
7. Bonneau, J., Miller, A., Clark, J., Narayanan, A., Kroll, J.A., Felten, E.W.: SoK: research perspectives and challenges for Bitcoin and cryptocurrencies. In: 2015 IEEE Symposium on Security and Privacy, pp. 104–121. IEEE (2015)
8. Chiesa, A., Green, M., Liu, J., Miao, P., Miers, I., Mishra, P.: Decentralized anonymous micropayments. In: Coron, J.-S., Nielsen, J.B. (eds.) EUROCRYPT 2017 Part II. LNCS, vol. 10211, pp. 609–642. Springer, Cham (2017). https://doi.org/10.1007/978-3-319-56614-6_21
9. Decker, C., Wattenhofer, R.: A fast and scalable payment network with bitcoin duplex micropayment channels. In: Pelc, A., Schwarzmann, A.A. (eds.) SSS 2015. LNCS, vol. 9212, pp. 3–18. Springer, Cham (2015). https://doi.org/10.1007/978-3-319-21741-3_1
10. INVESTOPEDIA. Bitcoin Exchange. https://www.investopedia.com/terms/b/bitcoin-exchange.asp
11. Krupp, J., Schröder, D., Simkin, M., Fiore, D., Ateniese, G., Nuernberger, S.: Nearly optimal verifiable data streaming. In: Cheng, C.-M., Chung, K.-M., Persiano, G., Yang, B.-Y. (eds.) PKC 2016 Part I. LNCS, vol. 9614, pp. 417–445. Springer, Heidelberg (2016). https://doi.org/10.1007/978-3-662-49384-7_16

12. Nakamoto, S.: Bitcoin: a peer-to-peer electronic cash system (2008). https://bitcoin.org/bitcoin.pdf
13. Noether, S.: Ring signature confidential transactions for Monero. Cryptology ePrint Archive, Report 2015/1098 (2015). http://eprint.iacr.org/
14. Pass, R., Shelat, A.: Micropayments for decentralized currencies. In: Proceedings of the 22nd ACM SIGSAC Conference on Computer and Communications Security, pp. 207–218. ACM (2015)
15. Pass, R., Shelat, A.: Micropayments for decentralized currencies (2016). http://eprint.iacr.org/2016/332
16. Poon, J., Dryja, T.: The Bitcoin lightning network: scalable off-chain instant payments. Technical report, Technical Report Draft v. 0.5.9.2 (2016) https://lightning.network/lightning-network-paper.pdf
17. Reid, F., Harrigan, M.: An analysis of anonymity in the Bitcoin system. In: 2011 IEEE Third International Conference on Privacy, Security, Risk and Trust and 2011 IEEE Third International Conference on Social Computing, pp. 1318–1326. IEEE (2011)
18. Rivest, R.L.: Electronic lottery tickets as micropayments. In: Hirschfeld, R. (ed.) FC 1997. LNCS, vol. 1318, pp. 307–314. Springer, Heidelberg (1997). https://doi.org/10.1007/3-540-63594-7_87
19. Ruffing, T., Kate, A., Schröder, D.: Liar, liar, coins on fire! Penalizing equivocation by loss of Bitcoins. In: Proceedings of the 22nd ACM SIGSAC Conference on Computer and Communications Security, pp. 219–230. ACM (2015)
20. Sasson, E.B., Chiesa, A., Garman, C., Green, M., Miers, I., Tromer, E., Virza, M.: Zerocash: decentralized anonymous payments from Bitcoin. In: 2014 IEEE Symposium on Security and Privacy, pp. 459–474. IEEE (2014)
21. Schöder, D., Simkin, M.: VeriStream – a framework for verifiable data streaming. In: Böhme, R., Okamoto, T. (eds.) FC 2015. LNCS, vol. 8975, pp. 548–566. Springer, Heidelberg (2015). https://doi.org/10.1007/978-3-662-47854-7_34
22. Schröder, D., Schröder, H.: Verifiable data streaming. In: Proceedings of the 2012 ACM Conference on Computer and Communications Security, pp. 953–964. ACM (2012)
23. Sompolinsky, Y., Zohar, A.: Secure high-rate transaction processing in Bitcoin. In: Böhme, R., Okamoto, T. (eds.) FC 2015. LNCS, vol. 8975, pp. 507–527. Springer, Heidelberg (2015). https://doi.org/10.1007/978-3-662-47854-7_32
24. Trillo, M.: Stress Test Prepares VisaNet for the Most Wonderful Time of the Year (2013). http://www.visa.com/blogarchives/us/2013/10/10/stress-test-prepares-visanet-for-the-most-wonderful-time-of-the-year/index.html
25. Wheeler, D.: Transactions using bets. In: Lomas, M. (ed.) Security Protocols 1996. LNCS, vol. 1189, pp. 89–92. Springer, Heidelberg (1997). https://doi.org/10.1007/3-540-62494-5_7

Z-Channel: Scalable and Efficient Scheme in Zerocash

Yuncong Zhang, Yu Long(✉), Zhen Liu(✉), Zhiqiang Liu(✉), and Dawu Gu(✉)

Department of Computer Science and Engineering, Shanghai Jiao Tong University,
Dongchuan Rd. 800, Minhang District, Shanghai 200240, China
{shjdzhangyuncong,longyu,liuzhen,ilu_zq,dwgu}@sjtu.edu.cn

Abstract. Decentralized ledger-based cryptocurrencies like Bitcoin present a way to construct payment systems without trusted banks. However, the anonymity of Bitcoin is fragile. Many altcoins and protocols are designed to improve Bitcoin on this issue, among which Zerocash is the first full-fledged anonymous ledger-based currency, using zero-knowledge proof, specifically zk-SNARK, to protect privacy. However, Zerocash suffers two problems: poor scalability and low efficiency. In this paper, we address the above issues by constructing a micropayment system in Zerocash called Z-Channel. First, we improve Zerocash to support multisignature and time lock functionalities, and prove that the reconstructed scheme is secure. Then we construct Z-Channel based on the improved Zerocash scheme. Our experiments demonstrate that Z-Channel significantly improves the scalability and reduces the confirmation time for Zerocash payments.

1 Introduction

Decentralized ledger-based cryptocurrencies like Bitcoin [1] present a way to construct payment systems without trusted banks. After Bitcoin, many digital currencies try to improve it in different aspects, including functionality [2–5], consensus scheme [3,6], scalability and efficiency [2,7], and privacy [8,9], etc.

Privacy protection in ledger-based digital currencies has attracted tremendous attention [10]. Bitcoin has been thoroughly analyzed and its privacy is deemed fragile [11]. Analyzing the transaction graph, values and dates in the ledger possibly link Bitcoin addresses with real world identities. *Mixes* are designed to break the linkability in Bitcoin system. A mix is a trusted party who mixes coins from many users and gives different coins back to them. However, coin mixing is time-consuming and centralized, so a mix is required to be trustworthy. Therefore, decentralized mixes are constructed like TumbleBit [12], CoinSwap [13], CoinParty [14], CoinShuffle [15] and CoinJoin [16], and altcoins such as Zerocoin [17], BlindCoin [8], Mixcoin [18] and Pinocchio coin [19], etc. However, these solutions still suffer drawbacks: (1) Insufficient performance. Most of them require more than one round of interactions between many parties. (2) Lack of functionality. They allows "washing" coins from time to time, but fail to hide everyday transactions.

W. Susilo and G. Yang (Eds.): ACISP 2018, LNCS 10946, pp. 687–705, 2018.
https://doi.org/10.1007/978-3-319-93638-3_39

In comparison, Zerocash [20] completely conceals the user identity and amount of payment in each and every transaction. Zerocash uses zero-knowledge proof, specifically zero-knowledge Succinct Non-interactive ARguments of Knowledge (zk-SNARKs) [21,22], to protect privacy. However, zero-knowledge proof worsens the scalability and efficiency problems which are already serious in ledger-based currencies. In fact, Zerocash transactions are even larger than those of Bitcoin, and verifying zk-SNARK proof takes longer than verifying a Bitcoin transaction.

For other ledger-based digital currencies, works have been trying to solve the scalability and efficiency issues. Changing the blocksize [23] straightforwardly increases the scalability, while compromising efficiency by higher network latency and longer verification time. The block merging proposed in MimbleWimble [24] requires a special structure for the blocks and transactions, sacrificing a majority of the digital currency functionalities. Currently, micropayment channel [25] is the most promising solution to both scalability and efficiency problems. Micropayment channel enables Bitcoin users to conduct payments securely off-chain, promising to support billions of users. However, nobody has proposed to construct a micropayment system on Zerocash[1].

1.1 Our Contribution

In this work we address the above problems by the following contributions: We develop a micropayment scheme over Zerocash, *Z-Channel*. Z-Channel allows numerous users to perform high-frequency transactions off-chain in day-to-day routine, conducting payments nearly instantly. Meanwhile, the Z-Channels are established and terminated with strong privacy guarantee.

To implement Z-Channel on Zerocash, we improve the Distributed Anonymous Payment (DAP) scheme of Zerocash and propose a new scheme called *DAP Plus* (DAP+ for short). DAP+ enriches DAP with multisignature and time lock features needed by Z-Channel. We give the formal definition of the security of DAP+ scheme based on the original DAP scheme. We prove that DAP+ scheme is secure under this definition.

Moreover, we implement the zk-SNARK for the new NP statement, based on the code of ZCash, and instantiate the Z-Channel protocol. We benchmark the zero-knowledge proofs and the procedures in Z-Channel protocol. In our experiment, a payment can be issued within 3 milliseconds, which is significantly faster than the original Zerocash payment, which requires several minutes for generating zero-knowledge proof, and dozens of minutes for ledger confirmation.

1.2 Paper Organization

The remainder of the paper is organized as follows. Section 2 introduces the preliminaries needed for understanding our work. Section 3 presents DAP+ scheme.

[1] The work of BOLT (Blind Off-chain Lightweight Transactions) [26] mentions Zerocash, claiming that if a BOLT is built on Zerocash, it would provide better channel privacy than built on other currencies. However, BOLT focuses on solving the linkability issue in channels, and does not specify the concrete construction over Zerocash.

In Sect. 4, we describe the construction of Z-Channel. Section 5 analyzes the performance of Z-Channel. Section 6 concludes this paper.

2 Preliminaries

2.1 Background on Zk-SNARKs

The zero-knowledge proving scheme in Zerocash is zk-SNARK (Succinct Non-interactive ARguments of Knowledge) [22]. Suppose Alice has an NP problem instance x and its witness w. She is proving to Bob that x is a valid instance, without revealing w to Bob. She inputs x and w in zk-SNARK to generate a proof π, and sends π instead of w to Bob. Bob then inputs x and π in zk-SNARK and is told if π is a valid proof of x. Let C be a circuit verifying an NP language $\mathcal{L}_C$. C takes as input an instance x and witness w, and outputs b indicating if w is a valid witness for x.

A zk-SNARK is a triple of algorithms (KeyGen, Prove, Verify) fulfilling the above procedure. The algorithm $\mathsf{KeyGen}(C)$ outputs a *proving key* pk and a *verification key* vk. The algorithm Prove takes as input an instance x, a witness w, and pk, and generates a non-interactive proof π for the statement $x \in \mathcal{L}_C$. The algorithm Verify takes as input the instance x, the proof π, and vk, and outputs b indicating if he is convinced that $x \in \mathcal{L}_C$.

A zk-SNARK has the property of

1. **Correctness.** If the honest prover can convince the verifier;
2. **Proof-of-knowledge.** If the verifier accepting a proof implies the prover knowing the witness;
3. **Perfect zero-knowledge.** If there exists a simulator which can always generate the same results for any instance $x \in \mathcal{L}_C$ without knowing witness w.

The work of Zerocash is based on the zk-SNARK implementation proposed in [27].

2.2 The Zerocash Scheme

Zerocash is constructed by overlaying a Decentralized Anonymous Payment (DAP) scheme over Bitcoin or any other ledger-based cryptocurrencies, which we call the basecoin.

DAP introduces a new kind of coin called *shielded coin* (by contrast, we call the unspent outputs in basecoin *transparent coins*), denoted by $\mathbf{c} = (\mathsf{cm}, v, \rho, a_{\mathsf{pk}}, r, s)$, where cm is an information-hiding trapdoor commitment, ρ is a random string for generating the unique serial number sn for this coin. ρ together with the denomination v and *shielded address* a_{pk} of the owner are concealed in cm. r and s are the trapdoors used in commitment.

DAP introduces two types of transactions to handle shielded coins: a *mint* transaction $\mathsf{tx}_{\mathsf{Mint}}$ transforms transparent coins into a shielded coin, and a *pour* transaction $\mathsf{tx}_{\mathsf{Pour}}$ conducts payments between shielded coins. $\mathsf{tx}_{\mathsf{Pour}}$ could also transform part of the input shielded coins back to transparent coins.

A mint transaction $\mathsf{tx}_{\mathsf{Mint}} = (\mathsf{cm}, v, k, s)$ takes transparent coins as input, and produces one shielded coin $\mathbf{c} = (\mathsf{cm}, v, a_{\mathsf{pk}}, r, s)$ [2]. The commitment is conducted in two steps: all the data except v are committed into an intermediary commitment k (with trapdoor r), which is then committed together with v to obtain cm (with trapdoor s). The second commitment is opened, i.e. k, s and v are appended in $\mathsf{tx}_{\mathsf{Mint}}$ for others to verify v, while other information are concealed in k.

A pour transaction $\mathsf{tx}_{\mathsf{Pour}} = (\mathsf{sn}_1^{\mathsf{old}}, \mathsf{sn}_2^{\mathsf{old}}, \mathsf{cm}_1^{\mathsf{new}}, \mathsf{cm}_2^{\mathsf{new}}, v_{\mathsf{pub}}, \pi_{\mathsf{POUR}}, *)$ takes two shielded coins $\mathbf{c}_1^{\mathsf{old}}$ and $\mathbf{c}_2^{\mathsf{old}}$ as input, and produces two newly generated shielded coins $\mathbf{c}_1^{\mathsf{new}}$ and $\mathbf{c}_2^{\mathsf{new}}$, and a (possibly zero-value) transparent coin of value v_{pub}. $\mathsf{tx}_{\mathsf{Pour}}$ reveals the commitments to new shielded coins, i.e. $\mathsf{cm}_1^{\mathsf{new}}$ and $\mathsf{cm}_2^{\mathsf{new}}$, and the serial numbers of the old coins to prevent trying to spend them again. The validity of $\mathsf{tx}_{\mathsf{Pour}}$ is proved by zero-knowledge proof π_{POUR} for the following statement: $\mathsf{sn}_1^{\mathsf{old}}$ and $\mathsf{sn}_2^{\mathsf{old}}$ are valid serial numbers whose ρ_i^{old} are respectively committed in $\mathsf{cm}_1^{\mathsf{old}}$ and $\mathsf{cm}_2^{\mathsf{old}}$ that exist on the ledger, and I can open the commitments; I can open $\mathsf{cm}_1^{\mathsf{new}}$ and $\mathsf{cm}_2^{\mathsf{new}}$; the input and the output are balanced, i.e. $v_1^{\mathsf{old}} + v_2^{\mathsf{old}} = v_1^{\mathsf{new}} + v_2^{\mathsf{new}} + v_{\mathsf{pub}}$; I am owner of the input coins, i.e. for each $i \in \{1, 2\}$, I know secret key $a_{\mathsf{sk},i}^{\mathsf{old}}$ corresponding to the address $a_{\mathsf{pk},i}^{\mathsf{old}}$ committed in $\mathbf{c}_i^{\mathsf{old}}$.

Above are the main ideas of Zerocash. [20] mentions and solves many other issues in implementing Zerocash, we only provide a brief description due to space limitation.

1. To prove the existence of a coin commitment cm on the ledger, all commitments are maintained in a Merkle-tree with root rt.
2. To protect all the public information in $\mathsf{tx}_{\mathsf{Pour}}$ (for example, the address of v_{pub}) from forgery, $\mathsf{tx}_{\mathsf{Pour}}$ is protected by a signature σ, whose verification key $\mathsf{pk}_{\mathsf{sig}}$ is generated on the fly, and protected by zero-knowledge proof.

Finally, the formal definition of DAP scheme consists of algorithms (Setup, CreateAddress, Mint, Pour, Verify, Receive). The Setup algorithm initializes a DAP instance by invoking the initializers in all the cryptographic building blocks (for example, KeyGen in zk-SNARK); the CreateAddress algorithm is executed by each user to generate a shielded address and its key $(a_{\mathsf{pk}}, a_{\mathsf{sk}})$; the Mint algorithm outputs a mint transaction and the resulting shielded coin; the Pour algorithm outputs a pour transaction and the new shielded coins; the Verify algorithm checks the validity of a mint or pour transaction; finally, the Receive algorithm scans a ledger and outputs all the shielded coins belonging to a given shielded address.

2.3 Micropayment Channel

Micropayment channel [25] allows two parties to make payments to each other without publishing transactions on the ledger. A basic micropayment channel

[2] We neglect the transaction fees.

scheme consists of three protocols: establish channel, update channel, and close channel. For convenience, we use Alice and Bob in the following description of a complete execution of a micropayment channel. We use A and B in the subscript for a coin of address Alice or Bob (AB for a coin in shared address). We use α and β to differentiate different versions of the same transaction, i.e. symmetric up to Alice and Bob.

Next, we present the execution procedure of a micropayment channel.

1. **Establish channel.**
   (a) Alice and Bob agree on (v_A, v_B), the currency they are willing to devote into the channel, and a shared address $\mathsf{addr}^{\mathsf{shr}}$.
   (b) They agree on a *sharing transaction* $\mathsf{tx}^{\mathsf{shr}}$, which transforms values v_A and v_B from Alice and Bob, to a coin $\mathbf{c}^{\mathsf{shr}}_{AB}$ in address $\mathsf{addr}^{\mathsf{shr}}$ of value $v_A + v_B$.
   (c) Alice signs a *closing transaction* $\mathsf{tx}^{\mathsf{cls}}_{\beta}$ for Bob, and Bob signs $\mathsf{tx}^{\mathsf{cls}}_{\alpha}$ for Alice. $\mathsf{tx}^{\mathsf{cls}}_{\alpha}$ transforms $\mathbf{c}^{\mathsf{shr}}_{AB}$ to two coins $\mathbf{c}^{\mathsf{cls}}_{\alpha,A}$ and $\mathbf{c}^{\mathsf{cls}}_{\alpha,B}$ of value v_A and v_B to Alice and Bob respectively. $\mathsf{tx}^{\mathsf{cls}}_{\beta}$ transforms $\mathbf{c}^{\mathsf{shr}}_{AB}$ to two coins $\mathbf{c}^{\mathsf{cls}}_{\beta,A}$ and $\mathbf{c}^{\mathsf{cls}}_{\beta,B}$ in the same way.
   (d) Finally, they publish $\mathsf{tx}^{\mathsf{shr}}$, and the channel is established. The *balance* of a new channel is (v_A, v_B).

   Remarks:
   - In case they do not have coins of the exact value before creating $\mathsf{tx}^{\mathsf{shr}}$, they can optionally conduct a funding procedure to prepare the coins. In this case, the input coins to $\mathsf{tx}^{\mathsf{shr}}$ are called *funding coins*, denoted by $\mathbf{c}^{\mathsf{fund}}_{A}$ and $\mathbf{c}^{\mathsf{fund}}_{B}$ respectively.
   - They sign $\mathsf{tx}^{\mathsf{cls}}$ before $\mathsf{tx}^{\mathsf{shr}}$, so that neither of them can lock the other's currency in the shared address forever.
   - The implementation of shared address varies for different cryptocurrencies. For Bitcoin, this is implemented by paying to multiple addresses. For Zerocash, however, this functionality is not implemented, and is what our work aims to provide.
2. **Update channel.** If Alice pays Bob by Δ, the balance of the channel should be updated to $(v_A - \Delta, v_B + \Delta)$. This procedure is executed without interacting with the ledger.
   (a) Alice signs a new closing transaction $\mathsf{tx}^{\mathsf{cls}'}_{\beta}$ for Bob, and Bob signs $\mathsf{tx}^{\mathsf{cls}'}_{\alpha}$ for Alice. $\mathsf{tx}^{\mathsf{cls}'}_{\alpha}$ transforms $\mathbf{c}^{\mathsf{shr}}_{AB}$ to two coins $\mathbf{c}^{\mathsf{cls}'}_{\alpha,A}$ and $\mathbf{c}^{\mathsf{cls}'}_{\alpha,B}$ of value $v_A - \Delta$ and $v_B + \Delta$ to Alice and Bob respectively; similar for $\mathsf{tx}^{\mathsf{cls}'}_{\beta}$.
   (b) Alice signs a *revoking transaction* $\mathsf{tx}^{\mathsf{rev}}_{B}$ for Bob, and Bob signs $\mathsf{tx}^{\mathsf{rev}}_{A}$ for Alice. $\mathsf{tx}^{\mathsf{rev}}_{B}$ transforms $\mathbf{c}^{\mathsf{cls}}_{\alpha,A}$ to a coin $\mathbf{c}^{\mathsf{rev}}_{B}$ for Bob; $\mathsf{tx}^{\mathsf{rev}}_{A}$ transforms $\mathbf{c}^{\mathsf{cls}}_{\beta,B}$ to a coin $\mathbf{c}^{\mathsf{rev}}_{A}$ for Alice.

   Remarks:
   - Each update is associated with a sequence number which increases by one with each update. And the sequence number of the transactions in each update are identical to that of the update.
   - After an update, the previous closing transactions are rendered obsolete. The revoking transactions prevents any of the parties from publishing obsolete closing transaction, by giving all his/her coin in the channel to the other party.

- To prevent the revoking transaction from being surpassed by a transaction immediately following the obsolete closing transaction, the coin $\mathbf{c}^{\mathsf{cls}}_{\alpha,A}$ is locked by time T after $\mathsf{tx}^{\mathsf{cls}}_{\alpha}$ is published, while $\mathsf{tx}^{\mathsf{rev}}_{B}$ overrides the time lock. Implementation of such fine access control over a coin is left to the cryptocurrencies. For Bitcoin, the pay-to-script feature suffices to do the job. For Zerocash, the current scheme cannot accomplish this, which is another issue solved in our work.

3. **Close channel.** Either Alice or Bob can close the channel any time after the channel is established, without interacting with the other party. To close the channel, Alice or Bob publishes his/her own (alpha or beta) version of the most updated closing transaction, and waits for time T before redeeming his/her closing coin. The transactions taking the closing coin are called redeem transactions.

Figure 1 presents an example of execution of micropayment channel.

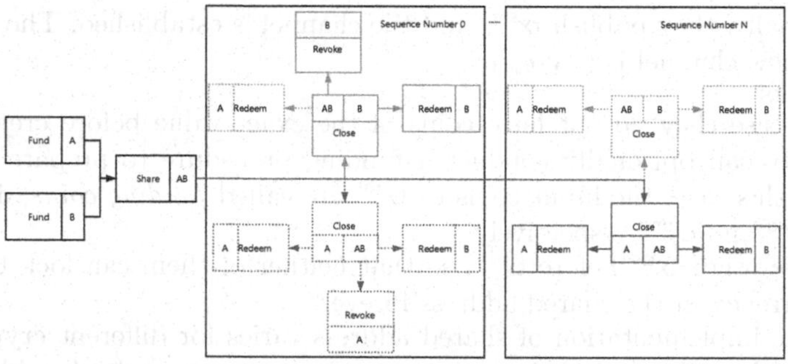

Fig. 1. Transactions and coins in a closed micropayment channel. The transactions that are finally confirmed on the ledger are represented in solid. This figure presents two examples: (1) (Blue) Bob publishes the latest beta version ending the channel in legal way or (2) (Red) Alice publishes an outdated alpha version, and Bob taking away all the coins for punishment. (Color figure online)

The establish and closing of a channel involves interaction with the ledger. They are comparably slow but conducted only once in the lifetime of a channel. Meanwhile, the update procedure is executed each time a payment is made, and it can be executed with high frequency.

2.4 Distributed Signature Generation Scheme

The naive implementation of multisignature scheme in Bitcoin, i.e. counting the number of signatures, reveals some data which compromises the privacy if used in Zerocash. We implement the multisignature feature in an alternative way, namely the *distributed signature generation scheme* [28]. Specifically, we require the scheme to support the following operations:

1. **Distributed key generation**. Multiple parties cooperate to generate a pair of public/private keys pk and sk. After the protocol is done, pk is known by all the parties, while sk is invisible to every one. Each party holds a share sk_i of the private key.
2. **Distributed signature generation**. Given a message M, the parties holding the pieces sk_i of the private key cooperate to generate a signature σ on M. Specifically, each party generates a share σ_i of the signature alone and broadcasts it to other parties. Anyone obtaining all the shares can recover the complete signature σ. This signature can be verified by pk and is indistinguishable from the signatures directly signed by sk.

3 DAP Plus: Improved Decentralized Anonymous Payment Scheme

Our construction of Z-Channel relies on two functionalities: multisignature and time lock. However, they are not provided by the original Zerocash scheme, i.e. DAP scheme. To solve this issue, we present DAP Plus, which is an improvement to the DAP scheme, with support to multisignature and time lock features.

3.1 Main Idea of DAP Plus Scheme

In this subsection, we present the improvements of DAP+ compared to the original DAP scheme. For convenience, we assume that the involved parties are Alice and Bob, and Alice is trying to send a coin to Bob.

Commit to a Public Key Lock in the Coin. In Zerocash, a shielded coin **c** consists of a commitment cm and some secret data necessary for opening cm. The commitment involves the following data: the shielded address a_{pk} owned by Bob, the denomination v and a random string ρ (used for generating serial number sn). In DAP+, we require Alice to additionally commit a *public key lock* pklk into cm. pklk is a properly encoded public key of some public signature scheme. For implementing multisignature functionality, we suggest that it is a *distributed signature generation scheme* described in last section, to enable multiple users to share a public key which is indistinguishable from a public key generated by a single user. For now we simply assume that Bob generates a pair of keys locally and sends the public key pklk to Alice for her to commit into cm. To fix the length of the committed data in cm, Alice commits the hash of pklk, denoted by pkh = Hash(pklk) instead of pklk. When Bob tries to spend this coin, he has to append to the transaction a signature σ which is verified by pklk. We denote the data protected by this signature (for example, the entire transaction, or a short fixed string) by a function ToBeLocked(), and leave it to be determined by the application that builds on top of DAP+ scheme.

To allow other parties to verify the signature, pklk should be disclosed as the coin is spent. The anonymity of Bob against Alice is thus compromised, since

Alice would immediately perceive when Bob spends the coin, by identifying pklk published in the transaction. To solve this problem, we let Bob commit pkh into a commitment pkcm, with his secret key a_{sk} as trapdoor, and sends pkcm to Alice. Therefore, Alice does not know either pklk or its hash pkh, but she is still able to commit pkh into cm in an indirect way, i.e. committing pkcm into cm. We modify the zero-knowledge NP statement POUR in [20] for the pour transaction so that Alice only needs to prove that she knows pkcm for the new coins. When Bob spends his coin, however, he has to prove that the revealed pkh is correctly committed in the coins to spend, with his knowledge of a_{sk}.

Commit a Time Lock in Coin. Next, we commit a time lock tlk into the coin. To avoid the clock synchronizing issue, we use the block height as the clock. For simplicity, we denote the height of the block containing a coin commitment cm by $\mathsf{BH}(\mathsf{cm})$. We then require that Alice appends a *minimum block height* MBH in the pour transaction. A transaction is considered invalid if its MBH is larger than the height of the block containing it, thus cannot get on the ledger until the block height reaches MBH. For each input coin, Alice should prove that $\mathsf{BH}(\mathsf{cm}) + \mathsf{tlk} < \mathsf{MBH}$ in zero-knowledge.

There is, however, a tricky issue about $\mathsf{BH}(\mathsf{cm})$, since it is somehow independent from cm, i.e. there is no computational relationship between them. Therefore, it is hard to prove in zero-knowledge that Alice has input the correct $\mathsf{BH}(\mathsf{cm})$ as a secret input to the zk-SNARK prover. In the meantime, $\mathsf{BH}(\mathsf{cm})$ cannot be disclosed, as this would compromise the privacy of Alice.

We solve this issue by noting that Alice does not have to prove that $\mathsf{BH}(\mathsf{cm}) + \mathsf{tlk} < \mathsf{MBH}$, but $\mathsf{BH}(?) + \mathsf{tlk} < \mathsf{MBH}$ where $\mathsf{BH}(?)$ is the block height of something that is guaranteed to be later than cm on the ledger and safe to be disclosed. The best candidate for this is the Merkle-tree root rt, which is used to prove the existence of the input coin commitment. Each time when a new coin commitment is appended on a ledger, the root is updated to a new one, thus there is a one-to-one correspondence between the list of commitments and the history of roots. We then naturally define the block height of a Merkle-root rt as that of the corresponding commitment and denote it by $\mathsf{BH}(\mathsf{rt})$.

Logical Relationship Between Public Key Lock and Time Lock. If a coin commits a public key lock pklk and time lock tlk, we say the coin is *locked* by pklk with tlk blocks. If tlk is set to the maximum time lock MTL, then we say the coin is locked by pklk forever. We denote a pair of public key commitment and time lock by $\mathsf{lock} = (\mathsf{pkcm}, \mathsf{tlk})$, and a pair of public key lock and signature by $\mathsf{unlock} = (\mathsf{pklk}, \sigma)$. We say unlock *unlocks* a lock if pklk is a correct opening of pkcm and the contained signature is valid.

We decide to take the "OR" relationship between the public key lock and the time lock. That is to say, the transaction is valid either when the time lock expires or a valid unlock is provided. To say it in another way, a coin is locked by tlk blocks unless overridden by the signature.

We accomplish this by adding a *overriding* boolean flag ovd as a public input to zk-SNARK, which is true if and only if a valid unlock is appended in the transaction. Then, Alice only has to prove in zero-knowledge that $\mathsf{ovd} || (\mathsf{BH}(\mathsf{rt}) + \mathsf{tlk} < \mathsf{MBH})$ is true, where $||$ means logical OR.

Note that this logic can be easily modified, without modifying the NP statement POUR. For example, by always setting ovd to false and requiring a valid unlock, the logic between the locks then becomes "AND". Similarly, always setting ovd to true totally neglects the time lock. We will use a slightly modified version of logic in Z-Channel, but for simplicity, we only describe constructing with basic OR logic in this section.

3.2 Construction of DAP Plus Scheme

A *DAP Plus scheme* is a tuple of polynomial-time algorithms (Setup, $\mathsf{CreateAddress}$, $\mathsf{CreatePKCM}$, $\mathsf{MintPlus}$, $\mathsf{PourPlus}$, $\mathsf{VerifyPlus}$, $\mathsf{ReceivePlus}$). Apart from the improvements mentioned in the previous subsection, the definition and construction of the algorithms in the DAP+ scheme are similar to the original DAP scheme in [20]. To save space, we only present the differences in the construction of these algorithms compared to the corresponding ones in the original DAP scheme. For interested readers we refer the complete construction to the full version of this paper [20,29].

We first present the cryptographic building blocks mentioned subsequently.

- Information hiding trapdoor commitment COMM.
- Collision resistance and flexible-input-length hash function Hash.
- Distributed public signature scheme $(\mathcal{G}_{\mathsf{dst}}, \mathcal{K}_{\mathsf{dst}}, \mathcal{S}_{\mathsf{dst}}, \mathcal{V}_{\mathsf{dst}})$, where $\mathcal{G}_{\mathsf{dst}}$ is for generating global public parameter $\mathsf{pp}_{\mathsf{dst}}$, $\mathcal{K}_{\mathsf{dst}}$ is the key generation algorithm, $\mathcal{S}_{\mathsf{dst}}$ is the signing algorithm and $\mathcal{V}_{\mathsf{dst}}$ is the verification algorithm.

Next, we present the detailed difference in the construction of the algorithms in DAP+ scheme compared to those in DAP scheme. For simplicity, we use subscript 1..2 to represent a pair each with subscript 1 and 2. For example, $\mathbf{c}^{\mathsf{old}}_{1..2}$ represents $\mathbf{c}^{\mathsf{old}}_1, \mathbf{c}^{\mathsf{old}}_2$.

System Setup. Given security parameter λ, the algorithm Setup generates a set of public parameters pp. It is executed by a trusted party only once at the startup of the ledger, and made public to all parties. Afterwards, no trusted party is needed.

Apart from the executions mentioned in the original Setup algorithm in DAP scheme, in DAP+ this algorithm does the following:

1. Compute $\mathsf{pp}_{\mathsf{dst}} = \mathcal{G}_{\mathsf{dst}}()$.
2. Add $\mathsf{pp}_{\mathsf{dst}}$ to pp.

Create Address. Given public parameter pp, the algorithm $\mathsf{CreateAddress}$ outputs a new shielded address and its secret key in a pair $(a_{\mathsf{pk}}, a_{\mathsf{sk}})$. The construction of $\mathsf{CreateAddress}$ in DAP+ is exactly the same to that in DAP.

Create Public Key Commitment. Given public parameter pp and address secret key $\mathsf{addr_{sk}}$, the algorithm $\mathsf{CreatePKCM}$ generates a key pair for the distributed signature scheme, and a commitment for the public key.

This algorithm is new in DAP+ scheme, so we present the complete construction as follows:

1. Compute $(\mathsf{pk_{dst}}, \mathsf{sk_{dst}}) = \mathcal{K}_{\mathsf{dst}}(\mathsf{pp_{dst}})$.
2. Compute $\mathsf{pkh} := \mathsf{Hash}(\mathsf{pk_{dst}})$.
3. Parse $\mathsf{addr_{sk}}$ as $(a_{\mathsf{sk}}, \mathsf{sk_{enc}})$, compute $\mathsf{pkcm} := \mathsf{COMM}_{a_{\mathsf{sk}}}(\mathsf{pkh})$.
4. Output $\mathsf{pk_{dst}}, \mathsf{sk_{dst}}, \mathsf{pkcm}$.

For complete anonymity, each time Alice tries to generate a coin (via $\mathsf{MintPlus}$ or $\mathsf{PourPlus}$ algorithm introduced later) for Bob, Bob invokes $\mathsf{CreatePKCM}$ algorithm to generate a fresh public key commitment pkcm and sends the pkcm to Alice. For privacy, each generated pkcm must be used only once. It is recommended that a user stores the output tuples in the wallet, and whenever a new coin is received, mark the tuple containing the corresponding pkcm as already used. A coin that uses a pkcm already used should be considered invalid.

Mint Coin. The $\mathsf{MintPlus}$ algorithm outputs a shielded coin and a mint transaction, which transforms some transparent coins into shielded coins with equal value.

Compared to the Mint algorithm in DAP scheme, the $\mathsf{MintPlus}$ algorithm behaves differently in the following respects.

1. Additionally take as input a lock lock.
2. Additionally commit lock into the intermediary coin commitment, i.e. compute
$$k := \mathsf{COMM}_r(a_{\mathsf{pk}}, \rho, \mathsf{lock}).$$
3. Add lock to the output coin $\mathbf{c}$.

Pour Algorithm. The $\mathsf{PourPlus}$ algorithm outputs two shielded coins and a pour transaction, which transfers values from two input shielded coins into two new shielded coins, and optionally transfers part of the input value back to a transparent coin.

Compared to the Pour algorithm in DAP scheme, the $\mathsf{PourPlus}$ algorithm makes the following modifications.

- Input:
  1. Additionally take as input the minimal block height MBH.
  2. Input two Merkle-roots $\mathsf{rt}_{1..2}$ instead of one rt, i.e. use separate roots for two old coins.
  3. For each new coin $\mathbf{c}_i^{\mathsf{new}}$ additionally input a lock $\mathsf{lock}_i^{\mathsf{new}}$.
  4. Each old coin $\mathbf{c}_i^{\mathsf{old}}$ additionally contains a lock $\mathsf{lock}_i^{\mathsf{old}}$.
  5. For each old coin $\mathbf{c}_i^{\mathsf{old}}$ additionally input a (possibly empty) secret key $\mathsf{sk}_{\mathsf{dst},i}$.

- Procedure:
  1. Replace the part of generating new coin with the procedure of MintPlus.
  2. Replace the zero-knowledge proof with one of the new statement (see paragraph "NP statement").
  3. In the part of preventing forgery, add the following to the message to be protected: $\mathsf{MBH}, \mathsf{pklk}^{\mathsf{old}}_{1..2}$.
  4. Add the unlock procedure:
     i. Compute $\mathsf{msg} := \mathsf{ToBeLocked}()$.
     ii. Let $\mathsf{ovd}_i := \mathsf{BH}(\mathsf{rt}_i) + \mathsf{tlk}^{\mathsf{old}}_i \geq \mathsf{MBH}$.
     iii. Compute[3] $\sigma_i := \mathcal{S}_{\mathsf{dst}}(\mathsf{sk}_{\mathsf{dst},i}, \mathsf{msg})$ if ovd_i, or let $\sigma_i := \perp$ if not ovd_i.
     iv. Let $\mathsf{unlock}_i := (\mathsf{pklk}^{\mathsf{old}}_i, \sigma_i)$.
- Output:
  1. In each output coin $\mathbf{c}^{\mathsf{new}}_i$, add the lock $\mathsf{lock}^{\mathsf{new}}_i$.
  2. Add to the pour transaction $\mathsf{MBH}, \mathsf{unlock}_{1..2}$.

Verify Transactions. Given public parameters pp, a transaction tx and a ledger L, the VerifyPlus algorithm outputs a bit b indicating if a given transaction is valid on a ledger.

If tx is a mint transaction, VerifyPlus behaves exactly as the Verify algorithm in DAP scheme.

If tx is a pour transaction, VerifyPlus behaves differently in the following respects.

1. Check the minimum block height MBH, if it is larger than the current block height, output $b := 0$ and exit.
2. In the part of preventing forgery, add the following to the message against which the signature is verified: MBH and $\mathsf{pklk}^{\mathsf{old}}_{1..2}$.
3. Check the validity of unlock:
   (a) If the signature σ_i in unlock_i is empty, set ovd_i to **false**, for $i = 1, 2$.
   (b) If the signature σ_i in unlock_i is not empty, compute $\mathsf{msg} = \mathsf{ToBeLocked}()$ and check $\mathcal{V}_{\mathsf{dst}}(\mathsf{pklk}_i, \mathsf{msg}, \sigma_i)$ for $i = 1, 2$. If any check fails, output $b := 0$ and exit.
4. Check the zero-knowledge proof according to the new NP statement.

Receive Coins. Given public parameter pp, a shielded address and its key $(a_{\mathsf{pk}}, a_{\mathsf{sk}})$, and a ledger L, the ReceivePlus algorithm scans the ledger and outputs coins on the ledger belonging to a given shielded address.

Compared to the Receive algorithm in DAP scheme, after finding out a coin belonging to the given address, the ReceivePlus algorithm additionally checks the pkcm in the coin to make sure that it is in the wallet and not marked as already used.

[3] This procedure may be executed distributedly, where the input $\mathsf{sk}_{\mathsf{dst},i}$ is shared by more than one parties, and σ_i is synthesized from the shared signatures.

NP Statement. We modify the NP statement POUR as follows:

- Public input:
  1. Use two Merkle-roots $\mathsf{rt}_{1..2}$ instead of one rt.
  2. Add minimum block height MBH.
  3. For each old coin, add $\mathsf{pkh}_i^{\mathsf{old}} = \mathsf{Hash}(\mathsf{pklk}_i^{\mathsf{old}})$ and ovd_i computed as in PourPlus and VerifyPlus algorithm.
- Private input: add the locks $\mathsf{lock}_i^{\mathsf{old}}$ and $\mathsf{lock}_i^{\mathsf{new}}$ in the corresponding coins.
- Statement:
  1. For each new coin, replace the commitment validity check with the following equation

$$\mathsf{cm}_i^{\mathsf{new}} = \mathsf{COMM}_{s_i^{\mathsf{new}}}(v_i^{\mathsf{new}}, \mathsf{COMM}_{r_i^{\mathsf{new}}}(a_{\mathsf{pk},i}^{\mathsf{new}}, \rho_i^{\mathsf{new}}, \mathsf{lock}_i^{\mathsf{new}})).$$

  2. For each old coin, replace the commitment validity check with the following equation

$$\mathsf{cm}_i^{\mathsf{old}} = \mathsf{COMM}_{s_i^{\mathsf{old}}}(v_i^{\mathsf{old}}, \mathsf{COMM}_{r_i^{\mathsf{old}}}(a_{\mathsf{pk},i}^{\mathsf{old}}, \rho_i^{\mathsf{old}}, \mathsf{COMM}_{a_{\mathsf{sk},i}^{\mathsf{old}}}(\mathsf{pkh}_i^{\mathsf{old}}), \mathsf{tlk}_i^{\mathsf{old}})).$$

  3. For each old coin, the time lock either expires or is overridden, i.e.

$$\mathsf{ovd}_i || (\mathsf{BH}(\mathsf{rt}_i) + \mathsf{tlk}_i^{\mathsf{old}} < \mathsf{MBH})$$

3.3 Security of DAP Plus Scheme

The security of DAP+ scheme is defined in a similar way as that of DAP scheme. We refer to the full version of this paper [29] for the complete security definition and the security proof.

4 Z-Channel

We present the micropayment system over Zerocash, which we call *Z-Channel*. Z-Channel follows the structure of micropayment channel presented in Sect. 2.3. We first give the main idea of Z-Channel, then present the complete protocol.

4.1 Main Idea of Z-Channel

In the micropayment scheme, the parties generate many transactions during each update. In Zerocash, due to zero-knowledge proof, this will be slow. We consider letting the parties hold a summary of the transaction instead of a complete one. Define the *note* of a pour transaction to be the tuple $(\mathsf{sn}_1^{\mathsf{old}}, \mathsf{sn}_2^{\mathsf{old}}, \mathsf{cm}_1^{\mathsf{new}}, \mathsf{cm}_2^{\mathsf{new}}, *)$, where $*$ is data of the public output[4]. The note specifies the behavior of the pour transaction. Recall that we left the ToBeLocked() function in DAP+ scheme to be defined by the application. We let this function to return the note of the pour transaction.

[4] In Z-Channel, the public output is always zero, so we neglect it in the sequel.

Context of a Z-Channel. If Alice and Bob negotiate the random data (namely $r, s, \rho, (a_{\mathsf{sk}}, a_{\mathsf{pk}})$) needed in every coin in the channel, the communication cost is tremendous. We consider letting them negotiate a random string seed, and generate all random data with a pseudorandom function. We assign a unique tag to each random string for distinction. We use the superscripts and subscripts of the coin to denote the tag, for example, $\mathsf{tag}^{\mathsf{cls}}_{\beta,A}$ denotes the tag of $\mathbf{c}^{\mathsf{cls}}_{\beta,A}$.

In the protocol, only a limited number of transactions (six, to be specific) will be published on the ledger, a limited number of public keys suffice to ensure the uniqueness of public key locks in each published transaction. They can be determined at the start of the protocol. We define the *context* of a Z-Channel ctx to be a tuple of seed and all the public key locks. Given the context and the denomination, each coin in the Z-Channel is completely determined, i.e. we can define the procedure $\mathbf{c} := \mathsf{GetCoin}(\mathsf{ctx}, v, \mathsf{tag})$ where tag specifies which coin to compute.

Relationship Between Time Lock and Public Key Lock. The closing coins $\mathbf{c}^{\mathsf{cls}}_{\alpha,A}$ and $\mathbf{c}^{\mathsf{cls}}_{\beta,B}$ are locked by T blocks, by the default specification of DAP+ scheme, the coin is spendable when either lock is resolved, so both Alice and Bob can spend the coins after T blocks. We have to modify the logic relationship between time lock and public key lock. We define two functions $\mathsf{ToBeLockedS}() := 0\|\mathsf{ToBeLocked}()$ and $\mathsf{ToBeLockedW}() := 1\|\mathsf{ToBeLocked}()$. We require that a valid pour transaction contains a signature verified by the public key lock on either $\mathsf{ToBeLockedS}()$ or $\mathsf{ToBeLockedW}()$. Furthermore, if the signature is verified on $\mathsf{ToBeLockedS}()$, we call it a *strong signature*, otherwise it is *weak*; we specify that only a strong signature can override the time lock.

When Alice signs $\mathsf{tx}^{\mathsf{cls}}_{\beta}$ for Bob, she simultaneously signs $\mathsf{tx}^{\mathsf{rdm}}_{B}$ which sends $\mathbf{c}^{\mathsf{cls}}_{\beta,B}$ to $\mathbf{c}^{\mathsf{rdm}}_{B}$ owned by Bob, with a weak signature. Denote the procedure of signing the notes for the other party in the update of sequence number seq with balance (v_A, v_B) by $(\sigma_1, \sigma_2) := \mathsf{SignNote}(v_A, v_B, \mathsf{seq})$. When Bob signs $\mathsf{tx}^{\mathsf{rev}}_{A}$ for Alice, which sends $\mathbf{c}^{\mathsf{cls}}_{\beta,B}$ to $\mathbf{c}^{\mathsf{rev}}_{A}$, he signs with strong signature. Therefore, if the closing coin is not revoked, after publishing $\mathsf{tx}^{\mathsf{cls}}_{\beta}$, Bob can wait T blocks before publishing $\mathsf{tx}^{\mathsf{rdm}}_{B}$ and get his coin back, while Alice can never get $\mathbf{c}^{\mathsf{cls}}_{\beta,B}$. If a revoked $\mathsf{tx}^{\mathsf{cls}}_{\beta}$ is published, Alice publishes $\mathsf{tx}^{\mathsf{rev}}_{A}$ which immediately takes $\mathbf{c}^{\mathsf{cls}}_{\beta,B}$ away. Table 1 summarizes all the public keys and time locks of each coin.

Table 1. Coin lock specifications in Z-Channel. The public keys with single subscript are generated by the corresponding parties locally and sent to the other. Those with double subscripts are generated in distributed way. MTL is the maximum time lock.

c	pklk	tlk	c	pklk	tlk	c	pklk	tlk	c	pklk	tlk
$\mathbf{c}^{\mathsf{fund}}_{A}$	$\mathsf{pk}^{\mathsf{fund}}_{A}$	MTL	$\mathbf{c}^{\mathsf{fund}}_{B}$	$\mathsf{pk}^{\mathsf{fund}}_{B}$	MTL	$\mathbf{c}^{\mathsf{shr}}$	$\mathsf{pk}^{\mathsf{shr}}_{AB}$	MTL			
$\mathbf{c}^{\mathsf{cls}}_{\alpha,A,i}$	$\mathsf{pk}^{\mathsf{cls}}_{AB}$	T	$\mathbf{c}^{\mathsf{cls}}_{\beta,A,i}$	$\mathsf{pk}^{\mathsf{cls}}_{A}$	MTL	$\mathbf{c}^{\mathsf{cls}}_{\beta,B,i}$	$\mathsf{pk}^{\mathsf{cls}}_{AB}$	T	$\mathbf{c}^{\mathsf{cls}}_{\alpha,B,i}$	$\mathsf{pk}^{\mathsf{cls}}_{B}$	MTL
$\mathbf{c}^{\mathsf{rdm}}_{A}$	$\mathsf{pk}^{\mathsf{rdm}}_{A}$	MTL	$\mathbf{c}^{\mathsf{rdm}}_{B}$	$\mathsf{pk}^{\mathsf{rdm}}_{B}$	MTL	$\mathbf{c}^{\mathsf{rev}}_{A}$	$\mathsf{pk}^{\mathsf{rev}}_{A}$	MTL	$\mathbf{c}^{\mathsf{rev}}_{B}$	$\mathsf{pk}^{\mathsf{rev}}_{B}$	MTL

4.2 Construction of Z-Channel Protocol

A Z-Channel Protocol ZCP is a tuple of subprotocols (Establish, Update, Close). We present the construction of the subprotocols in Algorithms 1, 2 and 3. In Algorithms 1 and 2 we divide (by horizontal rule) the procedures into groups. In each group the procedures are executed regardless of the presented order, while different groups should be finished in sequence. For clarity, we omit the description of sending data to the other party, or checking the correctness, etc. In each group, if they fall into dispute, any of them can immediately abort the protocol[5].

Establish the Channel. Alice and Bob agree on the context (seed and all public keys) of a Z-Channel. After that, they publish the funding coins and the share coin. This protocol is formalized in Algorithm 1.

Algorithm 1: Establish Protocol

Alice and Bob agree on seed, v_A and v_B;
Alice and Bob distributedly generate $\mathsf{pk}^{\mathsf{shr}}_{AB}$ and $\mathsf{pk}^{\mathsf{cls}}_{AB}$;

Alice generates $\mathsf{pk}^{\mathsf{fund}}_A, \mathsf{pk}^{\mathsf{cls}}_A, \mathsf{pk}^{\mathsf{rdm}}_A, \mathsf{pk}^{\mathsf{rev}}_A$;
Bob generates $\mathsf{pk}^{\mathsf{fund}}_B, \mathsf{pk}^{\mathsf{cls}}_B, \mathsf{pk}^{\mathsf{rdm}}_B, \mathsf{pk}^{\mathsf{rev}}_B$;

Let $\mathsf{ctx} := (\mathsf{seed}, \mathsf{pk}^{\mathsf{fund}}_A, \mathsf{pk}^{\mathsf{cls}}_A, \mathsf{pk}^{\mathsf{rdm}}_A, \mathsf{pk}^{\mathsf{rev}}_A, \mathsf{pk}^{\mathsf{fund}}_B, \mathsf{pk}^{\mathsf{cls}}_B, \mathsf{pk}^{\mathsf{rdm}}_B, \mathsf{pk}^{\mathsf{rev}}_B, \mathsf{pk}^{\mathsf{shr}}_{AB}, \mathsf{pk}^{\mathsf{cls}}_{AB})$;
Alice computes $\mathsf{SignNote}(v_B, v_A, 0)$;
Bob computes $\mathsf{SignNote}(v_A, v_B, 0)$;

Alice signs $(\mathsf{sn}^{\mathsf{fund}}_{\mathsf{A}}, \mathsf{sn}^{\mathsf{fund}}_{\mathsf{B}}, \mathsf{cm}^{\mathsf{shr}}, \mathsf{cm}^{\mathsf{dmy}})$;
Bob signs $(\mathsf{sn}^{\mathsf{fund}}_{\mathsf{A}}, \mathsf{sn}^{\mathsf{fund}}_{\mathsf{B}}, \mathsf{cm}^{\mathsf{shr}}, \mathsf{cm}^{\mathsf{dmy}})$;

Alice publishes $\mathbf{c}^{\mathsf{fund}}_A := \mathsf{GetCoin}(\mathsf{ctx}, v_A, \mathsf{tag}^{\mathsf{fund}}_A)$
Bob publishes $\mathbf{c}^{\mathsf{fund}}_B := \mathsf{GetCoin}(\mathsf{ctx}, v_B, \mathsf{tag}^{\mathsf{fund}}_B)$

Alice/Bob publishes $\mathbf{c}^{\mathsf{shr}}$;

Update the State of Channel. To update the channel, Alice and Bob sign notes for new closing transactions for each other. After that, they sign revocations for each other to revoke the old version of closing transactions. This protocol is formalized in Algorithm 2.

[5] When the channel is already established, to abort means executing the Close protocol.

Algorithm 2: Update Protocol

Alice and Bob agree on $v_{A,i}$ and $v_{B,i}$;

Alice computes $\mathsf{SignNote}(v_{B,i}, v_{A,i}, i)$;
Bob computes $\mathsf{SignNote}(v_{A,i}, v_{B,i}, i)$;

Alice signs $(\mathsf{sn}^{\mathsf{cls}}_{\alpha,A,i}, \mathsf{sn}^{\mathsf{dmy}}, \mathsf{cm}^{\mathsf{rev}}_{B}, \mathsf{cm}^{\mathsf{dmy}})$;
Bob signs $(\mathsf{sn}^{\mathsf{cls}}_{\beta,B,i}, \mathsf{sn}^{\mathsf{dmy}}, \mathsf{cm}^{\mathsf{rev}}_{A}, \mathsf{cm}^{\mathsf{dmy}})$;

Close the Channel. Let Alice be the party that actively closes the channel. Alice publishes the most updated closing transaction. Then they publish redeeming transactions to take away their coins. Alice waits for T blocks before publishing the redeeming transaction. This protocol is formalized in Algorithm 3.

Algorithm 3: Close Protocol

Alice publishes $\mathbf{c}^{\mathsf{cls}}_{\alpha}$;
Bob publishes $\mathbf{c}^{\mathsf{rdm}}_{B}$;
Alice waits T blocks and publishes $\mathbf{c}^{\mathsf{rdm}}_{A}$;

4.3 Security of Z-Channel Protocol

Due to space limitation, we refer to the full version of this paper [29] for the security definition and proof.

5 Performance Analysis

5.1 Instantiation of DAP Plus and Z-Channel

Instantiation of DAP Plus. Our implementation of DAP+ is based on that of ZCash [30], which is the most popular implementation of DAP scheme. ZCash follows the idea of DAP scheme, but modifies the algorithms and data structures dramatically. Despite that, our improvements in DAP+ can be applied directly to ZCash. For details of ZCash we refer interested readers to [30].

We implement the distributed signature generation scheme with EC-Schnorr signature [28]. We take SHA256 as the public key hash function Hash. We compute pkcm with trapdoor a_{sk} (which is 252-bit string in ZCash), by taking the SHA256 compression of their concatenation $a_{\mathsf{sk}} \| \mathsf{pkh}$ prefixed by four zero-bits. The time lock is set as a 64-bit integer. As in ZCash, we abandon the trapdoor s and compute the coin commitment as the SHA256 of the concatenation of all the coin data.

Instantiation of Z-Channel. For the distributed generation of Schnorr keys and signature, we take the following simple procedures:

1. For key generation, Alice generates random big integer a and computes $A = aG$ locally, where G is the generator of the elliptic curve group used in the EC-Schnorr signature scheme, and Bob generates b and $B = bG$; Alice commits A to Bob, Bob sends B to Alice, and Alice sends A to Bob; finally, the shared public key is $A + B$, and the shared secret key is $a + b$.
2. For signature generation, they first run a key generation procedure to agree on $K = k_1G + k_2G$, and Alice computes signature share by $e = H(x_K \| M)$, $s_1 = k_1 - ae$, $\sigma_1 = (e, s_1)$, where H is hash function and M is the message to sign; Bob computes σ_2 similarly; the complete signature is $\sigma = (e, s_1 + s_2)$.

For the consensus of secret seed, assume Alice and Bob have a secure communication channel. Alice and Bob generate random 256-bit strings a and b; Alice commits a to Bob, Bob sends b to Alice, and Alice sends a to Bob; the seed is $\mathsf{seed} = a \oplus b$.

5.2 Performance of Zero-Knowledge Proof in DAP Plus

We construct the circuit of the new NP statement for zk-SNARK based on the code of ZCash. Table 2 shows the performance of the zero-knowledge proof procedures, in comparison with that of the original DAP scheme. The modifications introduced in DAP+ scheme slightly (around 0.1% to 8%) increase the key sizes and the time consumption, as expected.

Table 2. Performance of zero-knowledge proof

	#Repeat	Mean	Std	Max	Min		
Platform	Ubuntu 16.04 LTS 64 bit on Intel Core i7-5500U @ 2.40 GHz 7.7 GB Memory					DAP PK size	465 MB
						DAP+ PK size	516 MB
DAP KeyGen time	5	340.44 s	6.2270 s	348.15 s	333.38 s	DAP VK size	773 B
DAP+ KeyGen time	5	367.48 s	4.3756 s	372.48 s	362.76 s	DAP+ VK size	932 B
Platform	Ubuntu 17.04 64 bit on Intel Core i5-4590 @ 3.30 GHz 3.6 GB Memory						
DAP Prove time	15	98.06 s	0.4914 s	99.490 s	97.558 s		
DAP+ Prove time	15	101.22 s	2.5206 s	107.52 s	98.089 s		
DAP Verify time	1500	23.43 ms	0.509 ms	25.4 ms	23.3 ms		
DAP+ Verify time	1500	23.46 ms	0.128 ms	26.3 ms	23.4 ms		

5.3 Performance of Z-Channel Protocol Between Single Pairs

In testing performance of a single Z-Channel, we run the Z-Channel clients on localhost to minimize the effect of real network latency, and simulate different network latencies. Table 3 shows the result.

Table 3. Performance of Z-Channel

	#Repeat	Mean	Std	Max	Min		
Platform	Ubuntu 17.04 64 bit on Intel Core i5-4590 @ 3.30 GHz 3.6 GB Memory					Establish time	26.59 ms
Update time	1000	3.778 ms	1.238 ms	22.5 ms	3.467 ms	Close time	0.3749 ms

6 Conclusion

We develop Z-Channel, a micropayment channel scheme over Zerocash. In particular, we improve the original DAP scheme of Zerocash and propose DAP Plus, which supports multisignature and time lock functionalities that are essential in implementing micropayment channels. We then construct the Z-Channel protocol, which allows numerous payments conducted and confirmed off-chain in short periods of time. The privacy protection provided by Z-Channel ensures that the identities of the parties and the balances of the channels and even the existence of the channel are kept secret. Finally, we implement Z-Channel protocol, and our experiments demonstrate that Z-Channel significantly improves the scalability and reduces the average payment time of Zerocash.

Acknowledgement. The authors are supported by the National Natural Science Foundation of China (Grant No. 61572318, 61672339, 61672347).

References

1. Nakamoto, S.: Bitcoin: a peer-to-peer electronic cash system (2008)
2. Eyal, I., Gencer, A.E., Sirer, E.G., Van Renesse, R.: Bitcoin-NG: a scalable blockchain protocol. In: 13th USENIX Symposium on Networked Systems Design and Implementation (NSDI 16), pp. 45–59. USENIX Association (2016)
3. King, S., Nadal, S.: PPCoin: peer-to-peer crypto-currency with proof-of-stake. self-published paper, 19 August 2012
4. Garay, J., Kiayias, A., Leonardos, N.: The Bitcoin backbone protocol: analysis and applications. In: Oswald, E., Fischlin, M. (eds.) EUROCRYPT 2015 Part II. LNCS, vol. 9057, pp. 281–310. Springer, Heidelberg (2015). https://doi.org/10.1007/978-3-662-46803-6_10
5. Kroll, J.A., Davey, I.C., Felten, E.W.: The economics of Bitcoin mining, or Bitcoin in the presence of adversaries. In: Proceedings of WEIS. Citeseer (2013)
6. Sompolinsky, Y., Zohar, A.: Accelerating Bitcoin's transaction processing. Fast money grows on trees, not chains. IACR Cryptology ePrint Archive 2013/881 (2013)
7. Wood, G.: Ethereum: a secure decentralised generalised transaction ledger. Ethereum Project Yellow Paper 151 (2014)
8. Valenta, L., Rowan, B.: Blindcoin: blinded, accountable mixes for Bitcoin. In: Brenner, M., Christin, N., Johnson, B., Rohloff, K. (eds.) FC 2015. LNCS, vol. 8976, pp. 112–126. Springer, Heidelberg (2015). https://doi.org/10.1007/978-3-662-48051-9_9

9. Kosba, A., Miller, A., Shi, E., Wen, Z., Papamanthou, C.: Hawk: the blockchain model of cryptography and privacy-preserving smart contracts. In: 2016 IEEE Symposium on Security and Privacy (SP), pp. 839–858, IEEE (2016)
10. Bonneau, J., Miller, A., Clark, J., Narayanan, A., Kroll, J.A., Felten, E.W.: SoK: research perspectives and challenges for Bitcoin and cryptocurrencies. In: 2015 IEEE Symposium on Security and Privacy (SP), pp. 104–121 IEEE (2015)
11. Reid, F., Harrigan, M.: An analysis of anonymity in the Bitcoin system. In: Altshuler, Y., Elovici, Y., Cremers, A., Aharony, N., Pentland, A. (eds.) Security and Privacy in Social Networks, pp. 197–223. Springer, Heidelberg (2013). https://doi.org/10.1007/978-1-4614-4139-7_10
12. Heilman, E., Baldimtsi, F., Alshenibr, L., Scafuro, A., Goldberg, S.: TumbleBit: an untrusted tumbler for Bitcoin-compatible anonymous payments. IACR Cryptology ePrint Archive 2016/575 (2016)
13. Maxwell, G.: Coinswap: transaction graph disjoint trustless trading (2013)
14. Ziegeldorf, J.H., Grossmann, F., Henze, M., Inden, N., Wehrle, K.: CoinParty: secure multi-party mixing of Bitcoins. In: Proceedings of the 5th ACM Conference on Data and Application Security and Privacy, pp. 75–86. ACM (2015)
15. Ruffing, T., Moreno-Sanchez, P., Kate, A.: CoinShuffle: practical decentralized coin mixing for Bitcoin. In: Kutyłowski, M., Vaidya, J. (eds.) ESORICS 2014 Part II. LNCS, vol. 8713, pp. 345–364. Springer, Cham (2014). https://doi.org/10.1007/978-3-319-11212-1_20
16. Maxwell, G.: CoinJoin: Bitcoin privacy for the real world. In: Post on Bitcoin Forum (2013)
17. Miers, I., Garman, C., Green, M., Rubin, A.D.: Zerocoin: anonymous distributed e-cash from Bitcoin. In: 2013 IEEE Symposium on Security and Privacy (SP), pp. 397–411. IEEE (2013)
18. Bonneau, J., Narayanan, A., Miller, A., Clark, J., Kroll, J.A., Felten, E.W.: Mixcoin: anonymity for Bitcoin with accountable mixes. In: Christin, N., Safavi-Naini, R. (eds.) FC 2014. LNCS, vol. 8437, pp. 486–504. Springer, Heidelberg (2014). https://doi.org/10.1007/978-3-662-45472-5_31
19. Danezis, G., Fournet, C., Kohlweiss, M., Parno, B.: Pinocchio coin: building zerocoin from a succinct pairing-based proof system. In: Proceedings of the First ACM workshop on Language support for privacy-enhancing technologies, pp. 27–30. ACM (2013)
20. Sasson, E.B., Chiesa, A., Garman, C., Green, M., Miers, I., Tromer, E., Virza, M.: Zerocash: decentralized anonymous payments from Bitcoin. In: IEEE Symposium on Security and Privacy, pp. 459–474 (2014)
21. Ben-Sasson, E., Chiesa, A., Genkin, D., Tromer, E., Virza, M.: SNARKs for C: verifying program executions succinctly and in zero knowledge. In: Canetti, R., Garay, J.A. (eds.) CRYPTO 2013 Part II. LNCS, vol. 8043, pp. 90–108. Springer, Heidelberg (2013). https://doi.org/10.1007/978-3-642-40084-1_6
22. Gennaro, R., Gentry, C., Parno, B., Raykova, M.: Quadratic span programs and succinct NIZKs without PCPs. In: Johansson, T., Nguyen, P.Q. (eds.) EUROCRYPT 2013. LNCS, vol. 7881, pp. 626–645. Springer, Heidelberg (2013). https://doi.org/10.1007/978-3-642-38348-9_37
23. Andresen, G.: Blocksize Economics (2014). bitcoinfoundation.org
24. Jedusor, T.: Mimblewimble (2016). Defunct hidden service
25. Poon, J., Dryja, T.: The Bitcoin lightning network: scalable off-chain instant payments (2016)

26. Green, M., Miers, I.: Bolt: anonymous payment channels for decentralized currencies. Cryptology ePrint Archive, Report 2016/701 (2016). http://eprint.iacr.org/2016/701
27. Ben-Sasson, E., Chiesa, A., Tromer, E., Virza, M.: Succinct non-interactive arguments for a von neumann architecture. IACR Cryptology ePrint Archive 2013/879 (2013)
28. Gennaro, R., Jarecki, S., Krawczyk, H., Rabin, T.: Secure distributed key generation for discrete-log based cryptosystems. In: Stern, J. (ed.) EUROCRYPT 1999. LNCS, vol. 1592, pp. 295–310. Springer, Heidelberg (1999). https://doi.org/10.1007/3-540-48910-X_21
29. Zhang, Y., Long, Y., Liu, Z., Liu, Z., Gu, D.: Z-channel: scalable and efficient scheme in zerocash. Cryptology ePrint Archive, Report 2017/684 (2017). https://eprint.iacr.org/2017/684
30. Hopwood, D., Bowe, S., Hornby, T., Wilcox, N.: Zcash protocol specification (2017)

Revisiting the Incentive Mechanism of Bitcoin-NG

Jiayuan Yin[1], Changren Wang[2], Zongyang Zhang[1,3(✉)], and Jianwei Liu[1]

[1] School of Cyber Science and Technology, Beihang University, Beijing, China
{yinjiayuan,zongyangzhang,liujianwei}@buaa.edu.cn

[2] School of Automation Science and Electrical Engineering, Beihang University, Beijing, China
14231017@buaa.edu.cn

[3] State Key Laboratory of Information Security, Institute of Information Engineering, Chinese Academy of Sciences, Beijing, China

Abstract. Recently, due to the inherent restriction of Bitcoin design, the throughput of Bitcoin blockchain protocol fails to meet the daily needs, leaving the scalability technology in dire need to provide better efficiency. To address this issue, numerous solutions have been proposed, including blocksize expansion, off-chain transactions and block structure modification. Among them, Bitcoin-NG, a scalable blockchain protocol introduced by Eyal et al. in USENIX 2016, improves scalability while simultaneously avoiding the deterioration of other metrics in the network. Bitcoin-NG has two types of blocks: key blocks for leader election and microblocks that contain ledger entries. Eyal et al. assert that the proportion of fee allocation of transactions in microblocks is bounded by miners' mining power ratio out of all mining power in the system. Specifically, the upper bound is determined by the incentive sub-mechanism of longest chain extension, while the lower bound determined by the incentive sub-mechanism of transaction inclusion. We revisit the incentive mechanism of Bitcoin-NG. We point out that Eyal et al. neglect on the calculation of lower bound and manifest the over-simplification in the analysis of upper bound in detail. After that, the correct incentive mechanism is derived. Finally, we put forward an optimal proportion of transaction fee distribution.

Keywords: Bitcoin · Bitcoin-NG · Blockchain
Incentive mechanism · Scalability

1 Introduction

Bitcoin, a decentralized digital cryptocurrency, was created by Nakamoto in 2008 [9]. Transactions in Bitcoin are broadcast to a peer-to-peer network, where records are kept by miners in a data structure called blockchain [10]. The blockchain technology provides a decentralized, open, untampered ledger, that

W. Susilo and G. Yang (Eds.): ACISP 2018, LNCS 10946, pp. 706–719, 2018.
https://doi.org/10.1007/978-3-319-93638-3_40

promises to become the infrastructure for many real-word applications, such as asset management, insurance and payments.

Despite its potential, Bitcoin blockchain suffers significantly from the scalability problem. Increasing scalability results in the deterioration of other metrics and the damage of system security. While the transaction processing speed failing to meet the daily needs, the scaling of Bitcoin blockchain has become a hot research area. Andresen [1] advocated for an increase of the block size limit in a predictable way for a period of time. By increasing the size of individual blocks, more transactions could be accommodated. Poon and Dryja [12] claimed to achieve frequent micropayments off-chain through pre-established channels to avoid a large number of small transactions occupying blockchain capacity. No matter how many off-chain transactions there are, no more burden will be imposed on the on-line blockchain. Croman et al. [3] discussed the challenges of the scalability of the blockchain in Bitcoin in general, and conclude that to maximize the amount of transactions that the Bitcoin blockchain can process, the basic structure of the blockchain needs to be redesigned.

Recently, Eyal et al. [4] introduced a scalable blockchain protocol, which is called Bitcoin-NG. Its latency is limited only by the propagation delay of the network, and its bandwidth is limited only by the processing capacity of the individual nodes. It can improve the scalability of the system to a certain extent, while maintaining other system metrics, such as performance and security, at a relatively good level. Bitcoin-NG is able to provide consensus mechanisms to demanding applications around the globe, including online payments, digital asset transactions and smart contracts.

The Bitcoin-NG incentive mechanism contains three sub-mechanisms: heaviest chain extension, transaction inclusion and longest chain extension. The incentive sub-mechanism of heaviest chain extension encourages miners to expand the chain that contains the most amount of work (the main chain), while punishing miners who extend the non-heaviest branch by deducting remuneration. The incentive sub-mechanism of transaction inclusion encourages miners to put new transactions into their own microblock and publicize it by allocating the transaction fee to the current leader and the next leader according to a certain proportion. The incentive sub-mechanism of longest chain extension also allows certain allocation of the transaction fee to motivate the miners to extend the longest chain by mining on the last microblock produced by the current leader. However, Eyal et al. fail to take into account the possibility that current leader might continue mining to become the next leader after putting a transaction into a microblock. Consequently, there is a negligence in the calculation of incentive sub-mechanism of transaction inclusion. Meanwhile, Eyal et al. over-simplify an important parameter in the calculation of incentive sub-mechanism of longest chain extension.

We revisit the Bitcoin-NG incentive mechanism in detail. We point out the errors in the analysis of two incentive sub-mechanisms, which are the negligence in transaction inclusion and the over-simplification in longest chain extension, and present a refined analysis. Finally, we propose an optimal proportion of transaction fee distribution, which is more reasonable compared to that claimed by Eyal et al.

In this paper, we make the following key contributions:

- We describe the Bitcoin-NG incentive mechanism in the form of schematic diagrams and visually represent the principle of three incentive sub-mechanisms in detail, which greatly facilitate the understanding of Bitcoin-NG.
- We point out the negligence in the analysis of incentive sub-mechanism of transaction inclusion, which ignores the possibility that current leader can continue mining and become the next leader after it puts transactions into microblocks. This negligence not only misleads their analysis of the incentive mechanism, but also results in an unreasonable proportion of transaction fee distribution in Bitcoin-NG protocol.
- We point out the over-simplification in the analysis of incentive sub-mechanism of the longest chain extension. The correct calculation is presented instead, laying a solid foundation for the analysis of optimal allocation of transaction fee.
- We give a correct analysis of Bitcoin-NG incentive mechanism in detail and propose an optimal proportion of transaction fee allocation using rigorous logical deductions.

1.1 Related Work

Since the original proposition of Bitcoin-NG blockchain protocol, researchers have made a series of subsequent improvements. Kokoris-Kogias et al. [6] combined the consensus mechanism of practical byzantine fault tolerance (PBFT) algorithm and the collective signing of CoSi [14] with Bitcoin-NG, designing the ByzCoin, which enables the reduction of the consensus delay and simultaneously realizes the enhancement of the transaction throughput. Luu et al. [8] further designed ELASTICO, a new scalable agreement protocol with identity exchange, partition confirmation and commission agreement mechanism and tolerates byzantine adversaries. ELASTICO increases the transaction throughput almost linearly with the computational power of the network. It also solves the problem of the significant increase in the consensus delay caused by scaling in Bitcoin-NG. On the basis of ELASTICO, a new distributed protocol OmniLedger is deisigned by Kokoris-kogias et al. [7], realizing fast verification, continuous transaction processing and atomic cross-shard transaction. In this way, the disadvantages of ELASTICO such as poor bias, high failure rate and atomicity of transaction cost are overcome.

Organization. In Sect. 2, we contrast Bitcoin-NG blockchain and the Bitcoin blockchain. In Sect. 3, we recall the Bitcoin-NG incentive mechanism, consisting of three contains three sub-mechanisms, which are heaviest chain extension, transaction inclusion and longest chain extension. In Sect. 4, we point out and correct the errors in the analysis of the Bitcoin-NG. In Sect. 5, we propose a refined analysis of the optimal proportion of transaction fee distribution. Finally, we give a conclusion in Sect. 6.

2 Contrasting Bitcoin-NG Blockchain and Bitcoin Blockchain

This section mainly contrasts Bitcoin-NG blockchain with Bitcoin blockchain. The readers are referred to [2,4] for more detailed information.

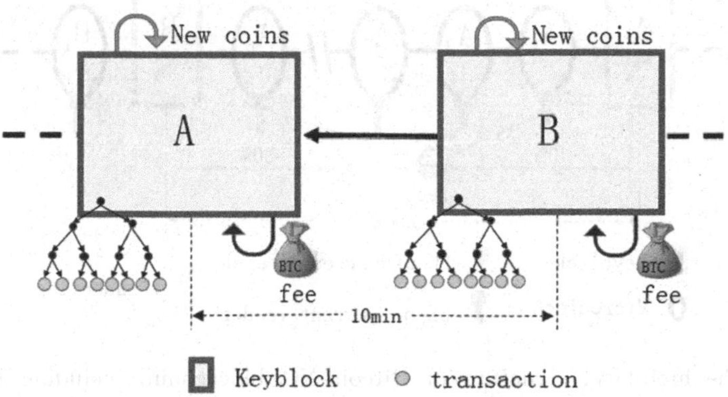

Fig. 1. The high-level structure of Bitcoin blockchain, including basic structure, mining reward and transaction structure.

Bitcoin Blockchain. In Bitcoin blockchain protocol [9], A and B are two blocks, as shown in Fig. 1. Any node in Bitcoin P2P network can become a miner mining for reward. Miners group transactions into a block and keep trying to find a nonce in order to make the hash value of the block header smaller than the target value set by the system. This process is called proof-of-work. The system adjusts the difficulty of proof-of-work by changing the target value so that the interval between the two blocks are approximately 10 min. Miners who successfully mine blocks receive two kinds of remuneration as compensation for recording transactions, which are generation of new coins and transaction fee. Each miner receives full transaction fee for all transactions included in his block. There are many transactions in each block, and transaction structure is a relatively large Merkle tree.

Bitcoin-NG Blockchain. There are two types of blocks in Bitcoin-NG protocol [4]: key blocks and microblocks, as shown in Fig. 2. Key blocks require proof-of-work with a 10-min interval between two key blocks, which is called an epoch. A miner who succeeds in mining a key block becomes the leader of current epoch, before the next key block is published. There is no transaction except for coinbase transaction in key blocks. In addition, a public key of the leader is stored in a key block. Leaders are allowed to generate microblocks at a set rate lower than a predefined maximum, recording transactions. Each microblock needs a signature of the current leader, which uses the private key that matches the public key in the latest key block in the chain. There are fewer transactions in each microblock, and transaction structure is a relatively small Merkle tree. About 40% of all transactions fees in all microblocks in an epoch are distributed to the current leader and 60% to the next leader.

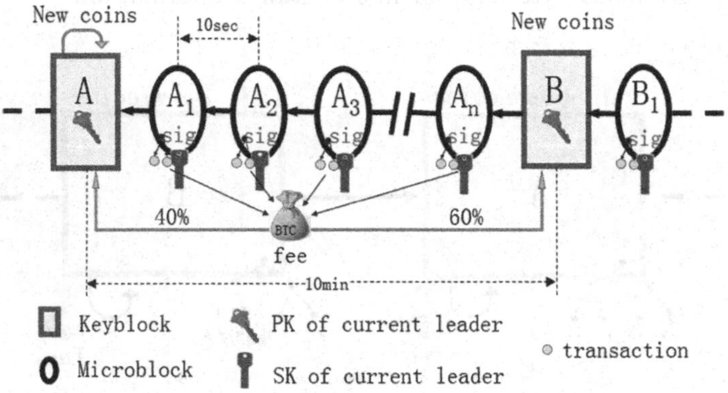

Fig. 2. The high-level structure of Bitcoin-NG blockchain, including key blocks, microblocks, mining reward, proportion of transaction fee allocation and transaction structure.

3 Bitcoin-NG Incentive Mechanism

Eyal et al. [4] made the following statements about the incentive mechanism of Bitcoin-NG. Miners with less than 25% of the total computational power network are incentivized to follow the protocol. Specifically, miners are motivated to do three things: (1) extend the heaviest chain; (2) include transactions in their microblocks; (3) extend the longest chain.

The heaviest chain [13] refers to the chain with the largest amount of proof-of-work. In Bitcoin, the heaviest chain indicates the chain with the most blocks, while in Bitcoin-NG, it means the chain with the most *key blocks*. The longest chain refers to the chain containing the largest number of blocks. In Bitcoin, the heaviest chain is equivalent to the longest chain. Unlike Bitcoin, the heaviest chain does not equal to the longest chain in Bitcoin-NG, as shown in Fig. 3, since only key blocks taking up weight require proof-of-work, microblocks do not. Accordingly, chain 1 and chain 2 have the same weight but different length.

Assume a miner whose mining power ratio out of all mining power in Bitcoin-NG system is α. The allocation mechanism of the transaction fee is set as following: r_{leader} for the current leader and $(1 - r_{leader})$ for the next leader. Eyal et al. set $r_{leader} = 40\%$.

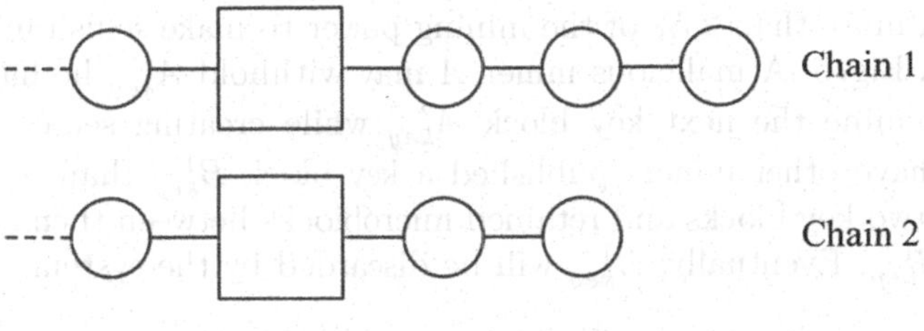

Fig. 3. Two chains with the same weight but different length. Both have the same weight as only key blocks have weight. Since chain 1 has one more microblock, chain 1 is longer than chain 2.

3.1 Heaviest Chain Extension

Bitcoin-NG has the same incentive mechanism as Bitcoin for the heaviest chain extension. Honest miners always extend the heaviest chain. If malicious miners are the majority, they can arbitrarily switch to any branch to expand the blockchain and gain advantage. Suppose that a minority chooses to mine on a branch, the miner will not catch up with the speed of honest majority expanding the main chain and therefore lose the remuneration. Thus rational miners will extend the heaviest chain to ensure its revenues.

In Bitcoin-NG, microblocks are designed to be weightless (no proof-of-work) because the risk of the system being attacked by selfish mining [11] greatly increases when microblocks are given weight. If microblocks have weight, the current leader A can keep a secret microblock A_{n+1} and gain advantage by mining the next key block A^2_{key} on unpublished microblocks A_{n+1}, as shown in Fig. 4. When other miners mine a key block B^1_{key}, the leader A immediately publishes his microblock A_{n+1} and key block A^2_{key}, isolating the key block B^1_{key}. Note that the solid blocks represent historical work and the dotted blocks indicate the work might be updated in the future.

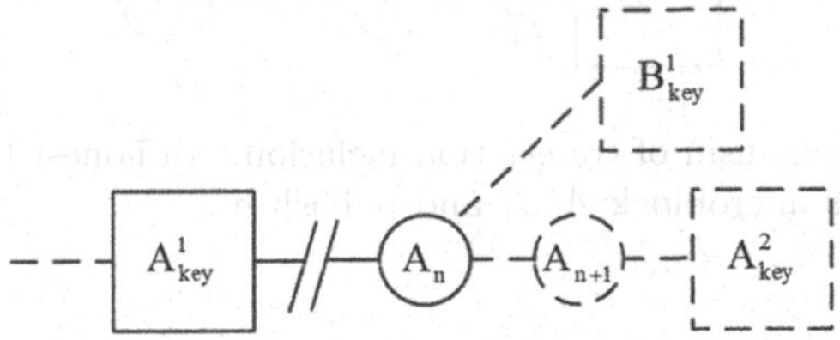

Fig. 4. Selfish mining under the assumption that microblocks have weight. The current leader A can get an advantage over other miners by mining on his unpublished microblocks.

Since Bitcoin-NG does not introduce a new vulnerability to selfish mining, Bitcoin-NG is resilient to selfish mining against attackers with less than 25% of the total mining power of then network. However, it is still profitable for the miners with more than 25% of the mining power to make selfish mining attack, as shown in Fig. 5. A malicious miner A may withhold A^1_{key} he has mined and continue to mine the next key block A^2_{key} while creating secret microblocks. No sooner have other miners published a key block B^1_{key} than A immediately publish his two key blocks and retained microblocks between them, isolating the key block B^1_{key}. Eventually, B^1_{key} will be discarded by the system.

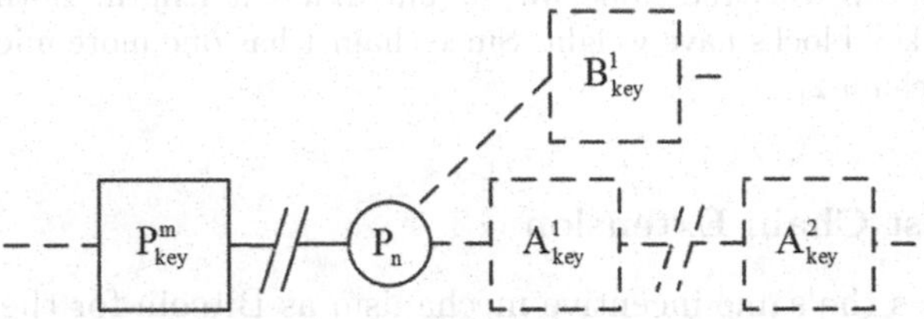

Fig. 5. Selfish mining in Bitcoin-NG. A leader A can simultaneously publish two key blocks, which results in B's key block being discarded by the system.

3.2 Transaction Inclusion

Assume a leader A has published A^1_{key} he had mined. In his epoch, a node broadcasts a transaction M. If the leader A abides by the agreement, he will create a microblock A_{n+1} with M and publish. Then he becomes the current leader of transaction M, obtaining r_{leader} transaction fee, as shown in Fig. 6.

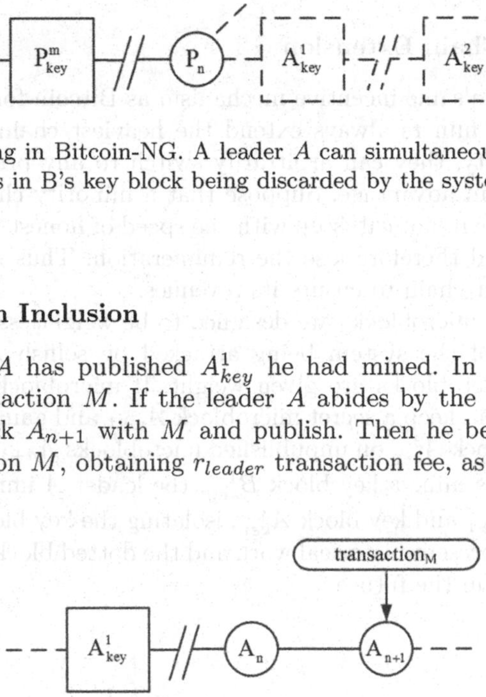

Fig. 6. Abide by mechanism of transaction inclusion. An honest leader A should place transaction M in his microblock A_{n+1} and publish it.

However, if the leader A does not abide by the agreement, he can potentially increase his average remuneration by taking certain measures. First, A creates a microblock A_{n+1} with transaction M without publishing it, as shown in Fig. 7.

Then, A tries to mine on top of A_{n+1}, while other miners mining on A_n. If the leader A succeeds in mining the subsequent key block $A^{'}_{key}$(with probability α), he becomes both the current leader and the next leader of transaction M,

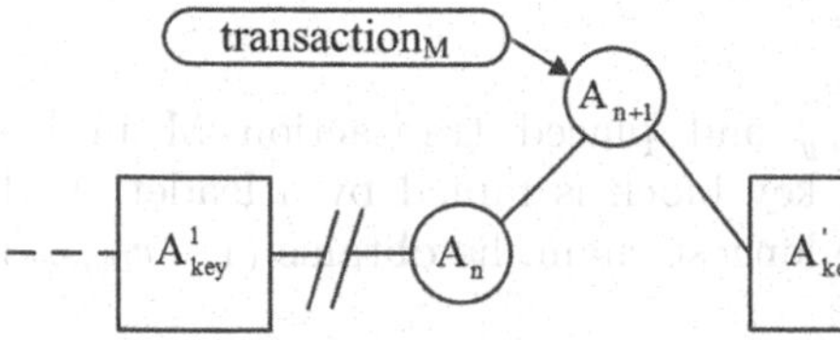

Fig. 7. Creation of microblock without publishing. A dishonest leader may place transaction M in an unpublished microblock for more rewards.

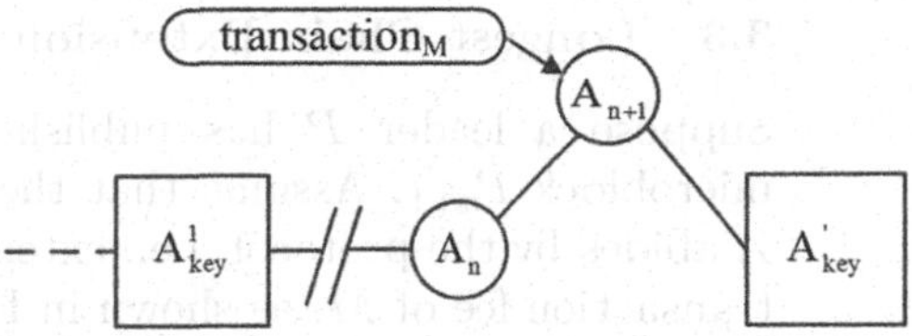

Fig. 8. Successfully mining the subsequent key block. A dishonest leader may obtain more rewards by publishing his microblock A_{n+1} and his new key block simultaneously.

obtaining all the transaction fees, as shown in Fig. 8. If other miners mine the next key block B_{key} (with probability $1 - \alpha$), the miner A will wait for the transaction M to be placed in a microblock by any other miner and try to mine on top of it, as shown in Fig. 9. Here, the dotted blocks indicate the behaviors of honest miners, which are abandoned by dishonest miners. If A successfully mines A_{key}^2 (with probability α), he becomes the next leader of transaction M, earning $(1 - r_{leader})$ transaction fee of M. The value of r_{leader} has to be such that the average revenue of a miner withholding microblocks is smaller than his revenue correctly executing the protocol:

$$\alpha + (1 - \alpha)\alpha(1 - r_{leader}) < r_{leader} \tag{1}$$

therefore

$$r_{leader} > 1 - \frac{1 - \alpha}{1 + \alpha - \alpha^2} \tag{2}$$

Assume that the power of an attacker is bounded by 25% of the mining power, we obtain $r_{leader} > 37\%$.

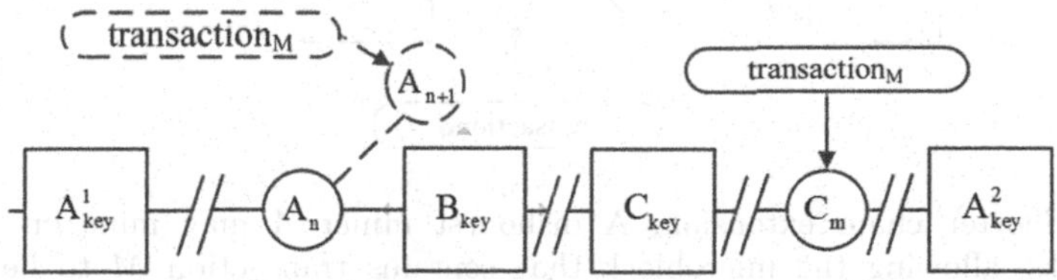

Fig. 9. Mining on the microblock C_m which contains transaction M. Assume that other miners mine the next key block B_{key}. The dishonest miner A may try to mine on the microblock containing transaction M.

3.3 Longest Chain Extension

Suppose a leader P has published P_{key} and placed transaction M in his microblock P_{n+1}. Assume that the next key block is mined by a leader A. If A abides by the protocol, i.e., extend the longest chain, he obtains $(1 - r_{leader})$ transaction fee of M, as shown in Fig. 10.

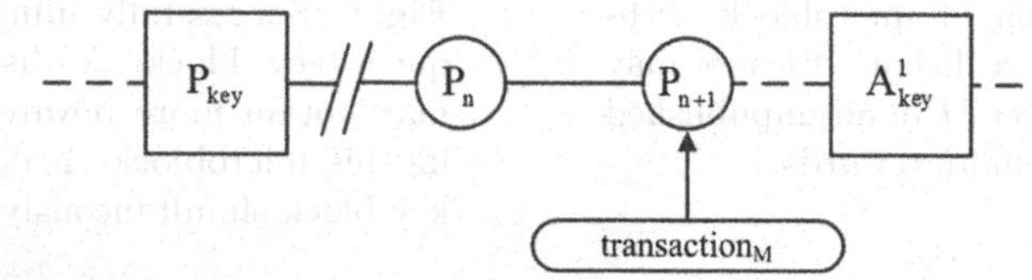

Fig. 10. Abide by longest chain extension. Honest miners should mine on the latest microblock.

However, if A does not abide by the agreement, he can potentially increase his average remuneration by avoiding M's microblock P_{n+1} and mining on a previous block P_n. Then he will place M in his own microblock A_n and try to mine the subsequent key block A^2_{key}, as shown in Fig. 11. As the current leader, A obtains r_{leader} transaction fee of M. Meanwhile, he earns $(1 - r_{leader})$ as the next leader with a probability of α. The value of r_{leader} has to be such that the average revenue of a miner extending short chain is smaller than his revenue correctly executing the protocol:

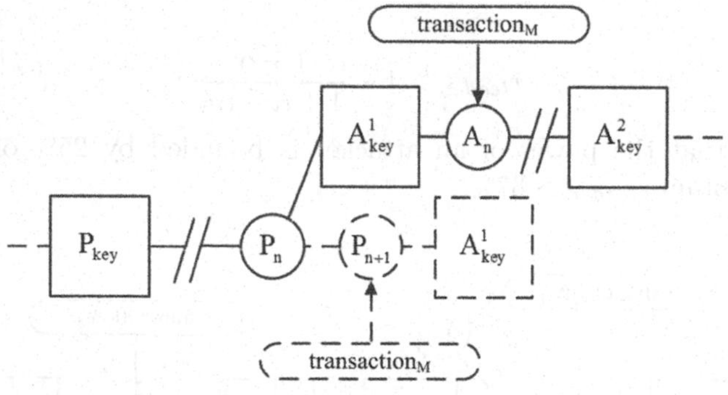

Fig. 11. Shorter chain extension. A dishonest miner A may mine on non-recent microblocks, allowing the microblock that contains transaction M to be discarded by the system. Then A places M in his own microblock and tries to mine the next key block.

$$r_{leader} + \alpha(1 - r_{leader}) < 1 - r_{leader}, \tag{3}$$

therefore

$$r_{leader} < \frac{1-\alpha}{2-\alpha}. \tag{4}$$

Combining the two incentive sub-mechanisms of transaction inclusion and longest chain extension, Eyal et al. obtained

$$1 - \frac{1-\alpha}{1+\alpha-\alpha^2} < r_{leader} < \frac{1-\alpha}{2-\alpha}. \tag{5}$$

For attackers larger than 29%, the intersection of the two conditions is empty. Therefore, Eyal et al. assert that incentive compatibility cannot be maintained in Bitcoin-NG for an attacker larger than about 29%.

4 Amendment of the Original Bitcoin-NG Protocol

4.1 Negligence in Transaction Inclusion Inequation and Its Amendment

A leader is encouraged to withhold the latest microblock if the average revenue of this attack is larger than that of abiding the rules. To keep a healthy mining ecosystem, the inequation (1) must hold true. However, there is a manifest error in the right side.

The average revenue for a current leader to include transactions in his epoch is not r_{leader}. This misconception ignores the probability of re-election of the incumbent leader in the next epoch. Instead, the revenue is $r_{leader}+\alpha(1-r_{leader})$.

The amended inequation will be

$$\alpha + (1-\alpha)\alpha(1-r_{leader}) < r_{leader} + \alpha(1-r_{leader}), \tag{6}$$

therefore

$$r_{leader} > \frac{\alpha}{1-\alpha}.$$

Taking the upper bound into consideration, the rational interval of r_{leader} is

$$\frac{\alpha}{1-\alpha} < r_{leader} < \frac{1-\alpha}{2-\alpha}. \tag{7}$$

4.2 Over-Simplification in Longest Chain Extension Inequation and Its Improvement

A leader-candidate might ignore the last microblock, mine on the previous microblock to become the next leader, and then place the transactions in the ignored preceding leader's microblock in his own microblock. This happens under the circumstance that the average revenue of this attack is larger than that of abiding the rules. To preserve the healthy mining order, the inequation (3) must hold true. However, the analysis is over-simplified, neglecting the parameter α.

The inequation (6) is the constraint for a incumbent leader in an epoch, while the inequation (3) is the constraint for a leader-candidate who wants to solve the mining puzzle to become the next leader. In reality, the average revenue for a leader-candidate who extends short chains is not the items at the left side of the inequation (3). $r_{leader} + \alpha(1 - r_{leader})$ is the average revenue for a leader-candidate who is fortunate enough to become the next leader, not the average revenue for a leader-candidate whose future is undetermined. Taking the uncertainty into account, the true average revenue for a dishonest leader-candidate is $\alpha(r_{leader} + \alpha(1 - r_{leader}))$. For the same reason, the true average revenue for an honest leader-candidate is $\alpha(1-r_{leader})$. Therefore, the inequation before simplification is

$$\alpha(r_{leader} + \alpha(1 - r_{leader})) < \alpha(1 - r_{leader}). \tag{8}$$

The detailed explanation above compensates the over-simplification of the original inequation (3), but the final upper bound for the parameter r_{leader} is identical to that in the paper [4] by detracting α simultaneously from both sides of the inequation (8).

5 Analysis of the Optimal Proportion of Transaction Fee Distribution

5.1 The Definition of the Optimal r_{leader}

Eyal et al. [4] selected r_{leader} by arbitrarily choosing 40% from the interval (37%, 43%) without detailed explanation. Unfortunately, the lower bound is incorrect due to the error presented in Sect. 4. The correct lower bound is much smaller than what Eyal et al. suggested. So the selection interval of r_{leader} is much larger, making the selection to be of greater significance.

As illustrated in Sect. 4, the average profit earned by behaving honestly must be larger than that earned by launching an attack. Therefore, the smaller the difference between honest and dishonest average profit is, the worse the mining ecosystem will be. In an extreme situation, two kinds of profit become equal and no distinction of revenue between honest miners and dishonest miners is presented. In this case, there is no incentive for honest miners to behave themselves. Consequently, in order to strengthen our mining ecosystem, it is of great necessity to set a lower bound for the difference between honest and dishonest average profit, defined as "safety margin".

There are two constraining inequations for a miner. The inequation (6) is for an incumbent leader in an epoch. The inequation (8) is for a leader-candidate who is eager to solve the mining puzzle to become the next leader. Therefore, there are two profit differences Δ_1 and Δ_2 for corresponding inequation by subtracting the left side of the inequation (i.e. the average profit for dishonest miners) from the right side of the inequation (i.e. the average profit for honest miners).

$$\begin{aligned}\Delta_1 &= [r_{leader} + \alpha(1 - r_{leader})] - [\alpha + (1-\alpha)\alpha(1 - r_{leader})] \\ &= (1-\alpha^2)r_{leader} - \alpha + \alpha^2 \end{aligned} \tag{9}$$

$$\begin{aligned}\Delta_2 &= [\alpha(1 - r_{leader})] - [\alpha(r_{leader} + \alpha(1 - r_{leader}))] \\ &= (\alpha^2 - 2\alpha)r_{leader} + \alpha - \alpha^2 \end{aligned} \tag{10}$$

Notice that the remuneration earned by a miner as well as the profit differences are approximately proportional to his mining power. Thus the safety margin is defined as the lower bound of the profit difference, where the miner's mining power should be considered. This means that the safety margin is not a constant for any miner but proportionally correlated to a miner's mining power. We define m to be the safety margin proportional coefficient, and M to be safety margin. We get $M = m\alpha$. Recall that the definition of safety margin is the lower bound of profit difference. Then we conclude

$$\Delta_1 \geq M \tag{11}$$

$$\Delta_2 \geq M \tag{12}$$

Finally, the ultimate goal of the optimization of parameter r_{leader} is to maximize m while subjecting to inequations (11) and (12) for all miners whose mining power α are in the interval $(0, 0.25)$. The upper bound 0.25 is set to avoid selfish mining [5]. This optimization aims to maximize the safety margin for any miner with the mining power $\alpha \in (0, 0.25)$ to obtain the most robust mining ecosystem.

5.2 Calculation of the Optimal r_{leader}

To deduce the optimal r_{leader}, we necessarily obtain the interval of r_{leader} from inequations (11), (12) ($\forall \alpha \in (0, 0.25)$) first.

$$\begin{aligned} &\Delta_1 \geq M, \quad \forall\alpha \in (0, 0.25) \\ \iff r_{leader} &\geq \frac{(m+1)\alpha - \alpha^2}{1-\alpha^2}, \quad \forall\alpha \in (0, 0.25) \\ \iff r_{leader} &\geq \max_{\alpha\in(0,0.25)} \frac{(m+1)\alpha - \alpha^2}{1-\alpha^2} = \frac{4m+3}{15} \end{aligned} \tag{13}$$

$$\begin{aligned} &\Delta_2 \geq M, \quad \forall\alpha \in (0, 0.25) \\ \iff r_{leader} &\leq \frac{1-\alpha-m}{2-\alpha}, \quad \forall\alpha \in (0, 0.25) \\ \iff r_{leader} &\leq \min_{\alpha\in(0,0.25)} \frac{1-\alpha-m}{2-\alpha} = \frac{3-4m}{7} \end{aligned} \tag{14}$$

Therefore, we get

$$\frac{4m+3}{15} \leq r_{leader} \leq \frac{3-4m}{7} \tag{15}$$

It is straightfoward that only when $r_{leader} = \frac{3}{11}$, the coefficient m can obtain its maximal value $\frac{3}{11}$. In summary, $r_{leader} = \frac{3}{11}$ is optimal according to our definition and assumption (Fig. 12).

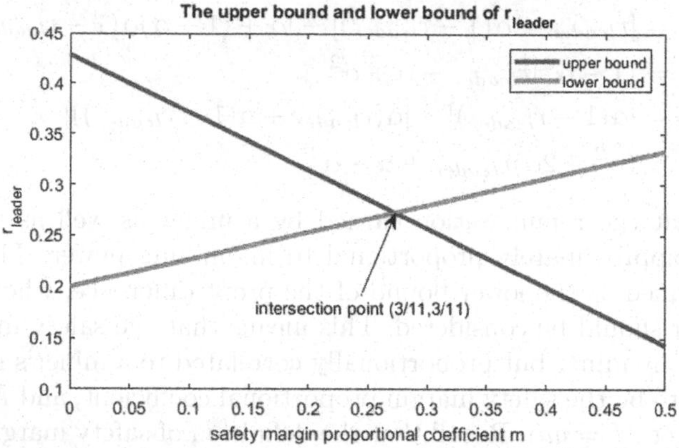

Fig. 12. The upper bound and lower bound of r_{leader} as functions of the safety margin proportional coefficient m. The safety margin proportional coefficient m takes its maximum value at the intersection point of upper bound and lower bound.

6 Conclusion

Bitcoin-NG protocol improves scalability and simultaneously maintains the system stability at a higher level. However, there are some errors in the incentive mechanism analysis, including the negligence calculating the lower bound and the over-simplification calculating the upper bound, directly leading to an unreasonable proportion of transaction fee allocation. This paper points out the errors of Eyal et al., and gives the correct analysis of the Bitcoin-NG incentive mechanism. We consummate the Bitcoin-NG blockchain protocol as a result of logically deducing the optimal proportion of transaction fee allocation. Specifically, the current leader earns 3/11 of transaction fee, leaving 8/11 to the subsequent leader.

On the basis of Bitcoin-NG, researchers have made a series of improvements and innovations and proposed protocols such as ByzCoin, ELASTICO and OmniLedger. In order to address the issue of Bitcoin scalability, more and more research will be conducted in the future. Hopefully, the optimal proportion of transaction fee distribution that we proposed in this paper can serve as a crucial reference for both future researches and applications.

Acknowledgements. The author thank Ying Gao and Feng Wang for their valuable comments on earlier versions of this manuscript. Zongyang Zhang is supported by National Key R&D Program of China (2017YFB1400700), by Beijing Natural Science Foundation (4182033), by the fund of the State Key Laboratory of Information Security, Institute of Information Engineering, Chinese Academy of Sciences, under grant No. 2017-MS-02, and the fund of the Beihang Jinhua Beidou Application Research Institute under grant No. BARI1702.

References

1. Andresen, G.: Increase maximum block size (bip 101) (2015). https://github.com/bitcoin/bips/blob/master/bip-0101.mediawiki
2. Antonopoulos, A.M.: Mastering Bitcoin: Programming the Open Blockchain. O'Reilly Media Inc., Sebastopol (2017)
3. Croman, K., et al.: On scaling decentralized blockchains. In: Clark, J., Meiklejohn, S., Ryan, P.Y.A., Wallach, D., Brenner, M., Rohloff, K. (eds.) FC 2016. LNCS, vol. 9604, pp. 106–125. Springer, Heidelberg (2016). https://doi.org/10.1007/978-3-662-53357-4_8
4. Eyal, I., Gencer, A.E., Sirer, E.G., Van Renesse, R.: Bitcoin-NG: a scalable blockchain protocol. In: 13th USENIX Symposium on Networked Systems Design and Implementation, NSDI 2016, pp. 45–59 (2016)
5. Eyal, I., Sirer, E.G.: Majority is not enough: bitcoin mining is vulnerable. In: Christin, N., Safavi-Naini, R. (eds.) FC 2014. LNCS, vol. 8437, pp. 436–454. Springer, Heidelberg (2014). https://doi.org/10.1007/978-3-662-45472-5_28
6. Kogias, E.K., Jovanovic, P., Gailly, N., Khoffi, I., Gasser, L., Ford, B.: Enhancing bitcoin security and performance with strong consistency via collective signing. In: 25th USENIX Security Symposium (USENIX Security 16), pp. 279–296 (2016)
7. Kokoris-Kogias, E., Jovanovic, P., Gasser, L., Gailly, N., Ford, B.: Omniledger: a secure, scale-out, decentralized ledger. In: 39th IEEE Symposium on Security and Privacy. IEEE (2018)
8. Luu, L., Narayanan, V., Zheng, C., Baweja, K., Gilbert, S., Saxena, P.: A secure sharding protocol for open blockchains. In: Proceedings of the 2016 ACM SIGSAC Conference on Computer and Communications Security, pp. 17–30. ACM (2016)
9. Nakamoto, S.: Bitcoin: a peer-to-peer electronic cash system (2008). https://bitcoin.org/bitcoin.pdf
10. Narayanan, A., Bonneau, J., Felten, E., Miller, A., Goldfeder, S.: Bitcoin and Cryptocurrency Technologies: A Comprehensive Introduction. Princeton University Press, Princeton (2016)
11. Nayak, K., Kumar, S., Miller, A., Shi, E.: Stubborn mining: generalizing selfish mining and combining with an eclipse attack. In: 2016 IEEE European Symposium on Security and Privacy (EuroS&P), pp. 305–320. IEEE (2016)
12. Poon, J., Dryja, T.: The bitcoin lightning network: scalable off-chain instant payments (2015). https://lightning.network/lightning-network-paper.pdf
13. Sompolinsky, Y., Zohar, A.: Secure high-rate transaction processing in bitcoin. In: Böhme, R., Okamoto, T. (eds.) FC 2015. LNCS, vol. 8975, pp. 507–527. Springer, Heidelberg (2015). https://doi.org/10.1007/978-3-662-47854-7_32
14. Syta, E., Tamas, I., Visher, D., Wolinsky, D.I., Jovanovic, P., Gasser, L., Gailly, N., Khoffi, I., Ford, B.: Keeping authorities "honest or bust" with decentralized witness cosigning. In: 2016 IEEE Symposium on Security and Privacy (SP), pp. 526–545. IEEE (2016)

Decentralized Blacklistable Anonymous Credentials with Reputation

Rupeng Yang[1,2], Man Ho Au[2(✉)], Qiuliang Xu[1(✉)], and Zuoxia Yu[2]

[1] School of Computer Science and Technology, Shandong University, Jinan 250101, China
orbbyrp@gmail.com, xql@sdu.edu.cn

[2] Department of Computing, The Hong Kong Polytechnic University, Hung Hom, Hong Kong
csallen@comp.polyu.edu.hk, zuoxia.yu@gmail.com

Abstract. Blacklistable anonymous credential systems provide service providers with a way to authenticate users according to their historical behaviors, while guaranteeing that all users can access services in an anonymous and unlinkable manner, thus are potentially useful in practice. Traditionally, to protect services from illegal access, the credential issuer, which completes the registration with users, must be trusted by the service provider. However, in practice, this trust assumption is usually unsatisfied.

In this paper, we solve this problem and present the decentralized blacklistable anonymous credential system with reputation (DBLACR), which inherits nearly all features of the BLACR system presented in Au et.al. (NDSS'12) but does not need a trusted party to register users. The new system also has extra advantages. In particular, it enables blacklist (historical behaviors) sharing among different service providers and is partially resilient to the blacklist gaming attack, where dishonest service providers attempt to compromise the privacy of users via generating blacklist maliciously.

Technically, the main approach to achieve DBLACR system is a novel use of the blockchain technique, which serves as a public append-only ledger. The system can be instantiated from three different types of cryptographic systems, including the RSA system, the classical DL system, and the pairing based system. To demonstrate the practicability of our system, we also give a proof of concept implementation for the instantiation under the RSA system. The experiment results indicate that when authenticating with blacklists of reasonable size, our implementation can fulfill practical efficiency demands.

1 Introduction

There always exists a conflict between users and service providers (SP) on the Internet. On the one hand, the SPs need to protect their services from illegal

R. Yang—This work was mainly done when doing the internship at The Hong Kong Polytechnic University.

W. Susilo and G. Yang (Eds.): ACISP 2018, LNCS 10946, pp. 720–738, 2018.
https://doi.org/10.1007/978-3-319-93638-3_41

users and users with misbehaviors, thus hope to know the exact identity and historical behaviors of each user. On the other hand, the users would like to protect their privacy, and thus hope to access services in an anonymous and unlikable manner.

The blacklistable anonymous credential system [9,25] is a good attempt to address this conflict. In this system, each SP maintains a blacklist to record users with misbehaviors, and a user attempting to access services of a SP is required to prove that he is legitimately registered and that he is not in the blacklist of the SP. Both the authentications and the maintenance of the blacklists are conducted in an anonymous and unlinkable fashion, thus privacy of users are well protected. Compared to traditional anonymous credential systems [8,10–14,16], the blacklistable anonymous credential system supports revocation of users, thus can protect SPs from users with misbehaviors. Moreover, compared to some other revocable anonymous credential systems [10,11], this is achieved without relying on a trusted third party, so in practice the blacklistable anonymous credential system is preferable.

Subsequently, there are a series of works following this line of research. Some of them consider how to improve the efficiency [24,26,31], and some others consider how to utilize historical behaviors of users in a cleverer way [5,6,27,29]. In particular, in [6], an anonymous credential system supporting fine-grained "blacklist" is proposed. In this system, instead of merely putting misbehaved users into the blacklist, the SP will rate behaviors of users in using the services. The rated scores can be either positive or negative for good and bad behaviors respectively, and belong to different categories based on types of behaviors rated. When authenticating, SPs can set complex policies about these scores, and a user attempting to access services of a SP needs to prove that he is legitimately registered and that his scores satisfy the policy of the SP. Likewise, all those operations are conducted in an anonymous and unlinkable fashion. For simplicity of notation, in this section, we still use the word "blacklist" to denote this fine-grained type of "blacklists".

To better explain how these blacklistable anonymous credential systems work, we illustrate the workflow for them in Fig. 1a. Generally speaking, a user who wants to access services of a SP first registers himself to the credential issuer and gets a credential back. Then he requests a policy from the SP and proves to the SP that he has a valid credential and that he satisfies the policy of the SP each time he wants to access the services of a SP. Behaviors of the user will be rated by the SP after he finishes using the services.

Note that to protect services from illegal access, the credential issuer must be trusted by the SP. Therefore, it is usually suggested that the credential issuer should be acted by the SP itself. However, in practice, this suggestion is often contradicted. Considering a SP who runs a forum about alcohol abuse, anyone who registers for this service runs the risk of revealing his drinking problem to the SP. So, at worst, no one would register for using this forum. As a result, the SP faces the dilemma of either trusting a third party credential issuer and suffering potential attacks or insisting on issuing credentials all by itself and suffering a loss of potential users. A similar dilemma occurs when we consider the blacklist management. More precisely, services will be better protected if the SP can refer to blacklists of other SPs and further evaluate a user according to his historical behaviors when using other services, but it may bring additional security issues if the shared blacklists are fake. Besides these two problems, current blacklistable anonymous credential systems are also vulnerable to the blacklist gaming attack, where a malicious SP attempts to learn the identity of the user via providing a maliciously generated blacklist during the authentication.

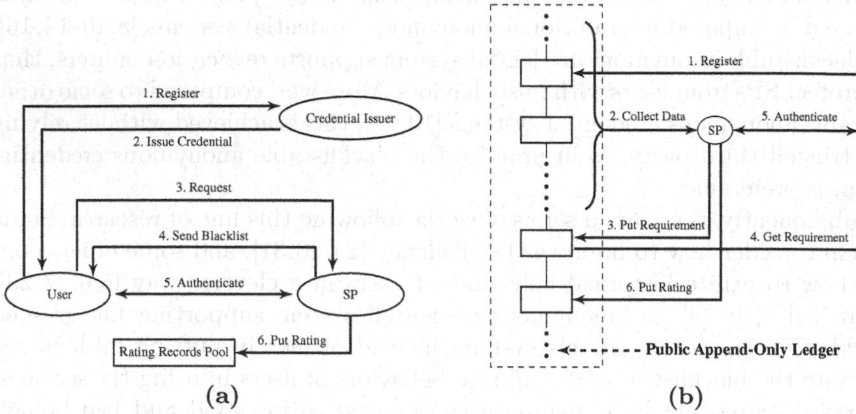

Fig. 1. Workflows of the traditional blacklistable anonymous credential systems (left) and our new decentralized blacklistable anonymous credential system with reputation (right).

The first problem, namely the requirement of a trusted credential issuer, is partially solved in [20], in which a decentralized anonymous credential system is constructed. In particular, in [20], a blockchain based public append-only ledger is employed to replace the credential issuer, and to register in the system, a user just needs to put his personal information attached with his credential to the ledger. When authenticating, a user proves to a SP that his credential belongs to a set, which is selected by the SP from credentials of all registered users. However, in [20], revocation of users is not considered, and it is unknown whether their techniques can be applied to decentralize current blacklistable anonymous credential systems. Besides, the other two problems, namely the blacklist management problem and the blacklist gaming attack, are still open.

1.1 Our Results

In this paper, we solve these open problems by presenting the decentralized blacklistable anonymous credential system with reputation (DBLACR), whose workflow is illustrated in Fig. 1b. More precisely, similar to that in [20], in our new system, there is no central credential issuer, and a user registers via uploading his credential together with his personal information to the public append-only ledger, which can be instantiated with the blockchain technique. Each SP collects data from the ledger automatically and put its requirement, including the selected candidate users set and the blacklist, to the ledger regularly. When a user wants to access a service of a SP, he first gets the latest requirement of the SP from the ledger, then he checks its validity and whether he satisfies it. If both tests are passed, he then proves to the SP that he satisfies its requirement. The user can access the service if the proof is valid, and scores for his behavior in using the service will be rated and put on the ledger by the SP then.

The DBLACR system can achieve enhanced security guarantee in the following three aspects. We also give a comparison between our system and existing blacklistable (or decentralized) anonymous credential systems in Table 1.

- *The registration is decentralized.* In our new system, no trusted credential issuer is needed, and each SP can select candidate users by itself. Thus, security for the SPs is improved. Note that the user does not need to indicate which service he would like to access when registering and only the fact that he wants to access at least one service in the system is revealed. Thus, the real purpose of the user is well hidden if there are some common and insensitive services in the system. Therefore, our solution will not compromise the privacy of users.
- *There is a consistency between the used blacklist and the shared blacklist for any SP.* This is because a SP will put his own used blacklist in the public append-only ledger, thus cannot share a fake blacklist without being caught. The property implies that to refer to blacklists of other SPs, a SP only needs to trust that they will not *use* a fake blacklist when conducting their own authentication protocols instead of trusting that they will not *share* a fake blacklist. So, to a great extent, the SP can employ blacklists of other SPs safely and makes better evaluations for users.
- *The system is partially resilient to the blacklist gaming attacks, thus provides a better protection for the privacy of users during the authentication.* This is achieved in two aspects. First, as in our system SPs update their blacklists regularly, a malicious SP can only make a less powerful passive blacklist gaming attack in each time period, where it fixes a blacklist in the beginning. Besides, in our system, a user can learn whether he could pass the verification in advance and will not attempt to launch an authentication if he does not satisfy the requirement, thus less information is leaked from authentication results. We give a more detailed discussion on how these two modifications could boost the security in Sect. 3.

Our Techniques. We construct decentralized blacklistable anonymous credential system with reputation by introducing the blockchain technique to current blacklistable anonymous credential systems and employ it as a public append-only ledger to store credentials and blacklists. However, there exists issues when integrating the blockchain technique and current (blacklistable) anonymous credential systems. To see this, recall that in a blockchain-based (blacklistable)

Table 1. The comparison.

	Decentralized registration	Blacklist supporting	Blacklist sharing	Blacklist-Gaming resilience
BLAC[25]	✗	†	‡	✗
EPID[9]	✗	†	‡	✗
PEREA[26]	✗	†	✗	✗
PE(AR)^2[31]	✗	†	✗	✗
FAUST[24]	✗	†	✗	✗
BLACR[6]	✗	✓	‡	✗
EXBLACR[27]	✗	✓	‡	✗
PERM[5]	✗	✓	✗	✗
FARB[29]	✗	✓	✗	✗
DAC[20]	✓	✗	-	-
Ours	✓	✓	✓	✓*

† : only a basic blacklist is supported.
‡ : blacklists can be shared if SPs trust each other.
✓* : the system is partially resilient to the blacklist gaming attacks.

decentralized anonymous credential system, users registers by putting its credential to the ledger. Then, to argue that he is legitimately registered, a user just proves that he knows the secret key for a credential stored in the ledger. To make the proof size constant, cryptographic accumulator is desired to accumulate all credentials in the ledger. However, in most (if not all) current (blacklistable) anonymous credential systems, credentials are commitments of the users' secret keys, thus are either (1) points in an elliptical curve, which cannot be accumulated using existing number-theory-based accumulators or (2) exponential in the users' secret keys (i.e., $C = g^s h^r$ where s is a secret key, C is the corresponding credential, r is a random number, and g, h are group elements), which bring expensive double discrete logarithm proof[1]. In both cases, the practicability of the system are reduced.

In this work, we solve these issues by presenting a new method to construct credential systems. In particular, the secret key of a user is two large primes p, q and his credential is another prime $n = 2pq + 1$. The credential can be accumulated by a strong-RSA assumption based accumulator and one can efficiently prove that his secret key relates to a credential in an accumulator. As a result, the efficiency of the system is boosted. The experiment result in Sect. 6 demonstrates that our new system is quite practical. Especially, it implies a decentralized anonymous credential system that is as much as 30 times faster for a user to generate an authentication, when compared with the decentralized anonymous credential sytem in [20].

[1] The decentralized anonymous credential system in [20] also suffers from this problem.

2 Notation

For a finite set $\mathcal{S}$, we use $\|\mathcal{S}\|$ to denote the size of $\mathcal{S}$ and write $x \xleftarrow{\$} \mathcal{S}$ to indicate that x is sampled uniformly from $\mathcal{S}$. We write $negl(\cdot)$ to denote a negligible function. For two random variables $\mathcal{X}$ and $\mathcal{Y}$, we write $\mathcal{X} \overset{c}{\approx} \mathcal{Y}$ to denote that $\mathcal{X}$ and $\mathcal{Y}$ are computationally indistinguishable. We will use a few cryptographic assumptions, including the strong RSA assumption, the LD-RSA assumption, the discrete logarithm assumption, the DDH assumption, and the DDH-II assumption. We will also use cryptographic primitives, such as zero-knowledge proof of knowledge, commitment scheme, dynamic accumulator, CL signature, and public append-only ledger. Note that all zero-knowledge proofs of knowledge used in this paper are non-interactive and admit an additional message as input, thus it is also called signature proof of knowledge (SPK), and is usually written as $SPK\{(w) : \mathcal{S}\}[m]$, for a statement $\mathcal{S}$ with witness w and additional message m. Due to lack of space, we do not provide detailed descriptions for the used assumptions and cryptographic primitives and refer the readers to the full version of this paper [30] for more details.

3 Syntax and Security Goals

3.1 The Syntax

There are two types of entities, namely the users and the service providers, and a public ledger in the DBLACR system, and the system consists of the following protocols:

- **Setup.** To setup the system, a trusted party is employed to generate the public parameter of the system. Note that this party is only used in the setup phase and we only need to trust that it will generate the public parameter honestly and will erase all the internal states of the generation process.
- **Registration.** In this protocol, a user registers himself to the system. To complete this task, a user just needs to put some information to a public ledger, which should include some auxiliary proof data and his attributes to aid the SPs in deciding whether to accept the user as a valid candidate user for accessing their services.
- **Authentication.** This protocol is executed between a user and a SP. The user attempts to access services of the SP in an anonymous and unlinkable fashion, and the SP will accept the user if and only if the user fulfills its requirement. Here, the requirement includes three parts, namely the candidate users set $\mathcal{C}$, the policy $\mathcal{P}_R$ and the rating records list $\mathcal{L}$. Our system can support a policy of any DNF formula, whose inputs are accumulated scores for a user's behaviors in different category. We refer the readers to the full version of this paper [30] for a more detailed explaination of the requirement.
- **Interaction with The Ledger.** The public ledger in this system is public and accessible to every participant, including the users and the SPs. In addition, the SPs can put data to the ledger. In particular, it can upload

its requirement to the ledger regularly. Besides, it can submit a rating for the anonymous user in an authentication event and submit a revocation of a rating record submitted by itself.

3.2 The Security

We refer the readers to the full version of this paper [30] for a formal security definition of our decentralized blacklistable anonymous credential system with reputation. Here, we only highlight a few security properties of the system that are most concerned in practice:

- **Authenticity.** The authenticity property guarantees that SPs are assured to accept authentication events only from users satisfying their requirements.
- **Anonymity.** The anonymity property guarantees that all a SP learns from an authentication is if the authenticating user satisfies its current requirement.
- **Non-frameability.** The non-frameability property guarantees that if a SP is honest, then users satisfying the current requirement of this SP can always successfully authenticate to it.
- **Sybil-Attack Resilience.** The Sybil attack [18] allows users to get new credentials after their current credentials are blacklisted, thus may expose services to users with misbehaviors. In our new system, since users register to the system via uploading their identities to the public ledger, the Sybil attack can be prevented if SPs only select users whose identities have not been uploaded previously as candidate users.
- **Authenticity of Registration.** This property guarantees that SPs can decide which users are legitimate directly and do not have to resort to a third party. The property can provide a better protection for SPs.
- **Privacy of Registration.** This property guarantees that only the fact that the registered user hopes to access at least one service supported by the system can be learned from a registration event. As personal information is usually required in registration, this property is significant in protecting the privacy of users.
- **Consistency of Blacklists.** This property guarantees that each rating record selected by a SP will be honestly assessed unless there exist SPs hoping to expose their services to possible malicious users. The property can greatly reduce the requirement of trust when using rating records from other SPs.
- **Blacklist-Gaming Attack Resilience.** The blacklist gaming attack [26] allows a SP to compromise the privacy of users via generating blacklists (requirements) maliciously. Our new system is partially resilient to the blacklist gaming attack and this is achieved in the following two aspects:
  - First, in our new system, the SPs can only update their requirements regularly, thus in each time period, the requirement used in authentication protocols is fixed. Compared to that in previous systems, where the malicious SP can use an adaptively chosen blacklist during each authentication event, the privacy of users is better protected now. To demonstrate this, we consider the following scenario. Via some auxiliary information,

a SP conjectures that the next authentication event is launched by the same user who launches a previous authentication event with identifier "t". In current blacklistable anonymous credential systems, the SP can definitely verify its conjecture via providing a blacklist with merely "t" in it. However, this attack is not applicable in our system since no SP is able to use a temporary blacklist in an authentication.

- Next, in our new system, as a user could obtain the latest requirement of a SP from the public ledger, he can check whether he is able to pass the verification in advance and will not attempt to launch the authentication protocol if he does not satisfy the requirement. To see why this can better protect the privacy of users, we consider the following scenario. Again, via some auxiliary information, a SP learns that the following authentication events will be launched by one of two lists of users. It also learns whether each user in these two lists satsifies a pre-defined requirement. Previously, even restricting the malicious SP to the pre-defined requirement, it can still determine the list of users in use if there exists an index i that the ith users in the two lists are different in satisfying the requirement. In contrast, in our new system, the malicious SP can learn nothing if the numbers of users satisfying the requirement in these two lists are identical.

We remark that the first four properties are already achieved in current blacklistable anonymous credential systems. The property "authenticity of registration" and the property "privacy of registration" have also been achieved previously, but no system has these two properties simultaneously, and our system is the first one that can protect both the security of the SPs and that of the users in the registration. The last two properties are new security properties that are only available in our new system.

4 General Construction

In this section, we provide a general framework for constructing the decentralized blacklistable anonymous credential system with reputation. We start by introducing a few algorithms and protocols used for building the system. Then we describe how to combine these components to complete the construction.

4.1 Building Blocks

Our DBLACR system can be instantiated from various public key systems, and for each public key system, we need the following sub-protocols to help build our system:

A Key Generation Algorithm. On input a security parameter 1^λ, the key generation algorithm returns a public key/secret key pair, namely, $(pk, sk) \leftarrow KeyGen(1^\lambda)$. In our system, the public key is the credential of a user, and the secret key is the witness for it. So we require that the key generation algorithm has the following properties:

- *Verifiability.* There exists a polynomial-time algorithm T s.t. $T(pk, sk) = 1$ iff the pair (pk, sk) is a legal key pair of the public key system.
- *Onewayness.* Given the public key pk, it is computationally hard to compute a secret key sk such that $T(pk, sk) = 1$.
- *Collision Resistance.* It is computationally hard to find a pair of different secret keys (sk_1, sk_2) and a public key pk such that $T(pk, sk_1) = T(pk, sk_2) = 1$.

A Ticket Generation Algorithm. On input a secret key sk, the ticket generation algorithm generates a ticket for sk, namely, $\tau \leftarrow TicketGen(sk)$. In our system, each ticket will be the representation of an authentication event, and an authentication event with a ticket τ will be regarded as launched by the owner of a secret key sk iff $S(sk, \tau) = 1$. So we require that the ticket generation algorithm has the following properties:

- *Verifiability.* There exists a polynomial-time algorithm S s.t. $S(sk, \tau) = 1$ iff τ is a valid ticket of sk.
- *Indistinguishability.* Let $(pk, sk) \leftarrow KeyGen(1^\lambda)$, then for any probabilistic polynomial time adversary $\mathcal{A}$, $\Pr[b \xleftarrow{\$} \{0,1\}; b \leftarrow \mathcal{A}^{\mathcal{O}_b}(pk)] \leq 1/2 + negl(\lambda)$, where $\mathcal{O}_0$ outputs a ticket of sk each time invoked, and $\mathcal{O}_1$ outputs a random element in the range of the ticket generation algorithm each time.
- *Verifying Consistency.* For any secret keys sk_1, sk_2, if there exists a τ s.t. $S(sk_1, \tau) = S(sk_2, \tau) = 1$, then for any τ' in the range of the ticket generation algorithm, we have $S(sk_1, \tau') = S(sk_2, \tau')$.
- *Connectivity.* Let $(pk, sk) \leftarrow KeyGen(1^\lambda)$, $\tau \leftarrow TicketGen(sk)$, and sk' be a secret key s.t. $S(sk', \tau) = 1$, then given (pk, sk'), one can efficiently compute sk.

An SPK System Proving the Possession of the Secret Key. We need a SPK system to prove that the prover possesses the secret key sk of a given public key pk. Formally, the prover needs to prove $SPK\{(sk) : T(pk, sk) = 1\}$.

An SPK System Proving the Validity of a Public Key and a Ticket. We need a SPK system proving that the prover possesses a secret key sk for a given ticket τ and the secret key is associated with a public key in a given set $\mathcal{C}$. Formally, the prover needs to prove $SPK\{(sk, pk) : S(sk, \tau) = 1 \wedge T(pk, sk) = 1 \wedge pk \in \mathcal{C}\}$.

An SPK System Proving the Fulfilment of a Policy. We also need a SPK system proving that the prover possesses a secret key sk for a given ticket τ and the secret key represents a user whose scores evaluated according to a policy $\mathcal{P}_R$ and a rating records list $\mathcal{L}$ satisfies $\mathcal{R}_R$. For simplicity of description, in this section, we define a boolean function $\mathcal{E}$ that outputs 1 iff the latter condition is satisfied. Then, the prover needs to prove $SPK\{(sk) : S(sk, \tau) = 1 \wedge \mathcal{E}(\mathcal{P}_R, \mathcal{L}, sk) = 1\}$.

4.2 The Construction

Now, we present the general construction of our DBLACR system, which is built on the sub-protocols shown in Sect. 4.1 and a public append-only ledger with ideal functionality $\mathcal{F}_{BB}^{\star}$, whose formal definition is given in the full version [30]. Formally, we have:

Setup. On input a security parameter 1^{λ}, a trusted party runs the setup algorithm for each sub-protocol of each public key system and outputs all those generated public parameters as the public parameter for the DBLACR system.

Registration. To register himself to the system, a user with auxiliary proof data aux and attributes $attr$ first generates his public key/secret key pair $(pk, sk) \leftarrow KeyGen(1^{\lambda})$ for one of the supported public key systems. Then he computes $\Pi_R \leftarrow SPK\{(sk) : T(pk, sk) = 1\}[aux \| attr]$. Finally, he stores the tuple $(Nym, pk, \Pi_R, attr, aux)$ to the public ledger via $\mathcal{F}_{BB}^{\star}$, where Nym is his pseudonym in the public ledger. We remark that here the user can use a temporary pseudonym and not a permanent one.

Authentication. In this protocol, a user uid attempts to authenticate with a service provider sid. Interactions between these two parties are summarized in Fig. 2. For the clarity of presentation, here we assume that there are k public key systems employed in our system, and denote them as $\Psi_1, \ldots, \Psi_k$ respectively. All algorithms in Ψ_i will be labeled with a superscript "(i)", and w.l.o.g. we assume that the user uid chooses the first public key system when registering.

In more detail, in this protocol, the user uid first downloads the requirement $(\mathcal{C}, \mathcal{P}_R, \mathcal{L})$ for accessing services of sid from the public ledger. Then he verifies the validity of this requirement. If the requirement is valid, the user then checks whether he satisfies the requirement. If not, he aborts the protocol even without communicating with sid. Otherwise, uid sends a request to sid and gets a challenge $m \| sid'$ back, where m is a randomly chosen bit string whose length is polynomial in the security parameter. Then, uid checks whether $sid = sid'$ and if so he generates a ticket $\mathcal{T}$ and a proof Π_A, and sends $(\mathcal{T}, \Pi_A)$ to sid. More precisely, to generate the ticket $\mathcal{T}$, the user computes $\tau_1 \leftarrow TicketGen^{(1)}(sk)$, randomly samples τ_i in the range of $TicketGen^{(i)}(\cdot)$ for $i \in [2, k]$, and sets $\mathcal{T} = \{\tau_1, \ldots, \tau_k\}$. To generate the proof Π_A, the user computes $\Pi_A = SPK\{(sk, pk) : \bigvee_{i=1}^{k} (T^{(i)}(pk, sk) = 1 \wedge pk \in \mathcal{C}_i \wedge S^{(i)}(sk, \tau_i) = 1 \wedge \mathcal{E}^{(i)}(\mathcal{P}_R, \mathcal{L}^{(i)}, sk) = 1)\}[m \| sid]$, which is constructed by employing the technique in [15] to combine the proof of "validity of a public key and a ticket" and the proof of "fulfillment of a policy" for each public key system, where $\mathcal{C}_i$ consists of all public keys of Ψ_i that are in $\mathcal{C}$, and $\mathcal{L}^{(i)}$ consists of all rating records in $\mathcal{L}$ but for each record the ticket $\mathcal{T}' = (\tau'_1, \ldots, \tau'_k)$ is replaced with τ'_i. Upon receiving the response $(\mathcal{T}, \Pi_A)$, sid verifies the proof and sends the result, which will be "accept" iff the proof is valid, back to uid.

Interaction with Ledger. To obtain data from the public ledger, a participant just needs to submit a "retrieve" request to $\mathcal{F}_{BB}^{\star}$. To put data to the public ledger, a SP just needs to submit a "store" request together with its permanent pseudonym and its data to $\mathcal{F}_{BB}^{\star}$. The submitted data vary depending on the

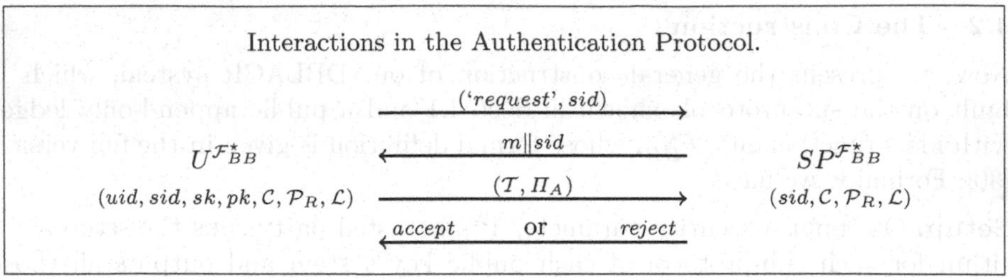

Fig. 2. Interactions in the authentication protocol. Here, we use "U" to denote the user, and "SP" to denote the service provider.

purpose of the SP. In particular, when a SP would like to submit a rating s, it needs to put a tuple $(rid, \mathcal{T}, s, \Gamma)$ to the public ledger, where rid is a unique string identifying this rating record, $\mathcal{T}$ is the ticket for the rated authentication event, and Γ is the transcript of this authentication event, which is used to prove that the rated authentication event can be accepted by this SP. When a SP would like to submit a revocation of a rating record rid, it needs to put a tuple $(\text{'}revoke\text{'}, rid)$ to the public ledger. When a SP would like to publish a new requirement, it first generates a valid requirement $(\mathcal{C}, \mathcal{P}_R, \mathcal{L})$, then puts it to the public ledger. To generate a valid requirement, apart from meeting those demands listed in Sect. 3.1, the SP should further ensure that each selected user in $\mathcal{C}$ is attached with a valid proof Π_R. We remark that all those data uploaded to the public ledger will not be verified in this phase, instead, the verification will be postponed until the data are used.

The Security. Security of our system is guaranteed by Theorem 4.1 stated as following. We refer the readers to the full version of this paper [30] for proof of Theorem 4.1.

Theorem 4.1. *The system presented in Sect. 4.2 is a secure DBLACR system if each sub-protocol has the properties demanded in Sect. 4.1.*

5 The Instantiations

To demonstrate the utility of our general framework, in this section, we instantiate sub-protocols defined in Sect. 4.1. The sub-protocols can be instantiated under three different types of public key systems, namely, the classical DL system, the pairing based system, and the RSA system. Here, we only present a high-level idea on how to instantiate the system from the RSA system and refer readers to the full version [30] for detailed instantiations from all three systems.

Our RSA based sub-protocols works in a quadratic residue group QR_N with a generator $\mathfrak{g}$, where N is the product of two big safe prime numbers. The secret key of the system is two safe primes p and q that $2pq + 1$ is also a prime and the public key is $n = 2pq + 1$. To generate a ticket $\tau = (b, t)$, one first samples $r \xleftarrow{\$} \mathbb{Z}_N$, then computes $b = \mathfrak{g}^r \mod N$ and $t = b^{p+q} \mod N$.

To prove the possession of a secret key $sk = (p, q)$ for a properly generated public key $pk = n$, the user works in two steps. First, the prover proves that $(n-1)/2$ is a product of two *primes*. This can be accomplished by employing a variant the proof system proposed in [21]. Then, the prover needs to prove that he knows two numbers p, q with identical lengths that satisfy $2pq + 1 = n$. To instantiate this proof system, we apply the framework presented in [23], which provides a simple method to prove knowledge of discrete logs that are in an interval and fulfil a set of equations over groups of unknown order.

Then, to construct the SPK system proving that a user possesses a secret key $sk = (p, q)$ associated with a public key $pk = n$ in a given set $\mathcal{C}$, we apply the approach presented in [17], which also builds on the framework of [23]. More precisely, the prover first accumulates public keys in $\mathcal{C}$ with a dynamic accumulator, then proves in zero-knowledge the possession of the secret key of a public key in the accumulator. To further prove that a given ticket $\tau = (b, t)$ is also generated from the same secret key, the prover just plugs the equation $t = b^p b^q$ into the above statement.

Finally, to prove the fulfilment of a policy, we exploit the idea in [6] to construct the proof system, but will employ RSA-based cryptographic primitives instead of those pairing-based ones. In particular, we will apply strong-RSA assumption based additive homomorphic commitment scheme [19] and CL signature scheme [12], and we will also apply the framework in [23] to construct our proof system.

6 The Implementation

To demonstrate the practicability of our system, in this section, we provide a proof of concept implementation for it. The implementation includes two relatively independent parts, namely, the public ledger part and the credential system part, and we describe the results for them in Sect. 6.1 and in Sect. 6.2 respectively.

6.1 The Public Ledger

First, we explore how the public ledger could be realized. Recall that the public ledger can be instantiated via the blockchain technique. So, we choose the Bitcoin and the Ethereum, which are the two most popular blockchain technique instantiations currently, as the test object. The test is conducted on a personal computer with a 3.16 GHz Intel(R) Core(TM)2 Duo Processor E8500, 8 GB RAM and 500 GB disk, running ARCHLinux version 4.10.6. The Bitcoin client run in the experiment is Bitcoin Core Version 0.14.0 and the Ethereum client is go-ethereum 1.5.9. The result is summarized in Table 2.

The row "Market Cap" indicates the market capitalizations of each instantiation, and the data come from [1]. This can reflect the robustness of the blockchain to some extent. The row "Initial Data Size" and the row "Initial Sync Time" indicates the disk space and time needed before one could employ

Table 2. Comparison of public ledger instantiations.

	Bitcoin	Ethereum
Market Cap	19257718797 USD	4376127411 USD
Initial Data Size	118 GB	15 GB
Initial Sync Time	9 h	5 h
Ease of Use	Difficult	Easy
Data Size Limit	80bytes	*
Cost	0.5342 USD	0.0225 USD
Confirmation Time	6 min/70 min	a few seconds/3 min

the public ledger. The row "Ease of Use" and the row "Data Size Limit" indicates the accessibility of using blockchain as a public ledger. For Bitcoin, in each transaction, there exists a field OP_RETURN allowing one to put up to 80 bytes arbitrary data [3] on it, but it seems that the Bitcoin community do not hope people to use this field, and the client Bitcoin Core also does not provide a convenient way to implement this functionality. Thus, we test this facility via a third party open source project on GitHub [22]. For Ethereum, putting data in a transaction is natively supported. There is also no explicit limits on the size of data put in a transaction, but for each block, there is a block gas limit, which is about 4 millions for current blocks. As it will consume gas to attach data to a transaction, one could only put dozens to hundreds kilobytes data in one transaction now according to the content of the data. The row "Cost" indicates the amount of money cost to put data on the blockchain. For Bitcoin, this is the transaction fee for rewarding the miners. According to statistics (data from [4]), to hope miners to deal with the transaction immediately, the transaction fee should be above 1.8×10^{-6} BTC per byte, and for our purpose, which will send a transaction of about 250 bytes (about 200 bytes for the basic transaction and about 50 bytes for the attached data), the transaction fee should be 0.00045 BTC, which is about 0.5342 USD according to the price of 1 BTC at April 14th, 2017. For Ethereum, the cost comes from the gas consumed. Currently, each gas is about 2×10^{-8} Ether, and according to the yellow paper of Ethereum [28], a transaction will cost 21000 gas for itself, and each non-zero byte put in the data field will cost 68 gas. In our experiment, we put 32 bytes in a transaction and this cost us 0.00047 Ether, or about 0.0225 USD according to the price of 1 Ether at April 14th, 2017. The row "Confirmation Time" indicates the time needed to wait for the transactions and the data to be confirmed. For Bitcoin, on average, it will take 10 min to generate a new block, so on average, it will take about 5 min to see the data appear on the blockchain, and about 1 h to confirm that the data are put in the blockchain (6 confirmation). For Ethereum, the new block appears every a few seconds, so the data will appear on the blockchain immediately. As claimed by the Ethereum Blog [2], 10 confirmation in Ethereum is enough to achieve a similar degree of security as that of 6 confirmation in Bitcoin, so it may take about 3 min to wait for the confirmation of the transaction/data.

From the experiment result, we observe that neither the Bitcoin nor the Ethereum can support large data storage. So in practice, to use them as a public ledger, one should first upload the data to some public cloud, then put the link (40 to 60 bytes for a dropbox link and 10 to 20 bytes if google url shorten service is used) and hash value of the data (32 bytes if SHA-256 is used) to the blockchain. In this way, the functionality of the public ledger still reserves. Another problem is that while it is quite easy for a service provider to sync and maintain a Bitcoin blockchain or an Ethereum blockchain in its server, this is not the case for a normal user. To tackle this problem, we suggest users with constrained devices to use a lightweight client or refer to an online service to complete interactions with the public ledger (they could exploit multiple approaches to retrieve data to boost the security), and this will not harm the security as long as there exists services providing correct Bitcoin or Ethereum blockchain information. When comparing the Bitcoin and the Ehtereum, it seems that the Bitcoin blockchain is more robust, while the Ethereum is also very secure and is much more convenient to use. Thus, in practice, Ethereum seems a better choice and we prefer to employ Ethereum to realize our system.

6.2 The Credential System

Then we examine the practicality of the credential system part of our system. The implementation is for the RSA-based instantiation. To simplify the criterion for evaluating the experiment result, we only consider a simple policy with a single category, threshold 0, and no adjusting factor, and a rating records list with one blacklist. The experiment is conducted on a Macbook Pro with 8 GB of 1866 MHz LPDDR3 onboard memory and a 2.7 GHz dual-core Intel Core i5 processor, running OSX 10.12.4. The test code is written in C based on the OPENSSL library (version 1.0.2).

There are two main operations, namely the registration and the authentication, in the system, thus our experiment also focuses on the performance of these two protocols. First, we test the performance of the registration protocol, including the time for a user to generate a credential, the time for a service provider to verify a credential, and the credential size. As the user may already have a key pair when joining the system, the time consumption for generating a credential is tested in two modes, namely the normal mode, where the user needs to generate both the key pair and the proof, and the pre-computation mode, where credential is generated on a given public key/secret key pair. Then, we test the performance of the authentication protocol, including the time for generating a proof, the time for verifying a proof, and the size of the proof. Since the user can access the requirement in advance and precompute some parts, we will test the times for generating a proof both with and without pre-computation.

The experiment performance is measured under different parameters, including the security parameter, the candidate users set size, and the blacklist size. In more detail, we will consider security parameters of 1024 bits, 2048 bits, and 3072 bits, which can achieve a security strength of about 80 bits, 112 bits, and 128 bits respectively (according to [7]), and summarize the performance of our system under different security parameters in Table 3. we will consider candidate users set size of 10000, 20000, 50000 100000, and 200000, and blacklist size of 1000, 2000, 3000, 4000, and 5000, and summarize the performance of the authentication protocol under these parameters in Fig. 3. When analyzing the relation between the performance and one particular parameter, the other two parameters will be set as default, and the default values of the security parameter, the candidate users set size, and the blacklist size are 2048 bits, 50000, 3000 respectively. Besides, we also test the performance for the setting with an empty blacklist, which is exactly the scenario considered in [20], and compare our results with theirs in Fig. 4.

Table 3. The performance of the registration protocol and the authentication protocol under different security parameters with 50000 users and 3000 blacklist records.

	GC	GC-P	VC	CS	GP	GP-P	VP	PS
1024 bits	1.316 s	0.153 s	0.047 s	70.1 KB	10.878 s	0.021 s	5.686 s	3.1 MB
2048 bits	19.296 s	0.932 s	0.295 s	139.9 KB	51.917 s	0.036 s	29.289	6.2 MB
3072 bits	69.578 s	2.959 s	0.910 s	209.8 KB	142.123 s	0.047 s	84.872 s	9.3 MB

Here, we use GC, GC-P, and VC to denote time consumed in generating a credential, generating a credential with pre-computation, and verifying the validity of a credential respectively; we use GP, GP-P, and VP to denote time consumed in generating a proof, generating a proof with pre-computation, and verifying a proof respectively; and we use CS and PS to denote the size of a credential and an authentication proof respectively.

From the experiment results, we can conclude that our system is quite practical when deployed in practice. First, at the user side, the time consumption is extremely low if pre-computation is enabled. At the service provider side, it is also fairly fast to verify the validity of a credential, but it seems time-consuming to verify the validity of a proof. Nonetheless, the service provider often controls more computation resources, so it will take less time to wait for the verification in real world applications. Besides, the size of the credential and the proof is also not very large, thus the communication cost of our system is also quite low. One advantage of our system is that both the communication cost and the computation cost hardly increase with the increasing of the candidate users, i.e. it is scalable in the number of supported users. This is important for the usefulness of our system, since a large number of registered users is always desired to protect the privacy of particular users. However, this is not the case for the blacklist size, as both the communication cost and the computation cost grow linearly

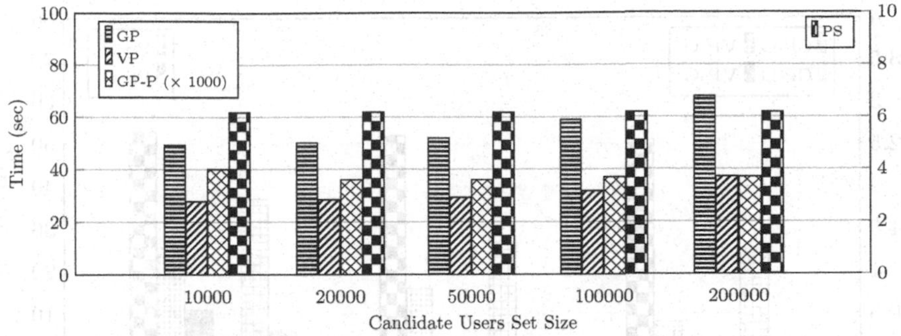

(a) Performance for the authentication protocol under different candidate users set size with security parameter 2048 bits and 3000 blacklist records. GP, GP-P and VP are times for generating a proof without pre-computation, generating *1000* proofs with pre-computation, and verifying a proof respectively, and PS is the size of the authentication proof.

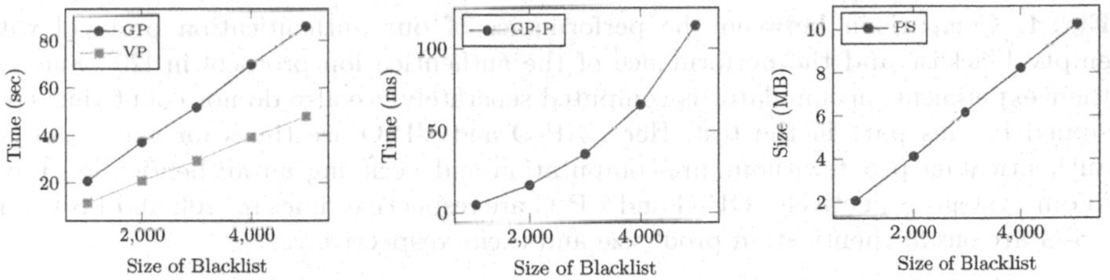

(b) Time for generating and verifying a proof under different blacklist size with security parameter 2048 bits and 50000 users. GP and VP are times for generating (without pre-computation) and verifying a proof respectively.

(c) Time (in milliseconds) for generating a proof with pre-computation under different blacklist size with security parameter 2048 bits and 50000 users.

(d) Size (in Megabyte) of an authentication proof under different blacklist size with security parameter 2048 bits and 50000 users.

Fig. 3. Performance of our system under different candidate users set size and blacklist size.

with the size of the blacklist. So, it is better to employ our system in settings with a small blacklist. We leave how to upgrade the system to scalable in the size of the blacklist as an open problem.

When comparing the efficiency of our system with that in [20], we observe that our efficiency is much better than theirs. More precisely, our system can be as much as 30 times faster than theirs for a user to generate an authentication, and can be as much as 4 times faster for a service provider to verifiy. Also, the communication cost of our system is only about 15% to 45% of theirs. Thus our system is preferable even in scenarios that no revocation is needed.

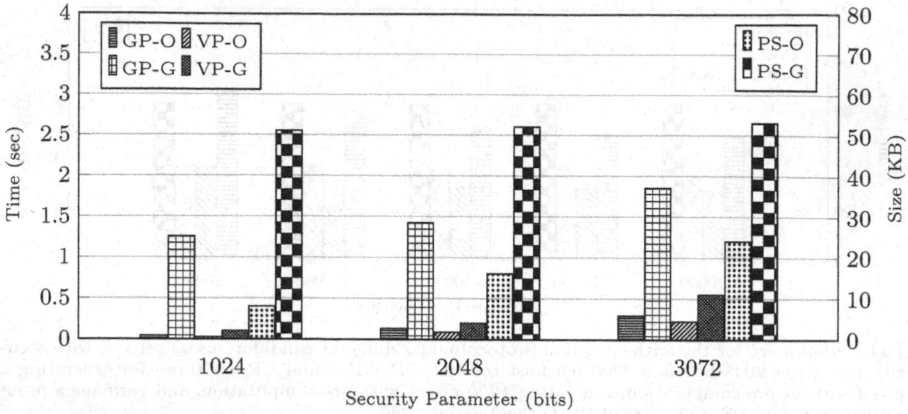

Fig. 4. Comparison between the performance of our authentication protocol with empty blacklist and the performance of the authentication protocol in [20]. Since in their experiment, accumulator is computed separately, we also do not count time consumed by this part in the test. Here, GP-O and VP-O are times for generating an authentication proof without pre-computation and verifying an authentication proof in our system respectively; GP-G and VP-G are respective times in [20]; and PS-O and PS-G are our authentication proof size and theirs respectively.

7 Conclusion

In this paper, we explore how to employ the blockchain technique to solve several open problems for previous anonymous credential systems, including trust of the credential issuer and the blacklist gaming attack. Note that, our system is only partially resilient to the blacklist gaming attack. Especially, a malicious verifier can still learn information such as the number of successfully authenticated users in a time period and may use this information to compromise the privacy of users. We leave how to construct a blacklistable anonymous credential system that is fully resilient to the blacklist gaming attack as an open problem.

Acknowledgement. We appreciate the anonymous reviewers for their valuable suggestions. Part of this work was supported by the National Natural Science Foundation of China (Grant No. 61602396, U1636205, 61572294, 61632020, 61602275), the MonashU-PolyU-Collinstar Capital Joint Lab on Blockchain and Cryptocurrency Technologies, and from the Research Grants Council of Hong Kong (Grant No. 25206317).

References

1. Cryptocurrency market capitalizations. https://coinmarketcap.com/. Accessed 15 Apr 2017
2. On slow and fast block times. https://blog.ethereum.org/2015/09/14/on-slow-and-fast-block-times/
3. Op_return. https://en.bitcoin.it/wiki/OP_RETURN. Accessed 15 Apr 2017

4. Predicting bitcoin fees for transactions. https://bitcoinfees.21.co/. Accessed 14 Apr 2017
5. Au, M.H., Kapadia, A.: PERM: practical reputation-based blacklisting without TTPs. In: CCS, pp. 929–940. ACM (2012)
6. Au, M.H., Kapadia, A., Susilo, W.: BLACR: TTP-free blacklistable anonymous credentials with reputation. In: NDSS (2012)
7. Barker, E.: Recommendation for key management-part 1: general (revision 4) (2015)
8. Belenkiy, M., Chase, M., Kohlweiss, M., Lysyanskaya, A.: P-signatures and non-interactive anonymous credentials. In: Canetti, R. (ed.) TCC 2008. LNCS, vol. 4948, pp. 356–374. Springer, Heidelberg (2008). https://doi.org/10.1007/978-3-540-78524-8_20
9. Brickell, E., Li, J.: Enhanced privacy id: a direct anonymous attestation scheme with enhanced revocation capabilities. In: Proceedings of the 2007 ACM Workshop on Privacy in Electronic Society, pp. 21–30. ACM (2007)
10. Camenisch, J., Lysyanskaya, A.: An efficient system for non-transferable anonymous credentials with optional anonymity revocation. In: Pfitzmann, B. (ed.) EUROCRYPT 2001. LNCS, vol. 2045, pp. 93–118. Springer, Heidelberg (2001). https://doi.org/10.1007/3-540-44987-6_7
11. Camenisch, J., Lysyanskaya, A.: Dynamic accumulators and application to efficient revocation of anonymous credentials. In: Yung, M. (ed.) CRYPTO 2002. LNCS, vol. 2442, pp. 61–76. Springer, Heidelberg (2002). https://doi.org/10.1007/3-540-45708-9_5
12. Camenisch, J., Lysyanskaya, A.: A signature scheme with efficient protocols. In: Cimato, S., Persiano, G., Galdi, C. (eds.) SCN 2002. LNCS, vol. 2576, pp. 268–289. Springer, Heidelberg (2003). https://doi.org/10.1007/3-540-36413-7_20
13. Camenisch, J., Lysyanskaya, A.: Signature schemes and anonymous credentials from bilinear maps. In: Franklin, M. (ed.) CRYPTO 2004. LNCS, vol. 3152, pp. 56–72. Springer, Heidelberg (2004). https://doi.org/10.1007/978-3-540-28628-8_4
14. Chaum, D.: Security without identification: transaction systems to make big brother obsolete. Commun. ACM **28**(10), 1030–1044 (1985)
15. Cramer, R., Damgård, I., Schoenmakers, B.: Proofs of partial knowledge and simplified design of witness hiding protocols. In: Desmedt, Y.G. (ed.) CRYPTO 1994. LNCS, vol. 839, pp. 174–187. Springer, Heidelberg (1994). https://doi.org/10.1007/3-540-48658-5_19
16. Damgård, I.B.: Payment systems and credential mechanisms with provable security against abuse by individuals. In: Goldwasser, S. (ed.) CRYPTO 1988. LNCS, vol. 403, pp. 328–335. Springer, New York (1990). https://doi.org/10.1007/0-387-34799-2_26
17. Dodis, Y., Kiayias, A., Nicolosi, A., Shoup, V.: Anonymous identification in *ad hoc* groups. In: Cachin, C., Camenisch, J.L. (eds.) EUROCRYPT 2004. LNCS, vol. 3027, pp. 609–626. Springer, Heidelberg (2004). https://doi.org/10.1007/978-3-540-24676-3_36
18. Douceur, J.R.: The sybil attack. In: Druschel, P., Kaashoek, F., Rowstron, A. (eds.) IPTPS 2002. LNCS, vol. 2429, pp. 251–260. Springer, Heidelberg (2002). https://doi.org/10.1007/3-540-45748-8_24
19. Fujisaki, E., Okamoto, T.: Statistical zero knowledge protocols to prove modular polynomial relations. In: Kaliski, B.S. (ed.) CRYPTO 1997. LNCS, vol. 1294, pp. 16–30. Springer, Heidelberg (1997). https://doi.org/10.1007/BFb0052225
20. Garman, C., Green, M., Miers, I.: Decentralized anonymous credentials. In: NDSS (2014)

21. Gennaro, R., Micciancio, D., Rabin, T.: An efficient non-interactive statistical zero-knowledge proof system for quasi-safe prime products. In: CCS, pp. 67–72. ACM (1998)
22. Greenspan, G.: Project php-op_return. https://github.com/coinspark/php-OP_RETURN. Accessed 15 Apr 2017
23. Kiayias, A., Tsiounis, Y., Yung, M.: Traceable signatures. In: Cachin, C., Camenisch, J.L. (eds.) EUROCRYPT 2004. LNCS, vol. 3027, pp. 571–589. Springer, Heidelberg (2004). https://doi.org/10.1007/978-3-540-24676-3_34
24. Lofgren, P., Hopper, N.: FAUST: efficient, TTP-free abuse prevention by anonymous whitelisting. In: Proceedings of the 10th Annual ACM Workshop on Privacy in the Electronic Society, pp. 125–130. ACM (2011)
25. Tsang, P.P., Au, M.H., Kapadia, A., Smith, S.W.: Blacklistable anonymous credentials: blocking misbehaving users without TTPs. In: CCS, pp. 72–81. ACM (2007)
26. Tsang, P.P., Au, M.H., Kapadia, A., Smith, S.W.: PEREA: towards practical TTP-free revocation in anonymous authentication. In: CCS, pp. 333–344. ACM (2008)
27. Wang, W., Feng, D., Qin, Y., Shao, J., Xi, L., Chu, X.: ExBLACR: extending BLACR system. In: Susilo, W., Mu, Y. (eds.) ACISP 2014. LNCS, vol. 8544, pp. 397–412. Springer, Cham (2014). https://doi.org/10.1007/978-3-319-08344-5_26
28. Wood, G.: Ethereum yellow paper (2014)
29. Xi, L., Feng, D.: FARB: fast anonymous reputation-based blacklisting without TTPs. In: Proceedings of the 13th Workshop on Privacy in the Electronic Society, pp. 139–148. ACM (2014)
30. Yang, R., Au, M.H., Xu, Q., Yu, Z.: Decentralized blacklistable anonymous credentials with reputation. IACR Cryptology ePrint Archive, vol. 2017, p. 389 (2017)
31. Yu, K.Y., Yuen, T.H., Chow, S.S.M., Yiu, S.M., Hui, L.C.K.: PE(AR)^2: privacy-enhanced anonymous authentication with reputation and revocation. In: Foresti, S., Yung, M., Martinelli, F. (eds.) ESORICS 2012. LNCS, vol. 7459, pp. 679–696. Springer, Heidelberg (2012). https://doi.org/10.1007/978-3-642-33167-1_39

Short Papers

Revocable Certificateless Encryption with Ciphertext Evolution

Yinxia Sun[1](✉), Futai Zhang[1], and Anmin Fu[2]

[1] School of Computer Science and Technology, Nanjing Normal University, Nanjing 210023, China
bela_suno@163.com

[2] School of Computer Science and Engineering, Nanjing University of Science and Technology, Nanjing 210094, China

Abstract. The user revocation of certificateless cryptosystems is an important issue. One of the existing solutions is to issue extra time keys periodically for every non-revoked user. However, since the scheme requires different time keys to decrypt data for different time periods, the user needs to hold a long list of time keys (linear growth with time), which is inefficient in practical applications. Moreover, the ciphertexts produced before revocation are still available to the revoked users, which is not acceptable in most applications such as cloud storage. To overcome these shortcomings, in this paper, we present an efficient solution called *revocable certificateless encryption with ciphertext evolution*. In our scheme, a current time key together with a private key are enough for the decryptions by non-revoked users. Meanwhile, revoked users cannot make decryptions on ciphertexts in the past any more. We give formal security proofs based on the IND-CPA model under the standard BDH problem.

Keywords: Certificateless · Revocable · Ciphertext evolution Cloud storage

1 Introduction

In a traditional public key cryptosystem, the CA has to do complicated certificate management which is costly. To address the problem, in 1984, Shamir proposed the famous notion called "Identity-based Cryptography" (IBC) [16]. In IBC, the user public key is no longer generated by the user himself but using a unique identity such as email address. So there is no need to issue a certificate to guarantee the authenticity of the user public key. However, the user private key is fully computed by a trusted third party called Private Key Generator (PKG). The PKG can do anything on behalf of the user which is not acceptable in some practical applications. In order to solve the inherent key escrow problem in IBC, in 2003, Al-Riyami and Paterson introduced certificateless public key cryptosystem (CLPKC) [2]. The CLPKC can be viewed as a combination of the

W. Susilo and G. Yang (Eds.): ACISP 2018, LNCS 10946, pp. 741–749, 2018.
https://doi.org/10.1007/978-3-319-93638-3_42

traditional public key cryptosystem and the IBC. In CLPKC, the user private key contains two parts, one of which is from a trusted third party called Key Generation Center (KGC), the other from the user himself. So, the KGC cannot access the full private key.

The user revocation is an important issue in a public key cryptosystem. The traditional public key system employs such as the technique of CRL for the revocation. However, these revocation methods are not suitable for IBC or CLPKC. In 2001, Boneh and Franklin [3] suggested a trivial way to revoke users that the PKG updates the private keys for all non-revoked users at every time period. In [10], the revocation is done by a third party called SEM (SEcurity Mediator). The first scalable and practical identity based revocation scheme is presented by Boldyreva et al. [4], which was then improved by Libert and Vergnaud [11] to reach a strong security level. In [14], Seo and Emura proposed the notion of decryption key exposure (DKE) and gave a DKE-resistant revocable identity based encryption scheme with provable security in the standard model.

The revocation problem in CLPKC is similar to that in IBC. The third party assistant SEM revocation method [5,9] is not an ideal solution in lots of applications, because the users cannot decrypt or sign independently. A natural trivial way is to update user partial private keys periodically [1]. But the need for secret channels to transmit all partial private keys consumes much computation and bandwidth. In 2015, Sun et al. gave an efficient solution to the revocation problem in CLPKC by constructing a revocable certificateless encryption scheme with provable security in the standard model [17]. The scheme updates time keys for non-revoked users over public channels and can resist the thereat of decryption key exposure. Other related works are such as [7,12,13,18,19].

Certificateless encryption can be applied in scenarios such as cloud storage to protect the privacy of data in the cloud [8,15]. But few consider the user revocation in applications. Directly applying a revocable certificateless encryption scheme might suffer from some drawbacks. For example, revoked data users can still decrypt the data encrypted before revocation; data users have to maintain all the time keys by himself (linear growth with time). Therefore, it is desirable to make some improvements when putting a revocable certificateless encryption scheme in applications e.g. cloud storage.

Our Contributions. In this paper, we provide a solution to those problems mentioned above by introducing a new notion called *revocable certificateless encryption with ciphertext evolution* (RCLE-CE). Suppose the system involves a data owner, a cloud server and a data user. After the data owner uploads data into the cloud, the data user can download to use the data. When the data user is revoked, the cloud server does ciphertext evolution to prevent the revoked user decrypting ciphertexts generated before revocation. As to the non-revoked users, they can ask the cloud server for ciphertext evolution to minimize their time key lists. We define the security model to meet the requirement of RCLE-CE and give a concrete construction with provable security against the attacks in the proposed model. The ciphertext evolution is simple and easy to realize.

The remaining sections are organized as follows. In Sect. 2, we give some preliminaries including the definition of revocable certificateless encryption with ciphertext evolution, the security model and complexity problems. The concrete construction with formal security proofs and efficiency analysis is presented in Sect. 3. Finally, we conclude this paper in the last section.

2 Definition and Security Model

2.1 Revocable Certificateless Encryption with Ciphertext Evolution

A revocable certificateless encryption scheme with ciphertext evolution is made up of the following algorithms:

- Setup: Taking a security parameter k as input, the algorithm outputs a master secret key msk and a list of public parameters params.
- Extract-Partial-Private-Key: Taking params, msk and a user identity ID as input, the algorithm outputs a partial private key D_{ID}. This is done by the KGC who then transmits D_{ID} to the user via a secret channel.
- Set-Secret-Value: Taking an identity ID as input, the algorithm outputs a secret value SV_{ID}. This is done by the user.
- Set-Public-Key: Taking an identity ID and the secret value SV_{ID} as input, the algorithm outputs a public key PK_{ID}.
- Update-Time-Key: Taking params, msk, an identity ID and a time tag t as input, this algorithm outputs a time key $\mathsf{TK}_{ID,t}$. This is done by the KGC who transmit $\mathsf{TK}_{ID,t}$ to the user via a public channel.
- Encrypt: Taking params, a data user identity ID, the current time t and a message M as input, this algorithm outputs a ciphertext C. This is done by the data owner who stores C in the cloud.
- Decrypt: Taking params, the data user identity and time key $(\mathsf{PSK}_{ID}, \mathsf{TK}_{ID,t})$ and the ciphertext C as input, the data user decrypts C to recover the message M.
- Revoke: Taking a user identity ID as input, the KGC stops computing time keys for the user.
- Ciphertext-Evolve: The cloud server transforms a ciphertext C of (ID, t) to a new ciphertext C' of (ID, t').

2.2 The Security Model

The security model of RCLE-CE is very similar to the security model of RCLE. Because the cloud server only use *public* user time keys to do ciphertext evolution. We allow ciphertext evolution queries by adversaries during the attacks.

Three types of adversaries are considered. A type I adversary $\mathcal{A}_I$ knows both partial private key and secret value, but does not have time key. $\mathcal{A}_I$ is a malicious revoked user. A type II adversary $\mathcal{A}_{II}$ has access to partial private key and time key, but does not know the secret value. $\mathcal{A}_{II}$ is the malicious KGC. A type III adversary $\mathcal{A}_{III}$ has access to secret value and time key, but does not know partial private key. $\mathcal{A}_{II}$ replaces the secret value with a new value of his choice.

We define the IND-CPA security of revocable certificateless encryption with ciphertext evolution via the following game interacting between the challenger and the adversary $\mathcal{A}$ ($\mathcal{A} \in \{\mathcal{A}_I, \mathcal{A}_{II}, \mathcal{A}_{III}\}$).

At the beginning, the challenger runs the setup algorithm to provide public parameters `params` to the adversary $\mathcal{A}$. If $\mathcal{A} = \mathcal{A}_{II}$, the challenger also gives the master secret key `msk` to the adversary; otherwise, the challenger keeps `msk` secret.

After that, $\mathcal{A}$ may make some queries (PPK: Partial Private Key query, SV: Secret Value query, PKR: Public Key Replacement query, PK: Public Key query, TK: Time Key query, CE: Ciphertext Evolution query) to the challenger.

Query	$\mathsf{PPK}_{\mathcal{A}_I,\mathcal{A}_{III}}$	SV	$\mathsf{PKR}_{\mathcal{A}_{III}}$	PK	TK	CE
Adversary	ID	ID	$(ID, \mathsf{PK}_{ID}, \mathsf{PK}'_{ID})$	ID	(ID, t)	$(C_{ID,t}, t')$
Challenger	D_{ID}	SV_{ID}	(ID, PK'_{ID})	PK_{ID}	$\mathsf{TK}_{ID,t}$	$C_{ID,t'}$

Challenge: $\mathcal{A}$ outputs two messages M_0 and M_1 of the same length, an identity ID^* and a time t^*. The challenger randomly chooses β from $\{0, 1\}$ and encrypts M_β to output a challenge ciphertext C^*.

$\mathcal{A}$ continues to make queries as before, subject to the constrain that $\mathcal{A}_I$ cannot make a time key query on (ID^*, t^*); $\mathcal{A}_{II}$ cannot make a secret value query on ID^*; $\mathcal{A}_{III}$ cannot request the partial private key of ID^*.

Guess: At the end of the game, $\mathcal{A}$ outputs a guess $\beta' \in \{0, 1\}$.

The adversary $\mathcal{A}$'s advantage is defined by $\Pr(\beta' = \beta) - 1/2$. An RCLE-CE scheme is said to be secure in the sense of indistinguishability against chosen plaintext attacks (IND-CPA secure) if no probabilistic polynomial-time adversary has non-negligible advantage in the above game.

2.3 Bilinear Paring and Complexity Problem

Bilinear paring. Suppose $\mathbb{G}_1$ is an additive cyclic group and $\mathbb{G}_2$ is a multiplicative cyclic group with the same prime order q. P is a generator of $\mathbb{G}_1$. A *bilinear pairing* is a map $e : \mathbb{G}_1 \times \mathbb{G}_1 \rightarrow \mathbb{G}_2$ satisfying three basic properties below.

- Bilinear: given $a, b \in \mathbb{Z}_q$, $e(aP, bP) = e(P, P)^{ab}$;
- Non-degenerate: $e(P, P) \neq 1_{\mathbb{G}_2}$;
- Computable: $e(U, V)$ can be computed efficiently.

The security of our scheme is based on the standard Computable Diffie-Hellman problem and Bilinear Diffie-Hellman problem.

Computable Diffie-Hellman (CDH) problem. *Given a random instance* $(aP, bP \in \mathbb{G}_1)$ *with* $a, b \in_R \mathbb{Z}_q^*$, *to compute* abP.

Bilinear Diffie-Hellman (BDH) problem. *Given a random instance* $(aP, bP, cP \in \mathbb{G}_1)$ *with* $a, b, c \in_R \mathbb{Z}_q^*$, *to compute* $e(P, P)^{abc}$.

3 Revocable Certificateless Encryption with Ciphertext Evolution

3.1 The Construction

- Setup: Take a security parameter k as input. $\mathbb{G}_1$ is an additive cyclic group and $\mathbb{G}_2$ is a multiplicative cyclic group. They are of the same order q. Suppose P is a generator of $\mathbb{G}_1$. $e : \mathbb{G}_1 \times \mathbb{G}_1 \rightarrow \mathbb{G}_2$ is a bilinear pairing. Choose $s \in \mathbb{Z}_q^*$ at random and compute $P_0 = sP$. Select four hash functions: $H_1 : \{0,1\}^* \rightarrow \mathbb{G}_1$, $H_2 : \{0,1\}^* \rightarrow \mathbb{G}_1$, $H_3 : \mathbb{G}_2 \rightarrow \{0,1\}^l$ and $H_4 : \mathbb{G}_2 \rightarrow \{0,1\}^l$.
The system parameters $\mathtt{params}$ are $\langle \mathbb{G}_1, \mathbb{G}_2, q, P, P_0, e, H_1, H_2, H_3, H_4 \rangle$. The master secret key $\mathtt{mk}$ is s.
- Extract-Private-Key: Taking $\mathtt{params}$, $\mathtt{mk}$ and ID as input, this algorithm computes $Q_{ID} = H_1(ID)$ and then calculates $D_{ID} = sQ_{ID}$ as the private key of user ID.
- Set-Secret-Value: Taking a user identity ID as input, choose $x_{ID} \in \mathbb{Z}_q^*$ at random. Output the secret value $\mathsf{SV}_{ID} = x_{ID}$.
- Set-Public-Key: Taking a user's identity ID and secret value x_{ID} as input, compute $\mathsf{PK}_{ID} = x_{ID}P$ as the user's public key.
- Time-Key-Update: Taking $\mathtt{params}$, $\mathtt{mk}$, ID and a time tag t as input, this algorithm computes $Q_{ID,t} = H_2(ID, t)$ and then calculates $\mathsf{TK}_{ID,t} = sQ_{ID,t}$ as the time key of the user ID at the time t.
- Encrypt: To encrypt a message M at the time t, this algorithm takes as input the receiver's identity ID and public key PK_{ID}, the time t and the message M, then does the following:
  - choose $r_0, r_1 \in Z_q^*$ at random and compute $U_0 = r_0P, U_1 = r_1P$;
  - compute $V = M \oplus H_3(e(Q_{ID}, P_0)^{r_0}, r_0\mathsf{PK}_{ID}) \oplus H_4(e(Q_{ID,t}, P_0)^{r_1})$;
  - output the ciphertext $C = (U_0, U_1, V)$.
- Decrypt: To decrypt a ciphertext $C = (U_0, U_1, V)$, this algorithm computes the plaintext $M = V \oplus H_3(e(D_{ID}, U_0), x_{ID}U_0) \oplus H_4(e(\mathsf{TK}_{ID,t}, U_1))$.
- Revoke: If the user with identity ID needs to be revoked at the time t, the KGC stops generating the time key $\mathsf{TK}_{ID,t}$ for the user.
- Ciphertext-Evolve: To transform a ciphertext $C = (U_0, U_1, V)$ of ID at the time t into a new ciphertext at the current time t', the cloud does the following.
  - Choose $r_1' \in Z_q^*$ at random and compute $U_1' = r_1'P$;
  - The cloud computes $V' = V \oplus H_4(e(\mathsf{TK}_{ID,t}, U_1)^{-1}) \oplus H_4(e(Q_{ID,t'}, P_0)^{r_1'})$;
  - Update the ciphertext to be $C = (U_0, U_1', V')$.

3.2 The Security

Theorem 1. *Suppose the hash functions H_1, H_2, H_3 and H_4 are random oracles. If there exists a type I adversary $\mathcal{A}_I$ against the IND-CPA security of our RCLE-CE scheme with advantage ϵ, making q_2 times H_2 queries and q_4 times H_4 queries, then there exists an algorithm $\mathcal{B}$ that can solve the BDH problem with advantage not less than ϵ/q_2q_4.*

Proof. $\mathcal{B}$ is a BDH problem solver with instance (P, aP, bP, cP, e). It will act as the challenger to compute $e(P,P)^{abc}$ by interacting with the adversary $\mathcal{A}_I$.

Taking the security parameter k as input, $\mathcal{B}$ chooses a bilinear group $(\mathbb{G}_1, \mathbb{G}_2, e)$ with q the order of both $\mathbb{G}_1$ and $\mathbb{G}_2$. P is a generator of $\mathbb{G}_1$. Set $P_0 = aP$ as the master public key. Select four hash functions H_1, H_2, H_3 and H_4 as required. The system parameters $\mathtt{params}$ are $\langle \mathbb{G}_1, \mathbb{G}_2, q, P, P_0, e, H_1, H_2, H_3, H_4 \rangle$. $\mathcal{B}$ randomly chooses $I^* \in [1, q_2] \cap \mathbb{Z}$.

Then the adversary may make some queries described as follows. All the hash functions are viewed as random oracles. Hash queries and answers are maintained in the related hash lists with tuples of the form: (ID, z, zP) for H_1, $(ID, t, z', z'P)$ for H_2, (x_0, x_1, h_3) for H_3 and (y, h_4) for H_4. If any query below is made, we always suppose that the related hash query-answer has existed in the list.

Especially, when $\mathcal{A}_I$ makes the ith query to the H_2 oracle, if $i = I^*$, $\mathcal{B}$ returns bP as the answer; otherwise, $\mathcal{B}$ randomly chooses $z' \in \mathbb{Z}_q^*$ and computes $z'P$ as the answer. Suppose the I^*th H_2 query is on the identity and time (ID^*, t^*).

Partial private key extraction query: When $\mathcal{A}_I$ makes a partial private key extraction query on the identity ID, $\mathcal{B}$ searches the H_1 list for a tuple (ID, z, zP). Compute $D_{ID} = zP_0$ and return D_{ID} to $\mathcal{A}_I$.

Time key query: When $\mathcal{A}_I$ makes a time key query on (ID, t), $\mathcal{B}$ searches the H_2 list for a tuple $(ID, t, z', z'P)$. Compute $\mathsf{TK}_{ID,t} = z'P_0$ and return $\mathsf{TK}_{ID,t}$ to $\mathcal{A}_I$. Note that if $(ID, t) = (ID^*, t^*)$, abort the game.

Secret value query: When $\mathcal{A}_I$ requests the secret value of the user with identity ID, $\mathcal{B}$ chooses a random $x_{ID} \in \mathbb{Z}_q^*$ and returns it to $\mathcal{A}_I$.

Public key query: When $\mathcal{A}_I$ requests the public key of the user ID, $\mathcal{B}$ checks the secret value list for x_{ID} and then computes $\mathsf{PK}_{ID} = x_{ID}P$ as the public key returned to $\mathcal{A}_I$.

Ciphertext evolution query: When $\mathcal{A}_I$ makes a ciphertext evolution query with $(C = (U_0, U_1, V), ID, t, t')$, $\mathcal{B}$ firstly searches the time key list for $\mathsf{TK}_{ID,t}$, then chooses $r_1' \in Z_q^*$ at random, computes $U_1' = r_1'P$ and $V' = V \oplus H_4(e(\mathsf{TK}_{ID,t}, U_1)^{-1}) \oplus H_4(e(Q_{ID,t'}, P_0)^{r_1'})$, finally returns $C' = (U_0, U_1', V')$ as the new ciphertext to $\mathcal{A}_I$.

Challenge: $\mathcal{A}_I$ selects two messages (M_0, M_1) of the same length as well as an identity ID^* and a time tag t^* to be challenged. $\mathcal{B}$ randomly chooses $\beta \in \{0,1\}$ and does the following:

- choose $r_0^* \in Z_q^*$, compute $U_0^* = r_0^*P$ and set $U_1^* = cP$;
- randomly choose $V^* \in \{0,1\}^l$;
- search the H_3 list for a tuple $(e(Q_{ID^*}, P_0)^{r_0^*}, r_0^*\mathsf{PK}_{ID^*}, h_3^*)$, then compute $h_4^* = V^* \oplus M_\beta \oplus h_3^*$ and set $H_4(e(P,P)^{abc}) = h_4^*$ (actually $\mathcal{B}$ doesn't know $e(P,P)^{abc}$);
- return (U_0^*, U_1^*, V^*) to $\mathcal{A}_I$ as the challenge ciphertext.

$\mathcal{A}_I$ may make more queries as before, subject to the constrain that the time key TK_{ID^*,t^*} query is not allowed.

Guess. At last, A_I outputs its guess $\beta \in \{0,1\}$. $\mathcal{B}$ randomly chooses a tuple (x, h_4) from the H_4 list and outputs x as the solution to the BDH problem.

Analysis. It is obvious that $\mathcal{B}$'s advantage to break the IND-CPA security of our scheme is not less than ϵ/q_2q_4.

Theorem 2. *Suppose the hash functions H_1, H_2, H_3 and H_4 are random oracles. If there exists a type II adversary $\mathcal{A}_{II}$ against the IND-CPA security of our RCLE-CE scheme with advantage ϵ, making q_2 times H_2 queries and q_4 times H_4 queries, then there exists an algorithm $\mathcal{B}$ that can solve the CDH problem with advantage not less than ϵ/q_1q_3.*

Theorem 3. *Suppose the hash functions H_1, H_2, H_3 and H_4 are random oracles. If there exists a type I adversary $\mathcal{A}_{III}$ against the IND-CPA security of our RCLE-CE scheme with advantage ϵ, making q_1 times H_1 queries and q_3 times H_3 queries, then there exists an algorithm $\mathcal{B}$ that can solve the BDH problem with advantage not less than ϵ/q_1q_3.*

Due to space limitation, we omit the proofs of Theorems 2 and 3. For details, please refer to the full version of this paper.

3.3 The Comparison

We choose two representative RCLE schemes to make comparisons. In the following table, "TK-list size" indicates the size of time key list that the user needs to maintain. "P1" means Problem 1: linearly growing time key list; "P2" means Problem 2: ciphertexts before revocation can be decrypted by the revoked user. "ST" and "RO" are short for standard model and random oracle model, respectively. $\mathbb{G}_1$ is the cyclic group of symmetric bilinear pairing. $|\mathbb{G}_1|$ and $|M|$ are the length of the element in $\mathbb{G}_1$ and the message, respectively. "p" is pairing computation and "e" is exponential computation.

Scheme	TK-list size	Encrypt	Decrypt	Ciphertext size	P1	P2	Model
[17]	$O(t)$	3p+5e	5p	$4\lvert\mathbb{G}_1\rvert + \lvert M\rvert$	No	No	ST
[19]	$O(t)$	1p+3e	1p+1e	$\lvert G_1\rvert + 2\lvert M\rvert$	No	No	RO
Ours	1	2p+4e	2p+1e	$2\lvert\mathbb{G}_1\rvert + \lvert M\rvert$	Yes	Yes	RO

The above comparison shows that our scheme solves two problems P1 and P2 inherent in conventional time-updating RCLE constructions. Our scheme is more applicable in e.g. cloud data sharing than the existing RCLE schemes.

4 Conclusion

We introduced the notion of *revocable certificateless encryption with ciphertext evolution* (RCLE-CE) with a concrete construction. The revocation is achieved via time key updating. The ciphertext evolution is operated by a third party e.g. the cloud server. Compared with conventional revocable certificateless encryption, our RCLE-CE is more practical. Because it saves a lot of storage resources for the users and makes the data in the cloud strongly secure against revoked users. We gave both the definition and the security model of RCLE-CE. The scheme is provably IND-CPA secure in the random oracle model assuming the BDH problem is hard.

Acknowledgements. This work is supported by the Nature Science Foundation of China (grant numbers 61502237, 61672289, 61572255).

References

1. Al-Riyami, S.S.: Cryptographic schemes based on elliptic curve pairings. Ph.D. thesis, Royal Holloway, University of London (2004)
2. Al-Riyami, S.S., Paterson, K.G.: Certificateless public key cryptography. In: Laih, C.-S. (ed.) ASIACRYPT 2003. LNCS, vol. 2894, pp. 452–473. Springer, Heidelberg (2003). https://doi.org/10.1007/978-3-540-40061-5_29
3. Boneh, D., Franklin, M.: Identity-based encryption from the weil pairing. In: Kilian, J. (ed.) CRYPTO 2001. LNCS, vol. 2139, pp. 213–229. Springer, Heidelberg (2001). https://doi.org/10.1007/3-540-44647-8_13
4. Boldyreva, A., Goyal, V., Kumar, V.: Identity-based encryption with efficient revocation. In: CCS 2008, pp. 417–426. ACM (2008)
5. Chow, S.S.M., Boyd, C., Nieto, J.M.G.: Security-mediated certificateless cryptography. In: Yung, M., Dodis, Y., Kiayias, A., Malkin, T. (eds.) PKC 2006. LNCS, vol. 3958, pp. 508–524. Springer, Heidelberg (2006). https://doi.org/10.1007/11745853_33
6. Dent, A.W., Libert, B., Paterson, K.G.: Certificateless encryption schemes strongly secure in the standard model. In: Cramer, R. (ed.) PKC 2008. LNCS, vol. 4939, pp. 344–359. Springer, Heidelberg (2008). https://doi.org/10.1007/978-3-540-78440-1_20
7. Hung, Y.H., Tseng, Y.M., Huang, S.S.: Lattice-based revocable certificateless signature. Symmetry **9**, 242 (2017). https://doi.org/10.3390/sym9100242
8. He, D., Kumar, N., Wang, H., et al.: Privacy-preserving certificateless provable data possession scheme for big data storage on cloud. Appl. Math. Comput. **314**, 31–43 (2017)
9. Ju, H.S., Kim, D.Y., Lee, D.H., Lim, J., Chun, K.: Efficient revocation of security capability in certificateless public key cryptography. In: Khosla, R., Howlett, R.J., Jain, L.C. (eds.) KES 2005. LNCS (LNAI), vol. 3682, pp. 453–459. Springer, Heidelberg (2005). https://doi.org/10.1007/11552451_60
10. Libert, B., Quisquater, J.J.: Efficient revocation and threshold pairing based cryptosystems. In: Symposium on Principles of Distributed Computing-PODC 2003, pp. 163–171 (2003)

11. Libert, B., Vergnaud, D.: Adaptive-ID secure revocable identity-based encryption. In: Fischlin, M. (ed.) CT-RSA 2009. LNCS, vol. 5473, pp. 1–15. Springer, Heidelberg (2009). https://doi.org/10.1007/978-3-642-00862-7_1
12. Nguyen, K., Wang, H., Zhang, J.: Server-aided revocable identity-based encryption from lattices. In: Foresti, S., Persiano, G. (eds.) CANS 2016. LNCS, vol. 10052, pp. 107–123. Springer, Cham (2016). https://doi.org/10.1007/978-3-319-48965-0_7
13. Qin, B., Deng, R.H., Li, Y., Liu, S.: Server-aided revocable identity-based encryption. In: Pernul, G., Ryan, P.Y.A., Weippl, E. (eds.) ESORICS 2015. LNCS, vol. 9326, pp. 286–304. Springer, Cham (2015). https://doi.org/10.1007/978-3-319-24174-6_15
14. Seo, J.H., Emura, K.: Revocable identity-based encryption revisited: security model and construction. In: Kurosawa, K., Hanaoka, G. (eds.) PKC 2013. LNCS, vol. 7778, pp. 216–234. Springer, Heidelberg (2013). https://doi.org/10.1007/978-3-642-36362-7_14
15. Seo, S.H., Nabeel, M., Ding, X., Bertino, E.: An efficient certificateless encryption for secure data sharing in public clouds. IEEE Trans. Knowl. Data Eng. **26**(9), 2107–2119 (2014)
16. Shamir, A.: Identity-based cryptosystems and signature schemes. In: Blakley, G.R., Chaum, D. (eds.) CRYPTO 1984. LNCS, vol. 196, pp. 47–53. Springer, Heidelberg (1985). https://doi.org/10.1007/3-540-39568-7_5
17. Sun, Y., Zhang, F., Shen, L., Deng, R.H.: Efficient revocable certificateless encryption against decryption key exposure. IET Inf. Secur. **9**(3), 158–166 (2015)
18. Sun, Y., Zhang, Z., Shen, L.: A revocable certificateless encryption scheme with high performance. Int. J. High Perform. Comput. Netw. **11**(1), 83–91 (2018)
19. Tsai, T.T., Tseng, Y.M.: Revocable Certificateless Public Key Encryption. IEEE Syst. J. **9**(3), 824–833 (2015)

A New Encryption Scheme Based on Rank Metric Codes

Terry Shue Chien Lau(✉) and Chik How Tan

Temasek Laboratories, National University of Singapore, 5A Engineering Drive 1, #09-02, Singapore 117411, Singapore
{tsltlsc,tsltch}@nus.edu.sg

Abstract. We propose a rank metric codes based encryption based on the hard problem of rank syndrome decoding problem. We distort the matrix used for our encryption by adding a random distortion matrix over $\mathbb{F}_{q^m}$. We show that IND-CPA security is achievable for our encryption under assumption of Decisional Rank Syndrome Decoding problem. Our proposal allows the choice of the error terms with rank up to $r/2$, where r is the error-correcting capability of a code. Our encryption based on Gabidulin codes has public key size of 13.68 KB, which is 82 times smaller than the public key size of McEliece Cryptosystem based on Goppa codes. For similar post-quantum security level of 2^{140} bits, our encryption scheme has smaller public key size than key size suggested by LOI17 Encryption [7].

Keywords: Code-based cryptography · Public-key encryption McEliece · Provable security

1 Introduction

In 1978, McEliece [8] proposed a public-key cryptosystem based on Goppa codes in Hamming metric. Although the original McEliece cryptosystem is still considered secured today, the large key size of Goppa codes (approximately 1 MB) is less practical in application. As an alternative for Hamming metric, Gabidulin introduced the rank metric and the Gabidulin codes over finite field with q^m elements, $\mathbb{F}_{q^m}$ and construct the first rank-based cryptosystem (GPT) [2] with much smaller key size compared to McEliece on Goppa codes. However, due to the weakness of Gabidulin codes containing huge vector space invariant under Frobenius automorphism, the GPT and other Gabidulin codes cryptosystems were proved to be insecure by different structural attacks (for instances [6,9]). In addition, some general rank syndrome decoding attacks (for instances [4,10]) are able to attack these cryptosystems with their parameters in polynomial time.

In 2017, there were two new attempts in rank metric encryption scheme. The first one is proposed by Gaborit et al. [3], namely RankPKE in their construction of a code-based identity-based encryption scheme. The second attempt is a McEliece type encryption proposed by Loidreau (LOI17) [7], which considers

W. Susilo and G. Yang (Eds.): ACISP 2018, LNCS 10946, pp. 750–758, 2018.
https://doi.org/10.1007/978-3-319-93638-3_43

a scrambler matrix P with its inverse P^{-1} over V, a λ-dimensional subspace of $\mathbb{F}_{q^m}$. The term $\boldsymbol{c}P^{-1} = \boldsymbol{m}SGPP^{-1} + \boldsymbol{e}P^{-1}$ has error $\boldsymbol{e}P^{-1}$ with $\boldsymbol{e}$ of rank t and $\boldsymbol{m}$ as plaintext. In other words, the matrix P^{-1} amplifies the rank of $\boldsymbol{e}$, and this leads to larger public key size as t has to be λ times smaller than r.

Our Contributions. In this paper, we propose an encryption scheme based on the hard problem of rank syndrome decoding problem. We hide the structure of the generator matrix of the code by adding a distortion matrix of column rank n, with an error of rank larger than r being added into the ciphertext. We show that our encryption scheme has IND-CPA security under assumption of Decisional Rank Syndrome Decoding (DRSD) problem. We propose Gabidulin codes as a choice of decodable code in our encryption. Furthermore, for similar post quantum security level of 2^{140} bits, our encryption scheme has smaller public key size as compared to key size suggested by LOI17 Encryption [7].

In the remainder of this paper, we review some preliminaries for rank metric, circulant matrix and the hard problems which our encryption is based on in Sect. 2. In Sect. 3 we describe our proposed cryptosystem and prove that our encryption scheme has IND-CPA security under assumption of DRSD in Sect. 4. In Sect. 5 we propose Gabidulin codes as a choice for the decodable code $\mathcal{C}$ in our encryption with its security analyzed and propose some parameters. We give our final considerations for this paper in Sect. 6. Due to page limitations, please refer to the extended version of this paper for the complete proofs of some results in this paper.

2 Preliminaries

We recall the definition of rank metric and the hard problems in coding theory which our encryption is based on.

Given a matrix M with coefficients in a field $\boldsymbol{F}$, the rank of M, $\text{rk}(M)$ is the dimension of the row span of M as a vector space over $\boldsymbol{F}$. We denote the row span of a matrix M over $\boldsymbol{F}$ by $\langle M \rangle_{\boldsymbol{F}}$, or $\langle M \rangle$ when the context is clear. Let $\mathbb{F}_{q^m}$ be a finite field with q^m elements and $\{\beta_1, \dots, \beta_m\}$ be a basis of $\mathbb{F}_{q^m}$ over $\mathbb{F}_q$, where q is a power of a prime.

Definition 1. Let $\boldsymbol{x} = (x_1, \dots, x_n) \in \mathbb{F}_{q^m}^n$ and $M \in \mathbb{F}_{q^m}^{k \times n}$. The *rank* of $\boldsymbol{x}$ in $\mathbb{F}_q$, denoted by $\text{rk}_q(\boldsymbol{x})$ is the rank of the matrix $X = (x_{ij}) \in \mathbb{F}_q^{m \times n}$ where $x_j = \sum_{i=1}^m x_{ij}\beta_i$. The *column rank* of M over $\mathbb{F}_q$, denoted by $\text{colrk}_q(M)$ is the maximum number of linearly independent columns over $\mathbb{F}_q$. The *support* of $\boldsymbol{x}$, $\text{supp}(\boldsymbol{x})$ is the $\mathbb{F}_q$-vector space of $\mathbb{F}_{q^m}$ generated by $x_1, \dots, x_n$.

Lemma 1 ([6]). Let $\boldsymbol{x} \in \mathbb{F}_{q^m}^n$ such that $\text{rk}_q(\boldsymbol{x}) = r$, there exists $\hat{\boldsymbol{x}} \in \mathbb{F}_{q^m}^r$ with $\text{rk}_q(\hat{\boldsymbol{x}}) = r$ and $U \in \mathbb{F}_q^{r \times n}$ with $\text{rk}(U) = r$ such that $\boldsymbol{x} = \hat{\boldsymbol{x}}U$. We call U a *Grassman support matrix* for $\boldsymbol{x}$ and $\text{supp}_{\text{Gr}}(\boldsymbol{x}) = \langle U \rangle_{\mathbb{F}_{q^m}}$ the *Grassman support* of $\boldsymbol{x}$.

Lemma 2 ([9]). Let $M \in \mathbb{F}_{q^m}^{k \times n}$ and $\text{colrk}_q(M) = s < n$. Then there exists $M' \in \mathbb{F}_{q^m}^{k \times s}$ with $\text{colrk}_q(M') = s$ and K an invertible $n \times n$ matrix over $\mathbb{F}_q$ such that $MK = \left[M' \mid \boldsymbol{0}_{k \times (n-s)}\right]$.

Definition 2. Let $\boldsymbol{x} = (x_0, \ldots, x_{n-1}) \in \mathbb{F}_{q^m}^n$. The *circulant matrix* induced by $\boldsymbol{x}$ is defined as $\mathrm{Cir}_n(\boldsymbol{x}) := \left[x_{(i-j) \bmod n}\right]_{i,j} \in \mathbb{F}_{q^m}^{n \times n}$. The *k-partial circulant matrix*, $\mathrm{Cir}_k(\boldsymbol{x})$ induced by $\boldsymbol{x}$ is the first k rows of $\mathrm{Cir}_n(\boldsymbol{x})$.

We now describe the hard problems which our cryptosystem is based on.

Definition 3 Rank Syndrome Decoding Problem (RSD). Let H be a full rank $(n-k) \times n$ matrix over $\mathbb{F}_{q^m}$, $\boldsymbol{s} \in \mathbb{F}_{q^m}^{n-k}$ and w an integer. The *Rank Syndrome Decoding Problem* $\mathsf{RSD}(q, m, n, k, w)$ needs to determine $\boldsymbol{x} \in \mathbb{F}_{q^m}^n$ such that $\mathrm{rk}_q(\boldsymbol{x}) = w$ and $H\boldsymbol{x}^T = \boldsymbol{s}^T$.

The RSD problem is analogous to the classical syndrome decoding problem with Hamming metric. Recently, the RSD problem has been proven to be hard with a probabilistic reduction to the Hamming setting [5].

Given $G \in \mathbb{F}_{q^m}^{k \times n}$ a full rank parity-check matrix of H in an RSD problem and $\boldsymbol{y} \in \mathbb{F}_{q^m}^n$. Then the dual version of $\mathsf{RSD}(q, m, n, k, w)$ is to determine $\boldsymbol{m} \in \mathbb{F}_{q^m}^k$ and $\boldsymbol{x} \in \mathbb{F}_{q^m}^n$ such that $\mathrm{rk}_q(\boldsymbol{x}) = w$ and $\boldsymbol{y} = \boldsymbol{m}G + \boldsymbol{x}$.

If X is a finite set, we write $\boldsymbol{x} \xleftarrow{\$} X$ to denote assignment to $\boldsymbol{x}$ of an element randomly sampled from the distribution on X. We now give the definition of Decisional version of RSD problem in its dual form:

Definition 4 Decisional RSD Problem (DRSD). Let G be a full rank $k \times n$ matrix over F_{q^m}, $\boldsymbol{m} \in \mathbb{F}_{q^m}^k$ and $\boldsymbol{x} \in \mathbb{F}_{q^m}^n$ of rank r. The *Decisional RSD Problem* $\mathsf{DRSD}(q, m, n, k, w)$ needs to distinguish the pair $(\boldsymbol{m}G + \boldsymbol{x}, G)$ from $(\boldsymbol{y}, G)$ where $\boldsymbol{y} \xleftarrow{\$} \mathbb{F}_{q^m}^n$.

It was proved that DRSD is hard in the worst case [3]. Therefore, the hardness of our cryptosystem relies on the DRSD problem (refer to Sect. 4).

There are generally two types of generic attacks on the RSD problem, namely the combinatorial attack and algebraic attack.

Combinatorial Attack. The combinatorial approach depends on counting the number of possible supports of size r for a rank code of length n over $\mathbb{F}_{q^m}$, which corresponds to the number of subspaces of dimension r in $\mathbb{F}_{q^m}$. These attacks are more efficient for small values of q (typically $q = 2$). The complexity of the best combinatorial attack has been updated to $(n-k)^3 m^3 q^{r\lfloor \frac{(k+1)m}{n} \rfloor - m}$ [1].

Algebraic Attack. The nature of the rank metric favors algebraic attacks using Gröbner bases, as they are largely independent of the value q. These attacks became efficient when q increases. In this paper, since our q is taken to be small ($q = 2$), the complexity of algebraic attacks is greater than the cost of combinatorial attacks [4].

3 A New Encryption Scheme

We propose our new encryption scheme which consists of a public matrix distorted by a matrix of column rank n. We will discuss some strengths of this encryption after the description of the scheme.

Presentation of the Encryption Scheme, $\mathsf{PE} = (\mathcal{S}_{\mathsf{PE}}, \mathcal{K}_{\mathsf{PE}}, \mathcal{E}_{\mathsf{PE}}, \mathcal{D}_{\mathsf{PE}})$.

Setup, $\mathcal{S}_{\mathsf{PE}}$: Generate global parameters $m > n > k > k' \geq 1$, $k' = \lfloor \frac{k}{2} \rfloor$ and $r \leq \lfloor \frac{n-k}{2} \rfloor$. The plaintext space is $\mathbb{F}_{q^m}^{k'}$. Outputs parameters $= (m, n, k, k', r)$.

Key Generation, $\mathcal{K}_{\mathsf{PE}}$: Generate $S \overset{\$}{\leftarrow} \mathrm{GL}_k(F_{q^m})$. Generate a generator matrix $G \in \mathbb{F}_{q^m}^{k \times n}$ of a linear code $\mathcal{C}_G$ (with efficient decoding algorithm $\mathcal{C}_G.\mathfrak{Dec}(\cdot)$ of error-correcting capabilities r). Generate $\boldsymbol{u} \overset{\$}{\leftarrow} \mathbb{F}_{q^m}^{n}$ with $\mathrm{rk}_q(\boldsymbol{u}) = n$. Generate $T \overset{\$}{\leftarrow} \mathrm{GL}_n(\mathbb{F}_q)$. Outputs public key $\kappa_{pub} = (G_{pub} = SG + \mathrm{Cir}_k(\boldsymbol{u})T, \boldsymbol{u})$ and private key $\kappa_{sec} = (S, G, T)$.

Encryption, $\mathcal{E}_{\mathsf{PE}}(\kappa_{pub}, \boldsymbol{m})$: Let $\boldsymbol{m} \in \mathbb{F}_{q^m}^{k'}$ be the message to be encrypted. Generate $\boldsymbol{m_s} \overset{\$}{\leftarrow} \mathbb{F}_{q^m}^{k-k'}$ satisfying $\mathrm{rk}_q((\boldsymbol{m}\|\boldsymbol{m_s})\mathrm{Cir}_k(\boldsymbol{u})) > \lceil \frac{3}{4}(n-k) \rceil$. Generate $\boldsymbol{e}_1, \boldsymbol{e}_2 \overset{\$}{\leftarrow} \mathbb{F}_{q^m}^{n}$ such that $\mathrm{rk}_q(\boldsymbol{e}_1) = r_1 \leq \frac{r}{2}$ and $\mathrm{rk}_q(\boldsymbol{e}_2) = r_2 \leq \frac{r}{2}$. Compute $\boldsymbol{c}_1 = (\boldsymbol{m}\|\boldsymbol{m_s})\mathrm{Cir}_k(\boldsymbol{u}) + \boldsymbol{e}_1$ and $\boldsymbol{c}_2 = (\boldsymbol{m}\|\boldsymbol{m_s})G_{pub} + \boldsymbol{e}_2$. Output $\boldsymbol{c} = (\boldsymbol{c}_1, \boldsymbol{c}_2)$.

Decryption, $\mathcal{D}_{\mathsf{PE}}(\kappa_{sec}, \boldsymbol{c})$: Returns $(\boldsymbol{m}\|\boldsymbol{m_s}) = (\mathcal{C}_G.\mathfrak{Dec}(\boldsymbol{c}_2 - \boldsymbol{c}_1 T))\, S^{-1}$.

Correctness. The correctness of our encryption scheme relies on the decoding capability of the code $\mathcal{C}$. Using the private keys, we have $\boldsymbol{c}_2 - \boldsymbol{c}_1 T = (\boldsymbol{m}\|\boldsymbol{m_s})G_{pub} + \boldsymbol{e}_2 - ((\boldsymbol{m}\|\boldsymbol{m_s})\mathrm{Cir}_k(\boldsymbol{u}) - \boldsymbol{e}_1)T = (\boldsymbol{m}\|\boldsymbol{m_s})SG + \boldsymbol{e}_2 - \boldsymbol{e}_1 T$. Since $\mathrm{rk}_q(\boldsymbol{e}_2 - \boldsymbol{e}_1 T) \leq \mathrm{rk}_q(\boldsymbol{e}_2) + \mathrm{rk}_q(\boldsymbol{e}_1 T) \leq r$, then we can retrieve $(\boldsymbol{m}\|\boldsymbol{m_s})S = \mathcal{C}_G.\mathfrak{Dec}(\boldsymbol{c}_2 - \boldsymbol{c}_1 T)$. Finally, compute $(\boldsymbol{m}\|\boldsymbol{m_s}) = (\boldsymbol{m}\|\boldsymbol{m_s})SS^{-1}$.

Strengths of the Proposed Encryption. In McEliece type encryption, the generator matrix G is scrambled so that the matrix for encryption will appear random. LOI17 Encryption applied this approach with the payoff that the error included in the message must have rank λ times smaller than r. Nevertheless, in our construction, we can choose $\boldsymbol{e}_1$ and $\boldsymbol{e}_2$ with rank $r_1 \leq r/2$ and $r_2 \leq r/2$ respectively. Furthermore, the matrix G in our encryption is scrambled into $G_{pub} = SG + X$ where $X = \mathrm{Cir}_k(\boldsymbol{u})T$ has column rank n:

Proposition 1. *Let $\boldsymbol{u} \in \mathbb{F}_{q^m}^{n}$ such that $\mathrm{rk}_q(\boldsymbol{u}) = n$. Then for any invertible $T \in \mathbb{F}_q^{n \times n}$, $\mathrm{colrk}_q(\mathrm{Cir}_k(\boldsymbol{u})T) = n$.*

Proof. We first show that $\mathrm{colrk}_q(\mathrm{Cir}_k(\boldsymbol{u})) \geq n$. Suppose that $\mathrm{colrk}_q(\mathrm{Cir}_k(\boldsymbol{u})) < n$, then there exists at most $n-1$ columns of $\mathrm{Cir}_k(\boldsymbol{u})$ that are linearly independent over $\mathbb{F}_q$. Then at most $n-1$ elements in the first row of $\mathrm{Cir}_k(\boldsymbol{n})$ are linearly independent over $\mathbb{F}_q$. Then $\mathrm{rk}_q(\boldsymbol{u}) \leq n-1$, a contradiction to $\mathrm{rk}_q(\boldsymbol{u}) = n$. Therefore $\mathrm{colrk}_q(\mathrm{Cir}_k(\boldsymbol{u})) \geq n$. Also, we have $\mathrm{colrk}_q(\mathrm{Cir}_k(\boldsymbol{u})) \leq n$. Since $T \in \mathrm{GL}_n(\mathbb{F}_q)$, then $\mathrm{colrk}_q(\mathrm{Cir}_k(\boldsymbol{u})T) = \mathrm{colrk}_q(\mathrm{Cir}_k(\boldsymbol{u})) = n$. □

By Proposition 1, $\mathrm{Cir}_k(\boldsymbol{u})T$ has column rank n instead of $t < n$. This will make the reduction of X into the form $XK = [X' \mid \boldsymbol{0}]$ (as in Lemma 2) impossible.

The second approach in constructing rank metric code based encryption is to publish the generator matrix G and introduces an error $\boldsymbol{e}$ with $\mathrm{rk}_q(e) > r$ to ensure the decoding to retrieve plaintext is hard. In our construction, the error term $(\boldsymbol{m}\|\boldsymbol{m_s})\mathrm{Cir}_k(\boldsymbol{u})T + \boldsymbol{e}_2$ in the ciphertext $\boldsymbol{c}_2$ has error larger than r:

Proposition 2. Let $\boldsymbol{u} \in \mathbb{F}_{q^m}^n$ such that $\text{rk}_q(\boldsymbol{u}) = n$. Given $\hat{\boldsymbol{m}} = (\boldsymbol{m} \| \boldsymbol{m}_s) \in \mathbb{F}_{q^m}^k$ such that $\text{rk}_q(\hat{\boldsymbol{m}}\text{Cir}_k(\boldsymbol{u})) > \lceil \frac{3}{4}(n-k) \rceil$. Then for any $\boldsymbol{e}_2 \in \mathbb{F}_{q^m}^n$ such that $\text{rk}_q(\boldsymbol{e}_2) = r_2$, we have $\text{rk}_q(\hat{\boldsymbol{m}}\text{Cir}_k(\boldsymbol{u})T + \boldsymbol{e}_2) > r$.

Proof. We have $\text{rk}_q(\hat{\boldsymbol{m}}\text{Cir}_k(\boldsymbol{u})T + \boldsymbol{e}_2) \geq \text{rk}_q(\hat{\boldsymbol{m}}\text{Cir}_k(\boldsymbol{u})T) - \text{rk}_q(\boldsymbol{e}_2) > r$. □

By Proposition 2, $\text{rk}_q((\boldsymbol{m}\|\boldsymbol{m}_s)\text{Cir}_k(\boldsymbol{u})T + \boldsymbol{e}_2) > r$. The adversary is not able to recover the plaintext $\boldsymbol{m}$ from $\boldsymbol{c}_2$ even he knows the structure of the generator matrix G. However in practicality, G is remained unknown to the adversary.

4 IND-CPA Secure Encryption

The desired security properties of a public-key encryption scheme is indistinguishability under chosen plaintext attack (IND-CPA). This is normally defined by a security game which is interacting between a challenger and an adversary $\mathcal{A}$. In the security game, the challenger is given a security parameters and first runs the key generation algorithm and send κ_{pub} to $\mathcal{A}$. $\mathcal{A}$ chooses two equal length plaintexts $\boldsymbol{m}_0$ and $\boldsymbol{m}_1$ and sends these to the challenger. The challenger chooses a random $b \in \{0, 1\}$, computes a challenge ciphertext $\boldsymbol{c} = \mathcal{E}_{\text{PE}}(\kappa_{pub}, \boldsymbol{m}_b)$ and returns $\boldsymbol{c}$ to $\mathcal{A}$. $\mathcal{A}$ outputs a bit $b' \in \{0, 1\}$. $\mathcal{A}$ wins if $b' = b$. The advantage of an adversary $\mathcal{A}$ is defined as $\mathsf{Adv}_{\text{PE},\mathcal{A}}^{\text{IND-CPA}}(\lambda) = \left|\Pr[b' = b] - \frac{1}{2}\right|$.

A secure public-key encryption scheme against CPA is formally defined as:

Definition 5. A public-key encryption scheme $\text{PE} = (\mathcal{S}_{\text{PE}}, \mathcal{K}_{\text{PE}}, \mathcal{E}_{\text{PE}}, \mathcal{D}_{\text{PE}})$ is (t, ϵ)-IND-CPA secure if for any probabilistic t-polynomial time adversary $\mathcal{A}$ has the advantage less than ϵ, that is, $\mathsf{Adv}_{\text{PE},\mathcal{A}}^{\text{IND-CPA}}(\lambda) < \epsilon$.

We need the following result to acheive IND-CPA security for our encryption:

Lemma 3. Given $m \geq n$, $k \geq 1$ and $r < \frac{n}{2}$. Let $\boldsymbol{x}, \boldsymbol{y} \in \mathbb{F}_{q^m}^n$ such that $\text{rk}_q(\boldsymbol{x}) = a$ and $\text{rk}_q(\boldsymbol{y}) = b$. Then there exists $\boldsymbol{e} \in \mathbb{F}_{q^m}^n$ with $\text{rk}_q(\boldsymbol{e}) = r' \leq \frac{r}{2}$ such that $\text{rk}_q(\boldsymbol{x} + \boldsymbol{e}) \geq r' + 1$ and $\text{rk}_q(\boldsymbol{y} + \boldsymbol{e}) \geq r' + 1$.

The proof is omitted due to page limitations. It will be included in the extended version of this paper.

Now, suppose the challenger adversary chooses two equal length plaintexts $\boldsymbol{m}_0, \boldsymbol{m}_1 \in \mathbb{F}_{q^m}^{k'}$ and sent these to the challenger. The challenger is able to choose a random $\boldsymbol{m}_s \in \mathbb{F}_{q^m}^{k-k'}$, $\boldsymbol{e}_1, \boldsymbol{e}_2 \in \mathbb{F}_{q^m}^n$ such that the conditions (1)–(3) are satisfied:

Lemma 4. Given $\boldsymbol{m}_0, \boldsymbol{m}_1 \in \mathbb{F}_{q^m}^{k'}$ and $\boldsymbol{m}_s \in \mathbb{F}_{q^m}^{k-k'}$, let $\hat{\boldsymbol{m}} = (\boldsymbol{0}_{k'} \| \boldsymbol{m}_s)$ and $\bar{\boldsymbol{m}} = (\boldsymbol{m}_0 + \boldsymbol{m}_1 \| \boldsymbol{m}_s)$, there exists $\boldsymbol{e}_1, \boldsymbol{e}_2 \in \mathbb{F}_{q^m}^n$ such that

$$\text{rk}_q(\boldsymbol{e}_1) = r_1 \leq r/2, \quad \text{rk}_q(\boldsymbol{e}_2) = r_2 \leq r/2, \tag{1}$$

$$\text{rk}_q(\hat{\boldsymbol{m}}\text{Cir}_k(\boldsymbol{u}) + \boldsymbol{e}_1) \geq r_1 + 1, \quad \text{rk}_q(\bar{\boldsymbol{m}}\text{Cir}_k(\boldsymbol{u}) + \boldsymbol{e}_1) \geq r_1 + 1, \tag{2}$$

$$\text{rk}_q(\hat{\boldsymbol{m}}G_{pub} + \boldsymbol{e}_2) \geq r_2 + 1, \quad \text{rk}_q(\bar{\boldsymbol{m}}G_{pub} + \boldsymbol{e}_2) \geq r_2 + 1. \tag{3}$$

Proof. Let $\text{rk}_q(\hat{\boldsymbol{m}}\text{Cir}_k(\boldsymbol{u})) = a_1$ and $\text{rk}_q(\bar{\boldsymbol{m}}\text{Cir}_k(\boldsymbol{u})) = b_1$, $\text{rk}_q(\hat{\boldsymbol{m}}G_{pub}) = a_2$ and $\text{rk}_q(\bar{\boldsymbol{m}}G_{pub}) = b_2$. Then apply Lemma 3 accordingly. □

Without knowing any information on $\boldsymbol{m}_s$, $\mathcal{A}$ is unable to distinguish between $\boldsymbol{c}_1 + (\boldsymbol{m}_0\|\boldsymbol{0})\text{Cir}_k(\boldsymbol{u})$ and $\boldsymbol{c}_1 + (\boldsymbol{m}_1\|\boldsymbol{0})\text{Cir}_k(\boldsymbol{u})$, between $\boldsymbol{c}_2 + (\boldsymbol{m}_0\|\boldsymbol{0})G_{pub}$ and $\boldsymbol{c}_2 + (\boldsymbol{m}_1\|\boldsymbol{0})G_{pub}$, as $\boldsymbol{e}_1$, $\boldsymbol{e}_2$ are chosen such that (1)–(3) are satisfied.

Notation. Denote $E_{cir}(\boldsymbol{m}_0, \boldsymbol{m}_1, \boldsymbol{m}_s)$ and $E_{G_{pub}}(\boldsymbol{m}_0, \boldsymbol{m}_1, \boldsymbol{m}_s)$ as the set of all elements in $\mathbb{F}_{q^m}^n$ that satisfy (1), (2) and (1), (3) respectively.

Definition 6 Decisional Rank Syndrome Decoding (DRSD) assumption. Let $\mathcal{D}_M$ be a distinguishing algorithm with input $(\boldsymbol{x} \in \mathbb{F}_{q^m}^n, M \in \mathbb{F}_{q^m}^{k\times n})$ and outputs a bit. The DRSD advantage of $\mathcal{D}_M$ is defined as $\mathsf{Adv}_{M,n,k}^{\mathtt{DRSD}}(\mathcal{D}_M) = |\Pr_{M,\boldsymbol{v},\boldsymbol{e}}[\mathcal{D}_M(\boldsymbol{v}M + \boldsymbol{e}, M) = 1] - \Pr_{M,\boldsymbol{y}}[\mathcal{D}_M(\boldsymbol{y}, M) = 1]|$, where $M \xleftarrow{\$} \mathbb{F}_{q^m}^{k\times n}$, $\boldsymbol{v} \xleftarrow{\$} \mathbb{F}_{q^m}^k$, $\boldsymbol{e} \xleftarrow{\$} \mathbb{F}_{q^m}^n$ with $\text{rk}_q(\boldsymbol{e}) = w$, $\boldsymbol{y} \xleftarrow{\$} \mathbb{F}_{q^m}^n$. The DRSD_M assumption is the assumption that $\mathsf{Adv}_{M,n,k}^{\mathtt{DRSD}}(\mathcal{D})$ is negligible for any $\mathcal{D}_M$, i.e., $\mathsf{Adv}_{M,n,k}^{\mathtt{DRSD}}(\mathcal{D}_M) < \varepsilon_M$.

Now, we prove that our encryption is `IND-CPA` secure under $\mathsf{DRSD}_{\text{Cir}_k(\boldsymbol{u})}$ and $\mathsf{DRSD}_{G_{pub}}$ assumptions.

Theorem 1. *Under the $\mathsf{DRSD}_{\text{Cir}_k(\boldsymbol{u})}$ and $\mathsf{DRSD}_{G_{pub}}$ assumptions, the proposed public-key encryption scheme* `PE` *is* `IND-CPA` *secure.*

Proof. To prove the security of the scheme, we are using a sequence of games.

Game $\mathcal{G}_0$: This is the real `IND-CPA` attack game against an adversary $\mathcal{A}$ in the definition of semantic security. We run the following attack game algorithm:

$$
\begin{array}{|l|}
\hline
S \xleftarrow{\$} \text{GL}_k(\mathbb{F}_{q^m}),\ \boldsymbol{u} \xleftarrow{\$} \mathbb{F}_{q^m}^n,\ T \xleftarrow{\$} \text{GL}_n(\mathbb{F}_q),\\
\kappa_{pub} \leftarrow (SG + \text{Cir}_k(\boldsymbol{u})T, \boldsymbol{u}),\ \kappa_{sec} \leftarrow (S, G, T)\\
(\boldsymbol{m}_0, \boldsymbol{m}_1) \xleftarrow{\$} \mathcal{A}(\kappa_{pub})\\
b \xleftarrow{\$} \{0,1\},\ \boldsymbol{m}_s \xleftarrow{\$} \mathbb{F}_{q^m}^{k-k'},\ \boldsymbol{e}_1 \xleftarrow{\$} E_{cir}(\boldsymbol{m}_0, \boldsymbol{m}_1, \boldsymbol{m}_s),\ \boldsymbol{e}_2 \xleftarrow{\$} E_{G_{pub}}(\boldsymbol{m}_0, \boldsymbol{m}_1, \boldsymbol{m}_s),\\
\boldsymbol{c}_1 \leftarrow (\boldsymbol{m}_b\|\boldsymbol{m}_s)\text{Cir}_k(\boldsymbol{u}) + \boldsymbol{e}_1,\ \boldsymbol{c}_2 \leftarrow (\boldsymbol{m}_b\|\boldsymbol{m}_s)G_{pub} + \boldsymbol{e}_2\\
\hat{b} \leftarrow \mathcal{A}(\kappa_{pub}, \boldsymbol{c}_1, \boldsymbol{c}_2)\\
\textbf{if } \hat{b} = b \textbf{ then } \text{return } 1 \textbf{ else } \text{return } 0\\
\hline
\end{array}
$$

Denote S_0 the event that $\mathcal{A}$ wins in Game $\mathcal{G}_0$. Then $\mathsf{Adv}_{\mathtt{PE},\mathcal{A}}^{\mathtt{IND-CPA}}(\lambda) = \left|\Pr[S_0] - \frac{1}{2}\right|$.

Game $\mathcal{G}_1$: We now make one small change to $\mathcal{G}_0$. In this game, we pick a random vector $\boldsymbol{y} \xleftarrow{\$} \mathbb{F}_{q^m}^n$ and replace $\boldsymbol{c}_1$ in $\mathcal{G}_0$ for $\mathcal{E}_{\mathtt{PE}}(\kappa_{pub}, (\boldsymbol{m}_b\|\boldsymbol{m}_s))$ by $\boldsymbol{c}_1 \leftarrow \boldsymbol{y}$. We denote S_1 the event that $\mathcal{A}$ wins in Game $\mathcal{G}_1$. Under the $\mathsf{DRSD}_{\text{Cir}_k(\boldsymbol{u})}$ assumption, the two games $\mathcal{G}_1$ and $\mathcal{G}_0$ are indistinguishable with $|\Pr[S_1] - \Pr[S_0]| \leq \varepsilon_{\text{Cir}_k(\boldsymbol{u})}$.

Game $\mathcal{G}_2$: We now make one small change to $\mathcal{G}_1$. In this game, we pick a random vector $\boldsymbol{z} \xleftarrow{\$} \mathbb{F}_{q^m}^n$ and replace $\boldsymbol{c}_2$ in $\mathcal{G}_1$ for $\mathcal{E}_{\mathtt{PE}}(\kappa_{pub}, (\boldsymbol{m}_b\|\boldsymbol{m}_s))$ by $\boldsymbol{c}_2 \leftarrow \boldsymbol{z}$. We denote S_2 the event that $\mathcal{A}$ wins in Game $\mathcal{G}_2$. Under the $\mathsf{DRSD}_{G_{pub}}$ assumption, the two games $\mathcal{G}_2$ and $\mathcal{G}_1$ are indistinguishable with $|\Pr[S_2] - \Pr[S_1]| \leq \varepsilon_{G_{pub}}$.

As the ciphertext challenge $\boldsymbol{c} = (\boldsymbol{c}_1, \boldsymbol{c}_2)$ is perfectly random, b is hidden to any $\mathcal{A}$ without any advantage, therefore $\Pr[S_2] = \frac{1}{2}$. We have $\mathsf{Adv}_{\mathtt{PE},\mathcal{A}}^{\mathtt{IND-CPA}}(\lambda) =$

$|\Pr[S_0] - \frac{1}{2}| = |\Pr[S_0] - \Pr[S_2]| \leq |\Pr[S_0] - \Pr[S_1]| + |\Pr[S_1] - \Pr[S_2]| \leq \varepsilon_{\mathrm{Cir}_k(\boldsymbol{u})} + \varepsilon_{G_{pub}}$. Therefore, under the $\mathsf{DRSD}_{\mathrm{Cir}_k(\boldsymbol{u})}$ and $\mathsf{DRSD}_{G_{pub}}$ assumption, the proposed public-key encryption scheme PE is IND-CPA secure. □

5 Our Encryption Based on Gabidulin Codes

We propose Gabidulin code as the decodable code $\mathcal{C}$ in our encryption. We analyze the security of the scheme by considering possible structural attacks to cryptanalyze the system based on Gabidulin code.

Definition 7. A matrix $G = [G_{i,j}] \in \mathbb{F}_{q^m}^{k\times n}$ is called a *Moore matrix* induced by $\boldsymbol{g}$ if there exists a vector $\boldsymbol{g} = (g_1, \ldots, g_n) \in \mathbb{F}_{q^m}^n$ such that $G = \left[g_j^{[i-1]}\right]$ for $i = 1, \ldots, k$, where $[i] := q^i$ is the ith Frobenius power. We define $G^{([l])} = \left[G_{i,j}^{[l]}\right]$ by raising each entries of G to the lth Frobenius power.

Definition 8. Let $\boldsymbol{g} \in \mathbb{F}_{q^m}^n$ with $\mathrm{rk}_q(\boldsymbol{g}) = n$. The $[n,k]$-*Gabidulin code* $\mathrm{Gab}_{n,k}(\boldsymbol{g})$ over $\mathbb{F}_{q^m}$ of dimension k and generator vector $\boldsymbol{g}$ is the code generated by a Moore matrix G induced by $\boldsymbol{g}$.

Note that the error-correcting capability of $\mathrm{Gab}_{n,k}(\boldsymbol{g})$ is $r = \lfloor \frac{n-k}{2} \rfloor$.

Due to page limitations, we only present some brief reasons our proposal resists some existing structural attacks against Gabidulin codes cryptosystems.

Key Recovery Attack. Consider $G_{pub}, \ldots, G_{pub}^{[m-1]}$, there are mkn equations with $mk^2 + mn$ unknown variables over $\mathbb{F}_{q^m}$ and n^2 unknown variables over $\mathbb{F}_q$. Solving these equations is equivalent to solving a multivariate quadratic problem.

Reduction Attack [9]. By Proposition 1, $\mathrm{colrk}_q(\mathrm{Cir}_k(\boldsymbol{u})T) = n$, thus the adversary is not able to rewrite $\mathrm{Cir}_k(\boldsymbol{u})T$ in the form of Lemma 2 which has columns of zero. Therefore, G_{pub} could not be reduced into components of random matrix $\bar{X}$ and Moore matrix $\bar{G}$ of the form $S(\bar{X} \mid \bar{G})Q$ where $Q \in \mathrm{GL}_n(\mathbb{F}_q)$.

Moore Decomposition Attack [6]. By Proposition 1, $\mathrm{colrk}_q(\mathrm{Cir}_k(u)T) = n$. Consider a minimal column rank Moore decomposition for $S^{-1}\mathrm{Cir}_k(u)T = M_{\mathrm{Moore}} + W$ where W is a non-Moore component which has the lowest possible column rank s. Since $t = n$ and $d_R^{\min}(\mathrm{Gab}_{n,k}(\boldsymbol{g})) = n - k + 1 < s + n + 2$, the condition to apply [6, Corollary 3.12] is not satisfied. Thus, [6, Theorem 4.1] could not be used to recover the encrypted message.

Proposed Parameters. We propose two sets of parameters for our encryption scheme. We consider $m > n$ and $r_1 = r_2 = \lfloor r/2 \rfloor$. For the first set (PC-I to PC-IV), we use the complexities in Sect. 2 as the lower bound of the complexity and follows Loidreau's application [7] of Grover's algorithm to square root the exponential term in the decoding complexity. For the second set, we compare our parameters (PC-V, PC-VI) and LOI17 parameters for similar post-quantum security level (PQ. Sec), by including the formula $m^3 2^{\frac{1}{2}(r-1)\lfloor \frac{k \min\{m,n\}}{n} \rfloor}$ in the lower bounds as it was used in [7] to evaluate the complexities. The following table gives our parameters and LOI17's parameters:

	q	m	n	k	r_1	r_2	r	Public key size	PQ. Sec
PC-I	2	71	67	22	11	11	22	13.68 KB	133
PC-II	2	85	83	16	16	16	33	14.99 KB	134
PC-III	2	103	101	29	18	18	36	39.01 KB	262
PC-IV	2	113	107	26	20	20	40	40.81 KB	268

	q	m	n	k	r_1	r_2	r	Public key size	PQ. Sec
PC-V	2	75	73	21	13	13	26	15.06 KB	141
PC-VI	2	85	83	18	16	16	32	16.76 KB	144
LOI17-I	2	128	90	24			11	21.50 KB	140
LOI17-II	2	128	120	80			4	51.00 KB	141

Our encryption has larger rank error r_1 and r_2. At similar security, our key size (15.06 KB) is smaller than the key size of LOI17 (21.50 KB). Our encryption scheme can provide better post quantum security with smaller key size.

6 Conclusion

This paper has proposed a new rank metric encryption with `IND-CPA` security under the $\mathsf{DRSD}_{\mathrm{Cir}_k(\boldsymbol{u})}$ and $\mathsf{DRSD}_{G_{pub}}$ assumptions. Our public matrix is distorted by $\mathrm{Cir}_k(\boldsymbol{u})T$ of column rank n. For similar post-quantum security level of 2^{140} bits, our encryption using Gabidulin codes has smaller public key size than the key size of LOI17.

References

1. Aragon, N., Gaborit, P., Hauteville, A., Tillich, J.P.: Improvement of Generic Attacks on the Rank Syndrome Decoding Problem (2017). <hal-01618464>
2. Gabidulin, E.M., Paramonov, A.V., Tretjakov, O.V.: Ideals over a non-commutative ring and their application in cryptology. In: Davies, D.W. (ed.) EUROCRYPT 1991. LNCS, vol. 547, pp. 482–489. Springer, Heidelberg (1991). https://doi.org/10.1007/3-540-46416-6_41
3. Gaborit, P., Hauteville, A., Phan, D.H., Tillich, J.-P.: Identity-based encryption from codes with rank metric. In: Katz, J., Shacham, H. (eds.) CRYPTO 2017. LNCS, vol. 10403, pp. 194–224. Springer, Cham (2017). https://doi.org/10.1007/978-3-319-63697-9_7
4. Gaborit, P., Ruatta, O., Schrek, J.: On the complexity of the rank syndrome decoding problem. IEEE Trans. Inf. Theory **62**(2), 1006–1019 (2016)
5. Gaborit, P., Zémor, G.: On the hardness of the decoding and the minimum distance problems for rank codes. IEEE Trans. Inf. Theory **62**(12), 7245–7252 (2016)

6. Horlemann-Trautmann, A., Marshall, K., Rosenthal, J.: Extension of Overbeck's Attack for Gabidulin Based Cryptosystems. CoRR, abs/1511.01549 (2015)
7. Loidreau, P.: A new rank metric codes based encryption scheme. In: Lange, T., Takagi, T. (eds.) PQCrypto 2017. LNCS, vol. 10346, pp. 3–17. Springer, Cham (2017). https://doi.org/10.1007/978-3-319-59879-6_1
8. McEliece, R.J.: A public-key cryptosystem based on algebraic coding theory. The Deep Space Network Progress Report 42–44, Jet Propulsion Laboratory, Pasedena, pp. 114–116 (1978)
9. Otmani, A., Kalachi, H.T., Ndjeya, S.: Improved Cryptanalysis of Rank Metric Schemes Based on Gabidulin Codes. CoRR abs/1602.08549 (2016)
10. Ourivski, A.V., Johansson, T.: New technique for decoding codes in the rank metric and its cryptography applications. Probl. Inf. Trans. **38**(3), 237–246 (2002)

Enhancing Intelligent Alarm Reduction for Distributed Intrusion Detection Systems via Edge Computing

Weizhi Meng[1], Yu Wang[2(✉)], Wenjuan Li[1,3], Zhe Liu[4], Jin Li[2], and Christian W. Probst[5]

[1] Department of Applied Mathematics and Computer Science, Technical University of Denmark, Kongens Lyngby, Denmark
weme@dtu.dk

[2] School of Computer Science, Guangzhou University, Guangzhou, China
{yuwang,lijin}@gzhu.edu.cn

[3] Department of Computer Science, City University of Hong Kong, Kowloon Tong, Hong Kong

[4] Nanjing University of Aeronautics and Astronautics, Nanjing, China

[5] Unitec Institute of Technology, Auckland, New Zealand

Abstract. To construct an intelligent alarm filter is a promising solution to help reduce false alarms for an intrusion detection system (IDS), in which an appropriate algorithm can be selected in an adaptive way. Taking the advantage of cloud computing, the process of algorithm selection can be offloaded to the cloud, but it may cause communication delay and additional burden on the cloud side. This issue may become worse when it comes to distributed intrusion detection systems (DIDSs), i.e., some IoT applications might require very short response time and most of the end nodes in IoT are energy constrained things. In this paper, with the advent of edge computing, we propose a framework for improving the intelligent false alarm reduction for DIDSs based on edge computing devices (i.e., the data can be processed at the edge for shorter response time and could be more energy efficient). The evaluation shows that the proposed framework can help reduce the workload for the central server and shorten the delay as compared to the similar studies.

Keywords: Intrusion detection · Intelligent false alarm filtration
Edge computing · Distributed environment · Cloud computing

1 Introduction

With the rapid development of computer networks, intrusions have become a big threat for network security [14]. To mitigate this issue, intrusion detection systems (IDSs) [16] are widely implemented worldwide to defend against different kinds of attacks (either host-based attacks or network-based attacks). Generally, IDSs can be categorized into three types based on their deployment manner:

W. Susilo and G. Yang (Eds.): ACISP 2018, LNCS 10946, pp. 759–767, 2018.
https://doi.org/10.1007/978-3-319-93638-3_44

host-based IDSs (HIDSs), network-based IDSs (NIDSs) and distributed IDSs (DIDSs). In particular, HIDSs are responsible for detecting anomalies in a local system, NIDSs focus on figuring out network attacks and threats, and DIDSs can aggregate the information from various IDS agents to improve the detection performance of a single IDS.

Motivation. Current IDSs including either signature-based or anomaly-based IDSs would suffer from the issue of false alarms in real-world applications [9]. To construct an intelligent false alarm filter is a promising solution, which can reduce false alarms and keep filtration accuracy by selecting an appropriate machine learning algorithm in an adaptive way [10]. One major issue is that such intelligent filter requires additional workload for performing the process of intelligent algorithm selection. Taking advantage of cloud computing, it is feasible to mitigate this issue and improve the performance of an IDS. However, in a distributed system like IoT environments, some applications might require very short response time, and some applications might cause a heavy load for networks by producing a large quantity of data. As a result, cloud computing may be not efficient enough to support these applications.

Contributions. With the advent of edge computing, there is a chance to mitigate this issue via edge computing devices. Edge computing allows the computation to be performed at the edge of the network, on downstream data on behalf of cloud services and upstream data on behalf of IoT services [18]. In this paper, we thus propose a framework for improving the intelligent false alarm reduction in distributed intrusion detection environments via edge computing devices. The contributions of our work can be summarized as below:

- We propose a framework for improving the intelligent false alarm reduction in distributed intrusion detection environments by means of edge computing. The rationale of edge computing is that computing should happen at the proximity of data sources, which could loose the workload of a cloud server and reduce the communication delay.
- As a study, we conduct an evaluation by comparing our approach with the previous related work. The experimental results indicate that our approach can greatly reduce the workload for a central server on the cloud and shorten the communication delay caused by selecting an algorithm.

The remaining parts of this paper are organized as follows. Section 2 describes the background of edge computing and presents our proposed framework. Section 3 shows our evaluation and discusses the results. We review related studies on cloud-based intrusion detection in Sects. 4 and 5 concludes our work with future directions.

2 Our Approach

2.1 Edge Computing

As mentioned earlier, edge computing refers to the enabling technologies allowing computation to be performed at the edge of the network, on downstream data

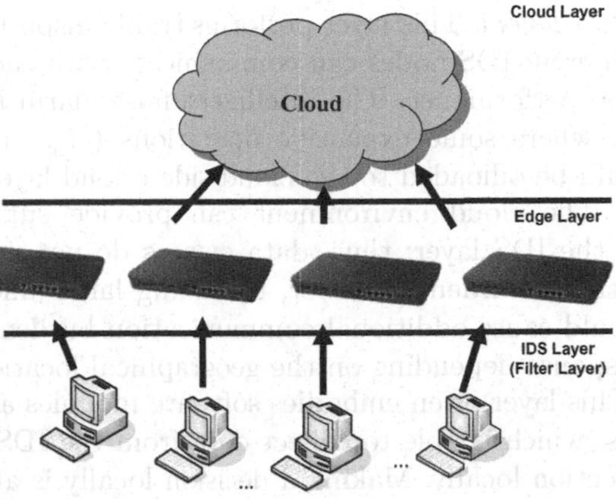

Fig. 1. The proposed framework for improving intelligent false alarm filter using edge (computing) devices.

on behalf of cloud services and upstream data on behalf of IoT services [18]. As compared to fog computing [3], they are interchangeable, but edge computing focuses more toward the things side, while fog computing focuses more on the infrastructure side. The rationale of edge computing is that computing should happen at the proximity of data sources. At the edge, the things can not only request service and content from the cloud but also perform the computing tasks from the cloud, including computing offloading, data storage, as well as distribute request and delivery service from cloud to user.

Edge computing can provide many benefits. For example, the edge computing paradigm can be flexibly expanded from a single home to community, or even city scale. For applications that require predictable and low latency such as health emergency or public safety, edge computing is an appropriate paradigm since it could save the data transmission time as well as simplify the network structure. Decision and diagnosis could be made from the edge of the network, which is more efficient compared with collecting information and making decision at central cloud. For geographic-based applications such as transportation and utility management, edge computing exceeds cloud computing due to the location awareness. In edge computing, data could be collected and processed based on geographic location without being transported to cloud.

2.2 Our Framework

As edge computing can help process the data with a shorter response time, more efficient processing and smaller network pressure, it has a potential to lighten the burden of deploying intelligent false alarm reduction for distributed intrusion detection environments. Figure 1 describes the proposed framework that aims to improve the intelligent false alarm filtration by means of edge (computing) devices. There are three major layers:

- *IDS layer (filter layer).* This layer performs traffic inspection and false alarm reduction. Different IDS nodes can communicate with each other to improve their detection performance. The intelligent false alarm filter is also located at this layer, where some expensive operations (e.g., intelligent algorithm selection) could be offloaded to the cloud side (cloud layer).
- *Cloud layer.* The cloud environment can provide sufficient computation resources for the IDS layer; thus, data owners do not need to worry about the computational burden. However, uploading large amount of data to the cloud side would cause additional communication burden and cannot ensure an instant response depending on the geographical locations.
- *Edge layer.* This layer often embodies software modules and embedded operating systems, which is able to collect data from the IDS layer and perform algorithm selection locally. Making a decision locally is an important way to reduce latency, and improve the efficiency of false alarm reduction.

Constructing an intelligent false alarm filter can help choose an efficient machine learning algorithm to conduct false alarm reduction. The previous work [10] showed that by adaptively selecting the most appropriate algorithm, the false alarm filter could achieve good results, whereas the workload is a concern for real-world implementation. While by means of the computing resources provided by a cloud, it becomes feasible to deploy such intelligent false alarm filter in a cloud environment, which can reduce false alarms according to specific IP sources [11]. When the connection is established among IDS nodes, edge devices and cloud environment, an IDS node can send data to the corresponding edge device for data processing at first and then the edge device forwards the data and results to the cloud side. For each edge device, an *Edge Manager (EM)* is adopted as a core component to manage all communications and handle other components including *Data Standardization*, *Machine Learning Algorithm Selection*, *Control System* and *Alarm Process System*.

In particular, the component of *Machine Learning Algorithm Selection* is used to select the most appropriate machine learning algorithm from a pool of algorithms by training with a number of labeled alarms. The most appropriate algorithm is denoted as the algorithm with the best *classification rate* and *precision rate*. The *Control System* is mainly responsible for comparing the performance of different machine learning algorithms and deciding the most appropriate algorithm used for alarm reduction. The *Alarm Process System* is mainly responsible for reducing false alarms based on the selected algorithm and maintaining a scheme-database for different IP sources. With the increase of labeled training data, the selected algorithm for a specific IP source may be varied. The outputs of the *Alarm Process System* are considered as true alarms.

3 Evaluation

3.1 Experimental Settings

The evaluation was performed in a company network including 20 Snort nodes [17]. Based on previous work [10], Snort alarms can be extracted and represented using a 8-feature set (*description*, *classification*, *priority*, *packet type*, *source IP address*, *source port number*, *destination IP address* and *destination port number*). During the algorithm training, all the features will be marked with their appearance possibility to ensure the correct operations of algorithms. Similar to [11], the algorithm pool contains seven specific machine learning algorithms: *ZeroR*, *KNN (IBK)*, *SVM (LibSVM)*, *NaiveBayes*, *NN (RBFNetwork)*, *DT (J48)* and *DT (RandomTree)*. All the algorithms were extracted from the WEKA platform [20], which provides a set of algorithms, in order to avoid implementation bias. We used two measures in deciding the performance of algorithms as below:

$$Classification\ accuracy = \frac{N_1}{N_2}. \tag{1}$$

$$Precision\ of\ false\ alarm = \frac{N_3}{N_4}. \tag{2}$$

where N_1 represents the number of correctly classified alarms, N_2 represents the total number of alarms, N_3 represents the number of alarms classified as false alarm, N_4 represents the number of false alarms. Ideally, a desirable algorithm is expected to have a classification accuracy of 1 and a precision of false alarm of 1, but there is a balance should be considered in practical deployment. Similar to [10,11], we define a *decision value* to determine the best algorithm. The calculation is described as below:

$$decision\ value = 0.4 \times CA + 0.6 \times PFA \tag{3}$$

where *CA* represents the *classification accuracy* and *PFA* represents the *precision of false alarm*.

3.2 Experimental Results

In this experiment, we randomly selected six IDS nodes and collected a real five-day alarm dataset from the deployed distributed IDS network. A node could generate around 5400 alarms on average each day. All alarms were labeled by expert knowledge with three network administrators from the same company.

Algorithm Selection. Table 1 presents the algorithm selection process for different IDS nodes (six nodes) and days (five days). It is noticeable that the algorithm selection performs in an intelligent way, in which the best algorithm could be selected for each day based on the collected data. Taking *IDS-1* as an example, the selected algorithm is SVM (LibSVM), DT (J48), DT (J48), DT (J48), and KNN (IBK) for respective day. These results indicate that the adaptive false alarm reduction can perform well in a cloud environment.

Workload and Delay Improvement. To explore the performance of our approach, we compare it with the previous work [11], where the intelligent false alarm filter was deployed in a cloud environment. Figure 2 depicts the reduced workload on average for the central server on the cloud, and the delay improvement for the data communication and algorithm selection. It is found that our proposed

Table 1. The process of algorithm selection varied with different IDS nodes and days.

Day	*IDS-1*	*IDS-2*	*IDS-3*
1	SVM (LibSVM)	DT (J48)	DT (J48)
2	DT (J48)	SVM (LibSVM)	DT (J48)
3	DT (J48)	KNN (IBK)	DT (RandomTree)
4	DT (J48)	SVM (LibSVM)	KNN (IBK)
5	KNN (IBK)	SVM (LibSVM)	DT (J48)
Day	*IDS-4*	*IDS-5*	*IDS-6*
1	KNN (IBK)	DT (RandomTree)	DT (J48)
2	SVM (LibSVM)	DT (RandomTree)	DT (J48)
3	SVM (LibSVM)	KNN (IBK)	KNN (IBK)
4	KNN (IBK)	KNN (IBK)	KNN (IBK)
5	KNN (IBK)	KNN (IBK)	DT (J48)

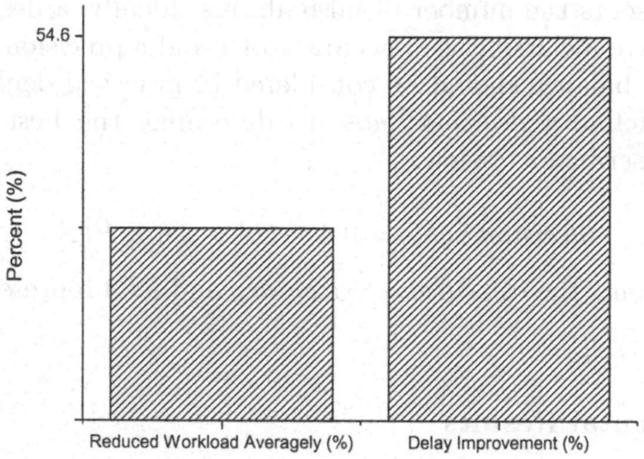

Fig. 2. The reduced workload for the cloud central server and the delay improvement, as compared to the previous work [11].

framework can help reduce the workload for the central server and shorten the delay by nearly 27% and 55%, respectively. The experimental results demonstrate the efficiency of the proposed framework.

4 Related Work

Cloud computing, which refers to both the applications delivered as services over the Internet and the hardware and systems software in the data centers that provide those services [2], has been applied to many fields. In turn, cloud environment is easily becoming a target for intruders looking for possible vulnerabilities [19]. For instance, an attacker can use cloud resources maliciously by impersonating legitimate cloud users. To protect the cloud environment from various attacks, intrusion detection systems have been widely investigated and deployed in such an environment.

To better deploy an IDS in a cloud environment, Roschke *et al.* [15] proposed and implemented an extensible IDS management architecture for different kinds of users and different kinds of requirements. Their management architecture was mainly composed of several sensors and a central management unit. By combining the virtualization technology and known VM monitor approaches, they indicated that this management system could handle most existing VM-based IDSs. Then, Vieira *et al.* [19] proposed a Grid and Cloud Computing Intrusion Detection System (CCCIDS) to detect both network-based and host-based attacks by employing an audit system with both knowledge and behavior analysis. In particular, each node could identify local events that represented security violations by interacting with other nodes.

To address the security issues in a cloud environment, Doelitzscher *et al.* [4] proposed an autonomous agent-based incident detection system with the purpose of solving new cloud specific security issues (i.e., the abuse of cloud resources). Specifically, their proposed Security Audit as a Service (SAaaS) detection system was built on intelligent, autonomous agents for collecting data, analyzing information and distributing underlying business process. Similarly, Alharkan and Martin [1] presented an Intrusion Detection System as a Service (IDSaaS) to enhance the cloud provider's security infrastructure. To enhance the performance of a single IDS, distributed IDSs enable various IDS nodes to collect useful information from others, which can be suitable for a cloud environment. Several related studies regarding distributed IDSs and cloud security issues can refer to [5–8, 12, 13].

5 Conclusion

In this paper, we propose a framework for improving the intelligent false alarm reduction in a distributed environment based on edge computing devices (i.e., the data can be processed at the edge for shorter response time and could be more energy efficient). We conducted a study and found that our proposed approach can further reduce the workload for the cloud central server and reduce the delay by nearly 27% and 55%, respectively, as compared to the similar work. To our knowledge, this is the first work in discussing the deployment of intelligent false alarm reduction through edge computing. The future work could include conducting more experiments to investigate the framework performance in the aspects of algorithm selection and communication burden.

References

1. Alharkan, T., Martin, P.: IDSaaS: intrusion detection system as a service in public clouds. In: Proceedings of the 12th IEEE/ACM International Symposium on Cluster, Cloud and Grid Computing, pp. 686–687 (2012)

2. Armbrust, M., Fox, A., Griffith, R.: Above the clouds: a berkeley view of cloud computing. Technical report, EECS Department, University of California, Berkeley (2009)
3. Bonomi, F., Milito, R., Zhu, J., Addepalli, S.: Fog computing and its role in the internet of things. In: Proceedings of the First Edition of the MCC Workshop on Mobile Cloud Computing (MCC), pp. 13–16 (2012)
4. Doelitzscher, F., Reich, C., Knahl, M., Clarke, N.: An autonomous agent based incident detection system for cloud environments. In: Proceedings of the 2011 IEEE 3rd International Conference on Cloud Computing Technology and Science (CloudCom), pp. 197–204 (2011)
5. Li, W., Meng, Y., Kwok, L.-F.: Enhancing trust evaluation using intrusion sensitivity in collaborative intrusion detection networks: feasibility and challenges. In: Proceedings of the 9th International Conference on Computational Intelligence and Security (CIS), pp. 518–522 (2013)
6. Li, W., Meng, W.: Enhancing collaborative intrusion detection networks using intrusion sensitivity in detecting pollution attacks. Inf. Comput. Secur. **24**(3), 265–276 (2016)
7. Li, W., Meng, Y., Kwok, L.-F., Ip, H.H.S.: PMFA: toward passive message fingerprint attacks on challenge-based collaborative intrusion detection networks. In: Proceedings of the 10th International Conference on Network and System Security (NSS), pp. 433–449 (2016)
8. Li, W., Meng, Y., Kwok, L.-F., Ip, H.H.S.: Enhancing collaborative intrusion detection networks against insider attacks using supervised intrusion sensitivity-based trust management model. J. Netw. Comput. Appl. **77**, 135–145 (2017)
9. McHugh, J.: Testing intrusion detection systems: a critique of the 1998 and 1999 DARPA intrusion detection system evaluations as performed by Lincoln laboratory. ACM Trans. Inf. Syst. Secur. **3**(4), 262–294 (2000)
10. Meng, Y., Kwok, L.-F.: Adaptive false alarm filter using machine learning in intrusion detection. In: Wang, Y., Li, T. (eds.) Practical Applications of Intelligent Systems, pp. 573–584. Springer, Heidelberg (2011). https://doi.org/10.1007/978-3-642-25658-5_68
11. Meng, Y., Li, W., Kwok, L.-F.: Towards adaptive false alarm reduction using cloud as a service. In: Proceedings of the 8th International Conference on Communications and Networking in China (ChinaCom 2013), pp. 420–425, August 2013
12. Meng, W., Li, W., Xiang, Y., Choo, K.-K.R.: A Bayesian inference-based detection mechanism to defend medical smartphone networks against insider attacks. J. Netw. Comput. Appl. **78**, 162–169 (2017)
13. Modi, C., Patel, D., Borisaniya, B., Patel, H., Patel, A., Rajarajan, M.: A survey of intrusion detection techniques in cloud. J. Netw. Comput. Appl. **36**(1), 42–57 (2013)
14. Microsoft Security Intelligence Report (SIR), vol. 11 (2011). http://www.microsoft.com/security/sir/default.aspx
15. Roschke, S., Cheng, F., Meinel, C.: Intrusion detection in the cloud. In: Proceedings of 8th IEEE International Conference on Dependable, Autonomic and Secure Computing (DASC), pp. 729–734 (2009)
16. Scarfone, K., Mell, P.: Guide to Intrusion Detection and Prevention Systems (IDPS). NIST Special Publication 800–894, February 2007

17. Snort, The Open Source Network Intrusion Detection System. http://www.snort.org/
18. Shi, W., Cao, J., Zhang, Q., Li, Y., Xu, L.: Edge computing: vision and challenges. IEEE Internet Things J. **3**(5), 637–646 (2016)
19. Vieira, K., Schulter, A., Westphall, C.B., Westphall, C.M.: Intrusion detection for grid and cloud computing. IT Prof. **12**(4), 38–43 (2010)
20. WEKA - Waikato Environment for Knowledge Analysis (Open source). http://www.cs.waikato.ac.nz/ml/weka/

Live Path CFI Against Control Flow Hijacking Attacks

Mohamad Barbar[1(✉)], Yulei Sui[1], Hongyu Zhang[2], Shiping Chen[3], and Jingling Xue[4]

[1] University of Technology Sydney, Sydney, Australia
mbarbar@runbox.com
[2] University of Newcastle, Callaghan, Australia
[3] CSIRO/Data61, Sydney, Australia
[4] University of New South Wales, Sydney, Australia

Abstract. Through memory vulnerabilities, control flow hijacking allows an attacker to force a running program to execute other than what the programmer has intended. Control Flow Integrity (CFI) aims to prevent the adversarial effects of these attacks. CFI attempts to enforce the programmer's intent by ensuring that a program only runs according to a control flow graph (CFG) of the program. The enforced CFG can be built statically or dynamically, and Per-Input Control Flow Integrity (PICFI) represents a recent advance in dynamic CFI techniques. PICFI begins execution with the empty CFG of a program and lazily adds edges to the CFG during execution according to concrete inputs. However, this CFG grows monotonically, i.e., edges are never removed when corresponding control flow transfers become illegal. This paper presents LPCFI, Live Path Control Flow Integrity, to more precisely enforce forward edge CFI using a dynamically computed CFG by both adding and removing edges for all indirect control flow transfers from indirect callsites, thereby raising the bar against control flow hijacking attacks.

Keyword: Control Flow Integrity

1 Introduction

Programs written in low-level languages, such as C and C++, make up the majority of performance-critical system software (e.g., web browsers and language runtimes) running on most computing platforms. In some domains, like embedded systems, these languages are almost ubiquitous. However, these unsafe languages are prone to memory corruption vulnerabilities (e.g., use-after-free and buffer overflows). An attacker may leverage these vulnerabilities to launch control flow hijacking attacks by changing the target of an indirect branch instruction to force a running program to execute at a location of the attacker's choice. In realistic scenarios, attackers may be able to perform Turing complete computation by abusing memory vulnerabilities and using techniques like return oriented programming [1] and counterfeit object-oriented programming [2].

W. Susilo and G. Yang (Eds.): ACISP 2018, LNCS 10946, pp. 768–779, 2018.
https://doi.org/10.1007/978-3-319-93638-3_45

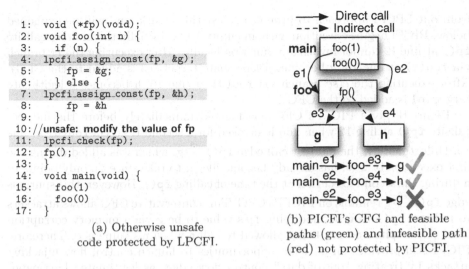

```
void (*fp)(void);
void foo(int n) {
  if (n) {
lpcfi_assign_const(fp, &g);
    fp = &g;
  } else {
lpcfi_assign_const(fp, &h);
    fp = &h
  }
//unsafe: modify the value of fp
lpcfi_check(fp);
fp();
}
void main(void) {
  foo(1)
  foo(0)
}
```

(a) Otherwise unsafe code protected by LPCFI.

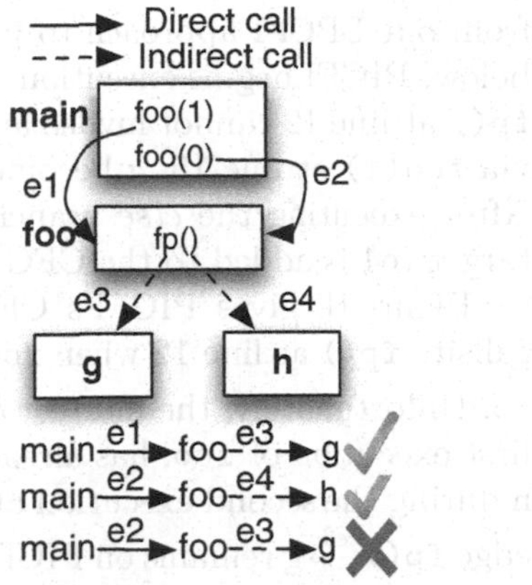

(b) PICFI's CFG and feasible paths (green) and infeasible path (red) not protected by PICFI.

Fig. 1. A motivating example to demonstrate the limitation of PICFI. (Colour figure online.)

Control Flow Integrity (CFI) has been proposed to prevent control flow hijacking [3]. CFI typically works by enforcing a control flow graph (CFG), which represents the programmer's intent - or rather, what can be inferred as legal and illegal control flow from the program. Edges in the CFG represent control flow transfers, and CFI aims to protect indirect control flow edges from being taken illegally. The protection offered by CFI is more effective if a more precise CFG is used. The CFG can be computed statically and this does not consider the fact that the legal status of indirect control flow transfers constantly changes during runtime. For example, when a function pointer is reassigned to a new value, an indirect call via that function pointer will call a new function target and calling the previous target would be illegal.

Insights. Per-Input Control Flow Integrity (PICFI) [4] represents a recent dynamic approach to forward edge CFI. PICFI first pre-computes a static CFG as the upper bound for its dynamic one. PICFI starts with the empty CFG of a program, and during runtime, once a function address is taken (e.g., `p = &func`), it will add an edge from each indirect callsite to `func` if this edge is also found in the static CFG. Hence PICFI provides better security guarantees than CFI techniques which enforce a statically computed CFG. However, PICFI's dynamic CFG grows monotonically, i.e, edges added to the CFG are never removed. Hence, edges become permanently legal to take regardless of whether their legality changes over time. The conservatively constructed dynamic CFG used by PICFI leaves an attack surface: when an indirect transfer remains on the monotonically growing CFG but can never be legally executed again.

Motivating Example. Figure 1 illustrates this limitation of PICFI via a proof-of-concept attack. Note that the lines marked in blue are instrumentation calls from our LPCFI approach to protect against this attack, and will be explained below. PICFI begins execution with an empty CFG. Initially the indirect callsite `fp()` at line 12 cannot invoke any function legally. After executing the *if* branch via `foo(1)` at line 15, `g` becomes a legitimate target (e3 is added to the CFG). After executing the *else* branch via `foo(0)` at line 16, `h` becomes a legitimate target (e4 is added to the CFG).

Figure 1b gives PICFI's CFG constructed immediately before the indirect callsite `fp()` at line 12 when `foo` is invoked for a second time via `foo(0)` at line 16. Unfortunately, the indirect call edge $\texttt{fp()} \xrightarrow{e3} \texttt{g}$, which was added during the first execution of `foo`, has already become illegal to take since `fp` only points to `h` during the second execution at the time of calling `fp()`. However, this spurious edge $\texttt{fp()} \xrightarrow{e3} \texttt{g}$ remains on PICFI's CFG. This conservative CFG allows attackers to redirect `fp()` to `g` by modifying `fp`'s value to be `g` via a memory corruption error [5], despite `foo` not being allowed to call `g` when `n`'s value is 0. Therefore, PICFI still provides an attacker opportunities to launch control flow hijacking attacks by treating "out-of-date" control flow edges as legitimate. This paper presents LPCFI, Live Path Control Flow Integrity, which aims to overcome this limitation of PICFI by both adding and removing CFG edges, allowing at most one outgoing forward edge from every indirect callsite at any one program point.

Let us revisit the example in Fig. 1 whilst taking into consideration LPCFI's instrumentation (highlighted in blue). During the first call to `foo`, $\texttt{fp()} \xrightarrow{e3} \texttt{g}$ is added to the CFG via `lpcfi_assign_const`. A check is then performed to ensure that the indirect call transfer from `fp()` will reach the only legitimate target `g`. During the second call to `foo`, `lpcfi_assign_const` in the *else* branch updates the CFG by first removing invalid edge $\texttt{fp()} \xrightarrow{e3} \texttt{g}$ from the CFG, and then adding $\texttt{fp()} \xrightarrow{e4} \texttt{h}$. This removal is important since the second call to `foo` via `foo(0)` is not allowed to call `g`, which PICFI ignores. LPCFI ensures only one legitimate (live) function target is allowed at any call path to an indirect callsite.

Challenges. Designing a CFI technique that overcomes the aforementioned limitation is challenging. Firstly, precise static analysis is required to find statements which may require instrumentation as the precision of static analysis directly correlates with the overhead reduction achieved. Only the statements which may modify or read the value of a function pointer should be identified by static pointer analysis for instrumentation. Secondly, function pointer values need to be correctly maintained in safe memory and the metadata data structure needs to be well designed to ensure efficient lookup and runtime checks.

Our Solution. LPCFI aims to ensure only edges which are currently "live" - can be legally taken - exist within the CFG. We have designed and implemented a new instrumentation approach which tracks function pointers and the address-taken function which they point to at any program point. A function pointer may only ever point to a single function object, so our instrumentation correctly updates which pointers point to which function objects in an efficient data structure in safe memory. We apply pointer analysis [6] to identify all statements which may potentially access the value of a function pointer, and instrument only those statements to minimise runtime overhead. Any callsite from a function pointer is checked to ensure the runtime value matches the value stored in safe memory.

This paper makes the following key contributions:

- We present LPCFI, a new dynamic control flow integrity technique that can protect against attacks undetected by the conservative monotonically growing CFG used by PICFI.
- We propose a new instrumentation approach coupled with a data structure to allow only one function to be a legal target for any indirect callsite.
- We have developed a proof-of-concept attack and defence to demonstrate the effectiveness of LPCFI in mitigating control flow attacks which are not protected by PICFI. This is publicly available at https://github.com/mbarbar/lpcfi.

2 Related Works

Often, CFI implementations determine policy (i.e. valid targets for an indirect control flow transfer at a particular time) according to only static information. This is limited in that some properties are impossible to determine statically, for example, the value of a function pointer reliant on user input.

Per-Input Control Flow Integrity (PICFI) is a CFI implementation which uses dynamic information to gradually build the CFG [4]. PICFI begins execution with an empty CFG; all indirect transfers of control are illegal. The CFG is gradually constructed by discovering valid targets for indirect control flow transfers during runtime according to program inputs. For example, when a function is called, that callsite becomes a valid target of return instructions, or when a function pointer is assigned a value, that value becomes a valid target for indirect callsites (constrained by the static CFG). However, these additions to the CFG are permanent; the CFG grows *monotonically.* This means that changes in target legality are not reflected in the CFG, and hence not enforced by PICFI. A target which is made legal by PICFI is regarded as legal for the rest of execution.

Offering improvements over PICFI, PittyPat [7], a very recent work, uses dynamic path-sensitive points-to analysis to further restrict the set of allowed function pointers at indirect callsites during runtime. Rather than considering just address activation, or the static points-to sets at a particular program point, PittyPat considers the points-to set of a function pointer at a particular program point only based on the *executed* program path. Hence PittyPat avoids PICFI's limitation of keeping previously legal targets which have become illegal. However, PittyPat has a strong dependency on specific hardware and a modified kernel. In contrast, LPCFI is a portable purely software-based approach without any hardware dependency.

A shadow stack is a *second* stack existing in memory used to ensure return instructions jump to the correct address [8,9]. Shadow stacks work by mirroring return addresses pushed onto the execution stack. Upon returning, the value on top of the shadow stack is compared with that on the execution stack, and if the comparison fails, an error is detected. If the shadow stack is safe from manipulation, shadow stacks perfectly protect return transfers. However, shadow stacks only protect backward edges but not forward edges like virtual calls.

CFI techniques have recently been used to protect against virtual table hijacking attacks in low-level object-oriented languages like C++. VTV [10], VTrust [11], and SafeDispatch [12] apply Class Hierarchy Analysis (CHA) to analyse virtual calls to enforce CFI. ShrinkWrap [13] aims to improve CHA based CFI by considering multiple and diamond inheritance. VIP [14] is a recent CFI technique that enforces a more precise call graph than CHA based approaches by using pointer analysis and a fast index-based instrumentation.

This work builds on an earlier version of our work [15].

3 LPCFI Approach

This section details our Live Path Control Flow Integrity approach designed to reduce the attack surface left by PICFI. Section 3.1 describes the program representation of a C/C++ program. Section 3.2 introduces the *fp-table*, the internal metadata design. Finally, Sect. 3.3 describes the instrumentation which operates on the *fp-table* to precisely update the dynamic CFG at runtime.

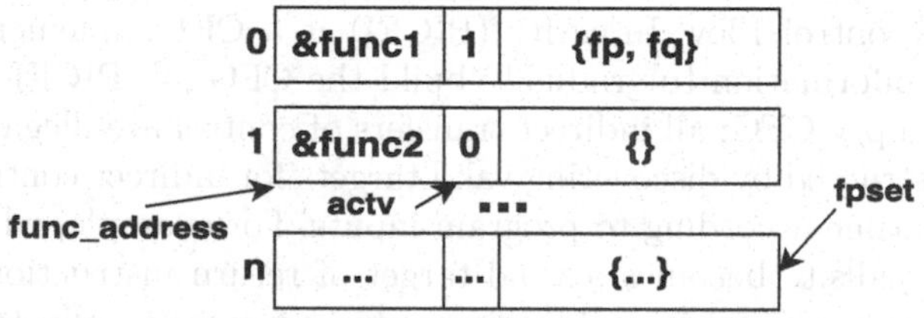

Fig. 2. Internal representation of the fp-table.

3.1 Program Representation

We represent programs in LLVM's SSA form following [6,16]. The set of all variables is separated into two subsets: top-level pointers (registers) whose addresses are not taken, and all potential targets, i.e., all address-taken objects of a pointer. In SSA, a program is represented by five statement types: `const (p = &o)`, `copy (p = q)`, `store (*p = q)`, `load (p = *q)`, and `call (fp(...))`. Passing arguments into and returning results from functions are modeled by copies. A global variable initialisation is translated into one of the four types of assignments and analysed immediately at the beginning of the main function. For a `const` statement `p = &o` (allocation sites), `o` is a stack or global variable, or a dynamically created abstract heap object. We only analyse statements which access (modify or read) the value of a function pointer according to static pointer analysis [6].

3.2 Data Structures

LPCFI needs to store metadata in the *fp-table* (Fig. 2) to perform bookkeeping to update the dynamic CFG. The metadata is stored in a safe memory region which is accessed frequently for both reading and writing following [11].

LPCFI maintains the fp-table as shown in Fig. 2, which is a fixed size array (size is the number of address-taken functions in the program) where each element holds: (1) the address of a function `func_address`, (2) an *activation* bit `actv`, and (3) a set `fpset` of function pointers which legally point to `func_address` at a particular program point during runtime. `pt(fp_table, fp)` returns the function that pointer `fp` points to. Overloaded `lookup(fp_table, &func)` returns the index of `&func` in the `fp_table`, and `lookup(fp_table, &fp)` returns the index of the function which `&fp` points to in the `fp_table`.

The fp-table is a simple yet efficient solution for fast lookup using a one dimensional array. The fp-table uses function addresses as keys for various reasons. Firstly, it can be a fixed size since functions which may have their addresses taken (`const` statements) at runtime are known statically. Secondly, the checking operation can perform lookups on the function that is about to be called (the runtime value) and retrieve its `fpset`. Finally, a data structure with function addresses as the key is required regardless to keep track of whether functions have been address-taken (activated) to guarantee a lower security bound of PICFI.

3.3 Instrumentation

LPCFI's instrumentation is placed immediately before the five statement types. We insert instrumentation for an assignment **only if** it may read/write a function pointer value as determined by Andersen's pointer analysis [6]. All instrumentations except the checking instrumentation write to the fp-table.

```
update(fp, &o) {
    // Check function object
    if(o not a function obj) return;
    // Search for index of object which fp points to
    oldInd = lookup(fp_table, &pt(fp_table,fp));
    // Remove fp from set of fp_table[oldInd]
    if (oldInd!=-1) remove(fp_table[oldInd].fpset, fp);
    // Search the index of function o in fp_table
    newInd = lookup(fp_table, &o);
    if (newInd==-1) error('not found');
    // Add fp to the new function pointer set
    add(fp_table[newInd].fpset, fp);
}
```

Fig. 3. Helper function `update` to remove and add pointers in the fp-table.

The four assignment instrumentations share helper function `update(fp, &o)` in Fig. 3 which updates a function pointer `fp` to correctly point to function `o` by removing `fp` from the `fpset` of `fp`'s old points-to target (if it is a member) at line 7, and adding `fp` to `o`'s `fpset` at line 12. Note that pointer analysis is always an over-approximation. A pointer `q` resolved to point to a function statically, may not point to such at runtime. LPCFI will not perform any runtime update if the right hand side expression of an assignment (e.g., `... = q`) does not refer to a function object as shown at line 3 in Fig. 3.

Handling Constant Assignments `fp=&func`: This case, as carried out by `lpcfi_assign_const` shown in Fig. 4, is simple as it is a direct assignment of a function address `func` to a function pointer `fp`. Upon executing this statement, LPCFI requires that, (1) `func` be regarded as activated, and (2) `fp` exclusively points to `func` in the fp-table.

Assignments of this form may execute multiple times for the same RHS value. Hence, functions will be *activated* multiple times. This does not affect correctness and runtime overhead for the activation operation is negligible.

```
lpcfi_assign_const(fp, &func) {
    // Search the index of &func in fp_table
    ind = lookup(fp_table, &func);
    if(ind==-1) error('not found');
    // Mark func as activated
    fp_table[ind].actv_bit = 1;
    // Update fp to point to func
    update(fp, &func);
}
fp = &func;
```

Fig. 4. Handling `const` statements using `lpcfi_assign_const`.

Handling Copy Assignments `p = q`: Represented by `lpcfi_assign_copy`, the second case is also straightforward as shown in Fig. 5. First, we obtain `pt(fp_table,q)`, the points-to target `o` of the RHS pointer `q` derived from the fp-table. Then, `p` is made to exclusively point to `q`'s pointee `o` if `o` is a function object, so both `p` and `q` are put into the `fpset` of object `o`.

```
lpcfi_assign_copy(p, q) {
    // Get the object that q points to in fp_table
    o = pt(fp_table, q);
    // Update p to point to o only if o is a function
    update(p, &o);
}
p = q;
```

Fig. 5. Handling `copy` statements using `lpcfi_assign_copy`.

Handling Load Assignments `p = *s`: `lpcfi_assign_load`'s implementation is shown in Fig. 6. Similar to handling the copy case, we first retrieve points-to target o of *s from the fp-table. o is checked to ensure that it has been activated (lines 5–8) (for a lower bound protection of PICFI, further discussed in Sect. 4.3). Then, p is made to exclusively point to the object o (line 10).

```
1:  lpcfi_assign_load(p, *s) {
2:      // Get the object that *s points to
3:      o = pt(fp_table,*s);
4:      // Search for the index of &o in fp_table
5:      ind = lookup(fp_table, &o);
6:      if(ind==-1) error('not found');
7:      // Ensure o has been activated
8:      assert(fp_table[ind].actv);
9:      // Update p to point to o
10:     update(p, &o);
11: }
    p = *s;
```

Fig. 6. Handling `load` statements using `lpcfi_assign_load`.

Handling Store Assignments `*r = q`: `lpcfi_assign_store`'s implementation is shown in Fig. 7. This case is similar to the `copy` case. The points-to target o of the RHS pointer q is retrieved via `pt(fp_table, q)`. Then, runtime value `*r` is made to exclusively point to the same as that which q does in the fp-table.

```
lpcfi_assign_store(*r, q) {
    // Get the object that *r points to
    o = pt(fp_table,q);
    // Update q to point to o
    update(*r, &o);
}
*r = q;
```

Fig. 7. Handling `store` statements using `lpcfi_assign_store`.

Handling Calls `fp(...)`: As shown in Fig. 8, whenever a call is made from a function pointer, the runtime value of the function pointer needs to be checked against its saved value in the fp-table. Furthermore, a check confirming that a callsite-to-target edge is within the static CFG must also be performed to guarantee a security lower bound of PICFI. If either check fails, LPCFI will report an error indicating an attempted illegal control flow transfer.

4 Implementation

We have developed a prototype with a step-by-step live demo to illustrate examples (those in Figs. 1 and 9) that can be protected by LPCFI but not by PICFI. They are publicly available at https://github.com/mbarbar/lpcfi.

```
lpcfi_check(fp, callsite) {
    // Get the object that fp points to
    o = pt(fp_table,fp);
    // Enforce control flow integrity
    assert(runtimeVal(*fp) == &o
        && edge(callsite, &o) ∈ static CFG);
}
fp(...);
```

Fig. 8. Handling `call` statements using `lpcfi_check`.

4.1 Instrumentation and Data Structure

In our open-source prototype, LPCFI's data structure (Fig. 2) and its instrumentation are implemented in an equivalent yet less efficient manner as a standalone library (i.e., `lpcfi.h`, `lpcfi.c`, `fptable.h` and `fptable.c`). In order to demonstrate the key idea and techniques easily, our prototype performs manual instrumention for the motivating example (Fig. 1) as available in `demo.c`.

At indirect callsites, a lookup operation through `lpcfi_check` is performed as discussed in Sect. 4.2. Assignment instrumentations are not idempotent so PICFI's optimsation strategy of patching out instrumentation can not be achieved. `lpcfi_assign_const` performs both function activation (which is idempotent) and fp-table modification. Function activation results in a bit being set and is negligible to the total runtime overhead.

Andersen's pointer analysis [6] is used to check whether pointer dereferences can read or write a function pointer value. This is conservative, so any statement determined to not access such a value is safe without runtime bookkeeping.

4.2 Lookup Operation on the fp-table

The lookup operation is important to LPCFI's metadata manipulation. This happens often, especially since checking function pointer callsites requires this search. During initialisation, the fp-table is sorted according to the `func_address` field for efficient searching. Then, a binary search can be performed on the fp-table with the `func_address` field as the key, an $O(\log n)$ operation.

Overhead mainly comes from the `update` helper function due to the search operation on the `fp-table` for assignment instrumentations. Optimisations can be implemented to improve the performance of the search, e.g., caching common searches with a hash map.

4.3 Security Guarantee

LPCFI guarantees security at a lower bound of PICFI but reduces the attack surface by removing spurious CFG edges during runtime. Following PICFI, LPCFI only allows an indirect call to target a function whose address has been taken (activated) if such callsite-target edge exists in the static CFG. However, LPCFI places a further restriction: that function pointers hold their last assigned value.

Calling a function pointer after it has been modified outside the standard assignment statements results in a raised assertion because assignment instrumentations are the only way to write to the fp-table, which the check operation relies on. Like PICFI, LPCFI enforces control flow integrity, not data flow integrity [17,18]. LPCFI does not ensure memory safety for code and data pointers (e.g., the pointers dereferenced in `load`/`store` statements are unprotected).

```
#include "privileges.h"
/* The header file contains function pointers                              */
/* 'volatile (void)(*priv)(void)' and 'volatile (void)(*nopriv)(void)' */
/* for accessing privileged and non-privileged system methods.          */
int main(void) {
    (void)(*op)(void);
    char password[7];
    while (true) {
        fgets(password, 7, stdin);
        if (strcmp(password, "secret") == 0) {
            lpcfi_assign_copy(op, priv);
            op = priv;
        } else {
            lpcfi_assign_copy(op, nopriv);
            op = nopriv;
        }
        // memory corruption vulnerability: modify the value of op
        lpcfi_check(op);
        op();
    }
}
```

Fig. 9. Password verification cope that is safe with LPCFI, but not with PICFI. (Colour figure online.)

5 Proof-of-Concept Attack and Defence

Figure 9 demonstrates LPCFI's effectiveness over PICFI with a proof-of-concept example in the presence of loops. This is a permission access scenario that allows a user to access a privileged or non-privileged call depending upon the password entered. This demo (including `extended-demo.c`, `privileges.c`, and `privileges.h`) is publicly available in the `extended-demo` folder in our release.

LPCFI's instrumentation is shown in blue (discussed below). In an infinite loop, a user is prompted for a password. If correct, function pointer `op` is set to function pointer `priv`, a privileged operation. If not, `op` is set to function pointer `nopriv`, a non-privileged operation. Finally, `op` is called and the loop begins anew. A memory vulnerability before the call allows an attackers to modify `op`.

If not instrumented, an attacker may change the value of `op` to any value, and the call will target that location. If the code was instrumented by PICFI, initially, the `op` call is deemed unable to target any location legally. The first time the password is entered incorrectly, the `op` call may reach the value pointed to by `nopriv`. Similarly, the first time the password is entered correctly, the `op` call may reach the value pointed to by `priv`. When *both* possible values have been activated, PICFI will see the `op` call as being able to legally take on either value until program exit. If a user enters the password incorrectly, they may modify the value of `op` to be that of the privileged function pointer, and PICFI will allow this call to be made. This is a problem when a malicious user uses the system after a privileged user.

When the code is instrumented with LPCFI (as shown in blue), this problem is remedied. When `op` is set to `priv` at line 12, the `op` call will only succeed if `op` retains the value it was assigned (`priv`). Similarly, when `op` is set to `nopriv` at line 15, for the `op` call to succeed, `op` must retain its value (`nopriv`). The fp-table is storing a **single** value - the most recently assigned value.

6 Conclusion

This paper presents LPCFI, a new dynamic control flow integrity technique that can protect against attacks undetected when using the monotonically growing CFG used by PICFI. LPCFI achieves a lower bound security guarantee of that promised by PICFI but reduces the attack surface left by PICFI using a new instrumentation approach and, with a specially designed data structure, ensures that indirect callsites from function pointers can only target at most one function.

References

1. Shacham, H.: The geometry of innocent flesh on the bone: return-into-libc without function calls (on the x86). In: CCS 2007, pp. 552–561 (2007)
2. Schuster, F., Tendyck, T., Liebchen, C., Davi, L., Sadeghi, A.-R., Holz, T.: Counterfeit object-oriented programming: on the difficulty of preventing code reuse attacks in C++ applications. In: S&P 2015, pp. 745–762 (2015)
3. Abadi, M., Budiu, M., Erlingsson, Ú., Ligatti, J.: Control-flow integrity principles, implementations, and applications. ACM Trans. Inf. Syst. Secur. **13**(1), 4:1–4:40 (2009)
4. Niu, B., Tan, G.: Per-input control-flow integrity. In: CCS 2015 (2015)
5. Evans, I., Long, F., Otgonbaatar, U., Shrobe, H., Rinard, M., Okhravi, H., Sidiroglou-Douskos, S.: Control jujutsu: on the weaknesses of fine-grained control flow integrity. In: CCS 2015, pp. 901–913 (2015)
6. Sui, Y., Xue, J.: SVF: interprocedural static value-flow analysis in LLVM. In: CC 2016, pp. 265–266 (2016)
7. Ding, R., Qian, C., Song, C., Harris, B., Kim, T., Lee, W.: Efficient protection of path-sensitive control security. In: USENIX Security 2017, pp. 131–148 (2017)
8. Sinnadurai, S., Zhao, Q., Wong, W.-F.: Transparent runtime shadow stack: protection against malicious return address modifications (2008)
9. Erlingsson, Ú., Abadi, M., Vrable, M., Budiu, M., Necula, G.C.: XFI: software guards for system address spaces. In: OSDI 2006, pp. 75–88 (2006)

10. Tice, C., Roeder, T., Collingbourne, P., Checkoway, S., Erlingsson, Ú., Lozano, L., Pike, G.: Enforcing forward-edge control-flow integrity in GCC & LLVM. In: USENIX Security 2014, pp. 941–955 (2014)
11. Zhang, C., Carr, S.A., Li, T., Ding, Y., Song, C., Payer, M., Song, D.: VTrust: regaining trust on virtual calls. In: NDSS 2016 (2016)
12. Jang, D., Tatlock, Z., Lerner, S.: SafeDispatch: securing C++ virtual calls from memory corruption attacks. In: NDSS 2014 (2014)
13. Haller, I., Göktaş, E., Athanasopoulos, E., Portokalidis, G., Bos, H.: ShrinkWrap: VTable protection without loose ends. In: ACSAC 2015, pp. 341–350 (2015)
14. Fan, X., Sui, Y., Liao, X., Xue, J.: Boosting the precision of virtual call integrity protection with partial pointer analysis for C++. In: ISSTA 2017, pp. 329–340 (2017)
15. Barbar, M., Sui, Y., Zhang, H., Chen, S., Xue, J.: Live path control flow integrity. In: ICSE 2018 (2018)
16. Sui, Y., Xue, J.: On-demand strong update analysis via value-flow refinement. In: FSE 2016, pp. 460–473 (2016)
17. Castro, M., Costa, M., Harris, T.: Securing software by enforcing data-flow integrity. In: OSDI 2016, pp. 147–160 (2016)
18. Kuznetsov, V., Szekeres, L., Payer, M., Candea, G., Sekar, R., Song, D.: Code-pointer integrity. In: OSDI 2014, pp. 147–163 (2014)

Security Analysis and Modification of ID-Based Encryption with Equality Test from ACISP 2017

Hyung Tae Lee[1], Huaxiong Wang[2], and Kai Zhang[3,4](✉)

[1] Division of Computer Science and Engineering, College of Engineering, Chonbuk National University, Jeonju, Republic of Korea
[2] Division of Mathematical Sciences, School of Physical and Mathematical Sciences, Nanyang Technological University, Singapore, Singapore
[3] Department of Information Security, College of Computer Science and Technology, Shanghai University of Electric Power, Shanghai, China
kzhang@shiep.edu.cn
[4] Co-Innovation Center for Information Supply & Assurance Technology, Anhui University, Hefei, China

Abstract. At ACISP 2017, Wu et al. provided an identity-based encryption scheme with equality test that considers to prevent insider attacks. In this paper, we demonstrate that their scheme does not achieve the claimed security requirement by presenting an attack. Subsequently, we provide a modification of their construction.

1 Introduction

Identity-based encryption with equality test (IBEET) is a special kind of identity-based encryption (IBE) that allows to perform equality tests between ciphertexts under different identities as well as the same identity. This feature enables us to apply IBEET to various scenarios in practice, such as keyword search on encrypted databases and efficient encrypted data management on the cloud. Due to wide availability in practice, several IBEET constructions [2,3,5,6] have been proposed. On the other hand, supporting equality tests makes the security of IBEET schemes weaken. If the adversary can have a trapdoor for equality test on the target ciphertext, he can generate a ciphertext of any message by herself and perform equality tests between the target ciphertext and the ciphertext generated by himself. We call this type of attacks *insider attack* [7]. To avoid insider attacks, the previous IBEET schemes assumed that the size of message space is exponential in the security parameter and the min-entropy of message distribution is as high as the security parameter.

At ACISP 2017, Wu et al. [7] proposed an IBEET scheme which considers to prevent insider attacks. To this end, they first established a variant of the traditional IBEET model: In their IBEET system, anyone can perform equality tests between any two ciphertexts publicly without trapdoors. Instead, only group members who have a token for a receiver's identity can generate a ciphertext.

W. Susilo and G. Yang (Eds.): ACISP 2018, LNCS 10946, pp. 780–786, 2018.
https://doi.org/10.1007/978-3-319-93638-3_46

Hence, testers who do not have a token cannot perform insider attacks. Thereafter, Wu et al. constructed an IBEET scheme using bilinear map groups under the proposed model. To analyze the security of their scheme, they introduced a new security notion, which is slightly weaker than the indistinguishability under adaptive identity and chosen ciphertext attacks (IND-ID-CCA2) for traditional IBE; a main difference between two security models is that messages m_0, m_1 submitted by the adversary at the challenge phase cannot be queried to the encryption oracle before and after the challenge phase in the security game for the new model. (Note that the challenger in the security game for the new model should provide an encryption oracle to the adversary because he does not have a token required for encryption, whereas the adversary for the traditional security model of IBE can encrypt a message by himself.) Then, they claimed that their proposed scheme achieves this new security notion under the Bilinear Diffie-Hellman (BDH) assumption in the random oracle model.

In this paper, we demonstrate that their construction does not satisfy their security notion by presenting an attack. Our attack algorithm is very simple: Once the adversary has the challenge ciphertext and a pair of message and ciphertext after the challenge phase, he generates a valid part for equality test of submitted messages at the challenge phase by manipulating the received ciphertext. Then, he can distinguish which message is contained in the challenge ciphertext between two candidates by performing an equality test between the challenge ciphertext and the ciphertext manipulated by himself. It takes one exponentiation to manipulate a ciphertext to obtain a valid part for equality test and two bilinear map evaluations to perform an equality test.

Next, we modify Wu et al.'s construction so that it achieves the security notion which was presented in the original paper [7]. To avoid our attack presented in this paper, we exploit a keyed permutation, and let group users share the same key for the exploited keyed permutation and use it as a token for encryption. Moreover, we also employ a message authentication code (MAC) to prevent an adversary from reusing an output of the exploited keyed permutation by manipulating other parts. As a result, we obtain a modification that achieves Wu et al.'s original security notion if the exploited keyed permutation is strong pseudorandom, the employed MAC is existentially unforgeable, and the BDH assumption holds in the random oracle model.

Organization of the Paper. In Sect. 2, we provide a description of Wu et al.'s construction [7]. Section 3 presents our attack algorithm for their IBEET scheme and Sect. 4 gives our modification. Due to the space limitation, we relegate security analysis of our modification to the full version [4].

2 Wu et al.'s IBEET Scheme

In this section, we review Wu et al.'s IBEET scheme [7]. The description of their IBEET construction is as follows.

- $\mathsf{Setup}(\lambda)$: On input a security parameter λ, generate two multiplicative cyclic groups $\mathbb{G}_1, \mathbb{G}_2$ of prime order $p = p(\lambda)$ and a bilinear map $e : \mathbb{G}_1 \times \mathbb{G}_1 \to \mathbb{G}_2$.

Pick a random generator g of $\mathbb{G}_1$. Select two random elements α, β from $\mathbb{Z}_p^*$, and set a master secret key MSK and a master token key MTK as

$$\text{MSK} = \alpha \quad \text{and} \quad \text{MTK} = \beta.$$

Compute $P_{pub} = g^\alpha$. Generate three cryptographic hash functions

$$\mathsf{H} : \{0,1\}^t \to \mathbb{Z}_p^*, \quad \mathsf{H}_1 : \{0,1\}^* \to \mathbb{G}_1, \text{ and } \mathsf{H}_2 : \mathbb{G}_1^3 \times \mathbb{G}_2 \to \{0,1\}^{t+\ell},$$

where t denotes the bit-length of messages and ℓ denotes the bit-length of randomness utilized in the encryption algorithm, i.e., $\ell = \lceil \log_2 p \rceil$ where $\lceil a \rceil$ denotes the smallest integer that is larger than or equal to a for $a \in \mathbb{R}$. Finally, output a system public parameter

$$\text{PP} = (\lambda, p, t, \ell, g, \mathbb{G}_1, \mathbb{G}_2, P_{pub}, e, \mathsf{H}, \mathsf{H}_1, \mathsf{H}_2)$$

and a pair of the master secret and master token keys (MSK, MTK).

- $\mathsf{Extract}(\mathsf{ID}, \text{MSK}, \text{MTK})$: On input an identity ID, the master secret key $\text{MSK} = \alpha$, and the master token key $\text{MTK} = \beta$, the key generation center (KGC) computes

$$g_{\mathsf{ID}} = \mathsf{H}_1(\mathsf{ID}), \quad d_{\mathsf{ID}} = g_{\mathsf{ID}}^\alpha \text{ and } \mathsf{tok}_{\mathsf{ID}} = g_{\mathsf{ID}}^\beta,$$

and outputs $(d_{\mathsf{ID}}, \mathsf{tok}_{\mathsf{ID}})$.
- $\mathsf{Enc}(\text{PP}, m, \mathsf{ID}, \mathsf{tok}_{\mathsf{ID}})$: It takes the system public parameter PP, a message m, an identity ID, and the token $\mathsf{tok}_{\mathsf{ID}}$ for identity ID as inputs and picks two random elements r_1, r_2 from $\mathbb{Z}_p^*$. Then, it computes

$$C_1 = \mathsf{tok}_{\mathsf{ID}}^{r_1 \mathsf{H}(m)}, \quad C_2 = g_{\mathsf{ID}}^{r_1}, \quad C_3 = g^{r_2},$$
$$C_4 = (m \| r_1) \oplus \mathsf{H}_2(C_1 \| C_2 \| C_3 \| e(P_{pub}, g_{\mathsf{ID}})^{r_2})$$

where $g_{\mathsf{ID}} = \mathsf{H}_1(\mathsf{ID})$. Finally, it outputs a ciphertext $\text{CT} = (C_1, C_2, C_3, C_4)$.
- $\mathsf{Test}(\text{CT}_A, \text{CT}_B)$: It takes two ciphertexts $\text{CT}_A = (C_{A,1}, C_{A,2}, C_{A,3}, C_{A,4})$ and $\text{CT}_B = (C_{B,1}, C_{B,2}, C_{B,3}, C_{B,4})$ for identities ID_A and ID_B, respectively, as inputs. Check whether

$$e(C_{A,1}, C_{B,2}) = e(C_{B,1}, C_{A,2}).$$

If it holds, output 1. Otherwise, output 0.
- $\mathsf{Dec}(\text{CT}, d_{\mathsf{ID}}, \mathsf{tok}_{\mathsf{ID}})$: It takes a ciphertext $\text{CT} = (C_1, C_2, C_3, C_4)$, a decryption key d_{ID} and a token $\mathsf{tok}_{\mathsf{ID}}$ for user ID as inputs, and computes

$$m' \| r_1' = C_4 \oplus \mathsf{H}_2(C_1 \| C_2 \| C_3 \| e(C_3, d_{\mathsf{ID}})).$$

Then, check whether

$$C_1 = \mathsf{tok}_{\mathsf{ID}}^{r_1' \mathsf{H}(m')} \text{ and } C_2 = g_{\mathsf{ID}}^{r_1'}.$$

where $g_{\mathsf{ID}} = \mathsf{H}_1(\mathsf{ID})$. If both hold, return m'. Otherwise, return $\perp$.

3 Our Attack Against Wu et al.'s IBEET Scheme

In this section, we provide our attack algorithm against Wu et al.'s IBEET construction.

Description of Our Attack Algorithm. The description of our attack algorithm is as follows.

1. Once $\mathcal{A}$ receives a system public parameter, $\mathcal{A}$ issues an encryption oracle query with a message m and an identity ID. Then, it returns a ciphertext $\text{CT} = (C_1, C_2, C_3, C_4)$ of message m under identity ID such that
$$C_1 = \mathsf{tok}_{\mathsf{ID}}^{r_1 \mathsf{H}(m)}, \quad C_2 = g_{\mathsf{ID}}^{r_1}, \quad C_3 = g^{r_2},$$
$$C_4 = (m \| r_1) \oplus \mathsf{H}_2(C_1 \| C_2 \| C_3 \| e(P_{pub}, g_{\mathsf{ID}})^{r_2})$$
where $r_1, r_2 \in \mathbb{Z}_p^*$ are random elements chosen by the encryption algorithm and $g_{\mathsf{ID}} = \mathsf{H}_1(\mathsf{ID})$.
2. At the challenge phase, $\mathcal{A}$ submits a target identity ID^* and two messages m_0, m_1 of the same-length such that $\mathsf{H}(m_0) \neq \mathsf{H}(m_1)$. Then, $\mathcal{C}$ returns the challenge ciphertext $\text{CT}^*_{\mathsf{ID}^*,b} = (C_1^*, C_2^*, C_3^*, C_4^*)$ such that
$$C_1^* = \mathsf{tok}_{\mathsf{ID}^*}^{r_1^* \mathsf{H}(m_b)}, \quad C_2^* = g_{\mathsf{ID}^*}^{r_1^*}, \quad C_3^* = g^{r_2^*},$$
$$C_4^* = (m_b \| r_1^*) \oplus \mathsf{H}_2(C_1^* \| C_2^* \| C_3^* \| e(P_{pub}, g_{\mathsf{ID}^*})^{r_2^*})$$
where b is a random bit chosen by $\mathcal{C}$, $r_1^*, r_2^* \in \mathbb{Z}_p^*$ are random elements chosen by the encryption algorithm and $g_{\mathsf{ID}^*} = \mathsf{H}_1(\mathsf{ID}^*)$.
3. Once receiving the challenge ciphertext $\text{CT}^*_{\mathsf{ID}^*,b} = (C_1^*, C_2^*, C_3^*, C_4^*)$ from $\mathcal{C}$, $\mathcal{A}$ first computes
$$C_1' = (C_1^{\mathsf{H}(m)^{-1} \bmod p})^{\mathsf{H}(m_1)} \tag{1}$$
using the ciphertext $\text{CT} = (C_1, C_2, C_3, C_4)$ of message m obtained at Step 1. Then, $\mathcal{A}$ checks whether
$$e(C_1', C_2^*) \stackrel{?}{=} e(C_1^*, C_2)$$
If it holds, it returns 1. Otherwise, it returns 0.

Correctness of Our Attack Algorithm. The correctness of our attack algorithm is straightforward. First, from Eq. (1), we have
$$C_1' = (C_1^{\mathsf{H}(m)^{-1} \bmod p})^{\mathsf{H}(m_1)} = ((\mathsf{tok}_{\mathsf{ID}}^{r_1 \mathsf{H}(m)})^{\mathsf{H}(m)^{-1} \bmod p})^{\mathsf{H}(m_1)} = \mathsf{tok}_{\mathsf{ID}}^{r_1 \mathsf{H}(m_1)}.$$
Thus,
$$e(C_1', C_2^*) = (\mathsf{tok}_{\mathsf{ID}}^{r_1 \mathsf{H}(m_1)}, g_{\mathsf{ID}^*}^{r_1^*}) = e(g_{\mathsf{ID}}, g_{\mathsf{ID}^*})^{\beta r_1 r_1^* \mathsf{H}(m_1)}$$
since $\mathsf{tok}_{\mathsf{ID}} = g_{\mathsf{ID}}^{\beta}$. On the other hand,
$$e(C_1^*, C_2) = e(\mathsf{tok}_{\mathsf{ID}^*}^{r_1^* \mathsf{H}(m_b)}, g_{\mathsf{ID}}^{r_1}) = e(g_{\mathsf{ID}^*}, g_{\mathsf{ID}})^{\beta r_1 r_1^* \mathsf{H}(m_b)}$$
since $\mathsf{tok}_{\mathsf{ID}^*} = g_{\mathsf{ID}^*}^{\beta}$. Therefore, they are the same if $b = 1$ and different if $b = 0$ and so our attack algorithm outputs the correct answer with probability 1. We note that our attack algorithm succeeds regardless of whether $\mathsf{ID} = \mathsf{ID}^*$ or not.

4 Our Modification

Now, we present our modification of Wu et al.'s IBEET construction.

Building Blocks. We employ a keyed permutation and a MAC for our modification. Their definitions are as follows.

Definition 1 (Keyed Permutation [1]**).** *Let* $F : \{0,1\}^\kappa \times \{0,1\}^n \to \{0,1\}^n$ *be a length-preserving, keyed function, that is,* F *is a two input function where the first input is called the key and the second input is called just the input. We say that a keyed function* F *is a keyed permutation if for every key* $k \in \{0,1\}^\kappa$*, the function* $F_k(\cdot) := F(k, \cdot)$ *is one-to-one.*

Definition 2 (Message Authentication Code (MAC)). *A message authentication code* MAC *consists of the following three polynomial time algorithms:*

- $\mathsf{G}(\lambda)$*: On input a security parameter* λ*, it returns a secret key* K*.*
- $\mathsf{S}(K, m)$*: Given the secret key* K *and a message* m*, it returns a tag* T*.*
- $\mathsf{V}(K, m, T)$*: Given the secret key* K*, a message* m*, and a tag* T*, it returns 1 or 0.*

Note that we do not exploit the verification algorithm V in our modification, but we assume that the signing algorithm S is deterministic.

Description of Our Modification. The description of our modification is as follows:

- $\mathsf{Setup}(\lambda)$: It generates parameters p, $\mathbb{G}_1$, $\mathbb{G}_2$, $e : \mathbb{G}_1 \times \mathbb{G}_1 \to \mathbb{G}_2$, $\text{MSK} = \alpha$, and $P_{pub} = g^\alpha$ by the same manner as in Wu et al.'s setup algorithm. Choose a keyed permutation $F : \{0,1\}^\kappa \times \{0,1\}^n \to \{0,1\}^n$ for positive integers $\kappa = \kappa(\lambda)$ and $n = n(\lambda)$. Select a random value K_1 from $\{0,1\}^\kappa$. Generate a MAC scheme $\mathsf{MAC} = (\mathsf{G}, \mathsf{S}, \mathsf{V})$ and obtain K_2 by running $\mathsf{G}(\lambda)$. Set the master token key $\text{MTK} = (K_1, K_2)$. Generate three cryptographic hash functions

  $\mathsf{H} : \{0,1\}^t \to \{0,1\}^n$, $\mathsf{H}_1 : \{0,1\}^* \to \mathbb{G}_1$, and $\mathsf{H}_2 : \mathcal{T} \times \mathbb{G}_1 \times \mathbb{G}_2 \to \{0,1\}^{t+\ell}$,

  where t denotes the bit-length of messages, ℓ denotes the bit-length of randomness utilized in the encryption algorithm and $\mathcal{T}$ denotes the range of outputs of S. We remark that the image of H and the domain of H_2 are slightly modified from those of the original scheme. Finally, output a system public parameter

  $$\text{PP} = (\lambda, p, t, \ell, g, \mathbb{G}_1, \mathbb{G}_2, P_{pub}, e, F, \mathsf{MAC}, \mathsf{H}, \mathsf{H}_1, \mathsf{H}_2)$$

  and a pair of the master secret and master token keys (MSK, MTK).
- $\mathsf{Extract}(\mathsf{ID}, \text{MSK}, \text{MTK})$: While d_{ID} is generated by the same manner as in Wu et al.'s extract algorithm, $\mathsf{tok}_{\mathsf{ID}}$ is set to $\text{MTK} = (K_1, K_2)$, and it outputs $(d_{\mathsf{ID}}, \mathsf{tok}_{\mathsf{ID}})$.

- $\mathsf{Enc}(\text{PP}, m, \mathsf{ID}, \mathsf{tok}_{\mathsf{ID}})$: Given the system public parameter PP, a message m, an identity ID, and the token $\mathsf{tok}_{\mathsf{ID}} = (K_1, K_2)$ for identity ID as inputs, pick a random element r from $\mathbb{Z}_p^*$. Then, it computes

$$C_1 = F(K_1, \mathsf{H}(m)),\ C_2 = g^r,\ C_3 = (m\|r) \oplus \mathsf{H}_2(T\|C_2\|e(P_{pub}, g_{\mathsf{ID}})^r) \quad (2)$$

  where $T \leftarrow \mathsf{S}(K_2, C_1)$ and $g_{\mathsf{ID}} = \mathsf{H}_1(\mathsf{ID})$. Finally, it outputs a ciphertext $\text{CT} = (C_1, C_2, C_3)$.
- $\mathsf{Test}(\text{CT}_A, \text{CT}_B)$: On input two ciphertexts $\text{CT}_A = (C_{A,1}, C_{A,2}, C_{A,3})$ and $\text{CT}_B = (C_{B,1}, C_{B,2}, C_{B,3})$ for identities ID_A and ID_B, respectively, check whether $C_{A,1} = C_{B,1}$. If it holds, output 1. Otherwise, output 0.
- $\mathsf{Dec}(\text{CT}, d_{\mathsf{ID}}, \mathsf{tok}_{\mathsf{ID}})$: Given a ciphertext $\text{CT} = (C_1, C_2, C_3)$, a decryption key d_{ID} and a token $\mathsf{tok}_{\mathsf{ID}} = (K_1, K_2)$ for user ID as inputs, compute

$$m'\|r' = C_3 \oplus \mathsf{H}_2(T\|C_2\|e(C_2, d_{\mathsf{ID}})).$$

  where $T \leftarrow \mathsf{S}(K_2, C_1)$. Then, it checks whether $C_1 = F(K_1, \mathsf{H}(m'))$ and $C_2 = g^{r'}$. If both hold, return m'. Otherwise, return $\perp$.

Correctness of Our Modification. Let $\text{CT} = (C_1, C_2, C_3)$ be a valid ciphertext of message m with respect to identity ID, i.e., it satisfies Eq. (2) for some r. Then, for $T \leftarrow \mathsf{S}(K_2, C_1)$ with a deterministic algorithm S,

$$\begin{aligned} m'\|r_1' &= C_3 \oplus \mathsf{H}_2(T\|C_2\|e(C_2, d_{\mathsf{ID}})) \\ &= (m\|r) \oplus \mathsf{H}_2(T\|C_2\|e(P_{pub}, g_{\mathsf{ID}})^r) \oplus \mathsf{H}_2(T\|C_2\|e(C_2, d_{\mathsf{ID}})) = m\|r \end{aligned}$$

since $e(P_{pub}, g_{\mathsf{ID}})^r = e(g^\alpha, g_{\mathsf{ID}})^r = e(g^r, g_{\mathsf{ID}}^\alpha) = e(C_2, d_{\mathsf{ID}})$. Moreover, it holds both $C_1 = F(K_1, \mathsf{H}(m'))$ and $C_2 = g^{r'}$. Thus, our decryption algorithm returns m correctly.

Suppose that two valid ciphertexts $\text{CT}_A = (C_{A,1}, C_{A,2}, C_{A,3})$ and $\text{CT}_B = (C_{B,1}, C_{B,2}, C_{B,3})$ of messages m_A and m_B for identities ID_A and ID_B, respectively, are given. Then,

$$C_{A,1} = F(K_1, \mathsf{H}(m_A)) \text{ and } C_{B,1} = F(K_1, \mathsf{H}(m_B))$$

and so the test algorithm always outputs 1 if $m_A = m_B$ and outputs 0 if $m_A \neq m_B$ with overwhelming property when the exploited hash function H is collision-resistant. Therefore, our modification is correct.

Security Analysis of Our Modification. We note that our modification achieves the security requirement, which was claimed that the original We et al.'s scheme achieved, in the random oracle model if the BDH assumption holds, the exploited F is a strong pseudorandom permutation and the employed MAC scheme is existentially unforgeable under chosen message attack. Due to the space limitation, we relegate the formal security analysis to the full version [4].

5 Conclusion

In this paper, we presented an attack on the identity-based encryption scheme with equality test against insider attack, proposed by Wu et al. [7]. Then, we provided a modification of their scheme that achieves the weak indistinguishability under adaptive identity and chosen ciphertext attacks, which was claimed to be achieved in the original paper.

Acknowledgements. We would like to thank the authors of [7] and the anonymous reviewers of ACISP 2018 for their valuable comments and discussions. Hyung Tae Lee would also like to thank Jae Hong Seo for the helpful discussion about a keyed permutation in our modification. Hyung Tae Lee was supported by Basic Science Research Program through the National Research Foundation of Korea (NRF) funded by the Ministry of Science and ICT (No. NRF-2018R1C1B6008476). Huaxiong Wang was supported by Singapore Ministry of Education under Research Grant MOE2016-T2-2-014(S) and RG133/17-(S). Kai Zhang was supported by the Open Foundation of Co-Innovation Center for Information Supply & Assurance Technology (No. ADXXBZ201701).

References

1. Katz, J., Lindell, Y.: Introduction to Modern Cryptography. Chapman & Hall/CRC, London (2008)
2. Lee, H.T., Ling, S., Seo, J.H., Wang, H.: Semi-generic construction of public key encryption and identity-based encryption with equality test. Inf. Sci. **373**, 419–440 (2016)
3. Lee, H.T., Ling, S., Seo, J.H., Wang, H., Youn, T.: Public key encryption with equality test in the standard model. IACR Cryptol. ePrint Archive **2016**, 1182 (2016)
4. Lee, H.T., Wang, H., Zhang, K.: Security analysis and modification of ID-based encryption with equality test from ACISP 2017. IACR Cryptol. ePrint Archive **2018**, 369 (2018)
5. Ma, S.: Identity-based encryption with outsourced equality test in cloud computing. Inf. Sci. **328**, 389–402 (2016)
6. Wu, L., Zhang, Y., Choo, K.R., He, D.: Efficient and secure identity-based encryption scheme with equality test in cloud computing. Future Gener. Comp. Syst. **73**, 22–31 (2017)
7. Wu, T., Ma, S., Mu, Y., Zeng, S.: ID-based encryption with equality test against insider attack. In: Pieprzyk, J., Suriadi, S. (eds.) ACISP 2017. LNCS, vol. 10342, pp. 168–183. Springer, Cham (2017). https://doi.org/10.1007/978-3-319-60055-0_9

Improving the BKZ Reduction Algorithm by Quick Reordering Technique

Yuntao Wang[1,2,3](✉) and Tsuyoshi Takagi[2,3]

[1] Graduate School of Mathematics, Kyushu University, Fukuoka, Japan
y-wang@math.kyushu-u.ac.jp

[2] Graduate School of Information Science and Technology, The University of Tokyo, Tokyo, Japan
takagi@mist.i.u-tokyo.ac.jp

[3] CREST, Japan Science and Technology Agency, Kawaguchi, Japan

Abstract. In this paper, we propose a simple method to improve the BKZ algorithm with small blocksize. At first, we observe that reordering the LLL-reduced basis vectors by increasing norm will change the distribution of search nodes in the enumeration tree, which gives a chance to reduce the enumeration search nodes with non-negligible probability. Thus the runtime of enumeration algorithm is accelerated approximately by a factor of two. We explain this phenomenon from a theoretical point of view, which follows the Gama-Nguyen-Regev's analysis [6]. Then we apply this reordering technique on the BKZ algorithm and implement it in the open source library NTL. Our experimental results in dimensions 100–120 with blocksize 15–30 show that on LLL-reduced bases, our modified NTL-BKZ outputs a vector shorter than the original NTL-BKZ with probability 40%–46% with LLL Lovász constant $\delta_{LLL} = 0.99$. Furthermore, in the instances where the improved BKZ found a same or shorter vector, the runtime is up to 2.02 times faster when setting the blocksize $\beta = 25$ with $\delta_{LLL} = 0.99$.

Keywords: Lattice · BKZ reduction · Enumeration · GSA
Quick reordering technique

1 Introduction

Lattice-based cryptography is considered as one of the most competitive post-quantum candidates. The security of lattice-based cryptosystems is related to the hardness of some problems in lattice theory such as the shortest vector problem (SVP), the closest vector problem (CVP) and their variants. The evaluation for the asymptotic and the concrete hardness of these hard problems are required before these cryptosystems are adequate to the reality. There is a series of enumeration algorithms (ENUM) for solving SVP or approximate SVP directly. In 1994, Schnorr and Euchner proposed their enumeration algorithm (SE-ENUM) [12]. Besides, lattice reduction is one of the most remarkable

W. Susilo and G. Yang (Eds.): ACISP 2018, LNCS 10946, pp. 787–795, 2018.
https://doi.org/10.1007/978-3-319-93638-3_47

algorithms for lattice-based cryptanalysis. Namely lattice reduction runs in polynomial time on generating a "better" basis and find relatively short vectors, to solve SVP or appr-SVP. The LLL reduction algorithm due to Lenstra et al. is usually used to generate an almost orthogonal basis with shorter basis vectors [9]. In our work, we use a floating point version of LLL [10] which is implemented in the open source library NTL [13]. The well known BKZ reduction algorithm was proposed by Schnorr and Euchner in the same paper of SE-ENUM [12]. Generally, BKZ is a block model of Korkin-Zolotarev reduction in [8] and it is a hybrid algorithm of the LLL reduction and the SE-ENUM search algorithm. Moreover, some fast implementations of BKZ are given in some softwares such as Magma [2] and NTL [13].

Our Contributions. In our work, we propose a simple approach to improve the BKZ algorithm with small blocksize. We firstly apply the quick reordering technique (QRT) on the "LLL then SE-ENUM" for small dimensions from 10 to 30. It shows that with non-negligible probability p, the SE-ENUM search nodes can be reduced by more than 10% (upto 95.88% maximally and 47.57% on average). We then integrate QRT into the BKZ function implemented in NTL (NTL-BKZ). The experimental results in high dimensions (100–120) show that by a limit on the number of SE-ENUM search nodes, our modified NTL-BKZ (modi-NTL-BKZ) can output a shorter vector than the original NTL-BKZ with probability 40.91%–45.73% by setting blocksize from 15 to 30 and $\delta = 0.99$. Further, our modified algorithm is around 2 times faster than NTL-BKZ by setting the blocksize $\beta = 25$ when $\delta = 0.99$.

2 Preliminaries

A *lattice* L is generated by a *basis* B which is a set of linearly independent vectors $\mathbf{b}_1, \ldots, \mathbf{b}_n$ in $\mathbb{R}^m$ such that $L(\mathbf{b}_1, \ldots, \mathbf{b}_n) = \{\sum_{i=1}^{n} x_i \mathbf{b}_i, x_i \in \mathbb{Z}\}$. Here n is the *rank* of L and m is the *dimension* of L. The *fundamental domain* for L corresponding to this basis is the set $\mathcal{F}(\mathbf{b}_1, \ldots, \mathbf{b}_n) = \{t_1\mathbf{b}_1 + t_2\mathbf{b}_2 + \cdots + t_n\mathbf{b}_n : 0 \leq t_i < 1\}$. Then the volume of $\mathcal{F}(B)$ is called the *determinant* of L (or the *volume* of L) which is denoted by $\det(L)$ (or $\mathrm{vol}(L)$) and can be written by $\det(L) = \mathrm{vol}(L) = \sqrt{\det(B^\top B)}$ in symbols. A *shortest vector* of L is one of the $\lambda_1(L)$-length vectors. Given a lattice basis B, the *shortest vector problem* (SVP) is to find a shortest non-zero vector of $L(B)$.

Gram-Schmidt Orthogonalization (GSO). Given a lattice basis $B = (\mathbf{b}_1, \ldots, \mathbf{b}_n)$, we denote by $B^* = (\mathbf{b}_1^*, \ldots, \mathbf{b}_n^*)$ the associated *Gram-Schmidt orthogonal basis* which can be computed as: $\mathbf{b}_1^* = \mathbf{b}_1$ and $\mathbf{b}_i^* = \mathbf{b}_i - \sum_{j=1}^{i-1} \mu_{ij}\mathbf{b}_j^*$, for all $2 \leq i \leq n$ where $\mu_{ij} = \frac{<\mathbf{b}_i, \mathbf{b}_j^*>}{\|\mathbf{b}_j^*\|^2} (1 \leq j < i \leq n)$. The volume of $L(B)$ can also be calculated by $\mathrm{vol}(L(B)) = \prod_{i=1}^{n} \|\mathbf{b}_i^*\|$. Let $\pi_i : \mathbb{R}^n \mapsto span(\mathbf{b}_1, \ldots, \mathbf{b}_{i-1})^\perp$, $\pi_i(\mathbf{b}_k) = \mathbf{b}_k - \sum_{j=1}^{i-1} \mu_{ij}\mathbf{b}_j^* (1 \leq j < i \leq k \leq n)$ be the projection of $\mathbf{b}_k$ onto the orthogonal complement of $L(\mathbf{b}_1, \ldots, \mathbf{b}_{i-1})$.

Root Hermite Factor. We can evaluate the performance of reduction algorithms on n-dimensional lattice by the *root Hermite Factor* (rHF) [5] with $\mathrm{rHF}(\mathbf{b}_1, \ldots, \mathbf{b}_n) = (\|\mathbf{b}_1\|/\mathrm{vol}(L)^{1/n})^{1/n}$.

Gaussian Heuristic. Given a lattice L and a vector set S, we can estimate the number of points in $S \cap L$ approximately $\mathrm{vol}(S)/\mathrm{vol}(L)$, which is called the *Gaussian Heuristic*. By a "nice" set S, this heuristic can be proved in some cases.

LLL-Reduced Basis [9]. A basis $B = (\mathbf{b}_1, \ldots, \mathbf{b}_n) \in \mathbb{R}^{m \times n}$ is *LLL-reduced* if $|\mu_{i,j}| = \frac{|\mathbf{b}_i \cdot \mathbf{b}_j^*|}{\|\mathbf{b}_j^*\|^2} \leq 1/2$ and $\|\mathbf{b}_i^*\|^2 \geq (\delta - \mu_{i,i-1}^2)\|\mathbf{b}_{i-1}^*\|^2$ for all $1 \leq j < i \leq n$ and *Lovász constant* $3/4 \leq \delta < 1$. In this paper, we call it "LLL then SE-ENUM" model when using the LLL algorithm [9] as a preprocessing for SE-ENUM.

Geometric Series Assumption (GSA). The *geometric series assumption* (GSA) [11] says that the norms of GSO vectors $\|\mathbf{b}_i^*\|$ in the LLL-type reduced basis decline geometrically with quotient q such as $\|\mathbf{b}_i^*\|^2/\|\mathbf{b}_1\|^2 = q^{i-1}$ for $i = 1, \ldots, n$ and $q \in [3/4, 1)$. Here q is called the *GSA constant*. In our work, we use linear *Least Squares Fitting* (LSF) to calculate the slope of GSO vectors.

Quick Reordering Technique (QRT). We reorder the output reduced basis vectors by their increasing or decreasing norms in our method. Indeed, we use the classical *quicksort algorithm* (denoted by QRT in this paper) published by Tony Hoare in 1962 [7]. To reorder n items, QRT takes $O(n \log n)$ comparisons averagely and often faster than other $O(n \log n)$ algorithms [14]. Hence, the complexity of QRT is negligible, comparing to $2^{O(n^2)}$ of SE-ENUM.

SE-ENUM Algorithm [12]. We present the basic idea of Schnorr-Euchner's *enumeration algorithm* (SE-ENUM) for solving SVP [12]. Given a lattice $L \subset \mathbb{R}^m$ with basis $B = (\mathbf{b}_1, \ldots, \mathbf{b}_n)$, the inputs of SE-ENUM are GSO coefficients $(\mu_{i,j})_{1 \leq j \leq i \leq n}$, the square norms $\|\mathbf{b}_1^*\|^2, \ldots, \|\mathbf{b}_n^*\|^2$ of B^*, and an initial search bound R. The output is a shortest vector $\mathbf{v} = \sum_{i=1}^{n} u_i \mathbf{b}_i$, where u_i are integer coefficients which SE-ENUM searches in a tree. The Gaussian heuristic estimates the number of nodes at depth k is:

$$H_k(R) = \frac{1}{2} \cdot \frac{V_k(R)}{\mathrm{vol}(\pi_{n+1-k}(L))} = \frac{1}{2} \cdot \frac{V_k(R)}{\prod_{i=n+1-k}^{n} \|\mathbf{b}_i^*\|}. \tag{1}$$

Then the heuristic number of total SE-ENUM search nodes is $N = \sum_{k=1}^{n} H_k(R)$. Due to [6], $H_k(R)$ is maximal around the middle depth $k \approx n/2$ (see an example in Fig. 1). If the bases are LLL-reduced, the bound on N is at most $2^{O(n^2)}$.

BKZ Algorithm [12]. The *BKZ algorithm* was originally proposed as a way of computing bases that are almost β-reduced [12]. For a given basis $B = (\mathbf{b}_1, \ldots, \mathbf{b}_n)$, one sets a proper blocksize $\beta \geq 2$, which impacts both the runtime and the output quality. Assume j is the first index of each local block $B_{[j, \min(j+\beta-1, n)]}$. BKZ iteratively performs the LLL reduction and the SE-ENUM algorithm on each local block for j from 1 to $n-1$. We call it "1 round" from $j = 1$ to $j = n-1$. For each "LLL then SE-ENUM" subroutine, it outputs linear coefficients to make a shortest vector in the local projected lattice. The execution stops when no updating of GSO vectors occurs during a tour. Further details may be found in [12].

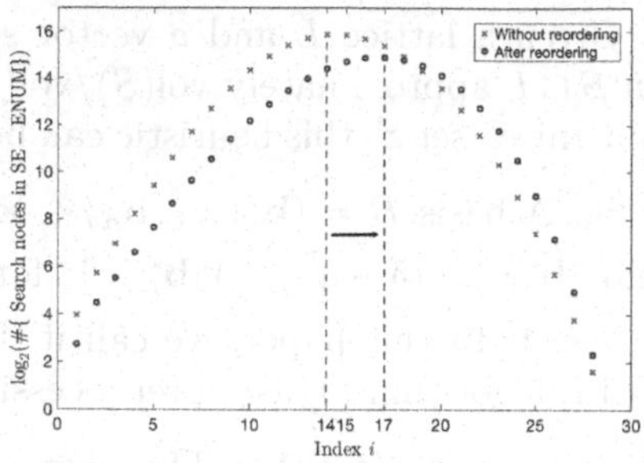

Fig. 1. Number of nodes at each level in SE-ENUM tree (average value of 100 cases of 28-dimensional random lattices).

3 Our Proposed Method

3.1 SE-ENUM with Quick Reordering Technique

We use a Quick Reordering Technique (QRT) to process the LLL-reduced basis before inputting them into SE-ENUM. Firstly we reorder the sequence of vectors of the LLL-reduced basis B by their norms:

$$(\mathbf{b}'_1, \ldots, \mathbf{b}'_n) = Reorder(\mathbf{b}_1, \ldots, \mathbf{b}_n),$$

while in the case of increasing order: $\|\mathbf{b}'_1\| \leq \|\mathbf{b}'_2\| \leq \cdots \leq \|\mathbf{b}'_{n-1}\| \leq \|\mathbf{b}'_n\|$, or the decreasing order: $\|\mathbf{b}'_1\| \geq \|\mathbf{b}'_2\| \geq \cdots \geq \|\mathbf{b}'_{n-1}\| \geq \|\mathbf{b}'_n\|$.

Experiment Overview. We run LLL and SE-ENUM on bases of dimensions from 10 to 30, which can be used as efficient blocksize for preprocessing in BKZ. For each dimension, we generate 10,000 random lattice bases (from seed 0 to 9,999) from the TU Darmstadt SVP Challenge [4]. Our implementation is using C language and running on Intel(R) Xeon(R) CPU E5-2697 v2 @ 2.70GHz. Here is a simple enunciation of our experiment procedure.

1. We process the original bases by LLL reduction algorithm using different Lovász constants $\delta \in \{0.80, 0.85, 0.90, 0.95, 0.99\}$.
2. Then for each lattice basis, we reorder their vectors by increasing and decreasing norm orders using QRT respectively.
3. Finally, we use SE-ENUM to find a shortest vector of each lattice by three different bases: original without reordering, increasing norm order, and decreasing norm order. For the sake of fairness, the initial SE-ENUM search bound is the same as the first vector's norm in the original basis.

Experimental Results. We calculate the probability that the average of $\|\mathbf{b}^*_{\lceil n/2 \rfloor -1}\|$, $\|\mathbf{b}^*_{\lceil n/2 \rfloor}\|$, $\|\mathbf{b}^*_{\lceil n/2 \rfloor +1}\|$ is bended larger after reordering the basis. The increasing reordering model can derive a much higher probability to bend the bases and reduce the amount of SE-ENUM search nodes successfully. Thus we will use the **increasing QRT** in the following work and just write it as

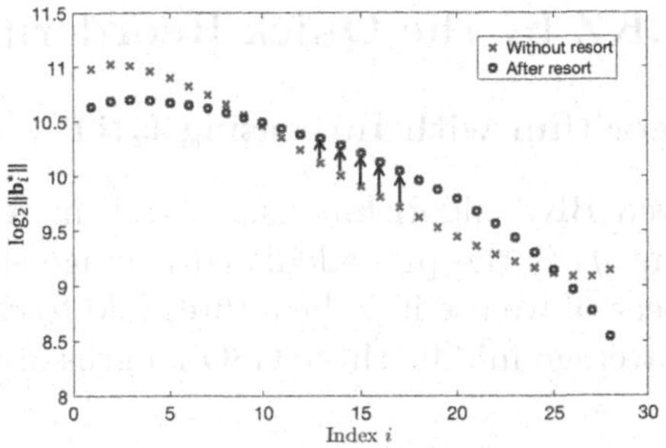

Fig. 2. Distribution of increasing QRT applied $\|\mathbf{b}_i^*\|$ (average value of 100 cases of 28-dimensional random lattices).

QRT if there is no specification. We count all of the cases including all of the dimensions but separated by $\delta = (0.80, 0.85, 0.90, 0.95, 0.99)$ in our experiments, the maximal value of acceleration by applying QRT on SE-ENUM are $(95.88\%, 91.91\%, 84.50\%, 77.65\%, 72.55\%)$ and respectively the average values are $(47.57\%, 32.83\%, 23.49\%, 18.31\%, 13.37\%)$. On the other side, the failed case may also increase the SE-ENUM search nodes by almost double. Therefore we should carefully handle the threshold when we adapt QRT to BKZ improvement in Sect. 4.

3.2 Theoretical Estimation

The index of maximal search nodes is slightly shifted (by 3 in the 28-dimensional example in Fig. 1), when the LLL-reduced basis is reordered. Moreover, the dominant number of search nodes are significantly reduced, such that the total search nodes are reduced by around 47.57% in average. We explain this phenomenon using the GH and the GSA of input GSO basis. According to Gama-Nguyen-Regev [6]'s analysis on the Eq. (1) from GH, the total SE-ENUM search nodes N is

$$N = \sum_{k=1}^{n} H_k(R) \approx \sum_{k=1}^{n} q^{(n-k)k/2} 2^{O(n)}. \tag{2}$$

Here q is the GSA constant. Our experimental results show that there is a non-negligible probability that q becomes smaller by "bending" the GSO elements $\log(\|\mathbf{b}_i^*\|)$ "flatter" due to the QRT procedure. From Fig. 2 we can see that after reordering the input basis, the associated $\log(\|\mathbf{b}_i^*\|)$ is bended "taller" around the centre index and "lower" at two ends. Namely, QRT can change the GSA distribution in the middle indices. According to the Eq. (2), the reduction of q can greatly influence the total number of nodes in the SE-ENUM tree.

4 Improving BKZ by the Quick Reordering Technique

4.1 The BKZ Algorithm with Increasing QRT

We show the improved BKZ algorithm using QRT in Algorithm 1. Since the additive GSA constant q_β is the pre-calculated average slope in the succeeded cases using QRT in Sect. 3, we use it to be a threshold to call QRT for optimization. At step 11, the average middle three GSO lengths are computed as follows respectively.

Algorithm 1. The BKZ algorithm with increasing QRT.

Input: A basis $B = (\mathbf{b}_1, \ldots, \mathbf{b}_n)$, the blocksize $\beta \in \{2, \ldots, n\}$, the GSO elements μ and $\|\mathbf{b}_1^*\|^2, \ldots, \|\mathbf{b}_n^*\|^2$, success slope q_β from sec. 3.
Output: A BKZ-reduced basis B^{QRT} for $L(B)$.
1: $z \leftarrow 0$; $j \leftarrow 0$; $\mathrm{LLL}(\mathbf{b}_1, \ldots, \mathbf{b}_n, \mu)$;
2: **while** $z < n-1$ **do**
3: $j \leftarrow (j \bmod (n-1)) + 1$; $k \leftarrow \min(j + \beta - 1, n)$;
4: $h \leftarrow \min(k+1, n)$; $\beta' = k - j + 1 = min(\beta, n - j + 1)$;
5: **if** $\beta' \geq 10$ **then**
6: Compute the slope $q_{curr}$of current GSO vector lengths by LSF;
7: **end if**
8: **if** $q_{curr} < q'_\beta$ **then**
9: Compute $\pi_j(L'_\beta) = \pi_j(\mathbf{b}_j), \pi_j(\mathbf{b}_{j+1}), \ldots, \pi_j(\mathbf{b}_k)$;
10: Reorder $\pi_j(L'_\beta)$ to increasing norm order by QRT;
11: Compute the average norm $AveGSO_{\pi_j(L'_\beta)}$ (and$AveGSO_{local(\mathbf{b}_i^*)}$) of middle three GSO vectors of $\pi_j(L'_\beta)$ (and local block respectively);
12: **if** $AveGSO_{\pi_j(L'_\beta)} > AveGSO_{local(\mathbf{b}_i^*)}$ **then**
13: Replace the local basis $(\mathbf{b}_j, \ldots, \mathbf{b}_k) = \mathrm{QRT}(\mathbf{b}_j, \ldots, \mathbf{b}_k)$;
14: Update the GSO informations by the reordered one: $(\mu_{[j,k]}, \|\mathbf{b}_j^*\|^2, \ldots, \|\mathbf{b}_k^*\|^2) = \mathrm{QRT}((\mu_{[j,k]}, \|\mathbf{b}_j^*\|^2, \ldots, \|\mathbf{b}_k^*\|^2))$;
15: **end if**
16: **end if**
17: $\mathbf{u} \leftarrow \mathrm{SE-ENUM}(\mu_{[j,k]}, \|\mathbf{b}_j^*\|^2, \ldots, \|\mathbf{b}_k^*\|^2)$;
18: **if** $\mathbf{u} \neq (1, 0, \ldots, 0)$ **then**
19: $z \leftarrow 0$; $\mathrm{LLL}(\mathbf{b}_1, \ldots, \sum_{i=j}^{k} u_i \mathbf{b}_i \mathbf{b}_j, \ldots, \mathbf{b}_h, \mu)$;
20: **else**
21: $z \leftarrow z + 1$; $\mathrm{LLL}(\mathbf{b}_1, \ldots, \mathbf{b}_h, \mu)$;
22: **end if**
23: **end while**

$$AveGSO_{\pi_j(L'_\beta)} = (\|\pi_i(\mathbf{b}_{j+\lceil\beta'/2\rfloor-1})\| + \|\pi_i(\mathbf{b}_{j+\lceil\beta'/2\rfloor})\| + \|\pi_i(\mathbf{b}_{j+\lceil\beta'/2\rfloor+1})\|)/3$$
$$AveGSO_{local(\mathbf{b}_i^*)} = (\|\mathbf{b}^*_{j+\lceil\beta'/2\rfloor-1}\| + \|\mathbf{b}^*_{j+\lceil\beta'/2\rfloor}\| + \|\mathbf{b}^*_{j+\lceil\beta'/2\rfloor+1}\|)/3$$

The GSO informations (μ_{iq} and $\|\mathbf{b}_i^*\|(j \leq q < i \leq k)$) will be updated at step 14, if the reordered GSO vectors qualify convex in the middle part at step 13.

We denote by "NTL-BKZ" the original floating point version BKZ_XD in NTL [13] and denote by "QRT-BKZ" the adaptation with QRT. Our experiments run on $n = \{100, 102, 104, \ldots, 120\}$-dimensional bases generated from TU Darmstadt SVP Challenge [4] (100 samples for each dimension). We process all of the bases by NTL-BKZ and preserve the necessary information in each i–th case $1 \leq i \leq 100$: the total number of SE-ENUM search nodes N_{ni}; the root Hermite Factor rHF(L_{ni}) when the last $\|\mathbf{b}_1\|_{ni}$ is updated; the SE-ENUM search nodes N_{ni} and the run time t'_{ni} until the last update. Similarly, we denote the SE-ENUM search nodes in QRT-BKZ version by N_{ni}^{QRT} and denote the run time by t_{ni}^{QRT}. For the sake of fairness, we set three terminating conditions:

(1) if the total number of SE-ENUM search nodes $N_{ni}^{QRT} > N_{ni}$;
(2) if the processing rHF of QRT-BKZ rHF(L_{ni}^{QRT}) < rHF(L_{ni});
(3) if there is no update for one tour (as the condition at step 2 in Algorithm 1).

We define the probability $p_{succLen}$ that our QRT-BKZ outputs a smaller rHF(L) (namely a shorter first vector) successfully than that from NTL-BKZ.

4.2 Experimental Results

4.2.1 Deriving a Smaller rHF by Probability $p_{succLen}$

We calculate all of the cases differing from the balocksize β and the δ used in LLL subroutine. The results are given in Table 1. For the blocksize from 15 to 25, the success probability $p_{succLen}$ is around 45%. Simultaneously, the $p_{succLen}$ is generally descending by increasing the blocksize.

Table 1. The rate of getting shorter $\mathbf{b}_1$ by QRT-BKZ than the original NTL-BKZ output, while QRT-BKZ is bounded by the same SE-ENUM serch nodes as latter.

β	$p_{succLen}(\delta = 0.90)$	$p_{succLen}(\delta = 0.95)$	$p_{succLen}(\delta = 0.99)$
15	44.64%	48.45%	**45.73%**
20	45.45%	43.82%	**45.55%**
25	41.82%	38.73%	**40.55%**
30	17.64%	34.36%	**41.45%**

4.2.2 Reducing the SE-ENUM Subroutine Cost

Further, we give the average runtime for each cases in Table 2. From this table we can see that the improved QRT-BKZ are 2.02 and 1.92 faster than the original NTL-BKZ, when setting the blocksize $\beta = 25$ and 30 respectively with $\delta = 0.99$. In practice, we suggest using blocksize $20 \leq \beta \leq 30$ and set LLL Lovász constant $\delta \geq 0.95$ in QRT-BKZ.

Table 2. Average runtime of NTL-BKZ and QRT-BKZ working on $n \in \{100, 102, \ldots, 120\}$-dimensional bases with $\delta \in \{0.90, 0.95, 0.99\}$ and $\beta \in \{20, 25, 30\}$. The QRT-BKZ performs better than NTL-BKZ for bigger δ, e.x. QRT-BKZ can reach around 2 times faster than NTL-BKZ for $\delta = 0.99$.

Runtime[*sec*]	$\delta = 0.90$			$\delta = 0.95$			$\delta = 0.99$		
	$\beta = 20$	$\beta = 25$	$\beta = 30$	$\beta = 20$	$\beta = 25$	$\beta = 30$	$\beta = 20$	$\beta = 25$	$\beta = 30$
$T_{\mathrm{NTL-BKZ}}$	7.79	15.98	80.60	10.69	31.33	335.29	22.67	**310.53**	**8911.02**
$T_{\mathrm{QRT-BKZ}}$	7.01	13.21	63.64	8.88	20.99	198.64	15.29	**153.39**	**4651.55**

5 Conclusion

In this work, firstly we introduced the quick reordering technique (QRT) applied in the "LLL then SE-ENUM" model to reduce the SE-ENUM search nodes by non-negligible probability. Our experimental results show that the reduced rate depends on the input basis quality. Then we improved the BKZ algorithm with QRT for small blocksize and modified the BKZ function in the open source library NTL (QRT-BKZ). Within some fairness limitations, the QRT-BKZ with small blocksize can output a smaller root Hermite factor than that of the original NTL-BKZ, with probability 40.91%–45.73% by setting $\delta = 0.99$. Further, for the instances that QRT-BKZ found a same or shorter vector, the runtime is up to 2.02 times faster than the original NTL-BKZ. Since our proposed QRT gives an improvement on BKZ with small blocksize, it is expectant to apply the QRT in the preprocessing subroutine of other algorithms such as BKZ 2.0 [3] or progressive BKZ [1]. Also a precise theoretic analysis for the phenomenon should be given in the future works.

Acknowledgement. We thank Dr. Atsushi Takayasu and Thomas Wunderer for their helpful comments. This work was supported by JSPS KAKENHI Grant Number JP17J01987 and JST CREST Grant Number JPMJCR14D6, Japan.

References

1. Aono, Y., Wang, Y., Hayashi, T., Takagi, T.: Improved progressive BKZ algorithms and their precise cost estimation by sharp simulator. In: Fischlin, M., Coron, J.-S. (eds.) EUROCRYPT 2016. LNCS, vol. 9665, pp. 789–819. Springer, Heidelberg (2016). https://doi.org/10.1007/978-3-662-49890-3_30
2. Bosma, W., Cannon, J., Playoust, C.: The magma algebra system I: the user language. J. Symbolic Comput. **24**(3), 235–265 (1997). http://magma.maths.usyd.edu.au/magma/
3. Chen, Y., Nguyen, P.Q.: BKZ 2.0: better lattice security estimates. In: Lee, D.H., Wang, X. (eds.) ASIACRYPT 2011. LNCS, vol. 7073, pp. 1–20. Springer, Heidelberg (2011). https://doi.org/10.1007/978-3-642-25385-0_1
4. Darmstadt, T.: SVP challenge (2017). https://www.latticechallenge.org/svp-challenge

5. Gama, N., Nguyen, P.Q.: Predicting lattice reduction. In: Smart, N.(ed.) EUROCRYPT 2008. LNCS, vol. 4965, pp. 31–51. Springer, Heidelberg (2008). https://doi.org/10.1007/978-3-540-78967-3_3
6. Gama, N., Nguyen, P.Q., Regev, O.: Lattice enumeration using extreme pruning. In: Gilbert, H. (ed.) EUROCRYPT 2010. LNCS, vol. 6110, pp. 257–278. Springer, Heidelberg (2010). https://doi.org/10.1007/978-3-642-13190-5_13
7. Hoare, C.A.R.: Quicksort. Comput. J. **5**(1), 10–16 (1962)
8. Korkine, A., Zolotareff, G.: Sur les forms quadratiques. Math. Ann. **6**, 581–583 (1873)
9. Lenstra, A., Lenstra, H., Lovász, L.: Factoring polynomials with rational coefficients. Math. Ann. **261**, 515–534 (1982)
10. Schnorr, C.: A more efficient algorithm for lattice basis reduction. J. Algorithms **9**(1), 47–62 (1988)
11. Schnorr, C.P.: Lattice reduction by random sampling and birthday methods. In: Alt, H., Habib, M. (eds.) STACS 2003. LNCS, vol. 2607, pp. 145–156. Springer, Heidelberg (2003). https://doi.org/10.1007/3-540-36494-3_14
12. Schnorr, C., Euchner, M.: Lattice basis reduction: improved practical algorithms and solving subset sum problems. Math. Program. **66**, 181–199 (1994)
13. Shoup, V.: NTL, a library for doing number theory (2017). http://www.shoup.net/ntl/
14. Skiena, S.: The Algorithm Design Manual, 2nd edn. Springer, London (2008)

ANTSdroid: Automatic Malware Family Behaviour Generation and Analysis for Android Apps

Yeali S. Sun[1(✉)], Chien-Chun Chen[1], Shun-Wen Hsiao[2], and Meng Chang Chen[3]

[1] Department of Information Management, National Taiwan University, Taipei, Taiwan
sunny@ntu.edu.tw
[2] Department of Information Management, National Cheng-chi University, Taipei, Taiwan
[3] Institute of Information Science, Academia Sinica, Taipei, Taiwan

Abstract. Malware developers often use various obfuscation techniques to generate polymorphic and metamorphic versions of malwares. Keeping up with new variants and creating signatures for each individuals in a timely fashion has been an important problem but tedious works that anti-virus companies face all the time. It motivates us the idea of no more dancing with variants. In this paper, we aim to find a malware family's main characteristic operations directly related to its intent. We propose global execution sequence alignment and segmentation algorithms to generate the execution stage chart of a malware family which presents a simple and easy-to-understand overview of the lifecycle as well as common and different operations that individual variants perform at a stage. We also present an automated dynamic Android malware profiling and family security analysis system in which we focus on the execution sequences of sensitive and permission-related API calls referred to as motifs of variants of malware family. To achieve the goal, we modify Android Debug Bridge (ADB) tool to add on several new features including enabling the recording of parameters and return value of an API call, the support of UID-based profiling to capture all the processes and threads to gain complete understanding of the activities of target malware app, and per thread trace generation. Finally, we use real-world dataset to validate the proposed system and methods. The generated family stage chart and motifs can provide security analysts semantics-rich understanding of what and how a malware family is designed and implemented. The main characteristic API call sequences of malware families can be used as signatures for effective and efficient malware detection in the future.

Keywords: Android malware family behaviour analysis
Execution sequence alignment and segmentation · Dynamic analysis
Android security

W. Susilo and G. Yang (Eds.): ACISP 2018, LNCS 10946, pp. 796–804, 2018.
https://doi.org/10.1007/978-3-319-93638-3_48

1 Introduction

Smartphones have become a vital part of our lives. Recent reports indicate that there is an arising proliferation of installs of unwanted software by commercial pay-per-install (PPI) where software developers bundle third-party apps as part of their installation process in return for a payout [1]. Many malicious software such as Trojan, backdoor and aggressive adware, are thus downloaded into user's device. Meantime, we observe that malware developers often use various obfuscation techniques to generate polymorphic and metamorphic versions of malwares. As a result, variants of a malware family generally exhibit resembling behaviour. Most importantly, they possess certain common essential codes so to achieve the same designed purpose.

In this paper we propose a novel automatic dynamic Android malware profiling and family security analysis system which focuses on execution sequences of the sensitive and permission-related API calls referred to as motifs of the variants of a malware family. We propose a global execution sequence alignment algorithm and a segmentation algorithm for malware family behaviour analysis to find the common and main characteristic motifs of the family.

In the past, a number of methods have been proposed in malware behaviour analysis. Basically there are two approaches: static and dynamic analysis. For static analysis, the subjects are mainly the APK file, DEX file, AndroidManifest.xml file and the permissions used by apps. By analyzing the information embedded in the files (such as permissions used [2–6] and taint information [7, 8]), researchers could assess the threat of an app. On the other hand, the dynamic analysis tools collect runtime execution information (e.g., system calls and API calls) [9–13] in a controlled environment to profile and examine the behaviour of an app. Different from these works, this paper focuses on automated generation of Android malware family's common and main characteristic security-related API call sequences from the filtered execution traces of its variants. The generated common or characteristic API call sequences of malware families can be used as signatures for effective malware detection in the future.

Our contributions include (1) designing and implementing an automated profiling and family behaviour analysis system for Android apps; (2) modifying Android Debug Bridge (ADB) tool to add on new features including enabling the recording of parameters and return value of an API call, support of UID-based profiling mode to capture all the processes and threads spawned from the main process to gain complete understanding of the activities of target malware app, and per thread trace generation; (3) compilation of a set of sensitive and permission-related APIs essential and necessary to capture security related activities of apps; (4) design and implementation of a global execution sequence alignment algorithm and a segmentation algorithm to generate the execution stage chart of a malware family which presents a simple and easy-to-understand overview of the lifecycle as well as common and different operations of individual variants at each stage; and (5) using real dataset to validate the proposed system to identify common and main characteristic operations (API call sequences) of malware families for effective detection use.

The remainder of the paper is organized as follows. In Sect. 2, we briefly review related works of Android malware behaviour analysis. In Sect. 3, we describe the design and implementation of the proposed automated profiling and family behaviour analysis system. In Sect. 4 we take an Android malware dataset to validate the proposed system and algorithms. Finally, Sect. 5 gives the conclusion.

2 Related Work

Barrera et al. [3] use self-organizing map to analyze the permission-based security model of Android. Pscout [4] discusses the relationship between the permissions and the Java APIs. VetDroid [5] is a dynamic analysis platform that can reveal how apps use permissions to access sensitive system resources, and how these acquired resources are further utilized by the app. Appsplayground [6] performs dynamic analysis in an Android emulator based on taint tracing of privacy-sensitive information, sensitive API monitoring and kernel-level tracking to identify known exploits and unwanted functionality. Apposcopy [7] focuses on static taint analysis of inter-component call graph for malware family classification. TaintDroid [8] adopts the taint analysis technique and provides a system-wide dynamic taint tracking system capable of tracking multiple sources of sensitive data.

Peiravian et al. [9] use static analysis to extract permissions and API calls of Android apps and apply machine learning techniques to detect malicious Android apps. DroidAPIMiner [10] extracts malware features at the API level, and adopts machine learning method to classify APIs used by malicious and benign apps, as well as those in common use. Droidmat [11] also applies machine learning algorithms on the features in app's manifest file and the API calls to distinguish Android malware. DroidScope [12] employs virtual machine introspection (VMI) technique to inspect an Android app in a virtual machine. In CopperDroid [13], the authors also apply VMI technique to perform system call-centric analysis and generate detailed behavioural profiles that abstract a large stream of low-level system calls into concise, high-level semantics. However, these works do not pay attention to the thread structure of an app and Java API call sequences as we do.

3 System Design

In our proposed dynamic malware profiling and family behaviour analysis system, the first step is to profile the execution of a target malware app. The main issue here is to determine what information to record so that the trace contains sufficiently detailed information without missing any suspicious or malicious operations. Meantime we also do not want every detail to introduce a lot of unnecessary noises. Figure 1 presents the architecture of the proposed profiling and family behaviour analysis system. The profiling and analysis process consists of three phases.

3.1 Generate All_APIs Execution Trace per Thread

We first make use of the Android SDK command "am profile" to obtain the initial trace for an app. However, this command only provides the class name, method name, thread name and parameter type. We modify the Android Debug Bridge (ADB) code to add on several new features: (*a*) enabling the recording of parameters and return value of an API call; (*b*) changing the PID-based profiling mode to UID-based so to capture all the processes and threads spawned from the main process to have complete view of the activities of target app; and (*c*) separation and generation of API call trace per thread.

Broadcast Messages: Triggering Malware Behaviour. In dynamic analysis, how to trigger most target malware behaviour is an issue. Here, we implement a broadcast message mechanism in our profiling system to ensure behaviour of a malware APK would be triggered as much as possible. In our experiments, 29 out of 49 malware families monitor the BOOT_COMPLETED event and 21 families listen to the SMS_RECEIVED event. It is also observed that most malware apps register multiple events. By doing so, we raise the activation rate of service components from 0.009 to 0.74 in the experiments.

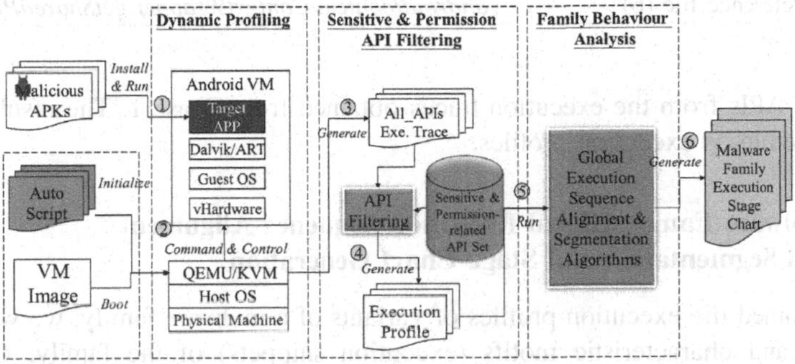

Fig. 1. The architecture of the Android app profiling and family behaviour analysis system.

3.2 Filtering for Sensitive and Permission-Related APIs

The trace obtained from Phase 1 include all APIs invoked in the app's execution. Because not all of them are relevant to suspicious or malicious activities, we thus focus on APIs that require user permission to invoke and APIs that are related to sensitive actions.

APIs Requiring Permissions. Because Google does not provide official specification documentation of the permission requirements for all APIs, to find out permission-required APIs, we implement a program which crawls Android Developer Website [14] in April 2016 and find 4382 classes, 35033 APIs and 135 permissions. Among them 265 APIs require permissions and only 36 of them are published on the website. The others are commonly referred to as undocumented APIs. In PScout [4] the authors develop a tool to extract the permission specification from four versions of the Android OS source codes (2.2 to 4.0) and compiled a list of permission-API mappings. From them, we focus on a selected set of 2456 APIs with 40 distinct permissions.

Sensitive APIs. In addition to APIs requiring permissions, we also identify 530 APIs whose uses require no permissions but are often invoked by malware [10, 15]. They are classified into nine use categories as shown in Table 1. The APIs totalled 2986, are used as the set of sensitive and permission-related APIs in this work to filter out

Table 1. The set of sensitive APIs.

Category (API count)	APIs with no permission required
File management (440)	*java/io/File, DataOutputStream, DataInputStream, etc.*
Java reflection (3)	*java/lang/Class.getName, forName, getMethod*
Execute command (2)	*java/lang/Runtime.exec, getRuntime*
Encryption/decryption (3)	*javax/crypto/Cipher.getInstance, doFinal*
Code loading (3)	*dalvik/system/DexClassLoader.loadClass, <init>, PathClassLoader.<init>*
String manipulation (4)	**java/lang/StringBuffer.append, subString, java/lang/StringBuilder.append, subString*
Database query (65)	*android/content/CursorWrapper (40), android/content/ContentProvider (24)*
Common network library & network-related API (4)	*org/apache/http/impl/client/AbstractHttpClient.execute, org/apache/http/client/utils/URLEncodedUtils.encode*
Shared preference file (6)	*android/content/ContextWrapper.getSharedPreference*

irrelevant APIs from the execution traces obtained from Phase 1. The resulting traces are referred to as execution profiles.

3.3 Malware Family Global Execution Sequence Alignment and Segmentation and Stage Chart Generation

Once obtained the execution profiles of variants of a malware family, we want to find common and characteristic motifs (execution snippets) of the family. Consider a malware family F_M with variants $\{v_1, v_2, \ldots, v_N\}$ and their execution profiles $\{P_1, P_2, \ldots P_N\}$. We design and develop a Global API call Sequence Alignment algorithm called API_GSA. In the algorithm, we first randomly select an execution profile as the baseline denoted as P(B). Pairwise global sequence alignment is then performed for each execution profile with the baseline. The algorithm is designed to align every API call in each execution profile to find the best matches so the similarities of the two profiles can be optimized. A segmentation algorithm is also developed to segment the matrix of aligned API call sequences into *stages* and produce family execution stage chart. From it, we now have complete view of what individual variants perform at a stage. Most importantly from the chart one can easily identify common stages where all variants have the same motifs, i.e., perform identical call sequences. By concatenating motifs of all common stages we obtain the common execution sequence of the family.

4 Evaluation

Our automated Android malware app profiling and family behaviour analysis system is built on QEMU and KVM. The physical machine has an Intel i7-3770S 3.1 GHz quad-core CPU with 8 GB RAM running Ubuntu 14.04. We take a dataset of ten families of 2568 malware samples from the Drebin Project [16]. However, in our experiments, not all samples are runnable.

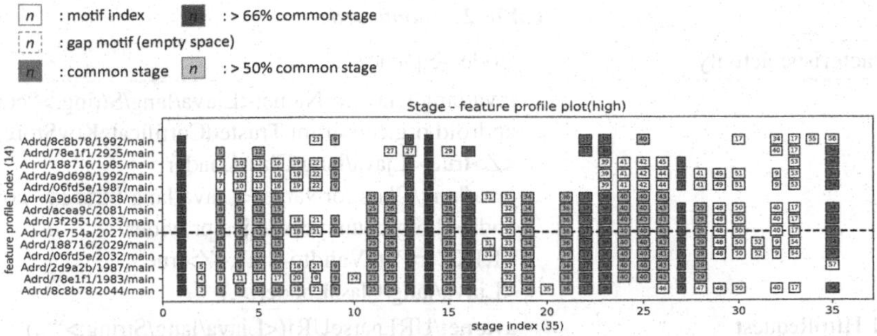

Fig. 2. The execution stage chart of a cluster (14 main threads).

Characteristic Security API Sequence Analysis. First, we show that our selected sensitive and permission related API set is sufficient to reveal major characteristic activities of a malware family. Due to the limit of pages, we take malware family ADRD as an example for illustration. ADRD is a Trojan family and one of its main characteristic behaviour is to steal device information and periodically send the data out. In the Drebin dataset, there are 25 runnable variant samples labelled as family ADRD. They all create 64 processes where a sample may spawn zero to three child processes in addition to the main process, and 94 threads. We apply UPGMA, an agglomerative hierarchical clustering method to roughly classify their operations, then run the proposed global execution sequence alignment and segmentation algorithms for in-depth characteristic behaviour analysis of each cluster. Figure 2 presents the generated execution stage chart of one of the resulting cluster. In Table 2, we present a mapping of technical descriptions of ADRD family and the main characteristic API calls identified in our family behaviour analysis. One main feature such as retrieving IMSI and IMEI appear in most variants. An interesting finding here is the set up app's activation date and time through the use of "oldtime" and update_flag.xml and configure alarm to periodically activate background component.

Table 2. Summary of main characteristic behaviour of ADRD family.

Characteristic activity	Code sequence
Encryption & certification	java/lang/Class.forName(<Ljava/lang/String;>"com.adroid.org.conscrypt.KeyManagerFactryImpl", <Z>true,<Ljava/lang/ClassLoader;>,) java/lang/Class.forName(<Ljava/lang/String;>"com.android.org.bouncycastle.jcajce.provider.keystore.bc.BcKeyStoreSpi$Std",<Z>true, <Ljava/lang/ClassLoader;>,) java/lang/Class.forName(<Ljava/lang/String;>"com.android.org.conscrypt.TrustManagerFactoryImpl", <Z>true,<Ljava/lang/ClassLoader;>,)

(continued)

Table 2. (*continued*)

Characteristic activity	Code sequence
	java/lang/Class.forName(<Ljava/lang/String;>"com.android.org.conscrypt.TrustedCertificateKeyStoreSpi", <Z>true,<Ljava/lang/ClassLoader;>,) java/lang/Class.forName(<Ljava/lang/String;>"com.android.org.bouncycastle.jce.provider.PKIXCertPathValidto-Spi",<Z>true, <Ljava/lang/ClassLoader;>,)
Send HttpRequest	ava/net/URI.parseURI(<Ljava/lang/String;>"",) java/net/URL.openConnection() java/net/URI.parseURI(<Ljava/lang/String;>"http://sd.3g.qq.com/g/softdown/util/apkskin.jsp",<Z>false,) org/apache/http/impl/client/AbstractHttpClient.execute (<Lorg/apache/http/client/methods/HttpUriRequest;>, <Lorg/apache/http/protocol/HttpContext;>,) org/apache/http/impl/client/AbstractHttpClient.execute(<Lorg/apache/http/HttpHost;>, <Lorg/apache/http/HttpRequest;>, <Lorg/apache/http/protocol/HttpContext;>,)
Retrieve IMSI, IMEI	android/content/ContextWrapper.getSystemService (<Ljava/lang/String;>"phone",) android/telephony/TelephonyManager.getDeviceId() android/telephony/TelephonyManager.getSubscriberId()
Check internet conn.	android/content/ContextWrapper.getSystemService (<Ljava/lang/String;> "connectivity",) android/net/ConnectivityManager.getActiveNetworkInfo()
Activation date & time	android/content/ContextWrapper.getSharedPreferences (<Ljava/lang/String;>"update_flag",<I>0,)
	android/app/SharedPreferencesImpl.getLong (<Ljava/lang/String;>"oldtime",<J>0,) java/util/Date.getTime(); android/app/SharedPreferencesImpl.edit()
Configure alarm to periodically activate background component	android/content/ContextWrapper.getSystemService(<Ljava/lang/String;>"alarm",) android/content/Intent.setAction(<Ljava/lang/String;> "com.lz.myservicestart",) android/app/PendingIntent.getBroadcast (<Landroid/content/Context;>,<I>0, <Landroid/content/Intent;>,<I>0,) android/content/Intent.writeToParcel (<Landroid/os/Parcel;>,<I>0,) android/app/AlarmManager.set()

5 Conclusion and Future Work

The proliferation of malware variants makes the approach of creating signatures for each individuals in a timely fashion inefficient and costly. It motivates us the idea of no more dancing with variants. Different from previous works and tools on dynamic malware analysis, this paper focuses on automated generation of Android malware family's common and main characteristic security-related API call sequences from the filtered execution traces of its variants. We modify the source code of ADB to enable the recording of parameters and return value of an API call, support UID-based profiling mode so to capture all the processes and threads spawned from the main process to gain complete understanding of the activities of target malware app, and generate trace for each thread. We also propose global execution sequence alignment and segmentation algorithms to generate the execution stage chart of a malware family which presents a simple and easy-to-understand overview of the lifecycle as well as common and different operations that individual variants performed at each stage. The family stage chart and the motifs also provide security analysts semantics-rich understanding of what and how a malware family is designed and implemented. Our system and the generated malware family characteristic API call sequences can be used as signatures for effective and efficient malware detection in the future.

References

1. Thomas, K., et al.: Investigating commercial pay-per-install and the distribution of unwanted software. In: Proceedings of the 25th USENIX Security Symposium, pp. 721–738 (2016)
2. Tam, K., et al.: The evolution of android malware and android analysis techniques. ACM Comput. Surv. (CSUR) **49**(4), 76 (2017)
3. Barrera, D., et al.: A methodology for empirical analysis of permission-based security models and its app to android. In: Proceedings of the ACM Conference on Computer and Communications Security (CCS), pp. 73–84 (2010)
4. Au, K.W.Y., et al.: PScout: analyzing the android permission specification. In: Proceedings of the ACM Conference on Computer and Communications Security (CCS), pp. 217–228 (2012)
5. Zhang, Y., et al.: Vetting undesirable behaviours in android apps with permission use analysis. In: Proceedings of the ACM Conference on Computer and Communications Security (CCS), pp. 611–622 (2013)
6. Rastogi, V., et al.: AppsPlayground: automatic security analysis of smartphone apps. In: Proceedings of the ACM Conference on Data and App Security and Privacy, pp. 209–220 (2013)
7. Feng, Y., Anand, S., Dillig, I., Aiken, A.: Apposcopy: semantics-based detection of android malware. In: Proceedings of the ACM Foundations of Software Engineering (FSE), pp. 576–588 (2014)
8. Enck, W., et al.: TaintDroid: an information-flow tracking system for realtime privacy monitoring on smartphones. ACM Trans. Comput. Syst. **32**(2), 1–29 (2014)
9. Peiravian, N., et al.: Machine learning for android malware detection using permission and API calls. In: Proceedings of the IEEE 25th International Conference on Tools with Artificial Intelligence, pp. 300–305 (2013)

10. Aafer, Y., Du, W., Yin, H.: DroidAPIMiner: mining API-level features for robust malware detection in android. In: Zia, T., Zomaya, A., Varadharajan, V., Mao, M. (eds.) SecureComm 2013. LNICST, vol. 127, pp. 86–103. Springer, Cham (2013). https://doi.org/10.1007/978-3-319-04283-1_6
11. Wu, D.J., et al.: DroidMat: android malware detection through manifest and API calls tracing. In: Proceedings of the IEEE Asia Joint Conference on Information Security (Asia JCIS), pp. 62–69 (2012)
12. Yan, L.-K., Yin, H.: DroidScope: seamlessly reconstructing the OS and Dalvik semantic views for dynamic android malware analysis. In: Proceedings of the USENIX Security Symposium, pp. 569–584 (2012)
13. Tam, K., et al.: CopperDroid: automatic reconstruction of android malware behaviours. In: Proceedings of the Network and Distributed System Security Symposium (2015)
14. Android developer. https://source.android.com/security/index.html
15. Somarriba, O., et al.: Detection and visualization of android malware behaviour. J. Electr. Comput. Eng. **2016**, 1–17 (2016)
16. https://www.sec.cs.tu-bs.de/~danarp/drebin/

Constant-Size CCA-Secure Multi-hop Unidirectional Proxy Re-encryption from Indistinguishability Obfuscation

Junzuo Lai[1,2](✉), Zhengan Huang[3], Man Ho Au[4], and Xianping Mao[5]

[1] Jinan University, Guangzhou, China
laijunzuo@gmail.com
[2] State Key Laboratory of Cryptology, Beijing, China
[3] Guangzhou University, Guangzhou, China
[4] The Hong Kong Polytechnic University, Hung Hom, Hong Kong
[5] ZhongAn Information Technology Service Co., Ltd., Shanghai, China

Abstract. In this paper, we utilize the recent advances in indistinguishability obfuscation, overcome several obstacles and propose a multi-hop unidirectional proxy re-encryption scheme. The proposed scheme is proved to be CCA-secure in the standard model (i.e., without using the random oracle heuristic), and its ciphertext remains *constant-size* regardless of how many times it has been transformed.

Keywords: Multi-hop · Unidirectional proxy re-encryption
Chosen-ciphertext attack · Indistinguishability obfuscation

1 Introduction

Proxy re-encryption (PRE), introduced by Blaze et al. [5], allows a semi-trust proxy, who is given a re-encryption key, to transform a ciphertext under the public key of Alice (the delegator) into another ciphertext for Bob (the delegatee). The proxy, however, learns nothing about the underlying messages encrypted.

According to the direction of transformation, PRE can be classified into *unidirectional* PRE and *bidirectional* PRE [13]. In unidirectional PREs, the proxy can only transform ciphertexts from Alice to Bob. While in bidirectional PREs, the proxy can transform ciphertexts in both directions. Unidirectional PRE usually gains the advantage over bidirectional PRE, and any unidirectional scheme can be easily transformed to a bidirectional one by running the former in both directions. PRE can also be categorized into *multi-hop* PRE, in which the ciphertexts can be transformed from Alice to Bob and then to Charlie and so on, and *single-hop* PRE, in which the ciphertexts can only be transformed once [1,2]. A multi-hop PRE will be more desirable than a single-hop PRE in practice as it provides the flexibility of re-delegation, that is, the delegatee can re-delegate the ciphertexts to another users.

W. Susilo and G. Yang (Eds.): ACISP 2018, LNCS 10946, pp. 805–812, 2018.
https://doi.org/10.1007/978-3-319-93638-3_49

In their seminal paper, Blaze et al. [5] proposed the first bidirectional PRE scheme. In NDSS 2005, Ateniese et al. [1,2] proposed several single-hop unidirectional PRE schemes. All of these schemes are only secure against chosen-plaintext attacks (CPA). However, applications often require security against chosen-ciphertext attacks (CCA). To fill this gap, in ACM CCS 2007, Canetti and Hohenberger [6] presented a novel multi-hop bidirectional PRE scheme, and proved its CCA-security in the standard model. In PKC 2008, Libert and Vergnaud [14,15] proposed the first CCA-secure single-hop unidirectional PRE scheme in the standard model. Subsequently, several CCA-secure single-hop unidirectional PRE schemes have been proposed [7,10,12].

It is worth noting that, compared with traditional public key encryption, PRE has more parties involved and its CCA-security model is more subtle. Thus designing CCA secure PRE is quite challenging (In fact, a number of alleged CCA-secure PRE schemes have subsequently been found insecure, e.g., [16,19]). For CCA-secure multi-hop unidirectional PREs, this problem is particularly more challenging. In ACM CCS 2007, Canetti and Hohenberger [6] left an open problem of how to construct a CCA-secure multi-hop unidirectional PRE scheme[1]. Eight years have passed, and there still exists no such scheme. Below we briefly explain the subtleties in designing CCA-secure multi-hop unidirectional PRE schemes.

It is well known that for a CCA-secure encryption scheme, its ciphertext should not be malleable. For original ciphertexts, the non-malleability of each ciphertext component can be easily ensured. However, as to transformed ciphertexts, it is rather difficult to ensure the non-malleability of each ciphertext component, since some of these components are modified after the transformation. Unfortunately, if the non-malleability of a given transformed ciphertext component cannot be ensured, there might exists an adversary who can break the CCA-security of the scheme. For example, given the challenge ciphertext $\mathrm{CT}^* = \mathsf{Encrypt}(pk^*, m_\beta)$ under the target public key pk^*, the adversary first issues a re-encryption query to transform CT^* into a transformed ciphertext $\mathrm{CT}_i = (..., C_i, ...)$ under a *uncorrupted* user i's public key pk_i, where the non-malleability of ciphertext component C_i cannot be ensured. Next, the adversary modifies C_i to C_i' and obtains another (might invalid) ciphertext $\mathrm{CT}_i' = (..., C_i', ...)$, and then issues a re-encryption query to transform CT_i' into another (might invalid) ciphertext CT_j' under a *corrupted* user j's public key pk_j. Note that it is legal for the adversary to issue this query, since (pk_i, CT_i') is *not* a derivative of (pk^*, CT^*). Now, with the corrupted user j's private key sk_j, the adversary might derive the underlying bit β from ciphertext CT_j', and then break the CCA-security of the scheme.

Our Contributions. To propose a CCA-secure multi-hop unidirectional PRE scheme, we utilize the recent advances in indistinguishability obfuscation [9]. We here briefly explain our high-level idea: the well-formedness of the original

[1] We notice that some alleged CCA-secure (identity-based) multi-hop unidirectional PRE schemes have been proposed, e.g. [8,20,21]. However, these schemes were subsequently found either insecure or flawed in the security proofs.

ciphertext in our scheme can be publicly verified, and with the help of indistinguishability obfuscation, the transformed ciphertext has the same form as the original ciphertext. Thus the well-formedness of the transformed ciphertext can also be verified, and the aforementioned attack can be accordingly ruled out in our scheme. In Sect. 2, we shall present our main idea and the proposed scheme. We stress that, it is *non-trivial* to use indistinguishability obfuscation to design a CCA-secure multi-hop unidirectional PRE scheme, and we face with several obstacles to be overcome. Interestingly, the ciphertext in our scheme remains *constant-size* regardless of how many times it has been transformed.

Related Work. We review related literature about indistinguishability obfuscation.

Indistinguishability Obfuscation. Program obfuscation deals with the problem of how to protect a program from reverse engineering while preserving functionality. Unfortunately, Barak et al. [3,4] showed that the most natural simulation-based formulation of program obfuscation (a.k.a. "black-box obfuscation") is impossible to achieve for *general* programs in a very strong sense. Faced with this impossibility result, Barak et al. [3,4] suggested another notion of program obfuscation named *indistinguishability obfuscation.* Roughly speaking, an indistinguishability obfuscation scheme ensures that the obfuscations of any two functionally equivalent circuits are computationally indistinguishable. Recently, Garg et al. [9] proposed the first candidate construction of an efficient indistinguishability obfuscation ($i\mathcal{O}$) for *general* programs.

Recently, staring with [18] there has been much interest in investigating what can be built from $i\mathcal{O}$, since this model leads to poly-time obfuscation of unrestricted program classes, circumventing the known impossibility results of [3,4]. Subsequently, many papers [11,17,18] have shown a wide range of cryptographic applications of $i\mathcal{O}$. In this paper, we seek to discover new application that is not achievable prior to the introduction of secure obfuscation. We utilize $i\mathcal{O}$ to resolve an open problem in the area of PRE.

2 Our Proposed Scheme

In this section, we shall first explain the intuition of our unidirectional proxy re-encryption scheme from indistinguishability obfuscation, and then describe the concrete construction in detail.

In order to resist the aforementioned attack described in Sect. 1, we design our scheme such that, the well-formedness of the original ciphertext can be publicly verified, and for any message $m \in \mathcal{M}$ and re-encryption key $rk_{i \to j}$, the original ciphertext $\mathsf{Encrypt}(pk_j, m; R)$ and the transformed ciphertext $\mathsf{ReEncrypt}(rk_{i \to j}, \mathsf{Encrypt}(pk_i, m; R))$ have the same form. Thus the well-formedness of the transformed ciphertext can also be verified. Our first idea is to create an indistinguishability obfuscation of the program ReEnc-i-j given in Fig. 1 as $\mathbf{P}^{\mathsf{ReEnc\text{-}i\text{-}j}}$ and set the re-encryption $rk_{i \to j} = \mathbf{P}^{\mathsf{ReEnc\text{-}i\text{-}j}}$. Now, given a ciphertext CT_i under user i's public key pk_i and the re-encryption key $rk_{i \to j} = \mathbf{P}^{\mathsf{ReEnc\text{-}i\text{-}j}}$, the re-encryption algorithm run by a proxy, outputs the ciphertext $\mathrm{CT}_j = \mathbf{P}^{\mathsf{ReEnc\text{-}i\text{-}j}}(\mathrm{CT}_i, R)$, where randomness R is chosen by the proxy. Obviously, the scheme satisfies the above requirement. Unfortunately, it is easy to find an attack. Let $\mathrm{CT}^* \leftarrow \mathsf{Encrypt}(pk^*, m_\beta)$ be the challenge ciphertext. An adversary can issue the re-encryption key generation query $\langle pk^*, pk_j \rangle$ to obtain the re-encryption key $rk_{*\to j} = \mathbf{P}^{\mathsf{ReEnc\text{-}*\text{-}j}}$, where pk_j is the uncorrupted user j's public key. Then, it chooses randomness R and computes $\mathrm{CT}_j = \mathbf{P}^{\mathsf{ReEnc\text{-}*\text{-}j}}(\mathrm{CT}^*, R)$. Observe that, $\mathrm{CT}_j = \mathsf{Encrypt}(pk_j, m_\beta; R)$, and thus the adversary can determine the underlying bit β and break the CCA-security of the scheme, since R is known to it.

ReEnc-i-j:
Input: Ciphertext CT_i and randomness R.
Constants: User i's private key sk_i.
1. Compute $m = \mathsf{Decrypt}(sk_i, \mathrm{CT}_i)$.
2. If $m = \perp$, output $\perp$.
3. Output: $\mathsf{Encrypt}(pk_j, m; R)$.

Fig. 1. Program ReEnc-i-j

Enc:
Input: Message $m \in \mathcal{M}$ and randomness R.
Constants: PRF keys K.
1. Compute $\widetilde{R} = F(K, R)$.
2. Output: $\overline{\mathsf{Encrypt}}(\overline{pk}, m; \widetilde{R})$.

Fig. 2. Program Enc

We try to resist the above attack by the following modifications. The goal of the modifications is to make the sender not know the randomness used to encrypt the message. Let $(\overline{\mathsf{Setup}}, \overline{\mathsf{Encrypt}}, \overline{\mathsf{Decrypt}})$ be a secure public key encryption scheme. The user's public key of the modified unidirectional proxy re-encryption scheme is set to be $pk = (\overline{pk}, \mathbf{P}^{\mathsf{Enc}})$, where $(\overline{pk}, \overline{sk}) \leftarrow \overline{\mathsf{Setup}}$ and $\mathbf{P}^{\mathsf{Enc}}$ is an indistinguishability obfuscation of the program Enc which is given in Fig. 2. In this modified unidirectional proxy re-encryption scheme, given a message $m \in \mathcal{M}$ and a randomness R chosen by the sender, the encryption algorithm computes the ciphertext $\mathrm{CT} = \mathbf{P}^{\mathsf{Enc}}(m, R)$ under the user's public key pk. Observe that, $\mathrm{CT} = \overline{\mathsf{Encrypt}}(\overline{pk}, m; \widetilde{R})$, where the randomness $\widetilde{R}$ used to encrypt the message is unknown to the sender, and thus the modified scheme can resist the above-mentioned attack. However, there still exists another attack. The adversary also issues the re-encryption key generation query $\langle pk^*, pk_j \rangle$ to obtain the re-encryption key $rk_{*\to j} = \mathbf{P}^{\mathsf{ReEnc\text{-}*\text{-}j}}$, where pk_j is the uncorrupted user j's public key. Then, it chooses a randomness R, and computes $\mathrm{CT}_j = \mathbf{P}^{\mathsf{ReEnc\text{-}*\text{-}j}}(\mathrm{CT}^*, R)$ and $\mathrm{CT}'_j = \mathbf{P}_j^{\mathsf{Enc}}(m_0, R)$. Notice that, $\mathrm{CT}_j = \overline{\mathsf{Encrypt}}(\overline{pk}_j, m_\beta; \widetilde{R})$ and $\mathrm{CT}'_j = \overline{\mathsf{Encrypt}}(\overline{pk}_j, m_0; \widetilde{R})$. Since the ciphertexts CT_j and CT'_j are generated by the same randomness $\widetilde{R}$, the adversary can determine the underlying bit β easily and thus break the CCA-security of the scheme, even if the randomness $\widetilde{R}$ is unknown to it.

Now, we build our multi-hop unidirectional PRE scheme on a new witness-recovering CCA-secure PKE scheme. The input of program ReEnc-i-j only includes a ciphertext, and the randomness R used to encrypt the message m in the program is obtained from the input ciphertext.

Concretely, the proposed multi-hop unidirectional proxy re-encryption scheme consists of the following algorithms (Figs. 3 and 4):

GlobalSetup(κ): Given a security parameter κ, the global setup algorithm first generates a bilinear group $(p, \mathbb{G}, \mathbb{G}_T, e)$. Then, it chooses $g, u, v, d \in \mathbb{G}$ uniformly at random, and a collision-resistant hash function $H : \mathbb{G} \times \{0,1\}^{\ell_s} \times \{0,1\}^{\ell} \to \mathbb{Z}_p^*$.
It also chooses puncturable PRFs $F : \mathcal{K} \times \{0,1\}^{\ell_s} \to \{0,1\}^{\ell_s}$, $\widetilde{F} : \widetilde{\mathcal{K}} \times \{0,1\}^{\ell_s} \to \mathbb{Z}_p^*$, key derivation functions $\mathsf{KDF}_1 : \mathcal{DK}_1 \times \mathbb{G}_T \to \{0,1\}^{\ell_s}$, $\mathsf{KDF}_2 : \mathcal{DK}_2 \times \{0,1\}^{\ell_s} \to \{0,1\}^{\ell}$. Next, it chooses $dk_1 \leftarrow \mathcal{DK}_1$ and $dk_2 \leftarrow \mathcal{DK}_2$. The global parameters is published as

$$param = (p, \mathbb{G}, \mathbb{G}_T, e, g, u, v, d,\ H, F, \widetilde{F}, \mathsf{KDF}_1(dk_1, \cdot), \mathsf{KDF}_2(dk_2, \cdot)).$$

For brevity, we assume that $param$ is implicitly included in the input of the following algorithms.

KeyGen(κ): The key generation algorithm first chooses $x \in \mathbb{Z}_p^*$ uniformly at random and sets $h = g^x$. Then, it chooses puncturable PRF keys $K \leftarrow \mathcal{K}, \widetilde{K} \leftarrow \widetilde{\mathcal{K}}$, and creates an obfuscation of the program Enc-v0 as $\mathbf{P}^{\mathsf{Enc}} \leftarrow i\mathcal{O}(\kappa, \textsf{Enc-v0})$. The public key is set to be $pk = (h, \mathbf{P}^{\mathsf{Enc}})$ and the private key $sk = (pk, (x, K, \widetilde{K}))$.

ReKeyGen(sk_i, pk_j): Given user i's private key $sk_i = (pk_i = (h_i, \mathbf{P}_i^{\mathsf{Enc}}), (x_i, K_i, \widetilde{K}_i))$ and user j's public key $pk_j = (h_j, \mathbf{P}_j^{\mathsf{Enc}})$, the re-encryption key generation algorithm creates an obfuscation of the program ReEnc-i-j-v0 as $\mathbf{P}^{\textsf{ReEnc-i-j}} \leftarrow i\mathcal{O}(\kappa, \textsf{ReEnc-i-j-v0})$, and outputs the re-encryption key $rk_{i\to j} = \mathbf{P}^{\textsf{ReEnc-i-j}}$.

Encrypt(pk, m): Given a public key $pk = (h, \mathbf{P}^{\mathsf{Enc}})$ and a message $m \in \{0,1\}^{\ell}$, the encryption algorithm proceeds as follows.

1. Choose $r \in \mathbb{Z}_p^*$ and $\delta \in \{0,1\}^{\ell_s}$ uniformly at random.
2. Compute $(r, c_1, c_2, c_3, c_4) = \mathbf{P}^{\mathsf{Enc}}(m, r, \delta)$.
3. The output ciphertext is $\mathrm{CT} = (r, c_1, c_2, c_3, c_4)$.

ReEncrypt($rk_{i\to j}, \mathrm{CT}_i$): Given a re-encryption key $rk_{i\to j} = \mathbf{P}^{\textsf{ReEnc-i-j}}$ and a ciphertext CT_i under user i's public key pk_i, the re-encryption algorithm outputs the ciphertext $\mathrm{CT}_j = \mathbf{P}^{\textsf{ReEnc-i-j}}(\mathrm{CT}_i)$.

Decrypt(sk, CT): Given a private key $sk = (pk = (h, \mathbf{P}^{\mathsf{Enc}}), (x, K, \widetilde{K}))$ and a ciphertext $\mathrm{CT} = (r, c_1, c_2, c_3, c_4)$, the decryption algorithm proceeds as follows.

1. Compute $t = H(c_1, c_2, c_3)$.
2. Check whether $e(h, c_4) = e(c_1, u^t v^r d)$ holds. If not, output $\perp$.
3. Compute $\widetilde{\delta} = c_2 \oplus \mathsf{KDF}_1(dk_1, e(g, c_1)^{1/x})$, $m = c_3 \oplus \mathsf{KDF}_2(dk_2, \widetilde{\delta})$.
4. Output the message m.

It can be verified that our proposed scheme satisfies the correctness requirement of multi-hop unidirectional proxy re-encryption. Observe that, the transformed ciphertexts have the same form as the original ciphertexts, and they can be consecutively transformed. This means that our scheme is multi-hop. Note

Enc-v0:
Input: Message $m \in \{0,1\}^\ell$, randomness $r \in \mathbb{Z}_p^*$ and $\delta \in \{0,1\}^{\ell_\delta}$.
Constants: PRF keys K and $\widetilde{K}$.
1. Compute $\widetilde{\delta} = F(K, \delta)$ and $s = \widetilde{F}(\widetilde{K}, \widetilde{\delta})$.
2. Compute
$$c_1 = h^s,\ c_2 = \mathsf{KDF}_1(dk_1, e(g,g)^s) \oplus \widetilde{\delta},\ c_3 = \mathsf{KDF}_2(dk_2, \widetilde{\delta}) \oplus m.$$
3. Compute $t = H(c_1, c_2, c_3)$ and $c_4 = (u^t v^r d)^s$.
4. Output: (r, c_1, c_2, c_3, c_4).

Fig. 3. Program Enc-v0

ReEnc-i-j-v0:
Input: Ciphertext $\mathrm{CT} = (r, c_1, c_2, c_3, c_4) \in \mathbb{Z}_p^* \times \mathbb{G} \times \{0,1\}^{\ell_\delta} \times \{0,1\}^\ell \times \mathbb{G}$.
Constants: User i's secret value x_i.
1. Compute $t = H(c_1, c_2, c_3)$.
2. Check whether $e(h_i, c_4) = e(c_1, u^t v^r d)$ holds. If not, output $\perp$.
3. Compute $\widetilde{\delta} = c_2 \oplus \mathsf{KDF}_1(dk_1, e(g, c_1)^{1/x_i})$, $m = c_3 \oplus \mathsf{KDF}_2(dk_2, \widetilde{\delta})$.
4. Output: $\mathbf{P}_j^{\mathsf{Enc}}(m, r, \widetilde{\delta})$.

Fig. 4. Program ReEnc-i-j-v0

that the well-formedness of both original ciphertext and transformed ciphertext can be publicly verified, and hence our scheme can resist the attack mentioned in Sect. 1. It is worth noting that, our techniques proposed in this paper can be used to construct an identity-based multi-hop unidirectional PRE scheme with constant-size ciphertexts and CCA-security in the standard model. Since the construction is quite straightforward, we here do not present the detailed construction. Below, we state the security theorem of our proposed scheme and defer detailed security proof to the full version, due to page limit.

Theorem 1. *If our obfuscation scheme is indistinguishably secure, H is a collision-resistant hash function, $F, \widetilde{F}$ are secure punctured PRFs, KDF_1 and KDF_2 are secure key derivation functions, and the 1-DBDHI assumption holds in the bilinear group $(p, \mathbb{G}, \mathbb{G}_T, e)$, then the proposed multi-hop unidirectional proxy re-encryption scheme is IND-PRE-CCA secure.*

Acknowledgment. We are grateful to the anonymous reviewers for their helpful comments. The work of Junzuo Lai was supported by National Natural Science Foundation of China (No. 61572235) and Guangdong Natural Science Funds for Distinguished Young Scholar (No. 2015A030306045).

References

1. Ateniese, G., Fu, K., Green, M., Hohenberger, S.: Improved proxy re-encryption schemes with applications to secure distributed storage. In: NDSS 2005 (2005)
2. Ateniese, G., Fu, K., Green, M., Hohenberger, S.: Improved proxy re-encryption schemes with applications to secure distributed storage. ACM Trans. Inf. Syst. Secur. **9**(1), 1–30 (2006)
3. Barak, B., Goldreich, O., Impagliazzo, R., Rudich, S., Sahai, A., Vadhan, S., Yang, K.: On the (im)possibility of obfuscating programs. In: Kilian, J. (ed.) CRYPTO 2001. LNCS, vol. 2139, pp. 1–18. Springer, Heidelberg (2001). https://doi.org/10.1007/3-540-44647-8_1
4. Barak, B., Goldreich, O., Impagliazzo, R., Rudich, S., Sahai, A., Vadhan, S.P., Yang, K.: On the (im)possibility of obfuscating programs. J. ACM **59**(2), 6 (2012)
5. Blaze, M., Bleumer, G., Strauss, M.: Divertible protocols and atomic proxy cryptography. In: Nyberg, K. (ed.) EUROCRYPT 1998. LNCS, vol. 1403, pp. 127–144. Springer, Heidelberg (1998). https://doi.org/10.1007/BFb0054122
6. Canetti, R., Hohenberger, S.: Chosen-ciphertext secure proxy re-encryption. In: CCS 2007, pp. 185–194 (2007)
7. Chow, S.S.M., Weng, J., Yang, Y., Deng, R.H.: Efficient unidirectional proxy re-encryption. In: Bernstein, D.J., Lange, T. (eds.) AFRICACRYPT 2010. LNCS, vol. 6055, pp. 316–332. Springer, Heidelberg (2010). https://doi.org/10.1007/978-3-642-12678-9_19
8. Chu, C.-K., Tzeng, W.-G.: Identity-based proxy re-encryption without random oracles. In: Garay, J.A., Lenstra, A.K., Mambo, M., Peralta, R. (eds.) ISC 2007. LNCS, vol. 4779, pp. 189–202. Springer, Heidelberg (2007). https://doi.org/10.1007/978-3-540-75496-1_13
9. Garg, S., Gentry, C., Halevi, S., Raykova, M., Sahai, A., Waters, B.: Candidate indistinguishability obfuscation and functional encryption for all circuits. In: FOCS 2013, pp. 40–49 (2013)
10. Hanaoka, G., Kawai, Y., Kunihiro, N., Matsuda, T., Weng, J., Zhang, R., Zhao, Y.: Generic construction of chosen ciphertext secure proxy re-encryption. In: Dunkelman, O. (ed.) CT-RSA 2012. LNCS, vol. 7178, pp. 349–364. Springer, Heidelberg (2012). https://doi.org/10.1007/978-3-642-27954-6_22
11. Hohenberger, S., Sahai, A., Waters, B.: Replacing a random oracle: full domain hash from indistinguishability obfuscation. In: Nguyen, P.Q., Oswald, E. (eds.) EUROCRYPT 2014. LNCS, vol. 8441, pp. 201–220. Springer, Heidelberg (2014). https://doi.org/10.1007/978-3-642-55220-5_12
12. Isshiki, T., Nguyen, M.H., Tanaka, K.: Proxy re-encryption in a stronger security model extended from CT-RSA2012. In: Dawson, E. (ed.) CT-RSA 2013. LNCS, vol. 7779, pp. 277–292. Springer, Heidelberg (2013). https://doi.org/10.1007/978-3-642-36095-4_18
13. Ivan, A.-A., Dodis, Y.: Proxy cryptography revisited. In: NDSS 2003 (2003)
14. Libert, B., Vergnaud, D.: Unidirectional chosen-ciphertext secure proxy re-encryption. In: Cramer, R. (ed.) PKC 2008. LNCS, vol. 4939, pp. 360–379. Springer, Heidelberg (2008). https://doi.org/10.1007/978-3-540-78440-1_21
15. Libert, B., Vergnaud, D.: Unidirectional chosen-ciphertext secure proxy re-encryption. IEEE Trans. Inf. Theory **57**(3), 1786–1802 (2011)
16. Matsuda, T., Nishimaki, R., Tanaka, K.: CCA proxy re-encryption without bilinear maps in the standard model. In: Nguyen, P.Q., Pointcheval, D. (eds.) PKC 2010. LNCS, vol. 6056, pp. 261–278. Springer, Heidelberg (2010). https://doi.org/10.1007/978-3-642-13013-7_16

17. Ramchen, K., Waters, B.: Fully secure and fast signing from obfuscation. IACR Cryptology ePrint Archive 2014:523 (2014)
18. Sahai, A., Waters, B.: How to use indistinguishability obfuscation: deniable encryption, and more. In: STOC 2014, pp. 475–484 (2014)
19. Shao, J., Cao, Z.: CCA-secure proxy re-encryption without pairings. In: Jarecki, S., Tsudik, G. (eds.) PKC 2009. LNCS, vol. 5443, pp. 357–376. Springer, Heidelberg (2009). https://doi.org/10.1007/978-3-642-00468-1_20
20. Shao, J., Cao, Z.: Multi-use unidirectional identity-based proxy re-encryption from hierarchical identity-based encryption. Inf. Sci. **206**, 83–95 (2012)
21. Wang, H., Cao, Z., Wang, L.: Multi-use and unidirectional identity-based proxy re-encryption schemes. Inf. Sci. **180**(20), 4042–4059 (2010)

Practical Signatures from the Partial Fourier Recovery Problem Revisited: A Provably-Secure and Gaussian-Distributed Construction

Xingye Lu[1], Zhenfei Zhang[2], and Man Ho Au[1(✉)]

[1] The Hong Kong Polytechnic University, Hung Hom, Hong Kong
xingye.lu@connect.polyu.hk, mhaau@polyu.edu.hk
[2] Onboard Security, Wilmington, MA, USA
zzhang@onboardsecurity.com

Abstract. In this paper, we present a new lattice-based signature scheme, PASS_G, based on signatures from the partial Fourier recovery problem PASS_{RS} introduced by Hoffstein et al. in 2014. Same as PASS_{RS}, security of our construction relies on the average-case hardness of a special kind of Short Integer Solution (SIS) problem and the hardness of partial Fourier recovery problem. PASS_G improves PASS_{RS} in two aspects. Firstly, unlike PASS_{RS}, PASS_G comes with a reduction proof and is thus provably secure. Secondly, we adopt rejection sampling technique introduced by Lyubashevsky in 2008 to reduce the signature size and improve the efficiency. More concretely, signatures of PASS_G are Gaussian-distributed and is more space efficient. We also present another security parameter set based on best known attack using BKZ 2.0 algorithm introduced by Chen and Nguyen in 2011.

Keywords: Lattice-based cryptography · Digital signature
Partial fourier recovery problem

1 Introduction

In 2014, Hoffstein et al. [9] presented a signature scheme called PASS_{RS}. As a candidate of practical post-quantum signature schemes, the security of PASS_{RS} is based on a special hard problem known as partial Fourier recovery. The problem requires recovery of a ring element with small norm given an incomplete description of its Chinese remainder representation. Even though there is no known reduction from standard lattice problems to the partial Fourier recovery problem, [9] shows that there is a relationship between this problem and the Short Integer Solution (SIS) problem. By assuming the average-case hardness of a special SIS problem which is called Vandermonde-SIS, the security of PASS_{RS} is said to rest on the hardness of Vandermonde-SIS. However, no security reduction between PASS_{RS} and Vandermonde-SIS is provided in [9].

W. Susilo and G. Yang (Eds.): ACISP 2018, LNCS 10946, pp. 813–820, 2018.
https://doi.org/10.1007/978-3-319-93638-3_50

In this paper, we present PASS_G, an efficient lattice-based signature scheme based on PASS_{RS} that provides provable security along with more secure parameter sets comparing with the original PASS_{RS}.

1.1 Related Work

Early candidates of lattice-based signature schemes, such as GGH signature scheme [8], lack security proofs and have been broken subsequently due to transcript attacks.

The seminal work of Gentry et al. [7], known as the GPV framework, combines a hash-and-sign paradigm with a pre-image sampling function. The signature schemes obtained through this fashion enjoy a provable security based on the hardness of the SIS problem. In the GPV framework, the efficiency of a signature scheme (in terms of both speed and size) depends heavily on the preimage sampling function and the quality of secret basis produced by the trapdoor generating function. Improving performance of these functions becomes the research objective for the following studies. To the best of our knowledge, the most efficient construction following this direction while admitting a security proof is due to Micciancio and Peikert [13].

Besides GPV framework adopting "hash-and-sign" techniques, there are also lattice-based signature schemes built through Fiat-Shamir heuristics. Lyubashevsky and Micciancio [12] first presented a lattice-based one-time signature scheme based on the ring-SIS problem. Based on [12], Lyubashevsky [10] then proposed a lattice-based interactive identification scheme and converted the scheme into a signature scheme using Fiat-Shamir heuristics. In the scheme, an abortion technique is used to protect the secret key from leakage. This abortion techniques, usually known as rejection sampling, has flourished modern lattice based signatures. For example, by rejecting to a Gaussian distribution [11] or a Bimodal Gaussian distribution (BLISS) [4], one is able to reduce both the rejection rate and the size of the signatures. State-of-the-art following this direction is Dilithium [5], whose hardness is based on the learning with error problem over modular lattices.

Different from these previous lattice-based signature schemes, Hoffstein et al. [9] proposed PASS_{RS} based on the partial Fourier recovery problem. It adopts the same aborting technique used in [10] to decouple the signature from the secret key. Although the time efficiency of PASS_{RS} is comparable with BLISS, we note that there are still rooms for improvement. First of all, PASS_{RS} does not admit a formal reduction proof. Moreover, cryptanalysis has been developing very rapidly during the past 2 years due to a new model [1] of analyzing the cost of BKZ 2.0 lattice reduction algorithm [3]. As a consequence, the security level of the original PASS_{RS} will be significantly reduced. It is fair to say PASS_{RS} may not be secure if the originally suggested parameters are adopted. To solve these problems, we present a new signature scheme called PASS_G.

Our Contribution: Comparing with PASS_{RS}, our contributions can be summarized as follow:

- We apply the rejection sampling technique from [11] to PASS_{RS} to construct a new scheme known as PASS_G. The use of rejection sampling can reduce the signature size of PASS_{RS};
- Comparing with PASS_{RS}, PASS_G comes with a formal reduction proof;
- We further provide several sets of security parameters for our new scheme that are robust against new analysis.

2 Preliminary

2.1 Notation

Elements in $\mathbb{Z}_q$ are represented by integers in $[-\frac{q}{2}, \frac{q}{2})$. We use cyclotomic polynomial rings $\mathbb{Z}_q[x]/(x^N + 1)$ with N being a power of 2 and q being a prime congruent to 1 mod $2N$. An element $\mathbf{a} \in R_q$ is represented as a polynomial $\mathbf{a} = a_0 + a_1\mathbf{x} + a_2\mathbf{x}^2 + \cdots + a_{N-1}\mathbf{x}^{N-1}$ with coefficients $a_i \in \mathbb{Z}_q$. We can also use vector $[a_0, a_1, a_2, \cdots, a_{N-1}]^T$ to represent polynomial $\mathbf{a}$. We use $\star$ to denote the multiplication on R_q and $\odot$ to denote component-wise multiplication of vectors. For any β with $\gcd(\beta, q) = 1$, Fermat's little theorem says $\beta^{q-1} = 1(\mod q)$. Since $q = rN + 1$, we have $\beta^{rN} = 1 \bmod q$. We can define a ring homomorphism mapping $\mathbf{f} \to \mathbf{f}(\beta^{\mathbf{r}})$ for any $\mathbf{f} \in R_q$. For any $\mathbf{f}_1, \mathbf{f}_2 \in R_q$,

$$(\mathbf{f}_1 + \mathbf{f}_2)(\beta^r) = \mathbf{f}_1(\beta^r) + \mathbf{f}_2(\beta^r) \text{ and } (\mathbf{f}_1 \star \mathbf{f}_2)(\beta^r) = \mathbf{f}_1(\beta^r) \odot \mathbf{f}_2(\beta^r)$$

For distribution $\mathcal{D}$, $x \xleftarrow{\$} \mathcal{D}$ means uniformly sampling x according to distribution $\mathcal{D}$. $\|\mathbf{v}\|_1$ is the ℓ_1 norm of vector $\mathbf{v}$ and $\|\mathbf{v}\|$ is the ℓ_2 norm of $\mathbf{v}$.

The continuous normal distribution over $\mathbb{R}^N$ centered at $\mathbf{v}$ with standard deviation σ is defined as $\rho^N_{\mathbf{v},\sigma}(\mathbf{x}) = (\frac{1}{\sqrt{2\pi\sigma^2}})^N e^{\frac{-\|\mathbf{x}-\mathbf{v}\|^2}{2\sigma^2}}$. For simplicity, when $\mathbf{v}$ is the zero vector, we use $\rho^N_\sigma(\mathbf{x})$.

The discrete normal distribution over $\mathbb{Z}^N$ centered at $\mathbf{v} \in \mathbb{Z}^N$ with standard deviation σ is defined as $\mathcal{D}^N_{\mathbf{v},\sigma}(\mathbf{x}) = \frac{\rho^N_{\mathbf{v},\sigma}(\mathbf{x})}{\rho^N_{\mathbf{v},\sigma}(\mathbb{Z}^N)}$.

Lemma 1 (Rejection Sampling [4]**).** *Let V be an arbitrary set, and $h : V \to \mathbb{R}$ and $f : \mathbb{Z}^m \to \mathbb{R}$ be probability distributions. If $g_v : \mathbb{Z}^m \to \mathbb{R}$ is a family of probability distribution indexed by all $v \in V$ with the property that*

$$\exists M \in \mathbb{R} \text{ such that } \forall v \in V, \forall \mathbf{z} \in \mathbb{Z}^m, \Pr[M \cdot g_v(\mathbf{z}) \geq f(\mathbf{z})] \geq 1 - \varepsilon.$$

Then the output distribution of the following algorithm $\mathcal{A}$:

1. $v \xleftarrow{\$} h$; 2. $\mathbf{z} \xleftarrow{\$} g_v$; 3. output $(\mathbf{z}, v)$ with probability $\min\left(\frac{f(\mathbf{z})}{M \cdot g_v(\mathbf{z})}, 1\right)$.

is within statistical distance $\frac{\varepsilon}{M}$ of

1. $v \xleftarrow{\$} h$; 2. $\mathbf{z} \xleftarrow{\$} f$; 3. output $(\mathbf{z}, v)$ with probability $\frac{1}{M}$.

The probability of algorithm $\mathcal{A}$ output something is at least $\frac{1-\varepsilon}{M}$.

Lemma 2 ([11])**.**

1. *For any $k > 0$, $\Pr[\|\mathbf{z}\| > k\sigma\sqrt{N}; \mathbf{z} \xleftarrow{\$} \mathcal{D}^N_\sigma] < k^N e^{\frac{N}{2}(1-k^2)}$;*
2. *For any vector $\mathbf{v} \in \mathbb{R}^N$, $\sigma, r > 0$, $\Pr[|\langle\mathbf{z}, \mathbf{v}\rangle| > r; \mathbf{z} \xleftarrow{\$} \mathcal{D}^N_\sigma] \leq 2\exp(-\frac{r^2}{2\|\mathbf{v}\|^2\sigma^2})$.*

2.2 Digital Signatures

A digital signature scheme consists of three algorithms, namely, KeyGen, Signing, Verification, described as follows.

- $\mathsf{KeyGen}(1^\lambda) \to (\mathsf{sk}, \mathsf{pk})$: On input security parameter 1^λ, this key generation algorithm generates private signing key sk and public verification key pk.
- $\mathsf{Signing}(\mathsf{sk}, \mu) \to \sigma$: On input signing key sk and message μ, the signing algorithm outputs signature σ on μ.
- $\mathsf{Verification}(\mu, \sigma, \mathsf{pk}) \to$ *accept*/*reject*: On input message μ, signature σ and verification key pk, the verification algorithm outputs accept if σ is a signature on μ. otherwise, it outputs reject.

Security of a digital signature scheme can be defined by a Game held between a challenger $\mathcal{C}$ and a probabilistic polynomial-time forger $\mathcal{F}$. Game consists of three phases, namely, *Setup*, *Query* and *Output*.

- *Setup*. The challenger $\mathcal{C}$ runs KeyGen algorithm and obtains private signing key and public verification key pair (sk, pk). $\mathcal{C}$ sends verification key pk to the forger $\mathcal{F}$.
- *Query*. Forger $\mathcal{F}$ sends message μ_i to challenger $\mathcal{C}$. $\mathcal{C}$ signs μ_i using sk and returns the corresponding signature σ_i to $\mathcal{F}$. Forger $\mathcal{F}$ repeats the process n times where n is polynomial in λ and finally obtains a list of message and signature pair $((\mu_1, \sigma_1), (\mu_2, \sigma_2), \cdots, (\mu_n, \sigma_n))$.
- *Output*. The forger $\mathcal{F}$ outputs a forgery (μ^*, σ^*). $\mathcal{F}$ wins Game if

$$(\mathsf{Verification}(\mu^*, \sigma^*, \mathsf{pk}) \to \mathit{accept}) \wedge ((\mu^*, \sigma^*) \notin \{(\mu_1, \sigma_1), (\mu_2, \sigma_2), \cdots, (\mu_n, \sigma_n)\}).$$

Definition 1. *A signature scheme (*KeyGen, Signing, Verification*) is said to be strong unforgeable if for any polynomial-time forger $\mathcal{F}$, the probability of $\mathcal{F}$ winning* Game *is negligible.*

2.3 Hardness Assumption

Before introducing the hard problem used in our construction, we first introduce the *partial Fourier recovery* problem which requires recovering a signal from a restricted number of its Fourier coefficients.

Let ω be the primitive Nth root of -1 modulo q. We define the discrete Fourier transform over $\mathbb{Z}_q$ to be the linear transformation $\mathbf{Fx} = \hat{\mathbf{x}} : \mathbb{Z}_q^N \to \mathbb{Z}_q^N$ given by $(\mathbf{F})_{i,j} = \omega^{ij}$. The Fourier transform matrix $\mathbf{F}$ is a Vandermonde matrix. Let $\mathbf{F}_\Omega$ be the restriction of $\mathbf{F}$ to the set of t rows specified by an index set, Ω, $(\mathbf{F}_\Omega)_{ij} = \omega^{\Omega_i j}$. The partial Fourier recovery problem is that, given an evaluation $\hat{\mathbf{f}}|_\Omega \in \mathbb{Z}_q^t$, find $\mathbf{x}$ with small norm such that $\hat{\mathbf{x}}|_\Omega = \hat{\mathbf{f}}|_\Omega (\mod q)$. The solution $\mathbf{x}$ is required to be small since one can easily find a large $\mathbf{x}$ such that $\hat{\mathbf{x}}|_\Omega = \hat{\mathbf{f}}|_\Omega$. This problem has been well studied and considered to be hard in general.

We note that to date, there is no known reduction from lattice-based hard problem to *partial Fourier recovery* problem. However, finding a short preimage by a given evaluation and a transform matrix $\mathbf{F}_\Omega$ is known to be related to solving the Short Integer Solution (SIS) and the Inhomogeneous Short Integer Solution (ISIS) problem, two average-case hard problems which are frequently used in lattice-based cryptography constructions. So we define a new problem called Vandermonde-SIS problem. Here we assume that the hardness of SIS problem is not relied on the structure of the public matrix and the Vandermonde-SIS problem is hard in average-case. The security of our proposed signature scheme is based on the assumed average-case hardness of the Vandermonde-SIS problem.

Definition 2 (Vandermonde $-$ $\mathbf{SIS}^{\mathcal{K}}_{q,t,N,\beta}$ problem). *Given a Vandermonde matrix $\mathbf{F}_\Omega \in \mathbb{Z}_q^{t\times N}$ drawn according to some distribution $\mathcal{K}$, find a non-zero $\mathbf{v} \in \mathbb{Z}_q^N$ such that $\mathbf{F}_\Omega \mathbf{v} = \mathbf{0}$ and $\|\mathbf{v}\| \leq \beta$.*

The distribution $\mathcal{K}$ here refers to randomly samples t rows from discrete Fourier transform matrix $\mathcal{F}$.

3 Construction

In this section, we describe the construction of PASS_G in details. Our construction involves the following algorithms:

KeyGen: This algorithm generates polynomial $\mathbf{f} \in R_q$ with each coefficient independently and uniformly sampled from $\{-1, 0, 1\}$ as the secret key. The corresponding public key is $\hat{\mathbf{f}}|_\Omega = \mathbf{F}_\Omega \mathbf{f}$. As described in Sect. 2.3, $\mathbf{F}_\Omega$ is the restriction of $\mathbf{F}$ to the set of t rows. Thus, $\mathbf{F}_\Omega$ can be generated by randomly picking t rows from the original Fourier transform matrix $\mathbf{F}$.

Signing$(\mathbf{f}, \mu)$: To sign message μ, the signer first randomly samples polynomial $\mathbf{y}$ from discrete normal distribution $\mathcal{D}_\sigma^N$ and computes $\hat{\mathbf{y}}|_\Omega = \mathbf{F}_\Omega \mathbf{y}$. The signer then computes challenge $\mathbf{c} = \mathsf{FormatC}(\mathsf{Hash}(\hat{\mathbf{y}}|_\Omega, \mu))$ where FormatC and Hash are two public algorithms such that:

$$\mathsf{Hash} : \mathbb{Z}_q^t \times \{0,1\}^* \to \{0,1\}^\ell, \mathsf{FormatC} : \{0,1\}^\ell \to \{\mathbf{v} : \mathbf{v} \in \{-1,0,1\}^N, \|\mathbf{v}\|_1 \leq \kappa\}.$$

Finally, the signer computes $\mathbf{z} = \mathbf{f} \star \mathbf{c} + \mathbf{y}$ and outputs $(\mathbf{z}, \mathbf{c})$ with probability $\min(\frac{\mathcal{D}_\sigma^N(\mathbf{z})}{M\mathcal{D}^N_{\mathbf{f}\star\mathbf{c},\sigma}(\mathbf{z})}, 1)$ where $M = \exp(\frac{28\alpha+1}{2\alpha^2})$ and $\sigma = \alpha \cdot \kappa\sqrt{N}$.

Verification$(\mu, \mathbf{z}, \mathbf{c}, \mathbf{F}_\Omega, \hat{\mathbf{f}}|_\Omega)$: The verifier accepts the signature if and only if $\|\mathbf{z}\| \leq k\sigma\sqrt{N}$ and $\mathbf{c} = \mathsf{FormatC}(\mathsf{Hash}(\hat{\mathbf{z}}|_\Omega - \hat{\mathbf{f}}|_\Omega \odot \hat{\mathbf{c}}|_\Omega, \mu))$.

In the signing procedure, $\mathbf{z}$ is distributed according to $\mathcal{D}^N_{\mathbf{f}\star\mathbf{c},\sigma}$. Thus, for any $\mathbf{z}^* \in \mathbb{R}^N$, we have:

$$\begin{aligned}
\Pr[\mathbf{z} = \mathbf{z}^*] = \mathcal{D}^N_{\mathbf{f}\star\mathbf{c},\sigma} &= \frac{\rho_{\mathbf{f}\star\mathbf{c},\sigma}(\mathbf{z}^*)}{\rho_\sigma(\mathbb{Z}^N)} = \frac{1}{\rho_\sigma(\mathbb{Z}^N)} \exp(-\frac{\|\mathbf{z}^* - \mathbf{f}\star\mathbf{c}\|^2}{2\sigma^2}) \\
&= \mathcal{D}_\sigma^N \exp(-\frac{-2\langle \mathbf{z}^*, \mathbf{f}\star\mathbf{c}\rangle + \|\mathbf{f}\star\mathbf{c}\|^2}{2\sigma^2})
\end{aligned}$$

We have:

$$\frac{\mathcal{D}_{\sigma}^{N}}{\mathcal{D}_{\mathbf{f}\star\mathbf{c},\sigma}^{N}} = \frac{\mathcal{D}_{\sigma}^{N}}{\mathcal{D}_{\sigma}^{N}\exp(-\frac{-2\langle\mathbf{z}^*,\mathbf{f}\star\mathbf{c}\rangle+\|\mathbf{f}\star\mathbf{c}\|^2}{2\sigma^2})} = \exp(\frac{-2\langle\mathbf{z}^*,\mathbf{f}\star\mathbf{c}\rangle+\|\mathbf{f}\star\mathbf{c}\|^2}{2\sigma^2})$$

According to Lemma 2, when $r = 14\|\mathbf{v}\|\sigma$, with probability at least $1-2^{-128}$ we have $\langle\mathbf{z}^*,\mathbf{f}\star\mathbf{c}\rangle > -14\|\mathbf{f}\star\mathbf{c}\|\sigma$. Then, with probability at least $1-2^{-128}$, we have:

$$\exp(\frac{-2\langle\mathbf{z}^*,\mathbf{f}\star\mathbf{c}\rangle+\|\mathbf{f}\star\mathbf{c}\|^2}{2\sigma^2}) < \exp(\frac{28\|\mathbf{f}\star\mathbf{c}\|\sigma+\|\mathbf{f}\star\mathbf{c}\|^2}{2\sigma^2}).$$

Assume $\sigma = \alpha\cdot\kappa\sqrt{N}$. Then,

$$\exp(\frac{28\|\mathbf{f}\star\mathbf{c}\|\sigma+\|\mathbf{f}\star\mathbf{c}\|^2}{2\sigma^2}) \le \exp(\frac{28\kappa\sqrt{N}\sigma+(\kappa\sqrt{N})^2}{2\sigma^2}) = \exp(\frac{28\alpha+1}{2\alpha^2}).$$

According to Lemma 1, if we reject $\mathbf{z}$ with probability $\min(\frac{\mathcal{D}_{\sigma}^{N}(\mathbf{z})}{M\mathcal{D}_{\mathbf{f}\star\mathbf{c},\sigma}^{N}(\mathbf{z})}, 1)$ where $M = \exp(\frac{28\alpha+1}{2\alpha^2})$. The distribution of $\mathbf{z}$ should be identical to $\mathbf{y}$.

Theorem 1. *Assume there is a polynomial-time forger who can successfully forge a PASS$_G$ signature with non-negligible probability δ by making at most s queries to the signing oracle and h queries to the random oracle* $\mathsf{FormatC}\circ\mathsf{Hash}$*. Then, there exits a polynomial-time algorithm which can solve the* $\mathbf{Vandermonde-SIS}_{q,t,N,\beta}^{\mathcal{K}}$ *problem for $\beta = 2k\sigma\sqrt{N}+2\kappa\sqrt{N}$ with probability $\frac{\delta^2}{2(h+s)}$.*

We remark that details of the security proof are omitted from this version due to page limit and can be found in the full version.

4 Practical Instantiation

In this section, we present a practical instantiation with parameters chosen according to the lattice reduction algorithm BKZ 2.0. This gives us an approach to analyse the security of PASS$_G$ under best known attack. Two sets of parameters with 128-bit security will be presented. Based on the two sets of parameters, we can estimate the rejection rate and signature size of our PASS$_G$.

Table 1 gives two sets of parameters. Both sets provides 128 bit security against quantum attackers. The first set of parameters provides a similar security level as the original PASS$_{RS}$ signature scheme, and is performance oriented. The second set is security oriented and has a larger build in margin. This is to account for future advance in cryptanalysis.

The best known lattice attack against our scheme is to look for the unique shortest vector within a lattice spanned via the basis:

$$\mathbf{B} = \begin{bmatrix} q\mathbf{I}_t & 0 & 0 \\ \mathbf{F}_{\Omega} & \mathbf{I}_N & 0 \\ \hat{\mathbf{f}}|_{\Omega} & 0 & 1 \end{bmatrix}$$

Table 1. PASS$_{RS}$ signature scheme parameter

	Parameter 1	Parameter 2
N	512	1024
$q \equiv 1 \mod 2N$	$2^{16}+1$	$2^{16}+1$
$t = \lvert\omega\rvert$	256	512
k	13.3	13.3
σ	2000	1800
κ s.t. $2^\kappa \cdot \binom{N}{\kappa} \geq 2^{256}$	44	36
$M = \exp(\frac{2\tau\kappa\sigma+\kappa^2}{2\sigma^2})$	≈7.4	≈7.4
Lattice strength	1.0035	1.0017
Public key size $(\log_2 q + 2)t$	832 bytes	1664 bytes
Signature length ≈ $(\log_2 \sigma + 2)N + \min(\kappa \log_2 N, N)$	882 bytes	1709 bytes

where $\mathbf{I}_t$ is a t dimensional identity matrix. This lattice has a unique shortest vector $\langle 0, \mathbf{f}, 1\rangle$ with an l_2 norm of approximately $\sqrt{2N/3+1}$. On the other hand, it has been shown in [6] that the ability to locate a unique shortest vector in a lattice depends on the root Hermite factor of the lattice, which is the n-th root of

$$\frac{\text{Gaussian expected length}}{l_2 \text{ norm of the target vector}}$$

where $n = (N+t+1)$ is the dimension of the lattice. We known that the Gaussian expected length of this lattice is $\sqrt{\frac{N+t+1}{2\pi e}} q^{\frac{t}{N+t+1}}$. This results in

$$\left(\frac{\sqrt{\frac{N+t+1}{2\pi e}}q^{\frac{t}{N+t+1}}}{\sqrt{2N/3+1}}\right)^{\frac{1}{N+t+1}}$$

With $t \approx N/2$, this quantity is $\approx \left(\sqrt{9/(8\pi e)}q^{\frac{1}{3}}\right)^{\frac{2}{3N}}$.

For the parameter sets that we are suggesting, this yields 1.0035 and 1.0017, respectively. Applying the latest results of estimating the cost of the BKZ 2.0 algorithm with (quantum) sieving [1–3], we estimate the cost to recover this shortest vector requires at least 2^{129} and 2^{198} operations.

Acknowledgement. We appreciate the anonymous reviewers for their valuable suggestions. Part of this work was supported by the National Natural Science Foundation of China (Grant No. 61602396, U1636205), and from the Research Grants Council of Hong Kong (Grant No. 25206317).

References

1. Alkim, E., Ducas, L., Pöppelmann, T., Schwabe, P.: Post-quantum key exchange - a new hope. In: 25th USENIX Security Symposium, USENIX Security 2016, Austin, TX, USA, 10–12 August 2016, pp. 327–343 (2016)
2. Bai, S., Laarhoven, T., Stehle, D.: Tuple lattice sieving. Cryptology ePrint Archive, Report 2016/713 (2016). https://eprint.iacr.org/2016/713
3. Chen, Y., Nguyen, P.Q.: BKZ 2.0: better lattice security estimates. In: Lee, D.H., Wang, X. (eds.) ASIACRYPT 2011. LNCS, vol. 7073, pp. 1–20. Springer, Heidelberg (2011). https://doi.org/10.1007/978-3-642-25385-0_1
4. Ducas, L., Durmus, A., Lepoint, T., Lyubashevsky, V.: Lattice signatures and bimodal gaussians. In: Canetti, R., Garay, J.A. (eds.) CRYPTO 2013. LNCS, vol. 8042, pp. 40–56. Springer, Heidelberg (2013). https://doi.org/10.1007/978-3-642-40041-4_3
5. Ducas, L., Lepoint, T., Lyubashevsky, V., Schwabe, P., Seiler, G., Stehle, D.: Crystals - dilithium: digital signatures from module lattices. Cryptology ePrint Archive, Report 2017/633 (2017). https://eprint.iacr.org/2017/633
6. Gama, N., Nguyen, P.Q.: Predicting lattice reduction. In: Smart, N. (ed.) EUROCRYPT 2008. LNCS, vol. 4965, pp. 31–51. Springer, Heidelberg (2008). https://doi.org/10.1007/978-3-540-78967-3_3
7. Gentry, C., Peikert, C., Vaikuntanathan, V.: Trapdoors for hard lattices and new cryptographic constructions. In: Dwork, C. (ed.) Proceedings of the 40th Annual ACM Symposium on Theory of Computing, Victoria, British Columbia, Canada, 17–20 May 2008, pp. 197–206. ACM (2008)
8. Goldreich, O., Goldwasser, S., Halevi, S.: Public-key cryptosystems from lattice reduction problems. In: Kaliski Jr., B.S. (ed.) CRYPTO 1997. LNCS, vol. 1294, pp. 112–131. Springer, Heidelberg (1997). https://doi.org/10.1007/BFb0052231
9. Hoffstein, J., Pipher, J., Schanck, J.M., Silverman, J.H., Whyte, W.: Practical signatures from the partial fourier recovery problem. In: Boureanu, I., Owesarski, P., Vaudenay, S. (eds.) ACNS 2014. LNCS, vol. 8479, pp. 476–493. Springer, Cham (2014). https://doi.org/10.1007/978-3-319-07536-5_28
10. Lyubashevsky, V.: Fiat-shamir with aborts: applications to lattice and factoring-based signatures. In: Matsui, M. (ed.) ASIACRYPT 2009. LNCS, vol. 5912, pp. 598–616. Springer, Heidelberg (2009). https://doi.org/10.1007/978-3-642-10366-7_35
11. Lyubashevsky, V.: Lattice signatures without trapdoors. In: Pointcheval and Johansson [14], pp. 738–755 (2012)
12. Lyubashevsky, V., Micciancio, D.: Asymptotically efficient lattice-based digital signatures. In: Canetti, R. (ed.) TCC 2008. LNCS, vol. 4948, pp. 37–54. Springer, Heidelberg (2008). https://doi.org/10.1007/978-3-540-78524-8_3
13. Micciancio, D., Peikert, C.: Trapdoors for lattices: simpler, tighter, faster, smaller. In: Pointcheval and Johansson [14], pp. 700–718 (2012)
14. Pointcheval, D., Johansson, T. (eds.): EUROCRYPT 2012. LNCS. Springer, Heidelberg (2012). https://doi.org/10.1007/978-3-642-29011-4

CRT-KPS: A Key Predistribution Schemes Using CRT

Pinaki Sarkar(✉), Mayank Baranwal, and Sukumar Nandi

Department of CSE, Indian Institute of Technology Guwahati, Guwahati, India
pinakisark@gmail.com, baranwalm2002@gmail.com, sukumar.nandi@gmail.com

Abstract. Key Predistribution Schemes (KPS) are efficient key management solutions that are well suited to establish lightweight symmetric keys even in resource starved environments, like low cost Internet of Things (IoT). This paper uses Chinese Remainder Theorem (CRT) to propose an energy efficient and deterministic KPS for distributed ad hoc networks, that we name as CRT-KPS. We theoretically establish the effectiveness of CRT-KPS in term of crucial metrics. Comparative study establishes that our proposals have better balance in overall performance as compared to state-of-the-art schemes and should find wide applications in IoT systems (specially for resource starved end devices).

Keywords: IoT networks security · Energy efficient key management
Key Predistribution Scheme (KPS)
Chinese Remainder Theorem (CRT) · Isomorphism

1 Introduction

Internet of Things (IoT) is a new reality where all objects can sense, identify, connect and communicate themselves to a single system. IoT is transforming our physical world to a single large information system and has several scientific applications. Of notable interests are networks that deal with sensitive data like military networks where security is premium. A few prototype IoT networks are (static) Wireless Sensor Networks (WSN), Mobile Ad hoc NETwork (MANET) and Radio Frequency IDentification (RFID) systems. It is obvious that a widespread adaptation of IoT systems is not risk free because if any (low cost) IoT device's security is compromised, then a valid threat can widely dispense through the Internet. This paper provides a lightweight indigenous solution that uses a device's identity and supports large number of (pre-defined) network nodes; and so, is implementable in RFID-WSN integration platforms.

1.1 Security and Key Management Issues: Motivation

To ensure secure (confidential and authentic) communication and distribution of sensitive IoT data, we implement cryptosystems. Constraints in resources restrict

W. Susilo and G. Yang (Eds.): ACISP 2018, LNCS 10946, pp. 821–830, 2018.
https://doi.org/10.1007/978-3-319-93638-3_51

applications of heavyweight Public Key Cryptosystems (PKC) in resource constraint IoT devices (sensors, tags, etc.). Instead, we exploit faster implementable Symmetric Key Cryptographic (SKC) protocols [3]. A major concern while implementing SKC systems for (low cost) networks is their demand to assign the same (or easily derivable) cryptographic key(s) among the communicating parties (prior to exchanges of messages).

Inefficient computation and communication overheads prohibit implementations of online PKC protocols [12] to manage symmetric keys in low cost networks. Pairwise assignments of mutual keys overburden the memory of devices. Employing Trusted Authorities (TA) to distribute symmetric secrets is prohibited since devices (including TAs) are prone to compromise. This motivates implementations of efficient *Key Predistribution Schemes (KPS)* to secure communication of resource constraint IoT devices. A KPS, as conceptualized by Eschenauer and Gligor [5], executes the steps below:

1. *preload keys:* prior to deployment, a root authority assigns *blocks of keys* of an underlying SKC (AES-128 [3]) with unique *key identifiers (ids)* into devices to form their *keyrings* from a large collection of system keys, aka the *key pool* $\mathcal{K}$;
2. *key establishment:* preloaded keys are established by a two phase process, as below:
   - *Shared key discovery*: discovers the shared key(s) among two nodes.
   - *Path key establishment*: establishes an optimized path between a given pair of nodes that do not share any key. This step involves intermediate nodes.

Nodes 'equate' each others' *node ids* (function of entire preloaded set key ids [7,9,11]) after (broadcast) exchange of these lightweight packets during a *key establishment process (KEP)*. Aforesaid subprocesses that establish mutual shared key(s) between participants can be either probabilistic or deterministic and accordingly leads to:

1. *Random Key Predistribution Schemes (RKPS)* [5]: preload SKC keys [3] into devices to form keyrings in an arbitrary manner and obtain a random graphical model. Gennaro et al. [6] and references therein extends this RKPS [5] to a subset scheme and combines with an identity based system [13] to obtain a hybrid leaf resistant non-interactive linear hierarchical key agreement scheme (ni-L-H-KAS).
2. *Deterministic Key Predistribution Schemes (DKPS)* [2]: use *combinatorial designs* to model a network's (symmetric) key sharing graph. The works [1, 7,9,11] set out desirable criteria for combinatorial KPS and manifest that they have predictable parametric properties. Paterson and Stinson [11] unify constructions of *combinatorial KPS.* Works that rectify certain parametric deficits (resilience or connectivity, defined in Sect. 3), with nominal increment in a node's storage are eminent [1,4].

1.2 Contribution and Organization of Our Work

We construct a simple-minded Chinese Remainder Theorem based Key Predistribution Scheme (CRT-KPS) in Sect. 2. Next we analyze this indigenous proposal in Sect. 3 on the basis of crucial design parameters and compare with prominent schemes.[1]

2 Key Predistribution Schemes (KPS) Based on CRT

This section devises a novel Chinese Remainder Theorem based Key Predistribution Scheme (CRT-KPS). We commence by revisiting CRT for any two co-prime integers p, q and reconstruct an associated isomorphism between $\mathbb{Z}_{pq} \longmapsto \mathbb{Z}_p \times \mathbb{Z}_q$. We employ this isomorphism to construct our CRT-KPS for the case of two co-prime integers, p, q.

Result 1 (CRT for 2 co-primes and an isomorphism). *Given two co-prime integers p and q, the following system of equations has an unique solution* mod pq, *i.e.*, $x \in \mathbb{Z}_{pq}$.

$$x \equiv a (\text{mod } p) \tag{1}$$

$$x \equiv b (\text{mod } q) \tag{2}$$

As an immediate consequence, an isomorphism is set out from $\mathbb{Z}_p \times \mathbb{Z}_q \longmapsto \mathbb{Z}_{pq}$. Reducing x mod p *and x* mod q, *we obtain reverse direction, i.e., the above two equations.*

Proof. We refer our readers to a standard text on basic number theory for proof of CRT (Koblitz [8]). Here we only state the solution and use it to construct the isomorphism:

$$\text{An Unique Solution is: } \alpha \equiv bm_1p + an_1q \in \mathbb{Z}_{pq}. \tag{3}$$

where $m_1 \equiv m(\text{mod} p), n_1 \equiv n(\text{mod} q)$ such that $mp + nq =$ from Extended Euclidean Algorithm (EEA) since $gcd(p, q) = 1$. We construct a map between $\mathbb{Z}_p \times \mathbb{Z}_q \longmapsto \mathbb{Z}_{pq}$ as $(a, b) \equiv \alpha$, where α is the unique solution of $x \equiv a \bmod p$ and $x \equiv b \bmod q$ that we obtain through CRT. Now we establish that this map is an isomorphism:

- *homomorphism:* follows from standard computation that we exhibit now. Consider $(a_1, b_1) \in \mathbb{Z}_p \times \mathbb{Z}_q \equiv \alpha_1 \in \mathbb{Z}_{pq}, (a_2, b_2) \in \mathbb{Z}_p \times \mathbb{Z}_q \equiv \alpha_2 \in \mathbb{Z}_{pq}$. Then since $(a_1, b_1) + (a_2, b_2) \in \mathbb{Z}_p \times \mathbb{Z}_q = (a_1 + a_2, b_1 + b_2) \equiv \alpha_1 + \alpha_2 \in \mathbb{Z}_{pq}$ and $(a_1, b_1) \cdot (a_2, b_1) \in \mathbb{Z}_p \times \mathbb{Z}_q = (a_1a_2, b_1b_2) \equiv \alpha_1 \cdot \alpha_2 \in \mathbb{Z}_{pq}$, we have an induced homomorphism.
- *bijection:* of the aforesaid map is a consequence of (i) the uniqueness (so, one-to-one) and, (ii) the fact that both the domain set (Cartesian product) and the range set has same number of elements (pq) , i.e., the induced map is onto.

[1] We refer to an existing result as 'Result'; while a 'Theorem' or 'Corollary' are new outcomes.

- *reverse isomorphism:* Given an $\alpha \in \mathbb{Z}_{pq}$, $(\alpha \bmod p, \alpha \bmod q)$ gives the inverse isomorphism. We use both maps during construction and analyses of our CRT-KPS.

2.1 CRT-KPS: A Novel Distributed KPS Using CRT

Here we construct the indigenous CRT-KPS for two co-prime integers. These two co-primes p, q (system parameters) are chosen so that $pq > \mathscr{N} =$ expected number of nodes in the network. So, both p, q are considerably small unlike primes used for cryptographic purposes (PKC [12] or pseudo-random number generators [10]). Further, we do not impose any further restrictions on them (for instance, to be of almost equal sizes, like in RSA [12]). Rest of the construction is set out next:

1. we set the key pool to be the ring $\mathbb{Z}_{pq}$ for the chosen co-primes p, q;
2. nodes ids are set as $\alpha \equiv (a, b)$ where $\alpha \in \mathbb{Z}_{pq}$ such that $\alpha \equiv a \bmod p$ and $\alpha \equiv b \bmod q$. So the maximum number of blocks and hence, nodes $= \beta = pq$;
3. we use the isomorphism resulting from CRT to assign key ids to a node $\alpha \equiv (a, b)$ as: $\{(a, j), j = 1, 2, 3, \cdots, q-1\} \cup \{(i, b), i = 1, 2, 3, \cdots, p-1\}$. We have a repeat of one key: (a, b) that we consider only once. So keyring sizes $= k = p + q - 1$.

Computation of shared keys between two nodes with ids $\alpha_i \equiv (a_i, b_i), i = 1, 2$ is done by *key establishment process (KEP)*, the executes the simple and lightweight steps below:

1. broadcast exchange of node ids (as elements in $\mathbb{Z}_{pq}$);
2. "equate" these node ids to trace the common shared keys between nodes as below;
   - in case $a_i \neq a_2, b_i \neq b_2$, common keys between the nodes α_1, α_2 are (a_1, b_2) and (a_2, b_1) since keyrings of $\alpha_i = (a_i, y), y \in \mathbb{Z}_q, (x, b_i), x \in \mathbb{Z}_p$ $(a_i, b_i), i = 1, 2$.
   - in case $a_i \neq a_2$ but $b_i = b_2 = b$ (say), we compute the common keys between nodes α_1 and α_2 to be $(i, b), i = 0, 1, \cdots, p-1$.
   - in case $a_i = a_2 = a$ (say) and $b_i \neq b_2$, then by a similar logic, the common keys between nodes α_1 and α_2 are $(a, j), j = 0, 1, \cdots, q-1$.

A *shared session key* between the nodes α_1 and α_2 in all the three cases can be taken as an unique publicly known function (example: xor) of all their common shared keys. For the first case, Theorem 1 proves the uniqueness of this session key in the entire system and therefore eliminates masquerading attacks. For latter two cases, session keys are unique only up to a threshold since common keys are shared by other $p + q - 1$ nodes (Theorems 2 and 4). An interested reader may refer to Fig. 1 for an instance with $p = 5, q = 7$ where we represent keyrings and connectivity of nodes $17, 12, 19 (\bmod 35)$. We choose these three nodes as their key sharing covers all possible (three) cases that we state above and analyze in depth through the Theorems 1, 2, 4 and 3 in next Sect. 3.

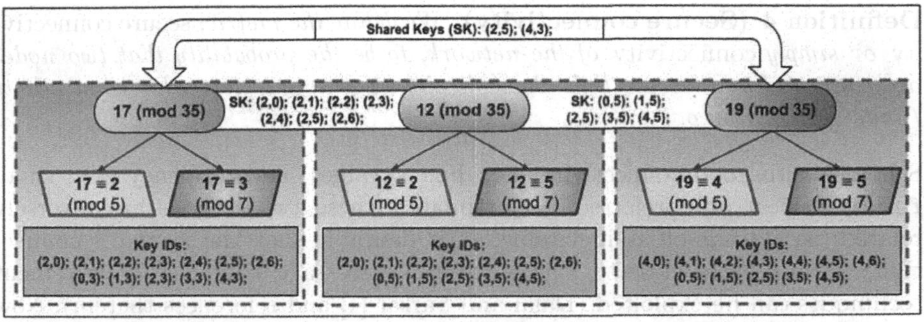

Fig. 1. Prototype connectivity between nodes due to (2 co-prime) CRT-KPS with $p = 5, q = 7$.

Remark 1 (Variant of $CRT - KPS$). CRT holds for any number of co-prime integers and potentially lead to constructions of generic CRT-KPS. Generalized CRT-KPS has more keys in intersections of keyrings at depth 1; and so facilitate subset construction. Due to limited scope of this shortened conference version and rigor of presentation of the generalized version, this paper studies the case of two co-prime integers only.

3 Analyses with Comparative Study

Here we scrutinize CRT-KPS in terms of crucial parameters. Like all (combinatorial) KPS, *energy requirement of CRT-KPS is less* and it *supports a network of pre-defined size (pq)*. Next we recall an active adversarial threat model, system's resiliency against it, the vital notions of secure connectivity and its trade-offs with resilience:

Definition 1 (Random Node Compromise attack). *is* random *capture or compromise of nodes [7, 9, 11] (without prior information about the network).*

Definition 2 (A Resilience Metric). $\mathtt{f}ail(s)$ *is defined as the probability of a link being compromised among the network of uncompromised nodes due to random compromise of s nodes. Notationally,* $\mathtt{f}ail(s) = \dfrac{c_s}{u_s}$*, where c_s is the number of compromised links and u_s is the total number of links in the remaining network of uncompromised nodes.*

We use $\mathtt{f}ail(1)$ to analyze our schemes and adapt during comparative study.

Definition 3 (Secure link). *A secure link is said to exist between nodes in a system designed by a KPS if they share at least one key of the underlying SKC [3]. In case of multiple (uniformly) shared keys between a pair of nodes, we construct a* shared session key *to be an unique (publicly known) function of all their common shared keys.*

Definition 4 (Secure connectivity). *We define the metric,* secure connectivity *or simply* connectivity *of the network, to be the probability that two nodes are connected by a secure link. Symbolically we denote a network's connectivity (under a KPS) by ρ.*

Schemes with good connectivity (i.e., high ρ values) and resiliency (i.e., small $\mathtt{f}ail(s)$ values) are preferred. Unfortunately these two metrics are inversely related; so a trade-off is inevitable. It is desirable that the system's connectivity ratio ρ be as close to 1 as possible. If necessary, resilience improvement techniques can be exploited (Dalai and Sarkar [4] and references therein). Now that the basic notions are formally set out, we analyze the key sharing graph of CRT-KPS through the theorems and corollaries, that follow:

Theorem 1. *Consider two nodes with ids $\alpha_i \in \mathbb{Z}_{pq}, i = 1, 2$ where $\alpha_i \equiv a_i(\bmod p)$ and $\alpha_i \equiv b_i(\bmod q)$ for $i = 1, 2$. So we consider the inverse isomorphism operation of CRT. Assume $a_1 \neq a_2, b_1 \neq b_2$. Then we can compute (a_1, b_2) and (a_2, b_1) to be the common shared keys between the nodes α_1 and α_2. Further these are the only two nodes in the system that share this pair keys. Therefore we arrive a case of absolute resilience.*

Proof. The fact that (a_1, b_2) and (a_2, b_1) are common shared keys between the nodes α_1 and α_2 is a direct consequence of our construction. Conversely, we use CRT and the method of "prove by contradiction" to ratify that these keys are jointly in no other nodes, i.e., $\alpha_z, z \neq i = 1, 2$. Suppose (a_1, b_2) and (a_2, b_1) in the same node $\alpha_z, z \in \mathbb{Z}_{pq}, z \neq i = 1, 2$. Then from our construction, keyring of the node α_z must contain: $(a_1, j); (l, b_2)$ or $(a_1, j); (l, b_2), (j = 1, 2, 3, \cdots, q-1, l = 1, 2, 3 \cdots, p-1$ in both cases); i.e., contain $\alpha_z \equiv (a_1, b_1)$ or $\alpha_z \equiv (a_2, b_2)$ since $a_1 \neq a_2$ and $b_1 \neq b_2$. This compels $\alpha_z = \alpha_1$ or $\alpha_z = \alpha_2$, which leads to a contradiction, and so our claim is true. □

Corollary 1. *Number of nodes pairs $< \alpha_1, \alpha_2 > \in \mathbb{Z}_{pq} \times \mathbb{Z}_{pq}$ that have perfect resilience against compromise of third party nodes $= \frac{pq(p-1)(q-1)}{2}$ (refer to Theorem 1).*

Proof. For a node $\alpha_1 \in \mathbb{Z}_{pq} \equiv (a_1, b_1) \in \mathbb{Z}_p \times \mathbb{Z}_q$, there are $(p-1)(q-1)$ possible $\alpha_2 \equiv (a_2, b_2) \in \mathbb{Z}_p \times \mathbb{Z}_q$ nodes with $a_1 \neq a_2, b_1 \neq b_2$. Now we can choose $\alpha_1 \in \mathbb{Z}_{pq}$ in pq ways since all choices of α_1 are stochastically independent. However in this process, we double count every pair of nodes in the form α_1, α_2 and α_2, α_1 (since α_1 is just a label). We divide by 2 to eliminate this double count and obtain the desired result. □

Theorem 2. *Consider $a_1 = a_2 = a$ (say) for two arbitrary nodes ids $\alpha_i \in \mathbb{Z}_{pq}(a_i, b_i) \in \mathbb{Z}_p \times \mathbb{Z}_q$ for $i = 1, 2$; so $b_1 \neq b_2$. Then there are q keys $(a, j), j = 0, 1, 2, 3, \cdots, q-1$ common between them. Similarly, the intersection of two arbitrary nodes α_1 and α_2 when $b_1 = b_2 = b$ (say), so that $a_1 \neq a_2$ has p keys: $(i, b), 1 = 0, 1, 2, 3, \cdots, p-1$.*

Proof. For nodes $\alpha_1 \neq \alpha_2 \in \mathbb{Z}_{pq}$ with $a = a_1 = a_2 \in \mathbb{Z}_p \Longrightarrow b_1 \neq b_2 \in \mathbb{Z}_q$. There cannot be any common key of the form $(i, b), b \in \mathbb{Z}_q$. This is because first co-ordinate is constant and second co-ordinate varies. So only possibility is to have common key of the form $(a, j), a \in \mathbb{Z}_p$. Our construction yields: $(a, j), j = 1, 2, 3, \cdots, q-1$ to be the set of q common keys as j varies over $\mathbb{Z}_q$. By symmetry, the other result follows. □

Corollary 2. *Number of nodes that contain the keys:* $(a, j), j = 0, 1, 2, \cdots, q-1$ *for a fixed* $a \in \mathbb{Z}_p$ *are* q. *So number of nodes that contains* $(a, j), j = 0, 1, 2, \cdots, q-1$ *for a varying* $a \in \mathbb{Z}_p = pq$. *Similarly the number of nodes that contain the keys:* $(i, b), i = 0, 1, 2, \cdots, p-1$ *for varying* $b \in \mathbb{Z}_q$ *are* qp.

Proof. From CRT-KPS construction and proof of previous Theorem 2, it is clear that for a fixed $a \in \mathbb{Z}_p$, the keys $(a, j), j = 0, 1, 2, \cdots, q-1$ jointly occur in the q nodes with ids: $(a, b), b = 0, 1, 2, \cdots, q-1$. Moreover, they are the only common keys among these nodes as second (key) co-ordinate varies for them only. Therefore, as a varies over $\mathbb{Z}_p$, number of nodes $= pq$ (q many for each $a \in \mathbb{Z}_p$). Proof of the other case is similar. □

Proof of the next theorem uses CRT-KPS construction and standard computations.

Theorem 3. *(Degree of CRT-KPS) Cycle of a given key* $(i, j) \in \mathbb{Z}_p \times \mathbb{Z}_q$ *(fixed* i, j*) has* $r = p + q - 1$ *nodes with ids* $(i, z_1), z_1 \in \mathbb{Z}_q \cup (z_2, j), z_2 \in \mathbb{Z}_p$ *(counting* (z_1, z_2) *once).*

Given the circumstantial importance of the structure of a KPS during parametric analyses, the next theorem formally classifies key sharing subgraph of a given node $\alpha \in \mathbb{Z}_{pq}$.

Theorem 4. *For an arbitrary node* $\alpha \in \mathbb{Z}_{pq} \equiv (a, b) \in \mathbb{Z}_p \times \mathbb{Z}_q$*, it has either:*

1. *precisely* 2 *distinct keys shared individually with* $(q-1)(p-1)$ *nodes (and no third node) whose* x *and* y *co-ordinates are simultaneously different from* α*;*
2. *exactly a set of* p *distinct shared keys with* p *node whose first co-ordinates varies in* $\mathbb{Z}_p$ *and second co-ordinate is same as* α*;*
3. *exactly a set of* q *distinct shared keys with* p *node whose first co-ordinate is same as* α *while second co-ordinates varies in* $\mathbb{Z}_q$.

CRT-KPS has full connectivity with multiple inter-nodal shared keys. Further compromise of a single node, yield $\texttt{fail}(1) = \dfrac{(q-1)(p-1) + p(p-1)/2 + q(q-1)/2)}{pq(pq-1)/2}$. *Further, CRT-KPS system has good resilience against* masquerading of internal nodes *since for a node,* $(q-1)(p-1)$ *nodes shares an unique session key.*

Proof. We observe that case 1 of this theorem corresponds to Theorem 1 and its Corollary 1; while cases 2 and 3 are covered in Theorem 2 and its Corollary 2. An obvious implication is an arbitrary node's connectivity with all nodes in the network with multiple common shared keys; and so, *the resultant network is fully connected.*

The statement about resilience of CRT-KPS requires deeper analysis, that we do now. Compromise of a node exposes all $p+q-1$ keys; each of which connect $p+q-1$ nodes individually but not independently. Since there are three types of connections in every node (cases 1, 2, 3), we count them separately. Our construction combines all shared keys between (a pair of) nodes to obtain a *shared session key* in each of the aforesaid case. So we count (i) a single link for each peer node corresponding to case 1, (ii) a cycle of length p for case 2 and (iii) a cycle of length q for case 3. Therefore there are $(q-1)(p-1)$ links corresponds to case 1 ($(q-1)(p-1)$ peer nodes), while cases 2 and 3 yield $\binom{p}{2}$ and $\binom{q}{2}$ links corresponding to p and q keys in respective cases (cycles of length p, q). Therefore, $\mathtt{fail}(1) = \dfrac{(q-1)(p-1) + p(p-1)/2 + q(q-1)/2)}{pq(pq-1)/2}$. □

Table 1. Comparison of asymptotic behavior of different schemes.

Scheme	No. of nodes	ρ	$\mathtt{fail}(1)$
$CRT-KPS$	$\mathcal{N} = pq$	1	$\dfrac{(q-1)(p-1) + \frac{p(p-1)}{2} + \frac{q(q-1)}{2}}{\frac{pq(pq-1)}{2}}$
$TD(2,k,p^t)$ [11] $\approxeq$	$\mathcal{N} = p^{2t}, t \in \mathbb{Z}$	z	$\frac{1}{p^t} = \mathcal{N}^{\frac{-1}{2}}$
$TD(k,p^t)$ [9], $k = zq$	(ext. of [9,11])	(z: variable)	
$TD(3,k,q), k = zq$	$\mathcal{N} = q^3, z < 1$	$\frac{z(2-z)}{2}$	$\frac{2(1-z)}{(2-z)}\mathcal{N}^{\frac{-1}{3}}$
$TD(3,k,q), k = q$	$\mathcal{N} = q^3$	1/2	$5\mathcal{N}^{\frac{-2}{3}}$
$TD(4,k,q), k = zq$	$\mathcal{N} = q^4$	$\frac{z(z^2-3z+6)}{6}$	$\frac{3(z^2-2z+2)}{z^2-3z+6}\mathcal{N}^{\frac{-1}{4}}$
$Symmetric\ BIBD$ [2]	$\mathcal{N} = q^2+q+1$	1	$\mathcal{N}^{\frac{-1}{2}}$

Comparative Study. We compare asymptotic behavior of CRT-KPS with prominent others in term of parameters defined in Sect. 3. We present the data in Table 1 and compare with SBIBD [2] and TD(t,k,q) [11] with intersection threshold $\eta = 1$.

4 Conclusion and Future Works

This paper proposes an energy efficient KPS, called CRT-KPS. Schematic analyses shows this deterministic CRT-KPS assigns multiple shared keys between nodes and has appreciable resilience against active node capture attacks. Comparative study show that our indigenous scheme outperforms state-of-the-art proposals.

We can construct a (deterministic) subset scheme with distributed CRT-KPS at top level. This subset scheme extends to a *strongly resistant hybrid ni-L-H-KAS* on combining with Sakai et al.'s distributed ni-KAS [13]. Being combinatorial, this decentralized KAS using bilinear pairing maps will have predictable design properties as opposed to Gennaro et al.'s random schemes [6] and so suit resourceful MANETs better.

Acknowledgement. We sincerely thank Ministry of Electronics and Information Technology, Government of India for funding the post doctoral tenure of Pinaki Sarkar through "ISEA" project.

References

1. Bag, S., Dhar, A., Sarkar, P.: 100% connectivity for location aware code based KPD in clustered WSN: merging blocks. In: Gollmann, D., Freiling, F.C. (eds.) ISC 2012. LNCS, vol. 7483, pp. 136–150. Springer, Heidelberg (2012). https://doi.org/10.1007/978-3-642-33383-5_9
2. Çamtepe, S.A., Yener, B.: Combinatorial design of key distribution mechanisms for wireless sensor networks. In: Samarati, P., Ryan, P., Gollmann, D., Molva, R. (eds.) ESORICS 2004. LNCS, vol. 3193, pp. 293–308. Springer, Heidelberg (2004). https://doi.org/10.1007/978-3-540-30108-0_18
3. Daemen, J., Rijmen, V.: The block cipher rijndael. In: Quisquater, J.-J., Schneier, B. (eds.) CARDIS 1998. LNCS, vol. 1820, pp. 277–284. Springer, Heidelberg (2000). https://doi.org/10.1007/10721064_26
4. Dalai, D.K., Sarkar, P.: Enhancing resilience of KPS using bidirectional hash chains and application on sensornet. In: Yan, Z., Molva, R., Mazurczyk, W., Kantola, R. (eds.) NSS 2017. LNCS, vol. 10394, pp. 683–693. Springer, Cham (2017). https://doi.org/10.1007/978-3-319-64701-2_54
5. Eschenauer, L., Gligor, V.D.: A key-management scheme for distributed sensor networks. In: Proceedings of the 9th ACM Conference on Computer and Communications Security, CCS 2002, pp. 41–47. ACM (2002)
6. Gennaro, R., Halevi, S., Krawczyk, H., Rabin, T., Reidt, S., Wolthusen, S.D.: Strongly-resilient and non-interactive hierarchical key-agreement in MANETs. In: Jajodia, S., Lopez, J. (eds.) ESORICS 2008. LNCS, vol. 5283, pp. 49–65. Springer, Heidelberg (2008). https://doi.org/10.1007/978-3-540-88313-5_4
7. Kendall, M., Martin, K.M.: Graph-theoretic design and analysis of key predistribution schemes. Des. Codes Crypt. **81**(1), 11–34 (2016)
8. Koblitz, N.: A Course in Number Theory and Cryptography. Springer, New York (1987). https://doi.org/10.1007/978-1-4684-0310-7
9. Lee, J., Stinson, D.R.: A combinatorial approach to key predistribution for distributed sensor networks. In: IEEE Wireless Communications and Networking Conference, WCNC 2005, pp. 1200–1205 (2005)
10. Naor, M., Reingold, O.: Number-theoretic constructions of efficient pseudo-random functions. J. Assoc. Comput. Mach. **51**(2), 231–262 (2004)

11. Paterson, M.B., Stinson, D.R.: A unified approach to combinatorial key predistribution schemes for sensor networks. Des. Codes Crypt. **71**(3), 433–457 (2014)
12. Rivest, R.L., Shamir, A., Adleman, L.M.: A method for obtaining digital signatures and public-key cryptosystems. Commun. ACM **21**(2), 120–126 (1978)
13. Sakai, R., Ohgishi, K., Kasahara, M.: Cryptosystems based on pairing. In: Symposium on Cryptography and Information Security – SCIS 2000 (2000). (In Japanese, English version available from the authors)

Correction to: Fast Lottery-Based Micropayments for Decentralized Currencies

Kexin Hu and Zhenfeng Zhang

Correction to: Chapter "Fast Lottery-Based Micropayments for Decentralized Currencies" in: W. Susilo and G. Yang (Eds.): *Information Security and Privacy*, LNCS 10946, https://doi.org/10.1007/978-3-319-93638-3_38

In the original version of this chapter the second affiliation was missing for both authors. This has now been corrected. The *University of Chinese Academy of Sciences* has been added as second affiliation.

The updated version of this chapter can be found at
https://doi.org/10.1007/978-3-319-93638-3_38

W. Susilo and G. Yang (Eds.): ACISP 2018, LNCS 10946, p. C1, 2020.
https://doi.org/10.1007/978-3-319-93638-3_52

Author Index

Ahmadi, Ahmad 598
Akand, Mamunur 598
Alberto Torres, Wilson Abel 558
Anada, Hiroaki 341
Au, Man Ho 502, 558, 720, 805, 813

Baranwal, Mayank 821
Barbar, Mohamad 768
Bhattacharjee, Nandita 558
Boyen, Xavier 245

Chen, Chien-Chun 796
Chen, Jiageng 417
Chen, Kefei 265
Chen, Meng Chang 796
Chen, Rongmao 376, 431
Chen, Shiping 768
Chen, Shuhui 431
Chen, Xiaofeng 417
Chen, Yuan 539
Cheng, Jacob 558
Cheon, Jung Hee 28
Chida, Koji 64
Cui, Jie 399, 649

David, Bernardo 45
Deng, Zhijun 619
Ding, Jintai 467
Ding, Ran 399
Dong, Liju 539
Dowsley, Rafael 45
Duong, Dung Hoang 487

Fluhrer, Scott 467
Fu, Anmin 741

Gu, Dawu 687

Haines, Thomas 245
Hamada, Koki 64
He, Jiantao 649
He, Shuangyu 304
Heys, Howard M. 135
Hsiao, Shun-Wen 796
Hu, Kexin 669
Hu, Lei 3
Hu, Ziyuan 265
Huang, Xinyi 417
Huang, Zhengan 805

Ikarashi, Dai 64
Ikematsu, Yasuhiko 487
Ito, Ryoma 154

Jeong, Jinhyuck 28
Jin, Hai 619

Kanaoka, Akira 341
Kikuchi, Ryo 64
Kılınç, Handan 579
Kim, Dongwoo 28
Kim, Eunkyung 101
Kuchta, Veronika 558
Kunihiro, Noboru 3

Lai, Junzuo 502, 805
Lai, Qiqi 539
Larangeira, Mario 45
Lau, Terry Shue Chien 750
Lee, Hyang-Sook 101
Lee, Hyung Tae 780
Lee, Jongchan 28
Leung, Hofung 431
Li, Bao 520
Li, Haoyu 455
Li, Jie 520
Li, Jin 759
Li, Shimin 284
Li, Wenjuan 759
Li, Xu 634
Li, Zhen 619
Liang, Bei 284
Lin, Dongdai 360
Liu, Chi 376
Liu, Dengzhi 417
Liu, Jianwei 304, 322, 706

Liu, Joseph K. 265, 558
Liu, Lin 431
Liu, Renzhang 455
Liu, Shengli 13, 265
Liu, Ximeng 431
Liu, Zhe 759
Liu, Zhen 687
Liu, Zhiqiang 687
Long, Yu 687
Lu, Xianhui 520
Lu, Xingye 813
Lu, Yao 3

Ma, Xuecheng 360
Mao, Xianping 805
Marrière, Nicolas 188
Matsuda, Takahiro 64
Matsuzaki, Natsume 341
Meng, Weizhi 759
Miyaji, Atsuko 154

Nachef, Valérie 188
Naito, Yusuke 225
Nandi, Sukumar 821
Nitaj, Abderrahmane 455

Pan, Yanbin 455
Park, Jeongeun 101
Paul, Souradyuti 114
Peng, Liqiang 3
Probst, Christian W. 759

Qin, Bo 304, 322

Rv, Saraswathy 467

Safavi-Naini, Reihaneh 598
Sakzad, Amin 558
Sarkar, Pinaki 821
Sarkar, Sumanta 207
Shen, Jian 417
Shrivastava, Ananya 114
Steinfeld, Ron 558
Su, Jinshu 431
Sui, Yulei 768
Sun, Liuying 83
Sun, Yeali S. 796
Sun, Yinxia 741
Syed, Habeeb 207

Takagi, Tsuyoshi 487, 787
Tan, Chik How 750
Tian, Tian 172

Vaudenay, Serge 579
Volte, Emmanuel 188

Wang, Changren 706
Wang, Dongcheng 634
Wang, Huaxiong 780
Wang, Xiaofeng 431
Wang, Xin 360
Wang, Yacheng 487
Wang, Yi 376
Wang, Yongjun 376
Wang, Yu 759
Wang, Yuntao 787
Watanabe, Yohei 341
Wen, Yunhua 13
Wu, Qianhong 304, 322

Xia, Zhe 83
Xu, Qikui 634
Xu, Qiuliang 502, 720
Xu, Yan 399, 649
Xue, Haiyang 520
Xue, Jingling 768
Xue, Rui 284

Yang, Bo 83, 539
Yang, Rupeng 502, 720
Yang, Xu 634
Ye, Chendong 172
Yin, Jiayuan 706
Yu, Yong 539
Yu, Zuoxia 502, 720

Zeng, Yali 634
Zhang, Daode 520
Zhang, Futai 741
Zhang, Hongyu 768
Zhang, Kai 520, 780
Zhang, Mingwu 83, 417

Zhang, Rui 3
Zhang, Yuncong 687
Zhang, Zhenfei 813
Zhang, Zhenfeng 669
Zhang, Zongyang 706
Zheng, Haibin 304, 322
Zhong, Hong 399, 649
Zhong, Lin 304, 322
Zhou, Yanwei 83
Zou, Deqing 619

Printed in the United States
By Bookmasters